C000143750

MILLER'S

Antiques
Shops, Fairs
& Auctions
in the UK & Ireland
2006

MILLER'S

Antiques Shops, Fairs & Auctions

in the UK & Ireland

2006

MILLER'S ANTIQUES SHOPS, FAIRS AND AUCTIONS IN THE UK & IRELAND 2006

Compiled, edited and designed by Miller's Publications Ltd
The Cellars, High Street, Tenterden, Kent TN30 6BN
Tel: 01580 766411 Fax: 01580 766100

First published in Great Britain in 2005 by Miller's,
a division of Mitchell Beazley, imprints of Octopus Publishing Group Ltd,
2–4 Heron Quays, London E14 4JP
Miller's is a registered trademark of
Octopus Publishing Group Ltd

ISBN 1 84533 147 8

A CIP catalogue record for this book is available from the British Library

Set in Frutiger

Printed and bound by Mackays of Chatham Ltd

Project Director Valerie Lewis
Executive Art Editor & Jacket Design Rhonda Fisher
Project Co-ordinator David Penfold, Edgerton Publishing Services
Principal Researchers Florence Buswell, Ailbhe Darcy, Clare Gillingham,
Camilla Mcoun, Caroline Petherick, Léonie Sidgwick,
Jessica Thompson, Elizabeth Watson, Carol Woodcock
Database entry Joanna Barry, Alice Cooke
Production Co-ordinator Philip Hannath
Designer Nick Harris
Production Controller Jane Rogers
Advertising Co-ordinator & Administrator Melinda Williams
Advertising Executive Emma Gillingham

Front cover illustrations:
l. A rosewood kettle stand, in the manner of Gillows,
19thC, 28¾in (73cm) high. **£680–810 / €1,000–1,200 / $1,250–1,500** ➤ G(B)

tr. A silver tankard, converted from a jug, with chased decoration,
London 1767, 8in (20.5cm) high. **£380–450 / €560–670 / $700–830** ➤ CHTR

br. A Staffordshire model of spaniel, late 19thC, 9½in (24cm) high.
£980–1,150 / €1,450–1,700 / $1,800–2,100 ➤ SWO

Scotland

North East

Northern Ireland

North West

Yorks & Lincs

Republic of Ireland

Midlands

East

Wales

Heart of England

West Country

South

South East

LONDON

Channel Islands

CONTENTS

8 HOW TO USE THIS BOOK

9 INTRODUCTION

11 ANTIQUE SHOPS, CENTRES & AUCTION HOUSES

12 SOUTH EAST
Kent, East Sussex

47 LONDON
East, North, South, West, Middlesex

115 SOUTH
Berkshire, Hampshire, Isle of Wight, Surrey, West Sussex

151 WEST COUNTRY
Cornwall, Devon, Dorset, Somerset, Wiltshire

201 EAST
Cambridge, Essex, Suffolk, Norfolk

230 HEART OF ENGLAND
Bedfordshire, Buckinghamshire, Gloucestershire, Herefordshire, Hertfordshire, Oxfordshire

269 MIDLANDS
Derbyshire, Leicestershire, Northamptonshire, Nottinghamshire, Rutland, Shropshire, Staffordshire, Warwickshire, West Midlands, Worcestershire

316 YORKS & LINCS
East Riding of Yorkshire, North Yorkshire, South Yorkshire, West Yorkshire, Lincolnshire

346 NORTH EAST
Co Durham, Northumberland, Tyne & Wear

353 NORTH WEST
Cheshire, Cumbria, Greater Manchester, Lancashire, Merseyside

379 WALES
Carmarthenshire, Ceredigion, Conwy, Denbighshire, Gwynedd, Flintshire, Isle of Angelsey, Mid Glamorgan, Monmouthshire, Pembrokeshire, Powys, South Glamorgan, West Glamorgan

395 SCOTLAND
Edinburgh, Glasgow, Aberdeenshire, Angus, Argyle & Bute, Dumfries & Galloway, East Ayrshire, East Lothian, Fife, Highland, Midlothian, Moray, North Ayrshire, Perth & Kinross, Renfrewshire, Scottish Borders, South Ayrshire, South Lanarkshire, Stirling, West Lothian

416 CHANNEL ISLANDS
Guernsey, Jersey

419 NORTHERN IRELAND
Co Antrim, Co Armagh, Co Down, Co Fermanagh, Co Londonderry, Co Tyrone

428 REPUBLIC OF IRELAND
Co Carlow, Co Cavan, Co Clare, Co Cork, Co Donegal, Co Dublin, Co Galway, Co Kerry, Co Kildare, Co Kilkenny, Co Laois, Co Leitrim, Co Limerick, Co Louth, Co Mayo, Co Meath, Co Offaly, Co Sligo, Co Tipperary, Co Waterford, Co Wexford, Co Wicklow

443 ASSOCIATED SERVICES

517 FAIRS

564 KEY TO MEMBER ORGANIZATIONS

565 INDEX OF ADVERTISERS

566 INDEX OF SPECIALISTS

583 INDEX OF PLACE NAMES

592 GENERAL INDEX

624 FORM FOR NEW ENTRIES

HOW TO USE THIS BOOK

It is our aim to make *Miller's Antiques Shops, Fairs & Auctions in the UK & Ireland 2006* simple to use. In order to make it easier to find entries, the book has been divided into three main sections: Dealers, Antiques Centres and Auction Houses; Associated Services; and Fairs.

The United Kingdom has been divided into geographical regions, which are listed in the Contents on page 7. There is also a section for the Republic of Ireland. Each region is divided into counties and within each county, cities, towns and villages are listed alphabetically. Indexes to company name and place name can be found at the end of this Directory.

YORKS & LINCS
SOUTH YORKSHIRE • BARLOW

SOUTH YORKSHIRE

BARLOW

⊞ **Byethorpe Antiques**
Contact John Gelsthorpe
✉ Shippen Rural Business Centre, Church Farm, Barlow, South Yorkshire, SI8 7TR 🅿
☎ 0114 289 9111
ⓦ www.byethorpe.com
Est. 1977 *Stock size* Medium
Stock Traditional oak and mahogany furniture
Open Mon–Sat 9am–5.30pm

BARNSLEY

⚒ **BBR Auctions**
Contact Mr Alan Blakeman
✉ Elsecar Heritage Centre, Barnsley, South Yorkshire, S74 8HJ 🅿
☎ 01226 745156 📠 01226 361561
✆ sales@onlinebbr.com
ⓦ www.onlinebbrauction.com
Est. 1979
Open Mon–Fri 9am–5pm
Sales Antique bottles and pot lids 4 per annum. Antique advertising every 6 months. Doulton, Beswick and 20thC pottery 2 per annum. Kitchenware 2 per annum. Breweriana and pub jugs 2 per annum. All sales Sun 11am, viewing full week prior 9am–5pm

Bentley, Doncaster, South Yorkshire, DN5 0EU 🅿
☎ 01302 873557
Est. 2002 *Stock size* Large
Stock Furniture, bureaux, desks, pottery, pictures, lamps, light fittings, mirrors
Open Tues–Sun 10am–5pm

CAWTHORNE

🏠 **Cawthorne Antique and Collectors Centre**
Contact Mr P Gates
✉ 2 Church Street, Cawthorne Village, Barnsley, South Yorkshire, S75 4HP 🅿
☎ 01226 792237
ⓦ www.cawthorneantiques centre.co.uk
Est. 1997 *Stock size* Large
No. of dealers 50
Stock Wide range of antiques, collectables, furniture
Open Mon–Sat 10am–4pm Sun 10.30am–4.30pm closed Wed
Services Tea room

FISHLAKE

⊞ **Fishlake Antiques**
Contact Fiona Trimingham
✉ Vine Cottage, Hay Green Corner, Fishlake, South Yorkshire, DN7 5LA 🅿
☎ 01302 841411
Est. 1979 *Stock size* Medium
Stock Country furniture, clocks

Each entry shows information such as address, phone number, opening hours, e-mail address and website, member organizations (eg LAPADA) and year established. Each **Dealer** entry contains details of stock and any services they provide. **Auction House** entries include information about their sales, frequency of sales and if catalogues are available. Entries for **Antiques Centres** include the number of dealers within the centre. **Associated Services** such as restorers, packers and valuers etc are listed alphabetically according to the service offered.

The **Fairs** section is divided into two parts. The first part gives an alphabetical list of fair organizers, while the second lists in date order, antiques fairs that will take place in the UK and Ireland throughout 2006. It is always advisable to contact the organizers in advance to check that information has not changed since going to press.

FAIRS: ORGANIZERS
CONTACT DETAILS

Abbey Fairs
Contact Nick Cox
⊠ PO Box 7482,
Nottingham,
NG16 2ZQ
☎ 01773 770422
✉ abbeyfairs@yahoo.co.uk
⊕ www.abbeyfairs.com
Fairs Art Deco Fairs in London, Warwick, Twickenham, Battersea and Kelam Hall, Newark

Adams Antiques Fairs
Contact Matthew Adams
☎ 020 7254 4054
⊕ www.adams-antiques-fairs.co.uk
Fairs Brocante and Decorative Living Show and Frock Me! at Kensington Town Hall. Adams Antiques Fairs at Kensington Town Hall and the Royal Horticultural Hall, London, 'Turn Out Your Attic', Battersea Arts Centre

Albany Fairs
Contact Robert Davison
☎ 0191 584 2934
Ⓜ 07976 619009
✉ enquiries@albanyfairs.com
⊕ www.albanyfairs.com

⊠ PO Box 119,
Cranbrook, Kent,
TN18 5WB
☎ 01797 252030
Fairs The LAPADA Antiques & Fine Art Fair

Antique Forum Group
☎ 01782 393660 Ⓕ 01782 393357
✉ info@antiqueforumgroup.com
⊕ www.antiqueforumgroup.com
Fairs Big Brum, Birmingham, Antiques Festivals, Trentham Gardens, and Uttoxeter 2-day Antiques Fair. Please phone for details. Also Antiques and Collectors Market, every Tuesday (8am–3pm), Newcastle-under-Lyme

Antiques & Collectors World
⊠ PO Box 129,
Tadworth, Surrey,
KT20 5YR
☎ 01737 812989
Ⓜ 07802 768364
✉ orchard.cottage@clara.co.uk
Fairs Antiques & Collectors Fairs, Goodwood Racecourse

FAIRS: CALENDAR
JANUARY

8

Antique & Collectors Fair
Organizer Blooms A1 Events
Location The Racecourse, Beverley, East Riding of Yorkshire ▣
Est. 2000
Open 9am–4pm
Entrance fee £1
Details 70 stands

Antiques & Collectables Fair
Organizer Take Five Fairs
Location Woking Leisure Centre, Kingfield Road, Woking, Surrey
Open 8.30am–4pm
Entrance fee £2
Details 175 stalls

Bob Evans Fair
Organizer Bob Evans Fairs
Location Leisure Centre, Holmer Road, Hereford (tel. 01432 278178) ▣
Est. 1974
Open 9.30am–4.30pm
Details 200 stalls

Deco Fair
Organizer Ann Zierold Fairs

Open 8.30am–5pm
Entrance fee 8.30am £4 10am £2.50
Details Up to 200 exhibitors

Midas Antiques Fair
Organizer Midas Fairs
Location Bellhouse Hotel, Beaconsfield, Buckinghamshire ▣
Open 10.30am–5pm
Entrance fee £1.50 children (6–16) 50p children under 6 free
Details Quality dateline stands

V&A Antiques & Collectors Fair
Organizer V&A Fairs
Location Park Royal Hotel, Stretton, Nr Warrington, Cheshire (M56 junction 10) ▣
Est. 2000
Open Trade (FWC) 8.30–10am public 10am–4.30pm
Details 100 stands, refreshment facilities, disabled facilities. Please note that this venue will be closed for two months at some point during the year. Please check with organisers

10–11

Key to Symbols

⊞ Dealer
🪓 Auction House
⌂ Antiques Centre
⊠ Address
▣ Parking
☎ Telephone No.
Ⓜ Mobile No.
Ⓕ Fax No.
✉ E-mail address
⊕ Web Address

There are Indexes of **Specialists, Place Names** and a **General Index,** which are to be found beginning on page 564.

9

Antiques Shops, Centres & Auction Houses

If you wish your company to be entered in the next edition of the Directory, please complete the form at the end of the book or go to our website: http://www.shopsfairsauctions.com

SOUTH EAST

EAST SUSSEX

BALCOMBE

🏹 Mid Sussex Auctions Ltd
Contact Lance Gibson
✉ Glebe Farm Estate,
Haywards Heath Road,
Balcombe, Haywards Heath,
East Sussex,
RH17 6NJ 🅿
☎ 01444 819100 📠 01444 819101
📧 sue@midsussexauctions.fsnet.co.uk
🌐 www.midsussexauctions.fsnet.co.uk
Est. 1998
Open Mon–Fri 9am–5.30pm
Sales Antiques and general sales
held at South of England
Showground, Ardingly,
East Sussex
Frequency Monthly
Catalogues Yes

BATTLE

⊞ Barnaby's of Battle
Contact Mr Barney Hance
✉ 50 High Street, Battle,
East Sussex,
TN33 0AN 🅿
☎ 01424 772221
Est. 1997 *Stock size* Medium
Stock Old pine, oak, hardwood
furniture
Open Mon–Sat 10am–6pm
Services Restoration

🏠 Battle Antiques Centre
Contact Andrew Polnik or
Christine Terry
✉ 91a High Street, Battle,
East Sussex,
TN33 0AQ 🅿
☎ 01424 773364
Est. 1963 *Stock size* Medium
No. of dealers 12
Stock General antiques
Open Mon–Sat 10am–5pm
Services Ceramic restoration,
caning, rushwork, gilding,
upholstery

🏹 Burstow & Hewett
Contact Mr R Ellin
✉ Abbey Auction Galleries &
Granary Salerooms,
Lower Lake, Battle,
East Sussex,
TN33 0AT 🅿
☎ 01424 772374 📠 01424 772302
📧 auctions@burstowandhewett.co.uk
🌐 www.burstowandhewett.co.uk
Est. 1790
Open Mon–Fri 9am–5.30pm
Sales Sales of general antiques.
Specialist sales of fine furniture,
paintings and ceramics
Frequency Monthly
Catalogues Yes

**⊞ Spectrum Fine
Jewellery Ltd (NAG, IPG)**
Contact Mr Keith Ingram

✉ 46 High Street, Battle,
East Sussex,
TN33 0EE 🅿
☎ 01424 774404 📠 01424 774404
Est. 1975 *Stock size* Medium
Stock Jewellery, silver
Open Tues–Sat 9.30am–5.30pm
Fairs NEC
Services Repairs, enamelling,
commissions, restoration of
antique jewellery

BEXHILL-ON-SEA

⊞ Acme Inc.
Contact Mrs Ruth Hardie
✉ 42 Sackville Road,
Bexhill-on-Sea, East Sussex,
TN39 3JE 🅿
☎ 01424 211848
📱 07973 402404
📧 ruth@acme-inc.com
🌐 www.acme-inc.com
Est. 1993 *Stock size* Large
Stock 19th–20thC decorative
arts, ceramics, glass, metalware,
furniture
Open Mon Thurs Fri 11am–noon
2.30–4pm Sat 3–5pm Sun 3–4pm
or by appointment

**⊞ Bexhill Museum
(Association of
Independent Museums)**
Contact Don Phillips
✉ Egerton Road,
Bexhill-on-Sea,
East Sussex,
TN39 3HL 🅿
☎ 01424 787950 📠 01424 787950
📧 museum@rother.gov.uk
🌐 bexhill-museum.co.uk
Est. 1914 *Stock size* Small
Stock Sculpture
Open Feb–Dec Tue–Fri 10am–5pm
Sat Sun Bank Holidays 2pm–5pm
Services Guided tours booked in
advance

**⊞ Bexhill Museum
(Association of
Independent Museums)**
Contact Mrs Pauline Bullock
✉ The Manor Gardens,
Upper Sea Road, Bexhill-on-Sea,
East Sussex,
TN40 7RL 🅿
☎ 01424 210045
📧 museum@rother.gov.uk
Est. 1972 *Stock size* Small
Stock Costume and social history
Open Apr–Oct daily except
Apr/May/Sept/Oct

♠ Gorringes Incorporating Julian Dawson (SOFAA, ISVA)
Contact Mr Ross Mercer
✉ Terminus Road,
Bexhill-on-Sea,
East Sussex,
TN39 3LR 🅿
☎ 01424 212994 ❶ 01424 224035
✉ bexhill@gorringes.co.uk
🌐 www.gorringes.co.uk
Est. 1926
Open Mon–Fri 8.30am–1pm
2–5pm Sat by appointment
Sales Fine art, antiques,
collectables, Tues Wed 10am,
viewing Fri 10am–5pm
Sat 9.30am–4pm
Frequency 6 weeks
Catalogues Yes

⊞ Elizabeth Morgan Antiques
Contact Mr H Jenkins
✉ 50 Western Road,
Bexhill-on-Sea, East Sussex,
TN40 1DY 🅿
☎ 01424 218343
Est. 1983 **Stock size** Medium
Stock General antiques
Open Mon–Sat 9am–5pm

⊞ Sivyer's
Contact Mrs V Sivyer
✉ 7 Sackville Road,
Bexhill-on-Sea, East Sussex,
TN39 3JB 🅿
☎ 01424 733821 ❶ 01424 734454
Est. 1990 **Stock size** Medium
Stock General antiques,
kitchenware
Open Mon–Sat 10am–5pm
Wed 10am–1pm
Services Auctions

⊞ Stocks Pine
Contact David Saunders
✉ 37 Devonshire Road,
Bexhill-on-Sea, East Sussex,
TN40 1BD 🅿
☎ 01424 211188 ❶ 01424 211188
⓾ 07768 797443
✉ saunders438@hotmail.co.uk
Est. 1993 **Stock size** Medium
Stock Indian furniture, reclaimed
antique pine, framed prints,
table lamps, clocks, accesories
Open Mon–Sat 10am–5pm
closed Wed
Fairs Ardingly, Newark,
Swinderby spring fair, NEC
Services After sales service,
export to France

BRIGHTON

⊞ Alexandria Antiques
Contact Mr A H Ahmed
✉ 3 Hanover Place, Brighton,
East Sussex,
BN2 2SD 🅿
☎ 01273 688793 ❶ 01273 688793
⓾ 07880 625558
✉ ahahmed52@yahoo.com
Est. 1978 **Stock size** Medium
Stock 18th–19thC furniture,
porcelain, bronzes, paintings,
decorative objects
Open Mon–Fri 9.30am–5.30pm
Sat Sun by appointment
Fairs Newark, Ardingly
Services Valuations, restoration

⊞ Ashton's Antiques
Contact Pearl or Bob Ashton
✉ 1 & 3 Clyde Road, Brighton,
East Sussex,
BN1 4NN 🅿
☎ 01273 605253 ❶ 01273 605253
⓾ 07775 736041
Est. 1970 **Stock size** Medium
Stock Antiques, collectables
Open Thurs–Sat 10am–4pm

⊞ Baba Bears
Contact Sheila Whittaker
✉ Brighton, East Sussex,
BN3 🅿
☎ 0845 257 6091
✉ baba.bears@virgin.net
🌐 www.bababears.co.uk
Est. 1988 **Stock size** Medium
Stock Antique teddy bears and
soft toys
Open By appointment
Fairs Hugglets winter Bearfest

⊞ Brighton Architectural Salvage
Contact Mr R L Legendre
✉ 33–34 Gloucester Road,
Brighton, East Sussex,
BN1 4AQ 🅿
☎ 01273 681656 ❶ 01273 681656
⓾ 07979 966245
Est. 1979 **Stock size** Large
Stock Restored architectural
antiques, fireplaces, reclaimed
flooring
Open Tues–Sat 10am–5pm
Services Fireplace installation

⊞ Brighton Books
Contact Paul Carmody
✉ 18 Kensington Gardens,
Brighton, East Sussex,
BN1 4AL

☎ 01273 693845 ❶ 01273 693845
Est. 1996 **Stock size** Large
Stock Rare, second-hand and
antiquarian books
Open Mon–Sat 10am–6pm
occasionally Sun noon–4pm
Services Valuations

⊞ Brighton Flea Market
Contact Mr A R Wilkinson
✉ 31a Upper St James's Street,
Brighton, East Sussex,
BN2 1JN
☎ 01273 624006 ❶ 01273 328665
⓾ 07884 267194
✉ arrw@btinternet.com
Est. 1988 **Stock size** Large
Stock Antiques, bric-a-brac,
collectables
Open Mon–Sat 10am–5.30pm
Sun Bank Holidays 10.30am–5pm

⊞ Brighton Lanes Antique Centre
Contact Peter Bryhon or
Alan Carden
✉ 12 Meeting House Lane,
Brighton, East Sussex,
BN1 1HB
☎ 01273 823121 ❶ 01273 726328
✉ antique-lighting@btinternet.com
🌐 brightonlanes-antiquescentre.co.uk
Est. 2001 **Stock size** Medium
Stock Jewellery, silver, furniture,
glass, lighting, porcelain
Open Mon–Sat 10am–5pm
Sun noon–4pm
Services Shipping, polishing,
rewiring lighting

⊞ Brighton Postcard Shop (PTA)
Contact Mr K Davies
✉ 38 Beaconsfield Road,
Brighton, East Sussex,
BN1 4QH 🅿
☎ 01273 600035 ❶ 01273 628660
✉ keith@brightonpostcardshop.co.uk
🌐 www.postcard.co.uk/flair
Est. 1987 **Stock size** Large
Stock Postcards, ephemera,
vintage glamour magazines
Open Tues–Sat 11am–4pm
Fairs Bloomsbury
Services Mail order

⊞ Tony Broadfoot Antiques (LAPADA)
Contact Tony Broadfoot
✉ 39 Upper Gardner Street,
Brighton, East Sussex,
BN1 4AN 🅿
☎ 01273 695457 ❶ 01273 620365

SOUTH EAST
EAST SUSSEX • BRIGHTON

07860 560325
Est. 1981 *Stock size* Large
Stock Commercial, shipping, general antiques, furniture
Trade only Yes
Open Mon–Fri 9am–5pm

C A R S (Classic Automobilia and Regalia Specialists)
Contact Mr G G Weiner
4–4a Chapel Terrace Mews, Kemp Town, Brighton, East Sussex, BN2 1HU
01273 622722 01273 622722
07890 836734
cars@kemptown-brighton.freeserve.co.uk
www.carsofbrighton.co.uk
Est. 1981 *Stock size* Medium
Stock Automobilia, collectors' car badges and mascots, hand-built collectors' and children's pedal cars
Open Mon–Sat 10am–6pm or by appointment
Fairs Classic car shows at NEC, Alexandra Palace
Services Valuations

Margaret Callaghan
Contact Margaret Callaghan
30a Upper St James's Street, Kemptown, Brighton, East Sussex, BN2 1JN
01273 681384
Est. 1983 *Stock size* Medium
Stock Textiles
Open Thurs–Sat 10.30am–5.30pm

Costume Jewellery
Contact Phillip Parfet
51 Upper North Street, Brighton, East Sussex, BN1 3FH
01273 202201 01273 202201
Est. 1985 *Stock size* Large
Stock Bakelite, costume jewellery
Open Wed–Sat 10am–5pm or by appointment
Fairs Alexandra Palace, Royal Horticultural Hall
Services Minor repairs

Decorative Arts
Contact Anthony White
27–28 Gloucester Road, Brighton, East Sussex, BN1 4AQ
01273 676486
07788 107101

info@decarts.net
www.decarts.net
Est. 1996 *Stock size* Medium
Stock Oak furniture 1880–1970, decorative arts, 1970s leather furniture
Open Mon–Sun 10am–5.30pm

Enhancements
Contact Lucille Robinson
1–1a Cavendish Street, Brighton, East Sussex, BN2 1RN
07778 233181 or 07919 453892
luerobinson@aol.com
Est. 1992 *Stock size* Medium
Stock Kitchenware, tools, beds, pine furniture, shabby chic furniture
Open Mon–Sat 10am–5.30pm
Services Free delivery

Hallmark Jewellers
Contact Mr J Hersheson
4 Union Street, The Lanes, Brighton, East Sussex, BN1 1HA
01273 725477 01273 725477
07885 298494
Est. 1959 *Stock size* Large
Stock Antique and modern silver, silver collectables, jewellery
Open Mon–Sat 9am–5pm
Sun 11am–4pm
Services Valuations

Dudley Hume (LAPADA)
Contact Mr D Hume
19 Abbey Road, Kemp Town, Brighton, East Sussex, BN2 1HS
01273 674283 01273 674283
07977 598627
dudley@dudleyhume.freeserve.co.uk
www.dudleyhumeantiques.co.uk
Est. 1973 *Stock size* Small
Stock 18th–19thC furniture, decorative items
Open By appointment only
Fairs Olympia, decorative fair Battersea

In My Room
Contact Oliver Learmonth
35 Gloucester Road, North Lane, Brighton, East Sussex, BN1 4AQ
01273 675506
www.inmyroom.co.uk
Est. 2003 *Stock size* Medium
Stock Furniture, decorative objects

Open Tues–Sat 10am–6pm
Sun 11am–4pm.
Services Lends furniture for photo shoots

The Lanes Armoury
Contact Mark or David Hawkins
26 Meeting House Lane, Brighton, East Sussex, BN1 1HB
01273 321357 01273 771125
enquiries@thelanesarmoury.co.uk
www.thelanesarmoury.co.uk
Est. 1992 *Stock size* Large
Stock Pre-Christian–WWII arms, armour, militaria and books
Open Mon–Sat 10am–5.15pm

Leoframes
Contact Stephen Round
70 North Road, Brighton, East Sussex, BN1 1YD
01273 695862
stephen@leoframes.com
Est. 1985 *Stock size* Medium
Stock Antique prints, maps
Open Mon–Sat 9am–5.30pm
Services Restoration, framing

Patrick Moorhead Antiques
Contact Mr P Moorhead
Spring Gardens, 76 Church Street, Brighton, East Sussex, BN1 1RL
01273 779696 01273 220196
info@patrickmoorhead.co.uk
Est. 1984 *Stock size* Large
Stock 18th–19thC furniture, European and Oriental ceramics, paintings, clocks
Open Mon–Fri 10am–5.30pm
Services Valuations, restoration

North Laine Antiques & Flea Market
Contact Mr A Fitchett
5a Upper Gardner Street, Brighton, East Sussex, BN1 4AN
01273 600894 01273 600894
07836 365411
market@fitchett.freeserve.co.uk
Est. 2002 *Stock size* Large
No. of dealers Approximately 70 including cabinets
Stock Wide range of antiques and collectables
Open Mon–Fri 10am–5.30pm
Sat 9am–5.30pm Sun 10am–4pm

SOUTH EAST
EAST SUSSEX • BRIGHTON

SOUTH EAST

⊞ Oasis
Contact Mr I Stevenson
✉ 39 Kensington Gardens,
Brighton, East Sussex,
BN1 4AL ▢
☎ 01273 683885
✉ anntmarch@yahoo.co.uk
Est. 1979 *Stock size* Medium
Stock Period lighting,
telephones, gramophones,
furniture, Art Deco, Art
Nouveau, watches, lighters,
glass, textiles, vintage clothing
Open Mon–Sat 10am–5.30pm

⊞ Odin Antiques
Contact Mr A Sjovold
✉ 43 Preston Street, Brighton,
East Sussex,
BN1 2HP ▢
☎ 01273 732738
Est. 1979 *Stock size* Medium
Stock Antique furniture,
maritime items, telescopes
Open Mon–Sat 10.30am–5.30pm

⊞ Colin Page Antiquarian Books (ABA)
Contact Mr J Loska
✉ 36 Duke Street, Brighton,
East Sussex,
BN1 1AG ▢
☎ 01273 325954
Est. 1969 *Stock size* Large
Stock Antiquarian and second-
hand books, antiquarian
literature, natural history, plate
books, bindings
Open Mon–Sat 9.30am–5.30pm
Fairs ABA, Olympia, Chelsea
Services Valuations

⊞ Dermot & Jill Palmer Antiques (LAPADA)
Contact Jill Palmer
✉ 7–8 Union Street, Brighton,
East Sussex,
BN1 1HA
☎ 01273 328669 ❶ 01273 777641
📱 07771 614331
✉ jillpalmer@maconlimited.net
Est. 1969 *Stock size* Large
Stock Mainly 19thC French and
English furniture
Open Mon–Sat 9.30am–5.30pm
or by appointment
Fairs Olympia, Decorative &
Textile Fair Battersea

⊞ Sue Pearson Antique Dolls & Teddy Bears
Contact Sue Pearson
✉ 18 Brighton Square, Brighton,
East Sussex,
BN1 1HD ▢
☎ 01273 329247 ❶ 01273 774851
✉ enquire@sue-pearson.co.uk
🌐 www.sue-pearson.co.uk
Est. 1981 *Stock size* Large
Stock Antique and modern
bears, soft toys, dolls
Open Mon–Sun 10am–5pm
Fairs Kensington Town Hall
Services Repair of dolls and bears

⊞ Rainbow Books
Contact Kevin Daly
✉ 28 Trafalgar Street, Brighton,
East Sussex,
BN1 4ED
☎ 01273 605101
Est. 1998 *Stock size* Large
Stock Antiquarian, second-hand
books
Open Mon–Sat 10.30am–6pm

⊞ Rin-Tin-Tin (ESoc)
Contact Mr Rick Irvine
✉ 34 North Road,
Brighton,
East Sussex,
BN1 1YB ▢
☎ 01273 672424 ❶ 01273 672424
✉ rick@rintintin.freeserve.co.uk
Est. 1982 *Stock size* Medium
Stock Old advertising,
promotional matter, magazines,
early glamour, games, toys,
plastics, 20thC fixtures and
fittings
Open Mon–Sat 11am–5.30pm
Fairs Alexandra Palace, Juke Box
Fairs
Services Framing

⌂ Snooper's Paradise
Contact Mr N Drinkwater
✉ 7–8 Kensington Gardens,
Brighton,
East Sussex,
BN1 4AL ▢
☎ 01273 602558 ❶ 01273 686611
✉ snoopersparadisebrighton@
btinternet.com
🌐 www.snoopersparadise.co.uk
Est. 1994 *Stock size* Large
No. of dealers 80
Stock China, pictures, 1970s
clothes and fabric, kitchenware,
ephemera, jewellery, watches,
records and CDs, phones and
electrical, Art Deco, glass, treen,
furniture, photographic, pens
and lighters, militaria etc
Open Mon–Sat 9.30am–5.30pm
Sun 11am–4pm

⤳ Southern Independent Auctions Ltd (NAVA)
Contact Daryl Taylor
✉ Regent House, The Hyde
Business Park, Lower Bevendean,
Brighton, East Sussex,
BN2 4JE ▢
☎ 01273 696545 ❶ 01273 624347
✉ info@sia-group.co.uk
🌐 www.sia-groupco.uk
Est. 2000
Open Mon–Fri 9am–5pm
Sales General antiques
Catalogues Yes

⊞ Step Back In Time (PTA)
Contact Robert Jeeves
✉ 125 Queens Road, Brighton,
East Sussex,
BN1 3WB
☎ 01273 731883 ❶ 01273 731883
Est. 1975 *Stock size* Large
Stock Postcards, prints,
ephemera
Open Mon–Sat 9am–6pm
Services Valuations

⊞ Studio Bookshop
Contact Mr P Brown
✉ 68 St James's Street, Brighton,
East Sussex,
BN2 1PJ ▢
☎ 01273 691253
✉ studiobookshop@btconnect.com
Est. 1995 *Stock size* Medium
Stock Reference books on glass,
art and antiques
Open Mon–Sat 10am–5.30pm
Fairs Glass fairs
Services Catalogue, telephone
orders

⊞ Trafalgar Bookshop
Contact David Boland
✉ 44 Trafalgar Street, Brighton,
East Sussex,
BN1 4ED
☎ 01273 684300
Est. 1979 *Stock size* Medium
Stock Antiquarian and second-
hand books
Open Mon–Sat 10am–5.30pm
Fri 11am–5.30pm

⊞ Valelink Ltd
Contact Mr J Trory
✉ 26 Queen's Road, Brighton,
East Sussex,
BN1 3XA ▢
☎ 01273 202906 ❶ 01273 202906
Est. 1970 *Stock size* Medium
Stock Collectables
Open Mon–Sat 10am–6pm

15

SOUTH EAST
EAST SUSSEX • BURWASH

⊞ Wardrobe
Contact Mr Clive Parks or
Philip Parfitt
✉ **51 Upper North Street,
Brighton, East Sussex,
BN1 3FH** 🅿
☎ 01273 202201 ✆ 01273 202201
📱 07802 483056
🌐 www.decoratif.co.uk
Est. 1986 **Stock size** Medium
Stock Vintage clothing and
accessories, textiles, jewellery, Art
Deco, Bakelite, collectable plastics
Open Wed–Sat 10am–5pm or by
appointment
Fairs Alexandra Palace,
Horticultural Hall

⊞ E & B White
Contact Elizabeth or Ben White
✉ **43 & 47 Upper North Street,
Brighton, East Sussex,
BN1 3FH**
☎ 01273 328706 ✆ 01273 207035
Est. 1965 **Stock size** Medium
Stock Antique and decorative
furniture
Open Mon–Fri 9.30am–5pm
Sat 9.30am–1pm

⊞ The Witch Ball
Contact Gina Daniels
✉ **48 Meeting House Lane,
Brighton, East Sussex,
BN1 1HB** 🅿
☎ 01273 326618
📱 07889 420524
📧 mg.daniels@btopenworld.com
Est. 1967 **Stock size** Large
Stock 1550–1850 prints and maps
Open Mon–Sat 10.30am–6pm
Sun by appointment
Services Lists on request

⊞ Tony Young Autographs
(UACC)
Contact Tony Young
✉ **138 Edward Street, Brighton,
East Sussex, BN2 0JL**
☎ 01273 732418
Est. 1984 **Stock size** Large
Stock Ephemera, autographs,
general antiques
Open Mon–Fri 10am–noon
2–5pm Sat 10am–12.15pm
Fairs Autographica
Services Valuations

BURWASH

⊞ Chateaubriand Antiques
Contact William Vincent
✉ **High Street, Burwash,**
**East Sussex,
TN19 7ES** 🅿
☎ 01435 882535
📧 info@chateaubriandantiques.co.uk
🌐 www.chateaubriandantiques.co.uk
Est. 1985 **Stock size** Medium
Stock Antique fine and country
furniture, maps, prints, pictures,
linen, lace, porcelain,
Staffordshire, oil lamps, silver,
rugs, carpets
Open Wed–Sat 10am–5pm
Sun noon–5pm
Services Valuations, shipping

CROWBOROUGH

⊞ Trowbridge Gallery
Contact Leslie Milne
✉ **Unit 16, Sybron Way,
Crowborough, East Sussex,
TN6 3DZ** 🅿
☎ 01892 667600 ✆ 01892 667007
🌐 www.trowbridgegallery.com
Stock size Large
Stock Antique framed prints
Open Mon–Fri 8.30am–6pm
Fairs NEC

⊞ Trudi's Treasures
Contact Trudi Blackman
✉ **The Old Post Office,
Crowborough Hill, Jarvis Brook,
Crowborough, East Sussex,
TN6 2EG** 🅿
☎ 01892 667671
📧 trudistreasures@hotmail.com
🌐 www.trudistreasures.co.uk
Est. 2001 **Stock size** Large
Stock Collectables, curios, pine,
painted furniture, china,
kitchenware
Open Mon–Sat 10am–5pm
Services Furniture painting

EASTBOURNE

⊞ 35 The Goffs
Contact Mrs Y Cole
✉ **35 The Goffs, Eastbourne,
East Sussex,
BN21 1HF** 🅿
☎ 01323 737272
Est. 2000 **Stock size** Medium
Stock Decorative antiques,
furniture, chandeliers
Open Tues–Fri 1.30–4.30 pm
Sat 10.30am–4.30pm

⊞ W. Bruford
Contact John Burgess
✉ **11–13 Cornfield Road,
Eastbourne, East Sussex,**
BN21 3NA 🅿
☎ 01323 725452 ✆ 01323 417873
Est. 1885 **Stock size** Small
Stock Jewellery, silver
Open Mon–Sat 9.30am–5pm
Services Valuations, restoråtion

⊞ Camilla's Bookshop
Contact Ms C Francombe or
Mr S Broad
✉ **57 Grove Road, Eastbourne,
East Sussex,
BN21 4TX** 🅿
☎ 01323 736001
📧 camillas@fsnet.co.uk
Est. 1975 **Stock size** Large
Stock Antiquarian and second-
hand books, postcards,
ephemera, children's books,
needlework, military, aviation
and nautical topics
Open Mon–Sat 10am–5.30pm
Services Valuations, book search

⊞ Collectors Dream
Contact Terence Kearns
✉ **38 Seaside, Eastbourne,
East Sussex,
BN22 7QJ** 🅿
☎ 01323 727147
📧 info@finechina4u.co.uk
🌐 www.finechina4u.co.uk
Est. 1986 **Stock size** Medium
Stock Collectables, Royal
Doulton, vintage clockwork tin
toys
Open Mon–Sat 9.30am–5.30pm
Services Valuations

⊞ John Cowderoy
Antiques Ltd (LAPADA)
Contact Mr Richard Cowderoy
✉ **42 South Street, Eastbourne,
East Sussex,
BN21 4XB** 🅿
☎ 01323 720058 ✆ 01323 410163
📱 07971 971387
📧 david@cowderoyantiques.co.uk
🌐 www.cowderoyantiques.co.uk
Est. 1973 **Stock size** Large
Stock General antiques,
collectables, clocks, musical
boxes
Open Mon–Sat 8.30am–5pm
closed Wed pm
Services Restoration of musical
boxes , clocks and barometers

⊞ Crest Collectables
Contact Mr C Powell
✉ **54 Grove Road, Eastbourne,
East Sussex,
BN21 4UD** 🅿

☎ 01323 721185
ⓦ www.teddy-collectables.co.uk
Est. 1986 *Stock size* Medium
Stock Teddy bears, dolls, soft
toys, collectables
Open Mon–Sat 10.30am–4pm
closed Wed

⊞ Crown Antiques
Contact Mark Simmons
✉ 1 Crown Street, Eastbourne,
East Sussex,
BN21 1NX ℗
☎ 01323 412985
ⓔ mark@crownantiques.fsnet.co.uk
Est. 1984 *Stock size* Medium
Stock Victorian–Edwardian
furniture
Open Tues Thur Fri Sat
10am–5.30pm
Services Valuations, restoration

⤳ Dreweatt Neate Eastbourne Salerooms (SOFAA)
Contact Jeremy Palmer
✉ 46–50 South Street,
Eastbourne, East Sussex,
BN21 4XB ℗
☎ 01323 410419 ℗ 01323 416540
ⓔ eastbourne@dnfa.com
ⓦ www.dnfa.com
Est. 1759
Open Mon–Fri 9am–5pm
Sales Fortnightly gallery sales of
general antiques, Thurs 10am,
viewing Wed 9am–8pm Thurs
9–10am, monthly specialist sections
of affordable pictures, decorative,
arts and collector's items
Frequency Fortnightly
Catalogues Yes

⌂ Eastbourne Antiques Market
Contact Irina Photiou
✉ 80 Seaside, Eastbourne,
East Sussex,
BN22 7QP ℗
☎ 01323 642233
Est. 1969 *Stock size* Large
No. of dealers 30
Stock Antiques, collectables
Open Mon–Fri 10am–5.30pm
Sat 10am–5pm

⤳ Eastbourne Auction Rooms
Contact Jeanette May
✉ Auction House, Finmere Road,
Eastbourne, East Sussex,
BN22 8QL ℗
☎ 01323 431444 ℗ 01323 417638

ⓔ enquiries@eastbourneauction.com
ⓦ www.eastbourneauction.com
Est. 1994
Open Mon–Fri 9am–5pm
Sales General antiques fortnightly
Sat 10am, viewing Fri 9am–7pm,
antiques and collectables every
six weeks Fri 10am, viewing
Wed,Thurs 9am–7pm
Catalogues Yes

⊞ Eastbourne Fine Art
Contact Mr Day
✉ 9 Meads Street, Eastbourne,
East Sussex,
BN20 7QY ℗
☎ 01323 725643
Est. 1964 *Stock size* Medium
Stock Primarily 19th–20thC
English continental paintings
and watercolours
Open By appointment
Services Valuations, restoration

⊞ Eastbourne Pine
Contact Mark Simmons
✉ 1 Crown Street, Eastbourne,
East Sussex,
BN21 1NX ℗
☎ 01323 412985
ⓔ mark@crownantiques.fsnet.co.uk
Est. 1984 *Stock size* Medium
Stock Antique pine
Open Tues Thur Fri Sat
10am–5.30pm
Services Valuations, restoration

⌂ The Enterprise Collectors Market
Contact Muriel Hide
✉ Enterprise Centre Car Park,
Station Parade, Eastbourne,
East Sussex,
BN21 1BD ℗
☎ 01323 732690
Est. 1990 *Stock size* Medium
No. of dealers 12
Stock General antiques,
collectables
Open Mon–Sat 9.30am–5pm

⊞ François (Postcard Society)
Contact François Celada
✉ 26 South Street, Eastbourne,
East Sussex,
BN21 4XB ℗
☎ 01323 644464 ℗ 01323 644464
Est. 1983 *Stock size* Medium
Stock Postcards, stamps, coins,
militaria, cigarette cards
Open Tues and Sat 10am–5pm
Services Valuations

⊞ Charles French
Contact Mr C McCleave
✉ 2 Kings Drive, Eastbourne,
East Sussex,
BN21 2NU ℗
☎ 01323 720128
Est. 1969 *Stock size* Medium
Stock General antiques
Open Mon–Fri 10am–5.30pm
Fairs Ardingly
Services House clearance

⊞ A & T Gibbard (PBFA)
Contact Mrs M T Gibbard or
Mr A Gibbard
✉ 30 South Street, Eastbourne,
East Sussex,
BN21 4XB ℗
☎ 01323 734128 ℗ 01323 734128
Est. 1910 *Stock size* Large
Stock Antiquarian and second-
hand books, specializing in
natural history, travel, topography,
leather-bound books
Open Mon–Sat 9.30am–5.30pm
Fairs Russell Hotel

⊞ More Than Music
Contact Mike Vandenbosch
✉ PO Box 2809, Eastbourne,
East Sussex,
BN21 2EA
☎ 01323 649778 ℗ 01323 649779
ⓔ morethnmus@aol.com
ⓦ www.mtmglobal.com
Est. 1995 *Stock size* Medium
Stock Vinyl, autographs, books,
magazines, posters etc
Open Mon–Fri 10am–5.30pm
Sat 10am–1pm
Services Worldwide mail order
service

⌂ The Old Town Antiques Centre
Contact Saff Baker
✉ 52 Ocklynge Road,
Eastbourne, East Sussex,
BN21 1PR ℗
☎ 01323 416016
ⓦ 07967 102325
Est. 1989 *Stock size* Large
No. of dealers 16
Stock Mixed antiques, furniture,
fine porcelain, glass, silver,
Beswick, Copenhagen figures etc
Open Mon–Sat 10am–5pm
Services Valuations, restoration

⊞ Timothy Partridge Antiques
✉ 46 Ocklynge Road,
Eastbourne, East Sussex,

BN21 1PP
☎ 01323 638731
Ⓜ 07860 864709
Est. 1982 *Stock size* Medium
Stock General pre-war goods, furniture, smalls
Open Mon–Fri 10am–5pm

🏠 **Seaquel Antiques & Collectors Market**
Contact Mrs P Mornington-West
✉ 37 Seaside Road, Eastbourne, East Sussex,
BN21 3PP 🅿
☎ 01323 645032
Est. 1998 *Stock size* Large
No. of dealers 16
Stock Furniture, collectables, bric-a-brac
Open Mon–Sat 10am–5pm
Sun 11am–4.30pm

⊞ **Shine's Antiques and Collectables**
Contact Brian Shine
✉ 8 Crown Street, Eastbourne, East Sussex,
BN21 1NX 🅿
☎ 01323 726261
Ⓔ brian.shine@ssmail.net
Est. 1999 *Stock size* Large
Stock Antiques, collectables
Open Mon–Sat 10am–5pm, flexible

🏠 **South Coast Collectables**
Contact Sylvia Redford
✉ 85 Seaside Road, Eastbourne, East Sussex,
BN21 3PL 🅿
☎ 01323 648811
Est. 1997 *Stock size* Large
No. of dealers 18
Stock Antiques, collectables, Georgian–Edwardian furniture
Open Tues–Sat 10am–5pm

⊞ **Tony's Antique Services Ltd**
Contact Tony King
✉ 85 Seaside Road, Eastbourne, East Sussex,
BN21 3PL
☎ 01323 733776 Ⓕ 01323 733776
Ⓜ 07752 201786
Est. 1977 *Stock size* Large
Stock Antique furniture
Open Tues–Sat 10am–5pm
Sun Mon by appointment
Services Restoration, export, search service

⊞ **World of Sport**
Contact Joanna Archibald
✉ Enterprise Shopping Centre, Station Parade, Eastbourne, East Sussex,
BN21 1BD 🅿
☎ 01323 411849
Est. 2002 *Stock size* Medium
Stock Sport and film memorabilia, historical prints
Open Mon–Sat 9.30am–4.30pm

🏠 **The Dandelion Clock**
Contact Mrs L Chapman
✉ Lewes Road, Forest Row, East Sussex,
RH18 5ES 🅿
☎ 01342 822335
Ⓔ centre@dandelion-clock.co.uk
Ⓦ www.dandelion-clock.co.uk
Est. 1994 *Stock size* Large
No. of dealers 12
Stock Pine and country furniture, antiques, collectables
Open Mon–Sat 10am–5pm
Services Local delivery available

⊞ **Pavilion**
Contact John Taylor
✉ Country House, Lewes Road, Forest Row, East Sussex,
RH18 5AN 🅿
☎ 01342 822199
Est. 1997 *Stock size* Medium
Stock Painted furniture, decorative antiques, gifts
Open Tues–Sat 10am–5.30pm

GOLDEN CROSS

⊞ **Golden Cross Antiques**
Contact Mrs R R Buchan
✉ A22, Golden Cross, Hailsham, East Sussex,
BN27 4AN 🅿
☎ 01825 872144 Ⓕ 01825 873408
Ⓜ 07957 224165
Ⓔ antiques@goldencross. fsbusiness.co.uk
Est. 1974 *Stock size* Medium
Stock Copper, brass, pewter, silver, furniture, collectables
Open Mon–Sat 9.30am–6pm
Sun 10am–6pm

GUESTLING

⊞ **Hearth & Home**
Contact Mr D Hance
✉ Rye Road, Guestling Green, Hastings, East Sussex,

TN35 4LS 🅿
☎ 01424 813220 Ⓕ 01424 813220
Ⓦ www.hearthandhomehastings.co.uk
Est. 1984 *Stock size* Medium
Stock Original Victorian and cast-iron fireplaces
Open Mon–Sat 9am–1pm 2–5pm
Services Advice, installation

HADLOW DOWN

⊞ **Hadlow Down Antiques**
Contact Mr Adrian Butler
✉ Hastingford Farm, Hastingford Lane, Hadlow Down, Uckfield, East Sussex,
TN22 4DY 🅿
☎ 01825 830707
Ⓜ 07951 817615
Ⓔ verandah@tesco.net
Est. 1989 *Stock size* Large
Stock Antiques, decorative furniture, accessories
Open Thurs–Sat 10am–5pm or by appointment
Services Valuations, restoration, custom-made oak furniture

HAILSHAM

⊞ **Football in Focus (2001) Ltd**
Contact Phil Cole
✉ Focus House, 12 Swan Farm Business Centre, Station Road, Hailsham, East Sussex,
BN27 2BY 🅿
☎ 01323 440800 Ⓕ 01323 445138
Ⓔ info@footballinfocus.co.uk
Ⓦ www.footballinfocus.co.uk
Est. 1998 *Stock size* Large
Stock Sporting memorabilia, film music
Open Mon–Fri 9am–5pm

⊞ **Original Old Pine Furniture**
Contact Mrs A Thompson
✉ Popes Farm House, Windmill Hill, Herstmonceux, Hailsham, East Sussex,
BN27 4RS 🅿
☎ 01323 832159
Est. 1970 *Stock size* Medium
Stock Victorian pine furniture
Open Mon–Fri 8.30am–5.30pm
Sat 8.30am–4pm
Services Valuations, restoration, pine stripping

⊞ **Stable Doors**
Contact Mr K Skinner or Mr B Skinner

✉ Market Street, Hailsham,
East Sussex,
BN27 2AE 🅿
☎ 01323 844033
✉ kevin@stabledoors.org.uk
🌐 www.stabledoors.org.uk
Est. 1996 *Stock size* Large
Stock Antiques, collectables
Open Mon–Sat 9am–5pm
Fairs Ardingly

⊞ Wealth of Weights (Cambridge Paperweight Circle)
Contact Mrs J Skinner or
Mr K Skinner
✉ Stable Doors, Market Street,
Hailsham, East Sussex,
BN27 2AE 🅿
☎ 01323 441150
✉ jaqui@weights.co.uk
🌐 www.weights.co.uk
Est. 1997 *Stock size* Large
Stock Largest selection of
paperweights in South England.
Registered PCA World Dealer
Open Mon–Sun 9am–5pm
Fairs Effingham Park, Copthorne,
Woking Glass Fair
Services Valuations, collections
bought

HASTINGS

⊞ Antiques
Contact Mrs H Philmore
✉ 7 George Street, Hastings,
East Sussex,
TN34 3EG
☎ 01424 445264
Est. 1985 *Stock size* Small
Stock Jewellery, Victorian to
modern
Open Mon–Sat 10am–5pm or by
appointment
Services Repair service

⊞ Coach House Antiques
Contact Mr R J Luck
✉ 42 George Street, Hastings,
East Sussex, TN34 3EA 🅿
☎ 01424 461849
📱 07710 234803
Est. 1979 *Stock size* Large
Stock Longcase clocks, Victorian
furniture, Dinky toys, Beswick
china
Open Mon–Sun 10am–5pm
Services Valuations, restoration

⌂ George Street Antiques Centre
Contact Mrs F McKay

✉ 47 George Street, Hastings,
East Sussex,
TN34 3EA 🅿
☎ 01424 429339
Est. 1984 *Stock size* Large
No. of dealers 8
Stock Collectables, antique
jewellery
Open Mon–Fri 11am–4pm
Sat 11am–4pm Sun 11am–4pm

⌂ High Street Retro Centre
Contact Jane Wilson-Smith
✉ 39 High Street, Hastings,
East Sussex,
TN34 3ER
☎ 01424 460068
Est. 1996 *Stock size* Large
No. of dealers 6
Stock Glass, furniture, antique
textiles, jewellery, lighting
Open Mon Tues Thurs Fri
10.30am–5pm Sat 10.30am–6pm
Sun noon–5.30pm
Services Valuations, restoration

⊞ Howes Bookshop Ltd (ABA, PBFA)
Contact Mr M Bartley
✉ Trinity Hall, Braybrooke
Terrace, Hastings, East Sussex,
TN34 1HQ 🅿
☎ 01424 423437 ☎ 01424 460620
✉ rarebooks@howes.co.uk
🌐 www.howes.co.uk
Est. 1946 *Stock size* Large
Stock Antiquarian and second-
hand books, arts and humanities
a speciality
Open Mon–Fri 9.30am–5pm
Fairs Olympia, Chelsea, Russell
Hotel
Services Valuations

⊞ Mollycoddles Collectables
Contact Gary Baker
✉ 24 George Street, Hastings,
East Sussex,
TN34 3EB 🅿
☎ 01424 433277
Est. 1995 *Stock size* Medium
Stock Collectables, pine
furniture, textiles, jewellery
Open Mon–Sun 10am–5pm

⊞ Nakota Antiques
Contact Mr Robert Mucci
✉ 12 Court House Street,
Hastings, East Sussex,
TN34 3AU 🅿
☎ 01424 438900
Est. 1969 *Stock size* Large

Stock General antiques, some
inexpensive non-European art
Open Mon–Sat 10.30am–1pm
2pm–4.30pm

⊞ Reeves & Son
Contact Mr C Hawkins
✉ 4–6 Courthouse Street,
Hastings, East Sussex,
TN34 3AU 🅿
☎ 01424 437672
📱 07778 311803
Est. 1818 *Stock size* Large
Stock Military collectables, china,
smalls, books
Open Mon–Sat 9am–5pm

⊞ Robert's Rumble
Contact Mr Robert Mucci
✉ 68 High Street, Hastings,
East Sussex,
TN34 3EW
☎ 01424 445340
Est. 1990 *Stock size* Medium
Stock Old-fashioned junk shop,
books, general collectables
Open Mon–Sun 11am–6pm
Services Identification of non-
European Art

⌂ Twinkled
Contact Luke Browne or Kevin
O'Doherty
✉ High Street Antiques Centre,
39 High Street, Hastings,
East Sussex,
TN34 3ER 🅿
☎ 01424 460068 or 020 7734 1978
📱 07940 471569
✉ info@twinkled.net or
limehouseblue47@aol.com
🌐 www.twinkled.net
Est. 1996 *Stock size* Large
No. of dealers 3
Stock Furniture, homeware,
textiles and vintage clothing
1950s–1980s
Open Mon–Wed Sat 11m–7pm
Thurs–Fri 11am–8pm Sun
noon–5pm
Services Propping, styling,
customized service for Japanese
dealers

HEATHFIELD

⊞ Botting & Berry
Contact John Botting or
David Berry
✉ 31 High Street, Heathfield,
East Sussex,
TN21 8HU
☎ 01435 813553

Est. 1990 *Stock size* Medium
Stock Victorian–Edwardian
furniture, effects, antiquarian,
second-hand books
Open Mon–Sat 10am–5pm

⌂ The Pig Sty
Contact Mrs Worton
⊠ 49 High Street, Heathfield,
East Sussex,
TN21 8HU ℗
☎ 01435 866671
Est. 1997 *Stock size* Medium
No. of dealers 10
Stock General antiques and
collectables
Open Mon–Sat 9am–4.30pm
Services Coffee shop

⊞ Graham Price Antiques Ltd
Contact Graham Price
⊠ Satinstown Farm, Burwash
Road, Broad Oak, Heathfield,
East Sussex,
TN21 8RT ℗
☎ 01892 523341 ☏ 01892 530382
⊕ 07768 330842
⊜ mail@upcountryantiques.co.uk
⊛ www.upcountryantiques.co.uk
Est. 1984 *Stock size* Large
Stock Decorative and antique
country furniture, rural artefacts
Open Mon–Fri 9am–5pm
Fairs Newark, Ardingly
Services Packing, shipping,
courier service

⌂ Toad Hall Antique Centre
Contact Patsy Quick
⊠ 57 High Street, Heathfield,
East Sussex,
TN21 8HU ℗
☎ 01435 863535
Est. 1996 *Stock size* Large
No. of dealers 16
Stock Furniture, general
antiques, collectables, fireplaces,
garden furniture
Open Mon–Sat 9am–5.30pm
Sun 11am–4pm
Services Referral to restorers and
valuers

HOVE

⋏ Bonhams
⊠ 19 Palmeira Square, Hove,
East Sussex,
BN3 2JN ℗
☎ 01273 220000 ☏ 01273 220335
⊜ hove@bonhams.com
⊛ www.bonhams.com

Est. 1793
Open Mon–Fri 9am–1pm 2–5pm
Sales Regional office. Regular
sales in London, New York, San
Francisco, Sydney, Geneva and
Los Angeles, as well as in
regional sales rooms across the
UK. Free auction valuations;
insurance and probate valuations

⊞ Simon Hunter Antique Maps (IMCOS)
Contact Mr Simon Hunter
⊠ 21 St Johns Road, Hove,
East Sussex,
BN3 2FB ℗
☎ 01273 746983 ☏ 01273 746983
⊜ simonhunter@fastnet.co.uk
⊛ www.antiquemaps.org.uk
Est. 1989 *Stock size* Large
Stock Antique maps
Open By appointment
Fairs London Map Fairs

⋏ Raymond P Inman
Contact Robert Inman
⊠ 98a Coleridge Street, Hove,
East Sussex,
BN3 5AA ℗
☎ 01273 774777 ☏ 01273 735660
⊜ r.p.inman@talk21.com
Est. 1929
Open Mon–Fri 9am–5pm
Sales General antiques sales
Frequency 10 a year
Catalogues Yes

⊞ Michael Norman Antiques (BADA)
Contact Michael Keehan
⊠ 61 Holland Road, Hove,
East Sussex,
BN3 1JN ℗
☎ 01273 329253/326712
☏ 01273 206556
⊜ antiques@michaelnorman.com
⊛ www.michaelnorman.com
Est. 1964 *Stock size* Large
Stock 18th–19thC English
furniture
Open Mon–Sat 9am–5.30pm
closed 1–2pm

⊞ Michael Norman Antiques (BADA)
Contact John Branch or
Armando Fava
⊠ 61 Holland Road, Hove,
East Sussex,
BN3 1JB ℗
☎ 01273 329253 ☏ 01273 206556
⊜ antiques@michaelnorman.com
⊛ www.michaelnorman.com

Est. 1965 *Stock size* Large
Stock Georgian and Regency
period furniture
Open Mon–Sat 9am–1pm 2–5pm
or by appointment
Services Restoration

⋏ Scarborough Perry Fine Arts
Contact Mr Andrew Scarborough
⊠ Hove Auction Rooms, Hove
Street, Hove, East Sussex,
BN3 2GL ℗
☎ 01273 735266 ☏ 01273 723813
⊜ enquiries@scarboroughperry.co.uk
⊛ www.scarboroughperry.co.uk
Est. 1897
Open Mon–Fri 9am–5pm
Sat 9am–noon
Sales General antique sales
Thurs–Fri 10.30am, viewing
Tues–Wed 10am–4.30pm Tues
6–8pm. Occasional special sales
Frequency 7 weeks
Catalogues Yes

⊞ Valentina Antique Beds
Contact Mrs Flechas
⊠ 212 Church Road, Hove,
East Sussex,
BN3 2DJ ℗
☎ 01273 735035
⊜ info@antiquebeds.com
⊛ www.antiquebeds.com
Est. 1992 *Stock size* Large
Stock French, Victorian brass and
iron bedsteads
Open Mon–Sat 10am–5pm

⊞ Yellow Lantern Antiques (LAPADA)
Contact B Higgins
⊠ 34 Holland Road, Hove,
East Sussex,
BN3 1JL ℗
☎ 01273 771572 ☏ 01273 455476
⊕ 07860 342976
Est. 1950 *Stock size* Medium
Stock Period English town
furniture pre-1840, ormolu and
bronzes
Open Mon–Fri 10am–5.30pm
Sat 10am–4pm
Fairs Olympia, Buxton
Services Valuations, restoration

HURST GREEN

⊞ Foxhole Antiques
Contact James Rourke
⊠ 79 London Road, Hurst Green,
East Sussex,
TN19 7PN ℗

☎ 01580 860317
ⓦ www.foxholeantiques.com
Est. 2003 *Stock size* Large
Stock English and French period furnishings for house and garden
Open Wed–Sat 9.30am–5.30pm

LEWES

⊞ Basically Bears
Contact Stan Lawrence
✉ 170a High Street, Lewes, East Sussex, BN7 1YB
☎ 01273 478847 ❶ 01273 478847
ⓦ www.basically-bears.com
Est. 2000 *Stock size* Medium
Stock Collectable bears
Open Thurs–Sat 9.30am–5pm

⊞ Bow Windows Bookshop (ABA, PBFA, ILAB)
Contact Alan or Jennifer Shelley
✉ 175 High Street, Lewes, East Sussex, BN7 1YE
☎ 01273 480780 ❶ 01273 486686
❸ rarebooks@bowwindows.com
ⓦ www.bowwindows.com
Est. 1964 *Stock size* Medium
Stock General antiquarian books, all subjects
Open Mon–Sat 9.30am–5pm
Fairs Russell Hotel, International Book Fairs London
Services Valuations, 3 or 4 catalogues per year

⊞ W.F. Bruce Antique Clocks
Contact W.F. Bruce
✉ 5 North Street, Lewes, East Sussex, BN7 2PA
☎ 01273 473123
❸ lewesclocks@btopenworld.com
ⓦ www.lewesclocks.com
Est. 1985 *Stock size* Medium
Stock Restored antique clocks
Open Mon–Sat 10am–4pm
Services Valuations, restoration, shipping

⌂ Church Hill Antique Centre Ltd
Contact Simon Ramm
✉ 6 Station Street, Lewes, East Sussex, BN7 2DA
☎ 01273 474842
❸ churchhilllewes@aol.com
ⓦ www.church-hill-antiques.com
Est. 1996 *Stock size* Large

No. of dealers 60
Stock Antiques and interiors
Open Mon–Sat 9.30am–5pm or by appointment
Services Valuations

⌂ Cliffe Antiques Centre
Contact The Manager
✉ 47 Cliffe High Street, Lewes, East Sussex, BN7 2AN
☎ 01273 473266 ❶ 01273 473266
Est. 1981 *Stock size* Medium
No. of dealers 15
Stock Wide range of antiques, collectables
Open Mon–Sat 9.30am–5pm

⊞ A & Y Cumming Ltd (ABA, PBFA)
Contact Andrew Cumming
✉ 84 High Street, Lewes, East Sussex, BN7 1XN
☎ 01273 472319 ❶ 01273 486364
❸ a.y.cumming@ukgateway.net
Est. 1976 *Stock size* Large
Stock Antiquarian and second-hand books on travel, natural history, colour plate books, first editions, leather bound
Open Mon–Fri 10am–5pm Sat 10am–5.30pm
Fairs Olympia (June), Chelsea Book Fair
Services Valuations

⌂ The Emporium Antiques Centre
Contact Michelle Doyle or Steven Madigan
✉ 42 Cliffe High Street, Lewes, East Sussex, BN7 2AN
☎ 01273 486866
Est. 1993 *Stock size* Large
No. of dealers 60
Stock General antiques, collectables, studio ceramics, toys, textiles, silver, jewellery, books, clocks, vintage clothes
Open Mon–Fri 10am–5pm Sat 9.30am–5.30pm Sun noon–4pm

⌂ The Emporium Antiques Centre Too
Contact Edmund Conway
✉ 24 High Street, Lewes, East Sussex, BN7 2LU
☎ 01273 477979
Est. 1989 *Stock size* Large
No. of dealers 100

Stock Antiques, collectables, furniture
Open Mon–Sat 9.30am–5pm Sun noon–5pm

⊞ The Fifteenth Century Bookshop (PBFA)
Contact Mrs Miraband
✉ 99–100 High Street, Lewes, East Sussex, BN7 1XH
☎ 01273 474160
Ⓜ 07751 487642
ⓦ www.15centurybookshop.co.uk
Est. 1930 *Stock size* Medium
Stock General stock, collectable children's books
Open Mon–Sat 10am–5.30pm Sun 10.30am–4pm
Services Book search for children's books, postal service

⚒ Gorringes Incorporating Julian Dawson (SOFAA, ISVA)
Contact Mr Julian Dawson
✉ Garden Street, Lewes, East Sussex, BN7 1TJ
☎ 01273 478221 ❶ 01273 487369
❸ auctions@gorringes.co.uk
ⓦ www.gorringes.co.uk
Est. 1920
Open Mon–Fri 9am–5.30pm Sat 9am–12.30pm
Sales Sales of general antiques and collectables Mon (not Bank Holidays) 10am, viewing Fri 10am–5pm Sat 9am–12.30pm
Frequency Weekly
Catalogues No

⚒ Gorringes Incorporating Julian Dawson (SOFAA, ISVA, BACA Award Winner 2002)
Contact Mr P Taylor
✉ 15 North Street, Lewes, East Sussex, BN7 2PD
☎ 01273 472503 ❶ 01273 479559
❸ auctions@gorringes.co.uk
ⓦ www.gorringes.co.uk
Est. 1926
Open Mon–Fri 8.30am–5.15pm Sat 9am–11.45am
Sales Fine art and antiques 3-day sale Tues–Thurs at 10am, viewing Fri 10am–5pm Sat 9.30am–4pm prior. Occasional house sales
Frequency 6 weeks
Catalogues Yes

⌂ Lewes Antique Centre
✉ 20 Cliffe High Street, Lewes,
East Sussex,
BN7 2AH ℗
☎ 01273 476148
Est. 1968 *Stock size* Large
No. of dealers 100
Stock Furniture, architectural
salvage, bric-a-brac, china, clocks,
metalware, glass, collectables.
Open Mon–Sat 9.30am–5pm
Sun Bank Holidays 12.30–4.30pm
Services Storage, delivery, pine
stripping, restoration, valuations

⊞ Lewes Book Centre
Contact John Tarry
✉ 38 Cliffe Street, Lewes,
East Sussex,
BN7 2AN ℗
☎ 01273 487053
✉ sales@lewesbookcentre.plus.com
Est. 1993 *Stock size* Medium
Stock History and military books
Open Mon–Fri 9am–4pm Sat
9am–5pm half day Wed
Fairs Military fairs, Farnham

⊞ Lewes Flea Market
Contact Mr A R Wilkinson
✉ 14a Market Street, Lewes,
East Sussex,
BN7 2NB ℗
☎ 01273 480328 ⊕ 01273 328665
⊗ 07884 267194
✉ arrw@btinternet.com
Est. 1993 *Stock size* Large
Stock Antiques, collectables, bric-
a-brac
Open Mon–Fri 10am–5pm
Sat Sun 10.30am–5pm

⊞ Pastorale Antiques
Contact Mr Soucek
✉ 15 Malling Street, Lewes,
East Sussex,
BN7 2RA
☎ 01273 473259 ⊕ 01273 473259
Est. 1980 *Stock size* Large
Stock English, French, East
European and pine furniture,
garden furniture and ornaments
Open Mon–Sat 10am–5pm
Services Restoration

⊞ Punzi
Contact Margherita Hale
✉ 27 Station Street, Lewes,
East Sussex,
BN7 2BB ℗
☎ 01273 475476
⊛ www.margheritahale.co.uk
Est. 2004 *Stock size* Large

Stock Semi-precious gemstone
jewellery, modern and
Impressionist paintings
Open Tues–Sat 10.30am–5pm
Services Bespoke jewellery

⊞ Star Gallery
Contact Hayley Brown
✉ Castle Ditch Lane,
Lewes,
East Sussex,
BN7 1YJ
☎ 01273 480218 ⊕ 01273 488241
✉ info@stargallery.co.uk
⊛ www.stargallery.co.uk
Est. 1989 *Stock size* Small
Stock Art exhibitions, Julian Opie
artworks, David Gerstein
sculpture
Open Mon–Sat 11am–5.30pm
Fairs Affordable Art Fairs,
London Art Fair, Brighton Art fair
Services Studio and workshops
to rent

⊞ Star Gallery 2
Contact Sarah O'Kane
✉ Southover Grange,
Southover Road,
Lewes,
East Sussex,
BN7 1TP ℗
☎ 01273 479565 ⊕ 01273 488241
✉ info@stargallery.co.uk
⊛ www.stargallery.co.uk
Est. 2005 *Stock size* Medium
Stock Contemporary art
Open Tues–Sat 10am–5pm
Fairs Affordable art fair,
Manchester art show
Services Studios to rent

⊞ Trade Antiques Centre
Contact Amanda Tollhurst
✉ 207 High Street, Lewes,
East Sussex,
BN7 2NS ℗
☎ 01273 486688
⊗ 07801 413783
Est. 2001 *Stock size* Large
Stock Pine, oak, mahogany
furniture, enamel ware, pictures,
jewellery, china and porcelain
Open Mon–Sat 10am–5.30pm
Sun noon–5pm

⊞ The Treasury
Contact Pamela Marshall
✉ 89 High Street, Lewes,
East Sussex,
BN7 1XN ℗
☎ 01273 480446 ⊕ 01273 838785
Est. 1986 *Stock size* Medium

Stock Collectables, small
antiques, out-of-production
figurines
Open Thurs Fri 10am–5pm

⋔ Wallis & Wallis
Contact Mr Roy Butler (militaria)
or Mr Glenn Butler (toys)
✉ West Street Auction Galleries,
Lewes, East Sussex,
BN7 2NJ ℗
☎ 01273 480208 ⊕ 01273 476562
✉ auctions@wallisandwallis.co.uk
(militaria) or
grb@wallisandwallis.co.uk (toys)
⊛ www.wallisandwallis.co.uk
Est. 1928
Open Mon–Fri 9am–5.30pm
closed 1–2pm
Sales 9 militaria, medals, coins,
arms and armour per annum
Tues 11am, 2 connoisseur arms
and armour per annum Tues Wed
11am, 8 die-cast and tinplate
toys per annum Mon 10.30am,
viewing prior Fri 9am–5pm
Sat 9am–1pm morning of sale
9am–10.30pm. Sales dates
available on request
Frequency 6 weeks
Catalogues Yes (2 to 3 weeks
before sales)

LITTLE HORSTEAD

⊞ Pianos Galore
Contact Jason Richards
✉ Little Horstead,
East Sussex,
TN22 5TT ℗
☎ 01825 750567 ⊕ 01825 750566
✉ info@pianosgalore.co.uk
⊛ www.pianosgalore.co.uk
Est. 1982 *Stock size* Large
Stock Pianos
Open Mon–Sat 9am–5pm
Sun 10am–noon

NEWHAVEN

⊞ Marion Bowen Vintage Clothes
Contact Marion Bowen
✉ 28 Manor Road,
Newhaven,
East Sussex,
BN9 0LS ℗
☎ 01273 512604
Est. 1986 *Stock size* Small
Stock Victorian–1950s vintage
clothes and accessories
Open By appointment
Fairs Kempton Park

🏠 **Newhaven Flea Market**
Contact Mr A R Wilkinson
✉ 28 Southway,
Newhaven,
East Sussex,
BN9 9LA 🅿
☎ 01273 517207/513435
📠 07884 267194
📧 arrw@btinternet.com
Est. 1979 *Stock size* Large
No. of dealers 40
Stock Furniture, collectables,
bric-a-brac
Open Mon–Sun 10am–5.30pm

NORTHIAM

⊞ **Northiam Antiques**
Contact Robert Bingham
✉ Station Road, Northiam,
East Sussex,
TN31 6QT 🅿
☎ 01797 252523 📠 01797 252523
📱 07881 611157
📧 robert.bingham2@btconnect.com
Est. 2004 *Stock size* Large
Stock 18th–19thC English
furniture
Open Mon–Sat 10am–6pm
Sun 10.30am–4pm
Fairs Ardingly, Newark
Services Valuations, shipping

NUTLEY

⊞ **Nutley Antiques**
Contact L Hall
✉ Libra House, High Street,
Nutley, East Sussex,
TN22 3NF 🅿
☎ 01825 713220
Est. 1986 *Stock size* Large
Stock Rustic, country and
decorative items
Open Mon–Sat 10am–5pm
Sun 1.30–5pm
Fairs Ardingly
Services Caning, rushing

PEACEHAVEN

⊞ **Hunters Antiques**
Contact Colin Ancell
✉ 348 South Coast Road,
Telscombe Cliffs,
Peacehaven,
East Sussex,
BN10 7EP 🅿
☎ 01273 588841 📠 01273 588841
📱 07710 611311
Est. 1970 *Stock size* Large
Stock General antiques, furniture
Open Mon–Fri 10.30am–5pm

Sat Sun 10.30am–2pm
Fairs Ardingly, Newark
Services Valuations

⊞ **June and Tony Stone
Fine Antique Boxes
(LAPADA)**
Contact Tony Stone
✉ PO Box 106, Bolney Avenue,
Peacehaven, East Sussex,
BN10 8AU 🅿
☎ 01798 812122 📠 01273 588908
📱 07092 106600 or 07768 382424
📧 jts@boxes.co.uk
🌐 www.boxes.co.uk
Est. 1990 *Stock size* Large
Stock 18th–19thC boxes, rare
and unusual tea caddies
Open By appointment
Fairs Olympia June, Fairs in New
York, Miami
Services Shipping included in
prices

PETT

⊞ **Norris of Blackheath**
Contact Paul Norris
✉ Dimpleshaven, Pett Road,
Pett, East Sussex,
TN35 4HE 🅿
☎ 01424 812129
🌐 www.norris-of-blackheath-
upholstery.co.uk
Est. 1945 *Stock size* Small
Stock Antique furniture
Open Mon–Fri 8am–6pm
Services Upholstery

PEVENSEY

⊞ **The Old Mint House**
Contact Mr Andrew Nicholson
✉ High Street, Pevensey,
East Sussex,
BN24 5LF 🅿
☎ 01323 762337 📠 01323 762337
📧 antiques@minthouse.co.uk
🌐 www.minthouse.co.uk
Est. 1903 *Stock size* Large
Stock General antiques
Open Mon–Fri 9am–5pm
Sat 10.30am–4pm
Services Shipping

POLEGATE

⊞ **Summers Antiques**
Contact Richard Millis
✉ 87 High Street, Polegate,
East Sussex,
BN26 6AE 🅿
☎ 01323 483834

Est. 2001 *Stock size* Small
Stock General antiques and
collectables
Open Mon–Fri 9am–5pm
Sat 9am–1pm
Fairs Ardingly

ROTHERFIELD

⊞ **6a Antiques**
Contact Mr B Samworth
✉ 6 High Street, Rotherfield,
Crowborough, East Sussex,
TN6 3LL 🅿
☎ 01892 852008
Est. 1979 *Stock size* Large
Stock Georgian–Victorian
furniture
Open Mon–Sat 10am–5pm

⊞ **Forge Interiors**
Contact Mr D Masham
✉ South Street, Rotherfield,
Crowborough, East Sussex,
TN6 3LN 🅿
☎ 01892 853000 📠 01892 853122
📧 douglas.masham@virgin.net
Est. 1999 *Stock size* Medium
Stock Asian and English
furniture, decorative items
Open Tues–Sat 10am–1pm 2–5pm
Services Cane and rush chairs
repaired

⊞ **David Hinton Antiques**
Contact David Hinton
✉ 5 The High Street,
Rotherfield,
East Sussex,
TN6 3LL 🅿
☎ 01892 852609
📱 07733 106882
📧 david.hinton@btconnect.com
Est. 1987 *Stock size* Medium
Stock General antiques
Open Mon–Fri 10.30am–5pm
Sat 10am–5pm Sun (May–Sept)
11am–4pm
Services Auctioneer and valuer

ROTTINGDEAN

🏠 **Farthings**
Contact Margaret Ixer
✉ 45 High Street,
Rottingdean,
East Sussex,
BN2 7HL 🅿
☎ 01273 309113
Est. 1996 *Stock size* Medium
No. of dealers 40
Stock General antiques and
collectables, furniture, jewellery

Open Mon–Sat 9.30am–5pm
Sun noon–5pm
Services Will buy and sell on
behalf of a customer

⊞ Grange Antiques
Contact Richard Payne
✉ 51 Marine Drive,
Rottingdean, Brighton,
East Sussex,
BN2 7HQ ℗
☎ 01273 390141
🖃 richard.payne@freedom255.com
Est. 1983 **Stock size** Small
Stock General, decorative
antiques
Open Mon–Sat 10am–4pm
Sun by appointment
Services Watch, clock, jewellery
repairs

⌂ Jordans of Rottingdean
Contact Mr Jordan Payne
✉ 98 High Street, Rottingdean,
Brighton, East Sussex,
BN2 7HF ℗
☎ 01273 302003
Est. 2001 **Stock size** Medium
No. of dealers 40
Stock Antiques, collectables, fine
china, jewellery
Open Mon–Sat 9.30–5pm
Sun noon–5pm

RYE

⊞ Bears Galore
Contact Richard Tatham
✉ c/o The Corner House,
27 High Street, Rye,
East Sussex,
TN31 7JF
☎ 01797 223187
🖃 bearsinrye@aol.com
ⓦ www.bearsgalore.co.uk
Est. 1979 **Stock size** Large
Stock Hand-made collectable
teddy bears
Open Mon–Sat 10am–4.30pm
Sun noon–4.30pm
Services Mail order, layaway
service

⊞ Black Sheep Antiques
Contact Mrs S Wright
✉ 72 The Mint, Rye,
East Sussex,
TN31 7EW ℗
☎ 01797 224508
Est. 1991 **Stock size** Medium
Stock Victorian china and glass
Open Mon–Sun 11am–5pm
Services China matching

⊞ Bragge & Sons
Contact Mr John Bragge
✉ Landgate House, Landgate,
Rye, East Sussex,
TN31 7LH ℗
☎ 01797 223358 ☏ 01797 223358
Est. 1849
Stock 18thC English furniture
and works of art
Open Mon–Sat 9am–5pm closed
Tues (advisable to ring first) or by
appointment
Services Valuations, restoration

⊞ Chapter & Verse
Booksellers
Contact Mr Spencer Rogers
✉ 105 High Street, Rye,
East Sussex,
TN31 7JE ℗
☎ 01797 222692
ⓜ 07970 386905
🖃 chapterandverse@btconnect.com
Est. 1976 **Stock size** Medium
Stock Antiquarian and out-of-
print books
Open Mon–Sat 9.30am–5pm
closed Tues
Services Free book search

⊞ Collectors Corner
Contact Mr. Woolveridge
✉ 2 Market Road, Rye,
East Sussex,
TN31 7JA ℗
☎ 01797 225796 ☏ 01797 229246
🖃 collectcor@hotmail.com
Est. 1994 **Stock size** Medium
Stock General antiques
Open Mon–Sun 10am–5pm

⊞ Country Ways
Contact Jane Wicks
✉ Strand Quay, Rye,
East Sussex,
TN31 7NX ℗
☎ 01797 227210
ⓜ 07754 308269
🖃 janes_kitchens@hotmail.com
Est. 1992 **Stock size** Medium
Stock Kitchen, garden and textile
collectables, oak and country
furniture
Open Mon–Sun 10am–5pm

⊞ French Treasures
Contact Terri Mcloughlin
✉ The Landgate Arch,
Tower Forge, Hilders Cliff,
Rye, East Sussex,
TN31 7LD ℗
☎ 01797 229447
🖃 frenchtreasures1@aol.com

Est. 2003 **Stock size** Small
Stock Antique white French
furniture, clocks, ironwork
Open Mon–Sun 10am–5pm
closed Tues
Services Valuations, restoration

⊞ Herbert G Gasson
Contact Mr T J Booth
✉ Lion Galleries, Lion Street,
Rye, East Sussex,
TN31 7LB ℗
☎ 01797 222208
ⓜ 07703 349431
🖃 hggassonantiques@hotmail.com
Est. 1909 **Stock size** Large
Stock Early oak, country, walnut,
mahogany furniture
Open Mon–Sat 10am–5pm

⌂ Heirloom Antiques
Contact Jan Byhurst
✉ 44 Cinque Ports Street,
Rye, East Sussex,
TN31 7AN ℗
☎ 01797 225827
Est. 1994 **Stock size** Medium
No. of dealers 6
Stock Dolls, teddies, porcelain,
prints, pictures, books,
Winstanley cats and dogs,
jewellery, furniture, militaria
Open Mon–Sat 10am–5pm
Sun 11am–5pm

⊞ Mint Antiques
Contact Mr Charles Booth
✉ 54 The Mint, Rye,
East Sussex,
TN31 7EN ℗
☎ 01797 224055
ⓜ 07719 547084
Est. 1984 **Stock size** Medium
Stock Antique furniture,
decorative items
Open Mon–Sun 11am–4pm

⌂ Mint Arcade
Contact Chris Viner, Lena
Baldock, Carole Fuggle or
Anthony Campion
✉ 71 The Mint, Rye,
East Sussex,
TN31 7EW ℗
☎ 01797 225952 ☏ 01797 224834
🖃 rameses@supanet.com
ⓦ www.ramases.supanet.com or
www.rye-tourism.com
Est. 1982 **Stock size** Large
No. of dealers 5
Stock Jewellery, dolls' house
furniture, hand-made military
figures, chess sets, picture frames

and mounts, cigarette and trade cards, framed sets of cards
Open Mon–Sat 10am–5pm

⌂ **Needles Antique Centre**
Contact Jenny King
✉ 15 Cinque Ports Street, Rye, East Sussex, TN31 7AD 🅿
☎ 01797 225064
🅴 needles.antiques@btinternet.com
🆆 www.btinternet.com/~needles _antiques_online/
Est. 1996 *Stock size* Large
No. of dealers 5
Stock Small antiques, collectables
Open Mon–Sun 10am–5pm

⌂ **Quay Antiques & Collectables**
Contact Norman Spratt
✉ 6 & 7 The Strand, Rye, East Sussex, TN31 7DB 🅿
☎ 01797 227321
Est. 1977 *Stock size* Large
No. of dealers 25
Stock General antiques and collectables
Open Sun–Mon 10.30am–5.30pm

⌂ **Quayside Antiques**
Contact G T D Niall
✉ The Corn Exchange, The Strand, Rye, East Sussex, TN31 7DB 🅿
☎ 01797 227088
🅴 quaysideantiques@aol.com
Est. 1997 *Stock size* Large
No. of dealers 6
Stock General antiques and collectables
Open Mon–Sun 10am–5.30pm

➢ **Rye Auction Galleries**
Contact Mr A Paine
✉ Rock Channel, Rye, East Sussex, TN31 7HL 🅿
☎ 01797 222124 🅵 01797 222126
🅜 07764 225457
🅴 sales@ryeauctions.fsnet.co.uk
Est. 1989
Open Mon–Fri 8.30am–5pm
Sales Antique and general sales 1st and 3rd Fri of each month 9.30am, viewing Thurs 9am–5pm, trade by appointment
Frequency Bi-monthly
Catalogues Yes

⊞ **Rye Old Books**
Contact Miss A Coleman
✉ 7 Lion Street, Rye,

East Sussex, TN31 7LB 🅿
☎ 01797 225410 🅵 01797 225410
🅴 ryeoldbooks@aol.com
🆆 www.ukbookworld.com/ members/ryeoldbooks
Est. 1993 *Stock size* Medium
Stock Antiquarian and second-hand books, illustrated, fine bindings
Open Mon–Sat 10.30am–5.30pm
Sun 2–5pm
Services Valuations

⊞ **Soldiers of Rye**
Contact Chris Viner
✉ The Mint Arcade, 71 The Mint, Rye, East Sussex, TN31 7EW
☎ 01797 225952
🅴 ramases@supanet.com
🆆 www.ryetourism.co.uk
Est. 1987 *Stock size* Medium
Stock Toy soldiers, cigarette cards and dolls' house miniatures
Open Mon–Sat 10am–5pm
Services Repair of old/damaged soldiers, framing of cigarette cards

⌂ **Strand Quay Antiques**
Contact Ann Marie Sutherland
✉ 1–2 The Strand, Rye, East Sussex, TN31 7DB 🅿
☎ 01797 226790
🅜 07775 602598
Est. 1994 *Stock size* Large
No. of dealers 12
Stock Victorian–Edwardian furniture, porcelain, glass, pictures, collectables
Open Mon–Sun 10am–5pm

⊞ **Suzette Antiques**
Contact Suzette Robson
✉ 32 High Street, Rye, East Sussex, TN31 7JG
☎ 01797 222475
Est. 1989 *Stock size* Medium
Stock General collectables
Open Mon–Fri 10am–5pm

⊞ **Wish Barn Antiques**
Contact Mr Robert Wheeler or Mr Joe Dearden
✉ Wish Street, Rye, East Sussex, TN31 7DA 🅿
☎ 01797 226797
Est. 1993 *Stock size* Large
Stock 19thC pine and country

furniture, 19thC mahogany furniture
Open Mon–Sat 10am–5pm
Sun 1–5pm

⊞ **Martin D Johnson Antiques**
Contact Martin Johnson
✉ 15–17 High Street, Seaford, East Sussex, BN25 1PE
☎ 01323 897777 🅵 01323 897777
🅜 07860 899774
🅴 info@martindjohnsonantiques.com
🆆 www.martindjohnsonantiques.com
Est. 1958 *Stock size* Large
Stock General antiques
Open Mon–Fri 9am–5pm
Sat 10am–12.30pm or by appointment

⊞ **The Little Shop**
Contact Mr C Keane
✉ 6 High Street, Seaford, East Sussex, BN25 1PG 🅿
☎ 01323 490742
Est. 1987 *Stock size* Large
Stock General curios, collectables, dolls' house furniture
Open Tues–Sat 9.30am–6pm

⊞ **The Old House (Antiques China Glass) Ltd**
Contact Mr S M Barrett
✉ 18 High Street, Seaford, East Sussex, BN25 1PG 🅿
☎ 01323 893795
Est. 1945 *Stock size* Large
Stock General antiques, furniture, china, glass, collectables
Open Mon–Sat 9am–5pm
Wed 9am–1pm
Services Valuations

⌂ **Bridge Garage Antiques**
Contact Lynn Scoones
✉ Main Street, The Street, Sedlescombe, Battle, East Sussex, TN33 0QB 🅿
☎ 01424 871424/870815
Est. 2000 *Stock size* Large
No. of dealers 13
Stock General antiques
Open Mon–Sun 10am–5pm

SOUTH EAST
EAST SUSSEX • ST LEONARDS-ON-SEA

ST LEONARDS-ON-SEA

⚹ Ascent Auction Galleries
Contact Paul Turner
✉ Mews Road,
St Leonards-on-Sea,
East Sussex,
TN38 0EA 🅿
☎ 01424 420275 📠 01424 460560
📧 auctions@ascent01.freeserve.co.uk
🌐 www.invaluables.com/ascent
Est. 1848
Open Mon–Fri 9am–5pm
Sales Antiques, fine art,
collectables, jewellery
Frequency Fortnightly
Catalogues Yes

⊞ The Book Jungle
Contact Mr M Gowen
✉ 24 North Street,
St Leonards-on-Sea,
East Sussex,
TN38 0EX 🅿
☎ 01424 421187
Est. 1990 *Stock size* Medium
Stock Antiquarian and second-
hand books
Open Mon–Sat 10am–5pm
closed Wed

⊞ Bookman's Halt
Contact Mr C Linklater
✉ 127 Bohemia Road,
St Leonards-on-Sea,
East Sussex,
TN37 6RL 🅿
☎ 01424 421413
Est. 1980 *Stock size* Medium
Stock Low-key general stock of
antiquarian and second-hand
books
Open Mon–Sat 10am–1pm
2.30pm–5pm closed Wed

⊞ Filsham Farmhouse
Antiques
Contact John York
✉ 111 Harley Shute Road,
St Leonards-on-Sea,
East Sussex,
TN38 8BY 🅿
☎ 01424 433109
📧 filshamfarmhouse@talk21.com
Est. 1962 *Stock size* Large
Stock Oak and shipping furniture
Open Mon–Fri 9am–5pm

🏠 Hastings Antiques
Centre
Contact Mr Robert Amstad
✉ 59–61 Norman Road,
St Leonards-on-Sea,

East Sussex,
TN38 0EG 🅿
☎ 01424 428561 📠 01424 428561
Est. 1982 *Stock size* Large
No. of dealers 15
Stock Continental decorative
furniture, sporting items,
luggage, English furniture and
general antiques
Open Mon–Sat 9am–5.30pm
Services Valuations

⊞ Monarch Antiques
Contact Mr Marcus King
✉ 371 Bexhill Road,
St Leonards-on-Sea,
East Sussex,
TN38 8AJ 🅿
☎ 01424 204141 📠 01424 204142
📱 07802 217842 or 07809 027930
📧 monarch.antiques@virgin.net
🌐 www.monarch-antiques.co.uk
Est. 1981 *Stock size* Large
Stock Victorian–Edwardian
furniture, pine, bamboo,
decorative items
Open Mon–Sat 8.30am–5.30pm
or by appointment
Fairs Newark
Services Valuations, restoration

STAPLECROSS

⊞ Claremont Antiques
Contact Mr A Broad
✉ Stockwood Farm,
Ellenwhorne Lane,
Staplecross, East Sussex,
TN32 5RR 🅿
☎ 01580 830650
📱 07786 262843
📧 antclaremont@aol.com
🌐 www.claremontantiques.com
Est. 1995 *Stock size* Large
Stock Pine, hardwood, painted
country furniture
Open By appointment

TICEHURST

⊞ Piccadilly Rare Books
(ABA, PBFA)
Contact Mr P Minet
✉ Church Street, Ticehurst,
East Sussex,
TN5 7AA 🅿
☎ 01580 201221 📠 01580 200957
📧 minet.royalty@btinternet.com
🌐 www.picrare.com
Est. 1968 *Stock size* Large
Stock Antiquarian and second-
hand books
Open Mon–Sat 10am–5pm

Fairs Chelsea, Royal National
(London)
Services Valuations

UCKFIELD

⊞ Ashdown Antiques
Restoration
Contact Robert Hale
✉ Old Forge Farm, Old Forge
Lane, Horney Common, Uckfield,
East Sussex,
TB22 3EL 🅿
☎ 01825 713003
📧 roberthale2@yahoo.com
Est. 1975 *Stock size* Medium
Stock General antiques, period
furniture
Open Mon–Sat 9am–6pm or by
appointment
Services Restoration

WADHURST

⊞ Browsers Barn
Contact Brian Langridge
✉ New Pond Farm, High Street,
Wallcrouch, Wadhurst,
East Sussex,
TN5 7JN 🅿
☎ 01580 200938 📠 01580 200885
📱 07809 836662
📧 sales@browsers-barn.co.uk
🌐 www.browsers-barn.co.uk
Est. 1973 *Stock size* Large
Stock General antiques and
collectables
Open Tues–Sat 9am–5pm
Sun 10.30am–4pm
Services Shipping

⊞ Park View Antiques
Contact Bunty Ross
✉ High Street, Durgates,
Wadhurst, East Sussex,
TN5 6DE 🅿
☎ 01892 783630 📠 01892 740264
📱 07970 202036
📧 info@parkviewantiques.co.uk
🌐 www.parkviewantiques.co.uk
Est. 1988 *Stock size* Medium
Stock Country furniture, stripped
pine, artefacts, rural items,
vintage tools, period oak
Open Wed–Sun 10am–4pm and
by appointment
Services Restoration

WINDMILL HILL

⊞ Popes Farm Antique
Pine & Stripping
Contact Peter Thompson

✉ Popes Farm, Windmill Hill,
Hailsham, East Sussex,
BN27 4RS 🅿
☎ 01323 832159
🄴 peter@popesfarm.co.uk
🔘 www.popesfarm.co.uk
Est. 1973 *Stock size* Medium
Stock Pine furniture
Open Mon–Fri 8.30am–6pm
Sat 8.30am–4pm
Services Pine stripping

KENT

APPLEDORE

⊞ Back 2 Wood
Contact Steve Fowler
✉ The Old Goods Shed,
Station Road,
Appledore, Kent,
TN26 2DF
☎ 01233 758109
🄴 pine@back2wood.com
🔘 www.back2wood.com
Est. 1987 *Stock size* Medium
Stock Antique pine furniture
Open Mon–Fri 9am–5pm
Sat 9am–4pm Sun 11am–5pm
Services Pine stripping

⌂ The Old Forge Antiques
Contact Anthony Unwin
✉ The Old Forge, 16 The Street,
Appledore, Kent,
TN26 2BX 🅿
☎ 01233 758585
Est. 2000
No. of dealers 18
Stock General antiques, china,
glass, furniture, garden items
Open Mon–Sat 10am–5pm
Sun 11am–5pm

ASHFORD

⋏ Hobbs Parker (RICS)
Contact Alan White
✉ Monument Way, Orbital Park,
Ashford, Kent,
TN24 0HB 🅿
☎ 01233 502222 🄵 01233 502211
🄴 antiques@hobbsparker.co.uk
🔘 www.hobbsparker.co.uk
Est. 1850
Open Mon–Fri 9am–5.30pm
Sales Antique furniture,
porcelain, pottery, glass, toys,
silver plate, jewellery, books,
coins, paintings, prints, clocks,
barometers, objets d'art
Frequency 6 weeks
Catalogues Yes

⊞ Richard Tozer Furniture
Workshop
✉ Unit 3, Wembdon Business
Centre, Bower Rod, Smeeth,
Ashford, Kent,
TN25 6SZ 🅿
☎ 01303 813824 🄵 01303 813824
🄼 07818 032088
🄴 asjanandruth@hotmail.com
Est. 1987 *Stock size* Small
Stock General antiques
Open By appointment
Services Restoration

ASHURST

⊞ The Architectural
Emporium
Contact Michael Roberts
✉ The Bald Faced Stag,
Ashurst, Kent,
TN3 9TE 🅿
☎ 01892 740877
🄴 mike@architecturalemporium.com
🔘 www.architectural emporium.com
Est. 2000 *Stock size* Large
Stock Architectural antiques,
garden statuary, sundials,
fountains, fireplaces, lighting
Open Tues–Sat 9.30am–5.30pm

BARHAM

⊞ Stablegate Antiques
Contact Michael Giuntini
✉ Barham, Kent,
CT4 6QD 🅿
☎ 01227 831639 🄵 01227 831639
🄼 07802 439777
🔘 www.stablegateantiques.co.uk
Est. 1981 *Stock size* Large
Stock Period furniture, pictures,
silver, silver plate, ceramics,
mirrors
Open Mon–Sun 10am–5pm
Fairs Claridges, NEC, Harrogate

BECKENHAM

⌂ Antiques & Collectors
Market
Contact Mrs Holley
✉ Public Hall, Beckenham,
Kent, BR3 5JE 🅿
☎ 020 8660 1369
Est. 1975 *Stock size* Medium
No. of dealers 12
Stock Antiques, collectables
Open Wed 8am–2pm

⊞ Pepys Antiques
Contact Sonia Elton
✉ 9 Kelsey Park Road,

Beckenham, Kent,
BR3 6LH 🅿
☎ 020 8650 0994
Est. 1968 *Stock size* Large
Stock Furniture, silver, porcelain,
paintings
Open Mon–Sat 10am–2pm
closed Wed
Services Valuations

BELLS YEW GREEN

⊞ Big Screen Collectabies
Contact Earl Brown
✉ Unit 4, Business Units,
Bayham Road,
Bells Yew Green,
Tunbridge Wells, Kent,
TN3 9BJ
☎ 01892 750066 🄵 01892 750077
🄴 earl.bigscreen@virgin.net
🔘 www.bigscreen.co.uk
Est. 1996 *Stock size* Medium
Stock Movie collectables
Open Mon–Fri 10am–6pm
Fairs NEC, Milton Keynes
Services Valuations

BENENDEN

⋏ Mervyn Carey
Contact Mr M Carey
✉ Twysden Cottage, Benenden,
Cranbrook, Kent,
TN17 4LD 🅿
☎ 01580 240283 🄵 01580 240283
Est. 1991
Sales Antiques sales at Church
Hall, Church Road, Tenterden,
Kent. Further details by post
Frequency Five per year
Catalogues Yes

BETHERSDEN

⊞ Stevenson Brothers
(British Toymakers Guild)
Contact Mark Stevenson or
Sue Russell
✉ The Workshop,
Ashford Road,
Bethersden,
Ashford, Kent,
TN26 3AP 🅿
☎ 01233 820363 🄵 01233 820580
🄴 sale@stevensonbros.com
🔘 www.stevensonbros.com
Est. 1982 *Stock size* Large
Stock Antique and new rocking
horses
Open Mon–Fri 9am–6pm
Sat 10am–1pm
Fairs The Game Fair, Burghley &

Blenheim Horse Trials, Country Living
Services Restoration of rocking horses and children's classic cars

⊞ Symonds Salvage Ltd (SALVO)
Contact Matthew Symonds
✉ Colts Yard, Pluckley Road, Bethersden, Ashford, Kent, TN26 3DD 🅿
☎ 01233 820724
📧 symondssalvage@aol.com
🌐 symondssalvage.co.uk
Est. 1975 **Stock size** Large
Stock Architectural salvage, original cast iron and marble fireplaces
Open Mon–Fri 7.30am–5.30pm Sat 8.30am–1pm
Services Restoration of pine furniture

BEXLEY

⊞ Bexley Antiques and Interiors
Contact Sue or Tony Armond
✉ 73 High Street , Bexley, Kent, DA5 1AA 🅿
☎ 01322 555496
📧 bexleyantiques@yahoo.co.uk
🌐 www.bexleyantiques.co.uk
Est. 2000 **Stock size** Medium
Stock Victorian–Art Deco furniture
Open Tues–Sat 9.30am–5pm
Fairs Art Deco Eltham Palace, May/Sept
Services Restoration

⊞ Ellenor Hospice Projects
Contact Jane Heaviside
✉ 18–20 High Street, Bexley, Kent, DA5 1AD 🅿
☎ 01322 553996
Est. 1996 **Stock size** Large
Stock General antiques. All profits raised support hospice care in North West Kent and London Borough of Bexley
Open Mon–Sat 9.30am–4.30pm Thurs 9.30am–1pm

BIDDENDEN

⊞ Period Piano Company
Contact David Winston
✉ Park Farm Oast, Hareplain Road, Biddenden, Nr Ashford, Kent,

TN27 8LJ 🅿
☎ 01580 291393 📠 01580 291393
📱 07778 652336
📧 periodpiano@talk21.com
🌐 www.periodpiano.com
Est. 1980 **Stock size** Medium
Stock 1760–1930 pianos, piano stools, music stands, music cabinets
Open By appointment
Services Valuations, restoration, shipping

BIGGIN HILL

⊞ Aviation Antiques & Collectables
Contact Dave Sutton
✉ 56 Scarborough Close, Biggin Hill, Kent, TN16 3YB 🅿
☎ 01959 576424 📠 01959 546424
📱 07973 885754
📧 sutt999@aol.com
Est. 1983 **Stock size** Large
Stock Aeronautica from the last 50 years, collectable model kits
Open By appointment
Fairs Shoreham Aero Jumble, Biggin Hill, Duxford, Redhill Airshows, Heathrow aviation fairs, War and Peace Show Kent

BILSINGTON

⊞ The Barn at Bilsington
Contact Gabrielle de Giles
✉ Swanton Lane, Bilsington, Ashford, Kent, TN25 7JR 🅿
☎ 01233 720917 📠 01233 720156
📱 07721 015263
📧 gabrielle@gabrielledegiles.com
🌐 www.gabrielledegiles.com
Est. 1985 **Stock size** Large
Stock Antique and country furniture, architectural items
Open By appointment
Fairs Battersea Decorative Antique & Textile Fair

BIRCHINGTON

⊞ Silvesters
Contact Mr S N Hartley
✉ Albion Chambers, 1 Albion Road, Birchington, Kent, CT7 9DN 🅿
☎ 01843 841524 📠 01843 845131
Est. 1954
Stock Decorative items, furniture, Georgian, Victorian,

silver, porcelain, glass
Open By appointment only
Services Valuations

BLUEWATER

⊞ Bears 'n' Bunnies
Contact Mrs K Sales or Mr L Sales
✉ Bluewater Shopping Centre, Upper Thames Walk, Greenhithe, Kent, DA9 9SR 🅿
☎ 01322 624997
📧 bearsnbunnies@btopenworld.com
Est. 1999 **Stock size** Large
Stock Collectable bears from leading manufacturers and artists
Open Mon–Fri 10am–9pm Sat 9am–8pm Sun 11am–5pm

⊞ Famously Yours Ltd
Contact Mr C Hales
✉ Upper Thames Walk, Unit U090B, Bluewater, Greenhithe, Kent, DA9 9SR 🅿
☎ 01322 427072 📠 01322 427072
📧 enquiries@famouslyyours.com
🌐 www.famouslyyours.com
Est. 1996 **Stock size** Large
Stock Autographed memorabilia
Open Mon–Fri 10am–9pm Sat 9am–8pm Sun 11am–5pm

BRASTED

⊞ David Barrington
Contact Mr D Barrington
✉ High Street, Brasted, Kent, TN16 1JL 🅿
☎ 01959 562537
Est. 1947 **Stock size** Medium
Stock General antiques
Open Mon–Sun 9am–5pm or by appointment

⊞ Cooper Fine Arts
Contact Mr Jonathan Hill-Reid
✉ Swan House, High Street, Brasted, Kent, TN16 1JJ 🅿
☎ 01959 565818
Est. 1980 **Stock size** Medium
Stock Paintings and furniture
Open Mon–Sat 10am–6pm
Services Framing, restoration of oils and watercolours

⊞ Courtyard Antiques
Contact Gill Whyman
✉ High Street, Brasted, Kent, TN16 1JA 🅿
☎ 01959 564483 📠 01732 454726

Ⓦ www.courtyardantiques.co.uk
Est. 1982 *Stock size* Large
Stock Silver, jewellery, ceramics, 19thC furniture including extending dining tables, chairs, Tunbridge ware, glass, copper, brass, watercolours, oils, prints, objets d'art
Open Mon–Sat 10am–5pm
Sun Bank Holidays 12.30–4.30pm
Services Furniture restoration, French polishing, releathering, upholstery

⊞ **Peter Dyke at The Old Bakery**
Contact Peter Dyke
✉ High Street, Brasted, Kent, TN16 1JA ℗
☎ 01959 565343
Ⓜ 07776 186819
Est. 1980 *Stock size* Medium
Stock Furniture, pictures, lighting, objets d'art
Open Mon–Sat 10.30am–5pm

⊞ **G A Hill Antiques**
Contact Mrs G A Hill
✉ 5 High Street, Brasted, Kent, TN16 1JA ℗
☎ 01959 565500
Est. 1999 *Stock size* Medium
Stock Georgian-period furniture, decorative French mirrors and chandeliers
Open Tues–Fri 10am–5pm Sat 10am–5.30pm or by appointment

⊞ **Keymer Son & Co Ltd**
Contact P T Keymer
✉ Swaylands Place, The Green, High Street, Brasted, Kent, TN16 1JY ℗
☎ 01959 564203 ❻ 01959 561138
Est. 1977 *Stock size* Small
Stock Small 19thC furniture
Open Mon–Fri 9.30am–5.30pm

⊞ **Roy Massingham Antiques (LAPADA)**
Contact Mr R Massingham
✉ The Coach House, High Street, Brasted, Kent, TN16 1JJ ℗
☎ 01959 562408 ❻ 01959 562408
Est. 1967 *Stock size* Large
Stock 18th–19thC furniture, pictures and objects
Open By appointment any time

⊞ **Southdown House Antique Galleries**
Contact Mr Graham Stead

✉ High Street, Brasted, Kent, TN16 1JE ℗
☎ 01959 563522
Est. 1978 *Stock size* Medium
Stock 18th–early 20thC furniture, porcelain, glass, metalware, Chinese embroidery
Open Mon–Sat 10am–5pm
Services Restoration, shipping

⊞ **W W Warner Antiques (BADA)**
Contact Mr Chris Jowitt
✉ The Green, High Street, Brasted, Kent, TN16 1JL ℗
☎ 01959 563698 ❻ 01959 563698
Ⓦ Gallery at www.bada.org
Est. 1957 *Stock size* Medium
Stock 18th–19thC porcelain, glass, pottery
Open Tues–Sat 10am–5pm

BROADSTAIRS

⊞ **Bee Antiques**
Contact Jane Burges
✉ 23b Albion Street, Broadstairs, Kent, CT10 1LU ℗
☎ 01843 864040
❸ theteddymaster@aol.com
Est. 1997 *Stock size* Medium
Stock Dolls, toys, teddybears, postcards, jewellery, collectables, musical instruments
Open Mon–Sun 11am–5pm
Services Valuations, restoration, shipping, lectures

⊞ **Broadstairs Antiques and Collectables**
Contact Penny Law
✉ 49 Belvedere Road, Broadstairs, Kent, CT10 1PF ℗
☎ 01843 861965
Est. 1992 *Stock size* Large
Stock Small collectable items, medium-sized furniture
Open Tues–Sat 10am–4.30pm

⊞ **Secondhand Department**
Contact Mr Alan Kemp
✉ 44–46 Albion Street, Broadstairs, Kent, CT10 1LX ℗
☎ 01843 862877 ❻ 01843 860084
❸ albionbooks@hotmail.com
Est. 1956 *Stock size* Large
Stock Antiquarian and second-

hand books
Open Mon–Sat 9am–5.30pm
Sun 10.30am–4.30pm

⊞ **UK Old Postcards Ltd (PTA)**
Contact Clive Baker
✉ 22 Brassey Avenue, Broadstairs, Kent, CT10 2DS ℗
☎ 01843 862707 ❻ 01843 862707
❸ info@clivebaker.co.uk
Ⓦ www.ukoldpostcards.co.uk
Est. 1990 *Stock size* Medium
Stock Vintage postcards, photographs, ephemera
Open By appointment

BROMLEY

⊞ **Patric Capon (BADA)**
Contact Patric Capon
✉ PO Box 581, Bromley, Kent, BR1 2WX ℗
☎ 020 8467 5722 ❻ 020 8295 1475
Ⓜ 07831 444924
❸ patric.capon@saqnet.co.uk
Est. 1975 *Stock size* Medium
Stock Antique clocks, marine chronometers, barometers
Open By appointment
Fairs Olympia (Summer)
Services Valuations, restoration, shipping

⊞ **Peter Morris (BNTA)**
Contact Mr P Morris
✉ 1 Station Concourse, Bromley North Station, Bromley, Kent, BR1 4EQ ℗
☎ 020 8313 3410 ❻ 020 8466 8502
❸ coins@petermorris.co.uk
Ⓦ www.petermorris.co.uk
Est. 1983 *Stock size* Large
Stock Coins, medals, bank notes, antiquities
Open Mon–Fri 10am–1pm 2–6pm Sat 9am–2pm closed Wed
Fairs BNTA Coinex
Services Mail order, 4 illustrated lists, valuations

⊞ **Studio Antiques**
Contact Mr Ian Burt
✉ 2 Sundridge Parade, Plaistow Lane, Bromley, Kent, BR1 4DT ℗
☎ 020 8466 9010
Est. 1998 *Stock size* Large
Stock Georgian–Edwardian

furniture, Art Deco, ceramics
Open Fri–Sat 11am–4.30pm or by
appointment

CANTERBURY

⊞ Antique & Design
Contact Mr S Couchman
✉ The Old Oast, Hollow Lane,
Canterbury, Kent,
CT1 3SA ℗
☎ 01227 762871 ✆ 01227 780970
ⓦ www.antiqueanddesign.co.uk
Est. 1987 *Stock size* Large
Stock English and Continental
pine furniture
Open Mon–Sat 9am–6pm
Sun 10am–4pm

⌂ Burgate Antiques
Contact Veronica Reeves
✉ 23a Palace Street,
Canterbury, Kent,
CT1 2DZ ℗
☎ 01227 456500
ⓔ vkreeves@burgate1.fsnet.co.uk
Est. 1988 *Stock size* Medium
No. of dealers 10
Stock Jewellery, furniture, silver,
porcelain, Art Deco china,
militaria, medals, toy soldiers,
prints
Open Mon–Sat 10am–5pm

⊞ Bygones Reclamation
(Canterbury) Ltd
Contact Bob Thorpe
✉ Nackington Road,
Canterbury, Kent,
CT4 7BA ℗
☎ 01227 767453 or 0800 043 3012
✆ 01227 762153
ⓜ 07802 278424
ⓔ bob@bygones.net
ⓦ www.bygones.net
Est. 1991 *Stock size* Large
Stock Victorian fireplaces, cast-
iron radiators, building
materials, architectural salvage
Open Mon–Sun 9am–5.30pm
Services Paint stripping,
spraying, sand blasting, welding
repairs

♪ The Canterbury Auction
Galleries (SOFAA)
Contact Christine Wacker
✉ 40 Station Road West,
Canterbury, Kent,
CT2 8AN ℗
☎ 01227 763337 ✆ 01227 456770
ⓔ auctions@thecanterbury
auctiongalleries.com

ⓦ www.thecanterburyauction
galleries.com
Est. 1911
Open Mon–Fri 9am–1pm 2–5pm
Sales 6 specialist sales a year.
Monthly sales of Victorian and
later furniture
Frequency Monthly
Catalogues Yes

⊞ The Canterbury Book
Shop (PBFA, ABA, ILAB)
Contact David Miles
✉ 37 Northgate,
Canterbury, Kent,
CT1 1BL ℗
☎ 01227 464773 ✆ 01227 780073
ⓔ canterburybookshop@
btconnect.com
Est. 1980 *Stock size* Medium
Stock Antiquarian and second-
hand books
Open Mon–Sat 10am–5pm
Fairs PBFA fairs, ABA London
Services Valuations

⊞ Chaucer Bookshop
(ABA)
Contact Robert Sherston-Baker
✉ 6–7 Beer Cart Lane,
Canterbury, Kent,
CT1 2NY ℗
☎ 01227 453912 ✆ 01227 451893
ⓔ chaucerbooks@btconnect.com
ⓦ www.chaucer-bookshop.co.uk
Est. 1957 *Stock size* Large
Stock Antiquarian and out-of-
print books
Open Mon–Sat 10am–5pm or by
appointment
Services Valuations, Shipping

⊞ W J Christophers
Contact Mr W Christophers
✉ 9 The Borough,
Canterbury, Kent,
CT1 2DR ℗
☎ 01227 451968
Est. 1970 *Stock size* Large
Stock General antiques
1720s–1950s, pottery, porcelain,
clocks, prints, books
Open Mon–Sat 9am–5pm

⌂ The Coach House
Antique Centre
Contact Manager
✉ 2a Duck Lane, Northgate,
Canterbury, Kent,
CT1 2AE ℗
☎ 01227 463117
Est. 1975 *Stock size* Large
No. of dealers 9 stalls

Stock General antiques,
collectables, pressed glass, linen,
tribal art, studio pottery
Open Mon–Sat 10am–4pm

⊞ Conquest House
Antiques
Contact Mrs C Hill
✉ 17 Palace Street,
Canterbury, Kent,
CT1 2DZ ℗
☎ 01227 464587 ✆ 01227 451375
ⓔ caroline@conquesthouse.co.uk
ⓦ www.conquesthouse.co.uk
Est. 1994 *Stock size* Large
Stock Georgian–Victorian
furniture, small items, paintings,
chandeliers, rugs
Open Mon–Sat 10am–5pm
Services Valuations, restoration

⊞ Stuart Heggie
(Photographic Collectors
Club)
Contact Mr Stuart Heggie
✉ 19 Kings Street,
Canterbury, Kent,
CT1 2AJ ℗
☎ 01227 471162
ⓜ 07833 593334
ⓔ heggie-cameras@yahoo.co.uk
Est. 1980 *Stock size* Medium
Stock Vintage cameras, optical
toys, photographic images
Open Fri–Sat 10am–5pm
Fairs South London Photographic
Fair, Photographica
Services Valuations, restoration

⊞ Housepoints
Contact Mr Robin Ross Hunt
✉ 13 The Borough,
Canterbury, Kent,
CT1 2DR ℗
☎ 01227 451350
ⓜ 07808 784638
Est. 1984 *Stock size* Medium
Stock French country pine
furniture, Victorian–Edwardian
pieces, painted items
Open Mon–Fri 10am–5pm
Sat 9.30am–5pm
Services Restoration, valuations

⊞ Kings Gallery (FATG)
Contact Sandra Christian
✉ 28 Palace Street,
Canterbury, Kent,
CT1 2DZ ℗
☎ 01227 786986 ✆ 01227 780532
ⓦ www.kingsgallery.co.uk
Est. 1993 *Stock size* Large
Stock Fine art, Lowry, Russell-

Flint, Terry Frost etc
Open Mon–Sat 9am–5.45pm
Services Valuations, restoration, framing

⊞ Nan Leith's Brocanterbury
Contact Nan Leith
✉ 68 Stour Street, Canterbury, Kent, CT1 2NZ ℙ
☎ 01227 454519
Est. 1982 **Stock size** Medium
Stock Small collectables
Open Mon Wed Fri Sat 1–6pm or by appointment

⊞ Pattinsons Galleries
Contact Alan Pattinson
✉ 25 Oaten Hill, Canterbury, Kent, CT1 3HZ ℙ
☎ 01227 780365
✉ pattinsonsgalleries@tiscali.co.uk
Est. 1975 **Stock size** Medium
Stock Fine art, antiques, collectables
Open Mon–Fri 9am–5pm
Sat by appointment
Services Valuations, restoration

⊞ The Neville Pundole Gallery
Contact Neville Pundole
✉ 8a & 9 The Friars, Canterbury, Kent, CT1 2AS ℙ
☎ 01227 453471 ☏ 01227 453471
☏ 07860 278774
✉ neville@pundole.co.uk
ⓦ www.pundole.co.uk
Est. 1986 **Stock size** Large
Stock William and Walter Moorcroft and contemporary pottery, glass, textiles, sculptures, pictures
Open Mon–Sat 10am–5pm or by appointment

⊞ Uniques
Contact Bob Shilling
✉ Parham Road, Canterbury, Kent, CT1 1DD ℙ
☎ 01227 479007
Est. 1996 **Stock size** Medium
Stock Collectables
Open Mon–Sat 10am–5pm
Sun 10am–4pm

⊞ The Victorian Fireplace
Contact John Griffith
✉ Thanet House,

92 Broad Street, Canterbury, Kent, CT1 2LU ℙ
☎ 01227 767723 ☏ 01227 767723
✉ info@victorianfireplace.co.uk
ⓦ www.victorian fireplace.co.uk
Est. 1986 **Stock size** Large
Stock Fireplaces
Open Tue–Sat 9am–5.30pm
closed Wed
Services Valuations, restoration

⊞ Whatever Comics
Contact Mr M Armario
✉ 2 Burgate Lane, Canterbury, Kent, CT1 2HH ℙ
☎ 01227 453226
ⓦ www.whatevercomics.co.uk
Est. 1988 **Stock size** Large
Stock Star Trek, Star Wars toys, movie-related items, sci-fi collectables, Beanie Babies, action figures, music related figures
Open Mon–Sat 10am–5.30pm

⊞ World Coins
Contact David Mason
✉ 35–36 Broad Street, Canterbury, Kent, CT1 2LR ℙ
☎ 01227 768887
✉ worldcoins@bigfoot.com
ⓦ www.worldcoins.freeservers.com
Est. 1970 **Stock size** Large
Stock Coins, medals, militaria, bank notes, stamps, medallions, tokens
Open Mon–Sat 9.30am–5pm
closed Thurs pm
Services Valuations, identification, quarterly catalogue

CHATHAM

⊞ The American Comic Shop
Contact Mr K Earl
✉ 1 Church Street, Chatham, Kent, ME4 4BS ℙ
☎ 01634 817410
Est. 1993 **Stock size** Large
Stock American imported comics, graphic novels, collectable toys, posters
Open Mon Wed–Fri 10am–5.30pm
Tues 10am–5pm Sat 9am–5.30pm
Services Valuations, mail order, standing orders

CHILHAM

⊞ Bagham Barn Antiques
Contact Peggy Boyd
✉ Canterbury Road, Chilham, Kent, CT4 8DU ℙ
☎ 01227 732522
☏ 07780 675201
✉ peggyboyd@baghambarn.com
ⓦ www.baghambarn.com
Est. 2002 **Stock size** Large
Stock 17th–18thC furniture, ceramics, clocks, collectables, arms, coins, notes, marine
Open Tues–Sun Bank Holiday Mon 10am–5pm
Fairs Ardingly, Detling
Services Restoration

⊞ Alan Lord Antiques
Contact Mr Russell Lord
✉ Bagham Barn Antiques Centre, Canterbury Road, Chilham, Kent, CT4 8DU ℙ
☎ 01303 253674 ☏ 01303 253674
✉ russell@lord8829.fsnet.co.uk
Est. 1953 **Stock size** Large
Stock 18th–19thC furniture, effects
Open Tues–Sun Bank Holiday Mon 10am–5pm
Services House clearance of antiques to 1930

CHISLEHURST

⊞ CCB Aviation Books and Prints
Contact Ian Brentnall
✉ 7 Holmdale Road, Chislehurst, Kent, BR6 1BY
☎ 020 8249 5540 ☏ 020 8249 5540
☏ 07855 350145
✉ ccbaviation@ntlworld.com
ⓦ www.ccbaviation.com
Est. 1999 **Stock size** Large
Stock WWII aviation memorabilia, books, prints
Open Mon–Sat 8am–5.30pm
Services Valuations, two catalogues per year

⊞ Chislehurst Antiques (LAPADA)
Contact Margaret Crawley
✉ 7 Royal Parade, Chislehurst, Kent, BR7 6NR ℙ
☎ 020 8467 1530
☏ 07773 345266

SOUTH EAST
KENT • CLIFTONVILLE

📧 margaret@chislehurstantiques.co.uk
🌐 www.antiquefurnishings.co.uk
Est. 1978 **Stock size** Large
Stock 1860–1910 lighting,
mirrors, 1760–1900 furniture
Open Sat 10am–5.30pm Sun
11am–4pm or by appointment

⊞ Michael Sim
Contact Mr M Sim
✉ 1 Royal Parade,
Chislehurst, Kent,
BR7 6NR 🅿
☎ 020 8467 7040 ✆ 020 8857 1313
Est. 1983 **Stock size** Large
Stock Clocks, barometers,
Georgian furniture
Open Mon–Sat 9am–6pm
Services Restoration

🏠 Wratten Antique &
Craft Mews
Contact Mrs M Brown
✉ 51–53 High Street,
Chislehurst, Kent,
BR7 5AF 🅿
☎ 020 8467 7400 ✆ 020 8295 2387
🌐 www.wrattens.co.uk
Est. 1996 **Stock size** Large
No. of dealers 45
Stock Antiques, collectables,
crafts
Open Mon–Sat 9.30am–5pm
Services Café

⊞ Cottage Antiques and
Lulu's
Contact Mr D J Emsley
✉ 172 Northdown Road,
Cliftonville, Margate, Kent,
CT9 2RB 🅿
☎ 01843 298214/299166
📱 07771 542872
Est. 1990 **Stock size** Large
Stock Georgian–1930s antiques,
oak, china, silver, smalls; vintage,
retro and designer clothing
Open Mon–Sat 10am–5pm
Services Valuations, house
clearances

⊞ Magpies Collectables
Gifts & Antiques
Contact Joanne Savage
✉ 161 North Down Road,
Cliftonville, Margate, Kent,
CT9 2PA 🅿
☎ 01843 223470
Est. 2003 **Stock size** Large
Stock Collectables
Open Tues–Sat 10am–5pm

COXHEATH

⊞ Farleigh Antiques
Contact John Gordon
✉ Homestead,
107 Heath Road,
Coxheath, Kent,
ME17 4PP 🅿
☎ 01622 747412
Est. 1981 **Stock size** Medium
Stock Period furniture
Open Fri Sat 10am–5pm
Mon–Thurs by appointment
Fairs Newark, Ardingly
Services Valuations, restoration

CRANBROOK

🏠 Antiques at Cranbrook
Contact Nick Everard
✉ 19 High Street,
Cranbrook, Kent,
TN17 3EE 🅿
☎ 01580 712173
📱 07885 690913
📧 nick@topdrawer.uk.com
Est. 1989 **Stock size** Large
No. of dealers 10
Stock 19thC country antiques,
silver, small items of furniture,
ceramics, prints
Open Mon–Sat 10am–5pm

🔨 Bentley's Fine Art
Auctioneers
Contact Mr Raj Bisram
✉ The Old Granary,
Waterloo Road,
Cranbrook, Kent,
TN17 3JQ 🅿
☎ 01580 715857 ✆ 01580 715857
📧 bentleyskent@aol.com
🌐 www.bentleysfineart
auctioneers.co.uk
Est. 1995
Open Mon–Fri 9am–5pm
Sat by appointment
Sales 1st Sat monthly antiques
and fine art sale at 11am,
viewing 2 days prior
9am–6.30pm. Specialist sales
throughout the year
Catalogues Yes

⊞ Bijou Art
Contact Jan Moloney
✉ Albert House, Stone Street,
Cranbrook, Kent,
TN17 3HG 🅿
☎ 01580 712720
Est. 2004 **Stock size** Medium
Stock General antiques
Open Mon–Sat 10am–5pm

⊞ Douglas Bryan (BADA,
LAPADA)
Contact Douglas Bryan
✉ The Old Bakery,
St David's Bridge,
Cranbrook, Kent,
TN17 3HN 🅿
☎ 01580 713103 ✆ 01580 712407
📱 07774 737303
Est. 1980 **Stock size** Medium
Stock 17th–18thC oak furniture,
associated items
Open By appointment only
Fairs Olympia, BADA

🔨 Desmond Judd
Auctioneers
Contact Jude McArdle
✉ Hazelden Farm Oast,
Marden Road,
Cranbrook, Kent,
TN17 2LP 🅿
☎ 01580 714522 ✆ 01580 715266
📧 desjudd@dial.pipex.com
Est. 1988
Open Mon–Fri 9 am–5pm
Sat 9.30–11.30am
Sales General antiques,
collectables, held at The Weald
of Kent Golf Club, Headcorn,
Kent Sun 11am, viewing Sat
10am–5pm
Frequency Monthly
Catalogues Yes

⊞ The Old Tackle Box
Contact Richard Dowson
✉ PO Box 55, High Street,
Cranbrook, Kent,
TN17 3ZU 🅿
☎ 01580 713979 ✆ 01580 713979
📱 07729 278293
📧 tackle.box@virgin.net
Est. 1994 **Stock size** Large
Stock Antique fishing tackle
Open By appointment
Services Valuations and mail
order

DARTFORD

⊞ Watling Antiques
Contact John Leitch
✉ 139 Crayford Road,
Dartford,
Kent,
DA1 4AS 🅿
☎ 01322 523620
Est. 1970 **Stock size** Small
Stock Shipping goods,
collectables
Open Mon–Sat 9.30am–5pm
Services Valuations

⊞ Wot-a-Racket (GCS [GB, USA], TCS)
Contact Mr B Casey
✉ 250 Shepherds Lane, Dartford, Kent, DA1 2PN 🅿
☎ 01322 220619 ✆ 01322 220619
📱 07808 593467
📧 wot-a-racket@talk21.com
Est. 1981 **Stock size** Large
Stock Sporting memorabilia
Open By appointment
Fairs Newark, Ardingly

DEAL

⊞ Decors
Contact Nicole Loftus-Potter
✉ 67a Beach Street, Deal, Kent, CT14 6HY 🅿
☎ 01304 368030 ✆ 01304 368030
Est. 1990 **Stock size** Medium
Stock 17th–19thC antiques, modern St Louis, Baccarat, non-renewable pieces, textiles
Open Mon–Sun 10am–7pm or by appointment
Services Restoration and valuations

⊞ McConnell Fine Books (ABA, PBFA)
Contact Mr Nick McConnell
✉ The Golden Hind, 85 Beach Street, Deal, Kent, CT14 6JB 🅿
☎ 01304 375086
📱 07977 573766
📧 mcconnellbooks@aol.com
Est. 1974 **Stock size** Medium
Stock Antiquarian and leather-bound books
Open Wed–Sat 11am–4pm or by appointment
Fairs Russell Square, Olympia

⊞ Quill Antiques
Contact Mr A J Young
✉ 12 Alfred Square, Deal, Kent, CT14 6LR 🅿
☎ 01304 375958
Est. 1969 **Stock size** Small
Stock General small antiques
Open Mon–Sat 9am–5pm

⊞ RSB Antiques
Contact Richard Baker
✉ 30 Dover Road, Walmer, Deal, Kent, CT14 7JW 🅿
☎ 01304 374082

📧 richardsbaker@yahoo.co.uk
Est. 1985
Stock Victorian pictures
Open By appointment
Services Restoration

⊞ Serendipity
Contact Marion Short or Jayne Eschalier
✉ 125 High Street, Deal, Kent, CT14 6BB 🅿
☎ 01304 369165 ✆ 01304 369165
📧 dipityantiques@aol.com
Est. 1979 **Stock size** Large
Stock Small furniture, ceramics, pictures
Open Mon–Sat 10am–1pm 2–4.30pm
Services Restoration of pictures

⊞ Toby Jug Collectables
Contact Mrs S Pettit
✉ South Toll House, Deal Pier, Beach Street, Deal, Kent, CT14 6HZ 🅿
☎ 01304 369917
Est. 1996 **Stock size** Large
Stock Royal Doulton, discontinued Toby and character jugs, other china collectables
Open Tues–Sun 11am–5.30pm closed 1.30–2.30pm
Fairs DMG Fair Detling, The Grand Hotel Folkestone

DOVER

⊞ Roman Painted House
Contact Mr Philp
✉ New Street, Dover, Kent, CT16 1HU 🅿
☎ 01304 240121
Est. 1975 **Stock size** Medium
Stock Architectural reproductions
Open Tues–Sun 10am–5pm
Services Guided house, workshops for young children

EAST PECKHAM

⊞ Desmond and Amanda North
Contact Desmond North
✉ The Orchard, 186 Hale Street, East Peckham, Kent, TN12 5JB 🅿
☎ 01622 871353 ✆ 01622 872998
Est. 1971 **Stock size** Medium
Stock Persian and other Oriental rugs, carpets, runners, and

cushions 1800–1939
Open Mon–Sun appointment advisable
Services Valuations, restoration

EDENBRIDGE

⊞ Lennox Cato Antiques (BADA, LAPADA, WKADA, CINOA, BACA Award Winner 2003)
Contact Lennox or Susan Cato
✉ 1 The Square, Church Street, Edenbridge, Kent, TN8 5BD 🅿
☎ 01732 865988 ✆ 01732 865988
📱 07836 233473
📧 cato@lennoxcato.com
🌐 www.lennoxcato.com
Est. 1979 **Stock size** Medium
Stock 18th–19thC furniture, works of art, accessories
Open Mon–Fri 9.30am–5.30pm Sat 10am–5.30pm or by appointment
Fairs Olympia, BADA, Harrogate
Services Valuations, consultancy, restoration

⊞ Chevertons of Edenbridge Ltd (LAPADA, BADA)
Contact Angus or David Adam
✉ 71–73 High Street, Edenbridge, Kent, TN8 5AL 🅿
☎ 01732 863196/863358
✆ 01732 864298
📱 07711 234010
📧 chevertons@msn.com
🌐 www.chevertons.com
Est. 1959 **Stock size** Large
Stock English and Continental antique and decorative furniture, accessories
Open Mon–Sat 9am–5.30pm
Fairs NEC, Olympia (June, Nov), BADA

EGERTON

⊞ Christine Swift Books
✉ Burnt Mill, Burnt Mill Lane, Egerton, Ashford, Kent, TN17 9AX 🅿
☎ 01233 713730
Est. 1975 **Stock size** Large
Stock Antique and local history books relating to Kent
Open By appointment
Fairs Kent Book Fair (Maidstone)
Services Valuations, Restoration, catalogues

ELHAM

Elham Antiques
Contact Mr Julian Chambers
✉ Cock Lane, Elham, Kent,
CT4 6TL 🅿
☎ 01303 840085
📧 elhamantiques@btopenworld.com
Est. 1989 *Stock size* Large
Stock Architectural antiques, old
metal toys, pine and country
furniture
Open By appointment
Fairs Sandown Park, Newark
Services Valuations

Old Bank Antiques
Contact Mrs J Swinbourne
✉ Bank Buildings, High Street,
Elham, Kent,
CT4 6TD 🅿
☎ 01303 840140
Est. 2001 *Stock size* Medium
Stock General antiques,
furniture, ceramics
Open Tues–Sat 10am–5.30pm
Sun 11am–4.30pm

ERIDGE GREEN

Kentdale Antiques
Contact Mr Bigwood
✉ Forge Road, Eridge Green,
Tunbridge Wells, Kent,
TN3 9LJ 🅿
☎ 01892 863840
📧 kentdale.antiques@ukgateway.net
Est. 1995 *Stock size* Medium
Stock Victoriana, furniture
Open By appointment only
Services Restoration

ERITH

Belmont Jewellers
Contact Mr S J Girt
✉ 5 Belmont Road,
Northumberland Heath,
Erith, Kent, DA8 1JY 🅿
☎ 01322 339646
Est. 1986 *Stock size* Small
Stock Jewellery, furniture, pictures,
silver, silver plate, general antiques
Open Mon–Sat 9am–5pm
Fairs Ardingly
Services Valuations, jewellery
repairs

FARNINGHAM

Peter Beasley
Contact Mrs R Beasley
✉ Forge Yard, High Street,
Farningham, Kent,
DA4 0DB 🅿
☎ 01322 862453
Est. 1964 *Stock size* Medium
Stock 17th–19thC furniture,
small items, brass, pewter
Open Mon–Sun 9am–5pm or by
appointment

Farningham Pine
Contact Mr P Dzierzek
✉ The Old Bull Stores,
Farningham, Kent,
DA4 0DG
☎ 01322 863230 📧 01322 863168
📧 info@pineandoak.co.uk
Est. 1987 *Stock size* Large
Stock Pine furniture, French oak,
country furniture
Open Mon–Sat 10am–5pm
Sun 11am–3pm closed Wed
Fairs Newark, Ardingly

FAVERSHAM

Ecomerchant Ltd
Contact Paul Whitlock or
Joe Hilton
✉ The Old Filling Station,
Head Hill Road, Goodnestone,
Faversham, Kent,
ME13 9BL 🅿
☎ 01795 530130 📧 01795 530430
📧 sales@ecomerchant.co.uk
🌐 www.ecomerchant.co.uk
Est. 1998 *Stock size* Medium
Stock Architectural antiques,
floor boards, stone, bricks,
wood/oak beams, conservation
building materials
Open Mon–Fri 8am–5pm
Sat 9am–4pm

Faversham Interiors
(PBFA)
Contact Mr Ralph Lane
✉ 7 Court Street,
Faversham, Kent,
ME13 7AN 🅿
☎ 01795 591471
📧 upleeslodge@aol.com
Est. 1997 *Stock size* Medium
Stock French decorative, books,
maps
Open Mon–Sat ring for times
Fairs Ardingly
Services Restoration of books

Squires Antiques
Contact Ann Squires
✉ 3 Jacob Yard, Preston Street,
Faversham, Kent,
ME13 8NY 🅿
☎ 01795 531503 📧 01795 591600
Est. 1985 *Stock size* Large
Stock General antiques
Open Mon Tues Fri Sat 10am–5pm

FOLKESTONE

Richard Amos Antiques
Contact Richard Amos
✉ 1 Darlinghurst Road, Cheriton,
Folkestone, Kent,
CT19 4PL
☎ 01303 274024
Est. 1999 *Stock size* Small
Stock General antiques
Open By appointment

The Folkestone Stamp
and Collectors Shop
Contact Brian Uden or
Richard Kennedy
✉ 8a The Old High Street,
Folkestone, Kent,
CT20 7RL
☎ 01303 850673 📧 01303 850687
📧 sales@internetstamps.co.uk
🌐 www.internetstamps.co.uk
Est. 1975 *Stock size* Large
Stock General collectables,
stamps
Open Mon–Fri 9am–5pm
Services Valuations for
insurance, magazine

Kent Auction Galleries
Ltd
Contact Melissa or David
✉ Unit C, Highfields Industrial
Estate, Warren Road,
Folkestone, Kent,
CT19 6DD 🅿
☎ 01303 246810 📧 01303 246256
📧 admin@kentauctiongalleriesltd.co.uk
🌐 www.kentauctiongalleriesltd.co.uk
Est. 1986
Open Mon–Fri 10am–6pm
Sales Victorian and later effects
2nd Sat of month, viewing Fri
10am–7pm, antiques and fine art
last Sat of month, viewing Thurs
10am–6pm Fri 10am–7pm
Frequency 2 sales a month
Catalogues Yes; see website

Lawton's Antiques
Contact Ian Lawton
✉ 26 Canterbury Road,
Folkestone, Kent,
CT19 5NG 🅿
☎ 01303 246418
📱 07833 946626
Est. 1987 *Stock size* Medium
Stock General antiques, good

second-hand furniture
Open Mon–Sat 9am–6pm
Services Valuations

⊞ Marrin's Bookshop (ABA, ILAB, PBFA)
Contact Patrick Marrin or John Powell
✉ 149 Sandgate Road, Folkestone, Kent, CT20 2DA 🅿
☎ 01303 253016 🖷 01303 850956
📱 07765 663808 or 07905 122182
🅔 sales@marrinbook.co.uk or marrinbook@clara.co.uk
🆆 www.marrinbook.com or www.marrinbook.co.uk
Est. 1947 **Stock size** Medium
Stock General antiquarian and second-hand books, specializing in Kent
Open Tues–Sat 9.30am–5.30pm
Fairs PBFA London Book Fair, Russell Hotel – monthly, major events in the UK and overseas
Services Valuations

⊞ Rennies Seaside Modern (ESoc)
Contact Mr P Rennie
✉ 47 The Old High Street, Folkestone, Kent, CT20 1RN 🅿
☎ 01303 242427
🅔 info@rennart.co.uk
🆆 www.rennart.co.uk
Est. 1990 **Stock size** Small
Stock 20thC art and design, inter-war period posters, graphics
Open Tues–Fri noon–6.30pm Sat noon–6pm
Services Valuations

⊞ Second Treasures
Contact Allen Fairbairn
✉ 69 Tontine Street, Folkestone, Kent, CT20 1JB 🅿
☎ 01303 223726 🖷 01303 246265
Est. 1994 **Stock size** Large
Stock General antiques
Open Mon–Fri 9am–5pm
Services Clock repairs, restoration

FOUR ELMS

⌂ Treasures
Contact Christine Evans
✉ Bough Beech Road, Four Elms, Kent, TN8 6NE 🅿
☎ 01732 700363

Est. 1974 **Stock size** Large
No. of dealers 8
Stock Antiques, collectables, bric-a-brac
Open Tue–Sat 10am–5.30pm (winter 5pm) Sun 2–5pm

GOUDHURST

⊞ Mill House Antiques
Contact Brad Russell
✉ Unit 3, Fountain House, High Street, Goudhurst, Kent, TN17 1AL 🅿
☎ 01580 212476
Est. 1991 **Stock size** Large
Stock Pine and country antiques, complementary items
Open Tues–Sat 10am–5pm
Services Valuations

GRAVESEND

⊞ Stamp and Hobbies
Contact Rob Atkinson
✉ 45 High Street, Gravesend, Kent, DA11 0AY
☎ 01474 534166
Est. 1959 **Stock size** Large
Stock Stamps, coins, medals
Open Mon–Sat 10am–5pm closed Wed
Services Valuations

HAMSTREET

⊞ Woodville Antiques
Contact Andrew MacBean
✉ The Street, Hamstreet, Ashford, Kent, TN26 2HG 🅿
☎ 01233 732981 🖷 01233 732981
📱 07932 5885979
🅔 woodvilleantique@yahoo.co.uk
Est. 1988 **Stock size** Medium
Stock Antique and collectable tools, glass, furniture
Open Tues–Sun 10am–5.30pm
Services Valuations

HERNE BAY

⊞ Brigsy's Antique Centre
Contact W. Briggs
✉ 75 High Street, Herne Bay, Kent, CT6 5LQ
☎ 01227 370621
Est. 1998 **Stock size** Large
Stock General antiques
Open Mon–Sat 10am–4pm
Fairs Newark, Swinderby

HIGH HALDEN

⊞ Rother Reclamation (SALVO)
Contact Mrs Symonds
✉ The Old Tile Centre, Ashford Road, High Halden, Tenterden, Kent, TN26 3BP 🅿
☎ 01233 850075 🖷 01233 850275
📱 07889 387136
Est. 1960 **Stock size** Medium
Stock Renovation materials, bricks, tiles, oak beams, flooring, doors, slate, stone, railway sleepers, garden statuary, pine furniture, sanitary ware etc
Open Mon–Sat 8am–5pm
Services Delivery (south east) & special requests

HYTHE

⊞ Alan Lord Antiques
Contact Mr Russell Lord
✉ 158 High Street, Canterbury Road, Hythe, Kent, CT21 5 JR 🅿
☎ 01303 264239/253674 🖷 01303 264239/253674
🅔 russell@lord8829.fsnet.co.uk
Est. 1952 **Stock size** Medium
Stock 18th–19thC furniture
Open Mon–Sat 9.30am–5pm Half day Wed
Services Valuations, restoration

⌂ Malthouse Arcade
Contact Mr or Mrs Maxtone Graham
✉ Malthouse Hill, Hythe, Kent, CT21 5BW 🅿
☎ 01303 260103
Est. 1974 **Stock size** Large
No. of dealers 24 on two floors
Stock General antiques
Open Fri Sat Bank Holiday Mon 9.30am–5.30pm
Services Café

⊞ Owlets (NAG)
Contact Mrs A Maurice
✉ 99 High Street, Hythe, Kent, CT21 5JH
☎ 01303 230333
🆆 www.owlets.co.uk
Est. 1955 **Stock size** Large
Stock Antique and estate jewellery, silver, costume jewellery

Open Mon–Sat 9.30am–5pm
closed Wed
Services Valuations, restoration,
jewellery repairs

⊞ Trouvailles
Contact Mr Alan Fairbairn
✉ 18 High Street,
Hythe,
Kent,
CT21 5AT ▣
☎ 01303 267801
Est. 1995 **Stock size** Large
Stock General antiques, clocks,
collectables
Open Mon–Sat 10am–5pm
closed Wed
Services Clock repair and
restoration

KESTON

⊞ Taurus Antiques
(BAFRA)
Contact Tim Akers
✉ 6 Heathfield Road,
Keston, Bromley,
Kent,
BR2 6BG ▣
☎ 020 8650 9179
📧 enquiries@akersofantiques.co.uk
ⓦ www.akersofantiques.co.uk
Est. 1980 **Stock size** Medium
Stock 18thC period furniture
Open By appointment
Fairs Battersea Park Antique and
Textile Fair
Services Restoration

LITTLEBOURNE

⊞ Canterbury Bears
Contact Maude Blackburn
✉ 1 Builders Square,
Court Hill, Littlebourne,
Canterbury,
Kent,
CT2 1XU ▣
☎ 01227 728630 📠 01227 728630
📧 maude.blackburn@btinternet.com
Est. 1979 **Stock size** Medium
Stock Antique bears
Open Mon–Fri 9am–5pm
Services Restoration

⊞ Good Golly Bear Dolly
Contact Kerstin Blackburn
✉ 1 Builders Square,
Court Hill, Littlebourne,
Canterbury,
Kent,
CT2 1XU ▣
☎ 01227 728028 📠 01227 710118

📧 kerstin.blackburn@btinternet.com
ⓦ www.goodgollybeardolly.com
Est. 2002 **Stock size** Small
Stock Antique bears, dolls,
rabbits, collectables, books
Open Mon–Fri 9am–5pm
Services Restoration

⊞ Jimmy Warren
Contact Mr J Warren
✉ Cedar Lodge,
28 The Hill, Littlebourne,
Canterbury, Kent,
CT3 1TA ▣
☎ 01227 721510 📠 01227 722431
📧 enquiries@jimmywarren.co.uk
ⓦ www.jimmywarren.co.uk
Est. 1973 **Stock size** Large
Stock Unusual antiques, garden
ornaments
Open Mon–Sun 10am–5pm
Services Valuations

LYMINGE

➹ Valley Auctions
Contact Mr E T Hall
✉ Claygate, Brady Road,
Lyminge, Folkestone, Kent,
CT18 8EU ▣
☎ 01303 862134 📠 01303 862134
Est. 1978
Open Mon–Fri 9am–5pm
Sales General antiques sale
Sun 9.30am, viewing Sat 1–6pm
Frequency Monthly except Aug,
Dec
Catalogues Yes

MAIDSTONE

⊞ Ad-Age Antique
Advertising
Contact Mike Standen
✉ Maidstone, Kent,
ME16 8JN ▣
☎ 01622 670595
Est. 1972 **Stock size** Medium
Stock Advertising signs, enamel,
tinplate, packaging, tobacco,
confectionary collectables
Open By appointment

⊞ Courtyard Curios
Contact Richard Attwell
✉ 6 Brewer Street,
Maidstone, Kent,
ME14 1RU ▣
☎ 01622 090479 📠 01622 090479
Est. 1995 **Stock size** Medium
Stock General antiques and
collectables
Open Mon–Sat 9am–5pm

⊞ Gem Antiques
Contact Mark Rackham
✉ 10 Gabriels Hill,
Maidstone,
Kent,
ME15 6JG ▣
☎ 01622 763344 📠 01622 844811
ⓦ www.gemantiques.com
Est. 1994 **Stock size** Medium
Stock Jewellery
Open Mon–Sat 9.30am–5pm
Services Repairs

⊞ Sutton Valence
Antiques (LAPADA,
CINOA)
Contact Nigel Mullarkey or
Tony Foster
✉ Unit 4,
Haslemere Parkwood Estate,
Sutton Road,
Maidstone, Kent,
ME15 9NL ▣
☎ 01622 675332 📠 01622 692593
📧 svantiques@aol.com
ⓦ www.svantiques.co.uk
Est. 1986 **Stock size** Large
Stock 18th–19thC furniture,
clocks, china, glass
Open Mon–Fri 9am–5pm
Sat 9am–1pm
Services Valuations, shipping

⊞ Whatever Comics
Contact Mr M Armario
✉ 5 Middle Row,
High Street, Maidstone,
Kent,
ME14 1TF
☎ 01622 681041
ⓦ www.whatevercomics.co.uk
Est. 1988 **Stock size** Medium
Stock American comics, *Star Trek*
and *Star Wars* toys, movie-
related items, sci-fi collectables,
Beanie Babies, action figures
Open Mon–Sat 10am–5.30pm

MARGATE

⊞ Heritage Antiques
Contact Brian Selman
✉ 105 Canterbury Road,
Margate,
Kent,
CT9 5AX
☎ 01843 209595
Est. 2000 **Stock size** Medium
Stock Antique furniture,
paintings, silver, bronzes, glass
Open Thur–Sat 10am–4pm
Services Valuations, informal
lectures

NEWENDEN

**⊞ Ingrid Nilson
(LAPADA)** *Contact* Ingrid Nilson
✉ Newenden, Kent,
TN18 🅿
☎ 01797 252030 ✆ 01797 252030
📱 07970 110370
📧 ingrid@ingridnilson.com
🌐 www.ingridnilson.com
Est. 1989 *Stock size* Small
Stock Decorative antique prints
Open By appointment only
Fairs Claridge's Antiques Fair
London, Northern Antiques Fair
Harrogate
Services Framing

NORTHFLEET

⊞ Northfleet Hill Antiques
Contact Martine Kilby
✉ 36 The Hill, Northfleet,
Gravesend, Kent,
DA11 9EX 🅿
☎ 01474 321521 ✆ 01474 350921
📱 07770 993906
Est. 1986 *Stock size* Medium
Stock Furniture, collectables,
glass, china
Open Mon Tues Fri 10am–5pm
Fairs Mainwarings Chelsea
Antiques Fair
Services Upholstery

ORPINGTON

⊞ In Retrospect
Contact David Holman
✉ 107–109 High Street,
Orpington, Kent,
BR6 0LG 🅿
☎ 01689 835900 ✆ 01689 891021
📧 info@retro.fsworld.co.uk
🌐 www.awards-uk.com
Est. 1996 *Stock size* Large
Stock Antiques, collectables
Open Mon–Fri 10am–5pm
Sat 9.30am–5pm closed Thur

**⊞ Priory Antiques &
Collectables**
Contact Mahshid Travers-Spencer
✉ 89 High Street, Orpington,
Kent, BR6 0LF 🅿
☎ 07785 705750
📱 07785 705750
📧 lesspencer7@hotmail.com
Est. 2003 *Stock size* Medium
Stock General antiques and
collectables
Open Tues–Fri 10am–6pm
Sat 9.30am–5.30pm

OTFORD

**⊞ Ellenor Hospice Care
Shop**
Contact Mrs Gill Saunderson
✉ 11a High Street,
Otford, Kent,
TN14 5PG 🅿
☎ 01959 524322
Est. 1995 *Stock size* Medium
Stock General antiques
Open Mon–Sat 10am–5pm
April–October 10am–4pm
November–March
Services Tea rooms

⊞ Mandarin Gallery
Contact Mr Joseph Liu
✉ The Mill Pond,
16 High Street,
Otford, Sevenoaks,
Kent,
TN14 5PQ 🅿
☎ 01959 522778 ✆ 01732 457399
Est. 1984 *Stock size* Medium
Stock Mainly Chinese Oriental
furniture, ivory, wood carvings,
silk, paintings
Open Tues–Sat 10am–5pm
Services Restoration

**🏠 Otford Antique and
Collectors Centre**
Contact Mr David Lowrie
✉ 26–28 High Street,
Otford, Sevenoaks,
Kent,
TN14 5PQ 🅿
☎ 01959 522025 ✆ 01959 525858
📧 info@otfordantiques.co.uk
🌐 www.otfordantiques.co.uk
Est. 1997 *Stock size* Large
No. of dealers 34
Stock General antiques,
collectables
Open Mon–Sat 10am–5pm
Sun 11am–4pm
Services Restoration, valuations,
upholstery

🔨 John M Peyto & Co Ltd
Contact John Peyto
✉ The Coach House,
Rowdow Lane, Otford Hills,
Sevenoaks, Kent,
TN15 6XN 🅿
☎ 01959 524022 ✆ 01959 522100
Est. 1992
Open Mon–Fri 7.30am–6pm
Sales General antiques 1st and 3rd
Sat 10am, viewing Fri 8am–6pm
Frequency Monthly
Catalogues Yes

PETTS WOOD

🏠 The Beehive
Contact Mr Johnson
✉ 22 Station Square,
Petts Wood,
Kent,
BR5 1NA 🅿
☎ 01689 890675
Est. 1996 *Stock size* Medium
No. of dealers 50
Stock Antiques and collectables
Open Mon–Sat 9.30am–5pm

⊞ Candlestick & Bakelite
Contact Martin Barnett
✉ The Beehive,
22 Station Square,
Petts Wood,
Kent,
BR5 1NA 🅿
☎ 020 8467 3743 ✆ 020 8467 3743
📧 candlestick.bakelite@mac.com
🌐 www.candlestickandbakelite.co.uk
Est. 1989 *Stock size* Small
Stock Collectable telephones
Open Mon–Sat 10am–5pm
Services Repairs

⊞ Memory Lane
Contact Mr R K Ludlam
✉ 105 Queensway,
Petts Wood,
Kent,
BR5 1DG 🅿
☎ 01689 826832
Est. 1972 *Stock size* Large
Stock General antiques and
collectables
Open Mon–Sat 9.30am–5.30pm
Fairs Ardingly
Services House clearance

PLUCKLEY

**⊞ Catchpole and Rye
(SALVO)**
Contact Diana Rabjohns or
Tony O'Donnell
✉ Saracen's Dairy,
Pluckley Road,
Pluckley,
Kent,
TN27 0SA 🅿
☎ 01233 840840 ✆ 01233 840444
📧 info@crye.co.uk
🌐 www.crye.co.uk
Est. 1991 *Stock size* Large
Stock Baths, basins, cisterns, taps,
sanitary ware
Open Mon–Fri 9am–5pm
Sat by appointment
Services Design service

37

RAINHAM

⊞ The Bookmark
Contact Mr G Harrison
✉ Unit 15c, Rainham Shopping
Centre, Rainham,
Gillingham, Kent,
ME8 7HW ▣
☎ 01634 365987
Est. 1992 *Stock size* Large
Stock Antiquarian, second-hand,
general books, fiction, non-
fiction
Open Mon–Sat 9.30am–5.30pm

RAMSGATE

⊞ B & D Collectors' Toys
Contact Mr R Smith
✉ 332 Margate Road,
Ramsgate, Kent,
CT12 6SQ ▣
☎ 01843 589606 ✆ 01843 589606
ⓦ www.banddcollectorstoys.com
Est. 1991 *Stock size* Large
Stock Old and obsolete toys,
Dinky, Corgi, new collectable
toys, *Star Wars*
Open Mon–Thur 9.30am–5.30pm
Wed 9.30am–1pm
Fri Sat 9.30am–6pm
Services Valuations, mail order

⊞ Granny's Attic
Contact Miss Penny Warn
✉ 2 Addington Street,
Ramsgate, Kent,
CT11 9JL ▣
☎ 01843 588955/596288
Ⓜ 07773 155339
ⓔ grannysattic@amserve.com
Est. 1986 *Stock size* Large
Stock Victorian, Edwardian, pre-
1930s furniture, china, silver,
glass, mirrors, pictures etc
Open Mon–Wed Fri–Sat
10am–5pm closed 1–2pm
Services Free local delivery,
delivery in UK and abroad can be
arranged

⊞ Thanet Antiques &
Marine Paraphernalia Ltd
Contact Mr Roy Fomison
✉ Archway 8, Military Road,
Ramsgate, Kent,
CT11 9LG ▣
☎ 01843 597336 ✆ 01843 597336
ⓦ www.thanetantiques.co.uk
Est. 1983 *Stock size* Large
Stock General antiques,
furniture, collectables, fireplaces
Open Mon–Sun 9am–5pm

⊞ Yesteryear Railwayana
Contact Patrick or Mary Mullen
✉ Stablings Cottage,
Goodwin Road,
Ramsgate,
Kent,
CT11 0JJ
☎ 01843 587283 ✆ 01843 587283
ⓔ mullen@yesrail.com or
mullen@yesrail.co.uk
ⓦ www.yesrail.com or
www.yesrail.co.uk
Est. 1980 *Stock size* Medium
Stock Out-of-print and scarce
books, illustrations,
documentation and printed
ephemera, both important and
trivial, relating to some aspect of
world railway history
Open Mail order or by
appointment
Services Catalogue monthly

ROCHESTER

⊞ Baggins Book Bazaar
Contact Mr Godfrey George
✉ 19 High Street,
Rochester, Kent,
ME1 1PY ▣
☎ 01634 811651 ✆ 01634 840591
ⓔ godfreygeorge@btinternet.com
ⓦ www.bagginsbooks.co.uk
Est. 1986 *Stock size* Large
Stock Antiquarian, rare, second-
hand books
Open Mon–Sun 10am–6pm
Services Book search, ordering
service

⊞ Cathedral Antiques
Contact Jeanette Dickson
✉ 83 High Street,
Rochester, Kent,
ME1 1LX ▣
☎ 01634 842735
Ⓜ 07944 870214
Est. 1974 *Stock size* Large
Stock 1600–1910 furniture
Open Mon–Sat 9.30am–5pm
Services Valuations for probate
and insurance

⊞ City Antiques Ltd
Contact Mr Brian Ware
✉ 78 High Street,
Rochester, Kent,
ME1 1JY ▣
☎ 01634 841278
Ⓜ 07855 388620
ⓔ wareclockmad@aol.com
Est. 1997 *Stock size* Large
Stock Clocks, barometers,

Georgian, Victorian, Edwardian
furniture
Open Mon–Sat 10am–5pm
closed some Wed
Services Clock and barometer
repair, furniture restoration

⊞ Cottage Style Antiques
Contact Mr W Miskimmin
✉ 24 Bill Street Road,
Frindsbury,
Rochester,
Kent,
ME2 4RB ▣
☎ 01634 717623
Est. 1982 *Stock size* Large
Stock Collectables, architectural
salvage, fireplaces, interesting
pieces
Open Mon–Sat 9.30am–5.30pm
Services Restoration, repairs

⊞ Dragonlee Collectables
Contact Janet Davies
✉ Memories,
128 High Street,
Rochester, Kent,
ME1 1JT ▣
☎ 01622 729502
Ⓜ 07761 400128
Est. 1995 *Stock size* Medium
Stock Noritake, ceramic
collectables, furniture
Open Mon–Sat 9am–5pm
Sun 11am–4pm
Fairs Detling

⊞ Fieldstaff Antiques
Contact Jane Staff or Jim Field
✉ 93 High Street,
Rochester,
Kent,
ME1 1LX ▣
☎ 01634 846144
ⓔ fieldstaffantiques@supanet.com
ⓦ www.fieldstaffantiques.com
Est. 1996 *Stock size* Large
Stock Antiques, collectables
Open Mon–Sat 10am–5pm
Services House clearance

⊞ Kaizen International Ltd
Contact Jason Hunt or Jo Olivares
✉ 88 The High Street,
Rochester,
Kent,
ME1 1JT ▣
☎ 01634 814132 ✆ 01634 827237
Est. 1997 *Stock size* Large
Stock Jewellery, silver, furniture,
wine-related items
Open Mon–Sat 10am–5pm
Services Valuations

⌂ **Memories**
Contact Mrs M Kilby
✉ **128 High Street,
Rochester, Kent,
ME1 1JT** 🅿
☎ 01634 811044
Est. 1985 *Stock size* Large
No. of dealers 12
Stock Small furniture, china,
general antiques
Open Mon–Fri 9.30am–5pm
Sat 9am–5pm Sun 11am–4.30pm

ROLVENDEN

⊞ **Barn Antiques**
Contact Cindy Knowles
✉ **Halden Lane, Rolvenden,
Cranbrook, Kent,
TN17 4BJ** 🅿
☎ 01580 240457
📱 07753 836305
✉ cindysantiques@hotmail.com
Est. 2005 *Stock size* Large
Stock French and English painted
furniture and accessories, soft
furnishings
Open Wed–Sat 10am–4pm
Fairs Ardingly

⊞ **Cindy's Antiques**
Contact Cindy Knowles
✉ **Trafalgar Barn,
Regent Street, Rolvenden,
Cranbrook, Kent,
TN17 4PB** 🅿
☎ 01580 240457
📱 07753 836305
✉ cindysantiques@hotmail.com
Est. 2000 *Stock size* Large
Stock Furniture, bric-a-brac
Open Tues–Sat 10am–4pm
Fairs Ardingly

⊞ **Falstaff Antiques**
Contact C M Booth
✉ **63–67 High Street,
Rolvenden, Kent,
TN17 4LP** 🅿
☎ 01580 241234
Est. 1964 *Stock size* Medium
Stock General antiques and
reproductions
Open Mon–Sat 10am–6pm

⊞ **J D and R M Walters**
Contact Mr John Walters
✉ **10 Regent Street,
Rolvenden, Kent,
TN17 4PE** 🅿
☎ 01580 241563
✉ waltersorchids@aol.com
Est. 1979 *Stock size* Medium

Stock 18th–19thC furniture
Open Mon–Fri 8am–6pm Sat
11am–4.30pm or by appointment
Services Restoration

SANDGATE

⊞ **Christopher Buck
Antiques (BADA)**
Contact Christopher Buck
✉ **56–60 Sandgate High Street,
Sandgate, Folkestone,
Kent,
CT20 3AP** 🅿
☎ 01303 221229 📠 01303 221229
📱 07836 551515
✉ cb@christopherbuck.co.uk
Est. 1983
Stock 18thC and early 19thC
English furniture and associated
items
Open Mon–Sat 9.30am–5pm
Fairs Olympia, BADA
Services Valuations, restoration

⊞ **Emporium Antiques**
Contact Mr West
✉ **31–33 Sandgate High Street,
Sandgate, Folkestone, Kent,
CT20 3AH** 🅿
📱 07860 149387
Est. 1984 *Stock size* Medium
Stock Antique and decorative
furniture
Open By appointment

⊞ **Finch Antiques**
Contact Mr Finch
✉ **40 Sandgate High Street,
Sandgate, Folkestone, Kent,
CT20 3AP** 🅿
☎ 01303 240725
Est. 1980 *Stock size* Medium
Stock Early 18thC–1930s
furniture
Open Mon–Sat 9.30am–5.30pm
Sun 10.30am–4pm
Services Restoration

⊞ **Michael W Fitch
Antiques (LAPADA)**
Contact Mr Michael Fitch
✉ **95, 97, 99 Sandgate High
Street, Sandgate,
Kent,
CT20 3BY** 🅿
☎ 01303 249600 📠 01303 249600
🌐 www.michaelfitchantiques.co.uk
Est. 1977 *Stock size* Large
Stock 18th–19thC and Edwardian
furniture, furnishings, clocks
Open Mon–Sat 10am–5.30pm
Services Valuations

⊞ **Freeman and Lloyd
Antiques (BADA, LAPADA)**
Contact Mr K Freeman or
Mr R Lloyd
✉ **44 Sandgate High Street,
Sandgate, Folkestone, Kent,
CT20 3AP** 🅿
☎ 01303 248986 📠 01303 241353
📱 07860 100073
✉ enquiries@freemanandlloyd.com
🌐 www.freemanandlloyd.com
Est. 1968 *Stock size* Large
Stock 18th–early 19thC furniture,
accessories, pictures, clocks,
bronzes
Open Tues Thurs–Sat 10am–5pm
Fairs Olympia (February, June,
November), BADA (March)
Services Valuations

⊞ **David Gilbert Antiques**
Contact Mr D Gilbert
✉ **30 Sandgate High Street,
Sandgate, Folkestone, Kent,
CT20 3AP** 🅿
☎ 01303 850491
Est. 1984 *Stock size* Large
Stock Victorian–Edwardian Arts
and Crafts
Open Mon–Sat 9.30am–4.30pm
or by appointment
Services Delivery

⊞ **Gabrielle de Giles**
Contact Gabrielle de Giles
✉ **21 Sandgate High Street,
Sandgate, Folkestone, Kent,
CT20 3BD** 🅿
☎ 01303 255600 📠 01233 720156
📱 07721 015263
✉ gabrielle@gabrielledegiles.com
🌐 www.gabrielledegiles.com
Est. 2002 *Stock size* Medium
Stock Antique and country
furniture, architectural items
Open Tue–Sat 10.30am–5.30pm
or by appointment
Fairs Battersea Decorative
Antique & Textile Fair, Antiques
& Audacity Arundel

⊞ **Jonathan Greenwall
Antiques (LAPADA)**
Contact Mr J Greenwall
✉ **61–63 Sandgate High Street,
Sandgate, Folkestone, Kent,
CT20 3AH** 🅿
☎ 01303 248987 📠 01303 248987
📱 07799 133700
Est. 1969 *Stock size* Large
Stock Jewellery, clocks, watches,
furniture, pictures, prints, glass
Open Mon–Sat 9.30am–5pm Sun

Bank Holidays by appointment
Services Valuations, watch, clock
and jewellery repair

David M Lancefield Antiques (LAPADA)
Contact David Lancefield
✉ 53 Sandgate High Street, Sandgate, Folkestone, Kent, CT 20 3AH 🅿
☎ 01303 850149 📠 01303 850149
📧 david@antiquedirect.freeserve.co.uk
🌐 www.davidmlancefield.co.uk
Est. 1976 *Stock size* Large
Stock General antiques
Open Mon–Sat 10am–6pm Sun
Bank Holidays 11am–5pm
Services Valuations, restoration

Old English Pine
Contact Andre Martin
✉ 100–102 Sandgate High Street, Sandgate, Folkestone, Kent, C72O 3BY
☎ 01303 248560 📠 01303 248560
Est. 1985 *Stock size* Large
Stock Old and new furniture and collectables
Open Mon–Sat 10am–6pm
Services Restoration

Sandgate Passage
Contact Mr John Rendle
✉ 82 Sandgate High Street, Sandgate, Folkestone, Kent, CT20 3BX 🅿
☎ 01303 850973
Est. 1987 *Stock size* Medium
Stock Old postcards, prints, books
Open Mon–Sat 10.30am–4pm
Fairs DMG Detling, York, Twickenham, Guildford, Woking
Services Valuations

SANDWICH

All Our Yesterdays
Contact Sandy Baker
✉ 3 Cattle Market, Sandwich, Kent, CT13 9AE 🅿
☎ 01304 614756
📧 chgramophones@aol.com
Est. 1994 *Stock size* Medium
Stock General antiques, collectables, unusual items
Open Mon–Sat 10.30am–2.30pm or by appointment closed Wed
Services Gramophone repairs

Chris Baker Gramophones (CLPGS)
Contact Mr Chris Baker
✉ 3 Cattle Market, Sandwich, Kent, CT13 9AE 🅿
☎ 01304 614756/375767
📠 01304 614696
📱 07808 831462
📧 chgramophones@aol.com
Est. 1996 *Stock size* Large
Stock Mechanical music
Open Mon–Sat 10.30am–2.30pm closed Wed
Services Repairs, stock list available on request

SEAL

Campbell and Archard (BADA)
Contact Paul Archard
✉ Lychgate House, Church Street, Seal, Kent, TN15 0AR 🅿
☎ 01732 761153
📧 campbellarchard@btclick.com
Est. 1970 *Stock size* Large
Stock Austro-Hungarian 1790–1850 clocks and regulators, English regulators and bracket clocks
Open By appointment only
Fairs Olympia, Duke of York's
Services Restoration

SEVENOAKS

Artworks Sculpture Gallery
Contact Simon Wheeler
✉ 3 The Shambles, Sevenoaks, Kent, TN13 1LJ
☎ 01732 450960
🌐 www.artworksgallery.co.uk
Est. 1995 *Stock size* Medium
Stock Bronze, resin, metal sculpture, figurative and abstract
Open Tues–Sun 10am–4pm closed Wed

Neill Robinson Blaxill (LAPADA)
Contact Neill Blaxill
✉ 21 St Johns Hill, Sevenoaks, Kent, TN13 3NX 🅿
☎ 01732 454179
🌐 www.hyperiondials.co.uk
Est. 2003 *Stock size* Medium
Stock Garden antiques,

decorative items, clocks, barometers
Open Mon–Sat 10am–6pm or by appointment
Fairs Hampton Court
Services Clock restoration

Bonhams
✉ 13 Lime Tree Walk, Sevenoaks, Kent, TN13 YH 🅿
☎ 01732 740310 📠 01732 741842
📧 sevenoaks@bonhams.com
🌐 www.bonhams.com
Est. 1793
Open Mon–Fri 8.30am–5pm
Sales Regional office. Regular sales in London, New York, San Francisco, Sydney, Geneva and Los Angeles, as well as in regional sales rooms across the UK. Free auction valuations; insurance and probate valuations
Catalogues Yes

Gem Antiques
Contact Mr M Rackham
✉ 122a High Street, Sevenoaks, Kent, TN13 1AP 🅿
☎ 01732 743540
🌐 www.gemantiques.com
Est. 1994 *Stock size* Medium
Stock Jewellery
Open Mon–Sat 9.30am–5pm
Services Clock repairs

Ibbett Mosely
Contact Mr Hodge
✉ 125 High Street, Sevenoaks, Kent, TN13 1UT 🅿
☎ 01732 456731 📠 01732 740910
📧 auctions@ibbettmosely.co.uk
🌐 www.ibbettmosely.co.uk
Est. 1935
Open Mon–Fri 9am–5.30pm
Sales General antiques, 9 sales a year, call for viewing times. Sales held at Otford Memorial Hall, Otford, Sevenoaks
Frequency 9 a year
Catalogues Yes

SISSINGHURST

Sissinghurst Antiques Gallery
Contact Jennifer Stubbs
✉ The Street, Sissinghurst, Kent, TN17 2JG 🅿
☎ 01580 712514

ⓜ 07786 255978
Est. 2002 *Stock size* Small
Stock Antique furniture, textiles, silver, jewellery, decorative items
Open Tues–Sat 10am–5pm
Services Valuations

SITTINGBOURNE

⊞ Past Sentence
Contact Mrs K Rowland
✉ 70 High Street,
Sittingbourne,
Kent,
ME10 4PB 🅿
☎ 01795 590000
🅔 enquiries@pastsentence.com
Est. 1997 *Stock size* Medium
Stock Second-hand and antiquarian books
Open Tues Thurs–Sat 9.30am–5.30pm

SNODLAND

⊞ AJC Antiquities
Contact Andrew Cooke
✉ 73 Lucas Road,
Snodland,
Kent,
ME6 5PZ 🅿
☎ 01634 352383
ⓜ 07787 101472
🅔 amjcook@blueyonder.co.uk
Est. 1999 *Stock size* Medium
Stock Art Deco, militaria, collectables, jewellery
Open Mon–Fri 9am–5pm

⚒ Amhuerst Auctions
Contact Andrew Cooke
✉ 73 Lucas Road,
Snodland,
Kent,
ME6 5PZ 🅿
☎ 01634 352383
ⓜ 07787 101472
🅔 amjcook@blueyonder.co.uk
🅦 www.amhuerstauctions.co.uk
Open Mon–Fri 9am–5pm
Sales Auction every second Saturday, antiques, furniture, collectables, clocks, jewellery
Catalogues Yes

STOCKBURY

⊞ Steppes Hill Farm Antiques (BADA)
Contact Mr William Buck
✉ Steppes Hill Farm, Stockbury,
Sittingbourne, Kent,
ME9 7RB 🅿

☎ 01795 842205 🅖 01795 842493
ⓜ 07931 594218
🅔 dwabuck@btinternet.com
Stock size Small
Stock General antiques, English porcelain, collectable silver
Open Mon–Fri 9am–5pm
Fairs Olympia, International Ceramics Fair, BADA Duke of York's
Services Valuations, restoration

SUTTON VALENCE

⊞ Sutton Valence Antiques (LAPADA, CINOA)
Contact Owen Marles
✉ North Street,
Sutton Valence,
Maidstone,
Kent,
ME17 3AP 🅿
☎ 01622 843333 🅖 01622 843499
🅔 svantiques@aol.com
Est. 1978 *Stock size* Large
Stock 18th–19thC furniture, clocks, china, glass
Open Mon–Fri 9am–5pm
Sat 10am–4pm
Services Valuations, shipping, container packing

TENTERDEN

⊞ Flower House Antiques
Contact Mr Q Johnson
✉ 90 High Street,
Tenterden,
Kent,
TN30 6JB 🅿
☎ 01580 763764 🅖 01580 291251
or 01797 270386
Est. 1995 *Stock size* Large
Stock 17th–early 19thC furniture, objets d'art, chandeliers, worldwide general antiques
Open Mon–Sat 9.30am–5.30pm
Sun by appointment
Services Valuations, restoration, items purchased

⊞ Gaby's Clocks and Things
Contact Gaby Gunst
✉ 140 High Street,
Tenterden,
Kent,
TN30 6HT 🅿
☎ 01580 765818
Est. 1969 *Stock size* Medium
Stock Clocks, barometers
Open Mon–Sat 10.30am–5pm
Services Clock and barometer restoration

⚒ Lambert and Foster
Contact Mrs G Brazier
✉ 102 High Street,
Tenterden,
Kent,
TN30 6HT 🅿
☎ 01580 762083 🅖 01580 764317
🅔 saleroom@lambertandfoster.co.uk
🅦 www.lambertandfoster.co.uk
Est. 1830
Open Mon–Fri 9am–5.30pm
Sales General antiques sale Thurs 9.30am, viewing Sun 10.30am–4pm Tues 9.30am–4.30pm
Frequency Monthly
Catalogues Yes

⊞ Memories
Contact Mr Mark Lloyds
✉ 74 High Street,
Tenterden, Kent,
TN30 6AU 🅿
☎ 01580 763416
Est. 1995 *Stock size* Large
Stock Antiques, collectables, small furniture
Open Mon–Sat 10am–5pm
Sun 11am–4pm

⊞ Tenterden Antique & Silver Vaults
Contact T Smith
✉ 66 High Street,
Tenterden, Kent,
TN30 6AU 🅿
☎ 01580 765885
Est. 1991 *Stock size* Large
Stock Clocks, silver, china, glass, collectables, jewellery
Open Mon–Sat 10am–5pm
Sun 11am–4pm
Services House clearance

⌂ Tenterden Antiques Centre
Contact Mick Ellin
✉ 66a High Street,
Tenterden, Kent,
TN30 6AU 🅿
☎ 01580 765655
ⓜ 07776 203755
Est. 1990 *Stock size* Large
No. of dealers 7
Stock Furniture, Art Deco, china, clocks, silver, jewellery, militaria, porcelain, bric-a-brac
Open Mon–Sat 10am–5pm
Sun 11am–5pm

⊞ Tussie Mussies
✉ The Old Stables,
2b East Cross, High Street,

Tenterden, Kent,
TN30 6AD
☎ 01580 766224
Est. 2002 *Stock size* Small
Stock General antiques, militaria,
home decorations and
collectables
Open Mon–Sat 9.30am–5.30pm
Sun 10am–4pm summer only

TEYNHAM

⊞ **Jackson-Grant Antiques**
Contact Mr David Jackson-Grant
✉ 133 London Road,
Teynham,
Sittingbourne,
Kent,
ME9 9QJ 🅿
☎ 01795 522027
📱 07831 591881
✉ david.jacksongrant@
btopenworld.com
Est. 1966 *Stock size* Large
Stock Antique furniture, small
items
Open Mon–Sat 10am–5pm
Sun 1–5pm closed Wed
Services Valuations

TONBRIDGE

⌂ **Barden House Antiques**
Contact Mrs Brenda Parsons
✉ 1 & 3 Priory Street,
Tonbridge,
Kent,
TN2 2AP 🅿
☎ 01732 350142
Est. 1959 *Stock size* Large
No. of dealers 4
Stock General antiques, prints,
watercolours, jewellery, china,
small pieces of furniture
Open Wed–Sat 10am–5pm

⊞ **Greta May Antiques**
Contact Mrs G May
✉ The New Curiosity Shop,
Tollgate Buildings,
Hadlow Road,
Tonbridge,
Kent,
TN9 1NX 🅿
☎ 01732 366730
✉ gretamayantiques@hotmail.com
Est. 1988 *Stock size* Medium
Stock Furniture, silver, silver
plate, china, glass, teddy bears
Open Tues Thurs–Sat
10am–4.30pm
Fairs Hollingbourne, Maidstone
Services Teddy bear repairs

⊞ **Derek Roberts Antiques
(BADA)**
Contact Mr Paul Archard
✉ 25 Shipbourne Road,
Tonbridge, Kent,
TN10 3DN 🅿
☎ 01732 358986 📠 01732 771842
✉ drclocks@clara.net
🖥 www.qualityantiqueclocks.com
Est. 1968 *Stock size* Large
Stock 17th–19thC clocks, books
written by Derek Roberts
Open Mon–Fri 9.30am–5pm
Sat 10am–4pm
Fairs Olympia (Nov), BADA,
Harrogate (Sept)
Services Valuations, annual
catalogues

TUNBRIDGE WELLS

⊞ **Aaron Antiques**
Contact Ron Goodman
✉ 77 St Johns Road,
Tunbridge Wells, Kent,
TN4 9TT 🅿
☎ 01892 517644
📱 07710 100407
Est. 1967 *Stock size* Large
Stock Coins, medals, clocks,
china, silver, paintings, prints,
scientific and musical instruments,
furniture, Chinese porcelain
Open By appointment

⊞ **Adams Arts & Antiques
Ltd**
Contact Mr M Adams
✉ Festival House,
Chapman Way, High Brooms,
Tunbridge Wells, Kent,
TN2 3EF 🅿
☎ 01892 557777 📠 01892 557777
Est. 1998 *Stock size* Medium
Stock Bronze garden statuary
Open Mon–Sun 9am–5pm

⊞ **Amadeus Antiques**
Contact Pat Davies
✉ 32 Mount Ephraim,
Tunbridge Wells, Kent,
TN4 8AU 🅿
☎ 01892 544406
Est. 1990 *Stock size* Medium
Stock China, lighting, furniture
Open Mon–Sat 10am–5pm
closed Tues

⊞ **The Architectural Stores**
Contact Nick Bates
✉ 55 St Johns Road,
Tunbridge Wells, Kent,
TN4 9TP 🅿

☎ 01892 540368
✉ nick@thearchitecturalstores.co.uk
Est. 1987 *Stock size* Medium
Stock Antique fireplaces, period
lighting, architectural
Open Tues–Sat 10am–5.30pm

⊞ **Henry Baines (LAPADA)**
Contact Mr H Baines
✉ 14 Church Road,
Southborough,
Tunbridge Wells, Kent,
TN4 0RX 🅿
☎ 01892 532099 📠 01892 532099
📱 07973 214406
Est. 1968 *Stock size* Large
Stock Oak, country furniture
Open Prior telephone call
advised

⊞ **Beau Nash Antiques**
Contact Mr David Wrenn
✉ 29 Lower Walk,
The Pantiles,
Tunbridge Wells,
Kent,
TN2 5TD 🅿
☎ 01892 537810
Est. 1990 *Stock size* Large
Stock Georgian–Edwardian
period furniture, associated
decorative items
Open Tues–Sat 11am–5pm

⊞ **Calverley Antiques**
Contact Mr P Nimmo
✉ 30 Crescent Road,
Tunbridge Wells,
Kent,
TN1 2LZ 🅿
☎ 01892 538254
✉ phil@calverleyantiques.com
Est. 1984 *Stock size* Large
Stock Pine, decorative and
painted furniture
Open Mon–Sun 9.30am–5.30pm
Fairs Ardingly
Services House clearance

⊞ **Chapel Place Antiques**
Contact Mrs J A Clare
✉ 9 Chapel Place,
Tunbridge Wells,
Kent,
TN1 1YQ
☎ 01892 546561 📠 01892 546561
Est. 1984 *Stock size* Large
Stock Antique and modern silver,
hand-painted Limoges boxes,
amber jewellery, silver photo
frames, old silver plate, claret jugs
Open Mon–Sat 9am–5.30pm
Services Valuations

Crescent Road Antiques
Contact Mr Twiddy
✉ 36 Crescent Road,
Tunbridge Wells, Kent,
TN1 2LZ 🅿
☎ 01892 537815
🌐 www.crescentantiques.com
Est. 1993 *Stock size* Medium
Stock General antiques
Open Mon–Sat 9am–5pm

Downlane Hall Antiques
Contact Mrs Hayes
✉ Culverden Down,
St Johns, Tunbridge Wells,
Kent,
TN4 9SA 🅿
☎ 01892 522440
🌐 www.downlanehall.co.uk
Est. 1980 *Stock size* Large
Stock Georgian–Victorian
furniture
Open Mon–Sat 9am–4pm
Services Restoration

➣ Dreweatt Neate Tunbridge Wells Salerooms (SOFAA)
Contact Daniel Bray
✉ Auction Hall,
The Pantiles,
Tunbridge Wells, Kent,
TN1 1UU 🅿
☎ 01892 544500 📠 01892 515191
📧 tunbridgewells@dnfa.com
🌐 www.dnfa.com
Est. 1759
Open Mon–Fri 9am–5pm
Sales Fine art and antiques sales
(7 a year), 2 Tunbridge ware,
Fri 10.30am, viewing Sat
9am–12.30pm Tues 9am–7pm
Wed 9am–5pm Thurs 9am–3pm
Fri 9–10am. Catalogues available
on website
Frequency 7 a year
Catalogues Yes

Glassdrumman
Contact Mr or Mrs G Dyson Rooke
✉ 7 Union Square,
The Pantiles,
Tunbridge Wells, Kent,
TN4 8HE 🅿
☎ 01892 538615
Est. 1989 *Stock size* Large
Stock Georgian, Victorian,
second-hand jewellery, silver,
pocket watches, decorative
items, furniture
Open Tues–Sat 10am–5.30pm
Services Repairs

Pamela Goodwin
Contact Pamela Goodwin
✉ 11 The Pantiles,
Tunbridge Wells, Kent,
TN2 5TD 🅿
☎ 01892 618200 📠 01892 618200
📱 07751 816443
📧 mail@goodwinantiques.co.uk
🌐 www.goodwinantiques.co.uk
Est. 1998 *Stock size* Large
Stock 18th–20thC furniture,
clocks, silver, English porcelain,
Moorcroft, Doulton, glass,
sewing collectables, Tunbridge
ware, musical boxes
Open Mon–Fri 9.30am–5pm
Sat 9.30am–5.30pm

➣ Gorringes Incorporating Julian Dawson (SOFAA)
Contact Mr Leslie Gillham
✉ 15 The Pantiles,
Tunbridge Wells, Kent,
TN2 5TD 🅿
☎ 01892 619670 📠 01892 619671
📧 tunbridge.wells@gorringes.co.uk
🌐 www.gorringes.co.uk
Est. 1926
Open Mon–Fri 8.30am–5.30pm
Sat 9am–noon
Sales Fine art and antiques sales
every 6 weeks Tues 11.30am,
viewing Mon prior noon–8pm
and day of sale 8.30–11am
Frequency Quarterly
Catalogues Yes

Hall's Bookshop
Contact Sabrina Izzard
✉ 20 Chapel Place,
Tunbridge Wells,
Kent,
TN1 1YQ
☎ 01892 527842
Est. 1898 *Stock size* Large
Stock Antiquarian and second-
hand books
Open Mon–Sat 9.30am–5pm

Peter Hoare Antiques
Contact Peter Hoare
✉ 35 London Road,
Southborough,
Tunbridge Wells,
Kent,
TN4 0PB 🅿
☎ 01892 524623
📧 phoare@nildram.co.uk
Est. 1983 *Stock size* Medium
Stock Arts and Crafts furniture
Open Tues–Sat 10am–5.30pm
Services Valuations

Howard Neville
Contact Mr H Neville
✉ 21 The Pantiles,
Tunbridge Wells,
Kent,
TN2 5TD 🅿
☎ 01892 511461 📠 020 7491 7623
📧 patrickboyd_carpenter@
hotmail.com
Est. 1986 *Stock size* Large
Stock Antiques and works of art
Open Mon–Sat 10am–5pm or by
appointment

Old Colonial
Contact Suzy Rees or Dee Martyn
✉ 56 St Johns Road,
Tunbridge Wells,
Kent,
TN4 9NY 🅿
☎ 01892 533993 📠 01892 513281
Est. 1994 *Stock size* Large
Stock Country antiques,
decorative items, painted
furniture
Open Tues–Sat 10am–5.30pm or
by appointment

Pantiles Antiques
Contact Mrs E M Blackburn
✉ 31 The Pantiles,
Tunbridge Wells,
Kent,
TN2 5TD 🅿
☎ 01892 531291 📠 01892 531291
Est. 1981 *Stock size* Medium
Stock Georgian and Edwardian
furniture, porcelain, decorative
pieces
Open Mon–Sat 9.30am–5pm
Services Restoration, upholstery

Pantiles Collectables
Contact Stephen Tewkesbury
✉ 1 The Corn Exchange,
The Pantiles,
Tunbridge Wells, Kent,
TN2 5TE 🅿
☎ 01892 538726
📧 carolineannefordham@
tiscali.co.uk
Est. 2001 *Stock size* Medium
Stock Post-war ceramics
Open Tues–Sat 10am–5pm
Sun by appointment
Services Valuations

Pantiles Spa Antiques
Contact Mrs J A Cowpland
✉ 4, 5 & 6 Union House,
The Pantiles, Royal Tunbridge
Wells, Kent,
TN4 8HE 🅿

☎ 01892 541377 🖶 01435 865660
🖂 psa.wells@btconnect.com
🌐 www.pantiles-spa-
antiques.co.uk
Est. 1987 *Stock size* Large
Stock Specialist dining room
tables and chairs, furniture, dolls,
porcelain, glass, prints,
watercolours, maps, clocks, silver
Open Mon–Fri 9.30am–5pm
Sat 9.30am–5.30pm
Services Free delivery within 30
mile radius

⊞ Phoenix Antiques
(WKADA)
Contact Robert Pilbeam,
Jane Stott or Peter Janes
🖂 51–53 St Johns Road,
Tunbridge Wells,
Kent,
TN4 9TP 🅿
☎ 01892 549099 🖶 01892 549099
🖂 shop@phoenixantiques.co.uk
🌐 www.phoenixantiques.co.uk
Est. 1989 *Stock size* Large
Stock 18th–19thC English and
French country furniture,
overmantel mirrors, associated
decorative items
Open Mon–Sat 10am–5.30pm or
by appointment

⊞ Sporting Antiques
Contact Mr L Franklin
🖂 10 Union Square,
The Pantiles,
Tunbridge Wells, Kent,
TN4 8HE 🅿
☎ 01892 522661 🖶 01892 522661
Est. 1993 *Stock size* Large
Stock Sporting antiques, arms,
armour, technical instruments,
tools
Open Mon–Sat 10am–5.30pm
telephone call advisable

⊞ John Thompson
Contact Mr J Thompson
🖂 27 The Pantiles,
Tunbridge Wells,
Kent,
TN2 5TD 🅿
☎ 01892 547215
Est. 1982 *Stock size* Medium
Stock 18th–early 19thC furniture,
late 17th–20thC paintings, glass,
porcelain
Open Tues–Sat 11am–5pm

⊞ Up Country Ltd
Contact Mr C Springett
🖂 The Old Corn Stores,

68 St Johns Road,
Tunbridge Wells,
Kent,
TN4 9PE 🅿
☎ 01892 523341 🖶 01892 530382
🖂 mail@upcountryantiques.co.uk
🌐 www.upcountryantiques.co.uk
Est. 1988 *Stock size* Large
Stock Antique and decorative
country furniture, rural artefacts
Open Mon–Sat 9am–5.30pm

⊞ Variety Box
Contact Penny Cogan
🖂 Tunbridge Wells,
Kent,
TN2
☎ 01892 531868
Est. 1982 *Stock size* Medium
Stock Tunbridge ware, hatpins,
fans, sewing and collectors' items
Open By appointment

⊞ World War Books
(OMRS, PBFA)
Contact Mr Tim Harper
🖂 Oaklands, Camden Park,
Tunbridge Wells, Kent,
TN2 5AE
☎ 01892 538465 🖶 01892 538465
🖂 wwarbooks@btinternet.com
Est. 1988 *Stock size* Large
Stock Military books including
manuals, weapon books,
regimental histories, maps,
photographs, diaries
Open Mail order or by
appointment
Fairs Arms and Armour Fair
(Birmingham), World War Book
Fair
Services Valuations, probate,
book search, catalogue

⊞ Yiju
Contact Wangtong
🖂 Yiju Ltd, 38 The Pantiles,
Tunbridge Wells,
Kent,
TN2 5TN 🅿
☎ 01892 517000 🖶 01892517000
🖂 yiju@netcomuk.co.uk
Est. 1998 *Stock size* Large
Stock Antique furniture and
ceramics
Open Tue–Sat 10am–5pm

⊞ Grandma's Attic
Contact S J Marsh
🖂 60 The Strand, Walmer, Kent,
CT14 7DP 🅿

☎ 01304 380121
Est. 1986 *Stock size* Medium
Stock Mirrors, Victoriana
Open Mon–Sat 9.45am–5.30pm
closed Thurs Sun by appointment
Services Restoration, gilding

WEST MALLING

⊞ The Old Clock Shop
Contact Mrs Sasha
🖂 63 High Street,
West Malling,
Kent,
ME19 6NA 🅿
☎ 01732 843246 🖶 01732 843246
🖂 theoldclockshop@tesco.net
🌐 www.theoldclockshop.co.uk
Est. 1975 *Stock size* Medium
Stock Clocks, barometers
Open Mon–Sat 9am–5pm
Services Restoration

WEST WICKHAM

🏛 Nightingale Antiques
and Craft Centre
Contact Maureen Haggerty
🖂 89–91 High Street,
West Wickham, Kent,
BR4 0LS 🅿
☎ 020 8777 0335 🖶 020 8776 2777
Est. 1998 *Stock size* Large
No. of dealers 20
Stock Victorian–Edwardian
furniture, 1930s oak, Royal
Doulton, Royal Crown Derby,
Moorcroft
Open Mon–Sat 10am–5pm

WESTERHAM

⊞ 20th Century Marks
Contact Mr M Marks
🖂 12 Market Square,
Westerham,
Kent,
TN16 1AW 🅿
☎ 01959 562221 🖶 01959 569385
📱 07831 778992
🖂 lambarda@btconnect.com
🌐 www.20thcenturymarks.co.uk
Est. 1960 *Stock size* Large
Stock Classic 20thC designs
Open Mon–Sat 10am–5.30pm
Services Valuations, restoration

⊞ Apollo Galleries
(LAPADA)
Contact Mr S M Barr
🖂 19–21 Market Square,
Westerham, Kent,
TN16 1AN 🅿

☎ 01959 562200 ✆ 01959 562986
✉ enq@apollogalleries.com
⊛ www.apollogalleries.com
Est. 1974 *Stock size* Large
Stock Mainly
Georgian–Edwardian furniture,
bronzes, oil paintings, mirrors,
objets d'art
Open Mon–Sat 9.30am–5.30pm
Fairs Olympia
Services Valuations for probate
and insurance

⌂ Castle Antique Centre Ltd
Contact Stewart Ward Properties
✉ 1 London Road,
Westerham,
Kent,
TN16 1BB ₱
☎ 01959 562492
Est. 1986 *Stock size* Large
No. of dealers 8
Stock 4 showrooms. Linen, tools,
silver, jewellery, china, glass,
books, 19thC clothing,
chandeliers, small furniture
Open Mon–Sun 10am–5pm
Services Valuations, advice,
house clearance

⊞ Clementines Antiques
Contact Jill Clark
✉ 3 The Green,
Westerham,
Kent,
TN16 1AS ₱
☎ 01959 562575
Est. 2000 *Stock size* Medium
Stock General antiques and
collectables
Open Mon–Sat 10am–5pm Sun
noon–5pm

⊞ The Design Gallery
Contact Chrissie Painell or
John Masters
✉ 5 The Green,
Westerham,
Kent,
TN16 1AS ₱
☎ 01959 561234 ✆ 01959 561234
⒨ 07785 503044
✉ sales@designgallery.co.uk
⊛ www.designgallery.co.uk
Est. 2002 *Stock size* Medium
Stock Art Deco, Art Nouveau,
Arts and Crafts, Gothic Revival
and the Aesthetic Movement
Open Mon–Sat 10am–5.30pm
Sun 1–5pm
Services Valuations, restoration,
shipping

⊞ The Green Antiques & Collectables
Contact Maria Lopez
✉ 3 The Green,
Westerham, Kent,
TN16 1AS ₱
☎ 01959 569393 ✆ 01959 569393
✉ greenantiques@btconnect.com
Est. 2003 *Stock size* Small
Stock Antiques, collectables,
Sir Winston Churchill
memorabilia, oak, old pine and
decorative furniture,
kitchenware, garden antiques.
Open Mon–Sat 10am–5.30pm
Sun noon–5pm
Services Main stockists for the
area of Burleigh china

⊞ Linden Antique Prints (PBFA)
Contact Mr M Synan
✉ First Floor, 149 Main Road,
Biggin Hill, Westerham,
Kent,
TN16 3JP ₱
☎ 01959 574306 ✆ 01959 574306
⒨ 078 017 08213
✉ martin@lindenprints.com
⊛ www.lindenprints.com
Est. 1997 *Stock size* Medium
Stock Antique prints, maps,
watercolours
Open Mon–Fri 10.30am–5.30pm
by appointment only
Fairs Royal National

⊞ London House Antiques
Contact Vivienne Graham
✉ 4 Market Square,
Westerham,
Kent,
TN16 1AW ₱
☎ 01959 564479 ✆ 01959 565424
Est. 1995 *Stock size* Large
Stock Furniture, clocks,
porcelain, glass
Open Mon–Sat 10am–5pm or by
appointment

⊞ Taylor-Smith Antiques (LAPADA)
Contact Ashton Taylor-Smith
✉ 4 The Grange,
High Street,
Westerham,
Kent,
TN16 1AH ₱
☎ 01959 563100
✉ ashton@taylor-smith.com
Est. 1974 *Stock size* Medium
Stock Fine 18th–early 19thC
furniture, objets d'art, Sir

Winston Churchill ephemera
Open Mon–Sat 10am–5pm
closed Wed

⊞ Vintage Jewels (WKADA)
Contact Mrs T Lawrence
✉ 2 Market Square,
Westerham, Kent,
TN16 1AW ₱
☎ 01959 561778 ✆ 01959 561778
Est. 1991 *Stock size* Medium
Stock Antique jewellery, portrait
miniatures, porcelain, fine
paintings
Open Wed–Sat 11am–5pm
Services Picture restoration

WESTGATE-ON-SEA

⊞ Berkeley House Antiques
Contact Barbara Croall
✉ 78 St Mildred's Road,
Westgate-on-Sea,
Kent,
CT8 8RF ₱
☎ 01843 833458
Est. 2001 *Stock size* Medium
Stock Decorative items, small
furniture, paintings, mirrors,
porcelain and reproduction
jewellery
Open Thurs–Sat 10am–5pm

⚒ Westgate Auctions
Contact Mr Colin Langston
✉ Rear of 70 St Mildred's Road,
Westgate-on-Sea,
Kent,
CT8 8RF ₱
☎ 01843 834891
Est. 1982
Open Mon–Sat 9am–5pm
auctions on Sun
Sales Antique and modern
furniture and effects Sun,
viewing Sat 9.30am–5pm
Frequency Every 3 weeks
Catalogues Yes

WHITSTABLE

⚒ Bonhams
✉ 95–97 Tankerton Road,
Whitstable Road,
Whitstable,
Kent,
CT5 2AJ ₱
☎ 01227 275007 ✆ 01227 266443
✉ whitstable@bonhams.com
⊛ www.bonhams.com
Est. 1793

45

Open Mon–Fri 9am–5.30pm
Sales Regional office. Regular sales in London, New York, San Francisco, Sydney, Geneva and Los Angeles, as well as in regional sales rooms across the UK. Free auction valuations; insurance and probate valuations
Catalogues Yes

⊞ Inside Out
Contact John Perry
✉ 6 Oxford Street,
Whitstable,
Kent,
CT5 1DD 🅿
☎ 01227 280111
📱 07850 365226
Est. 1985 *Stock size* Medium
Stock Country antiques, garden antiques, unusual decorative items

Open Mon–Sun 10.30am–5pm
Wed 10.30am–1pm
Fairs Ardingly, Kempton Park

⊞ Laurens Antiques
Contact Mr G Laurens
✉ 2 Harbour Street,
Whitstable, Kent,
CT5 1AG 🅿
☎ 01227 261940
Est. 1965 *Stock size* Medium
Stock General antiques
Open Mon–Sat 10am–5pm
closed Wed
Services Valuations

⊞ Tankerton Antiques (BHI)
Contact Mr Paul Wrighton
✉ 136 Tankerton Road,
Whitstable, Kent,
CT5 2AN 🅿
☎ 01227 266490

📱 07702 244064
Est. 1985 *Stock size* Medium
Stock Modern jewellery, clocks
Open Tues Thurs–Sat 10am–5pm
Wed 10.30am–1pm
Fairs Brunel Clock and Watch Fair, Ardingly
Services Clock repairs

WITTERSHAM

⊞ Old Corner House Antiques
Contact Gillian Shepherd
✉ 6 Poplar Road, Wittersham, Kent, TN30 7PG 🅿
☎ 01797 270236
Est. 1986 *Stock size* Medium
Stock Early English ceramics, needlework, carvings, country furniture
Open Wed–Sat 10am–5pm

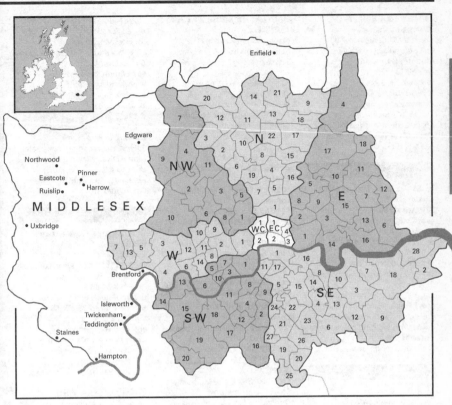

Enfield •
Edgware •
Northwood •
Eastcote •   Pinner •
Ruislip •   • Harrow
M I D D L E S E X
• Uxbridge
Brentford •
Isleworth •
Twickenham •
Teddington •
Staines •
Hampton •

NW
N
NW
W
WC EC
E
SE
SW

20 14 21
7   12 11 13 9 4
3   10 22 18
N
8   15 17 18
6   19 4   16 11
2   5   5   10 E
10 6   1   1   15 7
12 11 8   7   5   1   16 13
4   6   14 3   1   11 17 14 16 28
13 10 3   1   15 7 18 2
14 11 9   14 13 10 3
15 18 24 22 4 13 12 9
19 17 16 21 23 6
20 16 19 27 26 20
25

EAST

E1

🏠 **AA Antiques**
Contact Des King
✉ **14a Bacon Street,**
London,
E1 6LF 🅿
☎ 020 7739 4803
📱 07973 324814
Est. 1996 *Stock size* Medium
Stock Antique and shipping
furniture
Open Mon–Sat 10am–5pm

🏠 **La Maison**
Contact Mr Guillaume Bacou
✉ **107–108 Shoreditch High**
Street, London,
E1 6JN 🅿
☎ 020 7729 9646 📠 020 7729 6399
📧 gui@lamaison.com
🌐 www.@lamaison.com
Est. 1991 *Stock size* Medium
Stock French and Italian beds

Open Mon–Fri 10am–6pm
Sat 10.30am–6pm
Services Restoration, upholstery

🏠 **Town House (LAPADA)**
Contact Fiona Atkins
✉ **5 Fournier Street,**
London,
E1 6QE 🅿
☎ 020 7247 4745 📠 020 7247 4745
📱 07711 319237
📧 fiona@townhousewindow.com
🌐 www.townhousewindow.com
Est. 1984 *Stock size* Large
Stock Early and Georgian
furniture, decorative items
Open Thurs–Sat 10am–5pm
or by appointment

E2

🏠 **George Rankin Coin Co
Ltd**
Contact Mr G Rankin
✉ **325 Bethnal Green Road,**
London,

E2 6AH 🅿
☎ 020 7729 1280 📠 020 7729 5023
Est. 1969 *Stock size* Large
Stock Period jewellery, coins,
medals, banknotes
Open Tues–Sat 10am–6pm
closed Aug
Fairs Coinex, Cumberland and
Europa
Services Valuations

E4

🏠 **Record Detector**
Contact Mr J Salter
✉ **3 & 4 Station Approach,**
Chingford,
London,
E4 6AL 🅿
☎ 020 8529 6361
📧 nick@salter.co.uk
🌐 www.salter.co.uk
Est. 1991 *Stock size* Large
Stock Second-hand records, CDs,
1950–1990s, videos, magazines
Open Mon–Sat 9.30am–6pm

LONDON
EAST • E5

⊞ Nicholas Salter Antiques
Contact Mrs S Salter
✉ 8 Station Approach, Chingford, London, E4 6AL 🅿
☎ 020 8529 2938
📧 nick@salter.co.uk
🌐 www.salter.co.uk
Est. 1969 *Stock size* Large
Stock General antiques
Open Mon–Wed 10am–5pm Fri –Sat 10am–6pm

E5

⊞ M A Stroh Bookseller
Contact Mr M Stroh
✉ Riverside House, Leaside Road, London, E5 9LU 🅿
☎ 020 8806 3690 📠 020 8806 3690
📱 07974 413039
📧 patents@stroh.demon.co.uk
🌐 www.webspawner.com/users/buttonbook
Est. 1957 *Stock size* Medium
Stock Books, patents 1617–1970, journals, scientific papers, ephemera, old bindings, dissertations
Open By appointment

E9

⊞ Kelly Lordan
Contact Lesley Lordan or Christina Kelly
✉ 211a Victoria Park Road, London, E9 7JN 🅿
☎ 020 8985 7550
Est. 2002 *Stock size* Small
Stock Antiques, collectables, soft furnishings
Open Mon–Sat 10am–5pm closed Thurs

E11

⊞ I D Edrich
Contact Mr I Edrich
✉ 17 Selsdon Road, London, E11 2QF 🅿
☎ 020 8989 9541 📠 020 8989 9541
📧 idedrich@iderich.co.uk
🌐 www.idedrich.co.uk
Est. 1965 *Stock size* Large
Stock First editions, antiquarian books, literary periodicals, literature a speciality
Open By appointment

⊞ Brian Hawkins Antiques (LAPADA)
Contact Brian Hawkins
✉ 6–8 High Street, Wanstead, London, E11 2AJ
☎ 020 8989 2317 📠 020 8989 2317
📱 07831 888736
📧 brianhawkinsantiques@hotmail.com
Est. 1993 *Stock size* Medium
Stock General antiques
Open By appointment

⊞ The Old Cottage Antiques (LAPADA)
Contact Peter Blake
✉ 6 High Street, Wanstead, London, E11 2AJ 🅿
☎ 020 8989 2317 📠 020 8989 2317
📱 07710 031079
Est. 1973 *Stock size* Medium
Stock General antiques
Open By appointment

E17

⊞ Treasure World
Contact Ali Jewya
✉ 3 Central Parade, Hoe Street, Walthamstow, London, E17 4RT 🅿
☎ 020 8521 1255 📠 020 8521 1255
📱 07957 177283
Est. 2000 *Stock size* Medium
Stock Furniture, rugs
Open Mon–Sat 9.30am–6.30pm Sun 11am–5pm

E18

⊞ Albion Clocks (BHI)
Contact Colin Bent
✉ 4 Grove End, Grove Hill, South Woodford, London, E18 2LE 🅿
☎ 020 8530 5570
📧 colin.bent@btinternet.com
🌐 www.albionclocks.info
Est. 1963 *Stock size* Medium
Stock Antique clocks, furniture
Open Mon–Sun 9am–7pm by appointment

⊞ Victoria Antiques
Contact Mr M Holman
✉ 166a George Lane, London, E18 1AY 🅿
☎ 020 8989 1002
Est. 1998 *Stock size* Medium
Stock Silver, silver plate, brass, china, carved items, small furniture, coins, clocks

Open Mon–Sat 11am–5pm closed Tues Thurs
Services Valuations

⋏ Woodford Auctions
Contact Mrs D Green
✉ 209 High Road, South Woodford, London, E18 2PA 🅿
☎ 020 8553 1242
📱 07860 905667
Est. 1994
Open Mon 9am–5pm
Sales Antiques and general sale Mon 6.30pm, viewing Mon 4pm prior to sale
Frequency Fortnightly
Catalogues Yes

EC1

⊞ Antiques Consultant (GIA)
Contact Mr Williams
✉ 33–35 St John's Square, London, EC1M 4DS 🅿
📱 07956 604091
📧 sansdesign@hotmail.com
Est. 1988 *Stock size* Small
Stock Glass, furniture, jewellery and general antiques
Open Mon–Fri 10am–6pm
Fairs Earls Court, Olympia, NEC, London Museums
Services Valuations, consultancy

⊞ City Clocks (BHI)
Contact Jeffrey Rosson
✉ 31 Amwell Street, Clerkenwell, London, EC1R 1UN 🅿
☎ 020 7278 1154 📠 020 7476 7766
📱 07074 767766
📧 mail@cityclocks.co.uk
🌐 www.cityclocks.co.uk
Est. 1898 *Stock size* Medium
Stock Clocks
Open Tues–Fri 8.30am–5.30pm Sat 10am–3.30pm
Services Restoration, clock, watch repair

⊞ Frosts of Clerkenwell Ltd
Contact Mr G Redwood
✉ 60–62 Clerkenwell Road, London, EC1M 5PX 🅿
☎ 020 7253 0315
🌐 www.frostsofclerkenwell.co.uk
Est. 1938 *Stock size* Large
Stock Clocks, watches, cases, dials, movements
Open Mon–Fri 10am–5pm
Services Restoration

Hirsh London
Contact Ben Stevenson
✉ 10 Hatton Garden, London, EC1N 8AH 🅿
☎ 020 7405 6080 ⊕ 020 7430 0107
ⓦ www.hirsh.co.uk
Est. 1980 *Stock size* Large
Stock Fine antique jewellery, hand-made and designed diamond engagement rings
Open Mon–Fri 10am–5.30pm
Services Valuations

Planet Bazaar
Contact Maureen Silverman
✉ 397 St John Street, London, EC1V 4LD 🅿
☎ 020 7278 7793 ⊕ 020 7387 8326
ⓔ info@planetbazaar.co.uk
ⓦ www.planetbazaar.co.uk
Est. 1997 *Stock size* Medium
Stock 1950–1980 designer furniture, art, glass, lighting, ceramics, books, eccentricities
Open Tues–Sat 11.30am–7pm or by appointment

Andrew R Ullmann Ltd
Contact Mr J Ullmann
✉ 10 Hatton Garden, London, EC1N 8AH
☎ 020 7405 1877 ⊕ 020 7404 7071
ⓔ enquiries@aullmann.com
ⓦ www.aullmann.com
Est. 1950 *Stock size* Large
Stock Antique gold and gem jewellery, clocks, silver, objets d'art, watches
Open Mon–Fri 9am–5pm
Sat 9.30am–5pm
Services Restoration

EC2

LASSCO St Michael's (LAPADA, SALVO, BACA Award Winner 2001)
Contact Ferrous Auger or Anthony Reeve
✉ St Michael's Church, Mark Street (Off Paul Street), London, EC2A 4ER 🅿
☎ 020 7394 2100 ⊕ 020 7749 9941
ⓔ st.michaels@lassco.co.uk
ⓦ www.lassco.co.uk
Est. 1978 *Stock size* Large
Stock Architectural antiques, chimney pieces, overmantels, carved stonework, panelled rooms, statuary, garden ornaments and furniture, stained glass, metalwork

Open Mon–Fri 9.30am–5.30pm
Sat 10am–5pm
Services Shipping

Sport and Star Autographs (UACC, IADA)
Contact Steve Peacock
✉ 13 The Arcade, Liverpool Street, London, EC2M 7PN
☎ 020 7626 1818
ⓦ www.autographs.me.uk
Est. 2000 *Stock size* Medium
Stock Autographs, sport, film, music, signed memorabilia
Open Mon–Fri 9am–5.45pm
Services Valuations

Westland and Co (SALVO)
Contact Mr R Muirhead
✉ St Michael's Church, Leonard Street, London, EC2A 4ER 🅿
☎ 020 7739 8094 ⊕ 020 7729 3620
Ⓜ 07831 755566
ⓔ westland@westland.co.uk
ⓦ www.westland.co.uk
Est. 1969 *Stock size* Large
Stock Antique fireplaces, mantels, architectural elements, statuary, panelling
Open Mon–Fri 9am–6pm
Sat–Sun 10am–5pm
Services Valuations, restoration

EC3

Halcyon Days (BADA)
Contact Georgina Foster or Cheska Moon
✉ 14 Brook Street, London, EC3V 3LL 🅿
☎ 020 7629 8811 ⊕ 020 7283 1876
ⓔ info@halcyondays.co.uk
ⓦ www.halcyondays.co.uk
Est. 1950 *Stock size* Small
Stock Enamels, fans, snuff boxes, objects of virtue, tôle peinte, papier mâché, porcelain
Open Mon–Fri 10am–5.30pm
Fairs Grosvenor House

Searle & Co Ltd (NAG)
Contact Steve Carson
✉ 1 Royal Exchange, Cornhill, London, EC3V 3LL
☎ 020 7626 2456 ⊕ 020 7283 6384
ⓔ mail@searleandcoltd.uk
ⓦ www.searleandcoltd.uk
Est. 1893 *Stock size* Medium

Stock General antiques
Open Mon–Fri 9am–5pm
Services Valuations

NORTH

N1

After Noah
Contact Simon Tarr
✉ 121 Upper Street, London, N1 1QP 🅿
☎ 020 7359 4281 ⊕ 020 7359 4281
ⓔ mailorder@afternoah.com
ⓦ www.afternoah.com
Est. 1989 *Stock size* Medium
Stock Antique and contemporary furniture and houseware
Open Mon–Sat 10am–6pm
Sun noon–5pm
Services Restoration

Annie's Vintage Costume and Textiles
Contact Annie Moss
✉ 12 Camden Passage, Islington, London, N1 8ED 🅿
☎ 020 7359 0796 ⊕ 020 7359 2116
Est. 1975 *Stock size* Small
Stock 1900–1940s costume, linen, textiles
Open Mon Tues Thurs Fri Sun 11am–6pm Wed Sat 9am–6pm

The Antique Barometer Company
✉ 5 The Lower Mall, 359 Upper Street, London, N1 0PD 🅿
☎ 020 7226 4992 ⊕ 020 7226 4992
ⓔ sales@antiquebarometer.com
ⓦ www.antiquebarometer.com
Est. 1991 *Stock size* Large
Stock Barometers, barographs, similiar instruments
Open Mon Wed 8am–4pm Fri 10am–4pm Sat 9am–5pm
Services Valuations, restoration, shipping

The Antique Trader at the Millinery Works
Contact Brian Thompson, Derek Rothera or Jeff Jackson
✉ 85–87 Southgate Road, London, N1 3JS 🅿
☎ 020 7359 2019 ⊕ 020 7359 5792
ⓔ antiquetrader@millinery. demon.co.uk
ⓦ www.milleryworks.co.uk
Est. 1970 *Stock size* Large
Stock Arts and Crafts, furniture, effects

Open Tues–Sat 11am–6pm Sun
noon–5pm or by appointment
Services Valuations, bi-annual
exhibitions held

⊞ **R Arantes**
Contact R Arantes
✉ 27 The Mall, Camden Passage,
Islington, London,
N1 0PD ♿
☎ 020 7226 6367 ✆ 020 7253 5303
⓾ 07712 189160
✉ rlaliqueglass@btinternet.com
ⓦ www.laliqueglass.pnp.
blueyonder.co.uk
Est. 1987 *Stock size* Large
Stock Lalique glass
Open Wed Sat 8am–5pm or
by appointment
Services Valuations

⊞ **Kate Bannister
Antiques**
Contact Kate Bannister
✉ Angel Arcade, 116–118
Islington High Street, London,
N1 8EG ♿
✉ katebannister@aol.com
Est. 1990 *Stock size* Medium
Stock Decorative antiques
Open Wed 8am–4pm
Sat 10am–4pm

⌂ **Camden Passage
Antiques Market**
Contact Mrs S Lemkow
✉ 12 Camden Passage, London,
N1 8ED ♿
☎ 020 7359 0190 ✆ 020 7704 2095
Est. 1960 *Stock size* Large
No. of dealers 300
Stock General antiques and
specialist shops
Open Wed Sat 8am–3pm stalls
8am–5pm shops

⊞ **Camel Art Deco**
Contact Mrs E Durack
✉ 34 Islington Green,
London,
N1 8DU ♿
☎ 020 7359 5242
Est. 1996 *Stock size* Small
Stock Art Deco ceramics,
furniture, lighting
Open Wed Sat 9am–3.30pm
Fairs Specialist Art Deco fairs
Services French polishing,
upholstery of Lloyd Loom furniture

⊞ **Castle Gibson**
Contact Joyce Gibson
✉ 106a Upper Street, London,

N1 1QN ♿
☎ 020 7704 0927 ✆ 020 7704 0927
Stock size Large
Stock 19thC–1940s office furniture,
polished metal items, 1930s leather
chairs, sofas, early 20thC industrial
furniture, 1920s–1940s shop
fittings, garden furniture
Open Mon–Sat 10am–6pm
Sun noon–5pm
Services Deliveries within London

⊞ **Chancery Antiques Ltd**
Contact Mr R Rote
✉ 2 The Mall, 359 Upper Street,
London,
N1 0PD ♿
☎ 020 7359 9035 ✆ 020 7359 9035
Est. 1951 *Stock size* Medium
Stock Japanese porcelain,
pottery, ivory, 19thC Continental
works of art, cloisonné
Open Tues–Sat 10.30am–5pm or
by appointment closed Thurs

⊞ **Peter Chapman
Antiques and Restoration
(LAPADA, CINOA)**
Contact Peter Chapman or
Zac Chapman
✉ 10 Theberton Street, Islington,
London,
N1 0QX ♿
☎ 020 7226 5565 ✆ 020 8348 4846
⓾ 07831 093662
✉ pchapmanantiques@easynet.co.uk
ⓦ www.antiques-peterchapman.co.uk
Est. 1971 *Stock size* Medium
Stock English and Continental
furniture 1700–1900, mirrors,
Grand Tour souvenirs, bronzes,
spelters and other smalls,
paintings, lighting, hall lanterns,
stained glass, architectural,
garden and decorative items
Open Mon–Sat 9.30am–6pm or
by appointment
Services Valuations, restoration,
shipping

⊞ **Charlton House
Antiques**
Contact Mr S Burrows or
Mr R Sims
✉ 19 Camden Passage, Islington,
London,
N1 8EA ♿
☎ 020 7226 3141 ✆ 020 7226 1123
✉ charlhse@aol.com
Est. 1979 *Stock size* Large
Stock Antique furniture
Open Mon–Sat 9.30am–5pm
Services Shipping

⊞ **Chest of Drawers Ltd**
Contact Daniel Harrison or
Vincent Glanville
✉ 281 Upper Street, London,
N1 2TZ
☎ 020 7359 5909 ✆ 020 7704 6236
ⓦ www.chestofdrawers.co.uk
Est. 1986 *Stock size* Large
Stock Soft and hardwood old
furniture, wooden and metal
beds, sofas, armchairs, chests-of-
drawers, wardrobes
Open Mon–Sun 10am–6pm

⊞ **Cloud Cuckoo Land**
Contact Mrs C Harper
✉ 6 Charlton Place,
London,
N1 8AJ ♿
☎ 020 7354 3141
✉ cuckoolandmail@yahoo.co.uk.
Est. 1981 *Stock size* Medium
Stock Vintage clothes, accessories,
1850s–1950s, some later
Open Mon–Sat 11am–5.30pm

⊞ **Rosemary Conquest**
Contact Mrs R Conquest
✉ 27 Camden Passage,
London,
N1 8EA ♿
☎ 020 7359 0616
✉ rosemary@rosemaryconquest.com
ⓦ www.rosemaryconquest.com
Est. 1996 *Stock size* Large
Stock Continental and Dutch
lighting, decorative items
Open Tue Thurs Fri 11am–5.30pm
Wed–Sat 9am–5.30pm

⚒ **Criterion Auctioneers**
Contact Daniel Webster
✉ 53 Essex Road, Islington,
London,
N1 2SF ♿
☎ 020 7359 5707 ✆ 020 7354 9843
✉ info@criterion-auctioneers.co.uk
ⓦ www.criterion-auctioneers.co.uk
Est. 1989
Open Mon–Fri 9.30am–6pm
Sales Mon 5pm sale of antiques
and decorative furnishings,
viewing Fri 2–8pm Sat Sun
10am–6pm day of sale from 10am
Frequency Weekly
Catalogues Yes

⊞ **Carlton Davidson
Antiques**
Contact Mr Carlton Davidson
✉ 33 Camden Passage, London,
N1 8EA ♿
☎ 020 7226 7491 ✆ 020 7226 7491

Est. 1982 *Stock size* Medium
Stock Decorative French items,
including lighting
Open Wed Sat 10am–4pm

⊞ Eclectica
Contact Liz Wilson
✉ 2 Charlton Place,
London,
N1 8AJ 🅿
☎ 020 7226 5625 📠 020 7226 5625
🌐 www.eclectica.biz
Est. 1988 *Stock size* Large
Stock Vintage costume jewellery,
1920s–1960s
Open Sat 10am–6pm
Wed 9am–6pm Mon Tues Thurs
Fri 11am–6pm
Services Theatre and film hire

⊞ Fandango
Contact Jonathan Hathaway
✉ 50 Cross Street, Islington,
London,
N1 2BA 🅿
☎ 020 7226 1777 📠 020 7226 1777
📱 07979 650805
📧 shop@fandango.uk.com
🌐 www.fandango.uk.com
Est. 1997 *Stock size* Medium
Stock Post-war design lighting
and furniture
Open Tues–Sat noon–6pm
Services Valuations, interior design

⊞ Feljoy Antiques
Contact Mrs Joy Humphreys
✉ 3 Angel Arcade,
Camden Passage, London,
N1 8EA 🅿
☎ 020 7354 5336 📠 020 7831 3485
📧 joy@feljoy-antiques.demon.co.uk
🌐 www.chintz.net/feljoy
Est. 1985 *Stock size* Large
Stock Chintzware, textiles,
cushions, shawls, small decorative
furniture, decorative items
including beadwork cushions
Open Wed 8am–3.30pm
Sat 10am–4pm
Services Mail order

⊞ Vincent Freeman
Antiques
Contact Vincent Freeman
✉ 1 Camden Passage, Islington,
London,
N1 8EA
☎ 020 7226 6178 📠 020 7226 7231
📧 info@vincentfreemanantiques.com
🌐 www.vincentfreemanantiques.com
Est. 1966 *Stock size* Medium
Stock 19thC music boxes

Open Wed Sat 10am–5pm or by
appointment
Fairs Olympia

⊞ Furniture Vault
Contact Mr David Loveday
✉ 50 Camden Passage, London,
N1 8AE
☎ 020 7354 1047 📠 020 7354 1047
Est. 1984 *Stock size* Large
Stock 18th–19thC furniture
Open Tues–Sat 9.30am–4.30pm

⊞ Get Stuffed
Contact Robert Sinclair
✉ 105 Essex Road, Islington,
London,
N1 2SL 🅿
☎ 020 7226 1364 📠 020 7359 8353
📱 07831 260062
📧 taxidermy@thegetstuffed.co.uk
🌐 www.thegetstuffed.co.uk
Est. 1913 *Stock size* Large
Stock Victorian artefacts, birds,
animals, insects, butterflies and
glass domes
Open Telephone for appointment

⊞ Rosemary Hart
Contact Rosemary Hart
✉ London,
N1
📱 07946 576740
📧 contact@rosemaryhart.co.uk
Est. 1980 *Stock size* Small
Stock Small plated tableware
and silver pieces, decorative
pieces and mother-of-pearl
Open By appointment

⊞ Japanese Gallery Ltd
(Ukiyo-e Society)
Contact Mr C D Wertheim
✉ 23 Camden Passage, London,
N1 8EA 🅿
☎ 020 7226 3347 📠 020 7229 2934
📱 07930 411991
📧 info@japanesegallery.co.uk
🌐 www.japanesegallery.co.uk
Est. 1980 *Stock size* Large
Stock Japanese woodcut prints,
Japanese ceramics, sword
armour, Japanese dolls
Open Sun–Tues Thurs Fri
10am–6pm Wed Sat 9am–6pm
Services Restoration, free
authentification

⊞ Judith Lassalle (PBFA)
Contact Mrs J Lassalle
✉ 7 Pierrepoint Arcade, London,
N1 8EF 🅿
☎ 020 7607 7121

Est. 1765 *Stock size* Small
Stock Toys, games, books, optical
toys, ephemera, all pre-1914
Open Wed 7.30am–4pm Sat
9.30am–4pm or by appointment
Fairs English and American
ephemera fairs, PBFA Bookfair at
Russell Hotel

⊞ John Laurie Antiques
Ltd (LAPADA)
Contact Mr John Laurie
✉ 352 Upper Street, London,
N1 0PD 🅿
☎ 020 7226 0913 📠 020 7226 4599
📧 rdgewirtz@aol.com
Est. 1963 *Stock size* Large
Stock Antique and modern silver,
silver plate
Open Mon–Sat 9.30am–5pm
Services Restoration, re-plating

⊞ Leolinda
Contact Ms Leolinda Costa
✉ 3 The Mall, 359 Upper Street,
Camden Passage, London,
N1 0PD 🅿
☎ 020 7226 3450 📠 020 7209 0143
📱 07789 162972
📧 leolinda@hotmail.com
🌐 www.islington.co.uk/leolinda
Est. 1989 *Stock size* Small
Stock Old and new silver
jewellery, gemstone necklaces,
ethnic art, jewellery
Open Wed Sat 10am–5pm
Services After-sales service

⊞ Leons Militaria
Contact Leon
✉ Unit 8, The Mall Antiques
Arcade, 359 Upper Street,
Islington, London,
N1 0PD 🅿
☎ 020 7288 1070 📠 020 7288 1070
📱 07989 649972
📧 leonsmilitaria@yahoo.co.uk
Est. 1997 *Stock size* Large
Stock Commemorative ceramics,
porcelain, Victoriana, WW1, WWII
Open Tues Fri 11am–4.30pm
Wed 9am–4.30pm Thur by
appointment Sat 9am–5pm
Services Valuations, shipping

⊞ Leons Militaria
Contact Leon
✉ Unit 21, The Mall Antiques
Arcade, 359 Upper Street,
Islington, London,
N1 0PD 🅿
☎ 020 7288 1070 📠 020 7288 1070
📱 07989 649972

✉ leonsmilitaria@yahoo.co.uk
Est. 1997 *Stock size* Large
Stock Militaria, weapons, uniforms, naval, aviation and curios, Napoleonic–WWII
Open Tues Fri 11am–4.30pm Wed 9am–4.30pm Thur by appointment Sat 9am–5pm
Services Valuations, shipping

⌂ The Mall Antiques Arcade
Contact Neil Jackson
✉ 359 Upper Street, Camden Passage, London,
N1 0PD ☑
☎ 020 7351 5353 📠 020 7351 5350
✉ antique@dial.pipex.com
🌐 www.mallantiques.co.uk
Est. 1979 *Stock size* Large
No. of dealers 35
Stock Furniture, decorative antiques
Open Tues Thurs Fri 10am–5pm Wed 7.30am–5pm Sat 9am–6pm Sun 11am–4pm

⊞ Metro Retro
Contact Mr Saxon Durrant
✉ 1 White Conduit Street, London,
N1 9EL ☑
☎ 020 7278 4884 📠 020 7278 4884
📱 07850 319116
✉ sales@metroretro.co.uk
🌐 www.metroretro.co.uk
Est. 1994 *Stock size* Large
Stock Industrial style and stripped-steel furniture, lighting and design
Open Thurs–Sat 11am–6pm
Fairs Syon Park, Jukebox Madness, Chiswick, Battersea
Services Props hire, consultancy

⊞ Michel André Morin (LAPADA, CPTA)
Contact Brian Trotman
✉ 7 Charlton Place, Islington, London,
N1 8AQ ☑
☎ 020 7226 3803 📠 020 7704 0708
📱 07802 832496
✉ michelandremorin@aol.com
Est. 1989 *Stock size* Medium
Stock French decorative furniture, chandeliers, items for interior decorators
Open Wed–Sat 7.30am–4.30pm or by appointment
Fairs Olympia, Battersea Decorative Antiques and Textiles Fair
Services Valuations, restoration

⊞ Number 19
Contact Mr D Griffith
✉ 19 Camden Passage, London,
N1 8EA ☑
☎ 020 7226 1999 📠 020 7226 1126
Est. 1982 *Stock size* Large
Stock Decorative antiques, campaign furniture, vintage shop fittings, leather seating, decorative accessories
Open Tues–Sat 10am–5pm closed Thurs

⊞ Olde Hoxton Curios
Contact John Clarke
✉ 192 Hoxton Street, Shoreditch, London,
N1 5LH ☑
☎ 020 7729 7256
Est. 2003 *Stock size* Medium
Stock Antique collectables, curios
Open Mon–Fri noon–4pm Sat 10am–4.30pm

⊞ Origin Modernism
Contact Christopher Reen
✉ 25 Camden Passage, Islington, London,
N1 8EA
☎ 020 7704 1326
📱 07747 758852
✉ david@origin101.co.uk
🌐 www.origin101.co.uk
Est. 2001 *Stock size* Medium
Stock Modernist furniture,1930s–1950s. Designers from Northern Europe, Britain and USA
Open Wed–Sat noon–6pm
Fairs 20thC Design Fair

⊞ Out of Time
Contact Mr E Farlow
✉ 110 Elmore Street, Islington, London,
N1 3AH ☑
☎ 020 7354 5755 📠 020 7354 5755
✉ outoftime@btconnect.com
Est. 1969 *Stock size* Large
Stock 1940s–1950s homestyle furniture, glass, fridges, tables, chairs
Open Mon–Sun 10am–6pm
Fairs Jukebox Madness, Ascot
Services Valuations, restoration

⊞ Kevin Page Oriental Art Ltd (LAPADA)
Contact Mr K Page
✉ 2–6 Camden Passage, Islington, London,
N1 8ED ☑

☎ 020 7226 8558 📠 020 7354 9145
✉ kevin@kevinpage.co.uk
🌐 www.kevinpage.co.uk
Est. 1969 *Stock size* Large
Stock Oriental art, bronze, lacquer, porcelain, ivory
Trade only Trade and export only
Open Tues–Sat 10.30am–4.30pm

⊞ Phoenix Oriental Art (LAPADA)
Contact Elena Edwards
✉ 24–25 The Mall, 359 Upper Street, Islington, London,
N1 0PD ☑
☎ 07802 763518
✉ okinasan@aol.com
Est. 1981 *Stock size* Large
Stock Chinese and Japanese bronze from the last 1000 years
Open Wed Sat 10am–4pm or by appointment

⊞ Piers Rankin
Contact Mr P Rankin
✉ 14 Camden Passage, Islington, London,
N1 8ED ☑
☎ 020 7354 3349 📠 020 7359 8138
✉ piersrankin925@aol.com
Est. 1979 *Stock size* Large
Stock Silver, silver plate
Open Tues–Sat 9.30am–5.30pm
Services Packing for export

⊞ Rumours Decorative Arts (LAPADA)
Contact John Donovan
✉ 4 The Mall, 359 Upper Street, Camden Passage, Islington, London,
N1 0PD ☑
☎ 020 7704 6549
📱 07836 277274 or 07831 103748
✉ rumdec@aol.com
Est. 1988 *Stock size* Large
Stock Moorcroft pottery
Open Wed Sat 8am–4pm Sat 9am–5pm
Fairs NEC Antiques for Everyone
Services Valuations

⊞ Silver and Plate Centre
Contact M Leibovitz
✉ Unit 20, The Mall Antiques Centre, 359 Upper Street, London,
N1 0PD ☑
☎ 020 8802 7144
Est. 1975 *Stock size* Large
Stock Antique silver plate
Open Tues–Fri 10am–5pm

Sugar Antiques (CPTA)
Contact Mr T Sugarman
8–9 Pierrepoint Arcade,
Pierrepoint Row, London,
N1 8EF
020 7354 9896 020 7931 5642
07973 179980
tony@sugar-antiques.com
www.sugar-antiques.com
Est. 1990 *Stock size* Large
Stock Wristwatches, pocket
watches, pens, lighters, costume
jewellery
Open Wed–Sat 8am–3.30pm

**Tadema Gallery (BADA,
LAPADA, CINOA, BACA
Award Winner 2004)**
Contact Sonya or
David Newell-Smith
10 Charlton Place, Camden
Passage, Islington, London ,
N1 8AJ
020 7359 1055 020 7359 1055
07710 082395
info@tademagallery.com or
info@tademagalleryart.com
www.tademagallery.com or
www.tademagalleryart.com
Est. 1978 *Stock size* Large
Stock Art Nouveau, Arts and
Crafts, Art Deco jewellery
Open Wed Sat 10am–5pm or
by appointment
Fairs Grosvenor House

**Chris Tapsell Antiques
(CPADA)**
Contact Mr C Tapsell
16 Pierrepoint Row, Islington,
London,
N1 8EF
020 7354 3603
Est. 1993 *Stock size* Medium
Stock 18th–19thC English and
Continental furniture, Oriental
ceramics, Georgian–Victorian
mirrors
Open Wed Sat 9am–5pm
Services Valuations, restoration

Titus Omega
Contact John Harvey
London,
N1
07973 841846
john@titusomega.com
www.titusomega.com
Est. 1985 *Stock size* Medium
Stock Art Nouveau, Art Deco,
Arts and Crafts
Open By appointment
Fairs NEC, Olympia

Turn On Lighting
Contact Janet Holdstock
116–118 Islington High Street,
Camden Passage, Islington,
London,
N1 8EG
020 7359 7616 020 7359 7616
Est. 1976 *Stock size* Large
Stock Antique lighting
Open Tues–Fri 10.30am–6pm
Sat 9.30am–4.30pm
Services Museum work, interior
design

Vane House Antiques
Contact Michael Till
15 Camden Passage, Islington,
London,
N1 8EA
020 7359 1343 020 7359 1343
Est. 1962 *Stock size* Large
Stock 18th–early 19thC furniture
Open Tues Wed Fri and
Sat 10am–5pm

**The Waterloo Trading
Co**
Contact Robert Boys
North London Freight Centre,
York Way, Kings Cross, London,
N1 0AU
020 7837 4806 020 7837 4815
info@robertboysshipping.co.uk
Est. 1989 *Stock size* Large
Stock 10,000 sq ft of antique
furniture
Open Mon–Fri 8.30 am–5.30pm
Services Shipping

**Mike Weedon
(LAPADA, CPADA)**
7 Camden Passage, Islington,
London,
N1 8EA
020 7226 5319/7609 6826
0207 700 6389
info@mikeweedonantiques.com
www.mikeweedonantiques.com
Est. 1979 *Stock size* Large
Stock Art Nouveau, Art Deco,
general antiques, wholesale to
Japanese trade
Open Wed 9am–5pm Sat
10am–5pm or by appointment

Agnes Wilton
Contact Agnes Wilton
3 Camden Passage,
London,
N1 8EA
020 7226 5679 020 7226 0779
Est. 1972 *Stock size* Medium
Stock Furniture, silver,
decorative objects
Open Tues–Sat 10am–2pm
Services Valuations

**Woodage Antiques
(LAPADA)**
Contact Mr C Woodage
359 Upper Street, London,
N1 0PD
020 7226 4173 01753 529 047
woodage.antiques@btinternet.com
Est. 1995 *Stock size* Large
Stock 18th–20thC furniture
Open Wed 7.30am–5pm
Sat 9am–5pm

**www.buymeissen.com
(LAPADA)**
Contact Laurence Mitchell
20 The Mall, Camden Passage,
Islington, London,
N1 0PD
020 7359 7579
07968 065110
laurence@buymeissen.com
www.buymeissen.com
Est. 1974 *Stock size* Large
Stock 19thC Meissen, European,
Oriental works of art and ceramics
Open Tues–Sat 10am–5pm
Wed closed 4pm
Services Valuations, restoration

**York Gallery Ltd
(LAPADA)**
Contact Mr G Beyer
51 Camden Passage, Islington,
London,
N1 8EA
020 7354 8012 020 7354 8012
prints@yorkgallery.co.uk
www.yorkgallery.co.uk
Est. 1989 *Stock size* Large
Stock 17th–19thC engravings
Open Wed–Sat 10am–5pm
Services Picture framing

Michael Young
Contact M Young
21 Camden Passage, London,
N1 8EA
07768 233633
Est. 1985 *Stock size* Medium
Stock Marine models, pond
yachts, general antiquities
Open Wed Sat 9am–4pm
Services Valuations

N2

Martin Henham
Contact Mr M Henham
218 High Road, London,

N2 9AY 🅿
☎ 020 8444 5274
Est. 1963 *Stock size* Medium
Stock Victoriana, bronzes,
ceramics, porcelain
Open Mon–Sat 10am–6pm closed
Thurs or by appointment
Services Furniture restoration

N3

⊞ **Clifford Antiques**
Contact Simon Clifford
✉ 15 Long Lane, Finchley,
London,
N3 🅿
☎ 020 8343 0084
✉ cliffordantiques@btconnect.com
Est. 1960 *Stock size* Medium
Stock General antiques
Open Mon–Sat 9am–3pm
Services Restoration, painting

⊞ **Martin Gladman
Second-hand Books**
Contact Mr M Gladman
✉ 235 Nether Street, London,
N3 1NT 🅿
☎ 020 8343 3023
Est. 1991 *Stock size* Large
Stock Large range of rare and
antiquarian books through the
humanities, history, military
history
Open Sat 10am–6pm
Tues–Fri 11am–8pm
Services Valuations

⊞ **Intercol (ITA, Coin,
Banknote and Map
Collectors Societies)**
Contact Mr Yasha Beresiner
✉ 43 Templars Crescent,
London,
N3 3QR 🅿
☎ 020 8349 2207 ✆ 020 8346 9539
📱 07768 292066
✉ yasha@intercol.co.uk
🌐 www.intercol.co.uk
Est. 1981 *Stock size* Medium
Stock Maps, charts, books,
playing cards, currency
Open By appointment
Fairs Playing cards fairs, Map
Society fairs (phone for details)
Services Valuations

N4

⊞ **The Antique Shop**
Contact Michael Slade or
Michael Kairis
✉ 42 Quernmore Road, London,

N4 4QP 🅿
☎ 020 8341 3194 ✆ 020 8348 7652
📱 07973 800678
✉ michael.kairis@btinternet.com
or mikeslade@ntl.com
🌐 www.antiquesnorthlondon.co.uk
Est. 1982 *Stock size* Small
Stock Victorian–Edwardian
furniture
Open Tues–Fri 10am–6pm
Sat by appointment
Fairs Alexandra Palace
Services Restoration

⊞ **Kennedy Carpets**
Contact Michael Kennedy or
Vivien Eder
✉ Oriental Carpet Centre,
Building G, 105 Eade Road,
London,
N4 1TJ 🅿
☎ 020 8800 4455 ✆ 020 8800 4466
✉ kennedycarpets@ukonline.co.uk
🌐 www.cloudband.com/occ
/kennedycarpets
Est. 1972 *Stock size* Large
Stock Antique Oriental large
carpets and rugs
Open Mon–Fri 9.30am–6pm
Sat Sun by appointment
Services Valuations, restoration

⊞ **Joseph Lavian**
Contact Joseph Lavian
✉ 105 Eade Road, London,
N4 1TJ 🅿
☎ 020 8800 0707 ✆ 020 8800 0404
✉ lavian@lavian.com
🌐 www.lavian.com
Est. 1962 *Stock size* Large
Stock Oriental carpets and textiles
Open Mon–Fri 9.30am–5.30pm
Services Valuations, restoration

⊞ **Regent Antiques**
Contact Mr Tino Quaradeghini
✉ Manor Warehouse,
318 Green Lanes, London,
N4 1BX 🅿
☎ 020 8802 3900 ✆ 020 8809 9605
📱 07836 294074
✉ regentantiques@aol.com
Est. 1974 *Stock size* Large
Stock 18thC–Edwardian furniture
Open Mon–Fri 9am–5.30pm
Services Restoration of furniture

⊞ **The Rug Studio**
Contact Rachel Bassill
✉ First floor, Building A, Oriental
Carpet Centre, 105 Eade Road,
London,
N4 1TJ 🅿

☎ 020 8977 4403
✉ info@therugstudio.co.uk
🌐 www.therugstudio.co.uk
Est. 1994 *Stock size* Medium
Stock Antique, Oriental and
contemporary rugs
Open Mon–Sat by appointment
Fairs Antiques for Everyone,
Royal Horticultural Hall, BBC
Homes and Antiques
Services Restoration, rug search

N5

⊞ **Gathering Moss**
Contact Mrs S Murnane
✉ 193 Blackstock Road, London,
N5 2LL 🅿
☎ 020 7354 3034
Est. 1999 *Stock size* Medium
Stock Furniture, gifts, reclaimed
timber items
Open Wed–Fri 10.30am–5.30pm
Sat 10am–6pm Sun 11am–4pm

⊞ **Nicholas Goodyer
(PBFA, ABA)**
Contact Mr N Goodyer
✉ 8 Framfield Road, Highbury
Fields, London,
N5 1UU 🅿
☎ 020 7226 5682 ✆ 020 7354 4716
✉ email@nicholasgoodyer.com
Est. 1950 *Stock size* Medium
Stock Antiquarian and rare
books on architecture, travel,
design, illustrated, natural
history, colour-plate books
Open Mon–Fri by appointment,
prior call or e-mail advised
Fairs PBFA Russell, ABA
Services Valuations, restoration,
shipping, book search

⊞ **Sandby Fine Art**
Contact B Ashley
✉ 72 Mountgrove Road, London,
N5 2LT 🅿
☎ 020 7354 4759
Est. 1989 *Stock size* Medium
Stock General antiques,
fireplaces, paintings
Open Mon–Sat 9am–6pm

N6

⊞ **Fisher & Sperr (ABA)**
✉ 46 Highgate High Street,
London,
N6 5JB 🅿
☎ 020 8340 7244 ✆ 020 8348 4293
Est. 1945 *Stock size* Large
Stock General second-hand and

antiquarian books
Open Mon–Sat 10am–5pm
Services Valuations

⊞ Ripping Yarns (PBFA)
Contact Mrs C Mitchell
✉ **355 Archway Road, London,
N6 4EJ** ▣
☎ 020 8341 6111 ✆ 020 7482 5056
✉ yarns@rippingyarns.co.uk
ⓦ www.rippingyarns.co.uk
Est. 1982 **Stock size** Large
Stock General stock, antiquarian
and second-hand books
including children's fiction,
illustrated
Open Tues–Fri 11am–5pm
Sat 10am–5pm Sun 11am–4pm
Fairs PBFA
Services Book search, French and
Spanish spoken, annual
catalogue

N7

⊞ Back in Time
Contact Mr Demetriou
✉ **93 Holloway Road, London,
N7 8LT** ▣
☎ 020 7700 0744
✉ mario000@btclick.com
ⓦ www.backintime.com
Est. 1996 **Stock size** Large
Stock 1950s–1970s furniture,
metal wardrobes, decorative
items, metal kitchen furniture
Open Mon–Sat 10am–6pm
Services Valuations, restoration

**⊞ Dome Antiques
(LAPADA)**
Contact Mr A Woolf
✉ **40 Queensland Road, London,
N7 7AJ** ▣
☎ 020 7700 6266 ✆ 020 7609 1692
ⓜ 07831 805888
✉ info@domeantiques.com
ⓦ www.domeantiques.com
Est. 1974 **Stock size** Large
Stock 19thC decorative furniture
Open Mon–Fri 9am–5pm
Fairs NEC, Olympia
Services Restoration

⊞ Ooh-La-La
Contact David or Barry
✉ **147 Holloway Road, London,
N7 8LX** ▣
☎ 020 7609 6021
ⓜ 07970 007590
Est. 1997 **Stock size** Medium
Stock Leather Chesterfields,
contemporary sofas, furniture,

smalls, vintage clothing
Open Mon–Thurs 11am–5pm
Sat 10.30am–6pm
Services Valuations

N8

⚒ Hornsey Auctions Ltd
Contact Miss C Connoly
✉ **54–56 High Street, Hornsey,
London,
N8 7NX** ▣
☎ 020 8340 5334 ✆ 020 8340 5334
Est. 1983
Open Thurs Fri 9.30am–5.30pm
Sat 10am–4pm
Sales Antiques and general sale
Wed 6.30pm, viewing Tues
5–7pm Wed 10am–6.30pm prior
to sale
Frequency Weekly
Catalogues Yes

⊞ Of Special Interest
Contact Mr S Loftus
✉ **42–46 Park Road, London,
N8 8TD** ▣
☎ 020 8340 0909 ✆ 020 8374 6990
Est. 1988 **Stock size** Large
Stock Antique pine furniture,
porcelain, fabrics, garden
furniture, eastern European
furniture
Open Mon–Fri noon–7pm
Sat 10am–6pm Sun noon–4pm

⊞ Solomon
Contact Solomon
✉ **49 Park Road, London,
N8 8SY** ▣
☎ 020 8341 1817 ✆ 020 8341 1817
✉ solomon@solomonantiques.
fsnet.co.uk
Est. 1981 **Stock size** Medium
Stock 20thC design furniture,
collectables
Open Mon–Sat 9am–6pm
Services Restoration, French
polishing, upholstery, hand-
made furniture

N9

⊞ Anything Goes
Contact C J Bednarz
✉ **83 Bounces Road,
London,
N9 8LD** ▣
☎ 020 8807 9399
Est. 1978 **Stock size** Small
Stock Antiques, collectables
Open Tues–Sat 10am–5pm
Services Valuations

N10

⊞ Crafts Nouveau
Contact Laurie Strange
✉ **112 Alexandra Park Road,
Muswell Hill, London,
N10 2AE** ▣
☎ 020 8444 3300 ✆ 020 8815 9945
ⓜ 07958 448380
✉ info@craftsnouveau.co.uk
ⓦ www.craftsnouveau.co.uk
Est. 2003 **Stock size** Medium
Stock Art Nouveau, Arts and
Crafts furniture, decorative arts,
pewter, copperware, writing
accessories, books and print
Open Wed–Sat 10.30am–6.30pm
Tues–Sun by appointment

N11

⊞ A Pine Romance
Contact Mrs S Gray
✉ **111 Friern Barnet Road,
New Southgate, London,
N11 3EU** ▣
☎ 020 8361 5860 ✆ 020 8361 4697
Est. 1989 **Stock size** Medium
Stock British and Continental
pine furniture
Open Mon–Sat 10am–5.30pm
closed Wed
Services Valuations, restoration,
manufacturers of furniture from
reclaimed timber

N12

⊞ The New Curiosity Shop
Contact Mrs T Robins
✉ **211 Woodhouse Road,
Friern Barnet, London,
N12 9AY** ▣
☎ 020 8368 2117
Est. 1994 **Stock size** Medium
Stock Coins, stamps, banknotes,
sci-fi memorabilia, pop
memorabilia, *Star Wars* toys,
Corgi, Dinky, Matchbox
collectables, records, ceramics,
silver, jewellery
Open Mon–Sat 10am–5.00pm
Services Valuations

⚒ North London Auctions
Contact Mr Tarone
✉ **Lodge House, 9–17 Lodge
Lane, North Finchley,
London,
N12 8JH** ▣
☎ 020 8445 9000 ✆ 020 8446 6068
✉ info@northlondonauctions.com
ⓦ www.northlondonauctions.com

Est. 1977
Open Mon–Fri 9am–5.30pm
Sales Antiques and general sale
Mon 4pm, viewing Sun 9am–1pm
Mon 9am–4pm
Frequency Weekly
Catalogues Yes

⌂ Palmers Green Antiques Centre
Contact Michael Webb
✉ 472 Green Lane,
Palmers Green,
London,
N13 5PA 🅿
☎ 020 8350 0878
📱 07855 067544
Est. 1996 *Stock size* Large
No. of dealers 40+
Stock Furniture, clocks, pictures,
jewellery, porcelain, china, glass,
silver, lighting, general antiques
Open Mon Wed–Sat
10am–5.30pm Sun 11am–5pm
Services Valuations, house
clearance

N14

⊞ C J Martin Coins Ltd (LAPADA)
Contact Chris Martin
✉ 85 The Vale, Southgate,
London,
N14 6AT 🅿
☎ 020 882 1509 📠 020 886 5253
📧 ancientart@btinternet.com
🌐 www.ancientart.co.uk
Est. 1972 *Stock size* Large
Stock General antiquities and coins
Open By appointment
Services Valuations, restoration,
shipping, mail order

⋏ Southgate Auction Rooms
Contact Mr J Nolan
✉ 55 High Street, Southgate,
London,
N14 6LD 🅿
☎ 020 8886 7888 📠 020 8882 4421
📧 jmnolan@btinternet.com
🌐 www.southgateauction
rooms.com
Est. 1986
Open Mon–Fri 9am–5.30pm
Sales General and antiques sales
Mon 4pm, viewing Sat 9am–1pm
Mon 9am–4pm prior to sale
Frequency Weekly
Catalogues Yes

⊞ Richard Thornton Books (PBFA)
Contact Richard Thornton
✉ 25 Beechdale, Winchmore Hill,
London,
N21 3QE
☎ 020 8886 8202
📧 richard.thorntonbooks@
btinternet.com
Est. 1996 *Stock size* Medium
Stock Antiquarian, rare, used
books, large private bookrooms
to view with over 10,000 titles,
please ring to view
Open Mon–Fri 9am–6pm or
by appointment
Services Valuations

N15

⊞ Krypton Komics
Contact Mr G Ochiltree
✉ 252 High Road, Tottenham,
London,
N15 4AJ 🅿
☎ 020 8801 5378 📠 020 8376 3174
📧 gary.ochiltree@virgin.net
🌐 www.kryptonkomics.com
Est. 1980 *Stock size* Large
Stock 1950s–present day
American comics
Open Tues noon–5.30pm Wed
11am–6pm Thurs 10.30am–7pm
Fri Sat 10.30am–6pm
Fairs Comic Convention at the
Royal National Hotel
Services Valuations, mail order
catalogue

N16

⊞ The Cobbled Yard
Contact Carole Lucas
✉ 1 Bouverie Road, Stoke
Newington, London,
N16 0AH 🅿
☎ 020 8809 5286
📧 info@cobbled-yard.co.uk
🌐 www.cobbled-yard.co.uk
Est. 2002 *Stock size* Medium
Stock Furniture, pine, ceramics,
collectables, retro items
Open Wed–Sun 11am–6pm
Services Restoration, upholstery,
carpentry

⊞ I Ehrnfeld (NAWCC)
Contact Isaac Ehrnfeld
✉ 29 Leweston Place, London,
N16 6RJ 🅿
☎ 020 8802 4584 📠 020 8800 1364
📱 07966 136495
Est. 1989 *Stock size* Medium

Stock Watches, wristwatches
Open By appointment
Fairs Major antiques fairs,
clock/watch fairs
Services Shipping

N19

⊞ Chesney's Antique Fireplace Warehouse
Contact John Norman
✉ 734–736 Holloway Road,
London,
N19 3JF 🅿
☎ 020 7561 8280 📠 020 7561 8288
📧 sales@chesneys.co.uk
🌐 www.chesneys.co.uk
Est. 1985 *Stock size* Large
Stock Antique fireplaces
Open Mon–Fri 9am–5.30pm
Sat 10am–5pm
Services Shipping

⊞ Arthur Middleton Ltd (SIS)
Contact Mr A Middleton or
Miss Morgan
✉ 50 Whitehall Park, Archway,
London,
N19 3TN 🅿
☎ 020 7281 8445
📱 07887 481102
📧 arthur@antique-globes.com
🌐 www.antique-globes.com
Est. 1978 *Stock size* Medium
Stock Marine and scientific
instruments, globes
Open Mon–Fri 10am–6pm
Services Valuations

N21

⊞ Dollyland
✉ 864 Green Lanes,
Winchmore Hill, London,
N21 2RS 🅿
☎ 020 8360 1053 📠 020 8364 1370
📱 0780 821773
Est. 1986 *Stock size* Large
Stock Dolls, Steiff bears,
Scalextric, trains, die-cast toys
Open Tues Thurs–Sat
9.30am–4.30pm
Fairs Hugglets, Kensington Town
Hall

⊞ Past Present Toys
Contact Mr Jim Parsons
✉ 862 Green Lanes, London,
N21 2RS 🅿
☎ 020 8364 1370 📠 020 8364 1370
Est. 1986 *Stock size* Large
Stock Dinkys, Hornby railways,

tin-plate toys, Corgi, Matchbox
Open Tues Thurs–Sat
9.30am–4.30pm

NW1

✦ Archive Books and Music (Shepherds Book Directory)
Contact Mr T Meaker
✉ 83 Bell Street, Marylebone, London,
NW1 6TB ♿
☎ 020 7402 8212
Est. 1975 **Stock size** Medium
Stock Second-hand books, printed pop and classical music
Open Mon–Sat 10.30am–6pm

✦ Art Furniture
Contact Liam Scanlon
✉ 158 Camden Street, London,
NW1 9PA ♿
☎ 020 7267 4324 ☎ 020 7267 5199
✉ arts-and-crafts@artfurniture.co.uk
ⓦ www.artfurniture.co.uk
Est. 1989 **Stock size** Large
Stock Arts and Crafts furniture and objects including Liberty, Heals, Shapland and Petter
Open Mon–Sun noon–5pm
Services Shipping, restoration

✦ Benjamin Jewellery (LAPADA)
Contact Anita Benjamin
✉ PO Box 12656, London,
NW1 4WJ ♿
☎ 020 7486 5382 ☎ 020 7935 6134
Est. 1949 **Stock size** Medium
Stock Second-hand jewellery
Open By appointment
Fairs Miami Beach Show
Services Valuations

⚑ Comic Book Postal Auctions Ltd (Eagle Society)
Contact Malcolm Phillips
✉ 40–42 Osnaburgh Street, London,
NW1 3ND
☎ 020 7424 0007 ☎ 020 7424 0008
✉ comicbook@compuserve.com
ⓦ www.compalcomics.com
Est. 1992
Open By appointment
Sales Quarterly, British and American comics, 1900–1970s, also annuals, artwork, TV-related merchandise. Sales in March,

June, September, December
Frequency Quarterly
Catalogues Yes

✦ Laurence Corner
Contact Sales Manager
✉ 62–64 Hampstead Road, London,
NW1 2NU ♿
☎ 020 7813 1010 ☎ 020 7813 1413
ⓦ www.laurencecorner.com
Est. 1953 **Stock size** Large
Stock Militaria, uniforms
Open Mon–Sat 10.30am–6pm
Services Uniforms for hire

✦ Madeline Crispin Antiques
Contact Mrs M Crispin or David Thomas
✉ 95 Lisson Grove, London,
NW1 6UP ♿
☎ 020 7402 6845
ⓜ 07956 289906
✉ david@crispinantiques.fsnet.co.uk
Est. 1979 **Stock size** Medium
Stock Furniture, decorative items
Open Mon–Fri 10am–5.30pm Sat 10am–4pm
Services Valuations

✦ Decorative Arts
Contact Anthony White
✉ Unit 87, The Stables Market, Camden Market, London,
NW1 8AH ♿
☎ 01273 676486
ⓜ 07788 107101
✉ info@decarts.net
ⓦ www.decarts.net
Est. 2002 **Stock size** Medium
Stock Oak furniture 1880–1970, decorative arts, 1970s leather furniture
Open Fri–Sun 10am–6pm

✦ Elvisly Yours
Contact Mr Sid Shaw
✉ 233 Baker Street, London,
NW1 6XE ♿
☎ 020 7486 2005
✉ info@elvisly-yours.com
ⓦ www.elvisly-yours.com
Est. 1978 **Stock size** Large
Stock Elvis memorabilia
Open Mon–Sun 11am–6.30pm

✦ The Façade
Contact Gay Brown
99 Lisson Grove, London,
NW1 6UP ♿
☎ 020 7258 2017
ⓦ www.thefacade.co.uk

Est. 1975 **Stock size** Large
Stock Antique chandeliers, mirrors, decorative items
Open Tues–Sat 10.30am–5pm

✦ Carol Ketley Antiques (LAPADA)
Contact Carol Ketley
✉ PO Box 16199, London,
N1 7WD ♿
☎ 020 7359 5529 ☎ 020 7226 4589
ⓜ 07831 827284
Est. 1980 **Stock size** Large
Stock Drinking glasses and decanters, gilded decorative antiques especially mirrors
Open By appointment, see Sophie Ketley Antiques at Antiquarius (London SW3)
Fairs Olympia, Decorative Antiques and Textiles Fair

✦ Judith Michael
Contact Gillian Anderson or Judith Troldahl
✉ 73 Regent's Park Road, Primrose Hill, London,
NW1 ♿
☎ 01434 633165 ☎ 01434 633165
✉ info@judithmichael.com
ⓦ www.judithmichael.com
Est. 1989 **Stock size** Medium
Stock General antiques, decorative items, jewellery, small furniture, glass, china, gardening section
Open Tues–Sat 10am–5pm
Services Interior design

✦ The Relic Antiques Trade Warehouse
Contact Mr Gliksten
✉ 133–135 Pancras Road, London,
NW1 1JN ♿
☎ 020 7387 6039 ☎ 020 7388 2691
✉ malcolm.gliksten@blueyonder.co.uk
Est. 1972 **Stock size** Large
Stock Decorative antiques, folk art, fairground art, Black Forest carvings, country pieces, architectural, marine, trade signs, shop fittings
Open Mon–Fri 10am–6pm Sat by appointment
Services Valuations, framing, mirror restoration

✦ Travers Antiques
Contact Mr S Kluth
✉ 71 Bell Street, London,
NW1 6SX ♿

☎ 020 7723 4376
✉ spkluth@aol.com
Est. 1976 *Stock size* Large
Stock 1820–1920 furniture, decorative items
Open Mon–Sat 10.30am–5pm
Services Valuations, restoration

⊞ David J Wilkins
Contact Alex Wilkins
✉ 27 Princess Road, Regents Park, London, NW1 8JR 🅿
☎ 020 7722 7608 ☎ 020 7483 0423
✉ alexdwilkins@hotmail.com
ⓦ www.orientalrugexperts.com
Est. 1990 *Stock size* Large
Stock Antique Oriental rugs
Open Mon–Fri by appointment only

NW2

⊞ G and F Gillingham Ltd
Contact Mr Gillingham
✉ 62 Menelik Road, London, NW2 3RH
☎ 020 7435 5644 ☎ 020 7435 5644
ⓜ 07958 484140
Est. 1960
Stock 1750–1950 furniture
Open By appointment
Services Valuations, exports, restoration

⊞ Quality Furniture Warehouse
Contact Mr Anthony Dwyer
✉ Ionna House, Humber Road, London, NW2 6EN 🅿
☎ 020 8452 0074 ☎ 020 8450 9296
✉ info@qfw.co.uk
ⓦ www.qfw.co.uk
Est. 1981 *Stock size* Large
Stock Victorian–Edwardian furniture and earlier, quality used furniture, English and Continental, reproduction French and Italian ormolu furniture
Open Sat Sun 10.30am–5.30pm or by appointment
Fairs Newark, Wembley
Services Restoration, repairs

⊞ Sabera Trading Oriental Carpets & Rugs
Contact Nawrozzadeh
✉ Coles Green Road, London, NW2 7EU 🅿
☎ 020 8450 0012 ☎ 020 8450 0012
Est. 1992 *Stock size* Medium

Stock Oriental carpets, rugs, Chinese porcelain, jewellery
Open Mon–Sat 10am–6pm

NW3

⊞ Keith Fawkes
Contact Keith Fawkes
✉ 1–3 Flask Walk, Hampstead, London, NW3 1HJ 🅿
☎ 020 7435 0614
ⓜ 07939 000921
Est. 1967 *Stock size* Large
Stock Antiquarian and second-hand books
Open Mon–Sat 10am–5.30pm Sun 1.30–6pm
Services Valuations

⊞ Brian Fielden (BADA)
Contact Brian Fielden
✉ 7 Chalcot Gardens, London, NW3 4YB 🅿
☎ 020 7722 9192 ☎ 020 7722 9192
Est. 1965 *Stock size* Small
Stock English 18th–early 19thC furniture
Open By appointment

⊞ Gillian Gould Antiques
Contact Gill Gould
✉ 18a Belsize Park Gardens, London, NW3 4LH 🅿
☎ 020 7419 0500
ⓜ 07831 150060
✉ gillgould@dealwith.com
Est. 1989 *Stock size* Small
Stock Scientific, marine, general gifts
Open Mon–Wed Fri 9.30am–6.30pm Thurs 9.30am–7pm Sat 9.30am–5.30pm
Services Valuations, restoration

⌂ Hampstead Antique and Craft Emporium
Contact Mr John Martin
✉ 12 Heath Street, London, NW3 6TE 🅿
☎ 020 7794 3297
Est. 1967 *Stock size* Large
No. of dealers 20–30
Stock Furniture, jewellery, first-edition teddy bears, trimmings, buttons, paintings, prints, gifts, memorabilia, period jewellery, glass, porcelain, woollen goods. millinery
Open Tues–Fri 10.30am–5pm Sat 10am–6pm Sun 11am–5.30pm
Services Valuations

⊞ Sylvia Powell Decorative Arts (BADA, LAPADA)
Contact Mrs S Powell
✉ 400 Ceramic House, 573 Finchley Road, London, NW3 7BN 🅿
ⓜ 07802 714998
✉ dpowell909@aol.com
ⓦ www.sylvia-powell.com
Est. 1987 *Stock size* Large
Stock Art pottery, 20thC decorative arts
Open By appointment
Fairs Olympia, NEC, Harrogate, BADA
Services Valuations

⊞ Recollections Antiques
Contact Mrs June Gilbert
✉ The Courtyard, 12 Heath Street, Hampstead, London, NW3 6TE 🅿
☎ 020 7431 9907 ☎ 020 7794 9743
ⓜ 07930 394 014
✉ junal@recollectionsantiques.co.uk
ⓦ www.recollectionaantiques.co.uk
Est. 1991 *Stock size* Large
Stock Early 19thC blue and white transfer-printed pottery, early pine, miniature furniture, children's highchairs, kitchenware, collectors' teddy bears
Open Tues–Sat 10.30am–5pm

⊞ M & D Seligman (BADA)
Contact M or D Seligman
✉ 26 Belsize Park Gardens, London, NW3 4LH 🅿
☎ 020 7722 4315 ☎ 020 7722 4315
ⓜ 07946 634429
Est. 1947 *Stock size* Small
Stock Sophisticated 16th–early 19thC country furniture, associated works of art, antiquities
Open By appointment

⋏ Villa Grisebach Art Auctions
Contact Mrs Sabina Fliri
✉ 4 Evangelist Road, London, NW5 1UB
☎ 020 7431 9882 ☎ 020 7284 1746
✉ fliris@btconnect.com
ⓦ www.villa-grisebach.de
Est. 1986
Open By appointment
Sales 19th–20thC art and photography, telephone for details

Fairs Biennialle in Berlin
Frequency Twice a year
Catalogues Yes

NW4

⊞ Memories (PTA)
Contact Dave Smith
✉ 130–132 Brent Street, Hendon, London,
NW4 2DR 🅿
☎ 020 8202 9080
🔗 dave@mempics.demon.co.uk
🌐 www.memoriespostcards.co.uk
Est. 1975 *Stock size* Large
Stock Postcards
Open Mon–Sat 9.30am–5.30pm
Services Valuations, price guide catalogue

⊞ Murray Cards (International) Ltd
Contact Ian Murray
✉ 51 Watford Way, Hendon, London,
NW4 3JH
☎ 020 8202 5688 🖷 020 8203 7878
🔗 murraycards@ukbusiness.com
🌐 www.murraycards.com
Est. 1965 *Stock size* Large
Stock Cigarette and trading cards, albums, frames, books
Open Mon–Fri 9am–5pm
Fairs Murray Fair & Auction, Royal National Hotel, London
Services Annual catalogue, auction catalogue, Fair and Auction organiser

⊞ The Talking Machine
Contact Mr D Smith
✉ 30 Watford Way, London,
NW4 3AL 🅿
☎ 020 8202 3473
📱 07774 103139
🔗 davepaul50@hotmail.com
🌐 www.gramophones.endirect.co.uk
Est. 1975 *Stock size* Large
Stock Mechanical antiques, typewriters, radios, music boxes, photographs, sewing machines, juke boxes, calculators, televisions
Open Variable or by appointment
Services Valuations, restoration

NW5

⊞ The Orientalist
Contact M Fadaei
✉ 74–80 Highgate Road, London,
NW5 1PB 🅿
☎ 020 7482 0555 🖷 020 7267 9603
🔗 orientalist80@aol.com

🌐 www.orientalist.demon.co.uk
Est. 1985 *Stock size* Large
Stock Hand-made antique carpets, rugs
Open Mon–Sat 10am–6pm Sun 11am–5pm

NW6

⊞ Gallery Kaleidoscope incorporating Scope Antiques
Contact Mr K Barrie
✉ 64–66 Willesden Lane, London,
NW6 7SX 🅿
☎ 020 7328 5833 🖷 020 7624 2913
Est. 1970 *Stock size* Large
Stock Furniture, interior decorators' pieces, paintings, prints, sculptures, glass
Open Tues–Sat 10am–6pm Thur 1–7pm
Services Valuations, framing, silverwork

NW8

🏠 Alfies Antique Market
Contact Stefania Lategola
✉ 13–25 Church Street, London,
NW8 8DT 🅿
☎ 020 7723 6066 🖷 020 7724 0999
🔗 info@alfiesantiques.com
🌐 www.alfiesantiques.com
No. of dealers 100
Stock General antiques, collectables, 20thC design
Open Tues–Sat 10am–6pm
Services Restoration, bureau de change, rooftop restaurant

⊞ Beverley
Contact Beverley
✉ 30 Church Street, Marylebone, London,
NW8 8EP 🅿
☎ 020 7262 1576 🖷 020 7262 1576
📱 07776 136003
Est. 1958 *Stock size* Large
Stock 1850–1950 English ceramics, glass, metal, wood, pottery, collectables, decorative items
Open Mon–Fri 10.30am–6pm Sat 9.30am–6pm or by appointment
Fairs NEC, Peterborough Festival of Antiques
Services Mail order worldwide

⊞ Bizarre
Contact Mr V Conti or Mr A Taramasco
✉ 24 Church Street, London,

NW8 8EP 🅿
☎ 020 7724 1305 🖷 020 7724 1316
🔗 bizdec@aol.com
🌐 www.bizdec.co.uk
Est. 1982 *Stock size* Large
Stock Art Deco, Continental furniture, wrought iron, glass, ceramics
Open Mon–Fri 10am–5pm Sat 10am–4pm
Services Interior design

⊞ Canonbury Antiques
Contact Angela Martin
✉ 1 & 5 Church Street, London,
NW8 8EE
☎ 020 7724 7781 🖷 020 7724 7783
🔗 angela@canonburyantiques.co.uk
Est. 1976 *Stock size* Large
Stock Furniture, porcelain, bronzes, marble statues
Open Mon–Fri 10am–6pm Sat 10.30am–5pm
Services Valuations, restoration

⊞ Church Street Antiques
Contact Stuart Shuster
✉ 8 Church Street, London,
NW8 8ED 🅿
☎ 020 7723 7415 🖷 020 7723 7415
🔗 stuart@churchstreetantiques.net
Est. 1980 *Stock size* Large
Stock 18th–20thC furniture, decorative items
Open Tues–Sat 10am–6pm

⊞ Davidson Antiques
Contact Edward Davidson
✉ 5 Church Street, London,
NW8 8EE 🅿
☎ 020 7724 9236 🖷 020 7724 9387
🔗 enquiries@davidsonandmorgan.com
🌐 www.davidsonandmorgan.com
Est. 1958 *Stock size* Medium
Stock Furniture, decorative objects, clocks, chandeliers, lighting, architectural antiques
Open Mon–Sun 10am–6pm

⊞ Dodo
Contact Liz Farrow
✉ Alfies Antique Market, FO 73, 13–25 Church Street, London,
NW8 8DT 🅿
☎ 020 7706 1545 🖷 020 7724 0999
🔗 liz@dodoposters.co.uk
🌐 www.dodoposters.com
Est. 1960 *Stock size* Large
Stock Vintage posters, card signs, labels 1920–1940, food, drink, travel, entertainment
Open Tues–Sat 10.30am–5.30pm

LONDON
NORTH • NW8

Fairs Ephemera Society,
Russell Square Hotel
Services Restoration

⊞ Gallery 1930
Contact Nick Jones
✉ 18 Church Street, London,
NW8 8EP ℗
☎ 020 7723 1555
🖃 gallery1930@aol.com
Est. 1985 Stock size Medium
Stock Art deco, ceramics,
furniture, glass, lighting and
accessories
Open Tues–Sat 10am–5pm

⊞ The Girl Can't Help It
Contact Sparkle Moore or
Cad van Swankster
✉ Units G80, G90 & G100,
Alfies Antique Market,
13–25 Church Street,
London,
NW8 8DT ℗
☎ 020 7724 8984 📠 020 8809 3923
🖃 sparkle@sparklemoore.com
🌐 www.thegirlcanthelpit.com
Est. 1997 Stock size Medium
Stock 1930–1960 American
vintage clothing and accessories,
pin-up collectables
Open Tues–Sat 10am–6pm
Fairs Vintage Mayfair

⊞ Goldsmith & Perris
(LAPADA)
Contact Gloria Goldsmith
✉ Alfies Antique Market, 13–25
Church Street, London,
NW8 8DT ℗
☎ 020 7724 7051 📠 020 7724 7051
📱 07831 447432
🖃 gandpalfies@aol.com
Est. 1974 Stock size Large
Stock Antique silver, silver plate,
lamps, collectables, cocktail
shakers
Open Tues–Sat 10am–6pm

⊞ Ora Gordon (LAPADA,
CINOA)
Contact Ora Gordon
✉ London, NW8
☎ 020 7286 1306 📠 020 7286 1306
🖃 oragordon@onetel.com
Est. 1980 Stock size Medium
Stock English porcelain
18th–early 20thC export
Wedgwood
Open By appointment
Fairs NEC Antiques for Everyone
Services Shipping, valuations,
search specific items

⊞ Patricia Harvey
Antiques
Contact Mrs P Harvey
✉ 42 Church Street, London,
NW8 8EP
☎ 020 7262 8989 📠 020 7262 8989
🖃 info@patriciaharveyantiques.co.uk
🌐 www.patriciaharveyantiques.co.uk
Est. 1960 Stock size Large
Stock 18th–19thC English, French
furniture, decorative, paintings
Open Mon–Sat 10am–5.30pm
Fairs Decorative Antiques &
Textiles Fair (Jan, April, Sept)
Services Valuations

⊞ Just Desks
Contact Noelle Finch
✉ 20 Church Street, London,
NW8 8EP ℗
☎ 020 7723 7976
📠 020 7402 6416
Est. 1972 Stock size Small
Stock Desks, tables, chairs,
filing cabinets
Open Mon–Sat 9.30am–6pm

⊞ Magus Antiques
Contact David Juran
✉ 4 Church Street, London,
NW8 8ED
☎ 020 7724 1278 📠 020 7724 1278
Est. 1975 Stock size Large
Stock Furniture and general
antiques
Open Tues–Fri 10am–4.30pm
Sat 11am–5pm

⊞ Marie Antiques
✉ Stand G136–138, Alfies
Antique Market, 13–25 Church
Street, London,
NW8 8DT
☎ 020 7706 3727
🖃 marie136@globalnet.co.uk
🌐 www.marieantiques.co.uk
Est. 1987 Stock size Large
Stock Jewellery 1830–1930
Open Tues–Sat 10am–4.30pm
Services Valuations, restoration,
shipping

⊞ Andrew Nebbett
Antiques
Contact Andrew Nebbett
✉ 35–37 Church Street,
Marylebone, London,
NW8 8ES ℗
☎ 020 7723 2303
📱 07768 741595
🖃 anebbett@aol.com
🌐 www.andrewnebbett.com
Est. 1999 Stock size Large

Stock Simple, large, English and
Swedish oak furniture
17th–20thC
Open Tues–Sat 10am–5.30pm

⊞ Tara Antiques
Contact Mr G Robinson
✉ 6 Church Street, London,
NW8 8ED ℗
☎ 020 7724 2405
Est. 1984 Stock size Large
Stock Eclectic mix of decorative
furniture and items, ivories,
sculptures
Open Tues–Fri 10am–6pm
Sat 1.30–6pm
Fairs Decorative Textile Fairs,
Battersea

⊞ Tin Tin Collectables
Contact Mr P Pinnington or
Mr L Verrinder
✉ Ground Units 38–42, Alfies
Antique Market, 13–25 Church
Street, London,
NW8 8DT ℗
☎ 020 7258 1305
🖃 leslie@tintincollectables.com
🌐 www.tintincollectables.com
Est. 1995 Stock size Large
Stock Handbags, Victorian–
present day, decorative evening
bags, Victorian–1940s costume
Open Tues–Sat 10am–6pm
Services Valuations, film and
TV hire

⊞ Wellington Gallery
(LAPADA)
Contact Mrs M Barclay
✉ 1 St John's Wood High Street,
London,
NW8 7NG ℗
☎ 020 7586 2620 📠 020 7483 0716
Est. 1979
Stock Porcelain, silver, general
antiques
Open Mon–Fri 10.30am–6pm
Sat 10am–6pm
Services Valuations, restoration

⊞ Young & Son (LAPADA)
Contact Mr Young
✉ 12 Church Street, London,
NW8 8EP ℗
☎ 020 7723 5910
📱 07958 437043
🌐 www.youngandson.com
Est. 1990 Stock size Medium
Stock 18th–20thC antique
decorative furniture, 19thC
pictures, drawings, prints, fine
frames, lighting, mirrors, oddities

LONDON

Open Tues–Fri 10am–5.30pm
Sat 11am–5.30pm
Services Valuations

NW10

⊞ A D Carpets (LAPADA)
Contact Ahmad Gheiace
✉ 1 Chandos Road, Park Royal,
London,
NW10 6NF ▣
☎ 020 8838 3191 ❶ 020 8838 3191
❸ adcarpets@aol.com
Est. 1978 **Stock size** Large
Stock Antique oriental carpets
Open Mon–Fri 9.30am–6pm

**⊞ Retrouvius Architectural
Reclamation (SALVO)**
Contact Adam Hills
✉ 2A Ravensworth Road,
Kensal Green,
London,
NW10 5NR ▣
☎ 020 8960 6060
❶ 07778 210855
❸ mail@retrouvius.com
❿ www.retrouvius.com
Est. 1992 **Stock size** Medium
Stock Architectural antiques,
reclamation, design furniture
Open Thurs Fri 9.30am–6pm
or by appointment
Fairs Battersea Decorative Fair
Services Design service

**⊞ Willesden Green
Architectural Salvage**
Contact Mr D Harkin
✉ 189 High Road, Willesden,
London,
NW10 2SD ▣
☎ 020 8459 2947 ❶ 020 8451 1515
Est. 1994 **Stock size** Large
Stock Radiators, stained glass
windows, pine doors, lighting,
architectural salvage, fireplaces,
lead sash weights
Open Mon–Sat 9am–6pm

SOUTH

SE1

⊞ The Antiques Exchange
Contact Ray Gibbs
✉ 170–172 Tower Bridge Road,
London,
SE1 3LS ▣
☎ 020 7403 5568 ❶ 020 7378 8828
❸ info@AntiquesExchange.com
❿ www.AntiquesExchange.com
Est. 1966 **Stock size** Large

Stock Furniture, glass, china,
collectables, period style lighting
Open Mon–Fri 10am–6pm Sat
10.30am–6pm Sun 11am–5pm

**⊞ Sebastiano Barbagallo
Antiques**
Contact Mr S Barbagallo
✉ Universal House, 294–304 St
James's Road, London,
SE1 5JX ▣
☎ 020 7231 3680 ❶ 020 7231 3680
❸ sebastianobarbagallo@hotmail.com
Est. 1978 **Stock size** Large
Stock Chinese furniture, Indian
and Tibetan antiques, crafts
Open By appointment only

**⊞ Victor Burness
Antiques (SIS, PADA)**
Contact Mr V Burness
✉ Chelsea Gallery,
Portabello Road,
London
☎ 01732 454591
Est. 1975 **Stock size** Medium
Stock Scientific instruments
Open Sat 7am–3pm
Fairs Scientific Instrument Fair
Services Valuations, restoration

⊞ Capital Antiques Ltd
Contact Joan Carter
✉ 168a Tower Bridge Road,
London,
SE1 3LS ▣
☎ 020 7378 7263 ❶ 020 7378 7291
❸ joancarter@capitalantiques.
fsbusiness.co.uk
Est. 2002 **Stock size** Medium
Stock 17thC Edwardian antiques,
Arts and Crafts
Open Mon–Fri 10.30am–5.30pm
Sat 10.30-am–6pm
Sun 11am–5pm

**⊞ LASSCO Flooring
(SALVO, Timber Trade
Federation, TRADA)**
Contact Hamish Urquhart
✉ Brunswick House, 30
Wandsworth Road, Vauxhall,
London,
SW8 2LG ▣
☎ 020 7394 2100 ❶ 020 7501 7797
❸ flooring@lassco.co.uk
❿ www.lassco.co.uk
Est. 1978 **Stock size** Large
Stock Reclaimed timber flooring
in parquet strip and board
Open Mon–Fri 9am–5.30pm
Sat 10am–5pm
Services Shipping

⊞ LASSCO RBK (SALVO)
Contact Dan Neate
✉ Brunswick House, 30
Wandsorth Road, London,
SW8 2LG ▣
☎ 020 7394 2100 ❶ 020 7501 7797
❸ rbk@lassco.co.uk
❿ www.lassco.co.uk
Est. 1978 **Stock size** Large
Stock Reclaimed radiators,
bathrooms, kitchens
Open Mon–Sat 10am–5pm
Services Shipping

**⊞ Mayfair Carpet Gallery
Ltd**
Contact Mr A H Khawaja
✉ 301–303 Borough High Street,
London,
SE1 1JH ▣
☎ 020 7403 8228 ❶ 020 7407 1649
❸ aimz-kh@hotmail.com
Est. 1975 **Stock size** Large
Stock Fine antique Oriental
carpets, rugs
Open Mon–Sat 10.30am–6.30pm
Services Valuations, restoration

⊞ Radio Days
Contact Mrs C Layzell
✉ 87 Lower Marsh, London,
SE1 7AB ▣
☎ 020 7928 0800 ❶ 020 7928 0800
❿ www.radiodaysvintage.co.uk
Est. 1993 **Stock size** Large
Stock 1920s–1970s lighting,
telephones, radios, clothing,
magazines, cocktail bars, vintage
clothing and collectables
Open Mon–Thurs Sat 10am–6pm
Fri 10am–7pm or by
appointment
Services Valuations

⊞ Tower Bridge Antiques
Contact Joan Carter
✉ 71 Tanner Street, London,
SE1 3PL ▣
☎ 020 7403 3660 ❶ 020 7403 6058
❸ towerbridgeant@aol.com
Est. 1967 **Stock size** Large
Stock English, French and
American furniture
Open Mon–Fri 8am–5pm Sat
10am–6pm Sun 11am–5pm

⊞ G Viventi
Contact Giorgio
✉ 160 Tower Bridge Road,
London,
SE1 3LS ▣
☎ 020 7403 0022 ❶ 020 7277 5777

● viventi@btconnect.com
Est. 2000 *Stock size* Large
Stock Wide range of furniture,
styles and periods
Open Mon–Sat 9.30am–6pm

LONDON

SE3

⊞ **Beaumont Travel Books
(ABA, ILAB)**
Contact Mr G Beaumont
✉ **33 Couthurst Road,
Blackheath, London,
SE3 8TN** ▣
☎ 020 8293 4271
● JohnGabrielB@aol.com
Ⓦ www.abebooks.com/home
/beaumont
Est. 1996 *Stock size* Large
Stock Antiquarian, rare, second-
hand books, anthropology,
military, history, travel,
exploration a speciality
Open By appointment
Services Valuations, book search

⊞ **The Bookshop on the
Heath Ltd**
Contact Mr R Platt
✉ **74 Tranquil Vale, London,
SE3 0BW** ▣
☎ 020 8852 4786
Est. 2003 *Stock size* Large
Stock Antiquarian books,
prints, maps
Open Mon–Sat 10am–6pm
Sun noon–6pm
Services Valuations, book search

⊞ **Norris of Blackheath**
Contact Paul Norris
7a Tranquil Passage, Blackheath,
London,
SE3 0BJ ▣
☎ 020 8852 8725
Ⓦ www.norris-of-blackheath-
upholstery.co.uk
Est. 1945 *Stock size* Small
Stock Antique furniture
Open Mon–Fri 8am–6pm
Sat 9am–1pm
Services Upholstery

SE5

⊞ **Architectural Rescue**
Contact Mr J Powell
✉ **1 Southampton Way, London,
SE5 7JH** ▣
☎ 020 7277 0081 ● 020 7277 0081
Ⓜ 07930 416983
Est. 1993 *Stock size* Large
Stock Flooring, radiators,

sanitary ware, doors, door
furniture, fireplaces a speciality,
York stone
Open Mon–Sat 10am–5pm
Sun 10am–2pm
Fairs Newark, Swinderby

⊞ **Robert Hirschhorn
(BADA, LAPADA, CINOA)**
Contact Robert Hirschhorn
✉ **London, SE5**
☎ 020 7703 7443
Ⓜ 07831 405937
● hirschhornantiques@
macunlimited.net
Ⓦ www.hirschhornantiques.com
Est. 1978 *Stock size* Medium
Stock 18thC and earlier country
furniture, related objects
Open By appointment
Fairs Olympia, BADA
Services Valuations

SE6

⊞ **The Old Mill**
Contact Mr Sinclair
✉ **358 Bromley Road, Catford,
London,
SE6 2RT** ▣
☎ 020 8697 8006
Est. 1845 *Stock size* Medium
Stock Garden statuary, fireplaces
Open Mon–Sat 9.30am–5pm

⊞ **Wilkinson PLC**
Contact Jane Milnes
✉ **5 Catford Hill, London,
SE6 4NU** ▣
☎ 020 8314 1080 ● 020 8690 1524
● enquiries@wilkinson-plc.com
Ⓦ www.wilkinson-plc.com
Est. 1946 *Stock size* Large
Stock Lighting, chandeliers,
candelabra
Open Mon–Fri 9am–5pm
Services Restoration

SE7

⊞ **Ward's Antiques**
Contact Terry or Michael Ward
✉ **267 Woolwich Road, London,
SE7 7RB** ▣
☎ 020 8305 0963 ● 020 8305 2151
Ⓜ 07932 031936
Ⓦ www.wardantiquefireplaces.co.uk
Est. 1977 *Stock size* Large
Stock Victorian and Edwardian
fireplaces, general antiques
Open Mon–Sat 9am–6pm
Sun 11am–2pm
Services Restoration

SE8

⊞ **Antique Warehouse**
Contact Mrs Tillet
✉ **9–14 Deptford Broadway,
London,
SE8 4PA** ▣
☎ 020 8691 3062 ● 020 8469 0295
● martin@antiquewarehouse.co.uk
Ⓦ www.antiquewarehouse.co.uk
Est. 1983 *Stock size* Large
Stock General antiques
Open Mon–Sat 10am–6pm
Sun 11am–4pm
Services Valuations via website

SE10

⊞ **Creek Antiques**
Contact Dave
✉ **23 Greenwich South Street,
London,
SE10 8NW** ▣
☎ 020 8293 5721
Ⓜ 07778 427521
● www.creekantiques@aol.com
Est. 1986 *Stock size* Medium
Stock Jewellery, silver, enamel
signs, amusement machines
Open By appointment
Fairs Sandown

⊞ **Flying Duck Enterprises**
Contact Mr J Lowe or
Ms C Shrosbree
✉ **320–322 Creek Road,
Greenwich,
London,
SE10 9SW** ▣
☎ 020 8858 1964 ● 020 8852 3215
Ⓜ 07831 273303
● carolyn@flying-duck.com
Est. 1985 *Stock size* Large
Stock 1950–1970s items, cocktail
bars, furniture, lighting, fabrics,
dinette sets, glassware, china,
Open Tues–Fri 11am–6pm
Sat Sun 10.30am–6.30pm
Services Mail order

⋗ **Greenwich Auctions
Partnership**
Contact Marilyn Allen
✉ **47 Old Woolwich Road,
Greenwich, London,
SE10 9PP** ▣
☎ 020 8853 2121 ● 020 8293 7878
● greenwichauction@aol.com
Ⓦ www.greenwichauctions.co.uk
Est. 2000
Open Mon–Sat 9am–5pm
Sales Auction of antiques,
collectables, furniture,

memorabilia
Frequency Weekly
Catalogues Yes

⊞ Greenwich Gallery
Contact Richard Moy
✉ **9 Nevada Street, London, SE10 9JL** 🅿
☎ 020 8305 1666 ext 24
🅴 antiques@spreadeagle.org
🅦 www.spreadeagle.org
Est. 1957 *Stock size* Medium
Stock 18th–19thC watercolours, modern British art, prints
Open Mon–Sun 10.30am–5.30pm

⊞ The Junk Box
Contact Mrs M Dodd
✉ **47 Old Woolwich Road, Greenwich, London, SE10 9PP** 🅿
☎ 020 8293 5715
Est. 1988 *Stock size* Large
Stock Antiques, collectables, Victorian furniture, china, glass, copper, brass, kitchenware
Open Mon–Fri 10am–5pm
Services Valuations

⊞ The Junk Shop
Contact Tobias Moy
✉ **9 Greenwich South Street, London, SE10 8NW** 🅿
☎ 020 8305 1666 ext 25
🅦 www.spreadeagle.org
Est. 1985 *Stock size* Large
Stock Larger period furniture, architectural antiques, garden ornaments, decorative items
Open Mon–Sun 10.30am–5.30pm

⊞ Lamont Antiques Ltd (LAPADA)
Contact Mr F Llewellyn
✉ **Unit K, Tunnel Avenue Trading Estate, Greenwich, London, SE10 0QH** 🅿
☎ 020 8305 2230 🅕 020 8305 1805
🅴 lamontantiques@aol.com
🅦 www.lamontantiques.com
Est. 1974 *Stock size* Large
Stock Architectural items, stained glass, pub and restaurant fixtures, fittings
Open Mon–Fri 9.30am–5pm

⊞ Marcet Books (PBFA)
Contact Mr M Kemp
✉ **4a Nelson Road, Greenwich, London, SE10 9JB** 🅿
☎ 020 8853 5408

🅴 marcetbooks@btconnect.com
🅦 www.marcetbooks.co.uk
Est. 1980 *Stock size* Medium
Stock Antiquarian, rare, second-hand books, maritime, foreign travel, British topography, art, natural history, poetry specialities
Open Mon–Sun 10am–5.30pm
Fairs PBFA, Russell Hotel
Services Valuations

⊞ Minerva Antiques
Contact Jonathan Atkins
✉ **90 Royal Hill, Greenwich, London, SE10 8RT** 🅿
☎ 020 8691 2221 🅕 020 8691 2221
🅴 sales@minerva-antiques.co.uk
🅦 www.minerva-antiques.co.uk
Est. 1986 *Stock size* Medium
Stock Fully restored Georgian and Victorian antique furniture, English and French gilded mirrors
Open Tues–Sat 10am–6pm
Sun 11am–5pm
Services Valuation, restoration, upholstery

⊞ Rogers Turner Books (ABA, PBFA)
Contact Mr P Rogers
✉ **23a Nelson Road, Greenwich, London, SE10 9JB** 🅿
☎ 020 8853 5271 🅕 020 8853 5271
🅴 rogersturner@compuserve.com
Est. 1976 *Stock size* Medium
Stock Rare, antiquarian and second-hand books on experimental science, scientific instruments, horology, dialling a speciality
Open Thurs Fri 10am–6pm or by appointment
Fairs ABA Fairs, Olympia, PBFA London (monthly)
Services Valuations, catalogues

⊞ Spread Eagle Antiques
Contact Richard Moy
✉ **1 Stockwell Street, London, SE10 9JN** 🅿
☎ 020 8305 1666 ext 22
🅦 www.spreadeagle.org
Est. 1957 *Stock size* Medium
Stock Antique furniture, silver, decorative antiques, curios, ethnic art
Open Mon–Sun 10.30am–5.30pm

⊞ Spread Eagle Books
Contact Richard Moy
✉ **8 Nevada Street, London,**

SE10 9JL 🅿
☎ 020 8305 1666 ext 23
🅦 www.spreadeagle.org
Est. 1957 *Stock size* Medium
Stock Antiquarian books, collectables, ephemera
Open Mon–Sun 10.30am–5.30pm

⊞ The Warwick Leadlay Gallery (FATG)
Contact Mr Anthony Cross
✉ **5 Nelson Road, London, SE10 9JB** 🅿
☎ 020 8858 0317 🅕 020 8853 1773
🅴 info@warwickleadlay.com
🅦 www.warwickleadlay.com
Est. 1974 *Stock size* Large
Stock Antique maps, decorative maritime prints, fine arts, curios
Open Mon–Sat 9.30am–5.30pm
Sun 11am–5.30pm
Services Valuations, restoration, conservation, framing

⊞ Robert Whitfield (LAPADA)
Contact Mr R Whitfield
✉ **Unit K, Tunnel Avenue Trading Estate, Greenwich, London, SE10 0QH** 🅿
☎ 020 8305 2230 🅕 020 8305 1805
🅴 robertwhitfield@btinternet.com
Est. 1974 *Stock size* Large
Stock Oak, mahogany, walnut furniture
Trade only Yes
Open Mon–Fri 9am–5pm or by appointment

SE11

⊞ Nicholas Grindley (BADA)
Contact Ms Rebecca Gardner
✉ **London, SE11**
☎ 020 7437 5449 🅕 01449 614523
🅴 nick@nicholasgrindley.com
Est. 1993 *Stock size* Small
Stock Chinese works of art, sculptures, wall paintings, furniture etc
Open By appointment
Fairs Asian Art, London (Nov), Olympia
Services Valuations by mail

⊞ Kear of Kennington Antiques
Contact Mr S A Kear
✉ **4 Windmill Row, London, SE11 5DW** 🅿
☎ 020 7735 1304
Est. 1968 *Stock size* Small

Stock 18thC English drinking glasses, pottery, porcelain
Open By appointment

SE13

⊞ Robert Morley & Co Ltd (BADA)
Contact Julia Morley
✉ **34 Engate Street, London, SE13 7HA** 🅿
☎ 020 8318 5838
✉ jvm@morley-r.u-net.com
🌐 www.morleypianos.com
Est. 1881 **Stock size** Large
Stock Musical instruments
Open Mon–Sat 9.30am–5pm
Fairs Greenwich International Festival and Exhibition of Early Music
Services Restoration, tuning

SE15

⊞ CASA
Contact Mr M Tree
✉ **155 Bellenden Road, Peckham, London, SE15 4DH** 🅿
☎ 020 7732 3911
📱 07957 249722
✉ matt.tree@btopenworld.com
🌐 www.casaonline.co.uk
Est. 1993 **Stock size** Small
Stock Fireplaces, cast-iron radiators, doors, floorboards, stained glass windows, fixtures, fittings, sinks, basins, roll-top baths, taps, multi-fuel stoves, furniture, gardening antiques
Open Tues–Sat 10am–5pm or by appointement
Services Fireplace fitting, carpentry, plumbing, design

SE17

⊞ Pub Paraphernalia UK Ltd
Contact Mr M Ellis
✉ **Unit 13, Newington Industrial Estate, Crampton Street, London, SE17 3AZ** 🅿
☎ 020 7701 8913 ✆ 020 7277 4100
✉ sales@pub-paraphernalia.com
🌐 www.pub-paraphernalia.com
Est. 1980 **Stock size** Medium
Stock Water jugs, bar towels, beer mats, glassware, ashtrays, mirrors
Open Mon–Fri 9am–5pm by appointment
Fairs NEC (Spring)

SE19

⊞ The Book Palace
Contact Mr K Harman or Mr G West
✉ **Jubilee House, Bedwardine Road, London, SE19 3AP** 🅿
☎ 020 8768 0022 ✆ 020 8768 0563
✉ info@bookpalace.co.uk
🌐 www.bookpalace.com
Est. 1996 **Stock size** Large
Stock Histories of comics and popular media, art books, science fiction, film and TV biographies, Disney, animation, old US and UK comics, pulps, paperbacks, graphic novels
Open Mon–Fri 10am–6pm or by appointment
Fairs CIAMA, London Memorabilia Fair
Services Valuations, wanted titles list

SE20

⊞ Bearly Trading of London
Contact Cindy Hamilton-Aust
✉ **202 High Street, London, SE20 7QB** 🅿
☎ 020 8659 0500/8466 6696
✉ johom202@hotmail.com
Est. 1998 **Stock size** Large
Stock Old and new artists' teddy bears, rocking horses, antique furniture
Open Sat 10am–6pm or by appointment
Services Lay-away, mail order

SE21

⊞ Acorn Antiques
Contact Debbie
✉ **111 Rosendale Road, London, SE21 8EZ** 🅿
☎ 020 8761 3349
Est. 1977 **Stock size** Small
Stock Antiques and collectables
Open Mon–Fri 10am–6pm Sat 10am–5.30pm

⊞ Francis Jevons
Contact Mr F Jevons
✉ **80 Dulwich Village, London, SE21 7AJ** 🅿
☎ 020 8693 1991/020 8761 6612
Est. 1983 **Stock size** Small
Stock Antique furniture, china,

glass, interior design items
Open Mon–Fri 9.30am–1pm 2.30–5.30pm Sat 9.30– 5pm closed Wed
Services Valuations, restoration

SE22

⊞ Browns Antiques
Contact Erica Brown
✉ **149 Lordship Lane, East Dulwich, London, SE22 8HX** 🅿
☎ 020 8693 3000
Est. 2002 **Stock size** Medium
Stock Fine English furniture, glass, textiles
Open Mon–Sat 11am–6pm or by appointment
Services Restoration

⊞ Melbourne Antiques & Interiors
Contact Ian Peters
✉ **8 Melbourne Grove, London, SE22 8QZ** 🅿
☎ 020 8299 6565 ✆ 020 8299 4257
Est. 1998 **Stock size** Large
Stock French furniture, mirrors, chandeliers, armoires, linens, beds, commodes, fire surrounds
Open Mon–Sat 10am–6pm or by appointment

⊞ Middle of the Road
Contact Mr R Honour
✉ **52 Grove Vale, London, SE22 8DY** 🅿
☎ 020 8299 2515
Est. 1979 **Stock size** Large
Stock Oak and mahogany furniture, decorative items, lighting
Open Mon–Sat 10am–4pm

⊞ Timothy Millett Ltd (BADA)
Contact Timothy Millett
✉ **PO Box 20851, London, SE22 0YN** 🅿
☎ 020 8693 1111 ✆ 020 8299 3733
📱 07778 637898
✉ tim@historicmedals.com
🌐 www.historicmedals.com
Est. 2000 **Stock size** Large
Stock Historical medals, works of art
Open By appointment
Fairs Olympia June, Nov, BADA

SE26

⊞ Behind the Boxes – Art Deco
Contact Ray Owen
✉ 98 Kirkdale, London, SE26 4BG 🅿
☎ 020 8291 6116
🌐 mail@behindtheboxes-artdeco.co.uk
🌐 www.behindtheboxes-artdeco.co.uk
Est. 1991 *Stock size* Large
Stock Art Deco
Open Tues–Sat 10.30am–5pm

⊞ Bishops Furniture Stores
Contact Gareth Bishop
✉ 114 Sydenham Road, London, SE26 5JX 🅿
☎ 020 8778 9922
🌐 halldrive@aol.com
Est. 1971 *Stock size* Medium
Stock General antiques
Open Mon–Sat 9am–4.30pm
Services Upholstery

⊞ Grenadiers
Contact Mr C Chin-See
✉ 102 Sydenham Road, London, SE26 5JX 🅿
☎ 020 8659 1588 ❻ 020 8659 1588
📱 07887 571887
🌐 enquiries@grenadiers.co.uk
🌐 www.grenadiers.co.uk
Est. 1998 *Stock size* Medium
Stock Wide range of militaria
Open Mon–Fri 10am–4pm

⊞ Oola Boola Antiques London
Contact Mrs S Bramley
✉ 139–147 Kirkdale, London, SE26 4QJ 🅿
☎ 020 8291 9999 ❻ 020 8291 5759
📱 07956 261252
🌐 oola.boola@telco4u.net
Est. 1970 *Stock size* Large
Stock Victorian, Edwardian, Art Nouveau, Art Deco, Arts and Crafts furniture
Open Mon–Sat 10am–6pm
Sun 11am–5pm
Services Restoration, shipping

🏠 Sydenham Antiques Centre
Contact Mr P Cockton
✉ 48 Sydenham Road, London, SE26 5QF 🅿
☎ 020 8778 1706

Est. 1996 *Stock size* Large
No. of dealers 10
Stock Antiques, china, glass, furniture, jewellery, pictures, silver
Open Mon–Sat 10am–5pm

SE27

⚲ Rosebery Fine Art Ltd (ISVA)
Contact Angela Hayward
✉ 74–76 Knights Hill, London, SE27 0JD 🅿
☎ 020 8761 2522 ❻ 020 8761 2524
🌐 auctions@roseberys.co.uk
🌐 www.roseberys.co.uk
Est. 1987
Open Mon–Fri 9.30am–5.30pm
Sales Antiques and collectors' sale Tues Wed Thur 11am. viewing Sun 10am–2pm Mon 10am–7.30pm Tues Wed 9.30–10.45am. Quarterly select antiques, decorative arts and modern design, musical instruments, toys and collectors, books
Frequency Monthly
Catalogues Yes

SW1

⊞ After Noah
Contact Simon Tarr
✉ 4th Floor, Harvey Nichols, London, SW1X 7RJ 🅿
☎ 020 7235 5000
🌐 mailorder@afternoah.com
🌐 www.afternoah.com
Est. 1995 *Stock size* Medium
Stock Antique and contemporary furniture and houseware
Open Mon–Fri 10am–8pm
Sat 10am–7pm Sun noon–6pm
Services Restoration

⊞ Albert Amor (RWHA)
Contact Mark Law
✉ 37 Bury Street, London, SW1Y 6AU 🅿
☎ 020 7930 2444 ❻ 020 7930 9067
🌐 info@albertamor.co.uk
🌐 www.albertamor.co.uk
Est. 1899 *Stock size* Small
Stock 18th, early 19thC English porcelain
Open Mon–Thurs 10am–5pm or by appointment
Fairs Grosvenor House art and antiques fair
Services Valuations for insurance or ceramics

⊞ Anno Domini Antiques (BADA)
Contact Mr D Cohen
✉ 66 Pimlico Road, London, SW1W 8LS 🅿
☎ 020 7730 5496
Est. 1969 *Stock size* Large
Stock 18th–19thC furniture, mirrors, pictures, glass, porcelain
Open Mon–Fri 10am–1pm 2.15–5.30pm Sat 10am–3pm or by appointment
Services Valuations, restoration

⊞ Antiquus
Contact Elizabeth Amati
✉ 90–92 Pimlico Road, London, SW1W 8PL 🅿
☎ 020 7730 8681 ❻ 020 7823 6409
🌐 antiquus@antiquus-london.co.uk
🌐 www.antiquus-london.co.uk
Est. 1971 *Stock size* Large
Stock Gothic, Renaissance works of art, sculpture, textiles
Open Mon–Sat 9.30am–5.30pm

⊞ The Armoury of St James (OMRS)
Contact Mr Rawlins or Mr Davis
✉ 17 Piccadilly Arcade, London, SW1Y 6NH 🅿
☎ 020 7493 5082 ❻ 020 7499 4422
🌐 welcome@armoury.co.uk
🌐 www.armoury.co.uk
Est. 1969 *Stock size* Large
Stock Royal memorablilia, model soldiers, regimental brooches, side drums, bronzes
Open Mon–Fri 10am–6pm Sat noon–6pm
Services Valuations, world orders, decorations

⊞ Hilary Batstone Antiques (LAPADA)
Contact Hilary Batstone
✉ 8 Holbein Place, London, SW1W 8NL
☎ 020 7730 5335 ❻ 020 7730 5335
📱 07836 594908
🌐 hilary@hilarybatstone.com
🌐 www.hilarybatstone.com
Est. 1986 *Stock size* Medium
Stock 19th–20thC furniture, crystal chandeliers, Venetian mirrors, glass, stone, steel, natural textiles
Open Mon–Fri 10.30am–5.30pm Sat by appointment

⊞ Belgrave Carpet Gallery Ltd
Contact Mr Khawaja

LONDON
SOUTH • SW1

✉ **91 Knightsbridge, London, SW1X 7RV** 🅿
☎ 020 7235 2541 📠 020 7407 1649
Est. 1975 *Stock size* Large
Stock Antique Oriental carpets
Open Mon–Sat 10.30am–6.30pm

⊞ **Blanchard Ltd (LAPADA)**
Contact Mr Piers Ingall
✉ 86–88 Pimlico Road, London, SW1W 8PL
☎ 020 7823 6310 📠 020 7823 6303
✉ piers@jwblanchard.com
Est. 1950 *Stock size* Medium
Stock English and Continental furniture, decorative items, works of art, lighting
Open Mon–Fri 10am–6pm Sat 10am–3pm
Fairs Olympia (June)
Services Valuations, restoration, shipping

⊞ **N Bloom and Son (1912) Ltd (LAPADA, CINOA, BACA Award Winner 2001)**
Contact Ian Harris
✉ London, SW1
☎ 020 7629 5060 📠 020 7493 2528
✉ nbloom@nbloom.com
🌐 www.nbloom.com
Est. 1912 *Stock size* Large
Stock 1860–1960 jewellery, silver
Open By appointment
Fairs Olympia (June), LAPADA, Claridges (April), Miami (Jan)
Services Valuations, restoration, catalogue, jewellery consultant

⊞ **John Bly (BADA, CINOA)**
Contact Mr John Bly or Mr James Bly
✉ 27 Bury Street, London, SW1Y 6AL 🅿
☎ 01442 823030
✉ james@johnbly.com
🌐 www.johnbly.com
Est. 1891 *Stock size* Large
Stock 18th–19thC English furniture, works of art, objets d'art, paintings, silver, glass, porcelain, tapestries
Open By appointment
Fairs BADA (March), Palm Beach, Florida (Feb)
Services Valuations, restoration

⊞ **J H Bourdon-Smith Ltd (BADA, CINOA)**
Contact Mr J Bourdon-Smith
✉ 24 Masons Yard, Duke Street, St James's, London,

SW1Y 6BU 🅿
☎ 020 7839 4714 📠 020 7839 3951
Est. 1953 *Stock size* Large
Stock Georgian–Victorian silver, modern reproduction silver
Open Mon–Fri 9.30am–6pm
Fairs Grosvenor House, BADA, Olympia (Nov)

⊞ **John Carlton-Smith (BADA)**
Contact Mr J Carlton-Smith
✉ 19 Ryder Street, London, SW1Y 6PX 🅿
☎ 020 7930 6622 📠 020 7930 1370
📱 07967 180682
✉ jcarltonsm@aol.com
🌐 www.fineantiqueclocks.com
Est. 1968 *Stock size* Large
Stock Fine antique clocks and barometers
Open Mon–Fri 9am–5.30pm
Fairs March BADA, Grosvenor House
Services Valuations

⊞ **Chelsea Antique Mirrors**
Contact Mr A Koll
✉ 72 Pimlico Road, London, SW1W 8LS 🅿
☎ 020 7824 8024 📠 020 7824 8233
Est. 1980 *Stock size* Medium
Stock 18th–19thC mirrors, furniture
Open Mon–Fri 10am–6pm Sat 10am–2pm
Services Restoration

🎨 **Christie's**
✉ 8 King Street, London, SW1Y 6QT 🅿
☎ 020 7839 9060 📠 020 7839 1611
🌐 www.christies.com
Est. 1766
Open Mon–Fri 9am–5pm
Sales Sales throughout the year, except Aug and Jan, viewing 4 days prior to sales and weekends, evenings. Free verbal auction estimates
Catalogues Yes

⊞ **Ciancimino Ltd**
Contact Mr J Ciancimino
✉ 99 Pimlico Road, London, SW1W 8PH 🅿
☎ 020 7730 9950 📠 020 7730 5365
✉ info@ciancimino.com
🌐 www.ciancimino.com
Est. 1965 *Stock size* Medium
Stock Art Deco furniture, Oriental furniture, ethnography

Open Mon–Fri 10am–6pm Sat 10am–5pm
Fairs International Fine Art & Antique Dealers Show, New York

⊞ **Classic Bindings (ABA, PDFA)**
Contact Mr S Poklewski-Koziell
✉ 61 Cambridge Street, London, SW1V 4PS 🅿
☎ 020 7834 5554 📠 020 7630 6632
✉ info@classicbindings.net
🌐 www.classicbindings.net
Est. 1990 *Stock size* Large
Stock General antiquarian books, classic bindings
Open Mon–Fri 9.30am–5.30pm or by appointment
Fairs Olympia, New York book fair
Services Valuations

⊞ **Cobra & Bellamy**
Contact Tanya Hunter
✉ 149 Sloane Street, London, SW1X 9BZ 🅿
☎ 020 7730 9993 📠 020 7824 8996
✉ cobrabellamy@hotmail.com
Est. 1980 *Stock size* Medium
Stock Jewellery, amber, glass, ivory, coral
Open Mon–Fri 10.30am–6pm Sat 10.30am–5pm
Services Valuations

⊞ **Peter Dale Ltd (LAPADA)**
Contact Mr Robin Dale
✉ 12 Royal Opera Arcade, London, SW1Y 4UY 🅿
☎ 020 7930 3695 📠 020 7930 2223
📱 07785 580396
✉ robin@peterdaleltd.com
Est. 1960 *Stock size* Medium
Stock European antique arms, armour
Open Mon–Fri 9.15am–5pm
Services Valuations

⊞ **Alastair Dickenson Ltd (BADA)**
Contact Mr A Dickenson or Mrs M Cuchet
✉ 90 Jermyn Street, London, SW1Y 6JD 🅿
☎ 020 7839 2808 📠 020 7839 2809
📱 07976 283530
✉ adickensonsilver@btconnect.com
Est. 1996 *Stock size* Small
Stock 16th–19thC fine, rare English silver
Open Mon–Fri 9.30am–5.30pm
Services Valuations, restoration

LONDON

66

LONDON

⊞ Didier Aaron (London) Ltd (BADA)
Contact Didier Leblanc
✉ 21 Ryder Street, London, SW1Y 6PX 🅿
☎ 020 7839 4716 📠 020 7930 6699
📧 contact@didieraaronltd.com
Est. 2985 *Stock size* Medium
Stock 18thC–early 19thC
Continental furniture, old master drawings, paintings
Open Mon–Fri 11am–1pm 2–5pm and by appointment
Fairs Maastricht, Paris Bienniale

⊞ Druet Antiques
Contact Raphael Druet
✉ 33 Graham Terrace, London, SW1W 8JE
☎ 020 7259 0078 📠 020 7730 7878
📧 raphael@druet,net
🌐 www.druetdesign.com
Est. 2000 *Stock size* Medium
Stock 1950s–1970s Scandanavian design
Open By appointment
Fairs Les Pucesdu design (Paris), Bastille (Paris)
Services Valuations

⊞ Elizabeth Street Antiques and Restoration Services
Contact Mr Naik
✉ 35 Elizabeth Street, London, SW1W 9RP 🅿
☎ 020 7730 6777
📱 07973 909257
📧 info@elizabethstreetantiques.com
🌐 www.elizabethstreetantiques.com
Est. 1993 *Stock size* Medium
Stock General antiques
Open Mon–Sat 8am–7pm
Services Restoration

⊞ Filippa & Co
Contact Filippa Naess
✉ 51 Kinnerton Street, London, SW1X 8ED 🅿
☎ 020 7235 1722 📠 020 7245 9160
📧 filippa@dircon.co.uk
🌐 www.filippaandco.com
Est. 1998 *Stock size* Medium
Stock Swedish furniture, chandeliers, mirrors, decorative accessories
Open Mon–Fri 11am–5.30pm
Sat Sun by appointment
Services Shipping

⊞ N & I Franklin (BADA)
Contact Mr N Franklin or Mr I Franklin

✉ 11 Bury Street, London, SW1Y 6AB
☎ 020 7839 3131 📠 020 7839 3132
📧 neil@franklinsilver.com
Est. 1980 *Stock size* Large
Stock 17th–18thC English domestic silver
Open Mon–Fri 10am–5pm or by appointment
Fairs Grosvenor House
Services Valuations

⊞ J A L Franks and Co
Contact Mr G Franks
✉ 7 Allington Street, London, SW1E 5EB 🅿
☎ 020 7233 8433
📧 jalfranks@btinternet.com
🌐 www.jalfranks.btinternet.co.uk
Est. 1947 *Stock size* Medium
Stock 16th–19thC antique maps
Open Mon–Fri 10am–5pm
Fairs London Map Fair, IMCOS

⊞ Victor Franses Gallery (BADA)
Contact Graham Franses
✉ 57 Jermyn Street, St James's, London, SW1Y 6LX
☎ 020 7493 6284/7629 1144
📠 020 7495 3668
📧 bronzes@vfranses.com
🌐 www.vfranses.com
Est. 1972 *Stock size* Large
Stock 19thC animalier sculpture, paintings, drawings, watercolours
Open Mon–Fri 10am–5pm or by appointment
Fairs Grosvenor House
Services Valuations, restoration

⊞ Christopher Gibbs Antiques (LAPADA)
Contact Richenda Symonds
✉ 3 Dove Walk, Pimlico Road, London, SW1W 8PS
☎ 020 7730 8200 📠 020 7730 8420
📧 lucinda@christophergibbs.com or rollo@christophergibbs.com
Est. 1961 *Stock size* Large
Stock General antiques
Open Mon–Fri 9.30am–5.30pm

⊞ Nicholas Gifford-Mead (BADA, LAPADA)
Contact Mr N Gifford-Mead
✉ 68 Pimlico Road, London, SW1W 8LS 🅿
☎ 020 7730 6233 📠 020 7730 6239
Est. 1969 *Stock size* Medium

Stock Pre-1840 English and European chimney pieces, sculpture
Open Mon–Fri 9.30am–5.30pm
Services Valuations

⊞ Joss Graham Orientals
Contact Joss Graham
✉ 10 Eccleston Street, London, SW1W 9LT 🅿
☎ 020 7730 4370 📠 020 7730 4370
📧 jossgraham@btinternet.com
Est. 1982 *Stock size* Large
Stock Oriental antiques
Open Mon–Fri 10am–6pm
Services Valuations, restoration

⊞ Nicolas Guedroitz Ltd
Contact Simon Pugh
✉ 227 Ebury Street, London, SW1W 9NF 🅿
☎ 020 7730 3111 📠 020 7730 1441
📧 guedroitz@russianfurniture.co.uk
🌐 www.russianfurniture.co.uk
Est. 1996 *Stock size* Medium
Stock 18th–19thC Russian furniture
Open Mon–Fri 10am–6pm
Sat 11am–3.30pm

⊞ Nicolas Guedroitz Ltd
Contact Simon Pugh
✉ 24 Pimlico Road, London, SW1W 8JA 🅿
☎ 020 7730 3111 📠 020 7730 1441
📧 guedroitz@russianfurniture.co.uk
🌐 www.russianfurniture.co.uk
Est. 1996 *Stock size* Medium
Stock 18th–19thC Russian furniture
Open Mon–Fri 10am–6pm
Sat 11am–3.30pm

⊞ Ross Hamilton (Antiques) Ltd (LAPADA, CINOA)
Contact Mr C M Boyce
✉ 95 Pimlico Road, London, SW1W 8PH 🅿
☎ 020 7730 3015 📠 020 7730 3015
🌐 www.lapada.co.uk/rosshamilton/
Est. 1973 *Stock size* Large
Stock 17th–19thC fine English and Continental furniture, 16th–20thC paintings, Oriental porcelain, objets d'art, bronzes
Open Mon–Fri 9am–6pm
Sat 10.30am–5pm
Services Shipping worldwide

⊞ Brian Harkins
Contact Brian Harkins
✉ 3 Bury Street, St James's,

LONDON
SOUTH • SW1

London,
SW1Y 6AB 🅿
☎ 020 7839 3338 📠 020 7839 9339
🖃 info@brianharkins.co.uk
🌐 www.brianharkins.co.uk
Est. 1978
Stock Chinese and Japanese
antiques, scholars' items,
furniture, decorative items,
ceramics, bronzes, rocks, baskets
Open Mon–Fri 10am–6pm

⊞ Harris Lindsay (BADA, CINOA)
Contact Jonathan Harris or
Bruce Lindsay
🖃 67 Jermyn Street, London,
SW1Y 6NY 🅿
☎ 020 7839 5767 📠 020 7839 5768
🌐 www.harrislindsay.com
Est. 1967 *Stock size* Medium
Stock English, Continental and
Oriental works of art
Open Mon–Fri 9.30am–6pm or
by appointment
Fairs Grosvenor House,
International Show, New York
(Oct), TEFAF, Maastricht

⊞ Harvey & Gore (BADA)
Contact Nigel Norman
🖃 41 Duke Street, St James's,
London,
SW1Y 6DF 🅿
☎ 020 7839 4033 📠 020 7925 1213
🖃 nigel@harveyandgore.co.uk
🌐 www.harveyandgore.co.uk
Est. 1723 *Stock size* Large
Stock Jewellery, bijouterie, snuff
boxes, old Sheffield plate,
miniatures
Open Mon–Fri 9.30am–5pm
Fairs BADA
Services Valuations, restoration

⊞ Thomas Heneage Art Books (ABA, LAPADA)
Contact Ana Pereira
🖃 42 Duke Street, St James's,
London,
SW1Y 6DJ 🅿
☎ 020 7930 9223 📠 020 7839 9223
🖃 artbooks@heneage.com
🌐 www.heneage.com
Est. 1988 *Stock size* Large
Stock Art reference books
Open Mon–Fri 9.30am–6pm or
by appointment
Services Valuations

⊞ Hermitage Antiques PLC
Contact Mr Vieux-Pernon

🖃 97 Pimlico Road, London,
SW1W 8PH 🅿
☎ 020 7730 1973 📠 020 7730 6586
🖃 info@hermitage-antiques.co.uk
🌐 www.hermitage-antiques.co.uk
Est. 1970 *Stock size* Large
Stock Biedermeier and Russian
furniture, chandeliers, oil
paintings, decorative arts, bronzes
Open Mon–Fri 10am–6pm
Sat 10am–5pm
Fairs Olympia (June)
Services Consultancy

⊞ Appley Hoare Antiques
Contact Appley or Zoe Hoare
🖃 30 Pimlico Road, London,
SW1W 8LJ 🅿
☎ 020 7730 7070 📠 020 7730 8188
🖃 appley@appleyhoare.com
🌐 www.appleyhoare.com
Est. 1980 *Stock size* Large
Stock 18th–19thC French country
furniture, accessories
Open Mon–Fri 10.30am–6pm
Sat 11am–5pm
Services Shipping

⊞ John Hobbs Ltd (BADA)
Contact John Hobbs or
Dolores Hobbs
🖃 107a Pimlico Road, London,
SW1W 8PH 🅿
☎ 020 7730 8369 📠 020 7730 0437
📱 07831 694488
🖃 info@johnhobbs.demon.co.uk
🌐 www.johnhobbs.co.uk
Est. 1994 *Stock size* Large
Stock 18th–19thC Continental
and English furniture, objets
d'art, statuary
Open Mon–Fri 9am–6pm
Sat 11am–4pm

⊞ Christopher Hodsoll Ltd (BADA)
Contact Mr C Hodsoll
🖃 89–91 Pimlico Road, London,
SW1W 8PH 🅿
☎ 020 7730 3370 📠 020 7730 1516
🖃 info@hodsoll.com
🌐 www.hodsoll.com
Est. 1991 *Stock size* Large
Stock 18th–19thC furniture,
works of art
Open Mon–Fri 9.30am–6pm
Sat 10am–4pm
Services Finders service, interior
design

⊞ Hotspur Ltd (BADA)
Contact Mr R Kern
🖃 14 Lowndes Street, London,

SW1X 9EX 🅿
☎ 020 7235 1918 📠 020 7235 4371
🖃 robinkern@hotspurantiques.com
Est. 1924 *Stock size* Medium
Stock 18thC quality furniture,
chandeliers, clocks, works of art
Open Mon–Fri 9am–6pm
Sat by appointment
Fairs Grosvenor House
Services Valuations

⊞ Christopher Howe Antiques
Contact Christopher Howe or
Olivia Bishop
🖃 93 Pimlico Road, London,
SW1W 8PH 🅿
☎ 020 7730 7987 📠 020 7730 0157
🖃 christophe@howelondon.com
🌐 www.howelondon.com
Est. 1987 *Stock size* Large
Stock General antiques, furniture
Open Mon–Fri 9am–6pm
Sat 10.30am–4.30pm

⊞ Humphrey–Carrasco
Contact Mr David Humphrey or
Miss Marylise Carrasco
🖃 43 Pimlico Road, London,
SW1W 8NE 🅿
☎ 020 7730 9911 📠 020 7730 9944
🖃 hc@humphreycarrasco.demon.co.uk
Est. 1990 *Stock size* Medium
Stock English furniture,
18th–19thC lighting
Open Mon–Fri 10am–6pm
Sat by appointment
Fairs Olympia (Nov)

⊞ Iconastas Russian Works of Art
Contact Chris Martin
🖃 5 Piccadilly Arcade, London,
SW1Y 6NH
☎ 020 7629 1433 📠 020 7408 2015
🖃 info@iconastas.com
🌐 www.iconastas.com
Est. 1972 *Stock size* Large
Stock 10thC–1974 Russian works
of art
Open Mon–Fri 10am–6pm
Sat 2–5pm
Services Valuations

⊞ Isaac and Ede (BADA)
Contact David Isaac
🖃 1 Duke of York Street, London,
SW1Y 6JP 🅿
☎ 020 7925 1177 📠 020 7925 0606
🖃 info@isaacandede.com
🌐 www.isaacandede.com
Est. 1865 *Stock size* Medium
Stock Georgian, Regency prints

Open Mon–Fri 10am–5pm
appointment advisable
Fairs BADA, Olympia (June),
San Francisco Fall Antiques Show
Services Framing, restoration

⊞ Jeremy Ltd (BADA)
Contact Mr M Hill
⊠ **29 Lowndes Street, London,
SW1X 9HX** 🅿
☎ 020 7823 2923 🖷 020 7245 6197
🖲 jeremy@jeremique.ltd.uk
🌐 www.jeremy.co.uk
Est. 1946 *Stock size* Large
Stock 18th–early 19thC English
and Continental furniture, works
of art, clocks, antiques
Open Mon–Fri 8.30am–6pm
Sat by appointment
Fairs Grosvenor House, New York

⊞ Peter Jones/PJ2
Contact James Betts
⊠ **Sloane Square, London,
SW1W 8EL** 🅿
☎ 020 7730 3434 🖷 020 7808 4006
🌐 www.peterjones.co.uk
Est. 1915 *Stock size* Large
Stock 18th–19thC furniture, gilt
mirrors, accessories
Open Mon–Sat 9.30am–7pm
Services Shipping

⊞ Keshishian (BADA)
Contact Mr Arto or
Mr Eddy Keshishian
⊠ **73 Pimlico Road, London,
SW1W 8NE** 🅿
☎ 020 7730 8810
🖲 rujpics@yahoo.co.uk or
amale88@hotmail.com
Est. 1989 *Stock size* Large
Stock Aubussons, British Arts and
Crafts, Art Deco, antique and
modernist carpets and tapestries
Open Mon–Fri 9.30am–6pm
Sat 10am–5pm

⊞ John King (BADA)
Contact Mr J King,
Laila or Nicolette
⊠ **74 Pimlico Road,
London,
SW1W 8LS** 🅿
☎ 020 7730 0427 🖷 020 7730 2515
🖲 kingj896@aol.com
Est. 1967 *Stock size* Medium
Stock Period & 20thC decorative-
objects and furniture
Open Mon–Fri 10am–6pm
weekends by appointment
Services Advice on furnishing
homes

⊞ Knightsbridge Coins
(BNTA, ANA, PNG)
Contact Mr J Brown
⊠ **43 Duke Street, London,
SW1Y 6DD** 🅿
☎ 020 7930 8215 🖷 020 7930 8214
Est. 1975
Stock English and foreign
medieval–present day coins
Open Mon–Fri 10.15am–6pm
Fairs Coinex, London Coin Show
(Bloomsbury)
Services Valuations

⊞ Bob Lawrence Gallery
Contact Bob Lawrence
⊠ **93 Lower Sloane Street,
London,
SW1W 8DA** 🅿
☎ 020 7730 5900 🖷 020 7730 5902
🖲 bob@boblawrencegallery.fsnet.co.uk
Est. 1992 *Stock size* Medium
Stock 20thC decorative antiques
and furnishings
Open Mon–Fri 10am–6pm
Sat 10am–2pm

⊞ Jeremy Mason
Contact Mr J Mason
⊠ **145 Ebury Street, London,
SW1W 9QN** 🅿
☎ 020 7730 8331 🖷 020 7730 8334
🕻 07939 240884
Est. 1974 *Stock size* Small
Stock Oriental works of art from
all periods
Open By appointment only

⊞ Mayfair Carpet Gallery
Ltd
Contact Mr A H Khawaja
⊠ **91 Knightsbridge, London,
SW1X 7RB** 🅿
☎ 020 7235 2541 🖷 020 7245 9749
🖲 aimz-kh@hotmail.com
Est. 1975 *Stock size* Large
Stock Fine antique Oriental
carpets, rugs
Open Mon–Sat 10.30am–6.30pm
Services Valuations, restoration

⊞ Alexander von Moltke
Contact Alexander von Moltke
⊠ **46 Bourne Street,
London,
SW1W 8JD** 🅿
☎ 020 7730 9020 🖷 020 7730 2945
🖲 alexvonmoltke@btinternet.com
🌐 www.alexandervonmoltke.com
Est. 1992 *Stock size* Large
Stock French furniture
1920–1950, Italian lighting
Open Mon–Fri 10am–6pm

Sat 10am–4pm
Fairs Olympia, Decorative
Antiques & Textile Fair, Battersea

⊞ Peter Nahum at the
Leicester Galleries (BADA,
SLAD)
Contact Peter Nahum
⊠ **5 Ryder Street, London,
SW1Y 6PY** 🅿
☎ 020 7930 6059 🖷 020 7930 4678
🕻 07770 220851
🖲 peternahum@leicestergalleries.com
🌐 www.leicestergalleries.com
Est. 1984 *Stock size* Large
Stock Pre-Raphaelites,
Symbolists, 19th–20thC European
paintings, drawings, sculpture
Open Mon–Fri 9.30am–6pm
Fairs Grosvenor House Art and
Antiques Fair and International
Fine Art Fair, New York, 20/21
British Art Fair, London
Services Valuations, restoration,
shipping, book search

⊞ Odyssey Fine Arts Ltd
(LAPADA)
Contact Martin MacRodain
⊠ **24 Holbein Place, London,
SW1W 8NL**
☎ 020 7730 9942 🖷 020 7259 9941
🖲 odysseyfineart@aol.com
🌐 www.odysseyart.co.uk
Est. 1993 *Stock size* Large
Stock Decorative antiques
Open Mon–Fri 10.30am–5.30pm
Sat 10.30am–3.30pm
Fairs Olympia, Decorative
Antiques and Textiles

⊞ Ossowski (BADA)
Contact Mr M Ossowski
⊠ **83 Pimlico Road, London,
SW1W 8PH** 🅿
☎ 020 7730 3256 🖷 020 7823 4500
🖲 markossowski@hotmail.com
Est. 1960 *Stock size* Large
Stock 18thC English giltwood
mirrors, tables, decorative wood
carving
Open Mon–Fri 10am–6pm
Sat 10am–1pm
Fairs New York International (Oct)
Services Restoration

⊞ Pairs Antiques Ltd
Contact Iain Brunt
⊠ **57 Lupus Street, London,
SW1V 3EY** 🅿
☎ 020 7622 6446 🖷 020 7622 3663
🕻 07798 684694
🖲 mail@antiques.co.uk

W www.pairsantiques.co.uk
Est. 1995 *Stock size* Large
Stock Varied
Open By appointment

⊞ Trevor Philip & Son Ltd (BADA, BACA Award Winner 2004)
Contact Mr T Waterman
✉ 75a Jermyn Street, St James's, London, SW1Y 6NP ▣
☎ 020 7930 2954 **O** 020 7321 0212
e globe@trevorphilip.com
W www.trevorphilip.com
Est. 1972 *Stock size* Large
Stock Globes, ships' models, marine and navigation instruments
Open Mon–Fri 9.30am–6pm
Sat by appointment only
Fairs Grosvenor House
Services Valuations, restoration

⊞ Poloantiques
Contact Iain Brunt
✉ 57 Lupus Street, London, SW1V 3EY ▣
☎ 020 7622 6446 **O** 020 7622 3663
W 07798 684694
e mail@antiques.co.uk
W www.poloantiques.com
Est. 1995 *Stock size* Large
Stock Varied
Open By appointment

⊞ Priestley and Ferraro
Contact David Priestley
✉ 17 King Street, St James's, London, SW1Y 6QU ▣
☎ 020 7930 6228 **O** 020 7930 6226
e info@priestleyandferraro.com
W www.priestleyandferraro.com
Est. 1994 *Stock size* Medium
Stock Early Chinese art
Open Mon–Fri 9.30am–5.30pm
Fairs International Asian Art Fair, New York, Asian Art Fair, London

⊞ Pullman Gallery Ltd
Contact Mr S Khachadourian
✉ 14 King Street, St James's, London, SW1Y 6QU ▣
☎ 020 7930 9595 **O** 020 7930 9494
e sk@pullmangallery.com
W www.pullmangallery.com
Est. 1998 *Stock size* Large
Stock Cocktail shakers, bar accessories, smoking accessories, vintage Louis Vuitton and

Hermes luggage, motor racing posters, René Lalique glass, 1900–1940
Open Mon–Fri 10am–6pm
Services Usual gallery services

⊞ Mark Ransom Ltd
Contact Mr C Walker or Mr M James
✉ 62–64 & 105 Pimlico Road, London, SW1W 8LS ▣
☎ 020 7259 0220 **O** 020 7259 0323
e contact@markransom.co.uk
W www.markransom.co.uk
Est. 1992 *Stock size* Medium
Stock Russian and French Empire, Continental furniture, decorative items, objets d'art, prints, pictures
Open Mon–Sat 10am–6pm

⊞ The Silver Fund Ltd (LAPADA)
Contact A Crawford
✉ No 1 Duke of York Street, St James's, London, SW1Y 6JP ▣
☎ 020 7839 7664 **O** 020 7839 8935
e dealers@thesilverfund.com
W www.thesilverfund.com
Est. 1996 *Stock size* Large
Stock Georg Jensen silver
Open Mon–Fri 9am–6pm
Fairs Olympia June, November
Services Valuations

⊞ Sims Reed Ltd (ABA)
Contact Mr J Sims
✉ 43a Duke Street, St James's, London, SW1Y 6DD ▣
☎ 020 7493 5660 **O** 020 7493 8468
e info@simsreed.com
W www.simsreed.com
Est. 1977 *Stock size* Large
Stock Antiquarian, rare, second-hand books, including books illustrated by artists, books on fine and applied arts
Open Mon–Fri 10am–6pm or by appointment
Fairs ABA Olympia

⊞ Peta Smyth Antique Textiles (LAPADA, CINOA)
Contact Peta Smyth or Joseph Sullivan
✉ 42 Moreton Street, London, SW1V 2PB ▣
☎ 020 7630 9898 **O** 020 7630 5398

e petasmyth@ukonline.co.uk
Est. 1975 *Stock size* Large
Stock 16th–19thC European textiles, needlework, silks, velvets, tapestries, hangings, cushions
Open Mon–Fri 9.30am–5.30pm
Fairs Olympia (June, Nov)
Services Valuations

⊞ Somlo Antiques Ltd (BADA)
Contact Mr Paul Symons
✉ 7 Piccadilly Arcade, London, SW1Y 6NH ▣
☎ 020 7499 6526 **O** 020 7499 0603
e mail@somlo.com
W www.somloantiques.com
Est. 1970 *Stock size* Large
Stock Vintage wristwatches, antique pocket watches
Open Mon–Fri 10am–5.30pm
Fairs Olympia (Feb, June)
Services Valuations, repairs

⊞ Alexe Stanion Antiques
Contact Alexe Stanion
✉ 73 Elizabeth Street, London, SW1W 9PJ ▣
☎ 020 7824 8808 **O** 020 7824 8828
e alexestanion@aol.com
W www.alexestanion.com
Est. 1999 *Stock size* Medium
Stock Mid 20thC, post-war design and modernism
Open Mon–Sat 10am–6pm
Fairs Alexandra Palace

⊞ Westenholz Antiques Ltd
✉ 76–78 Pimlico Road, London, SW1W 8PL ▣
☎ 020 7824 8090 **O** 020 7823 5913
e shop@westenholz.co.uk
W www.westenholz.co.uk
Stock 18th–19thC English furniture, decorative items
Open Mon–Fri 8.30am–6pm
Services Interior design

⊞ www.antiques.co.uk
Contact Iain Brunt
✉ 57 Lupus Street, London, SW1V 3EY ▣
☎ 020 7622 6446 **O** 020 7622 3663
W 07798 684694
e mail@antiques.co.uk
W www.antiques.co.uk
Est. 1995 *Stock size* Large
Stock Varied
Open By appointment

LONDON

SW2

⊞ Chris Baron Antiques
Contact Chris Baron
✉ 87 Streatham Hill, London,
SW2 4UB 🅿
☎ 020 8671 8732 ● 020 8671 1984
✉ baronx3@aol.com
Ⓦ www.chrisbaroninteriors
Est. 1976 *Stock size* Medium
Stock Antiques furniture,
contemporary lights and
lighting, Arts and Crafts
Open Mon–Wed Fri
9.30am–5.30pm Thurs
9.30am–6.30pm Sat 9.30am–5pm
Services Valuations, restoration

SW3

⊞ Jaki Abbott
Contact Jaki Abbott
✉ Antiquarius,
131–141 King's Road,
London,
SW3 4PW 🅿
☎ 0777 486 4442
Stock size Small
Stock Antique and period jewellery
Open Mon–Sat 10am–6pm

**⊞ Norman Adams Ltd
(BADA, BACA Award
Winner 2001)**
Contact R G S Whittington or
C Claxton-Stevens
✉ 8–10 Hans Road (Opposite
West side of Harrods), London,
SW3 1RX 🅿
☎ 020 7589 5266 ● 020 7589 1968
✉ antiques@normanadams.com
Ⓦ www.normanadams.com
Est. 1923 *Stock size* Large
Stock Fine 18thC English
furniture, works of art, mirrors,
glass, paintings, chandeliers
Open Mon–Fri 9am–5.30pm
Sat Sun by appointment
Fairs BADA (March), Grosvenor
House (June)
Services Annual catalogue

⊞ Aesthetics (LAPADA)
Contact Philip A Jeffs
✉ Stand V1, Antiquarius,
131–141 King's Road, London,
SW3 4PW 🅿
☎ 020 7352 0395 ● 020 7376 4057
Est. 1983 *Stock size* Large
Stock Ceramics and silver
Open Mon–Sat 10am–6pm
Fairs Olympia (June)
Services Shipping

⊞ After Noah
Contact Simon Tarr
✉ 261 King's Road, London,
SW3 5EL 🅿
☎ 020 7351 2610
✉ mailorder@afternoah.com
Ⓦ www.afternoah.com
Est. 1995 *Stock size* Medium
Stock Antique and contemporary
furniture and houseware
Open Mon–Sat 10am–6pm
Sun noon–5pm
Services Restoration

⊞ Alexia Amato Antiques
Contact Alexia Amato
✉ Stand V8, Antiquarius,
131–141 King's Road, London,
SW3 4PW 🅿
☎ 020 7352 3666 ● 020 7352 3666
Ⓜ 07770 826254
✉ alexia@amato.freeserve.co.uk
Ⓦ www.amato.freeserve.co.uk
Est. 1993 *Stock size* Medium
Stock Continental 19thC glass,
especially French and Bohemian
Open Mon–Sat 10am–6pm
Services Shipping

⊞ Andipa Gallery (LAPADA)
Contact A Andipa
✉ 162 Walton Street,
Knightsbridge, London,
SW3 2JL
☎ 020 7589 2371 ● 020 7225 0305
✉ art@andipa.com
Ⓦ www.andipa.com
Est. 1953 *Stock size* Large
Stock Modern contemporary art
icons, old masters and works on
paper, classic masters
Open Mon–Fri 9.30am–6pm
`Sat 11am–6pm
Services Valuations, restoration

**🏛 Antiquarius Antique
Centre**
Contact Neil Jackson
✉ 131–141 King's Road, London,
SW3 4PW 🅿
☎ 020 7351 5353 ● 020 7351 5350
✉ antique@dial.pipex.com
Ⓦ www.antiquarius.co.uk
Est. 1969 *Stock size* Large
No. of dealers 80
Stock General and specialist
antiques of all periods
Open Mon–Sat 10am–6pm
Services Valuations

**⊞ Apter–Fredericks Ltd
(BADA)**
Contact Harry or Guy Apter

✉ 265–267 Fulham Road,
London,
SW3 6HY
☎ 020 7352 2188 ● 020 7376 5619
✉ antiques@apter-fredericks.com
Ⓦ www.apter-fredericks.com
Est. 1946 *Stock size* Large
Stock 18thC English furniture
Open Mon–Fri 9.30am–5.30pm
Fairs Grosvenor House,
International Art & Antiques Fair
New York

**⊞ Joanna Booth (BADA,
CINOA)**
Contact Joanna Booth
✉ 247 King's Road, London,
SW3 5EL 🅿
☎ 020 7352 8998 ● 020 7376 7350
✉ joanna@joannabooth.co.uk
Ⓦ www.joannabooth.co.uk
Est. 1966 *Stock size* Large
Stock Old master drawings, early
sculptures, tapestries, oak
furniture, textiles
Open Mon–Sat 10am–6pm
Fairs Olympia
Services Valuations, restoration

**🏛 Bourbon Hanby
Antique Centre**
Contact Mr I Towning
✉ 151 Sydney Street, London,
SW3 6NT 🅿
☎ 020 7352 2106/0870 142 3403
● 020 7565 0003
Ⓦ www.bourbonhanby.co.uk
Est. 1974 *Stock size* Large
No. of dealers 15
Stock China, glass, silver,
porcelain, jewellery, watches,
chandeliers, corkscrews
Open Mon–Sat 10am–6pm
Sun 11am–5pm
Services Restoration, jewellery
manufacturing, repairs

⊞ Brown & Kingston
Contact Alan Brown or
Dennis Kingston
✉ Antiquarius,
131–141 King's Road, London,
SW3 4PW 🅿
☎ 020 7376 8881 ● 020 7376 8881
Est. 1978 *Stock size* Large
Stock Japanese Imari, oil
paintings, George III furniture
Open Mon–Sat 10am–5pm
Services Shipping

**⊞ Jasmin Cameron
(Glass Circle)**
Contact Jasmin Cameron

✉ Stand M16, Antiquarius, 131–141 King's Road, London, SW3 4PW ℗
☎ 0207 351 4154 ℓ 0207 351 4154
Ⓜ 07774 871257
ℯ jasmin.cameron@mail.com
Est. 1980 *Stock size* Large
Stock 18th–19thC English and Irish drinking glasses, decanters, 19thC scent bottles, paperweights
Open Mon–Fri 10am–5.30pm
Sat 10am–5.45pm
Services Valuations, restoration

⊞ Chelsea Antique Rug Gallery (LAPADA)
Contact Noah Somnez
✉ Stand V19, Antiquarius, 131–141 King's Road, London, SW3 4PW
☎ 020 7351 6611 ℓ 020 7351 6611
ℯ chelseaarugs@aol.com
Est. 1978 *Stock size* Large
Stock Antique rugs, Aubusson tapestries
Open Mon–Sat 10am–6pm
Services Valuations, restoration

⊞ Chelsea Military Antiques
Contact Richard Black
✉ Stands N13–14, Antiquarius, 131–141 King's Road, London, SW3 4PW ℗
☎ 020 7352 0308 ℓ 020 7352 0308
ℯ richard@chelseamilitaria.com
Ⓦ www.chelseamilitaria.com
Est. 1996 *Stock size* Large
Stock British campaign medals, 19th and 20thC Allied and Axis militaria
Open Mon–Sat 10.30am–5.30pm
Fairs Britannia and South England Miitaria Fairs
Services Valuations, medal mounting

⊞ Classic Prints
Contact Mr Paul Dowling
✉ 265 King's Road, London, SW3 5EL
☎ 020 7376 5056 ℓ 020 7460 5356
Ⓜ 07770 431855
ℯ art@classicprints.com
Ⓦ www.classicprints.com
Est. 1983 *Stock size* Large
Stock Antique prints of all ages, maps
Open Mon–Sat 10am–6pm
Sun noon–5pm
Services Valuations

⊞ Adrian Cohen Antiques
✉ Stand A18–19 Antiquarius, 135 Kings Road, Chelsea, London, SW3 4PW
☎ 020 7352 7155
ℓ 07973 222520
ℯ silver@adrian-cohen.co.uk
Ⓦ www.adrian-cohen.co.uk
Est. 1987 *Stock size* Large
Stock Antique silver, silver plate
Open Mon–Sat 10am–6pm
Services Valuations, restoration

⊞ L and D Collins
Contact Louise Collins or David Collins
✉ London, SW3
☎ 020 7584 0712 ℓ 020 7584 0712
Est. 1994 *Stock size* Medium
Stock Paintings, fans, decorative objects
Open By appointment
Fairs Decorative Antiques and Textiles Fair, Penman Fairs

⊞ Richard Courtney Ltd (BADA)
Contact Mr R Courtney
✉ 114 Fulham Road, London, SW3 6HU ℗
☎ 020 7727 9105 ℓ 020 7370 4020
Est. 1965 *Stock size* Large
Stock Finest early 18thC English walnut furniture
Open Mon–Fri 9.30am–5.30pm
Fairs Grosvenor House, BADA Duke of York's

⊞ The Cufflink Shop
Contact Mr John Szwarc
✉ Stand G2, Antiquarius, 131–141 King's Road, London, SW3 4PW
☎ 020 7352 8201
Ⓜ 07715 381175
Est. 1990 *Stock size* Large
Stock Antique, vintage and modern cufflinks
Open Mon–Sat 10.30am–5.30pm

⊞ Robert Dickson and Lesley Rendall Antiques (BADA)
Contact Robert Dickson, Lesley Rendall or Justin Keating
✉ 263 Fulham Road, London, SW3 6HY ℗
☎ 020 7351 0330 ℓ 020 7352 0078
ℯ info@dicksonrendell-antiques.co.uk
Ⓦ www.dicksonrendall-antiques.co.uk
Est. 1969 *Stock size* Large
Stock Mid 18th–20thC up to

1960s furniture, works of art, lighting
Open Mon–Fri 9.30am–5.30pm
Sat 10am–4pm or
by appointment
Services Valuations, restoration

⊞ Drummonds Architectural Antiques Ltd (SALVO)
Contact Mr Drummond Shaw
✉ 78 Royal Hospital Road, Chelsea, London, SW3 4HN ℗
☎ 020 7376 4499
ℯ info@drummonds-arch.co.uk
Ⓦ www.drummonds-arch.co.uk
Est. 1989 *Stock size* Large
Stock Period bathrooms, oak and pine flooring, fireplaces, statues, garden furniture and lighting, brass door furniture and fittings, radiators, furniture, windows, doors, gates, railings, conservatories
Open Mon–Fri 9am–6pm
Sat 10am–5pm
Services Proper vitreous re-enamelling of cast-iron baths, restored antique bathrooms

⊞ Eclectic Antiques and Interiors
Contact Graham Tomlinson
✉ Stands T3–5, Antiquarius, 131–141 King's Road, London, SW3 4PW ℗
☎ 020 7286 7608 ℓ 020 7286 7608
Ⓜ 07778 470983
Est. 1993 *Stock size* Medium
Stock English and French decorative antiques and furniture
Open Mon–Sat 10am–6pm
Services Shipping, valuations

⊞ Edge (LAPADA)
Contact Donald Edge or James Smith
✉ W3, 135 King's Road, London, SW3 4PW ℗
☎ 020 7351 2333 ℓ 020 7352 2660
ℯ info@edgelondon.com
Est. 1991 *Stock size* Large
Stock Antique, bespoke jewels, diamonds set in platinum
Open Mon–Sat 11am–6pm
Services Valuations

⊞ Michael Foster (BADA)
Contact Margaret Susands
✉ 118 Fulham Road, Chelsea,

London,
SW3 6HU
☎ 020 7373 3636 ✆ 020 7373 4042
Est. 1967 *Stock size* Medium
Stock Fine 18th–early 19thC
furniture, works of art
Open Mon–Fri 9.30am–6pm
Services Valuations

⊞ Angelo Gibson
Contact Angelo Gibson
✉ Antiquarius,
131–141 King's Road,
London,
SW3 4PW 🅿
☎ 020 7352 4690
📱 07960 487010
📧 quicksilverangelo@zoom.com
Est. 1972 *Stock size* Small
Stock Antique silver and silver
plate
Open Mon–Sat 10am–6pm
Services Silver plating

⊞ Godson & Coles (BADA)
Contact Richard Godson or
Richard Coles
✉ 92 Fulham Road, London,
SW3 6HR 🅿
☎ 020 7584 2200 ✆ 020 7584 2223
📧 godsonandcoles@aol.com
📱 www.godsonandcoles.co.uk
Stock size Medium
Stock 18th–early 19thC furniture,
decorative works of art
Open Mon–Fri 9.30am–5.30pm
Fairs Grosvenor House, Olympia

⊞ James Hardy & Co
Contact Mr H P Ross
✉ 235 Brompton Road, London,
SW3 2EP 🅿
☎ 020 7589 5050 ✆ 020 7589 9009
Est. 1853 *Stock size* Medium
Stock Silver, jewellery
Open Mon–Sat 10am–5.30pm
Services Valuations, restoration

⊞ Robin Haydock Rare Textiles (LAPADA)
Contact Robin Haydock
✉ Antiquarius,
131–141 King's Road, London,
SW3 4PW
☎ 020 7349 9110 ✆ 020 7349 9110
📱 07770 931240
📧 robinhaydock@talk21.com
📱 www.robinhaydock.com
Est. 1996 *Stock size* Medium
Stock Antique textiles, mostly
18thC European and earlier,
decorative furnishings
Open Tues–Sat 10.30am–5.30pm

Fairs Olympia (June), Decorative
Antiques and Textile Fairs
Services Valuations, restoration

⊞ Hayman & Hayman
Contact Georgina Hayman
✉ Stand D6, Antiquarius,
131–141 King's Road,
London,
SW3 4PW 🅿
☎ 020 7351 6568 ✆ 020 8742 2262
Est. 1976 *Stock size* Large
Stock Photograph frames,
Limoges boxes, scent bottles
Open Mon–Sat 10am–5.30pm
Services Valuations, restoration,
shipping

⊞ Peter Herington Antiquarian Bookseller (ABA, PBFA)
Contact Peter Herington
✉ 100 Fulham Road, Chelsea,
London,
SW3 6HS 🅿
☎ 020 7591 0220 ✆ 020 7225 7054
📧 mail@peter-herington-books.com
📱 www.peter-herington-books.com
Est. 1969 *Stock size* Large
Stock Antiquarian books,
illustrated, fine bindings, English
literature, travel, children's etc,
modern first editions
Open Mon–Sat 10am–6pm
Fairs Olympia ABA, Chelsea ABA

⊞ Hill House Antiques & Decorative Arts
Contact S Benhalim
✉ PO Box 17320, 18 Chelsea
Manor Street,
London,
SW3 2WR
☎ 07973 842777
📧 info@hillhouse-antiques.co.uk
📱 www.hillhouse-antiques.co.uk
Est. 1999 *Stock size* Small
Stock Arts and Crafts, Art
Nouveau, small furniture,
metalware and decorative items
of the period
Open By appointment
Services Sourcing, design
consultancy

⊞ Michael Hughes (BADA)
Contact Michael Hughes
✉ 88 Fulham Road,
London,
SW3 6HR 🅿
☎ 020 7589 0660 ✆ 020 7823 7618
📧 info@michaelhughesantiques.co.uk
📱 www.michaelhughesantiques.co.uk

Est. 1995 *Stock size* Large
Stock 18th–early 19thC English
furniture and works of art
Open Mon–Fri 9.30am–5.30pm
Fairs Olympia
Services Valuations

⊞ Anthony James & Son Ltd (BADA, CINOA)
Contact James Millard
✉ 88 Fulham Road, London,
SW3 6HR 🅿
☎ 020 7584 1120 ✆ 020 7823 7618
📧 info@anthony-james.com
📱 www.anthony-james.com
Est. 1949 *Stock size* Large
Stock Fine 18th–19thC English
and Continental furniture,
decorative items
Open Mon–Fri 9.30am–5.30pm
Fairs Olympia (June, Nov)
Services Valuations, restoration

⊞ John Keil Ltd (BADA)
Contact Diana Yates-Watson
✉ First Floor,
154 Brompton Road, London,
SW3 1HX 🅿
☎ 020 7589 6454 ✆ 020 7823 8235
📧 antiques@johnkeil.com
Est. 1959 *Stock size* Medium
Stock 18thC English furniture
Open Mon–Fri 9.30am–5.30pm

⊞ Sophie Ketley Antiques (LAPADA)
Contact Carol Ketley
✉ Stands J9–11, Antiquarius,
131–141 King's Road, London,
SW3 4PW 🅿
☎ 020 7351 0005
📱 07831 827284
Est. 1980 *Stock size* Large
Stock Drinking glasses and
decanters, gilded decorative
antiques especially mirrors
Open Mon–Sat 10am–6pm
Fairs Olympia, Decorative
Antiques and Textiles Fair

⊞ Peter Lipitch Ltd (BADA)
Contact Melvyn Lipitch
✉ 120–124 Fulham Road,
London,
SW3 6HU 🅿
☎ 020 7373 3328 ✆ 020 7373 8888
📧 antiques@peterlipitch.com
📱 www.peterlipitch.com
Est. 1950 *Stock size* Medium
Stock 18thC English furniture
Open Mon–Fri 9.30am–5.30pm
Sat by appointment

⊞ **Little River Oriental Antiques**
Contact Mr D Dykes
✉ Antiquarius,
131–141 King's Road, London,
SW3 4PW 🄿
☎ 020 7349 9080 ☏ 01342 300131
Est. 1997 *Stock size* Large
Stock Chinese antiquities,
domestic ceramics
Open Mon–Sat 10am–6pm
Services Restoration

⊞ **The Map House
(BADA, ABA)**
Contact Mr P Stuchlik
✉ 54 Beauchamp Place, London,
SW3 1NY
☎ 020 7584 8559 ☏ 020 7589 1041
🅔 maps@themaphouse.com
🅦 www.themaphouse.com
Est. 1973 *Stock size* Large
Stock 15th–19thC antique maps,
16th–19thC decorative
engravings, globes, atlases
Open Mon–Fri 10am–6pm
Sat 10.30am–5pm
Services Valuations

⊞ **Mariad Antiques**
Contact Mrs H McClean
✉ Stand C38, Antiquarius,
131–141 King's Road, London,
SW3 4PW 🄿
☎ 020 7351 9526
Est. 1971 *Stock size* Large
Stock Georgian, Victorian,
Edwardian jewellery, cold-
painted Vienna bronzes, animal
subjects
Open Mon–Sun 10am–6pm
Fairs NEC
Services Valuations

⊞ **Gerald Mathias**
Contact Gerald Mathias
✉ Stands R5–6, Antiquarius,
131–141 King's Road, London,
SW3 4PW 🄿
☎ 020 7351 0484
🅔 info@geraldmathias.com
🅦 www.geraldmathias.com
Est. 1979 *Stock size* Large
Stock Antique boxes
Open Mon–Sat 10am–5.30pm

⊞ **McKenna & Co
(LAPADA, NAG)**
Contact Catherine McKenna
✉ 28 Beauchamp Place, London,
SW3 1NJ 🄿
☎ 020 7584 1966 ☏ 020 7225 2893
🅔 info@mckennajewels.com

Est. 1983 *Stock size* Large
Stock Antique, period and
contemporary jewellery
Open Mon–Sat 10.15am–5.45pm
Services Valuations, restoration

⊞ **C Negrillo Antiques and
Jewellery**
Contact C Negrillo
✉ Stands P1–3, Antiquarius,
131–141 King's Road, London,
SW3 4PW 🄿
☎ 020 7349 0038
🄌 07778 336781
🅔 negrilloc@aol.com
Est. 1994 *Stock size* Large
Stock Jewellery
Open Mon–Sat 10am–6pm

⊞ **Sue Norman**
Contact Sue Norman
✉ Antiquarius,
131–141 King's Road, London,
SW3 4PW 🄿
☎ 020 7352 7217 ☏ 020 8870 4677
🄌 07720 751162
🅔 sue@sue-norman.demon.co.uk
🅦 www.sue-norman.demon.co.uk
Est. Olympia *Stock size* Large
Stock Blue and white transfer ware
Open Mon–Sat 10.30am–5.30pm

⊞ **Rogers de Rin (BADA)**
Contact Mrs V de Rin
✉ 76 Royal Hospital Road, London,
SW3 4HN 🄿
☎ 020 7352 9007 ☏ 020 7351 9407
🅔 rogersderin@rogersderin.co.uk
🅦 www.rogersderin.co.uk
Est. 1965 *Stock size* Medium
Stock Collectors' items, snuff
boxes, enamels, Vienna bronzes,
Staffordshire, Scottish Wemyss
ware
Open Mon–Fri 10am–5.30pm
Sat 10am–1pm
Fairs Olympia (June, Nov), BADA
(March)
Services Shipping arranged

⊞ **Russell Rare Books
(ABA, PBFA, ILAB)**
Contact Charles Russell
✉ 239a Fulham Road, Chelsea
(at junction of Old Church
Street), London,
SW3 6HY 🄿
☎ 020 7351 5119 ☏ 020 7376 7227
🅔 crussell@russellrarebooks.com
🅦 www.russellrarebooks.com
Est. 1978 *Stock size* Medium
Stock Rare books, leather bound
books, library sets, illustrated

books, prints, maps
Open Mon–Fri 2pm–6pm
Fairs Olympia, Russell Hotel
Services Valuations

⊞ **Charles Saunders
Antiques**
Contact Mr Charles Saunders
✉ 255 Fulham Road, London,
SW3 6HY 🄿
☎ 020 7351 5242 ☏ 020 7352 8142
🅔 info@charlessaundersantiques.com
🅦 www.charlessaundersantiques.com
Est. 1987 *Stock size* Medium
Stock Antique lighting, English
and Continental 18th–early
19thC furniture, objects,
decorations, some 20thC
furniture, lighting, decorative
objects
Open Mon–Fri 9.30am–5.30pm

⊞ **Christine Schell**
Contact Ms Christine King
✉ 15 Cale Street, London,
SW3 3QS 🄿
☎ 020 7352 5563 ☏ 020 7589 7161
🄌 07836 330577
🅔 schellantiques@aol.com
Est. 1973 *Stock size* Medium
Stock Tortoiseshell, ivory, silver,
Arts and Crafts, decorative items,
mirrors
Open Mon–Sat 10am–5.30pm
Services Valuations, restoration

⊞ **Snap Dragon**
Contact Claire Taylor
✉ 247 Fulham Road, London,
SW3 6HY 🄿
☎ 020 7376 8889
🅔 snap.dragon@btconnect.com
🅦 www.snapdragoninteriors.co.uk
Est. 1995 *Stock size* Large
Stock 18th–19thC Chinese
furniture, chairs
Open Mon–Sat 10am–6pm

⊞ **Miwa Thorpe**
Contact Ms Miwa Thorpe
✉ Stands M8–9, Antiquarius,
131–141 King's Road, London,
SW3 4PW 🄿
☎ 020 7351 2911 ☏ 020 7351 6690
🄌 07768 455679
Est. 1987 *Stock size* Medium
Stock Jewellery and decorative
silver
Open Mon–Sat 10am–6pm

⊞ **Valerie Wade**
Contact Valerie Wade
✉ 108 Fulham Road, London,

SW3 6HS ♿
☎ 020 7225 1414 ✆ 020 7589 9029
✉ info@valeriewade.com
🌐 www.valeriewade.com
Est. 1983 *Stock size* Medium
Stock General antiques,
furniture, lighting
Open Mon–Sat 10am–6pm
Services Styling

⊞ Gordon Watson Ltd (LAPADA)
Contact Mr Sean Parks or
Dimenico Raimonbo
✉ 50 Fulham Road, London,
SW3 6HH ♿
☎ 020 7589 3108 ✆ 020 7584 6328
✉ gordonwatson@btinternet.com
Est. 1973 *Stock size* Medium
Stock Art Deco furniture,
lighting, 20thC decorative arts
Open Mon–Sat 11am–6pm
Fairs Olympia

⊞ O F Wilson Ltd (BADA, LAPADA)
Contact Mr P Jackson
✉ Queens Elm Parade, Old
Church Street, Chelsea, London,
SW3 6EJ ♿
☎ 020 7352 9554 ✆ 020 7351 0765
✉ ofw@email.msn.com
Est. 1949 *Stock size* Medium
Stock Continental furniture,
French chimney pieces, English
painted decorative furniture,
mirrors
Open Mon–Fri 9.30am–5.30pm
Sat 10.30am–1pm
Services Valuations

⊞ World's End Bookshop
Contact Mr S Dickson
✉ 357 King's Road, London,
SW3 5ES ♿
☎ 020 7352 9376
📱 07961 316 918
✉ stephen.dickson@virgin.net
Est. 1999 *Stock size* Medium
Stock Antiquarian, rare, second-
hand books, non-fiction, art,
literature etc
Open Mon–Sat 10am–6.30pm
Sun 10am–7pm
Fairs Royal National Hotel,
Bloomsbury (HD)
Services Valuations

⊞ Clifford Wright Antiques Ltd (BADA)
Contact Clifford Wright
✉ 104–106 Fulham Road,
London,

SW3 6HS ♿
☎ 020 7589 0986 ✆ 020 7589 3565
Est. 1960 *Stock size* Large
Stock English furniture early
18thC–Regency, English giltwood
furniture, period giltwood
mirrors
Open Mon–Fri 9am–6pm

SW4

⊞ Antiques and Things
Contact Mrs V Crowther
✉ London,
SW4
☎ 020 7498 1303 ✆ 020 7498 1303
📱 07767 262096
✉ info@antiquesandthings.co.uk
🌐 www.antiquesandthings.co.uk
Est. 1985 *Stock size* Medium
Stock Lighting, chandeliers,
curtain furniture, accessories,
French decorative furniture,
textiles
Open By appointment
Fairs Decorative Antiques and
Textiles Fair

⊞ Places and Spaces
Contact Paul Carroll or
Nick Hannam
✉ 30 Old Town, Clapham,
London,
SW4 0LB ♿
☎ 020 7498 0998 ✆ 020 7627 2625
✉ contact@placesandspaces.com
🌐 www.placesandspaces.com
Est. 1997 *Stock size* Large
Stock 20thC classic designs, 1950s
Scandinavian furniture, Italian
lighting, Eames, Panton
Open Tues–Sat 10.30am–6pm
Sun noon–4pm
Fairs 100% Design
Services Valuations, design
consultancy

SW6

⊞ 269 Antiques
Contact Mark Taylor
✉ 269 Lillie Road, London,
SW6 7LL
☎ 020 7610 1498
✉ www.antiques269@aol.com
Est. 2004 *Stock size* Medium
Stock 19th-20thC mirrors,
continental furniture
Open Mon–Sat 10.30am–5.30pm

⊞ 275 Antiques
Contact Mr D Fisher
✉ 275 Lillie Road, London,

SW6 7LL ♿
☎ 020 7386 7382 ✆ 020 7381 8320
Est. 1991 *Stock size* Large
Stock 1880s–1930s furniture,
decorative items, American
Lucite furniture, lighting,
1930s–1970s
Open Mon–Sat 10am–5.30pm

🏠 291
Contact The Manager
✉ 291 Lillie Road,
London,
SW6 7LL ♿
☎ 020 7381 5008 ✆ 020 7388 2691
📱 07831 785059
✉ malcolm.glikstein@blueyonder.co.uk
Est. 1972 *Stock size* Large
No. of dealers 4
Stock Decorative and general
antiques, collectables
Open Mon–Sat 10.30am–5.30pm
or by appointment
Services Valuations

⊞ Artefact
Contact Victoria Davar
✉ 273 Lillie Road, Fulham,
London,
SW6 7LL
☎ 020 7381 2500 ✆ 020 7381 8320
✉ artefact273@mac.com
Est. 2003 *Stock size* Medium
Stock 18th–20thC French, English
furniture, chandeliers
Open Mon–Sat 10.30am–5.30pm
Fairs Battersea Decorative and
Textile Fair

⊞ Sebastiano Barbagallo Antiques
Contact Mr S Barbagallo
✉ 661 Fulham Road, London,
SW6 5PZ ♿
☎ 020 7751 0691 ✆ 020 7751 0691
✉ sebastianobarbagallo@hotmail.com
Est. 1978 *Stock size* Large
Stock Chinese furniture, Indian
and Tibetan antiques, crafts
Open Mon–Sun 10am–6pm

⊞ Sebastiano Barbagallo Antiques
Contact Mr S Barbagallo
✉ 310 Wandsworth Bridge Road,
London,
SW6 2UA ♿
☎ 020 7751 0586 ✆ 020 7751 0586
✉ sebastianobarbagallo@hotmail.com
Est. 1978 *Stock size* Medium
Stock Chinese furniture and
objects
Open Mon–Sun 10am–6pm

⊞ Robert Barley
Contact Robert Barley
✉ 291 Lillie Road, London,
SW6 7LL 🄿
☎ 020 7381 5008 ✆ 020 7388 2691
Est. 1972 *Stock size* Medium
Stock Antiques, collectables
Open Mon–Sat 10.30am–5.30pm
or by appointment

⊞ Julia Boston Antiques (LAPADA, CINOA)
✉ 588 Kings Road, London,
SW6 2DX 🄿
☎ 020 7610 6783 ✆ 020 7610 6784
🌐 www.juliaboston.com
Est. 1968 *Stock size* Medium
Stock 17th–20thC Continental
furniture, 18th-19thC tapestry
cartoons, decorations
Open Mon–Sat 10am–6pm

⊞ I and J L Brown Ltd
Contact Mr S Hilton
✉ 634–636 King's Road, London,
SW6 2DU
☎ 020 7736 4141 ✆ 020 7736 9164
🄴 enquiries@brownantiques.com
🌐 www.brownantiques.com
Est. 1978 *Stock size* Large
Stock English country, French
provincial antique and
reproduction furniture, extensive
range of decorative items
including lighting
Open Mon–Sat 9am–5.30pm or
by appointment
Services Restoration, re-rushing

⊞ Alison Burdon
Contact Alison Burdon
✉ 291 Lillie Road, London,
SW6 7LL 🄿
☎ 020 7381 5008 ✆ 020 7388 2691
Est. 1972 *Stock size* Large
Stock Antiques, collectables
Open Mon–Sat 10.30am–5.30pm
or by appointment

⊞ Aurea Carter (LAPADA)
Contact Aurea Carter
✉ PO Box 44134, London,
SW6 3YX 🄿
☎ 020 7731 3486 ✆ 020 7731 3486
📱 07815 912477
🄴 aureacarter@englishceramics.com
🌐 www.englishceramics.com
Est. 1980 *Stock size* Large
Stock 18th–early 19thC English
pottery and porcelain
Open By appointment only
Fairs Olympia
Services Valuations, shipping

⊞ Rupert Cavendish Antiques
Contact Mr Francois Valcke
✉ 610 King's Road, London,
SW6 2DX 🄿
☎ 020 7731 7041 ✆ 020 7731 8302
🄴 rcavendish@aol.com
🌐 www.rupertcavendish.co.uk
Est. 1984 *Stock size* Large
Stock European 20thC paintings,
Empire, Biedermeier, Art Deco
furniture
Open Mon–Sat 10am–6pm

⊞ Cheyne Antiques
Contact G. Watson
✉ 314 Munster Road, London,
SW6 6BH
☎ 020 7610 0247
Est. 1996 *Stock size* Small
Stock General antiques
Open Mon–Sat 9am–6pm
Services Valuations, restoration

⊞ John Clay Antiques
Contact John Clay
263 New Kings Road, London,
SW6 4RB 🄿
☎ 020 731 5677 ✆ 020 731 5677
🄴 johnclayantiques@btconnect.com
Est. 1972 *Stock size* Medium
Stock Antique and decorative
furniture and smalls
Open Mon–Sat 9am–6pm
Services Valuations, restoration

⊞ Marc Costantini Antiques
Contact Mr M Costantini
✉ 313 Lillie Road, London,
SW6 7LL 🄿 ✆ 020 7610 2380
📱 07941 075289
Est. 1999 *Stock size* Large
Stock English and Continental
antique furniture
Open Mon–Sat 10.30am–5.30pm

⊞ Deans Antiques
Contact Mr D Gipson
✉ Core One, The Gas Works,
2 Michael Road, London,
SW6 2AN 🄿
☎ 020 7610 6997
📱 07770 231687
🄴 dean.antiques@virgin.net
Est. 1988 *Stock size* Large
Stock 18th–19thC French and
Italian decorative antiques
Open Wed–Fri 10am–6pm
Sat 11am–4pm or by
appointment
Fairs Battersea Decorative
Antiques and Textiles Fair

⊞ Decorative Antiques (LAPADA)
Contact Mr T Harley
✉ 284 Lillie Road, Fulham,
London,
SW6 7PX 🄿
☎ 020 7610 2694 ✆ 020 7386 0103
Est. 1992 *Stock size* Large
Stock 18th–19thC French
provincial furniture, Irish
furniture
Open Mon–Sat 10am–5.30pm

⊞ Charles Edwards (BADA, CINOA)
Contact Christina
✉ 19a Rumbold Road,
London,
SW6 2HX 🄿
☎ 020 7736 7172 ✆ 020 7731 7388
🄴 charles@charlesedwards2.
ademon.co.uk
🌐 www.charlesedwards.com
Est. 1969 *Stock size* Medium
Stock Antique lighting,
18th–19thC furniture, general
antiques
Open Mon–Fri 9.30am–6pm
Sat 10am–6pm

⊞ Nicole Fabre French Antiques
Contact Mrs N Fabre
✉ 592 King's Road,
London,
SW6 2DX 🄿
☎ 020 7384 3112 ✆ 020 7610 6410
🄴 antiques@nicolefabre.com
Stock size Medium
Stock French Provençale
furniture and beds, Provençale
quilts, linens, textiles,
18th–19thC toiles, decorative
items, antique fabrics
Open Mon–Fri 10am–6pm
Sat 11am–5pm
Fairs Decorative Antiques and
Textiles Fair

⊞ Hector Finch Lighting
Contact Mr H Finch
✉ 90 Wandsworth Bridge Road,
London,
SW6 2TF 🄿
☎ 020 7731 8886 ✆ 020 7731 7408
🄴 hector@hectorfinch.com
🌐 www.hectorfinch.com
Est. 1987 *Stock size* Large
Stock Specialist period lighting
shop, large range of antique and
contemporary decorative
lighting
Open Mon–Sat 10am–5.30pm

⊞ Birdie Fortescue Antiques (LAPADA)
Contact Birdie Fortescue
✉ Unit GJ, Cooper House,
2 Michael Road,
London,
SW6 2AD 🅿
☎ 01206 337557 🖷 01206 337557
🖩 07778 263467
🌐 birdie@birdiefortescueantiques.com
🌐 www.birdiefortescue.com
Est. 1991 *Stock size* Large
Stock 18th–early 20thC
Continental furniture
Open By appointment
Fairs Olympia

⊞ French House Antiques
Contact Marcus Hazell
✉ Unit A, Parsons Green Depot,
Parsons Green Lane,
London,
SW6 4HH 🅿
☎ 020 7371 7573
🌐 marcus@thefrenchhouse.co.uk
🌐 www.thefrenchhouse.co.uk
Est. 1998 *Stock size* Medium
Stock French furniture, beds,
mirrors
Open Mon–Sat 10am–6pm

⊞ Fulham Antiques
Contact Mr A Eves
✉ 320 Munster Road, London,
SW6 6BH 🅿
☎ 020 7610 3644
🌐 fulhamantique320@aol.com
Est. 1993 *Stock size* Large
Stock Antique and decorative
furniture, lighting, mirrors
Open Mon–Sat 10am–5.30pm

⊞ Judy Greenwood Antiques
Contact Ms J Greenwood
✉ 657–659 Fulham Road,
London,
SW6 5PY 🅿
☎ 020 7736 6037 🖷 020 7736 1941
🖩 07768 347669
🌐 judyg@dial.pipex.com
Est. 1978 *Stock size* Large
Stock 19th–20thC French
decorative items, beds, textiles,
lighting, furniture, mirrors, quilts
Open Mon–Fri 10am–5.30pm
Sat 10am–5pm
Services Restoration, painting

⊞ Guinevere Antiques Ltd
Contact Kevin Weaver
✉ 574–580 King's Road,
London,

SW6 2DY
☎ 020 7736 2917 🖷 020 7736 8267
🌐 info@guinevere.co.uk
🌐 www.guinevere.co.uk
Est. 1963 *Stock size* Large
Stock Classical–20thC antiques,
furniture and smalls
Open Mon–Fri 9.30am–6pm
Sat 10am–5.30pm
Fairs Olympia (Jun)
Palm Beach (Feb)

⊞ Gutlin Clocks & Antiques
Contact Mr Coxhead
✉ 606 King's Road, London,
SW6 2DX 🅿
☎ 020 7384 2439/2804
🖷 020 7384 2439
🖩 07973 123921
🌐 mark@gutlin.com
🌐 www.gutlin.com
Est. 1992 *Stock size* Medium
Stock Furniture, clocks,
chandeliers
Open Mon–Sat 10am–6.30pm
Services Restoration

⊞ H R W Antiques Ltd (LAPADA)
Contact Mr I Henderson-Russell
✉ 26 Sulivan Road, London,
SW6 3DT 🅿
☎ 020 7371 7995 🖷 020 7371 9522
🌐 ian@hrw-antiques.com
🌐 www.hrw-antiques.com
Est. 1988 *Stock size* Large
Stock 18th–19thC English and
continental furniture and
decorative items, 20thC Danish
designer furniture
Open Mon–Fri 9am–5pm

⊞ Roderick Haugh (BADA)
Contact Joe
✉ At Core 1, The Gasworks,
Gate-D, 2 Michael Road, London,
SW6 2AN 🅿
☎ 020 7371 5700
🌐 joe@roderickhaugh.com
Est. 1964 *Stock size* Large
Stock 18th–20th C furniture and
stone objects
Open Mon–Fri 10am–6pm
Fairs Olympia (Jun/Nov)
Services Restoration

⊞ Nigel Hindley
Contact Mr N Hindley
✉ 281 Lillie Road,
London,
SW6 7LL 🅿
☎ 020 7385 0706

Est. 1979 *Stock size* Large
Stock English period antiques,
French furniture, eccentricities,
lighting, mirrors
Open Mon–Sat 10.30am–5pm
Services Valuations

⊞ House of Mirrors
Contact Miss Witek
✉ 597 King's Road, London,
SW6 2EL
☎ 020 7736 5885 🖷 020 7610 9188
🌐 info@houseofmirrors.co.uk
🌐 www.houseofmirrors.co.uk
Est. 1972 *Stock size* Large
Stock 19thC English mirrors
Open Mon–Fri 9am–6pm
Sat 10am–6pm

⊞ Indigo
Contact Marion Bender
✉ 275 New King's Road,
London,
SW6 4RD 🅿
☎ 020 7384 3101 🖷 020 7384 3102
🌐 antiques@indigo-uk.com
🌐 www.indigo-uk.com
Est. 1982 *Stock size* Large
Stock Indian, Chinese and
Japanese furniture, decorative
items, handicrafts, Indonesian
furniture from recycled
teakwood
Open Mon–Sat 10am–6pm
Fairs House and Garden Fair

⊞ Christopher Jones Antiques
Contact Rene Sanderson
✉ 618–620 King's Road, London,
SW6 2DU 🅿
☎ 020 7731 4655 🖷 020 7371 8682
🌐 florehouse@msn.com
🌐 www.christopherjonesantiques.co.uk
Est. 1984 *Stock size* Large
Stock French furniture, mirrors,
screens, 1860–1890 Chinese
porcelain
Open Mon–Sat 10am–5.30pm

⊞ King's Court Galleries
Contact Mrs J Joel
✉ 949–953 Fulham Road,
London,
SW6 5HY 🅿
☎ 020 7610 6939 🖷 020 7731 4737
🌐 sales@kingscourtgalleries.co.uk
🌐 www.kingscourtgalleries.co.uk
Est. 1984 *Stock size* Large
Stock Antique maps, engravings,
sporting, decorative prints
Open Mon–Sat 10am–5.30pm
Services Framing

77

LONDON
SOUTH • SW6

⊞ Graham Kirkland
Contact Mr G Kirkland
✉ **271 Lillie Road, London, SW6 7LL** 🅿
☎ 020 7381 3195 ☏ 020 7381 3195
✉ sales@grahamkirkland.co.uk
⊕ www.grahamkirkland.co.uk
Est. 1978 *Stock size* Large
Stock Religious Victoriana, statues, chalices, sanctuary lamps, crucifixes, candlesticks
Open Mon–Fri 10am–5.30pm
Sat 11am–4pm

⊞ L & E Kreckovic
Contact Joanna Christopher
✉ **559 King's Road, London, SW6 2EB** 🅿
☎ 020 7736 0753 ☏ 020 7731 5904
Est. 1969 *Stock size* Large
Stock Early 18th–19thC furniture
Open Mon–Sat 10am–6pm
Services Valuations, restoration

⊞ Lunn Antiques Ltd
Contact Stephen Lunn
✉ **86 New Kings Road, Fulham, London, SW6 4OU**
☎ 020 7736 4638 ☏ 020 7371 7113
✉ lunnantiques@aol.com
⊕ www.lunnantiques.co.uk
Est. 1995 *Stock size* Medium
Stock Antique textiles, lace, linen
Open Mon–Sat 10am–6pm
Services Valuations, restoration

⊞ David Martin-Taylor Antiques (LAPADA)
Contact Mr Cavet
✉ **558 King's Road, London, SW6 2DZ** 🅿
☎ 020 7824 8200 ☏ 020 7824 8202
📱 07889 437306
✉ dmt@davidmartintaylor.com
⊕ www.davidmartintaylor.com
Est. 1965 *Stock size* Large
Stock 18th–19thC Continental and English furniture, objets d'art, decorative art, from the eccentric to the unusual
Open Mon–Fri 10am–6pm Sat 11am–4.30pm or by appointment
Fairs Olympia (June), London Decorative Arts

⊞ Ann May
Contact Mrs A May
✉ **80 Wandsworth Bridge Road, London, SW6 2TF** 🅿
☎ 020 7731 0862
Est. 1969 *Stock size* Medium

Stock Painted French furniture, decorative items
Open Mon–Sat 10am–6pm

⊞ Mark Maynard
Contact Mr M Maynard
✉ **651 Fulham Road, London, SW6 5PU** 🅿
☎ 020 7731 3533
⊕ www.markmaynard.co.uk
Est. 1985 *Stock size* Medium
Stock Painted French furniture, decorative items
Open Mon–Sat 10am–5pm

⊞ Mora & Upham Antiques
Contact Matthew Upham or Mark Punton
✉ **584 King's Road, London, SW6 2DX** 🅿
☎ 020 7731 4444 ☏ 020 7736 0440
✉ mora.upham@talk21.com
⊕ www.moraandupham.com
Est. 1996 *Stock size* Large
Stock Gilded French chairs, antique chandeliers, 18th–19thC English and Continental furniture, mirrors
Open Mon–Sat 10am–6pm

⊞ Nimmo & Spooner
Contact Myra Spooner or Catherine Nimmo
✉ **277 Lillie Road, London, SW6 7LL** 🅿
☎ 020 7385 2724 ☏ 020 7385 2724
Est. 1990 *Stock size* Medium
Stock Decorative antiques, unusual objects, 18thC French furniture, 20thC items
Open Mon–Sat 10.30am–5.30pm

⊞ Old Hat Vintage & Classic Clothing
Contact David Saxby
✉ **66 Fulham Road, High Street, Fulham, London, SW6 3LG** 🅿
☎ 020 7610 6558
Est. 1993 *Stock size* Large
Stock Vintage English gentleman's wardrobe
Open Mon–Sat 10.30am–6.30pm Sun 1.30pm–7pm

⊞ Old World Trading Co
Contact Mr R Campion
✉ **565 King's Road, London, SW6 2EB** 🅿
☎ 020 7731 4708 ☏ 020 7731 1291
✉ oldworld@btinternet.com
Est. 1970 *Stock size* Large

Stock 18th–19thC English and French chimney places, fire dogs, grates
Open Mon–Fri 9.30am–6pm
Sat 10am–3pm
Services Valuations, restoration

⊞ Orient Expressions Ltd (BABAADA)
Contact Amanda Leader or Patricia Wilkinson
✉ **Studio 3M1, 3rd Floor, Cooper House, 2 Michael Road, London, SW6 2ER** 🅿
☎ 020 7610 9311 ☏ 020 7610 6872
📱 07887 770406
✉ amanda@orientexpressions.com
⊕ www.orientexpressions.com
Est. 1996 *Stock size* Medium
Stock 19th–early 20thC Chinese furniture, French, Edwardian and Art Deco pieces
Open By appointment

⊞ M Pauw Ltd
Contact M Pauw
✉ **Cooper House, 2 Michael Road, Chelsea, London, SW6 2AD** 🅿
☎ 020 7731 4022 ☏ 020 7731 7356
✉ info@mpauw.com
⊕ www.mpauw.com
Est. 1985 *Stock size* Large
Stock Antique leather chairs
Open Mon–Sat 10am–6pm

⊞ Rainbow Antiques
Contact Mr Fabio Bergomi
✉ **329 Lillie Road, London, SW6 7NR** 🅿
☎ 020 7385 1323 ☏ 020 7385 4190
✉ rainbowlondon@aol.com
⊕ www.rainbowlondon.com
Est. 1998 *Stock size* Large
Stock Italian, French 1880–1940 period lighting, chandeliers, lamps, lanterns
Open Mon–Sat 10.30am–5.30pm or by appointment
Fairs Battersea Decorative Antiques Fair, House and Garden
Services Restoration, re-wiring

⊞ Rankin Conn Oriental Antiques (LAPADA)
Contact Ms Sara Reynolds
✉ **608 King's Road, London, SW6 2DX** 🅿
☎ 020 7384 1847 ☏ 020 7384 1847
📱 07774 487713
✉ daphnerankin@aol.com
⊕ www.rankin-conn-chinatrade.com

Est. 1979 *Stock size* Large
Stock 17th–19thC Japanese Imari, Chinese Export porcelain, Rose Mandarin, Blue Canton, tortoiseshell tea caddies, Dutch Delft
Open Mon–Sat 10.30am–6pm or by appointment
Fairs Olympia (June, Nov)

⊞ Relic Antiques
Contact Mr Malcolm Gliksten
⊠ 291 Lillie Road,
London,
SW6 7LL 🅿
☎ 020 7381 5008 📠 020 7388 2691
Ⓜ 07831 785059
📧 malcolm.gliksten@blueyonder.co.uk
Est. 1972 *Stock size* Large
Stock Decorative antiques, folk art, fairground art, country pieces, marine, architectural, trade signs, shop fittings
Open Mon–Sat 10.30am–5.30pm or by appointment
Fairs Battersea Decorative. Montpelier
Services Valuations

⊞ Rogers & Co (LAPADA)
Contact Christine or Michael Rogers
⊠ 604 Fulham Road, London,
SW6 5RP 🅿
☎ 020 7731 8504 📠 020 7610 6040
Ⓜ 07786 540355
📧 michael@sebeau.com
Est. 1971 *Stock size* Medium
Stock 19thC English antiques
Open Mon–Fri 10am–6pm
Sat 10am–5pm
Services Interior design, consultancy

⊞ Suzie Simons
Contact Suzie Simons
⊠ 291 Lillie Road, London,
SW6 7LL 🅿
☎ 020 7381 5008 📠 020 7388 2691
Est. 1972 *Stock size* Medium
Stock Antiques, collectables
Open Mon–Sat 10.30am–5.30pm or by appointment

⊞ Soo San
Contact Suzanna Murray
⊠ 598a King's Road,
London,
SW6 2DX
☎ 020 7731 2063 📠 020 7311 1566
📧 suze@soosan.co.uk
🌐 www.soosan.co.uk
Est. 1995 *Stock size* Large

Stock Oriental antiques and interiors
Open Mon–Sat 10am–6pm

⊞ Stephen Sprake Antiques
Contact Mr S Sprake
⊠ 283 Lillie Road, London,
SW6 7LL 🅿
☎ 020 7381 3209 📠 020 7381 9502
Ⓜ 07710 922225
Est. 1998 *Stock size* Medium
Stock 18th–20thC English and French furniture, lighting, unusual architectural pieces
Open Mon–Sat 10.30am–5.30pm

⊞ Trowbridge Gallery
Contact Martin
⊠ 555 King's Road, London,
SW6 2EB 🅿
☎ 020 7731 8733 📠 020 7371 8138
📧 gallery@trowbridge.com
🌐 www.trowbridgegallery.com
Est. 1983 *Stock size* Large
Stock Antique prints
Open Mon–Sat 9.30am–6pm Sat 10am–5.30 pm Sun noon–4pm

⊞ Leigh Warren
Contact Mr F Cochrane
⊠ 565 King's Road, London,
SW6 2EB 🅿
☎ 020 7736 9166
📠 020 77361 1291
📧 oldworld@btinternet.com
Est. 1979 *Stock size* Large
Stock 19th–20thC lighting
Open Mon–Fri 10am–5pm
Sat 10am–3pm

⊞ York Gallery Ltd
Contact Mr G Beyer
⊠ 569 King's Road, London,
SW6 2EB 🅿
☎ 020 7736 2260 📠 020 7736 2260
📧 prints@yorkgallery.co.uk
🌐 www.yorkgallery.co.uk
Est. 1989 *Stock size* Large
Stock Antique prints
Open Mon–Sat 10.30am–6pm
Services Picture framing

SW7

⚒ Bonhams
⊠ Montpelier Street, London,
SW7 1HH 🅿
☎ 020 7393 3900 📠 020 7393 3905
📧 info@bonhams.com
🌐 www.bonhams.com
Est. 1793
Open Mon–Fri 9am–4.30pm

Sun 11am–3pm
Sales Regular sales of pictures, frames, jewellery, silver, ceramics and glass, furniture, works of art, carpets and rugs, Oriental works of art, stamps, coins, arms and armour, sporting guns, collectables including toys, scientific instruments, rock 'n' roll and film memorabilia and the Vision 21 sale including modern design and 'antiques of the future', In addition Bonhams holds further sales in London (New Bond Street), New York, San Francisco, Sydney, Geneva and Los Angeles, as well as in regional salerooms across the UK. Free auction valuations; insurance and probate valuations
Catalogues Yes

⚒ Christie's South Kensington (BACA Award Winner 2002)
⊠ 85 Old Brompton Road,
London,
SW7 3LD
☎ 020 7930 6074 📠 020 7321 3311
🌐 www.christies.com
Est. 1766
Open Tues–Fri 9am–5pm
Mon 9am–7.30pm
Sales Weekly furniture sale Wed 10.30am. Fortnightly sale of silver Tues 2pm and ceramics Tues 10.30am and 2pm. Fortnightly jewellery sale Tues 2pm and pictures Thurs 10.30am, viewing Sun 1–4pm Mon 9am–7.30pm Tues–Fri 9am–5pm
Catalogues Yes

⊞ Gloucester Road Bookshop
Contact Vivi Gregory
⊠ 123 Gloucester Road, London,
SW7 4TE 🅿
☎ 020 7370 3503 📠 020 7373 0610
📧 manager@gloucesterbooks.co.uk
🌐 www.gloucesterbooks.co.uk
Est. 1983 *Stock size* Large
Stock Antiquarian, rare, second-hand books, modern literature, academic, art, first editions
Open Mon–Fri 9.30am–10.30pm
Sat Sun 10.30am–6.30pm
Services Catalogues, shipping, book search

⊞ M P Levene Ltd (BADA)
Contact Mr Martin Levene
⊠ 5 Thurloe Place, London,

79

SW7 2RR ▣
☎ 020 7589 3755 ✆ 020 7589 9908
✉ silver@mplevene.co.uk
ⓦ www.mplevene.co.uk
Est. 1889 *Stock size* Medium
Stock Antique and modern
English silver, silver cufflinks,
cutlery sets, hand-made silver
scale models
Open Mon–Fri 9am–6pm
Sat 9am–1.30pm
Services Valuations

⊞ Robert Miller
Contact Robert Miller
✉ 15 Glendower Place,
South Kensington, London,
SW7 3DR ▣
☎ 020 7584 4733
⑩ 07771 2657259
Est. 1968 *Stock size* Medium
Stock Furniture, pictures and
works of art
Open Mon–Fri 9am–5pm
Sat 2–6pm or by appointment
Fairs Olympia

⊞ Polonaise Gallery
(BADA)
Contact Mr Wojtek Grodzinski
✉ 35 Thurloe Place, London,
SW7 2HJ ▣
☎ 020 7589 8489 ✆ 020 7589 8189
⑩ 07831 455492
✉ polonaise@btconnect.com
Stock size Large
Stock Oriental and European
carpets and textiles, Islamic and
Indian art
Open Mon–Fri 9am–5.30pm
Services Valuations, restoration

⊞ Shanxi Ltd
Contact Gail Davidner
✉ 60 Gloucester Road,
Kensington, London,
SW7 4QT ▣
☎ 020 7581 3456
✉ info@shanxi.co.uk
ⓦ www.shanxi.co.uk
Est. 1994 *Stock size* Medium
Stock Antique Chinese furniture
and decorative items
Open Mon–Sat 10am–6pm
Sun 11am–5pm

SW8

⊞ Davies Antiques
(LAPADA)
Contact Hugh Davies
✉ c/o Cadogan Tate, 6–12
Ponton Road, Battersea, London,

SW8 5BA ▣
☎ 020 8947 1902 ✆ 020 8947 1902
✉ hugh.davies@btconnect.com
ⓦ www.antique-meissen.com
Est. 1975 *Stock size* Large
Stock Meissen porcelain
18thC–Art Deco period
Open By appointment

⊞ LASSCO Warehouse
(SALVO)
Contact Jesse Carrington
✉ Brunswick House, 30
Wandsworth Road, London,
SW8 2LG ▣
☎ 020 7394 2103
✉ warehouse@lassco.co.uk
ⓦ www.lassco.co.uk
Est. 1978 *Stock size* Large
Stock Architectural reclamation
and salvage
Open Mon–Sat 10am–5pm
Services Shipping

⊞ Paul Orssich (PBFA)
Contact Paul Orssich
✉ 2 St Stephens Terrace,
South Lambeth, London,
SW8 1DH ▣
☎ 020 7787 0030 ✆ 020 7735 9612
✉ paulo@orssich.com
ⓦ www.orssich.com
Est. 1980 *Stock size* Large
Stock Antiquarian, rare and out-
of-print books on Hispanic topics
Open By appointment
Services Valuations, book search

SW9

⊞ Collectable Furniture
Contact Robert Beckford
✉ 11 Rushcroft Road, Brixton,
London,
SW9 8LQ ▣
☎ 020 7738 4141
✉ robert@soulsofblackfolk.com
ⓦ www.soulsofblackfolk.com
Est. 1998 *Stock size* Large
Stock 1950s–1970s collectables
Open Mon–Sat noon–8pm
Sun noon–5pm
Services Valuations

⊞ More Than Just
Furniture
Contact Robert Beckford
✉ 407 Coldharbour Lane,
Brixton, London,
SW9 8LQ ▣
☎ 020 7738 4141
✉ robert@soulsofblackfolk.com
ⓦ www.soulsofblackfolk.com

Est. 1998 *Stock size* Large
Stock 1960s furniture, lighting
Open Mon–Sat noon–8pm
Sun noon–5pm
Services Valuations

SW10

⊞ Adam & Eve Books
Contact Mr S Dickson
✉ 18a Basement, Redcliffe
Square, London,
SW10 9JZ ▣
☎ 020 7370 4535
⑩ 07961 316 918
✉ stevdcksn@btinternet.com
Est. 1999 *Stock size* Small
Stock Antiquarian books, Middle
East, travel, first editions,
modern first editions a speciality
Open By appointment
Fairs Royal National Hotel Book
Fair

⊞ Paul Andrews Antiques
Contact Paul or Tycho Andrews
✉ The Furniture Cave,
533 King's Road, London,
SW10 0TZ ▣
☎ 020 7352 4584 ✆ 020 7351 7815
✉ mail@paulandrews.co.uk
ⓦ www.paulandrewsantiques.co.uk
Est. 1969 *Stock size* Large
Stock Eclectic furniture,
sculpture, paintings, works of
art, modern design
Open Mon–Sat 10am–6pm
Sun noon–5pm
Fairs Olympia Spring and
Summer

⊞ Alasdair Brown
Contact Mr A Brown
✉ Suite 150, 405 Kings Road,
London,
SW10 0BB ▣ ✆ 020 7384 3334
⑩ 07836 672857
✉ ab@ajcb.demon.co.uk
ⓦ www.alasdairbrown.com
Est. 1984 *Stock size* Medium
Stock 19th–20thC furniture,
lighting, upholstery, unusual
items
Open By appointment
Fairs Olympia
Services Valuations

⊞ Chelsea Gallery
(LAPADA)
Contact Mr S Toscani
✉ The Plaza, 535 King's Road,
Chelsea, London,
SW10 0SZ ▣

☎ 020 7823 3248 ✆ 020 7352 1579
✉ info@chelseagallery.co.uk
⊕ www.chelseagallery.co.uk
Est. 1978 *Stock size* Medium
Stock Antique illustrated books,
literature, prints, maps,
specializing in natural history,
travel, architecture, history
Open Mon–Sat 10.30am–7pm
Services Framing

⊞ The Classic Library
✉ 105 Pimlico Road,
London,
SW1W 8LJ
☎ 020 7259 0220 ✆ 020 7259 0323
Stock size Large
Stock Antiquarian books,
bookcases, library furniture,
prints
Open Mon–Sat 10am–6pm

⊞ L'Encoignure
Contact Thomas Kerr
✉ 517 King's Road, London,
SW10 0TX 🅿
☎ 020 7351 6465 ✆ 020 7351 4744
✉ kerrant@globalnet.co.uk
⊕ www.thomaskerrantiques.com
Est. 1994 *Stock size* Large
Stock 18th–19thC French
furniture, decorative items,
Continental furniture
Open Mon–Sat 10am–6pm
Services Interior design

⊞ Kenneth Harvey
Antiques (LAPADA)
Contact Mr K Harvey
✉ The Furniture Cave,
533 King's Road, London,
SW10 0TZ
☎ 020 7352 3775 ✆ 020 7352 3759
✉ mail@kennethharvey.com
⊕ www.kennethharvey.com
Est. 1982 *Stock size* Large
Stock English–French furniture,
chandeliers, mirrors, late
17th–20thC, leather armchairs
Open Mon–Sat 10am–6pm
Sun 11am–5pm

⊞ Simon Hatchwell
Antiques
Contact Mr A Hatchwell
✉ 533 King's Road,
London,
SW10 0TZ 🅿
☎ 020 7351 2344 ✆ 020 7351 3520
✉ hatchwells@btconnect.com
Est. 1961 *Stock size* Large
Stock English and Continental
furniture, early 19th–20thC

chandeliers, lighting, bronzes,
barometers, clocks including
longcase clocks
Open Mon–Sat 10am–6pm
Sun 11.30am–5pm
Fairs Olympia (June)
Services Valuations, restoration

⊞ Langfords Marine
Antiques (BADA, LAPADA)
Contact Mrs J Langford
✉ The Plaza, 535 King's Road,
London,
SW10 0SZ 🅿
☎ 020 7351 4881 ✆ 020 7352 0763
✉ langford@dircon.co.uk
⊕ www.langfords.co.uk
Est. 1950 *Stock size* Large
Stock Ships models, nautical
artefacts, steam engines
Open Mon–Fri 10am–5.30pm
Sat by appointment

⊞ Stephen Long
Contact Mr S Long
✉ 348 Fulham Road, London,
SW10 9UH 🅿
☎ 020 7352 8226
Est. 1966 *Stock size* Medium
Stock Painted furniture, small
decorative items, English pottery,
1780–1850
Open Mon–Fri 9.30am–1pm
2.15–5pm occasional
Sat 10am–12.30pm

⚲ Lots Road Galleries
Contact Melina Papadopolous
✉ 71–73 Lots Road, Chelsea,
London,
SW10 0RM 🅿
☎ 020 7376 6800 ✆ 020 7376 6899
✉ info@lotsroad.com
⊕ www.lotsroad.com
Est. 1979
Open Mon–Wed 9am–6pm
Thurs 9am–7pm Fri 10am–4pm
Sales Sun 1pm and 4pm, viewing
Wed 6–8pm Thurs 10am–7pm
Fri–Sat 10am–4pm Sun
10am–1pm
Frequency 2 per Sunday
Catalogues Yes

⊞ David Loveday
Antiques
Contact David Loveday
✉ First Floor, The Furniture Cave,
533 King's Road, London,
SW10 0TZ 🅿
☎ 020 7352 1100 ✆ 020 7351 5833
✉ davidloveday@aol.com
Est. 1965 *Stock size* Large

Stock 17th–19thC furniture
Open Mon–Sat 10am–6pm
Sun noon–5pm

⊞ James McWhirter
Contact James McWhirter
22 Park Walk, London,
SW10 0AQ 🅿
☎ 020 7351 5399 ✆ 020 7352 9821
✉ mail@jamesmcwhirter.com
⊕ www.jamesmcwhirter.com
Est. 1988 *Stock size* Medium
Stock 17th–20thC unusual
objects and furniture
Open Mon–Fri 9am–5.30pm

⊞ John Nicholas Antiques
Ltd
Contact John or Nicholas McAuliffe
✉ The Furniture Cave,
533 King's Road, London,
SW10 0TZ 🅿
☎ 020 7352 2046 ✆ 020 7352 3654
✉ mail@thecave.co.uk
⊕ www.thecave.co.uk
Est. 1999 *Stock size* Large
Stock Dining chairs, tables and
library furniture, contemporary
furniture
Open Mon–Sat 10am–6pm
Sun noon–5pm
Services Restoration

⊞ The Odd Chair Company
Contact Sue Cook
✉ The Plaza, Chelsea, London,
SW10
☎ 01772 691777 ✆ 01772 691888
✉ info@theoddchaircompany.com
⊕ www.theoddchaircompany.com
Est. 1969 *Stock size* Large
Stock 19thC antique chairs, sofas,
decorative furniture
Open Tues 10am–5pm
Sat 10am–6pm
Fairs Newark, Ardingly
Services Interior design,
upholstery, cabinet making

⊞ Orientation Antiques
(LAPADA)
Contact Evelyne Soler
2 Park Walk, London,
SW10 0AD
☎ 020 7351 0234 ✆ 020 7351 7535
📱 07774 445693
✉ evelynesoler@aol.com
⊕ www.orientationantiques.com
Est. 2000 *Stock size* Medium
Stock 18th–19thC Continental
furniture and works of art
Open Mon–Fri 10am–1pm
2pm–5.30pm Sat by appointment

LONDON

⊞ Phoenix Trading Co
Contact Mr T Shalloe
✉ The Furniture Cave,
533 King's Road, London,
SW10 0TZ 🅿
☎ 020 7351 6543 📠 020 7352 9803
📱 07768 825626
📧 mail@phoenixtrading.co.uk
🌐 www.phoenixtrading.co.uk.
Est. 1979 *Stock size* Large
Stock Antique and reproduction
decorative accessories, furniture,
porcelain, bronze, marble
Open Mon–Sat 10am–6pm
Sun 11am–5pm

⊞ H W Poulter & Son
Contact Mr D Poulter
✉ 279 Fulham Road,
London,
SW10 9PZ 🅿
☎ 020 7352 7268 📠 020 7351 0984
📧 hwpoulterandson@btconnect.co.uk
🌐 www.hwpoulterandson.co.uk
Est. 1946 *Stock size* Large
Stock 18th–19thC marble,
wooden, stone fireplaces,
accessories
Open Mon–Fri 9am–5pm
Sat 9am–noon
Services Restoration of marble

⊞ Christopher Preston Ltd (LAPADA)
Contact Christopher Preston
✉ The Furniture Cave,
553 King's Road, Chelsea,
London,
SW10 0TZ
☎ 020 7352 8587 📠 020 7376 3627
📧 christopherpreston@yahoo.co.uk
🌐 www.antiquebrasshandles.co.uk
Est. 1973 *Stock size* Large
Stock 18th–19thC furniture,
fireguards, fenders, brass door
furniture
Open Mon–Sat 10am–6pm
Services Restoration

⊞ Jane Sacchi Linens Ltd (LAPADA)
Contact Jane Sacchi
✉ World's End Studios,
132–134 Lots Road, Chelsea,
London,
SW10 0RJ 🅿
☎ 020 7349 7020 📠 020 7349 7049
📧 enquiries@janesacchi.com
🌐 www.janesacchi.com
Est. 1989 *Stock size* Medium
Stock 19thC–early 20thC bed and
table linen, 1930s furniture
Open Mon–Fri 10am–5pm

➤ Francis Smith Ltd
Contact Mr Norman Ashford
✉ 107 Lots Road, Chelsea,
London,
SW10 0RN 🅿
☎ 020 7349 0011 📠 020 7349 0770
🌐 www.wbauctioneers.com
Est. 1835
Open Mon–Fri 9am–6pm
Sales Antiques and general sale
Tues 6pm, viewing Sun
11am–4pm Mon 9am–7pm
Tues 9am–6pm prior to sale
Frequency Fortnightly
Catalogues Yes

⊞ John Thornton
Contact John or Caroline
Thornton
✉ 455 Fulham Road, London,
SW10 9UZ 🅿
☎ 020 7352 8810
Est. 1964 *Stock size* Medium
Stock Antiquarian and second-
hand books, Catholic and Anglo-
Catholic theology
Open Mon–Sat 10am–5.30pm

SW11

⊞ Banana Dance Ltd (LAPADA)
Contact Mr J Daltrey
✉ Unit 20, Northcote Road
Antiques Market, 155a
Northcote Road, Battersea,
London,
SW11 2QB 🅿
☎ 01634 364539
📧 jonathan@bananadance.com
🌐 www.bananadance.com
Est. 1988 *Stock size* Large
Stock Clarice Cliff, Art Deco,
ceramics, silver, silver plate
Open Mon–Sat 10am–6pm
Sun noon–5pm
Fairs Alexandra Palace
Services Valuations, mail order

⊞ Braemar Antiques
Contact Mrs Marlis Ramos
de Deus
✉ 113 Northcote Road, London,
SW11 6PW 🅿
☎ 020 7924 5628
🌐 www.braemar-antiques.com
Est. 1994 *Stock size* Medium
Stock Decorative antiques,
furniture, chandeliers, mirrors,
fabrics, armoires, secretaires,
commodes
Open Mon–Sat 10am–5.30pm
Fairs Chelsea Brocante

⊞ Chesney's Antique Fireplaces
Contact Henry Masterton
✉ 194–202 Battersea Park Road,
London,
SW11 4ND 🅿
☎ 020 7627 1410 📠 020 7622 1078
📧 sales@chesneys.co.uk
🌐 www.chesneys.co.uk
Est. 1985 *Stock size* Large
Stock Antique and reproduction
fireplaces
Open Mon–Fri 9am–5.30pm
Sat 10am–5pm
Fairs Decorex

➤ Criterion Riverside Auctions
Contact Addison Gelpey
✉ 41–47 Catford Road, Chatfield
Road, London,
SW11 3SE 🅿
☎ 020 7924 1723
📧 info@criterionriversideauctions.co.uk
🌐 www.criterionriversideauctions.co.uk
Est. 1990
Open Mon–Sun 10am–6pm
Sales General antiques
Frequency Weekly
Catalogues Yes

⊞ Eccles Road Antiques
Contact Mrs H Rix
✉ 60 Eccles Road, London,
SW11 1LX 🅿
☎ 020 7228 1638
📱 07885 172087
Est. 1985 *Stock size* Large
Stock Victoriana, pine and
mahogany furniture,
collectables, kitchenware
Open Tues–Sat 10am–5pm
Sun noon–5pm
Fairs Ardingly

⊞ Gideon Hatch Rugs & Carpets
Contact Gideon Hatch
✉ 1 Port House, Plantation
Wharf, London,
SW11 3GY 🅿
☎ 020 7223 3996
📱 07801 748962
🌐 www.gideonhatch.co.uk
Est. 1998 *Stock size* Medium
Stock Rugs and carpets
Open By appointment
Fairs Olympia
Services Restoration, cleaning

⊞ Jenny Hicks Beach (LAPADA)
Contact Jenny Hicks Beach

✉ **7 Battersea Church Road, London, SW11 3LY** 🅿
☎ 020 7228 6900 📠 020 7228 6900
📱 07778 794832
Est. 1995 *Stock size* Small
Stock Rugs, carpets, textiles
Open By appointment only
Fairs Olympia, Battersea Decorative Antiques and Textiles, HALI Antique Textile Art Fair
Services Search service

⊞ **The House Hospital**
Contact Mr J Brunton
✉ 14 Winders Road, London, SW11 3HE 🅿
☎ 020 7223 3179
📧 info@thehousehospital.com
🌐 www.thehousehospital.com
Est. 1983 *Stock size* Medium
Stock Fireplaces, cast-iron radiators, doors, handles, general architectural salvage
Open Tues–Sat 10am–5pm
Services Sandblasting

⌂ **Northcote Road Antiques Market**
Contact Mrs Gill Wilkins
✉ 155a Northcote Road, London, SW11 6QB 🅿
☎ 020 7228 6850
📧 antiques@spectrumsoft.net
🌐 www.spectrmsoft.net
Est. 1986 *Stock size* Large
No. of dealers 40
Stock Jewellery, prints, pictures, glass, Victoriana, Art Deco, furniture, lighting, silver, plate, studio pottery
Open Mon–Sat 10am–6pm
Sun noon–5pm
Services Café

⊞ **Overmantels**
Contact Seth Taylor
✉ 66 Battersea Bridge Road, London, SW11 3AG 🅿
☎ 020 7223 8151 📠 020 7924 2283
📧 seth@overmantels.co.uk
🌐 www.overmantels.co.uk
Est. 1982 *Stock size* Small
Stock Mirrors, console tables
Open Mon–Sat 9.30am–5.30pm

⊞ **Kate Thurlow and David Alexander Antiques (LAPADA, CINOA)**
Contact Rodney Robertson
✉ 29A Battersea Bridge Road,

London, SW11 3BA 🅿
☎ 020 7738 0792
📱 07836 588776
📧 katethurlow@onetel.com
Est. 1978 *Stock size* Medium
Stock 16th–17thC Continental and English furniture, associated wares
Open By appointment
Fairs Olympia
Services Restoration

⊞ **Wood Pigeon**
Contact Miss Lucy Kallim
✉ 71 Webbs Road, London, SW11 6SD 🅿
☎ 020 7223 8668
📱 07904 102442
🌐 www.woodpigeon.co.uk
Est. 1996 *Stock size* Medium
Stock French, country, painted, upholstered furniture, decorative items
Open Tues–Sat 10.30am–5.30pm

⊞ **Robert Young Antiques (BADA)**
Contact Robert or Josyane Young
✉ 68 Battersea Bridge Road, London, SW11 3AG 🅿
☎ 020 7228 7847 📠 020 7585 0489
📧 office@robertyoungantiques.com
🌐 robertyoungantiques.com
Est. 1975 *Stock size* Medium
Stock Country furniture, folk art, treen, naive and primitive paintings, Scandinavian objects
Open Tues–Fri 9.30am–6pm
Sat 10am–5pm
Fairs Olympia (June), San Francisco Fall, The New York Winter Antiques Show
Services In-house annual exhibition of Folk Art, May

SW13

⊞ **Christine Bridge Antiques (BADA, LAPADA, CINOA)**
Contact Christine Bridge or Darryl Bowles
✉ 78 Castelnau, London, SW13 9EX 🅿
☎ 020 8741 5501 📠 020 8255 0172
📱 07831 126668
📧 christine@bridge-antiques.com
🌐 www.abacil.com
Est. 1970 *Stock size* Medium
Stock 18thC collectors' glass, 19thC

coloured and decorative glass
Open By appointment only
Fairs BADA, Olympia, fairs in USA and Far East
Services Glass restoration, repairs, polishing, cleaning, website design (www.ABAC11.com)

⊞ **Simon Coleman Antiques**
Contact Simon Coleman
✉ 40 White Hart Lane, Barnes, London, SW13 0PZ 🅿
☎ 020 8878 5037
📧 colemansimon@aol.com
Est. 1977 *Stock size* Large
Stock Fully restored farmhouse tables, narrow serving tables
Open Mon–Fri 9.30am–6pm
Sat 9.30am–5pm

⊞ **The Dining Room Shop**
Contact David Hur
✉ 62–64 White Hart Lane, Barnes, London, SW13 0PZ 🅿
☎ 020 8878 1020 📠 020 8876 2367
📧 enquiries@thediningroomshop.co.uk
🌐 www.thediningroomshop.co.uk
Est. 1985 *Stock size* Medium
Stock Everything for formal and country dining rooms, furniture, china, glass, silver, linens, lighting, prints
Open Mon–Sat 10am–5.30pm
Fairs Olympia June
Services Valuations, restoration

⊞ **Theresa McCullough Ltd (BADA)**
Contact Theresa McCullough
✉ 80 Riverview Gardens, Barnes, London, SW13 8RA 🅿
☎ 020 8563 1680 📠 020 8563 1680
📱 07958 992374
📧 info@theresamccullough.com
🌐 www.theresamccullough.com
Est. 2000 *Stock size* Medium
Stock Indian, South East Asian works of art, predominantly sculpture, South East Asian gold jewellery
Open By appointment
Fairs International Asian Art Fair New York, Asian art London

⊞ **Joy McDonald Antiques**
Contact Ms Angela McDonald
✉ 50 Station Road, Barnes, London,

SW13 0LP 🅿
☎ 020 8876 6184 🔗 020 8876 6184
Est. 1966 *Stock size* Medium
Stock 18th–20thC mirrors,
chandeliers, lighting,
upholstered chairs, decorative
items
Open Tues–Sat 10.30am–5.30pm

⊞ Tobias & The Angel
Contact Angel Hughes
✉ 68 White Hart Lane, London,
SW13 0PZ
☎ 020 8878 8902 🔗 020 8296 0058
🔗 enquiries@tobiasandtheangel.com
🌐 www.tobiasandtheangel.com
Est. 1985 *Stock size* Large
Stock Country antiques,
furniture, lampshades, pictures,
mirrors, linen, pretty, useful
objects for the home
Open Mon–Sat 10am–6pm
Services Mail order, bespoke
furniture, printer of hand-
blocked fabric

SW14

⊞ Mary Cooke Antiques Ltd (BADA)
Contact Mary Cooke or
Neil Shepperson
✉ 12 The Old Power Station,
121 Mortlake High Street,
London,
SW14 8SN 🅿
☎ 020 8876 5777 🔗 020 8876 1652
📱 07836 521103
🔗 silver@marycooke.co.uk
🌐 www.marycooke.co.uk
Est. 1967 *Stock size* Medium
Stock 18thC silver, early 19thC
collectors' items
Open By appointment
Fairs Olympia, BADA

⊞ Paul Foster Books (ABA, PBFA)
Contact Paul Foster
✉ 119 Sheen Lane, East Sheen,
London,
SW14 8AE 🅿
☎ 020 8876 7424 🔗 020 8876 7424
🔗 paulfosterbooks@btinternet.com
Est. 1990 *Stock size* Medium
Stock Antiquarian, rare, second-
hand, out-of-print books
Open Wed–Sat 10.30am–6pm
Fairs Olympia, Chelsea

⊞ Pamela Godwin
Contact Pamela Godwin
✉ 136 Upper Richmond Road

West, East Cheam, London,
SW14 8DS 🅿
☎ 020 8878 8988
Est. 1964 *Stock size* Large
Stock General antiques,
Georgian, second-hand furniture
Open Mon–Sat 11am–5pm closed
Wed or by appointment
Services Valuations

SW15

⊞ 30th Century Comics
Contact Mr W Morgan
✉ 18 Lower Richmond Road,
London,
SW15 1JP 🅿
☎ 020 8788 2052
🔗 sales@30thcenturycomics.co.uk
🌐 www.30thcenturycomics.co.uk
Est. 1994 *Stock size* Large
Stock Vintage and new British
and American comics, annuals
Open Mon–Wed Sat
10.30am–6pm Thurs Fri
10.30am–7pm Sun 11am–5pm
Services Mail order, twice yearly
catalogue, valuations

⊞ The Clock Clinic Ltd (LAPADA)
Contact Mr R Pedler FBHI
✉ 85 Lower Richmond Road,
Putney, London,
SW15 1EU 🅿
☎ 020 8788 1407 🔗 020 8780 2838
🔗 clockclinic@btconnect.com
🌐 www.clockclinic.co.uk
Est. 1971 *Stock size* Medium
Stock Antique clocks,
barometers, all overhauled and
guaranteed
Open Tues–Fri 9am–6pm
Sat 9am–1pm
Fairs Olympia (Feb, June, Nov)
Services Valuations, restoration,
repairs

⊞ Hanshan Tang Books (ABA)
Contact Mr J Cayley
✉ Unit 3, Ashburton Centre,
276 Cortis Road,
London,
SW15 3AY 🅿
☎ 020 8788 4464 🔗 020 8780 1565
🔗 hst@hanshan.com
🌐 www.hanshan.com
Est. 1974 *Stock size* Medium
Stock East Asian art, archaeology
Open By appointment
Services Book search, library
purchases

SW16

⊞ H C Baxter & Sons (BADA, LAPADA)
Contact Mr G Baxter
✉ 40 Drewstead Road,
London,
SW16 1AB 🅿
☎ 020 8769 5969 🔗 020 8769 0898
🔗 partners@hcbaxter.co.uk
🌐 www.hcbaxter.co.uk
Est. 1928 *Stock size* Medium
Stock 18th–19thC English
furniture, decorative items
Trade only Public by
appointment only
Open Wed Thurs 9am–5pm
Fairs Olympia (Nov) BADA,
Duke of York, Grosvenor House
Services Valuations

⊞ A and J Fowle
Contact Mr A Fowle
✉ 542 Streatham High Road,
London,
SW16 3QF 🅿
☎ 020 8764 2896
📱 0796 8058790
Est. 1950 *Stock size* Medium
Stock General antiques,
furniture, silver, china, paintings,
decorative furniture
Open Mon–Sun 9am–6pm or
by appointment
Fairs Ardingly

⊞ Kantuta
Contact Mrs N Wright
✉ 1d Gleneagle Road,
London,
SW16 6AX 🅿
☎ 020 8677 6701
Est. 1986 *Stock size* Medium
Stock Antique furniture
Open Mon–Sat 10am–6pm
Services Restoration

SW17

⊞ Hudson Bay Trading Co Antiques
Contact David Hudson
✉ 6 Khama Road, Tooting,
London,
SW17 0EL 🅿
☎ 0870 606 6555
📱 07915 557700
🌐 www.hbtc.co.uk
Est. 1969 *Stock size* Medium
Stock General antiques, English
furniture, silver, collectables
Open By appointment
Services Valuations, restoration

Roger Lascelles Clocks
Contact Mr R Lascelles
✉ Unit 11, Wimbledon Stadium Business Centre, Riverside Road, London,
SW17 0BA [P]
☎ 020 8879 6011 ● 020 8879 1818
✉ info@rogerlascelles.com
Ⓦ www.rogerlascelles.com
Est. 1974 *Stock size* Large
Stock Longcase, mantel and traditional reproduction clocks
Open Mon–Fri 9am–5pm (telephone first) or by appointment

SW18

Bertie's
Contact Mrs B Ferguson
✉ 1st Floor, 284 Merton Road, London,
SW18 5JN [P]
☎ 020 8874 2520
✉ jamesferguson@beeb.net
Est. 1985 *Stock size* Small
Stock Antique and reproduction pine furniture, china, collectables
Open Tues–Sat 9.30am–5.30pm
Services Bespoke pine furniture

The Earlsfield Bookshop
Contact Mr C Dixon
✉ 513 Garratt Lane, Wandsworth, London,
SW18 4SW [P]
☎ 020 8946 3744
Est. 1994 *Stock size* Medium
Stock General books
Open Mon–Thurs 4–6pm Fri 11am–6pm Sat 10am–5pm
Fairs Kempton Park, Bloomsbury

Just a Second
Contact Mr J Ferguson
✉ 284 Merton Road, London,
SW18 5JN [P]
☎ 020 8874 2520
✉ jamesferguson@beeb.net
Est. 1980 *Stock size* Medium
Stock General antiques, good quality furniture
Open Tues–Sat 9.30am–5.30pm
Services Valuations, restoration

Lloyds International Auction Galleries Ltd
Contact Mr Mick Bown
✉ 9 Lydden Road, Earlsfield, London,
SW18 4LT [P]
☎ 020 8788 7777 ● 020 8874 5390

✉ valuations@lloyds-auction.co.uk
Ⓦ www.lloyds-auction.co.uk
Est. 1944
Open Mon–Fri 9.30am–5.30pm
Sales Furniture, paintings and collectables sale Sat 11am, viewing Fri 10.30am–7.30pm Sat 9am prior to sale. Jewellery sale Tues 11am, viewing Mon 9.30am–4pm. General Metropolitan Police 'Lost Property' sale Wed 2pm, viewing Wed 9.30am–1.45pm prior to sale
Frequency Fortnightly all sales
Catalogues Yes

SW19

Corfield Potashnick (LAPADA)
Contact Jonathan Fry
✉ 39 Church Road, Wimbledon Village, London,
SW19 5DG
☎ 020 8944 9022
📱 07974 565659
✉ jonfry@btopenworld.com
Ⓦ www.corfieldpotashnick.co.uk
Est. 1997 *Stock size* Medium
Stock 18th–19thC furniture
Open Mon–Sat 10am–6pm
Fairs LAPADA, Commonwealth Institute, London
Services Valuations, restoration

Mark J West (BADA)
Contact Mr M West
✉ Cobb Antiques Ltd, 39b High Street, London,
SW19 5BY [P]
☎ 020 8946 2811
✉ westglass@aol.com
Ⓦ www.markjwest-glass.com
Est. 1977 *Stock size* Large
Stock 18th–early 20thC English and Continental table glass
Open Mon–Sat 10am–5.30pm
Fairs Olympia, Grosvenor House

SW20

Antiques of Wimbledon
Contact WJ Russell
✉ 329 Kingston Road, London,
SW20 8JX [P]
☎ 020 8540 7669
Ⓦ www.antiquebuyer.co.uk
Est. 1978 *Stock size* Large
Stock Antiques and collectables
Open Mon–Sat 9am–9pm

W F Turk Fine Antique Clocks (BADA, LAPADA, CINOA)
Contact Mr W Turk
✉ 355 Kingston Road, London,
SW20 8JX [P]
☎ 020 8543 3231 ● 020 8543 3231
✉ sales@wfturk.com
Ⓦ www.fwturk.com
Est. 1979 *Stock size* Large
Stock Antique clocks, 17th–19thC longcase and bracket clocks, French decorative mantel and carriage clocks
Open Tues–Fri 9am–5.30pm Sat 9am–4pm
Fairs Olympia, LAPADA, NEC
Services Valuations, restoration, repairs, sales

WEST

W1

David Aaron
Contact Mr David Aaron
✉ 22 Berkeley Square, London,
W1J 6EH [P]
☎ 020 7491 9588 ● 020 7491 9522
✉ david_aaron@hotmail.com
Est. 1910 *Stock size* Large
Stock Worldwide ancient art, rare carpets
Open Mon–Fri 9am–6pm Sat by appointment only
Services Valuations, restoration

Aaron Gallery (ADA)
Contact Simon Aaron
✉ 125 Mount Street, London,
W1K 3NS [P]
☎ 020 7499 9434 ● 020 7499 0072
✉ simon@aarongallery.com
Ⓦ www.aarongallery.com
Est. 1910 *Stock size* Large
Stock Islamic, near Eastern, Greek, Roman, Egyptian ancient art
Open Mon–Fri 10am–5.30pm
Services Valuations, restoration

Emmy Abe Antiques
Contact Emmy Abe
✉ 58 Davies Street, London,
W1K 5LP
☎ 020 7629 1826
Est. 1982 *Stock size* Small
Stock Antique jewellery 1800–1960s
Open Mon–Fri 10am–5.30pm

ADC Heritage Ltd (BADA)
Contact Francis Raeymaekers or

LONDON
WEST • W1

Elisabeth Bellord
✉ **90 Mount Street,
London,
W1K 2ST** 🅿
☎ 020 7355 1444 **⊕** 020 7355 2444
Ⓜ 07788 720407
⊖ raeymaekers@aol.com or
elbellord@btinternet.com
ⓦ www.themetalgallery.com
Est. 1980 *Stock size* Small
Stock Antique English silver and
old Sheffield plate
Open By appointment only
Services Valuations, restoration

**⊞ Adrian Alan Ltd
(BADA, LAPADA)**
Contact Miss H Alan
✉ **66–67 South Audley Street,
London,
W1YK 2QX** 🅿
☎ 020 7495 2324 **⊕** 020 7495 0204
⊖ enquiries@adrianalan.com
ⓦ www.adrianalan.com
Est. 1964 *Stock size* Large
Stock Furniture, light fittings,
mirrors, objets d'art, paintings,
statues, garden furniture, pianos,
19thC Continental furniture a
speciality
Open Mon–Fri 9.30am–6pm
Fairs Olympia (June)
Services Restoration, shipping,
storage

**⊞ Altea Maps and Books
(PBFA, ABA, IMCoS)**
Contact Mr M De Martini
✉ **35 Saint George Street,
London,
W1S 2FN** 🅿
☎ 020 7491 0010 **⊕** 020 7281 0015
⊖ info@alteagallery.com
ⓦ www.alteagallery.com
Est. 1993 *Stock size* Medium
Stock 15th–19thC maps, atlases,
globes, sea charts, celestial charts
and town plans
Open Mon–Fri 10am–6pm
Sat by appointment
Fairs London Map Fairs, Miami
Map Fair
Services Valuations, sale on
commission

**⊞ Antiques by Jules
Ltd**
Contact Berte De Wit
✉ **45–46 New Bond Street,
London,
W1S 2RD**
☎ 020 7491 9193 **⊕** 020 7491 3349
⊖ antiquesbyjules@aol.com

Est. 2000 *Stock size* Large
Stock Antique diamond jewellery
Open By appointment

⊞ Argyll Etkin Ltd (PTS)
Contact Jim Hanson or
Ian Shapiro
✉ **1–9 Hills Place, Oxford Circus,
London,
W1F 7SA** 🅿
☎ 020 7437 7800
⊖ royalty@argyll-etkin.com
ⓦ www.argyll-etkin.com
Est. 1950 *Stock size* Large
Stock Royal memorabilia,
manuscripts, autographs, history
of the posts
Open Mon–Fri 8.30am–5pm
Fairs Olympia, Stampex

**⊞ Victor Arwas Gallery
(BACA Award Winner 2004)**
Contact Greta or Victor Arwas
✉ **3 Clifford Street, London,
W1S 2LF** 🅿
☎ 020 7734 3944 **⊕** 020 7437 1859
⊖ art@victorarwas.com
ⓦ www.victorarwas.com
Est. 1965 *Stock size* Large
Stock Original paintings, water
colours and graphics 1880–1980,
Art Nouveau, Art Deco, Arts and
Crafts
Open Mon–Fri 11am–6pm
Sat 11am–2pm
Services Valuations, restoration,
Victor Arwas is author of about
25 books on decorative arts and
related topics

⊞ ATLAS
Contact Mr B Burdett
✉ **49 Dorset Street, London,
W1U 7NF** 🅿
☎ 020 7224 4192 **⊕** 020 7224 3351
⊖ info@atlasgallery.com
ⓦ www.atlasgallery.com
Est. 1993 *Stock size* Medium
Stock Antiquarian, rare, second-
hand books, travel a speciality.
Fine art photographs from
vintage prints to limited edition
modern prints
Open Mon–Fri 9am–5.30pm
Fairs Bloomsbury, Phillips
Services Valuations, book search

**⊞ Aytac Antiques
(NAWCC)**
Contact Mr O Aytac
✉ **Stand 331–332, Grays
Antiques Market, 58 Davies
Street, London,**

W1Y 1LB 🅿
☎ 020 7629 7380 **⊕** 020 7629 7380
⊖ ossiemania@aol.com
Est. 1982 *Stock size* Large
Stock Vintage wristwatches,
clocks, 19thC French bronzes
Open Mon–Fri 10.30am–5pm
Services Wristwatch restoration,
repair

**⊞ J and A Beare Ltd
(BADA)**
Contact Simon Morris or
Frances Gilham
✉ **30 Queen Anne Street,
London,
W1G 8HX** 🅿
☎ 020 7307 9666 **⊕** 020 7307 9651
⊖ violins@beares.com
ⓦ www.beares.com
Est. 1892 *Stock size* Large
Stock Musical instruments of the
violin family
Open Mon–Fri 10am–12.30pm
1.30pm–5pm
Services Valuations

⊞ Linda Bee
Contact Linda Bee
✉ **The Mews Antique Market,
1–7 Davies Mews, London,
W1K 5AB** 🅿
☎ 020 7629 5921 **⊕** 020 7629 5921
Ⓜ 07956 276384
ⓦ www.emews.com
Est. 1992 *Stock size* Large
Stock Vintage fashion
accessories, handbags, perfume
bottles, powder compacts,
costume jewellery
Open Mon–Fri 1–6pm or
by appointment
Fairs Alexandra Palace
Services Valuations

⊞ Paul Bennett (LAPADA)
Contact Mr Dubiner
✉ **48A George Street, London,
W1H 5RF**
☎ 020 7935 1555
⊖ paulbennet@ukgateway.net
ⓦ www.paulbennet.ukgateway.net
Est. 1967
Stock Antique and modern silver,
Sheffield plate
Open Mon–Fri 10am–6pm
Fairs Olympia, Claridges
Services Valuations

**⊞ Daniel Bexfield
Antiques (LAPADA, BADA,
CINOA)**
Contact Mr D Bexfield

✉ **26 Burlington Arcade, Mayfair,
London,
W1J 0PU** 🅿
☎ 020 7491 1720 📠 020 7491 1730
📧 antiques@bexfield.co.uk
🌐 www.bexfield.co.uk
Est. 1981 *Stock size* Large
Stock 17th–20thC quality silver,
objects of virtue
Open Mon–Sat 9am–6pm
Services Valuations, restoration

⌂ **Biblion Ltd**
Contact Leo Harrison or
Stephen Poole
✉ Grays Antique Market,
1–7 Davies Mews,
London,
W1Y 2LP 🅿
☎ 020 7629 1374 📠 020 7493 7158
📧 info@biblion.co.uk
🌐 www.biblion.com
Est. 1999 *Stock size* Large
No. of dealers 100
Stock Antiquarian, rare books,
prints, modern first editions,
children's
Open Mon–Sat 10am–6pm
Services Book binding, book
search, shipping

⊞ **H Blairman & Sons Ltd
(BADA, BACA Award
Winner 2004)**
Contact Martin Levy, Patricia
Levy or Sara Sowerby
✉ 119 Mount Street,
London,
W1K 3NL 🅿
☎ 020 7493 0444 📠 020 7495 0766
📧 blairman@atlas.co.uk
🌐 www.blairman.co.uk
Est. 1884 *Stock size* Large
Stock 18th–19thC furniture,
works of art
Open Mon–Fri 9am–6pm or
by appointment
Fairs Grosvenor House Fair,
International Fine Art & Antique
Dealers Show, New York
Services Catalogues

⊞ **Blunderbuss Antiques**
Contact Mr C Greenaway
✉ 29 Thayer Street, London,
W1U 2QW 🅿
☎ 020 7486 2444 📠 020 7935 1645
📧 mail@blunderbuss-antiques.co.uk
🌐 www.blunderbuss-antiques.co.uk
Est. 1968 *Stock size* Large
Stock 16thC–WWII weapons,
militaria
Open Tues–Fri 9.30am–4.30pm

⌂ **The Bond Street
Antiques Centre**
Contact Mike Spooner
✉ 124 New Bond Street, London,
W1Y 9AE 🅿
☎ 020 7969 1500 📠 020 7351 5350
📧 antique@dial.pipex.com
Est. 1968 *Stock size* Large
No. of dealers 35
Stock Jewellery, silver, fine
vintage watches
Open Mon–Sat 10am–6pm
Services Valuations

➢ **Bonhams (BACA Award
Winner 2004)**
✉ 101 New Bond Street, London,
W1S 1SR 🅿
☎ 020 7447 7447 📠 020 7447 7400
📧 info@bonhams.com
🌐 www.bonhams.com
Est. 1793
Open Mon–Fri 9am–4.30pm
Sun 11am–3pm
Sales Regular sales of old master
and 19thC pictures, modern and
contemporary and 20thC British
art, watercolours and drawings,
prints, portrait miniatures,
jewellery, clocks and watches,
British and Continental ceramics
and glass, furniture, works of art,
books, Asian art, contemporary
ceramics, decorative arts, design,
musical instruments, wine,
antiquities, tribal art, Islamic,
motorcars, motorcyles and
automobilia. In addition
Bonhams hold further sales in
London (Knightsbridge), New
York, San Francisco, Sydney,
Geneva and Los Angeles, as well
as in regional salerooms across
the UK. Free auction valuations;
insurance and probate valuations
Catalogues Yes

⊞ **David Bowden Chinese
and Japanese Art**
Contact David Bowden
✉ Grays Antique Market,
58 Davies Street, London,
W1K 5LP 🅿
☎ 020 7495 1773
Est. 1980 *Stock size* Large
Stock Japanese netsuke, works
of art, Chinese works of art
Open Mon–Fri 10am–6pm
Fairs NEC

⊞ **Patrick Boyd-Carpenter
and Howard Neville**
Contact Mr P Boyd-Carpenter or

Mr H Neville
✉ Grays Antique Market,
58 Davies Street,
London,
W1Y 2LP 🅿
☎ 020 7491 7623 📠 020 7491 7623
📧 patrickboyd_carpenter@hotmail.com
Est. 1986 *Stock size* Large
Stock Wide range of antiques,
16th–18thC sculpture, paintings,
prints
Open Mon–Fri 10.30am–5.30pm
or by appointment
Services Valuations, restoration

⊞ **Brandt Oriental
Antiques**
Contact Robert Brandt
✉ 1st Floor, 29 New Bond Street,
London,
W1S 2RL 🅿
☎ 020 7499 8835 📠 020 7409 1882
📱 07774 989661
📧 brandt@nildram.co.uk
🌐 www.brandtorientalart.com
Est. 1980 *Stock size* Medium
Stock Japanese metalwork and
screens, the China trade
Open By appointment
Fairs June Olympia, New York

⊞ **Britannia**
Contact Rita Smythe
✉ Grays Antique Market, 58
Davies Street, London,
W1K 5JF
☎ 020 7629 6772 📠 020 8675 3120
Est. 1968 *Stock size* Medium
Stock 19thC decorative items
Open Mon–Fri 11am–6pm
Services Valuations

⊞ **John Bull (Antiques)
Ltd (LAPADA)**
Contact Elliot or Ken Bull
✉ 139a New Bond Street,
London,
W1S 2TN 🅿
☎ 020 7629 1251 📠 020 7495 3001
📧 sales@jbsilverware.co.uk
🌐 www.antique-silver.co.uk
Est. 1952 *Stock size* Medium
Stock Antique silver giftware
Open Mon–Fri 9am–5pm
Fairs Antiques for Everyone

⊞ **C and L Burman (BADA)**
Contact Charles Truman
✉ 5 Vigo Street, London,
W1S 3HF 🅿
☎ 020 7439 6604 📠 020 7439 6605
📧 charles-truman@lineone.net
Est. 2001 *Stock size* Medium

Stock Antiques and works of art including silver, glass, ceramics, furniture, sculpture
Open By appointment
Services Valuations, restoration

⊞ The Button Queen Ltd
Contact Martin Frith
⊠ 19 Marylebone Lane, London, W1U 2NF
☎ 020 7935 1505 ☏ 020 7935 1505
Ⓦ www.thebuttonqueen.co.uk
Est. 1950 *Stock size* Large
Stock Buttons
Open Mon–Wed 10am–5pm
Thur–Fri 10am–6pm
Sat 10am–4pm

⊞ Paul Champkins Oriental Art (BADA)
Contact Mr P Champkins
⊠ 41 Dover Street, London, W1X 3RB
☎ 020 7495 4600 ☏ 01235 751658
Ⓔ pc@paulchampkins.demon.co.uk
Est. 1995 *Stock size* Medium
Stock Chinese, Korean, Japanese porcelain, works of art
Open By appointment
Fairs Grosvenor House, New York Ceramics Fair, Olympia (winter)
Services Valuations, restoration, auction purchasing advice

⊞ Antoine Chenevière Fine Arts Ltd (BADA)
Contact Mr Chenevière
⊠ 27 Bruton Street, London, W1J 6QN
☎ 020 7491 1007 ☏ 020 7495 6173
Ⓔ finearts@antoinecheneviere.com
Stock size Medium
Stock 18th–19thC Russian, Austrian, German and Italian furniture, objets d'art
Open Mon–Sat 9.30am–6pm
Fairs Grosvenor House, The Armoury Fair

⊞ Classical Numismatic Group Inc. (BNTA)
Contact Irene Tilmont
⊠ 14 Old Bond Street, London, W1S 4PP
☎ 020 7495 1888 ☏ 020 7499 5916
Ⓔ cng@cngcoins.com
Ⓦ www.cngcoins.com
Est. 1990 *Stock size* Large
Stock Coins, Greek, Roman, Medieval, European to end of 18thC
Open Mon–Fri 9.30am–5.30pm

Fairs Coinex
Services Valuations, auctions, phone for details

⊞ Sibyl Colefax & John Fowler (LAPADA)
Contact Roger Jones
⊠ 39 Brook Street, London, W1K 4JE
☎ 020 7493 2231 ☏ 020 7355 4037
Ⓔ antiques@sibylcolefax.com
Ⓦ www.colefaxantiques.com
Stock size Large
Stock 18th–19thC Continental and English furniture, objects, pictures
Open Mon–Fri 9.30am–5.30pm
Fairs Olympia

⊞ Stuart Craig (PADA)
Contact Stuart Craig
⊠ Vintage Modes,
The Mews Antique Market, 1–7 Davies Mews, London, W1K 5AB
☎ 020 7221 8662
⑩ 07947 889012
Ⓔ info@vintagemodes.co.uk
Ⓦ www.vintagemodes.co.uk
Est. 1991 *Stock size* Medium
Stock Early 19thC–1950s antique ladies' clothing, accessories
Open Mon–Fri 10am–6pm or by appointment

⊞ Sandra Cronan Ltd (BADA)
Contact Sandra Cronan
⊠ 18 Burlington Arcade, London, W1J 0PN
☎ 020 7491 4851 ☏ 020 7493 2758
Ⓔ enquiries@sandracronan.com
Ⓦ www.sandracronan.com
Est. 1978 *Stock size* Medium
Stock 18th–early 20thC jewellery
Open Mon–Fri 10am–5pm
Fairs Grosvenor House, March BADA
Services Valuations, restoration, repairs, design commission

⊞ Adèle De Havilland
Contact Adèle De Havilland
⊠ The Bond Street Antique Centre, 124 New Bond Street, London, W1S 1DX
☎ 020 7499 7127
Est. 1971 *Stock size* Medium
Stock Oriental porcelain, netsuke, jade, ivory carvings,

bronze figures, objects of virtue
Open Mon–Sat 10am–4pm
Services Valuations

⋨ Dix Noonan Webb (BNTA, ANA, OMRS, OMSA)
Contact Mr C Webb
⊠ 16 Bolton Street, Piccadilly, London, W1J 8BQ
☎ 020 7016 1700 ☏ 020 7016 1799
Ⓔ auctions@dnw.co.uk
Ⓦ www.dnw.co.uk
Est. 1991
Open Mon–Fri 9am–5.30pm
Sales Coins, tokens, commemorative and war medals, orders, decorations, militaria, banknotes
Frequency 8 per annum
Catalogues Yes

⊞ Charles Ede Ltd (BADA, ADA, IADA)
Contact Mr J Ede
⊠ 20 Brook Street, London, W1K 5DE
☎ 020 7493 4944 ☏ 020 7491 2548
Ⓔ info@charlesede.com
Ⓦ www.charlesede.com
Est. 1976 *Stock size* Medium
Stock Egyptian, Greek, Roman classical and pre-classical antiquities
Open Tues–Fri 12.30–4.30pm or by appointment
Services Valuations, bidding at auction, mail order

⊞ Editions Graphiques (BACA Award Winner 2004)
Contact Gretha or Victor Arwas
⊠ 3 Clifford Street, London, W1S 2LF
☎ 020 7734 3944 ☏ 020 7437 1859
Ⓔ art@victorarwas.com
Ⓦ www.victorarwas.com
Est. 1965 *Stock size* Large
Stock Original paintings, water colours and graphics 1880–1980, Art Nouveau, Art Deco, Arts and Crafts
Open Mon–Fri 11am–6pm
Sat 11am–2pm
Services Valuations, restoration, Victor Arwas is author of about 25 books on decorative arts and related topics

⊞ Peter Edwards
Contact Mr P Edwards
⊠ 31 Burlington Arcade, London,

W1J 0PY ▣
☎ 020 7491 1589 ❺ 020 7408 2405
✉ peter@peter-edwards-jewels.co.uk
🌐 www.peter-edwards-jewels.co.uk
Est. 1966 *Stock size* Medium
Stock 20thC jewellery, signed
pieces
Open Mon–Sat 10am–6pm
Fairs Olympia, Harrogate
Services Valuations, restoration

⊞ Elisabeth's Antiques Ltd
Contact Elisabeth Hage
✉ Bond Street Antiques Centre,
124 New Bond Street, London,
W1S 1DY
☎ 020 7491 1723 ❺ 020 7629 8910
Est. 1978 *Stock size* Medium
Stock Antique and period
jewellery
Open Mon–Sat 10.30am–5.30pm
Fairs Olympia fairs

⊞ Emanouel Corporation (UK) Ltd (LAPADA)
Contact Emanouel Naghi
64–64a South Audley Street,
London,
W1K 2QT ▣
☎ 020 7493 4350 ❺ 020 7629 3125
Est. 1975 *Stock size* Large
Stock General antiques, works of
art
Open Mon–Fri 10am–6pm
Services Valuations, shipping

⊞ Eskenazi Ltd (BADA)
Contact Mr J Eskenazi
✉ 10 Clifford Street, London,
W1S 2LJ ▣
☎ 020 7493 5464 ❺ 020 7499 3136
✉ gallery@eskenazi.co.uk
🌐 www.eskenazi.co.uk
Est. 1960 *Stock size* Medium
Stock Early Chinese works of art
Open Mon–Fri 9am–5.30pm

⊞ John Eskenazi Ltd (BADA)
✉ 15 Old Bond Street, London,
W1S 4AX ▣
☎ 020 7409 3001 ❺ 020 7629 2146
✉ john.eskenazi@john-
eskenazi.com
🌐 www.john-eskenazi.com
Est. 1994 *Stock size* Medium
Stock South East Asian,
Himalayan and Indian works of
art, Oriental textiles and carpets
Open Mon–Fri 9.30am–6pm or by
appointment
Fairs International Asian Art Fair

⊞ Essie Carpets
Contact Mr Essie
✉ 62 Piccadilly, London,
W1J 0DZ ▣
☎ 020 7493 7766 ❺ 020 7495 3456
Est. 1766 *Stock size* Large
Stock Persian, Oriental rugs,
tapestries
Open Mon–Fri 9.30am–6pm Sun
Bank Holidays 10.30am–5.30pm

⊞ Simon Finch Rare Books (ABA)
Contact Mr S Finch
✉ 53 Maddox Street,
London,
W1S 2PN ▣
☎ 020 7499 0974 ❺ 020 7499 0799
✉ rarebooks@simonfinch.com
🌐 www.simonfinch.com
Est. 1982 *Stock size* Medium
Stock 15th–20thC books art,
architecture, literature, science,
medicine
Open Mon–Fri 10am–6pm
Fairs Olympia, Chelsea
Services Valuations, library
advice

⊞ Matthew Foster
Contact Mr M Foster
✉ Units 4–6, Bond Street
Antiques Centre,
124 New Bond Street,
London,
W1S 1DX ▣
☎ 020 7629 4977 ❺ 020 7629 4977
✉ info@matthew-foster.com
🌐 www.matthew-foster.com
Est. 1987 *Stock size* Large
Stock Large stock of Victorian
gold jewellery, Edwardian, Art
Deco gem set jewellery
Open Mon–Sat 10am–5.30pm
Fairs Olympia

⊞ Robert Frew Ltd (PBFA, ABA)
Contact Mr R Frew
✉ 31 Maddox Street,
London,
W1S 2PB ▣
☎ 020 7290 3800 ❺ 020 7290 3801
✉ shop@robertfrew.com
🌐 www.robertfrew.com
Est. 1976 *Stock size* Medium
Stock Antiquarian and rare
books, travel, literature, classics,
maps, prints
Open Mon–Fri 10am–6pm
Sat 10am–2pm
Fairs PBFA Bookfairs, Russell
Hotel, ABA Olympia Chelsea

⊞ Peter Gaunt
Contact Mr P Gaunt
✉ Stand 120, Grays Antique
Market, 58 Davies Street,
London,
W1K 5JF ▣
☎ 020 7629 1072 ❺ 020 7629 5253
✉ peter@ptgaunt.fsnet.co.uk
Est. 1978 *Stock size* Large
Stock 17th–19thC English and
Continental silver including
17thC candlesticks
Open Mon–Fri 10am–5.30pm

⊞ The Gilded Lily Jewellery Ltd (LAPADA, CINOA)
Contact Ms Korin Harvey
✉ Stand 145–146,
Grays Antique Market,
58 Davies Street, London,
W1K 5LP ▣
☎ 020 7499 6260 ❺ 020 7499 6260
✉ jewellery@gilded-lily.co.uk
🌐 www.graysantiques.com
Est. 1970 *Stock size* Large
Stock Glamorous jewellery,
signed pieces
Open Mon–Fri 10am–6pm
Fairs Olympia, LAPADA, Miami
Beach, Hong Kong

⊞ Gordon's Medals (OMRS)
Contact Mr M Gordon
✉ Stand G14–16,
The Mews Antique Market,
Davies Mews,
London,
W1K 5AB
☎ 020 7495 0900 ❺ 020 7495 0115
📱 07976 266293
✉ sales@cocollector.co.uk
🌐 www.cocollector.co.uk
Est. 1979 *Stock size* Large
Stock Militaria, uniforms,
headgear, badges, medals,
documents
Open Mon–Fri 10.30am–6pm
Fairs Brittania Fair, OMRS
Services Valuations

⊞ The Graham Gallery (LAPADA)
Contact Mr G Whittall
✉ 60 South Audley Street,
Mayfair, London,
W1K 2QW ▣
☎ 020 7495 3151 ❺ 020 7495 3171
Est. 1979 *Stock size* Large
Stock 18th–19thC furniture,
19thC oil paintings, objets d'art,
Art Deco furniture

LONDON

Open Mon–Fri 10.30am–6pm or by appointment
Fairs Olympia (June), LAPADA

⊞ Graus Antiques
Contact Jackie Stern
✉ 139a New Bond Street, London, W1S 2TN
☎ 020 7629 6680 ◐ 020 7499 8774
✉ eric@graus-antiques.com
Est. 1945 *Stock size* Large
Stock Antique pocket watches, jewellery
Open Mon–Fri 9am–5pm

⊞ Anita Gray (LAPADA)
Contact Mrs A Gray
✉ Grays Antique Market, 58 Davies Street, London, W1K 5LP P
☎ 020 7408 1638 ◐ 020 7495 0707
✉ info@chinese-porcelain.com
ⓦ www.chinese-porcelain.com
Est. 1975 *Stock size* Medium
Stock Asian and European porcelain, works of art, 16th–18thC
Open Mon–Fri 10am–6pm
Fairs Olympia (June)

⌂ Grays Antique Market
Contact William Griffith or Kirstine Wallace
✉ 58 Davies Street, London, W1K 5AB P
☎ 020 7629 7034 ◐ 020 7629 3279
✉ grays@clara.net
ⓦ www.graysantiques.com
Est. 1977 *Stock size* Large
No. of dealers 150
Stock Automata, British and Oriental ceramics, gems, precious stones, glass, Islamic jewellery, objects, prints, paintings, silver, textiles, lace, linen, watches
Open Mon–Fri 10am–6pm special hours at Christmas
Services Café, bureau de change, jewellery repair, glass and metal engraving, pearl stringing

⊞ Simon Griffin Antiques Ltd
Contact Mr S Griffin
✉ 3 Royal Arcade, 28 Old Bond Street, London, W1S 4SB P
☎ 020 7491 7367
Est. 1979 *Stock size* Medium

Stock Antique and modern silverware, old Sheffield plate
Open Mon–Sat 10.30am–5.30pm

⊞ Guest and Gray
Contact Anthony Gray
✉ The Mews Antique Market, 1–7 Davies Mews, London, W1K 5AB
☎ 020 7408 1252 ◐ 020 7499 1445
◍ 07968 719496
✉ info@chinese-porcelain-art.com
ⓦ www.chinese-porcelain-art.com
Est. 1970 *Stock size* Large
Stock Asian and European ceramics, works of art, reference books
Open Mon–Fri 10am–6pm
Fairs International Ceramics Fair, Olympia
Services Valuations

⊞ Claire Guest at Thomas Goode & Co. Ltd
Contact Claire Guest
✉ 19 South Audley Street, London, W1Y 6BH P
☎ 020 7499 2823/7243 1423
◐ 020 7629 4230/7792 5450
◍ 07974 767851
✉ claireguest130@hotmail.co.uk
Est. 1969 *Stock size* Medium
Stock Antique furniture, silver, silver plate, glass, china
Open Mon–Sat 10am–6pm

⊞ Hadji Baba Ancient Art Ltd (IADA, ADA)
Contact R Soleimani
✉ 34a Davies Street, London, W1K 4NE
☎ 020 7499 9363 ◐ 020 7493 5504
✉ info@hadjibaba.co.uk
ⓦ www.hadjibaba.co.uk
Est. 1979 *Stock size* Medium
Stock Islamic and Asian art
Open Mon–Fri 10am–6pm
Services Valuations

⊞ Hallmark Antiques
Contact Mr Ralph
✉ Stands 319 & 356, Grays Antique Market, Davies Street, London, W1K 5LP P
☎ 0207 629 8757
Est. 1979 *Stock size* Medium
Stock Victorian–Edwardian jewellery, amber, silver, silver photo frames
Open Mon–Fri 10am–6pm

⊞ Hancocks and Co (Jewellers) Ltd (BADA)
Contact Steven Burton, Duncan Semmens or Ian Morton
✉ 52–53 Burlington Arcade, London, W1J 0HH P
☎ 020 7493 8904 ◐ 020 7493 8905
✉ info@hancockslondon.com
ⓦ www.hancockslondon.com
Est. 1849 *Stock size* Large
Stock Jewellery, silver
Open Mon–Fri 9.30am–5pm
Sat by appointment
Fairs Grosvenor House, Maastricht, The Armoury, Palm Beach
Services Valuations, restoration, purchase of second-hand items

⊞ Brian Haughton Antiques (BACA Award Winner 2004)
Contact Brian Haughton
✉ 3b Burlington Gardens, London, W1S 3EP P
☎ 020 7734 5491 ◐ 020 7494 4604
✉ info@haughton.com
ⓦ www.haughton.com
Est. 1965 *Stock size* Large
Stock 18th–19thC English and Continental ceramics
Open Mon–Fri 10am–5pm
Fairs International Ceramics Fair and Seminar (June), The International Fine Art & Antique Dealers Show, New York (Oct)

⊞ Gerard Hawthorn Ltd (BADA)
Contact Mr G Hawthorn
✉ 104 Mount Street, London, W1K 2TL P
☎ 020 7409 2888 ◐ 020 7409 2777
◍ 07775 917487
✉ mail@gerardhawthorn.com
Est. 1996 *Stock size* Medium
Stock Oriental works of art
Open Mon–Fri 10.30am–late
Fairs 2 exhibitions at gallery (June, Nov), International Asian Art Fair, New York (March)
Services Valuations, restoration, photography

⊞ G Heywood Hill Ltd (ABA)
Contact Mr John Saumarez Smith
✉ 10 Curzon Street, London, W1J 5HH P

☎ 020 7629 0647 **ᗴ** 020 7408 0286
ᐃ books@gheywoodhill.com
ⓦ www.heywoodhill.com
Est. 1936 *Stock size* Medium
Stock Fiction, history, travel,
memoirs, children's antiquarian,
second-hand, new books
Open Mon–Fri 9am–5.30pm
Sat 9am–12.30pm
Services Book search

⊞ Hirsh London
Contact Ben Stevenson
✉ **56–57 Burlington Arcade,**
London,
W1J 0QN 🅿
☎ 020 7499 6814 **ᗴ** 020 7629 9946
ⓦ www.hirsh.co.uk
Est. 1980 *Stock size* Large
Stock Fine antique jewellery,
hand-made and designed
diamond engagement rings
Open Mon–Fri 10am–5.30pm
Services Valuations

⊞ Holmes Ltd
Contact Mr Eldred
✉ **24 Burlington Arcade, London,**
W1J 0PS
☎ 020 7629 8380
Est. 1923 *Stock size* Small
Stock Antique, modern jewellery
and silver
Open Mon–Sat 9.45am–5pm

⊞ C John Ltd (BADA)
Contact Mr L Sassoon
✉ **70 South Audley Street,**
London,
W1K 2RA 🅿
☎ 020 7493 5288 **ᗴ** 020 7409 7030
ᐃ cjohn@dircom.co.uk
ⓦ www.cjohn.com
Est. 1948 *Stock size* Large
Stock Persian, French, Russian,
Caucasian tapestries, Indian,
Turkish, Chinese carpets, rugs,
textiles
Open Mon–Fri 9.30am–5pm
Fairs Grosvenor House
Services Valuations, restoration

⊞ Johnson Walker Ltd
(BADA)
Contact Miss R Gill
✉ **64 Burlington Arcade, London,**
W1J 0QT 🅿
☎ 020 7629 2615/6
ᗴ 020 7409 0709
Est. 1849 *Stock size* Medium
Stock Jewellery, bijouterie
Open Mon–Sat 9.30am–5.30pm
Services Valuations, repairs

⊞ John Joseph (LAPADA, LJAJDA)
Contact Mr J Joseph
✉ **Stand 345–346,**
Grays Antique Market,
58 Davies Street,
London,
W1K 5LP
☎ 020 7629 1140 **ᗴ** 020 7629 1140
ᐃ jewellery@john-joseph.co.uk
ⓦ www.john-joseph.co.uk
Est. 1985 *Stock size* Medium
Stock Victorian, Edwardian, Art
Deco jewellery, gem set, gold,
platinum
Open Mon–Fri 10am–5pm
Fairs Olympia (June)

⊞ M & A Kaae (LAPADA)
Contact Minoo Kaae
✉ **The Mews Antique Market,**
1–7 Davies Mews,
London,
W1K 5AB 🅿
☎ 020 7629 1200 **ᗴ** 020 7629 1200
ᐃ andrekaae@aol.com
Est. 1981 *Stock size* Large
Stock Diamonds, antique
jewellery
Open Mon–Fri 10am–6pm

⊞ Daniel Katz Ltd (SLAD)
Contact Daniel Katz or
Stuart Lochhead
✉ **13 Old Bond Street,**
London,
W1S 4SX
☎ 020 7493 0688 **ᗴ** 020 7499 7493
ᐃ info@katz.co.uk
ⓦ www.katz.co.uk
Est. 1969 *Stock size* Large
Stock European sculpture
Open Mon–Fri 9am–6pm

⊞ Roger Keverne Ltd
(BADA)
Contact Mr R Keverne
✉ **2nd Floor, 16 Clifford Street,**
London,
W1S 3RG 🅿
☎ 020 7434 9100 **ᗴ** 020 7434 9101
ᐃ enquires@keverne.co.uk
ⓦ www.keverne.co.uk
Est. 1996 *Stock size* Large
Stock Chinese ceramics, jade,
lacquer, bronzes, enamels, hard
stones, ivory, bamboo
Open Mon–Fri 9.30am–5.30pm
Sat for exhibitions
Fairs Exhibition at 16 Clifford
Street (Jun, Nov), International
Asian Art Fair, New York (March)
Services Valuations, restoration

⊞ D S Lavender Antiques
Ltd (BADA)
Contact Mr D Lavender
✉ **26 Conduit Street, London,**
W1S 2XX 🅿
☎ 020 7629 1782 **ᗴ** 020 7629 3106
ᐃ dslavender@clara.net
Est. 1946 *Stock size* Large
Stock Gold, silver, enamel fine
snuff boxes, fine jewels,
16th–early 19thC portrait
miniatures
Open Mon–Fri 9.30am–5pm
Services Restoration

⊞ Michael Lipitch Ltd
(BADA)
Contact Mr M Lipitch
✉ **Mayfair, London,**
W1K 2TX 🅿
☎ 020 8441 4340 (evenings)
ᴹ 07730 954347
ᐃ michaellipitch@hotmail.com
Est. 1960 *Stock size* Large
Stock 18thC fine furniture and
objects
Open By appointment
Fairs Grosvenor House, BADA,
Olympia (Nov)
Services Specialist advice on
forming collections

⊞ Sanda Lipton (BADA,
CINOA, BACA Award
Winner 2003)
Contact Sanda Lipton
✉ **3rd Floor, Elliott House,**
28a Devonshire Street, London,
W1G 6PS 🅿
☎ 020 7431 0866 **ᗴ** 020 7431 3224
ᴹ 07836 660008
ᐃ sanda@antique-silver.com
ⓦ www.antique-silver.com
Est. 1979 *Stock size* Medium
Stock 16th–mid 19thC silver,
collectors items, early English
spoons, historical medals
Open By appointment
Fairs Olympia, March BADA
Services Valuations, restoration,
consultancy, bidding at auction

⊞ Michael Longmore and
Trianon Antiques Ltd
(LAPADA)
Contact Michael Longmore
✉ **Stand 378,**
Grays Antique Market,
58 Davies Street,
London,
W1K 5LP 🅿
☎ 020 7491 2764 **ᗴ** 020 7409 1587
ᐃ michaellongmore@aol.com

Est. 1974 *Stock size* Large
Stock Fine jewellery, objets d'art
Open Mon–Fri 10am–5.30pm

⊞ Maggs Bros Ltd (ABA, BADA, PBFA)
Contact Mr Edward F Maggs
✉ 50 Berkeley Square,
London,
W1J 5BA 🅿
☎ 020 7493 7160 🖷 020 7499 2007
✉ ed@maggs.com
⊕ www.maggs.com
Est. 1853 *Stock size* Large
Stock Military history, travel, natural history, science, modern literature, early English and Continental books, illuminated manuscripts, autographed letters
Open Mon–Fri 9.30am–5pm
Fairs Olympia
Services Catalogues issued by all departments

⊞ Mallett at Bourdon House Ltd (BADA, SLAD, CINOA, BACA Award Winner 2003)
✉ 2 Davies Street,
London,
W1K 3DJ 🅿
☎ 020 7629 2444 🖷 020 7499 2670
✉ info@mallettantiques.com
⊕ www.mallettantiques.com
Est. 1860 *Stock size* Large
Stock 18th–19thC English, continental furniture, objets d'art, glass, needlework, 18th–19thC pictures
Open Mon–Fri 9am–6pm
Sat by appointment
Fairs Grosvenor House, Olympia, Miami, New York, Maastricht, San Francisco

⊞ Mallett & Son (Antiques) Ltd (BADA, SLAD, CINOA, BACA Award Winner 2003)
✉ 141 New Bond Street,
London,
W1S 2BS 🅿
☎ 020 7499 7411 🖷 020 7495 3179
✉ info@mallettantiques.com
⊕ www.mallettantiques.com
Est. 1865 *Stock size* Large
Stock 18th–19thC English, continental furniture, objet d'art, glass, needlework, 18th–19thC pictures
Open Mon–Fri 9am–6pm
Sat 10am–4pm
Fairs Grosvenor House, Asian &

Ceramics Fair, Olympia, Miami, New York
Services Restoration

⊞ Map World (LAPADA)
Contact Jeffrey Sharpe
✉ 25 Burlington Arcade,
Piccadilly, London,
W1V 9AD
☎ 020 7495 5377 🖷 020 7495 5377
✉ info@map-world.com
⊕ www.map-world.com
Est. 1982 *Stock size* Large
Stock 15th–19thC antique maps
Open Mon–Sat 10am–5.30pm
Services Valuations

⊞ Marks Antiques (BADA, LAPADA)
Contact Anthony Marks
✉ 128 Mount Street, London,
W1K 3NU
☎ 020 7499 1788 🖷 020 7409 3183
✉ info@marksantiques.com
⊕ www.marksantiques.com
Est. 1921 *Stock size* Large
Stock Fine Antique silver, works of art, Fabergé
Open Mon–Fri 9.30am–6pm
Sat 9.30am–5pm
Fairs Olympia, Grosvenor House
Services Valuations, Shipping

⊞ Marlborough Rare Books Ltd (ABA)
Contact Jonathan Gestetner
✉ 4th Floor,
144–146 New Bond Street,
London,
W1S 2TR
☎ 020 7493 6993 🖷 020 7499 2479
✉ sales@mrb-books.co.uk
⊕ www.mrb-books.co.uk
Est. 1948 *Stock size* Medium
Stock Antiquarian and rare art, architecture, illustrated, colour plate, fine bindings, English literature, topography, books on London
Open Mon–Fri 9.30am–5.30pm
Fairs Olympia, Chelsea, California, New York
Services Valuations

⊞ Massada Antiques (LAPADA)
Contact Mr B Yacobi or Mrs C Yacobi
✉ Bond Street Antiques Centre, 124 New Bond Street, London,
W1S 1DX 🅿
☎ 020 7493 5610 🖷 020 7491 9852
✉ byacobi@aol.com
Est. 1970 *Stock size* Large

Stock Georgian–Edwardian wearable, decorative jewellery
Open Mon–Sat 10am–5.30pm
Fairs Olympia (June, Nov)
Services Valuations, repairs

⊞ Mayfair Gallery Ltd
Contact Mrs C Giese
✉ 39 South Audley Street,
London,
W1K 2PP 🅿
☎ 020 7491 3435/3436
🖷 020 7491 3437
✉ mayfairgallery@mayfairgallery.com
Est. 1974 *Stock size* Large
Stock 19thC antiques, decorative arts, bronzes, marbles, Continental porcelain, furniture
Open Mon–Fri 9.30am–6pm
Sat by appointment
Fairs Olympia, Miami Beach
Services Valuations, restoration

⊞ Melton's
Contact Cecilia Neale
✉ 27 Bruton Place, London,
W1J 6NQ
☎ 020 7409 2938 🖷 020 7495 3196
✉ sales@meltons.co.uk
⊕ www.meltons.co.uk
Est. 1980 *Stock size* Medium
Stock Antiques and collectables
Open Mon–Fri 9.30am–5.30pm

⌂ The Mews Antique Market
Contact William Griffith or Kirstine Wallace
✉ 1–7 Davies Mews, London,
W1K 5AB 🅿
☎ 020 7629 7034 🖷 020 7493 9344
✉ grays@clara.net
⊕ www.graysantiques.com
Est. 1978 *Stock size* Large
No. of dealers 150
Stock Asian, Islamic antiquities, books, perfume bottles, Bohemian glass, ceramics, handbags, carpets, jewellery, militaria, pewter, teddy bears, dolls, toys, clocks, timepieces
Open Mon–Fri 10am–6pm
Services Restoration, repairs, restaurant

⊞ Michael's Boxes (PADA)
Contact Michael Cassidy
✉ Unit L15, The Mews Antique Market, 1–7 Davies Mews, London,
W1K 5AB 🅿
☎ 020 7629 5716 🖷 020 8930 8318
✉ info@michaelsboxes.com

ⓦ www.michaelsboxes.com
Est. 1997 *Stock size* Large
Stock Limoges, enamel and
porcelain antique boxes
Open Mon–Fri 10am–5pm
Fairs Portobello
Services Personalized boxes

⊞ Moira
Contact Mrs S Lauder
✉ 11 New Bond Street,
London,
W1S 3SR
☎ 020 7629 0160 ✆ 020 7495 3343
✉ info@moira-jewels.com
Est. 1970 *Stock size* Large
Stock Antique, modern and own
design jewellery
Open Mon–Sat 10am–5pm

⊞ Sydney L Moss Ltd (BADA)
Contact Paul G Moss or
Mr M Rutherston
✉ 51 Brook Street,
London,
W1Y 1AU ℙ
☎ 020 7629 4670 ✆ 020 7491 9278
✉ pasi@slmoss.com
ⓦ www.slmoss.com
Est. 1904 *Stock size* Large
Stock Chinese and Japanese
antiques, works of art, paintings
Open Mon–Fri 10am–5.30pm
Fairs International Asian Art Fair
New York
Services Valuations

⊞ Richard Ogden Ltd (BADA)
Contact Robert Ogden
✉ 28–29 Burlington Arcade,
London,
W1J 0NX ℙ
☎ 020 7493 9136 ✆ 020 7355 1508
✉ admin@richardogden.com
Est. 1948 *Stock size* Medium
Stock Traditional antiques,
jewellery
Open Mon–Sat 9.30am–5pm
Services Valuations

⊞ Pelham Galleries Ltd (BADA, CINOA)
Contact Mr Alan Rubin
✉ 24 & 25 Mount Street,
London,
W1K 2RR ℙ
☎ 020 7629 0905 ✆ 020 7495 4511
✉ antiques@pelhamgalleries.com
ⓦ www.pelhamgalleries.com
Est. 1928 *Stock size* Large
Stock English and European

furniture, 16th–19thC works of
art, early keyboard instruments
Open Mon–Fri 9am–5.30pm Sat
by appointment
Fairs Grosvenor House,
Maastricht, IFAAD show at The
Armory, New York
Services Valuations, shipping

⊞ Pendulum of Mayfair (BADA)
Contact Mr J D Clements
✉ King House,
51 Maddox Street,
London,
W1S 2PH
☎ 020 7629 6606 ✆ 020 7629 6616
✉ pendulumclocks@aol.com
ⓦ www.pendulumofmayfair.co.uk
Est. 1995 *Stock size* Large
Stock Genuine pre-1800 clocks,
including longcase, bracket, wall,
Georgian period furniture
Open Mon–Fri 10am–6pm Sat
10am–5pm or by appointment
Services Servicing, restoration,
valuation

⊞ Ronald Phillips Ltd (BADA)
Contact Mr S Phillips
✉ 26 Bruton Street,
London,
W1J 6QL ℙ
☎ 020 7493 2341 ✆ 020 7495 0843
✉ advice@ronaldphillips.co.uk
ⓦ www.ronaldphillips.couk
Est. 1952 *Stock size* Large
Stock 18thC English furniture,
glass, clocks, barometers, mirrors
Open Mon–Fri 9am–5.30pm
Sat by appointment
Fairs Grosvenor House

⊞ S J Phillips Ltd (BADA)
✉ 139 New Bond Street, London,
W1A 3DL
☎ 020 7629 6261 ✆ 020 7495 6180
✉ enquiries@sjphillips.com
ⓦ www.sjphillips.com
Est. 1869 *Stock size* Large
Stock Antique–20thC jewellery,
18thC silver
Open Mon–Fri 10am–5pm
Fairs Grosvenor House, TEFAF,
Maastricht
Services Restoration

⊞ Pickering and Chatto (ABA, PBFA)
Contact Mr J Hudson
✉ 36 St George Street, London,
W1S 2FW ℙ
☎ 020 7491 2656 ✆ 020 7491 9161

✉ rarebook@pickering-chatto.com
ⓦ www.pickering-chatto.com
Est. 1820 *Stock size* Medium
Stock Antiquarian, rare, second-
hand books on economics,
philosophy, medicine, general
literature
Open Mon–Fri 9.30am–5.30pm or
by appointment
Fairs Olympia
Services Book search valuations

⊞ Pieces of Time (BADA)
Contact Mr J Wachsmann
✉ Units 17–19, The Mews
Antique Market,
1–7 Davies Mews, London,
W1K 5AB ℙ
☎ 020 7629 2422 ✆ 020 7409 1625
✉ info@antique-watch.com
ⓦ www.antique-watch.com
Est. 1973 *Stock size* Large
Stock Antique pocket watches,
Judaica
Open Mon–Fri 10.30am–5pm

⊞ Nicholas S Pitcher Oriental Art
Contact Mr N S Pitcher
✉ 1st Floor, 29 New Bond Street,
London,
W1S 2RL ℙ
☎ 020 7499 6621 ✆ 020 7499 6621
📱 07831 391574
✉ nickpitcher@aol.com
ⓦ www.asianart.com/pitcher
Est. 1990 *Stock size* Medium
Stock Early Chinese ceramics,
works of art
Open By appointment
Fairs Arts of Pacific Asia Show,
New York, Asian Art London, Nov
Services Valuations

⊞ Jonathan Potter Ltd (ABA, BADA, LAPADA, PBFA)
Contact Mr J Potter
✉ 125 New Bond Street, London,
W1S 1DY ℙ
☎ 020 7491 3520 ✆ 020 7491 9754
✉ jpmaps@attglobal.net
ⓦ www.jpmaps.co.uk
Est. 1974 *Stock size* Large
Stock History of cartography
books, atlases, maps,
reproduction globes
Open Mon–Fri 10am–6pm
Sat by appointment
Fairs ABA, Olympia, IMCoS,
International Map Fair
Services Valuations, restoration,
framing

⊞ **Nick Potter Ltd**
Contact Nick Potter
✉ **34 Sackville Street, Mayfair,**
London,
W1S 3ED 🅿
☎ 020 7439 4029 📠 020 7439 4027
📧 art@nickpotter.com
🌐 www.nickpotter.com
Est. 1997 *Stock size* Medium
Stock Fine sporting pictures
1750–1940, prints, memorabilia
Open Mon–Fri 10am–5.30pm or
by appointment
Services Valuations, restoration

⊞ **Pullman Gallery Ltd**
Contact Mr S Khachadourian
✉ **116 Mount Street, Mayfair,**
London,
W1K 3NH 🅿
☎ 020 7499 8080 📠 020 7499 9090
📧 sk@pullmangallery.com
🌐 www.pullmangallery.com
Est. 1998 *Stock size* Large
Stock Automobilia, vintage
luggage
Open Mon–Fri 10am–6pm

⊞ **Bernard Quaritch Ltd**
(PBFA, ABA, BADA)
Contact Mr I Smith
✉ **8 Lower John Street,**
London,
W1F 9AU
☎ 020 7734 2983 📠 020 7734 0967
📧 rarebooks@quaritch.com
🌐 www.quaritch.com
Est. 1847 *Stock size* Large
Stock Antiquarian books
Open Mon–Fri 9am–6pm
Fairs Olympia, California,
New York
Services Valuations

⊞ **Rare Jewellery**
Collections Ltd (LAPADA,
CINOA)
Contact Elizabeth Powell
✉ **45–46 New Bond Street,**
London,
W1S 2SF 🅿
☎ 020 7499 5414 📠 020 7499 6906
📧 info@rarejewellerycollections.com
🌐 www.rarejewellerycollections.com
Est. 1983 *Stock size* Medium
Stock Vintage jewellery
Open By appointment only

⊞ **David Richards & Sons**
Contact Mr Richards
✉ **10 New Cavendish Street,**
London,
W1G 8UL 🅿

☎ 020 7935 3206/0322
📠 020 7224 4423
📧 richards@thesilvershop.net
🌐 www.the-silvershop.co.uk
Est. 1970 *Stock size* Large
Stock Modern and antique silver
and silver plate, decorative
items, flatware, silver jewellery
Open Mon–Fri 9.30am–6pm
Sat 10am–5pm
Services Valuations, restoration

⊞ **Rossi & Rossi Ltd**
Contact Mr Fabio Rossi
✉ **13 Old Bond Street,**
London,
W1S 4SX 🅿
☎ 020 7355 1804 📠 020 7355 1806
📧 info@rossirossi.com
🌐 www.asianart.com/rossi
Est. 1986 *Stock size* Medium
Stock Asian art, sculpture,
paintings from India and the
Himalayas, Chinese textiles
Open Mon–Fri 10.30am–5.30pm

⊞ **Alistair Sampson**
Antiques Ltd (BADA,
BACA Award Winner 2002)
Contact Mr A Sampson or
Mr C Banks
✉ **120 Mount Street,**
London,
W1K 3NN 🅿
☎ 020 7409 1799 📠 020 7409 7717
📧 info@alistairsampson.com
🌐 www.alistairsampson.com
Est. 1969 *Stock size* Large
Stock English pottery, oak,
country furniture, metalwork,
needlework, pictures,
17th–18thC decorative items
Open Mon–Fri 9.30am–5.30pm
Sat by appointment
Fairs Olympia, Grosvenor House

⊞ **Seaby Antiquities**
(ADA)
Contact Peter Clayton
✉ **14 Old Bond Street, London,**
W1S 4PP 🅿
☎ 020 7495 2590 📠 020 7491 1595
📧 minerva@minervamagazine.com
🌐 www.royalathena.com
Est. 1942 *Stock size* Small
Stock Museum quality antiquities
Open Mon–Fri 10am–5pm
Services Valuations

⊞ **Bernard J Shapero Rare**
Books (ABA, PBFA, BADA)
Contact Lucinda Boyle
✉ **32 St George Street, London,**

W1S 2EA 🅿
☎ 020 7493 0876 📠 020 7229 7860
📧 rarebooks@shapero.com
🌐 www.shapero.com
Est. 1979 *Stock size* Large
Stock 16th–20thC guide books,
antiquarian and rare books,
English and Continental
literature, specializing in travel,
natural history, colour plates
Open Mon–Fri 9.30am–6.30pm
Sat 11am–5pm August Mon–Fri
10am–5pm
Fairs Olympia
Services Valuations, restoration

⊞ **Shapiro & Co. (LAPADA)**
Contact Sheldon Shapiro
✉ **Stand 380, Grays Antique**
Market, 58 Davies Street,
London,
W1K 5LP
☎ 020 74912710 📠 020 74912710
📱 07768 840930
Est. 1982
Stock Jewellery, silver, objets
d'art, Imperial Russian works of
art
Open Mon–Fri 10am–6pm
Fairs Olympia, NEC

⊞ **Shiraz Antiques**
(BADA)
Contact Mr Reza Kiadeh
✉ **127 Davies Mews,**
London,
W1K 5AB 🅿
☎ 020 7495 0635 📠 020 7495 0635
📧 rezkia7@hotmail.com
Est. 1990 *Stock size* Medium
Stock Asian art, antiquities, glass,
marble, pottery
Open Mon–Fri 10am–6pm
Fairs BADA

⊞ **W Sitch (Antique) Co Ltd**
Contact Mr Sitch
✉ **48 Berwick Street,**
London,
W1V 4JD 🅿
☎ 020 7437 3776 📠 020 7437 5707
📧 wsitch-co@hotmail.com
🌐 www.wsitch.co.uk
Est. 1776 *Stock size* Large
Stock Lighting
Open Mon–Sat 8am–6pm
Services Valuations, restoration,
shipping

⊞ **R Solaimany**
Contact Mr R Solaimany
✉ **Unit A16, The Mews Antique**
Market, 1–7 Davies Mews,

London,
W1K 5AB
☎ 020 7491 2562 ☎ 020 7493 9344
Est. 1981 *Stock size* Medium
Stock Oriental ceramics, bronzes,
Roman glass
Open Mon–Fri 10am–6pm

🏹 **Sotheby's (BACA Award
Winner 2003)**
✉ 34–35 New Bond Street,
London,
W1A 2AA
☎ 020 7293 5000
🌐 www.sothebys.com
Est. 1744
Open Mon–Fri 9am–5.30pm
Sales International auctioneer of
fine art, furniture, jewellery,
decorative arts, collectables and
more. Services include
restoration, valuation, financial
service, picture library, on-line
auctions, Sotheby's International
Realty and Sotheby's Bookshop
Frequency Varies by month
Catalogues Yes

⊞ **Henry Sotheran Ltd
(ABA, PBFA, ILAB)**
Contact Mr A McGeachin
✉ 2 Sackville Street, Piccadilly,
London,
W1S 3DP
☎ 020 7439 6151 ☎ 020 7434 2019
📧 sotherans@sotherans.co.uk
🌐 www.sotherans.co.uk
Est. 1761 *Stock size* Large
Stock Antiquarian books on
English literature, natural history,
travel, children's illustrated,
modern first editions, prints, art,
architecture
Open Mon–Fri 9.30am–6pm
Sat 10am–4pm

⊞ **Spectrum**
Contact Mrs S Spectrum
✉ Stand 372,
Grays Antique Market,
58 Davies Street, London,
W1K 5LB
☎ 020 7629 3501 ☎ 020 8883 5030
📱 07770 753302
Est. 1979 *Stock size* Large
Stock Georgian seedpearl
necklaces, brooches,
Georgian–Victorian jewellery,
Georg Jensen jewellery
Open Mon–Fri 10am–6pm
Fairs NEC
Services Valuations, repairs,
stringing, design

⊞ **A and J Speelman Ltd
(BADA)**
Contact Mr J Speelman
or J Mann
✉ 129 Mount Street, London,
W1K 3NX
☎ 020 7499 5126 ☎ 020 7355 3391
📧 enquiries@ajspeelman.com
🌐 www.ajspeelman.com
Est. 1976 *Stock size* Large
Stock Oriental furniture,
porcelain, works of art
Open Mon–Fri 10am–6pm
Fairs New York, Asian Art Fair
Services Valuations, restoration

⊞ **St Petersburg
Collection Ltd**
Contact Mr B Lynch
✉ 42 Burlington Arcade, London,
W1J 0QG
☎ 020 7495 2883 ☎ 01895 810566
📧 creations@stpetersburg
collection.com
🌐 www.stpetersburgcollection.com
Est. 1989 *Stock size* Medium
Stock English and French objets
d'art, boxes, 19th–20thC silver,
glass, ormolu
Open Mon–Sat 10am–5pm

⊞ **Stair & Company Ltd
(BADA, CINOA)**
Contact Mr R Luck
✉ 14 Mount Street,
London,
W1K 2RF
☎ 020 7499 1784 ☎ 020 7269 1050
📧 stairandcompany@talk21.com
🌐 www.stairandcompany.com
Est. 1911 *Stock size* Large
Stock 18thC fine English
furniture, works of art
Open Mon–Fri 9.30am–5.30pm
or by appointment
Fairs Grosvenor House, BADA
Services Valuations, restoration

⊞ **E Swonnell Ltd**
Contact Miss S Swonnell
✉ 37 South Audley Street,
London,
W1K 2PN
☎ 020 7629 9649 ☎ 020 7629 9649
Est. 1957 *Stock size* Large
Stock 17th–19thC silver and
plate, large decorative items
Open Mon–Fri 9am–6pm
Services Valuations, restoration

⊞ **Tagore Ltd**
Contact Mr R Falloon
✉ Stand 302, Grays Antique

Market, 58 Davies Street,
London,
W1Y 2LP
☎ 020 7499 0158 ☎ 020 7499 0158
📧 grays@clara.net
Est. 1977 *Stock size* Large
Stock 20thC drinking, smoking,
gambling collectors' items, silver,
glass, gentlemen's gifts
Open Mon–Fri 10am–6pm
Services Valuations

⊞ **Textile-Art: The Textile
Gallery (BADA)**
Contact Michael Franses or
Nicholas Waterhouse
✉ 12 Queen Street, Mayfair,
London,
W1J 5PG
☎ 020 7499 7979 ☎ 020 7409 2596
📱 07836 321461
📧 post@textile-art.com
🌐 www.textile-art.com
Est. 1972
Stock Textile art from China,
Central Asia, India and Ottoman
Empire, 300BC–1800AD, classical
carpets 1400–1700
Open Mon–Fri by appointment
10.30am–6pm
Fairs The European Fine Art Fair,
Maastricht, Summer Olympia
Services Conservation of
important textiles to museum
standards

⊞ **Toynbee-Clarke
Interiors Ltd**
Contact Mrs Daphne Toynbee-
Clarke
✉ 18 Cresswell Place,
London,
SW10 9RB
☎ 020 7373 6889
Est. 1959 *Stock size* Medium
Stock Continental furniture, works
of art, 18th–19thC Chinese hand-
painted export wallpapers, early
19thC French panoramic papers
Open Mon–Fri 11am–5.30pm or
by appointment
Services Restoration

⊞ **Trianon Antiques Ltd
(LAPADA, LJAJDA)**
Contact Miss L Horton
✉ Bond Street Antiques Centre,
124 New Bond Street,
London,
W1S 1DX
☎ 020 7629 6678 ☎ 020 7355 2055
📧 trianonantiques@hotmail.com
Est. 1974 *Stock size* Large

Stock Fine jewellery, objets d'art
Open Mon–Sat 10am–5.30pm
Fairs Olympia (June), Miami

⊞ Jan Van Beers Oriental Art (BADA)
Contact Mr J Van Beers
✉ 34 Davies Street,
London,
W1K 4NE 🅿
☎ 020 7408 0434 📠 020 7355 1397
📧 jan@vanbeers.demon.co.uk
🌐 www.janvanbeers.com
Est. 1978 *Stock size* Large
Stock Chinese and Japanese antiques, ceramics, works of art
Open Mon–Fri 10am–6pm
Fairs Asian Art Fair New York
Services Valuations

⊞ Vigo Carpet Gallery (LAPADA)
Contact Nadia Mair
✉ 6A Vigo Street, London,
W1S 3HF 🅿
☎ 020 7439 6971 📠 020 7439 2353
📧 vigo@btinternet.com
Est. 1980 *Stock size* Large
Stock Hand-made antique carpets
Open Mon–Fri 10am–6pm
Sat 11am–5pm
Fairs HALI Antique Textile Art Fair

⊞ Vinci Antiques
Contact Mr A Vinci
✉ 27 Avery Row, London,
W1K 4AY 🅿
☎ 020 7499 1041
Est. 1974 *Stock size* Large
Stock Objets d'art, objects of virtue, silver, porcelain, glass, paintings, jewellery, bronzes, miniatures
Open Mon–Sat 9am–7pm

⊞ Rupert Wace Ancient Art Ltd (ADA, IADAA, BADA)
Contact Mr R Wace
✉ 14 Old Bond Street,
London,
W1X 3DB 🅿
☎ 020 7495 1623 📠 020 7495 8495
📧 info@rupertwace.co.uk
🌐 www.rupertwace.co.uk
Est. 1987 *Stock size* Large
Stock Antiquities, Greek, Roman, ancient Egyptian, Near Eastern, Celtic, Dark Ages
Open Mon–Fri 10am–5pm or by appointment
Services Valuations

⊞ Westminster Group Antique Jewellery (LAPADA)
Contact Mr R Harrison
✉ Stand 150, Grays Antique Market, 58 Davies Street, London,
W1K 2LP 🅿
☎ 020 7493 8672 📠 020 7493 8672
Est. 1976 *Stock size* Large
Stock Victorian–Edwardian second-hand jewellery, watches
Open Mon–Fri 10am–6pm

⊞ Wheels of Steel
Contact Jeff Williams
✉ Stand A12–13, Unit B10, Basement, The Mews Antique Market, 1–7 Davies Mews, London,
W1Y 2LP
☎ 020 7629 2813
Est. 1976 *Stock size* Large
Stock Model trains
Open Mon–Fri 10.30am–6pm

⊞ Wilkinson PLC
Contact Mark Savin
✉ 1 Grafton Street, London,
W1S 4EA 🅿
☎ 020 7495 2477 📠 020 7491 1737
📧 enquiries@wilkinson-plc.com
🌐 www.wilkinson-plc.com
Est. 1946 *Stock size* Large
Stock Lighting, chandeliers, candelabra
Open Mon–Fri 9.30am–5pm
Services Restoration

⊞ Wimpole Antiques (LAPADA)
Contact Lyn Lindsay
✉ Stand 349, Grays Antique Market, 58 Davies Street, London,
W1Y 1LB
☎ 020 7499 2889 📠 020 7499 2889
📧 WimpoleAntiques@compuserve.com
Est. 1977 *Stock size* Large
Stock Affordable, wearable jewellery, 1780–1960, Victorian jewellery
Open Mon–Fri 10am–6pm
Fairs Olympia, NEC, LAPADA
Services Valuations, repairs, pearl stringing

⊞ Windsor House Antiques Ltd (LAPADA)
Contact Dr Kevin Smith
✉ 28–29 Dover Street, London,
WIS 4NA
☎ 020 7659 0340 📠 020 7499 6728
📧 sales@windsorhouseantiques.co.uk
🌐 www.windsorhouseantiques.co.uk
Est. 1958 *Stock size* Large
Stock 18th–19thC English furniture, decorative accessories
Open Mon–Fri 9.30am–6pm or by appointment
Fairs Claridges

⊞ Linda Wrigglesworth Ltd
Contact Gary Dickinson
✉ 34 Brook Street,
London,
W1K 5DN 🅿
☎ 020 7486 8990 📠 020 7935 1511
📧 info@lindawrigglesworth.com
🌐 www.lindawrigglesworth.com
Est. 1977
Stock Chinese court costumes, Tibetan and Korean textiles
Open Mon–Fri 11am–7pm by appointment
Fairs Grosvenor House

W2

⊞ Sean Arnold Sporting Antiques (PADA)
Contact Sean Arnold
✉ 21–22 Chepstow Corner, off Westbourne Grove, London,
W2 4XE 🅿
☎ 020 7221 2267 📠 020 7221 5464
Est. 1977 *Stock size* Large
Stock Sporting antiques, luggage, globes
Open Mon–Sat 10am–6pm or by appointment
Services Valuations, restoration

⊞ Gallery of Antique Costume & Textiles
Contact Justin Segal
✉ Connaught Street, London,
W2 🅿
☎ 020 7723 9981 📠 020 7723 9981
📧 info@gact.co.uk
🌐 www.gact.co.uk
Est. 1980 *Stock size* Medium
Stock Antique textiles, curtains, cushions, antique costumes, 1900–1960s vintage bridal wear
Open Tues–Sat by Appointment
Fairs HALI Antique Textile Art Fair, Olympia

⊞ Mark Gallery (BADA, CINOA)
Contact Helen Mark
✉ 9 Porchester Place, Marble Arch, London,
W2 2BS 🅿
☎ 020 7262 4906 📠 020 7224 9416

info@markgallery.co.uk
www.markgallery.co.uk
Est. 1970
Stock 16th–19thC Russian and
Greek icons, contemporary and
modern French lithographs and
etchings
Open Mon–Fri 10am–1pm 2–6pm
Sat by appointment 11am–1pm
Fairs Olympia, Cologne
Services Valuations, restoration

Reel Poster Gallery
Contact Mr Tony Nourmand
72 Westbourne Grove,
London,
W2 5SH
020 7727 4488 020 7727 4499
info@reelposter.com
www.reelposter.com
Est. 1989
Stock Original vintage film
posters
Open Mon–Fri 11am–7pm
Sat noon–6pm
Services Valuations, annual
catalogue

Zeitgeist Antiques
Contact Mr A Self
Notting Hill, London,
W2
020 7727 7660 020 7727 7660
07711 079708
adself@btinternet.com
www.zeitgeistantiques.com
Est. 1988 *Stock size* Small
Stock Art Nouveau, Art Deco,
glass, ceramics, metalware,
1940's antiques
Open By appointment only
Fairs Antiques for Everyone,
Glasgow and London

W3

Chiswick and West Middlesex Auctions
Contact Mr D Wells or
Mr T Keane
1 Colville Road,
London,
W3 8BL
020 8992 4442 020 8896 0541
www.chiswickauctions.co.uk
Est. 1992
Open Mon–Fri 10am–6pm
Sales Antiques and general
effects Tues noon, viewing
Sun noon–6pm Mon 10am–6pm
Tues 10am–noon
Frequency Weekly
Catalogues Yes

W4

Blackwood Cowell Antiques
Contact Jim Blackwood or
Anthony Cowell
61 South Parade, Chiswick,
London,
W4 5LG
020 8987 3117
Est. 2004 *Stock size* Large
Stock Period chandeliers and
lighting, fine English and
Continental furniture, mirrors,
paintings, quality decorative art
Open Tues–Sat 10.30am–6.30pm
of by appointment
Services Valuations, restoration

The Chiswick Fireplace Co
Contact Rosemary O'Grady
68 Southfield Road,
London,
W4 1BD
020 8995 4011 020 8995 4012
Est. 1990 *Stock size* Medium
Stock Original Art Nouveau,
Edwardian, Victorian fireplaces,
marble, limestone and wood
surrounds
Open Mon–Sat 9.30am–5pm

Chiswick Park Antiques
Contact Mr Azzariti
2 Chiswick Park Station,
London,
W4 5EB
020 8995 8930
Est. 1965 *Stock size* Medium
Stock Mirrors, furniture, clocks
Open Mon–Sat 11am–6pm
Services Restoration

David Edmonds Indian Furniture
Contact David Edmonds
1–4 Prince of Wales Terrace,
London,
W4 2EY
020 8742 1920 020 8742 3030
07831 666436
dareindia@aol.com
Est. 1987 *Stock size* Large
Stock Fine quality Indian furniture,
antiques, architectural items
Open Mon–Sat 10am–5pm
Sun by appointment
Services Valuations, repairs

W A Foster (PBFA)
Contact Mr Foster
183 Chiswick High Road,
London,
W4 2DR
020 8995 2768
Est. 1968 *Stock size* Medium
Stock Antiquarian, rare, second-
hand books, fine bindings,
illustrated children's books
Open Thurs–Sat 10.30am–5.30pm
Fairs PBFA Hotel Russell

Harmers of London Stamp Auctioneer Ltd (PTS)
Contact Dominic Savastano
111 Power Road, Chiswick,
London,
W4 5PY
020 8747 6100 020 8996 0649
auctions@harmers.demon.co.uk
www.harmers.com
Est. 1918
Open Mon–Fri 9am–5pm
(valuations 9.30am–4pm)
Sales Philatelic auctions every
6 weeks, ring for details
Catalogues Yes

Minerva Antiques
Contact Jonathan Atkins
160 Chiswick High Road,
London,
W4 1PR
020 8995 4166
sales@minerva-antiques.co.uk
www.minerva-antiques.co.uk
Est. 1986 *Stock size* Medium
Stock Fully restored Georgian
and Victorian antiques furniture,
English and French gilded mirrors
Open Tues–Sat 10am–6pm
Sun noon–5pm
Services Valuations, restoration,
upholstery

The Old Cinema
Contact Mr K Norris
160 Chiswick High Road,
London,
W4 1PR
020 8995 4166 020 8995 4167
theoldcinema@antiques-
uk.co.uk
www.theoldcinema.co.uk
Est. 1980 *Stock size* Large
Stock Furniture, clothing,
jewellery, decorative metal
and glass, Georgian–Art Deco
furniture, also retro, industrial,
vintage
Open Mon–Sat 9.30am–6pm
Sun noon–5pm
Services Upholstery, restoration,
transport

97

⊞ Strand Antiques
Contact Mrs A Brown
✉ **46 Devonshire Road,
London,
W4 2HD** 🅿
☎ 020 8994 1912
Est. 1977 *Stock size* Large
Stock English and French
furniture, glass, lighting,
jewellery, silver, garden items,
kitchenware, books, prints,
textiles, collectables
Open Tues–Sat 10.30am–5.30pm
Services Furniture restoration

W5

⊞ Harold's Place
Contact Miss Warner
✉ **148 South Ealing Road, Ealing,
London,
W5 4QJ** 🅿
☎ 020 8579 4825
Est. 1976 *Stock size* Medium
Stock Antique china, glass,
decorative items
Open Mon–Sat 9.30am–5.30pm

W8

⊞ Abstract/Noonstar
(LAPADA)
Contact Galya Aytac or
Juliette Boagers
✉ **58–60 Kensington Church
Street, London,
W8 4DB**
☎ 020 7376 2652 🖷 020 7376 2652
📱 07770 281301
📧 galya53@aol.com
🌐 www.abstract-antiques.com
Est. 1980 *Stock size* Medium
Stock 20thC decorative arts,
Art Nouveau, Art Deco
Open Mon–Sat 11am–5pm
Services Valuations, shipping

⊞ Antik West Oriental Art
& Antiques (CINOA)
Contact Mr J Robinson or
B Gremner
✉ **at Patrick Sandberg Antiques,
150–152 Kensington Church
Street, London,
W8 4BH** 🅿
☎ 020 7229 4115 🖷 020 7792 3467
📧 china@antikwest.com
🌐 www.antikwest.com
Est. 1980 *Stock size* Large
Stock Oriental porcelain, pottery
Open Mon–Fri 10am–6pm
Sat 10am–4pm
Fairs Gothenburg,

Sweden (Oct), Asian Art in
London (Nov)
Services Valuations, restoration

⊞ Artemis Decorative
Arts Ltd (LAPADA)
Contact Mr M Jones
✉ **36 Kensington Church Street,
London,
W8 4BX** 🅿
☎ 020 7376 0377 🖷 020 7376 0377
📧 artemis.w8@btinternet.com
Est. 1994 *Stock size* Medium
Stock Art Nouveau, Art Deco,
glass, bronze, ivory, furniture
Open Mon–Fri 10am–6pm
Sat 11am–5pm

⊞ Gregg Baker Asian Art
(BADA, LAPADA, CINOA)
Contact Mr G Baker
✉ **142 Kensington Church Street,
London,
W8 4BN** 🅿
☎ 020 7221 3533 🖷 020 7221 4410
📧 gregg@japanesescreens.com
🌐 www.japanesescreens.com
Est. 1984 *Stock size* Medium
Stock Japanese screens, Japanese
and Chinese works of art
Open Tues–Fri 10am–6pm
Sat 11am–4pm
Fairs Grosvenor House,
International Asian Art Fair,
New York

⊞ Eddy Bardawil (BADA)
Contact Mr E Bardawil
✉ **106 Kensington Church Street,
London,
W8 4BH** 🅿
☎ 020 7221 3967 🖷 020 7221 5124
🌐 Gallery at www.bada.org
Est. 1982 *Stock size* Medium
Stock 18th–19thC English
furniture, works of art
Open Mon–Fri 10am–6pm
Sat 10am–1pm
Services Restoration

⊞ David Brower (KCSADA,
BACA Award Winner 2004)
Contact Mr D Brower
✉ **113 Kensington Church Street,
London,
W8 7LN** 🅿
☎ 020 7221 4155 🖷 020 7221 6211
📱 07831 234343
📧 David@davidbrower-antiques.com
🌐 www.davidbrower-antiques.com
Est. 1969 *Stock size* Large
Stock Meissen, KPM, European
and Asian porcelain,

French bronzes, Japanese works
of art
Open Mon–Fri 10am–6pm
Sat by appointment
Fairs Olympia (June)

⊞ Butchoff Interiors
(LAPADA, BADA, CINOA,
BACA Award Winner 2004)
Contact Mr A Kaye
✉ **154 Kensington Church Street,
London,
W8 4BN** 🅿
☎ 020 7221 8174 🖷 020 7792 8923
📧 enquiries@butchoff.com
🌐 www.butchoff.com
Est. 1999 *Stock size* Large
Stock One-off items, textiles,
collectables, dining tables, chairs,
consoles, accessories, decorative
furniture
Open Mon–Fri 9.30am–6pm
Sat 9.30am–4pm

⊞ Cohen & Cohen (BADA,
KCSADA)
Contact Mr M Cohen or
Mrs E Cohen
✉ **101b Kensington Church
Street, London,
W8 7LN** 🅿
☎ 020 7727 7677 🖷 020 7229 9653
📧 info@cohenandcohen.co.uk
Est. 1973 *Stock size* Large
Stock Chinese export porcelain,
works of art
Open Mon–Fri 10am–6pm
Sat by appointment
Fairs Grosvenor House

⊞ Mrs M.E. Crick
Chandeliers
Contact Mr N Denton
✉ **166 Kensington Church Street,
London,
W8 4BN**
☎ 020 7229 1338 🖷 020 7792 1073
🌐 www.crick-chandeliers.co.uk
Est. 1897 *Stock size* Large
Stock French and English
chandeliers, lighting, table
lamps, 1750–1920
Open Mon–Fri 9.30am–5.30pm

⊞ Barry Davies Oriental
Art (BADA)
Contact Barry Davies
✉ **PO Box 34867,
London,
W8 6WH** 🅿
☎ 020 7408 0207 🖷 020 7352 9514
📧 bdoa@btopenworld.com
🌐 www.barrydavies.com

Est. 1976 *Stock size* Large
Stock Japanese works of art
Open By appointment

⊞ Decor Antique Chandeliers (KCSADA)
Contact John Slattery
✉ **125 Kensington Church Street,**
London,
W8 7LP 🅿
☎ 020 7221 1080 📠 020 7792 3404
Est. 1947 *Stock size* Large
Stock Chandeliers
Open Mon–Fri 11am–5pm, Sat,
Sun 10am–5pm

⊞ Denton Antiques
Contact Mr N Denton
✉ **156 Kensington Church Street,**
London,
W8 4BN 🅿
☎ 020 7229 5866 📠 020 7792 1073
🌐 www.denton-antiques.co.uk
Est. 1897 *Stock size* Large
Stock French and English
chandeliers, lighting, table
lamps, 1750–1920
Open Mon–Fri 9.30am–5.30pm

⊞ Didier Antiques (LAPADA)
Contact Didier Haspeslagh
✉ **58–60 Kensington Church**
Street, Kensington,
London,
W8 4DB 🅿
☎ 020 7938 2537 📠 020 7938 2537
📱 07973 800415
📧 didier.antiques@virgin.net.
🌐 www.didierantiques.com
Est. 1989 *Stock size* Large
Stock Late 19th–early 20thC Arts
and Crafts, Art Nouveau,
jewellery, silver, 1960s–1970s
designer jewellery
Open By appointment
Fairs Olympia (June, Nov)

⊞ C. Fredericks and Son (BADA, KCSADA)
Contact Richard Fredericks
✉ **142 Kensington Church Street,**
London,
W8 4BN 🅿
☎ 020 7727 2240 📠 020 7727 2240
📧 antiques@cfredericksandson.
freeserve.co.uk
🌐 www.cfredericksandson.com
Est. 1947 *Stock size* Medium
Stock 18thC English furniture
Open Mon–Fri 9.30am–5.30pm
Fairs BADA Olympia (Nov)
Services Restoration

⊞ Michael German Antiques Ltd (BADA, LAPADA)
Contact Mr M German or
Mr D Strickland
✉ **38b Kensington Church Street,**
London,
W8 4BX 🅿
☎ 020 7937 2771 📠 020 7937 8566
📧 info@antiquecanes.com or
info@antiqueweapons.com
🌐 www.antiquecanes.com or
www.antiqueweapons.com
Est. 1973 *Stock size* Large
Stock Antique walking canes,
antique arms, armour
Open Mon–Fri 10am–5pm
Sat 10am–1pm

⊞ Green's Antique Galleries
Contact Sidney Green
✉ **117 Kensington Church Street,**
London,
W8 7LN
☎ 020 7229 9618
Est. 1952 *Stock size* Medium
Stock General antiques
Open Mon–Sat 9.30am–5.30pm

⊞ Adrian Harrington (ABA, PBFA, ILAB)
Contact Adrian Harrington,
Jon Gilbert or Pierre Lambardini
✉ **64a Kensington Church Street,**
London,
W8 4DB 🅿
☎ 020 7937 1465 📠 020 7368 0912
📧 rare@harringtonbooks.co.uk
🌐 www.harringtonbooks.co.uk
Est. 1964 *Stock size* Large
Stock Antiquarian and rare
books, specializing in literature,
modern first editions, children's
books, library sets, travel
Open Mon–Sat 10am–6pm
Fairs Olympia, Chelsea Town Hall
Services Valuations

⊞ Haslam & Whiteway
Contact Helen Duntan
✉ **105 Kensington Church Street,**
London,
W8 7LN
☎ 020 7229 1145
Est. 1972 *Stock size* Medium
Stock 19thC British design
Open Mon–Fri 10am–6pm
Sat 10am–4pm

⊞ Jeanette Hayhurst (BADA)
Contact Mrs J Hayhurst

✉ **32a Kensington Church Street,**
London,
W8 4HA 🅿
☎ 020 7938 1539
Est. 1979 *Stock size* Medium
Stock 18thC glass, specializing in
English drinking glasses
Open Mon–Fri 10am–5pm Sat
noon–5pm or by appointment
Fairs BADA, Harrogate, NEC

⊞ Brian and Lynn Holmes (LAPADA)
Contact Brian or Lynn Holmes
✉ **London,**
W8
☎ 020 7368 6412 📠 020 7368 6412
Est. 1971 *Stock size* Medium
Stock Antique Georgian,
Victorian silver, gold and
jewellery, Scottish antique
jewellery
Open By appointment only

⊞ Hope & Glory (KCSADA)
Contact Mr J Pym
✉ **131a Kensington Church**
Street (Entrance in Peel Street),
London,
W8 7LP 🅿
☎ 020 7727 8424
Est. 1982 *Stock size* Large
Stock Commemorative ceramics,
Royal, political etc
Open Mon–Sat 10am–5pm

⊞ Jonathan Horne (BADA, CINOA)
Contact Mr S Westman or
Jonathan Horne
✉ **66c Kensington Church Street,**
London,
W8 4BY 🅿
☎ 020 7221 5658 📠 020 7792 3090
📧 jh@jonathanhorne.co.uk
🌐 www.jonathanhorne.co.uk
Est. 1968 *Stock size* Large
Stock Early English pottery,
medieval–1820
Open Mon–Fri 9.30am–5.30pm
Fairs BADA, Olympia (June, Nov),
Buxton (May)
Services Valuations

⊞ Iona Antiques (BADA)
Contact Stephen Joseph
✉ **PO Box 285, London,**
W8 6HZ 🅿
☎ 020 7602 1193
📠 020 7371 2843
📧 iona@ionaantiques.com
🌐 www.ionaantiques.com
Est. 1974 *Stock size* Large

Stock 19thC paintings of animals
Open By appointment
Fairs Grosvenor House, Olympia
(June)

⊞ **J A N Fine Art
(KCSADA)**
Contact F K Shimizu
✉ 134 Kensington Church Street,
Kensington,
London,
W8 4BH 🄿
☎ 020 7792 0736 🖷 020 7221 1380
🄴 fusashimizu@aol.com
Est. 1979 Stock size Medium
Stock Japanese, Chinese, Korean
ceramics, bronzes, works of art
Open Mon–Fri 10am–6pm
Sat by appointment

⊞ **Jag Applied and
Decorative Arts
(Decorative Arts Society)**
Contact C A Warner, G J Morgan
or G S Strickland
✉ 58–60 Kensington Church
Street, London,
W8 4DB 🄿
☎ 020 7938 4404 🖷 020 7938 4404
🄼 07974 567507
🄴 jag@jagdecorativearts.com
🄦 www.jagdecorativearts.com
Est. 1990 Stock size Medium
Stock Liberty pewter and silver,
Art Nouveau metal, glass
decorative items
Open Mon–Sat 11am–5pm

⊞ **Japanese Gallery Ltd
(Ukiyo-e Society)**
Contact Mr C D Wertheim
✉ 66d Kensington Church Street,
London,
W8 4BY 🄿
☎ 020 7229 2934 🖷 020 7229 2934
🄼 07930 411991
🄴 info@japanesegallery.co.uk
🄦 www.japanesegallery.co.uk
Est. 1978 Stock size Large
Stock Japanese woodcut prints,
Japanese ceramics, sword
armour, Japanese dolls
Open Mon–Sat 10am–6pm
Services Exhibitions every three
months of Japanese prints,
Japanese-speaking staff

⊞ **Roderick Jellicoe
(BADA, KCSADA, BACA
Award Winner 2001)**
✉ 3a Campden Street, off
Kensington Church Street,
London,

W8 7EP 🄿
☎ 020 7727 1571 🖷 020 7727 1805
🄴 jellicoe@englishporcelain.com
🄦 www.englishporcelain.com
Est. 1975
Stock 18thC English porcelain
Open Mon–Fri 10am–5.30pm
Sat by appointment
Fairs NY Ceramics fair

⊞ **John Jesse**
Contact John Jesse
✉ 160 Kensington Church Street,
London,
W8 4BN 🄿
☎ 020 7229 0312 🖷 020 7229 4732
🄼 07767 497880
🄴 jj@johnjesse.com
Est. 1963 Stock size Medium
Stock 20thC decorative arts,
sculpture, glass, ceramics, silver,
jewellery
Open Mon–Fri 10am–5.30pm
Sat 11am–4pm

⊞ **Howard Jones, The
Silver Shop (LAPADA)**
Contact Howard Jones
✉ 43 Kensington Church Street,
London,
W8 4BA 🄿
☎ 020 7937 4359 🖷 020 7937 4359
🄴 sjsilvershop@aol.com
🄦 www.silvershop.com
Est. 1979 Stock size Small
Stock Antique and modern silver,
trinket boxes, picture frames,
cufflinks, jewellery
Open Tues–Sat 10am–5.30pm

⊞ **Peter Kemp**
Contact Mr P Kemp
✉ 170 Kensington Church Street,
London,
W8 4BN 🄿
☎ 020 7229 2988 🖷 020 7229 2988
🄼 07836 282285
🄴 peterkemp@btinternet.com
Est. 1971 Stock size Large
Stock 18thC Oriental, European
porcelain, works of art
Open Mon–Fri 10.30am–5.30pm
or by appointment

⊞ **The Lacquer Chest**
Contact Mrs G Andersen
✉ 75 Kensington Church Street,
London,
W8 4BG 🄿
☎ 020 7937 1306 🖷 020 7376 0223
🄴 email@laquerchest.freeserve.co.uk
Est. 1959 Stock size Large
Stock Military chests, china,

clocks, samplers, lamps
Open Mon–Fri 9.30am–5.30pm
Sat 10.30am–4.30pm
Services Prop hire of antiques

⊞ **Lev Antiques Ltd**
Contact Alyson Lawrence
✉ 97a Kensington Church Street,
London,
W8 7LN 🄿
☎ 020 7727 9248
🄼 07768 470473
🄴 alyson@richardlawrence.co.uk
Est. 1882 Stock size Medium
Stock Jewellery, silver, paintings,
objets d'art, antiquities
Open Tues–Sat 10.30am–5.45pm
Mon noon–5.30pm
Services Oil painting restoration

⊞ **Libra Antiques**
Contact Mrs A Wolsey
✉ 131d Kensington Church
Street, London,
W8 7PT 🄿
☎ 020 7727 2990
Est. 1979 Stock size Large
Stock English blue and white
pottery 1790–1820, creamware
Open Mon–Fri 10am–5pm
Sat 10am–4pm

⊞ **London Antique Gallery**
Contact Mr C D Wertheim
✉ 66e Kensington Church Street,
London,
W8 4BY 🄿
☎ 020 7229 2934 🖷 020 7229 2934
🄼 07930 411991
🄴 sales@japanesegallery.co.uk
Est. 1996 Stock size Medium
Stock Meissen, Dresden,
Worcester, Minton, Shelley,
Sèvres, Lalique, bisque dolls
Open Mon–Sat 10am–6pm
Services Restoration, framing

⊞ **Mah's Antiques**
Contact Mr Mah
✉ 141 Kensington Church Street,
London,
W8 7LP 🄿
☎ 020 7229 9047 🖷 020 7229 9047
Est. 1994 Stock size Large
Stock Oriental and European
porcelain, works of art
Open Mon–Fri 10.30am–5.30pm
Services Valuations, restoration

⊞ **E and H Manners
(BADA)**
Contact Errol Manners
✉ 66a Kensington Church Street,

London,
W8 4BY 🅿
☎ 020 7229 5516 🖷 020 7229 5516
📱 07767 250763
📧 manners@europeanporcelain.com
🌐 www.europeanporcelain.com
Est. 1986 *Stock size* Medium
Stock 18thC European porcelain, pottery
Open Mon–Fri 10am–5.30pm
Fairs International Ceramics Fair

S Marchant & Son (BADA, KCSADA)
Contact Mr S Marchant or Mr R Marchant
✉ 120 Kensington Church Street, London,
W8 4BH 🅿
☎ 020 7229 5319 🖷 020 7792 8979
📧 gallery@marchantasianart.com
🌐 www.marchantasianart.com
Est. 1925 *Stock size* Large
Stock Chinese porcelain, works of art, snuff bottles, jade
Open Mon–Fri 9.30am–5.30pm
Fairs Grosvenor House, International Asian Art
Services Valuations

R & G McPherson Antiques (BADA)
Contact Robert McPherson
✉ 40 Kensington Church Street, London,
W8 4BX 🅿
☎ 020 7937 0812 🖷 020 7938 2032
📱 07768 432630
📧 rmcpherson@orientalceramics.com
🌐 www.orientalceramics.com
Est. 1987 *Stock size* Medium
Stock Chinese, Japanese ceramics before 1820
Open Mon–Fri 10.30am–5.30pm
Fairs Asian art exhibition
Services Valuations

Michael Coins
Contact Mr M Gouby
✉ 6 Hillgate Street, London,
W8 7SR 🅿
☎ 020 7727 1518 🖷 020 7727 1518
📧 michael@michael-coins.co.uk
🌐 www.michael-coins.co.uk
Est. 1966 *Stock size* Medium
Stock English and foreign, medieval–present day coins, banknotes
Open Mon–Fri 10am–5pm

Colin D Monk
Contact Mr C Monk
✉ 58–60 Kensington

Church Street, London,
W8 4DB 🅿
☎ 020 7229 3727 🖷 020 7376 1501
📧 colindmonk@yahoo.co.uk
Stock size Medium
Stock Oriental porcelain
Open Mon–Sat 11am–5pm

Nassirzadeh Antiques
Contact Mr Houshang
✉ 178 Kensington Church Street, London,
W8 4DP
☎ 020 7243 8262 🖷 020 7243 8262
📱 07958 626777
📧 houshang.nassirzadeh@btconnect.com
Stock size Large
Stock Porcelain, glass, textiles
Open Mon–Sat 11am–6pm

Pruskin Galleries
Contact Michael Pruskin
✉ 50 & 73 Kensington Church High Street, London,
W8 4BG 🅿
☎ 020 7937 1994 🖷 020 7376 1285
📧 pruskin@pruskingallery.demon.co.uk
Est. 1977 *Stock size* Large
Stock Decorative art, paintings, furniture, ceramics, jewellery, glass
Open Mon–Fri 10am–6pm
Sat 11am–5pm

Raffety & Walwyn Ltd (BADA, CINOA, LAPADA)
Contact Nigel Raffety or Howard Walwyn
✉ 79 Kensington Church Street, London,
W8 4BG 🅿
☎ 020 7938 1100 🖷 020 7938 2519
📧 raffety@globalnet.co.uk
🌐 www.raffetyantiqueclocks.com
Est. 1982 *Stock size* Medium
Stock Late 17th–18thC clocks, barometers, furniture
Open Mon–Fri 10am–6pm
Sat by appointment
Fairs BADA, Grosvenor House, Olympia (June)

Paul Reeves
Contact Mr Paul Reeves or Ms Sarah Barrett
✉ 32b Kensington Church Street, London,
W8 4HA
☎ 020 7937 1594 🖷 020 7938 2163
🌐 www.paulreeveslondon.com
Est. 1976 *Stock size* Large
Stock Victorian–Edwardian

furniture, artefacts, textiles, glass, ceramics, metalwork, Arts and Crafts, Aesthetic Movement, Gothic Revival
Open Mon–Fri 10am–5.30pm

Reindeer Antiques Ltd (BADA, LAPADA)
Contact Peter Alexander
✉ 81 Kensington Church Street, London,
W8 4BG 🅿
☎ 020 7937 3754 🖷 020 7937 7199
📧 pejwal@hotmail.com
🌐 www.reindeerantiques.co.uk
Est. 1969 *Stock size* Large
Stock Fine period English furniture, 17th–19thC mahogany, walnut, oak mirrors, paintings, objets d'art
Open Mon–Sat 9.30am–6pm
Fairs BADA (March), LAPADA (Oct), NEC
Services Valuations, restoration

Roderick Antique Clocks (LAPADA, KCSADA)
Contact Mr R Mee
✉ 23 Vicarage Gate, (Junction Kensington Church Street), London,
W8 4AA 🅿
☎ 020 7937 8517
📧 rick@roderickantiqueclocks.com
🌐 www.roderickantiqueclocks.com
Est. 1975 *Stock size* Large
Stock Antique clocks, 1700–1920, including bracket, Vienna, longcase, carriage, English, French, German
Open Mon–Fri 10am–5.30pm
Sat 10am–4pm
Services Valuations, repairs

Brian Rolleston Antiques Ltd (BADA)
Contact Mr B Rolleston
✉ 104a Kensington Church Street, London,
W8 4BU 🅿
☎ 020 7229 5892 🖷 020 7229 5892
Est. 1955 *Stock size* Medium
Stock 18thC English furniture
Open Mon–Fri 10am–1pm 2–5.30pm
Fairs Grosvenor House, Olympia (Nov), BADA

Patrick Sandberg Antiques (BADA, CINOA)
Contact Mr C Radford
✉ 150–152 Kensington Church Street,

London,
W8 4BN 🅿
☎ 020 7229 0373 ❶ 020 7792 3467
🄴 psand@antiquefurniture.net
🆆 www.antiquefurniture.net
Est. 1983 *Stock size* Large
Stock 18th–19thC English
furniture, mirrors, accessories
Open Mon–Fri 10am–6pm
Sat 10am–4pm
Fairs Spring BADA, Olympia
summer, winter

⊞ Santos (BADA)
Contact Mr A Santos
✉ **21 Old Court House,**
London,
W8 4PD 🅿
☎ 020 7937 6000 ❶ 020 7937 3351
🆆 www.santoslondon.com
Est. 1979 *Stock size* Small
Stock 17th–18thC Chinese export
porcelain
Open By appointment only
Fairs International Ceramics
Fair & Seminar London, The
International Asian Art Fair,The
New York Ceramics Fair, Lisbon
International Fair

⊞ B Silverman (BADA)
Contact Robin Silverman or
Bill Brackenbury
✉ **4 Campden Street,**
Off Kensington Church Street,
London,
W8 7EP 🅿
☎ 020 7985 0555 ❶ 020 7985 0556
🄴 silver@silverman-london.com
🆆 www.silverman-london.com
Est. 1925 *Stock size* Large
Stock 17th–19thC fine English
silverware, silver flatware
Open Mon–Fri 10am–5pm
Sat 10am–4pm
Fairs Olympia, BADA, Harrogate
Services Valuations

⊞ Simon Spero (BACA Award Winner 2003)
Contact Mr S Spero
✉ **109 Kensington Church Street,**
London,
W8 7LN 🅿
☎ 020 7727 7413 ❶ 020 7727 7414
Est. 1964 *Stock size* Large
Stock 18thC English porcelain,
enamels
Open Mon–Fri 10am–5pm
closed 1–2pm
Services Valuations, author of
5 reference books, lecturer

⊞ Stockspring Antiques (BADA, KCSADA)
Contact Mrs F Marno
✉ **114 Kensington Church Street,**
London,
W8 4BH
☎ 020 7727 7995 ❶ 020 7727 7995
🄴 stockspring@antique-porcelain.co.uk
🆆 www.antique-porcelain.co.uk
Est. 1979 *Stock size* Large
Stock 18th–early 19thC English
porcelain
Open Mon–Fri 10am–5.30pm
Sat 10am–1pm
Fairs Olympia (Nov, June)
Services Packing, shipping

⊞ Through The Looking Glass
Contact Sarah Link
✉ **137 Kensington Church Street,**
London,
W8 7LP
☎ 020 7221 4026
🄴 ttlg@btconnect.com
🆆 www.throughthelookingglass.co.uk
Est. 1988 *Stock size* Large
Stock 19thC mirrors
Open Mon–Sat 10am–5.30pm

⊞ Geoffrey Waters Ltd (BADA)
Contact Geoffrey Waters
✉ **133 Kensington Church Street,**
London,
W8 7LP 🅿
☎ 020 7243 6081
🄴 info@antique-chinese-porcelain.com
🆆 www.antique-chinese-porcelain.com
Est. 1992 *Stock size* Medium
Stock 16th–18thC Chinese
porcelain
Open Mon–Fri 10.15am–5.30pm
Sat 10.15am–4.30pm

⊞ Jorge Welsh (BADA, CINOA, Syndicat National des Antiquaires, Portugese Antique Dealers Association)
Contact Mr J Welsh
✉ **116 Kensington Church Street,**
London,
W8 4BH 🅿
☎ 020 7229 2140 ❶ 020 7792 3535
📱 07831 186224
🄴 uk@jorgewelsh.com
🆆 www.jorgewelsh.com
Est. 1997 *Stock size* Large
Stock Chinese porcelain,
particularly Chinese Export,
porcelain, Indo-Portugese art,
Namban, Japanese export

works of art
Open Mon–Fri 10am–5.30pm
Sat 10am–5pm
Fairs Olympia (June), Asian Art
in London, Lisbon and Paris
Bienniales, Maastricht, Palm
Beach, New York

⊞ Mary Wise & Grosvenor Antiques (BADA)
Contact Mrs M Wise
✉ **27 Holland Street,**
London,
W8 4NA 🅿
☎ 020 7937 8649 ❶ 020 7937 7179
📱 07850 863050
🄴 info@wiseantiques.com
🆆 www.wiseantiques.com
Est. 1970 *Stock size* Small
Stock Porcelain, small bronzes,
works of art, Chinese
watercolours on pith paper
Open Mon–Fri 10am–5pm
Fairs New York Ceramics Fair,
San Francisco Fall Antiques Show
Services Bid at auction

W9

⊞ Vale Antiques
Contact Mr P Gooley
✉ **245 Elgin Avenue, Maida Vale,**
London,
W9 1NJ 🅿
☎ 020 7328 4796
Est. 1973 *Stock size* Large
Stock Eclectic mix of antiques,
Victorian–1950s, pictures,
mirrors, silver, silver plate,
china, etc
Open Mon–Sat 10am–6pm
Services Restoration, pearl
stringing, clock and watch
repairs

W10

⊞ 88 Antiques
Contact Mr D Lucas
✉ **88 Golborne Road,**
London,
W10 5PS 🅿
☎ 020 8960 0827
Est. 1977 *Stock size* Large
Stock Antique pine, country
furniture
Open Tues–Sat 10am–6pm
Services Makers of tables from
reclaimed 100-year-old wood

⊞ Bazar
Contact Ms M Davis
✉ **82 Golborne Road, London,**

W10 5PS 🅿
☎ 020 8969 6262
Est. 1992 *Stock size* Medium
Stock French decorative country
furniture, beds, tables,
armchairs, kitchenware, garden
furniture etc
Open Tues–Thurs 10am–5pm
Fri 9.30am–5.30pm Sat
10am–5.30pm

W11

🏢 51 Antiques
Contact Mr Justin Raccanello
✉ 51 Ledbury Road,
London,
W11 2AA 🅿
☎ 020 7229 6153 📠 020 7229 6153
Est. 1975 *Stock size* Medium
Stock Italian ceramics,
1500–1900, Venetian glass
Open Mon–Fri 9.30am–5.30pm
Sat 9.30am–1pm

🏠 75 Portobello Road
Contact Gavin Douglas
75 Portobello Road,
London,
W11 2QB
☎ 020 7221 1121 📠 01825 724418
📧 gavin@antique-clocks.co.uk
Stock size Medium
No. of dealers 5
Stock 18th–19thC Continental
clocks, decorative gilt bronzes,
porcelain, 19th–20thC animal
subjects, Vienna, French bronzes,
Staffordshire, terracotta, tobacco
jars, chess sets, paperweights
Open Mon–Fri 10.30am–4.30pm
Sat 7.30am–5pm

🏠 Admiral Vernon Antiques Market (PADA)
Contact Angelo Soteriades
✉ 141–149 Portobello Road,
London,
W11 2DY
☎ 020 7727 5242 📠 020 7727 5242
📱 07956 277077
📧 info@portobello-antiques.com
🌐 www.portobello-antiques.com
Est. 1983 *Stock size* Large
No. of dealers Over 200
Stock Glass, treen, works of art,
Art Deco, Art Nouveau, jewellery
Open Sat 6am–5pm
Services Valuations

🏢 Chloe Alberry
Contact Chloe or Theo
✉ 84 Portobello Road,

London,
W11 2QD 🅿
☎ 020 7727 0707
🌐 www.alberry.co.uk
Est. 2002 *Stock size* Small
Stock Unique and exclusive
collection of door knobs and
cabinet fittings
Open Mon–Sun 9am–6pm
Services Delivery

🏢 Alice's
Contact Mr D Carter
✉ 86 Portobello Road,
London,
W11 2QD 🅿
☎ 020 7229 8187 📠 020 7792 2456
Est. 1887 *Stock size* Large
Stock Painted furniture,
decorative items, general
antiques
Open Tues–Fri 9am–5pm
Sat 7am–4pm

🏢 Anthea's Antiques
Contact A Mcilroy
✉ Burton's Arcade,
296 Westbourne Grove,
Portobello Market,
London,
W11 2PS 🅿
☎ 020 8690 7207
📱 07961 838780
Est. 1985 *Stock size* Medium
Stock 19thC English and
Continental glass and ceramics
Trade only Yes
Open Sat 7am–4pm
Fairs Newark, Ardingly
Services Will arrange shipping
if required

🏢 Appleby Antiques (PADA)
Contact Mike or Sue Witts
✉ Geoffrey Van Gallery,
105–107 Portobello Road,
London,
W11 2QB 🅿
☎ 01453 753126
📱 07778 282532
📧 mike@applebyantiques.net
🌐 www.applebyantiques.net
Est. 1986
Stock size Medium
Stock English pottery,
1750–1930, specializing in
Wedgwood, Lustreware,
culinary moulds in pewter,
copper, ceramic
Open Sat 6.45am–4pm
Fairs NEC
Services Shipping

🏢 Arbras Gallery
Contact Sandy
✉ 292 Westbourne Grove,
London,
W11 2PS 🅿
☎ 020 7229 6772 📠 020 7229 6772
📧 info@arbrasgallery.co.uk
🌐 www.arbrasgallery.co.uk
Est. 1973 *Stock size* Large
Stock Silver picture frames,
giftware
Open Mon–Fri 10am–4.30pm
Sat 7am–4.30pm
Services Mail order

🏢 Atlam Sales and Service (PADA)
Contact B Skogland-Kirk
✉ 111 Portobello Road,
London,
W11 2QB 🅿
☎ 020 7602 7573 📠 020 7602 2997
📧 info@atlam-watches.co.uk
🌐 www.atlam-watches.co.uk
or www.atlamsilver.com
Est. 1979 *Stock size* Large
Stock Silver and antique pocket
watches, decorative silver
Open Mon–Fri 9am–5pm
Sat 8am–5pm

🏢 B and T Antiques Ltd (LAPADA)
Contact Bernadette Lewis or
Vigi Sawdon
✉ 47 Ledbury Road,
London,
W11 2AA 🅿
☎ 020 7229 7001 📠 020 7229 2033
📧 bernadette@btantiques.
freeserve.co.uk
🌐 www.bntantiques.co.uk
Est. 1994 *Stock size* Large
Stock Decorative antiques,
Art Deco furniture and objects
Open Mon–Sat 10am–6pm
Services Restoration, gilding

🏢 Sebastiano Barbagallo Antiques
Contact Mr S Barbagallo
✉ 15 Pembridge Road,
London,
W11 3HG 🅿
☎ 020 7792 3320 📠 020 7792 3320
📧 sebastianobarbagallo@
hotmail.com
Est. 1978 *Stock size* Large
Stock Chinese furniture,
Indian and Tibetan antiques,
crafts
Open Mon–Fri 10.30am–6pm
Sat 9am–7pm Sun 10.30am–5pm

103

⊞ Barham Antiques (PADA)
Contact Mr M Barham
✉ 83 Portobello Road, London, W11 2QB 🅿
☎ 020 7727 3845 📠 020 7727 3845
📧 mchlbarham@aol.com
🌐 www.barhamantiques.co.uk
Est. 1970 *Stock size* Large
Stock Boxes, caddies, inkwells, clocks, glassware, inkstands, small furniture, silver plate
Open Mon–Fri 10am–4.30pm Sat 7am–5pm
Services Valuations, restoration

⊞ Berg Brothers Ltd
Contact Sean Berg
✉ 109 Freston Road, London, W11 4BD 🅿
☎ 020 7313 6590 📠 020 7313 6589
📧 bergbrothersltd@aol.com
🌐 www.bergbrothersltd.co.uk
Est. 2000 *Stock size* Medium
Stock 20thC design furniture and lighting
Open By appointment
Fairs Olympia, Battersea decorative

⊞ Book and Comic Exchange
Contact Mr R Brown
✉ 14 Pembridge Road, London, W11 3HL
☎ 020 7229 8420
Est. 1967 *Stock size* Medium
Stock Modern first editions, cult books, comics
Open Mon–Sun 10am–8pm

⊞ F E A Briggs Ltd
Contact Joan Wilson
✉ 77 Ledbury Road, London, W11 2AG 🅿
☎ 020 7727 0909 📠 023 8081 2595
📧 feabriggs@aol.com
Est. 1966 *Stock size* Small
Stock Victorian furniture
Open Mon–Fri 9am–5.30pm
Fairs Newark
Services Restoration

⊞ Jack Casimir Ltd (BADA, LAPADA)
✉ 23 Pembridge Road, London, W11 3HG 🅿
☎ 020 7727 8643

Est. 1931 *Stock size* Large
Stock 16th–19thC British and European domestic brass, copper, pewter, paktong
Open Mon–Sat 9.30am–5pm
Services Shipping

⊞ Chamade Antiques
Contact George Walters
✉ 65 Portobello Road, London, W11 2QB
☎ 020 8446 0130
Est. 1994 *Stock size* Medium
Stock Antique Rolex watches, Cartier watches
Open Sat 7am–3pm

⊞ Chelsea Clocks and Antiques
Contact Mr Peter Dickson
✉ 73 Portobello Road, Notting Hill, London, W11 2QB 🅿
☎ 020 7229 7762 📠 020 7274 5198
📧 info@chelseaclocks.co.uk
🌐 www.chelseaclocks.co.uk
Est. 1979 *Stock size* Large
Stock Clocks, scales, boxes, collectables, ink stands and wells
Open Mon–Fri 10am–4.30pm Sat 7am–4pm

⊟ Chelsea Galleries (PADA)
Contact Peter Dixon
✉ 67, 79 & 73 Portobello Road, London, W11 2QB 🅿
☎ 020 7733 3761 📠 020 7274 5198
📧 info@chelseaclocks.co.uk
🌐 www.chelseagalleries.co.uk
Est. 1975 *Stock size* Large
No. of dealers 55
Stock General antiques and collectables
Open Sat 7am–4pm

⊞ Sheila Cook Textiles
Contact Mrs S Cook
✉ 184 Westbourne Grove, London, W11 2RH 🅿
☎ 020 7792 8001 📠 020 7243 1744
📧 sheilacook@sheilacook.co.uk
🌐 www.sheilacook.co.uk
Est. 1970 *Stock size* Small
Stock Mid-18thC–1970s European costume, textiles, accessories
Open By appointment
Services Valuations

⊞ Julia Craig (PADA, BABAADA)
Contact Julia Craig
✉ Harris's Arcade, 163–165 Portobello Road, London, W11 2DY 🅿
☎ 01225 448202
📱 07771 786846
📧 julia@juliacraigcostume.com
🌐 www.juliacraigcostume.com
Est. 1980 *Stock size* Large
Stock Antique lace and linen, costumes, costume accessories
Open Fri–Sat 10am–5pm
Fairs P & A Fairs, Hammersmith
Services Valuations

⊟ Crown Arcade (ADA)
Contact Angelo Soteriades
✉ 119 Portobello Road, London, W11 2DY
☎ 020 7727 5242 📠 020 7727 5242
📱 07956 277077
📧 info@portobello-collections.co.uk
🌐 www.portobello-antiques.com
Est. 1983 *Stock size* Large
No. of dealers 21
Stock Glass, treen, works of art, jewellery, Art Deco, Art Nouveau
Open Sat 6am–5pm
Services Valuations

⊞ Cura Antiques
Contact Mr Cura
✉ 34 Ledbury Road, London, W11 2AB 🅿
☎ 020 7229 6880 📠 020 7792 3731
📧 mail@cura-antiques.com
🌐 www.cura-antiques.com
Est. 1969 *Stock size* Medium
Stock Continental works of art, furniture, old master paintings
Open Mon–Fri 10.30am–5.30pm Sat 10.30am–1pm
Fairs Olympia (June)
Services Restoration

⊟ John Dale Antiques (PADA)
Contact Mrs Jo Cairns
✉ 87 Portobello Road, London, W11 2QB 🅿
☎ 020 7727 1304
Est. 1960 *Stock size* Medium
No. of dealers 4
Stock Decorative antiques, books, prints
Open Sun Mon Fri 10am–5pm Sat 7am–6pm

LONDON

LONDON

⊞ Gavin Douglas
(LAPADA, PADA)
Contact Gavin Douglas
✉ 75 Portobello Road,
London,
W11 2QB 🅿
☎ 020 7221 1121 ✆ 01825 724418
✉ gavin@antique-clocks.co.uk
🌐 www.antique-clocks.co.uk
Est. 1992 *Stock size* Large
Stock Antique clocks, ormolu,
bronzes and porcelain
Open Mon–Sat 10.30am–4.30pm
Sat 7.30am–5pm
Fairs Olympia, LAPADA
Services Valuations, restoration

⊞ Fleurdelys Antiquités
Contact Ms Laurence Paul
✉ Gallery 289,
289 Westbourne Grove,
London,
W11 2QA
☎ 0207 636 2327 ✆ 0207 636 2327
📱 07798 600437
✉ info@fleurdelys.com
Est. 1997 *Stock size* Large
Stock Chinese antique wood
stands, Chinese porcelain
Open Sat 7am–5pm or by
appointment

⌂ Good Fairy Antique
Market (PADA)
Contact Stuart Pardoe
✉ 100 Portobello Road,
London,
W11 2DY
☎ 020 7385 2525
📱 07704 32169
✉ derekcarter@yahoo.com
🌐 www.goodfairyantiques.co.uk
Est. 1975 *Stock size* Large
No. of dealers 50
Stock Stamps, silver, glass, small
antiques, collectables,
memorabilia
Open Sat 5am–5pm

⊞ Henry Gregory
Contact Camy Gregory
✉ 82e Portobello Road,
London,
W11 2QD
☎ 020 7792 9221 ✆ 020 7792 9221
✉ shop@henrygregoryantiques.com
Est. 1970 *Stock size* Medium
Stock Antique silver, decorative
objects, vintage sports and
luggage
Open Mon–Fri 10am–5pm
Sat 8am–5pm
Services Shipping

⌂ Harris's Arcade
Contact Angelo Soteriades
✉ 161–163 Portobello Road,
London,
W11 2DY
☎ 020 7727 5242
📱 07956 277077
✉ info@portobello-antiques.com
🌐 www.portobello-antiques.com
Est. 2003 *Stock size* Medium
No. of dealers 35
Stock Collectables, textiles.
Oriental, English porcelain,
antiquities, travel
Open Sat 5am–5pm

⊞ Hart & Rosenberg
(PADA)
Contact Mrs E Hart
✉ Units L52–L53, Lower Trading
Hall, Admiral Vernon Antiques
Market, 141–149 Portobello
Road, London,
W11 2DY
☎ 020 8874 5250
🌐 www.enid_contact@yahoo.co.uk
Est. 1968 *Stock size* Large
Stock Oriental and Continental
ceramics, decorative items
Open Sat 9am–4pm
Services Valuations, restoration

⊞ Hirst Antiques
Contact Mrs S Hirst
✉ 59 Pembridge Road, London,
W11 3HN 🅿
☎ 020 7727 9364 ✆ 020 7460 6480
Est. 1969 *Stock size* Large
Stock General antique furniture,
antique beds, bronzes, sculpture,
pictures, costume jewellery
Open Mon–Sat 10am–6pm

⊞ Erna Hiscock (PADA)
Contact Erna Hiscock
✉ Chelsea Galleries,
69 Portobello Road,
London,
W11 2PS
☎ 01233 661407 ✆ 01233 661407
✉ erna@ernahiscockantiques.com
🌐 www.ernahiscockantiques.com
Est. 1975 *Stock size* Large
Stock 17th–19thC samplers,
needlework
Open Sat 7am–3pm
Fairs NEC
Services Valuations

⊞ Humbleyard Fine Art
(PADA)
Contact James Layte
✉ Unit 32, Admiral Vernon

Arcade, Portobello Road,
London,
W11 2DY 🅿
☎ 01362 637793 ✆ 01362 637793
📱 07836 349416
Est. 1974 *Stock size* Medium
Stock Scientific, medical,
decorative and collectors' items
Open Sat 6am–1.30pm
Fairs Olympia
Services Valuations

⊞ Kleanthous Antiques
Ltd (LAPADA)
Contact Mr C Kleanthous
✉ 144 Portobello Road, London,
W11 2DZ 🅿
☎ 020 7727 3649 ✆ 020 7243 2488
📱 07850 375501
✉ antiques@kleanthaus.com
🌐 www.kleanthous.com
Est. 1969 *Stock size* Medium
Stock Jewellery, wrist watches,
furniture, clocks, pocket watches,
porcelain, china, silver, works of
art, 20thC decorative items
Open Sat 8.30am–4pm or by
appointment
Fairs Olympia

⊞ M & D Lewis (PADA)
Contact Mr M Lewis
✉ 1 Lonsdale Road, London,
W11 2BY 🅿
☎ 020 7727 3908 ✆ 020 7727 3908
Est. 1959 *Stock size* Large
Stock English and Continental
furniture, Oriental porcelain
Open Mon–Fri 10am–5pm
Sat 10am–4pm

⊞ Andrew Lineham Fine
Glass (BADA, CINOA)
Contact Mr A Lineham
✉ Van Arcade, 105 Portobello
Road, London,
W11 2QB 🅿
☎ 020 7704 0195 ✆ 01243 576241
📱 07767 702722
✉ andrew@antiquecolouredglass.com
🌐 www.antiquecolouredglass.com
Est. 1979 *Stock size* Large
Stock 19th–20thC coloured glass,
European porcelain
Open Sat 8am–3pm
Fairs Olympia (Nov)
Services Restoration, commission
bidding, collectors services,
valuations, hire

⊞ Lunn Antiques Ltd
Contact Stephen Lunn
✉ Unit 8, Admiral Vernon

Arcade, Portobello Road,
London,
W11 2DY
☎ 020 7736 4638 ☏ 020 7371 7113
✉ lunnantiques@aol.co,
🌐 www.lunnantiques.co.uk
Est. 1995 *Stock size* Medium
Stock 17thC needlepoint,
Mechlin, 18thC Brussels,
Valenciennes
Open By appointment
Services Valuations, restoration

⊞ Caira Mandaglio
Contact Anne or Sharon
✉ **31 Pembridge Road,**
London,
W11 3HG 🅿
☎ 020 7727 5496 ☏ 020 7229 4889
📱 07836 354632
✉ caira_mandaglio@btopenworld.com
🌐 www.cairamandaglio.co.uk
Est. 1998 *Stock size* Large
Stock 20thC furniture, lighting,
glassware, objets d'art,
chandeliers
Open Wed–Fri 11am–5pm
Sat 10.30am–5.30pm

⊞ Mario's Antiques
(LAPADA, PADA)
Contact M Barazi
✉ **115 Portobello Road, London,**
W11 2DY 🅿
☎ 07919 254000 ☏ 020 8900 0810
📱 07956 580772
✉ marwan@barazi.screaming.net
🌐 www.marios-antiques.com
Est. 1986 *Stock size* Medium
Stock Porcelain, Meissen, Sèvres,
Vienna
Open Wed Fri 10am–4pm
Sat 7am–5pm
Fairs Olympia, LAPADA, NEC

⊞ Robin Martin Antiques
Contact Mr P Martin
✉ **44 Ledbury Road,**
London,
W11 2AB 🅿
☎ 020 7727 1301 ☏ 020 7727 1301
✉ paul.martin11@btconnect.com
Est. 1971 *Stock size* Medium
Stock Mirrors, Regency furniture,
Continental furniture, works of
art, lighting
Open Mon–Fri 10am–6pm
Sat 10am–1pm
Fairs Olympia (June, Nov)

⊞ Mayflower Antiques
(PADA)
Contact Mr John Odgers

✉ **117 Portobello Road, London,**
W11 2DY
☎ 020 7727 0381
📱 07860 843569
✉ antiques@johnodgers.com
Est. 1970 *Stock size* Medium
Stock Music boxes, clocks, dolls,
scientific instruments, pistols,
collectable items
Open Sat 7am–4pm
Fairs Newark, Ardingly

⊞ MCN Antiques
Contact Makoto Umezawa
✉ **183 Westbourne Grove,**
London,
W11 2SB 🅿
☎ 020 7727 3796 ☏ 020 7229 8839
Est. 1980 *Stock size* Large
Stock Japanese porcelain, works
of art
Open Mon–Fri 10am–6pm
Sat 11am–3pm

⊞ Mimi Fifi
Contact Rita Delaforge
✉ **27 Pembridge Road,**
Notting Hill Gate,
London,
W11 3HG 🅿
☎ 020 7243 3154 ☏ 020 7938 4222
📱 07956 222238
🌐 www.mimififi.com
Est. 1992 *Stock size* Large
Stock Collectors' and vintage
toys, Coca-Cola memorabilia,
Pokemon, perfume-related
items, vintage badges, tobacco
memorabilia, Michelin
memorabilia, Kewpie dolls,
Japanese collectables
Open Mon–Sat 11am–6pm
Services Overseas postal service

⊞ Myriad Antiques
Contact Mrs S Fenwick
✉ **131 Portland Road,**
London,
W11 4LW 🅿
☎ 020 7229 1709 ☏ 020 7221 3882
Est. 1975 *Stock size* Large
Stock French painted furniture,
garden furniture, faux bamboo,
Victorian–Edwardian
upholstered chairs, mirrors,
objets d'art
Open Tues–Fri 11am–6pm
Sat 10am–5pm

⊞ Polly Pallister (PADA)
Contact Polly Pallister
✉ **Geoffrey Van Gallery,**
105–107 Portobello Road,

London,
W11 2QB 🅿
☎ 020 7267 7864
🌐 www.polly-pallister-antiques.com
Est. 1996 *Stock size* Medium
Stock 18th–19thC decorative
antiques, 18thC engravings,
creamware, silk patchworks,
textiles
Open Sat 7am–2.30pm or
by appointment

⊞ Portobello Antique
Store
Contact Mr T J Evans
✉ **79 Portobello Road, London,**
W11 2QB 🅿
☎ 020 7221 1994 ☏ 020 7221 1994
Est. 1984 *Stock size* Large
Stock Silver, silver plate,
decorative items, flatware
Open Tues–Fri 10am–4pm
Sat 8.15am–4pm

🏛 Portobello Studios
(PADA)
Contact Angelo Soteriades
✉ **101–103 Portobello Road,**
London,
W11 2QB
☎ 020 7727 5242 ☏ 020 7727 5242
📱 07956 277077
✉ info@portobello-antiques.com
🌐 www.portobello-antiques.co.uk
Est. 1983
No. of dealers 40
Stock Treen, glass, works of art,
Art Deco, Art Nouveau, jewellery
Open Sat 6am–5pm
Services Valuations

🏛 Red Lion Antiques
Market (PADA)
Contact Angelo Soteriades
✉ **165–169 Portobello Road,**
London,
W11 2DY
☎ 020 7436 9416 ☏ 020 7727 5242
📱 07956 277077
✉ info@portobello-antiques.co.uk
🌐 www.portobello-antiques.co.uk
Est. 1983 *Stock size* Large
No. of dealers 40
Stock Glass, treen, Art Deco,
Art Nouveau, jewellery, cameras,
collectables, Oriental, African
art, jewellery
Open Sat 6am–5pm
Services Valuations, café

🏛 The Red Teapot Arcade
Contact Angelo Soteriades
✉ **101–103 Portobello Road,**

London,
W11 2QB
☎ 020 7727 5242
⦿ 07956 277077
℮ info@portobello-antiques.com
ⓦ www.portobello-antiques.com
Est. 2003 *Stock size* Medium
No. of dealers 40
Stock High quality antiques, watches, lighters, pens, silver
Open Sat 6am–5pm

🏠 **Rogers Antiques Gallery**
Contact Mike Spooner
✉ 65 Portobello Road, London,
W11 2QB
☎ 020 7969 1500 ⓕ 020 7969 1639
Est. 1969 *Stock size* Large
No. of dealers 65
Stock Wide range of antiques and collectables, specialist dealers in most fields
Open Sat 7am–4.30pm
Services Valuations

⊞ **Schredds of Portobello (LAPADA, CINOA)**
Contact George R Schrager
✉ 107 Portobello Road, London,
W11 2QB 🅿
☎ 020 8348 3314 ⓕ 020 8341 5971
℮ silver@schredds.demon.co.uk
ⓦ www.schredds.com
Est. 1972 *Stock size* Large
Stock Small pieces of pre-1880 silver
Open Sat 7am–2.30pm
Fairs Antiques for Everyone, Earl's Court, Penman fairs
Services Valuations, shipping

⊞ **Justin F Skrebowski Prints (PBFA, PADA)**
Contact Mr J Skrebowski
✉ Ground Floor,
177 Portobello Road, London,
W11 2DY 🅿
☎ 020 7792 9742 ⓕ 020 7792 9742
⦿ 07774 612474
℮ justin@skreb.co.uk
ⓦ www.skreb.co.uk
Est. 1979 *Stock size* Large
Stock 18–19thC decorative prints, 18th–20thC frames for prints and watercolours, oils, watercolours
Open Sat 9am–4pm or by appointment
Fairs PBFA, Russell Hotel
Services Folio stands, easels, display equipment

⊞ **Pam Taylor Antiques (PADA)**
Contact Mrs P Taylor
✉ Portobello Studios, The Red Teapot,
101 Portobello Road, London,
W11 2QB 🅿
⦿ 07850 416717
℮ pamlet@globalnet.co.uk
Est. 1982 *Stock size* Medium
Stock Late 19th–early 20thC ceramics, glass, oil lamps
Open Sat 6.30am–3.30pm
Fairs Antiques for Everyone

⊞ **Themes and Variations**
Contact Liliane Fawcett
✉ 231 Westbourne Grove, London,
W11 2SE 🅿
☎ 020 7727 5531 ⓕ 020 7221 6378
℮ go@themesandvariations.com
ⓦ www.themesandvariations.com
Est. 1984 *Stock size* Large
Stock Post-war Scandinavian, Italian furniture, decorative arts
Open Mon–Fri 10am–2pm Sat 2–6pm

⊞ **Philip Thomas Design**
Contact Philip Thomas
✉ 4a Ladbroke Grove, London,
W11 3BG 🅿
☎ 020 7229 4044 ⓕ 020 7229 4044
℮ info@pjthomas.com
Est. 1990 *Stock size* Medium
Stock Eclectic Continental furniture and design
Open Tues–Sat 10am–6pm

⊞ **Anthony Thompson Ltd**
✉ 7 Kensington Park Gardens, Notting Hill, London,
W11 3HB
☎ 020 7221 7729
℮ at@anthonythompsonltd.co.uk
ⓦ www.anthonythompsonltd.co.uk
Est. 1990 *Stock size* Small
Stock Antique rugs, carpets
Open By appointment
Services Valuations, restoration, packing, shipping

⊞ **Virginia**
Contact Mrs V Bates
✉ 98 Portland Road, London,
W11 4LQ 🅿
☎ 020 7727 9908 ⓕ 020 7229 2198
Est. 1971 *Stock size* Medium
Stock Vintage clothes, late 19thC–late 1930s
Open Mon–Fri 11am–6pm Sat by appointment only

⊞ **Trude Weaver (LAPADA)**
Contact Mr B Weaver
✉ 71 Portobello Road, London,
W11 2QB 🅿
☎ 020 7229 8738 ⓕ 020 7229 8738
⦿ 07768 551269
Est. 1968 *Stock size* Large
Stock 18th–19thC English and Continental furniture, complementary accessories
Open Wed–Sat 9.30am–5.30pm
Fairs Olympia (June, Nov)

W12

🎣 **Neil Freeman Angling Auctions**
Contact Mr N Freeman
✉ PO Box 2095, London,
W12 8RU 🅿
☎ 020 8749 4175 ⓕ 020 8743 4855
⦿ 07785 281349
℮ neil@anglingauctions.demon.co.uk
ⓦ www.thesaurus.co.uk/angling-auctions/
Est. 1990
Sales Angling auctions twice yearly, first Sat April noon, first Sat October noon, viewing The Grand Hall, Chiswick Town Hall, Heathfield Terrace, London W4 Fri 1.30–7pm Sat 8.30am to sale
Catalogues yes

W14

⊞ **Asenbaum Fine Arts Ltd**
Contact Paul Asenbaum or Isabella Croi
✉ 10 Carlton Mansions, Holland Park Gardens, London,
W14 8DW 🅿
☎ 020 7602 5373 ⓕ 020 7602 5373
℮ info@asenbaum.com
ⓦ www.asenbaum.com
Est. 1998 *Stock size* Medium
Stock Viennese decorative arts c1900, furniture, silver, glass, early 19thC Biedermeier
Trade only Yes
Open By appointment only

WC1

⊞ **Steven Burak Books**
Contact Steven Burak
✉ Ground Floor Shop, 18 Leigh Street, Bloomsbury, London,
WC1H 9EW 🅿
☎ 020 7388 1153
℮ stevenburaklondon@yahoo.com

Est. 2002 *Stock size* Medium
Stock Antiquarian, rare, out of
print books, ephemera,
manuscripts
Open Mon–Sat 11am–7pm
Services Valuations

⊞ Coincraft (ADA, IBNS, PNG, ANA)
Contact Mr B Clayden
✉ 44 & 45 Great Russell Street,
London,
WC1B 3LU ▣
☎ 020 7636 1188 ❻ 020 7323 2860
❸ info@coincraft.com
Ⓦ ww.coincraft.com
Est. 1955
Stock Greek, Roman, English,
medieval–present day coins,
British and foreign banknotes,
ancient artefacts
Open Mon–Fri 9.30am–5pm Sat
10am–2.30pm or by appointment
Services Catalogue of British coins

⊞ Collinge & Clark (PBFA)
Contact Mr O Clark
✉ 13 Leigh Street,
London,
WC1H 9EW
☎ 020 7387 7105 ❻ 020 7388 1315
❸ collingeandclarke@aol.com
Est. 1989 *Stock size* Medium
Stock Antiquarian, rare, second-
hand books, private press books,
limited editions, 18th–19thC
political and social history,
typography
Open Mon–Fri 11am–6.30pm
Sat 11am–3.30pm

⊞ Fine Books Oriental Ltd (PBFA)
Contact Mr J Somers
✉ 38 Museum Street, London,
WC1A 1LP ▣
☎ 020 7242 5288 ❻ 020 7242 5344
❸ oriental@finebooks.demon.co.uk
Ⓦ www.finebooks.demon.co.uk
Est. 1977 *Stock size* Medium
Stock Oriental, Middle Eastern,
South Asian and Indian,
out-of-print, rare books
Open Mon–Fri 9.30am–6pm
Sat 11am–6pm
Fairs PBFA, Russell Hotel
Services Valuations

⊞ R A Gekoski Booksellers (ABA, ILAB)
Contact Rick Gekoski or
Peter Grogan
✉ Pied Bull Yard, 15a

Bloomsbury Square, London,
WC1A 2LP ▣
☎ 020 7404 6676 ❻ 020 7404 6595
❸ gekoski@dircon.co.uk
Est. 1984 *Stock size* Small
Stock First editions, letters,
paintings, manuscripts
Open Mon–Fri 10am–5.30pm
Fairs ABA
Services Valuations

⊞ Griffith & Partners Ltd
Contact David Griffith
✉ 31–35 Great Ormond Street,
London,
WC1N 3HZ ▣
☎ 020 7430 1394
Est. 1992 *Stock size* Medium
Stock Antiquarian, rare, second-
hand books, London topography,
Middle East, poetry, Anglo and
Welsh topics a speciality,
Anglo literature
Open Mon–Fri noon–6pm
occasional Sat or by appointment
Services Valuations, book search,
catalogues, mail order

⊞ Jarndyce Antiquarian Booksellers (ABA, PBFA)
Contact Mr B Lake or
Ms Janet Nassau
✉ 46 Great Russell Street,
Bloomsbury,
London,
WC1B 3PA ▣
☎ 020 7631 4220 ❻ 020 7631 1882
❸ books@jarndyce.com
Ⓦ www.jarndyce.com
Est. 1969 *Stock size* Large
Stock Antiquarian, rare, second-
hand books on English language,
English literature, Dickens,
18th–20thC economic and social
history
Open Mon–Fri 10.30am–5.30pm
Fairs Olympia, Chelsea ABA,
York PBFA
Services Valuations, catalogues

⊞ Jessop Classic Photographic
Contact Martin Frost or
Steve Johnson
✉ 67 Great Russell Street,
London,
WC1B 3BN ▣
☎ 020 7831 3640 ❻ 020 7831 3956
Ⓦ www.jessops.com/classic
Est. 1989 *Stock size* Large
Stock 1900–1970 classic cameras
Open Mon–Sat 9am–5.30pm
Services Repairs

⊞ Photo Books International (PBFA)
Contact Bill Herbert
✉ 99 Judd Street,
London,
WC1H 9NE ▣
☎ 020 7813 7363 ❻ 020 7813 7363
❸ pbi@britishlibrary.net
Ⓦ www.pbi-books.com
Est. 1997 *Stock size* Large
Stock Books on photography
Open Wed–Sat 11am–6pm
Fairs London Photograph Fairs

⊞ Unsworths Booksellers Ltd (ABA, PBFA)
Contact Mr Charlie Unsworth
✉ 12 Bloomsbury Street,
London,
WC1B 3QA
☎ 020 7436 9836 ❻ 020 7637 7334
❸ books@unsworths.com
Ⓦ www.unsworths.com
Est. 1986 *Stock size* Large
Stock Antiquarian, second-hand
and remainder books on the
humanities
Open Mon–Sat 10.30am–8pm
Sun 11am–7pm
Fairs See website for details

⊞ Vortex Books
Contact Steven Lowe
✉ The Aquarium,
10 Woburn Walk,
London,
WC1H 0JL ▣
☎ 020 7387 8417
❸ info@aquariumgallery.co.uk
Ⓦ www.aquariumgallery.co.uk
Est. 2003 *Stock size* Medium
Stock Limited edition prints &
books, paintings and art
multiples
Open Mon–Sat 11am–6pm

WC2

⊞ Anchor Antiques Ltd
Contact Mrs Samne
✉ 26 Charing Cross Road,
London,
WC2H 0DG
☎ 020 7836 5686
Est. 1964 *Stock size* Medium
Stock European and Oriental
ceramics
Trade only Yes
Open By appointment

⊞ Any Amount of Books (PBFA, ABA, ILAB)
Contact Nigel Burwood

✉ **56 Charing Cross Road,
London,
WC2H 0QA** 🅿
☎ 020 7836 3597 ✆ 020 7240 1769
🖂 charingx@anyamountofbooks.com
🌐 www.anyamountofbooks.com
Est. 1975 *Stock size* Large
Stock Antiquarian, rare, second-hand books
Open Mon–Sat 10.30am–9.30pm
Sun 11.30am–8.30pm
Fairs PBFA Russell Hotel, Olympia
Services Shipping, appraisals,
book hire

⌂ The Apple Market
Contact Kate Lockyer
✉ **Covent Garden Market,
London,
WC2E 8RF**
☎ 020 7836 9136
🌐 www.coventgardenmarket.co.uk
Est. 1980 *Stock size* Small
No. of dealers 40
Stock 40 traders use the traditional
wrought iron stalls of the original
Covent Garden, jewellery, china,
small collectable items
Open Mon 10am–6pm

⊞ Argenteus Ltd (LAPADA)
Contact Mr M Feldman
✉ **Vault 2, The London Silver
Vaults, 53 Chancery Lane,
London,
WC2A 1QS** 🅿
☎ 020 7831 3637 ✆ 020 7430 0126
Est. 1991 *Stock size* Medium
Stock Antique silver, Sheffield
plate, flatware
Open Mon–Fri 9am–5.30pm
Sat 9am–1pm

⊞ A H Baldwin and Son (BADA, IAPN, BNTA)
Contact Tim Wilkes
✉ **11 Adelphi Terrace,
London,
WC2N 6BJ** 🅿
☎ 020 7930 6879 ✆ 020 7930 9450
🖂 coins@baldwin.sh
🌐 www.baldwin.sh
Est. 1872
Stock Coins, commemorative
medals, numismatic books
Open Mon–Fri 9am–5pm
Services Valuations

⊞ Belmont
Contact Alex Belmont
✉ **Vault 46, The London Silver
Vaults, 53–64 Chancery Lane,**

**London,
WC2A 1QT**
☎ 020 7242 3152
🖂 belmont@londonsilvervaults.
wanadoo.co.uk
🌐 www.belmontjewellery.com
Est. 1950 *Stock size* Medium
Stock Antique silver and gold,
silver jewellery
Open Mon–Fri 10.30am–4.30pm
Sat by appointment
Services Valuations, restoration,
repair

⊞ Malcolm Bord
Contact Mr M Bord
✉ **16 Charing Cross Road,
London,
WC2H 0HR** 🅿
☎ 020 7836 0631 ✆ 020 7240 1920
Est. 1970 *Stock size* Large
Stock Worldwide old silver
and bronze coins
Open Mon–Sat 10.30am–5.30pm
Services Valuations

⌂ Charing Cross Markets
Contact Rodney Bolwell
✉ **1 Embankment Place,
London,
WC2N 6NN** 🅿
☎ 01483 281771 ✆ 01483 281771
🖂 rodney@chicane.fsbusiness.co.uk
Est. 1974 *Stock size* Large
No. of dealers 35
Stock Stamps, postcards, coins
Open Sat 7.30am–3pm

⊞ Coins and Bullion (BNTA, ANA)
Contact Mr P Cohen
✉ **20 Cecil Court,
London,
WC2N 4HE**
☎ 020 7379 0615
Est. 1977
Stock British coins from 1500,
world coins
Open Mon–Fri 10.30am–5.30pm
Sat noon–5pm
Services Valuations

⊞ Paul Daniel (LSVA)
Contact Paul Daniel
✉ **51 & 68 The London Silver
Vaults, Chancery Lane,
London,
WC2A 1QS** 🅿
☎ 020 7430 1327 ✆ 020 7430 1327
📱 07831 338461
🖂 paveldaniel@aol.com
Est. 1979 *Stock size* Medium
Stock Commercial English and

Continental silver
Open Mon–Fri 10am–4pm
Services Valuations, restoration

⊞ Bryan Douglas (LAPADA)
Contact Mr B Douglas
✉ **12 & 14 The London Silver
Vaults, Chancery Lane,
London,
WC2A 1QS**
☎ 020 7242 7073 ✆ 020 7242 7073
🖂 sales@bryandouglas.co.uk
🌐 www.bryandouglas.co.uk
Est. 1971 *Stock size* Large
Stock Antique, vintage, modern
silver, silverplate, old Sheffield
plate
Open Mon–Fri 9.30am–5pm
Sat 9.30am–1pm
Services Valuations

⊞ Eat My Handbag Bitch
Contact George or Georgina Enoch
✉ **37 Drury Lane, Covent Garden,
London,
WC2B 5RR** 🅿
☎ 020 7836 0830 ✆ 020 7836 0890
🖂 gallery@eatmyhandbagbitch.com
🌐 www.eatmyhandbagbitch.co.uk
Est. 1998 *Stock size* Large
Stock Design of the modern
movements, 1840–1985, rare
furniture, decorative items,
ceramics, glass, art
Open Mon–Sat 11am–6pm
or by appointment
Fairs Olympia Fine Art (Spring)
Services Valuations, interior
design, shipping

⊞ R Feldman Ltd Antique Silver (LAPADA)
Contact Mr R Feldman
✉ **4 & 6 The London Silver
Vaults, 53 Chancery Lane,
London,
WC2A 1QS** 🅿
☎ 020 7405 6111 ✆ 020 7430 0126
🖂 rfeldman@rfeldman.co.uk
🌐 www.rfeldman.co.uk
Est. 1954 *Stock size* Large
Stock Antique Victorian silver,
old Sheffield plate
Open Mon–Fri 9am–5.30pm
Sat 9am–1pm
Services Valuations, repairs

⊞ I Franks (LAPADA)
Contact Eric Franks
✉ **The Vaults, 9–11 The London
Silver Vaults, Chancery Lane,
London,**

WC2A 1QS
☎ 020 7242 4035 ● 020 7242 4035
✉ sales@ifranks.com
⊕ www.ifranks.com
Est. 1958 *Stock size* Large
Stock Silver
Open Mon–Fri 9.30am–5pm
Sat 10am–1pm

⊞ **Fraser's Autographs (UACC)**
Contact Kerry Watson
✉ 399 The Strand, London, WC2R 0LX
☎ 020 7557 4404 ● 020 7836 7342
✉ sales@frasersautographs.co.uk
⊕ www.frasersautographs.com
Est. 1978 *Stock size* Large
Stock Signed photos, letters, documents, stage and film costumes and props, signed guitars, sports equipment
Open Mon–Sat 9.30am–5.30pm
Fairs Stanley Gibbons Fairs
Services Valuations, wants list, bi-monthly postal Internet autograph auction, lifetime authenticity guarantee

⋟ **Stanley Gibbons Auctions Ltd (PTS, ASDA)**
Contact Mr Colin Avery
✉ 399 Strand, London, WC2R 0LX
☎ 020 7836 8444 ● 020 7836 7342
✉ auctions@stanleygibbons.co.uk
⊕ www.stanleygibbons.com/auction
Est. 1856
Open Mon–Fri 9am–5pm
Sales 6 Postbid sales per year, 6 Collections & Ranges sales, occasional Web-only sales, viewing for all sales by appointment
Frequency Every 4–6 weeks
Catalogues Yes

⊞ **Gillian Gould Antiques**
Contact Gill Gould
✉ Ocean Leisure, 11–14 Northumberland Avenue, London, WC2N 5AQ
☎ 020 7419 0500
⊕ 07831 150060
✉ gillgould@dealwith.com
Est. 1989 *Stock size* Small
Stock Scientific, marine, general gifts
Open Mon–Fri 9.30am–6.30pm closed Wed Sat 9.30am–5.30pm
Services Valuations, restoration

⊞ **Anthony Green Antiques (NAWCC)**
Contact Anthony Green
✉ Vault 54, The London Silver Vaults, Chancery Lane, London, WC2A 1QS
☎ 0207 430 0038 ● 0207 430 0046
⊕ 07900 681469
✉ vintagewatches@hotmail.com
⊕ www.anthonygreen.com
Est. 1985 *Stock size* Large
Stock Antique and period jewellery, vintage wristwatches and antique pocket watches and objects of virtue
Open Mon–Fri 10am–5pm

⊞ **Grosvenor Prints**
Contact Ms McDiarmid
✉ 19 Shelton Street, Covent Garden, London, WC2H 9JN
☎ 020 7836 1979 ● 020 7379 6695
✉ grosvenorprints@btinternet.com
⊕ www.grosvenorprints.com
Est. 1976 *Stock size* Large
Stock Topographical, sporting, dogs, portraits, decorative prints
Open Mon–Fri 10am–6pm
Sat 11am–4pm
Fairs ABA Olympia, London

⊞ **Hamiltons**
Contact Mr M Hamilton
✉ 25 The London Silver Vaults, Chancery Lane, London, WC2A 1QS
☎ 020 7831 7030 ● 020 7831 5483
Stock size Large
Stock Antique silver, flatware services a speciality
Open Mon–Fri 9.30am–5.30pm
Sat 9.30am–1pm

⊞ **P J Hilton Books**
Contact Mr P Hilton
✉ 12 Cecil Court, London, WC2N 4HE
☎ 020 7379 9825
Est. 1986 *Stock size* Medium
Stock Antiquarian, second-hand, rare books, pre-1700 a speciality
Open Mon–Fri 10.30am–6pm
Sat 10.30am–5pm
Services Book search

⊞ **Raymond D Holdich (OMRS)**
Contact Mr R Holdich
✉ 7 Whitcomb Street, London, WC2H 7HA

☎ 020 7930 1979 ● 020 7930 1152
⊕ 07774 133493
✉ rdhmedals@aol.com
⊕ www.rdhmedals.com
Est. 1969 *Stock size* Large
Stock Cap badges, militaria including medals, orders, decorations
Open Mon–Fri 9.30am–3.30pm
Services Valuations, restoration

⊞ **Stephen Kalms Antiques (LAPADA)**
Contact Mr S Kalms
✉ The London Silver Vaults, Chancery Lane, London, WC2A 1QS
☎ 020 7430 1254 ● 020 7405 6206
✉ stephen@skalms.freeserve.co.uk
⊕ www.kalmsantiques.com
Est. 1990 *Stock size* Large
Stock Victorian–Edwardian silver, silver plate, decorative items
Open Mon–Fri 9am–5.30pm
Sat 9am–1pm
Fairs Olympia (June), New York (Jan), Miami (Jan)
Services Valuations, restoration, repairs

⊞ **Koopman Rare Art (London) Ltd (BADA, BACA Award Winner 2004)**
Contact Mr L Smith
✉ The London Silver Vaults, Chancery Lane, London, WC2A 1QS
☎ 020 7242 7624 ● 020 7831 0221
✉ rareart@compuserve.com
⊕ www.rareartlondon.com
Est. 1984 *Stock size* Large
Stock Antique silver
Open Mon–Fri 9am–5.30pm
Sat 10am–1pm
Fairs Olympia (June), IFAADS, New York

⊞ **Langfords (LAPADA)**
Contact Adam Langford
✉ 8 & 10 The London Silver Vaults, 53–64 Chancery Lane, London, WC2A 1QS
☎ 020 7242 5506 ● 020 7405 0431
✉ vault@langfords.com
⊕ www.langfords.com
Est. 1940 *Stock size* Medium
Stock Silver
Open Mon–Fri 9am–5.30pm
Sat 9am–1pm
Services Valuations, restoration, commissions, buys silver

LONDON
WEST • WC2

⊞ Nat Leslie Ltd
Contact Mr M Hyams
✉ 21 The London Silver Vaults, 53 Chancery Lane, London, WC2A 1QS 🅿
☎ 020 7242 4787
Est. 1947 *Stock size* Large
Stock Modern, antique, contemporary silverware, silver plate, flatware a speciality
Open Mon–Fri 9.30am–4.30pm

⊞ Linden & Co (Antiques) Ltd
Contact Mr S or Mr H Linden
✉ Vault 7, London Silver Vaults, Chancery Lane, London, WC2A 1QS 🅿
☎ 020 7242 4863 📠 020 7405 9946
📧 lindenandco@aol.com
🌐 www.lindenantiquessilver.co.uk
Est. 1960 *Stock size* Medium
Stock Silver, silver plate
Open Mon–Fri 10am–5.30pm
Services Engraving, repairs and valuations

⊞ C and T Mammon (LSVA)
Contact Mr C Mammon
✉ 55 & 64 The London Silver Vaults, Chancery Lane, London, WC2A 1QT 🅿
☎ 020 7405 2397 📠 020 7405 4900
📱 07785 325642
📧 claudemammon@btinternet.com
🌐 www.candtmammon.com
Est. 1969 *Stock size* Large
Stock Decorative silver, silver-plate items
Open Mon–Fri 9am–5.30pm or by appointment
Services Valuations

⊞ E W Marchpane Ltd (ABA, PBFA)
Contact K Fuller
✉ 16 Cecil Court, Charing Cross Road, London, WC2N 4HE
☎ 020 7836 8661 📠 020 7497 0567
📧 k_fuller@btclick.com
🌐 www.Marchpane.com
Est. 1989 *Stock size* Medium
Stock Antiquarian, rare, second-hand books, children's and illustrated books a speciality
Open Mon–Sat 11am–6pm

⊞ Colin Narbeth and Son (IBNS)
Contact Mr Simon Narbeth

✉ 20 Cecil Court, London, WC2N 4HE
☎ 020 7379 6975 📠 017 2 811244
📧 colin.narbeth@btinternet.com
🌐 www.colin-narbeth.com
Est. 1982 *Stock size* Large
Stock Banknotes, bonds, shares of all countries and periods
Open Mon Sat 10.30am–4pm
Tues–Fri 10am–5pm
Fairs Bonnington Paper Money Fair, IBNS (Oct)

⊞ Jeffrey Neal & Lynn Bloom (LAPADA)
Contact Jeffrey Neal or Lynn Bloom
✉ Vault 27, The London Silver Vaults, Chancery Lane, London, WC2A 1QS 🅿
☎ 020 7242 6189 📠 020 8421 8848
📱 07768 533055
📧 sales@bloomvault.com
🌐 www.bloomvault.com
Est. 1923 *Stock size* Large
Stock Silver, centrepieces, napkins, cutlery, miniature toys, collectables
Open Mon–Fri 10am–5pm
Sat 10am–1pm
Fairs NEC
Services Valuations, restoration

⊞ Notions Antiquaria
Contact T Alena Brett
✉ 24 Cecil Court, London, WC2N 4HE
☎ 020 7836 8222
Est. 1989 *Stock size* Small
Stock Antiquarian and second-hand books and prints, incuding Vanity Fair, maps, cartoons, early documents
Open By appointment

⊞ Percy's Ltd (LAPADA)
Contact Mr D Simons
✉ 16 The London Silver Vaults, Chancery Lane, London, WC2A 1QS 🅿
☎ 020 7242 3618 📠 020 7831 6541
📧 sales@percys-silver.com
🌐 www.percys-silver.com
Est. 1935 *Stock size* Large
Stock 18th–19thC decorative silver and plate
Open Mon–Fri 9.30am–5pm
Sat 10am–1pm
Fairs Olympia (June, Nov)
Services Valuations, repairs

⊞ Henry Pordes Books Ltd
Contact Mr G Della-Ragione
✉ 58–60 Charing Cross Road, London, WC2H 0BB
☎ 020 7836 9031 📠 020 7240 4232
📧 info@henrypordesbooks.com
🌐 www.henrypordesbooks.com
Est. 1983 *Stock size* Medium
Stock Remainders, second-hand, antiquarian books, art, literature, film, theatre, music Judaica a speciality
Open Mon–Sat 10am–7pm

⊞ Quinto Bookshop
Contact Miss Rebecca De Miguel
✉ 48a Charing Cross Road, London, WC2H 0BB
☎ 020 7379 7669 📠 020 7836 5977
Est. 1979 *Stock size* Medium
Stock General second-hand, books
Open Mon–Sat 9am–9pm
Sun noon–8pm

⊞ Bertram Rota Ltd (ABA, ILAB)
Contact Mr J Rota
✉ 1st Floor, 31 Long Acre, London, WC2E 9LT 🅿
☎ 020 7836 0723 📠 020 7497 9058
📧 bertramrota@compuserve.com
🌐 www.bertramrota.co.uk
Est. 1923 *Stock size* Small
Stock Antiquarian, rare, second-hand books, 1890–present day first editions of English and American literature
Open Mon–Fri 9.30am–5.30pm
Services Valuations, book search, catalogues (4–6 a year)

⊞ Silstar Antiques Ltd
Contact Mr B Stern
✉ 29 The London Silver Vaults, Chancery Lane, London, WC2A 1QS 🅿
☎ 020 7242 6740 📠 020 7430 1745
📧 silver@silstar.co.uk
Est. 1955 *Stock size* Large
Stock Antique and modern silver of all descriptions
Open Mon–Fri 10am–5pm

⊞ Jack Simons Antiques Ltd (LAPADA)
Contact Mr J Simons
✉ 16 The London Silver Vaults, Chancery Lane,

LONDON

London,
WC2A 1QS ▣
☎ 020 7242 3221 ✆ 020 7831 6541
Est. 1955 *Stock size* Large
Stock Fine antique English and
Continental silver, objets d'art
Open Mon–Fri 9.30am–5pm
Sat 10am–1pm
Services Valuations, restoration

⊞ Star Signings
Contact John or Mark
✉ 8 Upper St Martin's Lane,
Covent Garden,
London,
WC2H 9DL
☎ 020 7836 3013
✉ starsignings@btconnect.com
Est. 1998 *Stock size* Large
Stock Signed memorabilia,
photographs, programmes,
shirts, sporting, films, music
Open Mon–Sat 11am–6pm
Services Valuations

⊞ S & J Stodel (BADA)
Contact Mr S Stodel
✉ 24 The London Silver Vaults,
Chancery Lane,
London,
WC2A 1QS ▣
☎ 020 7405 7009 ✆ 020 7242 6366
✉ stodel@msn.com
⊕ www.chinesesilver.com
or www.stodelsilver.com
Est. 1973
Stock Chinese export silver,
Art Deco silver, antique silver
flatware
Open Mon–Fri 9.30am–5.30pm
Sat 9.30am–1pm
Fairs Olympia (June), (Nov)

⊞ Storeys Ltd
Contact T Kingswood
✉ 3 Cecil Court, Charing Cross,
London,
WC2N 4EZ
☎ 020 7836 3777 ✆ 020 7836 3788
✉ storeysltd@btinternet.com
Est. 1984 *Stock size* Large
Stock Antiquarian prints
Open Mon–Sat 10am–6pm

⊞ Tindley & Chapman
Contact James Tindley
✉ 4 Cecil Court,
London,
WC2N 4HE
☎ 020 7240 2161 ✆ 020 7379 1062
Est. 1972 *Stock size* Medium
Stock Antiquarian and second-
hand books, 20thC first editions,

literature, novels, poetry
Open Mon–Fri 10am–5.30pm
Sat 11am–5pm
Services Valuations

⊞ Tom Tom
Contact Gary Mitchell
✉ 42 New Compton Street,
London,
WC2H 8DA ▣
☎ 020 7240 7909 ✆ 020 7240 7909
✉ mail@tomtom.biz
⊕ www.tomtom.biz
Est. 1993 *Stock size* Large
Stock Post-war designer
furniture and technology, classics
by Eames, Jacobsen, Saarinen,
contemporary art
Open Tues–Fri noon–7pm Sat
11am–6pm or by appointment
Services Valuations

⊞ Travis & Emery Music
Bookshop (ABA, PBFA)
Contact Mr Coleman
✉ 17 Cecil Court,
off Charing Cross Road,
London,
WC2N 4EZ
☎ 020 7240 2129 ✆ 020 7497 0790
✉ maenq@travis-and-emery.com
Est. 1960 *Stock size* Medium
Stock Antiquarian sheet music,
prints, ephemera, books on music
Open Mon–Sat 11am–6pm Sun
noon–4pm or by appointment
Services Valuations

⊞ Vintage & Rare Guitars
(London)
Contact Adam Newman
6 Denmark Street,
London,
WC2H 8LX ▣
☎ 020 7240 7500 ✆ 020 7240 8900
✉ enquiries@vintageandrare
guitars.com
⊕ www.vintageandrareguitars.com
Est. 1981 *Stock size* Large
Stock Classic vintage American
guitars
Open Mon–Sat 10am–6pm
Sun noon–4pm
Services Valuations, restoration

⊞ William Walter
Antiques Ltd (BADA,
LAPADA)
Contact Miss E Simpson
✉ 3 The London Silver Vaults,
Chancery Lane,
London,
WC2A 1QS ▣

☎ 020 7242 3248 ✆ 020 7404 1280
✉ enq@wwantiques.prestel.co.uk
⊕ www.williamwalter.co.uk
Est. 1949 *Stock size* Large
Stock Georgian silver, decorative
silver, flatware etc
Open Mon–Fri 9.30am–5.30pm
Sat 9.30am–1pm
Services Valuations, repairs

⊞ Watkins Books Ltd
Contact Jeremy Cranswick
or Ricky James
✉ 19 Cecil Court,
London,
WC2N 4EZ ▣
☎ 020 7836 2182
✉ service@watkinsbooks.com
⊕ www.watkinsbooks.com
Est. 1894 *Stock size* Large
Stock Antiquarian books
specializing in mystical,
occult, Eastern religions
Open Mon–Fri 10am–8pm
Sat 10.30am–6pm
Services Shipping

⊞ Peter K Weiss
Contact Mr P Weiss
✉ 18 The London Silver Vaults,
Chancery Lane, London,
WC2A 8QS ▣
☎ 020 7242 8100
✉ peterweiss@mymailstation.com
Est. 1958 *Stock size* Large
Stock Antique clocks, watches,
objets d'art
Open Mon–Fri 10am–4pm
Sat 10am–1pm
Services Valuations, restoration

⊞ Nigel Williams Rare
Books (PBFA, ABA)
Contact Mr Nigel Williams
✉ 25 Cecil Court,
Charing Cross Road,
London,
WC2N 4EZ ▣
☎ 020 7836 7757 ✆ 020 7379 5918
✉ sales@nigelwilliams.com
⊕ www.nigelwilliams.com
Est. 1989 *Stock size* Medium
Stock Antiquarian, rare, second-
hand books, collectable
children's, illustrated,
19th–20thC first editions
Open Mon–Sat 10am–6pm
Fairs Olympia, Russell Hotel
Services Monthly catalogue

⊞ The Witch Ball
Contact Rosslyn Glassman
✉ 2 Cecil Court, London,

WC2N 4HE
☎ 020 7836 2922 🖷 020 7836 2922
📧 thewitchball@btinternet.com
🌐 www.thewitchball.co.uk
Est. 1967 *Stock size* Medium
Stock Antique prints, posters
of the performing arts
Open Mon–Sat 10.30am–7pm

MIDDLESEX

EASTCOTE

⊞ Eastcote Bookshop
Contact Mrs E May
✉ 156–160 Field End Road,
Eastcote,
Middlesex,
HA5 1RH 🅿
☎ 020 8866 9888 🖷 020 8985 9383
Est. 1994 *Stock size* Large
Stock General, antiquarian,
rare, second-hand books
Open Tues noon–4pm Thurs,
Fri 11am–4pm Sat 10am–5pm
Services Valuations

ENFIELD

⊞ Designer Classics
Contact Mr L Wilkin
✉ 70 Goat Lane, Enfield,
Middlesex,
EN1 4UB
☎ 020 8366 6006 🖷 020 8366 8788
📧 designerclassics@btconnect.com
🌐 www.designerclassic.co.uk
Est. 1998 *Stock size* Large
Stock 1950s–present day
classics by famous designers,
Bellini, Herman Miller, Verna
Panton, computers, hi-fi,
radios etc
Open By appointment

⊞ Gallerie Veronique
Contact Ms V Aslangul
✉ 66 Chase Side, Enfield,
Middlesex,
EN2 6NJ 🅿
☎ 020 8342 1005 🖷 020 8342 1005
📱 07770 410041
📧 antiques@gallerieveronique.co.uk
Est. 1993 *Stock size* Large
Stock Victorian, Edwardian,
1970s furniture
Open Mon–Fri 10am–3pm
Sat 10am–5pm closed Wed
Services Restoration, upholstery

⊞ Griffin Antiques
Contact Mr J Gardner
✉ 6 Chase Side, Enfield,

Middlesex,
EN2 6NF 🅿
☎ 020 8366 5959
📱 07837 950949
Est. 1970 *Stock size* Medium
Stock Wide range of antiques,
porcelain, silver, metalware,
scales, weights, measures,
candlesticks
Open Mon–Fri 10.30am–6pm
Sat 4.30am–6pm
Fairs Newark, Ardingly
Services Valuations

⊞ Period Style Lighting
(Lighting Association)
Contact Geoff Day
✉ 8–9 East Lodge Lane,
Botany Bay, Enfield,
Middlesex,
EN2 8AS 🅿
☎ 020 8363 9789 🖷 020 8363 2369
📧 sales@period-style-lighting.com
🌐 www.look4lights.com
Est. 1990 *Stock size* Large
Stock Antique, traditional lighting
Open Tues–Sun 10am–5pm
Services Valuations, restoration,
coffee shop

HAREFIELD

⊞ David Ansell (BHI,
BAFRA)
Contact David Ansell
✉ 48 Dellside, Harefield,
Middlesex,
UB9 6AX 🅿
☎ 01895 824648
📱 07812 841993
📧 davidansell@globalnet.co.uk
Est. 1990 *Stock size* Medium
Stock Clocks, photographica
Open Mon–Sun 8.30am–5.30pm
or by appointment
Fairs NEC, Newark
Services Restoration

HATCH END

⌂ A & C Antiques &
Collectables
Contact Mr Stevens or
Mrs Blagden
✉ 266 Uxbridge Road,
Hatch End,
Middlesex,
HA5 4HS 🅿
☎ 020 8421 1653
Est. 1994 *Stock size* Large
No. of dealers 12
Stock Doulton, Art Deco,
ceramics, small furniture,

collectables
Open Mon–Sat 10am–5.30pm
Sun 11.30am–4pm

RUISLIP

⚒ Alberts of Kensington
Contact Mr J A Wooster
✉ PO Box 147, Ruislip, Middlesex,
HA4 9WD
☎ 020 8869 9292 🖷 020 8869 9393
Est. 1964
Open Tues–Fri 10am–6pm
Sat 10am–4pm postal only
Sales 10–12 postal auctions of
cigarette cards and ephemera
per year
Catalogues Yes

⌂ The Old Trinket Box
Contact Eileen Cameron
✉ 1b High Street, Ruislip,
Middlesex,
HA4 7AU 🅿
☎ 01895 675658
Est. 1995 *Stock size* Medium
No. of dealers 8
Stock Wide range of collectables
Open Mon–Sat 10am–5pm
Sun 11am–3pm

STAINES

⊞ K W Dunster Antiques
Contact Mr K W Dunster
✉ 23 Church Street, Staines,
Middlesex,
TW18 4EN 🅿
☎ 01784 453297 🖷 01784 483146
📱 07831 649626
Est. 1973 *Stock size* Medium
Stock Brass, furniture, jewellery,
marine items
Open Mon–Sat 9am–4pm
Services Valuations, house
clearance

⊞ Staines Antiques
Contact Mr D Smith
✉ 145–147 Kingston Road,
Staines, Middlesex,
TW18 1PD 🅿
☎ 01784 461306 🖷 01784 461306
Est. 1978 *Stock size* Large
Stock Furniture, ceramics
Open Mon–Sat 9am–5.30pm
Services Valuations, restoration

TEDDINGTON

⊞ Waldegrave Antiques
Contact Mrs J Murray
✉ 197 Waldegrave Road,

LONDON
MIDDLESEX • TWICKENHAM

Teddington, Middlesex,
TW11 8LX 🅿
☎ 020 8404 0162
📱 07946 506145
Est. 1997 *Stock size* Large
Stock Wide selection of antiques,
furniture, silver, porcelain, glass etc
Open Mon–Sat 10.30am–5.30pm
Fairs Kempton Park
Services Valuations

TWICKENHAM

⊞ **Antique Interiors**
Contact Mr A Mundy
✉ 93 Crown Road, Twickenham,
Middlesex,
TW1 3EX 🅿
☎ 020 8607 9853
Est. 1995 *Stock size* Medium
Stock English, French and 19thC
mahogany and old pine
furniture, other quality English
items, garden items
Open Tues–Sat 10am–5.30pm
Services Restoration, upholstery

⊞ **Cheyne Galleries**
Contact Mrs C Cox
✉ 8 Crown Road, Twickenham,
Middlesex,
TW1 3EE 🅿
☎ 020 8892 6932
Est. 1977 *Stock size* Medium
Stock Wide range of antique and
second-hand items, collectables
Open Tues–Sat 10am–6pm
Services Valuations, house
clearance

⊞ **Anthony C Hall (ABA, PBFA)**
Contact Mr A C Hall
✉ 30 Staines Road, Twickenham,
Middlesex,

TW2 5AH 🅿
☎ 020 8898 2638 📠 020 8893 8855
📧 achallbooks@intonet.co.uk
🌐 www.hallbooks.co.uk
Est. 1966 *Stock size* Large
Stock Out-of-print and rare
books, Russian and eastern
European topics a speciality
Open Mon Thurs–Fri 10am–5pm
Fairs Richmond Book Fair
Services Mail order

⊞ **John Ives (PBFA)**
Contact Mr J Ives
✉ 5 Normanhurst Drive,
Twickenham,
Middlesex,
TW1 1NA 🅿
☎ 020 8892 6265 📠 020 8744 3944
📧 jives@btconnect.com
🌐 www.ukbookworld.com/
members/johnives
Est. 1979
Stock Reference books on
antiques and collecting, 1,000s of
titles in stock including scarce
items
Open By appointment
Services Mail order, catalogue

⊞ **The Twickenham
Antiques Warehouse**
Contact Mr A Clubb
✉ 80 Colne Road, Twickenham,
Middlesex,
TW2 6QE 🅿
☎ 020 8894 5555
📱 07973 132847
📧 and.clubb@aol.com
Est. 1984 *Stock size* Large
Stock English and Continental
furniture, 1700–1930s, decorative
items
Open Mon–Sat 9.30am–5pm
Services Valuations, restoration

UXBRIDGE

⊞ **Antiques Warehouse &
Restoration**
Contact Mr M Allenby
✉ 34 Rockingham Road,
Uxbridge, Middlesex,
UB8 2TZ 🅿
☎ 01895 256963
Est. 1979 *Stock size* Large
Stock 1800–1950 furniture,
collectables
Open Mon–Sat 10am–5pm
Services Restoration

WEST RUISLIP

🔨 **A Bainbridge & Co**
Contact Mr P Bainbridge
✉ The Auction House, Ickenham
Road, West Ruislip, Middlesex,
HA4 7DL 🅿
☎ 01895 621991 📠 01895 623621
Est. 1979
Open Mon–Fri 9am–5pm
Sales Antiques and general
effects Thurs 11am, viewing Wed
1–7pm Thurs from 9.30am
Frequency Every 6 weeks
Catalogues Yes

WRAYSBURY

⊞ **Wyrardisbury Antiques**
Contact Mr C Tuffs
✉ 23 High Street, Wraysbury,
Staines, Middlesex,
TW19 5DA 🅿
☎ 01784 483225 📠 01784 483225
Est. 1978 *Stock size* Medium
Stock All types, ages of clocks up
to Edwardian, small furniture,
barometers
Open Tues–Sat 10am–5pm
Services Valuations, repairs

SOUTH

BERKSHIRE

ALDERMASTON

⊞ Village Antiques Aldermaston

Contact Mrs Vivian Green
✉ The Old Dispensary,
The Street, Aldermaston,
Reading, Berkshire,
RG7 4LW ℗
☎ 0118 971 2370
Est. 1997 *Stock size* Large
Stock Clocks, architectural
antiques, furniture, china, glass,
silver, garden items
Open Tues–Sun 10am–5.30pm

⊞ Melnick House Antiques (ESoc)

Contact Mrs J Collins
✉ 306 Kings Road, Sunninghill,
Ascot, Berkshire,
SL5 8TS ℗
☎ 01344 628383 ℮ 01344 291800
ℯ antiquarian@melnick-
house.demon.co.uk
Est. 1972 *Stock size* Large
Stock Antique maps, prints,
decorative antiques
Open Mon–Sat 10am–5pm
Services Restoration, free
postage worldwide

⊞ Tempus Watches (LAPADA)

Contact John Wingate
✉ Sunninghill, Ascot, Berkshire,
SL5 ℗

☎ 01344 874007
ℯ john@tempus-watches.co.uk
ⓦ www.tempus-watches.co.uk
Est. 1978 *Stock size* Medium
Stock Antique clocks, vintage
wristwatches
Open By appointment
Services Restoration

ASHMORE GREEN

⚘ Law Fine Art Ltd

Contact Mr Mark Law
✉ Ash Cottage,
Ashmore Green Road,
Ashmore Green, Berkshire,
RG18 9ER ℗
☎ 01635 860033 ℮ 01635 860036
ℯ info@lawfineart.co.uk
ⓦ www.lawfineart.co.uk
Est. 2000
Open Mon–Fri 9am–5.30pm
Sales Eight sales a year including
five specialist ceramics and glass
sales
Frequency Monthly
Catalogues Yes

CAVERSHAM

⊞ Amber Antiques (TVADA)

Contact Clair Hughes
✉ 153 Bath Road, Reading,
Berkshire,
RG30 2BD
☎ 01189 567450
ⓜ 07977 499234
ⓦ www.amberantiques.co.uk

Est. 1990 *Stock size* Medium
Stock French antiques,
decorative items
Open Mon–Sat 10.30am–5.30pm
Fairs TVADA
Services Restoration, in-house
traditional upholstery

⊞ D Card

Contact D Card
✉ 1a Chester Street, Caversham,
Reading, Berkshire,
RG4 8JH ℗
☎ 01189 470777 ℮ 01189 470777
ℯ dncard@ntlworld.com
Est. 1971 *Stock size* Small
Stock Longcase, carriage, table
clocks and music boxes
Open Mon–Fri 9am–5pm
appointment preferred
Services Valuations, restoration

⊞ The Clock Workshop (LAPADA, TVADA, BHI)

Contact Mr J Yealland
✉ 17 Prospect Street, Caversham,
Reading, Berkshire,
RG4 8JB ℗
☎ 01189 470741
ℯ theclockworkshop@hotmail.com
ⓦ www.lapada.co.uk
Est. 1981 *Stock size* Medium
Stock English clocks, French
carriage, mantel clocks,
barometers
Open Mon–Fri 9.30am–5.30pm
Sat 10am–1pm
Fairs Olympia, LAPADA, TVADA
Services Valuations, restoration

SOUTH
BERKSHIRE • COOKHAM

COOKHAM

⊞ Cookham Antiques (TVADA)
Contact Mr G Wallis
✉ 35 Station Parade, Cookham, Maidenhead, Berkshire, SL6 9BR 🅿
☎ 01628 523224
📱 07778 020536
🌐 antiquedecorative.co.uk
Est. 1989 **Stock size** Large
Stock Furniture, decorative items, architectural, French and Continental painted furniture, country effects
Open Mon–Sat 10am–5pm Sun 11am–5pm or by appointment
Fairs Battersea

DONNINGTON

⚒ Dreweatt Neate (SOFAA, ARVA, BACA Award Winner 2004)
Contact Clive Stewart-Lockhart
✉ Donnington Priory, Donnington, Newbury, Berkshire, RG14 2JE 🅿
☎ 01635 553553 📠 01635 553599
📧 donnington@dnfa.com
🌐 www.dnfa.com
Est. 1759
Open Mon–Fri 9.30am–6pm Sat 9am–12.30pm
Sales General sales fortnightly Tues at 10am, antiques sales every six weeks Wed 10am, viewing Sat prior 9am–12.30pm Mon 9.30am–7pm and 9.30am–4pm for Wed sales
Catalogues Available on website

ETON

⊞ Art and Antiques (Eton Traders)
Contact Mrs V Rand
✉ 69 High Street, Eton, Windsor, Berkshire, SL4 6AA 🅿
☎ 01753 855727
📱 07903 921168
Est. 1982 **Stock size** Large
Stock Furniture, china, brass, silver plate, jewellery, collectors' items
Open Mon–Fri 10.30am–5.30pm Sat 10.30am–6pm Sun 2.30–6pm

⊞ Chobham & Eton Antique Clocks (BHI)
Contact Mike Morris
✉ 17 High Street, Eton, Windsor, Berkshire,
SL4 6AX 🅿
☎ 01276 682560
📱 07774 127098
📧 c10cks@aol.com
🌐 www.c10ck.com
Est. 1989 **Stock size** Medium
Stock Antique clocks, barometers
Open Mon–Sat 10am–5pm Sun 2pm–4pm
Services Valuations, restoration

⊞ Eton Antiques
Contact Mr M Procter
✉ 91 High Street, Eton, Windsor, Berkshire, SL4 6AF 🅿
☎ 01753 860752 📠 01753 818222
🌐 www.etonantiques.com
Est. 1969 **Stock size** Medium
Stock 18th–19thC English furniture, clocks
Open Mon–Sat 10am–5.30pm
Services Valuations, restoration, shipping

⊞ Marcelline Herald Antiques (LAPADA, TVADA)
Contact Marcelline Herald
✉ 41 High Street, Eton, Windsor, Berkshire, SL4 6BD 🅿
☎ 01753 833924
📱 07774 607443
📧 mail@marcellineherald.com
🌐 www.marcellineherald.com
Est. 1998 **Stock size** Medium
Stock 17thC shop in historic Eton High Street selling18th–19thC furniture, mirrors and decorative items, lighting
Open Tues–Sat 10am–5pm
Fairs Decorative Fair Battersea, TVADA
Services Valuations

⊞ Peter J Martin and Son (TVADA, LAPADA)
Contact Mr P Martin
✉ 40 High Street, Eton, Windsor, Berkshire, SL4 6BD 🅿
☎ 01753 864901
📱 07850 975889
📧 pjmartin.antiques@btopenworld.com
🌐 www.pjmartin-antiques.co.uk
Est. 1967 **Stock size** Large
Stock 18th–20thC furniture, copper, brass, mirrors
Open Mon–Fri 9am–5pm closed 1–2pm Sat 10am–1pm or by appointment
Services Restoration

⊞ Mostly Boxes
Contact Mr G Munday
✉ 93 High Street, Eton, Windsor, Berkshire, SL4 6AF
☎ 01753 858470 📠 01753 857212
Est. 1982 **Stock size** Large
Stock Ivory, tortoiseshell, wooden decorative antique boxes
Open Mon–Sat 10am–6.30pm
Fairs K & M London
Services Valuations

⊞ Studio 101
Contact Anthony Cove
✉ 101 High Street, Eton, Windsor, Berkshire, SL4 6AF 🅿
☎ 01753 863333
Est. 1959 **Stock size** Small
Stock General antiques
Open By appointment

⊞ Times Past Antiques (BHI)
Contact Mr P Jackson
✉ 59 High Street, Eton, Windsor, Berkshire, SL4 6BL 🅿
☎ 01753 856392 📠 01753 856392
📱 07768 454444
📧 phillipstimespast@aol.com
Est. 1974 **Stock size** Medium
Stock Clocks, barometers, small furniture
Open By appointment
Services Valuations, restoration

⊞ Turks Head Antiques
Contact Mrs A Baillie or Mr A Reeve
✉ 98 High Street, Eton, Windsor, Berkshire, SL4 6AF 🅿
☎ 01753 863939
Est. 1975 **Stock size** Medium
Stock Porcelain, silver, glass, pictures
Open Mon–Sat 10am–5pm
Services Restoration of porcelain, silver-plating

⌂ Windsor & Eton Antiques Centre
Contact Claudia Thomas or John French
✉ 17 High Street, Eton, Windsor, Berkshire, SL4 6AX 🅿
☎ 01753 840412 📠 01753 840412
Est. 2000 **Stock size** Large
No. of dealers 18
Stock General antiques and

collectables, clocks, porcelain
Open Mon–Fri 10.30am–5pm
Sun 2–4pm
Services Valuations

FIFIELD

⊞ Jan Hicks Antiques (TVADA, LAPADA)
Contact Jan Hicks
✉ Fifield, Near Windsor, Berkshire, SL4 🅿
☎ 01488 683986 ● 01488 681222
⊕ 07770 230686
● antiques@janhicks.com
Est. 1987 *Stock size* Large
Stock French and English country furniture, 18thC and earlier, oil paintings
Open By appointment
Fairs TVADA, Antiques & Audacity (Arundel Castle)

GORING ON THAMES

⊞ Barbara's Antiques and Bric-a-Brac
Contact Mrs M Bateman
✉ Wheel Orchard, Station Road, Goring on Thames, Reading, Berkshire, RG8 9HB 🅿
☎ 01491 873032
Est. 1981 *Stock size* Large
Stock Furniture, linen, lace, jewellery, china, brass, silver, plate, railwayana
Open Mon–Sat 10am–1pm 2.15–5pm

HUNGERFORD

⊞ Beedham Antiques Ltd (BADA)
Contact Herbert or Paul Beedham
✉ 26 Charnham Street, Hungerford, Berkshire, RG17 0EJ 🅿
☎ 01488 684141 ● 01488 684050
Est. 1971 *Stock size* Large
Stock 16th–17thC English and Continental oak furniture
Open Mon–Sat 11am–5pm or by appointment
Fairs Olympia June, Nov

⊞ Below Stairs of Hungerford
Contact Stewart Hofgartner
✉ 103 High Street, Hungerford, Berkshire, RG17 0NB 🅿
☎ 01488 682317 ● 01488 684294

● hofgartner@belowstairs.co.uk
⊚ www.belowstairs.co.uk
Est. 1972 *Stock size* Large
Stock Collectables, furniture, taxidermy, garden items, kitchenware, lighting, interior fittings, no reproductions
Open Mon–Sun 10am–6pm
Services Valuations

⊞ Sir William Bentley Billiards
Contact Travers Mettleton
✉ Standen Manor Farm, Hungerford, Berkshire, RG17 0RB 🅿
☎ 01488 681711 ● 01488 685197
⊚ www.billiards.co.uk
Est. 1976 *Stock size* Large
Stock Billiard tables, accessories, also builds contemporary and traditional billiard tables including convertible dining and billiard tables
Open Mon–Sun or by appointment
Fairs Daily Telegraph House and Garden, Ideal Homes
Services Valuations, restoration

⊞ Bowhouse Antiques
Contact Jo Preston
✉ 3–4 Faulkener Square, Charnham Street, Hungerford, Berkshire, RG17 0EP 🅿
☎ 01488 680826 ● 01488 680896
⊕ 07710 921331
● bowhouseantique@aol.com
Est. 2000 *Stock size* Large
Stock 19thC decorative interiors, contemporary furniture
Open Mon–Sat 10.00am–5.30pm Sun by appointment only
Services Upholstery

⊞ Bridge House Antiques & Interiors
Contact Kate Pols
✉ 7 Bridge Street, Hungerford, Berkshire, RG17 0EH 🅿
☎ 01488 681999 ● 01488 681999
● bridgehouse@kpols.fsnet.co.uk
Est. 1992 *Stock size* Large
Stock Antiques, decorative items for interiors
Open Tues–Sat 10am–5.30pm closed Fri
Services Shipping

⊞ Barry Cotton Antiques
Contact Barry Cotton
✉ Great Grooms Antique Centre,

Riverside House, Charnham Street, Hungerford, Berkshire, RG17 0EP 🅿
☎ 020 8563 9899 ● 020 8563 9899
● enquiries@barrycottonantiques.com
⊚ www.barrycottonantiques.com
Est. 1998 *Stock size* Medium
Stock 18th–19thC period furniture, associated items
Open Mon–Sat 9.30–5.30pm Sun 10am–4pm
Services Valuations

⊞ Countryside Books (PBFA)
Contact Mr Martin Smith
✉ The Hungerford Antiques Centre, High Street, Hungerford, Berkshire, RG17 0NB
☎ 01264 773943
Est. 1980 *Stock size* Medium
Stock Antiquarian, rare, second-hand books
Open Mon–Fri 9.15am–5.30pm Sat 9.15am–6pm Sun 11am–5pm
Fairs PBFA fair, Russell Hotel

⊞ Franklin Antiques
Contact Mrs L Franklin
✉ 25 Charnham Street, Hungerford, Berkshire, RG17 0EJ 🅿
☎ 01488 682404 ● 01488 686069
● antiques@lyndafranklin.com
Est. 1974 *Stock size* Large
Stock 18th–19thC Continental furniture
Open Mon–Sat 10am–5.30pm
Services Interior decoration and sourcing

⊞ Garden Art
Contact Mr Travers Nettleton
✉ Barrs Yard, 1 Bath Road, Hungerford, Berkshire, RG17 0HE 🅿
☎ 01488 686811 ● 01488 686801
● sales@gardenartplus.com
⊚ www.gardenartplus.com
Est. 1976 *Stock size* Large
Stock Architectural antiques for the garden including gates, neo-classical statuary, bronze
Open Mon–Sat 9am–6pm Sun 10am–4pm
Services Valuations, restoration, garden design

⌂ Great Grooms of Hungerford
Contact Mr J Podger
✉ Riverside House, Charnham

Street, Hungerford, Berkshire,
RG17 0EP 🅿
☎ 01488 682314 ✆ 01488 686677
📧 hungerford@greatgrooms.co.uk
🌐 www.greatgrooms.co.uk
Est. 1998 *Stock size* Large
No. of dealers 65
Stock General antiques,
furnishings, country furniture,
porcelain, clocks, silver, rugs,
glass, bronzes, lighting, pictures
Open Mon–Sat 9.30am–5.30pm
Sun 10am–4pm
Services Valuations, restoration

🏠 Hungerford Arcade
Contact Trevor Butcher
✉ 26 High Street, Hungerford,
Berkshire,
RG17 0ER 🅿
☎ 01488 683701
Est. 1973 *Stock size* Large
No. of dealers 85
Stock General antiques and
collectables
Open Mon–Sun 9.15am–5.30pm

⊞ Roger King Antiques
Contact Mrs A King
✉ 111 High Street, Hungerford,
Berkshire,
RG17 0NB 🅿
☎ 01488 682256
📧 annabel02@btconnect.com
🌐 www.kingantiques.co.uk
Est. 1974 *Stock size* Large
Stock Georgian–Victorian
furniture
Open Mon–Sat 9.30am–5pm
Sun 11am–5pm

⊞ M J M Antiques (Arms & Armour Society)
Contact Michael Mancey
✉ 13 Bridge Street, Hungerford,
Berkshire, RG17 0EH 🅿
☎ 01488 684905 ✆ 01488 684090
📱 07774 479997
📧 mike@oldguns.co.uk
🌐 www.oldguns.co.uk
Est. 1999 *Stock size* Medium
Stock Fine antique arms
Open Mon–Sat 10am–5pm
or by appointment
Fairs Arms & armour fairs
Services Valuations

⊞ The Old Malthouse (BADA, CINOA)
Contact Mr or Mrs P Hunwick
✉ 15 Bridge Street, Hungerford,
Berkshire, RG17 0EG 🅿
☎ 01488 682209 ✆ 01488 682209

📱 07771 862257
📧 hunwick@oldmalthouse
antiques.co.uk
Est. 1959 *Stock size* Large
Stock 18th–19thC furniture,
brass, mirrors, paintings,
decorative items
Open Mon–Sat 10am–5.30pm
Fairs Olympia, Chelsea
Services Valuations

⊞ Principia Fine Art
Contact Mr M Forrer
✉ 111d High Street, Hungerford,
Berkshire,
RG17 0NF 🅿
☎ 01488 682873
📱 07899 926020
🌐 www.antiquesportfolio.com
Est. 1970 *Stock size* Large
Stock Scientific instruments,
small furniture, Oriental art,
books, paintings, works of art
Open Mon–Fri 10.30am–5pm
Sat 2.30–5pm
Services Valuations, restoration,
shipping, book search

⊞ Styles Silver (LAPADA)
Contact Mr or Mrs Styles
✉ 12 Bridge Street, Hungerford,
Berkshire,
RG17 0EH 🅿
☎ 01488 683922 ✆ 01488 683488
📱 07778 769559
📧 george@styles-silver.co.uk
🌐 www.styles-silver.co.uk
Est. 1974 *Stock size* Large
Stock Silver of all periods,
flatware services a speciality,
collectables, christening, wedding
presents, silver birds and animals
Open Mon–Sat 9am–5.30pm
or by appointment
Services Restoration

⊞ Turpins Antiques (BADA, CINOA)
Contact Mrs J Sumner
✉ 17 Bridge Street, Hungerford,
Berkshire,
RG17 0EG 🅿
☎ 01488 681886/01672 870727
Est. 1959 *Stock size* Medium
Stock 18thC English and Regency
walnut furniture
Open Wed Fri Sat 10am–5pm or
by appointment
Fairs Olympia

⊞ Youll's Antiques
Contact Mr B Youll
✉ 27–28 Charnham Street,

Hungerford, Berkshire,
RG17 0EJ 🅿
☎ 01488 682046 ✆ 01488 684335
📧 bruce.youll@virgin.net
🌐 www.youll.com
Est. 1935 *Stock size* Large
Stock 17th–20thC English and
French furniture, porcelain,
silver, decorative items
Open Mon–Sun 10.30am–5.30pm
Fairs Newark
Services Valuations, restoration

KINGSCLERE

⊞ Wyseby House Books (PBFA)
Contact Dr Tim Oldham
✉ Kingsclere Old Bookshop,
2a George Street, Kingsclere,
Newbury, Berkshire,
RG20 5NQ 🅿
☎ 01635 297995 ✆ 01635 297677
📧 info@wyseby.co.uk
🌐 www.wyseby.co.uk
Est. 1977 *Stock size* Large
Stock General antiquarian, rare,
second-hand books, fine art,
decorative arts, architecture a
speciality
Open Mon–Sat 9am–5pm
Services Catalogue 10 times a year

LECKHAMPSTEAD

⊞ Hill Farm Antiques
Contact Mr M Beesley
✉ Hill Farm, Shop Lane,
Leckhampstead, Newbury,
Berkshire,
RG20 8QG 🅿
☎ 01488 638541/638361
✆ 01488 638541
📧 beesley@hillfarmantiques.
demon.co.uk
🌐 www.hillfarmantiques.co.uk
Est. 1987 *Stock size* Large
Stock 19thC extending dining
tables in mahogany, oak, walnut
Open By appointment

MIDGHAM

🔨 Cameo
Contact Jon King
✉ Kennet Home Farm, Bath Road,
Midgham, Reading, Berkshire,
RG7 5UX 🅿
☎ 01189 713772 ✆ 01189 710330
📧 office@cameo-auctioneers.co.uk
🌐 www.cameo-auctioneers.co.uk
Open Mon–Fri 9am–5pm
Sat by appointment

Sales Two-day sale of antiques, furniture, collectables, pictures
Frequency Monthly
Catalogues Yes

⚒ Special Auction Services
Contact Andrew Hilton
✉ **Kennetholme, Bath Road, Midgham, Reading, Berkshire, RG7 5UX** 🅿
☎ 0118 971 2949 ❶ 0118 971 2420
🄴 commemorative@aol.com
🅦 www.invaluable.com/sas
Est. 1991
Open 9am–5pm by appointment
Sales Special auctions of commemoratives, pot lids, Prattware, fairings, Goss & Crested, Baxter and Le Blond prints, toys for the collector. Held at The Courtyard Hotel, Padworth, Nr Reading. Please telephone for details
Frequency 8 per annum
Catalogues Yes

MORTIMER

⊞ Frank Milward (BNTA, ANA)
Contact Mr F Milward
✉ **2 Ravensworth Road, Mortimer, Reading, Berkshire, RG7 3UU** 🅿
☎ 0118 933 2843 ❶ 0118 933 2843
Est. 1975 *Stock size* Medium
Stock English and foreign coins, banknotes
Open By appointment
Fairs International Coin Fair, Coinex, London
Services Valuations

NEWBURY

⊞ Invicta Bookshop (PBFA)
Contact Mr S Hall
✉ **8 Cromwell Place, Newbury, Berkshire, RG14 1AF** 🅿
☎ 01635 31176
Est. 1969 *Stock size* Medium
Stock Antiquarian, rare and second-hand books, cookery, cricket, military topics a speciality
Open Mon–Sat 10.30am–5.30pm closed Wed
Fairs Oxford, Bath, York PBFA
Services Book search

⊞ Newbury Salvage Ltd
Contact Mr A Bromhead
✉ **Kelvin Road, Newbury,**

Berkshire, RG14 2DB 🅿
☎ 01635 528120 ❶ 01635 551007
❿ 07776 174875
Est. 1988 *Stock size* Large
Stock Bricks, tiles, slates, chimney pots, fireplaces, doors, windows, statuary, sanitary ware, oak beams
Open Mon–Fri 8am–5pm
Sat 9am–1pm

⊞ Alan Walker (BADA, TVADA)
Contact Mr A Walker
✉ **Halfway Manor, Halfway, Newbury, Berkshire, RG20 8NR** 🅿
☎ 01488 657670 ❶ 01488 657670
🅦 www.alanwalker-barometers.com
Est. 1987 *Stock size* Large
Stock 18th–19thC barometers, barographs, related instruments
Open By appointment
Fairs Olympia, BADA, Duke of York's
Services Valuations, restoration, barometers purchased

PANGBOURNE

⊞ R Butler
Contact Rita Butler
✉ **4 Station Road, Pangbourne, Berkshire, RG8 7AN** 🅿
☎ 0118 984 5522
❿ 07752 936327
🄴 rb@knappswood.co.uk
🅦 www.knappswood-antiques.co.uk
Est. 1999 *Stock size* Medium
Stock 17th–20thC small furniture, Victorian–Art Deco silver, 18th–19thC glass, fine ceramics
Open Tues–Sat 9.30am-5pm

READING

⊞ Addington Antiques
Contact Paul Schneiderman
✉ **41 Addington Road, Reading, Berkshire, RG1 5PZ** 🅿
☎ 0118 935 3435
Est. 1996 *Stock size* Small
Stock General antiques, 18thC–1960s design
Open Thurs–Sat 10am–6pm
Fairs Newark, Ardingly

⌂ Fanny's Antiques
Contact Fanny Lyons
✉ **1 Lynmouth Road, Reading, Berkshire,**

RG1 8DE 🅿
☎ 0118 950 8261
Est. 1993 *Stock size* Large
No. of dealers 29
Stock General antiques, furniture, smalls, garden antiques
Open Mon–Sat 10.30am–4pm
Sun noon–4pm

⊞ Graham Gallery
Contact John Steeds
✉ **Highwoods, Burghfield Common, Reading, Berkshire, RG7 3BG** 🅿
☎ 01189 831070 ❶ 01189 831070
🄴 jfsteeds@aol.com
Est. 1975 *Stock size* Medium
Stock 19th–20thC oils, watercolours, prints
Open By appointment

⊞ Rupert Landen Antiques (TVADA)
Contact Rupert Landen
✉ **Church Farm, Reading Road, Woodcote, Reading, Berkshire, RG8 0QX** 🅿
☎ 01491 682396
❿ 07974 7232472
🅦 www.rupertsantiques.com
Est. 1994 *Stock size* Small
Stock Late Georgian and Regency furniture
Open Mon–Fri 9am–6pm
Sat 10am–3pm
Services Restoration

⊞ Mid 20th Century
Contact Al Baynham
✉ **5 Tidmarsh Street, Reading, Berkshire, RG30 1HX**
☎ 0118 950 7224
🄴 info@mid20thcentury.co.uk
🅦 www.mid20thcentury.co.uk
Est. 2003 *Stock size* Medium
Stock Mid-20thC design, homewares, collectables
Open Mon–Sat 10am–6pm
Services Book search

⌂ Reading Collectors Centre
Contact John Willcocks
✉ **Unit 14–15, Harris Arcade, Station Road, Reading, Berkshire, RG1 1DN**
☎ 0118 932 0111 ❶ 0118 958 8666
Est. 2000 *Stock size* Medium
No. of dealers 3
Stock General antiques, memorabilia, records, toys,

model railways, militaria
Open Mon–Sat 10am–5.15pm
Services Valuations

SLOUGH

⊞ **Randtiques**
Contact Mr Tony Lowe
✉ 23 Stoke Road, Slough,
Berkshire,
SL2 5AH 🅿
☎ 01753 572512
📱 07770 407005
Est. 1984 *Stock size* Medium
Stock Furniture, china, glass,
pine, prints, watercolours
Open Mon–Sat 10am–5pm
Services Framing, paint stripping

SONNING-ON-THAMES

⊞ **Cavendish Fine Art
(BADA)**
Contact Janet Middlemiss
✉ Dower House, Pearson Road,
Sonning-on-Thames, Berkshire,
RG4 6UL 🅿
☎ 0118 969 1904
📱 07831 295575
📧 info@cavendishfineart.com
🌐 www.cavendishfineart.com
Est. 1973 *Stock size* Large
Stock Georgian furniture
Open By appointment
Fairs Olympia, BADA

TWYFORD

⊞ **Bell Antiques**
Contact Mr N Timms
✉ 2b High Street, Twyford,
Reading, Berkshire,
RG10 9AE 🅿
☎ 0118 934 2501
Est. 1989 *Stock size* Large
Stock General antiques,
collectables
Open Mon–Sat 9.30am–5.30pm
Sun 10am–5.30pm

⊞ **Stephen Brown Antiques**
Contact Stephen Brown
✉ Unit 6, Three Bridge Mill,
Twyford, Berkshire,
MK18 4DY 🅿
☎ 01296 730130 ☎ 01296 730196
📱 07770 380133
📧 sbrownantiques@btopenworld.com
🌐 www.stephenbrownantiques.co.uk
Est. 1997 *Stock size* Large
Stock Victorian–Edwardian
furniture
Trade only Yes

Open Mon–Fri 10am–5pm
or by appointment
Services Shipping

WARFIELD

⌂ **Moss End Antiques
Centre (TVADA)**
Contact Maureen Staite or
Maura Dorrington
✉ Moss End, Warfield, Berkshire,
RG42 6EJ 🅿
☎ 01344 861942
🌐 www.mossendantiques.co.uk
Est. 1988 *Stock size* Large
No. of dealers 20
Stock Antique furniture, clocks,
silver, glass, porcelain, linen,
collectables, Oriental furniture
Open Mon–Sun 10.30am–5pm
Services Restoration, coffee shop

WARGRAVE

⊞ **Rosina Antiques**
Contact Maxine Lucas
✉ 64 High Street, Wargrave,
Berkshire,
RG10 8BY 🅿
☎ 0118 947 3011 ☎ 0118 940 6299
📧 rosina-antiques@yahoo.com
🌐 www.rosina-antiques.co.uk
Est. 2001 *Stock size* Small
Stock General antiques, musical
instruments
Open Wed–Sun 10am–5pm

⊞ **Wargrave Antiques**
Contact Mr J Connell
✉ 66 High Street, Wargrave,
Berkshire,
RG10 8BY 🅿
☎ 0118 940 2914
Est. 1979 *Stock size* Large
Stock Furniture, porcelain, glass,
silver, copper, brass, 19thC
furniture a speciality
Open Wed–Sun 10am–5pm
Services Valuations, restoration

WINDSOR

⊞ **The Antique Wardrobe
Company**
Contact Mrs Dee Waghorn
✉ 89 Grove Road, Windsor,
Berkshire,
SL4 1HT 🅿
☎ 01753 865627
📧 dee@theantiquewardrobe
company.co.uk
🌐 www.theantiquewardrobe
company.co.uk

Est. 1979 *Stock size* Large
Stock Antique pine wardrobes,
chests-of-drawers
Open Tues–Sat 10am–6pm Sun
11am–3pm or by appointment

⊞ **Berkshire Antiques Co Ltd**
Contact Mr Sutton
✉ 42 Thames Street, Windsor,
Berkshire,
SL4 1PR 🅿
☎ 01753 830100 ☎ 01753 832278
📧 b.antiques@btconnect.com
🌐 www.jewels2go.co.uk
Est. 1981 *Stock size* Large
Stock Silver, dolls, jewellery,
furniture, pictures, porcelain,
Art Deco, Art Nouveau,
commemorative memorabilia,
royal commemoratives
Open Mon–Sat 10.30am–5.30pm
Sun by appointment
Services Valuations, restoration,
antique dolls hospital

⊞ **Norah's Antique Shoppe**
Contact Norah Brooks
✉ 51 Thames Street, Windsor,
Berkshire,
SL4 1TU
☎ 01753 851958
Est. 1987 *Stock size* Large
Stock General antiques,
collectables
Open Mon–Sat 10am–5.30pm
Sun noon–3pm
Services Valuations, restoration

⊞ **Old Barn Antiques**
Contact Mrs Sue Lakey
✉ Wyevale Garden Centre,
Dedworth Road, Windsor,
Berkshire,
SL4 4LH 🅿
☎ 01753 833099
🌐 www.estories.co.uk
Est. 1991 *Stock size* Large
Stock Furniture, porcelain,
jewellery, garden antiquities,
militaria, silver, dolls, glassware,
collectables
Open Mon–Sat 10am–5pm
Sun 10.30am–4.30pm

⊞ **Rule's Antiques (TVADA)**
Contact Miss Sue Rule
✉ 39 St Leonards Road, Windsor,
Berkshire,
SL4 3BP 🅿
☎ 01753 833210
Est. 1995 *Stock size* Medium
Stock Decorative pieces, brass,
lighting, door furniture and

SOUTH

fittings, Retro 1930–1979
Open Mon–Sat 10am–6pm
Fairs TVADA

⊞ **Supatra**
Contact Colin Macintosh
✉ The Old Coach House, Trinity
Yard, 59 St Leonards Road,
Windsor, Berkshire,
SL4 3BX ▣
☎ 01753 858885 ✆ 0870 62232
✉ info@supatra.com
Ⓦ www.supatra.com
Est. 2001 *Stock size* Large
Stock Antique Oriental furniture
Open Mon–Sat 10.30am–5.30pm
Sun 11am–4pm
Services Restoration

WOKINGHAM

⌂ **Barkham Antiques
Centre**
Contact Len or Mary Collins
✉ Barkham Street, Wokingham,
Berkshire,
RG40 4PJ ▣
☎ 0118 976 1355
Ⓦ www.neatsite.com
Est. 1984 *Stock size* Large
No. of dealers 51
Stock Collectables, toy specialists,
Doulton, general antiques,
architectural salvage
Open Mon–Sun 10.30am–5pm
Services Restoration

⊞ **K Faulkner**
Contact Kenneth Faulkner
✉ 65 Brookside, Wokingham,
Berkshire,
RG41 2ST ▣
☎ 0118 978 5255
✉ kfaulkner@bowmore.demon.co.uk
Ⓦ www.bowmore.demon.co.uk
Est. 1995 *Stock size* Medium
Stock Sale and purchase of
sporting memorabilia,
specializing in cricket
Open By appointment
Services Valuations, mail order

↗ **Martin & Pole**
Contact Mr G J R Lewis
✉ The Auction House, Milton
Road, Wokingham, Berkshire,
RG40 1DB ▣
☎ 0118 979 0460 ✆ 0118 977 6166
✉ a@martinpole.co.uk
Ⓦ www.martinpole.co.uk
Est. 1846
Open Mon–Fri 9am–5pm
Sales Monthly antiques and

collectables, also modern and
household. No sales in August.
Telephone for details
Frequency 2 per month
Catalogues Yes

WOOLHAMPTON

⊞ **The Old Bakery Antiques**
Contact Susan Everard
✉ Bath Road, Woolhampton,
Reading, Berkshire,
RG10 8BY ▣
☎ 0118 971 2116
Est. 1974 *Stock size* Medium
Stock Antique collectables,
country house, country
kitchenware, country gardenware
Open Mon–Sat 10am–5pm
Sun 1–5pm
Fairs Newark, Ardingly

HAMPSHIRE

ALDERSHOT

⊞ **Traders Antiques and
Country Pine Centre**
Contact Mrs J Burns
✉ Norfolk House, 131 Grosvenor
Road, Aldershot, Hampshire,
GU11 3EF ▣
☎ 01252 322055
✉ paul@traddoo.wanadoo.co.uk
Est. 1969 *Stock size* Large
Stock Furniture, fireplaces,
doors, pine, mahogany, oak,
collectables
Open Mon–Sat 10am–5.30pm
Services Restoration, French
polishing

⊞ **Artemesia**
Contact Mr Tim Wright
✉ 16 West Street, Alresford,
Hampshire,
SO24 9AT ▣
☎ 01962 732277
Est. 1969 *Stock size* Large
Stock English and Continental
furniture, ceramics, works of art
Open Mon–Sat 10am–1pm 2–5pm
Services Valuations

⊞ **Laurence Oxley Ltd
(ABA, FATG)**
Contact Anthony Oxley
✉ 17 Broad Street, Alresford,
Hampshire,
SO24 9AW ▣
☎ 01962 732188 ✆ 01962 732998
Ⓜ 07769 715510
✉ aoxley@freenet.co.uk

Est. 1950
Stock Victorian watercolours,
old maps, antiquarian books
Open Mon–Sat 9am–5pm
Fairs Chelsea Book Fair
Services Restoration, picture
framing

⊞ **Pineapple House**
Contact Peter Radford
✉ 49 Broad Street, Alresford,
Hampshire,
SO24 9AS ▣
☎ 01962 736575
Ⓜ 07973 254749
Est. 1979 *Stock size* Small
Stock 19th–20thC general
antiques especially walnut and
mahogany furniture
Open Thur 11am–3pm Fri Sat
11am–5pm Sun 11am–4pm
or by appointment

ALTON

⊞ **Appleton Eves Ltd**
Contact Richard Eves
✉ 30 Normandy Street, Alton,
Hampshire,
GU34 1BX ▣
☎ 01420 84422 ✆ 01420 84422
Est. 2001 *Stock size* Small
Stock Antiques, collectables, gifts
Open Mon–Sat 10am–5pm

⊞ **Jardinique (SALVO)**
Contact Mr Edward Neish
✉ Old Park Farm, Kings Hill,
Beech, Alton, Hampshire,
GU34 4AW ▣
☎ 01420 560055
✉ enquiries@jardinique.co.uk
Ⓦ www.jardinique.co.uk
Est. 1994 *Stock size* Large
Stock Statuary, sundials, urns,
garden items, seats, fountains,
stone troughs, staddle stones
Open Tues–Sat 10am–5pm
or by appointment
Services Valuations

ANDOVER

↗ **Pearsons Auction Rooms**
Contact Dominic Foster
✉ 41a London Street, Andover,
Hampshire,
SP10 2NU ▣
☎ 01264 364820 ✆ 01264 323402
✉ auctions@pearsons.com
Ⓦ www.pearsons.com
Est. 1979
Open Mon–Fri 8.30am–6pm

SOUTH

Sales General antiques, pictures, prints, silver and jewellery
Mon 10am, viewing Fri 9am–8pm
Sat 9am–5pm
Frequency Fortnightly
Catalogues Yes

ASH

⊞ Secondhand Land
Contact Elaine Barker
✉ 47 Ash Street, Ash, Hampshire, GU12 6OF 🅿
☎ 01252 332330
Est. 1992 **Stock size** Large
Stock General antiques
Open Mon–Sat 10am–5pm
closed Wed
Services Valuations

ASH VALE

⊞ The House of Christian
Contact Mrs Bail
✉ 5 Vale Road, Ash Vale, Aldershot, Hampshire, GU12 5HH 🅿
☎ 01252 314478
Est. 1975 **Stock size** Medium
Stock Pine furniture, general antiques and collectables
Open Mon–Fri 10am–5pm
Sat 12.30–3.30pm
Services Valuations, restoration

BASINGSTOKE

⊞ The Squirrel Antique & Collectors Centre
Contact Alan Stone
✉ Joyce's Yard, 9a New Street, Basingstoke, Hampshire, RG21 7DE 🅿
☎ 01256 464885
✉ ahs@squirrelsuk.fsnet.co.uk
Est. 1981 **Stock size** Large
Stock Antique jewellery, silver, dolls, teddy bears, Art Deco ceramics, china, furniture
Open Mon–Sat 10am–5.30pm
Services Valuations

BISHOPS WALTHAM

⊞ Something Else Antiques
Contact Selina Simpson
✉ 4 Basing Mews, Lower Basingwell Street, Bishops Waltham, Hampshire, SO32 1PA 🅿
☎ 01489 892179
Est. 1969 **Stock size** Large
Stock General antiques,

collectables
Open Mon–Sat 10am–5pm
or by appointment
Services Valuations, restoration

BOTLEY

⊞ The Furniture Trading Co
Contact Mr Davies
✉ The Old Flour Mills, Mill Hill, Botley, Hampshire, SO30 2GB 🅿
☎ 01489 788194 🖷 01489 797337
✉ mail@furnituretradingco.co.uk
🌐 www.furnituretradingco.co.uk
Est. 1984 **Stock size** Large
Stock General antiques, antique and contemporary furniture, accessories, porcelain, lighting, mirrors
Open Mon–Sat 10am–5pm
Sun 11am–4pm
Services Restoration

BROCKENHURST

⊞ Antiquiteas
Contact Mr R Wolstenholme
✉ 37 Brockley Road, Brockenhurst, Hampshire, SO42 7RB 🅿
☎ 01590 622120
✉ info@antiquiteas.co.uk
🌐 www.antiquiteas.co.uk
Est. 1999 **Stock size** Medium
Stock Pine furniture, copper, brass, porcelain. lamps, china, ceramics, glassware, bronzes, statues, mirrors
Open Mon–Sat 10am–5pm
Sun 10am–4pm

⊞ Squirrels
Contact Sue Crocket
✉ Lyndhurst Road, Brockenhurst, Hampshire, SO42 7RL 🅿
☎ 01590 622433
Est. 1989 **Stock size** Medium
Stock Antiques, collectables, stripped pine, furniture, Victoriana, Art Deco, Art Nouveau, kitchenware, garden items, pictures, mirrors
Open Wed–Sun 10am–5pm
winter 10am–4pm

BROOK

⊞ F E A Briggs Ltd
Contact Frank Briggs
✉ Birchenwood Farm, Brook, Hampshire,

SO43 7JA 🅿
☎ 023 8081 2595 🖷 023 8081 2595
📱 07831 315838
✉ feabriggs@aol.com
Est. 1966 **Stock size** Large
Stock Victorian furniture
Open Mon–Fri 9am–5.30pm
Fairs Newark
Services Restoration

CHANDLERS FORD

⊞ Bonan's Antique Glass
Contact Elaine Bonan
✉ Chandlers Ford, Hampshire, SO53 🅿
☎ 023 8027 3900
✉ info@bonansantglass.co.uk
🌐 www.bonansantglass.co.uk
Est. 1999 **Stock size** Small
Stock 18th–19thC glass
Open By appointment
Fairs NEC
Services Mail order

CRAWLEY

⊞ The Pine Barn (BADA)
Contact Mr P Chant
✉ Folly Farm, Crawley, Winchester, Hampshire, SO21 2PH 🅿
☎ 01962 776687 🖷 01962 776687
Est. 1987 **Stock size** Large
Stock Furniture made from oak and reclaimed pine, antique, reproduction pine
Open Mon–Sat 9am–5pm
Sun by appointment
Services Valuations, restoration, shipping, production of bespoke furniture – mostly oak

EAST COSHAM

⊞ Wayne Buckner Antiques
Contact Audrey Buckner
✉ Medina, East Cosham, Portsmouth, Hampshire, PO6 2AJ 🅿
☎ 02392 327584 🖷 02392 327584
📱 07801 254494
✉ wayne.buckner@virgin.net
Est. 1996 **Stock size** Medium
Stock Collectables, clocks, small items of furniture, music boxes, barometers, china toys, Meccano, steam engines, china, glassware, jewellery
Open Mon–Sat by appointment
Fairs Kempton, Goodwood
Services Valuations, restoration, house clearance

EASTLEIGH

⊞ Bonnons Antique Glass
Contact Elaine Bonnon
✉ 25 Randall Road, Chandlers Ford, Eastleigh, Hampshire, SO53 5AJ 🅿
☎ 023 8027 3900 📠 023 8027 3900
📱 07766 825414
📧 info@bonnonsantiqueglass.co.uk
🌐 www.bonnonsantiqueglass.co.uk
Est. 1995 *Stock size* Small
Stock Georgian, Victorian drinking glasses, decanters, rummers, decorative glassware
Open By appointment only
Fairs National Glass Collectors fair, Cambridge glass fair

EMSWORTH

⊞ Antique Bed Company
Contact Mr I Trewick
✉ 32 North Street, Emsworth, Hampshire, PO10 7DG 🅿
☎ 01243 376074 📠 01243 376074
📧 antiquebeds@aol.com
🌐 www.antiquebedsemsworth.co.uk
Est. 1992 *Stock size* Large
Stock Victorian–Edwardian brass, iron and wooden beds
Open Mon–Sat 9am–5.30pm
Services Valuations, restoration

⊞ Bookends
Contact Mrs C Waldron
✉ 7 High Street, Emsworth, Hampshire, PO10 7AQ 🅿
☎ 01243 372154
📱 07796 263508
📧 cawaldron@tinyworld.co.uk
Est. 1982 *Stock size* Medium
Stock Antiquarian, rare, second-hand books, sheet music
Open Mon–Sat 9.30am–5pm Sun 10.30am–3pm
Services Valuations, book search

🏠 Dolphin Quay Antique Centre
Contact Christopher or Lisa Creamer
✉ Queen Street, Emsworth, Hampshire, PO10 7BU 🅿
☎ 01243 379994
📧 chrisdqantiquesaol.com
Est. 1969 *Stock size* Large
No. of dealers 40+
Stock Fine antique furniture, porcelain, clocks, watches, jewellery, silver
Open Mon–Sat 10am–5pm Sun 10am–4pm
Services Restoration, furniture upholstery, clock clinic Wed 4–6pm

⊞ Tiffins Antiques
Contact Phyl Hudson
✉ 12 Queen Street, Emsworth, Hampshire, PO10 7BL 🅿
☎ 01243 372497
Est. 1989 *Stock size* Small
Stock General antiques, silver, oil lamps
Open Wed–Sat 9am–5pm

🏠 Eversley Barn Antiques
Contact Hilary Craven
✉ Church Lane, Eversley, Hampshire, RG27 0PX 🅿
☎ 0118 932 8518
📱 07811 934905
📧 eversleybarn@hotmail.com
🌐 eversleybarnantiques.co.uk
Est. 1998 *Stock size* Large
No. of dealers 20
Stock General antiques, collectables
Open Mon–Sun 10am–5pm
Services Delivery

FAREHAM

⊞ Wickham Square Gallery
Contact Emily MaCleane
✉ 13 The Square, Fareham, Hampshire, PO17 5JQ 🅿
☎ 01329 832329
🌐 www.wickhamsquaregallery.co.uk
Est. 2000 *Stock size* Large
Stock Jewellery, furniture
Open Mon–Sat 9am–4.30pm
Services Valuations, jewellery repairs

FARNBOROUGH

⊞ Clarice Cliff Ltd (ADDA)
Contact Mr J Motley
✉ The Clarice Cliff Nostalgia Store, Kingsmead, Farnborough, Hampshire, GU14 7SL 🅿
☎ 01252 372188 📠 01252 513671
📧 admin@claricecliff.net
🌐 www.claricecliff.co.uk
Est. 1973 *Stock size* Large
Stock Clarice Cliff, English 20thC ceramics
Open Mon–Sat 10am–5pm
Services Valuations, archive information, gallery

FORDINGBRIDGE

⊞ Bristow and Garland
Contact Mr David Bristow
✉ 45–47 Salisbury Street, Fordingbridge, Hampshire, SP6 1AB
☎ 01425 657337 📠 01425 657337
📧 davidbristow@bristowand garland.fsnet.co.uk
Est. 1960 *Stock size* Small
Stock Antiquarian, rare and second-hand books, manuscripts, ephemera
Open Mon Fri Sat 9.30am–5.30pm

⊞ West Essex Coin Investments (BNTA, IBNS)
Contact Mr R Norbury
✉ Croft Cottage, Station Road, Alderholt, Fordingbridge, Hampshire, SP6 3AZ
☎ 01425 656459 📠 01425 656459
Est. 1977 *Stock size* Medium
Stock English coinage medieval–present day including English milled, British colonial, coins of the USA
Open By appointment only
Fairs York Racecourse, BNTA Fairs
Services Valuations

GOSPORT

⊞ Easter Antiques
Contact Mr R Easter
✉ 333 Forton Road, Gosport, Hampshire, PO12 3HF 🅿
☎ 023 9250 3621
Est. 1984 *Stock size* Small
Stock Small decorative items
Open Thurs–Sat 10am–5pm

⊞ Former Glory
Contact Mr L Brannon
✉ 49 Whitworth Road, Gosport, Hampshire, PO12 3NJ 🅿
☎ 023 9250 4869
Est. 1986 *Stock size* Medium
Stock Victorian–Edwardian furniture, china
Open Mon–Sat 9am–5pm closed Wed
Services Restoration, traditional upholstery

HARTLEY WINTNEY

⊞ Nicholas Abbott (LAPADA)
Contact Mr C N Abbott
⊠ High Street,
Hartley Wintney,
Hampshire,
RG27 8NY ⊞
☎ 01252 842365 **●** 01252 842365
⊖ nicholasabbott@web-hq.com
⊛ nicholasabbott.com
Est. 1964 *Stock size* Medium
Stock 18thC furniture
Open Mon–Sat 10am–4.30pm or by appointment
Services Valuations, restoration

⊞ Anvil Antiques
Contact Andrew Pitter
⊠ The Old Forge Cottage,
The Green,
Hartley Wintney,
Hampshire,
RG27 8PG ⊞
☎ 01252 845403
⊛ 07778 934938
Est. 1980 *Stock size* Large
Stock General antiques
Open Mon–Sat 10am–5pm
Services Restoration china, pottery, porcelain

⌂ Cedar Antiques Centre Ltd
Contact Sally Green
⊠ High Street, Hartley Wintney,
Hampshire,
RG27 8NY ⊞
☎ 01252 843222 **●** 01252 842111
⊖ cac@cedar-antiques.com
⊛ www.cedar-antiques.com
Est. 1998 *Stock size* Large
No. of dealers 38
Stock Early English furniture, silver, glass, water colours, carpets, Art Deco, jewellery, paintings, prints, books, linen, porcelain, architectural fittings, clocks, hatware
Open Mon–Sat 10am–5.30pm
Sun Bank Holidays 11am–4pm
Services Café, Museum of T G Green pottery

⊞ Cedar Antiques Ltd
Contact Sally Green
⊠ High Street, Hartley Wintney,
Hampshire,
RG27 8NT ⊞
☎ 01252 843252 **●** 01252 842111
⊖ ca@cedar-antiques.com
⊛ www.cedar-antiques.com

Est. 1964 *Stock size* Large
Stock 17th–20thC English and Continental country furniture with colour
Open Mon–Sat 10am–5.30pm
Sun Bank Holidays 11am–4pm
Services Valuations, restoration

⊞ Bryan Clisby
Contact Mr B Clisby
⊠ Cedar Antique Centre,
High Street, Hartley Wintney,
Hampshire,
RG27 8NY ⊞
☎ 01252 716436/843222
⊖ bryanclisby@boltblue.co.uk
Est. 1978 *Stock size* Large
Stock Longcase, bracket, wall clocks, mantel clocks, barometers
Open Mon–Sun 10am–5.30pm
Services Restoration

⊞ Deva Antiques
Contact Mr A Gratwick
⊠ High Street, Hartley Wintney,
Hampshire,
RG27 8NY ⊞
☎ 01252 843538 **●** 01252 842946
⊖ devaants@aol.com
⊛ www.deva-antiques.com
Est. 1986 *Stock size* Medium
Stock 18th–19thC mahogany, walnut, country furniture, decorative accessories
Open Mon–Sat 9am–5.30pm
Services Collection from BR station by arrangement

⌂ Graham Dobinson Antiques
Contact Graham Dobinson
⊠ The Old Workshops,
Cricket Green, Hartley Wintney,
Hampshire,
RG27 8QB ⊞
☎ 01252 842115
Est. 1982 *Stock size* Small
No. of dealers 20
Stock Antique furniture
Open Mon–Fri 8.30am–5.30pm
Services Restoration

⊞ Sally Green Designs
Contact Sally Green
⊠ 63 High Street, Hartley Wintney, Hampshire,
RG27 8NT ⊞
☎ 01252 843252 **●** 01252 842111
⊛ 07786 543350
⊖ sg@cedar-ltd.demon.co.uk
⊛ www.cedar-antiques.com
Est. 1965 *Stock size* Medium
Stock 18th–19thC English and

Continental country furniture
Open Mon–Sat 10am–5.30pm
Sun 11am–4pm
Services Restoration and interior design

⊞ David Lazarus Antiques (BADA)
Contact Mr D Lazarus
⊠ High Street, Hartley Wintney,
Hampshire,
RG27 8NS ⊞
☎ 01252 842272 **●** 01252 842272
Est. 1973 *Stock size* Medium
Stock Furniture, sculpture, objets d'art
Open Mon–Sat 9.30am–5.30pm

HEADLEY

⊞ Victorian Dreams
Contact Mrs S Kay
⊠ The Old School, Crabtree Lane,
Headley, Bordon, Hampshire,
GU35 8QH ⊞
☎ 01428 717000 **●** 01428 717111
⊖ sales@victorian-dreams.co.uk
⊛ www.victorian-dreams.co.uk
Est. 1985 *Stock size* Large
Stock Brass, iron, wooden, upholstered and caned bedsteads
Open Tues–Sun 10am–4pm
Fairs Newark, Ardingly
Services Valuations, restoration, world and nationwide delivery

HIGHBRIDGE

⊞ Brambridge Antiques
Contact Mr D May
⊠ Bugle Farm, Highbridge Road,
Highbridge, Eastleigh,
Hampshire,
SO50 6HS ⊞
☎ 01962 714386
Est. 1973 *Stock size* Medium
Stock Mahogany, walnut furniture
Open Mon–Sat 9am–5pm
Services Restoration

HORNDEAN

⊞ The Goss & Crested China Club
Contact Lynda Pine
⊠ 62 Murray Road, Horndean,
Hampshire,
PO8 9JL ⊞
☎ 023 9259 7440 **●** 023 9259 1975
⊖ info@gosschinaclub.co.uk
⊛ www.gosscrestedchina.co.uk
Est. 1969 *Stock size* Large
Stock Over 5,000 pieces of Goss

and crested china, heraldic souvenir ware circa 1860–1939, specialist books
Open Mon–Sat 9am–4pm
Services Valuations

LISS

⊞ Plestor Barn Antiques
Contact Mr McCarthy
✉ Farnham Road, Liss, Hampshire, GU33 6JQ ▣
☎ 01730 893922
Ⓜ 07850 539998
🅔 craigmccarthy@btopenworld.com
Est. 1984 *Stock size* Medium
Stock Victorian–Edwardian stripped pine, 1920s furniture, used and reproduction soft furnishings
Open Mon–Fri 10am–4pm Sat 10am–2pm
Services Light removals service

LYMINGTON

⊞ Carlsen's Antiques and Fine Arts
Contact Mr D Carlsen
✉ 8 St Thomas Street, Lymington, Hampshire, SO41 9NA ▣
☎ 01590 676370
Est. 1987 *Stock size* Large
Stock Watercolours, pencils, etchings, mirrors, small Georgian–Victorian furniture
Open Mon–Sat 9.30am–5.30pm
Fairs Winchester, Lymington
Services Valuations

⊞ Century Fine Arts
Contact Victoria Roberts
✉ 120 High Street, Lymington, Hampshire, SO41 9AQ ▣
☎ 01590 673532 🅕 01590 678855
Est. 1995 *Stock size* Large
Stock Antique furniture, period paintings, prints, lamps, decorative items
Open Mon–Sat 9.30am–5.30pm

⊞ Corfield Ltd
Contact Mr A Roberts
✉ 120 High Street, Lymington, Hampshire, SO41 9AQ ▣
☎ 01590 673532 🅕 01590 678855
Est. 1995 *Stock size* Medium
Stock Decorative items, paintings, Regency–Victorian furniture
Open Mon–Sat 9.30am–5.30pm

⊞ Godleton Barn Antiques
Contact R Belfield
✉ Godleton Farm, Silver Street, Sway, Lymington, Hampshire, SO41 6DJ ▣
☎ 0203 8033 2293
Est. 1978 *Stock size* Medium
Stock Antique pine, salvage
Open Mon–Sat 9am–5pm
Services Restoration, paint stripping

➶ George Kidner
Contact Cherry L Lund
✉ The Lymington Saleroom, Emsworth Road, Lymington, Hampshire, SO41 9BL ▣
☎ 01590 670070 🅕 01590 675167
🅔 info@georgekidner.co.uk
Ⓦ www.georgekidner.co.uk
Est. 1991
Open Mon–Fri 9am–5pm
Sales Furniture and decorative items, silver, jewellery, paintings, collectors items. Sales Thurs, viewing Sat 9.30am–1pm, Tues 9.30am–4.30pm, Wed 9.30am–7pm and morning of the sale. Specialist sales of collectables toys, model railways and railwayana, books, maps, militaria, arms and armour
Frequency Quarterly
Catalogues Yes

⌂ Lymington Antique Centre
Contact Lisa Reeves
✉ 76 High Street, Lymington, Hampshire, SO41 9AL ▣
☎ 01590 670934
Est. 1990 *Stock size* Large
No. of dealers 30
Stock Furniture, porcelain, books, jewellery, silver, pictures
Open Mon–Fri 10am–5pm Sat 9am–5pm

⊞ Barry Papworth (NAG)
Contact Steve Park
✉ 28 St Thomas Street, Lymington, Hampshire, SO41 9NE ▣
☎ 01590 676422
Est. 1978 *Stock size* Medium
Stock Jewellery and silver
Open Mon–Sat 9.15am–5.15pm
Services Valuations, restoration

⊞ Pennyfarthing Antiques
Contact Roberta Payne
✉ Lymington Antique Centre,

76 High Street, Lymington, Hampshire, SO41 9AL ▣
☎ 023 8086 0846
Ⓜ 07970 847690
🅔 bobbypayne@lineone.net
Est. 1996 *Stock size* Large
Stock Georgian–Edwardian furniture, clocks, Oriental items, watches, barometers
Open Mon–Sat 10am–5pm
Services Valuations, restoration

⊞ Pod Interior Style
Contact Miss Polly Sturgess
✉ 15 St Thomas Street, Lymington, Hampshire, SO41 9NB ▣
☎ 01590 688769
Est. 1997 *Stock size* Medium
Stock Furniture, upholstery service
Open Mon–Fri 10am–6pm Sat 10am–5pm

⊞ Wick Antiques (LAPADA, CINOA)
Contact Mr Charlie Wallrock
✉ Fairlea House, 110–112 Marsh Lane, Lymington, Hampshire, SO41 9EE ▣
☎ 01590 677558 🅕 01590 677558
🅔 charles@wickantiques.co.uk
Ⓦ www.wickantiques.co.uk
Est. 1984 *Stock size* Large
Stock 18th–19thC English and French furniture
Open Mon–Fri 9am–5pm Sat by appointment
Fairs Olympia Fine Arts Fair, Fall Fair New York
Services Restoration

LYNDHURST

⌂ Forest Antique Centre
Contact Mr or Mrs J Brown
✉ 17 High Street, Lyndhurst, Hampshire, SO43 7BB ▣
☎ 023 8028 4545
Ⓜ 07971 355641
Est. 2004 *Stock size* Medium
No. of dealers 20
Stock General antiques
Open Mon–Sun 10am–5pm
Services Valuations

⊞ Lita Kaye Antiques
Contact Mr S Ferder
✉ 13 High Street, Lyndhurst, Hampshire, SO43 7BB ▣
☎ 023 8028 2337

Est. 1950 *Stock size* Large
Stock English period, 18thC
Regency furniture, porcelain,
decorative items
Open Mon–Sat 9.30am–5.30pm

🏠 **Lyndhurst Antique Centre**
Contact Mrs G Ashley
✉ 19–21 High Street, Lyndhurst, Hampshire, SO43 7BB 🅿
☎ 023 8028 4000
🌐 www.lyndhurstantiques.com
Est. 1998 *Stock size* Large
No. of dealers 50
Stock Collectables, furniture, militaria
Open Mon–Sun 10am–5pm

MATTINGLEY

🔨 **Odiham Auction Sales**
Contact Mr S R Thomas
✉ Unit 4, Priors Farm, West Green Road, Mattingley, Hampshire, RG29 8JU 🅿
☎ 01189 326824 ☎ 01189 326797
📱 07836 201764
📧 auction@dircon.co.uk
Est. 1989
Open Mon–Fri 9.30am–4pm
Sales General antiques sales Wed. Smalls sales at 2pm, furniture sales at 6.30pm, viewing Tues 6–9pm Wed 9am–2pm
Frequency Monthly
Catalogues Yes

MILFORD-ON-SEA

⊞ **Carringtons Antiques**
Contact Kerry Lee
✉ 100 High Street, Milford-on-Sea, Hampshire, SO41 0QE
☎ 01590 644665
Est. 2000 *Stock size* Medium
Stock General antiques, oil lamps and accessories
Open Mon–Sat 10am–5pm
Fairs Ardingly, Sandown Park, Newark
Services Oil lamp restoration

NEW MILTON

⊞ **Forest House Antiques**
Contact Mr K Plater
✉ 4 Winston Parade, Lymington Road, New Milton, Hampshire, BH25 6PT 🅿

☎ 01425 614441
📱 07740 644244
Est. 1984 *Stock size* Large
Stock 18th–19thC English furniture, ceramics, collectables
Open Mon–Fri 9am–4.30pm
Fairs Antiques for Everyone, Newark
Services Valuations, restoration

OLD BEDHAMPTON

⊞ **J F F Militaria & Fire Brigade Collectables**
Contact Mr J Franklin
✉ Ye Olde Coach House, Mill Lane, Old Bedhampton, Hampshire, PO9 3JH 🅿
☎ 023 9248 6485
📱 07786 012316
Est. 1995 *Stock size* Medium
Stock Militaria, brass fire helmets, medals, badges, cloth insignia, equipment, buttons
Open By appointment only
Fairs Stoneleigh, Beltring
Services Valuations

PETERSFIELD

⊞ **Folly Four Antiques & Collectables**
Contact Diane
✉ 10–12 College Street, Petersfield, Hampshire, GU31 4AD 🅿
☎ 01730 266650
Est. 1999 *Stock size* Small
Stock Antiques and collectables
Open Tues–Sat 10am–4.30pm

🔨 **Jacobs and Hunt Fine Art Auctioneers**
✉ 26 Lavant Street, Petersfield, Hampshire, GU32 3EF 🅿
☎ 01730 233933 ☎ 01730 262323
🌐 www.jacobsandhunt.co.uk
Est. 1895
Open Mon–Fri 9am–5pm
Sales General antiques sales Fri, viewing Wed 10am–4.30pm Thurs 10am–6.30pm morning of sale from 9am
Frequency Monthly
Catalogues Yes

⊞ **The Petersfield Bookshop (ABA, PBFA)**
Contact Frank Westwood
✉ 16a Chapel Street, Petersfield, Hampshire,

GU32 3DS 🅿
☎ 01730 263438 ☎ 01730 269426
📧 sales@petersfieldbookshop.com
🌐 www.petersfieldbookshop.com
Est. 1918 *Stock size* Large
Stock Antiquarian and modern books
Open Mon–Sat 9am–5.30pm
Fairs ABA, Olympia, Chelsea
Services Valuations, quarterly catalogues

PORTSMOUTH

⊞ **Good Day Antiques and Decor**
Contact Mrs G Day
✉ 22 The Green, Rowlands Castle, Portsmouth, Hampshire, PO9 6AB 🅿
☎ 023 9241 2924
📱 0795 8619413
📧 gillday@aol.com
Est. 1979 *Stock size* Medium
Stock Victorian furniture, small cabinets, jewellery, silver, porcelain, pottery, pictures
Open Thurs–Sun 11am–4pm
Services Silver-plating, gilding, engraving

🏠 **Alexandra Gray Antiques & Decorative Ideas**
Contact Alexandra Gray
✉ 129–131 Havant Road, Drayton, Portsmouth, Hampshire, PO6 2AA 🅿
☎ 023 9237 6379
📱 07752 781835
Est. 1997 *Stock size* Large
No. of dealers 15
Stock General antiques, chandeliers, French beds, china, especially Crown Derby, clocks, oil lamps
Open Mon–Sat 10am–5pm Sun noon–4pm closed Wed
Services Upholstery

⊞ **Petals in the Warehouse**
Contact Beverley Parker
✉ 17 Beck Street, Portsmouth, Hampshire, PO1 3AN 🅿
☎ 02392 737272
📧 salvage_warehouse@hotmail.com
Est. 2005 *Stock size* Large
Stock Architectural antiques, Victorian fireplaces, doors, baths, pine furniture, radiators, stained glass
Open Mon–Sat 10am–5pm

RINGWOOD

Black Cat Trading & Antiques
Contact Graham Sirl
✉ The Cross, Burley, Ringwood, Hampshire,
BH24 4AB
☎ 01425 404110
Est. 2000 *Stock size* Small
Stock General antiques and collectables
Open Tues–Sun 10.30am–5pm
Services Tea rooms

E Chalmers Hallam (PBFA)
Contact Mrs L Hiscock
✉ 9 Post Office Lane, St Ives, Ringwood, Hampshire,
BH24 2PG
☎ 01425 470060 ☏ 01425 470060
✉ laura@chalmershallam.freeserve.co.uk
Est. 1946 *Stock size* Large
Stock Antiquarian, rare, second-hand books, angling, field sports, travel, Africana
Open By appointment

The Magpie's Nest
Contact Mrs V A Batchelor or Mrs Favia Lister
✉ Ringwood Road, Burley, Ringwood, Hampshire,
BH24 4BU
☎ 01425 402404
Est. 1974 *Stock size* Small
Stock Porcelain, small collectables, jewellery, antique bric-a-brac, Delft ware, Russian figures, Royal Doulton, Wedgwood
Open Mon–Sun 9.30am–5pm
Services Repairs to jewellery including re-threading, silver plating

Millers Antiques Ltd (LAPADA)
Contact Mr A J Miller
✉ Netherbrook House, Christchurch Road, Ringwood, Hampshire,
BH24 1DR
☎ 01425 472062 ☏ 01425 472727
☏ 07806 711280
✉ mail@millers-antiques.co.uk
✇ www.millers-antiques.co.uk
Est. 1897 *Stock size* Large
Stock English and Continental country furniture, 19thC majolica, Quimper, treen,

decorative items
Open Mon 9.30am–1.30pm
Tue–Fri 9.30am–5pm Sat
10am–3pm
Fairs Decorative Antiques and Textiles Fair, Great Antiques Fair
Services Valuations, restoration, packing, shipping

Lorraine Tarrant Antiques
Contact Mrs L Tarrant
✉ 23 Market Place, Ringwood, Hampshire,
BH24 1AN
☎ 01425 461123
Est. 1991 *Stock size* Medium
Stock Furniture, carved oak, old pine, bears, collectors' items, tapestry cushions
Open Tues–Sat 10am–5pm

ROMSEY

Antique Enterprises
Contact Mr M Presterfield
✉ 19 Cavendish Close, Romsey, Hampshire,
SO51 7HT
☎ 01794 515589
Est. 1976 *Stock size* Medium
Stock Furniture, china, glass, collectables
Open By appointment

Bell Antiques (Gemmological Association)
Contact Mr M Gay
✉ 8 Bell Street, Romsey, Hampshire,
SO51 8GA
☎ 01794 514719
Est. 1979 *Stock size* Large
Stock Jewellery, silver, glass, china, small furniture, maps, topographical prints
Open Mon–Sat 9.30am–5.30pm closed Wed in winter

SHIPTON BELLINGER

May and Son
Contact Mr J May
✉ Unit 3, The Delta Works, Salisbury Road, Shipton Bellinger, Hampshire,
SP9 7UN
☎ 01980 846000 ☏ 01980 846000
☏ 07710 001660
✉ office@mayandson.com
✇ www.mayandson.com
Est. 1925

Open Mon–Fri 9am–5pm
Sat 9am–noon
Sales Antique furniture and effects 3rd Wed of the month at 10.30am, viewing Tues 8.30am–6pm morning of sale from 8.30am. Sales take place in Village Hall, Penton Mewsey, Andover. Periodic specialist auctions
Frequency Monthly
Catalogues Yes

SOUTHAMPTON

Amber Antiques
Contact Mr R Boyle
✉ 115 Portswood Road, Portswood, Southampton, Hampshire,
SO17 2FX
☎ 023 8058 3645 ☏ 023 8058 3645
Est. 1970 *Stock size* Large
Stock Furniture
Open Mon–Sat 9am–5pm
Sun 11am–3pm.
Services Restoration

Cobwebs
Contact Mr P Boyd-Smith
✉ 78 Northam Road, Southampton, Hampshire,
SO14 0PB
☎ 023 8022 7458 ☏ 023 8022 7458
✇ www.cobwebs.uk.com
Est. 1974 *Stock size* Large
Stock Ocean liner memorabilia including *Titanic* and White Star Line, aviation items, Royal and Merchant Navy items
Open Mon–Sat 10am–4pm closed Wed
Fairs Transportation 2000, British Titanic Convention
Services Valuations

Peter Rhodes Books
Contact Peter Rhodes
✉ 21 Portswood Road, Southampton, Hampshire,
SO17 2ES
☎ 023 8039 9003
☏ 07763 326440
✉ peterrhodes.books@virgin.net
Est. 1997 *Stock size* Large
Stock Antiquarian, rare, second-hand books, travel, history, archaeology
Open Tues–Sat 10am–5pm
Fairs HD Fairs
Services Valuations, book search, coffee bar

SOUTH
HAMPSHIRE • SOUTHSEA

SOUTHSEA

⊞ The Clock Shop
Contact M J Childs
✉ 155 Highland Road, Southsea,
Hampshire,
PO4 9EY 🅿
☎ 023 9285 1649
Est. 1999 *Stock size* Large
Stock Clocks, watches, jewellery,
general antiques
Open Thurs–Sat 9am–5pm
Fairs Kempton Park, DMG
Services Valuations, clock
restoration

⊞ Design Explosion
Contact Susan Mosely
✉ 2 Exmouth Road, Southsea,
Hampshire,
PO5 2QL 🅿
☎ 023 9229 3040 ☏ 023 9229 3040
Ⓜ 07850 131414
Ⓔ sue.moseley@btconnect.com
Ⓦ www.designexplosion.co.uk
Est. 1998 *Stock size* Medium
Stock 1950s–1970s china, glass,
lighting, furniture
Open Fri Sat 9am–5pm
Fairs Ardingly, Kempton,
Newark, Alexandra Palace and
Swinderby

⊞ A Fleming (Southsea) Ltd
Contact Mr Alfred Fleming
✉ The Clock Tower, Castle Road,
Southsea,
Hampshire,
PO5 3DE 🅿
☎ 023 9282 2934 ☏ 023 9229 3501
Ⓜ 07885 334545
Ⓔ mail@flemingsantiques.fsnet.co.uk
Ⓦ www.flemingsantiques.com
Est. 1908 *Stock size* Medium
Stock 18th–19thC English and
Continental furniture, silver,
boxes, barometers
Open Wed–Fri 9.30am–5.30pm
Fairs Goodwood, Petersfield
Services Valuations, furniture
and silver restoration

⊞ JBN Vanos Trading
Contact Frank Newland
✉ 143 Highland Road, Southsea,
Hampshire,
PO4 9EY 🅿
Est. 1975 *Stock size* Medium
Stock Georgian–Edwardian
furniture and smalls
Open Tues–Sat 9.30am–4.30pm
or by appointment
Services Restoration, upholstery

⊞ Kings Antiques
Contact Mr O'Riley
✉ 38 Albert Road, Southsea,
Hampshire,
PO5 2SJ 🅿
☎ 023 9286 2853
Est. 1990 *Stock size* Small
Stock Silver, general antiques
Open Mon–Fri 1.30–5.30pm
closed Wed

⊞ Langford Antiques
Contact Mr I Langford
✉ 70 Albert Road, Southsea,
Hampshire,
PO5 2SL 🅿
☎ 023 9283 0517
Est. 1982 *Stock size* Medium
Stock Victorian–20thC furniture,
collectables, silver, costume
jewellery
Open Mon–Fri 11am–5pm
Sat 10am–6pm closed Wed

➴ D M Nesbit & Co
Contact John Cameron MRICS,
ANAVA
✉ 7 Clarendon Road, Southsea,
Hampshire,
PO5 2ED 🅿
☎ 023 9229 5568 ☏ 023 9229 5522
Ⓔ auctions@nesbits.co.uk
Ⓦ www.invaluable.com/nesbits
Est. 1921
Open Mon–Fri 9.30am–5pm
Sales General antiques sale
monthly. Telephone for details
Catalogues Yes

⊞ Oldfield Gallery
Contact Ann Downs
✉ 76 Elm Grove, Southsea,
Hampshire,
PO5 1LN 🅿
☎ 023 9283 8042
Ⓔ oldfield-gallery@ntlworld.com
Ⓦ www.oldfield-antiquemaps.co.uk
Est. 1972 *Stock size* Large
Stock Antique maps and prints
Open Tues–Sat 10am–5pm
Fairs London Map Fairs
Services Valuations, framing

⊞ Ian Parmiter
Contact Mr I Parmiter
✉ 2 Exmouth Road, Southsea,
Hampshire,
PO5 2QL 🅿
☎ 023 9229 3040 ☏ 023 9229 3040
Ⓜ 07850 131414
Ⓔ info@ianparmiter.co.uk
Ⓦ www.ianparmiter.co.uk
Est. 1987 *Stock size* Medium

Stock Architectural antiques,
unusual items, doors, fireplace
spares, original tiles,
reproduction fireplaces, statues,
lighting, stained glass
Open Mon 11am–2.30pm Fri Sat
9am–5pm or by appointment
Fairs Kempton, Ardingly,
Newark, Swinderby
Services Finding service, house
clearance

⊞ Sabre Sales
Contact Mick Hall or
Richard Ingram
✉ 85–87 Castle Road, Southsea,
Hampshire,
PO5 3AY 🅿
☎ 023 9283 3394 ☏ 023 9283 7394
Ⓜ 07850 260148
Ⓔ sabre.sales@tiscali.co.uk
Ⓦ www.sabresales.co.uk
Est. 1987 *Stock size* Large
Stock Militaria Zulu war–present
day, weapons, uniforms, general
paraphernalia
Open Mon–Fri 9am–5pm
Sat 10am–4.30pm
Fairs Beltring, Farnham
Services Valuations, hire for film,
TV and theatre

STOCKBRIDGE

➴ Evans and Partridge
Contact John Partridge
✉ Agriculture House,
Stockbridge,
Hampshire,
SO20 6HF 🅿
☎ 01264 810702 ☏ 01264 810944
Ⓔ auctions@evansandpartridge.co.uk
Est. 1973
Open Mon–Fri 9am–5.30pm
Sat 9am–4pm
Sales Sales of early and modern
fishing tackle, sporting guns,
antique weapons, steam, tractors
and farming bygones
Frequency Annual
Catalogues Yes

⊞ Lane Antiques
Contact Mrs E Lane
✉ High Street,
Stockbridge, Hampshire,
SO20 6EU 🅿
☎ 01264 810435
Est. 1982 *Stock size* Medium
Stock 18th–19thC porcelain,
silver, glass, small furniture,
objets d'art
Open By appointment

⊞ Stockbridge Antiques Centre
Contact Tim Baker
✉ **Old London Road, Stockbridge, Hampshire, SO20 6EJ** 🅿
☎ 01264 811008
✉ rona@oakchairs.com
🌐 www.oakchairs.com
Est. 1978 **Stock size** Medium
Stock Pine and oak country furniture
Open Mon–Sat 10am–5pm
Sun 11am–2pm closed Wed

⊞ Fizzy Warren Decorative Antiques
Contact Fizzy Warren
✉ **High Street, Stockbridge, Hampshire, SO20 6EY** 🅿
☎ 01264 811137
Est. 1998 **Stock size** Medium
Stock Decorative antiques, 19thC French chandeliers, mirrors, furniture, fabrics
Open Mon–Sat 10.30am–5pm

WICKHAM

⚒ Solent Railwayana Auctions
Contact Nigel Maddock
✉ **Community Centre, Mill Lane, Wickham, Hampshire, PO17 5AL** 🅿
☎ 01489 574029
✉ nigel@solentrailwayana.com
🌐 www.solentrailwayana.com
Est. 1992
Open Sale 11am–5pm
Sales Railwayana auctions. Dates for 2006 18 March, 17 June, 21 October
Frequency 3 per annum
Catalogues Yes

WINCHESTER

⚒ Bonhams
Contact Sonya Wiebers or Clare Chalkey
✉ **The Red House, Hyde Street, Winchester, Hampshire, SO23 7DX** 🅿
☎ 01962 862515 ✆ 01962 865166
✉ winchester@bonhams.com
🌐 www.bonhams.com
Est. 1793
Open Mon–Fri 8.30am–1pm 2–5pm
Sales Regional office. Regular sales held in London and in our salerooms across the country. Free auction valuations; insurance and probate valuations

⊞ Boris Books (SOB)
Contact Mrs P Stevenson
✉ **Winnall Manor Farm, Wales Street, Winchester, Hampshire, SO23 0HA** 🅿
☎ 01962 890355
📱 07789 790949
✉ pam@borisbooks.fsnet.co.uk
🌐 www.borisbooks.co.uk
Est. 1995 **Stock size** Medium
Stock Antiquarian, rare, collectable, second-hand books, specializing in literature, music, children's, illustrated
Open By appointment

⊞ Burgess Farm Antiques
Contact Mr Brown
✉ **39 Jewry Street, Winchester, Hampshire, SO23 8RY** 🅿
☎ 01962 777546
Est. 1982 **Stock size** Large
Stock Antique pine and country furniture, general antiques
Open Mon–Sat 9.30am–5pm
Services Valuations, restoration

⊞ The Clock-Work-Shop (Winchester) (BHI, AHS)
Contact Mr P Ponsford-Jones
✉ **6a Parchment Street, Winchester, Hampshire, SO23 8AT** 🅿
☎ 01962 842331 ✆ 01962 878775
📱 07973 736155
🌐 www.clock-work-shop.co.uk
Est. 1997 **Stock size** Large
Stock Antique clocks, barometers
Open Mon–Sat 9am–5pm
Services Restoration of clocks and barometers

⊞ G E Marsh (Antique Clocks) Ltd (BADA, CINOA, CC, BHI, NAWCC)
Contact Mr D Dipper
✉ **32a The Square, Winchester, Hampshire, SO23 9EX** 🅿
☎ 01962 844443 ✆ 01962 844443
✉ gem@marshclocks.co.uk
🌐 www.marshclocks.co.uk
Est. 1947 **Stock size** Medium
Stock Carriage, English longcase , bracket and Continental clocks, barometers
Open Mon–Fri 9.30am–5pm

Sat 9.30am–1pm 2–5pm
Services Valuations, restoration, home visits

⊞ The Pine Cellars
Contact Mr N Brain
✉ **39 Jewry Street, Winchester, Hampshire, SO23 8RY** 🅿
☎ 01962 777546
Est. 1971 **Stock size** Large
Stock Antique pine, country furniture
Open Mon–Sat 9am–5.30pm
Services Restoration

⊞ Studio Coins (BNTA)
Contact Mr S Mitchell
✉ **16 Kilham Lane, Winchester, Hampshire, SO22 5PT** 🅿
☎ 01962 853156 ✆ 01962 624246
Est. 1987
Stock Old English coins
Open By appointment only
Fairs Coinex, Cumberland, York
Services Free list every 2 months

⊞ Todd & Austin Antiques & Fine Art
Contact Gerald Austin
✉ **2 Andover Road, Winchester, Hampshire, SO23 7BS** 🅿
☎ 01962 869824
Est. 1974 **Stock size** Medium
Stock 18th–early 20thC pottery, porcelain, glass paperweights 1845–60, decorative silver, boxes, silver plate, Oriental arts, 18th–19thC glass, objets d'art
Open Tues–Fri 9.30am–5pm
Sat 9am–noon
Services Valuations

⊞ Irene S Trudgett Collectables
Contact Irene S Trudgett
✉ **3 Andover Road, Winchester, Hampshire, SO23 7BS** 🅿
☎ 01962 854132/862070
Est. 1966 **Stock size** Medium
Stock Pottery, porcelain, cigarette cards, Goss and crested china, glass, collectables
Open Mon–Fri 9.30am–4pm
Thurs, Sat 9.30am–noon
Services Valuations, book search

⊞ Webb Fine Arts
Contact Mr Webb
✉ **38 Jewry Street, Winchester,**

SOUTH
ISLE OF WIGHT • BEMBRIDGE

Hampshire,
SO23 8RY ℗
☎ 01962 842273 ✆ 01962 880602
📧 davieswebb@hotmail.com
🌐 www.webbfinearts.co.uk
Est. 1972 *Stock size* Large
Stock Victorian paintings
Open Mon–Fri 9.30am–5pm
Sat 9.30am–2pm
Services Valuations, restoration

⊞ **The Winchester Bookshop**
Contact Mr M Green or
Mr R Brown
✉ 10a St George's Street,
Winchester, Hampshire,
SO23 8BG ℗
☎ 01962 855630
Est. 1991 *Stock size* Medium
Stock Antiquarian, rare, second-hand books, topography, sport, travel, literature
Open Mon–Sat 10am–5pm
Services Valuations, book search

ISLE OF WIGHT

BEMBRIDGE

⊞ **Cobwebs Antiques and Collectables**
Contact Mrs Sue Williams
✉ Foreland Road, Bembridge,
Isle of Wight,
PO35 5XN ℗
☎ 01983 874487
Est. 1997 *Stock size* Medium
Stock Bunnykins, Beatrix Potter, Doulton
Open Tues–Sat 10am–5pm

COWES

⊞ **Copperwheat Restoration (RICS)**
Contact Carole Copperwheat
✉ Rear of Pascall Atkey,
29–30 High Street, Cowes,
Isle of Wight,
PO31 7RX ℗
☎ 01983 281011
📱 07720 399670
Est. 1985 *Stock size* Small
Stock 17th–18thC furniture, metalware, ceramics
Open Any time by prior telephone call
Services Valuations, restoration

⊞ **Flagstaff Antiques**
Contact Mr T A M Cockram
✉ Tudor House,

Bath Road, Cowes,
Isle of Wight,
PO31 7RH ℗
☎ 01983 200138
Est. 1995 *Stock size* Medium
Stock Jewellery, porcelain, silver
Open Mon–Sat 10.30am–4pm
closed Wed
Fairs Miami, Florida
Services Valuations

⊞ **Gaby Goldscheider**
Contact Miss G Goldscheider
✉ The Library, Deep Eene,
Baring Road, Cowes,
Isle of Wight,
PO31 8DB
☎ 01983 293598
Est. 1974 *Stock size* Large
Stock Second-hand, antiquarian, rare books, prints, specializing in children's books, literature, fiction, topography, travel, nautical. About 15,000 books in stock
Open By appointment

⊞ **Royal Standard Antiques**
Contact Mrs C Bradbury
✉ 70–72 Park Road, Cowes,
Isle of Wight,
PO31 7LY ℗
☎ 01983 281672
📱 07890 962262
📧 caroline@royalstandardantiques.
fsbusiness.co.uk
🌐 www.royalstandardantiques.
fsbusiness.co.uk
Est. 1994 *Stock size* Medium
Stock Georgian–Edwardian English and French furniture, pictures, engravings, commemoratives, architectural antiques
Open Mon–Sat 10.30am–5.30pm
Wed 10.30am–1pm or by appointment
Services Furniture restoration, stained glass restoration, upholstery, chair caning

FRESHWATER

⊞ **The Old Village Clock Shop**
Contact Mr R Taylor
✉ 3 Moa Place, Freshwater,
Isle of Wight,
PO40 9DS ℗
☎ 01983 754193
Est. 1970 *Stock size* Medium
Stock 17th–19thC English longcase and dial clocks, Vienna

regulators, early German, English bracket, French ormolu, carriage clocks
Open Wed Fri Sat 9.30am–1pm
or by appointment
Services Valuations

NEWPORT

⊞ **Mike Heath Antiques**
Contact Mr M Heath
✉ 3–4 Holyrood Street, Newport,
Isle of Wight,
PO30 5AU ℗
☎ 01983 525748
Est. 1979 *Stock size* Medium
Stock Furniture, oil lamps, porcelain, glass, collectables
Open Mon–Sat 10am–5pm
closed Thurs
Services Metal restoration, polishing

⊞ **Kitch22**
Contact Fran Heath
✉ 3–4 Holyrood Street, Newport,
Isle of Wight,
PO30 5AU ℗
☎ 01983 525748
📧 info@kitch22.co.uk
Est. 2004 *Stock size* Small
Stock 1940s–1960s collectables
Open Mon–Sat 10am–5pm
closed Thurs

⊞ **Lugley Antiques and Interiors**
Contact Mr S Gratton
✉ 13 Lugley Street, Newport,
Isle of Wight,
PO30 5HD ℗
☎ 01983 523348
Est. 1991 *Stock size* Large
Stock Furniture, clocks, china, collectables, 19thC furniture a speciality
Open Mon–Fri 10am–4pm
Sat 10am–5pm closed Thurs
Services Valuations, restoration

⊞ **Online Antiques**
Contact Kim or Steve Snow
✉ 5 Watchbell Lane, Newport,
Isle of Wight,
PO30 5XU ℗
☎ 01983 526282
📧 vintage.uk@virgin.net
🌐 www.vintage-uk.com
Est. 2001 *Stock size* Small
Stock Anything old and interesting
Open Mon–Sat 10am–4pm
Services Online auction service

SOUTH

RYDE

⊞ Heritage Books
Contact Rev D H Nearn
✉ 7 Cross Street, Ryde,
Isle of Wight,
PO33 2AD ℗
☎ 01983 562933 ✆ 01983 812634
✉ dhnearn.heritagebooksryde@
virgin.net
Est. 1977 Stock size Medium
Stock General, Isle of Wight
antiquarian prints, books on
modern theology, history,
culture of Africa a speciality
Open Mon–Sat 10am–5pm
closed Thurs
Fairs Guildford Book Fair
Services Book search

⊞ Nooks and Crannies
Contact Mr D Burnett
✉ 60 High Street, Ryde,
Isle of Wight,
PO33 2RJ ℗
☎ 01983 568984
Est. 1984 Stock size Medium
Stock Collectables, lamps, 78 rpm
records, telephones, radios, glass,
china, furniture, gramophones
Open Mon–Sat 9.30am–1.30pm
2.30–5pm closed Thurs
Fairs Ardingly

⊞ Ryde Antiques
Contact Caroline Meeus
✉ 61 High Street, Ryde,
Isle of Wight,
PO33 2RJ ℗
☎ 01983 615025
Est. 1968 Stock size Medium
Stock General antiques
Open Mon–Sat 10am–4.30pm

↗ Ways Auction House
Contact Mr T L Smith
✉ The Auction House,
Garfield Road, Ryde,
Isle of Wight,
PO33 2PT ℗
☎ 01983 562255
✉ way@waysauctionrooms.
fsbusiness.co.uk
ⓦ www.waysauctionrooms.
fsbusiness.co.uk
Est. 1815
Open Mon–Fri 9am–5pm
Sales Antique and modern
furnishings sale on Thurs,
viewing day prior 10am–6pm.
No buyer's premium
Frequency Every 5 weeks
Catalogues Yes

SANDOWN

⊞ Lake Antiques
Contact Mrs J Marchant
✉ 18 Sandown Road, Sandown,
Isle of Wight,
PO36 9JP ℗
☎ 01983 406888
ⓜ 07710 067678
Est. 1982 Stock size Medium
Stock Antique furniture, clocks,
pictures, decorative items
Open Mon–Sat 10am–4pm closed
Wed or by appointment
Services Valuations, mainland
deliveries arranged

SHANKLIN

↗ Shanklin Auction Rooms (NAVA)
Contact Mr H Riches
✉ 79 Regent Street, Shanklin,
Isle of Wight,
PO37 7AP ℗
☎ 01983 863441 ✆ 01983 863890
✉ sales@shanklinauctionrooms.co.uk
ⓦ www.shanklinauctionrooms.co.uk
Est. 1850
Open Mon–Fri 9am–5pm
Sales Collectables monthly,
antiques quarterly. Telephone
for details
Frequency Monthly
Catalogues Yes

VENTNOR

⊞ Curios
Contact Mr M Gregory
✉ 3 Church Place, Chale, Ventnor,
Isle of Wight,
PO38 2HA ℗
☎ 01983 730230
ⓜ 07811 835159
Est. 1995 Stock size Large
Stock Taxidermy, architectural
antiques, fireplaces, staddle
stones, unusual curiosities
Open Mon–Sun noon–5.30pm
Services Valuations, house
clearance

⊞ Plumridge Antiques
Contact Mr R Plumridge
✉ Unit 2, Caxton House,
Ventnor Industrial Estate,
Ventnor, Isle of Wight,
PO38 1DX ℗
☎ 01983 856666 ✆ 01983 855325
ⓜ 07855 649297
✉ acornpianos@aol.com
Est. 1999 Stock size Large
Stock Pianos, furniture
Open Mon–Fri 8.30am–5pm
Sat 8.30am–1pm
Services Shipping, packing

⌂ Ventnor Antiques Centre
Contact Mr G Browne
✉ 66 High Street, Ventnor,
Isle of Wight,
PO38 1LU ℗
☎ 01983 855302
Est. 1994 Stock size Medium
No. of dealers 3
Stock General antiques,
collectables, furniture
Open Mon–Sat 10am–4.30pm
Services Delivery

⊞ Ventnor Junction
Contact Mr or Mrs P Dolby
✉ 48 High Street, Ventnor,
Isle of Wight,
PO38 1LT ℗
☎ 01983 853996
✉ shop@ventjunc.freeserve.co.uk
ⓦ www.ventjunc.freeserve.co.uk
Est. 1987 Stock size Large
Stock Old toys, collectables,
tin trains
Open Most mornings or by
appointment
Fairs Sandown Park Toy Fair, Esher
Services Mail order

YARMOUTH

⊞ Yarmouth Antiques and Books
Contact Mrs V Blakeley or
Mr M Coyle
✉ The House, The Square,
Yarmouth, Isle of Wight,
PO41 0NP ℗
☎ 01983 760046
✉ yarmouth-antiquesiow@
btopenworld.com
Est. 1996 Stock size Medium
Stock Antiquarian, second-hand
books, china, collectables
Open Mon–Sun 10am–5pm
Fairs Kempton Park, February

SURREY

ABINGER HAMMER

⊞ Stirling Antiques
Contact Mr V Burrell
✉ Aberdeen House, Guildford
Road, Abinger Hammer, Dorking,
Surrey,
RH5 6RY ℗

☎ 01306 730706
ⓜ 07748 005619
Est. 1968 *Stock size* Medium
Stock Architectural stained glass, metalware, furniture, jewellery, silver, curios
Open Mon–Sat 9.30am–6pm closed Thurs

ASHTEAD

⊞ **Bumbles**
Contact Mrs B Kay
✉ **90 The Street, Ashtead, Surrey, KT21 1AW** 🅿
☎ 01372 276219 ❷ 01798 875545
Est. 1978 *Stock size* Medium
Stock Clocks, porcelain, silver, cigarette cards
Open Mon–Sat 10am–5.30pm
Services Furniture restoration, upholstery

BAGSHOT

⊞ **Country & Town Antiques**
Contact Sue Summers
✉ **Pantiles, 20 London Road, Bagshot, Surrey, GU19 5HN** 🅿
☎ 01276 489499
❸ countryandtown@tiscali.co.uk
ⓦ www.affordable-antiques.net
Est. 1995 *Stock size* Medium
Stock Victorian–Edwardian furniture, glass, china, collectables
Open Mon–Sun 10am–5pm closed Wed

BETCHWORTH

⊞ **J G Elias Antiques Ltd (LAPADA, DADA)**
Contact Mr J G Elias
✉ **Stoney Croft Farm, Chalkpit Lane, Reigate Road, Betchworth, Surrey, RH3 7EY** 🅿
☎ 01737 845215
Est. 1990 *Stock size* Large
Stock Bookcases, furniture, oak, country furniture
Open Mon–Fri 9am–5.30pm
Sat 10.30am–5.30pm
Services Finding service

BLETCHINGLEY

⊞ **John Anthony**
Contact Mrs N Hart
✉ **71 High Street, Bletchingley,**

Redhill, Surrey, RH1 4LJ 🅿
☎ 01883 743197 ❷ 01883 742108
ⓜ 07836 221689
❸ johnanthonyantiques@hotmail.com
Est. 1974 *Stock size* Medium
Stock 18th–19thC furniture
Open By appointment only

⚒ **Lawrences Auctioneers Ltd**
Contact Miss S Debnam
✉ **Norfolk House, High Street, Bletchingley, Redhill, Surrey, RH1 4PA** 🅿
☎ 01883 743323 ❷ 01883 744578
❸ enquires@lawrences bletchingley.co.uk
ⓦ www.lawrencesbletchingley.co.uk
Est. 1960
Open Mon–Fri 9am–5pm
Sales General antiques sales on Tues Wed Thurs, viewing Fri Sat 10am–5pm
Frequency Every 6 weeks
Catalogues Yes

⊞ **Post House Antiques**
Contact Mr P Bradley
✉ **High Street, Bletchingley, Surrey, RH1 4PA** 🅿
☎ 01883 743317 ❷ 01883 743317
ⓦ www.antiquelightinguk.co.uk
Est. 1975 *Stock size* Large
Stock Antique lighting
Open Thurs–Sat 10am–5pm
Services Restoration

BRAMLEY

🏠 **Memories Antiques**
Contact Mrs P S Kelsey
✉ **High Street, Bramley, Guildford, Surrey, GU5 0HB** 🅿
☎ 01483 892205
ⓜ 07774 885014
Est. 1985 *Stock size* Medium
No. of dealers 8
Stock Georgian–Victorian French, pine furniture, silver, jewellery, porcelain, collectables, garden items, kitchenware, French antiques
Open Mon–Sat 10am–5pm
Services 'Wanted' service

BROCKHAM

⚒ **Cartels Auctioneers and Valuers**
Contact Mr Carter

✉ **2 Tanners Court, Middle Street, Brockham, Dorking (on A25), Surrey, RH3 7NH** 🅿
☎ 01737 844646 ❷ 01737 844646
ⓜ 07768 004293
❸ cartels@freenet.uk.net
Est. 1978
Open Mon–Fri 9.30am–5pm
Sales General antiques, fine art, pre-1930s Sat, viewing all day Fri 10am–7pm and morning of sale 8.30–10am
Frequency Monthly excluding August
Catalogues Yes

CARSHALTON

⊞ **Cherub Antiques**
Contact Mr M Wisdom
✉ **312 Carshalton Road, Carshalton, Surrey, SM5 3QB** 🅿
☎ 020 8643 0028
ⓜ 07764 275778
Est. 1985 *Stock size* Large
Stock Continental and English antique pine, mahogany, French decorative items
Open Mon–Sat 10am–5.30pm
Fairs Ardingly, Newark
Services Pine stripping, French polishing

⊞ **The Clock House (BWCG)**
Contact Mark Cocklin
✉ **75 Pound Street, Carshalton, Surrey, SM5 3PG** 🅿
☎ 020 8773 4844
ⓜ 07850 363317
❸ mark@theclockhouse.co.uk
ⓦ www.theclockhouse.co.uk
Est. 1989 *Stock size* Medium
Stock Antiquarian horology, longcase clocks
Open Tues–Fri 9.30am–4.30pm
Sat 9am–6pm or by appointment
Fairs Brunel University
Services Valuations, restoration, spares

⊞ **Hudson Bay Antiques**
Contact David
✉ **56 Wigmore Road, Carshalton, Surrey, SM5 1PH** 🅿
☎ 0870 6066555
ⓜ 07915 557700
Est. 2005 *Stock size* Large
Stock Furniture, silver, fine art

Open Mon–Sat 9am–5pm
Services Valuations, house clearance

CATERHAM

⊞ Caterham Clearance Centre
Contact John Simmons
✉ 63-65 Westway, Caterham, Surrey,
CR3 5TQ 🅿
☎ 01883 347267
📧 caterhamcc@btconnect.com
Est. 1975 **Stock size** Medium
Stock Furniture, smalls, cut glass, Cranberry glass
Open Thur–Sat 10am–4pm
Fairs Ardingly, Detling
Services Probate valuations, house clearances

⊞ Chaldon Books and Records
Contact Mr K Chesson
✉ 1 High Street, Caterham, Surrey,
CR3 5UE 🅿
☎ 01883 348583
Est. 1994 **Stock size** Medium
Stock Rare and second-hand books
Open Mon Tues 10am–2pm
Thurs–Sat 10am–5pm
Services Book search

CHARLWOOD

⊞ G D Blay Antiques (BADA)
Contact Geoffrey Blay
✉ The Old Dairy, Charlwood Place, Norwood Hill Road, Charlwood, Surrey,
RH6 0EB 🅿
📱 07785 767718
📧 gdblay@gdblayantiques.com
🌐 www.gdblayantiques.com
Stock size Medium
Stock Pre-1830s furniture, clocks, mirrors
Open Tues–Sat 10am–5pm or by appointment
Fairs Summer and Winter Olympia, BADA Chelsea

CHEAM

➶ Parkins
Contact Miss Wendy Zenthon
✉ 18 Malden Road, Cheam, Surrey,
SM3 8QF 🅿

☎ 020 8644 6633 📠 020 8255 4703
📧 info@parkinsauction.co.uk
🌐 www.parkinsauction.co.uk
Est. 1945
Open Mon–Fri 9am–1pm 2–5pm
Sales Antique furniture and effects 1st Mon of month 10am, general furniture and effects 2nd and 4th Mon of month 10am, viewing Fri 2–4pm Sat 10am–4pm. Smaller fine antiques and collectables monthly evening sale, viewing 2–7pm
Catalogues Yes

⊞ Village Antiques
Contact Miss S Jenner
✉ 16 Malden Road, Cheam, Sutton, Surrey,
SM3 8QF 🅿
☎ 020 8644 8567 📠 020 8644 8567
Est. 1986 **Stock size** Large
Stock Furniture, lighting, porcelain, glass, silver, jewellery, collectors' items
Open Mon–Sat 11am–5pm closed Tues Thurs
Services House clearance

CHERTSEY

⊞ Chertsey Antiques
Contact Mr R Ulisse
✉ 10 Windsor Street, Chertsey, Surrey,
KT16 8AS 🅿
☎ 01932 563313
Est. 1996 **Stock size** Large
Stock Porcelain, jewellery, furniture, books, lighting, plated ephemera, clocks, memorabilia
Open Mon–Fri 10am–5pm
Sat 10am–5.30pm
Fairs Alexandra Palace
Services Local delivery of furniture

⊞ D'Eyncourt Antiques
Contact Mr G D H Davies
✉ 21 Windsor Street, Chertsey, Surrey,
KT16 8AY 🅿
☎ 01932 563411
Est. 1970 **Stock size** Large
Stock Furniture, jewellery, china, collectables, fireplaces
Open Mon–Fri 10am–5.15pm
Sat 7am–5.30pm Sun 11am–4pm
Fairs London Photographic Fair
Services Valuations

➶ Wellers Auctioneers
Contact Mr Glen Snelgar FRICS or Mr Mark Longson

✉ 70 Guildford Street, Chertsey, Surrey,
KT16 9BB 🅿
☎ 01932 568678 📠 01932 568626
📧 auctions@wellers.co.uk
🌐 www.wellers-auctions.co.uk
Est. 1980
Open Mon–Fri 9am–5pm
Sales Antique sales Sat monthly at 9.30am, general sale every Tues
Catalogues Yes

CHIPSTEAD

⊞ Unique Collections of Chipstead
Contact Glen Chapman
✉ Old Chipstead Stores, 8 High Road, Chipstead, Surrey,
CR5 3QP 🅿
☎ 01737 555598 📠 01737 554846
📧 glen@uniquecollections.co.uk
🌐 www.uniquecollections.co.uk
Est. 1987 **Stock size** Medium
Stock Obsolete diecast Dinky toys, Corgi, Matchbox/Lesney, Triang, Spot-On/Minic ships, tinplate toys, William Britains, Timpo toy soldiers, Action Man
Open Tues–Sun 11am–5pm

CHOBHAM

⊞ Mimbridge Antiques and Collectables
Contact Mrs J Monteath Scott
✉ Mimbridge Garden Centre, Station Road, Chobham, Woking, Surrey,
GU24 8AS 🅿
☎ 01276 855736
📱 0771 862284
Est. 1987 **Stock size** Medium
Stock Small antiques, pictures, prints, maps, garden items, period furniture, decorative items, porcelain, glass, dolls
Open Mon–Sun 10am–5pm
Fairs Kempton
Services Picture framing

⊞ What-Not Antiques
Contact Carole Fisher
✉ 82 High Street, Chobham, Surrey,
GU24 8AF 🅿
☎ 01276 857622 📠 01276 856766
Est. 1984 **Stock size** Medium
Stock Antique pine and oak furniture, collectables, Disney
Open Mon–Sat 9am–5.30pm
Sun 10.30am–4pm

COBHAM

⊞ Village Antiques
Contact Mr N Tsangari
✉ 38 Portsmouth Road, Cobham, Surrey,
KT11 1HZ ⓟ
☎ 01932 589841
ⓜ 07973 549221
Est. 1998 *Stock size* Medium
Stock General antiques, small furniture, pictures, porcelain, glass
Open Mon–Fri 10am–6pm or by appointment
Services Picture restoration

COMPTON

⊞ Country Rustics
Contact Veronica Dewey
✉ 45 The Street, Compton, Guildford, Surrey,
GU3 1EG ⓟ
☎ 01483 810505
Est. 2001 *Stock size* Small
Stock Rustic furniture and collectables
Open Tues–Sat 10am–6pm Sun 1–4pm

⌂ Old Barn Antiques
Contact Mrs Chris Thurner
✉ Old Barn, The Street, Compton, Guildford, Surrey,
GU3 1EB ⓟ
☎ 01483 810819
Est. 1993 *Stock size* Small
No. of dealers 6
Stock Country items, blue and white, Victoriana, china, glass, collectables
Open Mon–Sat 10am–4pm

COULSDON

⊞ Decodream
Contact David Mobbs
✉ 233 Chipstead Valley Road, Coulsdon, Surrey,
CR5 3BY ⓟ
☎ 020 8668 5534 ⓕ 01737 556079
Est. 1987 *Stock size* Large
Stock Art Deco pottery
Open Mon–Sat by appointment
Services Valuations

CRANLEIGH

⊞ Dingly Dell Antiques & Collectables
Contact Susanna Wadey
✉ 8 Smithbrook Kilns (A281), Cranleigh, Surrey,
GU6 8JJ ⓟ
☎ 01483 268868
Est. 2002 *Stock size* Large
Stock Antiques, collectables
Open Tues–Sat 10am–5pm
Services Coffee shop

CROYDON

⌕ Croydon Coin Auctions
Contact Mr G J Monk
✉ PO Box 201, Croydon, Surrey,
CR9 7AQ ⓟ
☎ 020 8656 4583 ⓕ 020 8656 4583
ⓔ graeme@croydoncoinauctions.co.uk
ⓦ www.croydoncoinauctions.co.uk
Est. 1983
Open Mon–Fri 9am–5pm
Sales 6 sales a year of English, foreign and ancient coins, medallions, tokens and bank notes. Held at the United Reformed Church Hall, East Croydon Tues noon

⊞ Oscar Dahling Antiques
Contact Oscar Dahling
✉ 87 Cherry Orchard Road, East Croydon, Surrey,
CR0 6BE
☎ 0208 8681 8090
ⓔ oscar.dahling@virgin.net
Est. 1991 *Stock size* Medium
Stock General antiques
Open Tues–Thur 10.30am–6pm Sat 10.30am–4.30pm
Services Valuations

⊞ McNally Antiques
Contact I McNally
✉ 322 Brighton Road, South Croydon, Surrey,
CR2 6AJ ⓟ
☎ 020 8686 8387 ⓕ 020 8686 8387
Est. 1972 *Stock size* Large
Stock Oak, walnut, mahogany furniture
Open Mon–Fri 9am–5pm Sat 9am–1pm or by appointment
Services Shipping

⊞ Wood Be Good
Contact Mr Dennis Langford or John Ball
✉ 339 Limpsfield Road, Croydon, Surrey,
CR2 9BY ⓟ
☎ 020 8657 6606 ⓕ 020 8657 6610
ⓜ 07831 657357
ⓔ john.rw.ball@blueyonder.co.uk
Est. 1984 *Stock size* Medium
Stock Antique pine
Open Mon–Sat 9am–5pm
Fairs Ardingly
Services Restoration

DORKING

⊞ Antique Clocks by Patrick Thomas
Contact Mr P Thomas
✉ 62a West Street, Dorking, Surrey,
RH4 1BS ⓟ
☎ 01306 743661 ⓕ 01483 715289
ⓜ 07976 971024
ⓔ patrickthomas@btconnect.com
ⓦ www.antiqueclockshop.co.uk
Est. 1992 *Stock size* Large
Stock Clocks, scientific instruments, sporting antiques, desk accessories, original oils and watercolours
Open Mon–Sat 9.30am–5.30pm Sun 11am–4pm
Services Valuations, restoration

⊞ Nicholas Arkell Antiques Ltd (LAPADA)
Contact Nicholas Arkell
✉ 64–65 West Street, Dorking, Surrey,
RH4 1BS ⓟ
☎ 01306 742152 ⓕ 01306 742152
ⓜ 07973 819783
ⓔ nick@arkellantiques.co.uk
ⓦ www.arkellantiques.co.uk
Est. 1978 *Stock size* Large
Stock Georgian and Edwardian satinwood furniture, silver, lighting, garden statuary
Open Mon–Sat 10am–5pm
Fairs LAPADA, Guildford, Olympia

⊞ J and M Coombes
Contact Mr M Coombes
✉ 44 West Street, Dorking, Surrey,
RH4 1BU
☎ 01306 885479 ⓕ 01306 885479
Est. 1967 *Stock size* Large
Stock Victorian–Edwardian furniture
Open Mon–Fri 10am–5pm Sat 10am–5pm

⌕ Crows Auction Gallery
Contact Crows Auction Gallery
✉ Rear of Dorking Halls, Reigate Road, Dorking, Surrey,
RH4 1SG ⓟ
☎ 01306 740382 ⓕ 01306 881672
ⓜ 07713 382446
ⓔ enquiriescrows.co.uk
ⓦ www.crowsauctions.co.uk
Est. 1988

Open Mon–Fri 9am–4pm
Sat 9.30am–noon
Sales Antiques and collectables
sale last Wed in month 10am,
viewing Sat 9am–1pm Mon–Tues
9am–4pm and morning of sale
Frequency Monthly
Catalogues Yes

⊞ Dolphin Square Antiques
Contact Diana James
⊠ **42 West Street, Dorking,
Surrey,
RH4 1BU**
☎ 01306 887901
Est. 1995 *Stock size* Medium
Stock Georgian–Edwardian
furniture, clocks, mirrors,
Staffordshire, porcelain, glass,
copper, brass ware, bronzes
Open Tues–Sat 10.30am–5pm

⊞ Dorking Desk Shop
(LAPADA, DADA)
Contact J G Elias
⊠ **41 West Street, Dorking, Surrey,
RH4 1BU** 🅿
☎ 01306 883327 🖷 01306 875363
🄴 dorkingdesks@aol.com
🆆 www.desk.uk.com
Est. 1965 *Stock size* Large
Stock Desks and writing furniture
Open Mon–Fri 9am–5.30pm
Sat 10.30am–5.30pm
Services Desk finding service

⌂ Dorking House Antiques
Contact Mrs G Embury
⊠ **17–18 West Street, Dorking,
Surrey,
RH4 1BS** 🅿
☎ 01306 740915
Est. 1988 *Stock size* Large
No. of dealers 25
Stock Period furniture, silver,
porcelain, paintings, collectables,
treen, clocks
Open Mon–Sat 10am–5pm

⌂ Great Grooms of
Dorking
Contact Mr J Podger
⊠ **50–52 West Street, Dorking,
Surrey,
RH4 1BU** 🅿
☎ 01306 887076 🖷 01306 881029
🄴 dorking@greatgrooms.co.uk
🆆 www.greatgrooms.co.uk
Est. 1993 *Stock size* Large
No. of dealers 25
Stock Antique furniture,
collectables, jewellery, silver,
china, glass, pictures, lighting

Open Mon–Sat 9.30am–5.30pm
Sun 10am–4pm
Services Valuations, restoration,
interior design

⊞ The Howard Gallery
(LAPADA)
Contact Mrs F Howard
⊠ **5 West Street, Dorking, Surrey,
RH4 1BL** 🅿
☎ 01306 880022
🆆 www.thehowardgallery.co.uk
Est. 1989 *Stock size* Medium
Stock 17th–18thC early
Georgian, Queen Anne, Regency,
oak, country furniture, longcase,
bracket clocks
Open Tues–Sat 11am–5pm
Services Restoration, shipping

⊞ King's Court Galleries
(FATG)
Contact Mrs J Joel
⊠ **54 West Street, Dorking, Surrey,
RH4 1BS** 🅿
☎ 01306 881757 🖷 01306 875305
🄴 sales@kingscourtgalleries.co.uk
🆆 www.kingscourtgalleries.co.uk
Est. 1984 *Stock size* Large
Stock Antique maps, engravings,
sporting and decorative prints
Open Mon–Sat 9.30am–5.30pm
Services Bespoke framing,
mounting

⌂ Malthouse Antiques
Contact Mr C Waters
⊠ **49 West Street, Dorking,
Surrey, RH4 1BU** 🅿
☎ 01306 886169
Est. 1993 *Stock size* Large
No. of dealers 5
Stock 17th–20thC antiques
Open Mon–Sat 10am–5pm
Services Valuations, restoration,
shipping

⊞ Bruce Moss Antiques
Contact Bruce Moss
⊠ **Hampshires of Dorking
Antique Centre, 50–52 West
Street, Dorking, Surrey,
RH4 1BU** 🅿
☎ 01306 887076
Est. 2004 *Stock size* Medium
Stock Georgian furniture, silver
Open Mon–Sat 9.30am–5.30pm
Sun & Bank Holidays 10am–4pm

⌂ Pilgrims Antique Centre
Contact Mary Williams
⊠ **7 West Street, Dorking, Surrey,
RH4 1BL** 🅿

☎ 01306 875028
Est. 1990 *Stock size* Medium
No. of dealers 10
Stock Glass, furniture, paintings,
Art Deco, barometers, Jobling
glass, collectables, cutlery, silver,
glass, binoculars
Open Mon–Sat 10am–5pm
Sat 10am–5.30pm
Services Restaurant

⊞ Eric Tombs
Contact Mr Eric Tombs
⊠ **62a West Street, Dorking,
Surrey, RH4 1BS** 🅿
☎ 01306 743661
📱 07720 561680
🄴 ertombs@aol.com
Est. 1992 *Stock size* Medium
Stock Scientific instruments
Open Mon–Sat 9.30am–5.30pm
Sun 11am–4pm
Fairs Scientific Instruments Fair
Services Valuations, restoration

⊞ West Street Antiques
Contact Mr J G Spooner
⊠ **63 West Street, Dorking, Surrey,
RH4 1BS** 🅿
☎ 01306 883487 🖷 01306 883487
🄴 weststant@aol.com
🆆 www.antiquearmsandarmour.com
Est. 1986 *Stock size* Medium
Stock Arms, armour
Open Mon–Sat 9.30am–1pm
2.15–5.30pm or by appointment
Fairs London Arms Fair, Park
Lane Arms Fair
Services Valuations,
comprehensive on-line catalogue

⚒ P F Windibank
Contact Mr S Windibank
⊠ **Dorking Halls, Reigate Road,
Dorking, Surrey,
RH4 1SG** 🅿
☎ 01306 884556 🖷 01306 884669
🄴 sjw@windibank.co.uk
🆆 www.windibank.co.uk
Est. 1945
Open Mon–Fri 9am–5pm
Sat 10am–1pm
Sales Antique and quality sales
on Sat, viewing Thurs 5–9pm
Fri 9am–5pm
Frequency 4–6 weeks
Catalogues Yes

⊞ Books Bought and Sold
Ltd
Contact Mr P Sheridan

✉ 68 Walton Road, East Molesey,
Surrey,
KT8 0DL ℗
☎ 020 8224 3232 📠 020 8224 3576
📧 booksbought@yahoo.co.uk
Est. 1973 *Stock size* Medium
Stock Antiquarian, rare, second-
hand books, transport, collectable
children's books a speciality
Open Tues–Sat 10am–5pm
Fairs HD Book Fairs

⊞ Elizabeth R Antiques
Contact E L Mallah
✉ 39 Bridge Road, Hampton
Court, East Molesey, Surrey,
KT8 9ER ℗
☎ 020 8979 4004 📠 020 8979 4004
📧 lizaantiques@hotmail.com
Est. 1994 *Stock size* Large
Stock 18th–19thC furniture,
porcelain, glass, jewellery,
20thC dolls and toys
Open Tues–Sat 10am–4.30pm
Sun 11am–3pm closed Wed
Fairs Alexandra Palace, Sandown
Services Valuations, restoration

⌂ The Hampton Court
Emporium
Contact Mr A Smith
✉ 52–54 Bridge Road,
East Molesey, Surrey,
KT8 9HA ℗
☎ 020 8941 8876
🌐 www.hamptoncourtemporium.com
Est. 1992 *Stock size* Large
No. of dealers 38
Stock Cameras, books, jewellery,
lace, silver, brass, copper, toys,
war ephemera, French arts,
furniture
Open Mon–Sat 10am–5.30pm
Sun 11am–5.30pm

⌂ Journeyman Antique
Centre
Contact Mr or Mrs A Caplan
✉ 77 Bridge Road, East Molesey,
Surrey,
KT8 9WH
☎ 0208 979 7954
Est. 1974 *Stock size* Large
No. of dealers 9
Stock General antiques,
collectables, furniture, jewellery
Open Mon–Sat 10.30am–5.30pm
Sun noon–5pm

⌂ Palace Antiques
Contact John Prince
✉ 29–31 Bridge Road,
East Molesey, Surrey,

KT8 9ER
☎ 020 8979 2182 📠 020 8949 1153
Est. 2000 *Stock size* Large
No. of dealers 15
Stock General antiques and
bronzeware
Open Mon–Sun 10am–6pm

⊞ Alexis F J Turner
Antiques
Contact Mr Turner
✉ Antiques at 144a Bridge Road,
East Molesey, Surrey,
KT8 9HW ℗
☎ 020 8542 5926
📱 07770 880960
Est. 1992 *Stock size* Medium
Stock Natural history, taxidermy,
gentlemen's effects, curiosities
Open Sat 10am–2pm or by
appointment

EPSOM

⊞ Gavantiques
Contact Gavin Taylor
✉ 20 Stoneleigh Broadway,
Epsom, Surrey,
KT17 2HU ℗
☎ 0208 786 3484
📱 07836 561612
Est. 1988 *Stock size* Medium
Stock General antiques
Open Mon–Sat 10am–4pm
closed Thur

ESHER

⊞ Memento
Contact Michael Coshall
✉ 8b Church Street, Esher, Surrey,
KT10 8QS
☎ 01372 462121 📠 01372 462121
Est. 2004 *Stock size* Medium
Stock Decorative antiques,
including statues, for house and
garden
Open Tue–Sun 11am–6pm
Services Sourcing items for clients

EWELL

⊞ J W McKenzie Ltd
Contact John
✉ 12 Stoneleigh Park Road,
Ewell, Surrey,
KT19 0QR ℗
☎ 0208 393 7700 📠 0208 393 1694
📧 jwmck@net.comuk.co.uk
🌐 www.mckenzie-cricket.co.uk
Est. 1972 *Stock size* Large
Stock Antiquarian, rare books,
memorabilia

Open Mon–Fri 9am–5pm or
by appointment
Services Four catalogues per year

FARNHAM

⊞ Annie's Antiques
Contact Annie
✉ 1 Ridgway Parade,
Frensham Road, Farnham,
Surrey,
GU9 8UZ ℗
☎ 01252 713447
Est. 1982 *Stock size* Medium
Stock General antiques
Open Mon–Sat 10am–5.30pm

⌂ Bourne Mill Antiques
Contact Mrs Vicky Bowers
✉ 39–43 Guildford Road,
Farnham, Surrey,
GU9 9PY ℗
☎ 01252 716663
📱 07808 628440
Est. 1960 *Stock size* Large
No. of dealers 70
Stock Antiques, collectables in
38 rooms
Open Mon–Sat 9.30am–5pm
Sun 10am–5pm

⊞ Casque and Gauntlet
Militaria
Contact R L Colt or A Colt
✉ 55–59 Badshot Lea Road,
Badshot Lea, Farnham,
Surrey,
GU9 9LP ℗
☎ 01252 320745
📧 rayko37@msn.com
🌐 www.armsandarmour.co.uk
/dealers/casque/casque.htm
Est. 1972 *Stock size* Large
Stock Militaria, 15thC–modern
times including swords,
bayonets, armour
Open Mon–Sat 11am–5pm
Services Restoration of antique
weapons

⊞ Christopher's Antiques
Contact Mr C Booth
✉ 39a West Street, Farnham,
Surrey,
GU9 7DX ℗
☎ 01252 713794 📠 01252 713266
📧 cbooth7956@aol.com
Est. 1972 *Stock size* Large
Stock French provincial country
furniture
Open Mon–Fri 8am–5.30pm
Sat 8am–noon
Services Valuations, restoration

FERNHURST

⚲ John Nicholson Fine Art Auctioneers
Contact Mr John Nicholson
✉ The Auction Rooms, Longfield, Midhurst Road, Fernhurst, Haslemere, Surrey, GU27 3HA ⓟ
☎ 01428 653727 ❻ 01428 641509
❻ sales@johnnicholsons.com
ⓦ www.johnnicholsons.com
Est. 1992
Open Mon–Fri 9am–5.30pm
Sales Fine art auctions 6 weekly Wed Thurs. Paintings, prints, antiquarian books 3–4 times a year. 20thC decorative art, Russian paintings, sporting and gun sales
Catalogues Yes

GODALMING

⊞ The Antique Shop & Collectables
Contact Jillian Noble Jones
✉ 72 Ockford Road, Godalming, Surrey, GU7 7RF
☎ 01483 414428
Est. 1985 *Stock size* Medium
Stock General antiques and collectables
Open Mon–Sat 10am–4.30pm

⚲ Dreweatt Neate Godalming Salerooms
Contact Mark Stacey
✉ Baverstock House, 93 High Street, Godalming, Surrey, GU7 1AL ⓟ
☎ 01483 423567 ❻ 01483 426392
❻ godalming@dnfa.com
ⓦ www.dnfa.com
Est. 1759
Open Mon–Fri 9am–5.30pm
Sales Specialist sales of furniture, pictures, books, works of art, ceramics, silver and jewellery, objects of vertu, decorative arts, carpets on Wed 10.30am, viewing Sat 9am–12.30pm, Mon 9.30am–7pm, Tues 9.30am–5pm. Fortnightly gallery sales of general furniture and effects Tues 10.30am
Frequency 4 sales every 6–8 weeks
Catalogues Yes

⊞ Heath-Bullocks (BADA)
Contact Mrs Mary Heath-Bullock
✉ 8 Meadrow, Godalming, Surrey,

GU7 3HN ⓟ
☎ 01483 422562
❻ heathbullocks@aol.com
ⓦ www.heath-bullocks.com
or www.antiquescare.com
Est. 1925 *Stock size* Large
Stock 17th–19thC furniture
Open Mon–Sat 10am–5pm
Services Valuations, restoration, upholstery

🏠 Honeypot Antiques
Contact G Isenman
✉ Milford Road, Elstead, Godalming, Surrey, GU8 6HR ⓟ
☎ 01252 703614
ⓦ www.honeypotantiques.co.uk
Est. 1996 *Stock size* Large
No. of dealers 25
Stock General antiques and collectables
Open Mon–Sat 10am–5pm
Sun 11am–5pm

⊞ Milford Secondhand Services
Contact Mr Sudnick
✉ Hurst Farm Close, Milford, Godalming, Surrey, GU8 5ER ⓟ
☎ 01483 414404
Est. 1997 *Stock size* Medium
Stock Battleships–kitchen sink
Open Phone first
Services House clearance

GOMSHALL

⊞ The Coach House Antiques (LAPADA)
Contact Paul or Louise Reeves
✉ 60 Station Road, Gomshall, Guildford, Surrey, GU5 9NP ⓟ
☎ 01483 203838 ❻ 01483 202999
❻ coach_houseantiques@virgin.net
ⓦ www.coachhouseantiques.com
Est. 1984 *Stock size* Medium
Stock Regency–William IV furniture, clocks, pictures
Open Mon–Sat 9.30am–5pm
Sun noon–5pm
Fairs Guildford
Services Restoration

GREAT BOOKHAM

⊞ Roger A Davis Antiquarian Horologist
Contact Roger Davis
✉ 19 Dorking Road, Great Bookham, Surrey,

KT23 4PU ⓟ
☎ 01372 457655
Est. 1972 *Stock size* Medium
Stock Antique clocks
Open Tues Thurs Sat
9.30am–12.30pm 2–5pm
Services Restoration

⊞ Memory Lane Antiques
Contact Mrs J Westwood
✉ 30 Church Road, Great Bookham, Leatherhead, Surrey, KT23 3PW ⓟ
☎ 01372 459908
Est. 1984 *Stock size* Medium
Stock Antiques, toys
Open Mon–Fri 10am–5pm
Sat 10am–2pm closed Wed

GUILDFORD

⚲ Bonhams
✉ Millmead, Guildford, Surrey, GU2 4BE ⓟ
☎ 01483 504030 ❻ 01483 450205
❻ guildford@bonhams.com
ⓦ www.bonhams.com
Est. 1793
Open Mon–Fri 9am–5.30pm
Sales Regional office. Regular sales held in London and in our salerooms across the country. Free auction valuations; insurance and probate valuations

⚲ Clarke Gammon Wellers Auctioneers & Valuers (RICS)
Contact Gordon Patrick or Sarah Moran
✉ Bedford Road, Guildford, Surrey, GU1 4SJ ⓟ
☎ 01483 880915 ❻ 01483 880918
ⓦ www.invaluable.com/wellers
Est. 1919
Open Mon–Fri 9am–5.30pm
Sales Fine art, antiques and collectors' sales, viewing Sat 9am–noon Mon 9am–7pm prior to sale
Frequency 6 weeks
Catalogues Yes

⊞ Denning Antiques
Contact Mrs C Denning
✉ 1 Chapel Street, Guildford, Surrey, GU1 3UH ⓟ
☎ 01483 539595
Est. 1984 *Stock size* Large
Stock Silver, textiles, jewellery
Open Mon–Sat 10am–5pm

⊞ **Horological Workshops (BADA, BHI)**
Contact Mr M D Tooke
✉ **204 Worplesdon Road, Guildford, Surrey, GU2 9UY** 🅿
☎ 01483 576496 📠 01483 452212
✉ enquiries@horological workshops.com
🌐 www.horologicalworkshops.com
Est. 1968 *Stock size* Large
Stock Clocks, watches, barometers
Open Tues–Fri 8.30am–5.30pm
Sat 9am–12.30pm
Services Valuations, restoration, shipping, collection, delivery

⊞ **Perryhill Antiques**
Contact Dave Jenkins
✉ **Perry Hill, Worplesdon, Guildford, Surrey, GU3 3RD** 🅿
☎ 01483 236081
Est. 1985 *Stock size* Large
Stock 20thC furniture and related items, Arts and Crafts, 1950s–1960s items
Open Mon–Sun 9.30am–5.30pm
or by appointment
Fairs Newark, Kempton
Services House clearance

HASLEMERE

⊞ **West Street Antiques (LAPADA)**
Contact Mr M Holden
✉ **8–10 West Street, Haslemere, Surrey, GU27 2AB** 🅿
☎ 01428 644911 📠 01428 645201
✉ info@weststreetantiques.co.uk
🌐 www.weststreetantiques.co.uk
Est. 1998 *Stock size* Medium
Stock 17thC–early 20thC furniture, dinner services, maps, prints, Georgian and Victorian silver
Open Mon–Sat 9.30am–5pm
Services Valuations, restoration

⌂ **Woods Wharf Antiques Market**
Contact Mrs C Lunnon
✉ **56 High Street, Haslemere, Surrey, GU27 2LA** 🅿
☎ 01428 642125 📠 01428 642125
Est. 1975 *Stock size* Medium
No. of dealers 8
Stock Antiques, collectables
Open Mon–Sat 9.30am–5pm

HINDHEAD

⊞ **Albany Antiques**
Contact Mr T Winstanley
✉ **8–10 London Road, Hindhead, Surrey, GU26 6AF** 🅿
☎ 01428 605528 📠 01428 605528
📱 07931 672345
Est. 1949 *Stock size* Large
Stock Georgian furniture, 18thC brass, Victorian antiques, porcelain, statuary
Open Mon–Sat 9.30am–5pm
or by appointment

⊞ **Book Academy**
✉ **Crossways House, Crossways Road, Grayshott, Hindhead, Surrey, GU26 6HJ** 🅿
☎ 01428 609910 📠 01428 609904
Est. 1970 *Stock size* Large
Stock Antiquarian and new, reformed theology books including bibles, prayer, hymn books, Dickens, Hampshire a speciality
Open Mon–Fri 9.30am–4.30pm
Services Valuations, book repair, rebinding

⊞ **M J Bowdery (BADA)**
Contact Mr Malcolm John Bowdery
✉ **12 London Road, Hindhead, Surrey, GU26 6AF** 🅿
☎ 01428 606376
📱 07774 821444
Est. 1970 *Stock size* Small
Stock 18th–19thC furniture
Open Mon–Sat 9am–1pm
or by appointment
Services Valuations

⊞ **Drummonds Architectural Antiques Ltd (SALVO)**
Contact Mr Drummond Shaw
✉ **The Kirkpatrick Buildings, 25 London Road, Hindhead, Surrey, GU26 6AB** 🅿
☎ 01428 609444 📠 01428 609445
✉ info@drummonds-arch.co.uk
🌐 www.drummonds-arch.co.uk
Est. 1989 *Stock size* Large
Stock Period bathrooms, oak and pine flooring, fireplaces, statues, garden furniture and lighting, brass door furniture and fittings, radiators, furniture, windows, doors, gates, railings, conservatories

Open Mon–Fri 9am–6pm
Sat 10am–5pm
Services Proper vitreous re-enamelling of cast-iron baths, restored antique bathrooms

HORLEY

⊞ **Surrey Antiques**
Contact Mr M Bradnum
✉ **3 Central Parade, Massetts Road, Horley, Surrey, RH6 7PP** 🅿
☎ 01293 775522
Est. 1989 *Stock size* Large
Stock Antiques, collectables, furniture, silver, china, glass, brass, linen, pictures, books
Open Mon–Sat 10am–5pm
Services House clearance

KINGSTON-UPON-THAMES

⊞ **Glydon and Guess (NAG, NPA)**
Contact Mr A Fleckney
✉ **14 Applemarket, Kingston-upon-Thames, Surrey, KT1 1JE** 🅿
☎ 020 8546 3758 📠 020 8541 5743
✉ glydonandguess@finegem.co.uk
🌐 www.finegem.co.uk
Est. 1940 *Stock size* Medium
Stock Jewellery, antique and modern furniture, clocks, barometers
Open Mon–Sat 9.30am–5pm
Services Valuations, restoration, pawnbrokers

⌂ **The Kingston Antiques Centre**
✉ **29–31 Old London Road, Kingston-upon-Thames, Surrey, KT2 6ND** 🅿
☎ 020 8549 2004 📠 020 8549 3839
✉ enquiries@antiquesmarket.co.uk
🌐 www.kingstonantiquescentre.co.uk
Est. 1996 *Stock size* Large
No. of dealers 80+
Stock Furniture, jewellery, porcelain, silver, pictures, 20thC design, lighting, Oriental
Open Mon–Sat 9.30am–6pm
Sun 10.30am–6pm

MERSTHAM

⊞ **Geoffrey Van-Hay Antiques**
Contact Geoffrey Van-Hay
✉ **The Old Smithy, 7 High Street, Merstham, Surrey,**

RH1 3BA 🅿
☎ 01737 645131 📠 01737 645131
📧 olliev@hotmail.com
Est. 1992 *Stock size* Medium
Stock General antiques
Open Mon–Sat 9.30am–5.30pm
Services Valuations, restoration

NEW MALDEN

⊞ Coombe Antiques
Contact Sandra Sephton
✉ **25 Coombe Road, New Malden,
Surrey,
KT3 4PX** 🅿
☎ 020 8949 4238
📱 07970 718214
Est. 1980 *Stock size* Medium
Stock Furniture, china, textiles,
oil lamps, lighting, garden
furniture, silver
Open Mon–Sat 10am–5.30pm
Sun by appointment
Services Valuations, free deliveries

OCKLEY

⊞ Vintage Sewing Machines
Contact Dominic Macey
✉ **1 Heathfield Cottages,
Coles Lane, Ockley, Surrey,
RH5 5LS** 🅿
📱 07971 280479
📧 vintagesewingmachine@yahoo.com
🌐 www.vintagesewingmachine.com
Est. 2003 *Stock size* Medium
Stock Antique sewing machines
Open Mon–Sun 10am–6pm
Fairs Ardingly
Services Restoration

OXTED

⊞ The Second-Hand Bookshop
Contact Mr David Neal
✉ **27 Station Road West, Oxted,
Surrey,
RH8 9EE** 🅿
☎ 01883 715755
Est. 1994 *Stock size* Medium
Stock Rare, second-hand books,
mainly non-fiction
Open Mon–Sat 10am–5pm
Fairs HD, Titlepage

REDHILL

⊞ F G Lawrence and Son
Contact Mr C Lawrence
✉ **Rear of 89 Brighton Road,
Redhill, Surrey,**

RH1 6PS 🅿
☎ 01737 764196 📠 01737 764196
📱 07850 787873
📧 fglawrence@btopenworld.com
Est. 1890 *Stock size* Large
Stock Georgian–Edwardian,
1920s furniture
Open Mon–Fri 9am–5pm
Sat 9am–1pm
Fairs Newark, Ardingly
Services Valuations, restoration

REIGATE

⊞ Bertram Knoller
Contact Bertram Knoller
✉ **14a London Road, Reigate,
Surrey,
RH2 9HY** 🅿
☎ 01737 242548
Est. 1970 *Stock size* Small
Stock Copper, brass, silver,
fireplace accessories, lighting
Open Tues Thurs Sat 10am–5pm
Services Clock repairs, metal
repairs and polishing

⊞ Reigate Galleries (PBFA)
Contact J S Morrish
✉ **45a Bell Street, Reigate,
Surrey,
RH2 7AQ** 🅿
☎ 01737 246055
Est. 1958 *Stock size* Large
Stock Antiquarian, rare, second-
hand books, antique engravings
Open Mon–Sat 9am–5.30pm
Wed 9am–1pm
Fairs PBFA fairs in London

⊞ M & M White Antiques and Reproduction Centre
Contact Mr M White
✉ **57 High Street, Reigate, Surrey,
RH2 9AE** 🅿
☎ 01737 222331
📱 07974 172801
Est. 1994 *Stock size* Medium
Stock Regency, Victorian and
reproduction furniture
Open Mon–Sat 10am–5.30pm
Fairs Newark, Ardingly

RICHMOND

⊞ Antique Mart
Contact Mr G Katz
✉ **72–74 Hill Rise, Richmond,
Surrey,
TW10 6UB**
☎ 020 8940 6942 📠 020 8715 4668
📱 07775 626423
Est. 1963 *Stock size* Medium

Stock 18th–19thC furniture
Open Thurs–Sun 2–5.15pm or
by appointment

⊞ Hugo Austin Antiques
Contact Hugo Austin
✉ **128 Kew Road, Richmond,
Surrey,
TW9 2PN**
☎ 020 8332 2316
Est. 1993 *Stock size* Medium
Stock French country furniture
Open Mon–Sat 10.30am–6.30pm
Sun 2–6pm
Services Restoration

⊞ Andrew Davis Antiques
Contact Mr A Davis
✉ **6 Mortlake Terrace, Kew
Green, Richmond, Surrey,
TW9 3DT** 🅿
☎ 020 8948 4911
📱 07768 904041
Est. 1969 *Stock size* Medium
Stock General antiques, pictures,
prints
Open Most days and by
appointment
Services Valuations

⊞ The Gooday Gallery
Contact Mrs D Gooday
✉ **14 Richmond Hill, Richmond,
Surrey,
TW10 6QX** 🅿
☎ 020 8940 8652
📱 07710 124540
📧 goodaygallery@aol.com
Est. 1971 *Stock size* Medium
Stock Arts and Crafts,
Art Nouveau, Art Deco, post-
modernism, tribal art, African
and Oceanic masks
Open Thurs–Sat 11am–5pm
or by appointment
Services Valuations

⊞ Horton (LAPADA)
Contact David Horton
✉ **2 Paved Court, Richmond,
Surrey,
TW9 1LZ**
☎ 020 8832 1775
📧 richmond@hortonlondon.co.uk
🌐 www.hortonlondon.co.uk
Est. 1978 *Stock size* Small
Stock Antique jewellery
Open Mon–Sat 10am–5pm
Services Repairs

⊞ Lionel Jacobs (NAG)
Contact Tom French
✉ **12–14 Brewers Lane,**

SOUTH

Richmond, Surrey,
TW9 1HH
☎ 020 8940 8069 ✆ 020 8332 1841
✉ lioneljacobs@lioneljacobs.com
🌐 www. lioneljacobs.com
Est. 1977 *Stock size* Medium
Stock Antique fine jewellery,
silver, watches
Open Tues–Sat 10am–5pm
Services Valuations, jewellery
and watch repair

⊞ Marryat Antiques Ltd (LAPADA)
Contact Mrs M Samuels
✉ 88 Sheen Road, Richmond,
Surrey,
TW9 1UF 🅿
☎ 020 8332 0262
Est. 1990 *Stock size* Large
Stock Furniture, pictures, silver,
porcelain, Oriental antiques
Open Mon–Fri 10am–5.30pm
Sat 9.30am–5.30pm
Sun by appointment
Services Restoration

⊞ Richmond Hill Antiques
Contact Mrs M Hobson
✉ 72 Hill Rise, Richmond,
Surrey,
TW10 6UB 🅿
☎ 020 8940 5755 ✆ 020 8940 5755
📱 07909 912382
✉ richmondhillant@hotmail.com
Est. 1970 *Stock size* Medium
Stock Georgian and Victorian
furniture
Open Mon Thurs Fri noon–4pm
Sat 10.30am–5.30pm
Sun 1.30–5.30pm Tues Wed by
appointment
Services Valuations, restoration,
shipping

⊞ J Hartley Antiques Ltd (LAPADA)
Contact Mr J Hartley
✉ 186 High Street, Ripley,
Woking, Surrey,
GU23 6BB 🅿
☎ 01483 224318
Est. 1973 *Stock size* Medium
Stock Antique furniture
Open Mon–Fri 9am–6pm
Sat 9.30am–5pm
Services Free local delivery

⊞ The Lamp Gallery
Contact Graham Jones
✉ Talbot Walk Antique Centre,

Talbot Hotel, High Street, Ripley,
Surrey,
GU23 6BB 🅿
☎ 01483 211724 ✆ 01483 211724
Est. 1986 *Stock size* Medium
Stock Interior lighting, including
Art Nouveau and Art Deco lamps
Open Mon–Sat 10am–5pm Sun
11am–4pm or by appointment
Services Valuations, shipping

⊞ Sage Antiques & Interiors (LAPADA)
Contact Mr H Sage
✉ High Street, Ripley, Surrey,
GU23 6BB 🅿
☎ 01483 224396 ✆ 01483 211996
Est. 1973 *Stock size* Large
Stock 18thC mahogany, oak,
walnut furniture
Open Mon–Sat 9am–5.30pm

⌂ Talbot Walk Antique Centre
Contact Graham Jones
✉ Talbot Hotel, High Street,
Ripley, Surrey,
GU23 6BB 🅿
☎ 01483 211724 ✆ 01483 211724
Est. 1999 *Stock size* Medium
No. of dealers 40
Stock Interior lighting, including
Art Nouveau and Art Deco lamps,
general antiques, furniture
Open Mon–Sat 10am–5pm
Sun 11am–4pm
Services Valuations, restoration,
shipping

⊞ Anthony Welling (BADA)
Contact Mr A Welling
✉ Broadway Barn, High Street,
Ripley, Woking, Surrey,
GU23 6AQ 🅿
☎ 01483 225384 ✆ 01483 225384
Est. 1970 *Stock size* Medium
Stock Large 17th–18thC oak,
country furniture
Open Mon–Sat 10am–4.30pm
Sun and evenings by
appointment
Services Valuations, restoration

⌂ The Antiques Warehouse
Contact Mrs H Burroughs
✉ Badshot Farm, St Georges
Road, Runfold, Farnham,
Surrey,
GU9 9HY 🅿
☎ 01252 317590 ✆ 01252 879751
📱 07971 973289

🌐 www.theantiqueswarehouse.co.uk
Est. 1995 *Stock size* Large
No. of dealers 40
Stock Wide variety of antiques
including glass, silver, china,
17thC–1930s furniture, paintings,
prints, garden artefacts
Open Mon–Sun 10am–5.30pm
including Bank Holidays
Services Restoration, upholstery

⌂ The Packhouse Antiques Centre
Contact Alison Hougham
✉ Hewetts Kilns, Tongham Road,
Runfold, Farnham,
Surrey,
GU10 1PJ 🅿
☎ 01252 781010 ✆ 01252 783876
🌐 www.packhouse.com
Est. 1990 *Stock size* Large
No. of dealers 109
Stock Furniture, collectables,
garden artefacts, clocks,
paintings, mirrors
Open Mon–Fri 10.30am–5.30pm
Sat–Sun 10am–5.30pm
Services Delivery service, finders
file

⊞ Helena's Collectables
Contact Mrs H Lee
✉ Middle Street, Shere,
Guildford, Surrey,
GU5 9HF 🅿
☎ 01483 203039 ✆ 01483 203039
✉ helena@collectables.demon.co.uk
🌐 www.collectables.demon.co.uk
Est. 1996 *Stock size* Large
Stock Royal Worcester,
Wedgwood, Coalport, Doulton,
Beswick, classic Disney, porcelain,
collectable ceramics
Open Mon–Sat 9.30am–5.30pm
Sun 10.30am–4.30pm
Services Mail order service

⊞ Shere Antiques Centre
Contact Mrs Jean Watson
✉ Middle Street, Shere,
Guildford, Surrey,
GU5 9HF 🅿
☎ 01483 202846 ✆ 01483 830762
Est. 1987 *Stock size* Large
Stock Ceramics, clocks, chandeliers,
furniture, garden tools
Open Mon–Fri 11am–5pm
Sat Sun 11am–5pm or
by appointment
Services Restoration, shipping,
house clearance

SOUTH HOLMWOOD

⊞ Holmwood Antiques
Contact R Dewdney
✉ Charlwyns, Norfolk Road, South Holmwood, Dorking, Surrey, RH5 4LA ⓟ
☎ 01306 888468 ⓕ 01306 742636
Est. 1968 *Stock size* Medium
Stock General antiques
Open Mon–Fri 9am–6pm or by appointment
Services Restoration

SURBITON

⊞ Cockrell Antiques
Contact Peter or Sheila Cockrell
✉ 278 Ewell Road, Surbiton, Surrey, KT6 7AG ⓟ
☎ 020 8390 8290
ⓦ www.cockrellantiques.co.uk
Est. 1984 *Stock size* Large
Stock General antiques, mainly furniture
Open Mon–Sat 9am–6pm
Services Valuations

⊞ Maple Antiques
Contact Lynda or Geof Morris
✉ 4 Maple Road, Surbiton, Surrey, KT6 4AB ⓟ
☎ 020 8399 6718
Est. 1981 *Stock size* Medium
Stock Mahogany, pine, oak, walnut furniture, mirrors, rugs, garden art
Open Mon–Sat 10am–5.30pm
Fairs Ardingly, Kempton Park

⊞ Laurence Tauber Antiques
Contact Lauren J Tauber
✉ 131 Ewell Road, Surbiton, Surrey, KT6 6AL ⓟ
☎ 020 8390 0020
ⓜ 07710 443293
Est. 1975 *Stock size* Small
Stock 19thC–1930s Continental and decorative items, lighting
Trade only Mostly trade
Open Mon–Fri 10am–4.30pm by appointment

TADWORTH

⊞ Ian Caldwell (LAPADA)
Contact Mr I Caldwell
✉ 9a The Green, Dorking Road, Tadworth, Surrey, KT20 5SQ ⓟ
☎ 01737 813969
ⓔ caldwell.antiques@virgin.net
ⓦ www.lapada.co.uk/home pages/2486.htm
Est. 1978 *Stock size* Medium
Stock Town furniture William and Mary–Edwardian
Open Mon–Sat 10am–5pm closed Wed
Services Valuations, restoration

⊞ Diane France Antiques
Contact Diane France or Glen
✉ 43 Walton Street, Walton-on-the-Hill, Tadworth, Surrey, KT20 7RR ⓟ
☎ 01737 813747
ⓔ france-antiques@btopen world.com
Est. 2001 *Stock size* Small
Stock Furniture and ceramics
Open Mon–Sun 9am–5pm

THAMES DITTON

⊞ Clifford and Roger Dade
Contact Mr R Dade
✉ Boldre House, Weston Green, Hampton Court Way, Thames Ditton, Surrey, KT7 0JP ⓟ
☎ 020 8398 6293 ⓕ 020 8398 6293
ⓔ roger@dadeantiques.com
Est. 1937 *Stock size* Medium
Stock Georgian furniture, particularly mahogany
Open By appointment

WALTON-ON-THAMES

⊞ Antique Church Furnishings (SALVO)
Contact Mr L Skilling
✉ Rivernook Farm, Sunnyside, Walton-on-Thames, Surrey, KT12 2ET ⓟ
☎ 01932 252736 ⓕ 01932 252736
ⓔ info@churchantiques.com
ⓦ www.churchantiques.com
Est. 1989 *Stock size* Large
Stock Church furniture, fixtures and fittings
Open Mon–Fri 10am–6pm

⊞ Chancellors Church Furnishings (SALVO)
Contact Mr S Williams
✉ Rivernook Farm, Sunnyside, Walton-on-Thames, Surrey, KT12 2ET ⓟ
☎ 01932 230284 ⓕ 01932 252736

ⓜ 07973 139308
ⓔ info@churchantiques.com
ⓦ www.churchantiques.com
Est. 1992 *Stock size* Large
Stock All pre-war church furnishings, fixtures and fittings
Open Mon–Fri 10am–6pm

⊞ S & H Jewell Ltd
Contact Mr R Jewell or Mr G Korkis
✉ 17 Wolsey Drive, Walton-on-Thames, Surrey, KT12 3AY ⓟ
☎ 01932 222690
ⓜ 07973 406 255
Est. 1830 *Stock size* Large
Stock Quality English antique and period style 19th–20thC furniture
Open By appointment
Fairs Newark
Services Valuations, restoration

WEST BYFLEET

⊞ Academy Billiard Company
Contact Robert Donachie
✉ 5 Camp Hill Industrial Estate, Camp Hill Road, West Byfleet, Surrey, KT14 6EW ⓟ
☎ 01932 352067 ⓕ 01932 353904
ⓔ academygames@fsbdial.co.uk
ⓦ www.games-room.com
Est. 1983 *Stock size* Large
Stock Antique and modern games room equipment
Open By appointment
Services Valuations, restoration, shipping

WEYBRIDGE

⊞ Antiques & Decor
Contact Frances Jackson
✉ 8 York Road, Weybridge, Surrey, KT13 9DT ⓟ
☎ 01932 855427 ⓕ 01932 855427
Est. 1999 *Stock size* Medium
Stock Antiques, decor
Open Mon–Sat 9am–5pm

⊞ Church House Antiques
Contact Mary Foster
✉ 42 Church Street, Weybridge, Surrey, KT13 8DP ⓟ
☎ 01932 842190
Est. 1886 *Stock size* Medium
Stock Antique jewellery, furniture, silver, decorative accessories
Open Thurs–Sat 10am–5.30pm

⊞ The Clockshop
Contact Mr A Forster
✉ **64 Church Street, Weybridge, Surrey, KT13 8DL** 🅿
☎ 01932 855503 ❶ 01932 840407
Est. 1969 *Stock size* Large
Stock Antique clocks, barometers
Open Mon–Sat 10am–6pm
closed Wed
Services Restoration

⊞ Not Just Silver (NAG, BJA)
Contact Susan Hughes
✉ **16 York Road, Weybridge, Surrey, KT13 9DT** 🅿
☎ 01932 842468 ❶ 01932 830054
📱 07774 298151
📧 sales@not-just-silver.com
🌐 www.not-just-silver.com
Est. 1969 *Stock size* Medium
Stock Silver
Open Mon–Sat 9.30am–5.30pm
Services Valuations, restoration, silver and gold plating, watch repairs

WOKING

⚒ Barbers Fine Art Auctioneers (West Sussex Estate Agents, Surveyors and Auctioneers)
Contact Mr K Mansfield
✉ **Mayford Centre, Mayford Green, Woking, Surrey, GU22 0PP** 🅿
☎ 01483 728939 ❶ 01483 762552
📧 barbersfineart@btconnect.com
🌐 www.invaluable.com/barbers
Est. 1971
Open Mon–Sat 9am–1pm
Sales General and fine art sales. Please telephone for further details
Frequency Every 5–6 weeks
Catalogues Yes

⚒ Ewbank Fine Art Auctioneers (SOFAA, RICS)
Contact Mr C T J Ewbank FRICS
✉ **Burnt Common Auction Rooms, London Road, Send, Woking, Surrey, GU23 7LN** 🅿
☎ 01483 223101 ❶ 01483 222171
📧 antiques@ewbankauctions.co.uk
🌐 www.ewbankauctions.co.uk
Est. 1990
Open Mon–Fri 9.30am–5pm
Sales Sales held on first and third Thurs of every month, 4 antiques

sales and 20 sales of Victorian and later furnishings annually, viewing Tues week of sale 2–5pm and Wed 10am–8pm. Telephone for sale details
Catalogues Yes

⊞ Goldsworth Books and Prints (PBFA)
Contact Mr Brian Hartles
✉ **47 Goldsworth Road, Woking, Surrey, GU21 6JY** 🅿
☎ 01483 767670 ❶ 01483 767670
📧 brian@goldsworthbooks.com
Est. 1986 *Stock size* Medium
Stock Antiquarian, rare, second-hand books, antiquarian maps, books illustrated by Arthur Rackham a speciality
Open Tues–Fri 10am–5pm
Sat 9.30am–4.30pm
Fairs Russell Hotel, London, York National
Services Worldwide book search

WEST SUSSEX

ARDINGLY

🏠 Rocking Horse Antique Market
Contact Mrs J Livett or Mr P Livett
✉ **16 High Street, Ardingly, West Sussex, RH17 7TD** 🅿
☎ 01444 892205
Est. 1993 *Stock size* Large
No. of dealers 20
Stock Antiques, collectables, books, ephemera
Open Mon–Sat 9.30am–5.30pm
Sun 10am–5.30pm 5pm during winter

ARUNDEL

⊞ Antiquities
Contact Mr Ian Fenwick or Mrs Christina Fenwick
✉ **5–7 Tarrant Street, Arundel, West Sussex, BN18 9DG** 🅿
☎ 01903 884355 ❶ 01903 884355
📧 antiquities@btconnect.com
Est. 1991 *Stock size* Large
Stock 19thC English and French furniture, decorative items, majolica, blue and white, pond boats, French mirrors, chandeliers, lighting
Trade only Trade and export, public by appointment

🏠 Arundel Antiques Centre
✉ **51 High Street, Arundel, West Sussex, BN18 9AJ** 🅿
☎ 01903 882749
Est. 1975
No. of dealers 30
Stock Furniture, china, silver, porcelain, general antiques
Open Mon–Sun 10am–5pm
Services Valuations

⊞ The Arundel Bookshop
Contact G or A Shepherd
✉ **10 High Street, Arundel, West Sussex, BN18 9AB** 🅿
☎ 01903 882680
Est. 1977 *Stock size* Medium
Stock Rare, antiquarian, second-hand books
Open Mon–Sat 10am–5pm
Sun 10.30am–5pm

⊞ Arundel Bridge
Contact Lesley Barrett
✉ **6 High Street, Arundel, West Sussex, BN18 9AB**
☎ 01903 884164
Est. 1980 *Stock size* Medium
Stock General antiques
Open Mon–Sun 10am–5pm

⊞ Baynton-Williams
Contact Sarah or Roger Baynton-Williams
✉ **37a High Street, Arundel, West Sussex, BN18 9AG** 🅿
☎ 01903 883588
📧 gallery@baynton-williams.freeserve.co.uk
🌐 www.baynton-williams.com
Est. 1946 *Stock size* Medium
Stock Antiquarian maps, prints, decorative and botanical
Open Mon–Sat 10am–6pm or by appointment
Services Valuations

⊞ DecoGraphic Collectors Gallery
Contact G Cox
✉ **Arundel Antiques Centre, 51 High Street, Arundel, West Sussex, BN18 9AJ** 🅿
☎ 01243 787391

Est. 1994 *Stock size* Medium
Stock 1880–1960 toys, cameras, wirelesses, gramophones
Open Mon–Sun 10am–5pm
Services Restoration

⊞ Decorum
Contact Caroline Baker
✉ 9 Tarrant Street, Arundel, West Sussex, BN18 9DG ⓟ
☎ 01903 884436 ❶ 01903 889527
❸ caroline@decorum-arundel.co.uk
Ⓦ www.decorum-arundel.co.uk
Est. 1989 *Stock size* Medium
Stock French decorative furniture and antiques, antique linen, textiles, gardening antiques
Open Mon–Sun 10am–5pm

⊞ Mermaid Vintage
Contact Lisa Roake
✉ Ninevah House Antique Centre, Tarrant Street, Arundel, West Sussex, BN18 9DG ⓟ
⓪ 07979 906511
❸ enquiries@mermaidvintage.co.uk
Ⓦ www.mermaidvintage.co.uk
Est. 2000 *Stock size* Medium
Stock Vintage clothes, Victorian-thirties, forties, fifties, sixties & seventies, costume jewellery
Open Wed–Fri 10am–4pm Sat 10am–4.30pm or by appointment
Fairs Goodwood, vintage clothing fairs

⌂ The Old Cornstore Antiques Centre
Contact Peter Francis
✉ 31 High Street, Arundel, West Sussex, BN18 9AG ⓟ
☎ 01903 885456 ❶ 01903 885456
Est. 2001 *Stock size* Large
No. of dealers 30
Stock Georgian–Edwardian furniture, jewellery, ceramics, silver, paintings, clocks
Open Mon–Sat 10am–5pm Sun 11am–5pm closed Wed
Services Valuations, shipping

⊞ Old Maps
Contact Mr K R Goddard
✉ 59 High Street, Arundel, West Sussex, BN18 9AJ ⓟ
☎ 01903 882522
Est. 1975 *Stock size* Medium
Stock Maps, prints
Open Mon–Sun 10am–5pm
Services Valuations

⊞ Passageway Antiques
Contact J Saxon
✉ 18 High Street, Arundel, West Sussex, BN18 9AB ⓟ
☎ 01903 884602 ❶ 01903 884602
Est. 1994 *Stock size* Large
Stock Antiques, collectables
Open Mon–Sat 10am–5pm Sun 11am–5pm
Services Valuations

⊞ Spencer Swaffer (LAPADA, BACA Award Winner 2004)
Contact Spencer Swaffer
✉ 30 High Street, Arundel, West Sussex, BN18 9AB ⓟ
☎ 01903 882132 ❶ 01903 884564
❸ spencerswaffer@btconnect.com
Ⓦ www.spencerswaffer.com
Est. 1974 *Stock size* Large
Stock Eclectic mix of decorative items
Open Mon–Fri 9am–6pm Sat Sun 10am–6pm

⌂ Tarrant Street Antique & Collectors Centre
✉ Ninevah House, Tarrant Street, Arundel, West Sussex, BN18 9DL ⓟ
☎ 01903 884307
Est. 1989 *Stock size* Large
No. of dealers 14
Stock Antiques, craft and collectables
Open Mon–Fri 10am–5pm Sat 9.30am–5pm Sun 11am–5pm

⊞ The Walking Stick Shop
Contact Stuart Thompson
✉ 8 & 9 The Old Printing Works, Tarrant Street, Arundel, West Sussex, BN18 9JH ⓟ
☎ 01903 883796
Ⓦ www.walkingsticks.uk.com
Est. 1978 *Stock size* Large
Stock Walking sticks
Open Mon–Sat 9am–5.30pm

⊞ Woodall & Emery Ltd
Contact Mrs Chinn
✉ Haywards Heath Road, Balcombe, Haywards Heath, West Sussex, RH17 6PG ⓟ
☎ 01444 811608 ❶ 01444 819365
❸ enquiries@woodallandemery.co.uk

Ⓦ www.woodallandemery.co.uk
Est. 1844 *Stock size* Large
Stock Antique lighting, chandeliers, table lights, lanterns, wall lights
Open Mon–Sat 10am–5pm
Services Restoration, rewiring, cleaning, re-pining, polishing, conversion, bronzing, gilding, silvering, casting, gold leafing, wood carving, wrought iron, sand blasting

⊞ Howard's Reclamation
Contact Craig Howard
✉ Longfield Timber Mill, Lake Lane, Barnham, West Sussex, PO22 0AE ⓟ
☎ 01243 552095
❸ chowardsreclaim@aol.com
Est. 1971 *Stock size* Large
Stock Old and new planked timber floors, oak beams, oak sleepers, telegraph poles, bricks, doors, stone, fireplaces and architectural antiquities
Open Mon–Fri 9am–1pm 2–5pm Sat 8am–1pm closed Wed

⊞ Hereford House Interiors
Contact Jon Preedy
✉ Hereford House, 55 Station Road, Billingshurst, West Sussex, RH14 9SE ⓟ
☎ 01403 785379 ❶ 01403 785379
Est. 1995 *Stock size* Medium
Stock Furniture, lighting
Open By appoinment
Fairs Ardingly
Services Re-wiring of chandeliers, lamps and converting vases

⋏ Sotheby's South
✉ Summers Place, Billingshurst, West Sussex, RH14 9AD ⓟ
☎ 01403 833500 ❶ 01403 833696
Ⓦ www.sothebys.com
Est. 1744
Open Mon–Fri 9.30am–1pm 2.15–4.30pm (valuations Tues 9.30am–1pm)
Sales Garden statuary sales in May and September. Valuations given for items to be sold in London saleroom
Frequency Twice a year
Catalogues Yes

⊠ BOGNOR REGIS

⊞ Lauries Antiques
Contact Laurie Swarbrick
⊠ 62 Barnham Road, Barnham,
Bognor Regis, West Sussex,
PO22 0ES **P**
☎ 01243 533 387
Ⓜ 07891 042508
Est. 2004 *Stock size* Medium
Stock Quality 19th–20thC china,
pottery, porcelain, rocking chairs,
Lloyd Loom, small furniture,
mirrors
Open Mon–Sat 10am–5.30pm
closed Wed Sun 11am–4pm or
by appointment

⊞ Memory Lane
Contact David Crack
⊠ 79 Aldwick Road,
Bognor Regis, West Sussex,
PL21 2NW **P**
☎ 01243 841412
Est. 2004 *Stock size* Medium
Stock General antiques,
collectables
Open Mon–Sat 9.30am–5.30pm

⊠ BOSHAM

⊞ Mr Pickett's
Contact Mr M Pickett
⊠ The Lifestyle Centre, Bosham
Roundabout, Delling Lane,
Bosham, Nr Chichester,
West Sussex,
PO18 8NN **P**
☎ 01243 574573 ● 01243 574573
Ⓜ 07779 997012
❸ info@mrpicketts.co.uk
Ⓦ www.mrpicketts.co.uk
Est. 1991 *Stock size* Large
Stock Victorian pine furniture
Open Mon–Sun 10am–5pm but
phone first
Services Paint Stripping, sanding,
waxing, restoration, bespoke
items made to order from
original antique pine

⊠ BURGESS HILL

⊞ British Antique Replicas
⊠ 22 School Close,
Queen Elizabeth Avenue,
Burgess Hill, West Sussex,
RH15 9RX **P**
☎ 01444 245577 ● 01444 232014
Ⓦ www.1760.com
Est. 1963 *Stock size* Large
Stock English antique replica
furniture

Open Mon–Sat 9am–5.30pm
Services Restoration of antique
furniture

⊞ Recollect The Dolls Hospital
Contact Paul Jago
⊠ 17 Junction Road, Burgess Hill,
West Sussex,
RH15 0HR **P**
☎ 01444 871052 ● 01444 871052
❸ dollshopuk@aol.com
Est. 1973 *Stock size* Medium
Stock Antique dolls
Open Tues–Fri 10am–4pm Sat
10am–1pm or by appointment
Services Restoration of dolls

⊠ CHICHESTER

⚹ Henry Adams Auctioneers (RICS, SOFAA)
Contact Lynn Corbett
⊠ Baffins Hall, Baffins Lane,
Chichester, West Sussex,
PO19 1UA **P**
☎ 01243 532223 ● 01243 532299
❸ enquiries@henryadamsfineart.co.uk
Ⓦ www.henryadamsfineart.co.uk
Est. 2000
Open Mon–Fri 9am–5.30pm
Sales Antiques and fine art
Frequency Six weekly
Catalogues Yes

⊞ Antics
Contact Peter German
⊠ 19 The Hornet, Chichester,
West Sussex,
PO19 4JL **P**
☎ 01243 786327
Est. 1981 *Stock size* Small
Stock General antiques
Open Mon–Sat 9am–4pm

⊞ Barnett Antiques
Contact Mrs B Barnett
⊠ Unit 1, Almshouse Arcade,
19 The Hornet, Chichester,
West Sussex,
PO19 4JL **P**
☎ 01243 528089
Est. 1970 *Stock size* Medium
Stock Bric-a-brac, toys
Open Mon–Sat 10am–4.30pm

⊞ Canute Antiques
Contact Wendy Rowden
⊠ Bosham Walk, Bosham Lane,
Chichester, West Sussex,
PO18 8HX **P**
☎ 01243 576111
Est. 1977 *Stock size* Small

Stock Silver, jewellery, porcelain
and collectors' items
Open Mon–Sun 10am–5.30pm

⌂ Chichester Antiques Centre
Contact Michael Carter
⊠ 46–48 The Hornet, Chichester,
West Sussex,
PO19 4JG **P**
☎ 01243 530100
Est. 1994 *Stock size* Large
No. of dealers 40
Stock General antiques,
collectables, 18th–20thC
furniture, gramophones
Open Mon–Sat 10am–5pm
Sun 11am–4pm closed Tues
Services Valuations

⊞ The Chichester Bookshop
Contact Chris or Carol Lowndes
⊠ 39 Southgate, Chichester,
West Sussex,
PO19 1DP **P**
☎ 01243 785473
❸ redbooks@fsmail.net
Est. 1965 *Stock size* Large
Stock Rare, second-hand books,
Sussex books, maps, prints,
antiquarian books, music and
ephemera
Open Tues–Sat 10.30am–5.30pm
Services Book search

⊞ Collectors Corner
Contact Vivienne Barnett
⊠ Almshouse Arcade,
19 The Hornet, Chichester,
West Sussex,
PO19 7JL
☎ 01243 778126
Est. 1983 *Stock size* Medium
Stock Antiques, collectables,
toys, furniture, bric-a-brac
Open Mon–Sat 9am–4.30pm

⊞ Gems
Contact Maureen Hancock
⊠ 39 West Street, Chichester,
West Sussex,
PO19 1RP **P**
☎ 01243 786173 ● 01243 778865
Est. 1985 *Stock size* Large
Stock Edwardian furniture,
Staffordshire figures, European
porcelain, dolls, toys, optical
instruments
Open Tues–Sat 10am–1pm
2.30–5pm or by other
appointment
Services Restoration

⊞ Peter Hancock
Contact Peter Hancock
✉ 40 West Street, Chichester, West Sussex, PO19 1RP 🅿
☎ 01243 786173 📠 01243 778865
Est. 1965 *Stock size* Large
Stock A comprehensive range of antiques and collectables
Open Tues–Sat 10am–1pm 2.15–5.30pm or by appointment
Services Restoration

⊞ Heirloom Antiques
Contact Alan Hayes
✉ 57–58 Pound Farm Road, Chichester, West Sussex, PO19 2LU 🅿
☎ 01243 530489
📱 07970 396265
Est. 1986 *Stock size* Large
Stock Furniture, collectables, curios
Open Mon–Sat 9.30am–5pm
Fairs Goodwood, Kempton
Services House clearance

⊞ Heritage Antiques
Contact Mr D Grover
✉ 83 & 84 St Pancras, Chichester, West Sussex, PO19 4NL 🅿
☎ 01243 783796
Est. 1987 *Stock size* Medium
Stock Georgian–Edwardian, 1920s furniture
Open Mon–Sat 9am–5.30pm

⊞ Kim's Bookshop (PBFA)
Contact P Pegler
✉ 28 South Street, Chichester, West Sussex, PO19 1EL 🅿
☎ 01243 778477
Est. 1980 *Stock size* Medium
Stock Rare, antiquarian, second-hand books
Open Mon–Fri 10.30am–5pm Sat 9.30am–5.30pm

⊞ W D Priddy Antiques, Chichester Furniture Warehouse
Contact Mr W D Priddy
✉ Unit 6, Terminus Mill, Terminus Road, Chichester, West Sussex, PO19 2UN 🅿
☎ 01243 783960 📠 01243 783960
📱 07712 002371
📧 bill@priddyantiques.fsnet.co.uk
🌐 www.priddyantiques.co.uk
Est. 1983 *Stock size* Medium
Stock Georgian–Edwardian furniture

Open Mon–Fri 10am–4pm Sat 10am–5pm variable Sundays 11am–4pm or by appointment

⊞ Squirrel Antiques
Contact Lesley Hampshire
✉ 44 The Hornet, Chichester, West Sussex, PO19 7JG 🅿
☎ 01243 790904
Est. 1990 *Stock size* Small
Stock Collectables, curios
Open Mon–Sat 10am–12.30pm 1.30–4pm
Fairs Sandown Park

⊞ St Pancras Antiques
Contact Mr R Willatt
✉ 150 St Pancras, Chichester, West Sussex, PO19 5SH 🅿
☎ 01243 787645
Est. 1980 *Stock size* Medium
Stock Arms, armour, pre-1800 furniture, ceramics, numismatics, militaria
Open Mon–Sat 9.30am–5pm Thurs 9.30am–1pm
Services Valuations

🔨 Stride & Son
Contact Mr M Hewitt or Mr K Warne
✉ Southdown House, St Johns Street, Chichester, West Sussex, PO19 1XQ 🅿
☎ 01243 780207 📠 01243 786713
📧 enquiries@stridesauctions.co.uk
🌐 www.stridesauctions.co.uk
Est. 1890
Open Mon–Fri 9am–5.30pm closed 1–2pm
Sales Monthly sale of general antiques, periodic book auctions
Frequency Monthly
Catalogues Yes

⊞ Whitestone Farm Antiques
Contact Carey Mordue
✉ Whitestone Farm, Main Road, Birdham, Chichester, West Sussex, PO20 7HU 🅿
☎ 01243 513706
📧 antiques@whitestonefarm.force9.co.uk
Est. 1970 *Stock size* Medium
Stock 18th–20thC furniture, shabby chic
Open Mon–Sat 10am–5.30pm
Services Restoration

COCKING

⊞ The Victorian Brass Bedstead Co
Contact David Woolley
✉ Hoe Copse, Cocking, Midhurst, West Sussex, GU29 0HL 🅿
☎ 01730 812287
📧 toria@netcomuk.co.uk
Est. 1982 *Stock size* Large
Stock Brass and iron bedsteads, mattresses, bases, quilts
Open By appointment
Services Valuations, restoration

CUCKFIELD

⊞ David Foord-Brown Antiques (BADA)
Contact David Foord-Brown
✉ 3 Bank Buildings, High Street, Cuckfield, West Sussex, RH17 5JU 🅿
☎ 01444 414418
📱 07850 188250
📧 antiques@davidfoord-brown.com
🌐 www.davidfoord-brown.com
Est. 1988 *Stock size* Large
Stock 18th–19thC furniture, porcelain, silver, glass
Open Mon–Sat 10am–5.30pm or by appointment
Fairs BADA, Olympia

DITCHLING

⊞ Dycheling Antiques
Contact Mrs E A Hudson
✉ 34 High Street, Ditchling, West Sussex, BN6 8TA 🅿
☎ 01273 842929 📠 01273 842929
📱 07785 456341
📧 hudson@icsgroup.demon.co.uk
🌐 www.antiquechairmatching.com
Est. 1981 *Stock size* Large
Stock Sets of Georgian–Victorian dining furniture, upholstered furniture, chiffoniers
Open Sat 10.30am–5pm or by appointment
Services Chair search service

HASSOCKS

⊞ Vincent Reed Furniture
Contact Vincent
✉ 103a Keymer Road, Keymer, Hassocks, West Sussex, BN6 8QL 🅿
☎ 01273 845678
📱 07815 751005

@ info@vincentreed.com
ⓦ www.vincentreed.co.uk
Est. 1992
Stock 17–18thC country furniture
Open Mon–Fri 9am–5pm
Sat 10am–4pm

HENFIELD

⊞ Ashcombe Coach House Antiques (BADA, CINOA)
Contact Mr Roy Green
✉ PO Box No 2527, Henfield, West Sussex,
BN5 9SU ℗
☎ 01273 491630 ✆ 01273 492681
Ⓜ 07803 180098
@ sharon@anglocontinental. fsnet.co.uk
Est. 1953 *Stock size* Large
Stock 18th–early 19thC furniture, decorative objects
Open By appointment only
Fairs Olympia, BADA

⊞ Henfield Antiques and Home
Contact Mrs D Evans
✉ 2 Commercial Buildings, High Street, Henfield, West Sussex,
BN5 9DE ℗
☎ 01273 495300
Est. 1999 *Stock size* Medium
Stock Kitchenware, pine furniture, French decorative, chandeliers
Open Mon–Sat 10am–5pm
Services Verbal valuations

HORSHAM

⚲ Denham's
Contact Kate Tyekiff or Louise Shelley
✉ The Auction Galleries, Dorking Road (A24), Warnham, Horsham, West Sussex,
RH12 3RZ ℗
☎ 01403 255699 ✆ 01403 253837
@ enquiries@denhams.com
ⓦ www.invaluable.com/denhams
Est. 1884
Open Mon–Thurs 9am–5.30pm
Fri 9am–5pm Sat 9am–noon
Sales Sales of antiques and collectors' items every four weeks
Frequency Every 4 weeks
Catalogues Yes

⊞ Horsham Bookshop (PBFA)
Contact Mr Nick Costin

✉ 4 Park Place (off Piries Place), Horsham, West Sussex,
RH12 1DG ℗
☎ 01403 252187
✆ 07941 802954
@ sales@horshambookshop.com
ⓦ www.horshambookshop.com
Est. 1986 *Stock size* Large
Stock Rare, antiquarian, second-hand books, bindings, children's books, military, transport and collectable books
Open Tues–Sat 9.30am–5pm
Fairs PBFA
Services Valuations, book search

⌂ Queen Street Antique Centre
Contact Jonathon Dick
✉ 34 Queen Street, Horsham, West Sussex,
RH13 5AA ℗
☎ 01403 756644
Est. 2003 *Stock size* Large
No. of dealers 6
Stock Antique pine furniture, Georgian–modern, 20thC, architectural ironmongers, 1950s –1960s preowned clocks, radio, telephone, Beswick, china, glass. 1950s–1970s collectables
Open Tues–Sat 10am–5pm

HOUGHTON

⌂ Stable Antiques at Houghton
Contact Ian Wadey
✉ Main Road (B2139), Houghton, West Sussex,
BN18 9LW ℗
☎ 01798 839555 or 01903 740555
ⓦ www.stableantiques.co.uk
Est. 2000 *Stock size* Medium
No. of dealers 10
Stock Antiques, furniture and design
Open Tues–Sat 11am–4pm

HUNSTON

⊞ J and M Riley
Contact Mr J Riley
✉ Frensham House, Hunston, Chichester, West Sussex,
PO20 6NX ℗
☎ 01243 782660
Est. 1966 *Stock size* Medium
Stock 18thC English furniture
Open Mon–Sat 9am–6pm and by appointment

HURSTPIERPOINT

⊞ Graham Foster Antiques
Contact Graham Foster
✉ The Old Telephone Exchange, 41 Cuckfield Road, Hurstpierpoint, West Sussex,
BN6 9RW ℗
☎ 01273 833099
Ⓜ 07850 576434
@ graham.foster-antiques@ ukonline.co.uk
Est. 1982 *Stock size* Large
Stock Iron gates, furniture
Open Mon–Sat 8.30am–6pm
Fairs Ardingly, Newark
Services Valuations, restoration

⊞ Julian Antiques
Contact Mrs C Ingram or Mr J Ingram
✉ 124 High Street, Hurstpierpoint, West Sussex,
BN6 9PX ℗
☎ 01273 832145
Est. 1969 *Stock size* Medium
Stock 19thC French mirrors, clocks, candelabra, fireplaces, bronzes, sculptures, fenders, furniture
Open By appointment
Services Shipping

⊞ Samuel Orr (LAPADA)
Contact Mr S Orr
✉ 34–36 High Street, Hurstpierpoint, West Sussex,
BN6 9RG ℗
☎ 01273 832081 ✆ 01273 832081
Ⓜ 07860 230888
@ clocks@samorr.co.uk
ⓦ www.samorr.co.uk
Est. 1977 *Stock size* Large
Stock Antique clocks, barometers
Open Mon–Sat 10am–6pm or by appointment
Services Clock restoration

LINDFIELD

⊞ Lindfield Galleries (BADA)
Contact David Adam
✉ 62 High Street, Lindfield, West Sussex, RH16 2HL ℗
☎ 01444 483817 ✆ 01444 484682
@ david@davidadam.co.uk
ⓦ www.davidadam.co.uk
Est. 1973 *Stock size* Large
Stock Oriental carpets and tapestries
Open Tues–Fri 9.30am–5pm
Sat 10am–4pm
Services Valuations, restoration

LITTLEHAMPTON

⚲ Peter Cheney Auctioneers and Valuers (SSA)
Contact Mr P Cheney
✉ Western Road Auction Rooms, Western Road, Littlehampton, West Sussex, BH17 5NP 🅿
☎ 01903 722264/713418
🖷 01903 713418
Est. 1940
Open Mon–Fri 9am–1pm 2–5pm
Sales Monthly auction sales of antiques, furniture, pictures, silver, porcelain and collectors items. Valuations for insurance and probate. No buyer's premium
Catalogues Yes

⊞ Joan's Antiques
Contact Mrs J Walkden
✉ 1 New Road, Littlehampton, West Sussex, BN17 5AX 🅿
☎ 01903 722422
Est. 1977 *Stock size* Large
Stock China, glass, 1930s items, Victoriana, collectables
Open Thurs–Sat 10.30am–4.30pm
Fairs Goodwood

MIDHURST

⊞ Churchill Clocks (BHI)
Contact Mr W P Tyrell
✉ Rumbolds Hill, Midhurst, West Sussex, GU29 9BZ 🅿
☎ 01730 813891 🖷 01730 813891
🖂 info@churchillclocks.co.uk
🌐 www.churchillclocks.co.uk
Est. 1970 *Stock size* Medium
Stock Clocks, longcase, mantel, French bracket
Open Mon–Sat 9am–5pm closed Wed pm
Services Valuations, restoration, shipping

PETWORTH

⊞ Angel Antiques (LAPADA, PAADA)
Contact Nick or Barbara Swanson
✉ Lombard Street, Petworth, West Sussex, GU28 0AD 🅿
☎ 01798 343306 🖷 01798 342665
🖂 swansonantiques@aol.com
🌐 www.angel-antiques.com
Est. 1991 *Stock size* Medium

Stock Oak and country furniture, Mason's ironstone, ceramics, decorative items pictures
Open Mon–Sat 10am–5.30pm or by appointment
Services Shipping

⊞ Antiquated (PAADA)
Contact Vicki Emery
✉ 10 New Street, Petworth, West Sussex, GU28 0AS 🅿
☎ 01798 344011 🖷 01798 344011
🖂 info@antiquated.co.uk
🌐 www.antiquated.co.uk
Est. 1989 *Stock size* Medium
Stock 18th–19thC painted furniture, 19thC rocking horses
Open Mon–Sat 10am–5.30pm

⊞ Baskerville Antiques (BADA)
Contact Mr B Baskerville
✉ Saddlers House, Saddlers Row, Petworth, West Sussex, GU28 0AN 🅿
☎ 01798 342067
🖂 brianbaskerville@aol.com
Est. 1971 *Stock size* Medium
Stock Antiquarian horologist, clocks, barometers
Open Tues–Sat 10am–6pm

⊞ John Bird Antiques (PAADA)
Contact Mr Ian Miller
✉ High Street, Petworth, West Sussex, GU28 0AU 🅿
☎ 01798 343250 🖷 01798 343250
📱 07966 279761
🖂 abird.puttnam@virgin.net
Est. 1985 *Stock size* Large
Stock Furniture, fine art, decorative antiques
Open Mon–Sat 10.15am–5.15pm
Fairs Olympia, Bath

⊞ Bradley's Past and Present Shop (PAADA)
Contact Mr or Mrs M Bradley
✉ 21 High Street, Petworth, West Sussex, GU28 0AU 🅿
☎ 01798 343533
📱 07941 506232
Est. 1979 *Stock size* Medium
Stock Furniture and bygones, gramophones, metalware
Open Tues–Sat 10am–1pm 2–5pm Sun by appointment
Services Restoration of furniture, gramophones

⊞ Augustus Brandt Antiques (PADA)
Contact Augustus or Paula Parkinson
✉ Media House, Pound Street, Petworth, West Sussex, GU28 0DX 🅿
☎ 01798 344722
🖂 brandt@easynet.co.uk
🌐 www.augustus-brandt-antiques.co.uk
Est. 1975 *Stock size* Large
Stock 13th–19thC Swedish, Italian, German and French furniture, lighting, chaises longues, bath taps, architectural mirrors, 1920s Parisian desks, big picture frames
Open Mon–Sat 10am–5.30pm or by appointment
Fairs Battersea, France
Services Finding service, interior design, courier service, shipping to UK and Europe

⊞ Callingham Antiques Ltd
Contact Nigel Callingham
✉ Northchapel, Petworth, West Sussex, GU28 9HL 🅿
☎ 01428 707379
🖂 antiques@callingham.freeserve.co.uk
Est. 1979 *Stock size* Medium
Stock 17th–18thC English furniture
Open Mon–Sat 9am–5.30pm closed Wed
Services Restoration

⊞ Ronald G Chambers – Fine Antiques (LAPADA, CINOA, PAADA)
Contact Mr R G Chambers or Mrs J F Tudor
✉ Market Square, Petworth, West Sussex, GU28 0AH 🅿
☎ 01798 342305 🖷 01798 342724
📱 07932 161968
🖂 jackie@ronaldchambers.com
🌐 www.ronaldchambers.com
Est. 1985 *Stock size* Large
Stock Fine period furniture circa 1700–1910
Open Mon–Sat 10am–5.30pm Sun 10am–4.30pm
Services Valuations, restoration,

⊞ Oliver Charles Antiques Ltd (PAADA)
Contact Mr A Gardner
✉ Lombard Street, Petworth, West Sussex,

GU28 0AG 🅿
☎ 01798 344443
📧 olivercharles@aol.com
🌐 www.olivercharles.com
Est. 1987 *Stock size* Medium
Stock 18th–19thC English
furniture, related items, 19thC
paintings
Open Mon–Sat 10am–5.30pm
Sun by appointment

⊞ Cleall Antiques
Contact Damian Cleall
✉ 2 Leppards, High Street,
Petworth, West Sussex,
GU28 0AU 🅿
☎ 01798 343933 ℹ 01798 343933
📱 07831 869955
📧 damiancleall@hotmail.com
Est. 1976 *Stock size* Medium
Stock Decorative French and
English furniture and eclectic items
Open Mon–Sat 10.15am–5.15 pm
Fairs Battersea, Antiques &
Audacity Arundel
Services Courier service

⊞ Elliott's (PAADA)
Contact Mrs P Elliott
✉ 88a New Street, Petworth,
West Sussex,
GU28 0AB 🅿
☎ 01798 343408 ℹ 01798 872842
Est. 1993 *Stock size* Medium
Stock Georgian–Edwardian
furniture
Open Thur–Sat 10am–5pm
Services Valuations, upholstery

⊞ Richard Gardner
Antiques (LAPADA,
CINOA, PAADA, BACA
Award Winner 2002)
Contact Richard Gardner
✉ Market Square, Petworth,
West Sussex,
GU28 0AN 🅿
☎ 01798 343411
📧 rg@richardgardnerantiques.co.uk
🌐 www.richardgardnerantiques.co.uk
Est. 1990 *Stock size* Large
Stock Fine period furniture,
works of art including bronzes,
Staffordshire figures, paintings,
silver, mirrors, 18th–19thC
porcelain, etchings
Open Mon–Sat 10am–5.30pm
Sun 10am–5pm

⊞ John Giles (LAPADA)
Contact John Giles
✉ High Street, Petworth,
West Sussex,

GU28 0AU 🅿
☎ 01798 342136
📱 07770 873689
📧 gilesandhart@btinternet.com
Est. 1963 *Stock size* Medium
Stock 18th–early 20thC furniture,
decorative items
Open Mon–Sat 10am–5.30pm

⊞ John Harris Antiques
and Restorations
Contact Mr J Harris
✉ Stables, London Road,
Northchapel, Petworth,
West Sussex,
GU28 9EQ 🅿
☎ 01428 707667
Est. 1976 *Stock size* Medium
Stock 18th–19thC furniture,
decorative items
Open Mon–Sat 8am–5pm
Services Restoration

⊞ Heather Denham
Antiques
Contact Heather Denham
✉ 6 High Street, Petworth,
West Sussex,
GU28 0AU 🅿
☎ 01798 344622 ℹ 01798 343436
Est. 1981 *Stock size* Medium
Stock Decorative, painted
furniture, garden furniture,
English and French decorative
antique mirrors and lighting
Open Mon–Sat 10am–5.15pm

⊞ William Hockley
Antiques
Contact Val Thrower
✉ Tudor Rose Antique Centre,
East Street, Petworth,
West Sussex,
GU28 0AB 🅿
☎ 01403 701917 ℹ 01403 701917
📧 williamhockley@ocsl.co.uk
🌐 www.tudor-rose-antiques.co.uk
Est. 1982 *Stock size* Medium
Stock Early English oak, country
furniture and interiors
Open Mon–Sun 10am–5.30pm
Services Interior design

⊞ Lantiques
Contact Andrew Legere
✉ Dales House, Lombard Street,
Petworth,
West Sussex,
GU28 0AG 🅿
☎ 01798 344020
📧 info@lantiques.com
🌐 www.lantiques.com
Est. 1995 *Stock size* Medium

Stock French farmhouse tables,
painted furniture, lifestyle
elements
Open Mon–Sat 10am–5.30pm or
by appointment
Services Shipping

⊞ Octavia Antiques
(PAADA)
Contact Aline Bell
✉ East Street, Petworth,
West Sussex,
GU28 0AB 🅿
☎ 01798 342771
Est. 1972 *Stock size* Small
Stock Decorative antiques, small
furniture, mirrors, lamps, chairs,
blue and white china
Open Mon–Sat 10.30am–5.30pm
closed Fri

⌂ Petworth Antique
Centre & Market
Contact Mrs D M Rayment
✉ East Street, Petworth,
West Sussex,
GU28 0AB 🅿
☎ 01798 342073 ℹ 01798 344566
🌐 www.petworthantiquecentre.co.uk
Est. 1974 *Stock size* Large
No. of dealers 30
Stock English oak furniture,
silver, linen, books, soft
furnishings, porcelain, glass,
fans, general antiques
Open Mon–Sat 10am–5.30pm

⊞ Red Lion Antiques
(LAPADA)
Contact Karen Wilson
✉ New Street, Petworth,
West Sussex,
GU28 0AS 🅿
☎ 01798 344485 ℹ 01798 344439
📧 rod@redlion-antiques.com
🌐 www.redlion-antiques.com
Est. 1980 *Stock size* Large
Stock 17th–19thC furniture
Open Mon–Sat 10am–5.30pm or
by appointment
Fairs LAPADA

⊞ Riverbank Gallery Ltd
Contact Linda Burke White
✉ High Street, Petworth,
West Sussex,
GU28 0AU 🅿
☎ 01798 344401 ℹ 01798 343135
📧 rvrbnkg@aol.com
Est. 1997 *Stock size* Large
Stock Large English 18th–19thC
furniture, decorative items,
garden furniture, decorative

paintings, marine antiques,
vintage boats
Open Mon–Sat 10.30am–5.30pm

⊞ **Nicholas Shaw Antiques
(BADA, LAPADA, CINOA)**
Contact Nicholas Shaw
✉ Virginia Cottage, Petworth,
West Sussex,
GU28 0AG ▣
☎ 01798 345146 ❶ 01798 345157
⓿ 07885 643000
✉ silver@nicholas-shaw.com
⊕ www.nicholas-shaw.com
Est. 1992 **Stock size** Large
Stock Fine and rare antique silver
viewed by appointment only,
modern silver, gift items
Open Tues–Sat 10am–5pm
antiques by appointment only
Fairs BADA Fair, Olympia,
Antiques for Everyone, LAPADA
Services Valuations, restoration

⊞ **Thakeham Furniture**
Contact Tim and Belinda Chavasse
✉ Golden Square, Petworth,
West Sussex,
GU20 0AP ▣
☎ 01798 432333
⊕ www.thakehamfurniture.com
Est. 1979 **Stock size** Medium
Stock 18th–19thC English furniture
Open Mon–Sat 10am–5pm
Services Restoration

⌂ **Tudor Rose Antique
Centre**
Contact Elizabeth Lee
✉ East Street, Petworth,
West Sussex,
GU28 0AB ▣
☎ 01798 343621 ❶ 01798 344951
⓿ 07980 927331
✉ info@tudor-rose-antiques.co.uk
⊕ www.tudor-rose-antiques.co.uk
Est. 2001 **Stock size** Large
No. of dealers 12
Stock General antiques, brown
and decorative furniture, silver,
porcelain, blue and white, books,
reclamation, including William
Hockley, early country furniture
and interiors
Open Mon–Sat 10am–5.15pm
Sun 11am–4.15pm

⊞ **T G Wilkinson Antiques
Ltd (BADA, PAADA)**
Contact Mr Wilkinson
✉ Swan House, Market Square,
Petworth, West Sussex,
GU28 0AH ▣

☎ 01798 343638
Est. 1987 **Stock size** Large
Stock Oak, walnut, mahogany
furniture, country furniture,
silver, porcelain, decorative
items, paintings
Open Mon–Sat 10am–5pm
Services Valuations, restoration

PULBOROUGH

⊞ **Barn Antiques**
Contact Pam Borham
✉ Wyevale Garden Centre,
Storham Road, Pulborough,
West Sussex,
RH20 1DS ▣
☎ 01798 874782
Est. 1996 **Stock size** Large
Stock Bric-a-brac, pictures, books
Open Mon–Sat 10am–5pm
Sun 10.30am–4.30pm

🔨 **Rupert Toovey & Co
(RICS)**
Contact Alan Toovey
✉ Spring Gardens, Washington,
Pulborough, West Sussex,
RH20 3BS ▣
☎ 01903 891955 ❶ 01903 891966
✉ auctions@rupert-toovey.com
⊕ www.rupert-toovey.com
Est. 1995
Open Mon–Fri 9am–5pm
Sales Monthly sales of antiques,
fine art, collectables, silver,
jewellery, clocks and furniture.
Sales of books and postcards
2–3 times a year
Frequency Monthly
Catalogues Yes

🏠 **Traditions**
Contact Georgina Lott
✉ 9 & 11 High Street,
Pulborough, West Sussex,
RH20 4DR ▣
☎ 01903 740011 ❶ 01798 815004
⓿ 07831 449574
✉ georginalott@aol.com
Est. 2004
No. of dealers 30
Stock General antiques,
furniture, china
Open Mon–Sat 10am–5.30pm

SHOREHAM BY SEA

⊞ **Rodney Arthur Classics**
Contact Rodney Oliver
✉ Unit 5, Riverbank Business
Centre, Old Shoreham Road,
Shoreham by Sea,

West Sussex,
BN43 5FL ▣
☎ 01273 441606 ❶ 01273 441977
Est. 1979 **Stock size** Medium
Stock 19thC furniture
Open Mon–Sat 9am–5pm
Services Restoration

⊞ **Bookworms of
Shoreham**
Contact Mrs P A Liddell
✉ 4 High Street,
Shoreham by Sea, West Sussex,
BN43 5DA
☎ 01273 453856
Est. 1992 **Stock size** Medium
Stock Rare, second-hand books,
military, modern art
Open Tues–Sat 10am–5pm

STEYNING

⊞ **Curiouser & Curiouser**
Contact Deborah Pepper
✉ 50 The High Street, Steyning,
West Sussex,
BN44 3RD
☎ 01903 879483
Est. 1963 **Stock size** Medium
Stock General antiques
Open Mon–Sat 10.30am–5pm
closed Thurs

STORRINGTON

🏠 **Stable Antiques**
Contact Ian Wadey
✉ 46 West Street, Storrington,
West Sussex,
RH20 4EE ▣
☎ 01903 740555 or 01798 839555
❶ 01903 740441
⊕ www.stableantiques.co.uk
Est. 1993 **Stock size** Large
No. of dealers 35
Stock Antiques, furniture and
bric-a-brac
Open Mon–Sun 10am–6pm

STREAT

⊞ **Fisher Nautical (PBFA)**
Contact S D Fisher
✉ Huntswood House,
St Helena Lane, Streat, Hassocks,
West Sussex,
BN6 8SD
☎ 01273 890273 ❶ 01273 891439
✉ fishernautical@seabooks.fsnet.co.uk
⊕ www.fishernautical.co.uk
Est. 1963 **Stock size** Large
Stock Rare, antiquarian, second-
hand nautical books

Open Mail order Mon–Fri
9am–5pm
Services Mail order

TURNERS HILL

⊞ Albion House Antiques
Contact Janet Avery
⊠ Albion House, North Street,
Turners Hill, West Sussex,
RH10 4NS 🅿
☎ 01342 715670
Est. 1971 *Stock size* Medium
Stock 18th–19thC brass, copper,
furniture, collectables
Open Mon–Sun 9am–6pm
summer 9am–7pm

WEST GRINSTEAD

**⊞ Bedouin Antiques
(SALVO)**
Contact Chris Thornton
⊠ Partridge Barns, Floodgates
Farm, West Grinstead,
West Sussex,
RH13 8LH 🅿
☎ 01403 711441 🔗 01403 713382
🔗 info@bedouin.uk.com
🌐 www.bedouin.uk.com
Est. 2003 *Stock size* Small
Stock Unusual, decorative antiques
Open Tues–Sat 10am–4pm
Fairs Battersea Decorative
Antiques

WISBOROUGH GREEN

⋏ John Bellman Ltd
Contact John Ireland
⊠ New Pound,
Wisborough Green,
West Sussex,
RH14 0AZ 🅿
☎ 01403 700858 🔗 01403 700059
🔗 enquiries@bellmans.co.uk
🌐 www.bellmans.co.uk
Est. 1989
Open Mon–Fri 9am–5pm
Sales Monthly sales of antiques
and collectables Wed 1pm Thurs
10am and 2pm Fri 10am, viewing
Sat prior 9am–noon Mon
9am–4pm Tues 9am–7pm
Wed 9am–1pm
Frequency Monthly
Catalogues Yes

WORTHING

⊞ Acorn Antiques
Contact Henry Nicholls
⊠ 91 Rowlands Road, Worthing,
West Sussex,
BN11 3JX 🅿
☎ 01903 216926
🔗 hnick@ntlworld.com
Est. 1992 *Stock size* Large
Stock Georgian–Edwardian
furniture, china, silver, jewellery
Open Mon–Sat 9am–5.30pm
Services Valuations, restoration

⊞ Badgers Books
Contact Ray Potter
⊠ 8–10 Gratwicke Road,
Worthing, West Sussex,
BN11 4BH 🅿
☎ 01903 211816
Est. 1982 *Stock size* Large
Stock Rare, antiquarian, second-
hand books
Open Mon–Sat 9am–5.30pm

⊞ Chloe Antiques
Contact Mrs Dorothy Peters
⊠ 61 Brighton Road, Worthing,
West Sussex,
BN11 3EE 🅿
☎ 01903 202697
Est. 1967 *Stock size* Large
Stock Small collectables,
jewellery, china, glass
Open Mon–Sat 10am–4.30pm
closed Wed

⊞ Corner Antiques
Contact Richard Mihok
⊠ 9–10 Havercroft Building,
North Street, Worthing,
West Sussex,
BN11 1DY 🅿
☎ 01903 537669
Est. 1997 *Stock size* Small
Stock General antiques, textiles,
collectables
Open Mon–Sat 10am–5pm
Fairs Charmandan Centre
Worthing

⋏ Gorringes
Contact Clifford Lansberry
⊠ 44–46 High Street, Worthing,
West Sussex,
BN11 1LL 🅿
☎ 01903 238999
🔗 worthing@gorringes.co.uk
🌐 www.gorringes.co.uk
Est. 1928
Open Mon–Fri 9am–1pm 2–5pm
Sales Auctions of Edwardian–
Victorian furniture and
collectables, silver, paintings,
Oriental and rugs Thurs 10am,
viewing Sat 9am–12.30pm
Mon–Wed 9am–5pm day of sale

9–10am
Frequency Every 6 weeks
Catalogues Yes

⊞ Interiors and Antiques
Contact Pat or Janet Cassie
⊠ 162 Findon Road, Worthing,
West Sussex,
BN14 0EL 🅿
☎ 01903 261134
🔗 janet.cassie@btopenworld.com
Est. 1998 *Stock size* Medium
Stock Furniture, china, glass,
garden statues, bird baths
Open Thurs–Sat 10am–5pm

⊞ Wheelers (BHI, BWCG)
Contact Mr T P Wheeler
⊠ 14–16 Bath Place, Worthing,
West Sussex,
BN11 3BA 🅿
☎ 01903 207656 🔗 01903 207656
🌐 www.wheelersclocks.co.uk
Est. 1991 *Stock size* Small
Stock Clocks
Open Mon–Sat 9am–5pm
Services Restoration

**⊞ Wilsons Antiques
(LAPADA)**
Contact Mr F Wilson
⊠ 45–47 New Broadway,
Tarring Road, Worthing,
West Sussex,
BN11 4HS 🅿
☎ 01903 202059
📱 07778 813395
🔗 frank@wilsons-antiques.com
🌐 www.wilsons-antiques.com
Est. 1936 *Stock size* Medium
Stock Georgian–Edwardian
formal English furniture
Open Mon–Fri 10am–4.30pm or
by appointment
Fairs Olympia, NEC Antiques for
Everyone

**⋏ Worthing Auction
Galleries Ltd**
Contact Mr R Rood
⊠ Fleet House, Teville Gate,
Worthing,
West Sussex,
BN11 1UA 🅿
☎ 01903 205565 🔗 01903 214365
🔗 info@worthing-auctions.co.uk
🌐 www.worthing-auctions.co.uk
Est. 1964
Open Mon–Fri 8.30am–5pm
closed 1–2pm
Sales Monthly sales of general
antiques
Catalogues Yes

WEST COUNTRY

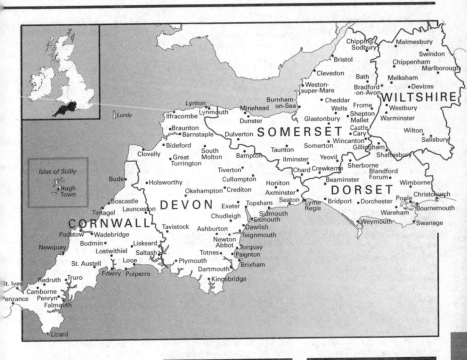

WEST COUNTRY

CORNWALL

BOSCASTLE

⊞ Atique
Contact Amanda Dawson
✉ Boscastle Old Mill,
Boscastle,
Cornwall,
PL35 0AQ 🅿
☎ 01840 250230
ⓦ www.boscastleoldmill.com
Est. 1999 *Stock size* Medium
Stock English, Continental
antiques and linens
Open Mon–Sun 10am–5pm
Nov–Feb by appointment

BUDE

⊞ Bluebells
Contact Denise Osbourne
✉ 36 Lansdown Road, Bude,
Cornwall,
EX23 8BA 🅿
☎ 01288 350230
ⓔ bluebellantiques@hotmail.com
Est. 2002 *Stock size* Medium
Stock Antiques, collectables, gifts
Open Mon–Sat 10am–4pm or by
appointment

CALLINGTON

**⊞ Country Living
Antiques**
Contact Ian Baxter CBE
✉ Weston House, Haye Road,
Callington, Cornwall,
PL17 7JJ 🅿
☎ 01579 382245
Est. 1988 *Stock size* Medium
Stock Country furniture and
effects
Open Mon–Sat 9.30am–5.30pm
Services Free valuations

CALSTOCK

⊞ Collectable Adge
Contact Adrian Jones
✉ 14 Church Lane, Calstock,
Cornwall,
PL18 9QH
☎ 01822 832231 🅕 01822 832231
ⓔ ag-jones1@talk21.com
Est. 1997 *Stock size* Large
Stock Football memorabilia
Open By appointment only
Fairs International Programme
Fair London
Services New catalogue every
two months

CAMELFORD

**⊞ Corner Shop Antiques
and Gallery**
Contact Mr P J Tillett
✉ 68 Fore Street, Camelford,
Cornwall,
PL32 9PG 🅿
☎ 01840 212573
Ⓜ 07884 456247
ⓔ tillett18@aol.com
Est. 1989 *Stock size* Medium
Stock General antiques,
collectables, Victorian
watercolours
Open Mon–Sat 10am–5.30pm

CHACEWATER

⊞ Chacewater Antiques
Contact Mrs J Bateman
✉ 5 Fore Street,
Chacewater, Truro,
Cornwall,
TR4 8PS 🅿
☎ 01872 561411
Est. 1992 *Stock size* Medium
Stock Georgian–Edwardian
furniture, paintings, 19thC
brassware, jewellery, silver
Open Tues–Sat 10am–5pm

151

WEST COUNTRY
CORNWALL • CHARLESTOWN

CHARLESTOWN

⊞ Charles Town Trading
Contact Pippa and Graham Kennedy
✉ The Old Workshop,
Charlestown,
St Austell,
Cornwall,
PL25 3NJ 🅿
☎ 01726 76018 📠 01726 76018
Est. 1992 *Stock size* Large
Stock China, furniture, garden statuary, coins, general antiques
Open Mon–Sun 10am–4.30pm
Services Valuations, house clearances

FALMOUTH

⊞ Browsers Bookshop
Contact Mr Floyd
✉ 13–15 St George's Arcade,
Church Street, Falmouth,
Cornwall,
TR11 3DH 🅿
☎ 01326 313464
Est. 1981 *Stock size* Medium
Stock Antiquarian, second-hand books, printed music
Open Mon–Sat 9.30am–5pm
Services Valuations

⊞ Isabelline Books
Contact Mr M Whetman
✉ 2 Highbury House,
8 Woodlane Crescent,
Falmouth, Cornwall,
TR11 4QS 🅿
☎ 01326 210412 📠 0870 051 6387
📧 mikann@beakbook.demon.co.uk
🌐 www.beakbook.demon.co.uk
Est. 1997 *Stock size* Small
Stock Antiquarian books on ornithology
Open By appointment
Services Valuations, 3 catalogues a year

⊞ Marine Instruments
Contact Alistair Heane
✉ The Wheelhouse,
Upton Slip, Falmouth,
Cornwall,
TR11 3DQ 🅿
☎ 01326 312414 📠 01326 211414
📧 info@marineinstruments.co.uk
🌐 www.marineinstruments.co.uk
Est. 1960 *Stock size* Large
Stock Marine-related charts, publications, sextants, compasses
Open Mon–Fri 9am–5pm
Sat 9am–1pm

Services Worldwide mail order, valuations, repair of sextants and compasses

⊞ Old Town Hall Antiques
Contact Terry Brandreth or Mary Sheppard
✉ Old Town Hall,
3 High Street,
Falmouth, Cornwall,
TR11 2AB 🅿
☎ 01326 319437
🌐 www.oldtownhallantiques.co.uk
Est. 1986 *Stock size* Large
Stock 18th–early 20thC furniture, general antiques and collectables
Open Mon–Sat 10am–5.30pm
Sun 10am–4pm
Services Deliveries abroad

FOWEY

⊞ Bookends of Fowey
Contact Mrs C Alexander
✉ 4 South Street, Fowey,
Cornwall,
PL23 1AR
☎ 01726 833361
📧 info@bookendsoffowey.com
🌐 www.bookendsoffowey.com
Est. 1987 *Stock size* Large
Stock Antiquarian and second-hand books
Open Mon–Sat 10am–5.30pm
Apr–Oct Sun 10am–5.30pm
Services Valuations, book search, publishers of Cornish literature books

GRAMPOUND

⊞ Pine & Period Furniture
Contact Simon Payne
✉ Fore Street,
Grampound, Cornwall,
TR2 4QT 🅿
☎ 01726 883117
📱 07850 318298
Est. 1971 *Stock size* Medium
Stock Pine and period furniture
Open Mon–Sat 10.30am–5pm

⊞ Radnor House Antiques
Contact Geoff or Penny Hodgson
✉ Fore Street, Grampound,
Truro, Cornwall,
TR2 4QT 🅿
☎ 01726 882921
Est. 1975 *Stock size* Medium
Stock Victorian, Edwardian and Georgian oak, pine and mahogany furniture
Open Mon–Sat 10am–6pm

HAYLE

⊞ Copperhouse Gallery
Contact Paul Dyer
✉ 14 Fore Street, Copperhouse,
Hayle, Cornwall,
TR27 4DY 🅿
☎ 01736 752787
Est. 1900 *Stock size* Large
Stock Victorian and early 20thC watercolours, art pottery
Open Tues–Sat 9am–5pm

HELSTON

⊞ Butchers Antiques
Contact Howard Jones
✉ Rear of 12 Wendron Street,
Helston, Cornwall,
TR13 8PS 🅿
☎ 01326 565117
Est. 1991 *Stock size* Medium
Stock Country and pine furniture, cottageware and very unusual items
Open Mon–Sat 8am–5pm

⊞ The Helston Bookworm (PBFA)
Contact Mr or Mrs Summers
✉ 9 Church Street,
Helston, Cornwall,
TR13 8TA 🅿
☎ 01326 565079
Est. 1994 *Stock size* Medium
Stock Antiquarian and second-hand books
Open Mon–Fri 10am–5.30pm
Sat 10am–2pm
Fairs PBFA, local fairs (telephone for details)
Services Restoration, book search

LAUNCESTON

⊞ Antique Chairs and Museum
Contact Alice or Tom Brown
✉ Colhay Farm, Polson,
Launceston, Cornwall,
PL15 9QS 🅿
☎ 01566 777485 📠 01566 777485
Est. 1987 *Stock size* Large
Stock Period chairs
Open Mon–Sun 9am–5.30pm
Services Restoration, upholstery

⊞ Todd's Antiques
Contact Mr T Mead
✉ 2 High Street,
Launceston, Cornwall,
PL15 8ER 🅿

☎ 01566 775007 ☏ 01566 775007
Est. 1997 *Stock size* Large
Stock Small furniture,
collectables, ceramics
Open Mon–Fri 9am–5pm
Thurs–Sat 9am–4pm

LELANT

⊞ Mike Read Antique Sciences
Contact Mr M Read
✉ 1 Abbey Meadow, Lelant,
St Ives, Cornwall,
TR26 3LL 🅿
☎ 01736 757237 ☏ 01736 757237
✉ mikeread@macmail.com
Est. 1978 *Stock size* Medium
Stock Scientific instruments,
maritime works of art and
nautical artefacts
Open By appointment
Fairs International Antique
Scientific and Medical
Instruments Fair, Marble Arch
Services Valuations

LISKEARD

⊞ Olden Days
Contact Hazel Young
✉ Five Lanes, Dobwalls,
Liskeard, Cornwall,
PL14 6JD 🅿
☎ 01579 321577 ☏ 01579 321804
📱 07879 814815
Est. 1989 *Stock size* Medium
Stock General antiques, old
furniture, new pine
Open Mon–Sat 9.30am–5.30pm
Sun 10am–4pm
Services Bespoke furniture,
upholstery, restoration

LOOE

⊞ Abbey Bears
Contact Mrs Barnes
✉ Fore Street,
Looe, Cornwall,
PL13 1DT 🅿
☎ 01503 265441
Est. 1999 *Stock size* Large
Stock Teddy bears
Open Mon–Sun 10am–6pm

⊞ Tony Martin
Contact Mr Tony Martin
✉ Fore Street, East Looe,
Looe, Cornwall,
PL13 1AE 🅿
☎ 01503 262734
Est. 1965 *Stock size* Medium

Stock General small furniture,
china, ceramics, pictures
Open Appointment advisable

LOSTWITHIEL

⊞ John Bragg Antiques
Contact Ann Bragg
✉ 35 Fore Street,
Lostwithiel, Cornwall,
PL22 0BN 🅿
☎ 01208 872827
📱 07798 941484
Est. 1973 *Stock size* Large
Stock Period furniture
Open Mon–Sat 10am–5pm
closed Wed pm
Services Valuations

⊞ Deja-Vu Antiques & Books
Contact Adrian or Marianne
Barratt
✉ 31 Fore Street,
Lostwithiel, Cornwall,
PL22 0BN 🅿
☎ 01208 873912
✉ antiquedejavu@hotmail.com
🌐 www.deja-vu-antiques-
lostwithiel.com
Est. 1998 *Stock size* Medium
Stock Rustic, country, painted
furniture, decorative arts,
selection of books
Open Mon–Sat 10am–5pm
closed Wed pm
Services Book search

⊞ The Higgins Press
Contact Doris Roberts
✉ South Street,
Lostwithiel,
Cornwall,
PL22 0BZ 🅿
☎ 01208 872755
Est. 1980 *Stock size* Medium
Stock Antiques and collectables
Open Mon–Sat 10am–4pm
closed Wed pm

➤ Jefferys
Contact Ian Morris
✉ 5 Fore Street,
Lostwithiel,
Cornwall,
PL22 0BP 🅿
☎ 01208 872245 ☏ 01208 873260
✉ lostwithiel@jefferys.uk.com
🌐 www.jefferys.uk.com
Est. 1865
Open Mon–Fri 9am–5.30pm
Sales Antique, fine art and
general household sales on a

regular basis, please call for
details and viewing times
Catalogues Yes

⊞ The Old Palace Antiques
Contact Mr J Askew
✉ Quay Street,
Lostwithiel,
Cornwall,
PL22 0BS 🅿
☎ 01208 872909
Est. 1979 *Stock size* Medium
Stock Pine furniture, china, brass,
prints, postcards
Open Tues–Sun 9am–5pm

⊞ Paraphernalia
Contact Gwyn Conner or
Michael Sharp
✉ 9 Fore Street,
Lostwithiel,
Cornwall,
PL22 0BP 🅿
☎ 01208 872344 ☏ 01208 872344
Est. 2004 *Stock size* Medium
Stock Old pine and country
furniture, rural bygones, general
antiques, complementary items
Open Mon–Sat 10am–4.30pm

MARAZION

⊞ Antiques
Contact Andrew S Wood
✉ The Shambles,
Market Place,
Marazion, Cornwall,
TR17 0AR 🅿
☎ 01736 711381
Est. 1988 *Stock size* Medium
Stock General antiques and
collectors' items, particularly
19th–20thC pottery, porcelain
and glass
Open 1 Apr–31 Oct Mon–Fri
10.15am–5.30pm 1 Nov–31 Mar
Mon–Sat 10.15am–5pm

MEVAGISSEY

⊞ Cloud Cuckoo Land
Contact Paul Mulvey
✉ 12 Fore Street,
Mevagissey,
St Austell, Cornwall,
PL26 6UQ 🅿
☎ 01726 842364
✉ paul@cloudcuckooland.biz
🌐 www.cloudcuckooland.biz
Est. 1993 *Stock size* Medium
Stock Autographs
Open Mon–Sun 11am–6pm

PADSTOW

⊞ Jacob & His Fiery Angel
Contact Debbie Morris-Kirby
⊠ 7 Middle Street, Padstow,
Cornwall,
PL28 8AP ⓟ
☎ 01841 532130 or 01841 533219
ⓔ debbie.morriskirby@tesco.net
ⓦ www.jacobandhisfieryangel.com
Est. 1992 **Stock size** Large
Stock Antiques, eccentricities,
angels, chandeliers, cats,
curiosities, taxidermy (birds)
Open Mon–Sat 11am–5pm
winter Mon Fri Sat 11am–4pm or
by appointment

PAR

⚒ Bonhams
⊠ Cornubia Hall, Eastcliffe Road,
Par, Cornwall,
PL24 2AQ
☎ 01726 814047 ⓔ 01726 817979
ⓔ par@bonhams.com
ⓦ www.bonhams.com/par
Open Mon–Fri 9am–5.30pm
Sales Regional Saleroom.
Frequent sales. Regular sales
held in London and in our
salerooms across the country.
Free auction valuations;
insurance and probate valuations

⊞ Tinkers Pine Stripping & Antiques
Contact Mark or Heidi Chapman
⊠ Unit 9, The Roundhouse,
Harbour Road, Par, Cornwall,
PL24 2BB ⓟ
☎ 01726 812812
Est. 2001 **Stock size** Medium
Stock Doors, architraves, skirting
boards, fire surrounds,
bannisters, spindles, cupboard
doors, mouldings, odd pieces of
furniture, stripped doors
Open Tues–Sat 9am–5pm
Services Pine stripping

PENRYN

⊞ The Old School Antiques
Contact Mr J Gavin
⊠ The Old School,
Church Road,
Penryn, Cornwall,
TR10 8DA ⓟ
☎ 01326 375092
ⓜ 07813 930813
Est. 1985 **Stock size** Large

Stock Antique furniture, glass,
china, clocks
Open Mon–Sun 9am–5.30pm
Services Clock repairs and
furniture restoration

⊞ Leon Robertson Antiques
Contact Mr L Robertson
⊠ Unit 2, The Old School,
Church Road, Penryn,
Cornwall,
TR10 8DA ⓟ
☎ 01326 372767
ⓜ 07971 171909
Est. 1973 **Stock size** Medium
Stock Furniture, paintings,
general antiques
Open Mon–Sun 9am–5.30pm
Services Valuations

PENZANCE

⊞ Antiques and Fine Art Ltd
Contact Elinor Davies or
Geoffrey Mills
⊠ 1–3 Queens Buildings,
The Promenade,
Penzance, Cornwall,
TR18 4HH ⓟ
☎ 01736 350509
ⓦ www.antiquesfineart.co.uk
Est. 1994 **Stock size** Medium
Stock 17thC–Edwardian furniture
Open Mon–Sat 10am–4pm
Services Valuations, restoration,
upholstery

⌂ Chapel Street Arcades
Contact Mr Bentley
⊠ 61–62 Chapel Street,
Penzance, Cornwall,
TR18 4AE ⓟ
ⓜ 07890 542708
Est. 1984 **Stock size** Medium
No. of dealers 25
Stock Furniture, brass, copper,
silver, glass, porcelain, pictures,
prints, linen, collectors' items
Open Mon–Sat 10am–5pm

⊞ R W Jeffery
Contact Mr R W Jeffery
⊠ Trebehor, St Levan,
Penzance,
Cornwall,
TR19 6LX ⓟ
☎ 01736 871263
Est. 1968 **Stock size** Large
Stock Coins, banknotes
Open By appointment
Services Mail order

⊞ Peter Johnson
Contact Mr P Johnson
⊠ 62 Chapel Street, Penzance,
Cornwall,
TR18 4AE ⓟ
☎ 01736 363267
Est. 1992 **Stock size** Medium
Stock Period lighting, Oriental
ceramics, furniture, hand-made
silk lampshades
Open Tues–Sat 9.30am–5pm
Services Valuations

⚒ W H Lane & Son, Fine Art Auctioneers and Valuers
Contact Graham J Bazley
⊠ Jubilee House, Queen Street,
Penzance, Cornwall,
TR18 4DF ⓟ
☎ 01736 361447 ⓔ 01736 350097
ⓔ info@whlane.co.uk
Est. 1934
Open Mon–Fri 9am–1pm 2–5.30pm
Sales 6 major picture sales per
annum, occasional country house
sales
Catalogues Yes

⚒ David Lays (BACA Award Winner 2003)
Contact Mr D Lay FRICS
⊠ The Penzance Auction House,
Alverton, Penzance,
Cornwall,
TR18 4RE ⓟ
☎ 01736 361414 ⓔ 01736 360035
ⓔ david.lays@btopenworld.com
ⓦ www.invaluable.com/davidlay
Est. 1985
Open Mon–Fri 9am–5pm
Sales Auctioneers and valuers.
General sales every 3 weeks Tues
10am, viewing Sat 9am–1pm
Mon 9am–5pm. Bi-monthly 2-day
antiques auctions Thurs Fri 10am,
viewing Sat, day prior, 9am–7pm,
and day of sale 8.30–10am.
Traditional contemporary art
auctions 3 per annum Feb June
Oct Thurs 11am, viewing Sat
9am–1pm, day prior, 9am–7pm,
day of sale 8.30–11am. Book and
Collectors' sales 2 per annum
Aug and April Tues 10am,
viewing Sat 9am–1pm day prior
9am–7pm, morning of sale
8.30–10am
Catalogues Yes

⊞ New Street Books
Contact Mr K Hearn
⊠ 4 New Street,

Penzance, Cornwall,
TR18 2LZ
☎ 01736 362758
✉ eankelvin@yahoo.com
Est. 1991 *Stock size* Medium
Stock Antiquarian and second-hand books, Cornish topics a speciality
Open Mon–Sat 10am–5pm
Fairs Morrab Library Book Fair
Services Book search

⊞ The Old Custom House
Contact Michelle Powell
✉ 53 Chapel Street,
Penzance, Cornwall,
TR18 4AF 🅿
☎ 01736 331030 ✆ 01736 331317
Est. 1997 *Stock size* Medium
Stock Glass, china
Open Mon–Sat 10am–5pm

⊞ Penzance Rare Books
Contact Pat Johnstone
✉ 43 Causewayhead,
Penzance, Cornwall,
TR18 2SS 🅿
☎ 01736 362140
✉ patricia.johnstone@btinternet.com
Est. 1991 *Stock size* Large
Stock Antiquarian and second-hand books
Open Mon–Sat 10.30am–5pm
Services Valuations

⊞ Shiver Me Timbers
Contact Mr T R E Gray
✉ Station Road, Long Rock,
Penzance, Cornwall,
TR20 9TT 🅿
☎ 01736 711338
Est. 1983 *Stock size* Medium
Stock Reclaimed materials
Open Mon–Sat 10am–5pm
Services Hire of materials to film companies, makes reproduction furniture

POLPERRO

⊞ Expectations
Contact John Walker
✉ Fore Street, Polperro,
Cornwall,
PL13 2QR
☎ 01503 272631
Est. 2001 *Stock size* Medium
Stock Furniture, lamps, brass, copper
Open Summer Mon–Sun winter Sat–Mon 10.30am–5.30pm
Services Search service for oil lamp parts

⊞ Gentry Antiques
Contact Pauline Black
✉ Little Green,
Polperro,
Cornwall,
PL13 2RF
☎ 01503 272361
✉ info@gentryantiques.co.uk
Est. 1998 *Stock size* Medium
Stock Pottery, porcelain and decorative items
Open Mon–Sun 10am–5pm
Fairs Battersea Antiques and Decorators Fair

REDRUTH

⊞ La Belle
Contact Danny Everard
✉ 52 Fore Street, Redruth,
Cornwall,
TR15 2AE 🅿
☎ 01209 216228
Est. 1991 *Stock size* Medium
Stock General antiques
Open Mon–Sat 9am–5pm
Services Valuations

⊞ Evergreen Antiques & Interiors
Contact Michele Jelf
✉ 38 Fore Street, Redruth,
Cornwall,
TR15 2AE 🅿
☎ 01209 215634
✉ evergreen@forestreet38.freeserve.co.uk
Est. 2000 *Stock size* Medium
Stock General antiques, interiors
Open Mon–Sat 10am–4.30pm

⊞ The Old Steam Bakery
Contact Mr Stephen Phillips
✉ 60a Fore Street, Redruth,
Cornwall,
TR15 2AF 🅿
☎ 01209 315099
Est. 1994 *Stock size* Large
Stock Late Victorian and Edwardian oak and pine furniture
Open Mon–Sat 10.30am–5pm

⚒ Pool Auctions
Contact Mr or Mrs Duncan
✉ Unit 1, Trevenson Road,
Pool, Redruth,
Cornwall,
TR15 3PH 🅿
☎ 01209 717111
Est. 1995
Open Mon–Fri 9am–3pm
Sales Antiques and general

household sale Tues 6pm, viewing Tues 9am–6pm prior to sale
Frequency Weekly
Catalogues No

⚒ Richards Son & Murdoch
Contact Mr Eddy
✉ Alma Place,
Redruth,
Cornwall,
TR15 2AT 🅿
☎ 01209 216367 ✆ 01209 314959
Est. 1876
Open Mon–Fri 9am–1pm 2–5pm Sat 9am–noon
Sales Tuesday, general antiques, household furniture, 11am
Frequency Every 5–6 weeks
Catalogues Yes

⊞ Romantiques
Contact Patrick Ludford
✉ Old Rectory, Churchtown,
Redruth, Cornwall,
TR15 3BT 🅿
📱 07980 500490
Est. 1999 *Stock size* Medium
Stock Period antiques and ornamental garden antiques, staddle stones, troughs
Open Mon–Sat 10am–5pm or by appointment

⊞ Thornleigh Trading Antique Lighting
Contact Mr Duncan
✉ 46 Fore Street,
Redruth,
Cornwall,
TR15 2AE 🅿
☎ 01209 315454
Est. 1992 *Stock size* Large
Stock Antique lighting, Victorian oil lamps
Open Mon–Sat 9.30am–5pm

ST COLUMB

⊞ M R Dingle
Contact Mr Dingle
✉ Station Yard,
Station Approach,
St Columb Road,
St Columb, Cornwall,
TR9 6QR 🅿
☎ 01726 861119
Est. 1989 *Stock size* Large
Stock Architectural antiques including reclaimed timber
Open Mon–Fri 8am–5pm Sat 8am–noon

ST IVES

⊞ Courtyard Collectables
Contact Janice Mosedale
✉ Cyril Noall Square,
Fore Street, St Ives,
Cornwall,
TR26 1HE
☎ 01736 798809
Est. 1994 *Stock size* Large
Stock General collectables
Open July–October Mon–Sun
10am–10pm Nov–June Mon–Sat
10am–5pm Sun noon–5pm

⊞ Dragons Hoard
Contact Chris Prescott
✉ 2 Tre-Pol-Pen, Street-an-Pol,
St Ives, Cornwall,
TR26 2DS
☎ 01736 798484 ☏ 01736 798417
✉ dragonshoard@dragonshoard.ws
⊛ www.dragonshoard.ws
Est. 1985 *Stock size* Small
Stock Collectables old and new,
Britain's figures, farm animals,
diecast models, Corgi, Matchbox,
playing cards, Kinder Surprise,
storage systems, advertising,
ephemera, curios
Open Mon–Fri 10.30am–5pm
Sat 10.30am–4pm
Fairs Newark

⊞ Tremayne Applied Arts
Contact Roger or Anne
Tonkinson
✉ Street-an-Pol, St Ives,
Cornwall,
TR26 2DS
☎ 01736 797779 ☏ 01736 793222
✉ tomkinson@btinternet.com
Est. 1997 *Stock size* Large
Stock 20thC antiques, 1960s, Arts
and Crafts, Art Deco, Art
Nouveau
Open Mon–Fri 10.30am–4.30pm
Sat 10am–1.30pm closed Wed

ST JUST

⊞ St Just Bygones
Contact H I Whitelaw
✉ 30 Fore Street, St Just,
Penzance, Cornwall,
TR19 7LX 🅿
☎ 01736 787860
Est. 1990 *Stock size* Large
Stock Furniture, general
antiques, bric-a-brac
Open Mon–Sat 10am–5.30pm,
summer months open daily
Services House clearance

ST JUST-IN-ROSELAND

L Edscer
Contact L Edscer
✉ Lanzeague House,
St Just-in-Roseland,
Cornwall,
TR2 5JD 🅿
☎ 01326 270845 ☏ 01326 270845
✉ laurenceedscer@prs17495.
demon.co.uk
⊛ www.autosportcollector.com
Est. 1989 *Stock size* Large
Stock Motor racing and rallying
memorabilia
Open Mon–Sun 9am–6pm
Fairs Goodwood events, Beaulieu
Fair
Services Valuations

TIDEFORD

⊞ Cutcrew Antiques
Contact Miss Nicola Stewart
✉ Cutcrew Sawmills,
Tideford, Cornwall,
PL12 5JS 🅿
☎ 01752 851402
Est. 1984 *Stock size* Large
Stock Georgian–Edwardian
furniture situated in an 18thC
water mill
Open Mon–Sun 9am–5.30pm

TINTAGEL

⊞ Atique
Contact Amanda Dawson
✉ Bath House,
Fore Street, Tintagel,
Cornwall,
PL34 0DD 🅿
☎ 01840 779009
✉ antique.interiors@virgin.net
⊛ www.boscastleoldmill.com
Est. 1999 *Stock size* Medium
Stock English, Continental
antiques and linens,
contemporary art
Open Mon–Sun 10am–5pm
Nov–Feb by appointment

**⊞ The House That Jack
Built**
Contact Sam Rowe
✉ Hollybush Studio,
Fore Street, Tintagel,
Cornwall,
PL34 ODB
☎ 01840 770055
Est. 2003 *Stock size* Small
Stock Antiques, collectables
Open By appointment

TRURO

⊞ The Bear Shop – Truro
Contact John Barnes
✉ 4 New Bridge Street,
Truro, Cornwall,
TR1 2AA 🅿
☎ 01872 225545
✉ enquiries@cornwallbearshop.co.uk
⊛ www.cornwallbearshop.co.uk
Est. 2000 *Stock size* Large
Stock Teddy bears
Open Mon–Sun 9am–5pm
Fairs Totally Teddies and
Hugglets

⊞ Alan Bennett Ltd
Contact Mr Alan Bennett or
Justin Bennett
✉ 24 New Bridge Street,
Truro, Cornwall,
TR1 2AA 🅿
☎ 01872 273296
Est. 1954 *Stock size* Large
Stock Furniture pre-1910,
general antiques
Open Mon–Sat 9am–5.30pm
Services Valuations

**⊞ Blackwater Pine
Antiques**
Contact Linda Cropper
✉ Blackwater, Truro,
Cornwall,
TR4 8ET 🅿
☎ 01872 560919
Est. 1989 *Stock size* Large
Stock Antique pine and country
furniture
Open Mon–Sat 10am–5.30pm
closed Wed
Services Valuations, restoration

⊞ Bonython Bookshop
Contact Mrs R Carpenter
✉ 16 Kenwyn Street,
Truro, Cornwall,
TR1 3BU
☎ 01872 262886
✉ bonythonbooks@btconnect.com
Est. 1996 *Stock size* Small
Stock Antiquarian, second-hand
and art books, Cornish interest a
speciality
Open Mon–Sat 10.30am–4.30pm
Services Valuations, book search

⌁ Philip Buddell
Contact Linda Buddell
✉ The Elms, Tresillian,
Truro, Cornwall,
TR2 4BA
☎ 01872 250173

📱 07974 022893
✉ lulubudd@aol.com
Est. 1989
Open Mon–Sat 10am–5pm
Sales Auctions and viewing at a hall in Ladock. Antiques and general household sale 3-weekly on Sat 10am, viewing Fri 2–8pm. Specialist wine sale, toy sale and book sale quarterly. Telephone for details
Catalogues Yes

⊞ Philip Buddell Antiques
Contact Philip or Linda Buddell
✉ The Elms, Tresillian,
Truro, Cornwall,
TR2 4BA 🅿
☎ 01872 520173
📱 07974 022893
✉ lulubudd@aol.com
Est. 2000 *Stock size* Medium
Stock Fine furniture, paintings
Open Mon–Sat 10am–5pm
Services Valuations, auctions

⌂ Coinage Hall Antique Centre
Contact David Taylor
✉ 1 Princes Street, Truro,
Cornwall,
TR1 2QU 🅿
☎ 01872 262336
Est. 1996 *Stock size* Medium
No. of dealers 3
Stock Fine furniture, collectables, general antiques, fabrics, fine art, postcards, cigarette cards
Open Mon–Sat 10am–3.30pm
Services Valuations

⊞ Collectors Corner
Contact Alan McLoughlin
✉ Unit 45–46, Pannier Market,
Back Quay, Truro, Cornwall,
TR1 2LL 🅿
☎ 01872 272729
✉ almacmedal@aol.com
🌐 www.militarycollectables.co.uk
Est. 1997 *Stock size* Medium
Stock Coins, banknotes, medals, militaria, stamps, postcards, cigarette cards
Open Mon–Sat 9.30am–4.30pm
Services Valuations, medal mounting

⊞ Count House Antiques
Contact Mrs M Such
✉ Coinage Hall, 1 Princes Street,
Truro, Cornwall,
TR1 2ES 🅿
☎ 01872 264269

Est. 1998 *Stock size* Medium
Stock General antiques
Open Mon–Sat 10am–4.30pm
Fairs Exeter

⊞ Just Books
Contact Jenny Wicks
✉ 9 Pydar Mews, Truro,
Cornwall,
TR1 2UX 🅿
☎ 01872 242532
Est. 1986 *Stock size* Medium
Stock Antiquarian, collectable, second-hand and out-of-print books, Cornwall a speciality
Open Mon–Sat 10am–5pm
Services Valuations, book search, repairs referral

⋋ Lodge and Thomas
Contact Mr Lodge
✉ 58 Lemon Street, Truro,
Cornwall,
TR1 2PY
☎ 01872 272722 ☏ 01872 223665
✉ info@lodgeandthomas.co.uk
🌐 www.lodgeandthomas.co.uk
Est. 1892
Open Mon–Fri 9am–5.30pm
Sat 9am–noon
Sales General antiques and collectables sale, viewing 9–11am prior to sale. Telephone for details. Sales held at Ludgvan Community Hall, Ludgvan, Penzance, Cornwall
Frequency 8 per year
Catalogues Yes

⊞ Once Upon A Time
Contact Graham Kennedy
✉ The Coinage Hall, 1 Princes Street, Truro, Cornwall,
TR1 2QU 🅿
☎ 01872 262520
✉ pbootantiques@btconnect.com
Est. 1996 *Stock size* Medium
Stock General antiques, English, French and Continental furniture, paintings, sculpture
Open Mon–Sat 10am–4pm
Services Restoration, upholstery

⊞ Taylor's Collectables
Contact Mr D Taylor
✉ The Coinage Hall,
1 Princes Street,
Truro, Cornwall,
TR1 2QU 🅿
☎ 01872 262336
📱 07775 811686
Est. 1994 *Stock size* Medium
Stock Postcards, cigarette cards,

toys, general antiques
Open Mon–Sat 10am–3.30pm
Fairs Newark, West Point, Twickenham
Services Valuations

VERYAN

⊞ Granny's Attic
Contact A K Gray
✉ Village Centre,
Veryan, Truro,
Cornwall,
TR2 5QA 🅿
☎ 01872 501637
Est. 2000 *Stock size* Medium
Stock Antiques, country items, collectables, second-hand clothes
Open Fri Sat 10am–4.30pm or by appointment

WADEBRIDGE

⊞ Acorn Antique Interiors
Contact Brian or Margaret
✉ Eddystone Road,
Wadebridge, Cornwall,
PL27 7AL 🅿
☎ 01208 812815
Est. 1982 *Stock size* Medium
Stock Antique pine furniture
Open Mon–Sat 9am–5pm
Services Restoration

⊞ D Holmes
Contact Mr D Holmes
✉ Port Gaverne,
Cornwall,
W8 6EE 🅿
☎ 01208 880254
📱 07790 431895
Est. 1965 *Stock size* Small
Stock 18th–19thC English mahogany furniture, silver, fine antiques
Open By appointment only
Services Also showrooms at Oudenaarde, Belgium

⋋ Lambrays
Contact Richard J Hamm
✉ Polmorla Walk, The Platt,
Wadebridge, Cornwall,
PL27 7AE 🅿
☎ 01208 813593 ☏ 01208 814986
✉ lambrays@freeuk.com
Est. 1981
Open Mon–Fri 9am–5.30pm
Sat 9am–noon (prior to sale)
Sales Quarterly specialist antique sales. Victoriana sales fortnightly Mon 11am
Catalogues Yes

WEST COUNTRY
DEVON • ASHBURTON

⊞ Polmorla Bookshop
Contact Joan Buck
✉ 1 Polmorla Road,
Wadebridge, Cornwall,
PL27 7NB 🅿
☎ 01208 814399
Est. 1991 *Stock size* Large
Stock Antiquarian, rare, second-hand and out-of-print books
Open Mon–Sat 10.30am–5pm
Services Valuations, book search

⊞ Relics
Contact Mr K Brenton
✉ 4 Polmorla Road,
Wadebridge, Cornwall,
PL27 7NB 🅿
☎ 01208 815383
Est. 1991 *Stock size* Large
Stock Furniture, china, brass, kitchenware, pictures
Open Mon–Sat 10am–5pm

⊞ Victoria Antiques
Contact Mr Daly
✉ 21 Molesworth Street,
Wadebridge, Cornwall,
PL27 7DD 🅿
☎ 01208 814160 ✆ 01208 814160
Est. 1974 *Stock size* Large
Stock General antiques, clocks, barometers, period furniture
Open Mon–Sat 9am–5pm

DEVON

ASHBURTON

⊞ Adrian Ager
Contact Adrian Ager
✉ Ashburton Marbles,
Great Hall, North Street,
Ashburton,
Newton Abbott, Devon,
TQ13 7QD 🅿
☎ 01364 653189 ✆ 01364 653189
📧 afager@tinyworld.co.uk
🌐 www.adrianager.co.uk
Est. 1975 *Stock size* Large
Stock Victorian furnishings, interior fittings, fireplaces, dining room tables, garden statuary, garden ornaments
Open Mon–Fri 8am–5pm Sat 10am–4pm
Services Valuations, restoration

⊞ The Dartmoor Bookshop Ltd (PBFA)
Contact Mr Paul Heatley
✉ 2 Kingsbridge Lane,
Ashburton,
Newton Abbot, Devon,

TQ13 7DX 🅿
☎ 01364 653356
📧 dartmoorbks@aol.com
🌐 www.dartmoorbks.dabsol.co.uk
Est. 1974 *Stock size* Large
Stock Antiquarian, second-hand, rare and out-of-print books
Open Wed–Sat 9.30am–5.30pm

⊞ Kessler Ford Antiques
Contact Matthew Ford or Elizabeth Kessler
✉ 9 North Street, Ashburton,
Newton Abbot, Devon,
TQ13 7QJ 🅿
☎ 01364 654310 ✆ 01364 654141
📱 07770 782402
📧 Matt@kessler-ford.co.uk
Est. 1998 *Stock size* Medium
Stock 17th–18thC English oak and mahogany furniture, sculpture, paintings
Open Tues–Sat 10am–5pm or by appointment

⊞ Memories
Contact Julia Walters
✉ Globe Buildings, 15 North Street, Ashburton, Newton Abbot, Devon,
TQ13 7QH 🅿
☎ 01364 654681
📱 07773 795777
📧 julieann.walters@btopenworld.com
Est. 1996 *Stock size* Medium
Stock A varied range of Georgian–Edwardian furniture, collectables
Open Mon–Sat 10am–4pm closed Wed pm

⊞ Moor Antiques
Contact Mr or Mrs Gatland
✉ 19a North Street, Ashburton,
Newton Abbot, Devon,
TQ13 7QH 🅿
☎ 01364 653767
📱 07720 183414
📧 moorantiques@aol.com
Est. 1984 *Stock size* Medium
Stock Fine early English porcelain 1750–1840, small pieces of antique English silver
Open Mon–Sat 10am–4pm Wed 10am–1pm
Services Valuations

⊞ Pennsylvania Pine Company
Contact Stephen Robinson
✉ 18 East Street,
Ashburton, Devon,
TQ13 7AZ

☎ 01364 652244 ✆ 01364 652244
🌐 www.pennsylvaniapine.co.uk
Est. 2000 *Stock size* Medium
Stock Antique English pine
Open Mon–Sat 10.30am–4.30pm closed Wed
Services Valuations, restoration

⚒ Rendells (RICS, CAAV)
Contact Mr Clive Morgan
✉ Stonepark, Ashburton,
Newton Abbot, Devon,
TQ13 7RH 🅿
☎ 01364 653017 ✆ 01364 654251
📧 stonepark@rendells.co.uk
🌐 www.rendells.co.uk
Est. 1816
Open Mon–Fri 9am–5.30pm
Sales Antiques and selected items monthly Thurs Fri 10am, viewing Tues 10am–7pm Wed 10am–5pm
Frequency monthly
Catalogues Yes

⌂ The Shambles
Contact Mrs Spendlove or Mrs Keith
✉ 24 North Street,
Ashburton,
Newton Abbot, Devon,
TQ13 7QD 🅿
☎ 01364 653848
Est. 1986 *Stock size* Large
No. of dealers 6
Stock Furniture, collectables, marine antiques, textiles, pictures, rugs, silver, Staffordshire figures
Open Mon–Sat 10am–5pm

⊞ The Snug
Contact Ros Gregg or Carol Dant
✉ 15 North Street,
Ashburton,
Newton Abbot, Devon,
TQ13 7QN 🅿
☎ 01364 653096
Est. 1991 *Stock size* Medium
Stock Antiques, textiles, interiors
Open Mon–Sat 10am–4.30pm

⊞ Taylors
Contact Wendy Taylor
✉ 5 North Street, Ashburton,
Newton Abbot, Devon,
TQ13 7QJ 🅿
☎ 01364 652631
Est. 1985 *Stock size* Medium
Stock 18thC–Edwardian oak furniture, 18thC blue and white Chinese porcelain
Open Tues–Sat 10am–5pm

AXMINSTER

⚒ Axminster Auctions
Contact John Bloxham
✉ Coombe Lane,
Axminster,
Devon,
EX13 5AY ▣
☎ 01297 35693 ✆ 01297 35693
Est. 1858
Open Mon–Fri 9am–5pm
Sales General antiques sale
second Wed of the month 10am,
viewing Tues 10am–8pm
Frequency Monthly

⊞ South Street Antiques
Contact Philip Atkins
✉ South Street,
Axminster,
Devon,
EX13 5AD ▣
☎ 01297 33701
Est. 1987 *Stock size* Medium
Stock General antiques
Open Mon–Sat 9.30am–4.30pm
closed Wed pm
Fairs Shepton Mallet
Services Valuations

BAMPTON

⊞ Bampton Gallery
Contact Gerald Chidwick
✉ 2–4 Brook Street, Bampton,
Devon,
EX16 9LY ▣
☎ 01398 331119/331354
✆ 01398 331119
📧 bampton.gallery@bampton.org.uk
🌐 www.bampton.org.uk
Est. 1997 *Stock size* Medium
Stock Antique porcelain, glass,
small furniture, pictures
Open Mon–Thurs 9.30am–3pm
Sat 9am–noon or by
appointment
Services Restoration, upholstery

BARNSTAPLE

⊞ The Barn Antiques
Contact Mr T Cusack
✉ 73 Newport Road,
Barnstaple,
Devon,
EX32 9BG ▣
☎ 01271 323131
Est. 1987 *Stock size* Large
Stock General antiques
Open Mon–Sat 9.30am–5pm
closed Wed pm
Services Valuations, restoration

⚒ Barnstaple Auctions
Contact Amy Waddington-Smith
✉ Pilton Quay,
Barnstaple,
Devon,
EX31 1PB ▣
☎ 01271 342952 ✆ 01271 342952
Est. 1993
Open Mon–Fri 9.30am–4.30pm
Sales General antiques sale last
Thurs of month 6.30pm, viewing
Wed 4–7pm
Frequency Monthly
Catalogues Yes

⊞ Medina Gallery
Contact Richard Jennings
✉ 80 Boutport Street,
Barnstaple, Devon,
EX31 1SR ▣
☎ 01271 371025
Est. 1973 *Stock size* Medium
Stock Antique prints, maps, oils,
watercolours
Open Mon–Sat 9.30am–5pm

⌂ North Devon Antiques Centre
Contact Patrick Broome
✉ The Old Church, Cross Street,
Barnstaple, Devon,
EX31 1BD ▣
☎ 01271 375788
📱 07967 930917
📧 broome72@tiscali.co.uk
🌐 www.northdevonantiques
centre.co.uk
Est. 1998 *Stock size* Large
No. of dealers 27
Stock Georgian to contemporary
furniture, Royal Worcester,
Clarice Cliff, crested china ware,
Barum and Brannam, militaria,
clocks, architectural salvage,
pictures and prints, Art Deco
Open Mon–Sat 10am–4.30pm
Services Restoration, café also
open 6 days

⊞ Tarka Books (BA)
Contact Fiona Broster
✉ 5 Bear Street,
Barnstaple,
Devon,
EX32 7BU ▣
☎ 01271 374997
📧 info@tarkabooks.co.uk
🌐 www.tarkabooks.co.uk
Est. 1987 *Stock size* Large
Stock Second-hand books, Henry
Williamson titles a speciality
Open Mon–Sat 9.45am–5pm
Services Book search

BEER

⊞ Beer Collectables
Contact Mr Forkes
✉ Dolphin Hotel, Fore Street,
Beer, Seaton, Devon,
EX12 3EQ ▣
☎ 01297 24362
Est. 1993 *Stock size* Medium
Stock Collectables, china, glass,
fishing tackle, jewellery
Open Mon–Sun 10am–5pm
Fairs Exeter Livestock, Salisbury,
T&T Fairs

BIDEFORD

⊞ J. Collins & Son Fine Art (BADA, LAPADA, CINOA)
Contact Mr John Biggs
✉ PO Box 119, Bideford, Devon,
EX39 1WX ▣
☎ 01237 473103 ✆ 01237 475658
📧 biggs@collinsantiques.co.uk
🌐 www.collinsantiques.co.uk
Est. 1953 *Stock size* Large
Stock Victorian–Edwardian oil
paintings, watercolours
Open By appointment
Fairs BADA, Olympia (Nov)
Services Restoration of oil
paintings and watercolours

⊞ J Collins & Son (BADA, LAPADA, CINOA)
Contact Mr Jonathan Biggs
✉ PO Box 119, Bideford, Devon,
EX39 1WX ▣
☎ 01237 473103 ✆ 01237 475658
📧 biggs@collinsantiques.co.uk
🌐 www.collinsantiques.co.uk
Est. 1953 *Stock size* Large
Stock Georgian and Regency
furniture
Open By appointment
Fairs BADA, Olympia (Nov)
Services Restoration of English
furniture

⊞ Peter Hames (PBFA)
Contact Mr P Hames
✉ Old Bridge Antiques Centre,
Market Place,
Bideford, Devon,
EX39 2DR ▣
☎ 01237 421065 ✆ 01237 421065
📧 peterhames@hotmail.com
Est. 1979 *Stock size* Medium
Stock Small selection of general
books, jazz and North Devon
books a speciality
Open Mon–Sat 9am–5.30pm
Fairs PBFA

WEST COUNTRY

WEST COUNTRY
DEVON • BOVEY TRACEY

⊞ Medina Gallery
Contact Caroline Jennings
✉ 55 Mill Street, Bideford,
Devon,
EX39 2JR 🅿
☎ 01237 476483
Est. 1973 *Stock size* Medium
Stock Antique prints, maps, oils,
watercolours
Open Mon–Sat 9.30am–5pm

BOVEY TRACEY

⊞ Albion House Antiques
Contact Anthony Seed
✉ 75a Fore Street,
Bovey Tracey, Devon,
TQ13 9HB
☎ 01626 835650
🖳 antseeds@aol.com
Est. 1998 *Stock size* Medium
Stock Antiques, collectables
Open By appointment
Services Valuations

BRIXHAM

**⊞ Brixham's King Street
Rooms**
Contact Mr Dean
✉ King Street Rooms,
King Street, Brixham, Devon,
TQ5 9TF 🅿
☎ 01803 858303
Est. 1971 *Stock size* Medium
Stock Early motoring, clocks,
general antiques
Open Mon–Sat 10am–5pm

**⊞ Commotions Antique,
Electric & Turret Clocks**
Contact Dr Paul Strickland
✉ Ye Olde Coffin House,
King Street, Brixham, Devon,
TQ5 9TF 🅿
☎ 01803 856307
🖳 info@got2town.co.uk
🌐 www.got2town.co.uk
Est. 2002 *Stock size* Large
Stock Clocks, related tools, books
Open Mon–Sun 9am–5pm
Services Restoration

⊞ John Prestige Antiques
Contact Mr Prestige
✉ Greenswood Court,
Greenswood Road,
Brixham, Devon,
TQ5 9HN 🅿
☎ 01803 856141 📠 01803 851649
🖳 sales@john-prestige.co.uk
🌐 www.john-prestige.co.uk
Est. 1971 *Stock size* Large

Stock Furniture, pictures, mirrors,
ceramics
Trade only Yes
Open Mon–Fri 8.45am–6pm or by
appointment
Services Valuations, restoration

BUDLEIGH SALTERTON

⊞ B & T Thorn and Son
Contact Mr Thorn
✉ 2 High Street,
Budleigh Salterton,
Devon,
EX9 6LQ 🅿
☎ 01395 442448
Est. 1950 *Stock size* Medium
Stock Ceramics, English pottery
and porcelain
Open Tues Fri Sat 10am–1pm
Services Valuations

CALLINGTON

**➤ Eric Distin Auctioneers
& Chartered Surveyors
(RICS)**
Contact Mr E Distin
✉ 72 Mutley Plain,
R/O 7 New Road,
Callington,
Devon,
PL17 7BE 🅿
☎ 01752 663046 or 01579 383322
📠 01752 257342
🖳 eric@distin.fsbusiness.co.uk
Est. 1973
Sales Antiques and collectables
Sat 10.30am, viewing morning of
sale or afternoon prior
Frequency Fortnightly
Catalogues Yes

CATTEDOWN

**➤ Plymouth Auction
Rooms**
Contact Mr P Keen
✉ Edwin House,
St John's Road, Cattedown,
Plymouth, Devon,
PL4 0NZ 🅿
☎ 01752 254740 📠 01752 254740
🖳 info@plymouthauctions.co.uk
🌐 www.plymouthauctions.co.uk
Est. 1992
Open Mon–Thur 9am–1pm
2–5pm, Fri 9am–1pm
Sales Antiques and collectables
three weekly Wed 10.30am,
viewing Tues 10am–7pm
Wed 9–10.30am.
Catalogues Yes

CLYST HONITON

⊞ Pennies Antiques
Contact Mrs Clark
✉ Home Farm, Clyst Honiton,
Devon,
EX25 2LX 🅿
☎ 01392 444491
🌐 www.penniesantiques.co.uk
Est. 1979 *Stock size* Medium
Stock General antiques
Open Mon–Sat 10am–5pm

COLYTON

⌂ Colyton Antique Centre
Contact R C Hunt
✉ Dolphin Street, Colyton,
Devon,
EX24 6LU 🅿
☎ 01297 552339 📠 01297 552339
📱 07973 678989
🖳 colytonantiques@model
garage.co.uk
🌐 www.modelgarage.co.uk
Est. 1988 *Stock size* Medium
No. of dealers 30
Stock Antiques and collectables
Open Summer Mon–Sat
10am–5pm Sun Bank Holidays
11am–4pm winter Mon–Sat
10am–4pm Sun 11am–4pm

COMBE MARTIN

⊞ Sherbrook Selectables
Contact Mr T Pickard
✉ 1a Hangman Path, Combe
Martin, Ilfracombe, Devon,
EX34 0DE 🅿
☎ 01271 889060
📱 07887 806493
🖳 trevor@sherbrook1.fsbusiness.co.uk
Est. 1999 *Stock size* Medium
Stock General antiques, glass,
ceramics, small furniture,
collectables
Open Sat–Tues 10am–5.30pm

CREDITON

**⊞ Musgrave Bickford
Antiques (BHI)**
Contact Dennis Bickford
✉ 15 East Street, Crediton,
Devon,
EX17 3AT 🅿
☎ 01363 775042
Est. 1987 *Stock size* Medium
Stock Clocks, barometers
Open By appointment
Fairs Westpoint
Services Valuations, restoration

160

CULLOMPTON

Cobweb Antiques
Contact Richard Holmes
✉ The Old Tannery, Exeter Road, Cullompton, Devon, EX15 1DT 🅿
☎ 01884 38476 🖷 01884 38476
🅔 tannery@cullompton-antiques.co.uk
🌐 www.cullompton-antiques.co.uk
Est. 1986 *Stock size* Large
Stock General antiques, country furniture
Open Mon–Sat 10am–5pm

Cullompton Old Tannery Antiques
Contact George Mills
✉ The Old Tannery, Exeter Road, Cullompton, Devon, EX15 1DT 🅿
☎ 01884 38476 🖷 01884 38476
🅔 tannery@cullompton-antiques.co.uk
🌐 www.cullompton-antiques.co.uk
Est. 1987 *Stock size* Large
Stock Antique country furniture, English, French and European clocks, mirrors, decorative items
Open Mon–Sat 10am–5pm
Services Shipping, courier

Oaks & Partners
✉ The Old Tannery, Exeter Road, Cullompton, Devon, EX15 1DT 🅿
☎ 01884 35848 🖷 01884 38000
🅔 auctionsoaksandpartners.co.uk
🌐 www.invaluable.com/oaksandpartners
Est. 1979
Open Mon–Fri 9am–4pm closed Wed
Sales Antiques and general sale Sat 10.30am, viewing Thurs 9am–5pm Fri 9am–8pm
Frequency 3-weekly
Catalogues Yes

DARTMOUTH

Looking Back
Contact Paddy Distin
✉ 32 Lower Street, Dartmouth, Devon, TQ6 9AN 🅿
☎ 01803 832615
Est. 1990 *Stock size* Medium
Stock General antiques
Open Summer Mon–Sun 10am–5.30pm
Services House clearance

Pennyfarthing Antiques
Contact Jill Williams
✉ 11 Lower Street, Dartmouth, Devon, TQ6 9AN
☎ 01803 839411
Est. 2000 *Stock size* Medium
Stock Antique furniture, ceramics, prints, collectables of interest
Open Mon–Fri 10am–4.30pm Sat 10am–5pm Sun 11am–4pm

EXETER

Bearne's (SOFAA)
Contact N J Saintey
✉ St Edmund's Court, Okehampton Street, Exeter, Devon, EX4 1DU 🅿
☎ 01392 207000 🖷 01392 207007
🅔 enquiries@bearnes.co.uk
🌐 www.bearnes.co.uk
Est. 1945
Open Mon–Fri 9.30am–5pm
Sales Antiques & collectables sales every 3 weeks on a Tuesday. Seasonal fine art sales every 3/4 months on Tues/Wed. Viewing before the sale 9.30am–1pm, Monday before the sale 9.30am–7pm, Telephone for details
Catalogues Yes

Lisa Cox Music (ABA, PADA)
Contact Lisa Cox
✉ The Coach House, Colleton Crescent, Exeter, Devon, EX2 4DJ 🅿
☎ 01392 490290 🖷 01392 277336
🅔 music@lisacoxmusic.co.uk
🌐 www.lisacoxmusic.co.uk
Est. 1984 *Stock size* Large
Stock Antiquarian music, pictures, ephemera, autographs
Open By appointment
Services Valuations

Eclectique
Contact Sue Bellamy
✉ 26–27 Commercial Road, The Quay, Exeter, Devon, EX2 4AE 🅿
☎ 01392 250799
Est. 1994 *Stock size* Medium
Stock Antique and painted furniture, ceramics, lamps, objets d'art, collectables
Open Mon–Sun 11am–5.30pm
Services Interior design

Exeter Antique Lighting
Contact Julian Wood
✉ Cellar 15, The Quay, Exeter, Devon, EX2 4AP 🅿
☎ 01392 490848
🖷 07702 969438
🌐 www.antiquelightingcompany.com
Est. 1990 *Stock size* Large
Stock Antique lighting, fireplaces, iron beds
Open Mon–Sun 11am–5pm or by appointment
Fairs Newark, Ardingly
Services Valuations, restoration

Exeter Rare Books (ABA, PBFA)
Contact Mr R C Parry
✉ 13a Guildhall Shopping Centre, Exeter, Devon, EX4 3HG 🅿
☎ 01392 436021
Est. 1974 *Stock size* Medium
Stock Antiquarian, rare, second-hand books
Open Mon–Sat 10am–1pm 2–5pm
Fairs Chelsea ABA

Exeter's Antiques Centre on the Quay
Contact Patsy Bliss
✉ The Quay, Exeter, Devon, EX2 4AN 🅿
☎ 01392 493501
🌐 www.exeterquayantiques.co.uk
Est. 1984 *Stock size* Large
No. of dealers 21
Stock Antiques, collectables, books, postcards, jewellery, tools, records, coins
Open Mon–Sun summer 10am–6pm winter 10am–5pm
Services Restaurant

McBains Antiques (LAPADA)
Contact Mr Martin McBain
✉ Exeter Airport Industrial Estate, Exeter, Devon, EX5 2BA 🅿
☎ 01392 446304 🖷 01392 446304
🖷 07831 381236
🅔 mcbain.exports@zetnet.co.uk
Est. 1980 *Stock size* Large
Stock Georgian, Victorian, Edwardian furniture, also selection of French and Continental furniture
Open Mon–Fri 9am–6pm Sat 10am–1pm closed Bank Holiday weekends

WEST COUNTRY
DEVON • EXMINSTER

Fairs Newark
Services Shipping, full container and export facility

⊞ Mortimers
Contact Ian Watson
✉ 87 Queen Street,
Exeter, Devon,
EX4 3RP 🅿
☎ 01392 279994
📱 07812 998896
Est. 1970 *Stock size* Large
Stock Antique jewellery, watches, clocks and silver
Open Mon–Sat 9.30am–5pm
Services Valuations, restoration

⊞ Pennies Antiques
Contact Mrs Clark
✉ 6 Marsh Green Road,
Marsh Barton, Exeter, Devon,
EX2 8NY 🅿
☎ 01392 276532
🌐 www.penniesantiques.co.uk
Est. 1979 *Stock size* Medium
Stock General antiques
Open Mon–Sun 10am–5pm

⌂ Phantique
Contact Mrs Bliss
✉ Unit 5–7, 47 The Quay,
Exeter, Devon,
EX2 4AN 🅿
☎ 01392 498995
🌐 www.phantique.co.uk
Est. 1996 *Stock size* Large
No. of dealers 9
Stock General antiques and collectables, prints, books, Torquay pottery, Dinky toys, costume jewellery, Oriental ceramics
Open Summer Mon–Fri 10.30am–5.30pm
Sat Sun 10.30am–6pm
winter 10.30am–5pm

⊞ The Quay Gallery Antiques Emporium
Contact Mark Davis
✉ 43 The Quay, Exeter, Devon,
EX2 4AN 🅿
☎ 01392 213283
Est. 1984 *Stock size* Large
Stock Fine mahogany and oak furniture, porcelain, silver, glass, paintings, prints, general antiques, antiquities, clocks, Art Deco, 20thC furniture
Open Mon–Sun 10am–5pm
Fairs West Point, Shepton Mallet, Cooper Fairs
Services Valuations

⊞ Tredantiques (LAPADA)
Contact Jon Tredant
✉ The Antiques Complex,
Exeter Airport Industrial Estate,
Exeter, Devon,
EX5 2BA 🅿
☎ 01392 447082
📱 07967 447082
🌐 www.tredantiques.com
Est. 1982 *Stock size* Large
Stock Good quality furniture and decorative items
Open Mon–Fri 9am–5.30pm
Sat 10am–1.30pm

⊞ Victoriana Antiques and Kents Jewellers
Contact Mr Kent
✉ 68 Sidwell Street,
Exeter, Devon,
EX4 6PH 🅿
☎ 01392 275204/275291
Est. 1945 *Stock size* Medium
Stock General antiques, porcelain, jewellery, silver
Open Mon Tues Thurs–Sat 9.30am–5pm
Services Jewellery, silver and porcelain restoration and repair

EXMINSTER

⊞ Tobys (SALVO)
Contact Mr P Norrish
✉ Station House,
Station Road, Exminster,
Exeter, Devon,
EX6 8DZ 🅿
☎ 01392 833499 📠 01392 833429
🌐 www.tobysreclamation.co.uk
Est. 1983 *Stock size* Large
Stock Architectural antiques, sanitary ware, fireplaces, reclaimed building materials
Open Mon–Fri 8.30am–5pm
Sat 9.30am–4.30pm Sun Bank Holidays 10.30am–4.30pm
Services House clearance, nationwide delivery

EXMOUTH

⊞ Browsers
Contact Mr or Mrs Spiller
✉ 1–2 The Strand,
Exmouth,
Devon,
EX8 1HL
☎ 01395 265010
Est. 1988 *Stock size* Large
Stock Collectables, toys, advertising, books, china
Open Mon–Sat 10.30am–6pm

⌖ Martin Spencer-Thomas (NAVA)
Contact Mr M Spencer-Thomas
✉ Bicton Street Auction Rooms,
Bicton Street, Exmouth, Devon,
EX8 2RT
☎ 01395 267403 📠 01395 222598
📧 martin@martinspencerthomas. co.uk
🌐 www.martinspencerthomas.co.uk
Est. 1984
Open Mon–Fri 9am–5pm
Sales Antiques sale Mon noon, viewing Thurs 9am–5pm
Fri 9am–5pm Sat 10am–4pm
Frequency 8 weeks
Catalogues Yes

HATHERLEIGH

⊞ Hatherleigh Antiques (BADA)
Contact Michael Dann
✉ 15 Bridge Street,
Hatherleigh, Devon,
EX20 3HU 🅿
☎ 01837 810159
Est. 1980 *Stock size* Large
Stock Gothic and Renaissance furniture
Open By appointment
Services Valuations, restoration

HELE

⊞ Fagins Antiques
Contact Jean Pearson
✉ Old Whiteways Cider Factory,
Hele, Exeter, Devon,
EX5 4PW 🅿
☎ 01392 882062 📠 01392 882194
📧 info@faginsantiques.com
🌐 www.faginsantiques.com
Est. 1978 *Stock size* Large
Stock Stripped pine, dark wood, general antiques, china, architectural antiques
Open Mon–Fri 9.15am–5pm
Sat 11am–5pm Bank Holidays 11am–4pm
Services Pine stripping

HOLSWORTHY

⊞ Baileys
Contact Sarah Stewart
✉ Bude Road,
Holsworthy, Devon,
EX22 6HZ 🅿
☎ 01409 254800
Est. 1996 *Stock size* Large
Stock Pine, mahogany and oak furniture, general antiques

Open Mon–Fri 10am–5pm
Sat 10am–4pm
Services Restoration, pine
stripping, upholstery

HONITON

⊞ **Antique Toys**
⊠ **38 High Street, Honiton,
Devon,
EX14 1PJ** 🅿
☎ 01404 41194
🄴 hattoys@hotmail.com
Est. 1976 *Stock size* Large
Stock Toys, teddies, dolls
Open Wed Fri Sat 10.30am–5pm
Services Dolls' hospital

⊞ **Asian Art.co.uk Ltd**
Contact The Manager
⊠ **Yarrow, 155 High Street,
Honiton, Devon,
EX14 1LJ** 🅿
☎ 01404 44399
🄴 james@asianart.co.uk
🅦 www.asianart.co.uk
Est. 1982 *Stock size* Large
Stock Oriental antiques,
furniture, kilims, carpets
Open By appointment

⊞ **Jane Barnes Antiques
and Interiors**
Contact Mrs Barnes
⊠ **35 High Street, Honiton,
Devon,
EX14 1PW** 🅿
☎ 01404 41712/861300
🄴 01404 861300
🅜 07971 328618
Est. 1985 *Stock size* Medium
Stock General antiques, Victorian
and Edwardian
Open Mon–Sat 10am–4pm
closed Wed or by appointment
Services Chairs copied to order

⊞ **Bell Antiques (LAPADA)**
Contact Nick Ball
⊠ **The Grove Antiques Centre,
High Street, Honiton, Devon,
EX14 1PW** 🅿
☎ 01404 890185 🄴 01404 890185
🄴 nick.ball2@tesco.net
Est. 1983 *Stock size* Medium
Stock Glass
Open Mon–Sat 10am–5pm
Services Valuations

⋏ **Bonhams**
⊠ **Dowell Street,
Honiton, Devon,
EX14 1LX**

☎ 01404 41872 🄴 01404 43137
🄴 honiton@bonhams.com
🅦 www.bonhams.com/honiton
Open Mon–Fri 9am–5.30pm
Sales Regional Saleroom.
Frequent sales. Regular sales
held in London and in our
salerooms across the country.
Free auction valuations;
insurance and probate valuations

⊞ **Roderick Butler (BADA)**
Contact Mr R Butler or
Mrs V Butler
⊠ **Marwood House,
Honiton, Devon,
EX14 1PY** 🅿
☎ 01404 42169
Est. 1948 *Stock size* Large
Stock 17th–18thC Regency
furniture, works of art and
metalwork
Open Mon–Sat 9.30am–5pm
August by appointment only
Services Restoration

⊞ **C J Button-Stephens
Antiques**
Contact Christopher Button-
Stephens
⊠ **59 High Street,
Honiton, Devon,
EX14 1PW**
☎ 01404 42640
Est. 1966 *Stock size* Small
Stock General antiques
Open Mon–Sat 10am–4pm

⊞ **Collectables**
Contact Mr Chris Guthrie
⊠ **134b High Street,
Honiton, Devon,
EX14 1JP** 🅿
☎ 01404 47024
🄴 chris@collectableshoniton.co.uk
🅦 www.collectableshoniton.co.uk
Est. 1995 *Stock size* Medium
Stock Annuals, breweriana,
cameras, ceramics, cigarette
cards, commemorative, militaria,
mugs, phonecards, postcards,
railwayana, toys, games
Open Mon–Sat 10am–4.45pm
closed Thurs

⋏ **Dreweatt Neate
Honiton Salerooms
(SOFAA)**
Contact Nigel Trevelyan
⊠ **205 High Street,
Honiton, Devon,
EX14 1LQ** 🅿
☎ 01404 42404 🄴 01404 46510

🄴 honiton@dnfa.com
🅦 www.dnfa.com
Est. 1759
Open Mon–Fri 9am–5pm
Sales Monthly fine art and
antiques Fri 10.30am, viewing
Mon–Thurs 9am–5pm Thurs Fri
9–10am. Twice yearly sales of
steam, model engineering, works
of art and railwayana. Twice
yearly sales of West Country
pictures
Catalogues Available on website

⊞ **Evans Emporium**
Contact Bob Evans
⊠ **140 High Street,
Honiton, Devon,
EX14 1JP** 🅿
☎ 01404 47869
Est. 2002 *Stock size* Medium
Stock Antiques, collectables,
music and instruments
Open Mon–Sat 10am–5pm

⊞ **Leigh Extence Antique
Clocks (BHI, LAPADA)**
Contact Mr Leigh Extence
⊠ **The Grove, 55 High Street,
Honiton, Devon,
EX14 1PW** 🅿
☎ 01404 549047
🅜 07967 802160
🄴 clocks@extence.co.uk
🅦 www.extence.co.uk
Est. 1981 *Stock size* Medium
Stock Antique clocks and
barometers
Open Mon–Sat 10am–5pm,
phone first for a personal
appointment
Services Valuations, restoration,
clock research, consultancy

🛋 **Fountain Antiques**
Contact Ann Barten or
Caroline Bushell
⊠ **132 High Street,
Honiton, Devon,
EX14 1JP** 🅿
☎ 01404 42074
🅜 07709 216282
🄴 phil@philannteeks.fsnet.co.uk
Est. 1988 *Stock size* Large
No. of dealers 23
Stock Linen, books, cutlery,
telephones, china, furniture,
lighting
Open Mon–Sat 9.30am–5.30pm

🛋 **The Globe Antiques &
Art Centre**
Contact A J Littler

163

✉ High Street, Honiton, Devon,
EX14 1LQ 🅿
☎ 01404 549372
📧 theglobe@honitonantiques.com
🌐 www.honitonantiques.com
Est. 2000 *Stock size* Large
No. of dealers 25
Stock Period furniture, Art Deco,
silver, porcelain, glass, lamps,
ephemera, collectables, bespoke
furniture, Oriental rugs, clocks,
jewellery, pictures
Open Mon–Sat 10am–5pm
Services Restoration, permanent
art exhibition

🏠 **The Grove Antique
Centre**
Contact Lesley Phillips
✉ 55 High Street,
Honiton, Devon,
EX14 1PW 🅿
☎ 01404 43377 📠 01404 43390
📱 07866 440408
📧 info@groveantiquescentre.com
🌐 www.groveantiquescentre.com
Est. 1998 *Stock size* Medium
No. of dealers 27
Stock Bears, silver, porcelain,
18th–20thC furniture,
collectables, paintings, clocks,
barometers, rugs, decorative
items, china, glassware, beds
Open Mon–Sat 10am–5pm
Services Shipping deliveries

⊞ **Hermitage Antiques**
Contact Ray Kirk
✉ 37 High Street,
Honiton, Devon,
EX14 1PW 🅿
☎ 01884 820944 📠 01404 42471
📱 07968 553172
📧 raykirk04@aol.com
Est. 1980 *Stock size* Large
Stock General antiques, furniture
Open Mon–Sat 10am–5pm
Sun 1–5pm
Services Valuations, buying and
selling

⊞ **High Street Books
(PBFA)**
Contact Geoff Tyson
✉ 150 High Street,
Honiton, Devon,
EX14 8JX 🅿
☎ 01404 44570 📠 01404 45570
📱 07930 171380
📧 tysonsbooks@hotmail.com
Est. 1982 *Stock size* Medium
Stock Antiquarian books, maps
and prints

Open Mon–Sat 10am–5pm
Fairs PBFA
Services Valuations

🏠 **Honiton Antique Centre**
Contact Nick Thompson
✉ Abingdon House,
136 High Street,
Honiton, Devon,
EX14 8JP 🅿
☎ 01404 42108
Est. 1982 *Stock size* Large
No. of dealers 20
Stock Early 17th–20thC furniture,
metalware, sporting, ceramics,
china, glass, paintings, militaria
Open Mon–Sat 9.30am–5.30pm
Sun 11am–4pm
Services Valuations, restoration,
delivery

⊞ **Honiton Old Book Shop
(PBFA, ABA)**
Contact Roger Collicott or Adele
✉ Felix House, 51 High Street,
Honiton, Devon,
EX14 1PW 🅿
☎ 01404 47180 📠 01404 47180
Est. 1978 *Stock size* Small
Stock Antiquarian, rare and
second-hand books, leather
bindings, antiquarian maps and
prints
Open Mon–Sat 10am–5pm
Fairs PBFA, Russell, ABA, Chelsea
Town Hall, Olympia (June)
Services Valuations

⊞ **Kingsway House
Antiques**
Contact Mrs M Peache
✉ 3 High Street, Honiton, Devon,
EX14 8PR 🅿
☎ 01404 46213
🌐 www.kingsway-antiques.com
Est. 1981 *Stock size* Medium
Stock Georgian furniture, china,
clocks
Open Mon–Sat 10am–5pm or by
appointment

⊞ **Merchant House
Antiques**
Contact Christian Giltsoff
✉ 19 High Street, Honiton,
Devon,
EX14 1PR 🅿
☎ 01404 42694
📧 merchant-house@btconnect.com
🌐 www.merchanthouseantiques.co.uk
Est. 1980 *Stock size* Large
Stock Fine furniture, general
antiques and collectables

Open Mon–Sat 10am–5pm
Services Valuations and interior
design

⊞ **Otter Antiques**
Contact Kate Skailes
✉ 69 High Street,
Honiton, Devon,
EX14 1PW
☎ 01404 42627 📠 01404 43337
📧 otterantiques@jspencer.co.uk
🌐 www.jspencer.co.uk
Est. 1979 *Stock size* Large
Stock Fine and antique silver,
silver plate
Open Mon–Sat 9.30am–5pm
Thurs 9.30am–1.30pm
Services Valuations, restoration,
silver plating, engraving

⊞ **Alexander Paul
Antiques**
Contact Dave Steele
✉ Fenny Bridges,
Honiton, Devon,
EX14 3BG 🅿
☎ 01404 850881
📱 07815 291470
📧 dave@alexanderpaulantiques.com
🌐 www.alexanderpaulantiques.com
Est. 2000 *Stock size* Medium
Stock French and English country
furniture, 1700s-1900, dining
tables a speciality
Open Mon–Fri 9am–5.30pm
Sat 10am–4pm
Fairs Shepton Mallet, Westpoint,
Bluilth Wells
Services Restoration

⊞ **Pilgrim Antiques
(LAPADA)**
Contact Mrs Mills
✉ 145 High Street,
Honiton, Devon,
EX14 1LJ 🅿
☎ 01404 41219 📠 01404 45317
📧 pilgriml@btconnect.com
🌐 www.pilgrimantiques.co.uk
Est. 1971 *Stock size* Large
Stock 17th–18thC English and
French oak and country
furniture, longcase clocks
Open Mon–Sat 9am–5.30pm
Services Valuations, shipping

⊞ **Plympton Antiques**
Contact Mr Button-Stephens
✉ 59 High Street,
Honiton, Devon,
EX14 8PW 🅿
☎ 01404 42640
Est. 1966 *Stock size* Medium

Stock Mostly mahogany furniture, copper, brass, porcelain
Open Mon–Sat 10am–4.30pm closed Thurs

⊞ Portland House Antiques and Collectables
Contact Mrs Gunilla Tanner
✉ 149 High Street, Honiton, Devon, EX14 1LJ 🅿
☎ 01404 45700
✉ jgtanner@btinternet.com
Est. 2002 **Stock size** Large
Stock Furniture, pictures, china, clocks, glass, Beswick, antique Honiton lace, kitchenware, all in a Georgian house fitted in period style
Open Mon–Sat 10am–5pm Sun in summer 11am–4pm
Services Restoration, upholstery, lacemaking demonstrations

⊞ Staffordshire Pride
Contact Sharon Racklyeft
✉ Abingdon House Antique Centre, 136 High Street, Honiton, Devon, EX14 1JP
☎ 01404 42108
📠 07958 453295
Est. 1975 **Stock size** Large
Stock 1790–1900 Staffordshire figures
Open Mon–Sun 9.30am–5.30pm

⊞ Jane Strickland & Daughters (LAPADA)
Contact Jane Strickland
✉ 71 High Street, Honiton, Devon, EX14 1PW 🅿
☎ 01404 44221 📠 01404 45309
✉ JSandDaughtersUK@aol.com
🌐 www.janestricklandand daughters.co.uk
Est. 1980 **Stock size** Medium
Stock 18th–19thC English and Continental furniture, upholstery, mirrors, lights, Aubussons, needlepoints
Open Mon–Sat 10am–5pm
Fairs Antiques and Decorative Fair Battersea
Services Re-upholstery

KINGSBRIDGE

⊞ Avon House Antiques
Contact Mr D Hayward
✉ 13 Church Street, Kingsbridge, Devon, TQ7 1BT 🅿
☎ 01548 853718
📠 07977 451223
✉ daymor@btopenworld.com
Est. 1969 **Stock size** Medium
Stock General antiques and collectables
Open Mon–Sat 10am–5pm Thurs Sat closed pm
Services Valuations, restoration

⊞ Salters Bookshelf 'The Bookshelf at the Top'
Contact Steve Salter
✉ 89 Fore Street, Kingsbridge, Devon, TQ7 1AB 🅿
☎ 01548 856176/857503
📠 01548 857503
Est. 1997 **Stock size** Medium
Stock Old picture postcards, postal history, postal stationery, accessories, ephemera
Open Mon–Sat 9am–5.30pm summer Sun 10am–2.30pm
Services Picture framing, booksearch agents

LYNTON

⊞ Farthings
Contact Jane or Lucy Farthing
✉ Church Hill House, Church Hill, Lynton, Devon, EX35 6HY 🅿
☎ 01598 753744 📠 01598 753483
✉ jane@farthings1.freeserve.co.uk
🌐 www.farthings.antiques.com
Est. 1984 **Stock size** Large
Stock Antiques, Oriental, Vienna bronzes, bronzes, 18th–20thC sporting art, Moorcroft, Mulberry bears, collectables, crafts
Open Mon–Sun 10am–4.30pm
Fairs Westpoint, Antiques for Everyone
Services Search service, delivery

⊞ Wood's Antiques
Contact Mr or Mrs Wood
✉ 29a Lee Road, Lynton, Devon, EX35 6BS 🅿
☎ 01598 752722
Est. 1995 **Stock size** Medium
Stock Antiques, collectables, furniture, clocks
Open Mon–Sun 9am–6pm closed Thurs

MERTON

⊞ Barometer World
Contact Philip Collins
✉ Quicksilver Barn, Merton, Okehampton, Devon, EX20 3DS 🅿
☎ 01805 603443 📠 01805 603344
✉ enquiries@barometerworld.co.uk
🌐 www.antiquebarometers.org.uk
Est. 1979 **Stock size** Large
Stock 1780–1930s barometers
Open Tues–Sat 9am–5pm
Services Valuations, restoration

MODBURY

⊞ Collectors Choice
Contact Allan Jenkins
✉ 27 Church Street, Modbury, Ivybridge, Devon, PL21 0QR 🅿
☎ 01548 831111
📠 07884 365361
Est. 1994 **Stock size** Medium
Stock Small furniture, ceramics, Bakelite, radios, general antiques
Open Mon–Sat 10am–5.30pm
Services Valuations, clock restoration

⊞ Wild Goose Antiques
Contact Kay or Ty Freeman
✉ 34 Church Street, Modbury, Devon, PL21 0QR 🅿
☎ 01548 830715
✉ wildgooseantiques@tiscali.co.uk
Est. 2000 **Stock size** Medium
Stock Antique pine, country furniture, decorative items, brass, iron beds
Open Mon–Sat 10am–5.30pm

MONKTON

⊞ Pugh's Antiques
Contact Guy Garner
✉ Pugh's Farm, Monkton, Honiton, Devon, EX14 9QH 🅿
☎ 01404 42860 📠 01404 47792
✉ sales@pughsantiques.com
🌐 www.pughsantiques.com
Est. 1987 **Stock size** Large
Stock Antiques, French beds, bedroom furniture
Open Mon–Sat 9am–5.30pm

NEWTON ABBOT

⊞ The Attic
Contact Mr Gillman
✉ 9 Union Street,

WEST COUNTRY

**Newton Abbot, Devon,
TQ12 2JX** 🅿
☎ 01626 355124
Est. 1976 *Stock size* Large
Stock General antiques and small
furniture
Open Tues–Sat 9am–5.30pm
closed Thurs
Services Valuations

🔨 Michael J Bowman
Contact Mr M Bowman
✉ 6 Haccombe House,
Netherton, Newton Abbot,
Devon,
TQ12 4SJ 🅿
☎ 01626 872890 ✆ 01626 872890
📱 07889 650 202
🌐 www.ukauctioneers.co.uk
Est. 1986
Open By appointment
Sales 7 antiques and effects sales
per annum Sat 2pm, viewing Fri
4.30–8.30pm. Held at Chudleigh
Town Hall, also free valuations
Mon 2–5pm at same venue
Catalogues Yes

🏛 St Leonard's Antiques and Craft Centre
Contact Mr Derick Wilson
✉ St Leonard's, Wolborough
Street, Newton Abbot, Devon,
TQ12 1JQ 🅿
☎ 01626 335666 ✆ 01626 335666
📱 07786 511367
Est. 1999 *Stock size* Large
No. of dealers 32
Stock General antiques,
furniture, jewellery
Open Mon–Sun 10am–4.30pm

⊞ Tobys (SALVO)
Contact Mr P Norrish
✉ Brunel Road, Newton Abbot,
Devon, TQ12 4PB 🅿
☎ 01626 351767 ✆ 01626 336788
🌐 www.tobysreclamation.co.uk
Est. 1985 *Stock size* Large
Stock General antiques,
reclaimed material
Open Mon–Fri 8.30am–5pm
Sat 9.30am–5pm
Sun 10.30am–4.30pm
Fairs Exeter Ideal Home, Devon
County Show
Services House clearance

OKEHAMPTON

⊞ Past & Present
Contact P Roche
✉ 14 & 15 The Victorian Arcade,

**Okehampton, Devon,
EX20 1EX**
☎ 01837 659238
Est. 1999 *Stock size* Medium
Stock General antiques,
collectables
Open Mon–Sat 10am–4pm
closed Wed

⊞ St James Street Antiques
Contact Jo Catling
✉ 1 St James Street,
Okehampton, Devon,
EX20 1DW 🅿
☎ 01837 659623
📠 07775 853583
Est. 2001 *Stock size* Medium
Stock General antiques,
furniture, Beswick china a
speciality
Open Mon–Sat 10am–4.30pm
Fairs Tavistock, Cornwall
Services Valuations

PAIGNTON

⊞ The Pocket Bookshop
Contact Mr L Corrall
✉ 159 Winner Street,
Paignton, Devon,
TQ3 3BP 🅿
☎ 01803 529804
Est. 1985 *Stock size* Large
Stock Antiquarian, second-hand
and out-of-print books
Open Summer Mon–Sat
10.30am–5.30pm winter
Wed–Sat 10.30am–5.30pm

PLYMOUTH

⊞ Anita's Antiques
Contact Anita Walker
✉ 27 New Street,
Plymouth, Devon,
PL1 2NB 🅿
☎ 01752 269622
Est. 1984 *Stock size* Large
Stock Furniture, silver, china,
jewellery, lighting, glass, clocks,
barometers, general antiques
Open Mon–Sat 9am–5pm
Services Valuations

⊞ Annterior Antiques
Contact Anne Tregenza
✉ 22 Molesworth Road, Stoke,
Plymouth, Devon,
PL1 5LZ 🅿
☎ 01752 558277 ✆ 01752 564471
📱 07815 618659
📧 sales@annterior.co.uk

🌐 www.annterior.co.uk
Est. 1984 *Stock size* Medium
Stock 19th and 20thC country
and pine furniture, selected
hardwood, painted and
decorative furniture and
accessories
Open Mon–Fri 9.30am–5.30pm
Sat 10am–5pm closed Tues
Services Restoration, finding
service

🏛 Barbican Antique Centre
Contact Clive Cooper
✉ 82–84 Vauxhall Street,
Plymouth, Devon,
PL4 0EX 🅿
☎ 01752 201752
Est. 1971 *Stock size* Large
No. of dealers 60
Stock Silver, jewellery, porcelain,
glass, pictures, furniture,
collectables
Open Mon–Sat 9.30am–5pm
Sun, Bank Holidays 10am–4pm

⊞ Grosvenor Chambers Restoration
Contact Robert Miller
✉ 180 Rendle Street, Plymouth,
Devon, PL1 1UQ 🅿
☎ 01752 257544
📧 robbie@grosvenor-restoration.
co.uk
Est. 1989 *Stock size* Large
Stock General architectural
antiques, pine furniture,
lighting, etc
Open Mon–Sat 9am–5.30pm
Services Valuations, restoration,
wood and metal stripping

🏛 New Street Antique and Craft Centre
Contact Mrs Cuthill
✉ 27 New Street, Barbican,
Plymouth, Devon,
PL1 2NB 🅿
☎ 01752 256265 ✆ 01752 256265
Est. 1980 *Stock size* Large
No. of dealers 11
Stock General collectables,
books, stamps, postcards, craft
materials, locally made crafts,
militaria
Open Mon–Sat Sun during
holiday season 10am–5pm
Services café

⊞ Parade Antiques
Contact Mr Cabello
✉ 27 New Street, The Barbican,

Plymouth, Devon,
PL1 2NB 🅿
☎ 01752 221443
⓪ 07765 408 063
✉ paradeantiques@hotmail.com
Est. 1999 *Stock size* Large
Stock General antiques, militaria
Open Mon–Sun 10am–5pm
Fairs Yates, Holsworthy

⚒ G S Shobrook and Co incorporating Fieldens (RICS)
Contact Roger Shobrook
⊠ **20 Western Approach, Plymouth, Devon, PL1 1TG** 🅿
☎ 01752 663341 ⓮ 01752 255157
✉ info@shobrook.co.uk
ⓦ www.shobrook.co.uk
Est. 1920
Open Mon–Fri 9am–5pm Sat 9–11am
Sales Monthly antiques and collectables sale Wed 1.30pm, viewing Tues 9am–5pm or by appointment. Weekly general household sale Wed 10am, viewing Tues 9am–5pm
Catalogues Yes

⊞ Michael Wood Fine Art
Contact Mr Michael Wood
⊠ **The Gallery, 17 The Parade, The Barbican, Plymouth, Devon, PL1 2JW** 🅿
☎ 01752 225533 ⓮ 01752 225770
⓪ 07764 377899
✉ michael@michaelwoodfineart.com
ⓦ www.michaelwoodfineart.com
Est. 1967 *Stock size* Large
Stock 1850–present day paintings, watercolours, original prints, sculptures, art pottery, studio glass
Open Tues–Sat 10am–5pm
Fairs NEC
Services Valuations, picture presentation and conservation

PLYMPTON

⚒ Eldreds Auctioneers and Valuers
Contact Anthony Eldred
⊠ **13–15 Ridge Park Road, Plympton, Plymouth, Devon, PL7 2BS** 🅿
☎ 01752 340066 ⓮ 01752 341760
✉ enquiries@eldreds.net
ⓦ www.eldreds.net
Est. 1992
Open Mon–Fri 8.30am–5pm

Sales Fortnightly 19th–20thC sales, 6–8 weekly antiques and specialist sales, telephone for details
Catalogues Yes

SEATON

⊞ Etcetera Antiques
Contact Mrs Rymer
⊠ **12 Beer Road, Seaton, Devon, EX12 2PA** 🅿
☎ 01297 21965
⓪ 07780 840507
Est. 1965 *Stock size* Large
Stock Furniture and small items
Trade only Yes
Open By appointment
Services Restoration, house clearances, shipping

🏠 The Green Dragon
Contact Mrs Denning
⊠ **4 Marine Crescent, Seaton, Devon, EX12 2QN** 🅿
☎ 01297 22039
ⓦ www.greendragonantiques.com
Est. 1991 *Stock size* Large
No. of dealers 47
Stock General antiques
Open Tues–Sun 10am–5pm

SIDMOUTH

⊞ The Lantern Shop Gallery
Contact Julia Creeke
⊠ **5 New Street, Sidmouth, Devon, EX10 8AP**
☎ 01395 578462 ⓮ 01395 578462
Est. 1977 *Stock size* Medium
Stock Porcelain, watercolours, oils
Open Mon–Sat 9.45am–4.45pm

⊞ The Old Curiosity Shop
Contact Mr or Mrs T Koch
⊠ **Old Fore Street, Sidmouth, Devon, EX10 8LP**
☎ 01395 515299
Est. 1995 *Stock size* Large
Stock General collectables
Open Mon–Sat 10am–5pm Sun 11am–5pm

🏠 Sidmouth Collectables
Contact Mr R Hair
⊠ **Devonshire House, All Saints Road, Sidmouth, Devon, EX10 8ES** 🅿

☎ 01395 512588
ⓦ www.sidmouthcolletables.com
Est. 1994 *Stock size* Medium
No. of dealers 10
Stock General antiques, antiquarian books
Open Mon–Sat 10am–5pm summer Sun 12.30–4pm
Services House clearance

⊞ The Vintage Toy & Train Shop
Contact David Salisbury
⊠ **Devonshire House, All Saints Road, Sidmouth, Devon, EX10 8ES** 🅿
☎ 01395 512588 ⓮ 01395 513399
Est. 1982 *Stock size* Medium
Stock Hornby Gauge O and Dublo trains, original Meccano, Dinky toys
Open Mon–Sat 10am–5pm

⊞ Sue Wilde
Contact Sue Wilde
⊠ **Ashcroft, Milford Road, Sidmouth, Devon, EX10 8DR** 🅿
☎ 01395 577966 ⓮ 01395 577988
✉ compacts@wildewear.co.uk
ⓦ www.wildewear.co.uk
Est. 1980 *Stock size* Medium
Stock Vintage fashion accessories, Art Deco period, beaded bags
Open By appointment

SOUTH BRENT

⊞ Patrick Pollak Rare Books (ABA)
Contact Patrick Pollak
⊠ **Moorview, Plymouth Road, South Brent, Devon, TQ10 9HT** 🅿
☎ 01364 73457 ⓮ 01364 649126
✉ patrick@rarevols.co.uk
ⓦ www.rarevols.co.uk
Est. 1973 *Stock size* Large
Stock Rare, antiquarian scholarly books
Open By appointment
Services Mail order

SOUTH MOLTON

⊞ C R Boumphrey
Contact Mr Boumphrey
⊠ **Finehay, Mariansleigh, South Molton, Devon, EX36 4LL** 🅿
☎ 01769 550419
✉ boumph@fhsinternet.com

Est. 1969 *Stock size* Medium
Stock 16th–18thC furniture
Open By appointment
Services Finds and orders stock

⊞ The Dragon
Contact Gerald Harris or
Jenny Aker
✉ 77 South Street,
South Molton, Devon,
EX36 4AG 🅿
☎ 01769 572374
📱 07712 079818
📧 snapdragonantiques@hotmail.com
🌐 www.nd1.co.uk/smtic/dragon.htm
Est. 1998 *Stock size* Medium
Stock Pine and country furniture,
books, farming bygones,
kitchenware
Open Mon–Sat 9.30am–5pm

⊞ Snapdragon
Contact Gerald Harris or
Jenny Aker
✉ 80 South Street,
South Molton, Devon,
EX36 4AG 🅿
☎ 01769 572374
📱 07712 079818
📧 snapdragonantiques@hotmail.com
🌐 www.snapdragondevon.co.uk.
Est. 1998 *Stock size* Medium
Stock Pine and country furniture,
roll-top baths, fireplaces,
agricultural bygones
Open Mon–Sat 9.30am–5pm

⊞ R M Young Bookseller
Contact Mr M Young
✉ 17 Broad Street,
South Molton, Devon,
EX36 3AQ 🅿
☎ 01769 573350
📧 rdyoung@lineone.net
Est. 1985 *Stock size* Large
Stock Antiquarian, second-hand,
rare and out-of-print books,
countryside topics a speciality
Open Mon–Sat 10am–5pm
Services Book search, book
binding

TAVISTOCK

⊞ Tavistock Furniture Store
Contact Shelley Barlow
✉ 142–146 Plymouth Road,
Tavistock, Devon,
PL19 9DS 🅿
☎ 01822 610274
📱 07833 925663
📧 shelley@tfs-doa.com

Est. 1999 *Stock size* Large
Stock English and French country
furniture and decorative items
Open Mon–Sat 10am–5pm Sun
by appointment

⚒ Ward and Chowen Auction Rooms
Contact Mrs Pat Smith
✉ Market Road,
Tavistock, Devon,
PL19 0BW 🅿
☎ 01822 612603 📠 01822 617311
📧 tavistockauctionrooms@ward
chowen.co.uk
Est. 1830
Open Mon–Fri 8.30am–4.30pm
Sales Quarterly antiques sale
Tues, viewing Mon 10am–6pm.
Fortnightly general household
sale Thurs 10am (no catalogue),
viewing Wed 1–6pm
Catalogues Yes

TEDBURN ST MARY

⊞ A E Wakeman and Sons Ltd
Contact Mr Wakeman
✉ Newhouse Farm,
Tedburn St Mary,
Exeter, Devon,
EX6 6AL 🅿
☎ 01647 61254 📠 01647 61254
📱 07836 284765/636525
Est. 1971 *Stock size* Medium
Stock 19thC furniture
Trade only Yes
Open Mon–Fri 8.30am–5.30pm or
by appointment
Fairs Newark

TEIGNMOUTH

⊞ Extence Antiques
Contact Mr T E or L E Extence
✉ 2 Wellington Street,
Teignmouth, Devon,
TQ14 8HH
☎ 01626 773353 📠 01626 777789
Est. 1928 *Stock size* Large
Stock Jewellery, silver and objets
d'art
Open Tues–Sat 10am–5pm
Services Repair and restoration
of jewellery and silver

⊞ Timepiece Antiques
Contact Clive or Willow Pople
✉ 125 Bitton Park Road,
Teignmouth, Devon,
TQ14 9BZ 🅿
☎ 01626 770275

Est. 1988 *Stock size* Medium
Stock Country, mahogany and
oak furniture, longcase clocks,
brass, copper, metalware,
gramophones, general antiques
Open Tues–Sat 9.30am–5.30pm

TIVERTON

⊞ Judith Christie
Contact Judith Christie
✉ 42 Gold Street, Tiverton,
Devon,
EX16 6PX 🅿
☎ 01884 258795
📱 07770 741885
Est. 1974 *Stock size* Medium
Stock General antiques, interiors
and decorative arts
Open Tues Fri Sat 10.30am–5pm

⊞ Guy Dennler Antiques & Interiors
Contact Mr G Dennler
✉ The Old Rectory Stables,
Rackenford, Tiverton, Devon,
EX16 8ED 🅿
☎ 01884 881250 📠 01884 881552
📱 07774 181071
📧 guydennler@btconnect.com
Est. 1979 *Stock size* Medium
Stock 18th–19thC English
furniture, decorative items
Open Mon–Fri 10am–4pm or by
appointment
Fairs Battersea Decorative Fair
Services Restoration, interior
design and decoration

⊞ Magnolia House Antiques
Contact Paul or Sarah
✉ Morley House, Angel Hill,
Tiverton, Devon,
EX16 6PE
☎ 01844 252649
Est. 1983 *Stock size* Large
Stock Victorian furniture
Open Mon–Sat 10am–6pm
Services Restoration

TOPSHAM

⊞ Bizarre!
Contact Alexandra Fairweather
✉ The Quay Antiques Centre,
The Quay, Topsham, Exeter,
Devon,
EX3 0JA 🅿
☎ 01392 874006
📧 office@quayantiques.com
🌐 www.quayantiques.com
Est. 1991 *Stock size* Large

Stock Vintage clothes, textiles and accessories
Open Mon–Sun 10am–5pm
Fairs Hammersmith Textile and Costume, Hyson Textile Fair

⊞ **Charis**
Contact Chris Evans
⊠ **The Quay Antiques Centre, The Quay, Topsham, Exeter, Devon,
EX3 0JA** 🅿
☎ 01392 874006
🄴 office@quayantiques.com
🅦 www.quayantiques.com
Est. 1993 *Stock size* Medium
Stock Old glass, crystal, china, jewellery
Open Mon–Sun 10am–5pm

⊞ **Gudrun Doel**
Contact Gudrun (Goody) Doel
⊠ **The Quay Antiques Centre, The Quay, Topsham, Exeter, Devon,
EX3 0JA** 🅿
☎ 01392 874006
🄴 office@quayantiques.com
🅦 www.quayantiques.com
Est. 1993 *Stock size* Medium
Stock Decorative items, porcelain, glass, pictures, silver, textiles
Open Mon–Sun 10am–5pm
Fairs Livestock Centre, Exeter

⊞ **Domani Antique & Contemporary**
Contact Caro Brewster or Jonathan Cull
⊠ **48 Fore Street, Topsham, Devon,
EX3 0HY**
☎ 01392 877899 🄵 01392 877899
🄴 shop@domani-topsham.com
🅦 www.domani-topsham.com
Est. 2003 *Stock size* Small
Stock Unusual antique and contemporary furniture, contemporary art, ceramics and glass
Open Tues–Sat 10am–5.30pm or by appointment
Fairs Olympia (Cull Antiques)

⊞ **Rob Gee**
Contact Rob Gee
⊠ **The Quay Antiques Centre, The Quay, Topsham, Exeter, Devon,
EX3 0JA** 🅿
☎ 01392 874006
🄴 office@quayantiques.com

🅦 www.quayantiques.com
Est. 1993
Stock Pot lids, Prattware, chemist items, steam and toy locomotives
Open Mon–Sun 10am–5pm

⊞ **Sheila Hyson**
Contact Sheila Hyson
⊠ **The Quay Antiques Centre, The Quay, Topsham, Exeter, Devon,
EX3 0JA** 🅿
☎ 01392 874006
🄼 07798 808701
🄴 shyson@freenetname.co.uk
🅦 www.quayantiques.com
Est. 1993 *Stock size* Large
Stock Kitchenware
Open Mon–Sun 10am–5pm
Fairs Hyson Fairs, Deco 1950s and 1960s Fair, Exmouth Fair

⊞ **Robin Jeffreys**
Contact Robin Jeffreys
⊠ **The Quay Antiques Centre, The Quay, Topsham, Exeter, Devon,
EX3 0JA** 🅿
☎ 01392 874006
🄴 office@quayantiques.com
🅦 www.quayantiques.com
Est. 1966 *Stock size* Large
Stock Ceramics and Oriental ware
Open Mon–Sun 10am–4pm
Fairs Hyson Pottery and Glass Fair, Chalford Antiques and Collectors' Fair

⊞ **Bart and Julie Lemmy**
Contact Bart or Julie Lemmy
⊠ **The Quay Antiques Centre, The Quay, Topsham, Exeter, Devon,
EX3 0JA** 🅿
☎ 01392 874006
🄼 07809 172468
🄴 rosettibrides@btinternet.com
🅦 www.quayantiques.com
Est. 1993
Stock Royal Doulton figurines
Open Mon–Sun 10am–5pm
Services Shipping furniture

⊞ **Betty Lovell**
Contact Betty Lovell
⊠ **The Quay Antiques Centre, The Quay, Topsham, Exeter, Devon,
EX3 0JA** 🅿
☎ 01392 874006
🄴 office@quayantiques.com
🅦 www.quayantiques.com

Est. 1993 *Stock size* Medium
Stock Linen and lace
Open Mon–Sun 10am–5pm
Fairs Hysons Textile Fair

⊞ **D Lovell**
Contact D Lovell
⊠ **The Quay Antiques Centre, The Quay, Topsham, Exeter, Devon,
EX3 0JA** 🅿
☎ 01392 874006
🄴 office@quayantiques.com
🅦 www.quayantiques.com
Est. 1986 *Stock size* Medium
Stock Silver and silver plate
Open Mon–Sun 10am–5pm

⊞ **Mere Antiques (LAPADA)**
Contact Mrs M Hawkins or Mrs M Reed
⊠ **13 Fore Street, Topsham, Exeter, Devon,
EX3 0HF** 🅿
☎ 01392 670373
🄼 07957 867751
🄴 bob@ntlbusiness.com
🅦 info@mereantiques.com
Est. 1986 *Stock size* Medium
Stock 18th–19thC porcelain, Japanese Satsuma ware, period furniture, paintings, silver
Open Mon–Sat 9.30am–5.30pm
Fairs NEC (LAPADA and Antiques for Everyone), Olympia
Services Appraisals, deliveries

⊞ **Number 38**
Contact Stuart Westaway
⊠ **The Quay Antiques Centre, The Quay, Topsham, Exeter, Devon,
EX3 0JA** 🅿
☎ 01392 874006
🄴 office@quayantiques.com
🅦 www.quayantiques.com
Est. 1993 *Stock size* Medium
Stock Restored period lighting
Open Mon–Sun 10am–5pm
Services Restoration

⊞ **Old Tools Feel Better!**
Contact Barry Cook
⊠ **The Quay Antiques Centre, The Quay, Topsham, Exeter, Devon,
EX3 0JA** 🅿
☎ 01392 874006 🄵 01392 874006
🄼 07799 054565
🄴 office@quayantiques.com
🅦 www.quayantiques.com
Est. 1993 *Stock size* Large

WEST COUNTRY

169

WEST COUNTRY
DEVON • TORQUAY

Stock Antique and collectable quality used tools
Open Mon–Sun 10am–5pm

⊞ Pennies Antiques
Contact Mrs Clark
✉ 40 Fore Street, Topsham, Exeter, Devon,
EX3 0HU 🄿
☎ 01392 877020
Ⓦ www.penniesantiques.co.uk
Est. 1979 *Stock size* Medium
Stock General antiques
Open Mon–Sat 10am–5pm
Sun 11am–4pm

⌂ The Quay Centre
Contact Beverley Cook
✉ The Quay,
Topsham,
Exeter, Devon,
EX3 0JA 🄿
☎ 01392 874006
Ⓔ office@quayantiques.com
Ⓦ www.quayantiques.com
Est. 1993 *Stock size* Large
No. of dealers 80
Stock Furniture, collectables, ephemera, Exeter silver, Torquay ware, studio pottery, jewellery, tools, period lighting, textiles
Open Mon–Sun 10am–5pm
Services Cards accepted, online buying, shipping advice

⊞ Nicky Russell
Contact Nicky Russell
✉ The Quay Antiques Centre, The Quay, Topsham, Exeter, Devon,
EX3 0JA 🄿
☎ 01392 874006
Ⓔ office@quayantiques.com
Ⓦ www.quayantiques.com
Est. 1993 *Stock size* Medium
Stock Decorative china, character jugs, Toby jugs
Open Mon–Sun 10am–5pm

⊞ Joel Segal Books
Contact Mrs Neal
✉ 27 Fore Street, Topsham, Exeter, Devon,
EX3 0HD 🄿
☎ 01392 877895
Ⓔ lily@segalbooks.com
Ⓦ www.segalbooks.com
Est. 1993 *Stock size* Large
Stock Antiquarian, rare and second-hand books
Open Mon–Sat 10.30am–1pm, 2–5pm

⊞ The Venerable Bead
Contact Daphne King
✉ The Quay Antiques Centre, The Quay, Topsham, Exeter, Devon,
EX3 0JA 🄿
☎ 01392 874006
Ⓜ 07787 561681
Ⓔ office@quayantiques.com
Ⓦ www.quayantiques.com
Est. 1993 *Stock size* Large
Stock Costume jewellery
Open Mon–Sun 10am–4pm
Fairs Westpoint, Shepton Mallet

⊞ S Vye
Contact S Vye
✉ The Quay Antiques Centre, The Quay, Topsham, Exeter, Devon,
EX3 0JA 🄿
☎ 01392 874006
Ⓔ s.vye@virgin.net
Ⓦ www.quayantiques.com
Est. 1993 *Stock size* Medium
Stock Furniture, ceramics, paintings, samplers
Open Mon–Sun 10am–5pm

⊞ Yesteryears
Contact Paul Gowing
✉ The Quay Antiques Centre, The Quay, Topsham, Exeter, Devon,
EX3 0JA 🄿
☎ 01392 874006
Ⓔ office@quayantiques.com
Ⓦ www.quayantiques.com
Est. 1993 *Stock size* Medium
Stock Furniture, including compactums, wardrobes, dressing tables
Open Mon–Sun 10am–5pm

TORQUAY

⊞ About Time Antiques (BWCG)
Contact David Jacobs
✉ 96 Belgrave Road, Torquay, Devon,
TQ2 5HZ 🄿
☎ 01803 200680 Ⓕ 01803 200680
Ⓜ 07771 580509
Ⓔ clockrepairs@hotmail.com
Ⓦ www.torbay.antiques.co.uk
Est. 1990 *Stock size* Medium
Stock Antique clocks, jewellery, gold, silver, glass, lighting, porcelain
Open Mon–Sat 9am–5pm
Services Longcase clock restoration

⊞ The Old Cop Shop
Contact Mr L Rolfe or Brian Harper
✉ Castle Lane, Torquay, Devon, TQ1 3AN 🄿
☎ 01803 294484
Est. 1974 *Stock size* Large
Stock General antiques
Open Mon–Sat 9am–5pm
Services Valuations

⊞ Tobys (SALVO)
Contact Mr P Norrish
✉ Newton Road, Torquay, Devon,
TQ2 5DD 🄿
☎ 01803 212222 Ⓕ 01803 200523
Ⓦ www.tobysreclamation.co.uk
Est. 1985 *Stock size* Large
Stock General antiques, furniture, architectural antiques, gifts
Open Mon–Sat 8.30am–5pm Sun Bank Holidays 10.30am–4.30pm
Fairs Exeter Ideal Home, Devon County Show
Services House clearance, nationwide delivery

⊞ Upstairs Downstairs
Contact Mrs Linda Nicholls
✉ 53 Fore Street, St Marychurch, Torquay, Devon,
TQ1 4PR 🄿
☎ 01803 313010 Ⓕ 01803 406777
Est. 1997 *Stock size* Large
Stock Antique and modern jewellery, glass, rocking horses, paintings, china, furniture
Open Mon–Sat 9am–5pm
Services Valuations, french polishing, upholstery

⊞ West Country Old Books (PBFA)
Contact Mr D Neil
✉ 215 Babbacombe Road, Torquay, Devon,
TQ1 3SX 🄿
☎ 01803 322712
Est. 1989 *Stock size* Small
Stock Antiquarian and good quality second-hand books, specializing in topography, and literature
Open By appointment only
Fairs PBFA
Services Valuations and books bought

⋗ West of England Auctions
Contact Mr Warren Hunt

✉ 3 Warren Road, Torquay,
Devon,
TQ2 5TQ 🅿
☎ 01803 211266 ☻ 01803 212286
🌐 www.west-of-england-auctions.com
Est. 1949
Open Mon–Fri 9am–1pm 2–5pm
Sales Sales of antiques, silver, jewellery Mon 10am, viewing Sat 9am–noon Sun 1–5pm Mon 9–10am prior to sale
Frequency Fortnightly
Catalogues yes

TOTNES

⊞ Bogan House Antiques
Contact Mr M Mitchell
✉ 43 High Street,
Totnes, Devon,
TQ9 5NP 🅿
☎ 01803 862075
Est. 1989 *Stock size* Large
Stock Silver, wood, brass, glass, Japanese woodblock prints
Open Tues noon–4.30pm Fri 10am–4.30pm Sat 10.30am–4.30pm

⌂ The Exchange
Contact John Caley
✉ 76 High Street,
Totnes, Devon,
TQ9 5SN
☎ 01803 866836
☻ bookworm1700@yahoo.com
Est. 1996 *Stock size* Large
No. of dealers 7
Stock Books, printed ephemera, tools, brass, china, stamps, toys, records, musical instruments, postcards, second-hand videos, spiritual items, music books
Open Mon–Sat 10am–5pm 5.30pm in summer
Services Valuations, restoration of instruments

⊞ Fine Pine Antiques
Contact Nick or Linda Gildersleve
✉ Woodland Road,
Harbertonford, Totnes, Devon,
TQ9 7SU 🅿
☎ 01803 732465
☻ info@fine-pine-antiques.co.uk
🌐 www.fine-pine-antiques.co.uk
Est. 1973 *Stock size* Medium
Stock Pine and country antiques
Open Mon–Sat 9.30am–5pm Sun 11am–4pm
Services Valuations, restoration and stripping

⊞ Pandora's Box
Contact Sarah Mimpriss
✉ 5b High Street,
Totnes, Devon,
TQ9 5NN 🅿
☎ 01803 867799
Est. 1999 *Stock size* Small
Stock Georgian–Edwardian furniture, mirrors, china, collectables
Open Fri Sat 10.30am–4pm

⊞ Pedlar's Pack Books
Contact Brenda Greysmith or Andy Collins
✉ 4 The Plains, Totnes, Devon,
TQ9 5DR 🅿
☎ 01803 866423
☻ books@thepedlarspack.co.uk
Est. 1983 *Stock size* Medium
Stock Antiquarian, second-hand, rare and modern books, art and history books a speciality
Open Mon–Sat 9am–5pm
Services Valuations, book search

TYTHERLEIGH

⌂ The Trading Post Antique Centre
Contact Mr M Remfry
✉ Main Road, Tytherleigh, Axminster, Devon,
EX13 7BE 🅿
☎ 01460 221330
Est. 1987 *Stock size* Large
No. of dealers 30
Stock General antiques, furniture, collectables
Open Mon–Sat 10am–4.30pm Sun 10am–4pm closed Tues
Services Valuations, restoration, clock repairs, repair of cane chairs, house clearance

UFFCULME

⊞ Country Antiques & Interiors
Contact Mr M C Mead
✉ The Old Brewery, High Street, Uffculme, Cullompton, Devon,
EX15 3AB 🅿
☎ 01884 841770 ☻ 01884 841770
📱 07768 328433
☻ mike@englishcountryantiques.co.uk
🌐 www.englishcountryantiques.co.uk
Est. 1994 *Stock size* Medium
Stock Country furniture, decorative items, contemporary
Open By appointment
Services Shipping arranged

YEALMPTON

⊞ Carnegie Paintings & Clocks
Contact Chris Carnegie
✉ 15 Fore Street, Yealmpton, Plymouth, Devon,
PL8 2JN 🅿
☎ 01752 881170
🌐 www.paintingsandclocks.com
Est. 1996 *Stock size* Medium
Stock Pre-1940s paintings, clocks, barometers
Open Thurs–Sat 10am–5.30pm
Services Restoration

DORSET

BERE REGIS

⊞ Dorset Reclamation (SALVO)
Contact David Kirk
✉ Cow Drove, Bere Regis, Wareham, Dorset,
BH20 7JZ 🅿
☎ 01929 472200 ☻ 01929 472292
☻ info@dorsetreclamation.co.uk
🌐 www.dorsetreclamation.co.uk
Est. 1992 *Stock size* Large
Stock Decorative architectural and garden antiques including flagstones, flooring, bathrooms, fittings, radiators, chimney pieces, traditional building materials, reconditioned Aga cookers
Open Mon–Fri 8am–5pm Sat 9am–4pm
Services Delivery

⊞ Legg of Dorchester
Contact Mrs H Legg
✉ The Old Mill, West Street, Bere Regis, Wareham, Dorset,
BH20 7HS 🅿
☎ 01929 472051
☻ jerry@leggofdorchester.co.uk
🌐 www.leggofdorchester.co.uk
Est. 1930 *Stock size* Large
Stock General, mostly furniture
Open Mon–Sat telephone to check times

BLANDFORD FORUM

⊞ Milton Antiques & Restoration
Contact Nigel Church
✉ Bere's Yard, Market Place, Blandford Forum, Dorset,
DT11 7HV 🅿
☎ 01258 450100

WEST COUNTRY
DORSET • BOURNEMOUTH

Est. 1989 *Stock size* Medium
Stock Period furniture
Open Mon–Sat 9am–5pm
Services Restoration

♪ Robert A Warry Auctioneer (FNAVA)
Contact Mr R Warry
✉ 1a Alfred Street, Blandford Forum, Dorset, DT11 7JJ 🅿
☎ 01258 452454 🖷 01258 452454
🖲 auctioneers@rwarry.freeserve.co.uk
🌐 www.rwarry.freeserve.co.uk
Est. 1956
Open Mon–Fri 9am–5pm
Sales Antique and collectables sale every three weeks, Fri 10am, viewing Wed 2–5pm Thurs 9.30am–7.30pm morning of sale
Frequency Every 3 weeks
Catalogues Yes

BOURNEMOUTH

⊞ Abbey Models
Contact Nick Powner
✉ 42 Littledown Drive, Littledown, Bournemouth, Dorset, BH7 7AQ 🅿
☎ 01202 395999 🖷 01202 395999
🖲 npowner@bournemouth.demon.co.uk
🌐 www.the-internet-agency.com/abbeymodels
Est. 1992 *Stock size* Large
Stock Old toys, Dinky, Corgi, Matchbox
Open By appointment
Fairs Sandown Park, NEC Toys
Services Valuations, mail-order catalogues available

⊞ Aladdins Antiques
Contact Paul
✉ Flat 3, 54 Lansdowne Road, Bournemouth, Dorset, BH1 1RS 🅿
☎ 01202 298805
🖷 07779 250940
🖲 paulboysen@cwcom.net
🌐 www.aladdinsantiques.cwc.net
Est. 1992 *Stock size* Small
Stock Furniture, ceramics
Open Mon–Sat 9am–6pm closed Wed

⊞ Books & Maps
Contact Mr R J Browne
✉ 1–3 Jewelbox Buildings, Cardigan Road, Winton, Bournemouth, Dorset,

BH9 2AD 🅿
☎ 01202 529403
🖲 sales@booksandmaps.freeserve.co.uk
🌐 www.finebooks.co.uk
Est. 1984 *Stock size* Large
Stock Antiquarian, rare, second-hand books, maps, books on Africa and dogs a speciality
Open Mon–Sat 9am–5.30pm
Fairs Royal National Hotel Fair
Services Valuations

⊞ Boscombe Militaria
Contact Mr E A Browne
✉ 86 Palmerston Road, Bournemouth, Dorset, BH1 4HU 🅿
☎ 01202 304250 🖷 01202 733696
Est. 1982 *Stock size* Medium
Stock 20thC militaria, uniforms, medals, badges
Open Mon–Sat 10am–1pm 2–5pm closed Wed
Fairs Farnham, Beltring

⊞ Boscombe Stamp Company
Contact Philip Clarke
✉ 20 North Road, Bournemouth, Dorset, BH7 6ET 🅿
☎ 01202 268672 🖷 01202 466205
Est. 2002 *Stock size* Large
Stock World wide stamps
Open Mon–Sat 8am–5.30pm
Services Valuations

⊞ Boscombe Toy Collectors
Contact Mr Harvey
✉ 802b Somerset Road, Boscombe, Bournemouth, Dorset, BH6 6DD 🅿
☎ 01202 398884
Est. 2001 *Stock size* Medium
Stock Trains, Action Man, *Star Wars*, die-cast and Dragon figures
Open Mon–Sat 10am–5pm closed Wed

⊞ Chorley–Burdett Antiques
Contact Ray Burdett
✉ 828 Christchurch Road, Bournemouth, Dorset, BH7 6DF 🅿
☎ 01202 423363 🖷 01202 423363
Est. 1992 *Stock size* Medium
Stock Victorian–Edwardian furniture, new and reclaimed pine
Open Mon–Sat 9am–5.30pm

⊞ Claire's Collectables
Contact Claire Castle
✉ Shop 6, Royal Arcade, Christchurch Road, Boscombe, Bournemouth, Dorset, BH1 4BT 🅿
☎ 01202 397558
Est. 1995 *Stock size* Large
Stock Collectables, china
Open Mon 10am–4pm Thurs–Sat 10am–5pm
Services Valuations, Poole pottery replacements

⊞ Classic Pictures (PTA)
Contact Betty Underwood
✉ 177 Tuckton Road, Bournemouth, Dorset, BH6 3LA 🅿
☎ 01202 433311
🖲 enquiries@classic-pictures.com
Est. 1989 *Stock size* Large
Stock Old postcards, Edwardian pictures, prints
Open Tues–Sat 9.30am–5pm
Fairs New Forest Show, Bournemouth International Centre
Services Valuations

⊞ Clobber
Contact Richard Mason
✉ 874 Christchurch Road, Bournemouth, Dorset, BH7 6DJ 🅿
☎ 01202 429794
🖷 07779 324109
🖲 richard@clobber.freeserve.co.uk
Est. 1997 *Stock size* Medium
Stock 1920–70s clothing
Open Mon–Sat 10.30am–5.30pm
Services Valuations

♪ Dalkeith Auctions Bournemouth
Contact Mr P Howard
✉ Dalkeith Hall, Dalkeith Steps, rear of 81 Old Christchurch Road, Bournemouth, Dorset, BH1 1YL 🅿
☎ 01202 292905 🖷 01202 292931
🖲 dalkeithauctions@ntlworld.com
🌐 www.dalkeithcatalogue.com
Est. 1992
Open Mon–Sat 8am–3pm
Sales Collectors' sales of ephemera and other collectors' items 1st Sat of month 11am, viewing week before 9am–3pm
Frequency Monthly
Catalogues Yes

⊞ Lionel Geneen Ltd (LAPADA)
Contact Mr Robert Geneen
✉ 811 Christchurch Road, Boscombe, Bournemouth, Dorset, BH7 6AP 🅿
☎ 01202 422961/520417
📠 01202 422961
📱 07770 596781
Est. 1902 *Stock size* Medium
Stock 19thC English, Continental, Oriental furniture, porcelain, bronzes, glass, ornamental decorative pieces, dessert services, tea and dinner services
Open Mon–Fri 9am–1pm 2–5pm Sat 9am–noon or by appointment
Services Valuations

⊞ Hardy's Collectables
Contact Mr J Hardy
✉ Boscombe, Bournemouth, Dorset, BH7 🅿
☎ 01202 473744
📱 07970 056858/613077
Est. 1987 *Stock size* Large
Stock 20thC collectables, mainly smalls, toys, metalware, ceramics
Open By appointment
Fairs Alexandra Palace, Kempton

⊞ Manor Antiques
Contact D R or T W Vendy
✉ 739 Christchurch Road, Bournemouth, Dorset, BH7 6AN 🅿
☎ 01202 392779
Est. 1969 *Stock size* Large
Stock General antiques, furniture, silver, porcelain
Open Mon–Sat 10am–1pm 2–5pm

⊞ Modern and Antique Fire Arms (GTA)
Contact Gillie Howe
✉ 147 Tuckton Road, Saltbourne, Bournemouth, Dorset, BH6 3JZ 🅿
☎ 01202 429369 📠 01202 426926
Est. 1971 *Stock size* Medium
Stock Firearms and accessories
Open Mon–Sat 10am–1pm 2–5.30pm Wed 10am–1pm
Fairs Midland Game Fair, Bisley Fair
Services Repair of classic and modern weapons

⊞ Mussenden & Sons, GB
Contact Gordon or David Mussenden
✉ 24 Seamoor Road, Westbourne, Bournemouth, Dorset, BH4 9AR
☎ 01202 764462
Est. 1970 *Stock size* Medium
Stock Antiques, jewellery, silver
Open Mon–Sat 9am–5pm closed Wed

⊞ Norman D Landing Militaria
Contact Mr Kenneth Lewis
✉ 76 Alma Road, Winton, Bournemouth, Dorset, BH9 1AN 🅿
☎ 01202 521944 📠 01202 521944
📱 07711 790044
✉ kenneth@44doughboy.fsnet.co.uk
🌐 norman-d-landing.com
Est. 1995 *Stock size* Large
Stock US Army uniforms and equipment 1910–1945
Open Thurs–Sat 10am–5pm, Mon–Wed by appointment
Fairs Stoneleigh, Warwicks (January), Beltring, Kent (July)
Services Valuations, mail order, hires to film and TV. Author of *Doughboy to GI*

⊞ George A Payne & Son Ltd
Contact Mr Payne
✉ 742 Christchurch Road, Boscombe, Bournemouth, Dorset, BH7 6BZ 🅿
☎ 01202 394954
Est. 1900 *Stock size* Medium
Stock Jewellery and silver
Open Mon–Sat 9.15am–5.30pm
Services Valuations, restoration

⌂ Pokesdown Antique Centre
Contact Mrs B Cook
✉ 848 Christchurch Road, Boscombe, Bournemouth, Dorset, BH7 6AP 🅿
☎ 01202 433263
Est. 1989 *Stock size* Large
No. of dealers 10
Stock Decorative antiques, wristwatches, lighting, pine, collectables (Georgian to modern), paintings
Open Mon–Sat 9am–5.30pm
Services Valuations, delivery, wristwatch repairs

⊞ Poole Pottery China Matching Service
Contact Claire Castle
✉ Shop 6, Royal Arcade, Christchurch Road, Boscombe, Bournemouth, Dorset, BH1 4BT 🅿
☎ 01202 397558
Est. 1995 *Stock size* Medium
Stock Poole, Denby, Mason's, Royal Albert, Royal Doulton, Wedgwood
Open Mon 10am–4pm Thurs–Sat 10am–5pm
Services China matching service

⊞ R E Porter
✉ 2–6 Post Office Road, Bournemouth, Dorset, BH1 1BA 🅿
☎ 01202 554289
Est. 1930 *Stock size* Large
Stock Silver, Baxter prints
Open Mon–Sat 9.30am–5pm
Services Valuations, restoration

⊞ Rawlinsons
Contact Mr M Rawlinson
✉ 884 Christchurch Road, Bournemouth, Dorset, BH7 6DJ 🅿
☎ 01202 433394
Est. 1983 *Stock size* Large
Stock General, smalls, furniture, glass, china, metalware, clocks, Art Deco
Open Mon–Sat 10am–5.30pm

⊞ H Rowan
Contact Mr H Rowan
✉ 459 Christchurch Road, Boscombe, Bournemouth, Dorset, BH1 4AD 🅿
☎ 01202 398820
Est. 1968 *Stock size* Large
Stock Antiquarian and second-hand books, maps, prints, local interest, art and antiques topics a speciality
Open Mon–Sat 9.30am–5.30pm
Services Valuations

⊞ Sainsburys Antiques Ltd (LAPADA)
Contact Jonathan Sainsbury
✉ 23–25 Abbott Road, Bournemouth, Dorset, BH9 1EU 🅿
☎ 01202 529271 📠 01202 510028
✉ sales@sainsburys-antiques.com
🌐 www.sainsburys-antiques.com
Est. 1918 *Stock size* Large

WEST COUNTRY
DORSET • BRIDPORT

Stock Antique furniture and accessories, exceptional replica chairs
Open By appointment
Services Antique timbers used to create replica furniture

⊞ **Sandy's Antiques**
Contact Michael Sandy
✉ 790–792 Christchurch Road, Boscombe, Bournemouth, Dorset, BH7 6DD 🄿
☎ 01202 301190 📠 01202 301190
📱 07836 367384
Est. 1970 Stock size Large
Stock Edwardian, Victorian, shipping, furniture
Open Mon–Sat 10am–5.30pm
Services Packing containers for export

⊞ **Sterling Coins and Medals (OMRS)**
Contact Mr V Henstridge
✉ 2 Somerset Road, Boscombe, Bournemouth, Dorset, BH7 6JH 🄿
☎ 01202 423881 📠 01202 423881
📧 agagia@aol.com
Est. 1985 Stock size Medium
Stock Medals
Open Mon–Sat 9am–3pm
Wed 9am–12.30pm
Services Valuations and medal mounting

⊞ **Victorian Chairman**
Contact Mrs M Leo
✉ 883 Christchurch Road, Bournemouth, Dorset, BH7 6AU 🄿
☎ 01202 420996
Est. 1977 Stock size Medium
Stock Victorian tables and chairs, wrought iron, glass tables
Open Mon–Sat 10am–5pm
Services Restoration of upholstery, French polishing

⊞ **Volume One Books and Records**
Contact Richard Cargill
✉ 1073 Christchurch Road, Boscombe East, Bournemouth, Dorset, BH7 6BE 🄿
☎ 01202 417652 📠 01202 483686
Est. 1989 Stock size Large
Stock Books, LP records, and CDs (classical, easy listening, jazz, stage and screen, country, rock and pop)

Open Mon Tues Fri 10am–5.30pm Wed Sat 10am–1pm closed 3rd Sat in each month
Fairs Midhurst Monthly Market, Sussex; others – please phone
Services Record search and mail order

⊞ **Wonderworld**
Contact Mr David Hern
✉ 540 Christchurch Road, Boscombe, Bournemouth, Dorset, BH1 4BE 🄿
☎ 01202 394918
📧 davejh4000@aol.com
🌐 www.wonderworld.uk.com
Est. 1977 Stock size Large
Stock Modern collectables, Star Wars, comics, Beanie Babies
Open Mon–Sat 9.30am–5.30pm

⊞ **Yesterdays Books (PBFA)**
Contact David Weir
✉ 6 Cecil Avenue, Bournemouth, Dorset, BH8 9EH 🄿
☎ 01202 522442
📱 07946 548420
📧 djl.weir@btinternet.com
Est. 1974 Stock size Medium
Stock Antiquarian books, African topics a speciality
Open By appointment
Fairs PBFA at London, Oxford and elsewhere, the London Travel Bookfair
Services Valuations, book search

BRIDPORT

🔨 **The Auction House Bridport**
Contact Michael Dark
✉ 38a St Michael's Trading Estate, Bridport, Dorset, DT6 3RR 🄿
☎ 01308 459400 📠 01308 459685
📱 07905 481388
📧 sales@theauctionhouse.dabsol.co.uk
🌐 www.theauctionhouse.dabsol.co.uk
Est. 1998
Open Mon–Fri 9.30am–5pm
Sales Antiques and modern sale last Fri each month 10am, viewing prior Wed Thurs 10am–5pm
Frequency Monthly
Catalogues Yes

⊞ **Batten's Jewellers**
Contact Gemma Batten
✉ 26 South Street,

Bridport, Dorset, DT6 3NQ 🄿
☎ 01308 456910
Est. 1978 Stock size Medium
Stock Jewellery, clocks, watches, silver
Open Mon–Fri 9am–5pm
Thurs Sat 9am–1pm

⊞ **Benchmark Antiques**
Contact Meg Standage
✉ West Allington, Bridport, Dorset, DT6 5BG 🄿
☎ 01308 420941 📠 01308 420941
📧 hohobird@netscape.net
Est. 1992 Stock size Medium
Stock 18thC furniture and related items
Open By appointment
Fairs NEC
Services Valuations

⊞ **Bridport Old Bookshop (PBFA)**
Contact Ms C MacTaggart
✉ 11 South Street, Bridport, Dorset, DT6 3NR 🄿
☎ 01308 425689
Est. 1998 Stock size Medium
Stock Antiquarian and second-hand books, children's illustrated, WWI, T E Lawrence, modern first editions, travel
Open Mon–Sat 10am–5pm
Fairs PBFA
Services Valuations

⊞ **Cast From The Past**
Contact David Coxhead
✉ Unit 57, Redbrick Studio, St Michael's Trading Estate, Bridport, Dorset, DT6 3RR 🄿
☎ 01308 426400
Est. 2002 Stock size Large
Stock Architectural antiques
Open Mon–Sat 8am–5pm
Services Valuations, restoration, demolition, clearance

⊞ **Jack's**
Contact Mr D Skeels
✉ 24 South Street, Bridport, Dorset, DT6 3NQ 🄿
☎ 01308 420700
Est. 1985 Stock size Medium
Stock Oriental rugs, furniture, antiques
Open Mon–Sat 10am–5pm
Services Restoration of rugs, cleaning

174

⊞ Ann Quested Antiques
Contact Ann Quested
✉ **59 East Street, Bridport,
Dorset,
DT6 3LB** 🅿
☎ 01308 422576/421551
Est. 1990 *Stock size* Medium
Stock Pine and country furniture,
brass
Open Wed–Sat 10.30am–5pm
Services Valuations

CHRISTCHURCH

⊞ H L B Antiques
Contact Mr H L Blechman
✉ **139 Barrack Road,
Christchurch, Dorset,
BH23 2AW** 🅿
☎ 01202 429252
Est. 1967 *Stock size* Medium
Stock General collectables,
gramophones, postcards,
walking sticks, Art Deco, ivory
Open Sat 9am–5pm or by
appointment
Fairs New Caledonian Market in
Bermondsey
Services Valuations, restoration

⊞ Gerald Hampton
Contact Gerald Hampton
✉ **12 Purewell, Christchurch,
Dorset,
BH23 1EP** 🅿
☎ 01202 484000
Est. 1930 *Stock size* Medium
Stock General antiques
Trade only Yes
Open By appointment

**⊞ M & R Lankshear
Antiques**
Contact Mike Lankshear
✉ **18 Plantation Drive, Walkford,
Christchurch, Dorset,
BH23 5SA** 🅿
☎ 01425 277332
📱 07811 018476
Est. 1977 *Stock size* Medium
Stock General antiques, military
items
Open Mon–Sat 9.30am–5pm
Services Valuations

⊞ Past 'n' Present
Contact Pete Woodford
✉ **4 St Catherine's Parade,
Fairmile Road, Christchurch,
Dorset,
BH23 2LQ** 🅿
☎ 01202 478900
Est. 1997 *Stock size* Large

Stock Collectables
Open Mon–Sat 9.30am–5pm
closed Wed pm
Services Valuations, restoration

**⊞ Pastime Antiques &
Collectables (FSB)**
Contact Jill Sirl
✉ **12a Castle Street,
Christchurch, Dorset,
BH23 1DT** 🅿
☎ 01202 485656
Est. 2005 *Stock size* Large
Stock General antiques,
collectables, fine art
Open Mon–Sat 9am–5pm Sun
10am–4pm
Services Valuations, restoration,
coffee lounge, house clearance

**⊞ Tudor House Antiques
(LAPADA)**
Contact Mrs P Knight or
Mrs D Burton
✉ **420 Lymington Road,
Highcliffe, Christchurch, Dorset,
BH23 5HE** 🅿
☎ 01425 280440
Est. 1940 *Stock size* Medium
Stock General
Open Tues–Sat 10am–5pm
closed Wed

CRANBORNE

⊞ Tower Antiques
Contact Mr P White
✉ **The Square, Cranbourne,
Dorset,
BH21 5PR** 🅿
☎ 01725 517552
Est. 1973 *Stock size* Small
Stock Georgian, Victorian
furniture
Open Mon–Sat 8.30am–5.30pm

DORCHESTER

⊞ Box of Porcelain
Contact Robert Lunn
✉ **51d Icen Way, Dorchester,
Dorset,
DT1 1EW** 🅿
☎ 01305 267110 ☎ 01305 263201
📱 07786 802113
📧 rlunn@boxofporcelain.com
🌐 www.boxofporcelain.com
Est. 1987 *Stock size* Large
Stock Collectables, Doulton,
Beswick, Royal Worcester, Spode,
Coalport, Lladrow, Moorcroft
Open Mon–Sat 10.30am–5pm
closed Thurs

⊞ Chattels
✉ Colliton Antique Centre,
3a Colliton Street, Dorchester,
Dorset,
DT1 1XH 🅿
☎ 01305 263620
Est. 1993 *Stock size* Large
Stock General, Edwardian,
Victorian furniture
Open Mon–Sat 9am–4pm

⌂ Colliton Antique Centre
Contact Tony Phillips
✉ **3a Colliton Street,
Dorchester, Dorset,
DT1 1XH** 🅿
☎ 01305 269398/260115
Est. 1983 *Stock size* Large
No. of dealers 6
Stock General Victorian,
Georgian, Edwardian furniture,
jewellery, silver, old pine
Open Mon–Sat 9am–5pm
Sun by appointment
Services Restoration of
metalwork, silver and jewellery
valuations

**⌂ De Danann Antiques
Centre**
Contact Mr J Burton
✉ **27 London Road,
Dorchester, Dorset,
DT1 1NF** 🅿
☎ 01305 250066/264123
☎ 01305 250113
🌐 www.dedanann.co.uk
Est. 1994 *Stock size* Medium
No. of dealers 20
Stock General antiques
Open Mon–Sat 9am–5pm

**⊞ The Dorchester
Bookshop**
Contact Michael Edmonds
✉ **3 Nappers Court,
Charles Street,
Dorchester, Dorset,
DT1 1EE** 🅿
☎ 01305 269919
Est. 1993 *Stock size* Medium
Stock Second-hand, antiquarian
books
Open Tues–Sat 10am–5pm
Services Valuations, restoration
and book search

⚒ Hy Duke & Son (SOFAA)
Contact Mr Guy Schwinge or
Mr Gary Batt
✉ **The Dorchester Fine Art
Salerooms, Weymouth Avenue,
Dorchester, Dorset,**

DT1 1QS ▣
☎ 01305 265080 ✆ 01305 260101
📱 07778 523962
✉ enquiries@dukes-auctions.com
🌐 www.dukes-auctions.com
Est. 1823
Open Mon–Fri some Sats
9am–1pm 2–5.30pm
Sales Specialist sales of paintings,
furniture, ceramics, silver,
jewellery and furniture, Thurs Fri
11am, viewing week prior Sat
9.30am–noon Mon 9.30am–5pm
Tues 9.30am–7pm Wed
9.30am–5pm morning of sale
Frequency 9 per annum
Catalogues Yes

✒ Hy Duke & Son (SOFAA)
Contact Garry Batt
✉ Grove Auctions, The Grove,
Dorchester, Dorset,
DT1 1ST ▣
☎ 01305 257544/ 0870 7771192
✆ 01305 259953
✉ enquires@dukes-auctions.com
Open Mon–Fri 9am–5.30pm
Sales Tues 10.30am, viewing Sat
9.30am–noon Mon 9.30am–7pm
the morning of sale
Frequency Every 3 weeks, phone
for details
Catalogues Yes

GILLINGHAM

⊞ Talisman (LAPADA)
Contact Mr Ken Bolan
✉ The Old Brewery, Wyke Road,
Gillingham, Dorset,
SP8 4NW ▣
☎ 01747 824423 ✆ 01747 823544
✉ shop@talismanantiques.com
🌐 www.talismanantiques.com
Est. 1979 *Stock size* Large
Stock Antiques and garden
statuary
Open Mon–Fri 9am–5pm
Sat 10am–4pm
Fairs Olympia June November

LYME REGIS

⊞ The Commemorative
Man
Contact Mr Harris
✉ Lyme Regis Antique & Craft
Centre, Marine Parade,
Lyme Regis, Dorset,
DT7 3JH ▣
☎ 01297 32682
Est. 1994 *Stock size* Large
Stock Political, royal and

sporting commemoratives
Open April–Oct Mon–Sun
11am–6.30pm Nov–Mar Fri Sat
Sun 11am–4.30pm
Services Mail order and search
service

⌂ Lyme Regis Antique &
Craft Centre
Contact Mr C Willis
✉ Marine Parade, Lyme Regis,
Dorset,
DT7 3JH ▣
☎ 01297 445053
Est. 1995 *Stock size* Large
No. of dealers 35
Stock Commemoratives, stamps,
postcards, china, jewellery, fossils
Open Apr–Oct Mon–Sun
11am–5pm Nov–Mar Fri Sat Sun
11am–4.30pm

LYTCHETT MINSTER

⊞ Old Button Shop
Contact Thelma Johns
✉ Dorchester Road, Lytchett
Minster, Dorset,
BH16 6JF ▣
☎ 01202 622169
✉ info@oldbuttonshop.fsnet.co.uk
Est. 1970 *Stock size* Small
Stock General and cottage
antiques, antique and Dorset
buttons
Open Tues–Fri 2–5pm Sat
11am–1pm
Services Valuations, restoration

MELBURY OSMOND

⊞ Hardy Country
Contact Mr S Groves
✉ Meadow View, Drive End,
Melbury Osmond, Dorchester,
Dorset,
DT2 0NA ▣
☎ 01935 83440
📱 07814 048449
✉ hardycountry@supanet.com
🌐 www.hardycountry.com
Est. 1972 *Stock size* Large
Stock Old pine
Open Mon–Sat 9am–6pm
Sun by appointment
Services Valuations, restoration

MELBURY SAMPFORD

⊞ Dynasty Antiques
Contact Nigel Hirst
✉ Hazel Farmhouse, Melbury
Sampford, Dorchester, Dorset,

DT2 0LN ▣
✆ 07787 561586
Est. 2000 *Stock size* Medium
Stock Chinese, Tibetan antique
furniture
Open By appointment

POOLE

⊞ Branksome Antiques
Contact Brian Neal
✉ 370 Poole Road, Branksome,
Poole, Dorset,
BH12 1AW ▣
☎ 01202 763324 ✆ 01202 763324
Est. 1972 *Stock size* Medium
Stock General antiques,
scientific, medical, marine, silver,
brass, copper
Open Mon Tues Thur Fri
10am–5pm
Fairs Scientific Fair, Portman
Hotel

⊞ Castle Books
Contact Mr Clark
✉ 2 North Street, Poole, Dorset,
BH15 1NX ▣
☎ 01202 660295
🌐 www.castlebooksofpoole.co.uk
Est. 1980 *Stock size* Medium
Stock Antiquarian, modern
second-hand, collectable books
Open Mon–Sat 10am–5pm
Services Valuations

✒ Davey & Davey (NAVA)
Contact Neil Davey
✉ 13 St Peters Road, Parkstone,
Poole, Dorset,
BH14 0NZ ▣
☎ 01202 748567 ✆ 01202 716258
🌐 www.daveyanddavey.com
Est. 1946
Open Mon–Fri 9am–1pm 2–5.30pm
Sales General antiques and
collectables every 2 months Tues
10am, viewing Mon 10am–4pm
Catalogues Yes

⊞ W A Howe
Contact Mr W A Howe
✉ 23 Cooke Road, Branksome,
Poole, Dorset,
BH12 1QB ▣
☎ 01202 743350
Est. 1999 *Stock size* Small
Stock Antiquarian, second-hand
books, modern first editions,
cookery, golf
Open Mon–Sun 8am–8pm
Fairs Local book fairs
Services Valuations

⊞ Laburnum Antiques & Interiors
Contact Mrs D Mills
✉ Lonbourne House,
250 Bournemouth Road,
Poole, Dorset,
BH14 9HZ ▣
☎ 01202 746222 ✆ 01202 736777
✉ enquiries@laburnumantiques.co.uk
⊕ www.laburnumantiques.co.uk
Est. 1997 *Stock size* Medium
Stock Georgian–Edwardian furniture, accessories, ottomans, stools and cushions, full range of interiors, soft furnishings
Open Tues–Sat 10am–5.30pm
Services Complete home furnishing service, fully qualified furniture restoration

⊞ Stocks and Chairs
Contact Mrs Carole Holding-Parsons
✉ 11 Bank Chambers,
Penn Hill Avenue,
Poole, Dorset,
BH14 9NB ▣
☎ 01202 718618
✆ 07970 010512
⊕ www.stockandchairsantiques.com
Est. 1979 *Stock size* Large
Stock 18th–19thC furniture, some smalls
Open Tues–Sat 10.30am–5pm
Services Restoration of hand-dyed leather

PUDDLETOWN

⊞ Antique Map and Bookshop (PBFA, ABA)
Contact Mrs H M Proctor
✉ 32 High Street,
Puddletown,
Dorchester, Dorset,
DT2 8RU ▣
☎ 01305 848633
✉ proctor@puddletown.demon.co.uk
⊕ www.puddletownbookshop.co.uk
Est. 1976 *Stock size* Medium
Stock Antique maps, antiquarian second-hand books
Open Mon–Sat 9am–5pm
Fairs Oxford, Russell Hotel (June) – PBFA
Services Valuations, restoration, book catalogues (4–6 a year)

PYMORE

⋏ William Morey & Son
Contact Malcolm Wilson
✉ The Sale Room, Unit 3,
Pymore Mills Estate,
Pymore, Dorset,
DT6 5PJ ▣
☎ 01308 422078 ✆ 01308 422078
✆ 07748 356376
✉ enquiries@wmoreyandson.co.uk
⊕ www.wmoreyandson.co.uk
Est. 1870
Open Mon–Fri 9am–5pm
Sales Antiques auction every 3 weeks Thurs 9.30am, viewing Wed 9am–4pm
Catalogues Yes

SEMLEY

⌂ Dairy House Antiques
Contact Andrew Stevenson
✉ Station Road, Semley,
Shaftesbury, Dorset,
SP7 9AN ▣
☎ 01747 853317
Est. 1998 *Stock size* Large
No. of dealers 9
Stock Antiques and collectables
Open Mon–Sat 9am–5pm

⊞ Robert Morgan Antiques
Contact Robert Morgan
✉ Unit 1a, Station Road,
Semley, Shaftesbury,
Dorset,
SP7 8AH ▣
☎ 01747 858770
✆ 07767 416106
✉ bobkate@barnhouse2.fsnet.co.uk
⊕ www.robertmorganantiques.co.uk
Est. 1985 *Stock size* Medium
Stock Small furniture, unusual items, medals, coins
Open By appointment
Fairs Kempton Park, Newark
Services Valuations

⋏ Semley Auctioneers
Contact Mr Simon Pearce
✉ Station Road, Semley,
Shaftesbury,
Dorset,
SP7 9AN ▣
☎ 01747 855122 ✆ 01747 855222
✉ simon.pearce@semley auctioneers.com
⊕ www.semleyauctioneers.com
Est. 1990
Open Mon–Fri 9am–5pm
Sales Sat 10am, viewing Friday prior 9am–9pm morning of sale. Items of higher quality appear in these sales about every 6 weeks
Frequency Fortnightly
Catalogues Yes

SHAFTESBURY

⌂ Mr Punch's Antique Market
Contact Mr C Jolliffe
✉ 33 Bell Street,
Shaftesbury, Dorset,
SP7 8AE ▣
☎ 01747 855775 ✆ 01747 855775
⊕ www.mrpunchs.co.uk
Est. 1994 *Stock size* Large
No. of dealers 20
Stock General, furniture, collectables, militaria, maps
Open Tue–Sat 10am–6pm
Services Valuations, restoration, pine stripping, house clearance, Punch museum

⊞ Shaston Antiques
Contact Mr J D Hine
✉ 14 & 16a Bell Street,
Shaftesbury, Dorset,
SP7 8AE
☎ 01747 850405
Est. 1996 *Stock size* Medium
Stock Georgian–Victorian quality furniture
Open Mon Tues Thurs Sat 9am–5pm Wed 9am–1pm
Services Restoration

SHERBORNE

⊞ Abbas Antiques
Contact Trevor F J Jeans
✉ Sherborne World of Antiques & Fine Art, Long Street,
Sherborne, Dorset,
DT9 3BS ▣
☎ 01935 816451 ✆ 01935 816240
Est. 1991 *Stock size* Medium
Stock 19thC furniture and smalls
Open Tue–Sat 9.30am–5pm
Services Valuations, restoration

⊞ Antiques of Sherborne (LAPADA, SAADA)
Contact Clive or Linda Greenslade
✉ 1 The Green, Sherborne,
Dorset,
DT9 3HZ ▣
☎ 01935 816549 ✆ 01935 816549
✆ 07971 019173
✉ clive@antiquesofsherborne. fsnet.co.uk
Est. 1988 *Stock size* Medium
Stock Georgian–Edwardian period town and country furniture, dining tables, chairs, sofas, wing chairs, linen, chess and mah jong sets

WEST COUNTRY

Open Mon–Sat 10am–5pm
Fairs Shepton Mallet
Services Upholstery, restoration,
deliveries worldwide

⊞ Chapter House Books
Contact Mr or Mrs Hutchison
⊠ Trendle Street, Sherborne,
Dorset,
DT9 3NT
☎ 01935 816262
🖃 chapterhousebooks@tiscali.co.uk
Est. 1988 *Stock size* Large
Stock Antiquarian books (mostly
hardback), out-of-print,
paperbacks
Open Mon–Sat 10am–5pm
Services Valuations, book repair,
book search

⊞ Greystoke Antiques
Contact Mr F Butcher
⊠ 4 Swan Yard, Cheap Street,
Sherborne, Dorset,
DT9 3AX 🅿
☎ 01935 812833
Est. 1974 *Stock size* Large
Stock Silver, Georgian and
Victorian, English blue transfer-
printed pottery 1800–1850
Open Mon–Sat 10am–4.30pm
closed Wed
Services Valuations, restoration

⊞ Pastimes
Contact Oliver Chisholm
⊠ Digby Road,
Sherborne,
Dorset,
DT9 3NL 🅿
☎ 01593 389666
🖃 info@pastimes-toys.co.uk
Est. 2000 *Stock size* Large
Stock Antique and collectable
toys
Open Thurs–Sat 9am–5pm

⊞ Phoenix (SAADA)
Contact Neil or Sally Brent Jones
⊠ 21 Cheap Street,
Sherborne,
Dorset,
DT9 3PU 🅿
☎ 01935 812788
🖃 phoenixantique@aol.com
Est. 1982 *Stock size* Medium
Stock 18th–20thC English and
Continental furniture,
mahogany, rosewood, painted
country furniture, furnishings
and lighting
Open Mon–Sat 9.30am–5.30pm
closed Wed or by appointment

⊞ Piers Pisani Ltd Antiques (SAADA)
Contact Mr Piers Pisani
⊠ The Court Yard, Newland,
Sherborne, Dorset,
DT9 3JG 🅿
☎ 01935 815209 🖷 01935 815209
🖃 antiques@pierspisani.sagehost.co.uk
🖳 www.pierspisani.com
Est. 1987 *Stock size* Large
Stock English and French
furniture, upholstery
Open Mon–Sat 10am–5pm
Services Valuations, restoration,
furniture copy

⊞ Renaissance
Contact Malcolm Heygate
Browne
⊠ South Street, Sherborne,
Dorset,
DT9 3NG 🅿
☎ 01935 815487 🖷 01935 815487
Est. 1984 *Stock size* Large
Stock 18th–19thC English
furniture, pottery, porcelain
Open Mon–Sat 10am–5pm
Sun 11am–3pm
Services Valuations, restoration

⊞ Timecraft Clocks (BHI)
Contact Mr G Smith
⊠ Unit 2, 24 Cheap Street,
Sherborne, Dorset,
DT9 3PX 🅿
☎ 01935 817771
Est. 1994 *Stock size* Small
Stock Clocks, barometers
Open Tue–Fri 10.30am–5.30pm
Sat 10am–2pm
Services Restoration, repairs

⊞ Wessex Antiques (SAADA)
Contact Frances Bryant
⊠ 6 Cheap Street, Sherborne,
Dorset,
DT9 3PX 🅿
☎ 01935 816816 🖷 01935 816816
🖃 sales@wessexantiques.com
🖳 www.wessexantiques.com
Est. 1986 *Stock size* Small
Stock Furniture, Staffordshire
figures, 19thC glass
Open Tues–Sat 10am–5pm

⊞ Henry Willis (Antique Silver)
Contact Henry Willis
⊠ 38 Cheap Street, Sherborne,
Dorset,
DT9 3PX 🅿
☎ 01935 816828

📱 07971 171818
Est. 1975 *Stock size* Medium
Stock English silver
medieval–1940
Open Mon–Sat 10am–5pm
Fairs Olympia (June)

STOURPAINE

➴ Onslow Auctions Ltd
Contact Patrick Bogue
⊠ The Coach House, Manor
Road, Stourpaine, Dorset,
DT11 8TQ 🅿
☎ 01258 488838
🖃 onslow.auctions@btinternet.com
🖳 www.onslows.uk
Est. 1984
Open Mon–Fri 9.30am–5pm by
appointment
Sales Collectors' sales, vintage
travel, aeronautical, posters,
railways, motoring, *Titanic*,
ocean liners, advisable to
telephone for details
Frequency 4 per annum
Catalogues Yes

SWANAGE

⊞ New, Secondhand & Antiquarian Books
Contact Mrs J Blanchard
⊠ 35 Station Road, Swanage,
Dorset,
BH19 1AD 🅿
☎ 01929 424088 🖷 01929 424088
🖃 info@editionone.co.uk
🖳 www.editionone.co.uk
Est. 1987 *Stock size* Large
Stock New and second-hand
books. First and pocket editions
Open Summer Mon–Sun
9.30am–5.00pm winter closed Sun

WAREHAM

➴ Cottees of Wareham
Contact Mr Bullock
⊠ The Market, East Street,
Wareham, Dorset,
BH20 4NR 🅿
☎ 01929 552826 🖷 01929 554916
🖃 auctions@cottees.fsnet.co.uk
🖳 www.auctionsatcottees.co.uk
Est. 1902
Open Mon–Fri 9am–5pm
closed 1–2pm
Sales General antique sales
fortnightly Tues 10am and 2pm,
viewing Mon 10am–1pm 2–5pm
6–8pm. Regular quality antique
and fine art sales. Poole pottery,

Clarice Cliff, Moorcroft pottery, Art Deco and collectable toy sales
Catalogues Yes

⊞ Heirlooms Antique Jewellers & Silversmiths
Contact Mr or Mrs Young
⊠ 21 South Street, Wareham, Dorset,
BH20 4LR ▣
☎ 01929 554207 ☏ 01929 554207
Est. 1985 *Stock size* Small
Stock Antique and period jewellery and silver
Open Mon–Sat 9.30am–5pm closed Wed
Services Jewellery, silver, watch, clock repair

WEYMOUTH

⊞ Books Afloat
Contact John Ritchie
⊠ 66 Park Street, Weymouth, Dorset,
DT4 7DE ▣
☎ 01305 779774
Est. 1983 *Stock size* Large
Stock Antiquarian, rare and second-hand books. Shipping, naval antiques and memorabilia, old postcards, ship models, paintings
Open Mon–Sat 9.30am–5.30pm

⊞ Books & Bygones
Contact Denise Nash
⊠ 26 Great George Street, Weymouth, Dorset,
DT4 7AS ▣
☎ 01305 777231
Est. 1985 *Stock size* Medium
Stock Antiques, collectables, out of print, rare and antiquarian books
Open Mon–Sun 2–5pm
Services Valuations

⊞ The Crows Nest
Contact Julia Marko
⊠ 3 Hope Square, Weymouth, Dorset,
DT4 8TR ▣
☎ 01305 786930 ☏ 01305 786930
Est. 1992 *Stock size* Large
Stock China, glass, pictures, farming, ship lamps, nautical, collectables
Open Mon–Sun 10am–5pm
Fairs Shepton Mallet, Exeter Livestock Market, Great Dorset Steam Fair
Services Restoration

⊞ The Curiosity Shop on the Quay
Contact David Pinches
⊠ 13 Trinity Road, Weymouth, Dorset,
DT4 8TJ ▣
☎ 01305 769988 ☏ 01305 769988
Est. 1990 *Stock size* Large
Stock General collectors' shop, Victoriana, collectables, Poole pottery and Pendelfin
Open Mon–Sun 10am–5pm
Fairs Shepton Mallet, Exeter West Point

⊞ Nautical Antique Centre
Contact Mr D C Warwick
⊠ 3a Cove Passage, off Hope Square, near Brewers Quay, Weymouth, Dorset,
DT4 8TR ▣
☎ 01305 777838/783180
☏ 07833 707247
✉ nauticalantiques@tinyworld.co.uk
🌐 www.nauticalantiques weymouth.co.uk
Est. 1988 *Stock size* Large
Stock Original maritime items, telescopes, sextants, clocks, barometers, logs, bells, lights, ships models, nautical collectables and memorabilia for collectors or commercial and domestic interior decor
Open Tues–Fri 10am–1pm 2–5pm (please phone in case shop is closed for fairs) evenings and weekends by appointment
Services Historical documentation on purchases

⊞ The Shrubbery
Contact Mrs Sally Dench
⊠ 15 Westham Road, Weymouth, Dorset,
DT4 8NS ▣
☎ 01305 768240
Est. 1997 *Stock size* Large
Stock Collectable dolls, dolls' houses, teddy bears, miniatures
Open Mon–Sat 10am–4pm
Fairs Weymouth

⊞ The Treasure Chest
Contact Mr P Barrett
⊠ 29 East Street, Weymouth, Dorset,
DT4 8BN ▣
☎ 01305 772757
Est. 1969 *Stock size* Medium
Stock Curios, coins, medals, local prints, brass, copper, china, army badges
Open Mon–Sat 10am–5pm
closed 1–2.30pm Wed 10am–1pm
Services Medal mounting, full size or miniature medals

WIMBORNE

⊞ Minster Books
Contact Mr or Mrs Child
⊠ 12 Cornmarket, Wimborne, Dorset,
BH21 1JL
☎ 01202 883355
Est. 1991 *Stock size* Large
Stock Antiquarian and second-hand books
Open Mon–Sat 10am–5pm
Services Valuations, restoration

⊞ The Wimborne Emporium
Contact Trisha Gurney
⊠ 9 West Borough, Wimborne, Dorset,
BH21 1LT ▣
☎ 01202 882980
Est. 1999 *Stock size* Large
Stock Antiques and collectables
Open Mon–Sat 9am–5pm closed Tues Wed

SOMERSET

BATH

⊞ Abbey Galleries (NAG, NPA)
Contact Richard Dickson
⊠ 9 Abbey Church Yard, Bath, Somerset,
BA1 1LY
☎ 01225 460565 ☏ 01225 484192
Est. 1950 *Stock size* Large
Stock Jewellery, Oriental porcelain, silver
Open Mon–Sat 10.30am–5pm
Services Restoration

♪ Aldridges of Bath
Contact Mr I Street
⊠ Newark House, 26–45 Cheltenham Street, Bath, Somerset,
BA2 3EX ▣
☎ 01225 462830 ☏ 01225 311319
🌐 www.invaluable.com/aldridges
Est. 1740
Open Mon–Fri 9am–5pm Sat 9am–noon
Sales All sales on Tues 10am, Victorian and general sales fortnightly, specialist antiques

WEST COUNTRY
SOMERSET • BATH

sales 6–8 weeks, collectors' sales
6–8 weeks
Catalogues Yes

⊞ Antique Glass (BABAADA)
Contact Margaret Hopkins
✉ 33 Belvedere, Lansdown Road,
Bath, Somerset,
BA1 5HR 🅿
☎ 01225 312367 ● 01225 312367
🄴 m.hopkins@antique-glass.co.uk
🆆 antique-glass.co.uk
Est. 1988 *Stock size* Medium
Stock Georgian glass, collectors'
drinking glasses, rummers, ales,
friggers, decanters, other
curiosities
Open Tues–Sat 10am–6pm
Services Searches

⊞ Antique Textiles and Lighting (BABAADA, BACA Award Winner 2002)
Contact Joanna Proops
✉ 34 Belvedere, Lansdown Road,
Bath, Somerset,
BA1 5HR 🅿
☎ 01225 310795
Est. 1970 *Stock size* Large
Stock Antique textiles, tapestries,
samplers, Paisleys, fans,
beadwork, linen, lace, wall and
ceiling lighting, chandeliers
Open Tues–Sat 10am–5pm
Fairs Bath Decorative Fair
Services Valuations

🏠 Assembly Antiques Centre (BABAADA)
Contact Lynda Brine
✉ 5–8 Saville Row, Bath,
Somerset,
BA1 2PP 🅿
☎ 01225 448488
🄴 lyndabrine@yahoo.co.uk
Est. 1969 *Stock size* Large
No. of dealers 3
Stock 18th–19thC furniture,
lighting, chess sets, tea caddies,
jewellery, scent bottles, porcelain
Open Mon–Sat 10am–5pm
Services Valuations, restoration

⊞ Bath Antiques Online
Contact Sue Turner
✉ Unit 3, 14 Fountain Buildings,
Lansdown Mews, Bath,
Somerset,
BA1 5DX 🅿
☎ 01225 311061 ● 0117 9608 309
🄴 info@bathantiquesonline.com
🆆 www.bathantiquesonline.com

Est. 1998 *Stock size* Large
Stock Antiques and collectables
Open Mon–Sat 10am–4pm

⊞ Bath Old Books (PBFA)
Contact Steven Ferdinando
✉ 9c Margaret's Buildings,
Bath, Somerset,
BA1 2LP 🅿
☎ 01225 422244
🄴 bathbooks@hotmail.com
Est. 1991 *Stock size* Medium
Stock Antiquarian and second-
hand books
Open Mon–Sat 10am–5pm
Fairs PBFA
Services Valuations, book
binding, book searches

⊞ George Bayntun (ABA)
Contact Mr Edward Bayntun-
Coward
✉ Manvers Street, Bath,
Somerset,
BA1 1JW 🅿
☎ 01225 466000 ● 01225 482122
🄴 ebc@georgebayntun.com
🆆 www.georgebayntun.com
Est. 1894 *Stock size* Large
Stock Antiquarian and rare
books, English literature first
editions, fine bindings
Open Mon–Fri 9am–1pm
2–5.30pm Sat 9.30am–1pm
Services Valuations, binding
service

⊞ Bedsteads (BABAADA)
Contact Nikki Ashton
✉ 2 Walcot Buildings,
London Road, Bath,
Somerset,
BA1 6AD 🅿
☎ 01225 339182
🆆 www.bedsteads-uk.co.uk
Est. 1990 *Stock size* Medium
Stock Antique bedsteads in iron,
brass and exotic woods
Open Tues–Sat 10am–5.30pm
Sun by appointment
Services Restoration

🔨 Bonhams
✉ 1 Old King Street, Bath,
Somerset,
BA1 2JT
☎ 01225 788988 ● 01225 446675
🄴 bath@bonhams.com
🆆 www.bonhams.com/bath
Open Mon–Fri 9am–5.30pm
Sales Regional Saleroom.
Regular sales held in London and
in our salerooms across the

country. Free auction valuations;
insurance and probate valuations
Catalogues Yes

⊞ Bonstow and Crawshay Antiques
Contact Simon Crawshay
✉ 46 Palace Avenue, Paignton,
Devon,
TQ3 3HF 🅿
☎ 01803 390850 ● 01803 390850
🆂 07989 418592
🄴 bonstowandcrawshay
antiques@talk21.com
Est. 1996 *Stock size* Medium
Stock Pre-1830 period English
furniture, decorative items,
marble, stonework, mirrors,
sculpture
Open By appointment
Fairs West Point
Services Valuations, restoration

⊞ Le Boudoir
Contact Sue Turner
✉ The Basement,
George Street Antiques Centre,
George Street,
Bath, Somerset,
BA1 2EE 🅿
☎ 01225 311061 ● 0117 9608 309
🄴 suemarie@blueyonder.co.uk
🆆 www.le-boudoir-online.com
Est. 1988 *Stock size* Large
Stock Perfume bottles, dolls,
decorative interior items,
jewellery, Art Deco ceramics,
Bakelite, petit point and beaded
purses, decoupage materials and
paper
Open Mon–Sat 9am–5pm
Wed 8am–5pm
Services Valuations, restoration
of ceramics

⊞ Lawrence Brass
✉ Apple Studio,
Bath, Somerset,
BA1 5YX 🅿
☎ 01225 852222
🆆 www.lawrencebrass.com
Est. 1973 *Stock size* Medium
Stock Furniture
Open Mon–Sat 9am–5pm
Services Valuations, restoration

⊞ Lynda Brine Antiques
Contact Lynda Brine
✉ Assembly Antiques,
5–8 Saville Row,
Bath, Somerset,
BA1 2QP 🅿
☎ 01225 448488 ● 01225 429661

☏ 077732 371233
✉ lyndabrine@yahoo.co.uk
Est. 1986 *Stock size* Large
Stock Perfume bottles, vinaigrettes, pomanders, objects of virtue, jewellery, silver
Open By appointment only
Fairs NEC, USA
Services Valuations

⊞ Camden Books (PBFA)
Contact Victor or Elizabeth Suchar
✉ 146 Walcot Street, Bath, Somerset, BA1 5BL ℙ
☏ 01225 461606 📠 01225 461606
✉ suchcam@msn.com
🌐 www.camdenbooks.com
Est. 1984 *Stock size* Large
Stock Antiquarian books, architecture, philosophy and science
Open Mon–Sat 10am–5pm
Fairs PBFA

⊞ Brian and Caroline Craik Ltd
Contact Mrs C Craik
✉ 8 Margaret's Buildings, Bath, Somerset, BA1 2LP ℙ
☏ 01225 337161
Est. 1962 *Stock size* Medium
Stock General portable items, china and metalwork
Open Mon–Sat 10am–4pm (resident on premises)

⊞ Mary Cruz Antiques (LAPADA, CINOA, BABAADA)
Contact Ms M Cruz
✉ 5 Broad Street, Bath, Somerset, BA1 5LJ ℙ
☏ 01225 334174 📠 01225 423300
Est. 1974 *Stock size* Large
Stock 18th–19thC English and French furniture, 18th–20thC paintings, bronze and marble statues
Open Mon–Sat 10am–7pm
Services Valuations, restoration

⊞ D & B Dickinson (BADA, BABAADA)
Contact Mr Dickinson
✉ 22 New Bond Street, Bath, Somerset, BA1 1BA
☏ 01225 466502
🌐 www.dickinsonsilver.co.uk

Est. 1917 *Stock size* Large
Stock Silver, jewellery, silver plate
Open Mon–Sat 9.30am–1pm 2–5pm

⊞ Frank Dux Antiques (BABAADA)
Contact Mr F Dux
✉ 33 Belvedere, Lansdown Road, Bath, Somerset, BA1 5HR ℙ
☏ 01225 312367 📠 01225 312367
✉ m.hopkins@antique-glass.co.uk
🌐 www.antique-glass.co.uk
Est. 1988 *Stock size* Medium
Stock 18th–19thC glass
Open Tues–Sat 10am–6pm
Services Search

⌂ George Street Antique Centre
Contact Paul Kembery
✉ 8 Edgar Buildings, George Street, Bath, Somerset, BA1 2QZ
☏ 01225 422322
📱 07850 623237
✉ kembery@kdclocks.co.uk
🌐 www.kdclocks.co.uk
Est. 2004 *Stock size* Small
No. of dealers 4
Stock Clocks, barometers, jewellery, music boxes, pocket watches, silver, porcelain
Open Mon–Sat 9.30am–5pm

⊞ Helios Gallery (ADA, PADA, BABAADA)
Contact Rolf Kiaer
✉ 14 Fountain Buildings Mews, Bath, Somerset, BA1 5DX ℙ 📠 01225 336097
📱 07711 955997
✉ heliosgallery@btinternet.com
🌐 www.heliosgallery.com
Est. 1995 *Stock size* Medium
Stock Roman, Greek, Egyptian, Chinese, ancient art
Open Sat 8am–4pm or by appointment
Fairs ADA Fair
Services Valuations, restoration, shipping

⊞ Jadis Antiques Ltd (BABAADA)
Contact Ms M Taylor
✉ 14 & 15 Walcot Buildings, London Road, Bath, Somerset, BA1 6AD ℙ
☏ 01225 333130 📠 01225 333130

☏ 07768 232133
✉ jadpalad@aol.com
🌐 www.jadis-ltd.com
Est. 1970 *Stock size* Large
Stock French furniture and decorative items
Open Mon–Sat 9.30am–6pm or by appointment
Fairs Bath Decorative and Antiques Fair
Services Design service, mural painting

⊞ Kembery Antique Clocks Ltd (BABAADA)
Contact Mr Paul Kembery
✉ George Street Antique Centre, 8 Edgar Buildings, Bath, Somerset, BA1 2EE ℙ
☏ 0117 9565281 📠 0117 9565281
📱 07850 623237
✉ kembery@kdclocks.co.uk
🌐 www.kdclocks.co.uk
Est. 1993 *Stock size* Medium
Stock Longcase, wall, mantel, bracket, carriage clocks and barometers
Open Mon–Sat 9.30am–5pm
Fairs NEC
Services Valuations, restoration, shipping

⊞ Ann King Antique Clothes
Contact Mrs Ann King
✉ 38 Belvedere, Lansdown Road, Bath, Somerset, BA1 5HR ℙ
☏ 01225 336245
Est. 1980 *Stock size* Medium
Stock Antique clothes, quilts, lace
Open Tues–Sat 10am–5pm
Services Valuations

⊞ Looking Glass of Bath
Contact Anthony Reed
✉ 94 Walcot Street, Bath, Somerset, BA1 5BG ℙ
☏ 01225 461969 📠 01225 316191
📱 07831 323878
✉ info@lookingglassofbath.co.uk
🌐 www.lookingglassofbath.co.uk
Est. 1968 *Stock size* Medium
Stock Antique and replica period mirrors, picture frames
Open Mon–Sat 9am–6pm
Fairs House & Garden Olympia
Services Valuations, restoration, shipping, manufacturers of mercury mirror plates

WEST COUNTRY

⊞ E P Mallory and Son Ltd (BADA)
Contact N Hall or P Mallory
✉ 1–5 Bridge Street, Bath, Somerset, BA2 4AP 🅿
☎ 01225 788800 📠 01225 442210
📧 mail@mallory-jewellers.com
🌐 www.mallory-jewellers.com
Est. 1898 *Stock size* Large
Stock Silver, jewellery
Open Mon–Fri 9.30am–5.15pm, Sat 9.30am–5.30pm
Services Valuations

⊞ S Millard Antiques (BABAADA)
Contact Simon Millard
✉ Bartlett Street Antiques Centre, 5–10 Bartlett Street, Bath, Somerset, BA1 2QZ 🅿
☎ 01225 469785
📧 tmillard@dircon.co.uk
Est. 1987 *Stock size* Medium
Stock Jewellery
Open Mon–Sun 10am–5pm Wed 8am–5pm

⊞ C Moss Clocks (Worshipful company of Clockmakers)
Contact Mr C Moss
✉ 59 Walcot Street, Bath, Somerset, BA1 5BN 🅿
☎ 01225 445892 📠 01225 445892
📱 07779 161731
📧 chris@chrismossclocks.co.uk
🌐 www.chrismossclocks.co.uk
Est. 1970 *Stock size* Medium
Stock Good English clocks
Open Mon–Sat 9am–5pm but please phone first
Services Clock case restoration

⌂ Old Bank Antiques Centre (BABAADA)
Contact David Moore
✉ 16, 17 & 20 Walcot Buildings, London Road, Bath, Somerset, BA1 6AD 🅿
☎ 01225 469282/338813
📧 alexatmontague@aol.com
🌐 www.oldbankantiquescentre.com
Est. 2002 *Stock size* Large
No. of dealers 9
Stock 17th–early 20thC English and Continental furniture, glass, ceramics, lighting, rugs, textiles, metalwork, paintings including English portraits
Open Mon–Sat 10am–6pm

Wed 8am–6pm closed Thur Sun 11am–4pm
Services Valuations, shipping

⊞ The Orientalist
Contact Steve Lee
✉ 10 Argyle Street, Bath, Somerset, BA2 4BQ 🅿
☎ 01225 469848 📠 01225 469849
📱 07932 189824
📧 enquiries@theorientalist.com
🌐 www.theorientalist.com
Est. 2002 *Stock size* Large
Stock Oriental antiques
Open Mon–Sat 10am–4.30pm
Services Restoration

⊞ Patterson Liddle (ABA, PBFA)
Contact John Patterson or Steve Liddle
✉ 10 Margarets Buildings, Brock Street, Bath, Somerset, BA1 2LP 🅿
☎ 01225 426722 📠 01225 426722
📧 mail@pattersonliddle.com
🌐 www.pattersonliddle.com
Est. 1982 *Stock size* Medium
Stock Antiquarian and second-hand books
Open Mon–Sat 10am–5.30pm

⊞ Piccadilly Antiques (BABAADA)
Contact John Davies
✉ 280 High Street, Batheaston, Bath, Somerset, BA1 2QZ 🅿
☎ 01225 851494 📠 01225 851120
📱 07785 966132
📧 piccadillyantiques@ukonline.co.uk
Est. 2001 *Stock size* Medium
Stock English and French furniture, decorative accessories aimed at the US market
Open Mon–Sat 9.30am–5.30pm or by appointment
Fairs Bath Decorative and Antiques Fair

⊞ Quiet Street Antiques (BABAADA)
Contact Mr Kerry Hastings-Spital
✉ 3 Quiet Street, Bath, Somerset, BA1 2JS 🅿
☎ 01225 315727 📠 01225 448300
📱 07860 818212
📧 kerry@quietstreetantiques.co.uk
🌐 www.quietstreetantiques.co.uk
Est. 1985 *Stock size* Large
Stock 18th–19thC furniture, clocks, tea caddies, boxes,

mirrors, Royal Worcester, works of art
Open Mon–Sat 10am–6pm
Services Valuations, free delivery within 100 miles, export services

⊞ Roland Gallery (BABAADA)
Contact Mike Pettitt
✉ 33 Monmouth Street, Bath, BA1 2AN 🅿
☎ 01225 312330/319464
📠 01225 312330
📱 07889 723272
📧 therolandgallery@aol.com
Est. 2000 *Stock size* Large
Stock Eclectic mix of 20thC design including silver, ivory, decorative items, paintings
Open Wed–Sat 11am–4pm or by appointment
Fairs NEC Birmingham, Newark, Sandown Park

⊞ Michael Saffell Antiques (BABAADA)
Contact Mr M Saffell
✉ 3 Walcot Buildings, London Road, Bath, Somerset, BA1 6AD 🅿
☎ 01225 315857 📠 01225 315857
📱 07941 158049
📧 michael.saffell@virgin.net
Est. 1975 *Stock size* Medium
Stock Advertising items, British tins (biscuit, tobacco, confectionery, mustard etc), decorative items
Open Mon–Fri 9am–5pm (telephone in advance) or by appointment
Fairs Newark, Bath Antiques & Decorative Fair
Services Valuations

⊞ Tim Snell Antiques (BABAADA)
Contact Tim Snell
✉ 5–6 Cleveland Terrace, Bath, Somerset, BA1 5DF
☎ 01225 423045 📠 01225 423045
Est. 1979 *Stock size* Large
Stock General antiques
Open Mon Thurs–Sat 10am–5pm
Services Valuations, restoration, house clearances

⊞ Source (BABAADA)
Contact Mr R Donaldson
✉ 11 Claverton Buildings, High Street, Widcombe,

WEST COUNTRY
SOMERSET • BRISTOL

Bath, Somerset,
BA2 4LD ⓟ
☎ 01225 469200
🅜 07831 734134
🅔 shop@source-antiques.co.uk
🅦 www.source-antiques.co.uk
Est. 1978 *Stock size* Medium
Stock Architectural antiques and
lights including 1950s aluminium
kitchens
Open Tues–Sat 10am–5pm
Fairs Bath Decorative and
Antiques Fair
Services Valuations

⊞ **Susannah (BABAADA,
The Textiles Society)**
Contact Mrs S Holley
✉ 25 Broad Street, Bath,
Somerset,
BA1 5LW ⓟ
☎ 01225 445069 🅖 01225 339004
Est. 1989 *Stock size* Medium
Stock General, decorative items,
textiles
Open Mon–Sat 10am–5pm please
telephone in advance
Fairs Bath Decorative and
Antiques Fair, The Textiles
Society Fair Manchester

⊞ **James Townshend
Antiques (BABAADA)**
Contact Mr Townshend
✉ 1 Saville Row,
Bath, Somerset,
BA1 2QP ⓟ
☎ 01225 332290 🅖 01225 332290
🅜 01225 332290
🅔 sales@jtownshendantiques.co.uk
🅦 www.jtownshendantiques.co.uk
Stock size Large
Stock 19thC furniture, decorative
items, mirrors
Open Mon–Sat 10am–5pm
Fairs Kempton
Services Valuations, restoration

⊞ **Vintage & Rare Guitars
(Bath) Ltd**
Contact Andy Lewis
✉ 7–8 Saville Row, Bath,
Somerset,
BA1 2QP ⓟ
☎ 01225 330 888 🅖 01225 335 999
🅔 enquiries@vintageandrareguit.com
🅦 www.vintageandrareguitars.com
Est. 1981 *Stock size* Large
Stock Classic vintage American
guitars
Open Mon–Sat 10am–6pm,
Sun noon–4pm
Services Valuations, restoration

⊞ **Vintage to Vogue
(BABAADA)**
Contact Teresa Langton
✉ 28 Milsom Street (entry in the
passage off Broad Street car
park), Bath,
BA1 1DG ⓟ
☎ 01225 337323
🅦 www.vintagetovogue.com
Est. 1994 *Stock size* Large
Stock 1850s–1950s period
clothing and accessories,
costume lace, white linens
Open Tues–Sat 10.30am–5pm

⊞ **Walcot Reclamation Ltd
(BABAADA)**
Contact Rick Knapp
✉ 108 Walcot Street, Bath,
Somerset,
BA1 5BG ⓟ
☎ 01225 444404 🅖 01225 448163
🅔 rick@walcot.com
🅦 www.walcot.com
Est. 1975 *Stock size* Large
Stock Architectural antiques
including bathrooms, radiators,
fireplaces, garden furniture and
reproductions of hard-to-find
items
Open Mon–Fri 9am–5.30pm
Sat 9am–5pm
Fairs The Country Living Fairs,
Business Design Centre Islington
(spring)
Services Restoration of marble,
stone and old radiators

⊞ **Waterfall Antiques
(BABAADA)**
Contact Mr or Mrs R D Waterfall
✉ 57 Walcot Street, Bath,
Somerset,
BA1 5BN ⓟ
☎ 01225 444201
🅜 07990 690240
Est. 1991 *Stock size* Medium
Stock Georgian, Victorian and
early 20thC furniture and
collectables
Open Mon–Sat 10.30am–5.30pm
Services Deliveries

BITTON

⊞ **Barrow Lodge Antiques**
Contact Derek Wookey
✉ Kings Square, Bitton, Bristol,
BS30 6HR ⓟ
☎ 0117 9324205
🅜 07836 293993
Est. 1975 *Stock size* Large
Stock Furniture, paintings, silver

Open By appointment
Fairs Newark, Ardingly
Services Restoration, stripping

BLACKFORD

⊞ **L D Watts**
Contact L D Watts
✉ Blackford County Old Primary
School, Sexey's Road, Blackford,
Wedmore, Somerset,
BS28 4NX ⓟ
☎ 01934 712372
Est. 1970 *Stock size* Medium
Stock 18th–19thC furniture
Open By appointment
Services Valuations

BRIDGWATER

⚒ **Tamlyn and Son**
Contact Julie Howard
✉ 56 High Street, Bridgwater,
Somerset, **TA6 3BN** ⓟ
☎ 01278 445251/458241
🅖 01278 458242
🅜 07850 335928
🅔 saleroom@tamlynandson.co.uk
🅦 www.tamlynandson.co.uk
Est. 1893
Open Mon–Fri 9am–5.30pm
Sales Antiques and general sales
monthly, 2 catalogue sales per
annum May and Nov, viewing
day before sale
Catalogues Yes

BRISTOL

⊞ **A & C Antique Clocks
(BWCG)**
Contact Mr David Andrews
✉ The Clock Shop,
86 Bryants Hill, Hanham, Bristol,
BS5 8QT ⓟ
☎ 0117 947 6141
🅔 info@antiquecorner.org.uk
🅦 www.antiquecorner.org.uk
Est. 1992 *Stock size* Large
Stock Clocks, barometers
Open Tues Thur Fri Sat please
telephone for hours
Services Clock repair service,
valuations, restoration, shipping

⊞ **The Antiques
Warehouse Ltd (RADS)**
Contact Chris Winsor
✉ 430 Gloucester Road, Horfield,
Bristol, **BS7 8TX** ⓟ
☎ 0117 942 4500 🅖 0117 942 4140
🅔 chriswinsor@theantiques
warehouseltd.co.uk

WEST COUNTRY

Ⓦ www.theantiqueswarehouse
ltd.co.uk
Est. 1994 *Stock size* Large
Stock Georgian–Edwardian and
post-Edwardian furniture,
carpets, mirrors
Open Tues–Sun 11am–5pm
Services Valuations, restoration
and upholstery

⊞ Arcadia Antiques & Interiors
Contact Julia Irish
✉ 4 Boyces Avenue, Clifton,
Bristol, BS8 4AA
☎ 0117 914 4479 ❺ 0117 923 9308
🅴 r.irish@phoenix-net.co.uk
Est. 1994 *Stock size* Small
Stock Furniture, collectables,
upholstery, prints, chandeliers
Open Mon–Sat 10am–5.30pm

⊞ Aristocratz
Contact Mr Zaid
✉ 115 Coldharbour Road,
Redlands, Bristol, Somerset,
BS6 7SD Ⓟ
☎ 0117 904 0091
Ⓜ 07770 393020
Ⓦ www.aristocratz.co.uk
Est. 1980 *Stock size* Medium
Stock General antiques
Open Mon–Sat 10am–5pm
Fairs Newark, Ardingly
Services Valuations, shipping

⊞ Au Temps Perdu (SALVO)
Contact Peter McGrain
✉ 28–30 Midland Road,
St Phillips, Bristol,
BS2 0JY Ⓟ
☎ 0117 929 9143
🅴 autempsperdu@autempsperdu.com
Ⓦ www.autempsperdu.com
Est. 1980 *Stock size* Medium
Stock Architectural antiques
Open Tues–Sat 10am–5pm

⊞ The Bed Workshop
Contact Dr Scott Jones
✉ The Old Pickle Factory,
Braunton Road, Bristol,
BS3 3AA Ⓟ
☎ 0117 963 6659
🅴 thebedworkshop@aol.com
Est. 1981 *Stock size* Large
Stock French antique furniture
Open Mon–Sat 9.30am–6pm

⊞ Bedsteads (BABAADA)
Contact Nicola Ashton
✉ Chelvey Court Barn,

Chelvey, Bristol,
BS48 4AA Ⓟ
☎ 01275 464 114 ❺ 01275 464 114
Ⓦ www.bedsteads-uk.co.uk
Est. 1990 *Stock size* Medium
Stock Antique bedsteads in iron,
brass and exotic woods
Open By appointment
Services Restoration

⊞ Bishopston Books
Contact Bill Singleton
✉ 259 Gloucester Road,
Bishopston, Bristol,
BS7 8NY Ⓟ
☎ 0117 944 5303
🅴 bishopstonbook@btinternet.com
Est. 1993 *Stock size* Small
Stock Antiquarian and second-
hand books
Open Tues–Fri 10am–5.30pm
Sat 9.30am–4.30pm Phone first
Services Book search

⊞ Bristol Bookbarn
Contact Mr Belton
✉ Central Trading Estate,
(A4 at Amos Vale, Brislington),
Bristol, Somerset,
BS4 3EH Ⓟ
☎ 01173 005400
🅴 bookbarn@bookbarn.co.uk
Ⓦ www.bookbarn.co.uk
Est. 1997 *Stock size* Large
Stock Antiquarian and second-
hand books
Open Mon–Sun 10am–6pm

⊞ Bristol Brocante
Contact David or Elizabeth
Durant
✉ 123 St Georges Road,
College Green,
Hotwells, Bristol,
BS1 5UW Ⓟ
☎ 0117 909 6688
Est. 1970 *Stock size* Large
Stock French antiques
Open Mon–Sat 1–6pm
Fairs Kensington Brocante (Sep)

⊞ Bristol Trade Antiques
Contact Mr L Dyke
✉ 192 Cheltenham Road,
Bristol,
BS6 5RB Ⓟ
☎ 0117 942 2790
Est. 1969 *Stock size* Medium
Stock Victorian and Edwardian
furniture
Open Mon–Sat 9am–5.30pm
Services Valuations, exports to
the USA

⊞ Caledonia Antiques
Contact Mrs M T Kerridge
✉ 6 The Mall, Clifton, Bristol,
BS8 4DR Ⓟ
☎ 0117 974 3582 ❺ 0117 946 7997
Ⓜ 07810 401261
Est. 1981 *Stock size* Medium
Stock Jewellery and silver
Open Mon–Sat 10am–5.30pm

⊞ Circle Books
Contact Mr Mike Piddock
✉ 65 North Street, Bedminster,
Bristol,
BS3 1ES Ⓟ
☎ 0117 966 2622
Est. 1999 *Stock size* Medium
Stock Antiquarian, second-hand,
rare and out-of-print books
Open Mon–Sat 10am–5.30pm
Services Valuations, café in shop

⊞ Clifton Hill Textiles
Contact Mrs Hodder
✉ 4 Lower Clifton Hill, Clifton,
Bristol,
BS8 1BT Ⓟ
☎ 0117 929 0644
🅴 cliftex@yahoo.com
Ⓦ www.cliftext.freeserve.co.uk
Est. 1984 *Stock size* Large
Stock Textiles, buttons, buckles
Open Mon–Fri noon–5pm
Sat 10am–5pm
Services Valuations

⊞ Cotham Antiques
Contact Susan Miller
✉ 39a Cotham Hill, Cotham,
Bristol,
BS6 6JZ Ⓟ
☎ 0117 973 3326
Est. 1983 *Stock size* Medium
Stock General
Open Tues–Sat 10.30am–5.30pm
Services Friendly advice

⚒ Dreweatt Neate Bristol Salerooms (SOFAA)
Contact Nick Ewing
✉ St John's Place, Apsley Road,
Clifton, Bristol,
BS8 2ST Ⓟ
☎ 0117 973 7201 ❺ 0117 973 5671
🅴 bristol@dnfa.com
Ⓦ www.dnfa.com
Est. 1759
Open Mon–Fri 8.45am–6pm
Sales Antiques and Fine Art,
Monthly sale Tues 10.30am,
viewing Sat 9.30am–1pm Mon
9.30am–7pm day of sale from
9am. General sale alternate

Thurs at Baynton Road, Ashton, Bristol. Collectors sale bi-monthly at Baynton Road
Catalogues Available on website

♪ Dreweatt Neate Bristol Salerooms (SOFAA)
Contact Simon Rayner
✉ Saleroom 2, Baynton Road, Ashton, Bristol, BS3 2EB 🅿
☎ 0117 953 1603 ❶ 0117 953 1598
✉ bristol@dnfa.com
ⓦ www.dnfa.com
Est. 1759
Open Mon–Fri 8.45am–6pm
Sales Victorian and modern furniture and effects sale, Thurs 10.30am, viewing Wed 11am–6pm day of sale from 9am
Frequency Fortnightly
Catalogues Yes

⊞ K Faulkner
Contact Kenneth Faulkner
✉ The Club Shop, Gloucestershire County Cricket Club, Neville Road, Bristol, BS9 EJ 🅿
☎ 0117 910 8020
✉ kfaulkner@bowmore.demon.co.uk
ⓦ www.bowmore.demon.co.uk
Est. 1995 *Stock size* Medium
Stock Sporting memorabilia, specializing in cricket
Open Mon–Fri 9am–5pm Sat 9am–1pm
Services Valuations, mail order

⊞ Focus on the Past
Contact Mrs Alison Roylance
✉ 25 Waterloo Street, Clifton Village, Bristol, BS8 4BT
☎ 0117 973 8080
Est. 1978 *Stock size* Large
Stock Furniture, pine, kitchenware, china, glass and books, advertising, 20thC collectables
Open Mon–Sat 9.30am–5.30pm Sun 11am–5.30pm
Fairs Ardingly, Newark

⊞ Grey-Harris & Co
Contact Mr Grey-Harris
✉ 12 Princess Victoria Street, Clifton, Bristol, BS8 4BP 🅿
☎ 0117 973 7365
Est. 1969 *Stock size* Large
Stock Antique jewellery, silver
Open Mon–Sat 9am–5pm
Services Valuations, restoration

⊞ Grimes Militaria
Contact Christopher or Hazel Grimes
✉ 13–14 Lower Park Row, Bristol, BS1 5BN 🅿
☎ 0117 929 8205
Est. 1967 *Stock size* Medium
Stock Scientific instruments, nautical memorabilia, militaria
Open Mon–Sat 11am–6pm
Fairs Exeter (Marsh Barton), Shepton Mallet, Newark
Services Valuations

⊞ David & Sally March Antiques (LAPADA, CINOA)
Contact David March
✉ Oak Wood Lodge, Stoke Leigh Woods, Abbots Leigh, Bristol, BS8 3QB 🅿
☎ 01275 372422 ❶ 01275 372422
ⓜ 07774 838376
✉ david.march@lineone.net
Est. 1973 *Stock size* Medium
Stock 18thC English porcelain figures, Plymouth and Bristol a speciality
Open By appointment only
Fairs LAPADA, NEC, Olympia
Services Valuations

⊞ Marlenes
Contact Marlene Risdale
✉ Clifton Antiques Centre, 23 The Mall, Clifton, Bristol, BS8 4JG 🅿
☎ 0117 973 7645
ⓜ 0797 1430831
Est. 1958 *Stock size* Medium
Stock Silver, jewellery
Open Tues–Sat 10am–6pm
Fairs Stafford
Services Valuations

⊞ Robert Mills Architectural Antiques (SALVO)
Contact Colin Scull
✉ Narroways Road, Eastville, Bristol, BS2 9XB 🅿
☎ 0117 955 6542 ❶ 0117 955 8146
✉ sales@rmills.co.uk
ⓦ www.rmills.co.uk
Est. 1970 *Stock size* Large
Stock Architectural antiques including Gothic church furnishings, stained glass windows, pub interiors, fittings
Open Mon–Fri 9am–5pm

⊞ Jan Morrison
Contact Jan Morrison
✉ 3 Clifton Arcade, Boyces Avenue, Clifton, Bristol, BS8 4AA 🅿
☎ 0117 970 6822 ❶ 0117 970 6822
ⓜ 07789 094428
Est. 1979 *Stock size* Medium
Stock 18th–19thC glass and silver, modern jewellery
Open Tues–Sat 10am–5.30pm
Services Valuations

⊞ Oldwoods
Contact Sid Duck
✉ 4 Colston Yard, Bristol, Somerset, BS1 5BD 🅿
☎ 0117 929 9023
Est. 1982 *Stock size* Small
Stock Victorian and pine furniture, decorative items
Open Mon–Fri 10am-5pm or by appointment
Services Restoration

⊞ Olliff's Architectural Antiques (SALVO)
Contact Marcus Olliff
✉ 26 Redland Court Road (office only), Redland, Bristol, Somerset, BS6 7EQ 🅿 ❶ 0117 924 4984
ⓜ 07850 235793
✉ marcus@olliffs.com
ⓦ www.olliffs.com
Est. 1993 *Stock size* Large
Stock Georgian–Edwardian marble, stone and timber fireplaces, garden statuary, garden decorative items, doors, door furniture, stone doorways and windows, gates, lighting, mirrors, oak flooring
Open By appointment only
Services Valuations, restoration, shipping

⊞ Pastimes (OMRS)
Contact Mr A H Stevens
✉ 22 Lower Park Row, Bristol, BS1 5BN 🅿
☎ 0117 929 9330
Est. 1974 *Stock size* Large
Stock Militaria
Open Mon–Sat 10.30am–1.45pm 2.45–5pm Wed 11am–5pm
Fairs Mark Carter Militaria and Medal Fairs
Services Medal mounting

⊞ Period Fireplaces
Contact John Ashton
✉ The Old Station Building,

185

Station Road, Montpelier,
Bristol, Somerset,
BS6 5EE ⓟ
☎ 0117 944 4449 ☻ 0117 942 4091
❸ enquiries@periodfireplaces.co.uk
ⓦ www.periodfireplaces.co.uk
Est. 1984 *Stock size* Large
Stock Fireplaces
Open Mon–Fri 9am–5pm
Sat 10am–4pm
Services Restoration

⊞ **Piano Export**
Contact Mr T W Smallridge
⊠ Bridge Road,
Kingswood,
Bristol,
BS15 4FW ⓟ
☎ 0117 956 8300
Est. 1982 *Stock size* Medium
Stock Grand pianos – Steinway,
Bechstein and decorative pianos
Open Mon–Fri 8am–5pm or by
appointment

⊞ **Porchester Antiques**
Contact Mrs Devonia Andrews
⊠ 58 The Mall, Clifton, Bristol,
BS8 4JG ⓟ
☎ 0117 373 0256 ☻ 01275 810629
ⓦ 07970 970449
❸ devonia@porchester-
collectables.co.uk
ⓦ www.porchester-collectables.co.uk
Est. 1978 *Stock size* Medium
Stock Moorcroft, enamels and
pottery, Sally Tuffin pottery, fine
jewellery
Open Tues–Sat 10am–6pm
Services Valuations

⊞ **Pride & Joy Antiques**
Contact Martin Williams
⊠ 25 North View,
Westbury Park,
Bristol,
BS6 7SD ⓟ
☎ 0117 973 5806
Est. 1994 *Stock size* Medium
Stock Victorian–Edwardian
furniture
Open Mon–Sat 10.30am–1pm
2–5pm
Services Upholstery

⊞ **Vincents of Clifton**
Contact Paul Risdale
⊠ Clifton Antique Centre,
23 The Mall, Clifton, Bristol,
BS8 4JG ⓟ
☎ 0117 973 7645
ⓦ 07792 927457
Est. 1984 *Stock size* Medium

Stock Jewellery, silver and gold
Open Tues–Sat 10am–6pm
Fairs Stafford

⌂ **Whiteladies Antiques &
Collectables**
Contact Kate Baker or
Lyn Stailygh
⊠ 49c Whiteladies Road,
Clifton, Bristol,
BS8 2LS ⓟ
☎ 0117 973 5766
Est. 2001 *Stock size* Large
No. of dealers 20
Stock Antiques and collectables,
small furniture, vintage clothes
Open Mon–Sat 10.30am–5pm

BRUTON

⊞ **The Antiques Shop
Bruton**
Contact David Gwilliam
⊠ 5 High Street, Bruton,
Somerset,
BA10 0AB ⓟ
☎ 01749 813264
Est. 1976 *Stock size* Medium
Stock Furniture, brass, copper,
jewellery, silver, china and
collectables
Open Thurs–Sat 10am–5.30pm
Services Jewellery repairs,
restringing, watch, clock repairs

⊞ **European Accent**
Contact Steve Green
⊠ Station Road, Bruton,
Somerset,
BA10 0EH ⓟ
☎ 01749 814961 ☻ 01749 814962
ⓦ 07977 496762
❸ enquiries@europeanaccent.co.uk
ⓦ www.europeanaccent.co.uk
Est. 1998 *Stock size* Medium
Stock Country decorative,
painted, pine and fruitwood
furniture, smalls
Open Mon–Fri 8.30am–5.30pm or
by appointment
Fairs Newark, Shepton Mallet
Services Valuations

⊞ **Michael Lewis Gallery**
Contact Mrs J L Lewis
⊠ 17 High Street, Bruton,
Somerset,
BA10 0AB ⓟ
☎ 01749 813557
Est. 1980 *Stock size* Large
Stock Antiquarian maps and prints
Open Mon–Sat 9.30am–5.30pm
closed Thurs 1pm

⊞ **M G R Exports**
Contact Mr M Read
⊠ Station Road,
Bruton,
Somerset,
BA10 0EH ⓟ
☎ 01749 812460 ☻ 01749 812882
❸ enquiries@mgrexports.co.uk
ⓦ www.mgrexports.co.uk
Est. 1979 *Stock size* Large
Stock General antiques
Open Mon–Fri 8.30am–5.30pm
Services Packing, container
packing and shipping

BURNHAM-ON-SEA

➢ **Adams Auctions**
Contact Mrs R Combes
⊠ 28 Adam Street,
Burnham-on-Sea,
Somerset,
TA8 1PQ ⓟ
☎ 01278 793709 ☻ 01278 793709
Est. 1993
Open Mon–Sat 10am–1pm
Sales Antique and general sales
monthly Wed 6pm, viewing Tues
2–6pm Wed 10am–6pm
Catalogues Yes

⊞ **The Burnham Model &
Collectors Shop**
Contact W Loudon
⊠ 3 College Court,
College Street,
Burnham-on-Sea,
Somerset,
TA8 1AR ⓟ
☎ 01278 780066 ☻ 01278 780066
❸ sambodys@hotmail.com
Est. 1994 *Stock size* Large
Stock Ephemera, postcards,
banknotes, coins, medals, die-
cast models, cigarette cards
Open Mon–Sat Sun in summer
holidays 9.30am–5pm
Services Valuations

⊞ **Heape's**
Contact Mrs M Heap
⊠ 39 Victoria Street,
Burnham-on-Sea,
Somerset,
TA8 1AN ⓟ
☎ 01278 782131 ☻ 01278 782131
Est. 1988 *Stock size* Large
Stock Porcelain, silverware, fine
art, glass, collectables, jewellery
Open Tues Thurs–Sat
10am–4.30pm Wed 10am–1pm
Services Bespoke framing,
specialist table lamps

CASTLE CARY

⊞ Antiquus
Contact Gerald Davison
✉ West Country House,
Woodcock Street, Castle Cary,
Somerset,
BA7 7BJ 🅿
☎ 01963 351246
📠 07968 810092
🌐 www.chinesemarks.com
Est. 2002 *Stock size* Medium
Stock English and Oriental
antiques
Open Tues Fri Sat 10am–5pm
Services Lectures on Chinese
ceramics

⊞ Johnsons Antiques
Contact Nicholas Johnson
✉ 6&7 Pithers Yard,
Castle Cary,
Somerset,
BA7 7AN 🅿
☎ 01963 351120 📠 01963 351030
Est. 1865 *Stock size* Medium
Stock Interesting and wacky
objects, 1950s –1960s retro pieces
Open Tues–Sun 9.30am–4pm

CHARD

🏛 Chard Antiques Centre
Contact Julie Hills or
Alistair Smith
✉ 23 High Street, Chard,
Somerset,
TA20 1QF 🅿
☎ 01460 63517
📧 info@chardantiques.co.uk
🌐 www.chardantiques.co.uk
Est. 1997 *Stock size* Medium
No. of dealers 7
Stock General antiques,
furniture, English pine and
decorative items
Open Mon–Sat 10am–5pm or by
appointment

CHEDDAR

⊞ Matthew Bayly Antiques
Contact Matthew Bayly
✉ Mark Hole Cottage,
The Cliffs, Cheddar,
Somerset,
BS27 3QH 🅿
☎ 01934 743990
Est. 1972 *Stock size* Small
Stock General small antiques
Open By appointment
Services Valuations, restoration

⊞ Cheddar Antiques & Upholstery
Contact Joy Maloney
✉ Barrows House, Tweentown,
Cheddar, Somerset,
BS27 3HU 🅿
☎ 01934 744816 📠 01934 744816
Est. 1976 *Stock size* Medium
Stock Antique upholstered
chairs, chaises longues, Victorian
furniture, Art Deco, ceramics,
china, glass
Open Tues–Sat 10am–6.30pm

CHILCOMPTON

⊞ Billiard Room Antiques (LAPADA, BABAADA, CINOA)
Contact Mrs J Mckeivor
✉ The Old School, Church Lane,
Chilcompton, Bath,
Somerset,
BA3 4HP 🅿
☎ 01761 232839 📠 01761 232839
📧 info@billiardroom.co.uk
🌐 www.billiardroom.co.uk
Est. 1990 *Stock size* Medium
Stock Billiard room furnishings
Open By appointment only
Fairs Olympia
Services Valuations, restoration
and shipping

CHIPPING SODBURY

⊞ Sodbury Antiques
Contact Millicent Brown
✉ 70 Broad Street,
Chipping Sodbury, Bristol,
BS37 6AG 🅿
☎ 01454 273369 📠 01454 273369
Est. 1989 *Stock size* Medium
Stock China, jewellery and bric-a-
brac
Open Mon–Sat 9.30am–5.30pm
closed Wed

CLEVEDON

⊞ Clevedon Books (PBFA)
Contact Mr or Mrs Douthwaite
✉ The Gallery, 29 Copse Road,
Clevedon, Somerset,
BS21 7QN 🅿
☎ 01275 790579/872304
📠 01275 342817
📧 clevedonbooks@globalnet.co.uk
Est. 1970 *Stock size* Medium
Stock Antiquarian books, maps
and prints, second-hand books,
history, science and technology a
speciality
Open Thurs–Sat 11am–4.30pm
Fairs PBFA
Services Print and map colouring

⚒ Clevedon Salerooms
Contact Marc Burridge
✉ The Auction Centre,
Kenn Road, Kenn,
Clevedon, Somerset,
BS21 6TT 🅿
☎ 01275 876699 📠 01275 343765
📧 clevedon-salerooms@blue
yonder.co.uk
🌐 www.clevedon-salerooms.com
Est. 1880
Open Mon–Fri 9am–5.30pm
Sales Fine art and antiques sales,
Thurs 10.30am, viewing Tues
2–5.30pm Wed 10am–6.30pm
9am morning of sale.
Fortnightly sales of Victorian
and later household furniture,
effects, Thurs 10am, viewing
Wed 10am–7.30pm morning of
sale 9am
Catalogues Yes

⊞ The Collector
Contact Malcolm or Tina
Simmonds
✉ 14 The Beach, Clevedon,
Somerset,
BS21 7QU 🅿
☎ 01275 875066
Est. 1992 *Stock size* Small
Stock Smalls and collectables
including Beatrix Potter figures
Open Mon–Sat 10am–5pm
Sun 11am–5pm closed Thurs
Fairs Malvern Three Counties,
Brunel Temple Meads, Bristol
Services Valuations

COXLEY

⊞ Mrs Mitchell
Contact Mrs Mitchell
✉ Clover Close House,
Main Road, Coxley, Somerset,
BA5 1QZ 🅿
☎ 01749 679533
Est. 1984 *Stock size* Medium
Stock General antiques
Open Mon–Sat 9am–5pm
Services Caning and upholstery

CREWKERNE

⊞ Antiques and Country Pine
Contact Mrs Wheeler
✉ 14 East Street,
Crewkerne, Somerset,

TA18 7AG ℗
☎ 01460 75623
Est. 1979 *Stock size* Medium
Stock Antique and country pine
furniture
Open Tues–Sat 10am–5pm

⊞ Books Galore
Contact Mrs Hall
✉ The Old Warehouse,
North Street, Crewkerne,
Somerset,
TA18 7AJ ℗
☎ 01460 74465 ℗ 01460 74465
⊕ 07957 986053
℮ hallbook@aol.com
Est. 1969 *Stock size* Large
Stock Second-hand books,
countryside topics a speciality
Open Mon–Sat 10am–1pm
2.30–5pm
Services Book search

⌂ Crewkerne Antiques
Contact Eddie Blewden
✉ 16 Market Street, Crewkerne,
Somerset,
TA18 7LA ℗
☎ 01460 77111 ℗ 01460 77111
Est. 1991 *Stock size* Large
No. of dealers 50
Stock General antiques, garden
section
Open Mon–Sat 9.30am–4.30pm
Services Valuations

⊞ Gresham Books (PBFA, ABA)
Contact James Hine
✉ 31 Market Street, Crewkerne,
Somerset,
TA18 7JU ℗
☎ 01460 77726 ℗ 01460 52479
℮ jameshine@gresham-books.
demon.co.uk
Est. 1972 *Stock size* Large
Stock Antiquarian and second-
hand books including early
cookery and architectural
Open Mon–Sat 10am–5pm
Fairs London Bookfair (monthly),
most major book fairs (phone for
details)
Services Valuations

♪ Lawrence Fine Art Auctioneers Ltd (ARVA, SOFAA)
Contact Leah Ferguson
✉ 4 Linen Yard, South Street,
Crewkerne, Somerset,
TA18 8AB ℗
☎ 01460 73041 ℗ 01460 270799

℮ enquiries@lawrences.co.uk
⊕ www.lawrences.co.uk
Est. 1900
Open Mon–Fri 9am–5pm
Sales 5 fine art sales a year.
General household sale every
Wed 9.30am, viewing Tues
9.30am–7pm
Catalogues Yes

⊞ Noah's
Contact Mrs Edmonds
✉ 41 Market Square,
Crewkerne,
Somerset,
TA18 7LP ℗
☎ 01460 77786
Est. 2001 *Stock size* Medium
Stock Fine art and antiques,
silver, jewellery
Open Mon–Sat 10am–4.30pm
Services Valuations

⊞ Phoenix Books
Contact Dennis Hann
✉ 5 The George Precinct,
Crewkerne, Somerset,
TA18 7LU ℗
☎ 01460 76579
Est. 1990 *Stock size* Medium
Stock Antiquarian and second-
hand books, crime, modern first
editions
Open Mon–Sat 10am–5pm

⊞ Newmans (BAFRA)
Contact Tony Newman
✉ Tithe Barn, Crowcombe,
Somerset,
TA4 4AQ ℗
☎ 01984 618367
⊕ 07717 682027
℮ tony@cheddon.fsnet.co.uk
Est. 1991 *Stock size* Small
Stock 18th–19thC furniture
Open Mon–Sun 9am–5pm but
phone first
Services Valuations, restoration

⊞ Acorn Antiques
Contact Peter Hounslow
✉ 39 High Street, Dulverton,
Somerset,
TA22 9DW ℗
☎ 01398 323286
℮ Peter@exmoorantiques.co.uk
⊕ www.exmoorantiques.co.uk
Est. 1988 *Stock size* Medium
Stock 18th–19thC furniture,

decorative items and general
antiques
Trade only Yes
Open Mon–Sat 9.30am–5.30pm
or Sun by appointment
Services Interior design

⊞ Anthony Sampson
Contact Mr A Sampson
✉ Holland House, Bridge Street,
Dulverton, Somerset,
TA22 9HJ ℗
☎ 01398 324247
⊕ 07767 842409
Est. 1968 *Stock size* Medium
Stock Furniture, general antiques
Open Mon–Sat 9.30am–5.30pm
Sun by appointment
Services Valuations

⊞ The Crooked Window
Contact Robert Ricketts
✉ 7 High Street, Dunster,
Somerset,
TA24 6SF ℗
☎ 01643 821606
⊕ 07787 722606
℮ icthus-fine-art@supanet.com
Est. 1987 *Stock size* Medium
Stock 17th–18thC English
furniture, Chinese and European
ceramics and works of art,
including jade, antique jewellery
Open Mon–Sat 10.30am–5.30pm
Fairs Wilton House
Services Valuations

⊞ Cottage Collectibles
Contact Mrs S Kettle
✉ 2 Pennard House,
East Pennard, Somerset,
BA4 6TP ℗
☎ 01749 860266 ℗ 01749 860732
⊕ 07967 713512
℮ sheila@cottagecollectibles.co.uk
⊕ www.cottagecollectibles.co.uk
Est. 1995 *Stock size* Medium
Stock English and Continental
country antiques, kitchenware,
pine furniture, garden and dairy
tools
Open Mon–Sat 10am–5pm
Services Restoration

⊞ Pennard House Antiques (BABAADA, LAPADA)
Contact Martin Dearden
✉ East Pennard, Shepton Mallet,

Somerset,
BA4 6TP P
☎ 01749 860731 📠 01749 860700
📱 07802 243569
📧 pennardantiques@ukonline.co.uk
🌐 www.pennardantiques.com
Est. 1979 *Stock size* Large
Stock French and English country
furniture and decorative items
Open Mon–Sat 9.30am–5.30pm
or by appointment
Fairs Bath Decorative and
Antiques Fair
Services Restoration, shipping
and deliveries

FRESHFORD

⊞ **Freshfords Fine Art
(LAPADA, CINOA,
BABAADA)**
Contact Mr Simon Powell
✉ High Street, Freshford,
Bath, Somerset,
BA2 7WF P
☎ 01225 722111 📠 01225 722991
📱 07720 838877
📧 antiques@freshfords.com
🌐 www.freshfords.com
Est. 1973 *Stock size* Large
Stock Regency period furniture
Open Mon–Fri 10am–5pm
Sat by appointment only
Fairs Olympia, Chelsea
Services Valuations, restoration,
shipping, book search

FROME

⌂ **Antiques and Country
Living**
Contact Mrs D M Williams
✉ 43–44 Vallis Way,
Frome, Somerset,
BA11 3BA P
☎ 01373 463015
📱 07808 933076
Est. 1994 *Stock size* Large
No. of dealers 4
Stock 18th–19thC pottery and
porcelain, Georgian–Edwardian
furniture, books
Open Mon–Sun 9.30am–5.30pm

⊞ **Steve Vee Bransgrove
Collectables**
Contact Steve
✉ 6 Catherine Hill,
Frome,
Somerset,
BA11 1BY
☎ 01373 453225
📱 07977 694537

Est. 1995 *Stock size* Medium
Stock Collectables, advertising,
vintage magazines, ephemera
and nostalgia
Open Mon–Sat 10am–5pm
Thurs closed in winter
10am–2pm in summer
Services Valuations

⚒ **Cooper and Tanner
Chartered Surveyors**
Contact Dennis Barnard
✉ The Agricultural Centre,
Standerwick, Frome,
Somerset,
BA11 2QB P
☎ 01373 831010 📠 01373 831103
📧 agricultural@cooperand
tanner.co.uk
Est. 1900
Open Mon 2.30–5pm Tues
9am–4pm Wed 8.30am–5.30pm
Thurs 9am–12.30pm
Sales Furniture, fine art and
antiques sale Wed 10.30am,
viewing Tues 9am–4pm Wed
8.30am prior to sale
Frequency Weekly
Catalogues No

⊞ **Frome Reclamation
(SALVO)**
Contact Karl or Steve Horler
✉ Station Approach,
Frome, Somerset,
BA11 1RE P
☎ 01373 463919 📠 01373 453122
📱 07729 263949 or 07836 277507
📧 info@fromerec.co.uk
🌐 www.fromerec.co.uk
Est. 1987 *Stock size* Large
Stock Architectural antiques,
including roofing, flooring,
period fireplaces, doors,
bathrooms, etc
Open Mon–Fri 8am–5pm
Sat 8am–4.30pm

GLASTONBURY

⊞ **Courtyard Books**
Contact Mr Mills
✉ 2–4 High Street,
Glastonbury,
Somerset,
BA6 9DU P
☎ 01458 835050 📠 08717 172155
📧 courtyard@speakingtree.co.uk
🌐 www.speakingtree.co.uk
Est. 1995 *Stock size* Large
Stock Antiquarian, esoteric, New
Age and magic books
Open Mon–Sun 9.30am–5.30pm

HINTON ST GEORGE

⊞ **David Carstairs**
Contact David Carstairs
✉ Hinton St George,
Somerset,
TA18 P
☎ 01460 54489 📠 01460 55407
🌐 www.davidcarstairs.co.uk
Est. 1986 *Stock size* Small
Stock 18th–19thC furniture and
works of art, lighting
Open By appointment
Fairs NEC
Services Valuations for probate
and insurance

ILCHESTER

⊞ **Gilbert and Dale**
Contact Roy Gilbert or Joan Dale
✉ The Old Chapel,
Church Street, Ilchester,
Yeovil, Somerset,
BA22 8LN P
☎ 01935 840464 📠 01935 841599
📧 roygilbertantiques.freeserve.co.uk
Est. 1969 *Stock size* Medium
Stock English and French country
furniture and accessories
Trade only Mainly trade
Open Mon–Fri 9am–5.30pm

ILMINSTER

⊞ **Stuart Interiors
Antiques Ltd (LAPADA)**
Contact Peter Russell
✉ Barrington Court,
Barrington, Ilminster,
Somerset,
TA19 0NQ P
☎ 01460 240349 📠 01460 242069
📧 design@studiointeriors.com
🌐 www.studiointeriors.com
Est. 1976 *Stock size* Large
Stock Early English oak and
decorative pieces
Open Mon–Fri 9am–5.30pm
Sat by appointment

KNOLE

⊞ **Knole Barometers**
Contact David Crawshaw
✉ Lower Knole Farm,
Knole, Long Sutton,
Longport,
Somerset,
TA10 9HZ P
☎ 01458 241015 📠 01458 241706
📱 07785 364567
📧 dccops@btconnect.com

WEST COUNTRY
SOMERSET • LANGPORT

Est. 1997 *Stock size* Medium
Stock Barometers, scientific instruments
Open Mon–Fri 9am–5pm
Services Valuations, restoration

LANGPORT

⊞ Oldnautibits
Contact Geoff Pringle
✉ PO Box 67, Langport, Somerset,
TA10 9WJ 🅿
☎ 01458 241816
Ⓜ 07947 277833
📧 geoff.pringle@oldnautibits.com
Ⓦ www.oldnautibits.com
Est. 2002 *Stock size* Medium
Stock Aeronautical, maritime collectables
Open Mon–Fri 9am–5pm
Fairs DNG Bath and West Showground

LYDEARD ST LAWRENCE

⌂ The Coach House
Contact Clare Roberts
✉ Handycross Farmhouse, Handycross, Lydeard St Lawrence, Taunton, Somerset,
TA4 3PL 🅿
☎ 01984 667568
Est. 1996 *Stock size* Large
No. of dealers 11
Stock A wide range of furniture, collectables, silver, ceramics
Open Thurs–Sun Bank Holidays 11am–5pm

MARTOCK

⊞ Castle Reclamation (SALVO)
Contact Mr A Wills
✉ Parrett Works, Martock, Somerset,
TA12 6AE 🅿
☎ 01935 826483 📠 01935 826791
📧 info@castlereclamation.com
Ⓦ www.castlereclamation.com
Est. 1989 *Stock size* Medium
Stock Architectural antiques, stone masonry, hand-carved natural stone fireplaces, oak flooring, 16th–17thC-style oak furniture, panelling
Open Mon–Fri 8.30am–5pm
Sat 10am–1pm
Fairs Bath and West, Dyrham Park, Kingston Lacy

MIDSOMER NORTON

⊞ Somervale Antiques (BADA, LAPADA, CINOA, BABAADA)
Contact Wing Commander Ron Thomas
✉ The Poplars, 6 Radstock Road, Midsomer Norton, Radstock, Somerset,
BA3 2AJ 🅿
☎ 01761 412686 📠 01761 412686
Ⓜ 07885 088022
📧 ronthomas@somervale antiquesglass.co.uk
Ⓦ www.somervaleantiquesglass.co.uk
Est. 1972 *Stock size* Large
Stock English 18th–19thC drinking glasses, decanters, cut and coloured, Bristol and Nailsea glass, scent bottles
Open By appointment. Trains to Bath met by arrangement
Services Valuations

MINEHEAD

⊞ Chris's Crackers
Contact Peter Marshall
✉ Townsend Garage, Main Road, Carhampton, Minehead, Somerset,
BA24 6LH 🅿
☎ 01643 821873
Ⓦ www.chriscrackers.net
Est. 1995 *Stock size* Large
Stock Reclamation, agricultural antiques, pine furniture, collectables
Open Mon–Sun 10.30am–5.30pm

NORTH CHERITON

⊞ Paper Pleasures (PBFA)
Contact Lesley Tyson
✉ Holt Farm, North Cheriton, Somerset,
BA8 0AQ 🅿
☎ 01963 33718
📧 books@paperpleasures.bchip.com
Ⓦ www.paperpleasures.com
Stock size Small
Stock Antiquarian and second-hand books
Open By appointment
Services Book search

NORTH PETHERTON

⊞ Hallidays (LAPADA)
Contact James Halliday
✉ 35 Fore Street, North Petherton, Somerset,

TA6 6PY 🅿
☎ 01278 662397 📠 01823 324073
Est. 1987 *Stock size* Medium
Stock 18th–19thC furniture, upholstery, ceramics
Open Mon–Sat 9am–5pm
Services Valuations, upholstery, furniture renovation

PORLOCK

⊞ Porlock Antiques and Gallery Ltd
Contact Sara Goodson
✉ High Street, Porlock, Somerset,
TA24 8PU 🅿
☎ 01643 862226
📧 porlockantiques@aol.com
Est. 2002 *Stock size* Medium
Stock Furniture, paintings
Open Mon–Sat 10am–5.30pm

⊞ Rare Books & Berry
Contact Michael Berry
✉ Lowerbourne House, High Street, Porlock, Somerset,
TA24 8PT 🅿
☎ 01643 863255 📠 01643 863092
📧 info@rarebooksandberry.co.uk
Ⓦ www.rarebooksandberry.co.uk
Est. 1982 *Stock size* Medium
Stock Antiquarian and second-hand books
Open Mon–Sat 9.30am–5pm
Services Book search

QUEEN CAMEL

⊞ Steven Ferdinando (PBFA)
Contact Mr Steven Ferdinando
✉ The Old Vicarage, Queen Camel, Yeovil, Somerset,
BA22 7NG 🅿
☎ 01935 850210
Est. 1978 *Stock size* Medium
Stock Antiquarian and second-hand books
Open Visitors welcome by appointment
Fairs PBFA
Services Valuations, book search

RADSTOCK

⊞ Notts Pine
Contact Jeff Nott
✉ Old Redhouse Farm, Stratton-on-the-Fosse, Radstock, Bath, Somerset,
BA3 4QE 🅿
☎ 01761 419911

Est. 1986 *Stock size* Medium
Stock Antique pine furniture
Open Mon–Fri 9am–6pm

SHEPTON MALLET

⊞ **Parkways Antiques**
Contact Pauline Brereton
⊠ **31 High Street,**
Shepton Mallet, Somerset,
BA4 5AQ ℗
☎ 01749 345065
Est. 1972 *Stock size* Small
Stock Period furniture
(mahogany, oak, walnut), china,
clocks, silver
Open Thurs–Fri 10am–4pm or by
appointment

SOMERTON

⊞ **John Gardiner**
Contact Mr John Gardiner
⊠ **Monteclefe House,**
Kirkham Street,
Somerton, Somerset,
TA11 7NL ℗
☎ 01458 272238 ❶ 01458 274329
Ⓜ 07831 274427
Est. 1968 *Stock size* Medium
Stock General antiques,
decorative items
Open Appointment advisable
Services Workshop facilities

⊞ **London Cigarette Card
Company Ltd**
Contact Mr Laker
⊠ **West Street, Somerton,**
Somerset,
TA11 6QP ℗
☎ 01458 273452 ❶ 01458 273515
❸ cards@londoncigcard.co.uk
Ⓦ www.londoncigcard.co.uk
Est. 1927 *Stock size* Large
Stock Cigarette cards, trade cards
Open Mon–Sat 9.30am–5pm
closed Wed Sat pm
Services Direct sales,
public/postal auctions. Publishes
catalogues, card collectors'
magazines, trade cards

⊞ **Simon's Books**
Contact Mr B Ives
⊠ **Broad Street, Somerton,**
Somerset,
TA11 7NH ℗
☎ 01458 272313
Est. 1979 *Stock size* Medium
Stock General antiquarian and
second-hand books
Open Mon–Sat 10am–4.30pm

⌂ **Somerton Antique
Centre**
Contact David Rogers
⊠ **Market Place, Somerton,**
Somerset,
TA11 7NB ℗
☎ 01458 274423 ❶ 01458 274423
Est. 1997 *Stock size* Large
No. of dealers 50
Stock General antiques including
paintings, linen, militaria, pine
and oak
Open Mon–Sat 10am–5pm

⊞ **Westville House
Antiques**
Contact Derek or Margaret
Stacey
⊠ **Westville House, Littleton,**
Somerton, Somerset,
TA11 6NP ℗
☎ 01458 273376 ❶ 01458 273376
❸ antique@westville.co.uk
Ⓦ www.westville.co.uk
Est. 1986 *Stock size* Large
Stock Antique country, pine, oak
and mahogany furniture
Open Mon–Sat 9am–5.30pm or
by appointment

STOKE SUB HAMDON

⊞ **R G Watkins (PBFA)**
Contact Mr R G Watkins
⊠ **9 North Street Workshops,**
Stoke sub Hamdon, Somerset,
TA14 6QR ℗
☎ 01935 822891 ❶ 01935 822891
❸ rgw@eurobell.co.uk
Ⓦ www.rgw.eurobell.co.uk
Est. 1985 *Stock size* Small
Stock Antiquarian books, prints,
portraits, books on art and
antiques a speciality
Open Fri 10am–5pm or by
appointment
Fairs PBFA
Services Valuations

TAUNTON

⊞ **Aarons Antiques**
⊠ **27–29 Silver Street,**
Taunton, Somerset,
TA1 3DH ℗
☎ 01823 698295
Est. 1982 *Stock size* Large
Stock Small antiques, collectables
Open Mon 9am–4pm

⊞ **Aarons Coins**
⊠ **27–29 Silver Street,**
Taunton, Somerset,

TA1 3DH ℗
☎ 01823 698295
Est. 1982 *Stock size* Large
Stock Coins and banknotes,
ancient and modern
Open Mon 9am–4pm

⌂ **Cider Press Antiques
Centre**
Contact Norman Clarke or
Mark Blake
⊠ **58 Bridge Street,**
Taunton, Somerset,
TA1 1UD ℗
☎ 01823 283050 ❶ 01823 283050
Ⓜ 07764 212520
Est. 2000 *Stock size* Large
No. of dealers 10
Stock Period furniture, ceramics,
jewellery, stamps, collectables,
vinyl records
Open Mon–Sat 10am–5pm
Sun 11am–4pm
Services Valuations

🖊 **Greenslade Taylor Hunt
Fine Art (SOFAA)**
Contact Luke Macdonald
⊠ **Magdalene House,**
Church Square, Taunton,
Somerset,
TA1 1SB ℗
☎ 01823 332525 ❶ 01823 353120
Ⓜ 07739 099989
❸ fine.art@gth.net
Ⓦ www.gth.net
Est. 1843
Open Mon–Fri 9am–5.30pm
Sales Bi-monthly fine art sales
second Tues 10.30am, viewing Fri
9.30am–4.30pm Sat 9.30am–1pm
Mon 9.30am–6pm. Also four
collectors' sales and two sporting
sales, viewing as for the fine art
sales
Catalogues Yes

⊞ **Hallidays (LAPADA)**
Contact James Halliday
⊠ **6 St James Street,**
Taunton, Somerset,
TA1 1JH ℗
☎ 01823 324073 ❶ 01823 324073
Est. 1987 *Stock size* Medium
Stock 18th–19thC furniture,
upholstery, ceramics
Open Mon–Sat 9am–5pm
Services Valuations, upholstery,
furniture renovation

⊞ **Selwoods Antiques**
Contact Mr J R Selwood
⊠ **Queen Anne Cottage,**

Mary Street, Taunton, Somerset,
TA1 3PE 🅿
☎ 01823 272780
Est. 1927 *Stock size* Large
Stock Furniture
Open Mon–Sat 9.30am–5pm

🏠 **Taunton Antiques Market**
Contact Mike Spooner
✉ 25–29 Silver Street, Taunton, Somerset, TA1 3DH 🅿
☎ 01823 289327 ☎ 01823 286555
Est. 1978 *Stock size* Large
No. of dealers 100
Stock General antiques and collectables including specialists in most fields
Open Mon 9am–4pm including Bank Holidays

TEMPLE CLOUD

⊞ **Bookbarn Ltd**
Contact Mr Belton
✉ White Cross, (10 miles south of Bristol Junction of A37 and A39), Temple Cloud, Somerset, BS39 6EX 🅿
☎ 01761 451777
🌐 bookbarn@bookbarn.co.uk
🌐 www.bookbarn.co.uk
Est. 1997 *Stock size* Large
Stock Antiquarian and second-hand books
Open Mon–Sun 10am–6pm

TIMSBURY

⊞ **Ministry of Pine**
Contact Tony or Susan Lawrence
✉ Timsbury Village Workshop, Unit 2, Timsbury Industrial Estate, Hayeswood Road, Timsbury, Bath, Somerset, BA2 0HQ 🅿
☎ 01761 472297
📱 07770 588536
🌐 info@ministryofpine.com
🌐 www.ministryofpine.com
Est. 1980 *Stock size* Large
Stock Antique pine furniture both painted and stripped
Open Mon–Fri 9am–6pm Sat 10am–4pm
Services Valuations, restoration and stripping

WATCHET

⊞ **Clarence House Antiques**
Contact Mr or Mrs Cotton
✉ 41 Swain Street, Watchet,

Somerset, TA23 0AE 🅿
☎ 01984 631389
Est. 1972 *Stock size* Medium
Stock Antiques, curios, collectables
Open Mon–Sat 11am–5.30pm

WELLINGTON

⊞ **Michael & Amanda Lewis Oriental Carpets and Rugs (LAPADA)**
Contact Amanda Lewis
✉ 8 North Street, Wellington, Somerset, TA21 8LT 🅿
☎ 01823 667430
🌐 rugmike@btopenworld.com
Est. 1981 *Stock size* Medium
Stock Antique and Oriental rugs
Open Tues–Fri 10.30am–1pm 2–5.30pm Sat by appointment
Services Valuations, restoration, cleaning

⊞ **Graham Sparks Restoration**
Contact Mr Graham Sparks
✉ Unit 63, Tone Mill, Tonedale, Wellington, Somerset, TA21 0AB 🅿
☎ 01823 663636 ☎ 01823 667393
🌐 grahamsparksrestoration@yahoo.co.uk
Est. 1979
Stock Desks, cabinets
Open Mon–Fri 8am–6pm Sat 8am–1pm
Services Restoration, cabinet making

WELLS

⊞ **Alcove Antiques**
Contact Nancy Alcock
✉ 1 Priest Row, Wells, Somerset, BA5 2PY 🅿
☎ 01749 672164 ☎ 01749 678925
Est. 1979 *Stock size* Medium
Stock China, brass, copper, pine, Victorian and Edwardian mahogany
Open Tues Thurs–Sat 10.30am–5pm Wed 10.30am–1pm
Services Restoration

⊞ **Country Brocante (BABAADA)**
Contact Tim Ovel
✉ Fir Tree Farm, Lower Godney, Wells, Somerset, BA5 1RZ 🅿

☎ 01458 833052 ☎ 01458 835611
📱 07970 719708
🌐 ovel@compuserve.com
Est. 1993 *Stock size* Large
Stock French furniture, chandeliers, early mirrors
Open By appointment
Fairs Newark, Shepton Mallet

⊞ **Bernard G House Longcase Clocks**
Contact Mr B G House
✉ 13 Market Place, Wells, Somerset, BA5 2RF 🅿
☎ 01749 672607 ☎ 01749 672607
🌐 www.antiqueclocksand barometers.co.uk
Est. 1971 *Stock size* Medium
Stock Longcase clocks, barographs, barometers, clocks, telescopes, scientific instruments
Open Mon–Sat 10am–5.30pm or by appointment
Services Repair and restoration of clocks and barometers

🔨 **Wells Auction Rooms**
Contact Nick Ewing or Cynthia Peak
✉ 66–68 Southover, Wells, Somerset, BA5 1UH 🅿
☎ 01749 678094/ 0117 973 7201
Est. 1845
Sales Sale monthly Wed 1.30pm, viewing Tues noon–5pm day of sale from 9am
Catalogues Yes

⊞ **Wells Reclamation Company**
✉ Coxley, Wells, Somerset, BA5 1RQ 🅿
☎ 01749 677087 ☎ 01749 671098
🌐 enquiries@wellsreclamation.com
🌐 www.wellsreclamation.com
Est. 1984 *Stock size* Large
Stock Architectural antiques, bricks, tiles, slates, fireplaces, doors, finials, pews, etc
Open Mon–Fri 8.30am–5.30pm Sat 9am–4pm
Services Oak studded doors made to order

WESTBURY-ON-TRYM

⊞ **Kemps**
Contact Michael Kemp
✉ 9 Carlton Court, Westbury-on-Trym, Somerset, BS9 3DF 🅿

ARTS AND CRAFTS LIVING

ARTS AND CRAFTS LIVING sells high quality home furnishings inspired by the style of the American Arts & Crafts era (c.1900 – 1930). Our products are handcrafted by artists and crafts people in the USA and are unique and original to the UK.

Our products include oak framed original prints, cushions, pottery, table placemats & runners, clocks, doormats and stationery.

www.artsandcraftsliving.co.uk

store@artsandcraftsliving.co.uk

Tel: 01799 531233

BEAUTIFUL :: **ELEGANT** :: **USEFUL**

☎ 0117 950 5090
Est. 1881 *Stock size* Medium
Stock Jewellery
Open Mon–Fri 9am–5.15pm
Sat 9am–1pm

WESTON-SUPER-MARE

⊞ **David Hughes Antiques**
Contact Mr Hughes
✉ 37 Baker Street,
Weston-super-Mare, Somerset,
BS23 3AD 🅿
☎ 01934 628007
📱 07860 964100
Est. 1974 *Stock size* Medium
Stock General antiques, Arts and
Crafts, Art Nouveau
Open Flexible times call first for
an appointment
Fairs Newark, Ardingly
Services House clearances

⊞ **Sterling Books (ABA,
PBFA)**
Contact Mr Nisbet
✉ 43a Locking Road,
Weston-super-Mare,
Somerset,
BS23 3DG 🅿
☎ 01934 625056
📧 sterling.books@talk21.com
Est. 1966 *Stock size* Large
Stock Antiquarian and second-
hand books on every subject
Open Tues–Sat 10am–5.30pm
Thurs 10am–1pm
Services Valuations, book
binding and picture framing

⊞ **Richard Twort**
Contact Richard Twort
✉ 12 Sand Road, Sand Bay,
Weston-super-mare,
Somerset,
BS22 9UH 🅿
☎ 01934 612439 📞 01934 641900
📱 07711 939789
📧 walls@mirage-interiors.com
Est. 1962 *Stock size* Medium
Stock Barographs,
thermographs, rain gauges, all
types of meteorological
instruments
Open By appointment

WINCANTON

⊞ **Green Dragon Antiques
and Crafts Centre**
Contact Sally Denning
✉ 24 High Street, Wincanton,
Somerset,

BA9 9JF 🅿
☎ 01963 34111
🌐 www.greendragonantiques.com
Est. 1991 *Stock size* Large
Stock General antiques,
jewellery, crafts
Open Tues–Sun 9am–5pm
Services Valuations, free gift
wrap, jewellery repairs

⊞ **The Old School Rooms
Antiques**
Contact Philip Broomfield
✉ 16 Mill Street, Wincanton,
Somerset,
BA9 9AP 🅿
☎ 01963 824259
📱 07768 726276
📧 oldschoolantiques@aol.com
Est. 1987 *Stock size* Large
Stock Furniture
Open Tues Wed Fri Sat
10am–4pm
Services Restoration

⊞ **Ottery Antique
Restorers Ltd (BABAADA)**
Contact Mr C James
✉ Wessex Way, Wincanton
Business Park, Wincanton,
Somerset,
BA9 9RR 🅿
☎ 01963 34572 📞 01963 34572
📱 07770 923955
📧 charles@otteryantiques.co.uk
🌐 www.otteryantiques.co.uk
Est. 1986 *Stock size* Medium
Stock Antique furniture
Open Mon–Fri 8am–5.30pm
Services Restoration

⊞ **Wincanton Antiques**
Contact Tony or Clare
✉ London House, 12 High Street,
Wincanton, Somerset,
BA9 9JL 🅿
☎ 01963 32223
Est. 1997 *Stock size* Large
Stock Georgian–Edwardian
furniture, beds, French antiques
Open Mon–Sat 9.30am–5pm
Services Upholstery

WIVELISCOMBE

⊞ **Yew Tree Antiques
Warehouse**
Contact N Nation
✉ Old Brewery, Wiveliscombe,
Taunton, Somerset,
TA4 2NT 🅿
☎ 01984 623950/623914
Est. 1997 *Stock size* Large

Stock Victorian, Edwardian and
French furniture, Lloyd Loom
Open Tue–Fri 11am–4.30pm Sat
10am–5pm

YEOVIL

⊞ **Yeovil Collectors Centre**
Contact Barry Scott
✉ 16 Hendford, Yeovil,
Somerset,
BA20 1TE 🅿
☎ 01935 433739 📞 01935 433739
Est. 1969 *Stock size* Small
Stock Militaria, postcards,
general collectables, animals,
blue and white, Toby jugs
Open Mon Wed–Sat 9am–5pm

WILTSHIRE

AVEBURY

⊞ **Avebury Antiques**
Contact Brian Sumbler
✉ High Street, Avebury,
Wiltshire,
SN8 1RF 🅿
☎ 01672 539436
Est. 1984 *Stock size* Small
Stock Antiques and collectables
Open Mon–Sun 10am–6pm

BRADFORD-ON-AVON

⊞ **Avon Antiques (BADA)**
Contact Andrew Jenkins
✉ 25, 26 & 27 Market Street,
Bradford-on-Avon,
Wiltshire,
BA15 1LL
☎ 01225 862052 📞 01225 868763
📧 avonantiques@aol.com
🌐 www.avon-antiques.co.uk
Est. 1963 *Stock size* Large
Stock 17th–mid 19thC furniture,
clocks, barometers, metalwork,
needlework, treen, English
furniture, folk art pictures
Open Mon–Sat 9.30am–5.30pm
Fairs Grosvenor House Antiques
Fair

⊞ **Andrew Dando (BADA,
BACA Award Winner 2002)**
Contact Andrew Dando
✉ 34 Market Street,
Bradford-on-Avon,
Wiltshire,
BA15 1LL 🅿
☎ 01225 865444
📧 andrew@andrewdando.co.uk
🌐 www.andrewdando.co.uk

Est. 1915 *Stock size* Large
Stock Pottery and porcelain
1750–1870
Open Tues–Sat 10am–5pm
Fairs Olympia (June)

⊞ Granary Pine
(BABAADA)
Contact Julia or Tony Chowles
⊠ The Granary, Pound Lane,
Bradford-on-Avon,
Wiltshire,
BA15 1LF ♿
☎ 01225 867781 🖷 01225 867781
🖳 tony@granarypine.co.uk
🌐 www.granarypine.co.uk
Est. 1987 *Stock size* Large
Stock Country pine furniture,
collectables
Open Mon–Sun 10am–5pm

⊞ Mac Humble Antiques
(BADA)
Contact Mr Humble
⊠ 7–9 Woolley Street,
Bradford-on-Avon, Wiltshire,
BA15 1AD ♿
☎ 01225 866329 🖷 01225 866329
📱 07702 501888
Est. 1979 *Stock size* Small
Stock 18th–19thC furniture,
needlework, samplers,
metalware and decorative items
Open Thurs–Fri 9.30am–5pm, Sat
10am–1pm or by appointment
Fairs Olympia (Nov), BADA
(March)
Services Valuations, restoration

⊞ Moxhams Antiques
(LAPADA, BABAADA)
Contact Roger, Jill or Nick
Bichard
⊠ 17 Silver Street,
Bradford-on-Avon, Wiltshire,
BA15 1JZ ♿
☎ 01225 862789 🖷 01225 867844
📱 07768 960295
🖳 info@moxhams-antiques.
demon.co.uk
🌐 www.moxhams-antiques.
demon.co.uk
Est. 1967 *Stock size* Large
Stock Good 17th–early 19thC
mahogany and oak furniture,
ceramics, tapestries and objects
Open Mon–Sat 9am–5.30pm
Fairs Olympia (June and Nov)
Services Furniture restoration

⊞ Revival
Contact Douglas Vallance
⊠ Unit 8, Tythebarn Workshops,

Pound Lane,
Bradford-on-Avon,
Wiltshire,
BA15 1LF ♿
☎ 01225 864780
Est. 1967 *Stock size* Medium
Stock Georgian–Edwardian
furniture
Open Tues–Sun 10am–5pm
Services Restoration

BRINKWORTH

⊞ North Wilts Exporters
Contact Caroline Thornbury
⊠ Farm Hill House, The Street,
Brinkworth, Swindon,
Wiltshire,
SN5 5AJ ♿
☎ 01666 510876
🖳 mike@northwilts.demon.co.uk
🌐 www.northwiltsantique
exporters.com
Est. 1974 *Stock size* Large
Stock Eastern European pine,
oak and mahogany furniture
Open Mon–Sat 9am–5pm or by
appointment
Fairs Newark
Services Packers and shippers

BROAD HINTON

⊞ Bookmark Children's
Books (PBFA)
Contact Leonora or Anne Excell
⊠ Fortnight, Wick Down,
Broad Hinton, Swindon,
Wiltshire,
SN4 9NR ♿
☎ 01793 731693 🖷 01793 731782
📱 07788 841305
🖳 leonora.excell@btinternet.com
Est. 1972 *Stock size* Medium
Stock Children's and illustrated
antiquarian books, nursery china,
toys, games
Open By appointment
Fairs PBFA
Services Book search

CALNE

⊞ Calne Antiques
Contact Malcolm Blackford
⊠ 2a London Road, Calne,
Wiltshire,
SN11 0AB ♿
☎ 01249 816311
Est. 1981 *Stock size* Large
Stock English and Continental
pine furniture
Open Mon–Sun 9.30am–5pm

CHERHILL

⊞ P A Oxley Antique
Clocks & Barometers
(LAPADA)
Contact Mr M Oxley
⊠ The Old Rectory, Cherhill,
Calne, Wiltshire,
SN11 8UX ♿
☎ 01249 816227 🖷 01249 821285
🖳 info@paoxley.com
🌐 www.british-
antiqueclocks.com
Est. 1971 *Stock size* Large
Stock Antique clocks and
barometers, longcase clocks a
speciality
Open Mon–Sat 9.30am–5pm
closed Wed Sun or by
appointment
Services Delivery and shipping

CHIPPENHAM

⊞ Ancient & Modern
Contact Ken Charles
⊠ 3 Club Building, Park Lane,
Chippenham, Wiltshire,
SN15 1LP ♿
☎ 01249 656477
Est. 2002 *Stock size* Medium
Stock General antiques,
collectables, bric-a-brac
Open Mon–Sat 10am–4pm
closed Wed
Services Valuations

⚒ Chippenham Auction
Rooms
Contact Richard Edmonds
⊠ St Mary's Street,
Chippenham, Wiltshire,
SN15 3JM ♿
☎ 01249 462222 🖷 01249 4654970
📱 07980 745441
🖳 richard@chippenhamauction
rooms.co.uk
Est. 2001
Open Mon–Fri 9am–1pm 2–6pm
Sales General antiques monthly
Sat 10am, viewing Thurs 4–9pm
Fri 10am–5pm Sat 8.30–10am.
Five fine art sales a year at
Lackham College, Lackham Tues
10am, viewing Sun noon–6pm
Mon 10am–5pm. Also garden
and farm machinery sales
Catalogues Yes

⊞ Collectors Corner
Contact Karen Groves
⊠ 36 The Causeway,
Chippenham, Wiltshire,

SN15 3DB 🅿
☎ 01249 461617
Est. 1990 *Stock size* Large
Stock Antiques, collectables,
musical instruments,
entertainment videos and DVDs
Open Mon–Sat 9am–5pm

⊞ Cross Hayes Antiques (LAPADA)
Contact David Brooks
✉ Unit 6 Westbrook Farm,
Draycot Cerne, Chippenham,
Wiltshire,
SN15 5LH 🅿
☎ 01249 720033 ☏ 01249 720033
✉ david@crosshayes.co.uk
🌐 www.crosshayes.co.uk
Est. 1976 *Stock size* Large
Stock Furniture
Open Mon–Fri 9am–5pm or by
appointment
Services Container packing
service

CHRISTIAN MALFORD

⊞ Harley Antiques
Contact Mr Harley
✉ The Comedy, Main Road,
Christian Malford,
Chippenham, Wiltshire,
SN15 4BS 🅿
☎ 01249 720112 ☏ 01249 720553
✉ thecomedy.wilts@ukonline.co.uk
Est. 1959 *Stock size* Large
Stock General antiques including
decorative and unusual items,
conservatory furniture and objects
Open Mon–Sun 9am–6pm

CODFORD

⊞ Tina's Antiques
Contact Tina Alder
✉ The High Street, Codford,
Warminster, Wiltshire,
BA12 0ND 🅿
☎ 01985 850828
Est. 1989 *Stock size* Medium
Stock General antiques
Open Mon–Sat 9am–5pm
Services Valuations

COOMBE BISSETT

⊞ Edward Hurst Antiques
Contact Edward Hurst
✉ The Battery,
Rockbourne Road,
Coombe Bissett,
Salisbury, Wiltshire,
SP5 4LP 🅿

☎ 01722 718859
📱 07768 255557
Est. 1985 *Stock size* Medium
Stock 17th–18thC British
furniture and associated works
of art
Open Open regularly please
telephone

CORSHAM

⊞ Automattic Comics
Contact Matthew Booker
✉ Unit 1, 17 Pickwick Road,
Corsham, Wiltshire,
SN13 9BQ 🅿
☎ 01249 701647
✉ automattic.comics@dsl.pipex.com
Est. 1995 *Stock size* Large
Stock American import comics,
old and new action figures, *Star
Wars* figures
Open Mon Tues noon–5pm
Thurs–Sat 10am–5pm
Fairs NEC Memorabilia (March,
Nov)

⊞ Matthew Eden
Contact Mrs M Eden or
Matthew Eden
✉ Pickwick End, Corsham,
Wiltshire,
SN13 0JB 🅿
☎ 01249 713335 ☏ 01249 713644
📱 07899 926076
✉ mail@mattheweden.co.uk
🌐 www.mattheweden.co.uk
Est. 1952 *Stock size* Large
Stock General antiques including
garden furniture
Open Mon–Sat 9am–6pm
Fairs Chelsea Flower Show

⤳ Gardiner Houlgate
Contact Nicholas Houlgate
✉ 9 Leafield Way,
Corsham,
Wiltshire,
SN13 9SW 🅿
☎ 01225 812912 ☏ 01225 811777
✉ auctions@gardiner-houlgate.co.uk
🌐 www.invaluable.com
Est. 1987
Sales Quarterly antiques and
works of art sales, 8 Victoriana
and later furnishings sales, Thurs
10.30am, viewing Tues Wed
9am–5.30pm morning of sale
9–11am. Also specialist sales of
clocks, musical instruments,
decorative art and silver
Catalogues Yes

CRUDWELL

⊞ Philip A Ruttleigh Antiques incorporating Crudwell Furniture
Contact Philip Ruttleigh
✉ Odd Penny Farm,
Crudwell, Wiltshire,
SN16 9SJ 🅿
☎ 01285 770970
📱 07989 250077
✉ enquiries@crudwellfurniture.co.uk
🌐 www.crudwellfurniture.co.uk
Est. 1987 *Stock size* Small
Stock General antique furniture
Open Mon–Fri 9am–5pm or by
appointment
Services Restoration, paint
removal from all wood types

DEVIZES

⤳ Henry Aldridge & Son
Contact Alan or Andrew
Aldridge
✉ Unit 1, Bath Road Business
Centre, Devizes,
Wiltshire,
SN10 1XA 🅿
☎ 01380 729199 ☏ 01380 730073
✉ andrew@henry-aldridge.co.uk
🌐 www.henry-aldridge.co.uk
Est. 1989
Open Mon–Fri 10am–4pm
Sales Fortnightly Victorian and
later effects sales, bi-monthly
antiques sales, bi-annual
maritime and Titanic sales held
on Sat
Catalogues Yes

⊞ Frantiques of Devizes
Contact Molly Hopkins
✉ 14a Bridewell Street,
Devizes, Wiltshire,
SN10 1NQ
☎ 01380 729901
✉ molly@frantiques.co.uk
🌐 www.frantiques.co.uk
Est. 1999 *Stock size* Medium
Stock Georgian–Victorian English
furniture, vintage clothing, silver,
jewellery, collectables
Open Mon–Sat 10am–5pm closed
Wed or by appointment
Services Valuations, restoration

⊞ Margaret Mead Antiques
Contact Mrs M Mead
✉ 19 Northgate Street,
Devizes, Wiltshire,
SN10 1JT 🅿

☎ 01380 721060 or 01793 533085
⊕ 07740 536560
Est. 1982 *Stock size* Medium
Stock General antiques, Victorian furniture, clocks, china, brass, lighting
Open Tues–Sat 10am–5pm closed Wed
Services Restoration

⊞ St Mary's Chapel Antiques (BABAADA)
Contact Richard Sankey
✉ St Mary's Chapel, Northgate Street, Devizes, Wiltshire, SN10 1DE ℗
☎ 01380 721399 ⊕ 01380 721399
⊖ richard@rsankey.freeserve.co.uk
Est. 1971 *Stock size* Large
Stock Original painted and country furniture, garden antiques and accessories
Open Mon–Sat 10am–6pm closed Wed
Fairs Bath Decorative and Antiques Fair
Services Selective restoration

⌂ Upstairs Downstairs
Contact Judy Coom
✉ 40 Market Place, Devizes, Wiltshire, SN10 1JG ℗
☎ 01380 730266 ⊕ 01380 730266
⊕ 07974 074220
⊖ judith.coom@btopenworld.com
Est. 2002 *Stock size* Large
No. of dealers 32
Stock Antiques and collectables, furniture, postcards, pictures, toys, dolls, china
Open Mon–Sat 9.30am–4.30pm Sun 9.30am–3pm closed Wed
Services Doll repair

⊞ Pillars Antiques
Contact Mr K Clifford
✉ 10 The Banks, Lyneham, Chippenham, Wiltshire, SN15 4NS ℗
☎ 01249 890632
⊖ enquiries@pillarsantiques.com
⊚ www.pillarsantiques.com
Est. 1986 *Stock size* Large
Stock Old pine, 1940s shipping oak, mahogany furniture, bric-a-brac
Open Mon–Sat 10am–5pm Sun 11am–5pm Wed by appointment closed Thurs

⊞ Athelstan's Attic
Contact Tim Harvey
✉ The Cross Hayes, Malmesbury, Wiltshire, SN16 9AU ℗
☎ 01666 825544/822678
⊖ tharvey@freeserve.co.uk
Est. 1997 *Stock size* Large
Stock General house clearance items, antique and garden effects
Open Mon Tue Wed Fri Sat 10am–4.30pm
Services House clearance

♪ Hilditch Auctioneers (NAVA)
Contact Mr Hilditch
✉ Gloucester Road Trading Estate, Malmesbury, Wiltshire, SN16 9JT ℗
☎ 01666 822577 ⊕ 01666 825597
⊖ sales@hilditchauctions.co.uk
⊚ www.hilditchauctions.co.uk
Est. 1990
Open Mon–Fri 8.30am–5pm
Sales General household sale fourth Sat of month 10am, viewing Fri 10am–7pm, call for alternate dates
Frequency Monthly
Catalogues Yes

⊞ Rene Nicholls
Contact Mrs I Nicholls
✉ 56 High Street, Malmesbury, Wiltshire, SN16 9AT
☎ 01666 823089
Est. 1979 *Stock size* Medium
Stock English pottery and porcelain
Open Mon–Sat 9.30am–6pm or by appointment
Services Valuations, restoration

⊞ Indigo
Contact Marion Bender or Richard Lightbown
✉ Dairy Barn, Maningford Bruce, Wiltshire, SN9 6JW ℗
☎ 01672 564722 ⊕ 01672 564733
⊕ 07867 982233
⊖ antique@indigo-uk.com
⊚ www.indigo-uk.com
Est. 1982 *Stock size* Large
Stock Antique Indian, Chinese, Japanese and Tibetan furniture

Trade only Yes
Open Mon–Fri 9am–5pm Sat 10am–4pm
Fairs House and Garden Fair
Services Restoration

⊞ Blanchard Ltd (LAPADA)
Contact Orlando Harris
✉ Froxfield, Marlborough, Wiltshire, SN8 3LD ℗
☎ 01488 680666 ⊕ 01488 680668
⊖ orlando@jwblanchard.com
Est. 1950 *Stock size* Large
Stock English and Continental furniture, decorative items, works of art, lighting
Open Mon–Fri 9.30am–5.30pm Sat 10am–5pm
Fairs Olympia June

⊞ Brocante Antiques
Contact A Morris
✉ 6 London Road, Marlborough, Wiltshire, SN8 1PH ℗
☎ 01672 516512 ⊕ 01672 516512
Est. 1995 *Stock size* Medium
Stock Furniture, ceramics, decorative items, books
Open Tues–Sat 10am–5pm
Services Valuations, pine stripping

⊞ The Cats Whiskers Antiques
Contact Sue Rumbold
✉ 44a Kingsbury Street, Marlborough, Wiltshire, SN8 1JE ℗
☎ 01672 511577
⊕ 07713 018543
Est. 2002 *Stock size* Medium
Stock Antiques, collectables, blue and white china, quilts, gardening items
Open Wed–Sat 10.30am–6pm

♪ Dreweatt Neate Marlborough Saleroom
Contact Edward Chetwynd
✉ The Marlborough Auction Rooms, Hilliers Yard, High Street, Marlborough, Wiltshire, SN8 1AA ℗
☎ 01672 516161 ⊕ 01672 512811
⊖ marlborough@dnfa.com
⊚ www.dnfa.com
Est. 1759
Open Mon–Fri 9.30am–5.30pm
Sales Antiques and fine art,

monthly sales of selected antiques and fine art Tues 10am, viewing Sat 10am–4pm, Sun 10am–4pm, Mon 10am–4pm. Two specialist sections of country sporting items a year
Catalogues Yes

⊞ Graylings Antiques
Contact Gail Young
⊠ Brocante Antiques Centre, 6 London Road, Marlborough, Wiltshire, SN8 1PH 🅿
☎ 01264 710077 📠 01264 710077
📱 07732 293302
✉ tremorfa1@onetel.com
🌐 www.staffordshire-figures.com
Est. 1995 *Stock size* Medium
Stock Staffordshire pottery
Open By appointment
Fairs Newark
Services Valuations

⊞ Katharine House Gallery
Contact Christopher Gange
⊠ Katharine House, The Parade, Marlborough, Wiltshire, SN8 1NE 🅿
☎ 01672 514040
✉ chrisgange@fsmail,net
Est. 1983 *Stock size* Medium
Stock Antiquarian and second-hand books, 20thC British pictures, general antiques and antiquities, British studio pottery
Open Tues–Sat 10am–5.30pm

⌂ The Marlborough Parade Antique Centre
Contact Gary Wilkinson or Penny Morgan
⊠ The Parade, Marlborough, Wiltshire, SN8 1NE 🅿
☎ 01672 515331
Est. 1985 *Stock size* Large
No. of dealers 50
Stock Small items, general antiques, very good quality
Open Mon–Sun 10am–5pm closed Christmas, Boxing Day and New Year's Day

⊞ The Old Rope Works
Contact Mr Newman
⊠ Rope Works, 20 Kennett Place, Marlborough, Wiltshire, SN8 1NG 🅿
☎ 01672 512111 📠 01672 512111
Est. 1999 *Stock size* Medium

Stock Antique and later furniture
Open Mon–Sat 10.30am–4.30pm closed Tues
Services Restoration

⊞ Anthony Outred Antiques Ltd (BADA)
Contact Anthony Outred
⊠ Blanchard, Froxfield, Marlborough, Wiltshire, SN8 3LD 🅿
☎ 01488 680666 📠 020 7371 9869
📱 07767 848132
✉ antiques@outred.co.uk
🌐 www.outred.co.uk
Est. 1977 *Stock size* Medium
Stock 18th–19thC English, Irish and Continental furniture, sculpture, lighting, oil paintings
Open By appointment
Fairs Olympia (June)

MELKSHAM

⊞ Peter Campbell Antiques
Contact Mr P Campbell
⊠ 59 Bath Road, Atworth, Melksham, Wiltshire, SN12 8JY 🅿
☎ 01225 709742
Est. 1976 *Stock size* Medium
Stock Country furniture and decorative items
Open Tues–Sat 10am–5pm Mon and Sun by appointment

⊞ Dann Antiques Ltd (BABAADA)
Contact Gary Low
⊠ Unit S1, New Broughton Road, Melksham, Wiltshire, SN12 8BS 🅿
☎ 01225 707329 📠 01225 790120
✉ sales@dannantiques.com
🌐 www.dannantiques.com
Est. 1984 *Stock size* Large
Stock English mahogany furniture, furniture accessories
Open Mon–Fri 8.30am–5.30pm Sat 9.30am–3.30pm or by appointment
Services Restoration

⊞ Jaffray Antiques (BABAADA)
Contact Mrs J Carter
⊠ 16 The Market Place, Melksham, Wiltshire, SN12 6EX 🅿
☎ 01225 702269 📠 01225 790413
✉ jaffray.antiques@fsmail.net
Est. 1955 *Stock size* Large

Stock 18th–19thC furniture, tallboys, desks, linen presses, bamboo, dining tables, chests-of-drawers, Staffordshire, metalware
Open Mon–Fri 9am–5pm or by appointment

⊞ King Street Curios
Contact Lizzie Board
⊠ 8–10 King Street, Melksham, Wiltshire, SN12 6HD 🅿
☎ 01225 790623
Est. 1987 *Stock size* Large
Stock General antiques, collectables, discontinued Denby
Open Mon–Sat 10am–5pm
Fairs Shepton Mallet, Royal Fairs, Malvern, Newark, Walcott Street

⊞ Polly's Parlour
Contact Pauline Hart
⊠ 4 King Street, Melksham, Wiltshire, SN12 6HD 🅿
☎ 01225 706418
Est. 1999 *Stock size* Large
Stock General antiques, collectables, decorative items
Open Mon–Sat 10am–4.30pm or by appointment

MERE

➴ Finan and Co
Contact Robert Finan
⊠ The Square, Mere, Wiltshire, BA12 6DJ 🅿
☎ 01747 861411 📠 01747 861944
✉ enquiries@finanandco.co.uk
🌐 www.finanandco.co.uk
Est. 1997
Open Tues Thurs Sat 10am–6pm or by appointment
Sales Two antiques sales April and October Sat, viewing Thurs Fri 10am–7pm Sat 9–11am prior to sale. 2 collectables sales January and July
Catalogues Yes

NORTH WRAXALL

⊞ Delomosne & Son Ltd (BADA, BABAADA)
Contact Mr T N M Osborne
⊠ Court Close, North Wraxall, Chippenham, Wiltshire, SN14 7AD 🅿
☎ 01225 891505 📠 01225 891907
✉ delomosne@delomosne.co.uk
🌐 www.delomosne.co.uk

Est. 1905 *Stock size* Large
Stock Glass, porcelain, pottery, enamels, needlework pictures, treen, bygones, period glass lighting
Open Mon–Fri 9.30am–5.30pm or by appointment
Fairs The Grosvenor House Art & Antiques, Winter Olympia
Services Valuations, restoration, commission buying

PEWSEY

⊞ Time Restored Ltd (BHI)
Contact J H Bowler-Reed
✉ 20 High Street, Pewsey, Wiltshire,
SN9 5AQ ▣
☎ 01672 563544
✉ time.restored@btopenworld.com
ⓦ www.timerestored.co.uk
Est. 1978 *Stock size* Medium
Stock Antique clocks, musical boxes, barometers
Open Mon–Fri 10am–6pm
Services Restoration and repairs

RAMSBURY

⊞ Heraldry Today (ABA)
Contact Mrs Henry
✉ Parliament Piece, Ramsbury, Wiltshire,
SN8 2QH ▣
☎ 01672 520617 ☏ 01672 520183
✉ heraldry@heraldrytoday.co.uk
ⓦ www.heraldrytoday.co.uk
Est. 1954 *Stock size* Large
Stock Antiquarian books on heraldry, geneaology and peerage
Open Mon–Fri 9.30am–4.30pm

⊞ Inglenook Antiques
Contact Dennis White
✉ 59 High Street, Ramsbury, Wiltshire,
SN8 2QN ▣
☎ 01672 520261
Est. 1969 *Stock size* Large
Stock Victorian oil lamps, longcase clocks
Open Tues Thur Fri Sat 10am–5pm or by appointment
Services Longcase clock restoration

⊞ D P White
Contact Mr White
✉ 59 High Street, Ramsbury, Wiltshire,
SN8 2QN ▣
☎ 01672 520261

Est. 1969 *Stock size* Large
Stock Victorian oil lamps, oil lamp spares (old and new stocked), 50 oil lamps always in stock, brass, copper, furniture, clocks
Open Tues–Sat 10am–1pm 2–5pm closed Wed or by appointment
Services Longcase clock mechanism restoration

SALISBURY

⊞ 21st Century Antics
Contact Ben Scott
✉ 13 Brown Street, Salisbury, Wiltshire,
SP1 1HE ▣
☎ 01722 337421 ☏ 01722 337421
Est. 1998 *Stock size* Large
Stock General furniture, antiques
Open Mon–Thurs Sat 9am–5.30pm Fri 9am–5pm
Services House clearance

⊞ The Barn Book Supply
Contact John Head
✉ 88 Crane Street, Salisbury, Wiltshire,
SP1 2QD ▣
☎ 01722 327767
Est. 1958 *Stock size* Large
Stock Antiquarian books, specializing in all field sports
Open By appointment
Services Book search

⊞ Robert Bradley Antiques
Contact Mr R Bradley
✉ 71 Brown Street, Salisbury, Wiltshire,
SP1 2BA
☎ 01722 333677 ☏ 01722 339922
Est. 1970 *Stock size* Medium
Stock 17th–18thC furniture
Open Mon–Fri 9.30am–5.30pm

⊞ Castle Galleries (OMRS)
Contact John Lodge
✉ 81 Castle Street, Salisbury, Wiltshire,
SP1 3SP ▣
☎ 01722 333734 ☏ 01722 333734
📱 07709 203745
✉ john.lodge1@tesco.net
Est. 1971 *Stock size* Medium
Stock Coins, medals, small items and jewellery
Open Tues Thurs Fri 9am–4.30pm Sat 9am–1pm
Services Valuations

⊞ Fisherton Antiques Market
Contact Nigel Roberts
✉ 53 Fisherton Street, Salisbury, Wiltshire,
SP2 7SU ▣
☎ 01722 422147
Est. 1997 *Stock size* Small
Stock Victorian and Edwardian furniture, jewellery, modern collectables (Doulton. Beswick etc)
Open Mon–Sat 9.30am–5pm

⊞ Jonathan Green Antiques
Contact Jonathan Green
✉ The Antiques Market, 37 Catherine Street, Salisbury, Wiltshire,
SP1 2DH ▣
☎ 01722 332635 ☏ 01722 332635
✉ jg@jonathangreenantiques.co.uk
Est. 1979 *Stock size* Medium
Stock Silver, silver plate and decorative items
Open Mon–Sat 10am–5pm

⊞ Edward Marnier Antiques (BABAADA)
Contact Mr E Marnier
✉ Bramble Cottage, East Knoyle, Salisbury, Wiltshire,
SP3 6BY ▣
☎ 01747 830878
📱 07785 110122
✉ emarnier@ukonline.co.uk
Est. 1989 *Stock size* Medium
Stock 17th–20thC furniture, pictures, mirrors, interesting items, antique rugs, carpets
Open By appointment
Fairs Olympia, Bath, Battersea
Services Valuations

⊞ Myriad
Contact Karen Montlake
✉ 48–54 Milford Street, Salisbury, Wiltshire,
SP1 2BP ▣
☎ 01722 413595/718203
☏ 01722 416395
✉ enquiries@myriad-antiques.co.uk
ⓦ www.myriad-antiques.co.uk
Est. 1994 *Stock size* Large
Stock Georgian–Victorian furniture in pine, mahogany, oak. Lamps, clocks, mirrors, rugs
Open Mon–Sat 9.30am–5pm Sun by appointment
Services Restoration, stripping, free collection and delivery to most areas within 80 miles, antique searches

⌂ **Salisbury Antiques Market**
Contact Peter Beck
✉ 37 Catherine Street, Salisbury, Wiltshire,
SP1 2DH 🅿
☎ 01722 326033
Est. 1988 *Stock size* Large
No. of dealers 70
Stock Antiques, collectables
Open Mon–Sat 10am–5pm

⌂ **Salisbury Antiques Warehouse Ltd**
Contact Kevin Chase
✉ 94 Wilton Road, Salisbury, Wiltshire,
SP2 7JJ 🅿
☎ 01722 410634 🖶 01722 410635
🌐 kevin@salisbury-antiques.co.uk
Est. 1965 *Stock size* Large
No. of dealers 12
Stock 18th–19thC furniture, paintings, clocks, bronzes, barometers
Open Mon–Fri 9.15am–5.30pm
Sat 10am–4pm

⊞ **Chris Wadge Clocks**
Contact Patrick Wadge
✉ 83 Fisherton Street, Salisbury, Wiltshire,
SP2 7ST 🅿
☎ 01722 334467
Est. 1985 *Stock size* Small
Stock Carriage clocks, Vienna regulators, dial and mantel clocks, 1890–1900
Open Tues–Sat 9am–4pm closed 1–2pm
Services Restoration

⤳ **Woolley and Wallis Salisbury Salerooms Ltd (SOFAA, BACA Award Winner 2002, 2003)**
Contact Sarah Bennie
✉ 51–61 Castle Street, Salisbury, Wiltshire,
SP1 3SU 🅿
☎ 01722 424500 🖶 01722 424508
🌐 enquiries@woolleyandwallis.co.uk
🌐 www.woolleyandwallis.co.uk
Est. 1884
Open Mon–Fri 9am–5.30pm
Sat 9am–noon
Sales Household sales generally fortnightly on Fri at 10am, viewing Thurs 10am–7pm. 30 specialist sales a year including furniture, ceramics, silver and jewellery, books and maps,

paintings, 20thC Decorative Arts, Art Deco, clocks and barometers
Catalogues Yes

SWINDON

⌂ **Penny Farthing Antiques**
Contact Ann Farthing
✉ Victoria Centre, 138–139 Victoria Road, Swindon, Wiltshire,
SN1 3BU 🅿
☎ 01793 536668
Est. 1999 *Stock size* Large
No. of dealers 9
Stock Antiques and collectables
Open Mon–Sat 10am–5pm
Services Valuations

⊞ **Sambourne House Antique Pine Ltd**
Contact Tim or Kim Cove
✉ Units 49–51, Brunel Shopping Centre, Swindon, Wiltshire,
SN1 1LF 🅿
☎ 01793 610855
🌐 tkcove34@globalnet.co.uk
🌐 www.sambourne-antiques.co.uk
Est. 1986 *Stock size* Large
Stock Antique and reproduction pine furniture, smalls, decorative items
Open Mon–Sun 9am–5pm
Services Hand-built kitchens

⊞ **Allan Smith**
Contact Mr A Smith
✉ Amity Cottage, 162 Beechcroft Road, Upper Stratton, Swindon, Wiltshire,
SN2 7QE 🅿
☎ 01793 822977 🖶 01793 822977
📱 07778 834342
🌐 allansmithclocks@lineone.net
🌐 www.allansmithantiqueclocks.co.uk
Est. 1988 *Stock size* Large
Stock 50–60 fully restored longcase clocks including Moonphase, automata, painted dial, brass dial, 30-hour, 8-day etc in mahogany, lacquer, walnut and marquetry plus a selection of other antique clocks
Open By appointment any time
Services Valuations and clockfinder service

⤳ **Dominic Winter Book Auctions**
Contact Admin Office
✉ The Old School,

Maxwell Street, Swindon, Wiltshire,
SN1 5DR 🅿
☎ 01793 611340 🖶 01793 491727
🌐 info@dominicwinter.co.uk
🌐 www.dominicwinter.co.uk
Est. 1988
Open Mon–Fri 9.30am–5.30pm
Sales General book sale Wed 11am, viewing day prior to sale 10am–7pm. Specialist single category sale Thurs 11am, viewing day prior to sale 10am–7pm
Frequency Every 5 weeks
Catalogues Yes

WARMINSTER

⊞ **Cassidy Antiques and Restorations (BABAADA)**
Contact Matthew Cassidy
✉ 7 Silver Street, Warminster, Wiltshire,
BA12 8PS 🅿
☎ 01985 213313 🖶 01985 213313
📱 07050 206806
🌐 mat_cassidy@yahoo.com
🌐 www.cassidyantiques.com
Est. 1994 *Stock size* Medium
Stock Georgian and Victorian furniture
Open Mon–Fri 9am–5pm
Sat 10am–5pm
Services Restoration

⊞ **Choice Antiques**
Contact Avril Bailey
✉ 4 Silver Street, Warminster, Wiltshire,
BA12 8PS 🅿
☎ 01985 218924
Est. 1987 *Stock size* Medium
Stock Small, unusual, furniture, decorative objects
Open Mon–Sat 10am–5pm
Services Valuations, shipping

⊞ **Collectable Interiors**
Contact David Swanton
✉ 33 Silver Street, Warminster, Wiltshire,
BA12 8PT 🅿
☎ 01985 217177
Est. 1967 *Stock size* Medium
Stock Furniture and accessories
Open Mon–Sat 10am–5pm

⊞ **Annabelle Giltsoff (TVADA)**
Contact Anabelle Giltsoff
✉ 3 Silver Street, Warminster, Wiltshire,

BA12 8PS 🅿
☎ 01985 218933
Est. 1984 *Stock size* Medium
Stock Paintings and frames
Open Mon–Sat 9.30am–1pm
2–5pm
Services Picture restoration and
gilding

⊞ **Isabella Antiques
(BABAADA)**
Contact Mr B W Semke
✉ 3 Silver Street, Warminster,
Wiltshire, BA12 8PS 🅿
☎ 01985 218933
Est. 1990 *Stock size* Medium
Stock 18th–19thC mahogany
furniture, 19thC gilt mirrors
Open Mon–Sat 10am–5pm

⊞ **Lewis Antiques &
Interiors**
Contact Sandie Lewis
✉ 9 Silver Street,
Warminster, Wiltshire,
BA12 8PS 🅿
☎ 01985 846222
⓿ 07764 576106
Est. 2004 *Stock size* Medium
Stock General antiques,
furniture, textiles, rugs, silver,
glass, ceramics
Open Wed–Sat 10am–5pm
Fairs Bath Decorative
Services Valuations, restoration,
shipping, antiques search

⊞ **Obelisk Antiques
(LAPADA, BABAADA)**
Contact Mr P Tanswell

✉ 2 Silver Street,
Warminster,
Wiltshire,
BA12 8PS 🅿
☎ 01985 846646 ✆ 01985 219901
⓿ 07718 630673
📧 all@obelisk-
antiques.freeserve.co.uk
Est. 1979 *Stock size* Large
Stock 18th–19thC French, English
and Continental furniture
Open Mon–Sat 10am–1pm
2–5.30pm

⌂ **Warminster Antique
Centre (BABAADA)**
Contact Mr P Walton
✉ 6 Silver Street, Warminster,
Wiltshire,
BA12 8PT 🅿
☎ 01985 847269 ✆ 01985 211778
⓿ 07860 584193
Est. 1993 *Stock size* Large
No. of dealers 15
Stock Wide range of antiques
and collectable items, furniture,
clocks, paintings, models, linens,
fabrics, etc
Open Mon–Sat 10am–5pm
Services Valuations

WEST YATTON

⊞ **Heirloom & Howard Ltd
(BABAADA)**
Contact David or Angela Howard
✉ Manor Farm, West Yatton,
Chippenham,
Wiltshire,
SN14 7EU 🅿

☎ 01249 783038 ✆ 01249 783039
Est. 1973 *Stock size* Medium
Stock Chinese armorial and other
export porcelain, armorial
paintings, coach panels, hall
chairs, portrait engravings
Open Mon–Fri 10am–6pm Sat
10am–6pm or by appointment
Services Bidding at auction

WILTON

⊞ **Bay Tree Antiques**
Contact Mrs J D Waymouth
✉ 26 North Street, Wilton,
Wiltshire,
SP2 0HJ
☎ 01722 743392 ✆ 01722 743392
⓿ 07980 921222
Est. 1997 *Stock size* Medium
Stock Period furniture,
decorative furniture and items
Open Mon–Sat 9am–5.30pm

⊞ **Hingstons of Wilton**
Contact Nick Hingston
✉ 36 North Street, Wilton,
Wiltshire,
SP2 0HJ 🅿
☎ 01722 742263
📧 nick@hingston-antiques.
freeserve.co.uk
🌐 hingston-antiques.
freeserve.co.uk
Est. 1976 *Stock size* Large
Stock 18th–early 20thC furniture,
clocks, pictures
Open Mon–Fri 9am–5pm
Sat 10am–4pm
Services Valuations

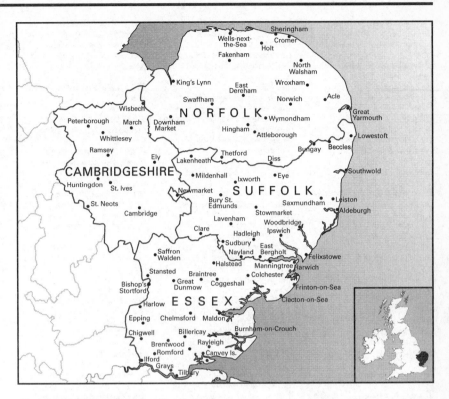

CAMBRIDGESHIRE

BALSHAM

⊞ **Ward-Thomas Antiques**
Contact Mr C R F Ward-Thomas
✉ **7 High Street, Balsham,
Cambridge, Cambridgeshire,
CB1 6DJ** 🅿
☎ 01223 892431 📠 01223 892367
📧 wtantiques@onetel.com
Est. 1997 *Stock size* Large
Stock Continental pine furniture,
furniture accessories
Open Mon–Fri 9am–5pm
Sat 10am–5pm Sun 10am–4pm
Fairs Newark, Kempton Park
Services Restoration, mail orders

BURWELL

⊞ **Peter Norman Antiques**
Contact Mr Peter Norman
✉ **55 North Street, Burwell,
Cambridge, Cambridgeshire,
CB5 0BA** 🅿
☎ 01638 616914

📧 amarpole@aol.com
🌐 www.peternormanantiques.co.uk
Est. 1978 *Stock size* Medium
Stock 18th–19thC furniture,
Oriental rugs, clocks, pictures,
prints
Open Mon–Sat 9am–5.30pm
Fairs Newmarket
Services Restoration

CAMBRIDGE

⊞ **Jess Applin (BADA)**
Contact Mr J Applin
✉ **8 Lensfield Road, Cambridge,
Cambridgeshire,
CB2 1EG** 🅿
☎ 01223 315168
Est. 1975 *Stock size* Medium
Stock 17th–19thC furniture,
works of art
Open Mon–Sat 9.30am–5.30pm

⊞ **John Beazor & Sons Ltd
(BADA)**
Contact Mr M Beazor
✉ **78–80 Regent Street,**
Cambridge, Cambridgeshire,
CB2 1DP
☎ 01223 355178 📠 01223 355183
📱 07774 123379
📧 martin@johnbeazorantiques.co.uk
🌐 www.johnbeazorantiques.co.uk
Est. 1875 *Stock size* Large
Stock English furniture late
17th–early 19thC furniture, clocks,
barometers, decorative items
Open Mon–Fri 9.15am–5pm
Sat 10am–4pm
Fairs Open weekend exhibitions
held on the premises in May,
November
Services Valuations

🔨 **Bonhams**
✉ **17 Emmanuel Road,
Cambridge, Cambridgeshire,
CB1 1JW**
☎ 01223 366523 📠 012223 300208
📧 cambridge@bonhams.com
🌐 www.bonhams.com
Open Mon–Fri 8.30am–5pm
Sales Regional office. Regular
sales held in London and in our

salerooms across the country.
Free auction valuations;
insurance and probate valuations

⊞ The Book Shop
Contact Mr P Bright or
Mr H Hardinge
✉ 24 Magdalene Street,
Cambridge, Cambridgeshire,
CB3 0AF
☎ 01223 362457
Est. 1996 Stock size Medium
Stock Antiquarian, second-hand,
out-of-print books
Open Mon–Sat 10.30am–5.30pm

⊞ Books & Collectables Ltd
Contact Mr A Doyle
✉ Unit 7–8, Railway Arches,
Coldhams Road, Cambridge,
Cambridgeshire,
CB1 3EW ℗
☎ 01223 412845 ✆ 01223 412845
℗ 07703 795206
✉ ask@booksandcollectables.com
Ⓦ www.booksandcollectables.com
Est. 1996 Stock size Large
Stock 16thC–modern books,
comics, toys, postcards, cigarette
cards, records, pop memorabilia,
magazines, china, furniture
Open Mon–Sat 9.30am–5pm
Sun 10am–4pm
Services Valuations, shipping

⊞ Buckies (NAG, LAPADA)
Contact Robin Wilson
✉ 31 Trinity Street, Cambridge,
Cambridgeshire,
CB2 1TB
☎ 01233 357910 ✆ 01233 357920
Est. 1953 Stock size Medium
Stock Jewellery, silver
Open Tues–Sat 9.45am–5pm
Services Valuations

⌂ Cambs Antique Centre
Contact Paul Cox
✉ Units 1 & 2, Dales Brewery,
Gwydir Street, Cambridge,
Cambridgeshire,
CB1 2LJ ℗
☎ 01223 356391
Est. 1987 Stock size Medium
No. of dealers 10
Stock Furniture, bric-a-brac,
collectables, decorative items
Open Mon–Sat 10am–5pm
Sun 11am–5pm

⋏ Cheffins
Contact J G Law, C B Ashton
or R Haywood

✉ Clifton House, 2 Clifton Road,
Cambridge, Cambridgeshire,
CB1 7EA ℗
☎ 01223 213343 ✆ 01223 271949
✉ fine.art@cheffins.co.uk
Ⓦ www.cheffins.co.uk
Est. 1824
Open Mon–Fri 9am–5pm
Sales 32 fine art and attic sales a
year, Catalogues and information
available on website
Frequency Fortnightly
Catalogues Yes

⊞ Peter Crabbe Antiques
Contact Mr P Crabbe
✉ 3 Pembroke Street,
Cambridge, Cambridgeshire,
CB2 3QY
☎ 01223 357117
Est. 1988 Stock size Large
Stock English furniture, Oriental
porcelain, works of art
Open Mon–Sat 9.30am–5pm
Services Valuations

⊞ G David (ABA, PBFA, BA)
Contact David Asplin, N T Adams
or B L Collings
✉ 16 St Edward's Passage,
Cambridge, Cambridgeshire,
CB2 3PJ
☎ 01223 354619 ✆ 01223 324663
Est. 1896 Stock size Large
Stock Antiquarian books, prints,
publishers' remainders, fine
antiquarian books a speciality
Open Mon–Sat 9am–5pm
Fairs Chelsea, London (June),
ABA (Nov)

⊞ Gabor Cossa Antiques
Contact David Theobald
✉ 34 Trumpington Street,
Cambridge, Cambridgeshire,
CB2 1QY ℗
☎ 01223 356049
✉ gaborcossa@yahoo.co.uk
Est. 1947 Stock size Large
Stock 18th–19thC ceramics,
small items, prints
Open Mon–Sat 10.30am–6pm
Fairs Horticultural Hall
Westminster

⊞ Gannochy Coins and Medals
Contact Mr A Hawk
✉ 46 Burleigh Street, Cambridge,
Cambridgeshire,
CB1 1DJ ℗
☎ 01223 361662
✉ gannochycoins@aol.com

Est. 1978 Stock size Large
Stock Coins and medals, bank notes
Open Mon–Sat 9am–5pm
Services Valuations, appraisals,
probate

⊞ The Haunted Bookshop (PBFA)
Contact Mrs Sarah Key
✉ 9 St Edward's Passage,
Cambridge, Cambridgeshire,
CB2 3PJ
☎ 01223 312913 ✆ 08700 0569392
✉ sarahkey@hauntedbooks.
demon.co.uk
Est. 1987 Stock size Medium
Stock Antiquarian, second-hand,
children's books, particularly
girls' school stories
Open Mon–Sat 10am–5pm
Fairs PBFA
Services Mail order worldwide,
book search for children's titles,
catalogues, valuations

⌂ The Hive
Contact Brenda Blakemore
✉ Unit 3, Dales Brewery,
Gwydir Street, Cambridge,
Cambridgeshire,
CB1 2LG ℗
☎ 01223 300269
Est. 1987 Stock size Medium
No. of dealers 10
Stock Antique pine, kitchenware,
collectables, period lighting,
pictures, Victorian–Edwardian
furniture, bric-a-brac, tiles
Open Mon–Sat 9.30am–5.30pm
Sun 11am–5pm
Services Commissions undertaken

⌂ The Old Chemist Shop Antique Centre
Contact Mrs J Tucker
✉ 206 Mill Road, Cambridge,
Cambridgeshire, CB1 3NF ℗
☎ 01223 247324
Est. 1996 Stock size Large
No. of dealers 5
Stock General antiques, collectables
Open Mon–Fri 10am–5pm
Sat 10am–5.30pm
Services Clock repair, house
clearance

⌂ Willroy Antiques Centre
Contact Mr Roy Williams
✉ Unit 5, Dales Brewery,
Gwydir Street, Cambridge,
Cambridgeshire, CB1 2LJ ℗
☎ 01223 311687
℗ 07921 152580

📧 rwilliams4@ntl.com
Est. 1985 *Stock size* Large
No. of dealers 6
Stock General antiques
Open Mon–Sat 10am–5pm
Sun noon–4pm
Services Restoration

CHATTERIS

⊞ **James Fuller and Son**
Contact Steven Fuller
✉ **51 Huntingdon Road,
Chatteris, Cambridgeshire,
PE16 6ED** 🅿
☎ 01354 692740
Est. 1919 *Stock size* Large
Stock Telephone and letter boxes
Open Mon–Fri 8am–12.30pm
1.30–5pm

CHITTERING

⊞ **Simon & Penny Rumble
Antiques**
Contact Mrs P Rumble
✉ **Causeway End Farmhouse,
School Lane, Chittering,
Cambridge, Cambridgeshire,
CB5 9PW** 🅿
☎ 01223 861831
📱 07778 917300
📧 prumble@beeb.net
Est. 1980 *Stock size* Small
Stock Early oak, country
furniture, woodcarving
Open By appointment
Fairs NEC

COMBERTON

⊞ **Comberton Antiques &
Interiors**
Contact Mrs Tunstall
✉ **5 Green End, Comberton,
Cambridgeshire, CB3 7DY**
☎ 01223 262674
📧 enquiries@combertonantiques.co.uk
🌐 www.combertonantiques.co.uk
Est. 1984 *Stock size* Large
Stock General furniture
including Continental pine, soft
furnishings
Open Mon Thurs–Sat 10am–5pm
Sun 2–5pm
Fairs Newark, Ardingly
Services Shipping

DUXFORD

⊞ **Riro D Mooney**
Contact Mr R Mooney
✉ **Mill Lane, Duxford,**

**Cambridgeshire,
CB2 4PS** 🅿
☎ 01223 832252
🌐 www.riromooney-antiques.com
Est. 1946 *Stock size* Large
Stock Victorian–Edwardian
furniture
Open Mon–Sat 9am–6.30pm
Sun 10am–noon 2.30–5pm
Services Restoration

ELY

⊞ **Cloisters Antiques
(PBFA)**
Contact Barry Lonsdale
✉ **1–1b Lynn Road, Ely,
Cambridgeshire,
CB7 4EG** 🅿
☎ 01353 668558
📱 07767 881677
Est. 1997 *Stock size* Medium
Stock General clocks, china,
second-hand and antiquarian
books, old postcards, mainly smalls
Open Mon–Sat 10.30am–4.30pm
Sun 12.30–4.30pm closed Tues
Services Valuations, picture
framing

⊞ **Griffin Antiques**
Contact E Griffin
✉ **13 Fore Hill, Ely, Cambridgeshire,
CB7 4AA**
☎ 01353 666672
📧 egriffinantiques@btconnect.com
Est. 2000 *Stock size* Medium
Stock General antiques
Open Mon–Sat 10am–5.30pm
Services Valuations, restoration

⊞ **Mrs Mills' Antiques Etc.**
Contact Mrs M Mills
✉ **1a St Mary's Street, Ely,
Cambridgeshire,
CB7 4ER** 🅿
☎ 01353 664268
Est. 1968 *Stock size* Large
Stock Porcelain, silver, jewellery
Open Mon–Sat 10am–5pm
closed Tues

🪝 **Rowley Fine Art**
Contact Diane White
✉ **8 Downham Road, Ely,
Cambridgeshire,
CB6 1AH** 🅿
☎ 01353 653020 📠 01353 653022
🌐 www.rowleyfineart.com.
Est. 1994
Open Mon–Fri 9am–5pm
Sales Fine art and antique sales,
specialist sales of film posters,

taxidermy, toys
Frequency 6 per annum
Catalogues Yes

⊞ **Valued History**
Contact Mr Paul Murawski
✉ **Club Mews, 7–9 Market Place,
Ely, Cambridgeshire,
CB7 4NP**
☎ 01353 654080 📠 01353 654080
📧 murawski@pmurawski.fsnet.co.uk
🌐 www.historyforsale.co.uk
Est. 1996 *Stock size* Medium
Stock Coins, antiquities
Open By appointment
Services Valuations

🏠 **Waterside Antiques**
Contact Mr G Peters
✉ **The Wharf, Waterside, Ely,
Cambridgeshire,
CB7 4AU** 🅿
☎ 01353 667066 📠 01353 667066
Est. 1985 *Stock size* Large
No. of dealers 68
Stock Furniture, collectables
Open Mon–Sat 9.30am–5.30pm
Sun 11.30am–5.30pm
Services Valuations, clearances

FORDHAM

⊞ **Phoenix Antiques**
Contact Mr K Bycroft
✉ **Homelands, 1 Carter Street,
Fordham, Ely, Cambridgeshire,
CB7 5NG** 🅿
☎ 01638 720363
Est. 1966 *Stock size* Medium
Stock Everything for a European
interior prior to 1750
Open By appointment
Services Valuations

GUYHIRN

⊞ **Ludovic Potts Antiques
(BAFRA)**
Contact Mr Ludovic Potts
✉ **Elm Tree Barns, Elm Tree Farm,
Parnell Road, Guyhirn,
Cambridgeshire,
PE13 4AQ** 🅿
☎ 01353 741537
📱 07889 341671
📧 mail@restorers.co.uk
🌐 www.restorers.co.uk
Est. 2001 *Stock size* Small
Stock Polished wood furniture,
upholstered chairs, sofas, soft
furnishings, porcelain, gilt mirrors
Open By appointment
Services Restoration

HADDENHAM

⊞ Hereward Books (PBFA)
Contact Mr R Pratt
✉ **17 High Street, Haddenham, Ely, Cambridgeshire, CB6 3XA** 🅿
☎ 01353 740821 🌐 01353 741721
📧 sales@herewardbooks.co.uk
🌐 www.herewardbooks.co.uk
Est. 1984 *Stock size* Medium
Stock Rare and collectable books, specializing in field sports and fishing
Open Mon Tues Thurs 10am–4pm
Fri Sat 10am–1pm
Fairs PBFA Russell Hotel, CLA Game Fair

HUNTINGDON

⊞ Houghton Antiques
Contact Jean Stevens
✉ **Thicket Road, Houghton, Huntingdon, Cambridgeshire, PE28 2BQ** 🅿
☎ 01480 461887
🌐 07803 716842
Est. 2000 *Stock size* Medium
Stock General antiques, small items of furniture, pottery, porcelain, silver, sporting items, prints
Open Mon–Sun 1–5.30pm
Fairs Alexandra Palace

🏠 Huntingdon Trading Post
Contact Mr John De'Ath
✉ **1 St Mary's Street, Huntingdon, Cambridgeshire, PE29 3PE** 🅿
☎ 01480 450998
📧 j.death@ntlworld.com
🌐 www.huntingdontradingpost.co.uk
Est. 2001 *Stock size* Large
No. of dealers 42
Stock General antiques, including furniture, clocks, collectables, brassware, pictures
Open Mon–Sat 9am–5pm
Sun 10am–2pm

IMPINGTON

⊞ Woodcock House Antiques
Contact Mr A M Peat
✉ **83–85 Station Road, Impington, Cambridge, Cambridgeshire, CB4 9NP** 🅿
☎ 01223 232858
Est. 1978 *Stock size* Large
Stock Late 19thC decorative

furniture, Aesthetic items, smalls, furniture
Open Mon–Fri 10am–5pm
or by appointment
Fairs Newark
Services Valuations, clearence

KIMBOLTON

⊞ Mark Seabrook Antiques (LAPADA)
Contact Mr M Seabrook
✉ **PO Box 396, Kimbolton, Huntingdon, Cambridgeshire, PE28 0ZA** 🅿
☎ 01480 861935
🌐 07770 721931
📧 enquiries@markseabrook.com
🌐 www.markseabrook.com
Est. 1996 *Stock size* Medium
Stock Early English oak, country furniture, metalware, treen, ceramics
Open By appointment 7 days
Fairs NEC, Kensington, Chelsea
Services Restoration

LANDBEACH

⊞ Cambridge Pianola Company and J V Pianos
Contact Tom Poole
✉ **The Limes, High Street, Landbeach, Cambridgeshire, CB4 8DR** 🅿
☎ 01223 861348 🌐 01223 441276
📧 ftpoole@talk21.com
🌐 www.cambridgepianola company.co.uk
Est. 1972 *Stock size* Medium
Stock Pianos, pianolas and player pianos
Open Appointment preferred
Services Restoration

PEAKIRK

⊞ Peakirk Bookshop
Contact Jeffrey Lawrence
✉ **St Pegas Road, Peakirk, Peterborough, Cambridgeshire, PE6 7NF** 🅿
☎ 01733 253182
📧 peakirkbooks@btinternet.com
🌐 www.peakirkbooks.com
Est. 1997 *Stock size* Medium
Stock Collectable and out-of-print books
Open Thurs Fri Sat 9.30am–5pm
Sun noon–4pm or by appointment
Services Catalogue on request

PETERBOROUGH

⊞ Antiques & Curios Shop
Contact Mr M Mason
✉ **249 Lincoln Road, Millfield, Peterborough, Cambridgeshire, PE1 2PL** 🅿
☎ 01733 314948
🌐 07749 876456
Est. 1989 *Stock size* Medium
Stock Mahogany, oak, pine, country furniture, fireplaces
Open Mon–Sat 10am–5pm
Fairs Newark, RAF Swinderby
Services Restoration

⊞ T V Coles
Contact Mr T V Coles
✉ **981 Lincoln Road, Peterborough, Cambridgeshire, PE4 6AH** 🅿
☎ 01733 577268
Est. 1980 *Stock size* Medium
Stock Antiquarian, out-of-print, second-hand books, militaria, ephemera, postcards etc
Open Mon–Sat 9am–4.30pm

RAMSEY

⊞ Abbey Antiques
Contact Mr J Smith
✉ **63 Great Whyte, Ramsey, Cambridgeshire, PE26 1HL** 🅿
☎ 01487 814753
Est. 1979 *Stock size* Medium
Stock General antiques, collectables
Open Tues–Sun 10am–5pm
Fairs Alexandra Palace
Services Valuations, Mabel Lucie Attwell Museum and Collectors' Club

⊞ Antique Barometers
Contact William Rae
✉ **Wingfield, 26 Biggin Lane, Ramsey, Cambridgeshire, PE26 1NB** 🅿
☎ 01487 814060 🌐 01487 814060
📧 antiquebarometers@talk21.com
Est. 1996 *Stock size* Medium
Stock Early stick and wheel barometers, barographs
Open By appointment
Fairs Hinchingbrook House, Putteridge Bury House
Services Valuations, restoration

SOHAM

🔨 Burwell Auctions
Contact Mr N Reed-Herbert
✉ **The Church Hall, High Street,**

Soham, Ely, Cambridgeshire,
CB7 5HD ▣
☎ 01353 727100 **☉** 01353 727101
Est. 1984
Open By appointment
Sales General antique sales,
viewing day prior to sale
9am–5pm and day of sale
9am–10.30am or by appointment
Catalogues Yes

ST IVES

🏹 **Hyperion Auction
Centre (ICOM)**
Contact Mrs Pat Bernard
✉ **Station Road, St Ives,
Huntingdon, Cambridgeshire,
PE27 5BH** ▣
☎ 01480 464140 **☉** 01480 497552
☉ enquiries@hyperion-auctions.co.uk
ⓦ www.hyperion-auctions.co.uk
Est. 1995
Open Mon–Sat 9.30am–5pm
Sales General antiques sale
2nd Mon monthly 10.30am,
viewing Sat prior 9.30am–5pm
Mon 9.30–10.30am
Catalogues Yes

⊞ **Quay Court Antiques**
Contact Mr M Knight
✉ **Bull Lane, Bridge Street,
St Ives, Huntingdon,
Cambridgeshire,
PE27 4AZ** ▣
☎ 01480 468295
☉ michaelknight9@hotmail.com
Est. 1972 *Stock size* Medium
Stock Pottery, porcelain, pictures,
jewellery, oil paintings, water
colours, prints
Open Mon noon–3pm Wed
10.30am–4pm Fri noon–3pm
Sat 11am–4.30pm
Services Valuations, talks to
antiques clubs

ST NEOTS

⊞ **Brentside Programmes**
Contact Mr Chris Ward
✉ **1 Dial Close, Little Paxton,
St Neots, Huntingdon,
Cambridgeshire,
PE19 4QN**
☎ 01480 474682 **☉** 01480 370650
☉ sales@brentside.co.uk
ⓦ www.brentside.co.uk
Est. 1974 *Stock size* Medium
Stock Football memorabilia,
mostly mail order
Open Mon–Fri 9am–5pm

WISBECH

⊞ **Steve Carpenter**
Contact Mr S Carpenter
✉ **95 Norfolk Street, Wisbech,
Cambridgeshire,
PE13 2LF** ▣
☎ 01945 588441 **☉** 01945 588441
Est. 1997 *Stock size* Medium
Stock 18th–19thC country
furniture, longcase clocks,
quality smalls
Open Mon–Sat 9am–5pm

⊞ **Peter A Crofts**
Contact Mrs Crofts
✉ **117 High Road, Wisbech,
Cambridgeshire,
PE14 0DN** ▣
☎ 01945 584614
Est. 1949 *Stock size* Large
Stock General antiques,
furniture, silver, china, jewellery
Open By appointment
Services Valuations

⊞ **Granny's Cupboard
Antiques**
Contact Mr R J Robbs
✉ **34 Old Market, Wisbech,
Cambridgeshire,
PE13 1NF** ▣
☎ 01945 589606/870730
Ⓜ 07721 616154
Est. 1985 *Stock size* Medium
Stock Victorian–Edwardian china,
glass and furniture to 1950s
Open Tues Thurs 10.30am–4pm
Sat 10.30am–3pm
Fairs The Maltings, Ely

🏹 **Grounds & Co**
Contact Mr R Barnwell
✉ **2 Nene Quay, Wisbech,
Cambridgeshire,
PE13 1AQ** ▣
☎ 01945 580713 **☉** 01945 580713
Ⓜ 07885 431520
☉ antiques@grounds-wisbech.co.uk
ⓦ www.grounds.co.uk
Est. 1792
Open Mon–Sat 1–5pm
Sales Antiques and collectors'
sales 4 times a year. Telephone
for details
Catalogues Yes

🏹 **Maxey & Son**
Contact John Maxey
✉ **Auction Hall, Cattle Market
Chase, Wisbech, Cambridgeshire,
PE13 1RD** ▣
☎ 01945 584609 **☉** 01945 589440

☉ mail@maxeyandson.co.uk
ⓦ www.maxeyandson.co.uk
Est. 1856
Open Mon–Fri 9am–5pm
Sat 9am–noon
Sales General sales with some
antiques and collectables twice
weekly on Wed and Sat 10am,
viewing any day. Occasional
special antiques sales
Catalogues No

⊞ **The Old Pine Shop**
Contact Kent or Adele Griffin
✉ **96 Norfolk Street, Wisbech,
Cambridgeshire,
PE13 2LS** ▣
☎ 01945 464555
Est. 1992 *Stock size* Medium
Stock Antique English and
Continental pine furniture
Open Fri–Sat 10am–4pm

ESSEX

BASILDON

⊞ **Bear Essentials**
Contact Kim Brown
✉ **64a Eastgate Shopping Centre,
Basildon, Essex,
SS14 1AF** ▣
☎ 01268 270154 **☉** 01268 270154
☉ hugs@companyofbears.com
ⓦ www.companyofbears.com
Est. 2000 *Stock size* Large
Stock Collectable bears, Steiff,
Dean's and Hermann Club store
Open Mon–Sat 10am–5.30pm

⊞ **Sport and Star
Autographs (UACC, IADA)**
Contact Toni McLennan
✉ **64 East Gate Shopping Centre,
Southernhay, Basildon, Essex,
SS14 1AF**
☎ 01268 524500
ⓦ www.autographs.me.uk
Est. 2000 *Stock size* Large
Stock Autographs, sport, film,
music, signed memorabilia
Open Mon–Sat 9.30am–5.30pm
Services Valuations

BATTLESBRIDGE

🏛 **Battlesbridge Antiques
Centre**
Contact Jim Gallie
✉ **Hawk Hill, Battlesbridge,
Wickford, Essex,
SS11 7RF** ▣
☎ 01268 575000 **☉** 01268 575001

EAST

ⓔ jim@battlesbridge.com
Ⓦ www.battlesbridge.com
Est. 1969 *Stock size* Large
No. of dealers 80
Stock General antiques, collectables
Open Mon–Sun 10am–5.30pm
Services Valuations

⊞ Battlesbridge Antiques Lighting (EADA)
Contact Mr Pettitt
✉ The Bones Lane Antiques Centre, The Green, Chelmsford Road, Battlesbridge, Wickford, Essex,
SS11 7RJ 🅿
☎ 01268 763500 ⊕ 01268 763500
ⓔ sales@battlesbridge-antiques.co.uk
Ⓦ www.battlesbridge-antiques.co.uk
Est. 1969 *Stock size* Medium
Stock Gas, oil and early electric lighting, gramophones
Open Tues–Sun 10am–4.30pm closed Thurs
Services Restoration of lighting and gramophones

⌂ The Bones Lane Antiques Centre
Contact Mr Pettitt
✉ The Green, Chelmsford Road, Battlesbridge, Wickford, Essex,
SS11 7RJ 🅿
☎ 01268 763500 ⊕ 01268 571157
ⓔ joe@battlesbridge-antiques.com
Ⓦ www.battlesbridge-antiques.com
Est. 1969 *Stock size* Medium
No. of dealers 12
Stock Collectables, militaria, lighting, furniture etc
Open Tues–Sun 10am–4.30pm closed Thurs
Services Restoration of lighting and gramophones

⊞ Jim Gallie Antiques
Contact Paul Elliott
✉ Muggeridge Farm, Maltings Road, Battlesbridge, Essex,
SS11 7RF 🅿
☎ 01268 769000 ⊕ 01268 769006
ⓔ jim@jimgallieantiques.com
Ⓦ www.jimgallieantiques.com
Est. 1969 *Stock size* Large
Stock General antiques
Open Mon–Sun 10am–5pm
Services Valuations

⌂ Harbour Traders Ltd
Contact Pat Stoneham
✉ Unit 2, Battlesbridge Harbour, Chelmsford Road, Battlesbridge, Nr Wickford, Essex,

SS11 8TR 🅿
☎ 01268 764382
Ⓜ 07941 179031
ⓔ vintage@collectibles99.freeserve.co.uk
No. of dealers 20
Stock General antiques
Open Mon–Sun 10am–5.30pm

⊞ Phoenix Fireplaces (National Fireplace Association)
Contact John or Cris
✉ Hawk Hill, Battlesbridge, Essex,
SS11 7RE 🅿
☎ 01268 768844 ⊕ 01268 768844
Ⓜ 07939 567672
Ⓦ www.phoenix-fireplaces.co.uk
Est. 1991 *Stock size* Large
Stock Fireplaces
Open Mon–Sun 10am–5.00pm
Services Restoration

⊞ Trails End Collectables Ltd
Contact Pat Stoneham
✉ Unit 2, Battlesbridge Harbour, Chelsford Road, Battlesbridge, Wickford, Essex,
SS11 8TR 🅿
☎ 01268 764682
Ⓜ 07941 179031
ⓔ vintage@collectibles99.freeserve.co.uk
Est. 1991 *Stock size* Small
Stock 20thC US collectables
Open Mon–Sun 10am–5.30pm

BENFLEET

⊞ E J & C A Brooks (BNTA, IBNS)
Contact Mr E J Brooks
✉ 44 Kiln Road, Thundersley, Benfleet, Essex,
SS7 1TB 🅿
☎ 01268 753835
Ⓜ 07850 262629
Est. 1974 *Stock size* Large
Stock Coins, English and foreign bank notes
Open By appointment
Fairs York, London
Services Free valuations

BRENTWOOD

⊞ Le-Potier
Contact Mr S Hall
✉ 42 King's Road, Brentwood, Essex,
CM14 4DW

☎ 01277 216310
Est. 1985 *Stock size* Small
Stock Collectables
Open Tues Wed Fri Sat 10am–5pm
Services China restoration

BRIGHTLINGSEA

⌂ Shipwreck Brightlingsea's Antique and Collectables Centre
Contact Mr Keel
✉ 22e Marshes Yard, Victoria Place, Brightlingsea, Colchester, Essex,
CO7 0BX 🅿
☎ 01206 307307
ⓔ info@theshipwreck.net
Ⓦ www.theshipwreck.net
Est. 1995 *Stock size* Large
No. of dealers 25
Stock Collectables, furniture, books, postcards, general antiques
Open Mon–Sun 10am–5pm

BROOMFIELD

⊞ Ruegavarret Ltd
Contact Mr I Honeywood
✉ 163 Main Road, Broomfield, Chelmsford, Essex,
CM1 7DJ 🅿
☎ 01245 363977
Est. 1994 *Stock size* Medium
Stock Antique pine furniture, ceramics, brass, pictures
Open Wed–Sun 10am–3pm
Services Free delivery

BURSTALL

⊞ Lion House Antiques Ltd (EADA)
Contact Mr P Young
✉ Fen Farm, Hadleigh Road, Burstall, Ipswich, Essex,
IP8 3EG 🅿
☎ 01473 652084
Ⓜ 07802 955829 or 07884 266901
ⓔ lionpy@aol.com
Est. 1991 *Stock size* Large
Stock 17th–19thC English furniture, chairs, oak farmhouse tables, hand-made replica furniture
Open By appointment
Fairs Newark, DMG fairs, Arthur Swallow fairs, High Point Furniture Market, North Carolina
Services Valuations, restoration, house clearance

CHELMSFIELD

⊞ Yesterdays Components Ltd
Contact Harry Edwards
⊠ Wellwood Farm, Lowestock Road, West Hanningfield, Chelmsfield, Essex, CM2 8UY
☎ 01277 840697 ❻ 01277 841185
Est. 1986 *Stock size* Large
Stock Spare parts for pre-war design Morris vehicles
Open By appointment
Services Mail order, item search

CHELMSFORD

⌂ Norton Heath Antiques & Collectables
Contact Mrs Bean
⊠ Chelmsford Road, Norton Heath, Chelmsford, Essex, CM4 0LN 🅿
☎ 01277 824848
Est. 1998 *Stock size* Medium
No. of dealers 20
Stock Clocks, barometers, furniture, jewellery, china, glass, porcelain, collectables, silver, silver plate, art pottery
Open Tues–Thurs Sat Sun 10am–4pm

⋟ S H Rowland
Contact Mr S H Rowland
⊠ 42 Mildmay Road, Chelmsford, Essex, CM2 0DZ 🅿
☎ 01245 354251 ❻ 01245 344466
⓪ 07768 344132
Est. 1946
Open Mon–Fri 9am–5.30pm
Sales General goods alternate weeks, antiques 2–3 a year on Wed, viewing Tues 9am–4.30pm Wed 9–10am
Catalogues Yes

COGGESHALL

⊞ English Rose Antiques
Contact Mr M Barrett
⊠ 7 Church Street, Coggeshall, Essex, CO6 1TU 🅿
☎ 01376 562683 ❻ 01376 563450
⓪ 07770 880790
❷ englishroseantiques@hotmail.com
Est. 1983 *Stock size* Large
Stock Antiques and country pine furniture
Open Mon–Sun 10am–5.30pm
Fairs Ardingly, Newark
Services Stripping, finishing

⊞ Partners in Pine
Contact Mr W T Newton
⊠ 63–65 West Street, Coggeshall, Colchester, Essex, CO6 1NS 🅿
☎ 01376 561972
Est. 1983 *Stock size* Medium
Stock Victorian pine furniture
Open Mon–Sun 10am–6pm closed Wed

COLCHESTER

⊞ Elizabeth Cannon Antiques
Contact Mrs E Cannon
⊠ 85 Crouch Street, Colchester, Essex, CO3 3EZ 🅿
☎ 01206 575817
Est. 1978 *Stock size* Large
Stock Antique glass, jewellery, silver, porcelain, furniture
Open Mon–Sat 9.30am–5.30pm

⊞ The Castle Book Shop (PBFA)
Contact Mr R Green
⊠ 40 Osborne Street, Colchester, Essex, CO2 7DB
☎ 01206 577520 ❻ 01206 577520
Est. 1947 *Stock size* Large
Stock Antiquarian and second-hand books, East Anglia, archaeology, modern first editions, maps, prints
Open Mon–Sat 9am–5pm
Fairs PBFA
Services Book search

⋟ Reeman Dansie
Contact Mr J Grinter
⊠ 8 Wyncolls Road, Severalls Business Park, Colchester, Essex, CO4 9HT 🅿
☎ 01206 754754 ❻ 01206 754750
❷ auctions@reemans.com
Est. 1881
Open Mon–Fri 9am–5.30pm, Sat 9am–1pm
Sales Victorian, Edwardian & later furnishings & general houehold goods, fine art & antique, specialist collectors's, classic car and property auctions
Frequency Fortnightly
Catalogues Yes

⋟ Stanfords
Contact Mr David Lord
⊠ The Cattle Market, Wyncells Road, Colchester, Essex, CO4 9Hu 🅿
☎ 01206 842156 ❻ 01206 852585
❷ info@stanfords-colchester.co.uk
Ⓦ www.stanfords-auctions.co.uk
Est. 1995
Open Mon–Fri 9am–5.30pm
Sales Quarterly fine art and collectables sales, weekly general and antique sales Sat 10am, antique furniture, collectables, viewing Fri 2–6pm Sat 8.30–10am
Frequency Weekly
Catalogues Yes

⊞ Totteridge Gallery (FATG)
Contact Ms J Clarke
⊠ 74 High Street, Earls Coine, Colchester, Essex, CO6 2QX 🅿
☎ 01787 220075
Ⓦ www.totteridgegallery.com
Est. 1985 *Stock size* Large
Stock Fine art, 18th–20thC British and Continental oil paintings, watercolours, drawings, limited-edition Sir William Russell Flint prints
Open Contact Totteridge Gallery for up-to-date opening hours or check website
Services Valuations, advice

DANBURY

⊞ Danbury Antiques (EADA)
Contact Mrs Southgate
⊠ Eves Corner, Danbury, Chelmsford, Essex, CM3 4QF 🅿
☎ 01245 223035
⓪ 07711 704652
Est. 1979 *Stock size* Large
Stock Jewellery, silver, ceramics, porcelain, furniture
Open Tues–Sat 10am–5pm
Services Restoration

DEBDEN

⌂ Debden Antiques (EADA)
Contact Mr Edward Norman
⊠ Elder Street, Debden, Saffron Walden, Essex, CB11 3JY 🅿
☎ 01799 543007 ❻ 01799 542482
❷ info@debden-antiques.co.uk
Ⓦ www.debden-antiques.co.uk
Est. 1999 *Stock size* Large
No. of dealers 30
Stock 17th–19thC furniture, paintings, jewellery, silver, glass, rugs, garden ornaments,

EAST

furniture
Open Tues–Sat 10am–5.30pm
Sun 11am–4pm
Services Valuations, restoration,
shipping

FINCHINGFIELD

⌂ Finchingfield Antiques Centre
Contact Mr Peter Curry
✉ **The Green, Finchingfield, Braintree, Essex, CM7 4JX** ℗
☎ 01371 810258
Est. 1996 **Stock size** Large
No. of dealers 30
Stock Furniture, silver, porcelain, antiquarian books, jewellery, collectables
Open Mon–Sun 10am–5pm

FRINTON-ON-SEA

⊞ Dickens Curios
Contact Miss M Wilsher
✉ **151 Connaught Avenue, Frinton-on-Sea, Essex, CO13 9AH** ℗
☎ 01255 674134
Est. 1970 **Stock size** Large
Stock Antiques, china, glass, pewter, copper, jewellery
Open Mon 11am–1pm
2pm–5.30pm Tues–Thurs
10am–1pm 2pm–5.30pm
Wed 10am–1pm Sat 10am–1pm
2pm–5pm closed Wed pm
Services Buying from public

⊞ No 24 of Frinton
Contact Mr C Pereira
✉ **24 Connaught Avenue, Frinton-on-Sea, Essex, CO13 9PR** ℗
☎ 01255 670505
ⓦ www.artdecoclassics.co.uk
Est. 1993 **Stock size** Large
Stock Art Deco, general antiques, original prints
Open Mon–Sat 10am–5pm
Sun 2–4pm closed Wed

⊞ Phoenix Trading
Contact Mr Tom Sheldon
✉ **130 Connaught Avenue, Frinton-on-Sea, Essex, CO13 9AD** ℗
☎ 01255 851094 ❻ 01255 851094
Est. 1996 **Stock size** Large
Stock Bespoke furniture
Open Mon–Sat 9.30am–5pm
closed Wed pm

GRAYS

⊞ Atticus Books
Contact Mr R Drake
✉ **8 London Road, Grays, Essex, RM17 5XY** ℗
☎ 01375 371200
Est. 1983 **Stock size** Large
Stock Antiquarian, out-of-print, second-hand books
Open Thurs–Sat 9am–4pm
Services Book search

GREAT BADDOW

⊞ The Antique Brass Bedstead Co Ltd
Contact Mr I Rabin
✉ **Baddow Antique Centre, Church Street, Great Baddow, Chelmsford, Essex, CM2 7JW** ℗
☎ 01245 471137
ⓦ www.llph.co.uk/bedsteads.htm
Est. 1978 **Stock size** Large
Stock Victorian brass and iron bedsteads
Open Mon–Sat 10am–5pm
Sun 11am–5pm
Services Restoration

⌂ Baddow Antique Centre (EADA)
✉ **The Bringey, Church Street, Great Baddow, Chelmsford, Essex, CM2 7JW** ℗
☎ 01245 476159
Est. 1974 **Stock size** Large
No. of dealers 20+
Stock 18th–20thC furniture, silver, glass, porcelain, paintings, Victorian brass and iron bedsteads
Open Mon–Sat 10am–5pm
Sun 11am–5pm
Services Valuations, restoration

GREAT DUNMOW

⚒ Mullucks Wells (NAVA)
Contact Mr Lloyd Rust
✉ **The Old Town Hall, Great Dunmow, Essex, CM6 1AU** ℗
☎ 01371 873014 ❻ 01371 878239
ⓔ trembathwelsh@ic24.net
ⓦ www.trembathwelchauctions.co.uk
Est. 1886
Open Mon–Fri 9am–5.30pm
Sat 10am–noon
Sales Chequers Lane, Great Dunmow, fine art and antiques sales quarterly, general sales every 2 weeks. Telephone for details
Catalogues Yes

⊞ F B Neill
Contact Mr F B Neill
✉ **Ivydene, Chelmsford Road, White Roding, Great Dunmow, Essex, CM6 1RG** ℗
☎ 01279 876376
Est. 1975 **Stock size** Medium
Stock Antique furniture
Open By appointment

⊞ Clive Smith
Contact Mr C Smith
✉ **Brick House, North Street, Great Dunmow, Essex, CM6 1BA** ℗
☎ 01371 873171 ❻ 01371 873171
ⓔ clivesmith@route56.co.uk
Est. 1975 **Stock size** Small
Stock Antiquarian books, British Isles, topography, military, natural history
Trade only Yes
Open By appointment
Services Mail order

⊞ The Stores
Contact Scott Saunders
✉ **The Stores, Great Waltham, Chelmsford, Essex, CM3 1DE** ℗
☎ 01245 360277
Est. 1975 **Stock size** Large
Stock English antique pine and country furniture
Open Wed–Sat 10am–5pm
Sun 11am–4pm
Services Deliveries

HAINAULT

⌂ Gallerie Antiques (EADA)
Contact Mrs Gregory
✉ **62–70 Fowler Road, Hainault, Essex, IG6 3XE** ℗
☎ 020 8501 2229 ❻ 020 8501 2209
Est. 1998 **Stock size** Large
No. of dealers 80
Stock Absolutely everything
Open Mon–Sat 10am–5.30pm
Sun 11am–5pm
Services Valuations, restoration, shipping

HALSTEAD

⊞ The Antique Bed Shop
Contact Mrs V McGregor
✉ **Napier House, Head Street, Halstead, Essex, CO9 2BT** ℗
☎ 01787 477346 ❻ 01787 478757

℗ 07801 626047
Est. 1976 *Stock size* Large
Stock Antique wooden beds
Open Thurs–Sat 9am–5pm or by appointment
Services Free delivery

⌂ **Townsford Mill Antiques Centre**
Contact Rosemary Bennett
✉ The Causeway, Halstead, Essex, CO9 1ET 🅿
☎ 01787 474451
Est. 1987 *Stock size* Large
No. of dealers 80
Stock Antiques, collectables, furniture, silver, porcelain, lace, copper, Beswick, Royal Doulton, kitchenware
Open Mon–Sat 10am–5pm
Sun Bank Holidays 11am–5pm

HARLOW

⊞ **West Essex Antiques**
Contact Mr C Dovaston
✉ Stone Hall, Down Hall Road, Matching Green, Harlow, Essex, CM17 0RA 🅿
☎ 01279 730609 📠 01279 730609
📧 chris@essexantiques.co.uk
🌐 www.essexantiques.co.uk
Est. 1975 *Stock size* Large
Stock Furniture
Open Mon–Fri 9am–5pm or by appointment

HARWICH

⌂ **Harwich Antiques Centre**
Contact Miss Karin Scholz
✉ 19 Kings Quay Street, Harwich, Essex, CO12 3ER 🅿
☎ 01255 554719
📧 hac@antiques-access-agency.com
🌐 www.antiques-access-agency.com
Est. 1997 *Stock size* Large
No. of dealers 35
Stock A wide range of antiques, collectables and decorative items
Open Tues–Sat 10am–4.30pm
Sun Bank Holidays 1–4.30pm or by appointment

HAVERING-ATTE-BOWER

⊞ **Robert Bush Antiques**
Contact Mr Robert Bush, Havering-atte-Bower, Essex, RM4 1PH
℗ 07836 236911
📧 bush.antiques@virgin.net

🌐 www.robertbushantiques.com
Stock Antique and decorative furniture, retro
Open By appointment

HOLLAND-ON-SEA

⊞ **Bookworm**
Contact Mr A Durrant
✉ 100 Kings Avenue, Holland-on-Sea, Essex, CO15 5EP 🅿
☎ 01255 815984 📠 01255 815984
📧 andy@adr-comms.demon.co.uk
🌐 www.bookwormshop.com
Est. 1995 *Stock size* Medium
Stock Antiquarian and general second-hand books, fiction, modern first editions
Open Mon–Sat 9am–5pm
Bank Holidays 10am–4pm
Services Free book search

ILFORD

⊞ **Goodwins**
Contact Mr C E Goodwin
✉ 773 Becontree Avenue, Dagenham, Essex, RM8 3HH 🅿
☎ 020 8590 4560/8595 7118
Est. 1964 *Stock size* Small
Stock General antiques
Open Mon–Sat 9am–6pm

INGATESTONE

⊞ **Hutchison Antiques and Interiors (EADA)**
Contact Mr Gavin Hutchison
✉ 60 High Street, Ingatestone, Essex, CM4 9DW 🅿
☎ 01277 353361 📠 01277 353361
Est. 1984 *Stock size* Large
Stock Furniture, paintings, antique and contemporary lamps
Open Mon–Sat 10am–5pm
Fairs NEC
Services Valuations, interior design service

⊞ **Megarry's Antiques (EADA, BACA Award Winner 2002)**
Contact Judy Wood
✉ Jericho Cottage, The Duckpond Green, Blackmore, Ingatestone, Essex, CM4 0RR 🅿
☎ 01277 821031
Est. 1994 *Stock size* Large
Stock General antiques, small

furniture, collectables, ceramics, blue and white china, prints, mirrors, small silver plate
Open Wed–Sun 11am–5pm
Services Valuations, restoration advice

KELVEDON

⊞ **Colton Antiques**
Contact Mr G Colton
✉ Station Road, Kelvedon, Colchester, Essex, CO5 9NP 🅿
☎ 01376 571504
Est. 1992 *Stock size* Small
Stock 18th–19thC furniture, Georgian, decorative furniture, art deco
Open Mon–Sat 8am–5pm
Services Restoration

LANGENHOE

⊞ **Lavender and Linen**
Contact Peter Godden or Sue Mason
✉ The Stables, Peat Hall, Langenhoe, Essex, CO5 7LN 🅿
☎ 01206 735650/790349
Est. 2002 *Stock size* Small
Stock French linen and ceramics, antique furniture
Open By appointment
Fairs NEC
Services Furniture restoration, repairs

LEIGH-ON-SEA

⊞ **Astoria Art Deco**
Contact Mr or Mrs R Taylor
✉ 80 Rectory Grove, Leigh-on-Sea, Essex, SS9 2HJ 🅿
☎ 01702 471800
℗ 07711 332148
📧 astoriaartdeco@aol.com
🌐 www.astoriaartdeco.com
Est. 1987 *Stock size* Large
Stock Furniture, mirrors, lighting, accessories
Open Thurs–Sat 10.30am–5pm or by appointment
Fairs Battersea, Hove
Services Polishing, upholstery

⊞ **Castle Antiques**
Contact Mrs Barbara Gair
✉ PO Box 1911, Leigh-on-Sea, Essex, SS9 1JG

☎ 01702 711390 ❻ 01702 475732
Ⓜ 07973 674355
❺ castle@enterprise.net
Ⓦ www.castle-antiques.com
Est. 1979 *Stock size* Large
Stock 19thC Staffordshire
figures, Ironstone wares, tribal
artefacts, good taxidermy
Trade only Yes
Open By appointment
Fairs NEC, Newark
Services Valuations

⚒ Chalkwell Auctions Ltd (EADA)
Contact Trevor or Simon
✉ The Arlington Rooms, 905
London Road, Leigh-on-Sea, Essex,
SS0 8NU
☎ 01702 710383 ❻ 01702 710383
Est. 1990
Sales Antiques and collectables
sale monthly, normally 2nd
Wed 6.30pm, viewing 4.30pm
Frequency Monthly
Catalogues Yes on the day

⊞ Deja Vu Antiques
Contact Mr S Lewis
✉ 876 London Road,
Leigh-on-Sea, Essex,
SS9 3NQ ☐
☎ 01702 470829
❺ info@deja-vu-antiques.co.uk
Ⓦ www.deja-vu-antiques.co.uk
Est. 1994 *Stock size* Large
Stock 18th–19thC French furniture
Open Mon–Sat 9.30am–5.30pm
Services Restoration

⊞ Othellos
Contact Mr F Bush or Mrs M Layzell
✉ 1376 London Road,
Leigh-on-Sea, Essex,
SS9 2UH ☐
☎ 01702 473334
Ⓜ 07710 764175
❺ othellos@hotmail.com
Est. 1999 *Stock size* Large
Stock Out-of-print and second-
hand books
Open Tues–Sat 9.30am–5pm

⊞ Paris-Art (EADA)
Contact N Rodgers
✉ 193 Leigh Road, Leigh-on-Sea,
Essex,
SS9 1JE ☐
☎ 01702 712832
❺ sales@paris-art.co.uk
Ⓦ www.paris-art.co.uk
Est. 1983 *Stock size* Large
Stock Late 19th-20thC furniture,

lighting, ceramics, sculptures,
paintings
Open Mon–Fri 9.30am–5pm
Sat 9.30am–6pm closed Wed
Services Valuations

⚒ John Stacey & Sons
Contact Mr P J Stacey
✉ 86–90 Pall Mall, Leigh-on-Sea,
Essex,
SS9 1RG ☐
☎ 01702 477051 ❻ 01702 470141
❺ jstacey@easynet.co.uk
Ⓦ www.jstacey.com
Est. 1946
Open Mon–Fri 9am–5.30pm
Sat 9am–1pm
Sales Antiques and collectables
sales every 3 weeks Tues
10.30am, viewing Sat 10am–4pm
Sun 10am–2pm Mon 10am–4pm
Fairs Newark, Ardingly
Catalogues Yes

⊞ John Stacey & Sons
Contact Mr P J Stacey
✉ 86–90 Pall Mall, Leigh-on-Sea,
Essex,
SS9 1RG ☐
☎ 01702 477051 ❻ 01702 470141
❺ jstacey@easynet.co.uk
Ⓦ www.jstacey.com
Est. 1946 *Stock size* Medium
Stock Victorian–Edwardian
furniture, clocks, ceramics
Open Mon–Fri 9am–5.30pm
Sat 9am–1pm
Fairs Newark, Ardingly
Services Adult education courses,
valuations, house clearance

⊞ J Streamer
Contact Mrs J Streamer
✉ 86 Broadway, Leigh-on-Sea,
Essex,
SS9 1AE
☎ 01702 472895
Est. 1963 *Stock size* Medium
Stock Jewellery, silver, small
furniture, art items
Open Mon–Sat 9am–5pm
closed Wed
Services Jewellery repair

LITTLE WALTHAM

⊞ Collectors' Corner
Contact Peter Workman or
Alasdair MacInnes
✉ 100 The Street, Little
Waltham, Chelmsford, Essex,
CM3 3NT ☐
☎ 01245 361166 ❻ 01245 361166

Est. 1987 *Stock size* Large
Stock Paper-type collectables,
postcards, cigarette cards,
ephemera, books
Open Mon–Sat 9am–5pm
Services Picture framing

LOUGHTON

⚒ Ambrose Auctioneers & Valuers
Contact Chrina Jarvis
✉ Ambrose House, Old Station
Road, Loughton, Essex,
IG10 4PE ☐
☎ 020 8502 3951 ❻ 020 8532 0833
❺ info@ambroseauction.co.uk
Ⓦ www.ambroseauction.co.uk
Est. 1900
Open Mon–Fri 9am–1pm
2–5.30pm
Sales General antiques
Frequency Monthly
Catalogues Yes

MALDON

⊞ All Books
Contact Mr K Peggs
✉ 2 Mill Road, Maldon, Essex,
CM9 5HZ ☐
☎ 01621 856214
❺ kevin@allbooks.demon.co.uk
Ⓦ www.allbooks.demon.co.uk
Est. 1975 *Stock size* Large
Stock Antiquarian and second-
hand books, especially sailing
and maritime history
Open Mon–Sat 10am–5pm
Sun 1.30–5pm
Services Valuations

⊞ The Antique Rooms (RADS)
Contact Mrs Ellen Hedley
✉ 104a High Street, Maldon, Essex,
CM9 5EG ☐
☎ 01621 856985
Est. 1977 *Stock size* Large
Stock 19th–20thC general antiques
Open Mon–Sat 10am–4pm
closed Wed
Services Scandinavian spoken

⊞ Clive Beardall Restoration Ltd (BAFRA, EADA)
Contact Mr Clive Beardall
✉ 104b High Street, Maldon, Essex,
CM9 7ET ☐
☎ 01621 857890 ❻ 01621 850753
❺ info@clivebeardall.co.uk
Ⓦ www.clivebeardall.co.uk

Est. 1982 *Stock size* Small
Stock 18th–20thC furniture
Open Mon–Fri 8am–5.30pm
Sat 9am–2pm
Services Valuations, restoration

MANNINGTREE

⊞ Out In The Sticks
Contact Paul Matthews
⊠ 2 The Lanes, Manningtree,
Essex,
CO11 1AW ▢
☎ 01206 391555
Est. 1999 *Stock size* Large
Stock General antiques,
reclamation kitchens
Open Mon–Sat 10am–5pm

NEWPORT

⊞ Omega Decorative Arts
Contact Mr Tony Phillips
or Mrs Sybil Hooper
⊠ High Street, Newport,
Saffron Walden, Essex,
CB11 3PF ▢
☎ 01799 540720
Est. 1985 *Stock size* Medium
Stock 1860–1960, Art Deco,
Arts and Crafts
Open Mon–Sat 10am–6pm
closed Thurs
Services Restoration

RAYLEIGH

**⊞ F G Bruschweiler
Antiques Ltd (LAPADA)**
Contact Mr F Bruschweiler
⊠ 41–67 Lower Lambricks,
Rayleigh, Essex,
SS6 8DA ▢
☎ 01268 773761/773932
🖷 01268 773318
🖃 info@fgbantiques.com
🌐 www.fgbantiques.com
Est. 1960 *Stock size* Large
Stock General antique furniture,
public house bars
Open Mon–Fri 8.30am–5pm
Services Restoration

ROMFORD

**⊞ Collectors Forum
(BNTA, PTS, BCCA)**
Contact Mr Thomas
⊠ 30 Victoria Road, Romford,
Essex,
RM1 2JH ▢
☎ 01708 723357 🖷 020 8590 0926
Est. 1970 *Stock size* Large

Stock Medals, coins, banknotes,
stamps
Open By appointment only
Services Valuations

SAFFRON WALDEN

⊞ Arts Decoratifs (EADA)
Contact Ann Miller
⊠ The Cockpit, Off Market Hill,
Saffron Walden, Essex,
CB10 1HQ ▢
☎ 01799 513666 🖷 0870 900 7997
📱 07774 003851
🖃 contactus@artsdecoratifs.co.uk
🌐 www.artsdecoratifs.co.uk
Est. 2002 *Stock size* Medium
Stock Small furniture, silver,
metalware, jewellery, ceramics,
glass, costume bags
Open Tues Wed 10am–4pm
Fri Sat 10am–5pm
Fairs Alexandra Palace

⊞ Ickleton Antiques
Contact Mr B Arbury
⊠ 4 Gold Street, Saffron Walden,
Essex,
CB10 1EJ
☎ 01799 513114
Est. 1995 *Stock size* Medium
Stock Militaria, postcards,
collectables WWI, WWII
Open Mon–Fri 10am–4pm
Sat 10am–5pm

**⊞ Lankester Antiques &
Books**
Contact Mr P Lankester
⊠ The Old Sun Inn, Church
Street, Saffron Walden, Essex,
CB10 1JW
☎ 01799 522685
Est. 1967 *Stock size* Large
Stock General antiques,
antiquarian and second-hand
books
Open Tues–Sat 10am–5pm

**⊞ Market Row Antiques &
Collectables**
Contact Mr P Bowyer or
Mr D Miller
⊠ 14 Market Row,
Saffron Waldon, Essex,
CB10 1HB
☎ 01799 516131
📱 07759 493613
Est. 1994 *Stock size* Small
Stock General antiques, clocks,
barometers, porcelain, militaria,
furniture
Open Mon–Sat 9.30am–5pm

Fairs London and Birmingham
clock fairs
Services Clock and watch repairs

**⊞ Maureen Morris (BADA,
LAPADA)**
Contact Maureen Morris
⊠ Saffron Walden, Essex
☎ 01799 521338 🖷 01799 522802
🖃 mm@antiqueembroidery.com
🌐 www.antiqueembroidery.com
Est. 1979 *Stock size* Small
Stock Samplers, embroidery, quilts
Open By appointment
Fairs Olympia
Services Shipping, book search

⊞ Reed & Son
Contact Martin Reed
⊠ 20 Church Street,
Saffron Walden, Essex,
CB10 1JW ▢
☎ 01799 527517
Est. 1881 *Stock size* Small
Stock General antiques
Open Mon–Sat 10am–5pm

**⌂ Saffron Walden
Antiques Centre**
Contact Mr G or Mrs M Wombwell
⊠ 1 Market Row, Saffron Walden,
Essex, CB10 1HA ▢
☎ 01799 524534
🌐 www.saffronantique.sco.uk
Est. 1997 *Stock size* Large
No. of dealers 50
Stock Huge range of antiques,
collectables, bygones, furniture,
silver, jewellery, porcelain,
lighting, pictures, sporting
memorabilia, railway
Open Mon–Sat 10am–5pm
Sun 11am–4pm

⚒ Saffron Walden Auctions
Contact Mr C Peeke-Voute
⊠ 1 Market Street,
Saffron Walden, Essex, CB10 1JB
☎ 01799 513281 🖷 01799 513334
🖃 info@saffronwaldenauctions.com
🌐 www.saffronwaldenauctions.com
Est. 1905
Open Tues Thurs Fri 10am–4pm
Sales Antiques sales Saturday
10am every 6 weeks, viewing
Fri 10am–5pm
Catalogues Yes

SIBLE HEDINGHAM

⊞ Hedingham Antiques
Contact Mrs P Patterson
⊠ 100 Swan Street,

Sible Hedingham, Halstead, Essex, CO9 3HP ℗
☎ 01787 460360 ❶ 01787 469109
Ⓜ 07802 265702
❺ patriciapatterson@totalise.co.uk
Ⓦ www.silberausengland.co.uk
Est. 1980 *Stock size* Medium
Stock Antique and early 20thC silver, silver plate, glass
Open By appointment
Services Silver and furniture restoration

⊞ Lennard Antiques (LAPADA)
Contact G Pinn
✉ 124 Swan Street, Sible Hedingham, Halstead, Essex, CO9 3HP ℗
☎ 01787 461127
Est. 1969 *Stock size* Medium
Stock Oak and country furniture, Delftware
Open Mon–Sat 9.30am–6pm
Fairs Olympia, Chelsea Spring and Autumn, Kensington

⊞ W A Pinn & Sons (LAPADA, BADA)
Contact Mr J Pinn or Mr K Pinn
✉ 124 Swan Street, Sible Hedingham, Halstead, Essex, CO9 3HP ℗
☎ 01787 461127
Ⓜ 0785 501 5104
Est. 1969 *Stock size* Medium
Stock 17th–early 19thC furniture, accessories
Open Mon–Sat 9.30am–6pm
Fairs Olympia, Chelsea Spring and Autumn, Kensington

SOUTH BENFLEET

⊞ Classique Antiques (EADA)
Contact Chris Elliott
✉ 356 High Road, South Benfleet, Essex, SS7 5HP ℗
☎ 01268 566695 ❶ 01268 566695
Est. 1999 *Stock size* Large
Stock General antiques, furniture, decorative arts, Clarice Cliff, Moorcroft, Staffordshire, Toby jugs
Open Mon–Sat 9am–4pm

SOUTH WOODHAM FERRERS

⊞ Rocking Horse Elite (Rocking Horse Guild)
Contact Jan Rushing or Debbie Walsh

✉ 9 Mount Pleasant Road, South Woodham Ferrers, Essex, CM3 5PA ℗
☎ 01245 320228
Ⓜ 07967 958074 /07808 767290
❺ rockinghorseelite.com
Ⓦ www.rockinghorseelite.com
Est. 1988 *Stock size* Large
Stock Rare rocking horses
Open By appointment
Services Specialist restoration, valuation on rocking horses and all moving toy horses

SOUTHEND-ON-SEA

⊞ CurioCity
Contact Sheila or Matt
✉ 333–335 Chartwell Square, Victoria Plaza, Southend-on-Sea, Essex, SS2 5SP ℗
☎ 01702 611350
Ⓦ www.curio-city.co.uk
Est. 1998 *Stock size* Large
Stock Wide range of antiques, collectables
Open Mon–Fri 10am–5pm Sat 9am–5pm
Services Cafe

⊞ David Morton
Contact Mr D Morton
✉ Rear of 61–69 Princes Street, Southend-on-Sea, Essex, SS1 1PT ℗
☎ 01702 354144
Est. 1967 *Stock size* Large
Stock 19thC furniture, general antiques
Trade only Yes
Open By appointment

⊞ R & J Coins (BNTA)
Contact Mr R Harvey
✉ 21b Alexandra Street, Market Place, Southend-on-Sea, Essex, SS1 1BX ℗
☎ 01702 345995
Est. 1967 *Stock size* Medium
Stock Coins, medals, bank notes, cap badges
Open Mon–Fri 10am–4pm Wed 10am–2pm Sat 10am–3pm

STANSTED MOUNTFITCHET

⊞ Linden House Antiques
Contact Mr A W Sargeant
✉ 3 Silver Street, Stansted Mountfitchet, Essex, CM24 8HA ℗

☎ 01279 812372
Est. 1962 *Stock size* Large
Stock 18th–19thC furniture, pictures
Open Mon–Sat 11am–4.30pm
Services Valuations

⚒ G E Sworder & Sons
Contact Mr Guy Schooling ASFAV FRICS
✉ 14 Cambridge Road, Stansted Mountfitchet, Essex, CM24 8BZ ℗
☎ 01279 817778 ❶ 01279 817779
❺ auctions@sworder.co.uk
Ⓦ www.sworder.co.uk
Est. 1782
Open Mon–Fri 9am–5pm
Sales Weekly sales of Victoriana Wed 11am, viewing Tues 2–5pm. Bi-monthly fine art sales Tues 10am, viewing Fri previous 10am–5pm Sat Sun 10am–1pm Mon 10am–5pm
Catalogues Yes

⊞ Valmar Antiques (BADA, LAPADA, CINOA)
Contact J A or M R Orpin
✉ Croft House Cottage, High Lane, Stansted Mountfitchet, Essex, CM24 8LQ ℗
☎ 01279 813201 ❶ 01279 816962
Ⓜ 07831 093701
❺ valmar-antiques@cwcom.net
Est. 1967 *Stock size* Large
Stock 18th–19thC furniture and accesssories, Arts and Crafts
Open By appointment only
Fairs Olympia BADA

THAXTED

⊞ Harris Antiques (BAFRA, EADA)
Contact Brian Harris
✉ 24 Town Street, Thaxted, Essex, CM6 2LA ℗
☎ 01371 832832
Est. 1956 *Stock size* Large
Stock 16th–20thC furniture, clocks, barometers
Open Mon–Sat 9am–5pm
Fairs NEC
Services Valuations, restoration

UPMINSTER

⌂ Collectors Fair
Contact Sally Reynolds
✉ 59 Station Road, Upminster, Essex, RM14 2SU ℗

EAST
NORFOLK • BURNHAM MARKET

☎ 01708 224410
Est. 2000 *Stock size* Medium
No. of dealers 15
Stock Antiques, collectables
Open Tues–Sat 10am–5pm
Services Valuations

⊞ It's About Time (EADA)
Contact Mr Paul Williams
✉ 863 London Road,
Westcliff-on-Sea, Essex,
SS0 9SZ 🅿
☎ 01702 472574 ✆ 01702 472574
✉ shop@antiqueclock.co.uk
🌐 www.antiqueclock.co.uk
Est. 1979 *Stock size* Medium
Stock Clocks, furniture
Open Tues–Sat 9am–5pm
or by appointment
Services Restoration

⊞ Les and Gary's
Contact Gary Bell
✉ 659 London Road,
Westcliff-on-Sea, Essex,
SS0 9PD 🅿
☎ 01702 300052 ✆ 01702 300050
🌐 www.les-and-gary.co.uk
Est. 1977 *Stock size* Large
Stock General antiques
Open Mon–Sun 9am–5pm

⊞ Prust & Sons Antique Furniture
Contact Mr Prust
✉ 9 West Road, Westcliff-on-Sea,
Essex,
SS0 9AU
☎ 01702 391093 ✆ 01702 391093
✉ sales@prust.co.uk
🌐 www.prust.co.uk
Est. 1987 *Stock size* Large
Stock General antiques
Open Mon–Sat 8.30am–5.30pm
Sun 10am–3pm
Services Restoration

⊞ Ridgeway Antiques (EADA)
Contact Trevor or Simon
✉ 66 The Ridgeway,
Westcliff-on-Sea, Essex,
SS0 8NU 🅿
☎ 01702 710383 ✆ 01702 710383
🌐 www.ridgeweb.co.uk
Est. 1987 *Stock size* Medium
Stock 18thC–pre-war furniture,
general antiques
Open Mon–Sat 10.30am–5pm
Fairs Hallmark, Ridgeway Fairs
Services Valuations

WOODFORD GREEN

⊞ Mill Lane Antiques
Contact Mr Wood
✉ 29 Mill Lane, Woodford Green,
Essex,
IG8 0UG 🅿
☎ 020 8502 9930
Est. 1987 *Stock size* Large
Stock Georgian–Victorian
furniture, lighting, chandeliers,
ironwork, collectables,
decorative items
Open Tues Thurs–Sat 10am–4pm
Fairs Kempton Park
Services House clearance

WRITTLE

⊞ Whichcraft Jewellery (EADA)
Contact Alan Turner
✉ 54–56 The Green, Writtle,
Chelmsford, Essex,
CM1 3DU 🅿
☎ 01245 420183 ✆ 01245 420030
Est. 1978 *Stock size* Large
Stock Antique and modern
jewellery, small silver items
Open Tues–Sat 9.30am–5.30pm
Services Jewellery repairs and
restoration

NORFOLK

ACLE

⌂ Horners Auctioneers (ISVA)
Contact Mr N Horner-Glister FRICS
✉ Acle Salerooms, Norwich Road,
Acle, Norwich, Norfolk,
NR13 3BY 🅿
☎ 01493 750225 ✆ 01493 750506
✉ auction@horners.co.uk
🌐 www.horners.co.uk
Est. 1900
Open Mon–Fri 9am–1pm 2–5pm
Sales General antiques sale
Thurs 10am, viewing
Wed 2–4pm, bi-monthly antiques
and collectables sale Sat 10am
Frequency Weekly
Catalogues Yes

AYLSHAM

⌂ Keys
Contact Mr D J Lines
✉ Aylsham Salerooms, Off
Palmers Lane, Aylsham, Norfolk,
NR11 6JA 🅿
☎ 01263 733195 ✆ 01263 732140

✉ info@gakey.co.uk
🌐 www.aylshamsalerooms.co.uk
Est. 1953
Open Mon–Fri 9am–5pm
closed 1–2pm Sat 9am–noon
Sales Weekly general sale,
antiques sale every 3 weeks Tues
Wed. Every 2 months book sale
Fri, collectors' sale Thurs, picture
sales Fri. Telephone for details
Catalogues Yes

⊞ Pearse Lukies Ltd
Contact The Manager
✉ The Old Vicarage, Aylsham,
Norfolk,
NR11 6HE 🅿
☎ 01263 734137
🌐 01263 734502
Est. 1974 *Stock size* Medium
Stock Pre-1800 antiques
Open By appointment

BRANCASTER STAITHE

⊞ Staithe Antiques
Contact Martin Allen
✉ Main Road, Brancaster Staithe,
Norfolk,
PE31 8BJ 🅿
☎ 01485 210600
Est. 2003 *Stock size* Medium
Stock Period oak and country,
walnut, mahogany furniture,
gardening antiques
Open Mon–Sun 10.30am–5pm
Services Collection, delivery

BURNHAM MARKET

⊞ Brazenhead Ltd
Contact David Kenyon
✉ Greenside, Market Place,
Burnham Market, King's Lynn,
Norfolk,
PE31 8HD 🅿
☎ 01328 730700 ✆ 01328 730929
✉ brazenheadbook@aol.com
Est. 1979 *Stock size* Large
Stock Antiquarian, second-hand,
out-of-print books, specializing
in childrens books, also books
concerning Nelson
Open Mon–Sat 9.30am–5pm
Services Valuations, book search

⊞ M & A Cringle
Contact Mr or Mrs Cringle
✉ The Old Black Horse, Market
Place, Burnham Market, Norfolk,
PE31 8HD 🅿
☎ 01328 738456
Est. 1965 *Stock size* Small

213

Stock Late 18thC furniture,
prints, maps, china, pottery
Open Mon–Sat 9am–1pm 2–5pm
closed Wed
Services Valuations

COLTISHALL

⊞ Roger Bradbury Antiques
Contact Roger Bradbury
✉ Church Street, Coltishall,
Norfolk,
NR12 7DJ 🅿
☎ 01603 737444 📠 01603 737018
📱 07860 372528
Est. 1967 *Stock size* Medium
Stock Chinese porcelain cargoes,
18th–19thC furniture, pictures,
objets d'art
Open Mon–Sat 9am–5pm
Sun 10am–4pm

CROMER

⊞ Bond Street Antiques (NAG, GAGTL)
Contact Mr M R T Jones
✉ 6 Bond Street, Cromer, Norfolk,
NR27 9DA 🅿
☎ 01263 513134
Est. 1970 *Stock size* Medium
Stock Silver, jewellery
Open Mon–Sat 9am–5pm
Services Valuations

⊞ Books Etc.
Contact Mr Kevin Reynor
✉ 15a Church Street, Cromer,
Norfolk,
NR27 9ES
☎ 01263 515501
🌐 bookskcr@aol.com
Est. 1997 *Stock size* Large
Stock Antiquarian and second-
hand books
Open Easter–Sept Sun–Mon
11am–4pm winter
Wed–Sat 11am–4pm

⊞ Collectors' World
Contact Mrs Irene Nockels
✉ 6 New Parade, Church Street,
Cromer, Norfolk, NR27 9EP 🅿
☎ 01263 515330/514174
🌐 nockels@25nr.fsnet.co.uk
Est. 1994 *Stock size* Large
Stock Furniture, general
antiques, collectables
Open Tues–Sat 10am–5pm
Fairs Norwich, Newark
Services Valuations, house
clearance

DEREHAM

⋀ Case & Dewing
Contact John Dewing
✉ Church Street, Dereham,
Norfolk,
NR19 1DJ 🅿
☎ 01362 692004 📠 01362 693103
🌐 info@case-dewing.co.uk
🌐 www.case-dewing.co.uk
Est. 1900
Open Mon–Fri 9am–5.30pm
Sat 9am–3.30pm
Sales General antiques and effects
Tues, viewing morning of sale
Frequency 2 weeks
Catalogues No

⋀ Tyrone R Roberts
Contact T R Roberts
✉ 10 Brunswick Close, Toftwood,
Dereham, Norfolk,
NR19 1XW 🅿
☎ 01362 691267 📠 01362 691267
📱 07702 642362
🌐 tyroneroberts@yahoo.co.uk
🌐 www.tyroneroberts.com
Est. 1970
Open Mon–Sun 9am–5pm
or by appointment
Sales General antiques
Frequency Monthly
Catalogues Yes

⊞ Village Books
Contact Mr Jack James
✉ 20a High Street, Dereham,
Norfolk,
NR19 1DR 🅿
☎ 01362 853066
🌐 villagebkdereham@aol.com
Est. 1996 *Stock size* Large
Stock General books, maps,
ephemera
Open Mon Tues Thurs Fri
9.30am–4.30pm Wed
9.30am–3pm Sat 9.30am–5pm
Services Free book search,
Readers' Club, postal sales

DISS

⌂ Antique and Collectors' Centre Diss
Contact Mr D Cockaday
✉ The Works, 3 Cobbs Yard,
St Nicholas Street, Diss, Norfolk,
IP22 4LB 🅿
☎ 01379 644472
Est. 1999 *Stock size* Large
No. of dealers 28
Stock General antiques,
1850–1970, Art Deco china and

glass, commemoratives
Open Mon–Thurs 10am–4.30pm
Fri 9am–4.30pm Sat
10am–4.30pm
Services Valuations

⊞ Diss Antiques & Interiors (LAPADA)
Contact Mr Brian Wimshurst
✉ 2–3 Market Place, Diss, Norfolk,
IP22 3JT 🅿
☎ 01379 642213 📠 01379 642213
📱 07770 477368
🌐 sales@dissantiques.co.uk
🌐 www.dissantiques.co.uk
Est. 1971 *Stock size* Medium
Stock Tudor–Edwardian
furniture, ceramics, silver,
antique jewellery
Open Mon–Sat 9am–5pm
Services Valuations, restoration

⋀ Thos Wm Gaze & Son
Contact Alan M Smith FRICS
✉ Diss Auction Rooms,
Roydon Road, Diss, Norfolk,
IP22 4LN 🅿
☎ 01379 650306 📠 01379 644313
🌐 sales@dissauctionrooms.co.uk
🌐 www.twgaze.com
Est. 1857
Open Mon–Fri 9am–5pm
Sat 9am–noon
Sales Weekly Fri sales of antiques
and collectables, Victorian pine
and shipping furniture, modern
furniture and effects. Periodic Fri
sales of decorative arts, modern
furniture and decor, 19th–20thC
paintings, books, ephemera.
Periodic Sat sales decorative arts,
modern furniture, decor, toys,
nostalgia, architectural salvage,
statuary, rural and domestic
bygones. Auction calendars
available, viewing Thurs 2–8pm
Fri Sat from 8.30am
Catalogues Yes

DOWNHAM MARKET

⊞ Antiques and Gifts
Contact Mrs Addirson
✉ 47 Bridge Street,
Downham Market, Norfolk,
PE38 9DW 🅿
☎ 01366 387700
Est. 1998 *Stock size* Medium
Stock Victorian–Edwardian
furniture, second-hand books,
china, glass, smalls, general
antiques
Open Mon–Sat 9am–5pm

⚹ Barry L Hawkins
Contact Mr B Hawkins FRICS
✉ **15 Lynn Road,**
Downham Market, Norfolk,
PE38 9NL ▣
☎ 01366 387180 ● 01366 386626
Ⓜ 07860 451721
✉ Barry@barryhawkins.co.uk
Ⓦ www.barryhawkins.co.uk
Est. 1840
Open Mon–Fri 9am–5pm
Sales Monthly antiques and
general sale of goods first Wed,
viewing morning of sale 8–11am.
Wine sales and Oriental carpet
sales, catalogued
Catalogues No

FAKENHAM

⚹ James Beck Auctions
Contact Mr James Beck
✉ **The Cornhall,**
Cattle Market Street, Fakenham,
Norfolk,
NR21 9AW ▣
☎ 01328 851557 ● 01328 851044
✉ jamesbeck@auctions18.fsnet.co.uk
Ⓦ www.jamesbeckauctions.co.uk
Est. 1840
Open Tues 10am–1pm
Thurs 10am–5pm Fri 10am–2pm
Sales General antiques sales on
Thurs at 11am, specialist sales
occasionally, viewing Wed 2–5pm
Thurs 9–11am
Frequency Weekly
Catalogues No

⌂ Fakenham Antiques
Centre
Contact Mandy Allen
or Julie Hunt
✉ **The Old Congregational**
Church, 14 Norwich Road,
Fakenham, Norfolk,
NR21 8AZ ▣
☎ 01328 862941
✉ norfolkantiques@tiscali.co.uk
Est. 1984 *Stock size* Large
No. of dealers 20
Stock Period furniture, antiques,
curios, collectables
Open Mon–Sat 10am–4.30pm
Services Restoration

⊞ Sue Rivett Antiques
Contact Sue Rivett
✉ **6 Norwich Road, Fakenham,**
Norfolk,
NR21 8AX ▣
☎ 01328 862924
Est. 1969 *Stock size* Small

Stock General antiques, Victorian
and pre-Victorian items
Open Mon–Sat 10am–1pm
closed Wed
Fairs Greshams
Services Valuations

GREAT YARMOUTH

⊞ Barry's Antiques
Contact Mr Barry Nichols
✉ **35 King Street,**
Great Yarmouth, Norfolk,
NR30 2PN ▣
☎ 01493 842713 ● 01493 745312
Ⓜ 07802 619579
Est. 1979 *Stock size* Large
Stock Jewellery, porcelain, silver
Open Mon–Sat 9.30am–4.30pm
closed Thurs
Services Jewellery repair,
insurance valuer and agent

⊞ Curiosity Too
Contact Mr or Mrs R Moore
✉ **163 Northgate Street,**
Great Yarmouth, Norfolk,
NR30 1BY ▣
☎ 01493 859690
Est. 1983 *Stock size* Medium
Stock China, glass, pictures,
general antiques, small furniture
Open Mon–Fri 10am–4.30pm Sat
10.30am–3.30pm closed Thurs
Services House clearance

⚹ Garry M Emms and Co Ltd
Contact Garry Emms
✉ **Great Yarmouth Salerooms,**
Beevor Road, Great Yarmouth,
Norfolk,
NR30 3PS ▣
☎ 01493 332668 ● 01493 728290
✉ g_emms@great-yarmouth-
auctions.com
Ⓦ www.great-yarmouth-
auctions.com
Est. 1994
Open Thurs–Fri 10am–4pm
accept goods for sale
Sales Weekly sales of antiques Wed
10am, viewing Tues 2–8pm Wed
9–10am. Quarterly special sales
Catalogues No

⊞ David Ferrow (ABA, PBFA)
Contact David Ferrow
✉ **77 Howard Street South,**
Great Yarmouth, Norfolk,
NR30 1LN ▣
☎ 01493 843800
Est. 1940 *Stock size* Large
Stock General antiquarian books,

local topography
Open Mon–Wed Fri Sat
10am–4.30pm closed Bank
Holidays
Services Valuations

HARLESTON

⊞ The Old Coach House
Contact David Burrough
✉ **Church Hill, Starston,**
Harleston, Norfolk,
IP2 9PT ▣
☎ 01379 852123
Est. 1990 *Stock size* Small
Stock Restored
Georgian–Victorian walnut and
mahogany furniture,
Open Mon–Sat 9am–5pm
Services Restoration

HINGHAM

⊞ Mongers Architectural
Salvage (SALVO)
Contact Mrs Sam Coster
✉ **15 Market Place, Hingham,**
Norwich, Norfolk,
NR9 4AF ▣
☎ 01953 851868 ● 01953 851870
✉ mongers@mongersofhingham.co.uk
Ⓦ www.mongersofhingham.co.uk
Est. 1997 *Stock size* Large
Stock Architectural salvage
Open Mon–Sat 9.30am–5.30pm
Services Stripping, fireplace
restoration

⊞ Past & Present
Contact Christine George
✉ **16a Fairland, Hingham,**
Norwich, Norfolk,
NR9 4NH ▣
☎ 01953 851471
Est. 1999 *Stock size* Large
Stock Fine art and antiques,
lighting
Open Tues–Sun 10am–5pm
Fairs Newark, Swindelby

HOLT

⊞ Baron Art
Contact Mr A Baron
✉ **9 Chapel Yard, Albert Street,**
Holt, Norfolk,
NR25 6HJ ▣
☎ 01263 713906 ● 01263 711670
✉ baronholt@aol.com
Est. 1990 *Stock size* Large
Stock Antiquarian books
Open Mon–Sat 9am–5pm
Services Framing

⊞ Baron Art
Contact Mr A Baron
✉ 17 Chapel Yard, Albert Street, Holt, Norfolk,
NR25 6HG 🅿
☎ 01263 713430 📠 01263 711670
📧 baronholt@aol.com
Est. 1990 *Stock size* Large
Stock Art Deco, paintings
Open Mon–Sat 9am–5pm

⊞ Cobwebs
Contact Ann Buchanan
✉ 2 Fish Hill, Holt, Norfolk,
NR25 6BD 🅿
☎ 01263 711955 📠 01328 829592
📱 0798 00 87889
Est. 1996 *Stock size* Large
Stock Bygones, collectables, woodworking and agricultural tools
Open Mon–Fri 10.30am–5pm
Sat 10.30am–6pm

⊞ Cottage Collectables
Contact Philip or Linda Morris
✉ Fish Hill, Holt, Norfolk,
NR25 6BD 🅿
☎ 01263 711707
Est. 1984 *Stock size* Large
Stock General antiques, jewellery
Open Mon–Sun 10am–5pm
Fairs Newark, The International Antique and Collectables Fair, RAF Swinderby, Peterborough and Norwich showgrounds
Services Restoration, house clearance

⊞ Anthony Fell Antiques & Works of Art (BADA, LAPADA)
Contact Anthony Fell
✉ Chester House, 47 Bull Street, Holt, Norfolk,
NR25 6HP
☎ 01263 712912
📧 afellantiques@tiscali.co.uk
Est. 1996 *Stock size* Medium
Stock 17th–18thC English furniture and works of art
Open Mon–Sat 10am–5pm
telephone call advisable
Services Valuations, restoration

⊞ Simon Finch Norfolk
Contact Mr Tristram Hull
✉ 3–5 Fish Hill, Holt, Norfolk,
NR25 6BD 🅿
☎ 01263 712650 📠 01263 711153
Est. 1974 *Stock size* Large
Stock General stock, antiquarian books
Open Mon–Sat 10am–5pm

⊞ Heathfield Antiques
Contact Stephen Heathfield
✉ Candlestick Lane,
Thornage Road, Holt, Norfolk,
NR25 6SU 🅿
☎ 01263 711609 📠 01263 711609
📧 info@antique-pine.net
🌐 www.antique-pine.net
Est. 1991 *Stock size* Large
Stock Antique pine, country items
Open Mon–Sat 8.30am–5pm
Services Restoration

⌂ Holt Antique Centre
Contact Mr D Attfield
✉ Albert Street, Holt, Norfolk,
NR25 6HX 🅿
☎ 01263 712097
Est. 1982 *Stock size* Large
No. of dealers 15
Stock Antiques, collectables
Open Mon–Sun 10am–5pm

⊞ Holt Antique Gallery
Contact Mrs J Holliday
✉ 2 Shire Hall Plain, Holt, Norfolk,
NR25 6HT
☎ 01263 711991 📠 01263 711991
Est. 1997 *Stock size* Large
Stock Antique furniture, china, brass, silver
Open Mon–Sun 10am–5pm
Fairs Newark, The International Antique and Collectables Fair, RAF Swinderby

⌂ Mews Antique Emporium
Contact Mr Howard Heathfield
✉ 17 High Street, Holt, Norfolk,
NR25 6BN
☎ 01263 713224
Est. 1998 *Stock size* Large
No. of dealers 14
Stock Furniture, pictures, pottery, china
Open Mon–Sat 10am–5pm
Sun 11am–4pm
Services Valuations, restoration

⊞ Past Caring
Contact Mrs Lynda Mossman
✉ 6 Chapel Yard, Albert Street, Holt, Norfolk,
NR25 6HG 🅿
☎ 01263 713771 📠 01362 680078
📧 mossmanlyn@btinternet.com
Est. 1987 *Stock size* Large
Stock Vintage clothing, accessories, costume jewellery 1800–1950
Open Mon–Sat 11am–5pm
Fairs Alexandra Palace

⊞ Richard Scott Antiques
Contact Mr Richard Scott
✉ 30 High Street, Holt, Norfolk,
NR25 6BH 🅿
☎ 01263 712479
Est. 1972 *Stock size* Large
Stock Ceramics, studio pottery, oil lamps
Open Tues–Fri 10am–5pm
Sat 10am–5pm closed Thurs
Fairs Newark
Services Advice on valuation, restoration

KING'S LYNN

⊞ Farm House Antiques
Contact P Philpot
✉ Whites Farm House,
Barkers Drove, Stoke Ferry,
King's Lynn, Norfolk,
PE33 9TA 🅿
☎ 01366 500588 📠 01366 500588
📱 07971 859151
Est. 1969 *Stock size* Small
Stock Antique furniture
Open By appointment
Services Restoration

⊞ The Old Curiosity Shop
Contact Mrs Wright
✉ 25 St James Street,
King's Lynn,
Norfolk,
PE30 5DA 🅿
☎ 01553 766591
📱 07802 348635
Est. 1984 *Stock size* Small
Stock General antiques, collectables, furniture
Open Mon–Sat 11am–5pm
Fairs Alexandra Palace, Lee Valley Park
Services Teddy bear restoration, clock, watch repairs, bead restringing

⌂ The Old Granary Antique Centre
Contact Mrs McKenna
✉ King's Staithe Lane,
King's Lynn, Norfolk,
PE30 1LZ 🅿
☎ 01553 775509
Est. 1979 *Stock size* Medium
No. of dealers 15
Stock General antiques, collectables, coins, medals, stamps, books
Open Mon–Sat 10am–5pm
(4.30pm in winter) Sundays in summer 11am–5pm
Services Valuations

⊞ Roderick Richardson (BNTA)
Contact Mr Roderick Richardson
✉ The Old Granary Antique Centre, Kings Staithe Lane, King's Lynn, Norfolk, PE30 1LZ 🅿
☎ 01553 670833 for coins only
☏ 01553 670833
📱 0778 637 2444
✉ roderickrichardson@yahoo.co.uk
🌐 www.roderickrichardson.com
Est. 1995 *Stock size* Large
Stock English hammered and early milled gold and silver
Open By appointment
Fairs Midland Coin Fair, London Coin Fair, Coinex
Services Valuations, buy on commission, illustrated circular

MARSHAM

⊞ Brian Watson Antique Glass (LAPADA)
Contact Brian Watson
✉ Foxwarren Cottage, High Street, Marsham, Norwich, Norfolk, NR10 5QA 🅿
☎ 01263 732519 ☏ 01263 732519
📱 07718 860535
✉ brian.h.watson@talk21.com
Est. 1991 *Stock size* Medium
Stock Georgian–Victorian drinking glasses, decanters and other glass of the period
Open By appointment
Fairs NEC, Penman fairs, Olympia
Services Valuations

MULBARTON

⊞ Junk and Disorderly
Contact Colin Whiting
✉ The Dell, Birchfield Lane, Mulbarton, Norfolk, NR14 8AA 🅿
☎ 01603 470495
📱 07903 323527
Est. 1976 *Stock size* Large
Stock General antiques
Open Sat 8am–4pm
Services House clearance, removals

NORTH WALSHAM

⊞ The Angel Bookshop (PBFA)
Contact Mr E Green
✉ 4 Aylsham Road, North Walsham, Norfolk, NR28 0BH
☎ 01692 404054

✉ angelbooks@onetel.net.uk
Est. 1989 *Stock size* Medium
Stock General antiquarian books, cycling, bicycles, Norfolk and natural history topics a speciality
Open Thurs Fri 9.30am–5pm
Sat 9.30am–3.30pm
Fairs PBFA
Services Book search

⊞ Cat Pottery
Contact Nick Allen
✉ 1 Grammar School Road, North Walsham, Norfolk, NR28 9JH 🅿
☎ 01692 402962 ☏ 01692 405822
🌐 www.winstanleycats.uk.com
Est. 1958 *Stock size* Large
Stock Ceramic cats
Open Mon–Fri 9am–5pm, Sat 11am–1pm

⚒ Horners Auctioneers (ISVA)
Contact Mr N Horner-Glister FRICS
✉ North Walsham Sales Rooms, Midland Road, North Walsham, Norfolk, NR28 9JR 🅿
☎ 01692 500603 ☏ 01692 500480
✉ auction@horners.co.uk
🌐 www.horners.co.uk
Est. 1993
Open Mon–Fri 9am–1pm 2–5pm
Sales Monthly antiques and collectables sale Sat 10am, viewing Fri 10am–8pm
Catalogues Yes

⊞ Park Lane Antiques
Contact Philip Sneddon
✉ 2 Park Lane, North Walsham, Norfolk, NR28 9JZ
☎ 01692 409775
🌐 www.parklaneantique.com
Est. 2002 *Stock size* Medium
Stock Antique furniture pre 1900
Open Wed–Sat 10.30am–4.30pm
Services Valuations, restoration

NORWICH

⊞ Antique Chair Shop
Contact Simon Hunt
✉ Kirstead Green, Norwich, Norfolk, NR15 1EB 🅿
☎ 01508 550051
✉ info@antiquechairshop.co.uk
🌐 www.antiquechairshop.co.uk
Est. 1985 *Stock size* Small
Stock Chairs

Open Mon–Sat 9am–5pm
Thur 9am–12.30pm
Services Restoration

⊞ Antiques & Interiors
Contact Patrick Russell-Davis
✉ 31–35 Elm Hill, Norwich, Norfolk, NR3 1HG 🅿
☎ 01603 622695 ☏ 01603 632446
✉ patrick.russelldavis@btopenworld.com
Est. 1996 *Stock size* Large
Stock Art Deco and Art Nouveau furniture, Arts and Crafts
Open Mon–Sat 10am–5pm, closed Thurs

⊞ James Brett Ltd (BADA)
Contact Mrs T Lotis
✉ 42 St Giles Street, Norwich, Norfolk, NR2 1LW 🅿
☎ 01603 628171 ☏ 01603 630245
Est. 1870 *Stock size* Large
Stock 17th–18thC furniture, fine art
Open Mon–Fri 9.30am–1pm 2–5pm
Fairs Olympia, BADA

⊞ The Collectors' Shop
Contact Mr L Downham
✉ 2 Angel Road, Norwich, Norfolk, NR3 3HP 🅿
☎ 01603 765672
Est. 1975 *Stock size* Large
Stock Stamps, postcards, coins, models, small items, collectables
Open Tues–Sat 9.30am–5.30pm closed Thurs
Services Valuations

⊞ Clive Dennett (BNTA, IBNS)
Contact Mr C Dennett
✉ 66 St Benedict's Street, Norwich, Norfolk, NR2 4AR 🅿
☎ 01603 624315 ☏ 01603 624315
Est. 1970 *Stock size* Large
Stock Coins, medals, banknotes, currency
Open Mon–Sat 9am–5pm closed Thurs
Fairs The Cumberland Coin Fairs

⊞ Elm Hill Antiques
Contact Mr Guyner
✉ 28 Elm Hill, Norwich, Norfolk, NR3 1HG 🅿
☎ 01603 667414
Est. 1993 *Stock size* Small

Stock Victorian furniture, china, linen
Open Mon–Sat 10am–4.30pm
closed Thurs

⊞ Nicholas Fowle Antiques (BADA)
Contact Mr N Fowle
✉ Websdales Court, Bedford Street, Norwich, Norfolk, NR2 1AR ⓟ
☎ 01603 219964 ⓕ 01692 630378
Ⓜ 07831 218808
ⓔ nicholas@nicholasfowle antiques.com
ⓦ www.nicholasfowleantiques.com
Est. 1995 *Stock size* Medium
Stock 18th–19thC furniture
Open Mon–Fri 9am–5.30pm
Sat by appointment
Fairs BADA
Services Restoration

⊞ Philip Hodge Antiques
Contact Philip Hodge
✉ Hall Farm Cottage, Easthill Lane, Kirby Bedon, Norwich, Norfolk,
NR14 7DZ ⓟ
☎ 01508 493136 ⓕ 07720 420655
Ⓜ 07801 007936
ⓔ philip@philiphodgeantiques.co.uk
ⓦ www.philiphodgeantiques.co.uk
Est. 1992 *Stock size* Medium
Stock Furniture
Open By appointment
Fairs Lomax Fairs

⋏ Knights Sporting Auctions
Contact Tim Knight
✉ Cuckoo Cottage, Town Green, Alby, Norwich, Norfolk,
NR11 7PR
☎ 01263 768488 ⓕ 01263 768788
ⓔ tim@knights.co.uk
ⓦ www.knights.co.uk
Est. 1993
Open Mon–Fri 9am–5pm
Sales Sporting memorabilia, especially cricket, football, at varied venues and dates, see website or call for details, viewing day prior to sale
Frequency Quarterly
Catalogues Yes

⊞ Leona Levine Silver Specialist (BADA)
Contact Leona Levine
✉ 2 Fishers Lane (off St Giles Street), Norwich, Norfolk,
NR2 1ET ⓟ

☎ 01603 628709 ⓕ 01603 628709
Est. 1865 *Stock size* Large
Stock Silver, old Sheffield plate
Open Tues Wed Fri 9.15am–5pm
or by appointment
Services Valuations, restoration

⊞ Maddermarket Antiques (NAG)
Contact Mr T Earl
✉ 18c Lower Goat Lane, Norwich, Norfolk,
NR2 1EL ⓟ
☎ 01603 620610 ⓕ 01603 620610
Est. 1984 *Stock size* Large
Stock Antique, second-hand and modern jewellery, silverware
Open Mon–Sat 9am–5pm
Services Restoration

⊞ The Movie Shop
Contact Mr P Cossey
✉ 11 St Gregory's Alley, Norwich, Norfolk,
NR2 1ER ⓟ
☎ 01603 615239
ⓔ pete.cossey@ntlworld.com
ⓦ www.thenorwichmovieshop.com
Est. 1985 *Stock size* Large
Stock General antiquarian books, movie, TV, theatre and vinyl
Open Mon–Sat 11am–5.30pm
Services Valuations

⊞ Norfolk Antiques
Contact Kevin Matthews
✉ Leopold Road, Norwich, Norfolk, NR4 7PG ⓟ
☎ 01508 499850
Est. 1970 *Stock size* Small
Stock General antiques
Open Mon–Sat 10am–2pm

⋏ Norwich Auction Rooms
Contact Mr J Sutton
✉ The Auction Centre, Bessemer Road, Norwich, Norfolk,
NR4 6DQ ⓟ
☎ 01603 666502 ⓕ 01603 666502
ⓔ jsauctioneer@aol.com
ⓦ www.easterncarauctions.co.uk
Est. 1983
Open Mon–Fri 9am–5pm
Sales Classic and normal car auctions, 3 times a week, Mon 6.30pm, Wed 1pm, Thurs 6.30pm. Viewing from 9am on the day
Frequency 3 times a week
Catalogues Yes

⊞ Timgems Jewellers
Contact Tim Snelling
✉ 30 Elm Hill, Norwich, Norfolk,

NR3 1HG ⓟ
☎ 01603 623296 ⓕ 01603 666183
ⓔ timgems@hotmail.co.uk
Est. 1969 *Stock size* Medium
Stock Antique jewellery, silverware
Open Tues–Sat 11am–4.30pm
closed Thurs
Services Valuations, restoration

⌂ Tombland Antiques Centre
Contact Nick Barker
✉ Augustine Stewart House, 14 Tombland, Norwich, Norfolk,
NR3 1HF ⓟ
☎ 01603 619129
Est. 1999 *Stock size* Large
No. of dealers 53
Stock A wide range of antiques and collectables
Open Mon–Sat 10am–5pm
Sun by appointment
Services Valuations

⊞ Tombland Bookshop
Contact Mr J Freeman
✉ 8 Tombland, Norwich, Norfolk,
NR3 1HF ⓟ
☎ 01603 490000 ⓕ 01603 760610
ⓔ tombland.bookshop@virgin.net
Est. 1973 *Stock size* Large
Stock Antiquarian, second-hand books
Open Mon–Fri 9.30am–5pm
Sat 9.30am–4.30pm

⊞ Malcolm Turner
Contact Mr M Turner
✉ 15 St Giles Street, Norwich, Norfolk, NR2 1JL ⓟ
☎ 01603 627007 ⓕ 01603 627007
Est. 1971 *Stock size* Large
Stock Mixed porcelain, bronze figures, silver, jewellery
Open Tues–Sat 10am–5pm
Services Valuations

RAVENINGHAM

⊞ M D Cannell
Contact Mr M Cannell
✉ Castell Farm, Beccles Road, Raveningham, Norfolk,
NR14 6NU ⓟ
☎ 01508 548406 ⓕ 01508 548406
Ⓜ 07801 416355
ⓔ mal@raveningham.demon.co.uk
Est. 1984 *Stock size* Large
Stock European decorative furniture, carpets, Oriental rugs
Open Fri–Mon 10am–6pm
or by appointment
Fairs Newark, Bath Decorative

REEPHAM

⚲ Bonhams
✉ The Market Place, Reepham,
Norwich, Norfolk,
NR10 4JJ
☎ 01603 871443 ❻ 01603 872973
❻ norfolk@bonhams.com
ⓦ www.bonhams.com
Est. 1793
Open Mon–Fri 9am–1pm 2–5pm
Sales Regional office. Regular
sales held in London and in our
salerooms across the country. The
specialist East Anglian View sale
is held in our Ipswich saleroom
annually. Free auction valuations;
insurance and probate valuations
Catalogues Yes

RINGSTEAD

⌂ Ringstead Village Antique & Collectors Centre
Contact Mr or Mrs Roberts
✉ 41 High Street, Ringstead,
Hunstanton, Norfolk,
PE36 5JU ▣
☎ 01485 525270
Est. 1998 *Stock size* Large
No. of dealers 30
Stock Antiques and collectables,
corkscrews, china, pottery, glass
Open Mon Thurs Fri Sun
8am–5.30pm Tues Wed
Sat 8am–1pm

SCRATBY

⊞ Keith Lawson Antique Clocks (BHI)
Contact Keith Lawson
✉ Scratby Garden Centre, Beach
Road, Scratby, Great Yarmouth,
Norfolk,
NR29 3AJ ▣
☎ 01493 730950 ❻ 01493 730658
Est. 1979
Stock Antique clocks
Open Mon–Sun 2–6pm
Services Valuations, restoration

SHERINGHAM

⊞ Dorothy's Antiques
Contact Mrs D E Collier
✉ 23 Waterbank Road,
Sheringham, Norfolk,
NR26 8RB ▣
☎ 01263 822319
Est. 1975 *Stock size* Medium
Stock Royal Worcester, Royal

Doulton, small furniture,
collectables
Open Mon–Sun 11.15am–3.30pm

STALHAM

⊞ Stalham Antique Gallery (LAPADA)
Contact Mr Mike Hicks
✉ 29 High Street, Stalham,
Norwich, Norfolk,
NR12 9AH ▣
☎ 01692 580636 ❻ 01692 580636
❻ mbhickslink@talk21.com
Est. 1970 *Stock size* Large
Stock Period furniture,
associated items
Open Mon–Fri 9am–5pm
Sat 9am–1pm or by appointment
Services Valuations, restoration

STIFFKEY

⊞ Stiffkey Lamp Shop
Contact David Mann
✉ Stiffkey, Norfolk,
NR23 1AJ ▣
☎ 01328 830460 ❻ 01328 830005
❻ enquiries@stiffkeylampshop.co.uk
ⓦ www.stiffkeylampshop.co.uk
Est. 1976 *Stock size* Medium
Stock Antique lighting
Open Mon–Sun 10am–5pm
Oct–Easter closed Wed Thur
Services Shipping

SWAFFHAM

⊞ Cranglegate Antiques
Contact Mrs R D Buckie
✉ 59 Market Place, Swaffham,
Norfolk,
PE37 7LE ▣
☎ 01760 721052
ⓦ www.buckie-antiques.com
Est. 1973 *Stock size* Medium
Stock Furniture, decorative,
small items
Open Tues Thurs Sat 10am–1pm
2–5.30pm
Fairs Newark

TACOLNESTON

⊞ Freya Books and Antiques
Contact Colin Lewsey
✉ St Marys Farm, Cheneys Lane,
Tacolneston, Norwich, Norfolk,
NR16 1DB ▣
☎ 01508 489252
Ⓜ 07799 401067
❻ freya.antiques@btinternet.com

ⓦ www.freyaantiques.co.uk
Est. 1971 *Stock size* Medium
Stock Furniture, books
Open Times vary so please call first
Fairs See website
Services Valuations, restoration,
book search, shipping, Freya Fair
Organizer

TOTTENHILL

⊞ Jubilee Antiques
Contact A J Lee
✉ Coach House,
Whincommon Road, Tottenhill,
King's Lynn, Norfolk,
PE33 0RS ▣
☎ 01553 810681 ❻ 01553 760128
Ⓜ 07899 753222
Est. 1971 *Stock size* Medium
Stock 18th–19thC furniture
Open Mon–Sun 9am–6pm
or by appointment
Services Restoration

WATTON

⊞ J C Books (PBFA)
Contact Mr J A Ball
✉ 55 High Street, Watton,
Thetford, Norfolk,
IP25 6AB ▣
☎ 01953 883488 ❻ 01953 883488
❻ j_c_books@lineone.net
Est. 1990 *Stock size* Medium
Stock General antiquarian books,
ephemera, Victorian and
Edwardian theatre a speciality
Open Mon–Wed Fri Sat
10am–4.30pm Thurs 10am–1pm
Fairs PBFA
Services Book search

⚲ Stephen Roberts (Auctioneer) Ltd
Contact Mr S Roberts
✉ Watton Salerooms, 10
Breckland Business Park, Norwich
Road, Watton, Thetford, Norfolk,
IP25 6JT ▣
☎ 01953 885676 ❻ 01953 885676
❻ watton.salerooms@eidosnet.co.uk
ⓦ www.thesalerooms.co.uk
Est. 1989
Open Mon 8am–8pm Tues
8am–6pm Wed–Fri 10am–3pm
Sat 10am–1pm
Sales 6 or 7 antiques sales yearly
(3 on Bank Holidays, others in
conjunction with Tues sale),
viewing day before the sale
3–7pm day of sale from 9am.
Also antiques and general

household Tues, viewing Mon
4–8pm and day of sale
Frequency Weekly
Catalogues On website

WELLS-NEXT-THE-SEA

⌂ **Wells Antique Centre**
Contact Mr Vallance
✉ The Old Mill, Maryland,
Wells-next-the-Sea, Norfolk,
NR23 1LY ℗
☎ 01328 711433
Est. 1989 *Stock size* Medium
No. of dealers 15
Stock General antiques, copper,
brass, porcelain, glass, rugs,
furniture, jewellery, linen,
collectables
Open Mon–Sun 10am–5pm

WOLFERTON

⚒ **Holt's (GTA)**
Contact Mr N Holt
✉ Church Farm Barns, Wolferton,
Norfolk,
PE31 6HA ℗
☎ 01485 542822 ● 01485 544463
● enquiries@holtandcompany.co.uk
ⓦ www.holtandcompany.co.uk
Est. 1993
Open Mon–Fri 9am–5pm
Sales Sales of fine modern and
antique guns and related items
in central London. See website
Frequency 4 per annum
Catalogues Yes

WROXHAM

⊞ **Eric Bates & Sons Ltd**
Contact Graham or Eric Bates
✉ Horning Road West, Hoveton,
Wroxham, Norfolk,
NR12 8QJ ℗
☎ 01603 781 771 ● 01603 781 773
● furniture@bates.fsnet.co.uk
ⓦ www.batesfurniture.co.uk
Est. 1982 *Stock size* Large
Stock General 19thC antiques,
Victorian chairs
Open Mon–Fri 9am–5pm
Sat 9am–4.30pm

⊞ **T C S Brooke (BADA)**
Contact Mr S T Brooke
✉ The Grange, Norwich Road,
Wroxham, Norfolk,
NR12 8RX ℗
☎ 01603 782644 ● 01603 782644
Est. 1936 *Stock size* Large
Stock General antiques, 18thC

furniture, Georgian items, 18thC
porcelain
Open Wed–Sat 9.15am–1pm
2.15pm–5.30pm appointment
advisable
Services Valuations of complete
house contents

⊞ **Bradley Hatch Jewellers**
Contact Mr Bradley Hatch
✉ Tunstead Road, Wroxham,
Norwich, Norfolk,
NR12 8QG ℗
☎ 01603 782233 ● 01603 784679
● sales@bradleyhatch.com
ⓦ www.bradleyhatch.com
Est. 1994 *Stock size* Medium
Stock Jewellery, watches, silver,
clocks, gifts, pocket watches
Open Mon–Sat 9am–5pm
Services Valuations, restoration,
shipping

WYMONDHAM

⊞ **Margaret King**
Contact Margaret King
✉ 16 Market Place,
Wymondham, Norfolk,
NR18 0AX ℗
☎ 01953 604758
Est. 1975 *Stock size* Large
Stock General antiques,
furniture, porcelain, glass, silver
Open Thurs–Sat 9am–1pm 2–4pm
Fairs Langley, Woolverstone, all
Lomax Fairs

⊞ **M and A C Thompson**
Contact Mr A C Thompson
✉ The Bookshop, 1 Town Green,
Wymondham, Norfolk,
NR18 0PN ℗
☎ 01953 602244
Est. 1981 *Stock size* Medium
Stock Antiquarian, general
second-hand books
Open Mon–Fri 10.30am–4.45pm
closed Wed

⌂ **Wymondham Antique
Centre**
Contact Kay Hipperson
✉ 3 Town Green, Wymondham,
Norfolk,
NR18 0PN ℗
☎ 01953 604817 ● 01603 811112
Est. 1987 *Stock size* Large
No. of dealers 23
Stock General antiques, china,
furniture, books, pictures
Open Mon–Sun 10am–5pm
Services Valuations

SUFFOLK

ALDEBURGH

⊞ **Mole Hall Antiques**
Contact Mr P Weaver
✉ 102 High Street, Aldeburgh,
Suffolk,
IP15 5AB
☎ 01728 452361
Est. 1981 *Stock size* Large
Stock General antiques
Open Mon–Sat 10am–5pm

BECCLES

⊞ **Besley's Books (PBFA,
ABA)**
Contact Piers or Gaby Besley
✉ 4 Blyburgate, Beccles, Suffolk,
NR34 9TA ℗
☎ 01502 715762 ● 01502 675649
● piers@besleysbooks.demon.co.uk
ⓦ www.besleysbooks.demon.co.uk
Est. 1970 *Stock size* Medium
Stock Antiquarian books,
gardening, natural history, art,
private press a speciality
Open Mon–Sat 9.30am–5pm
closed Wed
Fairs PBFA, ABA
Services Valuations, restoration,
booksearch, 2 catalogues a year

⊞ **Blyburgate Antiques**
Contact Mrs Kate Lee
✉ 27–29 Blyburgate, Beccles,
Suffolk, NR34 9TB ℗
☎ 01502 711174
● katherine.lee@lineone.net
Est. 1997 *Stock size* Medium
Stock General antiques, furniture
Open Tues–Sat 10am–4.30pm
closed Wed
Fairs Alexandra Palace
Services Valuations

⚒ **Durrants Auction Rooms**
Contact Mr Miles Lamdin
✉ The Old School House,
Peddars Lane, Beccles, Suffolk,
NR34 9UB
☎ 01502 713490 ● 01502 711039
● info@durrantsauctionrooms.com
ⓦ www.durrantsauctionrooms.com
Est. 1853
Open Mon–Fri 9am–4pm
Sat 9am–noon
Sales General antiques sales
every Fri. Special sale once every
6 weeks, viewing every Thurs and
sale day
Catalogues No

Fauconberges
Contact Mr R D Howard
or Mr R J Crozier
✉ 8 Smallgate, Beccles, Suffolk, NR34 9AD 🅿
☎ 01502 716147
Est. 1980 *Stock size* Medium
Stock 17th–19thC furniture, pictures, glass
Open Mon–Sat 10am–5pm
Fairs Lomax, Graham Turner (Long Melford)
Services Valuations for insurance and probate, sales on commission, decanter cleaning and renovation

BUNGAY

Black Dog Antiques
Contact Mr M Button
✉ 51 Earsham Street, Bungay, Suffolk, NR35 1AF 🅿
☎ 01986 895554
Est. 1985 *Stock size* Medium
Stock General, collectables, pine furniture
Open Mon–Sat 10am–5pm
Sun 11am–4.30pm

Cork Brick Antiques & Gallery
Contact Ken Skipper
✉ 6 Earsham Street, Bungay, Suffolk, NR35 1AG
☎ 01986 892875
✉ corkbrick2@tiscali.co.uk
Est. 1990 *Stock size* Medium
Stock Decorative antiques, country furnishings, contemporary art
Open Tues–Sat 10.30am–5pm

Friend or Faux
Contact Jane Cudlipp
or Kim Sisson
✉ 28 Earsham Street, Bungay, Suffolk, NR35 1AQ 🅿
☎ 01502 714246 ✆ 01502 714246
Est. 1989 *Stock size* Medium
Stock Antiques, decorative objects, murals, paintings, hand-painted furniture
Open Fri–Sat 10am–5pm
Services Restoration, faux finishes

One Step Back
Contact Mrs Diane Wells
✉ 4a Earsham Street, Bungay,

Suffolk, NR35 1AG 🅿
☎ 01986 896626
Est. 1998 *Stock size* Medium
Stock General antiques, furniture
Open Tues–Sat 10am–5pm
closed Wed
Services Restoration

BURES

Major Iain Grahame (ABA)
Contact Major Iain Grahame
✉ Daws Hall, Lamarsh, Bures, Suffolk, CO8 5EX 🅿
☎ 01787 269213 ✆ 01787 269634
✉ majorbooks@compuserve.com
🌐 www.iaingrahamerarebooks.com
or www.johngouldprints.com
Est. 1979 *Stock size* Medium
Stock Antiquarian books, especially sporting, natural history, Africana
Open By appointment

BURROUGH GREEN

R E and G B Way (ABA, PBFA)
Contact Mr G Way
✉ Brettons, Church Lane, Burrough Green, Newmarket, Suffolk, CB8 9NA 🅿
☎ 01638 507217 ✆ 01638 508058
✉ waybks@msn.com
🌐 www.geocititeis.com/regbway
Est. 1950 *Stock size* Large
Stock Antiquarian, out-of-print books, the sporting horse a speciality
Open Mon–Sat 9am–5pm
telephone to check
Fairs Russell Book Fair

BURY ST EDMUNDS

Chimney Mill Galleries
Contact Hilary Murfitt
✉ West Stow, Bury St Edmunds, Suffolk, IP28 6ER 🅿
☎ 01284 728234 ✆ 01284 728234
Est. 1976 *Stock size* Medium
Stock Antique stipped pine furniture
Open Wed–Sat 11am–5pm
or by appointment
Services Restoration

Lacy Scott & Knight (SOFAA)
Contact Edward Crichton

✉ 10 Risbygate Street, Bury St Edmunds, Suffolk, IP33 3AA 🅿
☎ 01284 748600 ✆ 01284 748620
✉ fineart@lsk.co.uk
🌐 www.lsk.co.uk
Est. 1869
Open Mon–Fri 9am–1pm
2–5.30pm
Sales Quarterly fine art sale and model and collectors' sales. Victoriana sales every 3–4 weeks, viewing Fri 3–7pm
Catalogues Yes

Marshall Buck and Casson
Contact Mr B Moss
✉ The Auction Rooms, Eastgate Street, Bury St Edmunds, Suffolk, IP33 1YQ 🅿
☎ 01284 756081/753361
✆ 01284 756081
📱 07768 324102
Est. 1999
Open Wed 8am–8pm
Sales Mixed antiques and general sales Sat, viewing Fri 2.30–8pm Sat 8–9am. Periodic special antiques sales
Frequency Every 3 weeks
Catalogues Yes

Thrift Cottage Antiques (BADA)
Contact Diane Oddy
✉ PO Box 113, Bury St Edmunds, Suffolk, IP33 2RQ 🅿
☎ 01284 702470
✉ thriftcottageantiques@british porcelain.com
🌐 www.britishporcelain.com
Est. 1984 *Stock size* Medium
Stock 18th–19thC British porcelain
Open By appointment
Fairs Olympia, NEC Antiques for Everyone

CAMPSEY ASH

Abbotts Auction Rooms
Contact Mrs Linda Coates
✉ Campsey Ashe, Woodbridge, Suffolk, IP13 0PS 🅿
☎ 01728 746323 ✆ 01728 748173
✉ auction.rooms@abbottscountry wide.co.uk
🌐 www.abbottsauctionrooms.co.uk
Est. 1920

Open Mon–Fri 9am–5.30pm Sat 9–11am
Sales General auction every Mon 11am, viewing Sat 9–11am day of sale 8.30–11am. Special antiques auctions (6 per annum) Wed 10am, viewing Sat 9am–11am Mon 2–8pm Tues 10am–4pm morning of sale from 8.30am
Catalogues Yes

⊞ Ashe Antiques Warehouse
Contact Mr G Laffling
✉ Station Road, Campsey Ash, Woodbridge, Suffolk, IP13 0PT ▣
☎ 01728 747255 ❺ 01728 747255
Est. 1987 *Stock size* Large
Stock 18thC oak furniture, Victorian smalls, mirrors etc
Open Mon–Sun 10.30am–5pm
Fairs The International Antique and Collectables Fair, RAF Swinderby, Newark
Services French polishing, upholstery, ceramic restoration

CLARE

⊞ Robin Butler
Contact Robin Butler
✉ The Old Bank House, Market Hill, Clare, Suffolk, CU10 8NN ▣
☎ 01787 279111
❿ 017830 194997
❷ robin.butler@btconnect.com
Ⓦ www.butlersantiques.com
Est. 1963 *Stock size* Large
Stock Antiques for the wine enthusiast
Open By appointment
Fairs Olympia, Bury St Edmunds, Snape
Services Valuations, lectures

⌂ Clare Antiques Warehouse
Contact Leonard Edwards
✉ The Mill, Malting Lane, Clare, Sudbury, Suffolk, CO10 8NW ▣
☎ 01787 278449 ❺ 01787 278449
Est. 1988 *Stock size* Large
No. of dealers 85
Stock General, pine, oak furniture
Open Mon–Sat 9.30am–5pm Sun 1–5pm
Services Restoration, shipping, valuations

⌁ Dyson & Son
Contact Mr M Dyson
✉ The Auction Rooms, Church Street, Clare, Sudbury, Suffolk, CO10 8PD ▣
☎ 01787 277993 ❺ 01787 277996
❷ info@dyson-auctioneers.co.uk
Ⓦ www.dyson-auctioneers.co.uk
Est. 1977
Open Mon–Fri 9am–5pm closed 1–2pm Sat 9am–1pm
Sales General antiques sales every 3 weeks Sat, 600–700 lots, viewing Fri 9am–9pm day of sale 9–11am. A yearly calendar is available on request
Catalogues Yes

⊞ F D Salter
Contact Mr F D Salter
✉ 1–2 Church Street, Clare, Sudbury, Suffolk, CO10 8PD ▣
☎ 01787 277693
Est. 1960 *Stock size* Medium
Stock 18th–19thC furniture, porcelain, glass
Open Mon–Sat 9am–5pm closed Wed
Fairs West London
Services Furniture restoration

⊞ Trinder's Fine Tools (PBFA)
Contact Mr P D Trinder
✉ Malting Lane, Clare, Sudbury, Suffolk, CO10 8NW ▣
☎ 01787 277130 ❺ 01787 277677
❷ peter@trindersfinetools.co.uk
Ⓦ www.trindersfinetools.co.uk
Est. 1974 *Stock size* Medium
Stock Woodworking tools including British infill planes by Norris, Spiers, Mathieson, Preston, second-hand, new books on furniture and woodworking, horology, architecture, art reference, collecting, metalworking, model engineering
Open Mon–Fri 10am–1pm 2–5pm Wed Sat 10am–1pm advisable to telephone to check times

DEBENHAM

⊞ Edward Bigden Fine Art
Contact Edward Bigden
✉ 48 High Street, Debenham, Suffolk, IP14 6QW ▣
☎ 01728 862065
❷ eb@edwardbigden.com
Ⓦ www.edwardbigden.com
Est. 2001 *Stock size* Medium
Stock Medieval to modern fine art
Open By appointment

⊞ Debenham Antiques
Contact Simon Sodeaux or Chris Bigden
✉ 73 High Street, Debenham, Suffolk, IP14 6QS ▣
☎ 01728 860707 ❺ 01728 860333
❿ 07836 260650
❷ info@debenhamantiques.com
Est. 1974 *Stock size* Large
Stock 17th–19thC furniture, paintings
Open Mon–Sat 9.30am–5.30pm

DRINKSTONE

⊞ Denzil Grant (BADA, LAPADA)
Contact Mr D Grant
✉ Drinkstone House, Gedding Rd, Drinkstone, Bury St Edmunds, Suffolk, IP30 9TG ▣
☎ 01449 736576 ❺ 01449 737679
❿ 07836 223312
❷ denzil@denzilgrant.com
Ⓦ www.denzilgrant.com
Est. 1979 *Stock size* Medium
Stock 17th–19thC country furniture
Open By appointment
Fairs LAPADA, BADA, Olympias

EXNING

⊞ Exning Antiques & Interiors
Contact Mrs M Tabbron
✉ 14–16 Oxford Street, Exning, Newmarket, Suffolk, CB8 7EW ▣
☎ 01638 600015 ❺ 01638 600073
Est. 1993 *Stock size* Small
Stock Beds, canopies, covers, drapes, mirrors, original lighting
Open Mon–Sat 10am–5pm
Fairs Newark
Services Restoring and cleaning lighting

EYE

⊞ English and Continental Antiques
Contact Mr Steven Harmer
✉ 1 Broad Street, Eye, Suffolk, IP23 7AF ▣

☎ 01379 871199 ❷ 01379 871199
✉ englishantiques@onetel.com
⊕ www.englishandcontinent
alantiques.com
Est. 1975 *Stock size* Medium
Stock 17th–19thC furniture
Open Wed–Sat 11am–5pm
Services Restoration, upholstery

FELIXSTOWE

⚐ **Diamond Mills &
Company (SVA)**
Contact Mr N J Papworth, FRICS
✉ 117 Hamilton Road,
Felixstowe, Suffolk,
1P11 7BL 🅿
☎ 01394 282281 ❷ 01394 671791
✉ diamondmills@btconnect.com
⊕ www.diamondmills.co.uk
Est. 1908
Open Mon–Fri 9am–6pm
Sat 9am–3pm
Sales Antiques sales monthly,
usually Wed, telephone for
details, 3 special sales annually
Catalogues Yes

⊞ **Poor Richard's Books
(PBFA)**
Contact Dick Moffat
✉ 17 Orwell Road, Felixstowe,
Suffolk,
IP11 7EP 🅿
☎ 01394 283138
✉ moffatsfx@aol.com
Est. 1997 *Stock size* Large
Stock General and antiquarian
books, modern first editions
Open Mon–Sat 9am–5pm
Fairs Norwich, Woodbridge,
Aldeburgh, Dedham, Oxford,
Cambridge
Services Valuations, restoration,
book search

⊞ **Tea and Antiques**
Contact David George
✉ 109 High Road East,
Old Felixstowe,
Suffolk,
IP11 9PS 🅿
☎ 01394 277789
Est. 2000 *Stock size* Medium
Stock Antiques, collectables,
furniture
Open Thurs–Sun Bank Holidays
10am–5pm
Services Tea shop

⊞ **The Treasure Chest
Books (PBFA)**
Contact Mr Robert Green

✉ **61 Cobbold Road, Felixstowe,
Suffolk,
IP11 7BH** 🅿
☎ 01394 270717
Est. 1981 *Stock size* Large
Stock Antiquarian and second-
hand books
Open Mon–Sat 9.30am–5.30pm

FINNINGHAM

⊞ **Abington Books**
Contact Mr J Haldane
✉ Primrose Cottage,
Westhorpe Road, Finningham,
Stowmarket, Suffolk,
IP14 4TW 🅿
☎ 01449 780303 ❷ 01449 780202
Est. 1971 *Stock size* Medium
Stock Antiquarian books on
Oriental and other carpets,
classical tapestries
Open By appointment
Services Valuations, restoration,
book search

FRAMLINGHAM

⊞ **Richard Goodbrey
Antiques**
Contact Mrs M Goodbrey
✉ 29 Double Street,
Framlingham, Woodbridge,
Suffolk,
IP13 9BN 🅿
☎ 01728 621191 ❷ 01728 724727
📱 07860 656333
✉ goodantiques29@yahoo.co.uk
Est. 1965 *Stock size* Large
Stock 18th–19thC Continental
and English furniture, sleigh
beds, painted furniture, pottery,
glass
Open Sat 9am–1pm 2–5.30pm or
by appointment
Fairs Newark, Ardingly

⊞ **The Green Room**
Contact Mrs J Shand Kydd
✉ 2 Church Street, Framlingham,
Woodbridge, Suffolk,
IP13 9BE 🅿
☎ 01728 723009
Est. 1986 *Stock size* Medium
Stock Antique textiles, quilts,
curtains, bed covers
Open Fri Sat 10.30am–4.45pm

🏛 **Honeycombe Antiques**
Contact Keith Honeycombe
✉ 8 Market Hill, Framlingham,
Suffolk,
IP13 9AN 🅿

☎ 01728 622011
✉ Keith.honeycombe@btopen
world.com
Est. 2002 *Stock size* Medium
No. of dealers 7
Stock Silver, furniture, jewellery,
guns
Open Mon–Sat 9.30am–5pm
Services Valuations

🏛 **The Theatre Antiques
Centre**
Contact Wig Darby
✉ 10 Church Street,
Framlingham,
Suffolk,
IP13 9BH 🅿
☎ 01728 621069
✉ wig@darbyw.freeserve.co.uk
⊕ www.darbyw.freeserve.co.uk
Est. 2002 *Stock size* Large
No. of dealers 8
Stock Country and fine furniture,
smalls
Open Mon–Sat 9.30–5.30pm

GLEMSFORD

⊞ **Seabrook Antiques**
Contact Mr John Tanner
✉ Lower Road, Glemsford,
Sudbury, Suffolk,
CO10 7QU 🅿
☎ 01787 281911
Est. 1978 *Stock size* Large
Stock 17th–19thC oak and
decorative furniture
Open Mon–Sat 10am–4pm or by
appointment
Services Interior design

HACHESTON

⊞ **Hardy's Antiques**
Contact Mrs Joyce Hardy
✉ Wisteria Cottage,
The Street, Hacheston,
Woodbridge, Suffolk,
IP3 0DS 🅿
☎ 01728 746485 ❷ 01728 746 568
Est. 1962 *Stock size* Medium
Stock Antique pine furniture,
wardrobes, dressers, chests of
drawers
Open Tues–Sat 10am–6pm
Fairs Ardingly, Ipswich

⊞ **Randolph Antiques
(BADA)**
Contact Mr Baden F Marston
✉ 97–99 High Street, Hadleigh,
Ipswich, Suffolk,
IP7 5EJ 🅿

EAST

☎ 01473 823789 ☏ 01473 823867
Est. 1929 *Stock size* Medium
Stock English furniture up to
1830, accessories
Open By appointment only

HALESWORTH

⊞ P & R Antiques Ltd
Contact Pauline Lewis
✉ Fairstead Farm Buildings,
Wash Lane, Spexhall,
Halesworth, Suffolk,
IP19 0RF 🅿
☎ 01986 873232 ☏ 01896 874682
📧 pauline@prantiques.com
🌐 www.prantiques.com
Est. 1996 *Stock size* Large
Stock 17th–19thC furniture
Open By appointment

IPSWICH

⊞ A Abbott Antiques
Contact Mr A Abbott
✉ 757 Woodbridge Road,
Ipswich, Suffolk,
IP4 4NE 🅿
☎ 01473 728900 ☏ 01473 728900
📱 07771 533413
📧 abbott_antiques@hotmail.com
Est. 1974 *Stock size* Medium
Stock General antiques,
furniture, smalls, clocks
Open Mon–Sat 9.30am–5pm
closed Wed
Fairs Newark, Ardingly

⋏ Bonhams
✉ 32 Boss Hall Road, Ipswich,
Suffolk,
IP1 5DJ
☎ 01473 740494 ☏ 01473 741091
📧 ipswich@bonhams.com
🌐 www.bonhams.com/ipswich
Open Mon 9am–7pm
Sat 9am–noon
Sales Regional Saleroom.
Frequent sales including the
specialist East Anglian View Sale
held annually. Regular sales held
in London and in our salerooms
across the country. Free auction
valuations; insurance and
probate valuations
Catalogues Yes

⊞ Claude Cox Books
(ABA, PBFA)
Contact Anthony Brian Cox
✉ 3–5 Silent Street, Ipswich,
Suffolk,
IP1 1TF 🅿

☎ 01473 254776 ☏ 01473 254776
📧 books@claudecox.co.uk
🌐 www.claudecox.co.uk
Est. 1974 *Stock size* Large
Stock Antiquarian and
second-hand books, fine
printing, private press,
catalogues issued, Suffolk maps
and prints a speciality
Open Wed–Sat 10am–5pm
or by appointment
Services Book binding, repairs

⊞ Hubbard's Antiques
Contact Mr Max Hubbard
✉ 16 St Margaret's Green,
Ipswich, Suffolk,
IP4 2BS 🅿
☎ 01473 233034 ☏ 01473 253639
📧 sales@hubbard-antiques.com
🌐 www.hubbard-antiques.com
Est. 1965 *Stock size* Large
Stock 18th–19thC antique
furniture, decorative items,
works of art
Open Mon–Sat 10am–6pm
or by appointment
Services Valuations by Internet

⊞ Lockdale Coins Ltd
(BNTA)
Contact Dan Daley
✉ 37 Upper Orwell Street,
Ipswich, Suffolk,
IP4 1HP 🅿
☎ 01473 218588 ☏ 01473 218588
📧 lockdales@shop1.freeserve.co.uk
🌐 lockdales.co.uk
Est. 1994 *Stock size* Medium
Stock British and foreign coins,
banknotes, metal detectors and
accessories
Open Mon–Sat 9.30am–4.30pm
Fairs Cumberland Hotel Show,
Olympia
Services Valuations,
auctioneering

⋏ Lockdale Coins Ltd
Contact Dan Daley
✉ 37 Upper Orwell Street,
Ipswich, Suffolk,
IP4 1HP 🅿
☎ 01473 218588 ☏ 01473 218588
📧 lockdales@shop1.freeserve.co.uk
🌐 www.lockdales.com
Est. 1996
Open Mon–Sat 9.30am–5pm
Sales Telephone for details of
sales. Coins, jewellery, medals,
militaria, ephemera, autographs
Frequency Bi-monthly
Catalogues Yes

⊞ Maud's Attic
Contact Mrs W Childs
✉ 25 St Peter's Street, Ipswich,
Suffolk,
IP1 1XF 🅿
☎ 01473 221057 ☏ 01473 221056
📧 maudsattic@hotmail.com
🌐 www.maudsatticantiques.com
Est. 1996 *Stock size* Large
Stock Antiques, collectables
Open Tues–Sat 10am–5pm

⊞ Merchant House
Antiques
Contact Mr G Childs
✉ 27–29 St Peter's Street,
Ipswich, Suffolk,
IP1 1XF 🅿
☎ 01473 221054 ☏ 01473 221056
📱 07768 068575
📧 merchanthouse@hotmail.com
🌐 www.merchanthouseantiques.com
Est. 2000 *Stock size* Medium
Stock Antiques and reclamation
Open Tues–Sat 10am–5pm

⊞ Mr Richard Anthony
Rush Antiques
Contact Mr R Rush
✉ Unit 5, Penny Corner,
Farthing Road, Ipswich, Suffolk,
IP1 5AP 🅿
☎ 01473 464609
📱 07939 220041
📧 info@antiquesandrestoration.co.uk
or admin@antiques.eu.com
🌐 www.antiques.eu.com
Est. 1997 *Stock size* Medium
Stock 18th–19thC furniture
Open Mon–Fri 8am–6pm
Sat 8am–1.30pm
Services Restoration

⊞ The Suffolk Antique
Bed Centre
Contact Mr A Sandham
✉ 273 Norwich Road, Ipswich,
Suffolk,
IP1 4BP 🅿
☎ 01473 252444
Est. 1985 *Stock size* Large
Stock Brass and iron bedsteads
Open Mon–Sat 9am–5.30pm
Services Hand-made mattresses

⊞ Suffolk Sci-fi Fantasy
Contact Mr M Milliard
✉ 17 Norwich Road, Ipswich,
Suffolk,
IP1 2ET 🅿
☎ 01473 400655
📧 symon@suffolksci-fi.com
🌐 www.suffolksci-fi.com

Est. 1992 *Stock size* Large
Stock Sci-fi collectables,
ephemera, collectable card
games, trade cards
Open Mon–Sat 8.30am–5.30pm

IXWORTH

⊞ E W Cousins & Son (LAPADA)
Contact Mr Robert Cousins
⊠ Old School, Thetford Road,
Ixworth, Bury St Edmunds,
Suffolk,
IP31 2HJ ▣
☎ 01359 230254 ✆ 01359 232370
✉ john@ewcousins.co.uk
ⓦ www.ewcousins.co.uk
Est. 1920 *Stock size* Large
Stock 18th–19thC furniture
Open Mon–Fri 8.30am–5pm
Sat 8.30am–1pm
Services Restoration, containers
packed

LAVENHAM

⊞ J & J Baker
Contact Mrs Joy Baker
⊠ 12–14 Water Street,
Lavenham, Sudbury, Suffolk,
CO10 9RW ▣
☎ 01787 247610
Est. 1970 *Stock size* Large
Stock General English antiques,
furniture, porcelain
Open Mon–Sat 10am–5.30pm
Sun by appointment

⌂ Timbers Antiques & Collectables
Contact Tom or Jenny White
⊠ High Street, Lavenham,
Sudbury, Suffolk,
CO10 9PT ▣
☎ 01787 247218
ⓦ www.timbersantiques.com
Est. 1996 *Stock size* Large
No. of dealers 48
Stock Antique furniture, silver,
glass, china, jewellery, clocks,
Open Mon–Fri 9.30am–5pm ,
Sat, Sun 10am–5pm

LEISTON

⊞ Leiston Trading Post
Contact Mrs L Smith
⊠ 17 High Street, Leiston,
Suffolk,
IP16 4EL ▣
☎ 01728 830081
ⓜ 0771 259 6005

Est. 1967 *Stock size* Large
Stock Shipping goods, general
antiques, china, bric-a-brac
Open Mon–Sat 9.30am–1pm
2–4.30pm half day Wed
Services Valuations

⊞ Warren Antiques
Contact Mr J Warren
⊠ 31 High Street, Leiston,
Suffolk,
IP16 4EL ▣
☎ 01728 831414 ✆ 01728 831414
ⓜ 07989 865598
✉ jrwantiques@aol.com
ⓦ www.warrenantiques.co.uk
Est. 1970 *Stock size* Medium
Stock Late 18thC–1930s furniture
Open Mon–Tues 9am–1pm
2–5pm Thurs–Sat 9am–12.30pm
Fairs Newark, Ardingly (DMG)
Services Restoration

LONG MELFORD

⊞ Sandy Cooke Antiques
Contact Mr Sandy Cooke
⊠ Hall Street, Long Melford,
Sudbury, Suffolk,
CO10 9JQ ▣
☎ 01787 378265 ✆ 01284 830935
✉ sandycooke@englishfurniture.co.uk
ⓦ www.englishfurniture.co.uk
Est. 1974 *Stock size* Large
Stock 1700–1830 English
furniture
Open Mon Fri Sat 10am–5pm

⊞ Cottage Antiques
Contact Mr R Jarman
⊠ Melford Antiques Warehouse,
Hall Street, Long Melford,
Sudbury, Suffolk,
CO10 9JB ▣
☎ 01268 764138 ✆ 01268 764138
ⓜ 07958 618629
✉ info@cottageantiquesfurniture.com
ⓦ www.cottageantiquesfurniture.com
Est. 1986 *Stock size* Large
Stock Georgian–Edwardian
items, mainly furniture,
collectables
Open Mon–Sun 10am–5.30pm
Services Furniture restoration,
French polishing, furniture
search

⌂ Long Melford Antiques Centre
Contact Mr Groves
⊠ Chapel Maltings,
Little St Mary's, Long Melford,
Sudbury, Suffolk,

CO10 9HX ▣
☎ 01787 379287 ✆ 01787 379287
Est. 1983 *Stock size* Medium
No. of dealers 43
Stock Antiques, collectables,
decorative items, glass, china
Open Mon–Sat 9.30am–5.30pm

⊞ Alexander Lyall Antiques
Contact Mr A J Lyall
⊠ Belmont House, Hall Street,
Long Melford, Sudbury, Suffolk,
CO10 9JF ▣
☎ 01787 375434 ✆ 01787 311115
✉ alex@lyallantiques.com
ⓦ www.lyallantiques.com
Est. 1977 *Stock size* Medium
Stock Georgian–Victorian
furniture
Open Mon–Sat 10am–5.30pm
closed Bank Holidays

⊞ Magpie Antiques
Contact Pat Coll
⊠ Hall Street, Long Melford,
Sudbury, Suffolk,
CO10 9JT ▣
☎ 01787 310581 ✆ 01787 310581
✉ collterry@hotmail.com
Est. 1984 *Stock size* Large
Stock Stripped old pine, country
collectables
Open Tues Thurs Fri 11am–4pm
Sat 11am–5pm

⌂ Melford Antiques Warehouse
Contact Mr Patrick Scholz
⊠ Hall Street, Long Melford,
Suffolk,
CO10 9JB ▣
☎ 01787 379638
✉ maw@antiques-access-agency.com
ⓦ www.antiques-access-agency.com
Est. 1990 *Stock size* Large
No. of dealers 125
Stock Antiques, collectables,
decorative items
Open Mon–Sat 10am–4.30pm,
Sun Bank Holidays 1pm–4.30pm
or by appointment

⊞ Noel Mercer Antiques
Contact Mr Noel Mercer
⊠ Aurora House, Hall Street,
Long Melford, Sudbury,
Suffolk,
CO10 9JR ▣
☎ 01787 311882
✉ info@noelmercerantiques.com
ⓦ www.noelmercerantiques.com
Est. 1991 *Stock size* Large

Stock Early English oak, walnut furniture
Open Mon–Sat 10am–5pm

⊞ The Stables
Contact Mrs P Gee
✉ Hall Street, Long Melford, Sudbury, Suffolk, CO10 9JB 🅿
☎ 01787 310754
Est. 1980 *Stock size* Medium
Stock Interiors, antiques, collectables
Open Mon–Sat 10am–4.30pm
Sun 11am–4.30pm closed Thurs

⊞ Matthew Tyler Antiques
Contact Matthew Tyler
✉ Hall Street, Long Melford, Suffolk, CO10 9JL 🅿
☎ 01787 377523 ❶ 01799 599978
Ⓜ 07770 496350
🅴 m.tyler1@btopenworld.com
Stock size Medium
Stock 17th–19thC English furniture and works of art
Open Mon Fri Sat 10am–5pm or by appointment
Fairs Snape, Lomax
Services Valuations, restoration, shipping

⊞ Village Clocks
Contact Mr J Massey
✉ Little St Mary's, Long Melford, Sudbury, Suffolk, CO10 0LQ 🅿
☎ 01787 375896
Est. 1989 *Stock size* Large
Stock Antique clocks
Open Mon–Sat 10am–4pm closed Wed
Services Restoration

LOWESTOFT

⊞ Lockdale Coins Ltd (BNTA)
Contact Dan Daley
✉ 168 London Road South, Lowestoft, Suffolk, NR33 0BB 🅿
☎ 01502 568468 ❶ 01502 568468
🅴 ddaley@lockdales.freeserve.co.uk
Ⓦ www.lockdales.co.uk
Est. 1998 *Stock size* Medium
Stock Gold, silver jewellery, British and world coins, banknotes, metal detectors, accessories
Open Mon–Sat 9.30am–4.30pm

Fairs Cumberland Hotel, Olympia
Services Valuations, jewellery, watch, clock repairs, auctioneering

⋌ Lockdale Coins Ltd
Contact Jean Daley
✉ 168 London Road South, Lowestoft, Suffolk, NR33 0BB 🅿
☎ 01502 568468 ❶ 01502 568468
🅴 ddaley@lockdales.freeserve.co.uk
Ⓦ www.lockdales.co.uk
Est. 1996
Open Mon–Sat 9.30am–4.30pm
Sales Telephone for details of sales in Ipswich. Coins, jewellery, medals, militaria, ephemera, autographs
Frequency Bi-monthly
Catalogues Yes

⋌ Lowestoft Auction Rooms
Contact Mr J Peyto
✉ Pinbush Road, South Lowestoft Industrial Estate, Lowestoft, Suffolk, NR33 7NL 🅿
☎ 01502 531532 ❶ 01502 531241
🅴 lowestoft@auctioneer.net
Est. 1985
Open Mon–Fri 8am–5.30pm
Sales Large house sales on site
Frequency Twice monthly
Catalogues Yes

⊞ M G Osborne
Contact Mr M G Osborne
✉ 140 High Street, Lowestoft, Suffolk, NR33 1HR 🅿
☎ 01502 508988
Est. 1988 *Stock size* Large
Stock General antiques
Open Mon–Sat 9.30am–4pm closed Thurs
Fairs The International Antique and Collectables Fair, RAF Swinderby

⊞ John Rolph
Contact Mr John Rolph
✉ Manor House, Pakefield Street, Lowestoft, Suffolk, NR33 0JT 🅿
☎ 01502 572039
Est. 1948 *Stock size* Medium
Stock 17thC–1950 antiquarian and second-hand books
Open Tues–Sat 11am–1pm 2.30–5pm closed Thurs

MARLESFORD

⊞ The Antiques Warehouse
Contact John or Lesley Ball
✉ The Old Mill, Main Road, Marlesford, Suffolk, IP13 0AG 🅿
☎ 01728 747438 ❶ 01728 747627
🅴 omtc@antiqueswarehouse.fsnet.co.uk
Est. 1989 *Stock size* Large
Stock Country furniture, mirrors, lighting, general antiques
Open Mon–Fri 7.30am–4.30pm Sat 10am–4.30pm Sun 11am–4.30pm

MARTLESHAM

⊞ Martlesham Antiques
Contact Mr R Frost
✉ Thatched Roadhouse, Main Road, Martlesham, Woodbridge, Suffolk, IP12 4RJ 🅿
☎ 01394 386732 ❶ 01394 382959
🅴 bob@martleshamantiques.com
Est. 1983 *Stock size* Large
Stock 18th–20thC furniture
Open Mon–Fri 9am–5pm Sat 10am–4pm

MIDDLETON

⊞ Marilyn Garrow Fine Textile Art (BADA, CINOA)
Contact Marilyn Garrow, Lydia Garrow or Tabitha Blyth
✉ Reckford Farmhouse, Middleton, Saxmundham, Suffolk, IP17 3NS 🅿
☎ 01728 648671 ❶ 01728 648496
Ⓜ 07774 842074
🅴 marilyn@marilyngarrow.com
Ⓦ www.marilyngarrow.com
Est. 1978 *Stock size* Large
Stock Textiles
Open By appointment
Services Valuations

NAYLAND

⊞ Town Prints
Contact Mr F E Jones
✉ Longwood Cottage, Nayland, Colchester, Suffolk, CO6 4HT 🅿
☎ 01206 262483
🅴 jonesnayland@tiscali.co.uk
Est. 1976 *Stock size* Medium
Stock Woodblock, copper and

steel engravings of Colchester and district
Open By appointment
Services Framing

NEEDHAM MARKET

⌂ Old Town Hall Antique & Collectors Centre
Contact Mr R Harrison
✉ Old Town Hall, High Street, Needham Market, Suffolk,
IP6 8AL 🅿
☎ 01449 720773
Est. 1979 *Stock size* Large
No. of dealers 30
Stock Antiques and collectables
Open Mon–Sat 10am–5pm

⊞ The Tool Shop (LAPADA)
Contact Mr Tony Murland
✉ 78 High Street, Needham Market, Ipswich, Suffolk,
IP6 8AW 🅿
☎ 01449 722992 ● 01449 722683
🖳 tony@antiquetools.co.uk
🌐 www.antiquetools.co.uk
Est. 1991 *Stock size* Large
Stock Antique woodworking tools, new quality French, Japanese, American
Open Mon–Sat 10am–5pm
Fairs All major national woodworking exhibitions

ORFORD

⊞ Castle Antiques
Contact Ms S Simpkin
✉ Market Hill, Orford, Woodbridge, Suffolk,
IP12 2LH 🅿
☎ 01394 450100 ● 01394 450536
🖳 stephanie@castle-estates.uk.com
Est. 1959 *Stock size* Small
Stock Furniture, lamps, pictures, glass, bric-a-brac
Open Mon–Sun 11am–4pm

PEASENHALL

⊞ Peasenhall Art & Antiques Gallery
Contact Mr M Wickens
✉ The Street, Peasenhall, Saxmundham, Suffolk,
IP17 2HJ 🅿
☎ 01728 660224
Est. 1972 *Stock size* Large
Stock 18th–early 20thC watercolours, oil paintings,

country furniture in all woods
Open Mon–Sun 9am–6pm
Services Restoration

RISBY

⌂ Past and Present
Contact Joe Aldridge
✉ The Risby Barn Complex, South Street, Risby, Bury St Edmunds, Suffolk,
IP28 6QU 🅿
☎ 01284 811480
Est. 1996 *Stock size* Large
No. of dealers 30
Stock Furniture, antique to present day china, silver, jewellery, bric-a-brac, pictures, books, glass, pine, Victorian–Edwardian furniture, European furniture, collectable toys
Open Mon–Sat 10am–5pm
Sun 10.30am–4.30pm
Services Restoration, coffee shop, garden centre

⌂ The Risby Barn Antique Centre
Contact Mr R Martin
✉ Risby Barn, South Street, Risby, Bury St Edmunds, Suffolk,
IP28 6QU 🅿
☎ 01284 811126 ● 01284 810783
🖳 r.martin@lineone.net
Est. 1980 *Stock size* Large
No. of dealers 30
Stock Victorian furniture, china, silver, clocks, rural bygones
Open Mon–Sat 9am–5.30pm
Sun Bank Holidays 10am–5pm
Services Coffee shop, restoration

SAXMUNDHAM

⊞ Keith A Savage
Contact Mr K A Savage
✉ 35 High Street, Saxmundham, Suffolk,
IP17 1AJ 🅿
☎ 01728 604538 or 01986 872231
Est. 1992 *Stock size* Medium
Stock Second-hand, collectors' books, second-hand ephemera, children's books a speciality
Open Mon Sat 10.30am–1pm
Tues Wed Fri 10.30am–5pm

SNAPE

⊞ Original Vintage Costume Jewellery
Contact Judy Portway
✉ Snape Antiques and Collectors

Centre, Snape, Saxmundham, Suffolk,
IP17 1SR 🅿
☎ 01449 775060
Est. 1989 *Stock size* Large
Stock Original vintage costume jewellery, compacts, handbags
Open Mon–Sun 10am–5pm

SOUTHWOLD

⊞ Architectural Artefacts
Contact Mr B Howard or Mrs J Twist
✉ The Rope House, Station Road, Southwold, Suffolk,
IP18 6AX 🅿
☎ 01502 723075 ● 01502 724346
🖳 aa@ropehouse.easynet.co.uk
Est. 1996 *Stock size* Small
Stock Stained glass, architectural antiques, taps, sinks, chimney pots
Open Mon–Fri 9am–5pm
Services Stained glass design

⊞ Puritan Values at the Dome
Contact Anthony Geering
✉ St Edmunds Business Park, St Edmunds Road, Southwold, Suffolk,
IP18 6BZ 🅿
☎ 01502 722211 ● 01502 722734
📱 07966 371676
🖳 sales@puritanvalues.com
🌐 www.puritanvalues.com
Est. 1985 *Stock size* Medium
Stock Arts and Crafts movement, Aesthetic Movement, Gothic Revival, important furniture
Open Mon–Sat 10am–6pm
Sun 11am–5pm
Fairs NEC, SEC, Olympia
Services Valuations, restoration

⊞ T Schotte Antiques
Contact Mrs Schotte
✉ Old Bakehouse, Blackmill Road, Southwold, Suffolk,
IP18 6AQ
☎ 01502 722083
Est. 1989 *Stock size* Small
Stock Antiques, decorative items
Open Mon–Sat 10am–4pm
closed Wed

⊞ S J Webster-Speakman (BADA)
Contact Mrs S J Webster-Speakman
✉ Southwold, Suffolk
☎ 01502 722252
Est. 1968 *Stock size* Medium

EAST
SUFFOLK • SPROUGHTON

Stock 18th–19thC furniture, clocks, Staffordshire animals
Open By appointment
Services Restoration of clocks

SPROUGHTON

⊞ Heritage Reclamations
Contact Mr Richard Howells
✉ 1a High Street, Sproughton, Ipswich, Suffolk,
IP8 3AF 🅿
☎ 01473 748519 📠 01473 748519
📧 heritage@reclamations.fsnet.co.uk
🌐 www.heritage-reclamations.co.uk
Est. 1985 *Stock size* Large
Stock Ironmongery, stoves, ranges, fireplaces, garden ornaments, stained glass, radiators, pews, sanitary ware
Open Mon–Fri 9am–5pm
Sat 9.30am–5pm Sun 10am–4pm
Fairs Newark, Ardingly, Swinderby, Kempton Park
Services Restoration

STOWMARKET

⊞ What-Not-Shop Antiques
Contact Mr F J Smith
✉ 28 Bury Street, Stowmarket, Suffolk,
IP14 1HH 🅿
☎ 01449 613126
Est. 1979 *Stock size* Medium
Stock Jewellery, china, glass, clocks
Open Mon–Sat 9am–4.30pm
Tues closed
Services Repairs

SUDBURY

⊞ Beckham Books (PBFA)
Contact Mrs Jenny Beckham
✉ Chilton Mount, Newton Road, Sudbury, Suffolk,
CO10 2RS 🅿
☎ 01787 373683 📠 01787 375441
📧 sales@beckhambooks.com or beckhambooks1@btconnect.com
🌐 www.beckhambooks.com
Est. 1996 *Stock size* Small
Stock Antiquarian, theological books, bibles
Open By appointment
Fairs PBFA Fairs
Services Book search

⊞ Napier House Antiques
Contact Mrs Veronica McGregor
✉ 3 Church Street, Sudbury,

Suffolk,
CO10 2BJ 🅿
☎ 01787 375280 📠 01787 478757
📠 07768 703406
Est. 1976 *Stock size* Large
Stock 18th–19thC mahogany furniture
Open Mon–Sat 10am–4.30pm closed Wed
Services Free delivery UK mainland

⊞ Neate Militaria & Antiques (OMRS)
Contact Gary Neate
✉ PO Box 3794, Preston St Mary, Sudbury, Suffolk,
CO10 9PX 🅿
☎ 01787 248168 📠 01787 248363
📧 gary@neatemedals.co.uk
🌐 www.neatemedals.co.uk
Est. 1984 *Stock size* Medium
Stock Worldwide orders, decorations, medals, with an emphasis on British material
Open Mon–Fri 9am–6pm
Fairs Brittania Medal Fair, Aldershot Medal Fair
Services Valuations, restoration, mail order catalogue

🪑 Olivers (SOFAA)
Contact Mr J Fletcher
✉ The Sale Room, Burkitts Lane, Sudbury, Suffolk,
CO10 1HB 🅿
☎ 01787 880305 📠 01787 880305
Est. 1766
Open Mon–Fri 9am–1pm 2–5pm
Sales Regular sales of antiques and works of art. Victorian, later furniture, household effects fortnightly Thurs 1pm, viewing day of sale from 9am
Catalogues Yes

⊞ Sasha
Contact Susan Bailey
✉ 79 Melford Road, Sudbury, Suffolk,
CO10 1JT 🅿
☎ 01787 375582
📠 07781 453250
Est. 1986 *Stock size* Medium
Stock Small furniture, ceramics, collectables, books
Open Mon–Sat 10.30am–5pm
Services Book search

⊞ Sitting Pretty Antiques
Contact Mr Darren Barrs
✉ 16 Friars Street, Sudbury, Suffolk,

CO10 2AA 🅿
☎ 01787 880908
📠 07974 689044
Est. 1987 *Stock size* Large
Stock Re-upholstered period furniture, 18thC–1930s
Open Mon–Sat 9.30am–5pm
Services Upholstery, interior design consultations

WOODBRIDGE

⊞ Blake's Books (PBFA)
Contact Mr R Green
✉ 88 The Thoroughfare, Woodbridge, Suffolk,
IP12 1AL
☎ 01394 380302
Stock Antiquarian and second-hand books, Suffolk and sailing books a speciality
Open Mon–Sat 9.30am–5pm
Fairs Woodbridge Book Fair

⊞ Dix-Sept Antiques
Contact Miss Sophie Goodbrey
✉ 17 Station Road, Woodbridge, Suffolk,
IP13 9EA 🅿
☎ 01728 621505 📠 01728 724884
Est. 1985 *Stock size* Medium
Stock French antiques, furniture, glass, pottery, textiles
Open Sat 10am–1pm 2–5.30pm or by appointment
Fairs Newark

⊞ David Gibbins (BADA)
Contact Mr David Gibbins
✉ The White House, 14 Market Hill, Woodbridge, Suffolk,
IP12 4LU 🅿
☎ 01394 383531 📠 01394 383531
📠 07702 306914
📧 david@gibbinsantiques.co.uk
Est. 1966 *Stock size* Medium
Stock 18thC furniture, Lowestoft porcelain
Open By appointment
Fairs The West London Antiques and Fine Art Fair, Louise Walker Harrogate Fair, BADA Fair
Services Valuations, restoration

⊞ Hamilton Antiques (LAPADA)
Contact Hamilton or Rosemary Ferguson
✉ 5 Church Street, Woodbridge, Suffolk,
IP12 1DH
☎ 01394 387222

© 07747 033437
@ enquiries@hamiltonantiques.co.uk
® www.hamiltonantiques.co.uk
Est. 1976 *Stock size* Large
Stock 18th–20thC furniture
Trade only Yes
Open Mon–Fri 8.30am–5pm
Sat 10am–5pm
Services Restoration, polishing

⊞ Anthony Hurst
Contact Mr Christopher Hurst
✉ **13 Church Street, Woodbridge,
Suffolk,
IP12 1DS** 🅿
☎ 01394 382500 **❶** 01394 382500
Est. 1968 *Stock size* Large
Stock 18th–19thC furniture,
mahogany, oak
Open Mon–Fri 10am–5pm
Sat 10.30am–1pm closed Wed

⊞ Raymond Lambert
Contact Mr Raymond Lambert
✉ **The Bull Ride, 70a New Street,
Woodbridge, Suffolk,
IP12 1DX** 🅿
☎ 01394 382380
@ mary@lamberts667.fsnet.co.uk
Est. 1963 *Stock size* Medium
Stock 19th–20thC furniture
Open Mon–Sat 9.30am–1pm
2–5pm closed Wed

**⊞ Sarah Meysey-
Thompson Antiques**
Contact Sarah Meysey-Thompson
✉ **10 Church Street, Woodbridge,
Suffolk,
IP12 1DH** 🅿
☎ 01394 382144
Est. 1961 *Stock size* Medium
Stock Georgian–Victorian
furniture, curios, decorative
pieces, textiles
Open Mon–Sat 10am–5pm
Fairs Battersea Park Decorative
Antique and Textile Fair

➢ Neal Sons & Fletcher
Contact Mr Edward Fletcher FRICS
✉ **26 Church Street, Woodbridge,
Suffolk,
IP12 1DP** 🅿
☎ 01394 382263 **❶** 01394 383030
@ enquiries@nsf.co.uk
® www.nsf.co.uk
Est. 1951

Open Mon–Fri 9am–5.30pm
Sat 9am–4pm
Sales General monthly antiques
sales, viewing day prior to sale
2.15–4.30pm 6.30–8pm sale day
9.30–10.30am. Bi- or tri-annual
specialist sales of period English
and Continental furniture,
pictures, books, carpets etc at
The Theatre Street Sale Room,
viewing Sat prior to sale
10am–1pm day preceding sale
11am–4.30pm 6.30–8pm sale day
9.30–10.30am
Catalogues Yes

**⊞ The Old Brewery
Antiques**
Contact Maurice Finch
✉ **Melton Road, Melton,
Woodbridge, Suffolk,
IP12 1PD** 🅿
☎ 01394 388836 **❶** 01394 388836
Est. 2003 *Stock size* Large
Stock General antiques,
collectables
Open Mon–Sat 9am–5pm
closed Wed

⊞ Isobel Rhodes
Contact Mrs I Rhodes
✉ **10 & 12 Market Hill,
Woodbridge, Suffolk,
IP12 4LS** 🅿
☎ 01394 382763
Est. 1964 *Stock size* Medium
Stock Oak, country furniture,
pewter, pottery, brass
Open Mon–Sat 10am–1pm
2–5pm

⊞ E F Wall
Contact Libby Wall
✉ **32 Church Street, Woodbridge,
Suffolk,
IP12 1DH** 🅿
☎ 01394 610511
@ efwall@msn.com
Est. 1979 *Stock size* Medium
Stock Decorative accesories
Trade only Yes
Open Mon–Sat 10am–5pm
closed Wed
Services Restoration

⊞ Woodbridge Gallery
Contact Mr David Bethell
✉ **23 Market Hill, Woodbridge,**

**Suffolk,
IP12 4LX** 🅿
☎ 01394 386500 **❶** 01394 386500
Est. 1998 *Stock size* Large
Stock Fine art gallery
Open Mon–Sat 10am–5.30pm
Wed 10am–1pm

WOOLPIT

⊞ John Heather
Contact John Heather
✉ **Old Crown, The Street,
Woolpit, Bury St Edmunds,
Suffolk,
IP30 9SA** 🅿
☎ 01359 240297
© 07715 282600
@ john@johnheather.co.uk
Est. 1946 *Stock size* Medium
Stock Late 18thC furniture
Open Mon–Sun 9am–6pm
Services Restoration

YOXFORD

⊞ Garden House Antiques
Contact Ann Gray or
Janet Hyde-Smith
✉ **High Street, Yoxford,
Saxmundham, Suffolk,
IP17 3ER** 🅿
☎ 01728 668044
© 07767 896401
Est. 1969 *Stock size* Large
Stock Antiques, vintage, decorative
and pretty things, books
Open Mon–Sat 10am–5pm
closed Wed

**⊞ Suffolk House Antiques
(BADA)**
Contact Mr A Singleton
✉ **High Street, Yoxford,
Saxmundham,
Suffolk,
IP17 3EP** 🅿
☎ 01728 668122 **❶** 01728 668122
© 07860 521583
@ andrew.singleton@suffolk-
house-antiques.co.uk
® www.suffolk-house-antiques.co.uk
Est. 1991 *Stock size* Large
Stock Early English furniture,
ceramics, associated works of art
Open Mon–Sat 10am–1pm
2.15–5.15pm closed Wed
Fairs BADA, Snape

EAST

HEART OF ENGLAND

BEDFORDSHIRE

AMPTHILL

⊞ **Ampthill Antiques and Collectables**
Contact Mr Shayler
✉ **Market Square, Church Street, Ampthill, Bedfordshire, MK45 2EH** 🅿
☎ 01525 403344
✉ ampthillantiques@btconnect.com
Est. 1980 *Stock size* Large
Stock General antiques
Open Mon–Sun 11am–6pm
Services Restoration, delivery

⌂ **Ampthill Antiques Emporium**
Contact Marc Legg
✉ **6 Bedford Street, Ampthill, Bedfordshire, MK45 2NB** 🅿
☎ 01525 402131   📠 01582 737527
📱 07831 374919
✉ info@ampthillantiques
emporium.co.uk
ⓦ www.ampthillantiques
emporium.co.uk
Est. 1979 *Stock size* Large
No. of dealers 40
Stock Georgian–Edwardian furniture, smalls, shipping goods
Open Mon–Sun 10am–5pm
closed Tues
Services Upholstery, valuations, shipping, furniture restoration, pine stripping, picture framing

⊞ **Antiquarius**
Contact Mr P Caldwell
✉ **107 Dunstable Street, Ampthill, Bedfordshire, MK45 2NG** 🅿
☎ 01525 841799
📱 07776 216907
✉ peter.caldwell@tesco.net
ⓦ www.antiquariusofampthill.com
Est. 1996 *Stock size* Medium
Stock Georgian–Edwardian sitting and dining room furniture
Open Mon–Sat 10.30am–5pm
Sun 1–5pm
Services Restoration, upholstery

⊞ **House of Clocks (BHI)**
Contact Mrs H Proud
✉ **98 Dunstable Street, Ampthill, Bedfordshire, MK45 2JP** 🅿
☎ 01525 403136
✉ houseofclocks@tiscali.co.uk
ⓦ www.houseofclocks.co.uk
Est. 1984 *Stock size* Large
Stock Fine-quality antiques, reproduction clocks
Open Mon–Sat 9am–5pm
closed Tues
Fairs Motorcycle Museum, NEC, Brunel University
Services Restoration

⊞ **David Litt Antiques**
Contact Mr D Litt
✉ **The Old Telephone Exchange, Claridges Lane, Ampthill,**
Bedfordshire, **MK45 2HU** 🅿
☎ 01525 404825   📠 01525 404563
📱 07802 449027
✉ litt@ntlworld.com
ⓦ www.davidlittantiques.co.uk
Est. 1967 *Stock size* Large
Stock French provincial, 19thC furniture
Open Mon–Fri 7am–4pm
Fairs Battersea, Olympia
Services Restoration

⊞ **Paris Antiques**
Contact Mr Paul Northwood
✉ **97b Dunstable Street, Ampthill, Bedfordshire, MK45 2NG** 🅿
☎ 01525 840488   📠 01525 840488
📱 07802 535059
Est. 1984 *Stock size* Medium
Stock 18th–early 20thC furniture and effects
Open Tues–Sun 9.30am–5.30pm
Services Valuations, restoration

⌂ **Pilgrim Antiques Centre**
Contact Gary Lester
✉ **111 Dunstable Street, Ampthill, Bedfordshire, MK45 2NE** 🅿
☎ 01525 633023
✉ garylesterbl@aol.com
Est. 1996 *Stock size* Large
No. of dealers 6
Stock General antiques,

Georgian–Edwardian furniture, glass, china, jewellery
Open Tues–Sat 10am–5pm
Sun 11am–4.30pm

BEDFORD

⊞ The Eagle Bookshop
Contact Mr Peter Budek
⊠ 103 Castle Road, Bedford, Bedfordshire,
MK40 3QP ▣
☎ 01234 269295
⊖ customers@eaglebookshop.co.uk
⊛ www.eaglebookshop.co.uk
Est. 1991 *Stock size* Large
Stock Rare, antiquarian and collectable books, books of a scholarly nature on most subjects, also a specialist stock of important scientific and mathematical books.
Open Mon–Sat 10am–5.30pm
Services Stock displayed on website, books bought

⊞ Goodrich House Antiques
Contact John Kromholc
⊠ 6 Goodrich Avenue, Bedford, Bedfordshire,
MK41 0DE ▣
☎ 01234 218206
⊛ 07989 759539
⊖ kromholc@btinternet.com
Est. 1995 *Stock size* Small
Stock Antiques, curios, collectables
Trade only Yes
Open Mon–Sun 10am–6pm
Fairs Woodgreen, Huntingdon

⚒ W & H Peacock
Contact Mark Baker
or Simon Rowell
⊠ 26 Newnham Street, Bedford, Bedfordshire,
MK40 3JR ▣
☎ 01234 266366 ⊖ 01234 269082
⊖ info@peacockauction.co.uk
⊛ www.peacockauction.co.uk
Est. 1901
Open Mon–Thurs 9am–5.30pm
Fri 9am–8.30pm Sat 8.30am–5pm
Sales General and antiques sale Sat 9.30am, viewing Fri 9am–8pm Sat 8.30am prior to sale, also Thurs 11am, viewing Wed 9am–8pm Thurs 8.30am prior to sale. Monthly antiques and collectables sale first Fri 10.45am, viewing Fri 5–8pm in week before Thurs 9am–6pm in week of sale and Fri

8.30–10.45am prior to sale
Frequency Weekly
Catalogues Yes

⊞ Victoria House
Contact Helen Felts
⊠ 70a Tavistock Street, Bedford, Bedfordshire,
MK40 2RP ▣
☎ 01234 320000
Est. 1998 *Stock size* Large
Stock Victorian–Edwardian furniture, antiques, reproduction and decorative pieces
Open Mon–Fri 11.30am–5pm
Sat 11am–5pm Sun 12.30–4.30pm
closed Wed
Services Interior design

BIGGLESWADE

⊞ Shortmead Antiques
Contact Mr S E Sinfield
⊠ 46 Shortmead Street, Biggleswade, Bedfordshire,
SG18 0AP ▣
☎ 01767 601780
Est. 1989 *Stock size* Medium
Stock Victorian–Edwardian furniture, china, silver, glass, general antiques
Open Tues Wed Fri Sat 10am–4.30pm

⊞ Simply Oak
Contact Anna Kilgarriff or Dick Sturman
⊠ Oak Tree Farm, Potton Road, Biggleswade, Bedfordshire,
SG18 0EP ▣
☎ 01767 601559 ⊖ 01767 312855
⊖ antiques@simplyoak.freeserve.co.uk
Est. 1997 *Stock size* Large
Stock Late Victorian–1930s restored oak furniture
Open Mon–Sat 10am–5pm
Sun 11am–4pm
Services Restoration

BROMHAM

⚒ Paperchase
Contact Brian Moakes
⊠ 77 Wingfield Road, Bromham, Bedford, Bedfordshire, MK43 8JY
☎ 01234 825942
⊖ brianmoakes@aol.com
Est. 1991
Open Mon–Fri 9am–5pm
Sales Postal auction of transport-related paper memorabilia
Frequency 6 per annum
Catalogues Yes

CHAWSTON

⊞ John Moore Antiques
Contact Mr J Moore
⊠ College Farm House Workshops, Chawston Lane, Chawston, Bedford, Bedfordshire,
MK44 3BH ▣
☎ 01480 214165
⊖ john@moorerestorations. freeserve.co.uk
⊛ www.jmooreantiques.co.uk
Est. 1975 *Stock size* Small
Stock High-quality period furniture 17th–20thC
Open Mon–Fri 9am–5pm
Services Restoration

DUNSTABLE

⊞ Bernard Gulley Antiques (BADA, CINOA)
Contact Bernard Gulley
⊠ Lancotbury Manor, Totternhoe, Dunstable, Bedfordshire,
LU6 1RG ▣
☎ 01582 606435
Est. 1969 *Stock size* Large
Stock Oak and country furniture, rural, naive and decorative period accessories
Open By appointment only
Fairs Olympia

EGGINGTON

⊞ Robert Kirkman Ltd (ABA, PBFA)
Contact Robert Kirkman
⊠ Kings Cottage, Eggington, Leighton Buzzard, Bedfordshire,
LU7 9PG ▣
☎ 01525 210647 ⊖ 01525 211184
⊖ robertkirkmanltd@btinternet.com
⊛ www.robertkirkman.co.uk
Est. 1988 *Stock size* Small
Stock Antiquarian books, specializing in English literature, Churchill, English Bibles, sets of standard authors
Open By appointment only
Fairs ABA, PBFA
Services Restoration, book binding, shipping

HENLOW

⊞ Hanworth House Antiques & Interiors
Contact Rose Jarvis

✉ 92 High Street, Henlow,
Bedfordshire,
SG16 6AB **P**
☎ 01462 814361 **✆** 01462 814361
✉ hanworthhouse@aol.com
Est. 2000 *Stock size* Large
Stock Antique furniture and
decorative smalls
Open Tues–Sat 11am–5.30pm
Sun noon–5.30pm
Services Antique search, framing

LEIGHTON BUZZARD

⊞ David Ball Antiques
Contact David Ball
✉ Leighton Buzzard,
Bedfordshire,
LU7 **P**
☎ 01525 210753
⊠ 07831 111661
Est. 1970 *Stock size* Medium
Stock Furniture, clocks,
barometers, 18th–early 20thC
porcelain
Open By appointment
Fairs Kempton Park

LOWER STONDON

⊞ Memory Lane Antiques
Contact Mrs Liz Henry
✉ 14 Bedford Road,
Lower Stondon, Henlow,
Bedfordshire,
SG16 6EA **P**
☎ 01462 812716
⊠ 07702 715477
Est. 1998 *Stock size* Medium
Stock Furniture, silver, porcelain,
crystal, collectables
Open Mon–Sun 10.30am–5pm
closed Wed Thurs
Services Appraisals

LUTON

⊞ Bargain Box
Contact Dean Dickinson
✉ 4 & 6a Adelaide Street, Luton,
Bedfordshire,
LU1 5BB **P**
☎ 01582 423809
Est. 1962 *Stock size* Medium
Stock Collectables
Open Mon–Sat 9.30am–5pm

POTTON

⊞ Wesley J West & Son
Contact Mr A West
✉ 58 King Street, Potton, Sandy,
Bedfordshire,

SG19 2QZ **P**
☎ 01767 260589
Est. 1931 *Stock size* Medium
Stock Georgian–Edwardian
furniture
Open Mon–Fri 9am–5pm
Sat 9am–noon
Services Restoration, upholstery

SHEFFORD

**⊞ S and S Timms Antiques
Ltd (LAPADA)**
Contact Sue Timms
✉ 2–4 High Street, Shefford,
Bedfordshire,
SG17 5DG **P**
☎ 01462 851051 **✆** 01462 817047
⊠ 07885 458541
✉ info@timmsantiques.com
⊛ www.timmsantiques.com
Est. 1976 *Stock size* Large
Stock 18th–19thC town and
country furniture
Open Mon–Fri 9.30am–5.30pm
Sat 11am–5pm or by
appointment
Fairs Chelsea, LAPADA, Olympia

WILSTEAD

**⊞ Manor Antiques and
Interiors**
Contact Mrs S Bowen
✉ The Manor House,
Cotton End Road, Wilstead,
Bedford, Bedfordshire,
MK45 3BT **P**
☎ 01234 740262 **✆** 01234 740262
⊠ 07831 419729
✉ brianmottram16@hotmail.com
Est. 1979 *Stock size* Large
Stock 19thC and Edwardian
furniture, antique and replica
mirrors, lighting
Open Mon–Sat 10am–5pm
Fairs House & Garden, Olympia

WOBURN

⊞ Geoffrey Hugall
Contact Mr G Hugall
✉ Woburn Abbey Antique
Centres, Woburn Abbey,
Bedfordshire,
MK17 9WA **P**
☎ 02078 380457 or 01525 290350
⊠ 07973 273485
Est. 1971 *Stock size* Medium
Stock General antiques, mirrors,
period furniture
Open Mon–Sun 10am–5.30pm
Services Valuations

**⊞ Walter Moores & Son
(LAPADA)**
Contact Peter Moores
✉ Woburn Abbey Antiques
Centre, Woburn, Bedfordshire,
MK7 9WA **P**
☎ 01525 290350
⊠ 07710 019045
✉ waltermoores@btinternet.com
⊛ www.waltermoores.co.uk
Est. 1925 *Stock size* Medium
Stock Georgian–Victorian
furniture, mainly mahogany
Open Mon–Sun 10am–5.30pm
including Bank Holidays, closed
Christmas holiday
Fairs Buxton (May), Harrogate
Antiques and Fine Art Fairs , NEC

⊞ Music Room Antiques
Contact Andrew Lancaster
✉ Woburn Abbey Antiques
Centre, Woburn, Bedfordshire,
MK7 9WA
☎ 01403 822189 **✆** 01403 823089
⊠ 07711 986926
✉ andrew@squarepiano.net
⊛ www.squarepiano.net
Est. 1986 *Stock size* Medium
Stock Square pianos and
associated music-related
antiques
Open Every day 10am–5.30pm
only closed Christmas holiday
Fairs BADA, Harrogate Antique
Fair
Services Restoration

**⋗ Charles Ross Fine Art
Auctioneers**
Contact Charles Ross
✉ The Old Town Hall, Woburn,
Bedfordshire,
MK17 9PZ **P**
☎ 01525 290502 **✆** 01525 290864
✉ info@charles-ross.co.uk
⊛ www.charles-ross.co.uk
Est. 1975
Open Mon–Fri 9am–5pm
Sales General antiques and fine
art
Frequency Monthly
Catalogues Yes

⊞ Christopher Sykes
Contact Mr C Sykes or
Mrs Sally Lloyd
✉ The Old Parsonage,
Bedford Street, Woburn,
Bedfordshire,
MK17 9QL **P**
☎ 01525 290259 **✆** 01525 290061
✉ sykes.corkscrews@sykes-

corkscrews.co.uk
ⓦ www.sykes-corkscrews.co.uk
Est. 1960 *Stock size* Large
Stock Items associated with
wine, speciality corkscrews,
scientific instruments
Open Mon–Sat 9am–5pm

⊞ Town Hall Antiques
Contact Mr or Mrs Groves
✉ Market Place, Woburn,
Bedfordshire,
MK17 9PZ ℗
☎ 01525 290950 ✆ 01525 292501
ⓔ info@townhallantiques.co.uk
ⓦ www.townhallantiques.co.uk
Est. 1993 *Stock size* Large
Stock Varied
Open Mon–Sat 10am–5.30pm
Sun 11am–5.30pm
Services Valuations

⌂ Woburn Abbey Antiques Centre
Contact Ian Osborn
✉ Woburn, Bedfordshire,
MK17 9WA ℗
☎ 01525 290350 ✆ 01525 292102
ⓔ antiques@woburnabbey.co.uk
ⓦ www.woburnabbey.co.uk/
Est. 1967 *Stock size* Large
No. of dealers 40
Stock Furniture (dateline 1910),
porcelain, silver, paintings
(dateline 1940)
Open 363 days a year
10am–5.30pm

⊞ Yew Tree
Contact Anna Maggs
✉ Woburn Abbey Antiques
Centre, Shop 7, Woburn,
Bedfordshire,
MK17 9WA ℗
☎ 01582 872514 ✆ 01582 873816
Est. 1983 *Stock size* Medium
Stock Farm and garden tools,
related rural items, 18th–20thC
decorative prints
Open 363 days a year
10am–5.30pm
Fairs NEC, Decorative Antiques &
Textiles Fair, Battersea

BUCKINGHAMSHIRE

AMERSHAM

⏶ The Amersham Auction Rooms (RICS)
Contact Pippa Ellis
✉ 125 Station Road, Amersham,
Buckinghamshire,

HP7 0AH ℗
☎ 08700 460606 ✆ 08700 460607
ⓔ info@amershamauctionrooms.co.uk
ⓦ www.amershamauctionrooms.co.uk
Est. 1877
Open Mon–Fri 9am–5.30pm
Sat 9–11.30am
Sales Antiques and collectors'
first Thurs of month. Victorian
and general furniture other
Thurs weekly 10.30am, viewing
Tues 2–5pm Wed 9.30am–8pm
Thurs 9–10.15am
Catalogues Yes

⏶ Old Amersham Auctions
Contact Mr M King
✉ 2 School Lane, Amersham,
Buckinghamshire,
HP7 0EL ℗
☎ 01494 722758 ✆ 01494 722758
ⓜ 07773 531010
ⓔ martinking8@hotmail.com
Est. 1979
Open Mon–Sat 9am–5pm
Sales General and antiques sale
Sat noon, viewing Sat 9am prior
to sale. Occasional house sales,
telephone for details
Frequency Fortnightly
Catalogues Yes

⊞ Pop Antiques
Contact Nicola Barwell
✉ 12 The Broadway, Amersham,
Buckinghamshire,
HP7 0HP ℗
☎ 01494 434443 ✆ 01494 434443
ⓜ 07768 366606
ⓦ www.popantiques.com
Est. 2001 *Stock size* Large
Stock Late 19thC French painted
furniture, mirrors
Open Mon–Sat 10am–5.30pm
Services Shipping

⊞ Liz Quilter
Contact Liz or Mike Quilter
✉ 38 High Street, Amersham,
Buckinghamshire,
HP7 0DJ ℗
☎ 01494 433723 ✆ 01494 433723
Est. 1969 *Stock size* Large
Stock Old pine collectables,
copper, brass, rustic furniture
Open Mon–Fri 10am–5pm
Sat 10am–5.30pm

⊞ Sundial Antiques
Contact Mr A Macdonald
✉ 19 Whielden Street,
Amersham, Buckinghamshire,
HP7 0HU ℗

☎ 01494 727955
ⓜ 07866 819314
Est. 1970 *Stock size* Medium
Stock 19thC copper and brass,
small furniture, ceramics
Open Mon–Sat 9.30am–5.30pm
closed Thurs

ASTON CLINTON

⊞ Dismantle & Deal Direct
Contact Mr T Pattison
✉ 108 London Road,
Aston Clinton, Buckinghamshire,
HP22 5HS ℗
☎ 01296 632300 ✆ 01296 631329
ⓔ info@ddd-uk.com
ⓦ www.ddd-uk.com
Est. 1992 *Stock size* Large
Stock Doors, entrance ways,
chimney pieces, lighting, stained
glass, mirrors, garden statuary,
other architecturally unusual
items
Open Mon–Sat 10am–5pm
Services Architectural
reclamation

AYLESBURY

⊞ Gillian Neale Antiques (BADA)
Contact Gillian Neale
✉ PO Box 247, Aylesbury,
Buckinghamshire,
HP20 1JZ ℗
☎ 01296 423754 ✆ 01296 334601
ⓔ gillianneale@aol.com
ⓦ www.gilliannealeantiques.co.uk
Est. 1980 *Stock size* Large
Stock English blue printed
pottery 1780–1900
Open By appointment
Fairs Olympia, BADA, NEC
Services Valuations, restoration,
export, search

BEACONSFIELD

⊞ Buck House Antique Centre
Contact Mrs B Whitby
✉ 47 Wycombe End,
Beaconsfield, Buckinghamshire,
HP9 1LZ ℗
☎ 01494 670714 ✆ 01494 670714
ⓔ bachantiques@supanet.com
Est. 1982 *Stock size* Medium
Stock Clocks, furniture,
metalware, ceramics, general
antiques
Open Mon–Sat 10am–5pm
closed Wed

⊞ Grosvenor House Interiors
Contact Mr T Marriott
⊠ 51 Wycombe End, Beaconsfield, Buckinghamshire, HP9 1LX 🅿
☎ 01494 677498 📠 01494 677498
📱 07747 014098
Est. 1978 *Stock size* Large
Stock 18th–19thC furniture, pictures, mirrors, clocks, fireplaces
Open Mon–Sat 10am–1pm 2–5pm closed Wed

⊞ Claudia Hill (BADA)
Contact Claudia Hill
⊠ Beaconsfield, Buckinghamshire, HP9 2DJ 🅿
☎ 01494 678880
📱 07720 317899
📧 claudia.hill@ellisonfineart.co.uk
🌐 www.ellisonfineart.com
Est. 2000 *Stock size* Large
Stock Portrait miniatures
Open By appointment
Fairs Olympia, Harrogate and Duke of York's barracks, Antiques and Fine Art fairs

⊞ Period Furniture Showrooms (TVADA)
Contact Mr R E W Hearne
⊠ 49 London End, Beaconsfield, Buckinghamshire, HP9 2HW 🅿
☎ 01494 674112 📠 01494 681046
📧 sales@periodfurniture.net
🌐 www.periodfurniture.net
Est. 1966 *Stock size* Large
Stock Victorian–Edwardian furniture
Open Mon–Sat 9am–5.30pm
Fairs TVADA Spring
Services Restoration of furniture

BOURNE END

🏠 Bourne End Antiques Centre
Contact Mr Simon Shepheard
⊠ 67 The Parade, Bourne End, Buckinghamshire, SL8 5SB 🅿
☎ 01628 533298
📱 07776 176876
Est. 1996 *Stock size* Large
No. of dealers 45
Stock General antiques, oak, pine, mahogany, silver, jewellery
Open Mon–Sat 10am–5.30pm Sun Bank Holidays noon–4pm

⤏ Bourne End Auction Rooms
Contact Mr S Brown
⊠ Station Approach, Bourne End, Buckinghamshire, SL8 5QH 🅿
☎ 01628 531500 📠 01628 522158
📧 be.auctions@lineone.net
🌐 www.bourneendauctionrooms.com
Est. 1992
Open Mon–Fri 9am–5pm Sat 9am–noon
Sales Weekly general sale Wed 10.30am, antiques sale 1st Wed monthly 10.30am, viewing Tues 9.30am–7pm Wed 9–10.30am
Catalogues Yes

⊞ La Maison (TVADA)
Contact Mr J Pratt
⊠ The Crossings, Cores End Road, Bourne End, Buckinghamshire, SL8 5AL 🅿
☎ 01628 525858 📠 01494 670363
📱 07885 209001
📧 jeremy@la-maison.co.uk
🌐 www.la-maison.co.uk
Est. 1994 *Stock size* Medium
Stock French mirrors, beds, tables, gifts, garden furniture and statuary, painted armoires
Open Mon 1–5.30pm Tues–Sat 10am–5.30pm Sun 11am–5pm
Fairs Ardingly
Services Upholstery, restoration

BUCKINGHAM

⊞ Buckingham Antiques Centre Ltd
Contact Mr P Walton
⊠ 5 West Street, Buckingham, Buckinghamshire, MK18 1HL 🅿
☎ 01280 824464
📱 07904 242877
📧 peterwalton@whsmithnet.co.uk
Est. 1992 *Stock size* Small
Stock General antiques, furniture, clocks, silver, china
Open Mon–Sat 9am–5pm closed Wed or by appointment
Services Valuations

⤏ Dickins Auctioneers
Contact Louise Gostelow
⊠ 1 Claydon Sale Room, Calvert Road, Buckingham, Buckinghamshire, MK18 2EZ 🅿
☎ 01296 714436 📠 01296 714492
📧 info@dickins-auctioneers.com
🌐 www.dickins-auctioneers.com
Est. 1999
Open Mon–Fri 9.30am–5.30pm
Sales County, sporting, fine art and general monthly antique sales
Catalogues Yes

⊞ Goodwin's Home & Garden
Contact Mr or Mrs M Goodwin
⊠ 2 High Street, Buckingham, Buckinghamshire, MK18 1NU 🅿
☎ 01280 813115
Est. 1978 *Stock size* Large
Stock Country pine furniture, accessories, garden items, lighting, mirrors, textiles
Open Mon–Sat 9.30am–5.30pm
Services Furniture made to order

CHALFONT ST GILES

⊞ Gallery 23 Antiques
Contact Mr F Vollaro
⊠ 5 High Street, Chalfont St Giles, Buckinghamshire, HP8 4QH 🅿
☎ 01494 871512 📠 01494 871512
Est. 1989 *Stock size* Large
Stock China, silver, furniture, glass, pictures, prints, clocks
Open Mon–Sat 10am–5pm
Services Valuations

⊞ St Giles Old Pine Company
Contact Toby Smith
⊠ The Furniture Village, London Road, Chalfont St Giles, Buckinghamshire, HP8 4RD 🅿
☎ 01494 873031
📱 07860 265130
📧 tobysmith@stgilesfurniture.com
Est. 1968 *Stock size* Large
Stock Antique, English and Continental oak and pine furniture
Open Mon–Sat 9am–5pm Sun noon–4pm

CHESHAM

⊞ The Attic
Contact Karen Page
⊠ 3 High Street, Chesham, Buckinghamshire, HP5 1BG 🅿
☎ 01494 794114
Est. 1998 *Stock size* Large
Stock Collectables, furniture, jewellery, paintings, pictures, china, pottery, clocks, brass, commemoratives

Open Mon–Sat 9.30am–5.30pm
Sun 11am–5pm

**⊞ Chess Antiques
(LAPADA)**
Contact Mr Wilder
✉ 85 Broad Street, Chesham,
Buckinghamshire,
HP5 3EF 🅿
☎ 01494 783043 📠 01494 791302
📱 07831 212454
📧 mike_wilder44@hotmail.com
Est. 1971 *Stock size* Medium
Stock Clocks
Open Mon–Fri 9am–5pm
Sat 10am–5pm
Services Valuations

⊞ A E Jackson
Contact Ann Jackson
✉ Queen Anne House,
57 Church Street, Chesham,
Buckinghamshire, HP5 1HY 🅿
☎ 01494 783811
Est. 1910 *Stock size* Medium
Stock Home antiques
Open Fri Sat 10am–12.30pm
1.30–5pm or by appointment

🏠 Stuff & Nonsense
Contact Helen or Elaine Robb
✉ 70 Broad Street, Chesham,
Buckinghamshire, HP5 3DX 🅿
☎ 01494 775988/782877
Est. 1998 *Stock size* Large
No. of dealers 20
Stock Collectables, books,
antiques, furniture
Open Mon–Sat 9.30am–5.30pm
Sun 11am–5.30pm closed Wed

**⊞ Hobday Toys (Dolls Club
of Great Britain)**
Contact Wendy Hobday
✉ Denham, Buckinghamshire,
UB9 5AD 🅿
☎ 01895 834348
📧 wendyhobday@freenet.co.uk
Est. 1985 *Stock size* Large
Stock Dolls houses and furniture,
tin-plate toys
Open By appointment
Fairs Sandown, Lyndhurst,
Pudsey, Stafford
Services Valuations

**⊞ Glade Antiques (BADA,
CINOA)**
Contact Sonia Vaughan

✉ PO Box 873, High Wycombe,
Buckinghamshire,
HP14 3ZQ
☎ 01494 882818
📱 07771 552328
📧 sonia@gladeantiques.com
Stock Oriental porcelain,
bronzes, jades, antiquities
Open By appointment
Fairs BADA, Olympia, LAPADA
Services Valuations

⊞ Yester-Year
Contact Mr P J Frost
✉ 12 High Street, Iver,
Buckinghamshire,
SL0 9NG 🅿
☎ 01753 652072
Est. 1968 *Stock size* Medium
Stock General antiques, furniture,
pictures, china, glass, metalwork
Open Mon–Sat 10am–6pm
Services Valuations, restoration,
picture framing, clock repairs

**🏹 Bosley's Military
Auctioneers (BACA Award
Winner 2004)**
Contact Mr S Bosley
✉ The White House, Marlow,
Buckinghamshire,
SL7 1AH 🅿
☎ 01628 488188 📠 01628 488111
🌐 www.bosleys.co.uk
Est. 1994
Open By appointment only
Sales Militaria sales Wed noon at
Court Gardens, viewing Wed
8am–noon prior to sale
Frequency Quarterly
Catalogues Yes

**⊞ Coldstream Military
Antiques (LAPADA)**
Contact Mr S Bosley
✉ The White House, Marlow,
Buckinghamshire,
SL7 1AH 🅿
☎ 01628 488188 📠 01628 488111
Est. 1978 *Stock size* Large
Stock Militaria including swords,
medals, pictures, campaign
furniture
Open By appointment only

**🏠 Marlow Antiques
Centre**
Contact Marilyn Short
✉ 35 Station Road, Marlow,

Buckinghamshire,
SL7 1NW 🅿
☎ 01628 473223 📠 01628 478989
📱 07802 188345
🌐 www.marlowantiques.com
Est. 1995 *Stock size* Large
No. of dealers 30+
Stock 18th–20thC furniture,
collectors' china, Staffordshire
figures, chandeliers, silver,
decorative glass, writing slopes,
tea caddies, postcards, pens,
collectables, fine china
Open Mon–Sat 10.30am–5pm
Sun 11am–4pm
Services Restoration, shipping

⊞ Grange Antiques Ltd
Contact Shuna Spencer
✉ The Market, Bell Walk,
Winslow, Milton Keynes,
Buckinghamshire
☎ 01296 713011
📱 07734 218935
📧 shuna@postmaster.co.uk
🌐 www.grangeantiques.com
Est. 1991 *Stock size* Large
Stock Victorian and earlier
furniture, smalls
Open Tues–Sun 10am–4pm
Fairs Gemsco, Bowman's
Services Upholstery

⊞ Off World
Contact Jamie
✉ Milton Keynes Shopping
Centre Market, MIlton Keynes,
Buckinghamshire,
LU1 2TP 🅿
☎ 01234 752485
📱 07774 867679
Est. 1995 *Stock size* Large
Stock Collectable toys, *Star Wars*,
Transformers, comics, cards etc
Open Mon–Sat 9am–5.30pm
Sun 10am–5pm

**⊞ Ken's Paper
Collectables (UACC,
Ephemera Society)**
Contact Ken Graham
✉ 29 High Street,
Newport Pagnell,
Buckinghamshire,
MK16 8AR 🅿
☎ 01908 210683/610003
📠 01908 610003
📧 ken@kens.co.uk
🌐 www.kens.co.uk

Est. 1983 *Stock size* Large
Stock Autographs, vintage
magazines, posters, historic
newspapers, British comics,
documents, printed, written
ephemera, show business
memorabilia
Open Mon–Wed Fri 9.30am–5pm
Sat 9.30am–4pm
Fairs Bloomsbury Postcard Fair,
ephemera fairs, film fairs

OLNEY

⌂ The Antique Centre at Olney
Contact Robert Sklar
✉ 13 Osborns Court,
off High Street South, Olney,
Buckinghamshire,
MK46 4LA 🄿
☎ 01234 710942 📠 01234 710947
🄴 webmaster@antiques-of-britain.co.uk
🄦 www.antiques-of-britain.co.uk
Est. 2001 *Stock size* Large
No. of dealers 80
Stock Furniture, jewellery, silver
china
Open Tues–Sat 10am–5pm Sun
11am–4pm

⊞ Pine Antiques
Contact Mrs Foster
✉ 10 Market Place, Olney,
Buckinghamshire,
MK46 4EA 🄿
☎ 01234 711065 📠 01234 711065
🄜 07711 917049
Est. 1990 *Stock size* Medium
Stock Pine furniture, giftware
Open Mon–Fri 10am–5pm Sat
9.30am–5.30pm Sun noon–5pm

⊞ Robin Unsworth Antiques
Contact Robin Unsworth
✉ 1a Weston Road, Olney,
Buckinghamshire,
MK46 5BD 🄿
☎ 01234 711210
🄜 07860 809584
Est. 1972 *Stock size* Large
Stock 18th–19thC furniture,
clocks
Open Mon–Sun 10am–4pm or by
appointment

PENN

⊞ Penn Barn
Contact Paul Hunnings
✉ By the Pond, Elm Road, Penn,

Buckinghamshire,
HP10 8LB 🄿
☎ 01494 815691
Est. 1968 *Stock size* Medium
Stock Antiquarian books, maps,
prints, watercolours, oil
paintings
Open Tues–Sat 10.30am–1pm
2–4pm

STONY STRATFORD

⊞ CIRCA Antiques & Art
Contact Victoria Holton
✉ 6 Church Street,
Stony Stratford,
Buckinghamshire,
MK11 1BD 🄿
☎ 01908 567100
🄴 info@circa-antiques.co.uk
🄦 www.circa-antiques.co.uk
Est. 2000 *Stock size* Medium
Stock Victorian–Edwardian
furniture, interesting pre-1939
pieces
Open Tues–Sat 10am–5pm
Fairs NEC
Services House clearance

⊞ Daeron's Books (SSBA)
Contact Mrs A Gardner
✉ 13 Market Square,
Stony Stratford, Milton Keynes,
Buckinghamshire,
MK11 1BE 🄿
☎ 01908 568989 📠 01908 266092
🄴 books@daerons.co.uk
🄦 www.daerons.co.uk
Est. 1993 *Stock size* Medium
Stock Fantasy, science fiction
books, Tolkien and C S Lewis a
speciality
Open Mon–Fri 9.30am–5.30pm
Sat 9am–5pm Sun by
appointment
Fairs Stony Stratford
Services Valuations, book search,
book fair organiser, suppliers of
English designed and made
portable bookcases

⊞ Periplus Books
Contact Mr J Phillips
✉ 2 Timor Court, High Street,
Stony Stratford, Milton Keynes,
Buckinghamshire,
MK11 1EJ 🄿
☎ 01908 263300
🄴 periplus@btconnect.com
Est. 1997 *Stock size* Small
Stock General second-hand,
antiquarian books
Open Tues–Sat 10.30am–5pm

Thurs by appointment
⊞ Stony Stratford Antiques
Contact M K Millen
✉ 1 Timor Court,
Stony Stratford, Milton Keynes,
Buckinghamshire,
MK11 1EJ 🄿
☎ 01908 568886
Est. 1998 *Stock size* Medium
Stock Furniture, collectables
Open Mon–Fri 10.30am–5pm
Sat 9.30am–5pm closed Thurs

WADDESDON

⊞ Farrelly Antiques
Contact Mr Paul Farrelly
✉ 68 High Street, Waddesdon,
Buckinghamshire,
HP18 0JD 🄿
☎ 01442 891905
🄜 07901 556587
Est. 1979 *Stock size* Medium
Stock Antique furniture up to
1900
Open Mon–Sun 10am–5pm
Services Restoration

WAVENDON

⊞ Jeanne Temple Antiques
Contact Mrs Temple
✉ Stockwell House,
1 Stockwell Lane, Wavendon,
Milton Keynes,
Buckinghamshire,
MK17 8LS 🄿
☎ 01908 583597 📠 01908 281149
Est. 1960 *Stock size* Medium
Stock Furniture, collectable
items, lighting
Open Tues–Sat 10am–5pm
Sun by appointment
Fairs Luton, Silsoe, Kempton
Park, Alexander Palace

WENDOVER

⌂ Antiques at Wendover
Contact Mrs N Gregory
✉ The Old Post Office,
25 High Street, Wendover,
Buckinghamshire,
HP22 6DU 🄿
☎ 01296 625335 📠 01296 620401
🄜 07712 032565
🄴 antiques@antiqueswendover.co.uk
🄦 www.antiqueswendover.co.uk
Est. 1987 *Stock size* Large
No. of dealers Over 30
Stock Town and country

antiques, furniture, silver, glass, rugs, English garden tools and statuary, kitchenware, architectural antiques, barometers, antiquities, guns, pocket watches, Art Deco (dateline 1940)
Open Mon–Sat 10am–5.30pm Sun Bank Holidays 11am–5pm
Services Restoration of caning, ceramics, metals, jewellery, furniture

⊞ Sally Turner Antiques (LAPADA)
Contact Sally Turner
✉ Hogarth House, High Street, Wendover, Buckinghamshire, HP22 6DU ℗
☎ 01296 624402 ✆ 01296 624402
⌖ 07860 201718
✉ majorsally@hotmail.com
Est. 1979 *Stock size* Large
Stock 18th–19thC furniture, decorative items, jewellery, works of art
Open Mon–Sat 10am–5pm closed Wed (before Christmas open every day)
Services Repairs

WHITCHURCH
⊞ Deerstalker Antiques
Contact Mrs L. Eichler
✉ 28 High Street, Whitchurch, Buckinghamshire, HP22 4JT ℗
☎ 01296 641505
Est. 1978 *Stock size* Small
Stock General country antiques
Open Tues–Thurs Sat 10am–6pm or by appointment
Fairs Milton Keynes
Services Restoration of period furniture only

WINSLOW
⌂ Winslow Antique Centre
Contact Mr Taylor
✉ 15 Market Square, Winslow, Buckinghamshire, MK18 3AB ℗
☎ 01296 714540 ✆ 01296 714556
Est. 1990 *Stock size* Large
No. of dealers 20
Stock Country antiques, Staffordshire, pottery
Open Mon–Sat 10am–5pm Sun 1–5pm closed Wed

GLOUCESTERSHIRE

ALMONDSBURY
⊞ Tower House Decorative Antiques (LAPADA)
Contact Graham Pendrill or Tony Yoe Smith
✉ Tower House, Almondsbury, Gloucestershire, BS32 4HA ℗
☎ 01454 626233 ✆ 01454 619203
Est. 2003 *Stock size* Large
Stock 19thC decorative antiques
Open By appointment
Services Valuations

ASTON SUBEDGE
⊞ Cottage Farm Antiques
Contact Tony or Ann Willmore
✉ Cottage Farm, Aston Subedge, Chipping Campden, Gloucestershire, GL55 6PZ ℗
☎ 01386 438263 ✆ 01386 438263
⌖ info@cottagefarmantiques.co.uk
⌖ www.cottagefarmantiques.co.uk
Est. 1986 *Stock size* Large
Stock Original Victorian–Edwardian furniture (mostly pine) unfitted kitchens
Open Mon–Sun 9am–5pm
Services Shipping

BERKELEY
⌂ Berkeley Market
Contact Mr Keith Gardener
✉ 11 The Market Place, Berkeley, Gloucestershire, GL13 9BD ℗
☎ 01453 511032
⌖ 07802 304534
Est. 1988 *Stock size* Large
No. of dealers 5
Stock Bric-a-brac, period furniture, general antiques
Open Tues–Sat 9.30am–5pm or by appointment
Services Free tea or coffee

⊞ Proudfoot Antiques (FATG)
Contact Peter or Penny Proudfoot
✉ 16–18 High Street, Berkeley, Gloucestershire, GL13 9BJ ℗
☎ 01453 811513 ✆ 01453 511616
⌖ 07802 911894
⌖ berkeley.framing@tesco.net
Est. 1956 *Stock size* Medium

Stock General antiques
Open Mon–Sun 9.30am–5.30pm
Services Valuations, picture framing

BISLEY
⊞ High Street Antiques
Contact Heather Ross
✉ Bisley, Stroud, Gloucestershire, GL6 7BA ℗
☎ 01452 770153
⌖ 07703 755841
Est. 1975 *Stock size* Small
Stock Oriental rugs, small furniture, collectables
Open Mon–Sat 2–6pm
Fairs Malvern

BOURTON-ON-THE-WATER
⚲ Humberts Incorporating Tayler & Fletcher
Contact Mr Martin Lambert
✉ London House, High Street, GL54 2AP ℗
☎ 01451 821666 ✆ 01451 820818
⌖ 07074 821666
⌖ bourton@humberts.co.uk
⌖ www.humberts.co.uk/fineart
Est. 1790
Open Mon–Fri 9am–5.30pm Sat 9am–12.30pm
Sales Monthly furniture sales held at The Royal British Legion Hall, Bourton-on-the-Water Sat 10am, viewing Fri 1–6pm morning of sale from 7.30am. Three fine art and antiques sales per annum held at The Frog Mill Hotel, Andoversford Tues 10.30am, viewing Mon 1–7pm morning of sale from 8am
Catalogues Yes

⊞ Hungry Ghost
Contact Mrs V Kern
✉ 2 Bourton Link, Bourton Industrial Park, Bourton-on-the-Water, Gloucestershire, GL54 2HQ ℗
☎ 01451 822988 ✆ 01451 822220
⌖ interiors@hungry-ghost.co.uk
⌖ www.hungry-ghost.co.uk
Est. 1998 *Stock size* Large
Stock Chinese furniture, Oriental china, gifts
Open Mon–Fri 9am–5pm Sat by appointment

⊞ The Looking Glass
Contact Mrs A P Jones
✉ Portland House, Victoria

237

Street, Bourton-on-the-Water,
Gloucestershire,
GL54 2BX
☎ 01451 810818
Est. 2001 *Stock size* Small
Stock Glass, small furniture,
collectables, silver, pottery, china,
studio pottery
Open Mon–Sun 10am–5pm

CHALFORD

⊞ Minchinhampton Architectural Salvage Co (SALVO)
Contact Jemma Colborne
✉ Cirencester Road,
Aston Down, Chalford, Stroud,
Gloucestershire,
GL6 8PE 🅿
☎ 01285 760886 📠 01285 760838
🌐 masco@catbrain.com
🌐 www.catbrain.com
Est. 1983 *Stock size* Large
Stock Architectural antiques,
statuary, garden ornaments,
reclaimed materials, metalwork,
gates, staddle stones, window
frames, chimney pieces
Open Mon–Fri 9am–5pm
Sat 9am–3pm Sun 11am–2pm
Fairs Gatcombe Horse Trials
Services Valuations, garden
design

CHARLTON KINGS

⊞ Latchford Antiques
Contact Mrs R Latchford
✉ 203 London Road,
Charlton Kings, Cheltenham,
Gloucestershire,
GL52 6HX 🅿
☎ 01242 226263 📠 01242 226263
Est. 1985 *Stock size* Medium
Stock Victorian and pine, period
furniture, jewellery, gifts
Open Mon–Sat 10am–5.30pm
Sun 11am–4pm

CHELTENHAM

⊞ Antique & Modern Fireplaces (SALVO)
Contact Martin Canning
✉ 41–43 Great Norwood Street,
Cheltenham, Gloucestershire,
GL50 2BQ 🅿
☎ 01242 255235 📠 01242 255235
📱 07976 678027
🌐 antfires@btconnect.com
Est. 1996 *Stock size* Large
Stock Antique and modern

fireplaces and accessories
Open Mon–Sat 10am–5pm
Fairs Newark, Olympia
Services Restoration

⊞ Bicks Jewellers & Antiques
Contact Mr Morris
✉ 5 Montpellier Walk,
Cheltenham, Gloucestershire,
GL50 1SD 🅿
☎ 01242 524738 📠 01242 524738
Est. 1895 *Stock size* Medium
Stock Antique jewellery and
silver, occasional smalls, glass and
paintings
Open Tues–Sat 10am–4pm
Services Valuations, restoration

🏠 Cheltenham Antique Market
Contact Mr K Shave
✉ 54 Suffolk Road, Cheltenham,
Gloucestershire,
GL50 2AQ
☎ 01242 529812
Est. 1979 *Stock size* Large
No. of dealers 5
Stock Victorian–20thC furniture,
chandeliers
Open Tues–Sat 10am–5pm
Services Valuations

🔨 The Cotswold Auction Co
Contact Mrs Elizabeth Poole
✉ Chapel Walk Sale Room,
Chapel Walk, Cheltenham,
Gloucestershire,
GL50 3DS
☎ 01242 256363 📠 01242 571734
🌐 info@cotswoldauction.co.uk
🌐 www.cotswoldauction.co.uk
Est. 1890
Open Mon–Fri 9am–5.30pm
Sales General and specialist sale
Tues 11am, viewing day prior
10am–5pm day of sale 9–11am
Frequency Monthly
Catalogues Yes

⊞ Giltwood Gallery
Contact Mr Jeff Butt or
Mrs Gill Butt
✉ 30 Suffolk Parade,
Cheltenham, Gloucestershire,
GL50 2AE
☎ 01242 512482 📠 01242 512482
Est. 1994 *Stock size* Medium
Stock Eclectic furniture, mirrors,
chandeliers, pictures
Open Mon–Sat 9am–5.30pm
Services Restoration, upholstery

⊞ Greens of Cheltenham Ltd (GAGTL)
Contact Mr S Reynolds
✉ 15 Montpellier Walk,
Cheltenham, Gloucestershire,
GL50 1SD 🅿
☎ 01242 512088 📠 01242 512088
🌐 steve@greensofcheltenham.co.uk
🌐 www.greensofcheltenham.co.uk
Est. 1947 *Stock size* Large
Stock Jewellery, Oriental works
of art
Open Mon–Sat 9am–1pm 2–5pm
Fairs Olympia (June), Miami
Beach (Jan)
Services Jewellery restoration,
repairs

⊞ Catherine Hunt Oriental Antiques (TADA)
Contact Catherine Hunt
✉ PO Box 743, Cheltenham,
Gloucestershire,
GL52 5ZB 🅿
☎ 01242 227794 📠 01242 227794
📱 07976 319344
🌐 cathyhunt@btinternet.com
Est. 1986 *Stock size* Large
Stock Chinese ceramics, Ming,
Qing, furniture, textiles from
Ming onwards
Open By appointment
Fairs Wilton House, Penman Fair
Petersfield

🔨 Mallams
Contact Robin Fisher
✉ Grosvenor Galleries,
26 Grosvenor Street,
Cheltenham, Gloucestershire,
GL52 2SG 🅿
☎ 01242 235712 📠 01242 241943
🌐 cheltenham@mallams.co.uk
🌐 www.mallams.co.uk/fineart
Est. 1788
Open Mon–Fri 9am–5.30pm
Sat 9am–noon
Sales Antiques and general sale
Thurs 11am, viewing Tues
9am–7pm Wed prior 9am–5pm.
Ceramics sales, 2 per annum
Thurs 11am, viewing Tues
9am–7pm Wed 9am–5pm
Frequency Monthly
Catalogues Yes

⊞ Montpellier Clocks (BADA, CINOA)
Contact Toby Birch
✉ 13 Rotunda Terrace,
Cheltenham, Gloucestershire,
GL50 1SW 🅿
☎ 01242 242178 📠 01242 242178

ℹ info@montpellierclocks.com
ⓦ www.montpellierclocks.com
Est. 1959 *Stock size* Medium
Stock Longcase clocks, bracket
clocks, chronometers,
barometers, carriage clocks
Open Mon–Sat 9am–5pm
Services Restoration,
conservation (BADA qualified)

⊞ Patrick Oliver Antiques
Contact Michael Oliver
✉ 4 Tivoli Street, Cheltenham,
Gloucestershire,
GL50 2UW **P**
☎ 01242 519538
Est. 1902 *Stock size* Medium
Stock General antiques
Open Mon–Fri 9am–1pm
Services Valuations

⊞ Q & C Militaria (OMRS)
Contact Mr John Wright
✉ 22 Suffolk Road, Cheltenham,
Gloucestershire,
GL50 2AQ **P**
☎ 01242 519815 **❶** 01242 519815
⓪ 07778 613977
ℹ john@qc-militaria.freeserve.co.uk
Est. 1994 *Stock size* Large
Stock Militaria
Open Tues–Sat 10am–5pm
Fairs Britannia Medal Fairs
Services Medal mounting

⊞ Michael Rayner Bookseller
Contact Michael Rayner
✉ 11 St Lukes Road, Cheltenham,
Gloucestershire,
GL53 7JQ **P**
☎ 01242 512806
Est. 1988 *Stock size* Medium
Stock Antiquarian and second-
hand books
Open Wed–Sat 10am–6pm or by
appointment
Services Valuations, restoration

⊞ Catherine Shinn Decorative Textiles
Contact Catherine Shinn
✉ 5–6 Well Walk, Cheltenham,
Gloucestershire,
GL50 3JX **P**
☎ 01242 574546 **❶** 01242 578495
ⓦ www.catherineshinn.com
Est. 1988 *Stock size* Large
Stock Decorative textiles,
antique cushions, furnishings,
accessories
Open Mon–Sat 10am–5pm
Services Advice

⊞ Tapestry Antiques
Contact Mrs G Hall
✉ 33 Suffolk Parade,
Cheltenham, Gloucestershire,
GL50 2AE **P**
☎ 01242 512191
Est. 1984 *Stock size* Large
Stock Decorative antiques, pine,
beds, garden furniture, mirrors
Open Mon–Sat 10am–5.30pm

⊞ Telephone Lines Ltd
Contact Malcolm Percival
✉ 304 High Street, Cheltenham,
Gloucestershire,
GL50 3JF **P**
☎ 01242 582699 **❶** 01242 690033
ℹ info@telephonelines.net
ⓦ www.telephonelines.net
Est. 1992 *Stock size* Large
Stock Collectable telephones
Open Mon–Sat 9am–5.30pm
Fairs NUCF
Services Valuations, restoration

⊞ Triton Gallery
Contact Mr L Bianco
✉ 27 Suffolk Parade,
Cheltenham, Gloucestershire,
GL50 2AE **P**
☎ 01242 510477
Est. 1984 *Stock size* Large
Stock Antique mirrors,
chandeliers, paintings,
Continental and decorative
furniture
Open Mon–Sat 9am–5pm

⊞ Woodward Antique Clocks (LAPADA)
Contact Patricia Woodward or
Chris Daines
✉ 21 Suffolk Parade,
Cheltenham, Gloucestershire,
Gl50 2AE **P**
☎ 01242 245667
⓪ 07745 101081
ℹ woodwardclocks@onetel.com
ⓦ www.woodwardclocks.com
Est. 1990 *Stock size* Large
Stock 18th–19thC longcase, wall,
mantle, carriage clocks,
decorative furnishings
Open Wed–Sat 11am–5pm or by
appointment
Fairs NEC, LAPADA Cheltenham
Services Valuations, restoration

CHIPPING CAMDEN

⊞ Draycott Books
Contact Mr R H McClement
✉ 2 Sheep Street, Chipping

Campden, Gloucestershire,
GL55 6DX
☎ 01386 841392
ℹ draycottbooks@hotmail.com
Est. 1981 *Stock size* Medium
Stock Second-hand and
antiquarian books
Open Mon–Fri 10am–1pm 2–5pm
Sat 10am–5.30pm
Services Valuations, book search

⊞ Schoolhouse Antiques
Contact Mr Hammond
✉ The Headmaster's House,
The Old School, High Street,
Chipping Camden,
Gloucestershire,
GL55 6HB **P**
☎ 01386 841474
ℹ hamatschoolhouse@aol.com
ⓦ www.schoolhouseantiques.co.uk
Est. 1969 *Stock size* Large
Stock 17th–19thC furniture,
pictures, clocks, Victorian oil
paintings, music boxes
Open Mon–Sun 10am–5pm
Oct–March closed Thurs
Services Valuations

CIRENCESTER

⌂ Cirencester Arcade
Contact Mr P Bird
✉ 25 Market Place, Cirencester,
Gloucestershire,
GL7 2NX **P**
☎ 01285 644214
Est. 1995 *Stock size* Large
No. of dealers 70
Stock Furniture, china, glass,
jewellery, coins, postcards
Open Mon–Sat 9.30am–5pm
Sun 11am–5pm
Services Shipping, book search,
clock repair

⚒ Corinium Auctions (PTA)
Contact Mr K Lawson
✉ 25 Gloucester Street,
Cirencester, Gloucestershire,
GL7 2DJ **P**
☎ 01285 659057 **❶** 01285 652047
Est. 1990
Open Mon–Fri 10am–1pm 3–7pm
Sales 3 sales in Jan June Oct selling
printed ephemera, cigarette
cards, books, postcards etc
Catalogues Yes

⊞ Corner Cupboard Curios
Contact P. Larner
✉ 2 Church Street, Cirencester,

Gloucestershire,
GL7 1LE ⓟ
☎ 01285 655476
Est. 1975 *Stock size* Medium
Stock General antiques and
collectables
Open By appointment

♪ The Cotswold Auction Co (RICS)
Contact Elizabeth Poole
✉ **The Coach House,**
9–13 West Market Place,
Cirencester, Gloucestershire,
GL7 2NH ⓟ
☎ 01285 642420 ❶ 01285 642400
❶ info@cotswoldauction.co.uk
Ⓦ www.cotswoldauction.co.uk
Est. 1890
Open Mon–Fri 9am–5.30pm
Sales Held at The Bingham Hall,
King Street, Cirencester. General
antiques and specialist sales
Fri 10am, viewing Thurs prior
10am–8pm day of sale 9–10am
Frequency Monthly
Catalogues Yes

⊞ Forum Antiques
Contact Mr Weston Mitchell
✉ **Springfield Farm, Perrott's**
Brook, Cirencester,
Gloucestershire,
GL7 7DT ⓟ
☎ 01285 831821
❶ enquiries@westonmitchell.com
Ⓦ www.westonmitchell.com
Est. 1985 *Stock size* Small
Stock 18thC and earlier veneered
walnut, early oak, Empire furniture
Open By appointment only

⊞ Hare's Antiques Ltd
Contact Allan Hare
✉ **4 Blackjack Street, Cirencester,**
Gloucestershire,
GL7 2AA ⓟ
☎ 01285 640077 ❶ 01285 653513
Ⓜ 07860 350097/6
❶ hares@hares-antiques.com
Ⓦ www.hares-antiques.com
Est. 1972 *Stock size* Large
Stock 18th–19thC English
furniture, Howard upholstery
Open Mon–Sat 10am–5.30pm or
by appointment
Fairs Olympia
Services Restoration, upholstery

♪ Moore, Allen & Innocent (FNAVA)
Contact Mrs Marjorie Williams
✉ **Norcote, Cirencester,**

Gloucestershire,
GL7 5RH ⓟ
☎ 01285 646050 ❶ 01285 652862
❶ fineart@mooreallen.co.uk
Ⓦ www.mooreallen.co.uk
Est. 1852
Open Mon–Fri 9am–5.30pm
Sat 9am–noon
Sales Selective antiques sale
quarterly Fri 10am. Sporting bi-
annually Fri 10am. Picture sale bi-
annually Fri 10am. General sale
every 2 weeks Fri 9.30am,
viewing day prior 10.30am–8pm
sale day 9am–3pm
Frequency Twice monthly
Catalogues Yes

⊞ Original Architectural Antiques Co Ltd (SALVO)
Contact John Rawlinson
✉ **Ermin Farm, Cricklade Road,**
Cirencester, Gloucestershire,
GL7 5PN ⓟ
☎ 01285 869222 ❶ 01285 862221
Ⓜ 07774 979735
❶ info@originaluk.com
Ⓦ www.originaluk.com
Est. 1980 *Stock size* Large
Stock Architectural antiques,
fireplaces, columns, limestone
troughs, oak doors
Open Mon–Sat 9am–5pm Sun
10am–4pm
Services Valuations, restoration

⊞ Parlour Farm Antiques
Contact Mr N Grunfeld
✉ **Unit 12b, Wilkinson Road,**
Love Lane Industrial Estate,
Cirencester, Gloucestershire,
GL7 1YT ⓟ
☎ 01285 885336 ❶ 01285 885338
❶ info@parlourfarm.com
Ⓦ www.parlourfarm.com
Est. 1994 *Stock size* Large
Stock Reclaimed pine furniture,
kitchens, garden furniture
Open Mon–Sun 10am–5pm
Services Furniture made to order

♪ Specialised Postcard Auctions (PTA)
Contact Mr K Lawson
✉ **25 Gloucester Street,**
Cirencester, Gloucestershire,
GL7 2DJ ⓟ
☎ 01285 659057 ❶ 01285 652047
Est. 1976
Open As per viewing
Sales Auctions in Feb, Apr, May,
July, Sept, Nov Mon 2pm,
viewing Mon–Fri prior

10am–1pm 3–7pm day of sale
10am–2pm
Frequency Every 5 weeks
Catalogues Yes

⊞ William H Stokes (BADA, CADA)
Contact Mr Peter Bontoft
✉ **The Cloisters,**
6–8 Dollar Street, Cirencester,
Gloucestershire,
GL7 2AJ ⓟ
☎ 01285 653907 ❶ 01285 653907
❶ williampost@stokes.com
Est. 1968 *Stock size* Medium
Stock Early oak furniture,
associated items
Open Mon–Fri 9.30am–5.30pm
Sat 9.30am–4.30pm

⊞ Patrick Waldron Antiques (CADA)
Contact Patrick Waldron
✉ **18 Dollar Street, Cirencester,**
Gloucestershire,
GL7 2AN ⓟ
☎ 01285 652880
Est. 1994 *Stock size* Medium
Stock 18th–early 19thC English
furniture
Open Mon–Sat 9.30am–6pm
Services Restoration

COLEFORD

⊞ Simon Lewis Transport Books
Contact Mr S Lewis
✉ **PO Box 9, Coleford,**
Gloucestershire,
GL16 8YF ⓟ
☎ 01594 839369 ❶ 01594 839369
❶ simon@simonlewis.com
Ⓦ www.simonlewis.com
Est. 1985 *Stock size* Medium
Stock 1910–present transport-
related books
Open By appointment

CUTSDEAN

⊞ Architectural Heritage (CADA)
Contact Alex Puddy
✉ **Taddington Manor,**
Taddington, Nr Cutsdean,
Cheltenham, Gloucestershire,
GL54 5RY ⓟ
☎ 01386 584414 ❶ 01386 584236
❶ puddy@architectural-heritage.co.uk
Ⓦ www.architectural-heritage.co.uk
Est. 1973 *Stock size* Large
Stock Garden ornaments,

chimneypieces, wood wall
panelling
Open Mon–Fri 9.30am–5.30pm
Sat 10.30am–4.30pm
Fairs Chelsea, Tatton Park Flower
Show, Decorex
Services Valuations, bespoke and
replica garden ornaments,
chimney pieces, panelling

FAIRFORD

⊞ Blenheim Antiques (CADA)
Contact Mr Neil Hurdle
✉ **Acacia House, Market Place,
Fairford, Gloucestershire,
GL7 4AB** 🅿
☎ 01285 712094
Est. 1973 *Stock size* Medium
Stock 18th–19thC town and
country furniture, clocks,
accessories
Open Mon–Sat 9am–6pm

⊞ Anthony Hazeldine Oriental Carpets
Contact Anthony Hazeldine
✉ **High Street, Fairford,
Gloucestershire,
GL7 4AD** 🅿
☎ 01285 713400 📠 01285 713400
✉ tonyhazrugs@aol.com
Est. 1982 *Stock size* Medium
Stock Antique Oriental rugs and
carpets
Open Mon–Sat 9.30am–5pm
Services Valuations, restoration,
cleaning

GLOUCESTER

➴ The Cotswold Auction Co
Contact Mrs Elizabeth Poole
✉ **4–6 Clarence Street,
Gloucester, Gloucestershire,
GL1 1DX**
☎ 01452 521177 📠 01452 305883
✉ info@cotswoldauction.co.uk
🌐 www.cotswoldauction.co.uk
Est. 1890
Open Mon–Fri 9am–5.30pm
Sales Antiques, collectables and
general sale at St Barnabas
Church Hall Tues 10am, viewing
Mon 9am–9pm
Frequency Every 2 months
Catalogues Yes

⊞ The Cottage
Contact Mrs Helen Webb
✉ **55 Southgate Street,**

Gloucester, Gloucestershire,
GL1 1TX
☎ 01452 526027
Est. 1999 *Stock size* Large
Stock Antiques, collectables, gifts
of distinction
Open Mon–Sat 9.30am–4.30pm
Wed closed
Services Ceramic repairs

⌂ Gloucester Antiques Centre
Contact Mr Cant
✉ **The Historic Docks,
1 Severn Road, Gloucester,
Gloucestershire,
GL1 2LE** 🅿
☎ 01452 529716 📠 01452 307161
✉ mail@antiques-center.com
🌐 www.antiques-center.com
Est. 1990 *Stock size* Large
No. of dealers 140
Stock General antiques,
collectables
Open Mon–Sat 10am–5pm
Sun 1–5pm
Services Valuations, shipping,
book search

⊞ M & C Cards
Contact Mr M W Cant
✉ **Shop 30, The Antiques Centre,
Severn Road, Gloucester,
Gloucestershire,
GL1 2LE** 🅿
☎ 01452 506361 📠 01452 307161
✉ mick@mandccards.co.uk
🌐 www.mandccards.co.uk
Est. 1991 *Stock size* Medium
Stock Postcards, cigarette cards,
advertising collectables
Open Mon–Thurs 10am–5pm
Sun 1–5pm
Fairs Cheltenham Race Course
Card Fair

⊞ M & C Stamps
Contact Mr M W Cant
✉ **Shop 30, The Antiques Centre,
Severn Road, Gloucester,
Gloucestershire,
GL1 2LE** 🅿
☎ 01452 506361 📠 01452 307161
✉ mick@mandcstamps.co.uk
Est. 1984 *Stock size* Medium
Stock Stamps, first day covers,
accessories
Open Thurs–Mon 10am–5pm
Sun 1–5pm
Fairs Stamp Fair Cheltenham
Town Hall
Services Valuations, new issue
service

⌂ Upstairs Downstairs
Contact Vic or Shirley Foster
✉ **2 The Cottage, Severn Road,
Gloucester, Gloucestershire,
GL1 2LE** 🅿
☎ 01452 421170
📱 07786 316060
Est. 1990 *Stock size* Large
No. of dealers 5
Stock General antiques, clocks,
18th–19thC English and French
furniture
Open Mon–Sun 10am–5pm

KEMPSFORD

⊞ Ximenes Rare Books Inc (ABA, PBFA)
Contact Mr Stephen Weissman
✉ **Kempsford House, Kempsford,
Fairford, Gloucestershire,
GL7 4ET** 🅿
☎ 01285 810640 📠 01285 810650
✉ steve@ximenes.com
Est. 1965 *Stock size* Medium
Stock Rare books
Open By appointment only
Fairs Olympia (June)
Services Catalogues

LECHLADE

⊞ Corner House Antiques
Contact Mr John Downes-Hall
✉ **No 1 Railway Terrace,
Burford Road, Lechlade,
Gloucestershire,
GL7 3EP** 🅿
☎ 01367 252007
✉ enquiries@corner-house-
antiques.co.uk
🌐 www.corner-house-antiques.co.uk
Est. 1995 *Stock size* Medium
Stock Antique silver, jewellery,
country furniture, porcelain,
objets d'art
Open By appointment
Services Restoration of old silver,
valuations

⌂ Jubilee Hall Antiques Centre
Contact Mr John Calgie
✉ **Oak Street, Lechlade,
Gloucestershire,
GL7 3AY** 🅿
☎ 01367 253777
✉ sales@jubileehall.co.uk
🌐 www.jubileehall.co.uk
Est. 1997 *Stock size* Large
No. of dealers 25
Stock Furniture, objets d'art,
metalware, pottery, porcelain

Open Mon–Sat 10am–5pm
Sun 11am–5pm
Services Shipping, delivery
arranged

⌂ Lechlade Arcade
Contact Mr J Dickson
✉ 5–7 High Street, Lechlade,
Gloucestershire,
GL7 3AD 🅿
☎ 01367 252832
📱 07949 130875
Est. 1990 *Stock size* Large
No. of dealers 39
Stock 40 rooms of china, smalls,
small furniture, cast-iron, farm
tools and implements, medals
Open Mon–Sun 9am–5pm
Services House clearance

⌂ The Old Ironmongers
Antiques Centre
Contact Mark Serle or
Geoff Allen
✉ 5 Burford Street, Lechlade,
Gloucestershire,
GL7 3AP 🅿
☎ 01367 252397
Est. 2000 *Stock size* Large
No. of dealers 40
Stock Tools, town and country
furniture, gramophones, iron,
copperware, architectural,
books, gardening bygones, pot
lids, china
Open Mon–Sun 10am–5pm
Services Restoration, shipping,
book search

MINCHINHAMPTON

⊞ Mick & Fanny Wright
Contact Mr M Wright
✉ The Trumpet, West End,
Minchinhampton, Stroud,
Gloucestershire,
GL6 9JA
☎ 01453 883027
Est. 1979 *Stock size* Medium
Stock General antiques, more
smalls than furniture, second-
hand books, watches, clocks
Open Wed–Sat 10.30am–5.30pm
Fairs Kempton

MORETON-IN-MARSH

⊞ Benton Fine Art and
Antiques (LAPADA)
Contact Matthew Benton
✉ Regent House, High Street,
Moreton-in-Marsh,
Gloucestershire,

GL56 0AX 🅿
☎ 01608 652153 📠 01608 652153
📧 bentonfineart@excite.com
🌐 www.bentonfineart.com
Est. 1972 *Stock size* Medium
Stock 19th–20thC oils and
watercolours, 19th–20thC fine
furniture
Open Mon–Sat 10am–5.30pm
Sun 11am–5.30pm closed Tues
Fairs LAPADA Birmingham, NEC

⊞ Berry Antiques
(LAPADA)
Contact Mr C Berry
✉ 3 High Street, Moreton-in-
Marsh, Gloucestershire,
GL56 0AH 🅿
☎ 01608 652929 📠 01608 652929
📧 chris@berryantiques.co.uk
🌐 www.berryantiques.co.uk
Est. 1984 *Stock size* Medium
Stock 18th–19thC furniture,
19thC oil paintings
Open Mon–Sat 10am–5.30pm
Sun 11am–5pm closed Tues

⊞ Paula Biggs (Silver
Society)
Contact Paula Biggs
✉ Windsor House Antiques
Centre, High Street, Moreton-in-
Marsh, Gloucestershire,
GL56 0AD 🅿
☎ 01993 869245 📠 01993 869247
📧 john@thebiggs.co.uk
Est. 1978 *Stock size* Large
Stock Antiques, collectable silver
items, objects of virtue
Open Mon–Sat 10am–5pm
Tues Sun noon–5pm

⊞ Chandlers Antiques
Contact Ian Kellam
✉ Chandlers Cottage, High
Street, Moreton-in-Marsh,
Gloucestershire,
GL56 0AD
☎ 01608 651347 📠 01608 651347
Est. 1984 *Stock size* Large
Stock All small porcelain, glass,
jewellery, silver
Open By appointment
Fairs Shepton Mallet, Newark,
Ardingly
Services Valuations

⊞ Cox's Architectural
Salvage Yard Ltd (SALVO)
Contact Mr P Watson
✉ 10 Fosse Way Industrial Estate,
Stratford Road, Moreton-in-
Marsh, Gloucestershire,

GL56 9NQ 🅿
☎ 01608 652505 📠 01608 652881
📧 info@coxsarchitectural.co.uk
🌐 www.coxsarchitectural.co.uk
Est. 1991 *Stock size* Large
Stock Architectural antiques,
doors, fireplaces, Gothic-style
windows, floorboards,
flagstones, radiators
Open Mon–Fri 9am–5pm
Sat 9am–4pm
Services Valuations, shipping

⊞ Dale House
Contact Nicholas Allen
✉ High Street, Moreton-in-
Marsh, Gloucestershire,
GL56 0AD 🅿
☎ 01608 652950 📠 01608 652424
Est. 1973 *Stock size* Large
Stock 18th–early 20thC furniture,
works of art, interior decorating
items
Open Mon–Sat 10am–5.30pm
Sun 11am–5pm
Services Valuations

⊞ Jeffrey Formby
Antiques (BADA)
Contact Mr J Formby
✉ Orchard Cottage, East Street,
Moreton-in-Marsh,
Gloucestershire,
GL56 0LQ 🅿
☎ 01608 650558
📱 07770 755546
📧 jeff@formby-clocks.co.uk
🌐 www.formby-clocks.co.uk
Est. 1994 *Stock size* Small
Stock English clocks, horological
books, longcase, bracket,
skeleton, lantern clocks
Open By appointment
Fairs Olympia, BADA

⊞ Jon Fox Antiques (CADA)
Contact Mr Jon Fox
✉ High Street, Moreton-in-
Marsh, Gloucestershire,
GL56 0AD 🅿
☎ 01608 650325
Est. 1983 *Stock size* Large
Stock Garden antiques,
furniture, country bygones
Open Mon–Sat 9.30am–5.30pm
closed Tues

⊞ Grimes House Antiques
& Fine Art
Contact Stephen or
Val Farnsworth
✉ High Street, Moreton-in-
Marsh, Gloucestershire,

HEART OF ENGLAND
GLOUCESTERSHIRE • NORTHLEACH

GL56 OAT 🅿
☎ 01608 651029
📧 grimes_house@cix.co.uk
🌐 www.cranberryglass.co.uk
or www.grimeshouse.co.uk
Est. 1977 *Stock size* Large
Stock Victorian and later
coloured glass, Royal Worcester
Open Mon–Sat 9.30am–5.30pm
closed 1–2pm
Services Valuations

⊞ Howards of Moreton-in-Marsh
Contact Robert Light
✉ 1 Old Market Way, High
Street, Moreton-in-Marsh,
Gloucestershire,
GL56 0AX 🅿
☎ 01608 650583 📠 01608 652540
📱 07850 066312
📧 robert.light@talk21.com
Est. 1989 *Stock size* Medium
Stock Antique and modern silver
and jewellery
Open Mon–Sat 10am–5.30pm
Services Valuations, restoration

⌂ London House Antique Centre
Contact Mr Brian Roberts
✉ London House, High Street,
Moreton-in-Marsh,
Gloucestershire,
GL56 0AH 🅿
☎ 01608 651084
🌐 www.london-house-antiques.co.uk
Est. 1979 *Stock size* Large
No. of dealers 11
Stock General antiques, Chinese
porcelain, furniture, silver,
porcelain, pictures
Open Mon–Sun 10am–5pm

⊞ Seaford House Antiques (LAPADA)
Contact Mr or Mrs D Young
✉ Seaford House, High Street,
Moreton-in-Marsh,
Gloucestershire,
GL56 0AD 🅿
☎ 01608 652423 📠 01608 652423
📱 07714 485632
Est. 1988 *Stock size* Medium
Stock 18th–early 20thC small
furniture, porcelain, pictures,
objets d'art
Open Wed–Sat 10am–5pm
Sun 1–4pm

⌂ Windsor House Antiques Centre
Contact Mr T Sutton

✉ High Street, Moreton-in-Marsh, Gloucestershire,
GL56 0AD 🅿
☎ 01608 650993 📠 01858 565438
📧 windsorhouse@btinternet.com
🌐 www.windsorhouse.co.uk
Est. 1992 *Stock size* Large
No. of dealers 40
Stock High-quality general
antiques, porcelain, glass, silver,
clocks, paintings, furniture
Open Mon–Sat 10am–5pm
Sun 11am–4pm
Services Shipping, delivery

⊞ Gary Wright Antiques Ltd
Contact Gary or Gill Wright
✉ 5 Fosseway Business Park,
Stratford Road, Moreton-in-Marsh, Gloucestershire,
GL56 9NQ 🅿
☎ 01608 652007 📠 01608 652007
📱 07831 653843
📧 garywrightantiques@fsbdial.co.uk
🌐 www.garywrightantiques.co.uk
Est. 1972 *Stock size* Large
Stock Georgian mahogany,
walnut, marquetry, unusual and
decorative objects. 17th–19thC
good-quality furniture from £500
to £20,000
Open Mon–Sat 9.30am–5.30pm
Services Valuations, buys at
auction

⌂ Copper Kettle Antiques Centre
Contact Susan Blackwell
✉ 51 George Street, Nailsworth,
Gloucestershire,
GL6 0AG 🅿
☎ 01453 832233
Est. 2000 *Stock size* Large
No. of dealers 15
Stock General antiques,
collectables
Open Mon–Sat 10am–5pm

⊞ Old Mother Hubbard
Contact Anne Russell
✉ Doys Mill, Old Market,
Nailsworth, Gloucestershire,
GL6 0BL 🅿
☎ 01453 835679 📠 01453 833590
Est. 1998 *Stock size* Large
Stock General antiques,
furniture, pine, mirrors, lighting
Open Mon–Sat 9.30am–5.30pm
Sun 11am–5pm
Fairs Swinderby, Ardingly
Services Restoration, shipping

NEWENT

⊞ Jillings (LAPADA, CINOA, BADA)
Contact John or Doro Jillings
✉ Croft House, 17 Church Street,
Newent, Gloucestershire,
GL18 1PU 🅿
☎ 01531 822100 📠 01531 822666
📱 07973 830110
📧 clocks@jillings.com
🌐 www.jillings.com
Est. 1987 *Stock size* Medium
Stock 18th–early 19thC English
and Continental clocks
Open Fri Sat 9.30am–5.30pm or
by appointment
Fairs BADA, LAPADA, Olympia,
Harrogate
Services Valuations, repair and
restoration to all fine antique
clocks

⊞ The Antique Shop
Contact Mrs Berry
✉ 11 High Street, Newnham,
Gloucestershire,
GL14 1AD 🅿
☎ 01594 516460
Est. 2000 *Stock size* Large
Stock China, silver, brass, copper,
furniture
Open Mon–Sat 10am–1pm
2–5pm closed Wed

⊞ Christopher Saunders (PBFA, ABA)
Contact Mr C Saunders
✉ Kingston House, High Street,
Newnham, Gloucestershire,
GL14 1BB 🅿
☎ 01594 516030 📠 01594 517273
📧 chrisbooks@aol.com
🌐 www.cricket-books.com
Est. 1980 *Stock size* Large
Stock Antiquarian cricket books,
memorabilia
Open By appointment only
Fairs PBFA

NORTHLEACH

⊞ Keith Harding's World of Mechanical Music
Contact Keith Harding
✉ The Oak House, High Street,
Northleach, Gloucestershire,
GL54 3ET 🅿
☎ 01451 860181 📠 10451 861133
📧 keith@mechanicalmusic.co.uk
🌐 www.mechanicalmusic.co.uk
Est. 1961 *Stock size* Medium
Stock Mechanical musical

antiques, clocks
Open Mon–Sun 10am–6pm
closed Christmas Day Boxing Day
Services Restoration, museum

NORTON

⊞ Ronsons
Contact Ron Jones
✉ Norton Barn, Wainlodes Lane, Sandhurst Lane, Norton, Gloucester, Gloucestershire, GL2 9LN ▯
☎ 01452 731236 ✆ 01452 731888
📱 07714 266414
✉ info@ronsonsreclamation.co.uk
🌐 www.ronsonsreclamation.com
Est. 1982 *Stock size* Large
Stock Architectural antiques
Open Mon–Sat 8am–5pm
Services Shipping

SOUTHAM

➶ BK Art & Antiques (SOFAA)
Contact Mr Simon Chorley
✉ The Tithe Barn Sale Room, Southam Lane, Southam, Cheltenham, Gloucestershire, GL52 3NY ▯
☎ 01452 880030 ✆ 01452 880088
✉ artantiques@bkonline.co.uk
🌐 www.bkonline.co.uk
Est. 1862
Open Mon–Fri 8.30am–5.30pm
Sales Art and antiques sales, telephone for details
Frequency Every 6 weeks
Catalogues Yes

STOW-ON-THE-WOLD

⊞ Yvonne Adams Antiques (BADA)
Contact Yvonne Adams
✉ The Coffee House, 3–4 Church Street, Stow-on-the-Wold, Gloucestershire, GL54 1BB ▯
☎ 01451 832015 ✆ 01451 833826
📱 07973 961101
✉ antiques@adames.demon.co.uk
🌐 www.antiquemeissen.com
Est. 1955 *Stock size* Large
Stock 18thC Meissen porcelain
Open By appointment
Fairs Olympia June
Services Valuations

⊞ Ashton Gower Antiques (LAPADA)
Contact Chris Gower

or Barry Ashton
✉ 9 Talbot Court, Market Square, Stow-on-the-Wold, Gloucestershire, GL54 1BQ ▯
☎ 01451 870699 ✆ 01451 870699
✉ ashtongower@aol.com
Est. 1987 *Stock size* Large
Stock Gilded mirrors, French decorative furniture, 20thC Lucite
Open Mon–Sat 10am–5pm
Services Valuations

⊞ Baggott Church Street Ltd (BADA, CADA)
Contact Mrs C Baggott
✉ Church Street, Stow-on-the-Wold, Gloucestershire, GL54 1BB ▯
☎ 01451 830370 ✆ 01451 832174
✉ info@baggottantiques.com
🌐 www.baggottantiques.com
Est. 1976 *Stock size* Large
Stock English 17th–19thC furniture, paintings, objects
Open Mon–Sat 9.30am–5.30pm
Services Annual exhibition in October

⊞ Duncan J Baggott (LAPADA, CADA)
Contact Mrs C Baggott
✉ Woolcomber House, Sheep Street, Stow-on-the-Wold, Gloucestershire, GL54 1AA
☎ 01451 830662 ✆ 01451 832174
✉ info@baggottantiques.com
🌐 www.baggottantiques.com
Est. 1967 *Stock size* Large
Stock English furniture, portraits, landscape paintings, domestic metalware, fireplace accoutrements, pottery, glass, garden statuary, ornaments
Open Mon–Sat 9.30am–5.30pm
Services Annual exhibition in October

⊞ Paula Biggs (Silver Society)
Contact Paula Biggs
✉ Durham House, Sheep Street, Stow-on-the-Wold, Gloucestershire, GL54 1AA ▯
☎ 01993 869245 ✆ 01993 869247
✉ john@thebiggs.co.uk
Est. 1978 *Stock size* Large
Stock Antiques, collectable silver items, objects of virtue
Open Mon–Sat 10am–5pm
Sun 11am–5pm

⊞ Bookbox (PBFA)
Contact Mrs C Fisher
✉ Chantry House, Sheep Street, Stow-on-the-Wold, Gloucestershire, GL54 1AA ▯
☎ 01451 831214
Est. 1977 *Stock size* Medium
Stock Antiquarian, second-hand books, 19th–20thC good literature, art, topography, hunting, shooting, fishing, drama, good mixed general stock
Open Mon–Sat 11am–1pm 2.15–5pm closed Wed (Jan–March Thurs–Sat only) phone first in winter

⊞ La Chaise Antiques
Contact Roger Clark
✉ Beauport Sheep Street, Stow-on-the-Wold, Gloucestershire, GL54 1AA ▯
☎ 01451 830582
✉ lachaise@tiscali.co.uk
Est. 1963 *Stock size* Medium
Stock Furniture
Open Mon–Sat 9am–6pm
Sun 10am–4pm

⊞ Christopher Clarke Antiques (LAPADA, CADA, BACA Award Winner 2004)
Contact Mr Simon Clarke
✉ The Fosseway, Stow-on-the-Wold, Gloucestershire, GL54 1JS ▯
☎ 01451 830476 ✆ 01451 830300
📱 07971 287733
✉ cclarkeantiques@aol.com
🌐 www.campaignfurniture.com
Est. 1961 *Stock size* Large
Stock Campaign, military and English furniture, travel items
Open Mon–Sat 9.30am–5.30pm or by appointment
Fairs Olympia (June November), CADA (October)

⊞ Country Life Antiques
Contact Ann or David Rosa
✉ Grey House, The Square, Stow-on-the-Wold, Gloucestershire, GL54 1AF ▯
☎ 01451 831564 ✆ 01451 831564
✉ grey.house@ukonline.co.uk
Est. 1974 *Stock size* Large
Stock Scientific instruments, decorative accessories, metalware, furniture, paintings
Open Mon–Sat 10am–5pm

⌂ Durham House
Contact Mr Alan Smith
✉ Sheep Street, Stow-on-the-Wold, Gloucestershire, GL54 1AA ℗
☎ 01451 870404
✉ durhamhousegb@aol.com
ⓦ www.durhamHouseGB.com
Est. 1994 *Stock size* Large
No. of dealers 30
Stock 4 large showrooms covering 2000 sq ft of general antiques, silver, clocks, oak, mahogany, porcelain, Derby, Worcester, Staffordshire, Mason's, linens, prints, paintings, samplers, sewing accessories, town and country furniture
Open Mon–Sat 10am–5pm Sun 11am–5pm

⌂ Fox Cottage Antiques
Contact Miss Sue London
✉ Digbeth Street, Stow-on-the-Wold, Gloucestershire, GL54 1BN ℗
☎ 01451 870307
Est. 1995 *Stock size* Medium
No. of dealers 10
Stock Pottery, porcelain, glassware, silver, plated ware, small furniture, decorative items, country goods, mainly pre-1910
Open Mon–Sat 10am–5pm

⊞ Grandfather Clock Shop
Contact Mr W J Styles
✉ The Little House, Sheep Street, Stow-on-the-Wold, Gloucestershire, GL54 1JS ℗
☎ 01451 830455 ✆ 01451 830455
✉ info@stylesofstow.co.uk
ⓦ www.stylesofstow.co.uk
Est. 1996 *Stock size* Large
Stock Clocks including longcase clocks, 18th–19thC furniture, 19th–20thC oil paintings and watercolours
Open Mon–Sat 10am–5pm or by appointment
Services Valuations, restoration

⊞ Keith Hockin Antiques (BADA, CADA)
Contact Mr K Hockin
✉ The Elms, The Square, Stow-on-the-Wold, Gloucestershire, GL54 1AF ℗
☎ 01451 831058
✉ keith.hockin@ruralsat.net
Est. 1973 *Stock size* Medium
Stock 17th–early 18thC English

oak furniture, pewter, early brass, 16th–17thC wood carvings
Open Thurs–Sat 10am–5pm closed 1–2pm or by appointment

⊞ Huntington Antiques Ltd (LAPADA, CADA, BACA Award Winner 2002)
✉ Church Street, Stow-on-the-Wold, Gloucestershire, GL54 1BE ℗
☎ 01451 830842 ✆ 01451 832211
✉ info@huntington-antiques.com
ⓦ www.huntington-antiques.com
Est. 1975 *Stock size* Large
Stock Early furniture and works of art, tapestries, English and Continental metalwork
Open Mon–Sat 9.30am–5.30pm
Fairs LAPADA London and Birmingham
Services Valuations, restoration, interior decoration

⊞ Roger Lamb Antiques and Works of Art (LAPADA, CADA)
Contact Roger Lamb
✉ The Square, Stow-on-the-Wold, Gloucestershire, GL54 1AB ℗
☎ 01451 831371 ✆ 01451 832485
ⓜ 07960 391959
Est. 1993 *Stock size* Medium
Stock 18th–early 19thC period furniture, decorative oil paintings, watercolours, antique lighting, accessories
Open Mon–Sat 10am–5pm
Fairs LAPADA

⊞ Malthouse Antiques
Contact Chris Mortimer
✉ The Malthouse, Digbeth Street, Stow-on-the-Wold, Gloucestershire, GL54 1BN ℗
☎ 01451 830592
✉ malthousestow@aol.com
ⓦ www.malthouseantiques.co.uk
Est. 2003 *Stock size* Large
Stock Furniture, paintings, specialist books, dental and medical items, wine-related material, ceramics, boxes and other interesting collectables
Open Mon–Sat 10am–5.30pm Sun in summer 11am–5pm closed Tues
Fairs NEC
Services Valuations, restoration, shipping, book search, coffee lounge

⊞ Simon Nutter and Thomas King-Smith
Contact Mr T M King-Smith or Mr S W Nutter
✉ Wraggs Row, Fosseway, Stow-on-the-Wold, Gloucestershire, GL54 1JT
☎ 01451 830658
ⓜ 07775 864394
Est. 1975 *Stock size* Medium
Stock 18th–19thC furniture, silver, porcelain
Open Mon–Sat 9.30am–5.30pm
Fairs Westonbirt
Services Valuations

⊞ Park House Antiques
Contact Mr George Sutton
✉ 8 Park Street, Stow-on-the-Wold, Gloucestershire, GL54 1AQ ℗
☎ 01451 830159
✉ teamsutton@btinternet.com
ⓦ www.thetoymuseum.com
Est. 1987 *Stock size* Large
Stock Old toys, textiles, small furniture, porcelain, pottery
Open Feb–Apr June–Oct Wed–Sat 10am–1pm 2–4.30pm other times by appointment
Services Repairs, toy museum, teddy bear repair

⊞ Antony Preston Antiques (BADA)
Contact Antony Preston
✉ The Square, Stow-on-the-Wold, Gloucestershire, GL54 1AB ℗
☎ 01451 831586
Est. 1977 *Stock size* Large
Stock Early 18th–19thC English furniture and objets d'art
Open Mon–Sat 9.30am–5.30pm
Fairs Grosvenor House, BADA

⊞ Michael Rowland Antiques
Contact Michael Rowland
✉ Stow-on-the-Wold, Gloucestershire, GL54 ℗
ⓜ 07779 509753
Est. 1991 *Stock size* Medium
Stock 17th–18thC oak and fruitwood country furniture
Open By appointment

⊞ Ruskin Decorative Arts (CADA)
Contact Mr or Mrs T W Morris
✉ 5 Talbot Court, Stow-on-the-Wold, Gloucestershire,

GL54 1DP 🅿
☎ 01451 832254 ☏ 01451 832167
🅴 william.anne@ruskindecarts.co.uk
Est. 1989 *Stock size* Small
Stock Decorative Arts 1880–1960,
Arts and Crafts, Art Nouveau, Art
Deco, the Cotswold Movement
including the Guild of
Handicraft, Gordon Russell,
Gimson and the Barnsleys, Heals
furniture, Scandinavian glass
Open Mon–Sat 10am–5.30pm
Fairs NEC, Antiques for Everyone
Services Valuations for insurance
and probate

Key to Symbols

⊞	=	Dealer
🏠	=	Antiques Centre
🔨	=	Auction House
✉	=	Address
🅿	=	Parking
☎	=	Telephone No.
Ⓜ	=	Mobile tel No.
☏	=	Fax No.
🅴	=	E-mail address
🆆	=	Website address

⊞ Arthur Seager Antiques
Contact Mr A Seager
✉ 50 Sheep Street,
Stow-on-the-Wold,
Gloucestershire,
GL54 1AA 🅿
☎ 01451 831605
🅴 arthur.seager@btconnect.com
🆆 www.arthurseager.co.uk or
www.arthurseager.moonfruit.com
Est. 1979 *Stock size* Medium
Stock 16th–17thC objects, oak
furniture, carvings
Open Thurs–Sat 10am–4pm

⊞ Stow Antiques (CADA, LAPADA, CINOA)
Contact Mrs H Hutton-Clarke
✉ The Square,
Stow-on-the-Wold,
Gloucestershire,
GL54 1AF 🅿
☎ 01451 830377 ☏ 01451 870018
🅴 hazel@stowantiques.demon.co.uk
Est. 1969 *Stock size* Large
Stock 18th–19thC mahogany
furniture, large tables, sets of
chairs, sideboards, bookcases
Open Mon–Sat 10am–5.30pm or
by appointment
Services Shipping

🏠 Tudor House
Contact Mr Peter Collingridge
✉ Sheep Street,
Stow-on-the-Wold,
Gloucestershire,
GL54 1AA 🅿
☎ 01451 830021 ☏ 01451 830021
Ⓜ 07860 581858
🆆 www.tudor-house-antiques.com
Est. 2001 *Stock size* Large
No. of dealers 22
Stock 18th–early 20thC furniture,
clocks, watercolours, porcelain,
metalware, fountain pens,
garden furniture, lighting, Arts
and Crafts
Open Mon–Sat 10am–5pm
Sun 11am–4pm

🏠 Twyford Antiques Centre
Contact Rob Pierce
✉ Wick Hill, Stow-on-the-Wold,
Gloucestershire,
GL54 1HY 🅿
☎ 01451 870003
Est. 1986 *Stock size* Large
No. of dealers 15
Stock General antiques,
collectables
Open Mon–Sat 9am–5pm
Sun 10am–4pm
Services Coffee shop

⊞ Vanbrugh House Antiques
Contact John or Monica Sands
✉ Vanbrugh House, Park Street,
Stow-on-the-Wold,
Gloucestershire,
GL54 1AQ 🅿
☎ 01451 830797
Est. 1978 *Stock size* Medium
Stock Early fine furniture,
musical boxes, early maps
Open Mon–Sat 10am–5.30pm
Services Valuations

STROUD

⊞ Ian Hodgkins & Co Ltd (ABA)
Contact Mr Simon Weager
✉ Upper Vatch Mill,
The Vatch, Stroud,
Gloucestershire,
GL6 7JY 🅿
☎ 01453 764270 ☏ 01453 755233
🅴 i.hodgkins@dial.pipex.com
enquiries@ianhodgkins.com
🆆 www.ianhodgkins.com
Est. 1974 *Stock size* Medium
Stock Antiquarian, 19thC art,

literature, children's books
Open By appointment
Fairs Chelsea Book Fair
(November)

⊞ Inprint
Contact Mr Mike Goodenough
✉ 31 High Street, Stroud,
Gloucestershire,
GL5 1AJ 🅿
☎ 01453 759731 ☏ 01453 759731
🅴 enquiries@inprint.co.uk
🆆 www.inprint.co.uk
Est. 1979 *Stock size* Medium
Stock Antiquarian, second-hand,
out-of-print books on fine,
applied and performing arts
Open Mon–Sat 10am–5pm
Services Book search

TETBURY

⊞ Philip Adler Antiques (CADA)
Contact Mr P Adler
✉ 27 Long Street, Tetbury,
Gloucestershire,
GL8 8AA 🅿
☎ 01666 505759 ☏ 01452 770525
Ⓜ 07710 477891
🅴 philipadlerantiques@hotmail.com
Est. 1979 *Stock size* Large
Stock Eclectic, general stock of
decorative and period antiques
Open Mon–Sat 10am–6pm or by
appointment
Fairs Bath Fair
Services Valuations, restoration

⊞ Alchemy Antiques
Contact Debbie Sayers
✉ The Old Chapel, Long Street,
Tetbury, Gloucestershire,
GL8 8AA
☎ 01666 505281
Est. 2004 *Stock size* Large
Stock Treen, metalware, English,
French furniture, oak, fruitwood
and mahogany furniture,
antiquities, silver, porcelain, glass,
lighting, gardening antiques
Open Mon–Sat 10am–5pm
Services Shipping

⊞ Alderson (BADA, CINOA)
Contact Mr C J Alderson
✉ 58 Long Street, Tetbury,
Gloucestershire,
GL8 8AQ 🅿
☎ 01666 500888
Est. 1976 *Stock size* Medium
Stock 18th–19thC furniture and

works of art
Open Mon–Sat 10am–5pm or by appointment
Fairs Olympia

⊞ The Ark Angel
Contact Arthur Smith
✉ 33 Long Street, Tetbury, Gloucestershire, GL8 8AA 🅿
☎ 01666 505820
Est. 2001 *Stock size* Large
Stock Decorative antiques, garden furniture
Open Mon–Sat 10am–5pm

⊞ Art Nouveau Lighting
Contact Jennie Horrocks
✉ Top Banana Antique Mall, 1 New Church Street, Tetbury, Gloucestershire, GL8 8DS 🅿
📱 07836 264896
📧 info@jenniehorrocks.plus.com
🌐 www.artnouveaulighting.co.uk
Est. 1978 *Stock size* Medium
Stock Art Nouveau and Edwardian lighting
Open Mon–Sat 10am–5.30pm
Sun 11am–5pm
Fairs NEC, Newark

⊞ Artique (TADA)
Contact George Bristow
✉ Talboys House, 17 Church Street, Tetbury, Gloucestershire, GL8 8JG
☎ 01666 503597 📠 01666 503597
📱 07836 337038
📧 george@artique.demon.co.uk
🌐 www.artique.uk.com
Est. 1990 *Stock size* Large
Stock Central Asian artefacts, rugs, jewellery, furniture, textiles, architectural items
Open Mon–Wed 10am–6pm
Thurs Fri 10am–8pm
Sun noon–4pm

⊞ Ball & Claw Antiques (TADA)
Contact Mr Chris Kirkland
✉ 45 Long Street, Tetbury, Gloucestershire, GL8 8AA 🅿
☎ 01666 502440
📱 07957 870423
🌐 www.ballandclaw.co.uk or www.antiquekitchentables.co.uk
Est. 1994 *Stock size* Medium
Stock 17th–19thC furniture, Arts and Crafts, engravings, pictures,

prints, ceramics, smalls
Open Mon–Sat 10am–5pm
Services Valuations

⊞ Paula Biggs (Silver Society)
Contact Paula Biggs
✉ Long Street Antiques, Stamford House, 14 Long Street, Tetbury, Gloucestershire, GL8 8AQ 🅿
☎ 01993 869245 📠 01993 869247
📧 john@thebiggs.co.uk
Est. 1978 *Stock size* Large
Stock Antiques, collectable silver items, objects of virtue
Open Mon–Sat 10am–5pm
Sun noon–5pm

➤ Bonhams
✉ 22a Long Street, Tetbury, Gloucestershire, GL8 8AQ
☎ 01666 502200 📠 01666 505107
📧 tetbury@bonhams.com
🌐 www.bonhams.com
Open Mon–Fri 9am–5.30pm
Sales Regional office. Regular sales held in London and in our salerooms across the country. Free auction valuations; insurance and probate valuations

⊞ Bread & Roses
Contact Rose Smith
✉ The Ark Angel, 33 Long Street, Tetbury, Gloucestershire, GL8 8AA 🅿
☎ 01666 505820
📱 07810 508804
Est. 1995 *Stock size* Large
Stock Kitchenware
Open Mon–Sat 10am–5pm
Fairs NEC, Newark

⊞ Breakspeare Antiques (LAPADA, CADA)
Contact Michael or Sylvia Breakspeare
✉ 36 Long Street, Tetbury, Gloucestershire, GL8 8AQ 🅿
☎ 01666 503122
📧 mark.breakspeare@hemscott.net
🌐 www.breakspeare-antiques.com
Est. 1962 *Stock size* Medium
Stock English period furniture, mahogany, 1750–1835, early veneered walnut, 1690–1740
Open Mon–Sat 10am–5pm

⊞ Geoffrey Breeze Antique Canes
Contact Mr Breeze

✉ Office 262, 3 Edgar Buildings, George Street, Bath, Somerset, BA1 2FL 🅿
📱 07740 534844
📧 geoffrey@geoffreybreeze.co.uk or info@antiquecanes.co.uk
🌐 www.antiquecanes.co.uk
Est. 1972 *Stock size* Medium
Stock Canes, walking sticks
Open By appointment
Fairs Antiques for Everyone, Battersea Decorative Arts

⊞ The Chest of Drawers (TADA)
Contact Mrs P Bristow
✉ 24 Long Street, Tetbury, Gloucestershire, GL8 8AQ 🅿
☎ 01666 502105
📱 07710 292064
Est. 1969 *Stock size* Medium
Stock English furniture, 17thC onwards
Open Mon–Fri 9.30am–5.30pm

⊞ Cottage Collectibles
Contact Mrs S Kettle
✉ Long Street Antiques, 14 Long Street, Tetbury, Gloucestershire, G18 8AQ 🅿
☎ 01666 500850
📱 07967 713512
📧 sheila@cottagecollectibles.co.uk
🌐 www.cottagecollectibles.co.uk
Est. 1995 *Stock size* Medium
Stock English and Continental country antiques, kitchenware, pine furniture, garden and dairy tools
Open Mon–Sat 10am–5pm
Sun noon–4pm
Fairs NEC, SECC
Services Restoration

⊞ Day Antiques (BADA, CADA)
Contact Mrs A or Roger Day
✉ 5 New Church Street, Tetbury, Gloucestershire, GL8 8DS 🅿
☎ 01666 502413 📠 01666 505894
📱 07836 565763
📧 dayantiques@lineone.net
🌐 www.dayantiques.com
Est. 1975 *Stock size* Medium
Stock Early oak, country furniture, related items
Open Mon–Sat 10am–5pm

⊞ The Decorator Source (TADA)
Contact Mr Colin Gee

HEART OF ENGLAND
GLOUCESTERSHIRE • TETBURY

⊠ **39a Long Street, Tetbury,
Gloucestershire,
GL8 8AA** 🅿
☎ 01666 505358 📠 01666 505358
Est. 1979 *Stock size* Large
Stock French and Italian
provincial furniture, accessories,
English country house furniture
and objects
Open Mon–Sat 10am–5.30pm or
by appointment
Services Shipping

⊞ **Jan Hicks Antiques
(TVADA, LAPADA)**
Contact Jan Hicks
⊠ **Top Banana,
32 Long Street, Tetbury,
Gloucestershire,
GL8 8AQ** 🅿
☎ 01488 683986 📠 01488 681222
📱 07770 230686
📧 antiques@janhicks.com
Est. 1987 *Stock size* Large
Stock 18thC and earlier French
and English country furniture,
oil paintings
Open Mon–Sat 10am–5.30pm
Sun (summer only) 11am–5pm
Fairs TVADA, Antiques &
Audacity (Arundel Castle)

⊞ **Jester Antiques
(TADA)**
Contact Mr Peter Bairsto
⊠ **10 Church Street, Tetbury,
Gloucestershire,
GL8 8JG** 🅿
☎ 01666 505125 📠 01666 505125
📱 07974 232783
📧 sales@jesterantiques.co.uk
🌐 www.jesterantiques.co.uk
Est. 1995 *Stock size* Medium
Stock Exciting, colourful stock
of furniture, decorative items,
lamps, mirrors, garden and
architectural antiques
Open Mon–Sun 10am–5.30pm
Services Shipping

⊞ **Lansdown Antiques
(BABAADA)**
Contact Chris or Ann Kemp
⊠ **1 New Church Street, Tetbury,
Gloucestershire,
GL8 8DS** 🅿
📱 07947 668279 or 07801 013663
📧 lansdown-antiques@lineone.net
Est. 1983 *Stock size* Medium
Stock Painted pine and country
furniture, metalware and
decorative items
Open Mon–Sat 10am–5.30pm

Sun 1–5pm
Fairs Bath Decorative and
Antiques Fair

🏠 **Long Street Antiques**
Contact Ray or Samantha White
⊠ **Stamford House, 14 Long
Street, Tetbury, Gloucestershire,
GL8 8AQ** 🅿
☎ 01666 500850 📠 01666 500950
📱 07876 793248
📧 longstantiques@aol.com
🌐 www.longstreetantiques.co.uk
Est. 2004 *Stock size* Large
No. of dealers 45–50
Stock Antiques, collectables,
works of art, kitchenware,
textiles, glass, silver, country and
antique furniture
Open Mon–Sat 10am–5pm
Sun Bank Holidays noon–4pm
Services Over 45 specialist
dealers displaying on two floors

⊞ **Merlin Antiques**
Contact Mr Brian Smith
⊠ **Shops 4 & 5, Chipping Court
Shopping Mall, Chipping Street,
Tetbury, Gloucestershire,
GL8 8ES** 🅿
☎ 01666 505008
Est. 1994 *Stock size* Large
Stock Mixed, china, pictures,
Victorian–Edwardian furniture,
costume jewellery, reproduction
furniture, garden stoneware
Open Mon–Sat 9.30am–5pm
Sun by appointment
Services Valuations, repairs,
items purchased, house clearance

⊞ **Bobbie Middleton
(TADA, CADA)**
Contact Bobbie Middleton
⊠ **Tetbury, Gloucestershire,
GL9** 🅿
📱 07774 192660
📧 bobbiemiddleton@lineone.net
🌐 www.bobbiemiddleton.com
Est. 1986 *Stock size* Medium
Stock Classic country house
furniture including painted
pieces, mirrors, decorative
accessories, upholstered furniture
Open By appointment
Services Antique search service,
interior design

⊞ **Peter Norden Antiques
(LAPADA, TADA)**
Contact Mr P Norden
⊠ **61 Long Street, Tetbury,
Gloucestershire,**

GL8 8AA 🅿
☎ 01666 503854 📠 01666 505595
📱 07778 013108
📧 peternorden_antiques@lineone.net
🌐 www.peter-norden-antiques.co.uk
Est. 1960 *Stock size* Medium
Stock Early oak and country
furniture, early wood carvings,
pewter, brass, treen
Open Mon–Sat 10am–5.30pm or
by appointment
Services Valuations

⊞ **Porch House Antiques
(TADA)**
Contact Mrs L A Woodburn
⊠ **42 Long Street, Tetbury,
Gloucestershire,
GL8 8AQ** 🅿
☎ 01666 502687
📱 07715 32793
Est. 1976 *Stock size* Large
Stock 17th–20thC furniture,
decorative items
Open Mon–Sat 10am–5pm most
Sundays

⊞ **Sieff (TADA)**
Contact Kirsty Sylvester
⊠ **49 Long Street, Tetbury,
Gloucestershire,
GL8 8AA** 🅿
☎ 01666 504477 📠 01666 504478
📧 sieff@sieff.co.uk
🌐 www.sieff.co.uk
Est. 1984 *Stock size* Large
Stock 18th–19thC French
provincial fruitwood, 20thC
furniture
Open Mon–Sat 10am–5.30pm
Fairs Decorative Antique &
Textile Fair

⊞ **Tetbury Old Books**
Contact Mr P M Gibbons
⊠ **4 The Chipping, Tetbury,
Gloucestershire,
GL8 8ET** 🅿
☎ 01666 504330
📧 oldbooks@tetbury.co.uk
Est. 1994 *Stock size* Medium
Stock Antiquarian and second-
hand books, prints and maps,
specialized collection of Black's
colourbooks
Open Mon–Sat 10am–6pm
Sun 11am–5pm

🏠 **Top Banana 1 Antiques
Mall**
Contact Sarah Townsend
⊠ **1 New Church Street, Tetbury,
Gloucestershire,**

GL8 8DS ☐
☎ 0871 288 1102 ✆ 0871 288 1103
✉ info@topbananaantiques.com
ⓦ www.topbananaantiques.com
Est. 2001 *Stock size* Large
No. of dealers 60
Stock A group shop of decorative antiques and interior inspiration, period brown furniture, painted original pine
Open Mon–Sat 10am–5.30pm
Sun (summer only) 11am–5pm
Services Packing, shipping

⌂ **Top Banana 2 Antiques Mall**
Contact Peter Bartholomew
✉ 32 Long Street, Tetbury, Gloucestershire,
GL8 8AQ ☐
☎ 08712 881110 ✆ 08712 881103
✉ info@topbananaantiques.com
ⓦ www.topbananaantiques.com
Est. 2002 *Stock size* Large
No. of dealers 15
Stock Decorative French furniture, antiquarian books, leather sofas, period brown and 1960s chrome furniture, country antiques
Open Mon–Sat 10am–5.30pm
Sun (summer only) 11am–5pm
Services Packing, shipping

⌂ **Top Banana 3 Antiques Mall**
Contact Julian Tatham-Losh
✉ 48 Long Street, Tetbury, Gloucestershire,
GL8 8AQ ☐
☎ 08712 883058
✉ info@topbananaantiques.com
ⓦ www.topbananaantiques.com
Est. 2002 *Stock size* Large
No. of dealers 8
Stock Antique and contemporary jewellery, English and French mirrors
Open Mon–Sat 10am–5.30pm
Sun (summer only) 11am–5pm
Services Packing, shipping, storage

⌂ **Top Banana 4 Antiques Mall**
Contact Julian Tatham-Losh
✉ 46 Long Street, Tetbury, Gloucestershire,
GL8 8AQ ☐
☎ 08712 883058 ✆ 08712 881103
✉ info@topbananaantiques.com
ⓦ www.topbananaantiques.com
Est. 2005 *Stock size* Large
No. of dealers 22
Stock Decorative French

furniture, antiquarian books, decorative smalls, pine and garden antiques
Open Mon–Sat 10am–5.30pm
Sun 11am–5pm
Services Packing, shipping, tearoom, garden

⊞ **Townsend Bateson (TADA)**
Contact Lynda Townsend-Bateson
✉ 51a Long Street, Tetbury, Gloucestershire,
GL8 8AA ☐
☎ 01666 505083 ✆ 01666 505083
✆ 07865 513856
✉ townsendbateson@btopenworld.com
ⓦ www.townsendbatesonantiques.com
Est. 1995 *Stock size* Medium
Stock French decorative, painted, fruitwood furniture, mirrors, lighting, etc
Open Mon–Sat 10am–5pm
Sun most Bank Holidays 1–5pm

⊞ **Westwood House Antiques (TADA)**
Contact R Griffiths
✉ 29 Long Street, Tetbury, Gloucestershire,
GL8 8AA ☐
☎ 01666 502328 ✆ 01666 502328
✉ westwoodhouseantiques@tinyworld.co.uk
ⓦ www.westwoodhouseantiques.com
Est. 1993 *Stock size* Large
Stock 17th–19thC oak, elm and ash country furniture, some French fruitwood furniture, decorative pottery, pewter, treen
Open Mon–Sat 10am–5.30pm

TEWKESBURY

⊞ **Cornell Books Ltd**
Contact Mr G Cornell
✉ 93 Church Street, Tewkesbury, Gloucestershire,
GL20 5RS ☐
☎ 01684 293337 ✆ 01684 273959
✉ gtcornell@aol.com
Est. 1996 *Stock size* Medium
Stock Antiquarian and second-hand books
Open Mon–Sat 10.30am–5pm

⊞ **Gainsborough House**
Contact A or B Hillson
✉ 81 Church Street, Tewkesbury, Gloucestershire,
GL20 5RX ☐

☎ 01684 293072
Est. 1962 *Stock size* Large
Stock Period furniture, porcelain, silver
Open Mon–Sat 10am–5pm
closed Thurs

⌂ **Tewkesbury Antiques Centre**
Contact Mrs Patricia Rose
✉ Tolsey Hall, Tolsey Lane, Tewkesbury, Gloucestershire,
GL20 5AE ☐
☎ 01684 294091 or 01531 822211
✆ 01531 822211
Est. 1991 *Stock size* Medium
No. of dealers 13
Stock Antiques, bric-a-brac, collectables, books, records, jewellery, furniture, radios, old tools
Open Mon–Sat 10am–5pm
Sun 11am–5pm

WICKWAR

⊞ **Bell Passage Antiques (LAPADA)**
Contact Mrs D Brand
✉ 36–38 High Street, Wickwar, Wotton-under-Edge, Gloucestershire,
GL12 8NP ☐
☎ 01454 294251
Est. 1966 *Stock size* Medium
Stock General antiques, furniture, glass, porcelain
Open Mon–Fri 9am–5pm
Sat 9am–3pm closed Wed or by appointment
Services Restoration, upholstery, caning

WINCHCOMBE

⊞ **Berkeley Antiques**
Contact Peter or Susan Dennis
✉ 3 Hailes Street, Winchcombe, Gloucestershire,
GL54 5HU ☐
☎ 01684 292034 ✆ 01684 292034
✆ 07836 243397
Est. 1974 *Stock size* Medium
Stock 17th–19thC brass, copper, china
Open Mon–Sat 10am–5.30pm
closed Thurs pm
Services Valuations, restoration

⊞ **Government House Quality Antique Lighting**
Contact Mr M Bailey

✉ St George's House,
High Street, Winchcombe,
Cheltenham, Gloucestershire,
GL54 5LJ ℗
☎ 01242 604562
📱 07970 430684
Est. 1980 *Stock size* Large
Stock Antique pre-1939 lighting
Open By appointment
Services Restoration

⊞ In Period Antiques
Contact John Edgeler
✉ Queen Anne House,
High Street, Winchcombe,
Gloucestershire,
GL54 5LJ ℗
☎ 01242 602319
📱 07816 193027
📧 john@cotswolds.uk.com
🌐 www.cotswolds.uk.com
Est. 1999 *Stock size* Medium
Stock 17th–19thC furniture,
period oak and walnut a
speciality, metalwork, glass,
porcelain, decorative items
Open Thurs–Sat 9.30am–5pm or
by appointment
Services Valuations, interior design

⊞ Newsum Antiques (CADA)
Contact Mark Newsum
✉ 2 High Street, Winchcombe,
Gloucestershire,
GL54 5HT
☎ 01242 603446
📱 07968 196668
📧 mark@newsumantiques.co.uk
🌐 www.newsumantiques.co.uk
Est. 1985 *Stock size* Medium
Stock Oak and country furniture,
treen, Swedish metalware,
Scandinavian folk art
Open Tues–Sat 10.30am–5pm
Fairs NEC, Penman Fairs
Kensington, Chelsea, Petersfield

⊞ Prichard Antiques (CADA)
Contact Keith and Debbie
Prichard
✉ 16 High Street, Winchcombe,
Gloucestershire,
GL54 5LJ ℗
☎ 01242 603566
📧 kanddprichard@msn.com
Est. 1979 *Stock size* Large
Stock 17th–19thC formal and
country furniture, clocks, treen,
boxes, metalware, decorative
items, garden furniture
Open Mon–Sat 9am–5.30pm

WOTTON-UNDER-EDGE

⌁ Wotton Auction Rooms Ltd
Contact Mr Philip Taubenheim
✉ Tabernacle Road, Wotton-
under-Edge, Gloucestershire,
GL12 7EB ℗
☎ 01453 844733 ✆ 01453 845448
📧 info@wottonauctionrooms.co.uk
🌐 www.wottonauctionrooms.co.uk
Est. 1991
Open Mon–Fri 9am–5pm
Sales Tues smalls, Wed furniture,
viewing Mon 10am–7pm
Tues 9–10.30am
Frequency Monthly
Catalogues Yes

HEREFORDSHIRE

ABBEY DORE

⊞ Ernest Howes
Contact Ernest Howes
✉ The Old Rectory, Abbey Dore,
Herefordshire,
HR20AA ℗
☎ 01981 240311
📧 howesdore@btopenworld.com
Est. 1975 *Stock size* Small
Stock Georgian country
furniture, mainly oak
Open Mon–Sat 9am–5pm
appointment advisable

HAY-ON-WYE

⊞ Addyman Annexe
Contact Mr Addyman
✉ 27 Castle Street, Hay-on-Wye,
Herefordshire,
HR3 5DF
☎ 01497 821600
📧 madness@hay-on-wyebooks.com
🌐 www.addyman-books.
demon.co.uk
Est. 1987 *Stock size* Medium
Stock Antiquarian books on all
subjects, modern first editions,
occult, myths and legends,
leather-bound sets
Open Mon–Sun 10.30am–5.30pm

⊞ Addyman Books
Contact Anne Brichto
✉ 39 Lion Street, Hay-on-Wye,
Herefordshire,
HR3 5AA
☎ 01497 821136 ✆ 01497 821732
📧 madness@hay-on-wyebooks.com
🌐 www.addyman-books.co.uk
Est. 1987 *Stock size* Medium

Stock Antiquarian and second-
hand books specializing in
English literature, modern first
editions
Open Mon–Sat 10am–6pm
Sun 10.30am–5.30pm

⊞ C Arden Bookseller (PBFA)
Contact Mrs C Arden
✉ Radnor House, Church Street,
Hay-on-Wye, Herefordshire,
HR3 5DQ ℗
☎ 01497 820471 ✆ 01497 820498
📧 info@ardenbooks.co.uk
🌐 www.ardenbooks.co.uk
Est. 1992 *Stock size* Large
Stock Antiquarian books on
natural history, gardening,
botany
Open Fri–Mon 10.30am–5.30pm
telephone call advisable
Fairs PBFA

⊞ Richard Booth's Bookshop Ltd
Contact Hope Booth
✉ Hay Castle, Hay-on-Wye,
Herefordshire,
HR3 5DL ℗
☎ 01497 820503 ✆ 01497 821314
📧 books@haycastle.co.uk
🌐 www.richardbooth.demon.co.uk
Est. 1961 *Stock size* Large
Stock Antiquarian, second-hand
and illustrated books, American
Indians, art and architecture,
cinema, crafts, humour,
photography and images,
transport, maps and prints
Open Mon–Sun 9.30am–5pm
Fairs Photography Book Fair,
London
Services Valuations

⊞ Richard Booth's Bookshop Ltd
Contact Mr R G W Booth
✉ 44 Lion Street, Hay-on-Wye,
Herefordshire,
HR3 5AJ ℗
☎ 01497 820322 ✆ 01497 821150
📧 postmaster@richardbooth.
demon.co.uk
🌐 www.richardbooth.demon.co.uk
Est. 1969 *Stock size* Large
Stock Antiquarian, second-hand
and illustrated books, literature,
military, topography, natural
history, children's fantasy and
science fiction, languages, law,
paperbacks, sport, science and
technology

Open Mon–Sat 9am–7pm
Sun 11.30am–5.30pm
Services Mail order

⊞ Boz Books (ABA)
Contact Peter Harries
✉ 13a Castle Street, Hay-on-Wye, Herefordshire, HR3 5DF ₽
☎ 01497 821277 🖷 01497 821277
✉ peter@bozbooks.demon.co.uk
🌐 www.bozbooks.co.uk
Est. 1989 *Stock size* Medium
Stock Antiquarian, rare, second-hand books, 19thC English literature
Open Mon–Sat 10am–5pm closed 1–2pm variable in winter
Services Book search

🏠 Bullring Antiques
Contact Mrs S Spencer or Marjorie Abel
✉ Bear Street, Hay-on-Wye, Herefordshire, HR3 5AN
☎ 01497 820467
Est. 1994 *Stock size* Medium
No. of dealers 4
Stock Wide general stock of good-quality antiques, furniture, ceramics, pictures, glass, silver
Open Mon–Sat 10am–5pm
Sun 11am–5pm

⊞ The Children's Bookshop
Contact Judith Gardener
✉ Toll Cottage, Pontvaen, Hay-on-Wye, Herefordshire, HR3 5EW ₽
☎ 01497 821083 🖷 01497 821083
✉ bob@childrensbookshop.com
🌐 www.childrensbookshop.com
Est. 1981 *Stock size* Medium
Stock 18th–20thC children's books
Open Mon–Sat 9.30am–5.30pm
Sun 10am–5pm
Services Book search, catalogue on website

⊞ davidleesbooks.com
Contact Julie Freeman
✉ Marches Gallery, 2 Lion Street, Hay-on-Wye, Herefordshire, HR3 5AA ₽
☎ 01497 822969
✉ enquiries@davidleesbooks.com
🌐 www.davidleesbooks.com
Est. 1986 *Stock size* Medium
Stock General secondhand books

Open Mon–Sun 11am–5pm
winter times may vary
Fairs Kinver Book Fair

⊞ Marijana Dworski Books
Contact Marijana Dworski
✉ Travel and Language Bookshop, PO Box 163, Hay-on-Wye, Herefordshire, HR3 5WX ₽
☎ 01497 820200 🖷 01497 820200
✉ info@dworskibooks.com
🌐 www.dworskibooks.com
Est. 1991 *Stock size* Medium
Stock Antiquarian books, specializing in Russia, Eastern Europe and minority languages
Open By appointment and mail order
Services 5 catalogues per year

🏠 Fleur de Lys Antiques & Collectables
Contact Sally A Harman
✉ Brook Street, Hay-on-Wye, Herefordshire, HR3 5BQ ₽
☎ 01497 821644
📱 07816 218338
✉ ladyharman@hotmail.com
Est. 2003
No. of dealers 5
Stock General antiques, rustic items
Open Mon–Sun 10am–5pm closed Tues in winter

⊞ Hancock & Monks
Contact Jerry Monks
✉ 6 Broad Street, Hay-on-Wye, Herefordshire, HR3 5DB ₽
☎ 01497 821784 🖷 01497 821784
✉ jerry@hancockandmonks.co.uk
🌐 www.hancockandmonks.co.uk
Est. 1974 *Stock size* Medium
Stock Antiquarian books on music, antiquarian sheet music
Open Mon–Sun 10am–5pm
Services Book search

🏠 Hay Antique Market
Contact Jenny Price
✉ 6 Market Street, Hay-on-Wye, Herefordshire, HR3 5AF ₽
☎ 01497 820175
Est. 1989 *Stock size* Large
No. of dealers 17
Stock China, glass, jewellery, linen, country furniture, period furniture, rural and rustic items, period clothing, lighting,

pictures, brass
Open Mon–Sat 10am–5pm
Sun 11am–5pm

⊞ Hay Cinema Bookshop (PBFA, ABA)
Contact Mr Greg Coombes
✉ The Old Cinema, Castle Street, Hay-on-Wye, Herefordshire, HR3 5DF ₽
☎ 01497 820071 🖷 01497 821900
✉ sales@haycinemabookshop.co.uk
🌐 www.haycinemabookshop.co.uk
Est. 1855 *Stock size* Large
Stock Antiquarian and second-hand books, leather-bound books, art, antiques topics a speciality, voyages, travel, naval, military, social sciences
Open Mon–Sat 9am–7pm
Sun 11.30am–5.30pm
Fairs PBFA, ABA

⊞ Hay on Wye Booksellers
Contact Mrs J Jordan
✉ 14 High Town, Hay-on-Wye, Herefordshire, HR3 5AE ₽
☎ 01497 820875 🖷 01497 847129
📱 07866 420741
✉ sales@hayonwyebooksellers.com
🌐 www.hayonwyebooksellers.com
Est. 1969 *Stock size* Large
Stock Antiquarian, second-hand, cut-price new books, publishers' returns
Open Mon–Sat 9am–6pm
Sun 9.30am–6pm

⊞ Lion Fine Arts & Books
Contact Mr Charles Spencer
✉ 19 Lion Street, Hay-on-Wye, Herefordshire, HR3 5AD ₽
☎ 01497 821726
✉ lionfinehearts@cma-int.demon.co.uk
🌐 www.hay-on-wye.co.uk/LionFine
Est. 1995 *Stock size* Medium
Stock Small antique furniture, porcelain, pottery, Georgian–early 19thC glass, old prints, treen, interesting collectables, antiquarian books
Open Mon Thurs Sat 10am–5pm other days variable, open most afternoons, telephone first

⊞ Lion Street Books
Contact Mr Mark Williams
✉ 1 St John's Place, Hay-on-Wye, Herefordshire, HR3 5BN ₽
☎ 01497 820121 🖷 01497 820121

☎ 07967 604732
✉ mark@boxingstuff.com
ⓦ www.boxingstuff.com
Est. 1993 *Stock size* Large
Stock Boxing memorabilia, books, programmes, magazines, photos
Open Mon–Sat 10am–5pm
Services Mail order catalogue

⊞ Murder & Mayhem
Contact Mr Addyman
✉ 5 Lion Street, Hay-on-Wye, Herefordshire, HR3 5AA
☎ 01497 821613 ☎ 01497 821732
ⓔ madness@hay-on-wyebooks.com
ⓦ www.hay-on-wyebooks.com
Est. 1997 *Stock size* Medium
Stock Antiquarian and second-hand books, specializing in detective fiction, crime, horror
Open Mon–Sat Sun in season 10.30am–5.30

⊞ Rose's Books
Contact Mrs M Goddard
✉ 14 Broad Street, Hay-on-Wye, Herefordshire, HR3 5DB
☎ 01497 820013 ☎ 01497 820031
ⓔ enquiry@rosesbooks.com
ⓦ www.rosesbooks.com
Est. 1984 *Stock size* Medium
Stock Rare, out-of-print, children's, illustrated books
Open Mon–Sun 9.30am–5pm
Services Regular e-mail or paper lists sent out for authors, illustrators or subjects of interest

⊞ Westwood Books Ltd (ABA, PBFA)
Contact Evelyn Westwood
✉ Grove House, High Town, Hay-on-Wye, Herefordshire, HR3 5AE
☎ 01497 820068 ☎ 01497 821641
ⓔ books@markwestwood.co.uk
Est. 1976 *Stock size* Medium
Stock Antiquarian, scholarly second-hand books on most subjects
Open Mon–Sun 10.30am–6pm
Fairs Oxford

HEREFORD

⊞ The Antique Tea Shop
Contact Miss J Cockin
✉ 5a St Peters Street, Hereford, Herefordshire, HR1 2LA

☎ 01432 342172
Est. 1990 *Stock size* Small
Stock Small items, pastry forks, afternoon tea knives, 1920s–1930s jewellery, French furniture, mirrors, ceramics
Open Tues–Sat 9.45am–5pm
Services Tea shop

⊞ I and J L Brown Ltd
Contact Mr Simon Hilton
✉ Whitestone Park, Whitestone, Hereford, Herefordshire, HR1 3SE
☎ 01432 851991 ☎ 01432 851994
ⓔ enquiries@brownantiques.com
ⓦ www.brownantiques.com
Est. 1978 *Stock size* Large
Stock English country, French provincial furniture
Open Mon–Sat 9am–5.30pm or by appointment
Services Re-rushing, restoration, makes reproduction furniture, especially Windsor chairs

⌂ Hereford Antique Centre
Contact Georgina Smith
✉ 128 Widemarsh Street, Hereford, Herefordshire, HR4 9HN
☎ 01432 266242
Est. 1989 *Stock size* Large
No. of dealers 35
Stock Furniture, pictures, fireplaces, china etc
Open Mon–Sat 10am–5pm Sun noon–5pm
Services Delivery

⊞ Hereford Map Centre Ltd (IMTA)
Contact Mr J Davey
✉ 24–25 Church Street, Hereford, Herefordshire, HR1 2LR
☎ 01432 266322 ☎ 01432 341874
ⓔ info@themapcentre.com
ⓦ www.themapcentre.com
Est. 1984 *Stock size* Large
Stock Old maps of varying scales, 1:10,000, 1:2,500, 1:500, tithe maps, hand-painted, County Series maps
Open Mon–Sat 9am–5.30pm
Fairs Royal Welsh show
Services Laminating, mounting

⌁ Sunderlands Sale Rooms
Contact David Probert
✉ Newmarket Street, Hereford,

Herefordshire, HR4 9HX
☎ 01432 266894 ☎ 01432 266901
ⓔ enquiries@sunderlandsfinearts.co.uk
ⓦ www.sunderlandsfinearts.co.uk
Est. 1868
Open Mon–Thurs 9am–5pm
Sales Regular general furniture and antique sales
Frequency Fortnightly
Catalogues No

KINGTON

⊞ Castle Hill Books
Contact Mr P Newman
✉ 12 Church Street, Kington, Herefordshire, HR5 3AZ
☎ 01544 231195 ☎ 01544 231161
ⓔ sales@castlehill.books.co.uk
ⓦ www.castlehillbooks.co.uk
Est. 1989 *Stock size* Medium
Stock New, antiquarian, out-of-print, second-hand books, general stock, most subjects covered, some specialist subjects including archaeology, British and Welsh topography
Open Mon–Fri 10.30am–1pm Sat 10.30am–1pm 2–4pm
Services Book search, valuations, restoration

⊞ Kington Antiques
Contact Paul Sheppard
✉ 15 High Street, Kington, Herefordshire, HR5 3AX
☎ 01544 340528
☎ 07773 216041
ⓔ office@kington-antiques.co.uk
ⓦ www.kington-antiques.co.uk
Est. 1976 *Stock size* Medium
Stock Collectables, memorabilia, art, antiques of Eastern European interest
Open Tues–Sat 11am–4pm closed Wed or by appointment
Services Valuations, shipping

LEDBURY

⊞ John Nash Antiques and Interiors (LAPADA, IDDA)
Contact John Nash
✉ 17c High Street, Ledbury, Herefordshire, HR8 1DS
☎ 01531 635714 ☎ 01531 635050
☎ 07831 382970
ⓦ www.johnnash.co.uk

Est. 1973 *Stock size* Medium
Stock 18th–19thC fine mahogany
and walnut furniture
Open Mon–Sat 9am–5.30pm
Sun by appointment

⚒ H J Pugh and Co
Contact Mr Howard Pugh
✉ Ledbury Sale Rooms,
Market Street, Ledbury,
Herefordshire,
HR8 2AQ 🅿
☎ 01531 631122 📠 01531 631818
📧 auctions@hjpugh.com
🌐 www.hjpugh.com
Est. 1990
Open Mon–Fri 9am–5.30pm
Sales General antiques sale Tues
6pm, viewing Tues 10am–6pm
prior to sale
Frequency Monthly
Catalogues Yes

⊞ Serendipity
Contact Mrs R Ford
✉ The Tythings,
Preston Court, Ledbury,
Herefordshire,
HR8 2LL 🅿
☎ 01531 660245 📠 01531 660689
📧 sales@serendipity-antiques.co.uk
🌐 www.serendipity-antiques.co.uk
Est. 1969 *Stock size* Large
Stock 18thC furniture, long
dining tables, four-poster beds,
Regency period furniture
Open Mon–Sat 9am–5pm
Fairs Olympia, Battersea,
Penman Antique Fairs Chelsea
Services Restoration

⊞ Keith Smith Books (PBFA)
Contact Mr K Smith
✉ 78b The Homend, Ledbury,
Herefordshire,
HR8 1BX 🅿
☎ 01531 635336
📧 keith@ksbooks.demon.co.uk
Est. 1989 *Stock size* Medium
Stock Antiquarian, general,
second-hand books, WWI poetry,
needlecrafts
Open Tues–Sat 10am–5pm
Fairs Churchdown

LEOMINSTER

⊞ 22 Broad Street
Contact Daphne Sturley
✉ 22 Broad Street, Leominster,
Herefordshire,
HR6 8BS 🅿

☎ 01568 620426
📱 07811 359473
Est. 1999 *Stock size* Medium
Stock French furniture, textiles,
decorative items, curtains,
mirrors
Open Mon–Sat 10.30am–5pm

⊞ The Barometer Shop
Contact Verity or Colin Jones
✉ New Street, Leominster,
Herefordshire,
HR6 8BT 🅿
☎ 01568 610200
🌐 www.thebarometershop.co.uk
Stock size Medium
Stock Antiques, collectables,
barometers, clocks
Open Mon–Fri 9am–5pm
Sat 10am–4pm
Services Restoration

⚒ Brightwells
Contact Roger Williams
✉ The Fine Art Sale Room,
Easters Court, Leominster,
Herefordshire,
HR6 0DE 🅿
☎ 01568 611122 📠 01568 610519
📧 fineart@brightwells.com
🌐 www.catalogs.icollector.com
/brightwells
Est. 1846
Open Mon–Fri 9am–5pm
Sales All sales on Wednesdays,
antiques and fine art sales every
four weeks; regular specialist:
silver, jewellery and coin sales;
ceramics and glass sales; English
and Continental paintings and
print sales; toys, dolls and textile
sales; vintage and classic
motorcars, motorcycles and
automobilia sales; books and
stamps; rock and pop and 20thC
design sales; animalia and
sporting items
Frequency 3–4 sales per month
Catalogues Yes

⊞ Courts Miscellany
Contact Mr G Court
✉ 48a Bridge Street, Leominster,
Herefordshire,
HR6 8DZ 🅿
☎ 01568 612995
Est. 1983 *Stock size* Medium
Stock Selection of collectables
and antiques relating to social
history, sporting, militaria,
breweriana, political
Open Mon–Sat 10.30am–5pm or
by appointment

⊞ Jeffery Hammond Antiques (LAPADA)
Contact Mr J Hammond
✉ Shaftesbury House,
38 Broad Street, Leominster,
Herefordshire,
HR6 8BS 🅿
☎ 01568 614876 📠 01568 614876
📱 07971 289367
📧 enquiries@jefferyhammond
antiques.co.uk
🌐 www.jefferyhammond
antiques.co.uk
Est. 1970 *Stock size* Medium
Stock Good quality 18th–early
19thC walnut, mahogany,
rosewood furniture, some clocks,
paintings, mirrors
Open Mon–Sat 9am–5.30pm or
by appointment
Services Valuations for
insurance, probate

🏛 Leominster Antique Centre
Contact Mr J Weston
✉ 34 Broad Street, Leominster,
Herefordshire,
HR6 8BS 🅿
☎ 01568 615505
Est. 1998 *Stock size* Large
No. of dealers 35
Stock Period furniture, early
porcelain, pottery, objets d'art,
antiquarian books, garden
furniture
Open Mon–Sat 10am–5pm
Sun 11am–4pm
Services Tea rooms, gardens

🏛 Leominster Antique Market
Contact Martin Cramp
✉ 14 Broad Street, Leominster,
Herefordshire,
HR6 8BS 🅿
☎ 01568 612189
Est. 1975 *Stock size* Large
No. of dealers 16
Stock Glass, china, pine,
furniture, collectables, jewellery
Open Mon–Sat 10am–5pm

⊞ Leominster Clock Repairs
Contact Ashley Prosser
✉ Unit 2, The Railway Station,
Worcester Road, Leominster,
Herefordshire,
HR6 8AR 🅿
☎ 01568 612298
Est. 2000 *Stock size* Small
Stock Georgian–Victorian

longcase and dial clocks
Open Mon–Sat 9am–6pm
Services Repairs, specialist in
longcase and early British
domestic clocks

🏠 **Linden House Antiques**
Contact Michael Clayton or
Caroline Scott Mayfield
✉ **1 Drapers Lane, Leominster,
Herefordshire,
HR6 8ND** 🅿
☎ 01568 620350
📱 07790 671722
Est. 1972 **Stock size** Large
No. of dealers 10
Stock Furniture, lighting, glass,
silver, porcelain, paintings, early
country pewter etc, collectables
Open Mon–Sat 10am–1pm
2–5pm Sun by appointment
Services Valuations (free if
brought to shop on Sat)

🏠 **Old Merchant's House
Antiques Centre &
Victorian Tearoom**
Contact Elaine Griffin
✉ **10 Corn Square, Leominster,
Herefordshire,
HR6 8LR** 🅿
☎ 01568 616141 ● 01568 616141
Est. 1997 **Stock size** Large
No. of dealers 18
Stock General antiques,
collectables
Open Mon–Sat 10am–5pm
Services Upholstery, tearoom

⊞ **The Old Shoe Box**
Contact Stacey Williams or Eric
Titchmarsh
✉ **2 Church Street, Leominster,
Herefordshire,
HR6 8NE** 🅿
☎ 01568 611414
📱 07980 286414
✉ staceycharleswilliams@yahoo.com
Est. 1997 **Stock size** Small
Stock Collectables, furniture,
soft furnishings, pictures,
books, antique lighting
Open Tues–Sat 10am–5pm
Services Book search, picture
valuation, restoration

⊞ **Tea Gowns & Textiles**
Contact Annie Townsend
✉ **28 & 30 Broad Street,
Leominster, Herefordshire,
HR6 8BS** 🅿
☎ 01568 612999 or 01982 560422
📱 07900 375410

Est. 2002 **Stock size** Medium
Stock Vintage clothing and
accessories
Open Mon–Sat 10am–5pm

⊞ **Utter Clutter**
Contact Mrs L M Mackenzie
✉ **16 West Street, Leominster,
Herefordshire,
HR6 8ES** 🅿
☎ 01568 611277
Est. 1995 **Stock size** Medium
Stock General antiques,
collectables, early toys, musical
instruments, textiles, curtains
Open Mon–Sat 10am–5pm
Services House clearance

LONGTOWN

⊞ **Abergavenny
Reclamation**
Contact Mr Simon Thomas
✉ **Lower Ponthendre, Longtown,
Herefordshire,
HR2 0NY** 🅿
☎ 01873 860633
📱 07970 318399
Est. 1993 **Stock size** Varies
Stock Architectural salvage,
reclaimed building materials
Open By appointment

PONTRILAS

🔨 **Nigel Ward & Co**
Contact Mr Nigel Ward
✉ **The Border Property Centre,
Pontrilas, Herefordshire,
HR2 0EH** 🅿
☎ 01981 240140 ● 01981 240857
✉ office@nigel-ward.co.uk
🌐 www.nigel-ward.co.uk
Est. 1988
Open Mon–Fri 9am–5.30pm
Sales Monthly sales of antique
and country furniture, porcelain
and collectables at Pontrilas Sale
Room
Catalogues Yes

ROSS-ON-WYE

⊞ **Fritz Fryer Antique
Lighting**
Contact Simon, Karen or Margaret
✉ **23 Station Street,
Ross-on-Wye, Herefordshire,
HR9 7AG** 🅿
☎ 01989 567416 ● 01989 566742
✉ enquiries@fritzfryer.co.uk
🌐 www.fritzfryer.co.uk
Est. 1982 **Stock size** Large

Stock Antique lighting
1820–1950, crystal chandeliers,
gasoliers, wall lights, table lights,
nickel and silver fittings,
industrial and post-modern lights
Open Mon–Sat 10am–5.30pm
Services Lighting design,
restoration, conversion, shipping,
removals and delivery

⊞ **Andy Gibbs**
✉ **29 Brookend Street,
Ross-on-Wye, Herefordshire,
HR9 7EE** 🅿
☎ 01989 566833
📱 07850 354480
✉ andygibbs@clara.co.uk
🌐 www.andygibbs-antiques.co.uk
Est. 1990 **Stock size** Large
Stock Furniture including dining
tables, chairs, reformed Gothic
and Gothic revival
Open Tues–Sat 10am–1pm
2–5.30pm
Services Valuations, restoration

🔨 **Morris Bricknell (RICS)**
Contact Mr Nigel Morris
✉ **Stroud House,
30 Gloucester Road,
Ross-on-Wye, Herefordshire,
HR9 5LE** 🅿
☎ 01989 768320 ● 01989 768345
✉ morrisbricknell@lineone.net
🌐 www.morrisbricknell.com
Est. 1989
Open Mon–Fri 9am–5.30pm
Sales General antiques sale
Sat 10.30am at the Memorial Hall
Whitchurch, viewing Sat 8.30am
prior to sale. Occasional special
and marquee sales (telephone
for details)
Frequency Monthly
Catalogues No

⊞ **Ross Old Books and
Print Shop (PBFA)**
Contact Mr P Thredder
✉ **51–52 High Street,
Ross-on-Wye, Herefordshire,
HR9 5HH** 🅿
☎ 01989 567458
✉ enquiries@rossoldbooks.co.uk
🌐 www.rossoldbooks.co,uk
Est. 1987 **Stock size** Medium
Stock Antique, second-hand, rare
books selling for £1–£1,000,
British county maps
Open Mon–Sat 10am–5pm closed
mid-Jan to mid-Feb
Fairs PBFA
Services Post inland and overseas

⊞ Ross-on-Wye Antique Gallery
Contact Mr Michael Aslanian
✉ Gloucester Road, Ross-on-Wye, Herefordshire, HR9 5BU 🅿
☎ 01989 762290 📠 01989 762291
📧 michael@rossantiquesgallery@btinternet.com
🌐 www.rossantiquesgallery.com
Est. 1996 *Stock size* Large
Stock Gothic-style church, period furniture, oak, mahogany, country furniture, oil paintings, silver, gold, jewellery, English and Continental porcelain, English and French glass, Oriental antiques, rugs, Art Deco, spoons, other cutlery, longcase clocks
Open Mon–Sat noon–5pm Sun Bank Holidays by appointment
Services Valuations

⊞ Waterfall Antiques
Contact Mr O McCarthy
✉ 43 High Street, Ross-on-Wye, Herefordshire, HR9 5HD 🅿
☎ 01989 563103
Est. 1991 *Stock size* Large
Stock Pine and country furniture
Open Mon–Sat 9.30am–5pm
Fairs Newark

⚒ Williams & Watkins Auctioneers Ltd
Contact Roger Garlick
✉ Ross-on-Wye Auction Centre, Overcross, Ross-on-Wye, Herefordshire, HR9 7QF 🅿
☎ 01989 762225 📠 01989 566082
📧 willwat@auctionmarts.com
Est. 1866
Open Mon–Fri 9am–5pm
Sales Wed 10am. General antiques sales, viewing Tues 1–7pm and day of sale 9–10am
Frequency Monthly
Catalogues Yes

HERTFORDSHIRE

BARNET

⊞ Antiques Little Shop
Contact Mrs F O'Gorman
✉ 2 Bruce Road, Barnet, Hertfordshire, EN5 4LS 🅿
☎ 020 8449 9282
Est. 1996 *Stock size* Medium

Stock Furniture, collectables, Georgian–1950s
Open Wed–Sat 10am–5pm Fri 11am–5pm
Services House clearance

⌂ Barnet Bygones
Contact Mrs M Phillips
✉ 2 Bruce Road, Barnet, Hertfordshire, EN5 4LS 🅿
☎ 020 8440 7304
Est. 1994 *Stock size* Large
No. of dealers 4
Stock Furniture, smalls, collectables
Open Mon Wed Fri Sat 9am–5pm
Services Valuations, painting and distressing furniture

⊞ C Bellinger Antiques
Contact Mr C Bellinger
✉ 91 Wood Street, Barnet, Hertfordshire, EN5 4BX 🅿
☎ 020 8449 3467
Est. 1971 *Stock size* Small
Stock General antiques
Open Thurs–Sat 10am–3pm

BERKHAMSTED

⊞ Country Life Interiors
Contact Mr Peter Myers
✉ 88 High Street, Berkhamsted, Hertfordshire, HP4 2BW 🅿
☎ 01442 387337 📠 01442 387338
📧 info@countrylifeinteriors.com
🌐 www.countrylifeinteriors.com
Est. 1982 *Stock size* Large
Stock Victorian pine, reproduction pine in old wood, oak furniture, painted furniture, giftware, fitted and free-standing kitchens
Open Mon–Sat 10am–5.30pm Sun 11am–4pm
Services Worldwide shipping arranged

⌂ Heritage Antique Centre
Contact Pauline Beales
✉ 24 Castle Street, Berkhamsted, Hertfordshire, HP4 2DW 🅿
☎ 01442 873819
Est. 1985 *Stock size* Medium
No. of dealers 22
Stock Bric-a-brac, Georgian furniture, garden furniture
Open Mon–Sun 10am–5.30pm

⌂ Home & Colonial Antique Centre
Contact Ali Reid-Davies
✉ 134 High Street, Berkhamsted, Hertfordshire, HP4 3AT 🅿
☎ 01442 877007
📧 homeandcolonial@btinternet.com
🌐 www.homeandcolonial.co.uk
Est. 1996 *Stock size* Large
No. of dealers 50
Stock English, French period furniture, clocks, pine and country furniture, Arts and Crafts, painted furniture, garden antiques, jewellery, collectables
Open Mon–Sat 10am–5.30pm Sun 11am–5pm closed Wed

BUNTINGFORD

⊞ Times Past
Contact Adrian Piggott
✉ 61 High Street, Buntingford, Hertfordshire, SG9 9AE 🅿
☎ 01763 274069
📧 timespast61@aol.com
Est. 1999 *Stock size* Large
Stock Continental, Victorian pine, ceramics
Open Mon–Sat 10am–5pm closed Wed or by appointment

BUSHEY

⊞ C and B Antiques
Contact Carol Epstein
✉ 22 Brooke Way, Bushey Heath, Watford, Hertfordshire, WD23 4LG 🅿
☎ 020 8950 1844 📠 020 8950 1844
📱 07831 647274
Est. 1979 *Stock size* Large
Stock 1790–1930 porcelain and small furniture, pictures
Open By appointment or at fairs
Fairs The Moat House, The Bell House, Shepton Mallet
Services Valuations

⊞ Country Life Interiors
Contact Mr Peter Myers
✉ 33a High Street, Bushey, Watford, Hertfordshire, WD23 1BD 🅿
☎ 020 8950 8575 📠 020 8950 6982
📧 info@countrylifeinteriors.com
🌐 www.countrylifeinteriors.com
Est. 1982 *Stock size* Large
Stock Victorian pine, reproduction pine in old wood, oak furniture, painted furniture,

giftware, fitted and free-standing kitchens
Open Mon–Sat 10am–5.30pm Sun 11am–4pm
Services Worldwide shipping arranged

⊞ Marcel Cards (Cartophilic Society)
Contact Marcel Epstein
✉ 22 Brooke Way, Bushey Heath, Watford, Hertfordshire, WD23 4LG 🅿
☎ 020 8950 1844 ❸ 020 8950 1844
📱 07887 648255
Est. 1991 **Stock size** Large
Stock Cigarette cards 1890–1939, new collectors' cards, tea, bubblegum cards
Open By appointment and at Marcel Fairs
Fairs Peterborough, Ardingly, Dunstable
Services Odd cards to complete sets, card search, valuations

CHORLEYWOOD

⊞ Douglas Roberts Antiques
Contact Andy Roberts
✉ 31 Lower Road, Chorleywood, Hertfordshire, WD3 5LQ 🅿
☎ 01923 283111
📱 07970 773917
❸ meta.roberts@btinternet.com
Est. 2004 **Stock size** Small
Stock Georgian–1930s furniture, pictures, glass
Open Tues–Sat 10am–5pm

DAGNALL

⊞ Ashridge Antique Flooring
Contact Richard Facer
✉ Mile Barn Farm, Hemel Hempstead Road, Dagnall, Berkhamsted, Hertfordshire, HP4 1QR 🅿
☎ 01442 843077
📱 07789 808085
Est. 1987 **Stock size** Large
Stock Reclaimed oak beams, flooring and furniture
Open Mon–Sat 9am–5pm

HEMEL HEMPSTEAD

⊞ Cherry Antiques
Contact Mr R S Cullen
✉ 101 High Street, Hemel Hempstead, Hertfordshire, HP1 3AH 🅿
☎ 01442 264358
📱 07720 263214
Est. 1981 **Stock size** Medium
Stock General antiques
Open Mon–Sat 9.30am–4.30pm Wed 9.30am–1pm
Services Valuations

⊞ Heritage Reclamation (SALVO)
Contact Mr L Leadbetter
✉ Wood Lane, Paradise Industrial Estate, Hemel Hempstead, Hertfordshire, HP2 4TL 🅿
☎ 01442 219936
🌐 www.heritagereclamation.co.uk
Est. 1998 **Stock size** Medium
Stock Victorian pews, roll-top baths, internal and external doors, stained glass, French burners, Victorian fireplaces, reclaimed bricks, tiles, floor boarding
Open Mon–Fri 9am–5pm Sat 9.30am–3.30pm
Services Supply timber and recommend floorers

⊞ The House of Elliott
Contact Michele
✉ 11 High Street, Hemel Hempstead, Hertfordshire, HP1 3AA 🅿
☎ 01442 405325
❸ michele@house-of-elliott.fsnet.co.uk
🌐 www.houseofelliott.org
Est. 2001 **Stock size** Small
Stock Pine furniture, clocks, fob watches, Victorian silver, jewellery, collectables
Open Mon–Sat 10am–5.30pm Sun 11am–4.30pm
Fairs Great Missenden, Kempton, Ardingly
Services Upholstery, clock repairs

⌂ Jordans Antique Centre
Contact Michael Porter
✉ 63 High Street, Old Town, Hemel Hempstead, Hertfordshire, HP1 3AF 🅿
☎ 01442 263451
🌐 www.thecollectorscompanion.co.uk/jordans.html
Est. 1998 **Stock size** Medium
No. of dealers 12
Stock China, glass, furniture, jewellery
Open Mon–Sun 10am–5pm

⊞ Libritz Stamps
Contact Mr R Hickman
✉ 70 London Road, Apsley, Hemel Hempstead, Hertfordshire, HP3 9SD 🅿
☎ 01442 242691 ❸ 01442 242691
❸ info@libritzstampshop.co.uk
🌐 www.libritzstampshop.co.uk
Est. 1967 **Stock size** Large
Stock Banknotes, stamps, coins, cigarette cards, accessories, albums, catalogues
Open Mon–Sat 10am–5pm
Services Want lists serviced

⌂ Off the Wall
Contact Michelle Smith
✉ 52 High Street, Hemel Hempstead, Hertfordshire, HP1 3AF 🅿
☎ 01442 218300
📱 07771 724700
❸ off_thewallantiques@hotmail.com
Est. 2001 **Stock size** Medium
No. of dealers 4
Stock Furniture, decorative items, glassware
Open Mon–Sat 10am–5.30pm Sun 11am–1pm

HERTFORD

⊞ Bazaar Boxes
Contact Andrew Grierson or Mark Brewster
✉ Hertford, Hertfordshire, SG14 🅿
☎ 01992 504454 ❸ 01992 504454
📱 07970 909204/909206
❸ bazaarboxes@hotmail.com
🌐 www.bazaarboxes.com
Est. 1998 **Stock size** Medium
Stock Tortoiseshell, ivory and mother-of-pearl tea caddies and boxes, objects of virtue, Oriental items
Open By appointment
Fairs Decorative Antique and Textile Fair, Olympia

⊞ Beckwith and Son incorporating Hertford Antiques
Contact Mr G Gray
✉ St Nicholas Hall, St Andrew Street, Hertford, Hertfordshire, SG14 1HZ 🅿
☎ 01992 582079
❸ sales@beckwithandson antiques.co.uk
🌐 www.beckwithandson antiques.co.uk

Est. 1903 *Stock size* Large
Stock 17thC–1930s mahogany, pine, oak furniture, silver, glass, pictures, metalware, general antiques, clocks
Open Mon–Sat 9am–5.30pm
Services Restoration, valuations

⊞ Gillmark Map Gallery
Contact Mr Mark Pretlove
✉ 25 Parliament Square, Hertford, Hertfordshire, SG14 1EX 🅿
☎ 01992 534444 📠 01992 554734
📧 gillmark@btinternet.com
🌐 www.gillmark.com
Est. 1997 *Stock size* Large
Stock Antique maps, prints, second-hand books
Open Tues–Sat 10am–5pm half day Thurs
Services Restoration, conservation, framing, hand-colouring

⊞ Tapestry Antiques
Contact Mrs P Stokes
✉ 27 St Andrew Street, Hertford, Hertfordshire, SG14 1HZ 🅿
☎ 01992 587438
📧 pjstokes27@yahoo.com
Est. 1974 *Stock size* Large
Stock General 18th–19thC furniture, brass, copper, porcelain, Staffordshire figures, lighting, mirrors
Open Mon–Sat 10am–5pm
Services Valuations for probate

HITCHIN

⊞ The Book Bug
Contact Mrs S Jevon
✉ 1 The Arcade, Hitchin, Hertfordshire, SG5 1ED 🅿
☎ 01462 431309
Est. 1984 *Stock size* Large
Stock General second-hand and antiquarian books
Open Mon–Sat 9am–5pm closed Wed

⊞ Michael Gander
Contact Mr M Gander
✉ 10 & 11 Bridge Street, Hitchin, Hertfordshire, SG5 2DE
☎ 01462 432678
📱 07885 728976
Est. 1974 *Stock size* Medium

Stock Period furniture, small items
Open Wed Thurs Sat 9am–5pm or by appointment Mon, Tues, Fri, 3–5pm

⊞ Eric T Moore
Contact John Leeson
✉ 24 Bridge Street, Hitchin, Hertfordshire, SG5 2DF 🅿
☎ 01462 450497
📧 booksales@erictmoore.co.uk
🌐 www.erictmoore.co.uk
Est. 1965 *Stock size* Large
Stock General, second-hand, antiquarian books, maps, loose prints
Open Mon–Sat 8.30am–6pm Sun 11am–5pm

⊞ Phillips of Hitchin Antiques Ltd (BADA)
Contact Mr J Phillips
✉ The Manor House, 26 Bancroft, Hitchin, Hertfordshire, SG5 1JW 🅿
☎ 01462 432067 📠 01462 441368
Est. 1884 *Stock size* Medium
Stock English furniture 1730–1830, unusual items such as campaign furniture, new and out-of-print reference books on antique furniture
Open Mon–Fri 9am–5.30pm

LEAVESDEN

⊞ Peter Taylor and Son
Contact Mr P Taylor
✉ 1 Ganders Ash, Leavesden, Watford, Hertfordshire, WD25 7HE 🅿
☎ 01923 663325
📧 taylorbooks@clara.co.uk
Est. 1973 *Stock size* Medium
Stock Tudor and medieval history antique books, documents
Open Catalogue order
Services Valuations

LETCHWORTH GARDEN CITY

⊞ The Barn Antiques
Contact Mr or Mrs Ryde
✉ 27 The Wynd, Letchworth Garden City, Hertfordshire, SG6 3EL 🅿
☎ 01462 678459
Est. 1997 *Stock size* Large
Stock Victorian–1940s hardwood furniture, china, Doulton, Beatrix Potter, Toby jugs, model boats

Open Mon Thurs–Sat 10am–5pm
Services Valuations, house clearance

⊞ Past & Present
Contact Paul Lawrence
✉ 18 Openshore Way, Letchworth Garden City, Hertfordshire, SG6 3ER 🅿
☎ 01462 485117
📱 07976 426704
Est. 1998 *Stock size* Medium
Stock Antiques, collectables
Open Mon–Sat 9.45am–5pm closed Wed
Fairs Newark, Swinderby
Services Valuations

PUCKERIDGE

⊞ St Ouen Antiques
Contact Jonathan Blake or Timothy Blake
✉ The Vintage Corner, Old Cambridge Road, Puckeridge, Ware, Hertfordshire, SG11 1SA 🅿
☎ 01920 821336 📠 01920 822506
Est. 1967 *Stock size* Large
Stock 18thC English furniture
Open Mon–Sat 9.30am–5pm
Services Valuations, restoration

REDBOURN

⊞ Bushwood Antiques (LAPADA, CINOA)
Contact Mr A Bush
✉ Stags End Equestrian Centre, Gaddesden Lane, Redbourn, Hemel Hempstead, Hertfordshire, HP2 6HN 🅿
☎ 01582 794700
📧 antiques@bushwood.co.uk
🌐 www.bushwood.co.uk
Est. 1967 *Stock size* Large
Stock 18th–19thC English and Continental furniture, accessories, objets d'art
Open Mon–Fri 8.30am–4pm Sat 10am–4pm

⊞ J N Antiques
Contact Mrs J Brunning
✉ 86 High Street, Redbourn, St Albans, Hertfordshire, AL3 7BD 🅿
☎ 01582 793603
Est. 1974 *Stock size* Large
Stock General antiques
Open Mon–Sat 9am–6pm
Services Valuations

HEART OF ENGLAND
HERTFORDSHIRE • RICKMANSWORTH

Tim Wharton (LAPADA)
Contact Mr T Wharton
✉ 24 High Street, Redbourn,
St Albans, Hertfordshire,
AL3 7LL ℗
☎ 01582 794371
📱 07850 622880
✉ tim@timwhartonantiques.co.uk
Est. 1973 *Stock size* Large
Stock 17th–19thC oak, country
furniture, some period
mahogany, metalware, treen,
country pictures
Open Tues Wed Fri 10am–5pm
Sat 10am–4pm Thurs by
appointment
Fairs LAPADA (Birmingham),
Olympia

RICKMANSWORTH

Country House Antiques
Contact Jane
✉ 251 Uxbridge Road,
Rickmansworth, Hertfordshire,
WD3 2DP ℗
☎ 01923 712666 01923 712666
✉ countryhouse@waitrose.com
Est. 1980 *Stock size* Medium
Stock Country furniture, mainly
pine, cast-iron fireplaces
Open Mon–Sat 10am–5pm
Fairs Newark

ROYSTON

Lovers of Blue and White
Contact Andrew Pye
✉ Steeple Morden, Royston,
Hertfordshire,
SG8 0RN ℗
☎ 01763 853800 01763 853700
✉ china@blueandwhite.com
🌐 www.blueandwhite.com
Est. 1995 *Stock size* Large
Stock British transfer ware
1780–present
Open By appointment
Services Valuations,
identification, mail order

SAWBRIDGE

Acorn Antiques & Collectors Centre
Contact Shirley Rowley
✉ The Maltings, Station Road,
Sawbridge, Hertfordshire,
CM21 9JX ℗
☎ 01279 722012
Est. 1993 *Stock size* Large
No. of dealers 80

Stock Antiques, collectables
Open Mon–Fri 10am–5pm
Sat Sun 10.30am–5.30pm

SAWBRIDGEWORTH

Arcane Antiques Centre (EADA)
Contact Mr Nigel Hoy
or Miss Nicola Smith
✉ The Maltings, Station Road,
Sawbridgeworth, Hertfordshire,
CM21 9JX ℗
☎ 01279 600562
📱 07957 551899
✉ nicola@charnwoodantiques.co.uk
Est. 1999 *Stock size* Large
No. of dealers 25
Stock Oriental and European
ceramics, 18thC glasses, silver,
oils, watercolours, prints,
jewellery, Georgian–Edwardian
furniture, longcase and other
clocks
Open Tues–Fri 10am–5pm
Sat Sun 11am–5pm
Services Antique furniture
restoration, cabinet-making,
upholstery, cabinet-lining, French
polishing, glass repair, picture
framing

The Herts & Essex Antique Centre
Contact Robert Sklar
✉ The Maltings, Station Road,
Sawbridgeworth, Hertfordshire,
CM21 9JX ℗
☎ 01279 722044 01279 725445
📱 07710 057750
✉ webmaster@antiques-of-britain.co.uk
🌐 www.antiques-of-britain.co.uk
Est. 1981 *Stock size* Large
No. of dealers 120
Stock Furniture, jewellery, silver
china
Open Mon–Fri 10am–5pm
Sat Sun 10.30am–5.30pm
Services Tea room

Riverside Antiques Centre
Contact John Barret
or Shirley Rowly
✉ Unit 1, The Maltings, Station
Road, Sawbridgeworth,
Hertfordshire,
CM21 9JX ℗
☎ 01279 600985
Est. 1998 *Stock size* Large
No. of dealers 300
Stock Probably the largest

antiques centre in Hertfordshire
and Essex. Antiques, collectables,
furniture, etc
Open Mon–Sun 10am–5pm
Services Restoration and repair
of furniture, glass, ceramics

ST ALBANS

James of St Albans
Contact Stephen James
✉ 11 George Street, St Albans,
Hertfordshire,
AL3 4ER ℗
☎ 01727 856996
Est. 1956 *Stock size* Small
Stock Victorian–Edwardian
furniture, collectables
Open Mon–Sat 10am–5pm
Thurs 10am–4pm

Magic Lanterns
Contact J A Marsden
✉ By George,
23 George Street, St Albans,
Hertfordshire,
AL3 4ES ℗
☎ 01727 865680
Est. 1987 *Stock size* Large
Stock 1800–1950 antique
lighting, mirrors, jewellery
Open Mon–Fri 10am–5pm
Sat 10am–5.30pm Sun 1–5pm
Services Lighting consultancy for
period houses

Paton Books
Contact Richard Child
✉ 34 Holywell Hill, St Albans,
Hertfordshire,
AL1 1DE ℗
☎ 01727 853984 01727 865764
✉ patonbooks@aol.com
🌐 www.patonbooks.co.uk
Est. 1962 *Stock size* Large
Stock General secondhand and
antiquarian books, specializing
in history, military history,
transport, art and craft, travel
Open Mon–Sat 9am–6pm
Sun 10am–6pm

Reg & Philip Remington (ABA)
Contact Mr R Remington
✉ 23 Homewood Road,
St Albans, Hertfordshire,
AL1 4BG
☎ 01727 893531 01727 893532
✉ philip@remingtonbooks.com
🌐 www.remingtonbooks.com
Est. 1979 *Stock size* Medium
Stock Antiquarian, rare, second-

hand books, voyage and travel books a speciality
Open By appointment
Fairs Olympia

TRING

⊞ John Bly (BADA)
Contact Mr Perris
⊠ The Old Billiards Room, Church Yard, Tring, Hertfordshire, HP23 5AG 🅿
☎ 01442 890802
Est. 1891 *Stock size* Large
Stock Georgian furniture, porcelain, silver, glass, other quality antiques
Open Tues–Sat 10am–4pm
Fairs Grosvenor House, Florida
Services Valuations, restoration

⊞ Country Clocks
Contact Mr Terry Cartmell
⊠ 3 Pendley Bridge Cottages, Tring Station, Tring, Hertfordshire, HP23 5QU 🅿
☎ 01442 825090
Est. 1976 *Stock size* Medium
Stock 18th–19thC wall, longcase, mantel clocks
Open Mon–Fri by appointment Sat 9am–5pm Sun 2–5pm
Services Valuations, restoration, repairs

⊞ New England House Antiques
Contact Mr S Munjee
⊠ 50 High Street, Tring, Hertfordshire, HP23 5AG 🅿
☎ 01442 827262 ✆ 01442 827262
📱 07711 224422
🌐 enquiries@newenglandhouse antiques.co.uk
🌐 www.newenglandhouse antiques.co.uk
Est. 1992 *Stock size* Large
Stock Georgian–Victorian furniture, silver, glass, paintings, clocks, table lamps
Open Tues–Sat 10.30am–5pm
Services Restoration, free search and find for furniture

TRINGFORD

⊞ Piggeries Pine
Contact Paul Brown
⊠ Tringford Road, Tringford, Hertfordshire,

HP23 4LH 🅿
☎ 01442 827961
🌐 piggeriespine@aol.com
🌐 www.piggeriespine.co.uk
Est. 1987 *Stock size* Large
Stock Pine furniture, kitchens, painted furniture
Open Mon–Sun 10am–5pm
Services Stripping

WARE

⚒ Amwell Auctions
Contact Marian Haldane
⊠ The Function Room, Hertford Rugby Football Club, Ware, Hertfordshire
☎ 01920 871901 ✆ 01920 871901
📱 07765 446976
Est. 1999
Open Mon–Fri 9am–7pm
Sat 9am–1pm
Sales General antiques
Frequency Monthly
Catalogues Yes

⚒ Ware Militaria Auctions
Contact Martin Greenfield
⊠ The Function Room, Hertford Rugby Football Club, Hoe Lane, Ware, Hertfordshire, SG12 2NZ 🅿
☎ 01920 871383 ✆ 01920 871901
📱 07747 860746
🌐 martin@ware-militaria-auction.com
🌐 www.ware-militaria-auction.com
Est. 1999
Open Mon–Fri 9am–7pm
Sat 9am–1pm
Sales Militaria
Frequency Bi-monthly
Catalogues Yes

WATFORD

⊞ Cards Inc
Contact Mr P Freedman
⊠ 31 Greenhill Crescent, Watford Business Park, Watford, Hertfordshire, WD18 8YB 🅿
☎ 01923 200138 ✆ 01923 200134
🌐 paul@cardsinc.com
🌐 www.cardsinc.com
Est. 1987 *Stock size* Small
Stock Collectable trading cards
Open By appointment

⊞ Collectors Corner
Contact Mr L Dronkes
⊠ Charter Place, Watford Market, Watford, Hertfordshire, WD1 2RN 🅿

☎ 01923 248855 or 020 8904 0552
Est. 1968 *Stock size* Small
Stock Coins, medals, bank notes, cigarette cards, small collectables
Open Tues Fri Sat 10am–5pm
Services Valuations, medal mounting

⊞ The Pine Furniture Store
Contact Ben
⊠ 304a High Street, Watford, Hertfordshire, WD12JE 🅿
☎ 01923 441604
Est. 1980 *Stock size* Large
Stock Eastern European, English pine furniture, pine and iron beds, mirrors, cast-iron fireplaces
Open Mon–Sat 10am–5pm or by appointment
Fairs Newark, Ardingly
Services Stripping

⊞ Quicktest
Contact Raffi Katz
⊠ PO Box 180, Watford, Hertfordshire, WD18 8PH 🅿
☎ 01923 220206
📱 07976 831953
🌐 info@quicktest.co.uk
🌐 www.quicktest.co.uk
Est. 1986 *Stock size* Large
Stock Testers, magnifiers, weighing machines, jewellery boxes, hand tools
Open Visitors welcome by appointment, map and directions on website
Fairs Newark, Alexandra Palace, Ardingly, Kempton, Shepton, Birmingham, Sandown

WHEATHAMPSTEAD

⊞ Collins Antiques
Contact Mr Michael Collins
⊠ Corner House, Church Street, Wheathampstead, Hertfordshire, AL4 8AP 🅿
☎ 01582 833111
Est. 1907 *Stock size* Medium
Stock 17th–19thC furniture, including oak and mahogany tables, chairs, chests-of-drawers
Open Mon–Sat 9am–1pm 2–5pm

⊞ The Old Bakery Antiques Ltd
Contact Mr Maurice Shifrin
⊠ 3 Station Road, Wheathampstead, Hertfordshire,

AL4 8BU 🅿
☎ 01582 831999 Ⓕ 01582 831555
Est. 1997 *Stock size* Large
Stock Made to order oak furniture, Oriental carpets
Open Mon–Sat 10am–5pm

Thomas Thorp (ABA, PBFA)
Contact Mr Jim Thorp
✉ **64 Lancaster Road, St Albans, Hertfordshire, AL1 4ET** 🅿
☎ 01727 864778 Ⓕ 01727 864778
Ⓔ thorpbooks@compuserve.com
Est. 1883 *Stock size* Small
Stock General antiquarian books, specializing in early printed English history, literature, modern, private press editions
Open By appointment
Fairs Olympia (Jun), Chelsea (Nov)

OXFORDSHIRE

ASCOTT-UNDER-WYCHWOOD

William Antiques
Contact Mr R Gripper
✉ **Manor Barn, Manor Farm, Ascott-under-Wychwood, Chipping Norton, Oxfordshire, OX7 6AL** 🅿
☎ 01993 831960 Ⓕ 01993 830395
Ⓔ robgripper@aol.com
Est. 1982 *Stock size* Medium
Stock Good-quality decorative antiques, Georgian–Victorian furniture
Open Mon–Fri 9am–5pm Sat pm by appointment
Services Restoration

BANBURY

Banbury Antiques Centre
Contact Veronica Hammond
✉ **18 Southam Road, Banbury, Oxfordshire, OX16 2EG** 🅿
☎ 01295 267800
Ⓜ 07968 870019
Est. 2003 *Stock size* Large
No. of dealers 40
Stock Clocks, furniture including pine, collectables, gardening antiques, silver, china, pictures, glass, linen
Open Mon–Sat 10am–5pm Sun 11am–4pm
Services Valuations

Bonhams
✉ **48 North Bar, Banbury, Oxfordshire, OX16 0TH**
☎ 01295 272723 Ⓕ 01295 272726
Ⓔ banbury@bonhams.com
Ⓦ www.bonhams.com
Open Mon–Fri 9am–5.30pm
Sales Regional Office. Regular sales held in London and in our salerooms across the country. Free auction valuations; insurance and probate valuations

Comic Connections
Contact Mr Glyn Smith
✉ **4a Parsons Street, Banbury, Oxfordshire, OX16 5LW** 🅿
☎ 01295 268989 Ⓕ 01295 268989
Ⓔ comicconnection@aol.com
Est. 1994 *Stock size* Large
Stock American comic books, graphic novels, action figures, science-fiction items, over 35,000 comics in stock
Open Mon–Fri 10.30am–5pm Sat 9.30am–5pm
Fairs Collector mania Milton Keynes
Services Standing order for comics, magazines, videos

Holloway's (LAPADA)
Contact Mr Nicholas Williams
✉ **49 Parsons Street, Banbury, Oxfordshire, OX16 5PF** 🅿
☎ 01295 817777 Ⓕ 01295 817701
Ⓔ enquiries@holloways auctioneers.co.uk
Ⓦ www.hollowaysauctioneers.co.uk
Est. 1970
Open Mon–Fri 9am–5.30pm Sat 9am–noon
Sales Fortnightly general sales Tues 11am, viewing Mon 9am–7pm Sat 9am–noon. Every 6/7 weeks specialist sales Tues 11am, viewing Fri 9am–5pm Sat 9am–noon Mon 9am–7pm and morning of sale
Catalogues Online

BICESTER

R A Barnes Antiques (LAPADA)
Contact John Langin
✉ **PO Box 82, Bicester, Oxfordshire, OX25 1RA** 🅿
☎ 01844 237388
Ⓔ AngeloUno2@aol.com
Est. 1970 *Stock size* Medium
Stock Continental glass, English and Continental porcelain, Art Nouveau, paintings, English metalware, 18th–19thC brass, Belleek, Wedgwood
Open By appointment Sat Royers Gallery
Fairs NEC, Little Chelsea
Services Valuations

Lisseters Antiques
Contact Mr M Lisseter
✉ **3 Kings End, Bicester, Oxfordshire, OX26 6DR** 🅿
☎ 01869 252402
Ⓜ 07801 667848
Est. 1959 *Stock size* Large
Stock Antiques, used furniture
Open Mon–Sat 9am–5pm
Services House Clearance

Mallams (SOFAA)
Contact C Turner
✉ **Pevensey House, 27 Sheep Street, Bicester, Oxfordshire, OX26 6JF** 🅿
☎ 01869 252901 Ⓕ 01869 320283
Ⓔ bicester@mallams.co.uk
Ⓦ www.mallams.co.uk/fineart
Est. 1788
Open Mon–Fri 9am–5pm Sat 9am–1pm on viewing days only
Sales General antiques sale Mon 11am, viewing Fri 9am–5pm Sat 9am–1pm morning of sale 9–11am. Valuations service
Frequency 16 per year
Catalogues Yes

BLEWBURY

Blewbury Antiques
Contact E Richardson
✉ **London Road, Blewbury, Didcot, Oxfordshire, OX11 9NX** 🅿
☎ 01235 850366
Est. 1970 *Stock size* Medium
Stock General, furniture, garden ornaments, books, glass, china, clocks
Open Mon–Sun 10am–6pm closed Tues Wed

BLOXHAM

Antiques of Bloxham
Contact Mr S Robinson
✉ **Church Street, Bloxham, Banbury, Oxfordshire,**

OX15 4ET 🅿
☎ 01295 721641
Est. 1996 *Stock size* Large
Stock General antiques
Open Wed Thurs 12.30–4.30pm,
Fri Sat 11am–4.30pm,
Sun noon–4.30pm
Services Delivery, clock repairs

BODICOTE

⊞ Blender Antiques
Contact Patsy Irana
✉ Cotefield Farm, Bodicote,
Banbury, Oxfordshire,
OX15 4AQ 🅿
☎ 01295 254754
📱 07969 922531
✉ blenderantiques@btopenworld.com
Est. 2003 *Stock size* Medium
Stock 18th–19thC Continental
furniture
Open Mon–Sat 10am–5pm

⤗ J S Auctions
Contact Joseph Smith
✉ Cotefield Farm Saleroom,
Oxford Road, Bodicote, Banbury,
Oxfordshire,
OX15 4EQ 🅿
☎ 01295 272488
📱 07775 848982
✉ joesmith@jsauctions.co.uk
🌐 www.jsauctions.co.uk
Est. 1994
Open Mon–Sat 9am–5pm
Sales Fortnightly general
antiques sale Sat 10am, viewing
Fri 9am–7pm. Two special sales
a year
Frequency Fortnightly
Catalogues Yes

BURFORD

⌂ Antiques @ The George
(The Cotswold Antiques
group)
Contact Coral Oswald
✉ 104 High Street, Burford,
Oxfordshire,
OX18 4QJ 🅿
☎ 01993 823319
✉ ask@antiquesatthegeorge.com
🌐 www.antiquesatthegeorge.com
Est. 1992 *Stock size* Large
No. of dealers 20
Stock Glass, furniture, treen,
books, pictures, rugs, silver,
silverplate, jewellery, teddy
bears, ceramics, brass and copper
Open Mon–Sat 10am–5pm
Sun noon–5pm

⊞ Bourton Bears
Contact Melvin Fabb
✉ Burford, Oxfordshire,
OX18 🅿
☎ 01993 824756   📠 01993 824756
📱 07748 123330
✉ help@bourtonbears.com
🌐 www.bourtonbears.com
Est. 2002 *Stock size* Large
Stock Antique–vintage bears
1902–1966
Open By appointment
Fairs Kensington Town Hall
Services Valuations

⊞ Burford Antiques Centre
Contact Mr G Viventi
✉ The Roundabout, Cheltenham
Road, Burford, Oxfordshire,
OX18 4JA 🅿
☎ 01993 823227
Est. 1988 *Stock size* Large
Stock General antiques,
1930s–modern, period furniture
Open Mon–Sat 10am–6pm
Sun noon–5pm

⊞ Bygones
Contact Mrs Jenkins
✉ 29 Lower High Street, Burford,
Oxfordshire,
OX18 4RN 🅿
☎ 01993 823588   📠 01993 704338
✉ sale@bygones-of-burford.co.uk
🌐 www.bygones-of-burford.co.uk
Est. 1986 *Stock size* Medium
Stock General collectables, curios
Open Mon–Sat 10am–1pm
2–5pm Sun noon–5pm

⊞ Jonathan Fyson
Antiques (CADA)
Contact Mr J Fyson
✉ 50–52 High Street, Burford,
Oxfordshire,
OX18 4QF
☎ 01993 823204   📠 01993 823204
✉ j@fyson.co.uk
Est. 1971 *Stock size* Large
Stock English and Continental
furniture, brass, lighting, fireplaces,
accessories, club fenders, papier
mâché, tôle, treen, porcelain,
glass, prints, jewellery
Open Mon–Fri 9.30am–5.30pm
closed 1–2pm Sat 10am–5pm
closed 1–2pm
Services Valuations

⊞ Gateway Antiques
(CADA)
Contact Mr Paul Brown
or Mr Michael Ford

✉ Cheltenham Road, Burford
Roundabout, Burford,
Oxfordshire,
OX18 4JA 🅿
☎ 01993 823678   📠 01993 823857
✉ enquiries@gatewayantiques.co.uk
🌐 www.gatewayantiques.co.uk
Est. 1985 *Stock size* Large
Stock 17th–20thC furniture, Arts
and Crafts, decorative objects,
accessories
Open Mon–Sat 10am–5.30pm
Sun 2–5pm
Services Shipping worldwide,
restoration, multi-lingual courier
service and driver,
accommodation, storage, stock
on website

⊞ Horseshoe Antiques
Contact Mr B Evans
✉ 97 High Street, Burford,
Oxfordshire,
OX18 4QA 🅿
☎ 01993 823244
📱 07711 525383
Est. 1979 *Stock size* Medium
Stock 17th–18thC furniture, oil
paintings, copper, brass, horse
brasses, clocks, longcase clocks
Open Mon–Sat 9am–4.30pm

⊞ David Pickup (BADA,
CADA)
Contact Mr D Pickup
✉ 115 High Street, Burford,
Oxfordshire,
OX18 4RG
☎ 01993 822555
Est. 1980 *Stock size* Medium
Stock Fine English furniture,
emphasis on the Cotswold Arts
and Crafts movement early 20thC
Open Mon–Fri 9.30am–5.30pm
Sat 10.30am–4.30pm
Fairs Olympia (Spring, Nov)

⊞ Manfred Schotten
Antiques (CADA, BACA
Award Winner 2002)
✉ 109 High Street, Burford,
Oxfordshire,
OX18 4RG 🅿
☎ 01993 822302   📠 01993 822055
✉ antiques@schotten.com
🌐 www.schotten.com
Est. 1976 *Stock size* Large
Stock Sporting antiques, prints,
library furniture, leather furniture
Open Mon–Sat 9.30am–5.30pm
Fairs Olympia
Services Exhibition held in Oct
every year

⊞ **Swan Gallery Antiques
(CADA)**
Contact Mr D Pratt
✉ 127 High Street, Burford,
Oxfordshire,
OX18 4RE ▣
☎ 01993 822244 ● 01993 822244
Est. 1977 *Stock size* Large
Stock Early oak and period
furniture
Open Mon–Sat 10am–5.30pm

CHALGROVE

⊞ **Hitchcox's Antiques**
Contact Rupert Hitchcox
✉ The Garth, Warpsgrove,
Chalgrove, Oxford, Oxfordshire,
OX44 7RW ▣
☎ 01865 890241 ● 01865 890241
ⓜ 07710 561505
● rupertsantiques@aol.com
ⓦ www.ruperthitchcoxantiques.co.uk
Est. 1957 *Stock size* Large
Stock 1650–1950 mainly English
furniture
Open Tues–Sat 10am–5pm or by
appointment
Services Valuations, buys at
auction

CHILTON

⌂ **Country Markets
Antiques & Collectables**
Contact Mr G Vaughan
✉ Wyevale Garden Centre,
Newbury Road, Chilton, Didcot,
Oxfordshire,
OX11 0QN ▣
☎ 01235 835125 ● 01235 833068
● country.markets.antiques@
breathemail.net
ⓦ www.countrymarkets.co.uk
Est. 1989 *Stock size* Large
No. of dealers 35
Stock Furniture, glass, jewellery,
cased fish, porcelain, ceramics etc
Open Mon 10.30am–5pm
Tues–Sat 10am–5.30pm Sun
Bank Holidays 10.30am–4.30pm
Services Valuations, restoration

CHINNOR

⊞ **Number 6**
Contact Pam Lievesley
✉ 6 Thame Road, Chinnor,
Oxfordshire, OX9 4QS ▣
☎ 01844 354344
Est. 1994 *Stock size* Small
Stock Antiques, decorative items
Open Mon–Sun 10am–5pm

CHIPPING NORTON

⊞ **Antique English
Windsor Chairs (BADA,
CINOA, CADA)**
Contact Michael Harding-Hill
✉ 9 Horse Fair, Chipping Norton,
Oxfordshire,
OX7 5AL ▣
☎ 01608 643322 ● 01608 644322
ⓜ 07798 653134
● michael@antique-english-
windsor-chairs.com
ⓦ www.antique-english-windsor-
chairs.com
Est. 1971 *Stock size* Large
Stock Antique English Windsor
chairs 18th–19thC, sets, singles
for collectors and everyday use
Open By appointment
Fairs Olympia (June, Nov)

⌂ **Chipping Norton
Antique Centre**
Contact Mr Wissinger
✉ Ivy House, Middle Row,
Chipping Norton,
Oxfordshire,
OX7 5NH ▣
☎ 01608 644212/641369
● 01608 641369
Est. 1986 *Stock size* Large
No. of dealers 15
Stock General antiques,
collectables,
Georgian–Edwardian furniture,
china, silver, kitchenware
Open 10am–5.30pm Mon–Sun
Services Tea room

⊞ **Cotswold Home
& Garden**
Contact Chris Holroyd
✉ 14 New Street,
Chipping Norton, Oxfordshire,
OX7 5LJ ▣
☎ 01608 644084
ⓜ 07770 904036
ⓦ kate@chippingnorton.fsworld.co.uk
Est. 1999 *Stock size* Medium
Stock Gardening antiques, eclectic
taste, benches, arches, urns,
gazebos, statuary, designer-led
Open Mon–Sat 10am–5pm most
Sun 10am–5pm closed Tues

⊞ **Georgian House
Antiques (LAPADA)**
Contact Sheila Wissinger
✉ 21 West Street,
Chipping Norton, Oxfordshire,
OX7 5EU ▣
☎ 01608 641369 ● 01608 641369

Est. 1986 *Stock size* Large
Stock Period oak, mahogany,
walnut furniture, paintings,
chairs, farmhouse furniture
Open Mon–Sun 10am–5pm or by
appointment
Services Delivery, shipping
arranged

⊞ **Kellow Books**
Contact Mr P Combellack
✉ 6 Market Place,
Chipping Norton, Oxfordshire,
OX7 5NA ▣
☎ 01608 644293
Est. 1998 *Stock size* Medium
Stock Antiquarian, rare, second-
hand collectable books
Open Mon–Sat 10am–4.30pm
Services Book search

⊞ **Key Antiques (CADA)**
Contact Jane or Keith Riley
✉ 11 Horsefair, Chipping Norton,
Oxfordshire,
OX7 5AL ▣
☎ 01608 643777
ⓜ 07860 650112
● info@keyantiques.com
ⓦ www.keyantiques.com
Est. 1976 *Stock size* Medium
Stock Period oak, country
furniture, related objects of
15th–18thC
Open Wed–Sat 10am–5.30pm
Services Valuations of period oak
and associated items

⌂ **Manchester House
Antiques**
Contact Mrs Shepherd
✉ Manchester House,
5 Market Place, Chipping Norton,
Oxfordshire,
OX7 5NA ▣
☎ 01608 646412
● msheperd@onetel.com
ⓦ www.chippingnorton.net
Est. 1997 *Stock size* Medium
No. of dealers 3
Stock Pine, oak furniture,
kitchenware, china, upholstered
chairs
Open Mon–Sun 10am–5pm

⊞ **Number 20**
Contact Chris Holroyd
✉ 20 New Street,
Chipping Norton, Oxfordshire,
OX7 5LJ ▣
☎ 01608 644084
ⓜ 07770 904036
ⓦ kate@chippingnorton.fsworld.co.uk

Est. 1999 *Stock size* Medium
Stock Gardening antiques,
eclectic taste, chandeliers,
benches, lighting – designer-led,
painted furniture
Open Mon–Sat most Sun
10am–5pm closed Tues

⌂ The Quiet Woman Antiques Centre
Contact Ann Marriott
✉ Southcombe,
Chipping Norton, Oxfordshire,
OX7 5QH 🅿
☎ 01608 646262 📠 01608 646262
📱 07860 889524
Est. 1998 *Stock size* Medium
No. of dealers 20
Stock Furniture, china, general
antiques, gardening antiques,
architectural
Open Mon–Fri 10am–6pm Sat
10am–5.30pm Sun 10am–5pm
Services Coffee shop

⌂ Station Mill Antiques Centre
Contact Jo Piperakis
✉ Station Road,
Chipping Norton, Oxfordshire,
OX7 5HX 🅿
☎ 01608 644563 📠 07092 310632
📧 info@stationmill.com
🌐 www.stationmill.com
Est. 1996 *Stock size* Large
No. of dealers 80
Stock Complete range of
antiques, collectables
Open Mon–Sun 10am–5pm
Services Tea room

CLEVELEY

⊞ A and E Foster Ltd (BADA, CINOA)
Contact Stephen Foster

✉ Quinton Cottage, Lidstone,
Oxfordshire,
OX7 4HL 🅿
☎ 01608 678731 📠 01608 678731
📱 07802 895146
📧 foster436@aol.com
Est. 1970 *Stock size* Medium
Stock European works of art and
sculpture
Open By appointment
Fairs Grosvenor House, Olympia
(spring and winter)

DEDDINGTON

⊞ Castle Antiques Ltd (LAPADA)
Contact John or Judy Vaughan
✉ Manor Farm, Clifton,
Deddington, Oxfordshire,
OX15 0PA 🅿
☎ 01869 338688
Est. 1972 *Stock size* Large
Stock General antiques,
furniture, metalware, silver,
reproduction garden furniture
Open By appointment

DEDDINGTON

⌂ Deddington Antique Centre (TVADA)
Contact Mrs Brenda Haller
✉ Laurel House, Bullring,
Deddington, Banbury,
Oxfordshire,
OX15 0TT 🅿
☎ 01869 338968 📠 01869 338916
📧 deddingtonantiquecentre@
yahoo.co.uk
Est. 1977 *Stock size* Large
No. of dealers 20
Stock Period furniture, silver,
porcelain, oil and watercolours,
jewellery, clocks, linen, glass
Open Mon–Sat 10am–5pm

Sun 11am–5pm
Services Porcelain, silver and
jewellery repairs, glass exports

DORCHESTER ON THAMES

⊞ Dorchester Antiques (TVADA, LAPADA)
Contact Mrs S or Jonty Hearnden
✉ The Barn, 3 High Street,
Dorchester on Thames,
Oxfordshire,
OX10 7HH 🅿
☎ 01865 341373 📠 01865 341373
Est. 1992
Stock Georgian furniture,
interesting country pieces
Open Tues–Sat 10am–5pm
Fairs TVADA
Services Finding service

⊞ Hallidays (Fine Antiques) Ltd (LAPADA, CINOA, TVADA)
Contact Mr E M Reily Collins
✉ High Street, Dorchester on
Thames, Oxfordshire,
OX10 7HL 🅿
☎ 01865 340028 📠 01865 341149
📧 antiques@hallidays.com
🌐 www.hallidays.com
Est. 1942 *Stock size* Large
Stock 17th–19thC English
furniture, decorative items,
paintings
Open Mon–Fri 9am–5pm
Sat 10am–4pm
Fairs Olympia, LAPADA (Jan)
Services Shipping

EAST HAGBOURNE

⊞ Craig Barfoot Clocks
Contact Craig Barfoot
✉ Tudor House, East Hagbourne,
Oxfordshire,

OX11 9LR
☎ 01235 818968 ❶ 01235 818968
Ⓜ 07710 858158
✉ craig.barfoot@tiscali.co.uk
Est. 1991 *Stock size* Medium
Stock Longcase, organ, musical
clocks
Open By appointment
Services Restoration, buys at
auction

⊞ E M Lawson and Co (ABA, ILAB)
Contact Mr J Lawson
✉ Kingsholm, Main Road,
East Hagbourne,
Oxfordshire,
OX11 9LN
☎ 01235 812033
Est. 1919 *Stock size* Small
Stock Rare and antiquarian
books, early English literature,
science, medicine, economics,
travel
Open Mon–Fri 9am–6pm or by
appointment

FARINGDON

⊞ Brushwood Antiques (TVADA)
Contact Nathan Sherriff
✉ 29 Marlborough Street,
Faringdon, Oxfordshire,
SN7 7JL
☎ 01367 244269
✉ nathan@brushwoodantiques.com
Ⓦ www.brushwoodantiques.com
Est. 1992 *Stock size* Medium
Stock 18th–19thC furniture
Open Tues–Sat 10am–5pm
appointment advisable
Fairs TVADA
Services Furniture restoration

HENLEY-ON-THAMES

⚘ Bonhams
✉ The Coach House,
66 Northfield End,
Henley-on-Thames,
Oxfordshire,
RG9 2JN
☎ 01491 413636 ❶ 01494 413637
✉ henley@bonhams.com
Ⓦ www.bonhams.com
Open Mon Fri 9am–5pm 1st
Sat of month 10am–1pm
Sales Regional office. Regular
sales held in London and in our
salerooms across the country.
Free auction valuations;
insurance and probate valuations

⊞ The Country Seat (TVADA, LAPADA, BACA Award Winner 2003)
Contact William Clegg
✉ Huntercombe Manor Barn,
Huntercombe, Henley-on-
Thames, Oxfordshire,
RG9 5RY
☎ 01491 641349 ❶ 01491 641533
✉ ferryandclegg@thecountryseat.com
Ⓦ www.thecountryseat.com
Est. 1971 *Stock size* Large
Stock Furniture designed by
architects 17th–20thC, post-war
furniture, art pottery,
metalwork, Whitefriars glass
Open Mon–Fri 9am–5pm
Sat 10am–5pm
Fairs TVADA

⌂ The Ferret (Friday Street Antiques Centre)
Contact Mrs D Etherington
✉ 4 Friday Street,
Henley-on-Thames, Oxfordshire,
RG9 1AH
☎ 01491 574104 ❶ 01491 641039
Est. 1984 *Stock size* Medium
No. of dealers 6
Stock Silver, furniture, china,
books, collectables, musical
instruments, stylized animals
Open Mon–Sat 10am–5.30pm
Sun noon–5.30pm

⌂ Henley Antique Centre
Contact Mr D Shepherd
✉ 2–4 Reading Road,
Henley-on-Thames, Oxfordshire,
RG9 1AG
☎ 01491 411468
Est. 1999 *Stock size* Large
No. of dealers 54
Stock Furniture, glass, china,
silver, coins, scientific
instruments, tools
Open Mon–Sat 10am–5pm
Sun noon–5pm

⚘ Jones and Jacob Ltd (RICS)
Contact Mr S Jones or
Miss M Share
✉ 32 Bell Street,
Henley-on-Thames, Oxfordshire,
RG9 2BH
☎ 01491 571111 ❶ 01491 579833
✉ info@jonesandjacob.com or
saleroom@jonesandjacob.com
Ⓦ www.jonesandjacob.com
Est. 1802
Open Mon–Fri 9am–5.30pm
Sat 9am–noon

Sales 8 sales of general antiques
per annum, valuations
Catalogues Yes

⊞ Jonkers Ltd (ABA, PBFA)
Contact Sam Jonkers
✉ 24 Hart Street,
Henley-on-Thames, Oxfordshire,
RG9 2AU
☎ 01491 576427 ❶ 01491 573805
✉ info@jonkers.co.uk
Ⓦ www.jonkers.co.uk
Est. 1990 *Stock size* Medium
Stock Antiquarian literature,
19th–20thC first editions,
illustrated and children's books
Open Mon–Sat 10am–5.30pm
Fairs Olympia
Services Valuations

⊞ Tudor House Antiques and Collectables
Contact Mr D Potter
✉ 49 Duke Street,
Henley-on-Thames, Oxfordshire,
RG9 1UR
☎ 01491 573680
Ⓜ 07717 132913
Est. 1996 *Stock size* Large
Stock General antiques,
collectables 1750s–2000
Open Mon–Sun 10am–5pm
Services Valuations, house
clearance

⊞ Ways Bookshop (ABA)
Contact Diana Cook
✉ 54b Friday Street,
Henley-on-Thames,
Oxfordshire,
RG9 1AH
☎ 01491 576663 ❶ 01491 576663
Est. 1977 *Stock size* Medium
Stock Rare and second-hand
books bought and sold
Open Mon–Sat 10am–5.30pm
Services Book search,
bookbinding, valuations

KINGHAM

⊞ Winson Antiques (BAFRA, LAPADA)
Contact Clive Payne
✉ Unit 11, Langstone Priory
Workshops, Station Road,
Kingham, Oxfordshire,
OX7 6UP
☎ 01608 658856
Ⓜ 07764476776
✉ clive.payne@virgin.net
Ⓦ www.clivepayne.co.uk
Est. 1986 *Stock size* Medium

Stock Period oak, Georgian mahogany
Open Mon–Fri 9am–5pm
Services Restoration

⊞ Winton Antiques (LAPADA, BAFRA)
Contact Clive Payne
✉ Unit 11 Langston Priory Workshops, Station Road, Kingham, Oxfordshire, OX7 6UP ℗
☎ 01608 658856 ℗ 01608 658856
Ⓜ 07764 476776
ⓔ clive.payne@virgin.net
Ⓦ www.clivepayne.co.uk
Est. 1986 *Stock size* Medium
Stock Period oak, Georgian mahogany, Mason's Ironstone china
Open Mon–Fri 9am–5pm
Services Antique furniture restoration

LONG WITTENHAM

⊞ Otter Antiques
Contact Mr P Otter
✉ Greenbank, High Street, Long Wittenham, Oxford, Oxfordshire, OX14 4QD ℗
☎ 01865 407396
Ⓦ www.otterantiques.co.uk
Est. 1994 *Stock size* Medium
Stock 18th–19thC boxes
Open By appointment
Services Restoration of boxes

MIDDLE ASTON

⊞ Cotswold Pine
Contact Mr Bob Prancks
✉ The Poultry Unit, Middle Aston, Bicester, Oxfordshire, OX25 5QL ℗
☎ 01869 340963 ℗ 01869 340963
Est. 1972 *Stock size* Large
Stock General antique furniture including mahogany, oak, pine
Open Mon–Sat 9am–6pm
Sun 10am–4.30pm
Services Restoration, stripping

⊞ Elizabeth Harvey-Lee (BACA Award winner 2003)
Contact Elizabeth Harvey-Lee
✉ 1 West Cottages, Middle Aston Road, North Aston, Oxfordshire, OX25 5QB ℗

☎ 01869 347164 ℗ 01869 347956
ⓔ north.aston@btinternet.com
Ⓦ www.elizabethharvey-lee.com
Est. 1989 *Stock size* Medium
Stock Old master prints, 19th–20thC artists' original etchings, wood engravings, etc
Open By appointment
Fairs London Original Print Fair, Olympia (Jun, Nov)
Services Catalogues by subscription

NORTHMOOR

⚒ Soames Country Auctioneers
Contact Gary Martin Soame
✉ Pinnocks Farm, Northmoor, Witney, Oxfordshire, OX29 5AY ℗
☎ 01865 300626 ℗ 01865 300432
ⓔ soame@msn.com
Ⓦ www.soamesauctioneers.co.uk
Est. 1991
Open By appointment
Sales General monthly antiques sales Sat 10.30am, viewing Thurs noon–6pm Fri 10am–8pm
Catalogues Yes

OXFORD

⌂ Antiques on High Ltd (TVADA)
Contact Mr P Lipson, J Lee or TS Wogett
✉ 85 High Street, Oxford, Oxfordshire, OX1 4BG ℗
☎ 01865 251075
Est. 1997 *Stock size* Large
No. of dealers 38
Stock Smalls, collectables, crafts, books
Open Mon–Sat 10am–5pm
Sun Bank Holidays 11am–5pm
Services Repairs, bookshops

⊞ Barclay Antiques
Contact Mr Colin Barclay
✉ 107 Windmill Road, Headington, Oxford, Oxfordshire, OX3 7BT ℗
☎ 01865 769551
ⓔ barclay-antiques@yahoo.com
Est. 1980 *Stock size* Large
Stock China, glass, silver, bronzes, lighting
Open Mon–Sat 10am–5.30pm closed Wed
Services Repairs to lighting

⊞ Blackwell's Rare Books (ABA, PBFA)
Contact Mr P Brown
✉ 48–51 Broad Street, Oxford, Oxfordshire, OX1 3BQ ℗
☎ 01865 333555 ℗ 01865 794143
ⓔ rarebooks@blackwell.co.uk
Ⓦ www.rarebooks.blackwell.co.uk
Est. 1879 *Stock size* Large
Stock Modern first editions, private press books, antiquarian English literature, juvenilia, general antiquarian books
Open Mon Wed–Sat 9am–6pm
Tues 9.30am–6pm
Fairs Olympia, 1 American fair per year east or west coast
Services Shipping, book search

⚒ Bonhams
✉ 39 Park End Street, Oxford, Oxfordshire, OX1 1JD
☎ 01865 723524 ℗ 01865 791064
ⓔ oxford@bonhams.com
Ⓦ www.bonhams.com/oxford
Open Mon–Fri 9am–5.30pm
Sales Regional saleroom. Regular sales held in London and in our salerooms across the country. Free auction valuations; insurance and probate valuations
Catalogues Yes

⊞ Reginald Davis (Oxford) Ltd (BADA, NAG)
Contact David Marcus
✉ 34 High Street, Oxford, Oxfordshire, OX1 4AN ℗
☎ 01865 248347
ⓔ finesilverware@aol.com
Est. 1966 *Stock size* Large
Stock Antique silverware and antique gemset gold jewellery
Open Tues–Fri 9am–5pm
Sat 10am–6pm
Services Valuations, repairs, restoration

⊞ Jericho Books (PBFA)
Contact Mr F Stringer
✉ 48 Walton Street, Oxford, Oxfordshire, OX2 6AD ℗
☎ 01865 511992
Ⓜ 07968 566591
ⓔ shop@jerichobooks.com
Ⓦ www.jerichobooks.com
Est. 1996 *Stock size* Medium
Stock Rare, antiquarian, general second-hand books

Open Mon–Sun 10am–6.30pm
Fairs Russell Square, London
Services Valuations, restoration,
book search

⊞ Liscious Interiors
Contact Fran or Walter
✉ 63 Banbury Road, Oxford,
Oxfordshire,
OX2 6PG ℗
☎ 01865 552232
⊕ 07973 479057
ⓦ www.liscious.co.uk
Est. 1995 *Stock size* Medium
Stock French mirrors, Italian
chandeliers, original painted
furniture, French country
antiques, Art Deco, 1950s
lighting, costumes, textiles
Open Mon–Sat 10.30am–6pm or
by appointment

⊞ Roger Little Antique
Pottery (English Ceramic
Circle)
Contact Roger Little
✉ White Lodge, Osler Road,
Headington, Oxford,
Oxfordshire,
OX3 9BJ ℗
☎ 01865 762317 ⊕ 01865 741595
ⓔ soxinfo@btclick.com
Est. 1985 *Stock size* Medium
Stock English and Continental
pottery, tiles,1650–1800
Open By appointment only
Fairs NEC
Services Valuations

⚒ Mallams
Contact Mr B Lloyd
✉ Bocardo House,
St Michael's Street, Oxford,
Oxfordshire,
OX1 2EB ℗
☎ 01865 241358 ⊕ 01865 725483
ⓔ oxford@mallams.co.uk
ⓦ www.mallams.co.uk
Est. 1788
Open Mon–Fri 9am–5.30pm
Sat 9am–1pm
Sales Sales of antiques, silver,
jewellery, books, pictures
Catalogues Yes

⊞ Oxford Furniture
Warehouse
Contact F & P K Mitchell
✉ 272 Abingdon Road, Oxford,
Oxfordshire,
OX1 4TA ℗
☎ 01865 202221 ⊕ 01865 202221
Est. 1992 *Stock size* Large

Stock Old pine, oak and general
furniture, some Continental
furniture
Open Mon–Sat 10am–5.30pm
Sun 11am–4.30pm

⊞ Payne and Son
(Goldsmiths) Ltd (BADA,
NAG)
Contact Judy Payne
✉ 131 High Street, Oxford,
Oxfordshire,
OX1 4DH ℗
☎ 01865 243787 ⊕ 01865 793241
ⓔ silver@payneandson.co.uk
ⓦ www.payneandson.co.uk
Est. 1790 *Stock size* Large
Stock 17thC–present day silver
including Arts and Crafts and
contemporary designs
Open Mon–Fri 9.30am–5.30pm
Sat 9am–5.30pm
Fairs BADA Chelsea, Olympia
Services Restoration

⊞ Sanders of Oxford
(PBFA)
Contact Sarah Boada-Momtahan
✉ 104 High Street, Oxford,
Oxfordshire,
OX1 4BW ℗
☎ 01865 242590 ⊕ 01865 721748
ⓔ sox-shop2@btclick.com
ⓦ www.sandersofoxford.com
Est. 1964 *Stock size* Large
Stock Antique prints, maps
especially Oxford related
Open Mon–Sat 10am–6pm
Fairs Original Print Fair (London,
Cork)

⊞ St Clements Antiques
Contact Mr G Power
✉ 93 St Clements Street, Oxford,
Oxfordshire,
OX4 1AR ℗
☎ 01865 727010 ⊕ 01865 864690
Est. 1999 *Stock size* Medium
Stock Town and country pieces
from home and abroad
Open Mon–Sat 10am–5pm
Services Valuations

PEPARD

⌂ Manor Farm Antiques
Contact Neil Bennett
✉ Manor Farm, Pepard Road,
Pepard, Oxfordshire,
RG9 5LA ℗
☎ 01491 628 448
ⓦ 07725 004449
Stock Furniture, glass,china,

silver, coins, scientific
instruments, tools
Open Mon–Sat 10am–5pm,
Sun noon–5pm

STANDLAKE

⊞ Manor Farm Antiques
Contact Charles Gower
✉ 159 Abingdon Road,
Standlake, Witney, Oxfordshire,
OX29 7RL ℗
☎ 01865 300303 ⊕ 01865 300153
Est. 1964 *Stock size* Large
Stock Brass, iron, wooden
bedsteads
Open Mon–Sat 10am–5pm

STEVENTON

⊞ Bennett and Kerr Books
(PBFA, ABA)
Contact Mr E Bennett
✉ Millhill Warehouse, Church
Lane, Steventon, Abingdon,
Oxfordshire,
OX13 6SW ℗
☎ 01235 820604
ⓔ bennettkerr@aol.com
Est. 1982 *Stock size* Medium
Stock Antique, scholarly books
on Middle Ages, Renaissance,
medieval studies
Open By appointment
Fairs PBFA, Oxford
Services Catalogues issued

TETSWORTH

⊞ Quillon Antiques of
Tetsworth (TVADA)
Contact Peter Magrath
✉ The Old Stores,
42a High Street,
Tetsworth, Nr Thame,
Oxfordshire,
OX9 7AS ℗
☎ 01844 281636
ⓔ quillonal@aol.com
Est. 1982 *Stock size* Medium
Stock Medieval armour
14th–19thC, period oak and
country furniture, French antiques
Open Tues Thurs Sat Sun
10am–6pm
Services Valuations

⌂ The Swan at Tetsworth
(TVADA, BACA Award
Winner 2004)
Contact Rita Woodman
✉ High Street, Tetsworth,
Nr Thame, Oxfordshire,

OX9 7AB 🅿
☎ 01844 281777
📧 antiques@theswan.co.uk
🌐 www.theswan.co.uk
Est. 1994 *Stock size* Large
No. of dealers 80
Stock 80 dealers in historic
Elizabethan coaching inn in 40
showrooms. Georgian–Art Deco
furniture, silver, mirrors, rugs,
glass, ceramics, jewellery, boxes,
garden statuary
Open Mon–Sun 10am–6pm
Services Renowned restaurant,
delivery arranged, events, shipping

THAME

⊞ Rosemary & Time
Contact Mr Tom Fletcher
✉ 42 Park Street, Thame,
Oxfordshire,
OX9 3HR 🅿
☎ 01844 216923
Est. 1983 *Stock size* Large
Stock Clocks
Open Mon–Sat 9am–5.30pm
Services Restoration, repairs

WALLINGFORD

⊞ Alicia Antiques
Contact Mrs A Collins
✉ Lamb Arcade, High Street,
Wallingford, Oxfordshire,
OX10 0BS 🅿
☎ 01491 833737
Est. 1979 *Stock size* Medium
Stock Silver, plate, glass, small
furniture
Open Mon–Sat 10am–5pm
Services Silver repairs

⊞ M & J De Albuquerque
Contact Mrs J De Albuquerque
✉ The Old Bakery, Thames Street
(car park), Wallingford,
Oxfordshire,
OX10 0BP 🅿
☎ 01491 832322 📠 01491 832322
📧 janedealb@tiscali.co.uk
Est. 1982 *Stock size* Medium
Stock 18th–19thC French and
English furniture, objects of the
period
Open By appointment
Fairs Brocante (Chelsea Town Hall)
Services Restoration, framing,
gilding

⊞ Toby English
Antiquarian &
Secondhand Bookshop

(PBFA)
Contact Mr T English
✉ 10 St Mary's Street,
Wallingford, Oxfordshire,
OX10 0EL 🅿
☎ 01491 836389 📠 01491 836389
📧 toby@tobyenglish.com
🌐 www.tobyenglish.com
Est. 1984 *Stock size* Large
Stock Art, architectural and
Renaissance literature, large
general stock
Open Mon–Sat 9.30am–5pm
Fairs PBFA
Services Book search, valuations,
catalogues issued

🏠 The Lamb Arcade
(TVADA)
Contact Mrs P Hayward
✉ 83 High Street, Wallingford,
Oxfordshire,
OX10 0BX 🅿
☎ 01491 835166 📠 01491 824247
📧 patriciantiques@aol.com
🌐 www.thelambarcade.co.uk
Est. 1979 *Stock size* Large
No. of dealers 45
Stock Everything from period
furniture to small items
Open Mon–Fri 10am–5pm
Sat 10am–5.30pm
Services Picture framing,
furniture restoration, local
delivery

⊞ O'Donnell Antiques
Contact Lin or Chris O'Donnell
✉ 26 High Street, Wallingford,
Oxfordshire,
OX10 0BU 🅿
☎ 01491 839332
Est. 1974 *Stock size* Large
Stock General antiques,
Georgian–early 20thC furniture,
taxidermy, rugs, English pine,
Oriental items, silver, Gaudy
Welsh, Staffordshire
Open Mon–Sat 9.30am–5pm

⊞ Phoenix Furniture
Contact David Belcher
✉ The Victorian Gallery,
3 Lamb Arcade, High Street,
Wallingford, Oxfordshire,
OX10 0BY 🅿
☎ 01491 833555
📱 07860 889524
Est. 1985 *Stock size* Large
Stock Antique pine,
Georgian–Victorian mahogany
furniture
Open Mon–Fri 10am–5pm

Sat 10am–5.30pm
Services Bespoke pine furniture,
restoration

⊞ Summers Davis
Antiques Ltd (TVADA,
LAPADA)
Contact Mr J Driver-Jones
✉ Calleva House, 6 High Street,
Wallingford, Oxfordshire,
OX10 0BP 🅿
☎ 01491 836284 📠 01491 833443
📧 antiques@summersdavis.co.uk
🌐 www.summersdavisantiques.co.uk
Est. 1915 *Stock size* Large
Stock 11 showrooms of
17th–19thC English and
Continental furniture
Open Mon–Fri 9am–5.30pm
Sat 9am–5pm Sun 11am–5pm
Fairs TVADA

⊞ Tooley, Adams and Co
(IMCOS, ABA, IAMA)
Contact Steve Luck
✉ PO Box 174, Wallingford,
Oxfordshire,
OX10 0YT 🅿
☎ 01491 838298 📠 01491 834616
📧 steve@tooleys.co.uk
🌐 www.tooleys.co.uk
Est. 1982 *Stock size* Large
Stock Antiquarian maps by
Blaeu, Bowen, Gibson, Fullarton,
Porcacchi, Saxton, Speed; Zatta
atlases
Open By appointment
Fairs London Map Fair (Olympia,
June), Bonnington Map Fair
(6 months per year), Miami
(February)
Services Valuations

WHEATLEY

⊞ Country Collections
Contact Mrs A Descenclos
✉ 47 High Street, Wheatley,
Oxford, Oxfordshire,
OX33 1XX 🅿
☎ 01865 875701
Est. 1992 *Stock size* Medium
Stock Small items, furniture,
general antiques
Open Mon–Sat 10am–4.30pm
Fairs Milton Keynes

WITNEY

⊞ Church Green Books
(PBFA)
Contact Margaret or Roger Barnes
✉ 46 Market Square, Witney,

Oxfordshire,
OX28 6AL 🅿
☎ 01993 700822
📧 books@churchgreen.co.uk
🌐 www.churchgreen.co.uk
Est. 1995 *Stock size* Medium
Stock General second-hand and
antiquarian books, books on
bellringing a speciality
Open Mon–Fri 10am–4pm
Services Book search

⊞ Julian Eade
✉ Witney, Oxon,
Oxfordshire,
OX29 🅿
📱 07973 542971
📧 julian.eade@cbre.com
Est. 1983 *Stock size* Medium
Stock Worcester, Minton, Derby,
Artist, Doulton stoneware
Open By appointment
Fairs NEC
Services Valuations

⊞ Colin Greenway Antiques (CADA)
Contact Jean Greenway
✉ 90 Corn Street, Witney,
Oxfordshire,
OX28 6BU 🅿
☎ 01993 705026 📠 01993 705026
📱 07831 585014
📧 jean_greenway@hotmail.com
🌐 www.greenwayantiques.viewing.at
Est. 1974 *Stock size* Medium
Stock 17th–early 20thC furniture,
general antiques, interesting and
unusual items, garden furniture,
gilt frames, rocking horses
Open Mon–Fri 9.30am–5.30pm
Sat 10am–4pm
Services Valuations

⊞ W R Harvey & Co (Antiques) Ltd (LAPADA, CADA)
Contact Mr David Harvey
✉ 86 Corn Street, Witney,
Oxfordshire,
OX28 6BU 🅿
☎ 01993 706501 📠 01993 706601
📧 antiques@wrharvey.co.uk
🌐 www.wrharvey.co.uk
Est. 1950 *Stock size* Large
Stock Important stock of English
furniture, clocks, pictures,
mirrors, works of art, 1680–1830
Open Mon–Sat 9.30am–5.30pm
Fairs Chelsea (spring, autumn),
Olympia (June)

Services Valuations, restoration,
conservation, buying at auction
for clients

⊞ Teddy Bears of Witney
Contact Ian Pout
✉ 99 High Street, Witney,
Oxfordshire,
OX28 6HY 🅿
☎ 01993 702616 📠 01993 702344
🌐 www.teddybears.co.uk
Est. 1985 *Stock size* Large
Stock Steiff, Merrythought,
Deans, Hermann, artists' bears
Open Mon–Fri 9.30am–5.30pm
Sat 9.30am–5pm
Sun 10.30am–4.30pm
Services Valuations

⊞ Witney Antiques (BADA, LAPADA, CADA)
Contact Mrs C J Jarrett
✉ 96–100 Corn Street, Witney,
Oxfordshire,
OX28 6BU 🅿
☎ 01993 703902 📠 01993 779852
📧 witneyantiques@community.co.uk
🌐 www.witneyantiques.com
Est. 1963 *Stock size* Large
Stock 17th–early 19thC furniture,
clocks, works of art, needlework,
probably the largest selection of
samplers in the UK
Open Wed–Sat 10am–5pm
Mon Tues by appointment
Fairs Grosvenor House, BADA
Services Restoration, catalogues

WOODSTOCK

⌂ Antiques at Heritage (TVADA)
Contact John Howard
✉ No 6 Market Place,
Woodstock, Oxfordshire,
OX20 1TA 🅿
☎ 01993 811332
📧 dealers@atheritage.co.uk
🌐 www.atheritage.co.uk
Est. 1984 *Stock size* Large
No. of dealers 4
Stock Textiles, books, silver,
ceramics, decorative arts,
luggage, lighting, pencil
drawings and pictures
Open Mon-Sat 10am–5pm
Sun 1–5pm

⊞ Chris Baylis Country Chairs (TVADA)
Contact Mr C Baylis

✉ 16 Oxford Street, Woodstock,
Oxfordshire,
OX20 1TS 🅿
☎ 01993 813887 📠 01993 812379
📧 rcwood@mcmail.com
🌐 www.realwoodfurniture.co.uk
Est. 1979 *Stock size* Large
Stock English country chairs
1780–present day, Windsor, rush-
seated ladder and spindleback
chairs, kitchen chairs etc
Open Tues–Sat 10.30am–5.30pm
Sun 11am–5pm

⊞ The Chair Set
Contact Allan James
✉ 18 Market Place, Woodstock,
Oxfordshire,
OX20 1TA 🅿
☎ 01428 707301 📠 01428 707457
📱 07801 754760
📧 allanjames@thechairset.com
🌐 www.thechairset.com
Est. 1985 *Stock size* Large
Stock 18th–19thC sets of chairs
and dining room antiques
Open Mon–Sun 10.30am–5.30pm
Services Valuations, search

⊞ John Howard (BADA, CADA, LAPADA)
Contact John Howard
✉ 6 Market Place, Woodstock,
Oxfordshire,
OX20 1TA 🅿
☎ 0870 444 0678 📠 0870 444 0678
📱 07831 850544
📧 john@johnhoward.co.uk
🌐 www.antiquepottery.co.uk
Est. 1976 *Stock size* Large
Stock British 18th–19thC pottery
Open Mon–Sat 10am–5pm
Sun 1–5pm
Fairs Olympia, New York
Ceramics Fair

YARNTON

⌂ Yarnton Antique Centre
Contact Mr M Dunseath
✉ within Yarnton Nurseries,
Sandy Lane, off A44, Yarnton,
Kidlington, Oxfordshire,
OX5 1PA 🅿
☎ 01865 379600
Est. 1998 *Stock size* Large
No. of dealers 70
Stock Furniture, silver, china,
brass, books, jewellery, lighting,
decorative items
Open Mon–Sun 10am–4.30pm

DERBYSHIRE

🏠 **Alfreton Antique Centre**
Contact Helen Dixon
✉ **11 King Street, Alfreton,
Derbyshire, DE55 7AF** ▣
☎ 01773 520781
Ⓜ 07970 786968
🅔 alfretonantiques@supanet.com
Ⓦ www.alfretonantiquescentre.com
Est. 1996 *Stock size* Large
No. of dealers 35
Stock General antiques,
collectables, furniture, clocks,
silver, militaria, books, postcards,
lighting
Open Mon–Sat 10am–4.30pm
Sun 11am–4.30pm
Services Derby replacement
service, ceramic restoration

🏛 **Curiosity Shop**
Contact Kenneth Allsop
✉ **37 King Street, Alfreton,
Derbyshire,**

DE55 7BY ▣
☎ 01773 832429
Ⓜ 07932 767463
Est. 1974 *Stock size* Medium
Stock General antiques, pine
furniture
Open Mon–Sat 9.30am–5pm

🏛 **steam-models.uk.com**
Contact Mr R Evison
✉ **31 South Street, Riddings,
Alfreton, Derbyshire,
DE55 4EJ** ▣
☎ 01773 541527 🅕 01773 541527
Ⓜ 07713 514320
🅔 raevison@aol.com
Ⓦ www.steammodels.uk.com
Est. 1990 *Stock size* Large
Stock Old and new live steam
models
Open Mon–Fri 9am–5pm

🏛 **Peter Bunting (LAPADA,
BADA, CINOA)**
Contact Mr P Bunting

✉ **Harthill Hall, Alport, Bakewell,
Derbyshire,
DE45 1LH** ▣
☎ 01629 636203 🅕 01629 636101
Ⓜ 07860 540870
🅔 peter@peterbunting.com
Ⓦ www.peterbunting.com
Est. 1975 *Stock size* Medium
Stock English oak and country
furniture, tapestries, portraits
Open By appointment
Fairs Olympia, NEC, CHELSEA

🏛 **Ashbourne Antiques Ltd**
Contact Robert Allsebrook
✉ **Blake House Farm, Shirley,
Ashbourne, Derbyshire,
DE6 3AS** ▣
☎ 01335 361236
Ⓜ 07970 094883
Est. 1975 *Stock size* Large
Stock 18th–20thC furniture
Open By appointment
Services Restoration, shipping,
removals, storage

⊞ **M G Bassett Pine &
Decorative Items
(Asbourne Antiques
Association)**
Contact Gill Bassett
✉ 38 Church Street, Ashbourne,
Derbyshire,
DE6 1AJ 🅿
☎ 01335 300 061 ❶ 01335 300 061
✉ mgbassett@aol.cpm
Est. 1980 *Stock size* Medium
Stock French and English
countrypine furniture, decorative
items
Open Mon–Sat 10am–5pm
closed Wed or by appointment
Services Restoration

⊞ **Daniel Charles Antiques**
Contact Keith Phillip-Small
✉ 33 Church Street,
Ashbourne,
Derbyshire,
DE6 1AE 🅿
☎ 01335 300002
Ⓜ 07775 862491
✉ keith@danielcharlesantiques.com
Ⓦ www.danielcharlesantiques.com
Est. 2000 *Stock size* Medium
Stock General antiques
Open Mon–Fri 9.30–5pm
closed Wed Sat 10am–5pm
Services Restoration

⊞ **Eclectica Interiors**
Contact Quinton Heyre
✉ 30 Clifton Road,
Ashbourne,
Derbyshire,
DE6 1DT 🅿
☎ 01335 346113 ❶ 01335 346113
Ⓜ 07971 660949
Est. 2003 *Stock size* Medium
Stock Continental and English
antiques, interior design
Open Mon–Sat 10.30am–4.30pm
closed Wed
Fairs Keddleston Hall

⊞ **J H S Antiques Ltd
(LAPADA, CINOA, Pewter
Society, Metalware Society)**
Contact Mr J H Snodin
✉ 45 & 47 Church Street,
Ashbourne, Derbyshire,
DE6 1AJ 🅿
☎ 01335 347733
Ⓜ 07810 122248
Est. 1970 *Stock size* Medium
Stock Period oak, metalware,
carving, treen
Open Tues–Sat 10am–5pm
closed Wed

⊞ **Prestwood Antiques**
Contact Mr Chris Ball
✉ 28b & 39 Church Street,
Ashbourne,
Derbyshire,
DE6 1AJ 🅿
☎ 01335 342198 ❶ 01335 342198
Ⓜ 07976 767629
✉ chris@spurrier-smith.fsnet.co.uk
Est. 1989 *Stock size* Large
Stock General antiques
Open Mon–Sat 10am–5pm
closed Wed
Services Restoration

⊞ **Rose Antiques**
Contact Mrs G Rose
✉ 37 Church Street,
Ashbourne,
Derbyshire,
DE6 1AE 🅿
☎ 01335 343822 ❶ 01335 343822
Est. 1984 *Stock size* Medium
Stock General antiques
Open Mon–Sat 10am–5pm
closed Wed

⊞ **Spurrier-Smith Antiques
(LAPADA, CINOA)**
Contact Mr I Spurrier-Smith
✉ 28b & 39 Church Street,
Ashbourne,
Derbyshire,
DE6 1AE 🅿
☎ 01335 343669 ❶ 01335 342198
Ⓜ 07831 454603
✉ ivanspurrier-smith@fsnet.com
Ⓦ www.spurrier-smith.co.uk
Est. 1974 *Stock size* Large
Stock General antiques, large
pine warehouse, furniture,
decorative items
Open Mon–Sat 10am–5pm
closed Wed
Services Valuations

⊞ **Top Drawer Antiques**
Contact Justin Flint
✉ 30 Church Street,
Ashbourne,
Derbyshire,
DE6 1AE 🅿
☎ 01335 343669
Ⓜ 07970 720133
✉ sarah@topdrawerantiques.
freeserve.co.uk
Est. 1990 *Stock size* Large
Stock General antiques, pine,
kitchenware, highly decorative
items
Open Mon–Sat 10am–5pm
closed Wed or by appointment
Services Restoration

BAKEWELL

⊞ **Allens**
Contact Mike or Mavis Allen
✉ Chappells Antiques Centre,
Bakewell, 1–4 King Street,
Bakewell, Derbyshire,
DE45 1DZ 🅿
☎ 01629 812496 ❶ 01629 411918
✉ books@allensbooks.co.uk
(books) or
mavis@allensbooks.co.uk
(ceramics)
Ⓦ www.allensbooks.co.uk
Est. 1996 *Stock size* Medium
Stock 20thC ceramics, quality
second-hand books
Open Mon–Sat 10am–5pm
Sun noon–5pm
Services Online sales

⊞ **Cambridge Fine Art
(LAPADA)**
Contact Nick Lury
✉ 33 Church Street,
Little Stelford, Cambridge,
CB2 5HG 🅿
☎ 01223 842866 ❶ 01223 842866
✉ cambridgefineart@aol.com
Est. 1973 *Stock size* Large
Stock Fine British and
Continental oil paintings
1750–1940
Open By appointment
Fairs Olympia, Chester, NEC

⌂ **Chappells Antiques
Centre, Bakewell**
Contact Mrs J Chappell
✉ 1–4 King Street, Bakewell,
Derbyshire,
DE45 1DZ 🅿
☎ 01629 812496 ❶ 01629 814531
✉ ask@chappellsantiquescentre.com
Ⓦ www.chappellsantiquescentre.com
Est. 1992 *Stock size* Large
No. of dealers 30
Stock 17th–20thC furniture,
decorative and collectors' items
Open Mon–Sat 10am–5pm Sun
noon–5pm
Services Restoration, valuation
for sale, wedding lists, finance

⊞ **Cottage Antiques**
Contact P Milling
✉ Chappells Antiques Centre,
Bakewell, 1–4 King Street,
Bakewell, Derbyshire,
DE45 1DZ 🅿
☎ 01283 562670 ❶ 01283 562670
✉ ask@chappellsantiquescentre.com
Ⓦ www.chappellsantiquescentre.com

Est. 1970 *Stock size* Large
Stock Late 19thC curtain
furniture, curtain poles, pelmets,
tie-backs, curtain rings, small
decorative antiques
Open Mon–Sat 10am–5pm
Sun noon–5pm
Fairs NEC, Harrogate, Chester
Spirit of Christmas, Daily
Telegraph House and Garden
Show Olympia

⊞ D J Green Antiques (LAPADA)
Contact D Green
✉ Chappells Antiques Centre, Bakewell, 1–4 King Street, Bakewell, Derbyshire, DE45 1DZ ℗
☎ 01629 812496
℡ 07768 832616
✉ antiques@dggreen.co.uk
ⓦ www.chappellsantiquescentre.com
Est. 1970 *Stock size* Medium
Stock 18–19thC furniture, desks, upholstered chairs and settees, dining tables, chests-of-drawers, decorative mirrors, furnishings
Open Mon–Sat 10am–5pm
Sun noon–5pm
Fairs Buxton, Newark

⊞ Stephanie Davison Antiques (LAPADA, CINOA)
Contact Stephanie Davison
✉ Chappells Antiques Centre, Bakewell, 1–4 King Street, Bakewell, Derbyshire, DE45 1DZ ℗
☎ 01629 812496 ⓖ 01629 814531
℡ 07771 564993
Est. 1999 *Stock size* Large
Stock Oak and country furniture, longcase clocks, treen, metalware and associated items
Open Mon–Sat 10am–5pm
Sun noon–5pm
Fairs NEC, Buxton, LAPADA, Cheltenham
Services Restoration of clocks and furniture

⊞ Roger DeVille Antiques (LAPADA)
Contact Roger DeVille
✉ Chappells Antiques Centre, Bakewell, 1–4 King Street, Bakewell, Derbyshire, DE45 1DZ ℗
☎ 01629 812496 ⓖ 01629 814531
℡ 07798 793857
✉ ask@chappellsantiquescentre.com
ⓦ www.chappellsantiquescentre.com

Est. 1980 *Stock size* Medium
Stock 18th–19thC pottery, Mason's Ironstone, Prattware, creamware, Delft, saltglaze, blue and white, printed wares, commemoratives, Staffordshire figures
Open Mon–Sat 10am–5pm
Sun noon–5pm
Fairs Kensington, Chelsea, Harrogate, NEC, Penman Fairs Chester
Services Valuations

⊞ J Dickinson Maps & Prints
Contact J Dickinson
✉ Stand 4, Chappells Antiques Centre, Bakewell, 1–4 King Street, Bakewell, Derbyshire, DE45 1DZ ℗
☎ 01629 812496 ⓖ 01629 814531
℡ 07885 174890
✉ ask@chappellsantiquescentre.com
ⓦ www.chappellsantiquescentre.com
Est. 1994 *Stock size* Large
Stock Antiquarian maps and engravings, mainly topographical, but also railway, children's and decorative prints, Derbyshire books and related items
Open Mon–Sat 10am–5pm
Sun noon–5pm
Fairs Louise Walker's Harrogate Fairs, NEC, datelined fairs, midlands and north of England
Services Map search, cleaning, restoring, mounting and fixing, valuations, restoration

⊞ Etceteras
Contact B Austin
✉ Chappells Antiques Centre, Bakewell, 1–4 King Street, Bakewell, Derbyshire, DE45 1DZ ℗
☎ 01629 812496 ⓖ 01629 814531
✉ ask@chappellsantiquescentre.com
ⓦ www.chappellsantiquescentre.com
Est. 1970 *Stock size* Small
Stock Vintage handbags, jewellery, bijouterie, compacts, linen
Open Mon–Sat 10am–5pm
Sun noon–5pm

⊞ G W Ford & Son Ltd (LAPADA)
Contact Ian Thomson
✉ Stands 1 and 2, Chappells Antiques Centre, 1–4 King Street, Bakewell, Derbyshire,

DE45 1DZ ℗
☎ 01246 410512 ⓖ 01246 419223
℡ 07740 025936
✉ enquiries@gwfordantiques.co.uk
ⓦ www.gwfordantiques.co.uk
Est. 1908 *Stock size* Medium
Stock 18th–early 20thC town and country furniture, sculpture, decorative items, treen, silver, old Sheffield plate, metalware
Open Mon–Sat 10am–5pm
Sun noon–5pm
Fairs Buxton
Services Restoration, commisioning

⊞ Martin and Dorothy Harper Antiques (LAPADA)
Contact Martin or Dorothy Harper
✉ King Street, Bakewell, Derbyshire, DE45 1DZ ℗
☎ 01629 814757
℡ 07885 347134
Est. 1971 *Stock size* Medium
Stock 18th–early 20thC furniture, metalware, decorative items
Open Tues Wed Fri Sat 10am–5pm or by appointment
Services Valuations

⊞ Brian L Hills (BADA, LAPADA)
Contact Brian L Hills
✉ Stands 5 and 6, Chappells Antiques Centre, Bakewell, 1–4 King Street, Bakewell, Derbyshire, DE45 1DZ ℗
☎ 01629 812496 ⓖ 01629 814531
℡ 07860 453940
✉ ask@chappellsantiquescentre.com
ⓦ www.chappellsantiquescentre.com
Est. 1978 *Stock size* Large
Stock 17th–19thC furniture, bronze sculpture, works of art, marble, treen, metalware, paintings, decorative objects, longcase and bracket clocks
Open Mon–Sat 10am–5pm
Sun noon–5pm

⊞ J Lawrence (BADA, LAPADA)
Contact J Lawrence
✉ Chappells Antiques Centre, Bakewell, 1–4 King Street, Bakewell, Derbyshire, DE45 1DZ ℗
☎ 01629 812496 ⓖ 01629 814531
✉ ask@chappellsantiquescentre.com
ⓦ www.chappellsantiquescentre.com

Est. 1980 *Stock size* Medium
Stock Silver and silver plate,
scent bottles, porcelain,
tortoiseshell and mother-of-pearl
card cases etc, vesta cases,
bijouterie
Open Mon–Sat 10am–5pm
Sun noon–5pm

⊞ Original Vintage Costume Jewellery
Contact Judy Portway
⊠ Chappells Antiques Centre,
Bakewell, 1–4 King Street,
Bakewell, Derbyshire,
DE45 1DZ ⚏
☎ 01629 812496 ● 01629 814531
● ask@chappellsantiquescentre.com
ⓦ www.chappellsantiquescentre.com
Est. 1989 *Stock size* Medium
Stock Original vintage costume
jewellery, compacts, handbags
Open Mon–Sat 10am–5pm
Sun noon–5pm
Fairs Snape

⊞ Paraphernalia
Contact Steve or Jo Bentley
⊠ Stand 11, Chappells Antiques
Centre, Bakewell, 1–4 King
Street, Bakewell, Derbyshire,
DE45 1DZ ⚏
☎ 01629 812496 ● 01298 71648
● stevebentley@btinternet.com
ⓦ www.chappellsantiquescentre.com
Est. 1992 *Stock size* Large
Stock Period lighting, Arts and
Crafts, metalware, small
furniture, decorative glass
Open Mon–Sat 10am–5pm
Sun noon–5pm
Fairs Buxton
Services Valuations, restoration,
fitting, delivery

⊞ Michael Pembery Antiques
Contact Michael Pembery
⊠ Peppercorn House, Kings
Street, Bakewell, Derbyshire,
DE45 1FD ⚏
☎ 01629 814161
Est. 1967 *Stock size* Medium
Stock 17th–18thC oak and
walnut furniture, blue john,
Ashford marble
Open Mon–Sat 10am–5pm
closed Thurs

⊞ Doug Pye
Contact Douglas Pye
⊠ Chappells Antiques Centre,
Bakewell, 1–4 King Street,

Bakewell, Derbyshire,
DE45 1DZ ⚏
☎ 01629 812496 ● 01629 814531
ⓜ 07890 328449
● douglas.pye@tesco.net
ⓦ www.chappellsantiquescentre.com
Est. 1975 *Stock size* Medium
Stock Early blue and white,
Ironstone china, copper lustre,
Flow blue, clocks and barometers
Open Mon–Sat 10am–5pm
Sun noon–5pm
Services Courier service, buying
advice

⊞ Scarlett Antiques
Contact Robert Furmage
⊠ Chappells Antiques Centre,
Bakewell, 1–4 King Street,
Bakewell, Derbyshire,
DE45 1DZ ⚏
☎ 01629 812496 ● 01629 814531
ⓜ 07813 701146
● ask@chappellsantiquescentre.com
ⓦ www.chappellsantiquescentre.com
Est. 1900 *Stock size* Medium
Stock Antique gemstone
jewellery, bracket clocks
Open Mon–Sat 10am–5pm
Sun noon–5pm
Services Restoration of jewellery
and clocks

⊞ Shirley May
Contact S M Smith
⊠ Chappells Antiques Centre,
Bakewell, 1–4 King Street,
Bakewell, Derbyshire,
DE45 1DZ ⚏
☎ 01629 812496 ● 01629 814531
● ask@chappellsantiquescentre.com
ⓦ www.chappellsantiquescentre.com
Est. 1985 *Stock size* Medium
Stock Cornish ware, Denby ware,
old linen and lace, interesting
bygones and kitchenware
Open Mon–Sat 10am–5pm
Sun noon–5pm

⊞ Sandra Wallhead
Contact Sandra Wallhead
⊠ Stand 14, Chappells Antiques
Centre, Bakewell, 1–4 King
Street, Bakewell, Derbyshire,
DE45 1DZ ⚏
☎ 01629 812496 ● 01629 814531
ⓜ 07748 005954
● ask@chappellsantiquescentre.com
ⓦ www.chappellsantiquescentre.com
Est. 1980 *Stock size* Medium
Stock Cranberry glass, music
boxes, hatpins, small Victorian
furniture, clocks and barometers,

silver, dolls, Clarice Cliff, scent
bottles
Open Mon–Sat 10am–5pm
Sun noon–5pm
Fairs Newark

⊞ N I Wilkinson
Contact Ian Wilkinson
⊠ Chappells Antiques Centre,
Bakewell, 1–4 King Street,
Bakewell, Derbyshire,
DE45 1DZ ⚏
☎ 01629 812496 ● 01629 814531
● ask@chappellsantiquescentre.com
ⓦ www.chappellsantiquescentre.com
Est. 1983 *Stock size* Small
Stock Pottery, metalware, treen,
gardening antiques, collectables,
textiles
Open Mon–Sat 10am–5pm
Sun noon–5pm

BAMFORD

⊞ High Peak Antiques
Contact Denise Shaw or
Richard Casey
⊠ High Peak Garden Centre,
Sickleholme, Bamford,
Derbyshire,
S33 0AH ⚏
☎ 01433 659595
ⓜ 07976 934007
ⓦ www.highpeakantiques.co.uk
Est. 1998 *Stock size* Large
Stock Sports memorabilia, books,
Victoriana, jewellery, Moorcroft,
toys, kitchenware, paintings,
furniture, linen, glass, china, silver
Open Mon–Sun 10am–4.30pm
Winter 10am–5pm Summer

BARLOW

⊞ Hackney House Antiques
Contact Mrs J M Gorman
⊠ Hackney House,
Hackney Lane, Barlow,
Dronfield, Derbyshire,
S18 7TF ⚏
☎ 0114 289 0248
Est. 1981 *Stock size* Medium
Stock Longcase and wall clocks,
Georgian–Edwardian furniture,
silver, pictures, porcelain, glass
Open Tues–Sun 9am–6pm

BASLOW

⊞ Antiques in Baslow
Contact Richard Crabtree
⊠ Barbrook House, Nether End,

Baslow, Bakewell, Derbyshire,
DE45 1SR 🅿
☎ 01246 583659
Ⓜ 07946 277814
Est. 1993 *Stock size* Medium
Stock General antiques, clocks,
barometers, children's toys,
rocking horses, pedal cars
Open Fri–Sat 10.30am–4.30pm
Sun 12.30–4.30pm or by
appointment
Services Clock restoration

BELPER

⊞ Best Secondhand Centre
Contact Simon Truin
✉ 118 Bridge Street, Belper,
Derbyshire,
DE56 1AZ 🅿
☎ 01773 828388
Est. 1997 *Stock size* Medium
Stock Furniture
Open Mon–Sun 9am–4.30pm

⊞ Derwentside Antiques
Contact Mr M J Adams
✉ Derwent Street, Belper,
Derbyshire,
DE56 1WN 🅿
☎ 01773 828008 ❻ 01773 828983
❸ enquiries@derwentsidehome
centre.co.uk
Ⓦ www.derwentsidehomecentre.co.uk
Est. 1994 *Stock size* Large
Stock General antiques
Open Mon–Sun 8.30am–5pm
Fairs Newark, Swinderby
Services Architectural salvage

⊞ Sweetings Antiques Belper
Contact Mr or Mrs Sweeting
✉ 1 & 1a The Butts, Belper,
Derbyshire,
DE56 1HX 🅿
☎ 01773 825930
Ⓜ 07973 658640
Est. 1972 *Stock size* Large
Stock General antiques, country
pine furniture, home accessories
Open Mon–Sat 9.30am–5.30pm
Sun 11am–4.30pm
Services Restoration and pine
stripping

BRADWELL

🏠 Bradwell Antiques Centre
Contact Mr N Cottam
✉ Newburgh Hall, Netherside,
Bradwell, Derbyshire,

S33 9JL 🅿
☎ 01433 621000 ❻ 01433 621000
❸ info@bradwellantiques.com
Ⓦ www.bradwellantiques.com
Est. 2000 *Stock size* Large
No. of dealers 47
Stock Furniture, paintings,
general antiques, collectables
Open Mon–Sat 10am–5pm
Sun 11am–5pm
Services Restoration, coffee shop

BUXTON

⊞ Antiques Warehouse
Contact Nigel Thompson
✉ 25 Lightwood Road, Buxton,
Derbyshire,
SK17 7BJ 🅿
☎ 01298 72967 ❻ 01298 22603
Ⓜ 07947 050552
Est. 1979 *Stock size* Large
Stock General antiques
Open Mon–Fri 10am–3pm Sat
10am–4pm Sun by appointment
Services Valuations, restoration

⊞ Back to Front
Contact Miss Simone Jordan-
Lomas
✉ 9–11 Market Street, Buxton,
Derbyshire,
SK17 6JY 🅿
☎ 01298 23969
Est. 1974 *Stock size* Large
Stock Antique textiles
Open Mon–Sun 10am–8pm
Fairs Newark, The International
Antique and Collectables Fair at
RAF Swinderby

⊞ A & A Needham
Contact Ann Needham
✉ 8 Cavendish Circus, Buxton,
Derbyshire,
SK17 6AT 🅿
☎ 01298 24546
Ⓜ 07941 436931
Est. 1953 *Stock size* Small
Stock French, Dutch, English
furniture, paintings, bronzes,
works of art
Open Mon–Sat 9am–5pm
Fairs Buxton, Tatton

⊞ What Now Antiques
Contact Mrs L or Mr Carruthers
✉ Unit 8, Cavendish Arcade,
The Crescent, Buxton,
Derbyshire,
SK17 6BQ 🅿
☎ 01298 27178
Est. 1987 *Stock size* Medium

Stock General 19th–20thC antiques
Open Mon–Sat 10am–5pm
Sun 1–4.30pm
Services Valuations

CASTLE DONINGTON

⊞ Once Removed
Contact Mrs Whiston
✉ 25 Borough Street, Castle
Donington, Derbyshire,
DE74 2LA 🅿
Ⓜ 07931 993251
Est. 1998 *Stock size* Small
Stock Furniture, glass, china
Open Mon Fri 9.30am–4pm Thurs
9.30am–3pm Sat 10am–1pm
Services Valuations

CASTLETON

⊞ Hawkridge Books
Contact Irene or Joe Tierney
✉ Cruck Barn, Cross Street,
Castleton, Derbyshire,
S33 8WH 🅿
☎ 01433 621999
Ⓦ www.hawkridge.co.uk
Est. 1995 *Stock size* Large
Stock Antiquarian, rare and
second-hand books, ornithology
Open Mon–Fri 10am–5pm Sat
10am–5.30pm Sun noon–5.30pm

CHESTERFIELD

🏠 Chesterfield Antiques Centre
Contact Chris
✉ 110–112 Saltergate,
Chesterfield, Derbyshire,
S40 1NE 🅿
☎ 01246 224345
Ⓜ 07855 966221
Est. 2005 *Stock size* Large
No. of dealers 50+
Stock General antiques and
collectables including furniture,
ceramics, glass, jewellery,
pictures and textiles
Open Mon–Sat 10am–5pm
Sun 10am–4pm
Services Valuations, restoration

⊞ Ian Morris
Contact Mr I Morris
✉ 479 Chatsworth Road,
Chesterfield, Derbyshire,
S40 3AD 🅿
☎ 01246 235120
Est. 1974 *Stock size* Medium
Stock General antiques
Open By appointment

Marlene Rutherford Antiques
Contact Mrs M Rutherford
⊠ 401 Sheffield Road, Whittington Moor, Chesterfield, Derbyshire, S41 8LS 🅿
☎ 01246 450209
📱 07885 665440
🌐 www.marlenerutherford.co.uk
Est. 1984 *Stock size* Large
Stock General antiques, upholstered furniture, oil lamps, clocks, porcelain, pottery
Open Mon Tues Fri Sat 1–4pm Thurs 10am–4pm
Fairs Jaguar fairs
Services Valuations

CLOWNE

Wartime Wardrobe
Contact Mr Barry Draycott
⊠ 105 Portland Street, Clowne, Chesterfield, Derbyshire, S43 4SA 🅿
📱 07966 450726
Est. 1995 *Stock size* Medium
Stock Military and civilian 1940s vintage clothing, general militaria
Open Any time by appointment
Fairs Most 1940s themed events throughout the UK, some military shows
Services Valuations, advice

CROMFORD

Antiques Loft
Contact Brendan Rogerson
⊠ Market Place, Cromford, Matlock, Derbyshire, DE4 3QH 🅿
☎ 01629 826565
Est. 1993 *Stock size* Large
Stock Victorian pine, shipping furniture
Open By appointment

DERBY

🔨 Bamfords Auctioneers & valuers (RICS)
Contact Simon Beresford
⊠ The Derby Auction House, Chequers Road, off Pentagon Island, Derby, Derbyshire, DE21 6EN 🅿
☎ 01332 210000
📱 01332 368424
📧 bamfords-auctions@tiscali.co.uk
🌐 www.bamfords-auctions.co.uk
Est. 2002

Open Mon–Fri 9am–5.30pm
Sales General sale fortnightly, fine art 6 times a year
Catalogues Yes

Cottage Antiques
Contact Roger Harrison
⊠ 34 Derby Road, Melbourne, Derby, Derbyshire, DE73 8FE 🅿
☎ 01332 862465 📱 01332 862465
Est. 1999 *Stock size* Medium
Stock Country furniture, general antiques
Open Please call for times
Services Valuations, restoration

A S Derrick
Contact Steven Derrick
⊠ 141 Normanton Lane, Littleover, Derby, Derbyshire, DE23 6LF 🅿
☎ 01332 773674
Est. 1983 *Stock size* Medium
Stock Clocks
Open Mon–Fri 9am–5pm
Services Restoration of clocks

Finishing Touches
Contact Lynne Robertson
⊠ 224 Uttoxeter Old Road, Derby, Derbyshire, DE1 1NF 🅿
☎ 01332 721717
📱 07789 727596
🌐 www.derbyantiques.co.uk
Est. 1994 *Stock size* Medium
Stock Georgian–Victorian fireplaces and fire surrounds, pine doors, locks, handles, window catches, pine furniture
Open Thur–Sat 10am–5.30pm or by appointment

Friargate Antiques Company
Contact Glyn or Daryl Richards
⊠ 120 Friargate, Derby, Derbyshire, DE1 1EX 🅿
☎ 01332 297966 📱 01332 297966
📱 07976 929456
📧 daryl@friargateantiques.co.uk
🌐 www.friargateantiques.co.uk
Est. 1978 *Stock size* Large
Stock General antiques, Royal Crown Derby
Open Mon–Fri 10am–4pm Sat 10am–5pm
Fairs Newark
Services Valuations, restoration

Friargate Pine Co Ltd
Contact John Marianszi
⊠ Old Pump House, Friargate Goods Wharf, Stafford Street, Derby, Derbyshire, DE1 1JL 🅿
☎ 01332 341215 📱 01332 341215
📧 enquiries@friargatepine.co.uk
🌐 www.friargatepine.co.uk
Est. 1984 *Stock size* Medium
Stock Antique, reproduction pine
Open Mon–Sat 9am–5pm
Services Made to measure

Melbourne Hall Furniture
Contact Mr N Collumbell
⊠ Old Saw Mill Craft Centre, Melbourne Hall, Melbourne, Derby, Derbyshire, DE73 8EN 🅿
☎ 01332 864131
Est. 2002 *Stock size* Small
Stock Georgian–Edwardian furniture, general bric a brac
Open By appointment
Services Restoration

DUFFIELD

Wayside Antiques
Contact Brian Harding
⊠ 62 Town Street, Duffield, Belper, Derbyshire, DE56 4GG 🅿
☎ 01332 840346
Est. 1976 *Stock size* Large
Stock 18th–19thC furniture
Open Mon–Sat 10am–6pm
Services Valuations, restoration

FURNESS VALE

Furness Vale Antiques
Contact Mrs K Thomas
⊠ 95 Buxton Road, Furness Vale, High Peak, Derbyshire, SK23 7PL 🅿
☎ 01663 747183
Est. 1980 *Stock size* Small
Stock General antiques
Open Thurs 10am–4pm

GLOSSOP

Chapel Antiques
Contact Mr Norman Pogsom
⊠ Glossop Antique Centre, 126 Brookfield, Glossop, Derbyshire, SK13 6JE 🅿
☎ 01457 866711
Est. 1984 *Stock size* Medium

MIDLANDS
DERBYSHIRE • NEW MILLS

MIDLANDS

Stock Clocks, barometers, pottery, general antiques
Open Thurs–Sun 10am–4pm

⊞ **Cottage Antiques**
Contact Mrs J Shapter
✉ Unit 13, Brookfield, Glossop, Derbyshire,
SK13 6JF
☎ 01457 863984
Est. 1979 Stock size Large
Stock General antiques
Open Thurs–Sun Bank Holidays 10am–5pm
Services Valuations, house clearance

⊞ **Derbyshire Clocks**
Contact Terry or Judith Lees
✉ 104 High Street West, Glossop, Derbyshire,
SK13 8BB
☎ 01457 862677
Est. 1971 Stock size Medium
Stock Clocks, barometers and other related items, pre-1880 longcase and wall clocks
Open Thurs–Sat 9am–5pm Sun noon–4.30pm
Services Restoration

⌂ **Glossop Antique Centre**
Contact Mr G Conway
✉ Brookfield, Glossop, Derbyshire,
SK13 6JE
☎ 01457 863904
Est. 1990 Stock size Medium
No. of dealers 12
Stock General antiques
Open Thurs–Sun 10am–5pm
Services Valuations, restoration, café

⊞ **O'Sullivan Antiques Ltd**
Contact Michael O'Sullivan
✉ Unit 3, Glossop Antique Centre, Brookfield, Glossop, Derbyshire,
SK13 6JE
☎ 01457 864488
⓿ 07834 478555
Est. 2003 Stock size Medium
Stock Victorian–Edwardian furniture, collectables
Open Thurs–Sun 10am–5pm

HAYFIELD

⊞ **Paul Pickford Antiques**
Contact Paul Pickford
✉ Top of the Town, Hayfield, High Peak, Derbyshire,

SK22 2JE
☎ 01663 747276/743356
⓿ 07887 585891
✉ paul@pickfordantiques.co.uk
⊕ www.pickfordantiques.co.uk
Est. 1974 Stock size Medium
Stock General antiques, furniture, stripped pine, light fittings
Open Tues Thurs Sat 11am–4pm Sun 1–5pm

HEANOR

⌂ **Heanor Antiques Centre**
Contact Jane Richards
✉ Church Square, 1–2 Ilkeston Road, Heanor, Derbyshire,
DE75 7AE
☎ 01773 531181
Est. 1997 Stock size Large
No. of dealers 120
Stock General antiques and small collectable items
Open Mon–Sun 10.30am–4.30pm
Services café

ILKESTON

⊞ **Flourish Farm Antiques**
Contact Joyce Mumford
✉ Dale Abbey, Ilkeston, Derbyshire,
DE7 4PQ
☎ 01332 667820
⓿ 07970 055151
Est. 1995 Stock size Medium
Stock Original pine furniture, cast-iron fireplaces, doors and door fittings
Open Tues–Sat 10am–5pm closed Wed pm
Services Wood stripping

⊞ **R Shelton**
Contact Raymond Shelton
✉ 1 Caroline Court, Greenwood Avenue, Ilkeston, Derbyshire,
DE7 5PW
☎ 0115 930 5801
Est. 1985 Stock size Medium
Stock General furniture
Open By appointment
Services Valuations, house clearances

MATLOCK

⊞ **Archway Antiques**
Contact Martin Powys
✉ 4 The Market Place, Wirksworth, Matlock, Derbyshire,

DE4 4ET
☎ 01629 825373
Est. 1990 Stock size Large
Stock Collectables, bric-a-brac, small items
Open Fri–Sat 11am–1pm 2–5pm or by appointment

⚒ **Bamfords (RICS)**
Contact Mr Simon Beresford
✉ Matlock Auction Gallery, The Old Picture Palace, Dale Road, Matlock, Derbyshire,
DE4 3LU
☎ 01629 57460 ⊕ 01629 580821
✉ bamfords-matlock@tiscali.co.uk
⊕ www.bamfords-auctions.co.uk
Est. 1923
Open Mon–Fri 9am–5.30pm
Sales General auction every 3 weeks, fine art 2 per year
Catalogues Yes

⊞ **R F Barrett Rare Books**
Contact Mr R Barrett
✉ 87 Dale Road, Matlock, Derbyshire,
DE4 3LU
☎ 01629 57644
Est. 1979 Stock size Medium
Stock Antique, rare and second-hand books
Open Mon–Sun 10am–5pm

⌂ **Matlock Antiques & Collectables**
Contact Miss Wendy Shirley
✉ 7 Dale Road, Matlock, Derbyshire,
DE4 3LT
☎ 01629 760808 ⊕ 01629 760808
⊕ www.matlock-antiques-collectables.cwc.net
Est. 1996 Stock size Large
No. of dealers 70+
Stock General antiques, collectables
Open Mon–Sun 10am–5pm
Services Delivery, riverside café

NEW MILLS

⊞ **Michael Allcroft Antiques**
Contact Michael Allcroft
✉ 203 Buxton Road, Newtown, New Mills, Nr Stockport,
SK12 2RA
☎ 01663 744014 ⊕ 01663 744014
⓿ 07798 781642
✉ alkrom@aol.com
Est. 1986 Stock size Large

275

Stock General antiques, Victorian–Edwardian and 1930s furniture, ideal for Japanese/Korean market
Open Tues–Thur Sat 11am–5pm closed Fri
Services Packing

⊞ Antiques & Pine Shop
Contact Mrs Pickering
⊠ **2 High Street, New Mills, Derbyshire, SK22 4AL** ℙ
☎ 01663 744710
Est. 1979 **Stock size** Medium
Stock Antique and pine furniture, bric-a-brac, giftware, pictures, glass
Open Thurs Fri Sat 9am–5.30pm or by appointment
Services House clearance

OCKBROOK

⊞ The Good Olde Days
Contact Mr S Potter
⊠ **6 Flood Street, Ockbrook, Derby, Derbyshire, DE72 3RF** ℙ
☎ 01332 544244
Est. 1995 **Stock size** Large
Stock General antiques
Open Tues–Sat 10am–5pm Wed noon–5pm
Fairs Swinderbury, Kettering, Kedlaston Hall
Services Valuations

RIPLEY

⌂ Memory Lane Antiques
Contact Jim Cullen
⊠ **1 Nottingham Road, Ripley, Derbyshire, DE5 3AS** ℙ
☎ 01773 570184
Ⓜ 07703 115626
❸ JamesGC1@aol.com
Est. 1993 **Stock size** Large
No. of dealers 40
Stock General antiques, collectables, shipping goods, kitchenware, Derby
Open Mon–Sun 10.30am–4pm only closed Christmas Day
Services Valuations, talks, house clearance. A permanent display of all 150+ Derby domestic ware patterns produced from 1940

⊞ Upstairs & Downstairs Antiques

Contact Mr C Lawrence
⊠ **8 Derby Road, Ripley, Derbyshire, DE5 3HR** ℙ
☎ 01773 745201
Ⓜ 07885 327753
Ⓦ www.upstairsdownstairs antiques.co.uk
Est. 1971 **Stock size** Large
Stock Edwardian–Victorian bedroom furniture, bookcases, pottery, china, pictures
Open Mon–Sat 10am–4pm
Services Vaulations, restoration, clock repair

SHARDLOW

⊞ Shardlow Antiques
Contact Nina or Nigel
⊠ **24 The Wharf, Shardlow, Derbyshire, DE72 2GH** ℙ
☎ 01332 792899
Est. 1977 **Stock size** Large
Stock Georgian furniture, general antiques
Open Mon–Thurs 10.30am–5pm Sat 10am–5pm Sun noon–5pm
Fairs Newark

SWADLINCOTE

⊞ Brewery House Antiques & Collectables
Contact Margi or David Morton
⊠ **32 High Street, Woodville, Swadlincote, Derbyshire**
☎ 01283 218681
Est. 2004 **Stock size** Medium
Stock Victoriana, Art Deco, wash stands, fireplaces, linen, collectables
Open Fri Sat 10am–6pm Sun 10am–4pm

⊞ Escolme House Antiques
Contact Shirley May Smith
⊠ **118 High Street, Woodville, Swadlincote, Derbyshire, DE11 7DU** ℙ
☎ 01283 216699
❸ escolmehouse@btopenworld.com
Est. 2003 **Stock size** Small
Stock Pine furniture, ceramics, kitchenware, Victorian–Edwardian glass
Open Tues Thurs–Sat 9am–5.30pm
Services Pine stripping service

WHALEY BRIDGE

⊞ George House
Contact Val Fallon
⊠ **21 George Street, Whaley Bridge, High Peak, Derbyshire, SK23 7NA** ℙ
☎ 01663 734 323
Est. 1997 **Stock size** Small
Stock Period furniture, kitchenware, etc
Open Mon–Sat 9am–5pm closed Wed Sun 1pm–4pm

⊞ Nimbus Antiques
Contact Mr H C Brobbin
⊠ **14 Chapel Road, Whaley Bridge, High Peak, Derbyshire, SK23 7JZ** ℙ
☎ 01663 734248 ❶ 01663 734248
❸ nimbusantiques@hotmail.com
Ⓦ www.antiques-atlas.com/ nimbus.htm
Est. 1979 **Stock size** Large
Stock General antiques, Georgian–Victorian furniture and clocks
Open Mon–Fri 9am–5.30pm Sat 10am–5.30pm Sun 2–5.30pm

LEICESTERSHIRE

ASHBY DE LA ZOUCH

⊞ Ashby Antiques
Contact Paul Logue
⊠ **4 Baker Court, Market Street, Ashby de la Zouch, Leicestershire, LE65 1AN** ℙ
☎ 01530 413015
Est. 2003 **Stock size** Large
Stock Clocks, specializing in longcase clocks, furniture
Open Mon–Sat 10am–5pm closed Wed

COALVILLE

⊞ Coalville Pine & Antiques
Contact Mr Truswell
⊠ **115–117 Belvoir Road, Coalville, Leicestershire, LE67 3PN** ℙ
☎ 01530 830099 ❶ 01530 830099
ⓂCO 07812 608654
Est. 2003 **Stock size** Medium
Stock Antique pine furniture, oak furniture
Open Tues–Sat 9am–5pm
Services Restoration

⊞ **Keystone Antiques (LAPADA)**
Contact Miss H McPherson FGA
✉ **66 London Road, Coalville, Leicestershire, LE67 3JA** 🅿
☎ 01530 835966 🖶 01530 817773
✉ keystone@heathermcpherson.co.uk
Est. 1980 *Stock size* Medium
Stock General antiques, jewellery, silver, small collectables
Open Mon–Wed by appointment Thurs–Sat 10am–5pm
Fairs NEC
Services Valuations for jewellery, silver

FINEDON

3 Church Street Antiques
Contact Bob Harrison
✉ **3 Church Street, Finedon, Northamptonshire, NN9 5NA** 🅿
☎ 01933 682515 🖶 01933 682210
📱 07860 679116
✉ sales@frenchbeds.com
🌐 www.frenchbeds.com
Est. 1985 *Stock size* Large
No. of dealers 4
Stock English, French furniture, decorative items, clocks, French beds, mirrors
Open Mon–Sat 9am–5.30pm Sun 11am–5pm
Services Valuations, restoration, shipping, nationwide delivery

GRIMSTON

⊞ **Ancient and Oriental Ltd (ADA)**
Contact Mr Alex Szolin
✉ **Park View, Grimston, Melton Mowbray, Leicestershire, LE14 3BZ** 🅿
☎ 01664 812044
✉ alex@antiquities.co.uk
🌐 www.antiquities.co.uk
Est. 1992
Stock Ancient art and items of archaeological interest from major world cultures, ancient–medieval
Open By appointment
Services Mail order, catalogues and website

HINCKLEY

⊞ **Bob Harrison Antiques**
Contact Bob Harrison
✉ **27 Burbage Road, Burbage,**

Hinckley, Leicestershire, **LE10 2TS** 🅿
☎ 01455 611689
🖶 07860 679116
✉ bob@bh-antiques.co.uk
🌐 www.3churchstreetantiques.co.uk
Est. 1985 *Stock size* Medium
Stock English & continental furniture, decorative items, clocks, mirrors, silver, ceramics
Trade only Yes
Open By appointment
Services Valuations, restoration

⊞ **House Things Antiques**
Contact P Robertson
✉ **44 Mansion Street, Trinity Lane, Hinckley, Leicestershire, LE10 0AU** 🅿
☎ 01455 618518
Est. 1976 *Stock size* Medium
Stock General antiques
Open Mon–Sat 10am–6pm closed Tues
Services Valuations, restoration

⊞ **Magpie**
Contact Michelle Johnson or David Wassell
✉ **126 Castle Street, Hinckley, Leicestershire, LE10 1DD** 🅿
☎ 01455 891819
📱 07713 099744
✉ michelle@magpieantiques.fsnet.co.uk
Est. 1985 *Stock size* Medium
Stock Georgian to pre-1950s household effects, kitchenware, toys
Open Mon–Sat 9am–5pm
Fairs Newark, Swinderby
Services House clearance

HOBY

⊞ **Withers of Leicester**
Contact Simon Frings
✉ **The Old Rutland, 6 Regent Road, Hoby, Leicestershire, LE14 3DU** 🅿
☎ 01664 434803
📱 07836 526595
Est. 1860 *Stock size* Medium
Stock 17th–early 20thC furniture
Open Mon–Sat telephone first
Services Valuations, restoration

KIBWORTH

⊞ **Kibworth Pine Co**
Contact Mrs Burdett
✉ **16 Harcourt Estate,**

Kibworth, Leicestershire, **LE8 0NE** 🅿
☎ 0116 279 3475
🌐 www.kibworthpinecompany.com
Est. 1981 *Stock size* Large
Stock Original antique pine furniture
Open Tues–Sat 9.30am–5pm

LEICESTER

⊞ **The Black Cat Bookshop (PBFA)**
Contact Mr P Woolley
✉ **90 Charles Street, Leicester, Leicestershire, LE1 1GE** 🅿
☎ 0116 251 2756 🖶 0116 281 3545
✉ blackcatuk@aol.com
🌐 www.blackcatbookshop.com
Est. 1987 *Stock size* Large
Stock Antiquarian, rare and second-hand books, British comics, magazines, printed ephemera
Open Mon–Sat 9.30am–5pm
Fairs Memorabilia Fair (NEC)
Services Worldwide mail order, book search, catalogues

⊞ **Brass and Wood Still Looking Good**
Contact Marcus Lee-Adams
✉ **Unit 3046, 20 Deacon Street, Leicester, Leicestershire, LE2 3EF** 🅿
📱 07973 294622
✉ marcusadams@btinternet.com
Est. 2000 *Stock size* Medium
Stock Brassware, furniture, lighting
Open By appointment
Fairs Adams Antique Fair, Royal Horticultural Hall
Services Restoration

🔨 **Churchgate Auctions Ltd**
Contact Mr D Dearman
✉ **66 Churchgate, Leicester, Leicestershire, LE1 4AL** 🅿
☎ 0116 262 1416 🖶 0116 251 7711
✉ info@churchgateauctions.co.uk
🌐 www.churchgateauctions.co.uk
Est. 1966
Open Mon–Fri 8.30am–6pm Sat 8.30am–noon
Sales General and antiques sales Fri 10am, viewing Thurs 2–6pm
Frequency Weekly
Catalogues Yes

⊞ Clarendon Books (PBFA)
Contact Mr J Smith
✉ 144 Clarendon Park Road, Leicester, Leicestershire, LE2 3AE 🅿
☎ 0116 270 1856 ✆ 0116 270 9020
📱 07803 174139
📧 clarendonbooks@aol.com
Est. 1986 *Stock size* Medium
Stock Antiquarian, rare and second-hand books
Open Mon–Sat 10am–5pm
Fairs PBFA

⊞ Corry's Antiques (LAPADA)
Contact Mrs E I Corry
✉ 26 Francis Street, Stoneygate, Leicester, Leicestershire, LE2 2BD 🅿
☎ 0116 270 3794 ✆ 0116 270 3794
📱 www.corrys-antiques.com
Est. 1964 *Stock size* Large
Stock General antiques, clocks, mirrors, porcelain, silver, furniture
Open Mon–Sat 10am–5pm
Fairs NEC
Services Restoration

⌂ Leicester Antiques Warehouse
✉ Clarkes Road, Wigston, Leicester, Leicestershire, LE18 2BG 🅿
☎ 0116 288 1315 ✆ 0116 281 1742
📧 webmaster@antiques-of-britain.co.uk
📱 www.antiques-of-britain.co.uk
Est. 2002 *Stock size* Large
No. of dealers 60
Stock General antiques, collectables
Open Tues–Sat 10am–5pm Sun noon–5pm

⊞ Oxford Street Antique Centre
Contact Mr P Giles
✉ 16–26 Oxford Street, Leicester, Leicestershire, LE1 5XU 🅿
☎ 0116 255 3006 ✆ 0116 255 5863
Est. 1987 *Stock size* Large
Stock Victorian–present-day furniture
Open Mon–Fri 10am–5.30pm Sat 10am–5pm Sun 2–5pm
Services Export, container packing

⊞ Retrobuy
Contact Mr Mark Williamson
✉ 62 Silver Arcade, Leicester, Leicestershire, LE1 5FB
☎ 0116 242 5949 ✆ 0116 242 5949
📧 retrobuy@ntlworld.com
📱 www.retrobuy.co.uk
Est. 1997 *Stock size* Large
Stock Retro toys, clothes, arcade, home, music, records
Open Mon–Sat noon–5pm
Fairs NEC, Donnington
Services Valuations, mail order

⊞ The Rug Gallery
Contact Mr R Short
✉ 50 Montague Road, Leicester, Leicestershire, LE2 1TH
☎ 0116 270 0085 ✆ 0116 270 0113
Est. 1987 *Stock size* Large
Stock Old and new Oriental rugs and kilims, antique Oriental furniture
Open Fri Sat 10am–4pm or by appointment

⊞ Treasure Trove Books
Contact Linda Sharman
✉ 21 Mayfield Road, Leicester, Leicestershire, LE2 1LR 🅿
☎ 0116 275 5933
📧 sales@treasuretrove-books.co.uk
Est. 1993 *Stock size* Medium
Stock Second-hand books, pop records, CDs, tapes
Open Mon–Sat 9.30am–5.30pm
Fairs Leicestershire, Missing Book Fair

⊞ White Elephant Antique and collectables
Contact Mr C Freedman
✉ 117 Clarendon Park Road, Leicester, Leicestershire, LE2 3AH 🅿
☎ 0116 270 1528 ✆ 0116 270 9279
📧 white-elephant1@btconnect.com
Est. 1996 *Stock size* Medium
Stock General antiques and collectables, specializing in the 1940s–1950s
Open Tues–Sat 9am–5pm

LOUGHBOROUGH

⊞ Loughborough Antiques Centre
Contact Richard or Carol Wesley
✉ 50 Market Street, Loughborough, Leicestershire, LE11 3ER
☎ 01509 239931
Est. 1979 *Stock size* Medium
Stock General antiques, jewellery, clocks
Open Tues Thurs–Sat 10am–5pm
Services Valuations

⊞ Charles Lowe & Sons Ltd
Contact Richard Lowe
✉ 37–40 Church Gate, Loughborough, Leicestershire, LE11 1UE 🅿
☎ 01509 212554/217876
Est. 1846 *Stock size* Medium
Stock General antiques, furniture
Open Mon–Fri 9am–5.30pm
Services Valuations, restoration

LUBENHAM

⊞ Oaktree Antiques
Contact Gillian Abraham
✉ The Drapers House, Main Street, Lubenham, Market Harborough, Leicestershire, LE16 9TF 🅿
☎ 01858 410041
📧 gillian@oaktreeantiques.co.uk
📱 www.oaktreeantiques.co.uk
Est. 1990 *Stock size* Large
Stock Town and country 17th–19thC furniture, longcase clocks, works of art
Open Wed–Sun 10am–6pm

MARKET HARBOROUGH

⊞ Aquarius Books
Contact Mr R Lack
✉ 8 St Marys Road, Market Harborough, Leicestershire, LE16 7DU
☎ 01858 431060
📧 raylack@btconnect.com
📱 www.aquariusbooks.co.uk
Est. 1989 *Stock size* Medium
Stock Antiquarian, rare and second-hand books
Open Mon–Sat 10am–5pm

➤ Bonhams
✉ 34 High Street, Market Harborough, Leicestershire, BN3 2JN 🅿
☎ 01858 438900 ✆ 01858 438909
📧 marketharborough@bonhams.com
📱 www.bonhams.com
Est. 1793
Open Mon–Fri 9am–1pm 2–5pm
Sales Regional office. Regular sales held in London and in our

salerooms across the country.
Free auction valuations;
insurance and probate valuations
Catalogues Yes

⊞ **The Furniture Barn**
Contact Richard Kimbell
⊠ **Rockingham Road,**
Market Harborough,
Leicestershire,
LE16 7QE 🅿
☎ 01858 433444 🖷 01858 461301
🌐 www.thefurniturebarn.com
Est. 1969 *Stock size* Medium
Stock Antique, pine and country
furniture, upholstery, end-of-line
fabrics
Open Mon–Wed Fri 10am–6pm
Thurs 10am–8pm Sat 9am–6pm
Sun 10.30am–4.30pm

⚒ **Gildings**
Contact John Gilding
⊠ **Roman Way,**
Market Harborough,
Leicestershire,
LE16 7PQ 🅿
☎ 01858 410414 🖷 01858 432956
🖀 sales@gildings.co.uk
🌐 www.gildings.co.uk
Est. 1980
Open Mon–Fri 9am–5pm
Sales Regular fine art, antiques,
specialist sales, weekly Victoriana
and collectables sales
Frequency Monthly
Catalogues Yes

⊞ **Edward Pritchard**
Antiques & 20thC
Furniture
Contact Edward Pritchard
⊠ **The Courtyard, Bennetts Place,**
30–31 High Street,
Market Harborough,
Leicestershire,

LE16 7NL 🅿
☎ 01858 439974
🖀 edwardpritchard@bennettsplace.
fsnet.co.uk
Est. 2002 *Stock size* Medium
Stock Antique and 20thC
furniture
Open Mon noon–5.30pm
Tues–Sat 10am–5.30pm
Fairs NEC

⊞ **J Stamp & Sons**
Contact Mark Stamp
⊠ **The Chestnuts, 15 Kettering**
Road, Market Harborough,
Leicestershire,
LE16 8AN 🅿
☎ 01858 462524 🖷 01858 465643
🖀 jstampandsons@btconnect.com
🌐 www.jstampandsons.co.uk
Est. 1946 *Stock size* Medium
Stock Georgian–Edwardian
furniture
Open Mon–Fri 8.30am–5.30pm
Sat 9am–1pm or by appointment
Services Valuations, restoration

⊞ **Flagstones Pine and**
Country Furniture
Contact Julie Adcock
⊠ **24 Burton Street,**
Melton Mowbray,
Leicestershire,
LE13 1AF 🅿
☎ 01664 566438
📱 07971 299206
🌐 www.flagstonespine.com
Est. 1984 *Stock size* Medium
Stock Pine and country furniture,
old and reproduction lighting,
accessories
Open Tues Sat 9.30am–5.15pm
Services Stripping service,
custom-built furniture

⊞ **David E Burrows**
Antiques (LAPADA)
Contact Mr David Burrows
⊠ **Manor House Farm,**
Osgathorpe, Loughborough,
Leicestershire,
LE12 9SY 🅿
☎ 01530 222218 🖷 01530 223139
📱 07702 059030
🖀 david.burrows2@virgin.net
Est. 1970 *Stock size* Large
Stock Pine, oak, mahogany and
walnut furniture, clocks, pictures
Trade only Yes
Open By appointment
Services Valuations, shipping

⚒ **David Stanley Auctions**
Contact David Stanley
⊠ **Stordon Grange, Osgathorpe,**
Loughborough, Leicestershire,
LE12 9SR 🅿
☎ 01530 222320 🖷 01530 222523
🖀 auctions@davidstanley.com
🌐 www.davidstanley.com
Est. 1979
Open Mon–Sat 8am–5pm
Sales Antique woodwork tools
(telephone for details)
Frequency Bi-monthly
Catalogues Yes

⊞ **J Green & Son**
Contact Mr R Green
⊠ **1 Coppice Lane,**
Queniborough, Leicestershire,
LE7 3DR 🅿
☎ 01162 606682 🖷 01162 606682
📱 07860 513121
🌐 www.jgreenantiques@
btinternet.com
Est. 1949 *Stock size* Medium

Stock Georgian and period furniture, 18th–19thC English furniture
Open By appointment
Services Valuations

QUORN

⊞ **Quorn Pine**
Contact Steven Yates or Steven Parker
✉ **The Mills, Leicester Road, Quorn, Leicestershire, LE12 8ES** 🅿
☎ 01509 416031 ● 01509 416051
Ⓦ www.quorn-pine.co.uk
Est. 1983 *Stock size* Large
Stock Mainly antique pine and country furniture, clocks, doors, fireplaces, reproduction furniture
Open Mon–Fri 9am–5.30pm Sat 9.30am–5.30pm Sun 2–5pm
Services Restoration, stripping

ROTHLEY

⊞ **Pooks Transport Bookshop**
Contact Barrie Pook
✉ **Fowke Street, Rothley, Leicestershire, LE7 7PJ** 🅿
☎ 0116 237 6222 ● 0116 237 6491
● pooks.motorbooks@virgin.net
Est. 1985 *Stock size* Large
Stock Car, commercial and motorcycle literature 1896–date
Open Mon–Fri 1am–5.30pm Sat by appointment
Fairs Goodwood
Services Valuations

SEAGRAVE

⌖ **Miller Services**
Contact Robert Miller
✉ **43–45 Swan Street, Seagrave, Leicestershire, LE12 7NL** 🅿
☎ 01509 812037 ● 01509 812037
Ⓜ 07708 086457
Est. 1986
Open Sun 9.30am
Sales Monthly antiques and jewellery sales, Seagrave Village Hall Sun 12.30pm, viewing 9.30am
Catalogues Yes

⊞ **Miller Services**
Contact Robert Miller
✉ **43–45 Swan Street, Seagrave,**
Leicestershire, LE12 7NL 🅿
☎ 01509 812037 ● 01509 812037
Ⓜ 07708 086957
Est. 1986
Stock Pottery, glass, silver, jewellery
Open Mon–Fri 9am–5pm Sat 10am–12.30pm
Fairs Arthur Swallow, DMG
Services Auctions, valuations

THURMASTON

⌂ **Thurmaston Antiques Centre**
Contact Mr Chapman
✉ **5 Garden Street, Thurmaston, Leicestershire, LE4 8DS** 🅿
☎ 0116 269 4477 ● 0116 269 4477
Ⓦ www.antiques@home.co.uk
Est. 1990 *Stock size* Large
No. of dealers 100
Stock 2 main halls, 5 rooms of cabinets, clocks, furniture, modern art, bronzes, coins, stamps, toys, militaria, telephones, oil lamps
Open Mon–Fri 9.30am–5.30pm Sat 9am–5pm Sun Bank Holidays 10am–5pm

WHITWICK

⊞ **Charles Antiques**
Contact Mr Haydon
✉ **Whitwick, Leicestershire, LE67** 🅿
☎ 01530 836932
Ⓜ 07831 204406
● charles.antiques@btopenworld.com
Est. 1973 *Stock size* Large
Stock Clocks, furniture
Open By appointment
Fairs Birmingham Motorcycle Museum

WIGSTON

⌂ **The Leicester Antiques Warehouse**
Contact Robert Sklar
✉ **Clarkes Road, Wigston, Leicestershire, LE18 2BG** 🅿
☎ 0116 288 1315 ● 0116 281 1742
Ⓜ 07778 171915
● webmaster@antiques-of-britain.co.uk
Ⓦ www.antiques-of-britain.co.uk
Est. 2002 *Stock size* Large

No. of dealers 60
Stock Furniture, jewellery, silver china, clocks, watches, architectural and collectables
Open Tues–Sat 10am–5pm Sun 11am–4pm

WYMESWOLD

⊞ **N F Bryan-Peach Antiques**
Contact Mr N Bryan-Peach
✉ **30 Brook Street, Wymeswold, Loughborough, Leicestershire, LE12 6TU** 🅿
☎ 01509 880425 ● 01509 880425
Ⓜ 07860 559590
● norm@bryanpeach.demon.co.uk
Est. 1974 *Stock size* Medium
Stock 18th–19thC furniture, clocks, barometers
Open By appointment
Services Valuations, restoration

WYMONDHAM

⊞ **The Old Bakery Antiques**
Contact Tina Bryan
✉ **The Old Bakery, Main Street, Wymondham, Melton Mowbray, Leicestershire, LE14 2AG** 🅿
☎ 01572 787472
Est. 1990 *Stock size* Medium
Stock Architectural and reclaimed items, door hardware, stained glass, doors, tiles, fireplaces, chimney pots, pine furniture, kitchenware, advertising items
Open Mon–Sat 10am–5.30pm closed Thur

NORTHAMPTONSHIRE

BRACKLEY

⌂ **The Brackley Antiques Cellar**
Contact Debbe Perry
✉ **Drayman's Walk, Brackley, Northamptonshire, NN13 6BE** 🅿
☎ 01280 841851 ● 01280 841851
Est. 2000 *Stock size* Large
No. of dealers 150+
Stock General antiques, smalls, collectables, furniture, militaria
Open Mon–Sun 10am–5pm
Services Tea room

⊞ Charlotte's Barn
Contact Sherley Sharp
✉ 3 Market Place, Brackley,
Northamptonshire,
NN13 7AB ℗
☎ 01280 704978
✉ sherley@charlottesbarn.co.uk
ⓦ www.charlottesbarn.co.uk
Est. 1995 *Stock size* Small
Stock Pine furniture and
complementary items
Open Tues Thurs Sat 10am–4pm
Fri 10am–2pm
Services Pine furntiure
restoration

**⊞ The Old Hall Bookshop
(ABA, PBFA, ILAB)**
Contact Tom Dixon
✉ 32 Market Place, Brackley,
Northamptonshire,
NN13 7DP ℗
☎ 01280 704146 ℗ 01280 705131
✉ books@oldhallbooks.com
ⓦ www.oldhallbooks.com
Est. 1977 *Stock size* Large
Stock A wide range of second-
hand and antiquarian books
Open Mon–Fri 9.30am–5.30pm
Sat 9.30am–1pm 2–5.30pm

Fairs ABA, PBFA
Services Book search for out-of-
print books

DAVENTRY

⊞ Bygone Days
Contact Sue Pratley
✉ 16 Sheaf Street, Daventry,
Northamptonshire,
NN11 4AB ℗
☎ 01327 878617
✉ susanbygonedays@aol.com
Est. 1999 *Stock size* Medium
Stock General antiques,
collectables, furniture, glass,
Worcester, Crown Derby
Open Mon–Sat 10am–5pm
Fairs Lamport Hall

DESBOROUGH

**⊞ Old Bus Station
Antiques Ltd**
Contact Fiona Kimbell
✉ The Old Bus Station,
Harborough Road,
Desborough,
Northamptonshire,
NN14 2QX ℗

☎ 01536 762093 ℗ 01536 763263
✉ enquiries@oldbus-antiques.com
Est. 1980 *Stock size* Large
Stock Painted antique pine,
architectural, decorative and
country furniture
Trade only Yes
Open Mon–Fri 9am–5pm or by
appointment
Services Container packing,
shipping, furniture made to
order

EVENLEY

⌂ Amors of Evenley
Contact Mr Amor
✉ Evenley, Brackley,
Northamptonshire,
NN13 5SB ℗
☎ 01869 811342
✉ amorsofevenley@hotmail.com
Est. 1960 *Stock size* Large
No. of dealers 6
Stock 17th–19thC furniture,
porcelain, ceramics, paintings
Open Mon–Sat 9am–5.30pm
Sun 10am–4pm
Services Valuations, house
clearance

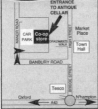

FINEDON

⌂ Aspidistra Antiques
Contact Patricia Moss
✉ 51 High Street, Finedon,
Wellingborough,
Northamptonshire,
NN9 5JN 🅿
☎ 01933 680196
📱 07768 071948
✉ info@aspidistra-antiques.com
🌐 www.aspidistra-antiques.com
Est. 1994 *Stock size* Medium
No. of dealers 6
Stock Specialist in decorative
arts, good selection of smalls and
furniture
Open Mon–Sat 10am–5pm
Sun 11am–5pm
Services Valuations, commission
sales, restoration

⊞ Simon Banks Antiques
Contact Mr S Banks
✉ 28 Church Street, Finedon,
Wellingborough,
Northamptonshire,
NN9 5NA 🅿
☎ 01933 680371
📱 07976 787539
Est. 1984 *Stock size* Large
Stock General antiques, dining
room furniture, clocks, silver,
silver plate, pottery, porcelain
Open Mon–Sat 10am–5.30pm
Sun 11am–4.30pm
Services Valuations

⊞ Michael Chapman Antiques (LAPADA)
Contact Michael Chapman
✉ 3 Church Street, Finedon,
Northamptonshire,
NN9 5NA 🅿
☎ 01933 682515
📱 07771 883060
✉ sales@finedonantiques.com
Est. 1973 *Stock size* Medium
Stock 18th–early 20thC English,
Continental furniture, clocks,
decorative items, shipping
goods, upholstery
Open Mon–Sat 9am–5.30pm
Sun 11am–5pm
Services Valuations

⊞ Robert Cheney Antiques
Contact Robert Cheney
✉ 11–13 High Street, Finedon,
Wellingborough,
Northamptonshire,
NN9 5JN 🅿
☎ 01933 681048

Est. 1992 *Stock size* Medium
Stock General antiques
Open Mon–Sat 9am–5pm
Sun 11am–4pm
Services Valuations and house
clearances

⊞ E K Antiques
Contact E Kubacki
✉ 37 High Street, Finedon,
Northamptonshire,
NN9 5JN 🅿
☎ 01933 681882
📱 07711 245530
Est. 1991 *Stock size* Medium
Stock General antiques
Open Mon–Sat 9.30am–5pm
Sun 11am–4pm
Fairs Hinchingbrooke, Hunts
Services Valuations, restoration,
house clearance

⊞ Finedon Antiques Ltd (LAPADA)
Contact Michael Chapman
✉ 3 Church Street, Finedon,
Wellingborough,
Northamptonshire,
NN9 5ND 🅿
☎ 01933 681260/682210
☎ 01933 682210
✉ sales@finedonantiques.com
🌐 www.finedonantiques.com
Est. 1972 *Stock size* Large
Stock 18th–19thC English and
French furniture, pottery,
porcelain, decorative items
Open Mon–Sat 9am–5.30pm
Sun 11am–5pm
Services Valuations, restoration

FLORE

⊞ Blockheads
Contact Richard Sear
✉ The Hunter Shields, Flore,
Northamptonshire,
NN7 4LZ 🅿
☎ 01327 340718 ☎ 01327 349263
Est. 1965 *Stock size* Large
Stock Restored wooden hat
blocks, restored, polished and
mounted as a decorative item
Open By appointment
Fairs Newark

⊞ Granary Antiques
Contact Richard Sear
✉ The Hunter Shields, Flore,
Northamptonshire,
NN7 4LZ 🅿
☎ 01327 340718 ☎ 01327 349263
Est. 1965 *Stock size* Large

Stock Early metalwork, country
furniture
Open By appointment
Fairs Newark

⊞ Christopher Jones Antiques
Contact Christopher Jones
✉ Flore House, The Avenue,
Flore, Northamptonshire,
NN7 4LZ 🅿
☎ 01327 342165 ☎ 01327 349230
✉ florehouse@msn.com
🌐 www.christopherjones
antiques.co.uk
Est. 1993 *Stock size* Large
Stock Decorative objects and
furniture 18th–early 20thC
Open Mon–Sat 10am–5pm
Fairs Olympia

HARPOLE

⊞ Inglenook Antiques
Contact Tony or Pamela Havard
✉ 23 High Street, Harpole,
Northamptonshire,
NN7 4DH 🅿
☎ 01604 830007
Est. 1971 *Stock size* Small
Stock Small country items,
copper, brass, Victoriana, general
antiques, clocks
Open Mon–Sat 9am–6.30pm
closed Wed
Services Longcase clock restoration

ISLIP

⊞ John Roe Antiques
Contact Mr John Roe
✉ Furnace Site, Kettering Road,
Islip, Kettering,
Northamptonshire,
NN14 3JW 🅿
☎ 01832 732937 ☎ 01832 732937
Est. 1969 *Stock size* Large
Stock General antique furniture
Open Mon–Fri 9am–6pm Sat
10am–5pm Sun by appointment
Fairs Newark
Services Shipping, packing

KETTERING

⊞ Dragon Antiques
Contact Sandra Hunt
✉ 85 Rockingham Road,
Kettering, Northamptonshire,
NN16 8LA 🅿
☎ 01536 517017
Est. 1982 *Stock size* Small
Stock General antiques, paintings

Open Mon–Sat 10am–4pm
closed Thurs
Services Picture framing,
restoration

NORTHAMPTON

⊞ Cave's
Contact Allan Cave
✉ 111 Kettering Road,
Northampton,
Northamptonshire,
NN1 4BA 🅿
☎ 01604 638278 ✆ 01604 230177
Est. 1879 *Stock size* Large
Stock Georgian furniture
Open Mon–Sat 9am–5.30pm
closed Thurs

⊞ Hampton Antiques
Contact Mark Goodger
✉ Northampton,
Northamptonshire,
NN7 🅿
☎ 01604 863979 ✆ 01604 863979
📱 07779 654879
✉ info@hamptonantiques.co.uk
🌐 www.hamptonantiques.co.uk
Est. 1998 *Stock size* Large
Stock Boxes and tea caddies
Open By appointment
Fairs Antiques for Everyone,
US fairs

⊞ Inglenook Antiques
Contact Mrs Hull
✉ 92 St Leonards Road,
Northampton,
Northamptonshire,
NN4 8DW 🅿
☎ 01604 708754
✉ inglenook98@btopenworld.com
🌐 www.inglenook.org.uk
Est. 1998 *Stock size* Medium
Stock Victorian and older
furniture
Open Mon–Sun 11am–4pm or by
appointment
Services Delivery within 150 mile
radius

⊞ Inglenook Antiques
Contact Tony or Pamela Havard
✉ 23 High Street, Harpole,
Northampton,
Northamptonshire,
NN7 4DH 🅿
☎ 01604 830007
Est. 1971 *Stock size* Medium
Stock General antiques
Open Mon–Sat 9am–7pm
closed Wed
Services Clock repairs

⊞ Giuseppe Miceli
(OMRS, BNTA)
Contact Mr Giuseppe Miceli
✉ 204 Bants Lane,
Northampton,
Northamptonshire,
NN5 6AH 🅿
☎ 01604 581533
Est. 1969 *Stock size* Medium
Stock Coins, medals
Open Mon–Sat 9am–6pm
Services Valuations

⊞ The Old Brigade
Contact Mr S Wilson
✉ 10a Harborough Road,
Kingsthorpe, Northampton,
Northamptonshire,
NN2 7AZ 🅿
☎ 01604 719389 ✆ 01604 712489
✉ theoldbrigade@btconnect.com
🌐 www.theoldbrigade.co.uk
Est. 1985 *Stock size* Medium
Stock 1850–1945 militaria, Third
Reich
Open Mon–Sat 10.30am–5pm by
appointment only
Services Valuations

OUNDLE

⊞ Harpurs of Oundle
Contact Nigel Hill
✉ 5a West Street,
Oundle,
Northamptonshire,
PE8 4EJ 🅿
☎ 01832 274050
✉ info@harpurjewellery.com
🌐 www.arms-and-armour-uk.com
Est. 1981 *Stock size* Medium
Stock Antique, contemporary
and new jewellery, small
collectables, watches, silver
Open Mon–Sat 10am–4.30pm
closed Wed

⊞ Geraldine Waddington
Books and Prints (PBFA)
Contact Geraldine Waddington
✉ 3 West Street,
Oundle,
Northamptonshire,
PE8 4EJ 🅿
☎ 01832 275028 ✆ 01832 275028
✉ mail@geraldine-waddington.com
🌐 www.geraldinewaddington.com
Est. 1999 *Stock size* Medium
Stock Books, illustrations,
contemporary wood engravings
Open Mon–Sat 10am–5pm
closed Wed
Fairs Fine Press Fair Oxford, PBFA

POTTERSPURY

⊞ Reindeer Antiques Ltd
(LAPADA, BADA)
Contact Nicholas Fuller
✉ 43 Watling Street, Potterspury,
Northamptonshire,
NN12 7QD 🅿
☎ 01908 542407/542200
✆ 01908 542121
📱 07711 446221
✉ nicholas.fuller@reindeer-
antiques.co.uk
🌐 www.reindeerantiques.co.uk
Est. 1969 *Stock size* Large
Stock Early 17thC–mid-19thC fine
English furniture,
17thC–contemporary works of art
Open Mon–Fri 9am–6pm
Sat 10am–5pm
Fairs BADA
Services Valuations, restoration

RUSHDEN

⊞ D W Sherwood Ltd
Contact Mrs S Sherwood
✉ 59 Little Street, Rushden,
Northamptonshire,
NN10 0LS 🅿
☎ 01933 353265
Est. 1959 *Stock size* Large
Stock General antiques,
paintings, clocks, furniture,
prints, maps, glass, china, lace
bobbins
Open Tues–Sat 11am–5pm
closed Thurs
Services Valuations

SILVERSTONE

⊞ Collectors Carbooks
Contact Mr C Knapman
✉ 2210 Silverstone Technology
Park, Silverstone Circuit,
Silverstone, Northamptonshire,
NN12 8TN 🅿
☎ 01327 855888 ✆ 01327 855999
✉ sales@collectorscarbooks.com
🌐 www.collectorscarbooks.com
Est. 1991 *Stock size* Large
Stock Rare, out-of-print, motoring
and motor-racing books,
magazines, posters, autographs,
programmes, new car-related
books, Menoshire books
Open Mon–Sat 9am–5pm Race
Saturdays 8.30am–2.30pm
Fairs All major historic race
meetings, classic car shows
Services Free book search,
international mail order

THRAPSTON

⊞ Granary Antiques
Contact Mr A H Cox
✉ The Old Granary, Manor House Farm, Addington Road, Woodford, Thrapston, Northamptonshire, NN14 4ES ℗
☎ 01832 732535
⓶ 07732 169884
Est. 2003 *Stock size* Large
Stock Pine, oak, walnut furniture, clocks, glass, china, general antiques
Open Mon–Sun 10am–5.30pm closed Thurs
Services Valuations, restoration

TOWCESTER

⊞ Ron Green
Contact M or N Green
✉ 227 & 239 Watling Street West, Towcester, Northamptonshire, NN12 6DD ℗
☎ 01327 350615 ⓕ 01327 350387
⓶ 07740 774152
⊜ ron@green227.freeserve.co.uk
⊛ www.rongreenantiques.com
Est. 1954 *Stock size* Medium
Stock General antiques, furniture, 18th–19thC Continental, English furniture
Open Mon–Sat 8.30am–5.30pm
Sun by appointment
Services Valuations for probate and insurance

⊞ Walter Moores & Son (LAPADA)
✉ The Reindeer Antique Centre, 43 Watling Street, Potterspury, Towcester, Northamptonshire, NN12 7QD ℗
☎ 01908 543704
⊛ www.waltermoores.co.uk
Est. 1925 *Stock size* Medium
Stock Georgian–Victorian furniture, mainly mahogany
Open Mon–Sun 10am–5pm
Fairs NEC, Harrogate, Buxton

⊞ Lorraine Spooner Antiques Ltd
Contact Lorraine Spooner
✉ 211 Watling Street West, Towcester, Northamptonshire, NN12 6BX ℗
☎ 01327 358777 ⓕ 01327 358777
⊜ lorraine@lsantiques.com
⊛ www.lsantiques.com

Est. 2003 *Stock size* Medium
Stock Furniture, clocks, silver, porcelain, glass, paintings, prints, linens, books
Open Mon–Sat 9.30am–5.30pm closed Wed 1.30pm

WEEDON

⊞ Helios and Co
Contact Mr B Walters
✉ 25–27 High Street, Weedon, Northamptonshire, NN7 4QD ℗
☎ 01327 340264 ⓕ 01327 342235
⊛ www.heliosantiques.com
Est. 1976 *Stock size* Large
Stock General antiques, reproduction 18thC-style oak furniture
Open Tues–Sat 9.30am–5pm
Sun 10.30am–4pm Mon by appointment
Services Valuations, restoration

⊞ Memories
Contact H Huizinga
✉ Heart of the Shires Shopping Village, Watling street, Weedon, Northamptonshire, NN7 4LB ℗
☎ 01327 342263
Est. 1998 *Stock size* Medium
Stock General antiques and collectables, all periods of furniture and collectables, Mackintosh and Tiffany style lamps
Open Tues–Sat 10am–5pm
Sun 11am–5pm

⊞ Rococo Antiques & Interiors
Contact Neville Griffiths
✉ Bridge Street, Lower Weedon, Northamptonshire, NN7 4PN ℗
☎ 01327 341288
⓶ 07939 212542
⊛ www.nevillegriffiths.co.uk
Est. 1983 *Stock size* Medium
Stock Antiques and architectural salvage
Open Mon–Sat 10am–5pm
Sun by appointment
Services Restoration, metal polishing, conservation of period property

⊡ The Village Market Antiques
Contact Mrs M Howard
✉ 62 High Street, Weedon,

Northamptonshire, NN7 4QD ℗
☎ 01327 342015
Est. 1981 *Stock size* Large
No. of dealers 40
Stock General antiques, collectables
Open Mon–Sun 10.30am–5.15pm including Bank Holidays

⊡ Weedon Antiques
Contact Nick Tillman
✉ 23 High Street, Weedon, Northamptonshire, NN7 4QD ℗
☎ 01327 349777
⓶ 07711 570798
⊜ weedonantiques@tiscali.co.uk
Est. 2000 *Stock size* Large
No. of dealers 21
Stock Porcelain, silver, glass, small range of furniture, pictures
Open Wed–Sat 10am–5pm
Sun 10.30am–4.30pm

WELLINGBOROUGH

⋔ Wilfords
Contact Mr S Wilford
✉ 76 Midland Road, Wellingborough, Northamptonshire, NN8 1NB ℗
☎ 01933 222760 ⓕ 01933 271796
Est. 1934
Open Mon Tues 9am–5pm
Wed 8am–6pm Thur Fri 8am–5pm Sat 8–11am
Sales General antiques weekly on Thurs 9.30am, viewing Wed 8–6pm
Frequency Weekly
Catalogues No

WEST HADDON

⊞ Paul Hopwell Antiques (BADA, LAPADA)
Contact Mr or Mrs P Hopwell
✉ 30 High Street, West Haddon, Northampton, Northamptonshire, NN6 7AP ℗
☎ 01788 510636 ⓕ 01788 510044
⓶ 07836 505950
⊜ paulhopwell@antiqueoak.co.uk
⊛ www.antiqueoak.co.uk
Est. 1969 *Stock size* Large
Stock 17th–18thC English oak furniture, metalware, treen, Delftware
Open Mon–Sat 10am–6pm

Sun by appointment
Fairs Olympia, Chelsea, NEC
Services Valuations, restoration

NOTTINGHAMSHIRE

BEESTON

⊞ Turner Violins
Contact Steve Turner
✉ 1–5 Lily Grove, Beeston,
Nottinghamshire,
NG9 1QL 🅿
☎ 0115 943 0333   📠 0115 943 0444
📧 info@turnerviolins.co.uk
🌐 www.turnerviolins.co.uk
Est. 1980 *Stock size* Large
Stock Violins, double basses,
violas, cellos, bows
Open Mon–Fri 9am–6pm
Sat 9am–5pm
Services Instrument and bow
repairs, valuations, consultations,
export

BOBBERSMILL

**⊞ Philips Traditional
Bathrooms**
Contact Philip Lucas
✉ 418–424 Alfreton Road,
Bobbersmill, Nottinghamshire,
NG7 5NG 🅿
☎ 0115 970 5552   📠 0115 841 3752
📧 shop@b-b-1.co.uk
🌐 www.b-b-1.co.uk
Est. 1997 *Stock size* Medium
Stock Antique bathrooms
Open Mon–Sat 9am–5pm

BUDBY

**🏛 Dukeries Antiques
Centre**
Contact John Coupe
✉ Thoresby Park, Budby,

Nottinghamshire,
NG22 9EX 🅿
☎ 01623 822252   📠 01623 822209
📱 07836 635312
📧 dukeriesantiques@aol.com
Est. 2001 *Stock size* Large
No. of dealers 18
Stock Antique furniture,
paintings, porcelain, glass, silver
Open Mon–Sun 10am–5pm
Services Valuations, restoration,
restaurant

FARNSFIELD

⊞ A B Period Pine
Contact Alan Baker
✉ The Barn, 38 Main Street,
Farnsfield, Newark,
Nottinghamshire,
NG22 8EA 🅿
☎ 01623 882288   📠 01623 883793
📧 alan@abperiodpine.fsnet.co.uk
🌐 www.periodpine.co.uk
Est. 1998 *Stock size* Large
Stock Pine
Open Mon–Sat 10am–5pm
Sun 11am–4.30pm
Services Farmhouse and painted
pine and oak kitchens

GOTHAM

**⚒ T Vennett-Smith
Auctioneers and Valuers**
Contact T or M A Vennett-Smith
✉ 11 Nottingham Road, Gotham,
Nottingham, Nottinghamshire,
NE11 0HE 🅿
☎ 0115 983 0541   📠 0115 983 0114
📧 info@vennett-smith.com
🌐 www.vennett-smith.com
Est. 1989
Open Mon–Fri 9am–5.30pm
Sales Autographs, postcards,
cigarette cards, 5 sales per year,

2 theatre, cinema memorabilia,
3 postal auctions of postcards and
cigarette cards, 2 sports auctions
including cricket, football, general
sports, 1 postal sports auction
Catalogues Yes

GRINGLEY ON THE HILL

**⚒ Peter Young
Auctioneers**
Contact Mr P Young
✉ Hillside, Beacon Hill Road,
Gringley on the Hill,
Nottinghamshire,
DN10 4RQ 🅿
☎ 01777 816609
📱 07801 079818
Est. 1961
Open Mon–Fri 9.30am–5.30pm
Sales Antiques and collectables
Sat 10am, viewing Fri 4–9pm
Sat 9–10am.
Frequency Quarterly
Catalogues Yes

KIRKBY IN ASHFIELD

⊞ Kyrios Books
Contact Mr K Parr
✉ 11 Kingsway, Kirkby in
Ashfield, Nottingham,
Nottinghamshire,
NG17 7BB 🅿
☎ 01623 452556
📧 keith@kyriosbooks.co.uk or
kyriosbooks@tiscali.co.uk
🌐 www.kyriosbooks.co.uk
Est. 1989 *Stock size* Large
Stock Rare and second-hand
Christian and philosophy books
Open Mon–Sat 9.30am–noon
1–4.30pm or by appointment
Services Mail order. Bi-monthly
catalogue available from
www.abebooks.com

LANGFORD

⊞ T Baker
Contact Mr T Baker
✉ Langford House Farm,
Langford, Newark,
Nottinghamshire,
NG23 7RR 🅿
☎ 01636 704026
Est. 1966 *Stock size* Medium
Stock Period and Victorian
furniture
Open Mon–Fri 8am–5pm or by
appointment

LONG EATON

⊞ Miss Elany
Contact Mr D Mottershead
✉ 2 Salisbury Street, Long Eaton,
Nottinghamshire,
NG10 1BA 🅿
☎ 0115 973 4835 ✆ 0115 973 4835
🌐 www.misselany.com
Est. 1977 *Stock size* Large
Stock Antiques and pianos
Open Mon–Sat 9am–5pm
Fairs Newark, Swinderby
Services Valuations

MANSFIELD

⊞ Mansfield Antique Centre
Contact Dave Buckinger
✉ 185 Yorke Street, Mansfield
Woodhouse, Mansfield,
Nottinghamshire,
NG19 2NJ 🅿
☎ 01623 661122 ✆ 01623 631738
Est. 1992 *Stock size* Medium
Stock General antiques
Open Thurs–Sun 10am–5.30pm
Fairs Newark, Swinderby

⊞ Tom's Clock Shop (BWCG)
Contact Mr Tom Matthews
✉ 20 Station Street, Mansfield
Woodhouse, Mansfield,
Nottinghamshire,
NG19 8AB 🅿
☎ 01623 476097
🕾 07752 735605
📧 tomclockrepairs@lineone.net
🌐 www.tomclockrepairs.co.uk
Est. 1974 *Stock size* Large
Stock Antique clocks, watches,
jewellery
Open Mon–Fri 8.45am–4.45pm
Sat 9am–2pm
Fairs Birmingham Clock Fair
Services Valuations, restoration
of clocks and jewellery

⊞ A H Antiques & House Clearance
✉ 9 Rutland Avenue, Newark,
Nottinghamshire,
NG24 4DL 🅿
☎ 01636 706582
Est. 1985 *Stock size* Large
Stock General antiques and
collectables
Open By appointment
Services Valuations, house
clearance

⊞ N F Bryan-Peach Antiques
Contact Mr N Bryan-Peach
✉ No. One Castlegate Antiques,
1–3 Castlegate, Newark,
Nottinghamshire,
NG24 1AZ 🅿
☎ 01636 701877
📧 norm@bryanpeach.demon.co.uk
Est. 1974 *Stock size* Medium
Stock 18th–19thC furniture,
clocks, barometers
Open Mon–Fri 9.30am–5pm
Sat 9.30am–5.30pm
Services Valuations, restoration

⌂ Castlegate Antique Centre
Contact John Dench
✉ 55 Castle Gate, Newark,
Nottinghamshire,
NG24 1BE 🅿
☎ 01636 700076 ✆ 01636 700144
Est. 1983 *Stock size* Large
No. of dealers 9
Stock General antiques
Open Mon–Sat 10am–5pm,
closed Tues
Services Valuations, restoration

⊞ The Curio Cafe and Antiques
Contact Emily Powell
✉ 57–59 Castle Gate, Newark,
Nottinghamshire,
NG24 1BE
☎ 01636 700716 ✆ 01636 525193
Est. 2004 *Stock size* Medium
Stock General antiques,
collectables
Open Mon–Fri 9am–4.30pm
Sat 9am–4.30pm Sun 1pm–4pm
Services Valuations, café

⊞ Galerie
Contact Gillian Jennison
✉ 18 Kirkgate, Newark,
Nottinghamshire,
NG24 1AB 🅿
☎ 01636 705899

🕾 07951 691487
Est. 2000 *Stock size* Small
Stock French furniture, lights,
mirrors, paintings, textiles
Open Mon–Sat 9.30am–5.30pm

⊞ Lawrence Books
Contact Mr A Lawrence
✉ Newark Antique Centre,
Lombard Street, Newark,
Nottinghamshire,
NG24 1XP 🅿
☎ 01636 701619
Est. 1987 *Stock size* Small
Stock Antiquarian, rare and
second-hand books
Open Mon–Sat 9.30am–4.30pm
Sun 11am–4pm
Services Valuations

⊞ R R Limb Antiques
Contact Mr R Limb
✉ 33 North Gate, Newark,
Nottinghamshire,
NG24 1HD 🅿
☎ 01636 674546
Est. 1955 *Stock size* Large
Stock General antiques, pianos
Open By appointment
Fairs Newark, Swinderby
Services Piano exporters

⊞ M B G Antiques (DGA)
Contact Margaret Begley-Gray
DGA
✉ 41b Castlegate, Newark,
Nottinghamshire,
NG24 1BE 🅿
☎ 01636 704442 ✆ 01636 679586
🕾 07702 209808
📧 margaretbegleygray@aol.com
Est. 1982 *Stock size* Medium
Stock Period jewellery, quality
pictures, diamond rings
Open Wed–Sat 11am–4pm
closed Thurs
Services Picture search

⌂ Newark Antiques Centre
Contact Mr M Tinsley
✉ Regent House, Lombard
Street, Newark,
Nottinghamshire,
NG24 1XP 🅿
☎ 01636 605504 ✆ 01636 605101
📧 thephoenixexperi@btintrnet.com
🌐 www.newarkantiquescentre.com
Est. 1988 *Stock size* Large
No. of dealers 101
Stock General antiques
Open Mon–Sat 9am–5pm
Sun Bank Holidays 11am–4pm

private viewings by appointment
Services Valuations, upholstery,
clock repairs, specialist book
service

⌂ Newark Antiques Warehouse Ltd
Contact Nick Mellors
✉ Kelham Road, Newark,
Nottinghamshire,
NG24 1BX 🅿
☎ 01636 674869 ☎ 01636 612933
📱 07974 429185
✉ enquiries@newarkantiques.co.uk
🌐 www.newarkantiques.co.uk
Est. 1984 *Stock size* Large
No. of dealers 80
Stock Good furniture,
collectables, smalls
Open Mon–Fri 8.30am–5.30pm
Sat 9.30am–4pm Sun at Newark
Antiques Fair 9am–7pm
Services Valuations

⌂ No. One Castlegate Antiques
✉ 1–3 Castlegate, Newark,
Nottinghamshire,
NG24 1AZ 🅿
☎ 01636 701877
Est. 1974 *Stock size* Large
No. of dealers 10
Stock 18th–19thC antique
furniture, clocks, barometers,
decorative items
Open Mon–Fri 9.30am–5pm
Sat 9.30am–5.30pm
Services Valuations, restoration
of clocks and barometers

⊞ Pearman Antiques & Interiors
Contact Jan Parnham
✉ 9 Castle Gate, Newark,
Nottinghamshire,
NG24 1AZ 🅿
☎ 01636 679158 or 01949 837693
Est. 2001 *Stock size* Medium
Stock Oak and mahogany
furniture
Open Tues–Sat 10am–4pm

⊞ Wickersley Antiques
Contact Sandra Butler
✉ Newark Antiques Warehouse,
Kelham Road, Newark,
Nottinghamshire,
NG24 1BX 🅿
☎ 0114 285 1486
✉ sandra@lowerbradfield.fsnet.co.uk
Est. 1971 *Stock size* Large
Stock Furniture, paintings,
clocks, pottery, porcelain, silver,

pewter, jewellery, linen and
textiles
Open Mon–Fri 9am–5pm
Sat 10am–4pm

⊞ Acanthus Antiques & Collectables
Contact Trak or Sandra Smith
✉ 140 Derby Road (off Canning
Circus), Nottingham,
Nottinghamshire,
NG7 1LR 🅿
☎ 0115 924 3226
✉ trak.e.smith@ntlworld.com
🌐 www.acanthusantiques.co.uk
Est. 1979 *Stock size* Medium
Stock General antiques
Open Mon–Fri 10am–2.30pm Sat
12.30–4pm Sun by appointment
Fairs Newark, Swinderby,
Donnington
Services Valuations, lectures and
teaching

⊞ Antiques Across the World (LAPADA)
Contact Mr Rimes
✉ James Alexander Buildings,
London Road, Manvers Street,
Nottingham, Nottinghamshire,
NG2 3AE 🅿
☎ 0115 979 9199 ☎ 0115 239 3134
📱 07785 777787
✉ tonyrimes@btinternet.com
Est. 1992 *Stock size* Large
Stock Georgian–Edwardian
furniture
Open Mon–Fri 9am–5pm
Sat 10am–2pm
Fairs Newark
Services Valuations, courier
service, antique finder service

⊞ The Autograph Collectors Gallery
Contact Mr or Mrs G Clipson
✉ 7 Jessops Lane, Gedling,
Nottingham, Nottinghamshire,
NG4 4BQ
☎ 0115 961 2956/987 6578
☎ 0115 961 2956
✉ sales@autograph-gallery.co.uk
🌐 www.autograph-gallery.co.uk
Est. 1990 *Stock size* Large
Stock Signed photographs,
documents, letters
Open Telephone 9am–8pm
Services Mail order only

⊞ Castle Antiques
Contact Mr L Adamson
✉ 78 Derby Road, Nottingham,
Nottinghamshire,

NG1 5FD 🅿
☎ 0115 947 3913
Est. 1979 *Stock size* Medium
Stock General antiques, pictures,
maps, prints, lighting
Open Mon–Sat 9.30am–5pm

⊞ Cathay Antiques
Contact Jenny Bu or Paul Shum
✉ 74 Derby Road, Nottingham,
Nottinghamshire,
NG1 5FD 🅿
☎ 0115 988 1216 ☎ 0115 988 1216
✉ jennybu8@hotmail.com or
paulshum8@hotmail.com
🌐 www.furniture-made-in-
china.co.uk
Est. 2000 *Stock size* Medium
Stock Chinese furniture,
porcelain, neolithic pottery,
Tibetan thangka, wooden
carvings, embroidery and other
collectables
Open Mon–Sat 11am–6pm not
Bank Holidays

⊞ Collectors World
Contact Mr M Ray
✉ 188 Wollaton Road, Wollaton,
Nottingham, Nottinghamshire,
NG8 1HJ 🅿
☎ 0115 928 0347 ☎ 0115 928 0347
Est. 1991 *Stock size* Large
Stock Coins, banknotes, cigarette
cards, postcards
Open Tues–Sat 10.30am–4.30pm
Fairs Specialist fairs
Services Valuations, currency
exchange, framing

⊞ Dutton & Smith Medals & Badges
Contact Mr A Dutton or
Mr T Smith
✉ 140 Derby Road, Nottingham,
Nottinghamshire,
NG7 1LR 🅿
☎ 0115 924 3226
✉ trak.e.smith83@ntlworld.com
🌐 www.acanthusantiques.co.uk
Est. 1991 *Stock size* Medium
Stock Campaign medals,
gallantry awards, militaria and
badges
Open Mon–Fri 10.30am–2pm
Sat 12.30–4pm
Fairs Newark, Swinderby,
Donnington
Services Valuations

⊞ Fourways Antiques
Contact Mr Peter Key
✉ 38 Owen Avenue,

Nottingham, Nottinghamshire,
NG10 2FS 🅿
☎ 0115 972 1830
📱 07850 973889
Est. 1974 *Stock size* Medium
Stock General antiques
Open By appointment
Fairs Newark, Swinderby

⊞ Gatehouse Workshops
Contact Mr S J Waine
✉ 163 Castle Boulevard,
Nottingham, Nottinghamshire,
NG7 1FS 🅿
☎ 0115 948 3954 🖷 0115 948 3954
🌐 www.gatehouseworkshops.co.uk
Est. 1979 *Stock size* Medium
Stock Architectural antiques,
stained glass
Open Mon–Fri 9.30am–4pm
Sat 9am–5pm
Services Pine stripping

⊞ Harlequin Antiques
Contact Peter Hinchley or
Holly Hinchley
✉ 79–81 Mansfield Road,
Daybrook, Nottingham,
Nottinghamshire,
NG5 6BH 🅿
☎ 0115 967 4590
🅔 sales@antiquepine.net
🌐 www.antiquepine.net
Est. 1994 *Stock size* Large
Stock Original 18th–19thC pine
and country furniture
Open Mon–Sat 9.30am–5pm
Sat 9am–5pm
Services Restoration of all period
furniture, door and furniture
stripping

⊞ Andy Holmes Books
(PBFA)
✉ 82 Highbury Avenue, Bulwell,
Nottingham, Nottinghamshire,
NG6 9DB 🅿
☎ 0115 979 5603 🖷 0115 979 5616
🅔 holmesbook@aol.com
Est. 1996 *Stock size* Large
Stock Antiquarian, rare and
second-hand books, 19thC travel,
gypsies, folklore and general
topics
Open By appointment only
Fairs London Royal National,
Buxton
Services Valuations, book search

⊞ D D & A Ingle (OMRS)
Contact Mr D Ingle
✉ 380 Carlton Hill, Carlton,
Nottingham, Nottinghamshire,

NG4 1JA 🅿
☎ 0115 987 3325 🖷 0115 987 3325
🅔 ddaingle@talk21.com
Est. 1968 *Stock size* Medium
Stock General antiques
Open Mon–Sat 9am–5pm
Services Valuations

⊞ Jeremy & Westerman
Contact Geoff Blore
✉ 203 Mansfield Road,
Nottingham, Nottinghamshire,
NG1 3FF
☎ 0115 947 4522
Est. 1981 *Stock size* Medium
Stock Antiquarian and second-
hand books
Open Mon–Sat 11am–5pm
Fairs HD Book fairs

⤳ Arthur Johnson & Sons
Contact Mr R Hammersley
✉ Nottingham Auction Centre,
Meadow Lane, Nottingham,
Nottinghamshire,
NG2 3GY 🅿
☎ 0115 986 9128 🖷 0115 986 2139
🅔 clientservices@arthur
johnson.co.uk.com
Est. 1899
Open Mon–Thurs 9am–1pm
2.15–5pm Fri 9am–12.45pm
2–6.45pm Sat 9am–2pm
Sales Antique and export
furniture and collectables
Sat 10am, viewing Fri 2–6.45pm
Sat from 9am
Frequency Weekly
Catalogues Yes

⊞ Lights, Camera, Action
(UACC)
Contact Mr N Straw
✉ 6 Western Gardens, Western
Boulevard, Nottingham,
Nottinghamshire,
NG8 5GP 🅿
☎ 0115 913 1116
📱 07970 342363
Est. 1998 *Stock size* Large
Stock Collectors' items,
autographs, *Titanic* memorabilia
Open By appointment
Fairs NEC, Olympia, Newark
Services Free valuations

⊞ Michael D Long Ltd
(GTA, BACA Award Winner
2001)
Contact Mr Robert Hedger
✉ 96–98 Derby Road,
Nottingham, Nottinghamshire,
NG1 5FB 🅿

☎ 0115 941 3307 🖷 0115 941 4199
🅔 sales@michaeldlong.com
🌐 www.michaeldlong.com
Est. 1964 *Stock size* Large
Stock Fine antique arms and
armour
Open Mon–Fri 9.30am–5.15pm
Sat 10am–4pm
Fairs London Arms Fair,
Birmingham, Nottingham
Services Valuations

⊞ Luna
Contact Paul Rose
✉ 23 George Street, Nottingham,
Nottinghamshire,
NG1 3BH 🅿
☎ 0115 924 3267
🅔 info@luna-online.co.uk
🌐 www.luna-online.co.uk
Est. 1993 *Stock size* Medium
Stock 1950s–1970s objects for
the home
Open Mon–Sat 10.30am–5.30pm
Fairs Newark
Services Sourcing items, hire

⤳ Mellors & Kirk (RICS)
Contact Nigel Kirk or
Martha Parvin
✉ The Auction House,
Gregory Street, Nottingham,
Nottinghamshire,
NG7 2NL 🅿
☎ 0115 979 0000 🖷 0115 978 1111
🅔 menquiries@mellorsandkirk.com
🌐 www.mellorsandkirk.com
Est. 1993
Open Mon–Fri 8.30am–5pm
Sat 9am–noon
Sales Weekly general sale on
Tues. Fine art sale every six to
eight weeks
Catalogues yes

⊞ Memory Lane
Contact Mrs E Ramskill
✉ 82 Longmoor Lane, Sandiacre,
Nottingham, Nottinghamshire,
NG10 5JP 🅿
Est. 2003 *Stock size* Medium
Stock General antiques,
furniture, pottery, porcelain
Open Mon–Sat 11am–6pm
Sun noon–6pm closed Wed

⤳ Neales Auctioneers
(SOFAA, ARVA)
Contact Bruce Fearn, ARICS
✉ 192 Mansfield Road,
Nottingham, Nottinghamshire,
NG1 3HU 🅿
☎ 0115 962 4141 🖷 0115 969 3450

✉ nottingam@dnfa.com
ⓦ www.dnfa.com/nottingham
Est. 1840
Open Mon–Fri 9am–5.30pm
Sat 9am–12.30pm
Sales Specialist antique and fine
art sales every 2–3 months plus
general antiques and collectables
sales
Frequency Weekly
Catalogues Yes

⊞ Nottingham Architectural Antiques & Reclamation (SALVO)
Contact Jo Sanders
✉ St Albans Works,
181 Hartley Road,
Radford, Nottingham,
Nottinghamshire,
NG7 3DW ℗
☎ 0115 979 0666 ℗ 0115 845 8936
✉ admin.naar@ntlworld.com
ⓦ www.naar.co.uk
Est. 2003 *Stock size* Medium
Stock Original period fireplaces,
architectural salvage, doors,
fireplaces, parquet flooring,
stained glass
Open Mon–Sat 9am–6pm
Services Restoration

⊞ The Poison Dwarf
Contact Andrew Kulka
✉ 111 Alfreton Road,
Nottingham,
Nottinghamshire,
NG7 3JL ℗
☎ 0115 970 5552 ℗ 0115 970 5553
✉ info@thepoisondwarf.com
ⓦ www.thepoisondwarf.com
Est. 2004 *Stock size* Small
Stock Antique Continental
furniture
Open Tues–Sat 11am–6pm
Sun 11am–5pm

⚒ John Pye & Sons Ltd (NAVA)
Contact Adam Pye FNAVA
✉ James Shipstone House,
Radford Road, Nottingham,
Nottinghamshire,
NG7 7EA ℗
☎ 0870 910 9000 ℗ 0115 942 0100
✉ info@johnpye.co.uk.
ⓦ www.johnpye.co.uk
Est. 1969
Open Mon–Fri 8am–4.30pm
Sales General sales every Thurs,
plant & machinery sales on third
Fri of every month
Catalogues Online

⊞ Top Hat Antiques
Contact Mrs J Wallis
✉ 62 Derby Road, Nottingham,
Nottinghamshire,
NG1 5FD ℗
☎ 0115 941 9143 ℗ 0115 877 4185
✉ info@tophat-antiques.co.uk
ⓦ www.tophat-antiques.co.uk
Est. 1979 *Stock size* Large
Stock Surprises from the past,
furniture, silver, glass, ceramics,
jewellery, pictures, metalware,
collectables
Open Mon–Sat 10am–5pm

RETFORD

⚒ Bonhams
✉ 20 The Square, Retford,
Nottinghamshire,
DN22 6XE ℗
☎ 01777 708 633 or 0115 947 4414
℗ 01777 706724
✉ retford@bonhams.com
ⓦ www.bonhams.com
Open Mon–Fri 9am–1pm 2–5pm
Sales Regional office. Regular
sales held in London and in our
salerooms across the country.
Free auction valuations;
insurance and probate
valuations.

⊞ Lynn Guest Antiques
Contact Lynn Guest
✉ 15 Mill Lane,
Rockley, Retford,
Nottinghamshire,
DN22 0QP ℗
☎ 01777 838498
Est. 1979 *Stock size* Medium
Stock General antiques and
collectables
Open Mon–Fri 9am–6pm or by
appointment
Fairs Newark
Services Valuations, house
clearance

SANDIACRE

⊞ The Glory Hole
Contact Mr or Mrs C Reid
✉ 14 Station Road,
Sandiacre, Nottingham,
Nottinghamshire,
NG10 5BG ℗
☎ 0115 939 4081 ℗ 0115 939 4085
Est. 1984 *Stock size* Medium
Stock Antique furniture,
fireplaces
Open Mon–Sat 10am–5.30pm
Services Restoration

SUTTON-IN-ASHFIELD

⚒ C B Sheppard & Son
Contact Mr B Sheppard
✉ The Auction Gallery,
87 Chatworth Street,
Sutton-in-Ashfield,
Nottinghamshire,
NG17 4GG
☎ 01623 556310
📱 07714 798244
Est. 1951
Open Fri (auction weeks Tues–Fri)
10am–4pm
Sales General antiques
Frequency Monthly
Catalogues Yes

⊞ Yesterday and Today
Contact Mr J Turner
✉ 82 Station Road,
Sutton-in-Ashfield,
Nottinghamshire,
NG17 5HB ℗
☎ 01623 442215
📱 07957 552753
Est. 1984 *Stock size* Medium
Stock Collectables, 1920s and
1930s oak furniture
Open Tues–Sat 9am–5pm
Fairs Newark, Swinderby

WEST BRIDGFORD

⊞ Portland Antiques & Curios
Contact Brendan or Carole
Sprakes
✉ 5 Portland Road,
West Bridgford,
Nottinghamshire,
NG2 6DN ℗
☎ 0115 914 2123
Est. 1999 *Stock size* Large
Stock General antiques
Open Wed–Sat 10am–5pm

RUTLAND

MANTON

⊞ David Smith Antiques
Contact Mr D Smith
✉ 20 St Mary's Road, Manton,
Oakham, Rutland,
LE15 8SY ℗
☎ 01572 737119
Est. 1952 *Stock size* Medium
Stock General antiques
Open Mon–Sat 9am–5pm or by
appointment
Fairs Kettering
Services Valuations, restoration

OAKHAM

⊞ Antiques & Curios
Contact Bob Smith
✉ 30 Northgate, Oakham,
Rutland,
LE15 6QS 🅿
☎ 01572 771436
📧 smithrob31smith@aol.com
Est. 1992 *Stock size* Small
Stock General antiques,
collectables
Open By appointment
Fairs Newark, Swinderby

⊞ Robert Bingley
Antiques (LAPADA)
Contact Robert Bingley
✉ Church Street,
Wing, Oakham,
Rutland,
LE15 8RS 🅿
☎ 01572 737725   📠 01572 737284
🌐 www.robertbingley.com
Est. 1980 *Stock size* Large
Stock George II–Victorian
furniture
Open Mon–Sat 9am–5pm
Services Valuations, restoration

⊞ Swans Antiques and
Interiors
Contact Mr Tom Scott
✉ 17 Mill Street,
Oakham,
Rutland,
LE15 6EA 🅿
☎ 01572 724364   📠 01572 755094
📱 07860 304084
📧 info@swansofoakham.co.uk
🌐 www.swansofoakham.co.uk
Est. 1986 *Stock size* Large
Stock Antique beds, English and
French decorative furniture
Open Mon–Sat 9am–5.30pm
Sun by appointment
Fairs Newark
Services Valuations, restoration,
retail

⊞ Treedale Antiques
Contact Mr G Warren
✉ 10b Mill Street,
Oakham,
Rutland,
LE15 6EA 🅿
☎ 01572 757521   📠 01572 757521
Est. 1968 *Stock size* Medium
Stock 17th–18thC furniture,
specializing in walnut and oak
Open Mon–Sat 9am–5.30pm
Sun by appointment
Services Restoration

UPPINGHAM

⊞ John Garner Antiques
(LAPADA)
Contact John Garner
✉ 51 & 53 High Street East,
Uppingham, Rutland,
LE15 9PY 🅿
☎ 01572 823607   📠 01572 821654
📱 07850 596556
📧 sales@johngarnerantiques.com
🌐 www.johngarnerantiques.com
Est. 1968 *Stock size* Large
Stock Antiques furniture 18th-
20thC paintings, engravings,
etching, prints, bronzes and
clocks
Open Mon–Fri 9am–5pm
Sat Sun by appointment
Services Valuations, restoration,
framemaking, export

⊞ Goldmark Gallery
Contact Ian Broughton
✉ 14 Orange Street, Uppingham,
Oakham, Rutland,
LE15 9SQ 🅿
☎ 01572 822694   📠 01572 821503
📧 Mike@mgoldmark.freeserve.co.uk
🌐 www.goldmarkart.com
Est. 1974 *Stock size* Large
Stock 20thC prints
Open Mon–Sat 9.30am–5.30pm
Sun 2.30–5.30pm

⌂ Rutland Antiques
Centre
Contact Wendy Grindley
✉ Crown Passage,
Uppingham,
Rutland,
LE15 9NB 🅿
☎ 01572 824011
📧 rutlandantiques@btconnect.com
Est. 2001 *Stock size* Large
No. of dealers 50
Stock Quality antiques of all
descriptions
Open 364 days a year

⊞ Tattersalls
Contact Mrs J Tattersall
✉ 14b Orange Street,
Uppingham,
Oakham, Rutland,
LE14 2AG 🅿
☎ 01572 821171
📧 janice_tattersall@hotmail.com
Est. 1985 *Stock size* Medium
Stock Antique and old Persian
rugs
Open Tues–Sat 9.30am–5pm
Services Restoration

⊞ Woodmans House
Antiques
Contact Mr or Mrs J Collie
✉ 35 High Street East,
Uppingham, Oakham, Rutland,
LE15 9PY 🅿
☎ 01572 821799
📧 woodmanshouse@aol.com
Est. 1992 *Stock size* Medium
Stock Georgian furniture,
designer fabrics
Open Mon–Sat 9.30am–5pm or
Sun by appointment
Fairs NEC, Olympia
Services Valuations, restoration,
reference library, complete
interior design service

SHROPSHIRE

ATCHAM

⊞ Mytton Antiques
Contact M A Nares
✉ Norton Crossroads, Atcham,
Shrewsbury, Shropshire,
SY4 4UH 🅿
☎ 01952 740229   📠 01952 440229
📱 07860 575639
📧 nares@myttonantiques.
freeserve.co.uk
🌐 www.myttonantiques.com
Est. 1979 *Stock size* Medium
Stock 18th–19thC furniture and
smalls, longcase clocks, country
furniture, restoration materials
Open Mon–Sat 10am–5pm or by
appointment
Services Valuations, restoration,
shipping, courier service

BISHOPS CASTLE

⊞ Autolycus
Contact Mr David Wilkinson
✉ 10 Market Square,
Bishops Castle,
Shropshire,
SY9 5BN 🅿
☎ 01588 630078   📠 01588 630078
📧 autolycusbc@aol.com
🌐 www.booksonline.uk.com
Est. 1996 *Stock size* Medium
Stock Antiquarian and quality
second-hand books, specializing
in modern first editions,
illustrated, children's, travel,
topography, fine sporting prints
and pictures, antiques,
decorative items
Open Mon–Thurs 11am–4.30pm
Fri 11am–5pm Sat 10.30am–5pm
Services Valuations, book search

⊞ Decorative Antiques
Contact Richard Moulson
⊠ 47 Church Street,
Bishops Castle,
Shropshire,
SY9 5AD 🅿
☎ 01588 638851 ❶ 01588 638851
✉ enquiries@decorative-
antiques.co.uk
ⓦ www.decorative-antiques.co.uk
Est. 1996 *Stock size* Medium
Stock Art Deco 1860–1910, Arts
and Crafts, pottery, glass,
jewellery, metalware, evening
bags, early plastics
Open Mon–Sat 9.30am–5.30pm
closed Wed pm
Services Identification and
informal valuations

⊞ The Book Passage
Contact Mr David Lamont
⊠ 57a High Street, Bridgnorth,
Shropshire,
WV16 4DX 🅿
☎ 01746 768767
✉ bookman@btconnect.com
ⓦ www.thebookpassage.co.uk
Est. 1999 *Stock size* Large
Stock Antiquarian and second-
hand books
Open Mon–Sat 9am–5.15pm
Services book search, valuation
and repairs

🏠 Bridgnorth Antiques Centre
Contact Mr Richard Lewis
⊠ Whitburn Street, Bridgnorth,
Shropshire,
WV16 4QP 🅿
☎ 01746 768055
Est. 1994 *Stock size* Large
No. of dealers 20 (6 rooms)
Stock Late Victorian, Edwardian
and 1930s furniture, collectables
Open Mon–Sat 10am–5pm
Sun 10.30am–4.30pm
Services Clock repairs

⊞ English Heritage
Contact Mrs M Wainwright
⊠ 2 Whitburn Street, Bridgnorth,
Shropshire,
WV16 4QN 🅿
☎ 01746 762097
Est. 1988 *Stock size* Medium
Stock Militaria, coins & general
antiques
Open Mon–Sat 10am–5pm
closed Thurs

⊞ Malthouse Antiques
Contact Mrs Susan Mantle
⊠ 6 Underhill Street, Bridgnorth,
Shropshire,
WV16 4BB 🅿
☎ 01746 763054 ❶ 01746 763054
Est. 1979 *Stock size* Large
Stock Victorian–Edwardian
furniture, chandeliers
Open Mon–Sat 10am–6pm
Sun 2–5pm closed Wed
Services Restoration

🏠 Old Mill Antique Centre
Contact Mr Dennis Ridgeway
⊠ 48 Mill Street, Bridgnorth,
Shropshire,
WV15 5AG 🅿
☎ 01746 768778 ❶ 01746 768944
Est. 1996 *Stock size* Large
No. of dealers 90
Stock Complete range of
antiques and collectables
Open Mon–Sun 10am–5pm
Services Restaurant

🔨 Perry & Phillips
Contact Dennis Ridgeway
⊠ Old Mill Auction Rooms,
Mill Street, Bridgnorth,
Shropshire,
WV15 5AG 🅿
☎ 01746 762248 ❶ 01746 768944
✉ sales@perryandphillips.co.uk
ⓦ www.perryandphillips.co.uk
Est. 1835
Open Mon–Fri 9am–5pm
Sales General antiques sales Tues
10.30am, viewing Sat 10am–2pm
Sun 10am–4pm Mon 10am–5pm.
Occasional special sales
Frequency Monthly
Catalogues Yes

⊞ North Shropshire Reclamation and Antique Salvage (SALVO)
Contact Mrs J Powell
⊠ Wackley Lodge Farm,
Wackley, Burlton,
Shrewsbury, Shropshire,
SY4 5TD 🅿
☎ 01939 270719 ❶ 01939 270895
📱 07802 315038
Est. 1997 *Stock size* Large
Stock Garden statuary, bricks,
baths, hand basins, tiles, doors,
architectural salvage of all types
Open Mon–Fri 9am–6pm
Sat Sun 9am–5.30pm
Services Paint stripping

⊞ Funnye Olde Worlde
Contact Brian Taylor
⊠ 54 The High Street,
Church Stretton, Shropshire,
SY6 🅿
☎ 01743 244626
📱 07754 084949
Est. 1991 *Stock size* Small
Stock Antiques, bygones, general
Open Tues Thurs Fri 10am–4pm
Sat 10.30am–4.30pm
Fairs Swinderby
Services Valuations

🏠 Stretton Antiques Market
Contact Terry or Lisa Elvins
⊠ 36 Sandford Avenue,
Church Stretton,
Shropshire,
SY6 6BH
☎ 01694 723718 ❶ 01694 723718
Est. 1985 *Stock size* Large
No. of dealers 60
Stock Wide range of antiques
and collectables
Open Mon–Sat 9.30am–5.30pm
Sun 10.30am–4.30pm
Services Tea room

⊞ Martin Quick Antiques (LAPADA)
Contact Mr C Quick
⊠ Unit 2, Long Lane, Cosford,
Shropshire,
TF11 8PJ 🅿
☎ 01902 754703
📱 07774 124859
✉ cqantiques@aol.com
Est. 1970 *Stock size* Large
Stock Georgian–Victorian and
later furniture, French furniture
Trade only Yes
Open By appointment or chance
Fairs Newark
Services Valuations

🔨 Walker, Barnett & Hill
Contact Christopher Sidebottom
⊠ Cosford Auction Rooms,
Long Lane, Cosford,
Shropshire,
TF11 8PJ 🅿
☎ 01902 375555 ❶ 01902 375566
✉ wbhauctions@lineone.net
ⓦ www.walker-barnett-hill.co.uk
Est. 1780
Open Mon–Fri 9.30am–4pm
Sales Fortnightly antique and

contemporary furniture sales,
fine art sales 6-weekly
Catalogues Yes

CRAVEN ARMS

⊞ Marine
Contact Mark Jarrold
✉ Lower House Farm,
Middlehope, Craven Arms,
Shropshire,
SY7 9JT ⊡
☎ 01584 841210
⊕ 07776 193193
✆ mark@markjarrold.plus.com
Est. 1989
Stock Binoculars, ships' models,
navigational instruments,
chronometers, clocks, optical
equipment
Open By appointment
Fairs Birmingham International
Arms Fair
Services Valuations, restoration

DITTON PRIORS

**⊞ Priors Reclamation
(SALVO)**
Contact Miss V Bale
✉ Unit 65, Ditton Priors
Industrial Estate,
Ditton Priors,
Bridgnorth, Shropshire,
WV16 6SS ⊡
☎ 01746 712450 ⊕ 01746 712450
⊕ 07989 302488
✆ vicki@priorsrec.co.uk
✇ www.priorsrec.co.uk
Est. 1998 *Stock size* Large
Stock Reclaimed flooring, new
oak flooring, reclaimed doors,
brass and iron door furniture
Open By appointment at any time
Services Delivery, doors made to
order from reclaimed timber

ELLESMERE

⅄ Bowen, Son & Watson
Contact Mr Eddie Bowen
✉ Wharf Road, Ellesmere,
Shropshire,
SY12 0EJ ⊡
☎ 01691 622534 ⊕ 01691 623603
✆ bsw.ellesmere@virgin.net
✇ www.bowensonandwatson.co.uk
Est. 1869
Open Mon–Fri 9am–5pm
Sat 9am–noon
Sales Antique and household
goods monthly Tues 11am,
viewing Mon 9am–5pm

Tues 9–11am
Frequency Monthly
Catalogues Yes

**⊞ Georgiana Antiques &
Interiors**
Contact Julie George
✉ Cambrian House,
Frankton, Ellesmere,
Shropshire,
SY12 9HE ⊡
☎ 01691 690307
⊕ 07745 373568
Est. 2003 *Stock size* Small
Stock General antiques for the
home
Open Flexible hours call for an
appointment
Services Interior design
consultancy and finding antiques
for the home

IRONBRIDGE

⊞ Bears on the Square
Contact Margaret Phillips
✉ 2 The Square, Ironbridge,
Telford, Shropshire,
TF8 7AQ ⊡
☎ 01952 433924 ⊕ 01952 433926
✆ bernie@bearsonthesquare.com
✇ www.bearsonthesquare.com
Est. 1991 *Stock size* Large
Stock Steiff, Deans, Hermann,
Spielwaren, Artist and second-
hand bears, Country Life, Boyds
Open Mon–Sun 10am–5pm
Services Worldwide mail order

⊞ Tudor House Antiques
Contact Mr Peter Whitelaw
✉ 11 Tontine Hill, Ironbridge,
Telford, Shropshire,
TF8 7AL ⊡
☎ 01952 433783
✆ tudoriron@aol.com
✇ www.tudorhouse.co.uk
Est. 1964 *Stock size* Large
Stock Coalport, Caughley,
general English ceramics
Open Mon–Sat 10am–5pm
Sun by appointment
Services Valuations

LUDLOW

⊞ Bayliss Antiques
Contact Mr A B Bayliss
✉ 22–24 Old Street,
Ludlow, Shropshire,
SY8 1NP ⊡
☎ 01584 873634 ⊕ 01584 873634
⊕ 07831 672211

Est. 1968 *Stock size* Medium
Stock Oak and mahogany
furniture, paintings
Open Mon–Sat 9am–6pm or by
appointment
Services Valuations

⊞ Bread & Roses
Contact Rose Smith
✉ Corve Street, Ludlow,
Shropshire,
SY8 1DA ⊡
☎ 01584 877200
⊕ 07810 508804
Est. 1995 *Stock size* Medium
Stock Kitchenware
Open Mon–Sat 10am–5pm
closed Thurs
Fairs NEC, Newark

**⊞ R G Cave & Sons Ltd
(LAPADA, BADA)**
Contact Mr R G Cave or
John Cave
✉ 17 Broad Street, Ludlow,
Shropshire,
SY8 1NG ⊡
☎ 01584 873568 ⊕ 01584 875050
Est. 1965 *Stock size* Medium
Stock Period furniture,
metalwork, works of art
Open Mon–Sat 10am–5.30pm
Services Valuations for probate
and insurance, shippers of
Bordeaux wine

⊞ Corve Street Antiques
Contact Mr Jones or Mr Mcavoy
✉ 141a Corve Street, Ludlow,
Shropshire,
SY8 2PG ⊡
☎ 01584 879100
Est. 2001 *Stock size* Medium
Stock Longcase clocks, oak,
country, mahogany furniture,
copper, brass, pictures,silver
Open Mon–Sat 10am–5pm
Services Valuations

⊞ Garrard Antiques
Contact Mrs C Garrard
✉ 139a Corve Street,
Ludlow, Shropshire,
SY8 2PG ⊡
☎ 01584 876727 ⊕ 01584 781277
⊕ 07971 588063
Est. 1985 *Stock size* Large
Stock Period pine, oak and
country furniture, pottery,
porcelain, glass, treen, books,
collectables
Open Mon–Fri 10am–1pm 2–5pm
Sat 10am–5pm closed Tues

⊞ Leon Jones
Contact Mr L Jones
⊠ Mitre House Antiques,
Corve Bridge, Ludlow,
Shropshire,
SY8 1DY ⓟ
☎ 01584 872138
ⓜ 07976 549013
Est. 1972 *Stock size* Large
Stock Country furniture,
mahogany, clocks
Open Mon–Sat 9am–5pm
Fairs Newark, Ardingly

⊞ Little Paws
Contact Mr Martin Rees-Evans
⊠ 4 Castle Street, Ludlow,
Shropshire,
SY8 1AT ⓟ
☎ 01584 875286
ⓦ www.littlepawsludlow.co.uk
Est. 1992 *Stock size* Medium
Stock Traditional teddy bears,
dolls
Open Mon–Sat 10am–5pm
Services Restoration on bears

⊞ Ludlow Antique Beds & Fireplaces
Contact Mr G Jones or
Mrs S Small
⊠ 142 Corve Street, Ludlow,
Shropshire,
SY8 2PG ⓟ
☎ 01584 875506
ⓜ 07850 841609
Est. 1987 *Stock size* Medium
Stock Pine country and garden
furniture, kitchen units, iron,
wooden beds
Open Mon Fri 11am–4pm
Sat 11am–5pm

⚒ McCartneys
Contact Mr Daniel Fielder
⊠ The Ox Pasture, Overton Road,
Ludlow, Shropshire,
SY8 4AA ⓟ
☎ 01584 872251 ⓕ 01584 875727
ⓔ fineart@mccartneys.co.uk
ⓦ www.maccartneys.co.uk
Est. 1874
Open Mon–Fri 9am–5.30pm
Sales Fine art, antiques and
household effects Fri 10.30am,
viewing Thurs 2–7pm day of sale
9–10.30am
Frequency Monthly
Catalogues By Email

⌂ K W Swift
Contact Mr K W Swift
⊠ 56 Mill Street, Ludlow,

Shropshire,
SY8 1BB ⓟ
☎ 01584 878571 ⓕ 01746 714407
ⓔ ken@onetel.net
Est. 1989 *Stock size* Medium
No. of dealers 20
Stock Book market, total circa
5,000 volumes (frequently
changed), antiquarian maps and
prints
Open Mon–Sat 10am–5pm
Services Mounting, framing

⊞ Zany Lady
Contact Sue Humphreys
⊠ Corve Street, Ludlow,
Shropshire,
SY8 1DA ⓟ
☎ 01584 877200
Est. 2001 *Stock size* Medium
Stock Decorative stock, country
furniture, textiles, French garden
furniture
Open Mon–Sat 10am–5pm
closed Thurs

⊞ Richard Midwinter Antiques
Contact Mr R Midwinter
⊠ Market Drayton,
Shropshire,
TF9 4EF ⓟ
☎ 01630 673901 ⓕ 01630 672289
ⓜ 07836 617361
ⓔ antiques@midwinter.fslife.co.uk
Est. 1972 *Stock size* Medium
Stock Town and country
furniture, longcase clocks,
samplers, needlework pictures,
decorative objects
Open By appointment
Fairs Olympia, NEC, Penman
Chester
Services Restoration

⊞ John King (BADA)
Contact Mr J King
⊠ Raynalds Mansion,
Much Wenlock,
Shropshire,
TF13 6AE ⓟ
☎ 01952 727456 ⓕ 01952 727456
ⓔ kingj896@aol.com
Est. 1967 *Stock size* Large
Stock Period furniture and
associated items
Open By appointment only
Services Advice on furnishing
homes

⊞ Corner Farm Antiques
Contact Mr Tim Dams
⊠ 102 Kings Street,
Weston Heath, Newport,
Shropshire,
TF11 8RX ⓟ
☎ 01952 691543 ⓕ 01952 691543
ⓜ 07971 578585
ⓦ www.antique-clocks.com
Est. 1995 *Stock size* Large
Stock Georgian–Victorian and
dining furniture, clocks,
barometers, longcase clocks,
collectables
Open Mon–Sun 10am–5pm
Services Restoration, clock
repairs, valuations

⚒ Davies, White & Perry
Contact Mr J P Davies
⊠ 45–47 High Street, Newport,
Shropshire,
TF10 7AT ⓟ
☎ 01952 811003 ⓕ 01952 811439
ⓔ newport@davieswhiteperry.co.uk
ⓦ www.davieswhiteperry.co.uk
Est. 1806
Open Mon–Fri 8.15am–5pm
Sat 9am–4pm closed noon–2pm
Sun 11am–4pm
Sales Occasional antiques sales
on site
Catalogues Yes

⊞ Brook Farm Antiques
Contact Mr Tucker or Mr James
⊠ Brook Farm, Gauntons Bank,
Norbury, Shropshire,
SY13 4HY ⓟ
☎ 01948 666043
ⓜ 07754 418777
Est. 1993 *Stock size* Medium
Stock Victorian–Edwardian
dining tables
Open Mon–Sun 9am–5pm
Fairs Stafford Bingley Hall
Services Restoration

⊞ Bookworld
Contact Mr J Cranwell
⊠ 32 Beatrice Street, Oswestry,
Shropshire,
SY11 1QG ⓟ
☎ 01691 657112 ⓕ 01691 657112
ⓔ jcbookworld@arrowweb.co.uk
ⓦ www.tgal.co.uk/bookworld
Est. 1995 *Stock size* Medium

Stock Antiquarian and second-hand books
Open Mon–Sat 9am–5pm
Services Book search

PREES HEATH

⊞ Whitchurch Antique Centre
Contact Mr John Simcox
✉ Heath Road, Prees Heath, Whitchurch, Shropshire,
SY13 2AD ℗
☎ 01948 662626 ℗ 01948 662604
ⓦ www.whitchurchantiques.co.uk
Est. 1979 *Stock size* Large
Stock French and English furniture and pine
Open Mon–Sun 9am–5pm
Services Packing, shipping

SHIFNAL

⚒ Davies, White & Perry
Contact Mr J P Davies
✉ 18 Market Place, Shifnal, Shropshire,
TF11 9AZ ℗
☎ 01952 460523
ⓦ www.davieswhiteperry.co.uk
Est. 1806
Open Mon–Fri 9am–5pm
closed 1pm–2pm Sat 9am–noon
Sales Occasional antiques sales on site
Catalogues Yes

SHREWSBURY

⊞ Antique Barometer & Clock Shop
Contact Clive Hickman
✉ 21a Castle Street, Shrewsbury, Shropshire,
SY1 2AZ
☎ 01743 360415
ℯ clocks.barometers@virgin.net
ⓦ www.thebarometershop.com
Est. 1999 *Stock size* Large
Stock Antique clocks, barometers
Open Tues Thurs–Sat 10.30am–5pm
Services Restoration

⊞ Bear Steps Antiques
Contact John or Sally Wyatt
✉ 2 Bear Steps, Fish Street, Shrewsbury, Shropshire,
SY1 1UR ℗
☎ 01743 344298
ⓜ 07743 118192
ⓦ www.bear-steps-antiques.co.uk
Est. 1990 *Stock size* Large

Stock 18th–early 19thC English porcelain
Open Mon–Sat 9am–5pm
Fairs NEC Antiques for Everyone

⊞ Candle Lane Books
Contact Mr J Thornhill
✉ 28 Princess Street, Shrewsbury, Shropshire,
SY1 1LW ℗
☎ 01743 365301
Est. 1965 *Stock size* Large
Stock Antiquarian and second-hand books
Open Mon–Sat 9.30am–1pm 2–4.45pm

⊞ Collectors Gallery (IBNS, IBSS, ANA, BNTA)
Contact Mr Veissid
✉ 24 The Parade, St Mary's Place, Shrewsbury, Shropshire,
SY1 1DL ℗
☎ 01743 272140 ℗ 01743 366041
ℯ m.veissid@btinternet.com
ⓦ www.collectors-gallery.co.uk
Est. 1976 *Stock size* Medium
Stock Coins, medals, stamps, bank notes, postcards, bonds and shares
Open Mon–Fri 9am–5.30pm
Sat 9.30am–5pm
Services Mail order

⊞ Collectors Place
Contact Mr Keith Jones or Mrs June Jones
✉ 29a Princess Street, Shrewsbury, Shropshire,
SY1 1LW ℗
☎ 01743 246150
ⓦ www.collectors-place.co.uk
Est. 1996 *Stock size* Large
Stock Antique bottles, pot lids, Wade, Beswick, Carlton ware, Art Deco, collectables
Open Tues–Sat 10am–4pm
Services Valuations on bottles

⊞ Deborah Paul
Contact Debbie or Paul
✉ Leebotwood, Church Streighton, Shropshire,
SY6 6LU ℗
☎ 01743 357696
ⓜ 07890 926530
ℯ pgurden@aol.com
Est. 2000 *Stock size* Medium
Stock Decorative and period furniture, oak and country decorations

Open Wed–Sat10am–5pm
Sat 10am–4pm
Services Clock restorer on site

⊞ Deja Vu Antiques
Contact Mr I Jones
✉ 48 High Street, Shrewsbury, Shropshire,
SY13 1EU ℗
☎ 01743 362251
ⓜ 07720 691939
ℯ dejavuantiques@lineone.net
ⓦ www.antiquephones.co.uk
Est. 1984 *Stock size* Medium
Stock Antique telephones, Art Deco, pine furniture, jewellery
Open Mon–Sat 9.30am–5pm usually closed Thurs
Fairs Chester, Leeds and Loughborough Art Deco fairs, Warwick
Services Valuations, restoration, repairs, mail order service

⊞ Expressions
Contact Mrs J Griffiths
✉ 17 Princess Street, Shrewsbury, Shropshire,
SY1 1LP ℗
☎ 01743 351731
Est. 1991 *Stock size* Medium
Stock Art Deco, furniture, pictures, glass, ceramics
Open Mon–Sat 10am–4pm

⚒ Halls Fine Art Auctions (ARVA, SOFAA, BACA Award Winner 2004)
Contact Richard Allen or Jeremy Lamond, RICS
✉ Welsh Bridge, Shrewsbury, Shropshire,
SY3 8LA ℗
☎ 01743 231212 ℗ 01743 246191
ℯ fineart@halls-auctioneers.ltd.uk
ⓦ www.hallsgb.com
Est. 1865
Open 9am–5pm
Sales Antiques sales every 6 weeks, general and collectors sales every Fri 10.30am, viewing Thurs 9.30am–7pm
Catalogues Yes

⊞ Brian James Antiques (FSB)
Contact Brian James
✉ Unit 9, Rodenhurst Business Park, Rodington, Shrewsbury, Shropshire,
SY4 4QU ℗
☎ 01952 770856 ℗ 01952 770856
ⓜ 07909 886903

📧 brianjamesantiques@yahoo.co.uk
🌐 www.brainjamesantiques.co.uk
Est. 1986 *Stock size* Medium
Stock Georgian–Edwardian
chests of drawers, TV and
entertainment cabinets
Open Mon–Fri 9am–6pm
Sat 9am–1pm or by appointment
Services Wholesale export,
conversion and manufacturing
specialist

⊞ The Little Gem (NAG)
Contact Mrs M A Bowdler
✉ 18 St Mary's Street,
Shrewsbury,
Shropshire,
SY1 1ED 🅿
☎ 01743 352085 📠 01743 352085
📧 mbowdler@littlegem.
freeserve.co.uk
🌐 www.thelittlegem.co.uk
Est. 1960 *Stock size* Medium
Stock Antique and second-hand
jewellery, modern Waterford
crystal, lighting, hand-made
jewellery
Open Mon–Sat 9am–5.15pm
Services Jewellery and watch
repair

⊞ F C Manser & Son Ltd (LAPADA)
Contact Paul Manser
✉ Coleham Head, Shrewsbury,
Shropshire,
SY3 7BJ 🅿
☎ 01743 351120 📠 01743 271047
📧 mansers@theantiquedealers.com
🌐 www.theantiquedealers.com
Est. 1944 *Stock size* Large
Stock Antiques, furniture,
porcelain, glassware
Open Mon–Sat 9am–5pm
Fairs LAPADA NEC
Services Valuations, restoration

⌂ Princess Antique Centre
Contact Mr John Langford
✉ 14a The Square, Shrewsbury,
Shropshire,
SY1 1LH
☎ 01743 343701
Est. 1984 *Stock size* Large
No. of dealers 100
Stock Complete range of
antiques and collectables
Open Mon–Sat 9.30am–5.15pm

⊞ Quayside Antiques
Contact Mr Chris Winter
✉ 9 Frankwell, Shrewsbury,
Shropshire,

SY3 8JY 🅿
☎ 01743 360490 or 01948 830363
📱 07715 748223
🌐 www.quaysideantiques
shrewsbury.co.uk
Est. 1974 *Stock size* Large
Stock Victorian and Edwardian
mahogany furniture, large
tables, sets of chairs
Open Tues–Sat 10am–4pm
closed Thurs
Fairs NEC
Services Restoration

⌂ Shrewsbury Antique Centre
Contact Mr John Langford
✉ 15 Princess House,
The Square, Shrewsbury,
Shropshire,
SY1 1JZ 🅿
☎ 01743 247704
Est. 1984 *Stock size* Large
No. of dealers 70
Stock Wide range of stock
Open Mon–Sat 9.30am–5.15pm

⊞ Shrewsbury Clock Shop (BHI)
Contact Mr A Donnelly
✉ The Clock Shop,
7 The Parade, St Mary's Place,
Shrewsbury, Shropshire,
SY1 1DL 🅿
☎ 01743 361388 📠 01743 361388
📧 clockshopshrewsbury@
btopenworldcom
🌐 www.clockshopshrewsbury.co.uk
Est. 1987 *Stock size* Medium
Stock Clocks, especially longcase,
and barometers
Open Mon–Fri 9.30am–4.30pm
Sat 10am–1pm closed Wed
Fairs NEC Spring
Services Clock and barometer
repairs and restoration

STANTON UPON HINE HEATH

⊞ Marcus Moore Antiques
Contact Mr M Moore
✉ Booley House, Booley,
Stanton upon Hine Heath,
Shrewsbury, Shropshire,
SY4 4LY 🅿
☎ 01939 200333 📠 01939 200333
📱 07976 228122
📧 mmooreantiques@aol.com
🌐 www.marcusmoore-antiques.com
Est. 1980 *Stock size* Large
Stock Georgian–Victorian oak,
country and mahogany furniture
and associated items

Open By appointment any time
Services Restoration, upholstery,
search, courier

WALL UNDER HEYWOOD

➶ Mullock & Madeley (RICS, ISVA)
Contact John Mullock or
Paul Madeley
✉ The Old Shippon,
Wall under Heywood,
Church Stretton, Shropshire,
SY6 7DS 🅿
☎ 01694 771771 📠 01694 771772
📧 info@mullockmadeley.co.uk
🌐 www.mullockmadeley.co.uk
Est. 1997
Sales Sporting memorabilia,
vintage fishing tackle, historical
documents, autographs. Regular
Internet sales of fishing tackle
and sporting memorabilia. Sales
venues Ludlow Race Course,
Sutton Coldfield Town Hall.
Specialist football, golf auctions
held in Midlands venues
Frequency Every 3 months
Catalogues Yes

STAFFORDSHIRE

BASFORD

⊞ The Pottery Buying Centre
Contact Mr P Hume
✉ 535 Etruria Road, Basford,
Stoke-on-Trent, Staffordshire,
ST4 6HT 🅿
☎ 01782 635453
📱 07971 711612
Est. 1997 *Stock size* Medium
Stock Fine ceramics, collectables,
Doulton, Moorcroft, Beswick,
small furniture
Open Mon–Sat 10am–4pm
Services Valuations, restoration
of ceramics

BREWOOD

⊞ Passiflora
Contact David, Paula or
Jim Whitfield
✉ 25 Stafford Street, Brewood,
Staffordshire,
ST19 9DX 🅿
☎ 01902 851557
📱 07711 682216
📧 paula.whitfield@ukonline.co.uk
Est. 1988 *Stock size* Large

Stock Antiques and collectables dating back to Victorian times, glass, china, pottery, copper, brass, cast-iron, curios, leather, ephemera, postcards, children's books, bric-a-brac, garden tools, garden statuary, small furniture, decorative items including Mabel Lucie Attwell
Open Very flexible, phone first
Fairs Stafford Bingley Hall, West Midlands Fairs
Services Valuations and house clearance

⊞ **Brearley's Antiques Corner Curios**
Contact James Brearley
✉ **54 New Street,
Burton-on-Trent, Staffordshire,
DE14 3QY** 🅿
☎ 01283 532600 📠 01283 532600
Est. 1984 **Stock size** Medium
Stock Antiques, collectables
Open Mon–Sat 10am–6pm
Services House clearance

⊞ **Burton Antiques**
Contact Mr M Rodgers
✉ **1–2 Horninglow Road,
Burton-on-Trent, Staffordshire,
DE14 2PR** 🅿
☎ 01283 542331
Est. 1978 **Stock size** Medium
Stock Antique pine and other antique furniture
Open Mon–Sat 9am–5pm
Sun 11am–4pm
Services Valuations, pine stripping, shipping

⊞ **Byrkley Books Ltd**
Contact Mrs P Tebbett
✉ **159 Station Street,
Burton-on-Trent, Staffordshire,
DE14 1BE** 🅿
☎ 01283 565900
Est. 1963 **Stock size** Medium
Stock Antiquarian, second-hand and remainder books, horse racing a speciality
Open Mon–Fri 9.30am–5pm
Sat 9am–5pm

⊞ **Roy C Harris (LAPADA)**
Contact Roy Harris
✉ **Burton-on-Trent,
Staffordshire,
DE14** 🅿
☎ 01283 520355
📱 07718 500961

🖃 rchclocks@aol.com
🌐 www.rch-antique-clocks.com
Est. 1983 **Stock size** Medium
Stock Lanterns, marine chronometers
Open By appointment
Fairs NEC
Services Valuations, restoration, shipping

⊞ **Gordon Litherland**
Contact Gordon Litherland
✉ **25 Stapenhill Road,
Burton-on-Trent, Staffordshire,
DE15 9AE** 🅿
☎ 01283 567213 📠 01283 517142
🖃 gordon@jmp2000.com
Est. 1975 **Stock size** Small
Stock Advertising, breweriana, whiskiana
Open By appointment
Services Mail order

⊞ **Alan Winson Antiques**
Contact Alan Winson
✉ **147 Derby Street,
Burton-on-Trent, Staffordshire,
DE14 2LG**
☎ 01283 510429
Est. 1987 **Stock size** Medium
Stock Decorative antiques
Open Mon–Fri 9am–5pm
Sat 10am–4pm

🪕 **Richard Winterton Auctioneers and Valuers**
Contact Mr A Rathbone or Mr R Winterton
✉ **School House Auction Rooms,
Hawkins Lane, Burton-on-Trent,
Staffordshire,
DE14 1PT** 🅿
☎ 01283 511224 📠 01283 568650
🖃 adrianrathbone@btconnect.com
🌐 www.invaluable.com/richard winterton
Est. 1864
Open Mon–Fri 9am–5pm
Tues 9am–6.30pm
Sales Weekly auctions of ceramics, glass, silver, fine art, jewellery, furniture, toys, sporting memorabilia, collectors items, antiquarian books, shipping furniture
Catalogues Yes

⊞ **P & K Turner Auctions**
Contact Phil Turner
✉ **Cannock Road, Heath Hayes,
Cannock, Staffordshire,**

WS12 3HA 🅿
☎ 01543 274176
🖃 philkt@btinternet.com
Est. 1986 **Stock size** Small
Stock English country oak furniture, desks, bookcases
Open Mon–Sat 9am–5pm or by appointment
Services Valuations, restoration

⊞ **Country Pine Trading Co**
Contact Mr S Beard
✉ **Unit 15, New Haden Yard,
Draycoft Cross Road, Cheadle,
Staffordshire,
ST10 2NP** 🅿
☎ 01538 756894 📠 01538 756894
📱 07959 585133
🌐 www.countrypinetrading.co.uk
Est. 1974 **Stock size** Large
Stock Country pine and antique pine furniture
Open Mon–Fri 8am–5pm
Sat 8am–1pm or by appointment
Fairs Newark
Services Restoration and pine stripping

⊞ **Cottage Collectibles**
Contact Mrs S Kettle
✉ **62 High Street,
Eccleshall,
Staffordshire,
ST21 6BZ** 🅿
☎ 01785 850210 📠 01785 850757
📱 07967 713512
🖃 sheila@cottagecollectibles.co.uk
🌐 www.cottagecollectibles.co.uk
Est. 1995 **Stock size** Medium
Stock English and Continental country antiques, kitchenware, pine furniture, garden and dairy tools
Open By appointment only
Services Restoration

⊞ **David J Cope**
Contact Mr D Cope
✉ **Fox Earth, Harriseahead Lane,
Harriseahead, Stoke-on-Trent,
Staffordshire,
ST7 4RF** 🅿
☎ 01782 511926 📠 01782 516931
📱 07712 880695
🖃 ceramicsinter@btconnect.com
Est. 1979 **Stock size** Medium
Stock Moorcroft, Royal

Worcester, Royal Doulton and porcelain
Open Mon–Sun 10am–5pm
Fairs Newark
Services Valuations

LEEK

⊞ Antique Mirrors
Contact Tony Williams
✉ 2 Duke Street, Leek, Staffordshire,
ST13 5LG 🅿
☎ 01538 372553
🌐 info@williamsantiquemirrors.co.uk
🌐 www.williamsantiquemirrors.co.uk
Est. 2005 **Stock size** Large
Stock 19thC French and English mirrors
Open Mon–Fri 9am–4pm
Fairs NEC, Earls Court
Services Export packing, restoration

⊞ The Antique Store
Contact Mrs Robinson
✉ 1 Clerk Bank, Leek, Staffordshire,
ST13 5HE 🅿
☎ 01538 386555 📠 01782 570119
📱 07775 582058
🌐 antiques@leek.aol.com
Est. 1979 **Stock size** Medium
Stock Traditional English decorative items, garden items, architectural antiques, silver
Open Wed Sat 10am–5pm

⊞ Antiques Within
Contact Mr R Hicks or Mrs K Hicks
✉ Ground Floor, Compton Mill, Compton, Leek, Staffordshire,
ST13 5NJ 🅿
☎ 01538 387848 📠 01538 387848
🌐 antiques.within@virgin.net
🌐 www.antiques-within.com
Est. 1994 **Stock size** Large
Stock Pine, oak, mahogany and Continental furniture, brass, copper, mirrors, collectables
Open Mon–Sat 10am–5.30pm
Sun 1–5pm
Fairs Newark, Swinderby and Ardingly
Services Container packing

⊞ Anvil Antiques
Contact Mr Jim Spooner
✉ Pretty Polly Mill, Buxton Road, Leek, Staffordshire,
ST13 6ES 🅿
☎ 01538 384522 📠 01538 385118

Est. 1975 **Stock size** Medium
Stock Reproduction and old pine furniture, Old French dark-wood furniture
Open Mon–Fri 9am–5pm Sat 10am–5pm Sun by appointment
Services Restoration, stripping

➴ Bury & Hilton
Contact John Hilton
✉ 6 Market Street, Leek, Staffordshire,
ST13 6HZ 🅿
☎ 01538 383344 📠 01538 371314
🌐 info@buryandhilton.co.uk
Est. 1887
Open Mon–Fri 9am–5.30pm
Sales Monthly antiques and general sales 1st Thurs 10am. Special antiques sales April and October
Catalogues No

⌂ Compton Mill Antique Emporium
Contact Mrs S K Butler
✉ Compton Mill, Compton, Leek, Staffordshire,
ST13 5NJ 🅿
☎ 01538 373396 📠 01538 399092
🌐 kelly.butler@ntlbusiness.co.uk
Est. 1996 **Stock size** Large
No. of dealers 30
Stock Wide range of antiques
Open Tues–Sat 10am–5.30pm
Sun 1–5pm
Services Pine furniture made from reclaimed timber

⊞ Coopers Furniture
Contact Tony or Ben Cooper
✉ Unit 10, Brooklands Way, Basford Lane Industrial Estate, Leek, Staffordshire,
ST13 7QF 🅿
☎ 01538 385930 📠 01538 385930
Est. 1980 **Stock size** Medium
Stock Irish country furniture
Open Mon–Sat 8.30am–5pm

⊞ Roger Haynes Antique Finder
Contact Mr R Haynes
✉ 54 Shoebridge Street, Leek, Staffordshire,
ST13 5JZ 🅿
☎ 01538 385161 📠 01538 385161
🌐 info@rogerhaynesantiquefinder.com
Est. 1959 **Stock size** Large
Stock Decorative English and French items, pine and country small items, collectables

Trade only Yes
Open By appointment only
Services Export trade

⊞ Johnsons Antiques Ltd
Contact Mr P Johnson
✉ Chorley Mill, 1 West Street, Leek, Staffordshire,
ST13 8AF 🅿
☎ 01538 386745 📠 01538 388375
📱 07714 288765
🌐 johnsonsantiques@btconnect.com
Est. 1976 **Stock size** Medium
Stock English and French country furniture, decorative accessories, unique objects
Open Mon–Fri 8am–5pm
Sat Sun by appointment
Services Suppliers to export market

⊞ Jonathan Charles Antiques
Contact Mr J Heath
✉ 6 Broad Street, Leek, Staffordshire,
ST13 5NS 🅿
☎ 01538 381883
Est. 1999 **Stock size** Medium
Stock Pine furniture, country furniture
Open Mon–Sat 11am–5pm
Services One-off pieces made to measure

⌂ Leek Antiques Centre (Barclay House)
Contact Mr P Lumley
✉ 4–6 Brook Street, Leek, Staffordshire,
ST13 5JE 🅿
☎ 01538 398475
📱 07721 413095
Est. 1969 **Stock size** Large
No. of dealers 7–8
Stock Wide range of antiques including dining tables, sets of chairs, bedroom furniture, chests of drawers, pottery, watercolours, oil paintings, pine
Open Mon–Sat 10.30am–5pm
Services Restoration, polishing and upholstery

⊞ Odeon Lighting (Lighting Association)
Contact Mr S Ford
✉ 76–78 St Edward Street, Leek, Staffordshire,
ST13 5DL 🅿
☎ 01538 387188 📠 01538 384235
📱 07973 317961
🌐 odeonantiques@hotmail.com

Ⓦ www.odeonantiques.co.uk
Est. 1990 *Stock size* Large
Stock Antique lighting, country furniture
Open Mon–Sat 11am–5pm
Services Restoration

⊞ Page Antiques
Contact Denis Page
✉ Antiques Within Ltd, Ground Floor, Compton Mill, Leek, Staffordshire,
ST13 5NJ ℗
☎ 01663 732358 ❶ 01663 732358
Ⓜ 07966 154993
Est. 1979 *Stock size* Medium
Stock General antiques, Georgian–Edwardian furniture
Open Mon–Sat 10am–5pm
Fairs Swinderby, Buxton
Services Valuations, exports

⊞ Richardson Antiques Ltd
Contact Mr Richardson
✉ Antiques Within, Compton Mill, Leek, Staffordshire,
ST13 5NJ ℗
☎ 01270 625963
Est. 1984 *Stock size* Medium
Stock Furniture, china
Open Mon–Sat 10am–5pm
Sun 1–5pm

⊞ Roberts & Mudd Antiques
Contact Mr C Mudd
✉ Compton Mill, Compton, Leek, Staffordshire,
ST13 5NJ ℗
☎ 01538 371284 ❶ 01538 371284
Ⓜ 07768 845942
❺ robertsmudd@compuserve.com
Ⓦ www.robertsandmudd.com
Est. 1993 *Stock size* Large
Stock French, pine and country furniture, decorative items, French and English furniture
Open Mon–Fri 8am–6pm
Sat 9am–noon
Services Restoration

⊞ Simpsons
Contact Mr M Simpson
✉ 39 St Edward Street, Leek, Staffordshire,
ST13 5DN ℗
☎ 01538 371515 ❶ 01538 371515
Est. 1989 *Stock size* Medium
Stock Original painted furniture and decorative items for the home and garden, antique mirrors
Open Mon–Sat 10am–5pm

Thurs 11am–4pm
Services Bespoke items made to customers' requirements

🏠 Curborough Hall Farm Antiques Centre
Contact Mr J Finnemore
✉ Unit 10, Curborough Hall Farm, Watery Lane, Lichfield, Staffordshire,
WS13 7SE ℗
☎ 01543 417100
Ⓜ 07885 285053
Est. 1995 *Stock size* Large
No. of dealers 31
Stock Furniture, china, collectables, jewellery, books, linen, pictures
Open Tues–Sun Bank Holidays 10am–4.30pm
Services Restaurant

⊞ The Essence of Time (BHI)
Contact Malcolm Hinton
✉ Unit 2, Curborough Antiques and Lichfield Craft Centre, Curborough Hall Farm, Watery Lane, Lichfield, Staffordshire,
WS13 8ES ℗
☎ 01543 418239 or 01902 764900 (evenings)
Ⓜ 07944 245064 (any time)
Est. 1990 *Stock size* Large
Stock Longcase, Vienna, wall, mantel and novelty clocks
Open Wed–Sun 10.45am–5pm

⊞ James A Jordan (BHI Qualified Member)
Contact Mr J Jordan
✉ 7 The Corn Exchange, Conduit Street, Lichfield, Staffordshire,
WS13 6JR ℗
☎ 01543 416221
Est. 1988 *Stock size* Large
Stock Jewellery, watches, clocks, silver, small antique furnishings
Open Mon–Sat 9am–5pm closed Wed
Services Watch, clock and barometer repairs

⊞ Milestone Antiques (LAPADA)
Contact Humphrey or Elsa Crawshaw
✉ 5 Main Street, Whittington, Lichfield, Staffordshire,
WS14 9JU ℗
☎ 01543 432248
Est. 1988 *Stock size* Medium

Stock Georgian–early Victorian traditional English furniture, 19thC English porcelain, decorative items
Open Thurs–Sat 10am–6pm Sun 11am–3pm or by appointment

⊞ Royden Smith
Contact Mr R Smith
✉ Church View House, Farewell Lane, Burntwood, Lichfield, Staffordshire,
WS7 9DP ℗
☎ 01543 682217
Est. 1973 *Stock size* Large
Stock General antiques, some furniture, collectables
Open Sat 10am–4pm Sun 10.30am–4pm or by appointment
Services Shipping

⊞ The Staffs Bookshop
Contact Miss S Hawkins
✉ 4 & 6 Dam Street, Lichfield, Staffordshire,
WS13 6AA ℗
☎ 01543 264093 ❶ 01543 264093
Ⓦ www.staffsbookshop.co.uk
Est. 1925 *Stock size* Large
Stock Children's, antiquarian, second-hand and new books, Samuel Johnson, 18thC literature, prints, maps
Open Mon–Sat 9.30am–5.30pm, summer Sun 1–5pm
Services Valuations

🔨 Wintertons Ltd (SOFAA)
Contact Charles Hanson
✉ Lichfield Auction Centre, Fradley Park, Lichfield, Staffordshire,
WS13 8NF ℗
☎ 01543 263256 ❶ 01543 415348
❺ enquiries@wintertons.co.uk
Ⓦ www.wintertons.co.uk
Est. 1864
Open Mon–Fri 9am–5.30pm
Sales Victorian and general sales, every 2 or 3 weeks Thurs 10.30am, viewing Wed 1–7pm. Bi-monthly 2-day fine art sale, Wed Thurs 10.30am, viewing Tues noon–8pm and day of sale
Catalogues Yes

PENKRIDGE

⊞ Golden Oldies
Contact Mr Knowles
✉ 5 Crown Bridge, Penkridge, Staffordshire,

ST19 5AA 📓
☎ 01785 714722
Est. 1973 *Stock size* Large
Stock Antique and reproduction stock mainly furniture and general antiques
Open Mon 9.30am–1.30pm, Tues–Sat 9.30am–5.30pm, Sun noon–4pm
Fairs Newark

RUGELEY

⌂ Rugeley Antique Centre
Contact Mr Thornhill
✉ 161 Main Road, Brereton, Rugeley, Staffordshire, **WS15 1DX** 📓
☎ 01889 577166 📠 01889 577166
📱 07980 756602
Est. 1980 *Stock size* Large
No. of dealers 20
Stock Antiques and collectables
Open Sun–Thurs 10am–4.30pm
Fri Sat 10am–5pm
Services Small parcel shipping

STAFFORD

⊞ Windmill Antiques
Contact Mr I Kettlewell
✉ 9 Castle Hill, Broad Eye, Stafford, Staffordshire, **ST16 2QB** 📓
☎ 01785 228505 📠 01785 228505
Est. 1992 *Stock size* Large
Stock Antiques, jewellery, decorative items, woodworking tools
Open Mon–Sat 10am–5pm
Services Valuations, ceramic restoration

⊞ Abacus Gallery
Contact Mr D Mycock
✉ 56–60 Millrise Road, Milton, Stoke-on-Trent, Staffordshire, **ST2 7BW** 📓
☎ 01782 543005
Est. 1980 *Stock size* Medium
Stock Antiquarian and second-hand books, postcards
Open Mon–Fri 9am–5pm
Sat 9am–4pm
Fairs Buxton Book Fair

⊞ Ann's Antiques
Contact Mrs A Byatte
✉ 26 Leek Road, Stockton Brook, Stoke-on-Trent, Staffordshire, **ST9 9NN** 📓
☎ 01782 503991
Est. 1969 *Stock size* Large

Stock Georgian–Edwardian furniture, cranberry glass, Victorian oil lamps, jewellery, pottery, porcelain, rocking horses, dolls' houses
Open Fri 10am–5pm, Sat noon–5pm or by appointment
Services Restoration of dolls' houses

⊞ Burslem Antiques and Collectables
Contact D Bradbury
✉ 11 Market Place, Burslem, Stoke-on-Trent, Staffordshire, **ST6 3AA** 📓
☎ 01782 577855 📠 01782 577222
📧 info@burslemantiques.co.uk
🌐 www.burslemantiques.co.uk
Est. 2000 *Stock size* Large
Stock Pottery and furniture
Trade only Yes
Open Mon–Sat 9.30am–5.30pm
Sun 10am–4pm
Services Valuations, tea room

⊞ Castle Antiques Warehouse
Contact K McMain
✉ 9 Rope Street, Stoke-on-Trent, Staffordshire, **ST4 6DJ** 📓
☎ 01782 626333
Est. 1999 *Stock size* Large
Stock Antique furniture, pottery
Open Mon–sat 10am–5pm

⊞ Ceramics International
Contact Christine Cope
✉ Unit 1, Top Bridge Works, Trubshaw Cross, Burslem, Stoke-on-Trent, Staffordshire, **ST6 4LR** 📓
☎ 01782 575545 📠 01782 814447
📱 07885 376699
📧 ceramicsinter@btconnect.com
🌐 www.ceramicsinternational.com
Est. 1996 *Stock size* Large
Stock English, imported ceramics, Worcester, Wedgewood, Moorcroft, chintz, Flow blue, Royal Doulton
Trade only Yes
Open Mon–Fri 9am–5.30pm
Fairs Newark, Swinderby, Ardingly, Detling

⊞ Checkley Interiors
Contact Mr S Clegg
✉ 496 Hartshill Road, Hartshill, Stoke-on-Trent, Staffordshire, **ST4 6AD** 📓
☎ 01782 717522 📠 01782 717522

Est. 1998 *Stock size* Medium
Stock Victorian and Edwardian upholstered and occasional furniture
Open Mon–Sat 9.30am–5pm
closed Thurs
Services Restoration, upholstery, room interior service

⊞ Peggy Davies Ceramics
Contact Rod Davies
✉ Formerly St Luke's School Lower, Wellington Road, Hanley, Stoke-on-Trent, Staffordshire, **ST1 3QH** 📓
☎ 01782 262002 📠 01782 284681
📧 rhys@peggydavies.com
🌐 www.peggydavies.com
Est. 1981 *Stock size* Small
Stock Collectables
Open Mon–Fri 9am–1pm 2–5pm

⊞ Harrison's
Contact Cyril Harrison
✉ Little Eaves, Stanley Road, Stockton Brook, Stoke-on-Trent, Staffordshire, **ST9 9LL** 📓
☎ 01782 502168
📧 dianedawhar@aol.com
Est. 1987 *Stock size* Small
Stock Collectable Doulton, Beswick pottery
Open Mon–Sat 9am–8pm
Services Valuations

⊞ On the Hill Antiques
Contact Ms Sue Bird
✉ 450 Hartshill Road, Stoke-on-Trent, Staffordshire, **ST4 7PL** 📓
☎ 01782 252249 📠 01782 252249
📱 07932 726035
Est. 1996 *Stock size* Large
Stock 1930s oak furniture, pottery, collectables
Open Mon–Fri 10am–5pm, Sat 10am–3pm
Fairs Bingley, Staffordshire
Services Valuations, house clearances

⊞ Potteries Antique Centre
Contact Ms K Ware
✉ 271 Waterloo Road, Cobridge, Stoke-on-Trent, Staffordshire, **ST6 3HR** 📓
☎ 01782 201455 📠 01782 201518
📧 katy@potteriesantiquecentre.com
🌐 www.potteriesantiquecentre.com
Est. 1990 *Stock size* Large
Stock Wedgwood, Doulton,

Beswick, Moorcroft, Crown Devon, Coalport, Minton, Clarice Cliff, Crown Derby, Wade, Shelley, Carlton ware
Open Mon–Sat 9am–5.30pm
Fairs Royal Doulton & Beswick Fairs
Services Valuations

⚲ Potteries Specialist Auctions
Contact Martyn Bullock
✉ 271 Waterloo Road, Cobridge, Stoke-on-Trent, Staffordshire, ST6 3HR ♿
☎ 01782 286622 • 01782 213777
🌐 enquiries@potteriesauctions.com
🌐 www.potteriesauctions.com
Est. 1986
Open Mon–Fri 9am–5.30pm
Sales Mainly British 20thC pottery, view 10am–4pm day prior morning of sale 9–11am. See website for sale dates
Frequency Monthly
Catalogues Yes

⚲ Louis Taylor Fine Art Auctioneers
Contact Mr C Hillier MRICS
✉ Britannia House, 10 Town Road, Hanley, Stoke-on-Trent, Staffordshire, ST1 2QG ♿
☎ 01782 214111 • 01782 215283
Est. 1877
Open Mon–Fri 9am–5pm closed 1–2pm
Sales Quarterly 2-day fine art sales Mon Tues 10am, viewing Thurs 10am–7pm Fri 10am–4pm day of sale from 9am. Specialist Doulton and Beswick quarterly, viewing as for fine art. General and Victoriana every two weeks Mon 10am, viewing Fri 10am–4pm Sat 9am–noon
Frequency Fortnightly
Catalogues Yes

⊞ The Tinder Box
Contact Mrs P Yarwood
✉ 61 Lichfield Street, Hanley, Stoke-on-Trent, Staffordshire, ST1 3EA ♿
☎ 01782 261368 • 01782 261368
📱 07946 445659
Est. 1969 **Stock size** Large
Stock Jewellery, pottery, silver, lamps, spares for oil lamps
Open Mon–Sat 9am–5.30pm
Services Valuations, restoration

⊞ Wooden Heart
Contact Mrs Y Quirke
✉ 51 Stoke Road, Shelton, Stoke-on-Trent, Staffordshire, ST4 2QN ♿
☎ 01782 411437
Est. 1995 **Stock size** Large
Stock Edwardian–Victorian mahogany furniture and decorative items
Open Mon–Fri 8.30am–5pm Sat 10.30am–3.30pm
Services Restoration

TAMWORTH

⊞ Janic Antiques
Contact Lincoln
✉ 4 King Street, Tamworth, Staffordshire, B79 7DB
☎ 01827 59333
Est. 1985 **Stock size** Medium
Stock General antiques
Open Mon–Fri 10am–4.30pm closed Wed Sat 10am–2.30pm
Services Valuations, jewellery repairs, silverplating

⊞ Patricks Antiques
Contact Patrick
✉ Mile Oak Farm, Plantation Lane, Tamworth, Staffordshire, B78 3DQ ♿
☎ 0121 749 3788
📱 07976 404876
🌐 patricksantiques@tiscali.co.uk
Est. 1988 **Stock size** Medium
Stock porcelain, glass,19thC furniture
Open By appointment
Fairs Newark
Services Restoration

TUTBURY

⊞ The Clock Shop (BHI)
Contact Ms A James
✉ 1 High Street, Tutbury, Burton-on-Trent, Staffordshire, DE13 9LP ♿
☎ 01283 814596 • 01283 814594
📱 07710 161949
🌐 sales@antique-clocks-watches.co.uk
🌐 www.antique-clocks-watches.co.uk
Est. 1987 **Stock size** Large
Stock Antique clocks, longcase clocks and watches, barometers
Open Mon–Sat 10am–5pm
Services Valuations, restoration and repair

⌂ Old Chapel Antiques & Collectables Centre
Contact Roger Clarke
✉ The Old Chapel, High Street, Tutbury, Burton-on-Trent, Staffordshire, PE13 9LP ♿
☎ 01283 815255
Est. 1996 **Stock size** Large
No. of dealers 30
Stock Antiques, collectables
Open Mon–Sun 10am–5pm

UTTOXETER

⌂ Country Homes and Antiques
Contact Mrs Vicky Jacques
✉ 8 Market Place, Uttoxeter, Staffordshire, ST14 8HP ♿
☎ 01889 567717 • 01889 567717
Est. 1999 **Stock size** Large
No. of dealers 10
Stock Wide range of antiques, specializing in original pine and painted furniture
Open Mon–Sat 9am–5pm
Services Sourcing service, design

WOODSEAVES

⊞ A D Antiques
Contact Alison Davey
✉ PO Box 2407, Woodseaves, Stafford, Staffordshire, ST15 8WY
📱 07811 783518
🌐 alison@adantiques.com
🌐 www.adantiques.com
Est. 1997 **Stock size** Medium
Stock Decorative arts, ceramics and metalware, Moorcroft, Doulton Lambeth, William de Morgan, Pilkington's lustre, Wedgwood
Open By appointment
Fairs NEC, Bingley Hall, Penman's Chester

YOXALL

⊞ H W Heron & Son Ltd (LAPADA)
Contact Mrs J Heron
✉ The Antique Shop, King Street, Yoxall, Burton-on-Trent, Staffordshire, DE13 8NF ♿
☎ 01543 472266 • 01543 473800
📱 07773 337809

@ shop@hwheronantiques.com
@ www.hwheronantiques.com
Est. 1949 *Stock size* Medium
Stock Period furniture, ceramics,
objects, paintings
Open Mon–Fri 9am–6pm
Sat 9am–5.30pm Sun by
appointment
Services Valuations

WARWICKSHIRE

ALCESTER

⌂ **Malthouse Antiques
Centre**
Contact Pat Alcock
✉ **4 Market Place, Alcester,
Warwickshire,
B49 5AE** 🅿
☎ 01789 764032
Est. 1984 *Stock size* Large
No. of dealers 10
Stock 18th–early 20thC furniture,
ceramics, silver, collectables etc
Open Mon–Sat 10am–5pm
Sun 1–4pm

⊞ **Justin Neales Antiques
& Interiors**
Contact Mr Justin Neales
✉ **3 Evesham Street, Alcester,
Warwickshire,
B49 5DS** 🅿
☎ 01789 766699
🕾 07771 560411
@ j.neales@btinternet.com
@ www.jneales.com
Est. 1987 *Stock size* Large
Stock Georgian, Victorian and
Edwardian furniture, painted
furniture, tapestry, cushions,
mirrors, silver picture frames
Open Mon–Fri 9am–5pm
Sat 10am–5pm
Fairs NEC
Services Restoration, upholstery

BIDFORD-ON-AVON

⌂ **Bidford Antiques &
Collectables**
Contact Thelma Hughes
✉ **94 High Street,
Bidford-on-Avon,
Warwickshire,
B50 4AF** 🅿
☎ 01789 773680
Est. 1980 *Stock size* Medium
No. of dealers 2
Stock Furniture, jewellery,
paintings, china
Open Thurs–Sat 11am–5pm

🔨 **Steven B Bruce
Auctioneers Ltd (NAVA,
SOFAA)**
Contact Mr S Bruce
✉ **Unit 5, Clayhall Farm,
Honeybourne Road,
Bidford-on-Avon, Warwickshire,
B49 5PD**
☎ 01789 490450
🕾 07778 595952
@ stevenbbruce@hotmail.com
@ www.stevenbbruce.co.uk.co.uk
Est. 1995
Open Mon–Sat 9.30am–5.30pm
Sales Regular sales held at
Stratford Racecourse and on-site
country house sales
Frequency Monthly
Catalogues Yes

BRINKLOW

⊞ **Annie's Attic**
Contact Martin Deakin
✉ **19a Broad Street, Brinklow,
Warwickshire,
CV23 0LS** 🅿
☎ 01788 833094
Est. 1998 *Stock size* Medium
Stock Clocks, small furniture,
metalwork, old and interesting
objects, period lighting
Open Sat 11am–5pm Sun
11am–4pm or by appointment
Services Clock restoration

DUNCHURCH

⊞ **Now & Then**
Contact Mike Best
✉ **6 The Green, Dunchurch,
Rugby, Warwickshire,
CV22 6NX** 🅿
☎ 01788 811211
Est. 2001 *Stock size* Large
Stock Antiques, collectables and
new furniture
Open Mon–Sat 10am–5pm
alternate Sundays 11–4 (phone
first)

EARLSWOOD

🔨 **P & K Turner Auctions**
Contact Phil Turner
✉ **Earlswood Village Hall, Shutt
Lane, Earlswood, Warwickshire**
☎ 01543 274176
@ philkt@btinternet.com
Est. 1988
Open Mon–Sat 9am–5pm
Sales General antiques
Frequency Monthly

HATTON

⌂ **The Stables Antique
Centre**
Contact Mr John Colledge
✉ **Hatton Country World,
Dark Lane, Hatton, Warwick,
Warwickshire,
CV35 8XA** 🅿
☎ 01926 842405 📠 01926 842023
Est. 1992 *Stock size* Large
No. of dealers 25
Stock Old clocks, furniture,
curios, china etc
Open Mon–Sun 10am–5pm
Services Craft centre, café, bar,
clock repairs

HENLEY-IN-ARDEN

⌂ **Henley Antiques &
Collectables Centre**
Contact Mrs Rosie Montague
✉ **Rear of Henley Bakery,
92 High Street, Henley-in-Arden,
Warwickshire,
B95 5BY** 🅿
☎ 01564 795979
🕾 07950 324376
Est. 2000 *Stock size* Large
No. of dealers 15–20
Stock Georgian–Edwardian
furniture, wide range of
antiques, ceramics, glass, silver,
collectables
Open Mon–Sat 10.30am–5pm
Sun Bank Holidays 11am–4pm

⊞ **The Purple Antique
Shop Centre**
Contact Chris Davison
✉ **86b High Street,
Henley-in-Arden, Warwickshire,
B95 5BY** 🅿
☎ 01564 795131
@ thepurpleantiqueshop@
blueyonder.co.uk
Est. 2002 *Stock size* Medium
Stock General antiques and
collectables
Open Mon–Sat 10am–5pm
Sun Bank hols 11am–4pm

ILMINGTON

⊞ **Peter Finer (BADA)**
Contact Peter Finer or
Nickki Eden
✉ **The Old Rectory, Ilmington,
Shipston-on-Stour,
Warwickshire,
CV36 4JQ**
☎ 01608 682267 📠 01608 682575

@ pf@peterfiner.com
@ www.peterfiner.com
Est. 1970 *Stock size* Large
Stock Arms, armour and related
objects
Open Strictly by appointment
Fairs International Fine Art New
York, Palm Beach International
Art & Antiques Fair
Services Restoration, displays

LEAMINGTON SPA

⊞ **Kings Cottage Antiques
(LAPADA)**
Contact Mr A Jackson
⊠ **4 Windsor Street,
Leamington Spa,
Warwickshire,
CV32 5EB** ⊡
☎ 01926 422927
Est. 1993 *Stock size* Medium
Stock Early oak and country
furniture
Open Mon–Fri 9am–5pm
Sat by appointment

⋏ **Locke & England (RICS)**
Contact Claire Thorp
⊠ **18 Guy Street,
Leamington Spa,
Warwickshire,
CV32 4RT** ⊡
☎ 01926 889100 ☏ 01926 470608
@ info@leauction.co.uk
@ www.leauction.co.uk
Est. 1834
Open Mon–Fri 9am–5.30pm
Sales Household and Victoriana
auctions weekly, antiques and
fine art auctions bi-monthly
Catalogues Yes

⊞ **Mortimers Curios**
Contact John Airey
⊠ **128 Warwick Street,
Leamington Spa,
Warwickshire,
CU32 4QY** ⊡
☎ 01962 887711
@ sales@mortimerscurios.enta.net
Stock size Medium
Stock Wrist and pocket watches,
clocks, curios, collectables
Open Wed–Sat 10am–5pm
Services Valuations, restorations

⊞ **Portland Books**
Contact Mr Martyn Davies or
Gareth Wyatt
⊠ **93 Warwick Street,
Leamington Spa, Warwickshire,
CV32 4RJ** ⊡

☎ 01926 888118 ☏ 01926 885305
@ twiceportlandbooks@
quicknetuk.com
@ www.portlandbooks.com
Est. 1974 *Stock size* Large
Stock Antiquarian, second-hand
and new books, Warwickshire
history a speciality, modern
books at discounted prices
Open Mon–Sat 9.30am–5.30pm
Services Valuations, book search

LONG MARSTON

⌂ **Barn Antique Centre**
Contact Bev or Graham Simpson
⊠ **Station Road, Long Marston,
Stratford-upon-Avon,
Warwickshire,
CV37 8RP** ⊡
☎ 01789 721399 ☏ 01789 721390
@ info@barnantique.co.uk
@ www.barnantique.co.uk
Est. 1978 *Stock size* Large
No. of dealers 40
Stock Huge barn full of antiques
and collectables,
Georgian–Edwardian furniture,
pine, fireplaces, silver,
kitchenware, porcelain
Open Mon–Sat 10am–5pm
Sun noon–6pm
Services Licensed restaurant

NUNEATON

⊞ **Bosworth Antiques**
Contact Mr J H Thorp
⊠ **12 Main Street, Market
Bosworth, Nuneaton,
Warwickshire,
CV13 0JW** ⊡
☎ 01455 292134
@ 07904 781760
Est. 1985 *Stock size* Medium
Stock General antiques
Open Wed–Sat 10am–1pm
2–5pm
Services Valuations

⊞ **The Granary Antiques**
Contact Gordon Stockdale
⊠ **Hoar Park, Craft Village,
Ansley, Nuneaton,
Warwickshire,
CV10 0QU** ⊡
☎ 024 7639 5551 ☏ 024 7639 4433
@ jl@hpcv.freeserve.co.uk
@ www.hpcv.freeserve.co.uk
Est. 1996 *Stock size* Large
Stock General antiques, pine,
kitchenware, Edwardian
furniture, porcelain and Mason's

Ironstone in a 17thC converted
building
Open Tues–Sun 10am–5pm
Services Restaurant

⊞ **G Payne Antiques**
Contact Mr G Payne
⊠ **25 Watling Street, Nuneaton,
Warwickshire,
CV11 6JJ** ⊡
☎ 024 7632 5178
@ 07836 754489
Est. 1991 *Stock size* Medium
Stock Mahogany and oak
furniture
Open Mon–Sat 8am–6pm
Services Valuations

POLESWORTH

⊞ **G & J Chesters (PBFA)**
Contact Mr G Chesters
⊠ **14 Market Street, Polesworth,
Warwickshire,
B78 1HW** ⊡
☎ 01827 894743
@ gandjchesters@bun.com
Est. 1970 *Stock size* Large
Stock Antiquarian and second-
hand books, maps, prints
Open Mon–Sat 9.30am–5.30pm
Wed 9.30am–9pm
Fairs NEC Antiques for Everyone

RUGBY

⋏ **M G Seaman &
Daughter**
Contact Mrs M or Miss L Seaman
⊠ **6 Paynes Lane, Rugby,
Warwickshire,
CV21 2UH** ⊡
☎ 01788 542367/543445
☏ 01788 570 425
Est. 1979
Sales General antiques Mon
7pm, viewing Sun 11am–3pm
Mon noon–7pm
Frequency Weekly
Catalogues Yes

SHENTON

⌂ **Whitemoors Antique
Centre**
Contact Mr Colin Wightman
⊠ **Main Street, Shenton,
Warwickshire,
CV13 6BZ** ⊡
☎ 01455 212250
Est. 1993 *Stock size* Large
No. of dealers 25
Stock Furniture, pottery, clocks,

bric-a-brac, paperweights
Open Mon–Sun summer
11am–5pm winter 11am–4pm

SHIPSTON-ON-STOUR

⊞ Church Street Gallery
Contact Mr Robert Field
✉ 24 Church Street,
Shipston-on-Stour,
Warwickshire,
CV36 4AP 🅿
☎ 01608 662431
✉ churchstgallery@aol.com
🌐 www.churchstreetgallery.co.uk
Est. 1979 *Stock size* Large
Stock Antique maps and prints,
late 19th–early 20thC
watercolours, oils, furniture, bric-
a-brac
Open Mon–Fri 9.30am–6pm
Thurs 9.30am–1pm Sat
10am–5.30pm
Services Picture framing,
restoration

⊞ The Richard Harvey Collection Ltd
Contact Mr C Harvey
✉ 28 Church Street,
Shipston-on-Stour,
Warwickshire,
CV36 4AP 🅿
☎ 01608 662168 ✆ 01608 662168
Est. 1973 *Stock size* Large
Stock Chinese antiques, painted
Gustavian furniture, leather
furniture, rugs, contemporary
lighting
Open Mon–Sat 9am–5.30pm or
by appointment

⊞ Pine and Things
Contact Mr R Wood
✉ Portobello Farm,
Campden Road,
Shipston-on-Stour,
Warwickshire,
CV36 4PY 🅿
☎ 01608 663849 ✆ 01608 663849
✉ mailus@pinethings.co.uk
🌐 www.pinethings.co.uk
Est. 1991 *Stock size* Large
Stock Victorian and earlier pine
furniture
Open Mon–Sat 9am–5pm

⊞ Time in Hand (BHI)
Contact FR Bennett
✉ 11 Church Street,
Shipston-on-Stour,
Warwickshire,
CV36 4AP 🅿

☎ 01608 662578 ✆ 01608 662578
✉ timeinhand1@aol.com
🌐 www.timeinhand.co.uk
Est. 1979 *Stock size* Large
Stock 18th–20th century clocks
and barometers
Open Mon–Fri 9am–1pm
2–5.30pm Sat 9am–5pm
Services Valuations and
restorations

SNITTERFIELD

➴ Phillips Brothers (NAVA)
Contact Robin Phillips
✉ The Sale Room,
Bearley Road, Snitterfield,
Stratford-upon-Avon,
Warwickshire,
CV37 0EZ 🅿
☎ 01789 731114 ✆ 01789 731114
Est. 1980
Open Mon–Fri 9.30am–5pm
Sales General and antiques sales
Sat 10am, viewing from 9am.
Frequency Fortnightly
Catalogues No

⊞ Arbour Antiques Ltd
Contact Mr Colwell
✉ Poets Arbour, Sheep Street,
Stratford-upon-Avon,
Warwickshire,
CV37 6EF
☎ 01789 293453
Est. 1954 *Stock size* Large
Stock 16th–19thC arms and
armour
Open Mon–Fri 9am–5pm

⊞ Thomas Crapper & Co (SALVO)
✉ Stable Yard, Alscot Park,
Stratford-upon-Avon,
Warwickshire,
CV37 8BL 🅿
☎ 01789 450522 ✆ 01789 450523
✉ wc@thomas-crapper.com
🌐 www.thomas-crapper.com
Est. 1861 *Stock size* Medium
Stock Victorian–Edwardian and
unusual bathroom fittings.
Open Mon–Fri 9.30am–5pm or by
appointment
Services Restoration, catalogues
(£5 refundable on purchase)

⊞ Goodbye To All That
Contact Mr Briggs
✉ 50 Henley Street,
Stratford-upon-Avon,
Warwickshire,
CV37 6QL 🅿

☎ 01789 262906
📱 07867 611923
Est. 1999 *Stock size* Small
Stock Firearms, scientific
instruments
Open Mon–Sun 10am–5.30pm

⊞ Henley Street Antique Centre
Contact Ian Harper
✉ 50 Henley Street,
Stratford-upon-Avon,
Warwickshire,
CV37 6QW
☎ 01789 296024
📱 07703 500419
Est. 2001 *Stock size* Large
Stock Jewellery, china, militia,
furniture, pictures, coins, medals
Open Mon–Sun 10am–5pm
Fairs NEC
Services Valuations

⊞ Pickwick Gallery
Contact Mr H D Dankenbring
✉ 32 Henley Street,
Stratford-upon-Avon,
Warwickshire,
CV37 6QW 🅿
☎ 01789 294861
✉ mm@meridienmaps.co.uk
🌐 www.meridenmaps.co.uk
Est. 1986 *Stock size* Medium
Stock Antique maps, sporting
prints, 1600–1880
Open Mon–Sat 10am–5pm Sun
Bank Holidays 11am–4.30pm

⊞ George Pragnell The Jeweller (NAG)
Contact Mary Machin
✉ 5 & 6 Woods Street,
Stratford-upon-Avon,
Warwickshire,
CV37 6JA 🅿
☎ 01789 267072 ✆ 01789 415131
✉ enquiries@pragnell.co.uk
🌐 www.pragnell.co.uk
Est. 1954 *Stock size* Medium
Stock Antique silver, jewellery
Open Mon–Sat 9.15am–5.30pm
Fairs NEC

⊞ Riverside Antiques
Contact Mr Richard Monk
✉ 60 Ely Street,
Stratford-upon-Avon,
Warwickshire,
CV37 6LN 🅿
☎ 01789 262090
📱 07931 512325
Est. 1996 *Stock size* Medium
Stock Clarice Cliff, antique and

designer jewellery
Open Mon–Sun 10am–5pm
Services Rings designed and made

⌂ Stratford Antiques and Interiors
Contact Mr or Mrs Kerr
✉ Dodwell Trading Estate, Evesham Road, Stratford-upon-Avon, Warwickshire, CV37 9SY 🅿
☎ 01789 297729 ⊕ 01789 297710
⊖ drewkerr@tiscali.co.uk
ⓦ www.stratfordantiques.co.uk
Est. 1995 **Stock size** Large
No. of dealers 20
Stock A wide range of antiques and collectables, home furnishings and decorative items
Open Mon–Sun 10am–5pm

⌂ Stratford Antiques Centre
Contact Mr Mike Conway
✉ 59–60 Ely Street, Stratford-upon-Avon, Warwickshire, CV37 6LN
☎ 01789 204180
Est. 1981 **Stock size** Large
No. of dealers 50
Stock Wide range of antiques and collectables. One of the largest antiques markets in the Midlands
Open Mon–Sun 10am–5pm
Services Restaurant

TIDDINGTON

⚒ Bigwood Auctioneers Ltd (SOFAA)
Contact Mr C Ironmonger
✉ The Old School, Tiddington, Stratford-upon-Avon, Warwickshire, CV37 7AW 🅿
☎ 01789 269415 ⊕ 01789 294168
⊖ sales@bigwoodauctioneers.co.uk
ⓦ www.bigwoodauctioneers.co.uk
Est. 1849
Open Mon–Fri 9am–12.45pm 2–5.30pm Sat 9am–noon
Sales Quarterly fine furniture and works of art, monthly antiques and collectables, sporting memorabilia (Mar Sept) wine sales (Mar June Sept Dec) collectables, games, toys (Apr Oct)
Frequency 50 per annum
Catalogues Yes

WARTON

⊞ Afford Decorative Antiques (LAPADA)
Contact Jan Afford
✉ Warton, Warwickshire, B79 🅿
☎ 01827 330042
⓪ 07831 114909
⊖ affordantiques@fsmail.net
ⓦ www.afforddecarts.com
Est. 1980 **Stock size** Medium
Stock All decorative arts 1870–1950
Open By appointment
Fairs Antiques for Everyone, LAPADA
Services Valuations, restoration

⊞ Duncan M Allsop (ABA)
Contact Mr D Allsop
✉ 68 Smith Street, Warwick, Warwickshire, CV34 4HU 🅿
☎ 01926 493266 ⊕ 01926 493266
⊖ duncan.allsop@btopenworld.com
ⓦ www.allsop-books.freeserve.co.uk
Est. 1966 **Stock size** Medium
Stock Varied stock of books including antiquarian, fine bindings and modern books
Open Mon–Sat 10am–4.30pm
Fairs Royal National

⊞ The Antique Cellar
Contact Carolyn Boylin
✉ 36a Market Place, Warwick, Warwickshire, CV34 4SH 🅿
☎ 01962 491546
⓪ 07785 237728
⊖ antiquecellar@btconnect.com
Est. 1990 **Stock size** Medium
Stock Furniture and decorative arts
Open Mon–Fri 10am–3pm Sat 10am–4pm
Services Valuations and restorations

⊞ Apollo Antiques Ltd (LAPADA, CINOA)
Contact Roger Mynott
✉ The Saltisford, Warwick, Warwickshire, CV34 4TD 🅿
☎ 01926 494746/494666
⊕ 01926 401477
⊖ mynott@apolloantiques.com
ⓦ www.apolloantiques.com
Est. 1968 **Stock size** Large
Stock English 18th–19thC furniture, sculpture, paintings, decorative items, Arts and Crafts,

Gothic revival
Open Mon–Fri 9.30am–5.30pm Sat by appointment
Services Free delivery service to London

⊞ W J Casey Antiques (LAPADA, CINOA)
Contact Mr Bill Casey
✉ 9 High Street, Warwick, Warwickshire, CV34 4AP 🅿
☎ 01926 499199
⓪ 07771 920475
Est. 1998 **Stock size** Large
Stock 18th–19thC furniture, especially dining room furniture, general furniture
Open Tues–Sat 10am–5pm or by appointment
Services Restoration

⊞ Castle Antiques (WADA)
Contact Julia Reynolds
✉ 24 Swan Street, Warwick, Warwickshire, CV34 4BJ 🅿
☎ 01926 401511
Est. 1998 **Stock size** Large
Stock Edwardian–Victorian furniture, small items, linen
Open Mon–Sat 10am–5pm
Services Restoration

⊞ Collectables, Nostalgia and Militaria
Contact Mark Goodwin
✉ 59 Smith Street, Warwick, Warwickshire, CV34 4HU 🅿
☎ 01926 411772
Est. 2004 **Stock size** Medium
Stock Collectable items, Dinky cars, annuals, ephemera, militaria
Open Mon–Sat 10am–6pm, Sun 11am–3pm
Fairs Bob Evans Skyblue

⊞ Dorridge Antiques
Contact Mrs P Spencer
✉ Warwick Antique Centre, 22–24 High Street, Warwick, Warwickshire, CV34 4AP 🅿
Est. 1981 **Stock size** Medium
Stock Silver, jewellery
Open Mon–Sat 10am–5pm

⊞ Russell Lane Antiques
Contact Mr Lane
✉ 2–4 High Street, Warwick,

Warwickshire,
CV34 4AP 🅿
☎ 01926 494494 ● 01926 492972
e russell.laneantiques@virgin.net
Est. 1974 *Stock size* Large
Stock Antique jewellery and
silver. Official jewellers to the
Royal Show
Open Mon–Sat 10am–5pm
Services Replacement insurance
claims

⊞ Patrick & Gillian Morley
(LAPADA)
Contact Mr P Morley
✉ 62 West Street,
Warwick,
Warwickshire,
CV34 6AW 🅿
☎ 01926 494464
Ⓜ 07768 835040
Est. 1969 *Stock size* Large
Stock Period decorative and
unusual furniture, works of art
Open Tues–Fri 10am–5.30pm
appointment advisable

⊞ Christopher Peters
Antiques
Contact Mr C or Mrs J Peters
✉ 28 West Street,
Warwick,
Warwickshire,
CV34 6AN 🅿
☎ 01926 494106 or 02476 303300
● 02476 303300
e enquiries@christopherpeters
antiques.co.uk
Ⓦ www.christopherpeters
antiques.co.uk
Est. 1985 *Stock size* Large
Stock 17th–19thC painted
fruitwood and country furniture,
design and installation of
original bespoke kitchens
Open Mon–Sat 10am–5.30pm or
by appointment
Fairs NEC (Spring, Summer)

⊞ Quinneys of Warwick
Contact James Reeve
✉ 9 Church Street,
Warwick,
Warwickshire,
CV34 4AB 🅿
☎ 01926 498113 ● 01926 498113
e jamesreeve@callnetuk.com
Est. 1865 *Stock size* Large
Stock 17th–19thC English
furniture
Open Mon–Fri 9.30am–5.30pm
Sat 9.30am–4pm
Services Valuations, restoration

⊞ Summersons
Contact Mr Peter Lightfoot
✉ 172 Emscote Road, Warwick,
Warwickshire,
CV34 5QN 🅿
☎ 01926 400630 ● 01926 400630
e clocks@summersons.com
Ⓦ www.summersons.com
Est. 1979 *Stock size* Medium
Stock Clocks, barometers
Open Mon–Fri 9am–5pm
Sat 10am–1pm
Services Restoration, repair of
clocks and barometers, sales of
materials for restoration

⊞ Tango Art Deco &
Antiques
Contact Jenny and Martin Wills
✉ 46 Brook Sreet, Warwick,
Warwickshire,
CV34 4BL 🅿
☎ 01926 496999 ● 0121 704 4969
Ⓜ 07889 046969
e info@tango-artdeco.co.uk
Ⓦ www.tango-artdeco.co.uk
Est. 1987 *Stock size* Large
Stock Decorative arts 1880–1940,
ceramics, furniture, accessories
Open Thurs–Sat 10am–5pm

⌂ Vintage Antiques
Centre (WADA)
Contact Mr Peter Sellors
✉ 36 Market Place, Warwick,
Warwickshire,
CV34 4SH 🅿
☎ 01926 491527
e vintage@globalnet.co.uk
Est. 1979 *Stock size* Large
No. of dealers 20
Stock Victorian glass, 19thC
ceramics, 20thC collectables,
1950s smalls, 19th–20thC
costume, agate, gemstone
jewellery
Open Mon–Sat 10am–5pm
Sun 11.30am–4.30pm

⌂ Warwick Antique
Centre
Contact Mr P Viola
✉ 22–24 High Street, Warwick,
Warwickshire,
CV34 4AP 🅿
☎ 01926 491382
Ⓜ 07770 897707
Est. 1971 *Stock size* Large
No. of dealers Over 30
Stock General antiques,
collectables, coins
Open Mon–Sat 10am–5pm
Services Valuations

⊞ John Williams Antique
& Collectables
Contact Mr John Williams
✉ Warwick Antiques Centre,
22–24 High Street, Warwick,
Warwickshire,
CV34 4AP 🅿
☎ 01926 419966
Ⓜ 07752 377680
e johnowilliams@hotmail.com
Ⓦ www.johnwilliams.co.uk
Est. 1981 *Stock size* Medium
Stock Cameras, toys, tools,
collectables, militaria, scientific
instruments
Open Mon–Sat 10am–4.30pm
Fairs Alexandra Palace,
Birmingham Rag Market, NEC,
Motorcycle Museum Birmingham
Services Valuations

WOOTEN WAWEN

⊞ Le Grenier Antiques
Contact Joyce Ellis or Clive Evans
✉ Yew Tree Farm, Stratford
Road, Wooten Wawen,
Henley-in-Arden, Warwickshire,
B95 6BY 🅿
☎ 01564 795401
Ⓜ 07712 126048
e info@legrenier.com
Ⓦ www.legrenier.com
Est. 1992 *Stock size* Medium
Stock French beds, armours
Open Tues–Fri 9am–5pm
Sat Sun 10am–5pm
Services Items sourced

WEST MIDLANDS

BIRMINGHAM

⊞ Acme Toy Company
Contact Mr P Hall
✉ 17 Station Road, Erdington,
Birmingham, West Midlands,
B23 6UB 🅿
☎ 0121 384 8835 ● 0121 321 1432
e pete36hall@aol.com
Ⓦ www.solnet.co.uk/acme
Est. 1995 *Stock size* Medium
Stock Antique and collectable
toys – TV, Sci-Fi, Action Man
Open Mon–Thurs 11am–3pm
Fri Sat 10.30am–5pm
Fairs D & G Fairs
Services Valuations

⊞ Albany Antiques
Contact Mr Hartland
✉ 133 Shard End Crescent,
Shard End, Birmingham,

**West Midlands,
B23 0JU** ℗
☎ 0121 783 8902
Ⓜ 07970 665891
Est. 1987 *Stock size* Medium
Stock General antique furniture
Open Mon–Sat 9am–5.30pm
Fairs Malvern, Newark
Services Valuations

⚒ Biddle & Webb Ltd
Contact Mr Thornton
✉ Icknield Square, Ladywood,
Middleway, Birmingham,
West Midlands,
B16 0PP ℗
☎ 0121 455 8042 ☏ 0121 454 9615
✉ antiques@biddleandwebb.
freeserve.co.uk
🌐 www.invaluable.com/biddle
andwebb.
Est. 1955
Open Mon–Fri 9am–5pm Thurs
10am–1pm free valuation service
Sales Pictures and prints 11am
1st Fri of month, viewing Sat
prior 9am–noon Wed Thur
10am–4pm. Antiques and later
furnishings, porcelain, glass sale
2nd Fri, viewing as previously.
Toys, juvenalia 3rd Fri alternate
months. Jewellery 4th Fri
Catalogues Yes

🏠 The Birmingham
Antique Centre
Contact Mr Baldock or
Mrs Arblafter
✉ 1407 Pershore Road,
Stirchley, Birmingham,
West Midlands,
B30 2JR ℗
☎ 0121 459 4587
✉ bhamantiquecent@aol.com
🌐 birminghamantiquecentre.co.uk
Est. 1994 *Stock size* Large
No. of dealers 65+
Stock Antique furniture, lightly
used furniture, bric-a-brac
Open Mon–Sat 9am–5pm
Sun 10am–4pm
Services Valuations, house
clearance

⊞ Birmingham Coins
Contact Mr D Harris
✉ 30 Shaftmoor Lane,
Acocks Green, Birmingham,
West Midlands,
B27 7RS ℗
☎ 0121 707 2808 ☏ 0121 707 2808
Est. 1996 *Stock size* Large
Stock General, world and British

coins and bank notes, collectors'
models, medals
Open Tues Thurs Fri 10.30am–5pm

⊞ Cambridge House
Antiques
Contact Mr T McIntosh
✉ 168 Gravelly Lane,
Birmingham, West Midlands,
B23 5SN ℗
☎ 0121 386 1346
Est. 1998 *Stock size* Large
Stock General antiques
Open Mon–Sat 10am–5.30pm
Fairs Newark, Birmingham Rag
Market

⊞ Chesterfield Antiques
Contact Mrs Mara Cirjanic
✉ 181 Gravelly Lane,
Birmingham, West Midlands,
B23 5SG ℗
☎ 0121 373 3876
Est. 1974 *Stock size* Large
Stock Victorian, Edwardian and
1930s furniture and sets of chairs
Open Mon–Sat 9.30am–5pm

⊞ Peter Clark Antiques
(LAPADA)
Contact Peter Clark
✉ 36 St Mary's Row, Moseley,
Birmingham, West Midlands,
B13 8JG ℗
☎ 0121 449 8245 ☏ 0121 449 7598
✉ peterclarkantiques@
btopenworld.com
🌐 www.peterclarkantiques.com
Est. 1969 *Stock size* Medium
Stock Georgian mahogany
furniture, mirrors, decorative
items
Open Mon–Sat 9am–5.30pm
Services Valuations, restoration

⚒ Fellows & Sons (BJA)
Contact Mr S Whittaker
✉ Augusta House,
19 Augusta Street, Birmingham,
West Midlands,
B18 6JA ℗
☎ 0121 212 2131 ☏ 0121 212 1249
✉ info@fellows.co.uk
🌐 www.fellows.co.uk
Est. 1876
Open Mon–Thurs 9am–5pm Fri
9am–4pm
Sales 10 Sales per annum of
antiques and later furniture,
porcelain, clocks, pictures, toys
and collectables. Fortnightly
sales of jewellery and watches
from pawnbrokers nationwide.

8 antique and modern jewellery,
watch and silver sales per annum
Catalogues Yes

⊞ Format Coins (IAPN,
BNTA)
Contact Mr D Vice
✉ 18–19 Bennetts Hill,
Birmingham, West Midlands,
B2 5QJ ℗
☎ 0121 643 2058 ☏ 0121 643 2210
Est. 1970 *Stock size* Medium
Stock Coins, medallions, bank
notes.
Open Mon–Fri 9.30am–5pm
Fairs London Coinex

⊞ The House of
Edgebaston
Contact Lord Cooke
✉ Donne House,
8–9 Calthorpe Road,
Birmingham, West Midlands,
B15 1QT ℗
☎ 0121 455 7111
Ⓜ 07762 428720
🌐 www.houseofedgbaston.com
Est. 2002 *Stock size* Medium
Stock Fine art, jewellery, general
antiques
Open Mon–Sat 10am–6.30pm
Sun 10am–4pm
Fairs London fairs, NEC
Services Valuations, restoration

⊞ Lindsay Architectural
Antiques
Contact Mr G Lindsay
✉ 25 Passfield Road, Stechford,
Birmingham, West Midlands,
B33 8EU ℗
☎ 0121 789 8295
Ⓜ 07966 221632
✉ glindsay@zoom.co.uk
🌐 www.authenticfireplaces.co.uk
Est. 1996 *Stock size* Large
Stock Architectural salvage,
fireplaces, quarry tiles, wrought-
iron gates, stained glass
Open By appointment
Fairs Newark, Swinderby
Services Restoration and fitting
service

⊞ MDS Ltd (SALVO)
Contact Mr R Wootton
✉ 14–16 Stechford Trading
Estate, Lyndon Road, Stechford,
Birmingham, West Midlands,
B33 8BU ℗
☎ 0121 783 9274 ☏ 0121 783 9274
Ⓜ 07836 649064
✉ sales@mdsltd.net

Ⓦ www.mdsltd.net
Est. 1992 *Stock size* Medium
Stock Architectural antiques
Open Mon–Fri 8am–6pm
Sat 8am–1pm

⊞ Moseley Emporium
Contact Miss G Dorney
✉ 116 Alcester Road, Moseley,
Birmingham, West Midlands,
B13 8EE 🅿
☎ 0121 449 3441 ❶ 0121 449 3441
Ⓜ 07973 156902
Est. 1993 *Stock size* Large
Stock Victorian, Edwardian and
period furniture, architectural
antiques
Open Mon–Sat 9.30am–6pm
Services Restoration

⊞ Turner Violins
Contact Marcus Coulter
✉ 1 Gibb Street, off Digbeth
High Street, Birmingham,
West Midlands,
B9 4AA 🅿
☎ 0121 772 7708
❸ birmingham@turnerviolins.co.uk
Ⓦ www.turnerviolins.co.uk
Est. 1980
Stock Violins, double basses,
violas, cellos, bows
Open Mon–Sat 9.30am–6pm
Services Instrument and bow
repairs, valuations, consultations,
export

⋌ Weller & Dufty Ltd
(GTA)
Contact Mr W Farmer
✉ 141 Bromsgrove Street,
Birmingham, West Midlands,
B5 6RQ 🅿
☎ 0121 692 1414 ❶ 0121 622 5605
❸ sales@welleranddufty.co.uk
Ⓦ www.welleranddufty.co.uk
Est. 1835
Open Mon–Fri 9am–4.30pm
Sales Arms and armour
Frequency 6–8 per annum
Catalogues Yes

⊞ Windworld
Contact Marcus Coulter
✉ 1 Gibb Street, off Digbeth
High Street, Birmingham,
West Midlands,
B9 4AA 🅿
☎ 0121 772 7889
❸ info@wind-world.co.uk
Est. 1980
Stock Wind instruments
Open Mon–Sat 9.30am–6pm

Services Instrument and bow
repairs, valuations, consultations,
export

⊞ Stephen Wycherley
(PBFA)
Contact Mr S Wycherley
✉ 508 Bristol Road, Selly Oak,
Birmingham, West Midlands,
B29 6BD 🅿
☎ 0121 471 1006
❸ s.wycherley@btopenworld.com
Est. 1971 *Stock size* Large
Stock Traditional general second-
hand and antiquarian bookshop
Open Mon–Sat 10am–5pm closed
Wed Jul Aug Thurs–Sat 10am–5pm
Fairs PBFA
Services Valuations

BRIERLEY HILL

⊞ Cast Offs
Contact Mr Terence Young
✉ Moor Street Industrial Estate,
Moor Street, Brierley Hill,
West Midlands,
DY5 3EH 🅿
☎ 01384 486456
Ⓜ 07711 661135
Est. 1996 *Stock size* Medium
Stock Quarry tiles, paviors, cast-
iron fireplaces, troughs, baths,
radiators, sinks, taps, doors,
furniture, chimney pots, gates,
fencing, bricks
Open Mon–Fri 9am–5pm
Sat 9am–2pm

COVENTRY

🏠 Antiques Adventure
Contact Lesley Lawrence
✉ Rugby Road, Binley Woods,
Coventry, West Midlands,
CV3 2AW 🅿
☎ 024 7645 3878 ❶ 024 7644 5847
❸ sales@antiquesadventure.com
Ⓦ www.antiquesadventure.com
Est. 2000 *Stock size* Large
No. of dealers 35+
Stock Antiques, collectables
Open Mon–Sun 10am–5pm
Services Shipping, delivery

⊞ Armstrong's Books &
Collectables
Contact Mr Colin Armstrong
✉ 178 Albany Road, Earlsdon,
Coventry, West Midlands,
CV5 6NG 🅿
☎ 024 7671 4344
Est. 1983 *Stock size* Medium

Stock General second-hand
books, paperbacks, first editions,
special sci-fi comics, annuals,
magazines, posters, postcards
Open Tues–Sat 10am–5pm

⊞ The Bookshop
Contact Mr A R Price
✉ 173 Walsgrave Road,
Coventry, West Midlands,
CV2 4HH 🅿
☎ 024 7645 5669
Est. 1990 *Stock size* Medium
Stock Antiquarian and second-
hand books on all subjects
Open Mon–Sat 9am–5pm
Services Valuations

🏠 Old Lodge Farm
Antiques
Contact Diane Wright
✉ Old Lodge Farm, Kenilworth
Road, Balsall Common, Coventry,
West Midlands,
CV7 7EY 🅿
☎ 01676 535282
Est. 1995 *Stock size* Large
No. of dealers 30
Stock 18th–20thC furniture,
glass, clocks, china, etc
Open Mon–Fri 11am–4pm
Sat Sun Bank Holidays 10am–5pm
or by appointment

⋌ Warwick Auctions
(NAVA)
Contact Mr R Beaumont
✉ 3 Queen Victoria Road,
Coventry, West Midlands,
CV1 3JS 🅿
☎ 024 7622 3377/30992
❶ 024 7622 0044
❸ sales@warwick-auctions.co.uk
Ⓦ www.warwickauctions.com
Est. 1947
Open Mon–Fri 9am–5pm
Sales General household goods
Wed 10am, viewing Tues
9am–4.30pm Wed 9–10am.
Antiques and collectables sales
first Wed of each month,
except Jan
Frequency Weekly
Catalogues Yes

DUDLEY

⋌ Black Country Auctions
Contact Chris Aston
✉ Baylies' Hall, Tower Street,
Dudley, West Midlands,
DY1 1NB 🅿
☎ 01384 250220 ❶ 08707 052948

MIDLANDS *(vertical tab)*

ⓔ info@blackcountryauctions.co.uk
ⓦ www.blackcountryauctions.co.uk
Est. 1989
Open Mon–Fri 10am–4pm
Sales General, collectables
weekly, Thurs 6.30pm, viewing
from noon, antiques fine art
quarterly, toys and dolls quarterly
Catalogues Online

HAGLEY

⚒ Walton & Hipkiss
Contact Mr J Carter
✉ 111 Worcester Road,
Hagley, Stourbridge,
West Midlands,
DY9 0NG 🅿
☎ 01562 886688 ✆ 01562 886655
ⓔ hagley@waltonandhipkiss.co.uk
ⓦ www.waltonandhipkiss.co.uk
Est. 1929
Open Mon–Fri 9am–5.30pm
Sat 9am–1.30pm
Sales 5 auctions per year, general
antiques, telephone for details
Catalogues Yes

HALESOWEN

⊞ Anvil Books
Contact Mr J K Maddison
✉ 52 Summer Hill,
Halesowen,
West Midlands,
B63 3BU 🅿
☎ 0121 550 0600
ⓔ jkm@anvilbookshalesowen.co.uk
ⓦ www.anvilbookshalesowen.co.uk
Est. 1997 *Stock size* Small
Stock General second-hand and
antiquarian books, local history,
transport and maritime topics
specialities
Open Tues Thurs Sat 10am–5pm
Fairs Kinver Book Fair, Waverley
Fairs
Services Book search

⊞ Tudor House Antiques
Contact Mr D J Taylor
✉ 68 Long Lane,
Halesowen,
West Midlands,
B62 9LS 🅿
☎ 0121 561 5563
Est. 1991 *Stock size* Medium
Stock Architectural antiques,
stripped pine furniture, bespoke
furniture
Open Tues–Sat 9.30am–5pm
Services Restoration, stripping,
reclaimed pine to order

KNOWLE

⚒ Bonhams (BACA Award Winner 2003)
✉ The Old House, Station Road,
Knowle, Solihull, West Midlands,
B93 0HT
☎ 01564 776151 ✆ 01564 778069
ⓔ knowle@bonhams.com
ⓦ www.bonhams.com
Open Mon–Fri 9am–5pm
Sales Regional Saleroom.
Regular sales held in London and
in our salerooms across the
country. Free auction valuations;
insurance and probate valuations
Catalogues Yes

OLDBURY

⊞ S J. Willder Antiques
Contact Mr S Willder
✉ 97 Stourbridge Road,
Halesowen, West Midlands,
B63 3UA 🅿
☎ 0121 550 8228 ✆ 0121 585 5611
Ⓜ 07860 820 221
ⓔ steve@sjwillderantiques.co.uk
ⓦ www.sjwillderantiques.co.uk
Est. 1975 *Stock size* Large
Stock General antiques, shipping
furniture, silver, china
Open Mon–Sat 9.30am–5.30pm
Fairs Stafford
Services Valuations

SOLIHULL

⊞ Alscot Bathroom Company (SALVO)
Contact Mr Cockroft
✉ 1 Oak Farm, Hampton Lane,
Catherine de Barnes, Solihull,
West Midlands,
B92 0JB 🅿
☎ 0121 709 1901 ✆ 0121 709 1800
ⓔ alscotbathrooms@tiscali.co.uk
ⓦ www.alscotbathrooms.co.uk
Est. 1960 *Stock size* Large
Stock Victorian–Edwardian and
Art Deco sanitary ware, roll-top
baths
Open By appointment
Services Restoration

⊞ Dalton Antiques
Contact Mr Martin Chandler
✉ 124 Sandy Hill Road, Shirley,
Solihull, West Midlands,
B90 2EX 🅿
☎ 0121 7456565
Ⓜ 07970 477 848
Est. 1978 *Stock size* Large

Stock General antiques,
architectural antiques
Open Mon–Fri 10am–6pm half
day Sat
Fairs Newark
Services Valuations, restoration

🏠 Dorridge Antiques & Collectables Centre
Contact Colleen Swift
✉ 7 Forest Court, Dorridge,
Solihull, West Midlands,
B93 8HN 🅿
☎ 01564 779336 or 01574 779768
Est. 1996 *Stock size* Large
No. of dealers 20
Stock Furniture, ceramics,
paintings, prints, glass, jewellery,
guns, swords, silver, bric-a-brac
Open Mon–Sat 11am–5.30pm
Services Valuations and
restoration advice

⊞ High Street Antiques
Contact Mrs Devlen
✉ 1582 High Street, Knowle,
Solihull, West Midlands,
B93 0LF 🅿
☎ 01564 779276
Est. 1998 *Stock size* Medium
Stock General antiques and
collectables
Open Mon–Fri 9am–5pm
Sat 9.30am–5.30pm

⊞ Yoxall Antiques & Fine Arts
Contact Mr Paul Burrows
✉ 68 Yoxall Road, Solihull,
West Midlands,
B90 3RP 🅿
☎ 0121 744 1744
Ⓜ 07860 168078
ⓔ sales@yoxallantiques.co.uk
ⓦ www.yoxallantiques.co.uk
Est. 1988 *Stock size* Large
Stock Period furniture, quality
porcelain, glassware, clocks,
barometers
Open Mon–Sat 9.30am–5pm or
by appointment
Fairs NEC
Services Restoration

STOURBRIDGE

⊞ Lye Antique Furnishings
Contact Paul Smith
✉ 206 High Street, Lye,
Stourbridge, West Midlands,
DY9 8JZ 🅿
☎ 01384 897513

Ⓜ 07976 765142
Est. 1980 *Stock size* Medium
Stock Antiques, collectables
Open Mon–Sat 9am–5pm
Fairs Swinderby Market,
Birmingham Rag Market
Services Valuations

⊞ Memory Lane Antiques
Contact Mr Paul Jones
⊠ 129 Brettell Lane,
Stourbridge,
West Midlands,
DY8 4BA ℗
☎ 01384 370348
Ⓜ 07801 139949
Est. 1989 *Stock size* Large
Stock Country furniture,
architectural antiques
Open Mon–Sat 10am–6pm
Fairs Newark, Ardingly,
Birmingham
Services House clearance

SUTTON COLDFIELD

⚒ Acres Fine Art Auctioneers & Valuers
Contact Mr I Kettlewell
⊠ 28 Beeches Walk,
Sutton Coldfield,
West Midlands,
B73 6HN ℗
☎ 0121 355 1133 ☏ 0121 354 5251
Ⓦ www.acres.co.uk
Est. 1992
Open Mon–Sat 9am–5.30pm
Sales Antiques sales. Telephone
for details
Frequency Quarterly
Catalogues Yes

⊞ Thomas Coulborn and Sons (BADA, CINOA)
Contact Jonathan Coulborn
⊠ Vesey Manor,
64 Birmingham Road,
Sutton Coldfield,
West Midlands,
B72 1QP ℗
☎ 0121 354 3974 ☏ 0121 354 4614
Ⓜ 07941 252299
℮ jc@coulborn.com
Ⓦ www.coulborn.com
Est. 1940 *Stock size* Large
Stock 18thC furniture and works
of art, 19th–20thC paintings and
watercolours
Open Mon–Fri 9.15am–1pm
2–5.30pm Sat evenings by
appoinment
Fairs BADA London
Services Valuations

⊞ S & J Antiques
Contact Mr Steve Dowling
⊠ 431 Birmingham Road,
Wylde Green,
Sutton Coldfield,
West Midlands,
B72 1AX ℗
☎ 0121 384 1595
Ⓜ 07850 099194
℮ candhdowling@aol.com
Est. 1988 *Stock size* Large
Stock Silver, silver plate, oak,
period and stripped-pine
furniture, coins
Open Mon–Sat 10am–5.30pm
Fairs Birmingham Rag Market,
Newark
Services Restoration, re-plating,
mirror re-silvering

WALSALL

⊞ Collectors Centre
Contact Mr Lance Warwood
⊠ 79 Bridge Street, Walsall,
West Midlands,
WS1 1JQ ℗
☎ 01922 625518
Ⓦ www.collectorsweb.co.uk
Est. 1979 *Stock size* Large
Stock Coins, medals, militaria,
postcards, cigarette cards, toys,
antique jewellery
Open Mon–Sat 9am–5pm
Thurs 9am–1pm

⊞ The Dog House
⊠ 309 Bloxwich Road, Walsall,
West Midlands,
WS2 7BD ℗
☎ 01922 630829 ☏ 01922 631236
Est. 1966 *Stock size* Large
Stock General antiques
Open Mon–Sat 9am–5.30pm

⊞ L P Furniture
Contact Mr P Farouz
⊠ The Old Brewery,
Short Acre Street,
Walsall, West Midlands,
WS2 8HW ℗
☎ 01922 746764 ☏ 01922 611316
Ⓜ 07860249097
℮ pierrefarouz@btconnect.com
Ⓦ www.lpfurniture.net
Est. 1982 *Stock size* Large
Stock Continental furniture and
exclusive reproduction French
furniture
Trade only Yes
Open Mon–Fri 9am–6.30pm or by
appointment
Fairs Newark, Swinderby

WEDNESBURY

⊞ Berry Street Bookshop
Contact Mr Lambert
⊠ 37 Lower High Street,
Wednesbury, West Midlands,
WS10 7AQ ℗
☎ 0121 502 4622
℮ geoffsandhurstdr@blueyonder.co.uk
Est. 1988 *Stock size* Medium
Stock General second-hand and
antiquarian books
Open Mon–Sat 9am–2pm
closed Wed
Services Book search

WOLVERHAMPTON

⊞ Don's Den
Contact Mr Relph
⊠ 54 Warstones Road,
Wolverhampton, West Midlands,
WV4 4LP ℗
☎ 01902 331892
Ⓜ 07710 180185
Est. 1975 *Stock size* Large
Stock Antiques and collectables
Open Mon–Sat 10am–5pm closed
Wed

⊞ Newhampton Road Antiques
Contact Mr R G Hill
⊠ 184–184a Newhampton Road
East, Wolverhampton,
West Midlands,
WV1 4PQ ℗
☎ 01902 334363
Ⓜ 07930 894719
Est. 1985 *Stock size* Large
Stock Antiques and collectables
Open Mon–Sat 9.30am–3.30pm
Fairs Newark, Swinderby
Services House clearance

⊞ No. 9 Antiques
⊠ 9 Upper Green, Tettenhall,
Wolverhampton,
West Midlands,
WV6 8QQ ℗
☎ 01902 755333
Est. 1995 *Stock size* Medium
Stock 19thC furniture, porcelain,
silver, watercolours
Open Wed–Sat 10am–5pm
Sat 9am–5.30pm

⊞ Old Book Shop
Contact Kate Lee
⊠ 53 Bath Road,
Wolverhampton, West Midlands,
WV1 4EL ℗
☎ 01902 421055 ☏ 01902 421055

e theoldbookshop@btopenworld.com
Est. 1975 *Stock size* Large
Stock Antiquarian and second-hand books
Open Tues–Wed 10am–3pm
Thurs–Fri 10am–4pm Sat
10am–5pm
Services Book search

⊞ Martin Taylor Antiques (LAPADA)
Contact Darrel
⊠ 140b Tettenhall Road,
Wolverhampton, West Midlands,
WV6 0BQ 🅿
☎ 01902 751166 ❻ 01902 746502
e enquiries@mtaylor-antiques.co.uk
ⓦ www.martintaylor-antiques.com
Est. 1975 *Stock size* Large
Stock 18th–20thC furniture
Open Mon–Fri 8.30am–5.30pm
Sat 10am–5pm or by
appointment
Fairs Newark, NEC
Services Restoration

⊞ Martin Taylor Antiques (LAPADA)
Contact Mr Martin Taylor
⊠ 323 Tettenhall Road,
Wolverhampton, West Midlands,
WV6 0BQ 🅿
☎ 01902 751166 ❻ 01902 746502
ⓜ 07836 636524
e enquiries@mtaylor-antiques.co.uk
ⓦ www.mtaylor-antiques.co.uk
Est. 1976 *Stock size* Small
Stock Antique furniture, gifts
Open Mon–Sat 10am–5.30pm

⊞ West Midlands Collectors Centre
Contact Mr S Moran
⊠ 9 Heaton House, Salop Street,
Wolverhampton, West Midlands,
WV3 0SQ 🅿
☎ 01902 772570
Est. 1983 *Stock size* Small
Stock Stamps, coins, medals,
bank notes, curios, die-cast models
Open Mon–Sat 9.30am–5pm
Services Valuations

⊞ Wood 'n' Things
Contact Mrs K Carter
⊠ 388 Penn Road,
Wolverhampton, West Midlands,
WV4 4DF 🅿
☎ 01902 333324
ⓜ 07808 444786
Est. 1983 *Stock size* Medium
Stock Antiques, collectables,
Victorian, Edwardian and 1920s

furniture
Open Mon–Sat 10am–5pm
Wed 10am–1pm
Services Restoration

WORCESTERSHIRE

BARNT GREEN

⊞ Barnt Green Antiques (BAFRA)
Contact Neville Slater
⊠ 93 Hewell Road, Barnt Green,
Birmingham, Worcestershire,
B45 8NL 🅿
☎ 0121 445 4942 ❻ 0121 445 4942
Est. 1977 *Stock size* Medium
Stock Furniture, clocks
Open Mon–Fri 9am–5.30pm
Sat 9am–1pm
Services Valuations, restoration

BEWDLEY

⌂ Bewdley Antiques
Contact Mrs A Hamilton
⊠ 62a Load Street, Bewdley,
Worcestershire,
DY12 2AP 🅿
☎ 01299 405636 ❻ 01299 841568
Est. 1999 *Stock size* Medium
No. of dealers 12
Stock 19th–20thC furniture,
collectables, small decorative
pieces
Open Mon–Sat 10am–5.30pm
Services Valuations, picture
framing, jewellery repairs

BROADWAY

⊞ Art Nouveau Originals (LAPADA)
Contact Mrs C Turner
⊠ The Bindery Gallery,
69 High Street, Broadway,
Worcestershire,
WR12 7DP 🅿
☎ 01386 854645 ❻ 01386 854645
ⓜ 07774 718096
e cathy@artnouveauoriginals.com
ⓦ www.artnouveauoriginals.com
Est. 1980 *Stock size* Medium
Stock An eclectic mix of items
from the decorative arts
1860–1930
Open Please telephone or e-mail
for opening times
Fairs NEC

⊞ Nicolaus Boston Antiques
Contact Mr N Boston

⊠ Cotswold Design Centre,
Kennel Lane, Broadway,
Worcestershire,
WR12 7DJ 🅿
☎ 01386 854999 ❻ 01386 854986
e info@majolica.co.uk
ⓦ www.majolica.co.uk
Est. 1983 *Stock size* Large
Stock Majolica, Christopher
Dresser, aesthetic pottery
Open Fri 10am–6pm or by
appointment
Fairs New York Ceramic Fair,
Palm Beach Jewellery & Antiques
Show, The New York Spring
International

⊞ Broadway Bears at the Bindery
Contact Mrs C Turner
⊠ 69 High Street, Broadway,
Worcestershire,
WR12 7DP 🅿
☎ 01386 854645 ❻ 01386 854645
ⓜ 07774 718096
e cathy@artnouveauoriginals.com
ⓦ www.artnouveauoriginals.com
Est. 2005 *Stock size* Medium
Stock Period teddy bears and
collectable Steiff items
Open Summer Mon–Sun
10am–5pm off season 6 days
please ring to check

⊞ Stephen Cook Antiques Ltd (BADA, CADA)
Contact Stephen Cook
⊠ 58 High Street, Broadway,
Worcestershire,
WR12 7DP 🅿
☎ 01386 854716 ❻ 01386 859360
e stephen@scookantiques.com
Est. 1986 *Stock size* Medium
Stock 17th–18thC oak and
walnut furniture
Open Mon–Sat 10am–5.30pm

⊞ Fenwick & Fenwick Antiques (CADA)
Contact Mr G Fenwick
⊠ 88–90 High Street, Broadway,
Worcestershire,
WR12 7AJ 🅿
☎ 01386 853227/841724
❻ 01386 858504
Est. 1980 *Stock size* Large
Stock 17th–early 19thC oak,
mahogany, walnut furniture and
works of art, treen, boxes,
pewter, lace bobbins, Chinese
porcelain, corkscrews, early
metalware
Open Mon–Sat 10am–6pm

⊞ Gallimaufry
Contact Chris Stone
✉ 51a High Street, Broadway,
Worcestershire,
WR12 7DT 🅿
☎ 01386 852898
Est. 1992 *Stock size* Medium
Stock China, glass, furniture,
pictures, collectables
Open Mon–Sun 10.30am–4.30pm

⊞ H W Keil Ltd (BADA, CADA)
Contact Mr Keil
✉ Tudor House, Broadway,
Worcestershire,
WR12 7DP 🅿
☎ 01386 852408 📠 01386 852069
📧 info@hwkeil.co.uk
🌐 www.hwkeil.co.uk
Est. 1932 *Stock size* Large
Stock Early 17th–early 19thC
furniture, works of art
Open Mon–Sat 9.15am–1.15pm
2.15–5.30pm
Services Restoration

⊞ John Noott Galleries (BADA, LAPADA, CADA)
Contact Kathryn Plume
✉ Dickens House, 20 High Street,
Broadway, Worcestershire,
WR12 7DT 🅿
☎ 01386 854868/858969
📧 info@john-noott.com
🌐 www.john-noott.com
Est. 1972 *Stock size* Large
Stock Paintings from the 19thC
to the present day
Open Mon–Sat 9.30am–1pm
2pm–5pm
Fairs NEC, Harrogate, Olympia
Services Valuations, restoration,
shipping

BROMSGROVE

⊞ Worcester Medal Service Ltd (OMRS)
Contact Mrs K McDermott
✉ 56 Broad Street, Sidemoor,
Bromsgrove, Worcestershire,
B61 8LL 🅿
☎ 01527 835375 📠 01527 576798
📧 wms@worcmedals.com
🌐 www.worcmedals.com
Est. 1988 *Stock size* Large
Stock Medals and medal
mountings
Open Mon–Fri 9am–5pm
Sat 8.30–noon
Services Suppliers of specialist
cases, medal mounting, valuations

CLEOBURY MORTIMER

⊞ M & M Baldwin
Contact Dr M Baldwin
✉ 24 High Street, Cleobury
Mortimer, Kidderminster,
Worcestershire,
DY14 8BY 🅿
☎ 01299 270110 📠 01299 270110
📧 mb@mbaldwin.free-online.co.uk
Est. 1978 *Stock size* Medium
Stock Second-hand and
antiquarian books, books on
transport, industrial history,
WWII intelligence and
codebreaking a speciality
Open Wed 2–6pm Fri
(Easter–October) Sat 10am–1pm
2–6pm or by appointment
Services Book search, valuations

DROITWICH SPA

⊞ Robert Belcher Antiques
Contact Mr R Belcher
✉ 128 Worcester Road,
Droitwich Spa, Worcestershire,
WR9 8AN 🅿
☎ 01905 772320
Est. 1984 *Stock size* Large
Stock Georgian–Victorian
furniture, paintings, fine art,
decorative items
Open Tues–Sat 9.30am–5.30pm
Fairs NEC
Services Furniture restoration,
picture framing

EVESHAM

⊞ Bookworms of Evesham (PBFA)
Contact Mr T Sims
✉ 81 Port Street, Evesham,
Worcestershire,
WR11 3LF 🅿
☎ 01386 45509
Est. 1971 *Stock size* Medium
Stock Second-hand and
antiquarian books on most
subjects, Gloucestershire and
Worcestershire topics specialities
Open Tues–Sat 10am–5pm
Fairs Churchdown,
Gloucestershire Book Fair (1st
Sunday of each month)
Services Valuations

⌂ Twyford Antiques Centre
Contact Andy Mayhew
✉ 86 High Street, Evesham,

Worcestershire,
WR11 4EV 🅿
☎ 01386 446923
📧 twyfordantiques@tiscali.co.uk
Est. 1999 *Stock size* Medium
No. of dealers 20
Stock General antiques from the
late Victorian period to 20thC
Open Mon–Sat 9.30am–5pm

⊞ Wizpan China & Collectables
Contact Mary Campbell
✉ Cadbury Courtyard,
Blackminster Business Park,
Evesham, Worcestershire,
WR11 7RE 🅿
☎ 01386 833894
📧 wizpan@surfree.co.uk
Est. 2004 *Stock size* Medium
Stock China
Open Mon–Sat 9am–4pm

HALLOW

⊞ Antique Map & Print Gallery
Contact Margaret Nichols
✉ Hallow, Worcestershire,
WR2 6LS 🅿
☎ 01905 641300
📧 antiquemap@aol.com
Est. 1983 *Stock size* Large
Stock Maps, illustrated books,
Vanity Fair prints
Open By appointment

KIDDERMINSTER

⊞ BBM Jewellery, Coins & Antiques (BJA)
Contact Mr W V Crook
✉ 9 Lion Street, Kidderminster,
Worcestershire,
DY10 1PT 🅿
☎ 01562 744118 📠 01562 829444
📧 williamvcrook@btinternet.com
Est. 1980 *Stock size* Large
Stock Antique and second-hand
jewellery, coins, medals,
porcelain, silver
Open Wed–Sat 10am–5pm
Services Restoration and repair

⊞ French Lavender
Contact Zara
✉ Well House, Shenstone,
Kidderminster, Worcestershire,
DY10 4DD 🅿
☎ 01562 777901
📱 07976 267869
🌐 www.frenchlavender.co.uk
Est. 2001 *Stock size* Medium

MIDLANDS

Stock French antiques including beds, armoires, chairs, tables and accessories
Open By appointment only
Fairs Swinderby, Kemptown, Ardingly, Newark

⌂ **Kidderminster Antique Centre**
Contact Mrs V Bentley
✉ 5–8 Lion Street, Kidderminster, Worcestershire, DY10 1PT ℗
☎ 01562 740389   ☏ 01562 740389
✆ theantiquecentre@btconnect.com
Est. 1980 *Stock size* Large
No. of dealers 8
Stock Furniture, china, glass, silver, jewellery, architectural salvage, cast-iron fireplaces, surrounds, tiles, books
Open Mon–Sat 10am–5pm
Services Jewellery and clock repairs, furniture and door stripping, furniture restoration

⋏ **Kidderminster Market Auctions**
Contact Mr B Cooke
✉ Wholesale Market, Comberton Hill, Kidderminster, Worcestershire, DY10 1QH ℗
☎ 01562 741303   ☏ 01562 865495
Est. 1957
Open Mon–Fri 9am–5pm
Sat 9am–1pm
Sales General antiques sale
Thurs 10.30am furniture 2.30pm, viewing Wed 4–8pm
Thurs from 7am
Frequency Weekly

⋏ **Phipps & Pritchard**
Contact Mr A Mayall
✉ 31 Worcester Street, Kidderminster, Worcestershire, DY10 1EQ ℗
☎ 01562 822244   ☏ 01562 825401
⋓ 07970 218140
✆ amayall@phippspritchard. demon.co.uk
Est. 1848
Open Mon–Fri 9am–5.15pm
Sat 9am–3.30pm
Sales General antiques and collectables Sat 10.30am, viewing Fri 3–6.30pm Sat from 8.30am. Sale held at Hartlebury Village Hall
Frequency Every 7–8 weeks
Catalogues Yes

MALVERN

⊞ **Carlton Antiques**
Contact Mr D W Roberts
✉ 43 Worcester Road, Malvern, Worcestershire, WR14 4RB ℗
☎ 01684 573092
✆ dave@carlton-antiques.com
⋓ www.carlton-antiques.com
Est. 1991 *Stock size* Medium
Stock Furniture, ephemera, postcards, bottles, die-cast toys, second-hand books etc
Open Mon–Sun 10am–5pm

⊞ **Foley Furniture**
Contact Mr D W Roberts
✉ Foley Bank, Malvern, Worcestershire, WR14 4QW ℗
☎ 01684 573092
✆ dave@carlton-antiques.com
⋓ www.carlton-antiques.com
Est. 1991 *Stock size* Medium
Stock Furniture of all periods, postcards, bottles, die-cast toys, books etc
Open Wed–Sun 10am–5pm

⌂ **Foley House Antiques**
Contact Roger Hales
✉ 28 Worcester Road, Great Malvern, Worcestershire, WR14 4QW ℗
☎ 01684 575750
☏ 07773 421143
Est. 2003 *Stock size* Large
No. of dealers 12
Stock Victorian–Edwardian furniture, collectables and just about everything
Open Mon–Sat 10am–5.30pm
Sun Bank Holidays 11am–5pm
Services Restoration, shipping

⊞ **Great Malvern Antiques**
Contact Mr R Rice or Mr L Sutton
✉ Salisbury House, 6 Abbey Road, Malvern, Worcestershire, WR14 3HG ℗
☎ 01684 575490
gma@dsl.pipex.com
✆ gmantiques@dial.pipex.com
Est. 1984 *Stock size* Medium
Stock Decorative furniture and furnishings, paintings
Trade only Yes
Open By appointment
Fairs Bath Decorative Antiques Fair, Decorative Antiques and Textiles Fair

⊞ **Kimber & Son**
Contact Mr E M Kimber
✉ 6 Lower Howsell Road, Malvern, Worcestershire, WR14 1EF ℗
☎ 01684 574339
Est. 1950 *Stock size* Medium
Stock 18th–early 20thC furniture, English, European and American markets
Open Mon–Fri 9am–5.30pm
Sat 9am–1pm

⋏ **Philip Laney**
Contact Mr P Laney
✉ Malvern Auction Centre, Portland Road, off Victoria Road, Malvern, Worcestershire, WR14 2TA ℗
☎ 01684 893933   ☏ 01684 577948
✆ philiplaney@aol.com
Est. 1969
Open Mon–Fri 9am–1pm
2–4.30pm
Sales General antiques and collectables sales
Frequency Monthly (14–15 a year)
Catalogues Yes

⊞ **Lechmere Antiquarian Books**
Contact Mr R Lechmere
✉ Primswell, Evandrine, Colwall, Malvern, Worcestershire, WR13 6DT
☎ 01684 540340
Est. 1945 *Stock size* Small
Stock Antiquarian, rare and second-hand books on Hereford, Worcester, Australia
Open Mail order only
Services Mail order

⊞ **The Malvern Bookshop**
Contact Howard Hudson
✉ 7 Abbey Road, Malvern, Worcestershire, WR14 3ES ℗
☎ 01684 575915   ☏ 01684 575915
✆ browse@malvernbookshop.co.uk
Est. 1954 *Stock size* Medium
Stock Antiquarian, rare and second-hand books, books on music and sheet music a speciality
Open Mon–Sat 10am–5pm
Services Book search

⊞ **Malvern Studios (BAFRA, UKIC, NCCR)**
Contact Jeff Hall
✉ 56 Cowleigh Road, Malvern, Worcestershire, WR14 1QD ℗

☎ 01684 574913 ❷ 01684 569475
Ⓦ www.malvernstudios.co.uk
Est. 1961
Stock 18th–20thC furniture
Open Mon Tues Thurs
9am–5.15pm Fri Sat 9am–4.45pm
Services Restoration

⊞ Miscellany Antiques
Contact R S or E A Hunaban
✉ 20 Cowleigh Road, Malvern,
Worcestershire,
WR14 1QD 🅿
☎ 01684 566671 ❷ 01684 560562
❸ liz.hunaban@virgin.net
Ⓦ www.freespace.virgin.net/
lizhunaban
Est. 1974 *Stock size* Medium
Stock Georgian–Edwardian
furniture, some country oak,
bronzes, ivories, silver, jewellery,
decorative items
Open Mon–Sat 9am–5pm
Services Valuations, restoration

⊞ Priory Books
Contact Mr L P Kelly
✉ Church Walk, Malvern,
Worcestershire,
WR14 2XH 🅿
☎ 01684 560258
Est. 1985 *Stock size* Medium
Stock Wide range of antiquarian
and second-hand books
Open Mon–Sat 9.30am–5.25pm
Services Valuations, book search

⊞ Promenade Antiques & Books
Contact Mark Servester
✉ 41 Worcester Road, Malvern,
Worcestershire,
WR14 4RB 🅿
☎ 01684 566876 ❷ 01684 566876
❸ promant@bigfoot.com
Est. 1997 *Stock size* Medium
Stock Victorian–Edwardian
furniture, collectables,
decorative items, reproduction
lamps, books
Open Mon–Sun 10.30am–6pm
Fairs Newark
Services Valuations, restoration

⚒ Philip Serrell Auctioneers & Valuers
Contact P Serrell FRICS
✉ Barnards Green Road,
Malvern, Worcestershire,
WR14 3LW 🅿
☎ 01905 26200 ❷ 01905 21202
❸ serrell.auctions@virgin.net
Ⓦ www.serrell.com

Open Mon–Fri 9am–5pm
closed 1–2pm
Sales General and fine art sales
at the Malvern Sale Room,
Malvern. Special sales of
Worcester porcelain
Frequency Fortnightly
Catalogues Yes

⊞ St James Antiques
Contact Mr Hans Van
Wyngaarden
✉ De Lys, Wells Road, Malvern,
Worcestershire,
WR14 4JL 🅿
☎ 01684 563404
❸ hansvanwyn@tiscali.co.uk
Est. 1992 *Stock size* Large
Stock General furniture, lighting,
decorative items, garden
Open Mon–Sat 10.30am–5pm
Services Valuations, house
clearance

PERSHORE

⊞ Coach House Books
Contact Mrs J S Ellingworth
✉ 17a Bridge Street, Pershore,
Worcestershire,
WR10 1AJ 🅿
☎ 01386 554633 ❷ 01386 554633
❸ sue.chb@virgin.net
Est. 1982 *Stock size* Medium
Stock Antiquarian, rare, new and
second-hand books, prints
Open Mon–Sat 9am–5pm or by
appointment
Services Book search

⊞ Hansen Chard Antiques (BHI)
Contact Mr P Ridler
✉ 126 High Street, Pershore,
Worcestershire,
WR10 1EA 🅿
☎ 01386 553423
Est. 1984 *Stock size* Large
Stock Clocks, barometers, old
and antique model steam
engines, scientific instruments
Open Tues–Sat 10am–4pm
closed Thurs or by appointment
Fairs Bracknell, Birmingham and
Brunel Clock Fairs
Services Valuations, restoration

⊞ Ian K Pugh Books
Contact Mr I Pugh
✉ 40 Bridge Street, Pershore,
Worcestershire,
WR10 1AT 🅿
☎ 01386 552681

❿ 07968 429112
Est. 1974 *Stock size* Medium
Stock Antiquarian, rare and
second-hand books on most
subjects. Antiques, fine art,
horticulture and military topics
specialities
Open Mon–Fri 10.30am–5pm
Sat 9.30am–5pm but check
during termtime
Services Valuations, book search

⊞ S W Antiques (LAPADA)
Contact Mr Adrian Whiteside
✉ Abbey Showrooms,
Newlands, Pershore,
Worcestershire,
WR10 1BP 🅿
☎ 01386 555580 ❷ 01386 556205
❸ catchall@sw-antiques.co.uk
Ⓦ www.sw-antiques.co.uk
Est. 1978 *Stock size* Large
Stock 19th–early 20thC furniture,
antique beds
Open Mon–Sat 9am–5pm
Services Valuations, restoration

REDDITCH

⊞ Angel Antiques
Contact Mrs C Manners
✉ 211 Mount Pleasant,
Redditch, Worcestershire,
B97 4JG 🅿
☎ 01527 545844
Est. 1989 *Stock size* Medium
Stock Georgian–Edwardian
antique furniture, decorative
items
Open Mon Tues Thurs Fri
10am–3.30pm Wed 10am–2pm
Sat 10am–5pm
Services Restoration

⚒ Arrow Auctions (SMA)
Contact Mr A Reeves
✉ Bartleet Road,
Washford, Redditch,
Worcestershire,
B98 0DG 🅿
☎ 01527 510923 ❷ 01527 510982
❸ enquiries@arrowauctions.co.uk
Ⓦ www.arrowauctions.co.uk
Est. 1982
Open Mon–Fri 8.30am–5pm
Sales General househld sale
every Tues 6pm, viewing from
9am. Specialist bi-annual fine art
sales Tues 11am. Free valuations.
Removal, collection and storage
facilities available. On-site
restaurant.
Catalogues Yes

MIDLANDS
WORCESTERSHIRE • UPTON-ON-SEVERN

UPTON-UPON-SEVERN

⊞ Boar's Nest Trading
Contact Mr G Smith
✉ 37a–37b Old Street,
Upton-upon-Severn, Worcester,
Worcestershire,
WR8 0HN 🅿
☎ 01684 592540
Est. 1992 *Stock size* Large
Stock Second-hand and
antiquarian books, non-fiction a
speciality
Open Mon–Sun 10am–5pm
Services Valuations

WHITBOURNE

⊞ Juro Farm and Garden Antiques
Contact Mr R Hughes
✉ Whitbourne, Worcester,
Worcestershire,
WR6 5SF 🅿
☎ 01886 821261 ❶ 01886 821261
🌐 info@juro.co.uk
🌐 www.juro.co.uk
Est. 1990 *Stock size* Large
Stock Garden antiques, staddle
stones, troughs, cider mills,
statuary, farming and garden
implements
Open Mon–Sat 9am–1pm
2pm–5pm
Fairs Newark, Hampton Court,
Malvern Spring Garden Show
Services Valuations

WORCESTER

⊞ Antiques & Curios
Contact Mr B Inett
✉ 50 Upper Tything, Worcester,
Worcestershire,
WR1 1JY 🅿
☎ 01905 25412 ❶ 01905 25412
Est. 1980 *Stock size* Large
Stock Victorian–Edwardian
furniture, mirrors, clocks,
porcelain, glass, decorative items
Open Mon–Sat 9.30am–5.30pm
Services Valuations, restoration

⊞ The Antiques Warehouse
Contact Mr D Venn
✉ 74 Droitwich Road (rear),
Worcester, Worcestershire,
WR1 8BW 🅿
☎ 01905 27493
Est. 1979 *Stock size* Large
Stock Pine furniture, Victorian
interior doors, antique and

reproduction fireplaces
Open Mon–Fri 8am–6pm
Sat 10am–5pm
Services Restoration, stripping

⊞ The Barbers Clock
Contact Graham Gopsill
✉ 37 Droitwich Road, Worcester,
Worcestershire,
WR3 7LG 🅿
☎ 01905 29022
🕾 07710 486598
🌐 Graham@barbersclock37@
fsnet.co.uk
Est. 1993 *Stock size* Medium
Stock Clocks from 1840–1930,
wind-up gramophones, Art Deco,
WWII uniforms, badges
Open Mon–Sat 9am–5pm
Services Valuations, gramophone
and clock repairs

⊞ B Browning & Son
Contact Mr A Browning
✉ 35a Wylds Lane, Worcester,
Worcestershire,
WR5 1DA 🅿
☎ 01905 355646
Est. 1904 *Stock size* Medium
Stock Modern and antique
general household furniture
Open Mon–Sat 9am–5pm
closed Thurs
Services House clearance

⊞ Bygones by the Cathedral (LAPADA, FGA)
Contact Gabrielle Bullock
✉ Cathedral Square, Worcester,
Worcestershire,
WR1 2JD 🅿
☎ 01905 25388 ❶ 01905 23132
Est. 1946 *Stock size* Medium
Stock Decorative antiques, silver,
jewellery, porcelain, furniture,
paintings, glass, metalwork
Open Mon–Fri 9.30am–5.30pm
Sat 9.30am–1pm 2–5.30pm

⊞ Bygones of Worcester (LAPADA, FGA)
Contact Gabrielle Bullock
✉ 55 Sidbury,
Worcester,
Worcestershire,
WR1 2HU 🅿
☎ 01905 23132 ❶ 01905 23132
Est. 1946 *Stock size* Medium
Stock 17th–20thC furniture,
paintings, bronzes, silver,
porcelain
Open Mon–Sat 9.30am–1pm
2–5.30pm

⚒ Andrew Grant Fine Art Auctioneers (RICS)
Contact Christopher Jarrey
✉ St Marks House,
St Marks Close, Worcester,
Worcestershire,
WR5 3DJ 🅿
☎ 01905 357547 ❶ 01905 763942
🌐 fine.arts@andrew-grant.co.uk
🌐 www.andrew-grant.co.uk
Est. 1980
Open Mon–Fri 9am–5.30pm
Sales Quarterly antiques and fine
art sale Thurs, viewing day prior
10am–7pm. Monthly Victoriana
and collectables sale Wed,
viewing day prior 10am–7pm
Catalogues Yes

⊞ Grays Antiques
Contact Mr D Gray
✉ 29 The Tiding, Worcester,
Worcestershire,
WR1 1JL
☎ 01905 724456 ❶ 01905 723433
🌐 enquiries@grays-antiques.com
🌐 www.grays-antiques.com
Est. 1984 *Stock size* Large
Stock Early 19th–early 20thC
furniture and furnishings and
decorative items including
chandeliers
Open Mon–Sat 8.30am–5.30pm
Services Restoration

⊞ Grenadiers
Contact Mr C Chin-See
✉ 13 Barbourne Road,
Worcester, Worcestershire,
WR1 1RS 🅿
☎ 01905 24455
🕾 07887 571887
🌐 enquiries@grenadiers.co.uk
🌐 www.grenadiers.co.uk
Est. 2004 *Stock size* Medium
Stock Wide range of militaria
Open Mon–Fri 10am–4pm

⊞ Heirlooms
Contact Mrs L Rumford
✉ 46 Upper Tything, Worcester,
Worcestershire,
WR1 1JZ 🅿
☎ 01905 23332
Est. 1988 *Stock size* Medium
Stock Antique and old
reproduction furniture, china,
glass, decorative items
Open Mon–Sat 9.30am–4.30pm

⊞ P J Hughes Antiques
Contact Mr P J Hughes
✉ 3 Barbourne Road, Worcester,

56
0

Worcestershire,
WR1 1RS 🅿
☎ 01905 610695
📱 07774 204127
Est. 1972 *Stock size* Large
Stock Jewellery, collectables,
china, silver, small furniture
Open Tues–Sat 9.30am–5pm
Services Valuations

⊞ M Lees & Son (LAPADA)
Contact Mr M Lees
✉ **Tower House,
1 Castle Place,
Severn Street, Worcester,
Worcestershire,
WR1 2NB** 🅿
☎ 01905 26620 📠 01905 26620
📱 07860 826218
📧 michael@leesandsons.fsnet.co.uk
Est. 1974 *Stock size* Medium
Stock Period furniture, china,
pictures, decorative items, mirrors
Open Mon–Fri 9.30am–4.45pm
Thurs 9.30am–12.45pm

Sat 10.30am–4pm and by
appointment
Services Valuations

⊞ The Old Toll House
Contact Mr D Askew
✉ **1 Droitwich Road, Worcester,
Worcestershire,
WR3 7LG** 🅿
☎ 01905 20608
📧 merylaskew@aol.com
Est. 1980 *Stock size* Medium
Stock Pine furniture, reclaimed
wooden doors, pottery,
porcelain, glass
Open Mon–Sat 10am–6pm
Services Restoration, stripping

⤳ Philip Serrell Auctioneers & Valuers
Contact P Serrell FRICS
✉ **Field House, 6 Sansome Walk,
Worcester, Worcestershire,
WR1 1NU** 🅿
☎ 01905 26200 📠 01905 21202
📧 serrell.auctions@virgin.net

🌐 www.serrell.com
Open Mon–Fri 9am–5pm
closed 1–2pm
Sales General and fine art sales
at the Malvern Sale Room,
Malvern. Special sales of
Worcester porcelain
Frequency Fortnightly
Catalogues Yes

🏛 Worcester Antiques Centre
Contact Mr S Zacaroli
✉ **Unit 15, Reindeer Court,
Mealcheapen Street, Worcester,
Worcestershire, WR1 4DS** 🅿
☎ 01905 610680
📧 worcsantiques@aol.com
Est. 1991 *Stock size* Large
No. of dealers 45
Stock Porcelain, early Worcester,
furniture, silver, jewellery, Art
Nouveau, Arts and Crafts,
militaria, scientific instruments
Open Mon–Sat 10am–5pm
December Sun 11am–4pm

EAST RIDING OF YORKSHIRE

▌BEVERLEY

⊞ **David Hakeney Antiques**
Contact David Hakeney
✉ PO Box 171, Beverley,
East Riding of Yorkshire,
HU17 7WH
☎ 01482 677006
📱 07860 507774
✉ dhakeney@aol.com
Est. 1970 *Stock size* Medium
Stock General antiques,

quality items
Open By appointment
Fairs NEC, Newark, Ardingly

🏠 **St Crispin Antiques & Collectors Centre**
Contact Chris Fowler
✉ 11 Butcher Row,
Beverley,
East Riding of Yorkshire,
HU17 0AA 🅿
☎ 01482 869583
📱 07951 252101
Est. 1997 *Stock size* Large
No. of dealers 70
Stock Antiques, collectables,

furniture, books
Open Mon–Sat 10am–5pm
Sun 10.30–4.30pm
Services Valuations, restoration

⊞ **Time and Motion (BHI, BWCG)**
Contact Mr Peter Lancaster
✉ 1 Beckside, Beverley,
East Riding of Yorkshire,
HU17 0PB 🅿
☎ 01482 881574
Est. 1984 *Stock size* Large
Stock Antique clocks and
barometers
Open Mon–Sat 10am–5pm

closed Thurs
Services Valuations, restoration
East Riding of Yorkshire, Beverley

⌂ Vicar Lane Antique Centre
Contact Chris Fowler
✉ The Old Granary, Vicar Lane, North Bar Within, Beverley, East Riding of Yorkshire, HU17 8DF ℗
☎ 01482 888088
☏ 07951 252101
Est. 2002 *Stock size* Medium
No. of dealers 20
Stock Pre-1910 furniture, small antiques
Open Mon–Sat 10am–5pm Sun 10.30am–4pm
Services Valuations, restoration

BRIDLINGTON

⊞ Dixon's Medals (OMRS)
Contact Mr C J Dixon
✉ 23 Prospect Street, Bridlington, East Riding of Yorkshire, YO15 2AE ℗
☎ 01262 603348/676877
☏ 01262 606600
✉ chris@dixonsmedals.co.uk
🌐 www.dixonsmedals.co.uk
Est. 1969 *Stock size* Large
Stock Medals from Peninsular war, Victorian campaigns to present day
Open Mon–Fri 9.30am–5pm
Fairs OMRS Convention
Services Restoration of medals, catalogue, mail order worldwide, Dixons Gazette

⊞ The Emporium
Contact Mr Burdall
✉ 59 St John Street, Bridlington, East Riding of Yorkshire, YO16 7NN ℗
☎ 01262 677560
☏ 07779 200335
Est. 1979 *Stock size* Large
Stock Sanitary ware, doors, radiators, pine furniture, cast-iron fires, French stoves, brass ware, reclaimed timber etc
Open Tues–Sat 10am–5.30pm or by appointment
Services Valuations, restoration, stripping

⌂ The Georgian Rooms
Contact David Rothwell
✉ 56 High Street, Bridlington, East Riding of Yorkshire, YO16 4QA ℗

☎ 01262 608600
🌐 www.kpkaren@aol.com
Est. 2000 *Stock size* Large
No. of dealers 15
Stock General antiques, silver, jewellery, furniture, paintings
Open Mon–Sat 10am–5pm Sun 10am–3pm

DRIFFIELD

⊞ The Crested China Co
Contact Mr David Taylor
✉ Highfield, Windmill Hill, Driffield, East Riding of Yorkshire, YO25 5YP ℗
☎ 0870 300 1 300 ☏ 01377 272759
✉ dt@thecrestedchinacompany.com
🌐 www.thecrestedchinacompany.com
Est. 1978 *Stock size* Large
Stock Goss and crested china
Open By appointment
Fairs Goss Collectors Club Fairs
Services Mail order, bi-monthly illustrated catalogue

➴ Dee, Atkinson and Harrison
Contact Owen Nisbet or Pippa Whiteley
✉ The Exchange, Driffield, East Riding of Yorkshire, YO25 6LD ℗
☎ 01377 253151 ☏ 01377 241041
✉ info@dahauctions.com
🌐 www.dahauctions.com
Est. 1880
Open Mon–Fri 9am–5.30pm
Sales 6 antique and collectors' sales per annum, 2 collectors' sports and toy sales per annum, fortnightly 19thC and modern sales
Catalogues Yes

⊞ Francis Scott
Contact Francis Scott
✉ Kirkburn Manor, Kirkburn, Driffield, East Riding of Yorkshire, YO25 9DU ℗
☎ 01377 232070
☏ 07870 704959
🌐 www.francis-scott.co.uk
Est. 2005 *Stock size* Small
Stock Victorian pine and collectables
Open Please call for an appointment

⊞ Smith & Smith Designs (Driffield) Ltd
Contact Mr D Smith
✉ 58a Middle Street North,

Driffield, East Riding of Yorkshire, YO25 6SU ℗
☎ 01377 256321 ☏ 01377 256070
☏ 07941 034446
✉ shop@pine-on-line.co.uk
🌐 www.pine-on-line.co.uk
Est. 1976 *Stock size* Medium
Stock Antique, replica antique and reproduction pine furniture, period furniture, clocks, decorative items, lighting, water features
Open Mon–Sat 9.30am–5.30pm or by appointment
Services Restoration

GOOLE

⌂ Arcadia Antiques Centre
Contact Mr Martin Spavin
✉ 10–14 The Arcade, Goole, East Riding of Yorkshire, DN14 5QT ℗
☎ 01405 720549 ☏ 01405 750549
☏ 07775 557499
Est. 1991 *Stock size* Medium
No. of dealers 20
Stock Collectables, costume jewellery, pictures, furniture etc
Open Mon–Sat 10am–5pm Sun by appointment
Services Valuations, clock and watch repairs

➴ Clegg & Son
Contact Mr C Clegg
✉ 68 Aire Street, Goole, East Riding of Yorkshire, DN14 5QE ℗
☎ 01405 763140 ☏ 01405 764235
✉ gooleoffice@cleggandson.co.uk
🌐 www.cleggandson.co.uk
Est. 1895
Open Mon–Fri 9am–5pm
Sales Antiques and household sale Sat am, viewing day of sale 9am–sale. Held at St Mary's Church Hall, Goole
Catalogues Yes

HORNSEA

⊞ Second Time Around
Contact Mr T Brown
✉ 61–61a Southgate, Hornsea, East Riding of Yorkshire, HU18 1AL
☎ 01964 532037
Est. 1981 *Stock size* Large
Stock General antiques, furniture, pottery, collectables, china

Open Mon–Sat 10am–4.30pm closed Wed
Fairs Newark, Birmingham
Services Restoration, upholstery

HOWDEN

⊞ Churchside Antiques
Contact Lorraine Barber
✉ 13 Churchside, Howden, East Riding of Yorkshire, DN14 7BS 🅿
☎ 01430 430077
🌐 www.churchside-antiques.co.uk
Est. 2005 *Stock size* Medium
Stock General antiques
Open Tues–Sat 10am–4.30pm

⊞ Kemp Booksellers (ABA, PBFA, BA)
Contact Mike Kemp
✉ 5–7 Vicar Lane, Howden, East Riding of Yorkshire, DN14 7BP 🅿
☎ 01430 432071 📠 01430 431666
📧 kemp.books@dial.pipex.com
🌐 www.kempbooksellers.co.uk
Est. 1979 *Stock size* Medium
Stock Mervyn Peake, modern first editions, Yorkshire and Lincolnshire topography
Open Mon–Sat 9am–5pm
Fairs ABA, PBFA, BA

HULL

⊞ Imperial Antiques
Contact M Langton
✉ 397 Hessle Road, Hull, East Riding of Yorkshire, HU3 4EH 🅿
☎ 01482 327439
Est. 1980 *Stock size* Medium
Stock Pine furniture
Open Mon–Sat 9am–5pm
Fairs Newark

⊞ Kilnsea Antiques
Contact Tony Smith
✉ The Old Barn, Kilnsea Road, Hull, East Riding of Yorkshire, HU12 0UB 🅿
☎ 01964 650311
📧 tsantiques@hotmail.com
Est. 1981 *Stock size* Medium
Stock Furniture and collectables from the late 1800s
Open Tues–Sun 10am–5pm

⊞ Mill Antiques
Contact John Mills
✉ 388–396 Beverley Road, Hull, East Riding of Yorkshire,

HU5 1LN 🅿
☎ 01482 342248
📧 johnay70@hotmail.com
🌐 www.millantiques.co.uk
Est. 1971 *Stock size* Medium
Stock Antique pine, brass beds, cast-iron fireplaces, architectural items
Open Mon–Sat 9am–5pm
Fairs Newark
Services Valuations, pine stripping

⊞ Pine-Apple Antiques
Contact Diane Todd
✉ 321–327 Beverley Road, Hull, East Riding of Yorkshire, HU5 1LD 🅿
☎ 01482 441384 📠 01482 441073
📱 07860 874480
📧 diane@pine-apple.co.uk
🌐 www.pine-apple.co.uk
Est. 1981 *Stock size* Large
Stock Architectural antiques, pine, oak, beech furniture, lighting, clocks, jewellery, pottery, curios, fireplaces, bathrooms, bespoke kitchens, soft furnishings, leather furniture
Open Mon–Sat 9am–5.30pm Sun 11am–4pm

MARKET WEIGHTON

⋏ R Hornsey & Sons
Contact Mr M Swann
✉ 33 High Street, Market Weighton, East Riding of Yorkshire, YO43 3AQ 🅿
☎ 01430 872551 📠 01430 871387
📱 07711 200854
📧 sales@hornseys.uk.com
🌐 www.hornseys.uk.com
Est. 1884
Open Mon–Fri 9am–5pm Sat 9am–noon
Sales General antiques
Frequency Periodic
Catalogues No

⌂ Mount Pleasant Antiques Centre
Contact Linda Sirrs
✉ 46 Cliffe Road, Market Weighton, East Riding of Yorkshire, YO43 3BP 🅿
☎ 01430 872872
🌐 www.mountpleasantantique scentre.co.uk
Est. 1999 *Stock size* Large

No. of dealers 20
Stock Good-quality furniture, collectables, 4,000 sq ft showroom
Open Mon–Sun 9.30am–5pm
Services Restoration

NORTH CAVE

⋏ Hawleys
Contact John Hawley
✉ Albion House, Westgate, North Cave, East Riding of Yorkshire, HU15 2NJ 🅿
☎ 01430 470654 📠 01430 422958
📱 07850 225805
📧 info@hawleys.info
🌐 www.hawleys.info
Est. 1966
Open By appointment
Sales Auctions are held at the Memorial Hall, Lairgate, Beverley, no set times

PATRINGTON

⊞ Clyde Antiques
Contact Ms S Nettleton
✉ 12a Market Place, Patrington, Hull, East Riding of Yorkshire, HU12 0RB 🅿
☎ 01964 630650
Est. 1980 *Stock size* Medium
Stock Wide range of antique stock from collectables to period furniture
Open Tues–Sat 10am–5pm closed Wed
Services Valuations

⋏ Frank Hill & Son
Contact Mr R E Ward
✉ 18 Market Place, Patrington, Hull, East Yorkshire, HU12 0RB 🅿
☎ 01964 630531 📠 01964 631203
📱 07980 864909
Est. 1926
Open Mon–Fri 9am–5pm Sat 9am–noon
Sales Antique and modern household furniture and effects quarterly, telephone for details, viewing morning of sale. Held at Church Hall, Ottringham
Frequency Quarterly
Catalogues Yes

THORNTON

⊞ Abacus Fireplaces
Contact Mr J White
✉ Common End Farm,

Thornton, Melbourne,
East Riding of Yorkshire,
YO42 4RZ
☎ 01759 318575 ❻ 01759 318136
Ⓜ 07703 517544
✉ abacus03@globalnet.co.uk
Est. 1969 *Stock size* Large
Stock Architectural antiques,
fireplaces, fireplace furnishings
Open Mon–Sat 9am–4.30pm
Services Restoration of all
antiques, custom-made castings

WITHERNSEA

⊞ **Mathy's Emporium**
Contact Mr M Quinn
✉ 2 Pier Road, Withernsea,
East Riding of Yorkshire,
HU19 2JS
☎ 01964 615739
Est. 1994 *Stock size* Large
Stock Brass, furniture, pottery,
Wade, collectables
Open Mon–Sun 10am–5pm
closed Wed
Services Valuations

NORTH YORKSHIRE

ASKRIGG

⚒ **J R Hopper & Co**
Contact Mr D Lambert
✉ Wood End Countersett,
Askrigg, North Yorkshire,
DL8 3DE
☎ 01969 650776 ❻ 01969 650893
✉ brian.carlisle@easynet.co.uk
Est. 1886
Open Possible to contact at all
times
Sales General antiques,
household furnishings
Frequency Monthly
Catalogues Yes

AUSTWICK

⊞ **Austwick Hall Books**
Contact Michael Pearson
✉ Townhead Lane,
Austwick, Nr Settle,
North Yorkshire,
LA2 8BS
☎ 01524 251794
✉ austwickhall@btinternet.com
Est. 2000 *Stock size* Medium
Stock Antiquarian, rare and
second-hand books, including
natural history and science
Open By appointment only
Services Book search

BEDALE

⊞ **Bedale Antiques**
Contact Mr or Mrs R C Stubley
✉ 2a Sussex Street, Bedale,
North Yorkshire,
DL8 2AJ
☎ 01677 427765
Est. 1998 *Stock size* Medium
Stock Period furniture, pottery
Open Mon–Sat 10am–4.30pm
closed Thurs

⊞ **Bennetts Antiques &
Collectables Ltd**
Contact Paul Bennett
✉ 7 Market Place, Bedale,
North Yorkshire,
DL8 1ED
☎ 01677 427900 ❻ 01677 426858
✉ info@bennetts.uk.com
Ⓦ www.bennetts.uk.com
Est. 1997 *Stock size* Large
Stock Furniture, clocks, works of
art, 19thC Yorkshire paintings,
collectables
Open Mon 9am–1pm Tues–Sat
9am–5pm Sun by appointment
Services Restoration, clock repair

⚒ **Bonhams**
✉ 14 Market Place, Bedale,
North Yorkshire,
DL8 1EQ
☎ 01667 424 114 ❻ 01677 424 115
✉ bedale@bonhams.com
Ⓦ www.bonhams.com
Open Mon–Fri 9am–1pm 2–5pm
Sales Regional office. Regular
sales held in London and in our
salerooms across the country.
Free auction valuations;
insurance and probate valuations

⚒ **M W Darwin & Son**
Contact Mr M W Darwin
✉ The Dales Furniture Hall,
Bridge Street, Bedale,
North Yorkshire,
DL8 2AD
☎ 01677 422846 ❻ 01609 779072
✉ mwdarwin1@estategazette.net
Est. 1959
Open Mon–Fri 9am–4.30pm
Thurs 9am–noon
Sales General antiques sales held
on Fri
Frequency Every 3 weeks
Catalogues No

⊞ **Dovetail Interiors of
Bedale**
Contact Brian Jutsum

✉ Bridge Street, Bedale,
North Yorkshire,
DL8 2AD
☎ 01677 426464 ❻ 01677 426464
Ⓦ www.dovetailinteriors.com
Est. 1997 *Stock size* Medium
Stock Antiques, bespoke
furniture, ethnic artefacts,
jewellery
Open Mon–Sat 10am–5.15pm
Sun 11.30am–4.30pm

BOLTON ABBEY

⊞ **Grove Rare Books
(PDFA)**
Contact Mr A Sharpe
✉ The Old Post Office, Bolton
Abbey, Skipton, North Yorkshire,
BD23 6EX
☎ 01756 710717
Ⓦ www.groverarebooks.co.uk
Est. 1997 *Stock size* Medium
Stock Antique, rare, and second-
hand books, local topography a
speciality
Open Tues–Sat 10am–5pm
variable during winter
Fairs PDFA
Services Restoration, book
search

BOROUGHBRIDGE

⚒ **Lister Haigh**
Contact Mr Paul Johnston
✉ 5 St James Square,
Boroughbridge,
North Yorkshire,
YO51 9AS
☎ 01423 322382 ❻ 01423 324735
✉ boroughbridge@listerhaigh.co.uk
Ⓦ www.listerhaigh.co.uk
Est. 1919
Open Mon–Fri 9am–5.30pm
Sat 9–11.30am
Sales General antiques and
periodic catalogue sales
Frequency Monthly
Catalogues Yes

⊞ **Mauleverer Antiques**
Contact Ms Caroline Louise
Forster
✉ The Old Goods Yard,
Milby Road, Boroughbridge,
North Yorkshire,
YO51 9BL
☎ 01423 340170 ❻ 01423 340170
Ⓜ 07974 255087
✉ mauleverer@tiscali.co.uk
Ⓦ www.earlyenglishoak.co.uk
Est. 1984 *Stock size* Medium

Stock 1650–1850 early English oak and country furniture
Open By appointment only
Fairs Tatton Park, NEC, The Northern Antique Fair, Harrogate

⊞ R S Wilson & Son
Contact Mr R Wilson
✉ PO Box 41, Boroughbridge, North Yorkshire, YO51 9WY ℗
☎ 01423 322417 📠 01423 322417
📱 07711 794801
📧 richard.wilsonantiques@virgin.net
Est. 1917 *Stock size* Small
Stock 17th–19thC furniture
Open By appointment

EASINGWOLD

⊞ Easingwold Antiques
Contact Jane Fish
✉ 108 Long Street, Easingwold, North Yorkshire, YO61 3HX ℗
☎ 01347 822977
📱 07968 088705 or 07977 108907
Est. 2003 *Stock size* Large
Stock Glass, silver, ceramics, linen, pre-20thC furniture
Open Tues–Sat 10am–5pm
Fairs Harrogate
Services Restoration

⊞ Milestone Antiques
Contact Mr A Streetley
✉ Farnley House, 101 Long Street, Easingwold, York, North Yorkshire, YO61 3HY ℗
☎ 01347 821608
📧 milestoneantiques-easingwold@fsmail.net
🌐 www.milestoneantiques.co.uk
Est. 1982 *Stock size* Medium
Stock Furniture, clocks
Open Mon–Sat 9am–5.30pm
Sun by appointment
Services Valuations

⊞ Vale Antiques (GADAR)
Contact J M Leach
✉ Mooracres, North Moor, Easingwold, York, North Yorkshire, YO61 3NB ℗
☎ 01347 821298 📠 01347 821298
📧 chris.leach@ukonline.co.uk
Est. 1990 *Stock size* Medium
Stock Georgian, Victorian and later furniture, collectables
Open Mon–Sun 9am–5.30pm
Services Furniture restoration

FLAXTON

⊞ Flaxton Antique Gardens (SALVO)
Contact Tim Richardson
✉ Glebe Farm, Flaxton, North Yorkshire, YO60 7RU ℗
☎ 01904 468468
🌐 www.salvo.co.uk/dealers/flaxton
Est. 1990 *Stock size* Large
Stock Garden antiques, terracotta urns, seats, Victorian edging, bird baths, troughs, sundials
Open By appointment
Services Valuations

GARGRAVE

⊞ Dickinson's Antiques Ltd
Contact H H or A E Mardall
✉ Estate Yard, West Street, Gargrave, Skipton, North Yorkshire, BD23 3RD ℗
☎ 01756 748257
Est. 1959 *Stock size* Medium
Stock Antique early furniture
Open Mon–Sat 9am–5.30pm or by appointment
Services Restoration

⊞ Gargrave Gallery
Contact Mr B Herington
✉ 48 High Street, Gargrave, Skipton, North Yorkshire, BD23 3RD ℗
☎ 01756 749641
Est. 1974 *Stock size* Medium
Stock General antiques, Georgian–Victorian furniture
Open Mon–Sat 10am–4pm

⊞ R N Myers & Son (BADA)
Contact Simon Myers
✉ Endsleigh House, High Street, Gargrave, Skipton, North Yorkshire, BD23 3LX ℗
☎ 01756 749587 📠 01756 749322
📱 07801 310126
📧 rnmyersson@aol.com
Est. 1890 *Stock size* Medium
Stock 17th–early 19thC furniture, ceramics, works of art
Open Mon–Sat 9am–5pm or by appointment
Services Valuations

GUISBOROUGH

⊞ Curiosity Corner
Contact Mr B Wilson
✉ 47 Church Street, Guisborough, Cleveland, North Yorkshire, TS14 6HG ℗
☎ 01287 636660
Est. 1987 *Stock size* Medium
Stock General antiques, longcase clocks
Open Mon–Sat 9am–4.30pm

HARROGATE

⊞ Armstrong Antiques (BADA)
Contact M A Armstrong
✉ 10–11 Montpellier Parade, Harrogate, North Yorkshire, HG1 2TJ ℗
☎ 01423 506843 📠 01423 506843
📱 07802 721815
Est. 1983 *Stock size* Medium
Stock Fine18th–early 19thC English furniture
Open Mon–Sat 10am–5.30pm
Fairs Olympia
Services Valuations

⊞ Richard Axe Books (PBFA)
Contact Mr R Axe
✉ 12 Cheltenham Crescent, Harrogate, North Yorkshire, HG1 1DH
☎ 01423 561867 📠 01423 561837
📧 rjaxe@tiscali.co.uk
Est. 1980 *Stock size* Large
Stock Antiquarian, rare, second-hand books, Yorkshire topics a speciality
Open Tues–Sat 10am–5.30pm

⊞ Carlton Hollis Ltd
Contact Paul Hollis
✉ 9 Montpellier Mews, Montpellier Street, Harrogate, North Yorkshire, HG1 2TQ ℗
☎ 01423 500216 📠 01423 500283
📱 07711 188565
📧 carltonhollis@btconnect.com
Est. 2000 *Stock size* Medium
Stock Antique silver and jewellery
Open Tues–Sat 10am–5pm
Fairs NEC
Services Valuations, restoration

⊞ Crown Jewellers of Harrogate
Contact Steve Kramer, FGA, DGA
✉ 23 Commercial Street, Harrogate, North Yorkshire, HG1 1UB ℗
☎ 01423 502000 📠 01423 502000
📧 sask@crownjewellers.freeserve.co.uk
Est. 2000 *Stock size* Medium

Stock Second-hand gold jewellery, new silver jewellery, porcelain, glass, silver
Open Mon–Sat 10am–5pm closed Wed
Services Valuations, jewellery repairs

⊞ John Daffern Antiques (LAPADA)
Contact John Daffern
✉ 38 Forest Lane Head, Harrogate, North Yorkshire, HG2 7TS 🅿
☎ 01423 889832
📱 07802 324202
✉ daffern@talk21.com
Est. 1968 *Stock size* Medium
Stock Fine 17th–18thC furniture, clocks, paintings
Open Mon Wed Fri Sat 10.30am–5.30pm

⊞ Dragon Antiques
Contact Mr Peter Broadbelt
✉ 10 Dragon Road, Harrogate, North Yorkshire, HG1 5DF 🅿
☎ 01423 562037
Est. 1964 *Stock size* Medium
Stock General antiques, ephemera, postcards
Open Mon–Sat 11am–6pm

⊞ Garth Antiques (LAPADA)
Contact Mr or Mrs J Chapman
✉ 16 Montpellier Parade, Harrogate, North Yorkshire, HG1 2TG 🅿
☎ 01423 530573 ✆ 01423 564084
✉ irenechapman@btconnect.com
Est. 1978 *Stock size* Medium
Stock General antiques
Open Mon–Sat 10am–5.30pm
Services Restoration

⌂ The Ginnel Antique Center
Contact Mrs P Stephenson
✉ The Ginnel, (off Parliament Street), Harrogate, North Yorkshire, HG1 2RB 🅿
☎ 01423 508857 ✆ 01423 508857
✉ enquiries@theginnel.com
🌐 www.theginnel.co.uk
Est. 1986 *Stock size* Large
No. of dealers 50
Stock Quality datelined antiques
Open Mon–Sat 9.30am–5.30pm selected Sundays to coincide with major fairs 10.30am–5pm
Services Café, licensed restaurant

⊞ Havelocks Pine and Antiques
Contact Philip Adam
✉ 13–17 Westmoreland Street, Harrogate, North Yorkshire, HG1 5AY 🅿
☎ 01423 506721 ✆ 01423 506721
📱 07802 914419
Est. 1986 *Stock size* Large
Stock General antiques
Open Mon–Sat 10am–5pm Sun 11am–4pm
Fairs Newark
Services Restoration, pine stripping, valuations

⊞ Charles Lumb & Sons Ltd (BADA)
Contact Mr A Lumb
✉ 2 Montpellier Gardens, Harrogate, North Yorkshire, HG1 2TF 🅿
☎ 01423 503776 ✆ 01423 530074
✉ info@harrogateantiques.com
🌐 www.harrogateantiques.com
Est. 1910 *Stock size* Medium
Stock 18th–19thC English furniture, works of art, metalware
Open Mon–Fri 9.30am–6pm closed 1–2pm Sat 9.30am–1pm

➴ Christopher Matthews
Contact Christopher Matthews
✉ 23 Mount Street, Harrogate, North Yorkshire, HG2 8DQ 🅿
☎ 01423 871756 ✆ 01423 879700
Est. 1989
Open Mon–Fri 9am–5pm
Sales Quarterly antiques auctions, telephone for details
Catalogues Yes

⌂ Montpellier Mews Antique Market
✉ Montpellier Street, Harrogate, North Yorkshire, HG1 2TQ 🅿
☎ 01423 530484
Est. 1987 *Stock size* Medium
No. of dealers 10
Stock General antiques, collectables, furniture, silver, china
Open Mon–Sat 10am–5pm

➴ Morphets of Harrogate (SOFAA)
Contact Elizabeth Pepper-Darling
✉ 6 Albert Street, Harrogate, North Yorkshire, HG1 1JL
☎ 01423 530030 ✆ 01423 500717

✉ enquires@morphets.co.uk
🌐 www.morphets.co.uk
Est. 1895
Open Mon–Fri 9am–5.30pm Wed 9am–6pm Sat 9am–noon
Sales Fine art and antiques sale quarterly Thurs 10am, viewing Tues 2–7pm Wed 10am–5pm Thurs 8.30–10am. Victorian and later furniture and effects twice monthly Thurs 10am, viewing Wed 10am–7pm Thurs 8.30–10am
Catalogues Yes

⊞ Paul Weatherell Antiques (LAPADA)
Contact Mr P Weatherell
✉ 30–31 Montpellier Parade, Harrogate, North Yorkshire, HG1 2TG 🅿
☎ 01423 507810 ✆ 01423 520005
Est. 2004 *Stock size* Large
Stock 18th–early 20thC English and Continental furniture, paintings, objets d'art, mirrors, lighting
Open Mon–Sat 9am–5.30pm
Services Restoration, shipping worldwide

⊞ Paul M Peters (LAPADA)
Contact Mr Paul Peters
✉ 15a Bower Road, Harrogate, North Yorkshire, HG1 1BE 🅿
☎ 01423 560118 ✆ 01423 560118
📱 07803 082378
Est. 1964 *Stock size* Large
Stock Chinese, Japanese, European ceramics, Oriental works of art
Open by appointment only
Fairs Olympia

⊞ Elaine Phillips Antiques Ltd (BADA)
Contact Elaine, Colin or Louise Phillips
✉ 1–2 Royal Parade, Harrogate, North Yorkshire, HG1 2SZ 🅿
☎ 01423 569745
📱 07710 793753
✉ elainephillips@heliscott.co.uk
Est. 1965 *Stock size* Medium
Stock 17th–18thC oak furniture, metalware, treen, some mahogany
Open Mon–Sat 9.30am–5.30pm or by appointment
Fairs Harrogate (Apr Sept)
Services Interior design

⊞ **Smiths the Rink Ltd**
Contact R T Smith
⊠ Dragon Road, Harrogate,
North Yorkshire,
HG1 5DR ℗
☎ 01423 557890 ❻ 01423 520416
ⓦ www.smithstherink.co.uk
Est. 1906 *Stock size* Medium
Stock General antiques
Open Mon–Sat 9am–5.30pm
Sun 11am–4.30pm

⊞ **St Julien**
Contact Mr J White
⊠ 4 Royal Parade, Harrogate,
North Yorkshire,
HG1 2SZ ℗
☎ 01423 526569 ❻ 01423 524999
⓪ 07703 517544
ⓔ abacus03@globalnet.co.uk
Est. 1998 *Stock size* Large
Stock Antique and period
lighting, door furniture,
fireplaces
Open Mon–Sat 10am–5.30pm
Fairs Newark
Services Restoration, light fittings,
custom-made brass castings

⚒ **Tennants Auctioneers**
Contact Mr N Smith
⊠ 34 Montpellier Parade,
Harrogate, North Yorkshire,
HG1 2TG ℗
☎ 01423 531661 ❻ 01423 530990
ⓔ harrogate@tennants-ltd.co.uk
ⓦ www.tennants.co.uk
Est. 1899
Open Mon–Fri 9am–5pm
Sales Almost weekly general
sales of antiques, Victorian and
later estate and house contents.
International Fine Art Catalogue
sales in spring, summer and
autumn. Specialist catalogue
sales of books, stamps, postcards
and coins are held regularly.
Special sections of decorative
arts, textiles, dolls, toys, militaria,
railwayana, general collectables,
cameras etc
Catalogues Yes

⊞ **Thorntons of Harrogate**
(LAPADA)
Contact Jason or Hugh Thornton
⊠ 1 Montpellier Gardens,
Harrogate, North Yorkshire,
HG1 2TF ℗
☎ 01423 504118 ❻ 01423 528400
ⓔ tofh@harrogateantiques.com
ⓦ www.harrogateantiques.com
Est. 1973 *Stock size* Medium

Stock 18th–19thC furniture, clocks,
barometers, decorative items
Open Mon–Sat 9.30am–5.30pm
or by appointment
Services Restoration, valuations

⊞ **Walker Galleries**
(BADA, LAPADA, CINOA)
Contact Ian Walker
⊠ 1 Crown Place, Harrogate,
North Yorkshire,
HG1 2RY ℗
☎ 01423 520599 ❻ 01423 536664
ⓔ walkermodern@aol.com
ⓦ www.walkerfineart.co.uk
Est. 1972 *Stock size* Large
Stock 20thC British paintings,
French impressionist paintings
Open Tues–Sat 9.30am–5.30pm
Fairs Olympia, BADA, Harrogate
Fine Art and Antique Fair
Services Valuations, restoration

⊞ **Walker Galleries**
(BADA, LAPADA, CINOA)
Contact Ian Walker
⊠ 6 Montpellier Gardens,
Harrogate, North Yorkshire,
HG1 2TF ℗
☎ 01423 567933 ❻ 01423 536664
ⓔ wgltd@aol.com
ⓦ www.walkerfineart.co.uk
Est. 1972 *Stock size* Large
Stock 18th–20thC British and
Continental watercolours and oil
paintings, small furniture,
bronzes
Open Mon–Sat 9.30am–5.30pm
Fairs Olympia, BADA, Harrogate
Fine Art and Antique Fair
Services Valuations, restoration

⊞ **Chris Wilde Antiques**
(LAPADA)
Contact Mr C Wilde
⊠ 134 Kings Road, Harrogate,
North Yorkshire,
HG1 5HY ℗
☎ 01423 525855 ❻ 01423 552301
⓪ 07831 543268
ⓔ chris@harrogate.com
ⓦ www.antiques.harrogate.com
or www.antiquescourses.co.uk
Est. 1995 *Stock size* Large
Stock Georgian–Victorian
furniture, longcase clocks,
pictures
Open Mon–Sat 10am–5pm
Fairs NEC Antiques for Everyone,
Bailey fair Harrogate
Services Valuations, restoration,
antique furniture appreciation
and appraisal courses

⊞ **Cellar Antiques**
Contact Mr Ian Iveson
⊠ Bridge Street, Hawes,
North Yorkshire,
DL8 3QL ℗
☎ 01969 667224
Est. 1987 *Stock size* Medium
Stock General antiques, country
oak period furniture, clocks,
longcase clocks
Open Mon–Sun 10am–5pm
Services Valuations, house
clearance

⊞ **Sturmans Antiques**
(LAPADA)
Contact Mr Peter Sturman
⊠ Main Street, Hawes,
North Yorkshire,
DL8 3QW ℗
☎ 01969 667742
ⓔ enquiries@sturmansantiques.co.uk
ⓦ www.sturmansantiques.co.uk
Est. 1984 *Stock size* Medium
Stock 18th–19thC furniture,
clocks, porcelain
Open Mon–Sat 10am–5.30pm
Sun 11am–5pm
Services Valuations, restoration,
nationwide delivery, overseas
shipping arranged

⊞ **Buckingham Antiques**
Contact Mrs H Wilson
⊠ 17 Bridge Street, Helmsley,
York, North Yorkshire,
YO62 5BG ℗
☎ 01439 771642
Est. 1997 *Stock size* Large
Stock General antiques, jewellery
Open Tues–Sat 10am–5pm
Services Sourcing

⊞ **Castle Gate Antiques**
Contact Mr D Hartshorne
⊠ 14 Castlegate, Helmsley, York,
North Yorkshire,
YO62 5AB ℗
☎ 01439 771580 ❻ 01439 770370
Est. 1999 *Stock size* Large
Stock General antiques
Open Mon–Sun 10.30am–5pm
Services Valuations

⊞ **Helmsley Antiquarian**
& Secondhand Books
Contact Mr M Moorby
⊠ Old Fire Station, Borogate,
Helmsley, North Yorkshire,

YO62 5BN 🅿
☎ 01439 770014
Est. 1985 *Stock size* Medium
Stock Antique, rare, and second-hand books, Yorkshire topography a speciality
Open Mon–Sat 10am–5pm
Sun noon–5pm

⊞ Westway Pine
Contact Mr J Dzierzek
✉ Carlton Lane, Helmsley, North Yorkshire, YO62 5HB 🅿
☎ 01439 771399 ☏ 01439 771401
🅔 westway-pine@btopenworld.com
Est. 1987 *Stock size* Large
Stock Antique pine, French and English oak furniture, antique pine
Open Mon–Fri 9am–5pm Sat 10am–5pm Sun 1–5pm closed Tues
Services Valuations, restoration

KILLINGHALL

⋏ Thompsons Auctioneers
Contact Mr B D Thompson
✉ The Dales Salesroom, Levens Hall Park, Lund Lane, Killinghall, Harrogate, North Yorkshire, HG3 2BG 🅿
☎ 01423 709086 ☏ 01423 709085
🅔 bryan@thompsonsauctions.co.uk
🅦 ww.thompsonsauctioneers.co.uk
Est. 1989
Open Mon–Fri 9am–5pm
Sat 9.30am–noon closed Thurs pm
Sales General antiques and collectables sale
Frequency Weekly on Fri, quarterly toys
Catalogues Yes

KNARESBOROUGH

⊞ Early Oak
Contact Mr André Gora
✉ Knaresborough, North Yorkshire, HG5
☎ 01904 627823
🅔 info@earlyoak.co.uk
🅦 www.earlyoak.co.uk
Est. 1985 *Stock size* Large
Stock Oak and country furniture, samplers, rugs, Delft and other ceramics, pewter, metalware
Open By appointment
Fairs Newark

⊞ Frantique
Contact Mr I Hughes
✉ 20 The High Street,

Knaresborough, North Yorkshire, HG5 0EQ 🅿
☎ 01423 797799 ☏ 01943 463380
Ⓜ 07802 740012
🅔 ivor@frantique.fsnet.co.uk
🅦 www.frantique.co.uk
Est. 1998 *Stock size* Medium
Stock Continental decorative arts, including faïence, kitchen antiques, clocks, bronzes, glass, metalware, enamelware
Open Mon–Sat 11am–4pm
Sun noon–4pm
Services Anglo-French antiques press relations and translation

⊞ John Thompson Antiques (LAPADA)
Contact Mr John Thompson
✉ Swadforth House, Gracious Street, Knaresborough, North Yorkshire, HG5 8DT 🅿
☎ 01423 864698 ☏ 01423 864698
Ⓜ 07831 899948
Est. 1967 *Stock size* Medium
Stock Fine 18th–19thC furniture, related decorative objects
Open Mon–Sat 9am–5.30pm or by appointment
Fairs Olympia

⋏ Thornton & Linley
Contact Mr I A Thornton
✉ 2–4 Jockey Lane, High Street, Knaresborough, North Yorkshire, HG5 0HG 🅿
☎ 01423 862271 ☏ 01423 862271
🅔 thornton.linley@virgin.net
Est. 1909
Open Tues–Fri 9am–5pm closed 1–2pm
Sales General antiques
Frequency Periodic
Catalogues Yes

LEALHOLM

⊞ Stepping Stones
Contact Mrs J Davies
✉ Lealholm, Whitby, North Yorkshire, YO21 2AJ 🅿
☎ 01947 897382
Est. 1974 *Stock size* Medium
Stock General antiques, books
Open Daily 10am–5pm please phone in winter

LEYBURN

⌂ Leyburn Antiques Centre
Contact Paul Ashford
✉ Harmby Road, Leyburn,

North Yorkshire, DL8 5NF 🅿
☎ 01969 625555 ☏ 01969 625507
Est. 2001 *Stock size* Large
No. of dealers 36
Stock General antiques, collectables
Open Mon–Sun 10.30am–4.30pm

⋏ Tennants Auctioneers (BACA Award Winner 2000, 2001)
Contact Mr Rodney Tennant
✉ The Auction Centre, Leyburn, North Yorkshire, DL8 5SG 🅿
☎ 01969 623780 ☏ 01969 624281
🅔 enquiry@tennants-ltd.co.uk
🅦 www.tennants.co.uk
Open Mon–Fri 9am–5pm
Sales Frequent general antiques sales. 3 fine art sales per annum, 3 book sales and collectors' sales per annum
Catalogues Yes

MALTON

⋏ Boulton & Cooper Fine Art (SOFAA)
Contact Mr A McMillan
✉ Forsyth House, Market Place, Malton, North Yorkshire, YO17 7LR 🅿
☎ 01653 696151 ☏ 01653 600311
🅔 antiques@boultoncooper.co.uk
Est. 1801
Open Mon–Fri 9am–5.30pm
Sat by appointment
Sales General antiques
Frequency Alternate months
Catalogues Yes

⋏ Cundalls (FAAV)
Contact Jackie Barker
✉ 15 Market Place, Malton, North Yorkshire, YO17 7LP
☎ 01653 697820 ☏ 01653 698305
🅔 malton@cundalls.co.uk
🅦 www.cundalls.co.uk
Est. 1860
Open Mon–Fri 9am–5.30pm
Sales General antiques sales, telephone for details
Catalogues Yes

⊞ Matthew Maw
Contact Mr M Maw
✉ 18 Castlegate, Malton, North Yorkshire, YO17 7DT 🅿
☎ 01653 694638 ☏ 01653 694638

Est. 1974 *Stock size* Small
Stock General antiques
Open Mon–Sat 9am–5pm

⊞ Old Talbot Gallery
Contact Mr David Smith
⊠ Old Talbot Gallery, 9 Market
Street, Malton, North Yorkshire,
YO17 7LY 🅿
☎ 01653 696142
Est. 1981 *Stock size* Medium
Stock Books, prints, pictures, maps
Open Please telephone
Services Valuations, restoration

MASHAM

⊞ Aura Antiques
⊠ Silver Street, Masham,
North Yorkshire,
HE4 4DX 🅿
☎ 01765 689315
🅔 robert@aura-antiques.co.uk
🆆 www.aura-antiques.co.uk
Est. 1986 *Stock size* Medium
Stock Georgian, Regency,
mahogany and oak furniture
Open Mon–Sat 10am–4.30pm
Services Delivery throughout UK

MIDDLEHAM

⊞ Middleham Antiques
Contact Mrs Angela Walton
⊠ The Corner Shop, Kirkgate,
Middleham, North Yorkshire,
DL8 4PF 🅿
☎ 01969 622982
🆆 07867 945360
🅔 angiwal@yahoo.com
Est. 1986 *Stock size* Small
Stock Victorian–Edwardian
collectables, decorative arts
Open Sat Sun 10am–5.30pm
telephone call before visiting
recommended or by
appointment

NORTHALLERTON

⚒ Northallerton Auctions Ltd
Contact Brian Weighell
⊠ Applegarth Sales Rooms,
Romanby Road, Northallerton,
North Yorkshire,
DL7 8LZ 🅿
☎ 01609 772034 🅕 01609 778786
🆆 07789 373095
🅔 northallerton@auctionmarts.com
🆆 www.northallertonauction.com
Est. 1920
Open Mon–Fri 9am–5pm

Sat 9am–noon
Sales General antiques
fortnightly, watercolours by
Yorkshire artists, Border Fine Arts
and Beswick, Yorkshire oak
furniture
Frequency Fortnightly
Catalogues Yes

NORTON

⊞ Northern Antiques Co
Contact Mrs Ashby-Arnold
⊠ 2 Parliament Street,
Scarborough Road, Norton,
Malton, North Yorkshire,
YO17 9HE 🅿
☎ 01653 697520 🅕 01653 690056
Est. 1990 *Stock size* Medium
Stock Georgian–Victorian
furniture, decorative accessories
Open Mon–Fri 9am–5pm closed
1–2pm Sat 9.30am–12.30pm

PATELEY BRIDGE

⊞ H S C Fine Arts Ltd
Contact David Hinchliffe
⊠ 45 High Street, Pateley Bridge,
North Yorkshire,
HG3 5LB 🅿
☎ 01423 712218
🅔 rhinch4426@aol.com
🆆 www.earlyantique-glass.co.uk
Est. 1997 *Stock size* Medium
Stock Small furniture, porcelain,
Royal Worcester, pictures, 18thC
wine glasses
Open By appointment

⊞ Brian Loomes (BACA Award Winner 2001)
Contact Brian Loomes
⊠ Calf Haugh Farm,
Pateley Bridge, Harrogate,
North Yorkshire,
HG3 5HW 🅿
☎ 01423 711163
🅔 clocks@brianloomes.com
🆆 www.brianloomes.com
Est. 1966 *Stock size* Large
Stock British clocks
Open By appointment
Services Restoration, valuation,
author of several books on
British clocks

⊞ Needfull Things Ltd
Contact Rebecca Hinchliffe
⊠ 32 High Street, Pateley Bridge,
North Yorkshire,
HG3 5JZ 🅿
☎ 01423 712851 🅕 01423 712851

🅔 rhinch4426@aol.com
Est. 1999 *Stock size* Medium
Stock Jewellery, glassware,
ceramics
Open Fri–Sun 10am–4pm or by
appointment

⊞ David South (HADA)
Contact James South or
David South
⊠ 15 High Street, Pateley Bridge,
North Yorkshire,
HG3 5AP 🅿
☎ 01423 712022 🅕 01423 712412
🅔 sales@davidsouth.co.uk
🆆 www.davidsouth.co.uk
Est. 1985 *Stock size* Medium
Stock Upholstered furniture
Open Mon–Sat 9am–5.30pm
Services Restoration

PICKERING

⊞ Country Collector
Contact Grahame Berney
⊠ 11–12 Birdgate, Pickering,
North Yorkshire,
YO18 7AL 🅿
☎ 01751 477481
🅔 enquiries@country-collector.co.uk
🆆 www.country-collector.co.uk
Est. 1992 *Stock size* Small
Stock Art Deco, ceramics, blue
and white china, glass, silver,
metalware, collectables
Open Mon–Sat 10am–5pm
closed Wed
Services Valuations

⊞ Inch's Books (PBFA, ABA)
Contact Mr P Inch
⊠ 6 Westgate, Pickering,
North Yorkshire,
YO18 8BA 🅿
☎ 01751 474928 🅕 01751 475939
🅔 inchs.books@dial.pipex.com
🆆 www.inchsbooks.co.uk
Est. 1982 *Stock size* Medium
Stock Antique and second-hand
books
Open By appointment
Fairs ABA Chelsea, PBFA June fair
Services Mail order, catalogues
(8 per year)

⌂ Pickering Antique Centre
Contact Mrs C Vance
⊠ Southgate, Pickering,
North Yorkshire,
YO18 8BN 🅿
☎ 01751 477210 🅕 01751 477210

sales@pickantiques.freeserve.co.uk
Est. 1998 *Stock size* Large
No. of dealers 40
Stock General antiques,
bedsteads, furniture, glass,
books, postcards, pictures,
collectables
Open Mon–Sun 10am–5pm
Services Valuations, metal
restoration service, pine
stripping, delivery

Pickering Antique Centre (Hawthorn House Antiques)
Contact D Lloyd Williams
✉ Unit 21, Southgate, Pickering,
North Yorkshire,
YO18 8BL
☎ 01653 693016
dlloydwilliams@btopenworld.com
Est. 1976 *Stock size* Medium
Stock Mixed cross section,
Georgian and Victorian
glassware, pictures, prints
Open Mon–Sun 10am–5pm
Services Valuations, restoration

C H & D M Reynolds
Contact Mr Colin Reynolds
✉ The Curiosity Shop,
122 Eastgate, Pickering,
North Yorkshire,
YO18 7DW
☎ 01751 472785
☏ 07714 355676
Est. 1949 *Stock size* Large
Stock General antiques,
furniture, curios
Open Mon–Sat 9.30am–5.30pm
Sun by appointment
Services Valuations

Stable Antiques
Contact Mrs Yvonne Kitching-
Walker

✉ Pickering Antique Centre,
Southgate, Pickering,
North Yorkshire,
YO18 8BN
☎ 01751 477210
Est. 1998 *Stock size* Medium
Stock General antiques
Open Mon–Sun 10am–5pm

RICHMOND

York House (Antiques)
Contact Mrs Christine Swift
✉ 60 Market Place, Richmond,
North Yorkshire,
DL10 4JQ
☎ 01748 850338
☏ 07711 307045
christina.swift@tiscali.co.uk
Est. 1997 *Stock size* Medium
Stock Oak, mahogany, pine
furniture, general antiques,
furnishings, chandeliers,
fireplaces
Open Mon–Sat 9.30am–5.30pm
Sun noon–4pm
Services Restoration, pine
stripping

RIPON

Hornsey's of Ripon
Contact Bruce, Susan or
Daniel Hornsey
✉ 3 Kirkgate, Ripon,
North Yorkshire,
HG4 1PA
☎ 01765 602878 ☏ 01765 601692
hornseys@ripon-internet.co.uk
Est. 1974 *Stock size* Large
Stock Antiques, collectables, rare
books, fine linen, lace, maps,
prints
Open Mon–Sat 9am–5.30pm or
by appointment
Services Valuations

Sigma Antiques
Contact Mr David Thomson
✉ The Old Opera House,
Water Skellgate, Ripon,
North Yorkshire,
HG4 1BH
☎ 01765 603163 ☏ 01765 603163
Est. 1964 *Stock size* Large
Stock General antiques
Open Mon–Sat 9am–5.30pm

Skellgate Curios
Contact Mrs J Wayne
✉ 2 Low Skellgate, Ripon,
North Yorkshire,
HG4 1BE
☎ 01765 601290
Est. 1975 *Stock size* Medium
Stock General antiques
Open Mon–Sat 11am–5pm
closed Wed

ROBIN HOOD'S BAY

John Gilbert Antiques
Contact John Gilbert
✉ King Street, Robin Hood's Bay,
Whitby, North Yorkshire,
YO22 4SY
☎ 01947 880528
Est. 1990 *Stock size* Medium
Stock 18th–19thC oak, country
furniture, treen
Open Mon Tues Thurs 2–4pm
telephone call advisable Sat
10am–1pm Sun 10am–4pm or by
appointment
Services Valuations, restoration

SALTBURN-BY-THE-SEA

Anderson Antiques
Contact Mrs K Anderson
✉ 20 Milton Street, Saltburn-by-the-
Sea, Cleveland, North Yorkshire,
TS12 1DG

☎ 01287 624810 ❶ 01287 625349
❿ 07798 587622
✉ andersak@fsbdial.co.uk
Est. 1996 *Stock size* Medium
Stock Furniture, pictures,
porcelain, jewellery, clocks, linen
Open Mon–Sat 10am–5pm
closed Wed
Services Valuations

⚒ J C Simmons & Son
Contact Mr TJ Aked
✉ Saltburn Salerooms, Diamond
Street, Saltburn-by-the-Sea,
North Yorkshire,
TS12 1EB ▣
☎ 01287 622366
❿ www.saltburnsalerooms.co.uk
Est. 1949
Open Viewing Sat and Mon
10am–4pm
Sales General antiques
Frequency Periodic
Catalogues Yes

⊞ Jösef Thompson
Contact Jösef Thompson
✉ Saltburn Bookshop,
3 Amber Street, Saltburn-by-the-
Sea, Cleveland, North Yorkshire,
TS12 1DT ▣
☎ 01287 623335
✉ joseftthompson@freeuk.com
Est. 1977 *Stock size* Large
Stock Second-hand books
Open March–Oct Mon–Sat
11am–1pm 2–5pm Nov–Feb
Mon–Sat 11am–1pm 2–4pm
Services Book search

⌂ Antique and Collector's
Centre (PTA)
Contact Colin Spink
✉ 35 St Nicholas Cliff,
Scarborough, North Yorkshire,
YO11 2ES ▣
☎ 01723 365221
❿ 07730 202405
✉ spink@collectors.demon.co.uk
❿ www.collectors.demon.co.uk
Est. 1965 *Stock size* Medium
Stock General antique jewellery,
ephemera, cigarette cards, coins,
postcards, antiques,
commemorative ware, etc
Open Mon–Sat 10am–4.30pm
Services Valuations

⊞ Bar Bookstore (The
Antiquary Ltd) (PBFA)
Contact Mr M Chaddock

✉ 4 Swan Hill Road,
Scarborough, North Yorkshire,
YO11 1BW ▣
☎ 01723 500141
✉ antiquary@btinternet.com
Est. 1976 *Stock size* Medium
Stock Antiquarian, rare and
second-hand books
Open Tues–Sat 10.30am–5pm
Fairs York, Harrogate, Darlington
Services Valuations, book search

⚒ David Duggleby Fine
Art
Contact Jane Duggleby
✉ The Vine Street Salerooms,
Scarborough, North Yorkshire,
YO11 1XN ▣
☎ 01723 507111 ❶ 01723 507222
✉ auctions@davidduggleby.com
❿ www.davidduggleby.com
Est. 1996
Open Mon–Fri 8.30am–5pm
Sales Fortnightly 500-lot house
contents and Victoriana sales,
700 lots of fine art and antiques
every 8 weeks. Picture sales Sept
and March at the Paddock
Salerooms, Whitby
Catalogues Yes

⊞ Now & Then Antiques
Contact Richard Ellis
✉ 7 The Crescent, Selby,
North Yorkshire,
YO8 4PD ▣
☎ 01757 708138 ❶ 01757 708138
❿ www.nowandthenuk.com
Est. 1992 *Stock size* Medium
Stock General antiques
Open Mon–Sat 9am–5pm
Services Valuations, restoration,
pine stripping

⊞ Potterton Books
Contact Mrs Clare Jameson
✉ The Old Rectory, Sessay,
Nr Thirsk, North Yorkshire,
YO7 3LZ ▣
☎ 01845 501218 ❶ 01845 501439
✉ enquiries@pottertonbooks.co.uk
❿ www.pottertonbooks.co.uk
Est. 1980
Stock Fine and decorative arts
books
Open Mon–Fri 9am–5pm
Fairs Fine Art Olympia, Decorex
International
Services Book search

⊞ Mary Milnthorpe
& Daughters
Contact Miss Judith Milnthorpe
✉ Market Place, Settle,
North Yorkshire,
BD24 9DX ▣
☎ 01729 822331 ❶ 01729 823062
Est. 1959 *Stock size* Medium
Stock Antique jewellery, silver
Open Mon–Sat 9.30am–5pm
closed Wed
Services Valuations, repairs

⊞ Nanbooks
Contact Mrs J L Midgley
✉ Roundabout,
41 Duke Street, Settle,
North Yorkshire,
BD24 9DJ ▣
☎ 01729 823324
✉ midglui@aol.com
Est. 1955 *Stock size* Medium
Stock English and Continental
ceramics, some 18th–19thC glass
Open Tues Fri Sat 11am–5pm
closed 12.30–2pm or by
appointment

⊞ Thistlethwaite
Antiques
Contact Mr E C Thistlethwaite
✉ Market Square, Settle,
North Yorkshire,
BD24 9EF ▣
☎ 01729 822460
Est. 1978 *Stock size* Medium
Stock 18th–19thC country
furniture, metalware
Open Mon–Sat 9am–5pm closed
Wed

⚒ Malcolms No 1
Auctioneers & Valuers
Contact Mr Malcolm Dowson
✉ The Chestnuts, 16 Park
Avenue, Sherburn-in-Elmet,
North Yorkshire,
LS25 6EF ▣
☎ 01977 684971 ❶ 01977 681046
❿ 07774 130784
✉ info@malcolmsno1auctions.co.uk
❿ www.malcolmsno1auctions.co.uk
Est. 1980
Open Mon–Fri 9am–5pm
Sales Antiques and collectables,
named ceramics (all periods),
viewing Mon 10am–6.15pm
Sun 1–6pm. Held at Trustees Hall,
High Street, Boston Spa,

Wetherby, West Yorkshire
Frequency Monthly
Catalogues Yes

SKIPTON

⌂ **Skipton Antiques
& Collectors Centre**
Contact Ann Hall
✉ The Old Foundry, Cavendish
Street, Skipton, North Yorkshire,
BD23 2AB ♿
☎ 01756 797667
Est. 1995 *Stock size* Large
No. of dealers 30
Stock General antiques and
collectables, Art Deco, clocks,
books, ceramics, pine, etc
Open Mon–Sat 10.30am–4.30pm
Sun 11am–4pm

SLEIGHTS

⊞ **Eskdale Antiques**
Contact Mr P Smith
✉ 164 Coach Road, Sleights,
Whitby, North Yorkshire,
YO22 5EQ ♿
☎ 01947 810297
Ⓜ 07813 589117
Est. 1979 *Stock size* Medium
Stock Antique stripped pine,
garden ornaments
Open Tues–Sun 9.30am–5pm
Services Valuations

SLINGSBY

⊞ **Tony Popek Antiques**
Contact Mr E Popek
✉ West View, Railway Street,
Slingsby, York, North Yorkshire,
YO62 4AH ♿
☎ 01653 628533/01751 430978
Ⓜ 07973 292956
Est. 1989 *Stock size* Medium
Stock General antiques
Open By appointment
Fairs Harrogate, Swinderby, Newark

STAITHES

⊞ **Staithes Antiques**
Contact Mrs Sweeting
✉ 28 High Street, Staithes,
North Yorkshire,
TS13 5BH ♿
☎ 01947 840313
Est. 1998 *Stock size* Medium
Stock Small furniture, general
antiques
Open Easter–October Tues–Sun
11am–5pm or by appointment

STOCKTON-ON-TEES

➤ **Vectis Auctions Ltd**
Contact Debbie Cockerill
✉ Fleck Way, Thornaby,
Stockton-on-Tees, Cleveland,
North Yorkshire,
TS17 9JZ ♿
☎ 01642 750616 🖷 01642 769478
📧 admin@vectis.co.uk
🌐 www.vectis.co.uk
Est. 1990
Open Mon–Fri 9am–5pm
Sales Collectable toy sales
Frequency Monthly
Catalogues Yes

STOKESLEY

➤ **Lithgow Sons
& Partners**
Contact Richard Storry
✉ The Auction Houses,
Station Road, Stokesley,
North Yorkshire,
TS9 7AB ♿
☎ 01642 710158 🖷 01642 712641
📧 info@lithgowsauctions.com
🌐 www.lithgowsauctions.com
Est. 1868
Open Mon–Fri 9am–5pm
Sales Weekly sale Wed 10.30am
viewing Tues noon–4pm
Catalogues Yes

⊞ **Mantle Antiques**
Contact Mr Derek Bushby
✉ 23 College Square, Stokesley,
North Yorkshire,
TS9 5DL ♿
☎ 01642 714313
Ⓜ 07713 155772
Est. 1973 *Stock size* Medium
Stock Victorian furniture,
architectural antiques
Open Tues Thurs–Sat 10am–4pm
Fairs Newark, Swinderby

⊞ **Alan Ramsey Antiques
(LAPADA)**
Contact Mr Alan Ramsey
✉ 7 Wainstones Court,
Stokesley Industrial Estate,
Stokesley, North Yorkshire,
TS9 5JY ♿
☎ 01642 713008
Ⓜ 07702 523246 or 07762 049848
📧 a.ramseyantiques@btinternet.com
🌐 www.alanramseyantiques.co.uk
Est. 1970 *Stock size* Large
Stock Georgian–Edwardian
furniture, clocks
Open By appointment

TADCASTER

➤ **Scarthingwell Auction
Centre**
Contact John Griffiths or
Christine Bridge
✉ Scarthingwell, Tadcaster,
North Yorkshire,
LS24 9PG ♿
☎ 01937 557955 🖷 01937 557955
Ⓜ 07778 520463
🌐 www.scarthingwellauctions.co.uk
Est. 1990
Open Mon–Fri 10am–5pm
Sales Antiques and general sales
Tues 5pm every 2–3 weeks,
viewing Sun prior to sale
noon–5pm Tues 2pm or by
appointment
Catalogues Yes

THIRSK

⊞ **Hambleton Books**
Contact Mr T F Parr
✉ 43 Market Place, Thirsk,
North Yorkshire,
YO7 1HA ♿
☎ 01845 522343
📧 hambooks@btinternet.com
Est. 1979 *Stock size* Medium
Stock Antique, rare and second-
hand books, books on cricket a
speciality
Open Mon–Sat 9am–5.30pm
Sun 10am–4pm

⊞ **Millgate Antiques**
Contact Tim Parvin
✉ Abel Grange, Newsham Road,
Thirsk, North Yorkshire,
YO7 4DB ♿
☎ 01845 523878 🖷 01845 523878
Ⓜ 07966 251609
📧 babs.jenkins@btinternet.com
Est. 1991 *Stock size* Large
Stock Pine furniture, panelled
doors
Open Mon–Sat 8.30am–5pm
Services Stripping, restoration

THORNTON-LE-DALE

⊞ **Cobweb Books**
Contact Mr Robin Buckler
✉ Ye Olde Corner Shoppe,
1 Pickering Road, Thornton-le-
Dale, North Yorkshire,
YO19 7LG ♿
☎ 01751 476638
📧 sales@cobwebbooks.co.uk
🌐 www.cobwebbooks.co.uk
Est. 1991 *Stock size* Medium

Stock Antiquarian, rare and second-hand books
Open Tues–Sun 10am–5pm
Fairs Royal National Hotel Book Fair, London
Services Book search

TOCKWITH

⊞ Tomlinson Antiques (LAPADA, CINOA)
Contact Sarah Worrall
⊠ Moorside, Tockwith, York, North Yorkshire, YO26 7QG ⓟ
☎ 01423 358833 ⓕ 01423 358188
ⓔ info@antique-furniture.co.uk
ⓦ antique-furniture.co.uk
Est. 1977 *Stock size* Large
Stock Quality Georgian–pre-war furniture, china, silver, silver plate, longcase clocks, rugs, Art Deco, reproduction furniture
Trade only Mon–Fri; retail club at weekends
Open Mon–Fri 9am–5pm
Sun 10am–4pm
Services Restoration, shipping, bespoke manufacturing service

UPPER POPPLETON

⌖ D Wombell & Son
Contact Mr W Rice
⊠ Northminster Business Park, Upper Poppleton, York, North Yorkshire, YO26 6QU ⓟ
☎ 01904 790777 ⓕ 01904 798018
ⓦ www.invaluable.com/wombell
Est. 1984
Open Mon–Fri 10am–5pm
Sales General antiques, monthly on Sat viewing on Fri 10am–7pm
Frequency Monthly
Catalogues Yes

WHITBY

⊞ Abbey Antiques
Contact Mr A L Barsby
⊠ 4 & 5 Grape Lane, Whitby, North Yorkshire, YO22 4DD ⓟ
☎ 01947 821424
Est. 1996 *Stock size* Large
Stock General antiques, collectables
Open Flexible, please telephone

⊞ Clewlow Antiques (PBFA)
Contact Mr A Clewlow
⊠ Sandringham House,

6–8 Skinner Street, Whitby, North Yorkshire, YO21 3AJ
☎ 01947 825508
ⓔ fiona.clewlow@ntlworld.com
Est. 1977 *Stock size* Large
Stock General antiques
Open Summer Mon–Sat 10am–5pm winter Fri Sat only

⊞ Curio Corner
Contact Mr A L Barsby
⊠ 7 Market Place, Whitby, North Yorkshire, YO22 4DD ⓟ
☎ 01947 821424
Est. 1969 *Stock size* Small
Stock General antiques, collectables
Open Flexible hours or by appointment

⊞ Endeavour Books
Contact Mrs L Allison
⊠ 1 Grape Lane, Whitby, North Yorkshire, YO22 4BA ⓟ
☎ 01947 821331
ⓔ linda@enbooks.co.uk
ⓦ www.enbooks.co.uk
Est. 1989 *Stock size* Medium
Stock Rare and second-hand books
Open Mon–Sun summer 10am–8pm winter 10.30am–5pm

⊞ Eskdale Antiques
Contact Mr P Smith
⊠ 85 Church Street, Whitby, North Yorkshire, YO22 4BH
☎ 01947 600512
Est. 1982 *Stock size* Medium
Stock Ceramics, pictures, bottles, advertisements
Open Easter–Oct Mon–Sun 10.30am–5pm or by appointment

⊞ Picfair Antiques
Contact Mr J Robertson
⊠ 67 Haggersgate, Whitby, North Yorkshire, YO21 3PP ⓟ
☎ 01947 602483
ⓔ picfair@amserve.net
ⓦ www.picfairantique.com
Est. 1987 *Stock size* Medium
Stock General antiques including glass, costume jewellery, porcelain
Open Mon–Sun noon–6pm
Services Valuations, advice to collectors

⊞ The Staffordshire Knot
Contact Ricky Clarke
⊠ The Shambles Market, Market Place, Whitby, North Yorkshire, YO22 4TY
ⓜ 07796 595465
Est. 2004 *Stock size* Medium
Stock Ceramics, glass, Art Deco
Open Mon–Sun 10am–5.30pm

YARM

⊞ Farthing
Contact Shirley Smith or Sybil Watson
⊠ 57a High Street, Yarm, Cleveland, North Yorkshire, TS15 9BH ⓟ
☎ 01642 785881
Est. 1977 *Stock size* Medium
Stock General antiques, prints, gifts
Open Mon–Sat 9.30am–5.30pm
Services Picture framing

YORK

⊞ Abacus
Contact Julian White
⊠ Common End Farm, Thornton, Melbourne, York, North Yorkshire, YO42 4RZ ⓟ
☎ 01759 318575 ⓕ 01759 318136
ⓔ abacus03@globalnet.co.uk
Est. 1975 *Stock size* Large
Stock Architectural, fireplaces
Open Mon–Sat 8.30am–4.30pm
Services Fitting service

⊞ Advena Antiques & Fairs
Contact Alan White
⊠ Cavendish Antique Centre, 44 Stonegate, York, North Yorkshire, YO1 8AS
☎ 01904 668785
ⓜ 07713 150510
ⓔ advena.antiques@ntlworld.com
Est. 1992 *Stock size* Medium
Stock Antique silver, jewellery
Open Mon–Sat 9am–6pm
Sun 10am–4pm
Services Valuations, repairs

⌂ The Antiques Centre York
Contact Liz Robson
⊠ 41 Stonegate, York, North Yorkshire, YO1 8AW ⓟ
☎ 01904 635888 ⓕ 01904 676342

ⓦ www.theantiquescentreyork.co.uk
Est. 1996 *Stock size* Large
No. of dealers 100
Stock General antiques, collectables
Open Mon–Sun 9am–6pm
Services Café

⊞ Bishopgate Antiques
Contact Mr R Wetherill
⊠ 23–24 Bishopgate, York,
North Yorkshire,
YO23 1JH **P**
☎ 01904 623893 **☉** 01904 626511
Est. 1965 *Stock size* Medium
Stock General antiques
Open Tues–Sat 9.15am–6pm

⊞ Brigantia Ltd (ADA)
Contact John Moor
⊠ The Red House Antiques
Centre, The Red House,
1 Duncombe Place, York,
North Yorkshire,
YO1 7ED **P**
☎ 01904 624062
☉ lindsay@ancientworldyork.co.uk
Est. 1975 *Stock size* Medium
Stock Ancient coins, antiquities
Open Mon–Fri 9.30am–5.30pm
Sat 9.30am–5pm Sun
10.30am–5.30pm July–Sep
Mon–Fri 9.30am–7pm
Fairs ADA

⊞ Barbara Cattle (BADA)
Contact Mr Richard Pool
⊠ 45 Stonegate, York,
North Yorkshire,
YO1 8AW
☎ 01904 623862
☉ info@barbaracattle.co.uk
ⓦ www.barbaracattle.co.uk
Stock Jewellery, silver, old
Sheffield plate
Open Mon–Sat 9am–5.30pm
Services Valuations, repairs,
restoration

⌂ Cavendish Antiques
& Collectors Centre
Contact Debbie or Mark Smith
⊠ 44 Stonegate, York,
North Yorkshire, YO1 8AS
☎ 01904 621666 **☉** 01904 675747
ⓦ www.cavendishantiques.co.uk
Est. 1999 *Stock size* Large
No. of dealers 60
Stock General antiques
Open Mon–Sun 9am–6pm

⊞ Mike Fineron Cigarette
Cards & Postcards
Contact Mike Fineron

⊠ 28 The Pastures,
Dringhouses, York,
North Yorkshire,
YO24 2JE **P**
☎ 01904 703911
☉ fineronmikef@yahoo.co.uk
Est. 1997 *Stock size* Medium
Stock Cigarette cards, postcards,
Yorkshire postcards a speciality
Open By appointment
Fairs Pudsey, Chester le Street,
Sheffield
Services Valuations, postal
service

⊞ Foss Gate Books
Contact Mr Alex Helstrip
⊠ 36 Fossgate, York,
North Yorkshire,
YO1 9TF **P**
☎ 01904 641389 **☉** 0870 420 4372
Est. 1984 *Stock size* Medium
Stock Antiquarian, scholarly and
second-hand books
Open Mon–Sat 10am–5.30pm

⊞ French House Antiques
Contact Steve
⊠ 74 Micklegate, York,
North Yorkshire,
YO1 6LF **P**
☎ 01904 624465 **☉** 01904 629965
☉ info@thefrenchhouse.co.uk
ⓦ www.thefrenchhouse.co.uk
Est. 1995 *Stock size* Large
Stock 18th-19thC chandeliers,
mirrors, beds
Open Mon–Sat 9.30am–5.30pm

⊞ Harpers Jewellers Ltd
Contact Nicholas Wiseman
⊠ 2–6 Minster Gates, York,
North Yorkshire,
YO1 7HL
☎ 01904 632634 **☉** 01904 673370
☉ info@vintage-watches.co.uk
ⓦ www.vintage-watches.co.uk
Est. 1990 *Stock size* Large
Stock Jewellery, watches
Open Mon–Sat 9am–5.30pm
Services Valuations

⊞ Hunts Pine (GADAR)
Contact Steve Evely
⊠ Unit 6a, Victoria Farm,
Water Lane, York,
North Yorkshire,
YO30 6PQ **P**
☎ 01904 690561 **☉** 01904 690561
☉ yorkvale@hotmail.com
Est. 1995 *Stock size* Medium
Stock Antique pine furniture
Open Mon–Fri 9am–5.30pm

Sat 9am–2pm
Fairs Newark
Services Stripping

⊞ Laurel Bank Antiques
Contact Mr K Lamb
⊠ 52 Clarence Street, York,
North Yorkshire,
YO31 7EW **P**
☎ 01904 676030
☉ sales@laurelbankantiques.co.uk
ⓦ www.laurelbankantiques.co.uk
Est. 1997 *Stock size* Medium
Stock General antiques,
collectables,
Georgian–Edwardian furniture,
longcase, wall and mantel clocks
Open Mon–Sat 10am–5pm
closed Tues
Services Restoration, French
polishing

⊞ Minstergate Bookshop
(PBFA)
Contact Mr N Wallace
⊠ 8 Minster Gates, York,
North Yorkshire,
YO1 7HL
☎ 01904 621812 **☉** 01904 622960
☉ rarebooks@minstergatebooks.co.uk
ⓦ www.minstergatebooks.co.uk
Est. 1977 *Stock size* Medium
Stock Books, children's and
illustrated books a speciality
Open Mon–Sun 10am–5.30pm
Services Valuations

⊞ Janette Ray Rare Books
(PBFA, ABA)
Contact Miss J Ray
⊠ 8 Bootham, York,
North Yorkshire,
YO30 7BL **P**
☎ 01904 623088 **☉** 01904 625528
☉ books@janetteray.co.uk
ⓦ www.janetteray.co.uk
Est. 1995 *Stock size* Medium
Stock Architectural and
decorative arts, rare and second-
hand books, landscape design,
gardens, specializing in 19thC
Arts and Crafts, Art Deco,
Modernism
Open Fri–Sat 10am–5.30pm other
times by appointment
Fairs York PBFA, London PBFA
Services Book search, valuations

⌂ The Red House
Antiques Centre
Contact Mrs P Stephenson
⊠ Duncombe Place, York,
North Yorkshire,

YO1 7ED 🅿
☎ 01904 637000 ✆ 01904 637000
✉ enquires@redhouseyork.co.uk
Ⓦ www.redhouseyork.co.uk
Est. 1999 *Stock size* Large
No. of dealers 60
Stock Datelined quality antiques, from antiques to the best of the 20thC decorative antiques
Open Mon–Fri 9.30am–5.30pm
Sat 9.30am–6pm Sun
10.30am–5.30pm July–Sep
Mon–Fri 9.30am–7pm

↗ John Simpson
Contact Mr John Simpson
✉ 4 Forest Grove, Stockton Lane, York, North Yorkshire, YO3 0BL 🅿
☎ 01904 424797
Est. 1984
Open By appointment
Sales General antiques
Frequency Quarterly
Catalogues Yes

⊞ J Smith (BNTA)
Contact Mr J Smith
✉ 47 Shambles, York, North Yorkshire, YO1 7LX
☎ 01904 654769 ✆ 01904 677988
Est. 1963 *Stock size* Large
Stock Coins, stamps, medals
Open Mon–Sat 9am–4pm
Services Valuations

⊞ Ken Spelman (ABA, PBFA, ILAB)
Contact P Miller or A Fothergill
✉ 70 Micklegate, York, North Yorkshire, YO1 6LF 🅿
☎ 01904 624414 ✆ 01904 626276
✉ rarebooks@kenspelman.com
Ⓦ www.kenspelman.com
Est. 1948 *Stock size* Large
Stock Antique, rare, second-hand books
Open Mon–Sat 9am–5.30pm
Fairs Olympia
Services Valuations, restoration, catalogues

⊞ Taikoo Books Ltd
Contact Mr David Chilton
✉ 46 Bootham, York, North Yorkshire, YO30 7BZ 🅿
☎ 01904 641213
Est. 1978 *Stock size* Large
Stock Books on Africa and the Orient
Open Mon–Fri 10am–5pm or by appointment

⌂ York Antiques Centre
Contact Mr S Revere
✉ 2a Lendal, York, North Yorkshire, YO1 8AA
☎ 01904 641445
Est. 1984 *Stock size* Large
No. of dealers 15
Stock General antiques
Open Mon–Sat 10am–5pm

⊞ York Vale Antiques (GADAR)
Contact Steve Evely
✉ Unit 6a, Victoria Farm, Water Lane, York, North Yorkshire, YO30 6PQ 🅿
☎ 01904 690561 ✆ 01904 690561
✉ yorkvale@hotmail.com
Est. 1995 *Stock size* Medium
Stock General antique furniture
Open Mon–Fri 9am–5.30pm
Sat 9am–2pm
Fairs Newark
Services Restoration, repairs

SOUTH YORKSHIRE

BARLOW

⊞ Byethorpe Antiques
Contact John Gelsthorpe
✉ Shippen Rural Business Centre, Church Farm, Barlow, South Yorkshire, SI8 7TR 🅿
☎ 0114 289 9111
Ⓦ www.byethorpe.com
Est. 1977 *Stock size* Medium
Stock Traditional oak and mahogany furniture
Open Mon–Sat 9am–5.30pm

BARNSLEY

↗ BBR Auctions
Contact Mr Alan Blakeman
✉ Elsecar Heritage Centre, Barnsley, South Yorkshire, S74 8HJ 🅿
☎ 01226 745156 ✆ 01226 361561
✉ sales@onlinebbr.com
Ⓦ www.onlinebbrauction.com
Est. 1979
Open Mon–Fri 9am–5pm
Sales Antique bottles and pot lids 4 per annum. Antique advertising every 6 months. Doulton, Beswick and 20thC pottery 2 per annum. Kitchenware 2 per annum. Breweriana and pub jugs 2 per annum. All sales Sun 11am, viewing full week prior 9am–5pm
Frequency Quarterly
Catalogues Yes

⌂ Elsecar Antiques Centre
Contact Graham Wilson
✉ The Elsecar Heritage Centre, Wath Road, Elsecar, Barnsley, South Yorkshire, S74 8HJ 🅿
☎ 01226 744425 ✆ 01226 361561
Ⓜ 07712 834895
✉ sales@elsecarantiques.co.uk
Ⓦ www.elsecarantiques.co.uk
Est. 2003 *Stock size* Large
No. of dealers 100
Stock Antiques, collectables, jewellery, dolls, furniture, pottery, glass, Chinese antiquities, collectors' books
Open Mon–Sun 10am–5pm

⊞ Past & Present
Contact Mrs C Wiggett
✉ 224 Aston Road, Bentley, Doncaster, South Yorkshire, DN5 0EU 🅿
☎ 01302 873557
Est. 2002 *Stock size* Large
Stock Furniture, bureaux, desks, pottery, pictures, lamps, light fittings, mirrors
Open Tues–Sun 10am–5pm

⊞ Phoenix Trading Company – South Yorkshire
Contact John A Hallam
✉ 127–129 Askern Road, Bentley, Doncaster, South Yorkshire, DN5 0JH 🅿
☎ 01302 872547
Ⓜ 07801 631072
Est. 1995 *Stock size* Large
Stock Georgian–Victorian furniture, shipping items, brass, copper, ceramics, silver, curios
Open Mon–Sat 9am–5pm
Fairs Newark, Harrogate
Services Restoration, repairs, valuations

CAWTHORNE

⌂ Cawthorne Antique and Collectors Centre
Contact Mr P Gates
✉ 2 Church Street, Cawthorne Village, Barnsley, South Yorkshire,

S75 4HP 🅿
☎ 01226 792237
🌐 www.cawthorneantiques
centre.co.uk
Est. 1997 *Stock size* Large
No. of dealers 50
Stock Wide range of antiques,
collectables, furniture
Open Mon–Sat 10am–4pm
Sun 10.30am–4.30pm closed Wed
Services Tea room

FISHLAKE

⊞ Fishlake Antiques
Contact Fiona Trimingham
✉ Vine Cottage, Hay Green
Corner, Fishlake, South Yorkshire,
DN7 5LA 🅿
☎ 01302 841411
Est. 1979 *Stock size* Medium
Stock Country furniture, clocks
Open Sun 1–4pm or by
appointment
Services Restoration

KILLAMARSH

⊞ Havenplan Ltd
Contact Mrs M Buckle
✉ The Old Station, Station Road,
Killamarsh, Sheffield,
South Yorkshire,
S21 1EN 🅿
☎ 0114 248 9972
📱 07720 635889
Est. 1972 *Stock size* Large
Stock Mainly Victorian pine
furniture, architectural items,
panelling, doors, fireplaces,
troughs, gates, lighting
Open Tues–Thurs Sat 10am–2pm
Services Prop hire

MALTBY

⊞ A J's Antiques
Contact Mr H Hall
✉ 14 Abbey Glen, Carr, Maltby,
Rotherham, South Yorkshire,
S66 8PS 🅿
☎ 01709 816312
🌐 www.internet-antiques.com
Est. 1993 *Stock size* Large
Stock Furniture
Open By appointment
Fairs Swinderby, Newark

MEXBOROUGH

⊞ Roger Appleyard Ltd
(LAPADA)
Contact Roger Appleyard

✉ Whitelea Grove,
Whitelea Industrial Estate,
Mexborough,
South Yorkshire,
S64 9QL 🅿
☎ 01709 590404
📧 roger@rogerappleyard.com
Est. 1971 *Stock size* Large
Stock Turn-of-the-century and
shipping furniture
Trade only Yes
Open Mon–Fri 8am–5pm
Services Shipping

PENISTONE

⊞ Penistone Pine
& Antiques
Contact Mr P W Lucas
✉ Unit 2–3, Sheffield Road,
Penistone, Sheffield,
South Yorkshire,
S36 6HG 🅿
☎ 01226 370018
📱 07891 193828
Est. 1985 *Stock size* Large
Stock Antique, original Victorian
pine furniture
Open Mon–Sat 9am–5pm
Services Restoration, stripping

ROTHERHAM

🏠 Fosters Antiques Centre
Contact Sally Foster
✉ Doncaster Road,
Thrybergh, Rotherham,
South Yorkshire,
S65 4BE 🅿
☎ 01709 850337
Est. 1997 *Stock size* Medium
No. of dealers 20
Stock General antiques,
colectables
Open Mon–Sat 10am–4.30pm
Sun 11am–5pm
Services Coffee shop, garden
centre, craft shop

⊞ John Shaw Antiques Ltd
Contact Mr John Shaw
✉ The Old Methodist Chapel,
Broad Street, Parkgate,
Rotherham, South Yorkshire,
S62 6DL 🅿
☎ 01709 522340
📧 jshaw_antiques@hotmail.com
🌐 www.jshaw-antiques.co.uk
Est. 1969 *Stock size* Large
Stock Wide range of
Victorian–Edwardian furniture,
clocks, pictures, mirrors etc
Open Mon–Fri 9am–5pm

Sat 9.30am–5pm
Services Free valuations
Sat 10am–noon

🏠 Wentworth Arts, Crafts
& Antiques
Contact Jan Sweeting
✉ The Old Builders Yard,
Cortworth Lane, Wentworth,
Rotherham, South Yorkshire,
S62 7SB 🅿
☎ 01729 822051
🌐 www.wentworthartscraftsand
antiques.co.uk
Est. 1999 *Stock size* Large
No. of dealers 53
Stock General antiques, collectables
Open Mon–Sun 10am–5pm
Services Wheelchair access,
coffee shop

SHEFFIELD

⊞ Abbeydale Antiques
Contact Mr D Barks
✉ 639 Abbeydale Road,
Sheffield, South Yorkshire,
S7 1TB 🅿
☎ 0114 255 5646 📠 0114 255 2555
Est. 1974 *Stock size* Large
Stock Pre-1950s furniture
Open By appointment
Fairs Newark, Swinderby

⊞ Acorn Antiques
Contact Mr B Priest
✉ 298 Abbeydale Road,
Sheffield, South Yorkshire,
S7 1FL 🅿
☎ 0114 255 5348 📠 0114 225 5348
📧 info@acornantique.co.uk
Est. 1988 *Stock size* Large
Stock General antiques, small
furniture, collectables
Open Mon–Sat 10am–6pm

🏠 Banners Collectors
& Antiques Centre
Contact Miss S Bates
✉ Banners Business Centre,
Attercliffe Road, Sheffield,
South Yorkshire,
S9 3QS 🅿
☎ 0114 244 0742
Est. 1997 *Stock size* Large
No. of dealers 40
Stock Wide range of antiques,
collectables, Wade, Beanies,
McDonald's, clocks etc
Open Mon–Fri 10am–4.30pm
Sat Sun 11am–4.30pm
Services Lists of goods wanted,
deliveries, collectables bought

331

YORKS & LINCS
SOUTH YORKSHIRE • SHEFFIELD

⌂ Barmouth Court Antique Centre (LAPADA)
Contact Annette, Norman or Chris Salt
✉ Barmouth Court, Barmouth Road, Sheffield, South Yorkshire, S7 2DH 🅿
☎ 0114 255 2711 📠 0114 258 2672
📱 07801 101363
Est. 1999 *Stock size* Large
No. of dealers 50
Stock Complete range of antiques, Art Deco, collectables
Open Mon–Sat 10am–5pm Sun 11am–4pm
Services Valuations

⊞ Beech House
Contact Mr M Beech
✉ 361 Abbeydale Road, Sheffield, South Yorkshire, S7 1FS 🅿
☎ 0114 250 1004 📠 0114 250 1004
📧 beech.house@lineone.net
Est. 1996 *Stock size* Medium
Stock Rustic country pine furniture, cupboards, tables, dressers, chairs, fine art, kitchens
Open Mon–Sat 10am–5pm closed Thurs or by appointment
Fairs Newark, Swinderby, Chatsworth

⌂ Chapel Antiques Centre
Contact Mrs Kate Bonshall
✉ 99 Broadfield Road, Sheffield, South Yorkshire, S8 0XH 🅿
☎ 0114 258 8288 📠 0114 258 8288
📧 info@antiquesinsheffield.com
🌐 www.antiquesinsheffield.com
Est. 1997 *Stock size* Medium
No. of dealers 20
Stock English and French antique furniture, mirrors, chandeliers, garden antiques, discounted upholstery fabrics
Open Mon–Sat 10am–5pm Sun Bank Holidays 11am–5pm
Services Restoration, upholstery, French polishing, custom-made furniture from reclaimed wood, paint effecting, finding service, picture framing

⌂ Courthouse Antiques Centre
Contact Mrs S M Grayson
✉ 2–6 Town End Road, Ecclesfield, Sheffield, South Yorkshire, S35 9YY 🅿
☎ 0114 257 0641

🌐 www.courthouseantiques.co.uk
Est. 1994 *Stock size* Large
No. of dealers 35
Stock Town and country furniture, jewellery, kitchenware, clocks, decorative items, mirrors, books, maps
Open Mon–Sat 10.30am–5pm Sun 11.30am–5pm
Services Tea room

⊞ The Door Stripping Company Ltd
Contact Mr B Findley
✉ 32 Main Road, Renishaw, Sheffield, South Yorkshire, S21 3UT 🅿
☎ 01246 435521
Est. 1984 *Stock size* Medium
Stock Pine furniture
Open Mon–Fri 9am–5pm Sat–Sun 11am–2pm
Services Stripping

⚒ A E Dowse & Son (NAVA)
Contact Michael Dowse ANAVA
✉ Cornwall Galleries, Scotland Street, Sheffield, South Yorkshire, S3 7DE
☎ 0114 272 5858 📠 0114 249 0550
📧 aedowse@aol.com
🌐 www.aedowseandson.com
Est. 1915
Open Mon–Fri 9.30am–5pm
Sales Antiques and collectables monthly. Fine art and antiques quarterly Wed 11am. Die-cast, tinplate and collectors' toys quarterly Sat 11am, viewing for Wed sales Mon 4–7pm Tues 10am–7pm Wed 9–11am, viewing for Sat sales Fri 2.30–7.30pm Sat 9.30–11am
Catalogues Yes

⊞ Earnshaw Antiques
Contact Mr Earnshaw
✉ 58 Abbeydale Road, Sheffield, South Yorkshire, S7 1FD 🅿
☎ 0114 258 1220
Est. 1990 *Stock size* Medium
Stock Furniture, chairs, wardrobes, fireplaces
Open Mon–Sat 10am–4pm or by appointment

⚒ ELR Auctions Ltd
Contact Liz Dashper
✉ The Nichols Building, Shalesmoor, Sheffield,

South Yorkshire, S3 8UJ 🅿
☎ 0114 281 6161 📠 0114 281 6162
📧 elrauctions@btconnect.com
🌐 www.elrauctions.com
Est. 1840
Open Mon–Fri 9am–5pm
Sales Specialist sales of coins, stamps, medals, postcards, cigarette cards, sporting memorabilia, football programmes. Quarterly antique and fine art sales. Please see website for details
Frequency Frequent
Catalogues Yes

⊞ Filibuster & Booth Ltd
Contact Mr A Booth
✉ 158 Devonshire Street, Sheffield, South Yorkshire, S3 7SG 🅿
☎ 0114 275 2311
Stock Unusual, eclectic mixture of genuine things
Open Please telephone, times irregular
Services Valuations

⊞ Just Military Ltd
Contact Dr or Mrs Jones
✉ 701 Abbeydale Road, Sheffield, South Yorkshire, S7 2BE 🅿
☎ 0114 255 0536
📱 07788 147550
Est. 1994 *Stock size* Large
Stock Militaria, WWI–Falklands, 1940s clothing, memorabilia, uniforms etc
Open Fri Sat 10am–5pm
Services Medal mounting

⌂ Langton's Antiques & Collectables
Contact Jill Mitchell
✉ 443 London Road, Sheffield, South Yorkshire, S2 4HJ 🅿
☎ 0114 258 1791
📱 07815 754880
Est. 1998 *Stock size* Large
No. of dealers 70
Stock General antiques, specializing in the 1950s–1970s
Open Mon–Sat 10am–5pm Sun 10.30am–4.30pm
Services Café

⌂ Nichols Antique Centre
Contact Mr M Vickers
✉ Nichols Building, Shalesmoor, Sheffield, South Yorkshire,

S3 8UJ ▣
☎ 0114 281 2811 ❶ 0114 278 7578
✉ nichols.antiques@btconnect.com
Est. 1994 *Stock size* Large
No. of dealers 60
Stock Wide range of antique
stock, specializing in Victorian
furniture
Open Mon–Sun 10.30am–5pm
Services In-house auctioneers

⊞ Paraphernalia
Contact W K Keller
✉ 66–68 Abbeydale Road,
Sheffield, South Yorkshire,
S7 1FD ▣
☎ 0114 255 0203
Est. 1969 *Stock size* Large
Stock Large range of antique
stock including porcelain, glass,
light fittings, brass, iron beds,
chimney pots, kitchenware
Open Mon–Sat 9.30am–5pm
closed Thurs

⊞ Renishaw Antique & Pine Centre
Contact Mr B Findlay
✉ 32 Main Road, Sheffield,
South Yorkshire,
S21 3UT ▣
☎ 01246 435521
Est. 1988 *Stock size* Medium
Stock Victorian–Edwardian and
1930s furniture, pine,
architectural items
Open Mon–Fri 8am–1pm
Sun 11am–2pm

⊞ N P and A Salt Antiques (LAPADA)
Contact Mrs Annette Salt
✉ Barmouth Court Antiques
Centre, Barmouth Road,
Sheffield, South Yorkshire,
S7 2DH ▣
☎ 0114 255 2711 ❶ 0114 255 5157
⑩ 07801 101363
Est. 1974 *Stock size* Large
Stock General antiques,
collectables, furniture, jewellery,
toys, scientific instruments, textiles
Open Mon–Sat 10am–5pm
Sun 11am–4pm
Services Restoration of furniture

⊞ Sarah Scott Antiques (LAPADA)
Contact Sarah Scott
✉ 6 Hutcliffe Wood Road,
Sheffield, South Yorkshire,
S8 0EX ▣
☎ 0114 236 3100

✉ sarahscottantiques@tiscali.co.uk
⑩ www.antiquefurnishings.co.uk
Est. 1998 *Stock size* Medium
Stock Mirrors, lighting, Georgian–
Edwardian town furniture
Open Tues–Sat 10am–5pm
Fairs Antiques for Everyone,
Buxton Pavilions

⊞ Michael J Taylor Antiques
Contact Michael Taylor
✉ Barmouth Court Antiques
Centre, Barmouth Road,
Sheffield, South Yorkshire,
S7 2DH ▣
☎ 01226 340595
⑩ 07970 437248
Est. 1995 *Stock size* Large
Stock Georgian–Edwardian
furniture, porcelain
Open Mon–Sat 10am–5pm
Sun 11am–4pm
Services Valuations

⊞ Tilleys Vintage Magazine Shop
Contact Mr A Tilley
✉ 281 Shoreham Street,
Sheffield, South Yorkshire,
S1 4SS ▣
☎ 0114 275 2442 ❶ 0114 275 2442
⑩ 07939 066872
✉ tilleys281@aol.com
⑩ www.tilleysmagazines.com
Est. 1978 *Stock size* Large
Stock Antique, rare, second-hand
books, magazines
Open Mon 1.30–4.30pm Tues–Fri
10am–4.30pm Sat 10am–1.30pm
3.15–4.30pm

⊞ Paul Ward Antiques
Contact Paul or Christine Ward
✉ Owl House, 8 Burnell Road,
Sheffield, South Yorkshire,
S6 2AX ▣
☎ 0114 233 5980 ❶ 0114 233 5980
⑩ 07702 309000
Est. 1977 *Stock size* Large
Stock Chairs
Open By appointment only
Fairs Swinderby
Services Valuations, restoration,
repolishing

THURCROFT

↗ Paul Beighton Auctioneers Ltd
Contact Miss S Lally
✉ Woodhouse Green, Thurcroft,
Rotherham, South Yorkshire,

S66 9AQ ▣
☎ 01709 700005 ❶ 01709 700244
✉ paul.beighton@btconnect.com
⑩ www.paulbeighton
auctioneers.co.uk
Est. 1987
Open Mon–Fri 9am–5pm
Sales Antiques, furniture and
fine art Sun 11am, viewing Fri
prior 11am–4pm Sun 9–11am.
Quarterly fine art sales
Sun 11am, see website
Frequency Fortnightly
Catalogues Yes

WENTWORTH

⊞ Holly Farm Antiques
Contact Mrs Linda Hardwick
✉ Holly Farm, Harley, Wentworth,
Rotherham, South Yorkshire,
S62 7UD ▣
☎ 01226 744077
Est. 1989 *Stock size* Medium
Stock Porcelain, Coalport,
Worcester, Rockingham, silver,
silver plate, jewellery, mirrors,
furniture, lamps
Open Sat Sun 10am–5pm
weekdays by appointment
Services Valuations

WEST YORKSHIRE

ABERFORD

⊞ Aberford Interiors
Contact Carol Robinson
✉ Hicklam House, Aberford,
Leeds, West Yorkshire,
LS25 3DP ▣
☎ 0113 281 3209 ❶ 0113 281 3121
✉ enquiries@aberfordinteriors.co.uk
⑩ www.aberfordinteriors.co.uk
Est. 1973 *Stock size* Medium
Stock Oak, painted furniture
Open Tues–Sat 9.30am–5pm
Sun 10am–5pm

BAILDON

⊞ Browgate Antiques
Contact Mrs D Shaw
✉ 13 Browgate, Baildon, Shipley,
West Yorkshire,
BD17 6BP ▣
☎ 01274 597494
Est. 1995 *Stock size* Medium
Stock Georgian–Victorian
furniture, clocks, porcelain
Open Mon–Sun 10.30am–5pm
closed Thurs
Services Valuations

BATLEY

⊞ Tansu
Contact Mr N Hall or Mr C Battye
⊠ Red Brick Mill, 218 Bradford Road, Batley Carr, Batley, West Yorkshire,
WF17 6JF 🅿
☎ 01924 460044/459441
✆ 01924 462844
✉ tansu@tansu.co.uk
⊕ www.tansu.co.uk
Est. 1992 *Stock size* Large
Stock Chinese, Japanese antique furniture, silk kimonos, dolls, scrolls, prints
Open Mon–Sat 9.30am–5.30pm Sun 11am–5pm
Fairs Ideal Homes
Services Storage, restoration, valuations, customer pick-up service, airports and train stations

⌂ Village Antiques
Contact Mr W Brown
⊠ Jessops Mill Complex, 10 Station Road, Bottom Soothill Lane, Batley, West Yorkshire,
WF17 5SU 🅿
☎ 01924 478002
✉ angie@jessops10.freeserve.co.uk
Est. 1996 *Stock size* Large
No. of dealers 28
Stock General antiques, collectables, music memorabilia
Open Mon–Sun 10am–4pm

⌔ Dale Wood & Co
Contact Martyn or Ann Sadler
⊠ 20 Station Road, Batley, West Yorkshire,
WF17 5SU 🅿
☎ 01924 479439 ✆ 01924 472291
⊕ 07711 645236
✉ dalewoodandco@hotmail.com
Est. 1989
Open Mon–Thurs 9am–5pm Fri 9am–4pm
Sales General antiques and general furnishings, fortnightly Tues 4pm
Frequency Fortnightly
Catalogues Yes

BRADFORD

⊞ The Baildon Furniture Co Ltd
Contact Mr Richard Parker
⊠ Showers Mill, 76 Frizinghall Road, Bradford, West Yorkshire,
BD9 4JB 🅿
☎ 01274 544644 ✆ 01274 414345
⊕ 07885 707462
✉ baildonfurniture@aol.com
⊕ www.antiquefurniture-uk.com
Est. 1974 *Stock size* Large
Stock General antique furniture
Open Mon–Fri 9.30am–5pm Sat 10.30am–5pm
Services Valuations, restoration

⌔ de Romes
Contact Mr S Le Blancq
⊠ 12 New John Street, Bradford, West Yorkshire,
BD1 2QY
☎ 01274 734116 ✆ 01274 729970
✉ deromes2000@yahoo.co.uk
Est. 1948
Open Mon–Fri 9am–5.15pm
Sales General antiques
Frequency Periodic
Catalogues Yes

⌔ Windle & Co
Contact Mr A Windle
⊠ 535 Great Horton Road, Bradford, West Yorkshire,
BD7 4EG 🅿
☎ 01274 572998 ✆ 01274 572998
Est. 1971
Open Mon–Thurs 9.15am–5.30pm Fri 9.15am–noon
Sales General antiques Wed 6.30pm, viewing Wed from 10am
Frequency Weekly

CASTLEFORD

⊞ Antique Clocks (Watch & Clockmakers Guild)
Contact Tom Robinson
⊠ 55a Healdfield Road, Castleford, West Yorkshire,
WF10 4LJ 🅿
☎ 01977 516704
⊕ 07721 092058
Est. 1975 *Stock size* Small
Stock Antique clocks
Open By appointment
Services Restoration

CROSS HILLS

⊞ Heathcote Antiques (BACA Award Winner 2004)
Contact Mr Michael Webster
⊠ Skipton Road Junction Crossroads, Cross Hills, Keighley, West Yorkshire,
BD20 7DS 🅿
☎ 01535 635250 ✆ 01535 637205
⊕ 07836 259640
✉ heathcote1@btopenworld.com
Est. 1974 *Stock size* Large
Stock General antiques, original English unstripped pine, pottery, porcelain
Open Wed–Sat 10am–5.30pm Sun 12.30–4.30pm
Services Most

DENBY DALE

⊞ Worlds Apart
Contact Mrs Sharon Dawson
⊠ Unit 6a, Springfield Mill, Norman Road, Denby Dale, Huddersfield, West Yorkshire,
HD8 8TH 🅿
☎ 01484 866713
⊕ 07801 349960
✉ shaz@chris216.fsnet.co.uk
Est. 1995 *Stock size* Large
Stock Antiques, collectables
Open Tues–Sat 10am–4.30pm Sun noon–5pm

FEATHERSTONE

⊞ A645 Trading Post
Contact Mr G Thomas
⊠ Chapel Works, Wakefield Road, Featherstone, Pontefract, West Yorkshire,
WF7 5HL 🅿
☎ 01977 695255
Est. 1982 *Stock size* Large
Stock Furniture, collectables, books, die-cast toys, ceramics
Open Fri–Sat 10am–5pm Sun 11am–5pm Mon 10am–5pm

HALIFAX

⊞ Art Deco Originals/Muir Hewitt
Contact Mr M Hewitt
⊠ Halifax Antique Centre, Queens Road Mills, Gibbet Street, Halifax, West Yorkshire,
HX1 4LR 🅿
☎ 01422 347377 ✆ 01422 347377
✉ muir.hewitt@virgin.net
⊕ www.muirhewitt.com
Est. 1982 *Stock size* Large
Stock Art Deco ceramics, decorative arts, furniture, lighting, mirrors, chrome
Open Tues–Fri 10.30am–4.30pm Sat 10.30am–5pm closed Bank Holidays please telephone for seasonal time changes
Fairs Chester, Leeds Art Deco fairs
Services Valuations

⊞ **Collectors Old Toy Shop**
Contact Simon Haley
✉ **89 Northgate, Halifax,
West Yorkshire,
HX1 1XF** 🅿
☎ 01422 822148/360434
✉ collectorsoldtoy@aol.com
Est. 1983 *Stock size* Medium
Stock Dinky, Corgi, die-casts, tin-plate toys, railways, money boxes
Open Tues Wed Fri Sat
10.30am–4.30pm
Fairs Sandown Park, Harrogate
International
Services Insurance valuations

⌂ **Halifax Antique Centre**
Contact Mr M Carroll
✉ **Queens Road, Halifax,
West Yorkshire,
HX1 4LR** 🅿
☎ 01422 366657 ❶ 01422 369293
Ⓦ www.halifaxantiques.co.uk
Est. 1981 *Stock size* Large
No. of dealers 30
Stock French and English furniture,
Art Deco, costume, kitchenware,
collectables, Italian chandeliers
Open Tues–Sat 10am–4.30pm
Services Valuations, restoration,
café

⊞ **Holmfirth Antiques**
Contact Ken Priestley
✉ **Halifax, West Yorkshire, HX1** 🅿
☎ 01484 686854
Ⓜ 07973 533478
✉ ken@fonograf.com
Ⓦ www.fonograf.com
Est. 1988 *Stock size* Medium
Stock Mechanical music,
gramophones, phonographs
Open By appointment
Services Valuations, restoration,
mail order

⊞ **Linen & Lace**
Contact Shirley Tomlinson
✉ **Halifax Antiques Centre,
Queens Raod/Gibbet Street,
Halifax, West Yorkshire,
HX1 4LR** 🅿
☎ 01484 540492 or 01422 366657
Est. 1989 *Stock size* Medium
Stock Antique textiles, costume
and accessories, Victorian–1960s
Open Tues–Sat 10am–4pm

HAWORTH

⊞ **Bingley Antiques**
Contact J B or J Poole
✉ **Springfield Farm Estate,**
Flappit, Haworth, Keighley,
West Yorkshire,
BD21 5PT 🅿
☎ 01535 646666 ❶ 01535 646666
✉ john@bingleyantiques.com
Ⓦ www.bingleyantiques.com
Est. 1969 *Stock size* Large
Stock 5 wharehouses of antiques
and architectural items,
1 warehouse specializing in
antique doors
Open Thurs Fri Sat 9am–5pm
Services Valuations

⊞ **Yorkshire Relics**
Contact Colin Ruff
✉ **11 Main Street, Haworth,
West Yorkshire,
BD22 8DA** 🅿
☎ 01535 642218/662093
❶ 01535 642218
Ⓜ 07808 757851
Est. 1987 *Stock size* Large
Stock Antiquarian and
collectable books, records,
general collectables
Open Mon–Fri noon–5pm
Sat Sun 11am–5pm

HEBDEN BRIDGE

⊞ **Cornucopia**
Contact Mr N Strophair
✉ **13 West End, Hebden Bridge,
West Yorkshire,
HX7 8JP** 🅿
☎ 01422 844497
Est. 1974 *Stock size* Medium
Stock General antiques,
collectables
Open Fri–Sun noon–5pm
Fairs Newark, Nottinghamshire

⊞ **G J Saville (BADA)**
Contact Graham Saville
✉ **Foster Clough, Hebden Bridge,
West Yorkshire,
HX7 5QZ** 🅿
☎ 01422 882808 ❶ 01422 882808
Ⓜ 07801 071710
✉ g.j.saville@btinternet.com
Est. 1968 *Stock size* Large
Stock 1750–1830 caricatures,
caricature reference books
Open By appointment
Fairs Olympia, BADA
Services Valuations

HOLMFIRTH

⊞ **Huddersfield Picture
Framing Co.**
Contact Miss P Ward
✉ **15 Greenfield Road, Holmfirth,
Huddersfield, West Yorkshire,
HD9 2LA** 🅿
☎ 01484 687598
Ⓦ www.huddpicfr.co.uk
Est. 1979 *Stock size* Medium
Stock Paintings, swept frames,
ovals, circles, mouldings etc
Open Wed–Fri 10am–6pm Sat
10am–1pm or by appointment
Services Restoration, framing

⊞ **Old Friendship Antiques**
Contact Mr C J Dobson
✉ **77 Dunford Road, Holmfirth,
Huddersfield, West Yorkshire,
HD9 3DT** 🅿
☎ 01484 682129
Est. 1984 *Stock size* Large
Stock Antique furniture, old
pine, clocks
Open Tue–Fri 9.30am–5.30pm
Sat 9am–3.30pm Sun 2–4pm
Fairs Newark, Swinderby
Services Pine stripping

⋔ **William Sykes & Son**
Contact Mr R Dixon
✉ **Sude Hill, New Mill, Holmfirth,
Huddersfield, West Yorkshire,
HD9 3JH** 🅿
☎ 01484 683543 ❶ 01484 683543
Ⓜ 07854 843228
✉ info@wmsykes.co.uk
Ⓦ www.wmsykes.com
Est. 1866
Open Mon–Fri 9am–5.15pm
Sat 9am–2pm Sun 11am–2pm
Sales General antiques every
3rd Friday, viewing Wed 7–9pm
Thurs 2-9pm Fri 12noon–sale

HONLEY

⊞ **Holme Valley
Warehouse**
Contact Paula Moss or
Michael Silkstone
✉ **11 Westgate, Honley,
Holmfirth, Huddersfield,
West Yorkshire,
HD9 1AA** 🅿
☎ 01484 667915 ❶ 01484 667915
Est. 1995 *Stock size* Large
Stock Pine furniture, quirky
items, artwork
Open Mon–Sun 10am–5pm
Services Restoration, stripping

⊞ **Honley Antiques & Pine**
Contact Mr P Brown
✉ **2 Woodhead Road, Honley,
Holmfirth, Huddersfield,**

West Yorkshire,
HD9 6PX ▣
☎ 01484 660806
✉ honleyantiques@onetel.net.uk
Est. 1997 *Stock size* Large
Stock Georgian–modern furniture,
silver, longcase clocks, paintings,
pine, collectables, jewellery
Open Tues–Sat 10am–5pm
Sun 11am–4pm
Services Valuations

HUDDERSFIELD

⊞ O'Briens Antiques
Contact Kim O'Brien
✉ 133 Church Street, Paddock,
Huddersfield, West Yorkshire,
HD1 4UJ ▣
☎ 01484 352424
Est. 1995 *Stock size* Medium
Stock Victorian & Edwardian
Antiques
Open Mon–Sun 9am–5pm
Fairs Newark

⊞ Old Field Antiques
Contact Peter
✉ 27–29 St Peters Street,
Huddersfield, West Yorkshire,
HD1 1RA ▣
☎ 01484 544171
⊕ 07778 060898
✉ allen.skrynnyk@btconnect.com
Est. 1989 *Stock size* Large
Stock General antiques and
collectables
Open Mon–Sat 12.30pm–4.30pm
Fairs Swinderby, Newark
Services Valuations, restoration,
house clearance

⊞ Serendipity Antiques
Contact Mr Franco
✉ 1 Bridge Street, Huddersfield,
West Yorkshire,
HD4 6EL ▣
☎ 01484 428223
⊕ 07967 919292
✉ samfranco59@hotmail.com
Est. 1988 *Stock size* Medium
Stock Situated in a Georgian
coach house, selling general
antiques, pine, porcelain,
Victorian–Edwardian furniture
Open Wed–Sat 10.30am–5pm
Services Valuations, restoration

ILKLEY

⊞ Beacon Antiques
Contact L Cousins
✉ 2 North View, Menston, Ilkley,

West Yorkshire,
LS29 6JU ▣
☎ 01943 872392
✉ les@beacon-antiques.co.uk
⊕ www.beacon-antiques.co.uk
Est. 1994 *Stock size* Medium
Stock 18th–19thC porcelain and
ceramics, silver, paintings
Open Tues–Sat 10am–5pm
Fairs Harrogate, Stafford

⊞ Coopers of Ilkley
(LAPADA)
Contact Charles Cooper
✉ 46–50 Leeds Road, Ilkley,
West Yorkshire,
LS29 8EQ ▣
☎ 01943 608020 ⊕ 01943 604321
✉ enquiries@coopersantiques
ilkley.co.uk
⊕ www.coopersantiquesilkley.co.uk
Stock size Medium
Stock Period and Victorian furniture
Open Mon–Fri 9am–1pm
2–5.30pm Sat 9am–5.30pm
Services Restoration

⋏ Andrew Hartley Fine
Arts (ISVA, SOFAA)
Contact Mr A D Hartley, ARICS
✉ Victoria Hall, Little Lane, Ilkley,
West Yorkshire,
LS29 8EA ▣
☎ 01943 816363 ⊕ 01943 817610
✉ info@andrewhartleyfinearts.co.uk
⊕ www.andrewhartleyfinearts.co.uk
Est. 1906
Open Mon–Fri 9am–5.30pm
Sat 9am–12.30pm
Sales Victorian and later every
Wed 10am, viewing Tues prior
9am–7pm. Antique and fine art
sale every two months Wed
Thurs 10am, viewing Sat prior
9.30am–12.30pm Mon Tues prior
9.30am–4.30pm day of sale
9–10am
Catalogues Yes

KEIGHLEY

⊞ Revival
Contact Peter Pryimuk
✉ 104–106 South Street,
Keighley, West Yorkshire,
BD21 1EH ▣
☎ 01535 606837
Est. 1987 *Stock size* Medium
Stock General antiques,
architectural items, pine,
bric-a-brac
Open Mon–Sat 10am–5pm
telephone call advisable

LEEDS

⋏ Abbey Auctions
(LAPADA)
Contact Mr S Smith
✉ 11 Morris Lane, Kirkstall,
Leeds, West Yorkshire,
LS5 3JT ▣
☎ 0113 275 8787 ⊕ 0113 275 8787
✉ simon@abbeyauctions.co.uk
Open Mon–Fri 8am–5pm Sat
8am–noon
Sales General antiques sales,
household furniture, bric-a-brac,
Doulton and Beswick figures,
viewing 10am–6pm
Frequency Fortnightly
Catalogues No

⊞ Aladdin's Cave
Contact Roberta Spencer
✉ 19 Queen's Arcade, Leeds,
West Yorkshire,
LS1 6LF ▣
☎ 0113 245 70903
✉ robertajspencer@hotmail.com
Est. 1985 *Stock size* Large
Stock Antique jewellery
Open Mon–Sat 10am–5pm
Services Valuations, repairs

⊞ Antique Boutique
Contact E Viol
✉ 56–59 Merrion Centre
Superstore, Merrion Centre,
Leeds, West Yorkshire,
LS2 8LY ▣
☎ 0113 244 4174
Est. 1981 *Stock size* Large
Stock Antique and modern fancy
dress, retro clothes, wigs,
theatrical accessories for sale and
hire
Open Mon–Sat 10am–5pm Wed
10am–2pm

⊞ Aquarius Antiques
Contact Peter McGlade
✉ Abbey Mills, Abbey Road,
Leeds, West Yorkshire,
LS5 3HP ▣
☎ 0113 278 9216
Est. 1979 *Stock size* Medium
Stock General antiques,
Georgian–Victorian furniture
Open Mon–Sat 9am–5pm
Services Repairs, restoration

⋏ Bonhams (BACA Award
Winner 2003)
✉ 17a East Parade, Leeds,
West Yorkshire,
LS1 2BH

☎ 0113 244 8011 ✆ 0113 242 9875
✉ leeds@bonhams.com
⊕ www.bonhams.com
Sales Regional Saleroom.
Frequent sales including the
specialist Yorkshire Sale held
annually. Regular sales held in
London and in our salerooms
across the country. Free auction
valuations; insurance and
probate valuations

⚲ **Gary Don Antiques**
Contact Gary Don
✉ Harrogate Road, Leeds,
West Yorkshire,
LS17 6PA ℗
☎ 0113 266 7434
✉ garydon@ntlworld.com
⊕ www.garydon.co.uk
Est. 1929
Open Mon–Fri 9am–5pm
Sales Call for details of upcoming
auctions

⌂ **Headrow Antiques**
Contact Sally Hurrell
✉ Level 3, The Headrow
Shopping Centre, The Headrow,
Leeds, West Yorkshire,
LS1 6JE ℗
☎ 0113 245 5344
⊕ www.headrowantiques.com
Est. 1992 *Stock size* Large
No. of dealers 17
Stock General antiques
Open Mon–Sat 10am–5pm
Nov Dec Sun 11am–4pm

⌂ **Kolekt**
Contact Hazel Gough
✉ Level 2, Unit 8 , The Headrow,
Leeds, West Yorkshire,
LS1 6PT ℗
☎ 0113 244 8485
⊕ 07919 118308
✉ kolekt@tiscali.co.uk
Est. 2005 *Stock size* Small
No. of dealers 21
Stock General antiques and
collectables
Open Mon–Sat 10am–5pm
Sun 11am–4pm
Services Valuations for insurance

⊞ **Swiss Cottage
Furniture**
Contact Mr J Howorth
✉ 85 Westfield Crescent, Burley,
Leeds, West Yorkshire,
LS3 1DJ ℗
☎ 0113 242 9994 ✆ 0113 245 0639
⊕ www.swisscottageantiques.com

Est. 1987 *Stock size* Large
Stock General antiques, salvage
yard
Open Mon–Sat 10am–5pm
closed Tues

⊞ **Toot-Sweet**
Contact Lily Bennett
✉ 1st Floor, 39 Call Lane, Leeds,
West Yorkshire,
LS1 7BT ℗
☎ 0113 244 6133
✉ leeds@toot-sweet.co.uk
Est. 1980 *Stock size* Medium
Stock Wind instruments
Open Mon–Sat 9.30am–6pm
Services Instrument and bow
repairs, valuations, consultations,
export

⊞ **Turner Violins**
Contact Lily Bennett
✉ 1st Floor, 39 Call Lane, Leeds,
West Yorkshire,
LS1 7BT ℗
☎ 0113 244 6133
✉ leeds@turnerviolins.co.uk
⊕ www.turnerviolins.co.uk
Est. 1980
Stock Violins, double basses,
violas, cellos, bows
Open Mon–Sat 10am–6pm
Services Instrument and bow
repairs, valuations, consultations,
export

⊞ **Woodstock Antiques**
Contact Mr R J Link
✉ 134 Woodhouse Street, Leeds,
West Yorkshire,
LS6 2JN ℗
☎ 0113 246 1296
Est. 1990 *Stock size* Medium
Stock General antiques
Open Mon–Sat 10am–5pm
Fairs Newark

⊞ **Works of Iron**
Contact Mr G Higgins
✉ Beaver Works,
36 Whitehouse Street, Leeds,
West Yorkshire,
LS10 1AD ℗
☎ 0113 234 0555 ✆ 0113 234 2555
Est. 1985 *Stock size* Large
Stock Antique beds
Open Wed–Sat 11am–5pm
Services Valuations, restoration

⊞ **Year Dot**
Contact Mr Adrian Glithro
✉ 41 The Headrow, Leeds,
West Yorkshire,

LS1 6PU ℗
☎ 0113 246 0860
Est. 1977 *Stock size* Medium
Stock General antiques, jewellery
Open Mon–Sat 9.30am–5pm

LEPTON

⊞ **K L M & Co**
Contact Mr K L Millington
✉ Wakefield Road, Lepton,
West Yorkshire,
HD8 0EL ℗
☎ 01484 607763 ✆ 01484 607763
⊕ 07860 671547
Est. 1981 *Stock size* Large
Stock Antiques, 1940s furniture
Open Mon–Sat 10.30am–5pm

MENSTON

⊞ **J Hanlon Antiques**
Contact Mrs J Hanlon
✉ 101 Bradford Road, Menston,
Ilkley, West Yorkshire,
LS29 6BU ℗
☎ 01943 877634/463693
Est. 1974 *Stock size* Small
Stock Small collectables, textiles,
jewellery, silver
Open Thurs–Sat 2.30–5pm
Fairs Newark

⊞ **Park Antiques**
Contact Brian O'Connell
✉ 2 North View, Menston, Ilkley,
West Yorkshire,
LS29 6JU ℗
☎ 01943 872392
⊕ 07811 034123
⊕ www.parkantiques.com
Est. 1980 *Stock size* Medium
Stock Early Georgian–Edwardian
paintings, ceramics, clocks,
furniture
Open Tues–Sat 10am–5pm
Services Restoration

OSSETT

⚲ **John Walsh & Co.
(NAVA)**
Contact Mr J Walsh
✉ Ashfield House Auction
Rooms, Illingworth Street,
Ossett, West Yorkshire,
WF5 8AL ℗
☎ 01924 264030 ✆ 01924 267758
⊕ 07976 241587
✉ auctions@john-walsh.co.uk
⊕ www.john-walsh.co.uk
Est. 1989
Open Mon–Fri 9am–5.30pm

Sales General antiques
Frequency 8 per annum
Catalogues Yes

OTLEY

⊞ **JT's Curios & Antiques**
Contact John Ramsey
✉ 5 Westgate, Otley,
West Yorkshire,
LS21 3AT 🅿
☎ 01943 468240
Est. 2002 *Stock size* Small
Stock General Antiques
Open Please call for an
appontment
Services Valuations, information

PUDSEY

⊞ **Geary Antiques**
Contact Mr J A Geary
✉ 114 Richardshaw Lane,
Pudsey, Leeds, West Yorkshire,
LS28 6BN 🅿
☎ 0113 256 4122
📱 07802 441245
📧 jag@t-nlbi.demon.co.uk
Est. 1933 *Stock size* Large
Stock General antique English
furniture
Open Mon–Sat 10am–5.30pm
Sun noon–4pm
Services Restoration, interior
design, furnishing fabrics,
wallpapers

SALTAIRE

⊞ **Mick Burt (Antique
Pine)**
Contact Andrew Draper
✉ The Victoria Centre,
3–4 Victoria Road, Saltaire,
Shipley, West Yorkshire,
BD18 3LA 🅿
☎ 01274 533722 📠 01274 533722
Est. 1994 *Stock size* Medium
Stock Restored antique pine
furniture
Open Sat 10.30am–5pm
Services Restoration

⊞ **John Lewis**
✉ The Victoria Centre,
3–4 Victoria Road,
Saltaire, Shipley,
West Yorkshire,
BD18 3LA 🅿
☎ 01274 533722 📠 01274 533722
Est. 1988 *Stock size* Large
Stock Burmantoft's art pottery
Open Mon–Sun 10.30am–5.30pm

Fairs NEC, Alexandra Palace
🏠 **Victoria Antiques**
Contact Mr A Draper
✉ 3–4 Victoria Road, Saltaire,
Shipley, West Yorkshire,
BD18 3LA 🅿
☎ 01274 533722
Est. 1995 *Stock size* Large
No. of dealers 30
Stock General antiques, country
furniture, paintings, clocks,
porcelain, silver
Open Tue–Sun 10.30am–5pm

SOWERBY BRIDGE

⊞ **Talking Point Antiques**
Contact Mr Paul Austwick
✉ 66 West Street, Sowerby
Bridge, West Yorkshire,
HX6 3AP 🅿
☎ 01422 834126
📧 tpagrams@aol.com
Est. 1985
Stock Gramophones, other
mechanical antiques
Open Thurs–Sat 10.30am–5.30pm
or by appointment
Fairs NEC Vintage
Communications Fair, Blackpool
Vintage Technology Fair

WETHERBY

⊞ **Elden Antiques**
Contact Elaine Broadley
✉ 23 Ashdale View,
Kirk Deighton, Wetherby,
West Yorkshire,
LS22 4DS 🅿
☎ 01937 584770
Est. 1980 *Stock size* Medium
Stock General antiques
Open Mon–Fri 9am–5pm
Sat Sun 11am–5pm

⊞ **French & Country
Living**
Contact Sara Qualter
✉ 11a Westgate, Wetherby,
West Yorkshire,
LS22 6LL 🅿
☎ 01937 586550 📠 01977 682673
📱 07971 693042
📧 theglasshouse@ic24.net
🌐 www.frenchandcountryliving.co.uk
Est. 2001 *Stock size* Medium
Stock Antiques and collectables,
oak and country furniture, pine,
20thC design
Open Mon–Sat 10am–5pm
Fairs Swinderby, Newark
Services Shipping

LINCOLNSHIRE

ALFORD

🏠 **Town and Country
Antiques Centres**
Contact Louise Chatterton
✉ 7–8 West Street, Alford,
Lincolnshire, LN13 9DG 🅿
☎ 01507 466953
📱 07771 718514
Est. 1999 *Stock size* Large
No. of dealers 24
Stock Antiques both small and large
Open Mon–Sun 10am–4.30pm

ALLINGTON

⊞ **Garth Vincent Antique
Arms and Armour (LAPADA)**
Contact Garth Vincent
✉ The Old Manor House,
Allington, Nr Grantham,
Lincolnshire,
NG32 2DH 🅿
☎ 01400 281358 📠 01400 282658
📱 077835 352151
📧 garthvincent@aolcom
🌐 www.guns.uk.com
Est. 1980 *Stock size* Large
Stock International guns, swords,
helmets, reproduction arms and
armour
Open By appointment only
Fairs Birmingham and London
Arms Fairs
Services Valuations

AYLESBY

⊞ **Robin Fowler Period
Clocks (LAPADA)**
Contact Mr R Fowler
✉ Washingdales, Washingdales
Lane, Aylesby, Grimsby,
Lincolnshire,
DN37 7LH 🅿
☎ 01472 751335 📠 01472 751335
📱 07949 141891
📧 periodclocks@washingdales
.fsnet.co.uk
Est. 1968 *Stock size* Large
Stock Antique clocks,
barometers, scientific instruments
Open By appointment
Fairs LAPADA, Bailey, Galloway
Services Valuations, restoration

BELTON

⊞ **Richard Ellory Furniture**
Contact Richard Ellory
✉ Unit 5, Sandtoft Industrial

Estate, Sandtoft Road, Belton,
Lincolnshire,
DN9 1PN 🅿
☎ 01427 874064 ❶ 01427 875055
Est. 1981 *Stock size* Medium
Stock English pine
Open Mon–Sat 9am–5pm

BOSTON

⊞ **Junktion Antiques**
Contact Mr Jack Rundle
✉ The Old Railway Station,
Main Road, New Bolingbroke,
Boston, Lincolnshire,
PE22 7LN 🅿
☎ 01205 480068 ❶ 01205 480132
Ⓜ 07836 345491
Est. 1983 *Stock size* Large
Stock Early toys, advertising,
bygones, architectural and
mechanical antiques 1880–1960
Open Wed Thurs Sat 10am–5pm
Fairs Newark, Swinderby

⊞ **Pennyfarthing Antiques**
Contact Mr Hale
✉ 1 Red Lion Street, Boston,
Lincolnshire,
PE21 6NY 🅿
☎ 01205 362988
Ⓦ www.pennyfarthingantiques.net
Est. 2000 *Stock size* Medium
Stock General antiques
Open Tues Wed Fri Sat
10am–4.30pm

BOURNE

⊞ **Antique and Second
Hand Traders**
Contact Mr Alan Thompson
✉ 39 West Street, Bourne,
Lincolnshire,
PE10 9N3 🅿
☎ 01778 394700 ❶ 01778 394700
Ⓜ 07548 941728
Est. 1969 *Stock size* Large
Stock Antique and second-hand
furniture
Open Mon–Sat 10am–5pm
closed Wed Thurs
Fairs Newark, Ardingly
Services House clearance,
removals

BRIGG

⋗ **DDM Auction Rooms**
Contact Robert Horner
✉ Old Courts Road, Brigg,
North Lincolnshire,
DN20 8JD 🅿

☎ 0845 230 4202 ❶ 01652 650085
Ⓜ 07970 126311
🄴 auctions@ddmauctionrooms.co.uk
Ⓦ www.ddmauctionrooms.co.uk
Est. 1889
Open Mon–Fri 9am–5.30pm
auction Sat
Sales Antiques and fine art sale
every 6 weeks Tues Wed 9.30am.
Fortnightly auction of
contemporary and antiques Sat
9.30am, ring for details, viewing
day prior 2–7pm day of auction
from 8.30am
Catalogues Yes

CLEETHORPES

⊞ **Cleethorpes
Collectables**
Contact Mr A Dalton
✉ 34 Alexandra Road,
Cleethorpes, Lincolnshire,
DN35 8LF 🅿
☎ 01472 291952 ❶ 01472 291952
Ⓦ www.cleethorpescollectables.co.uk
Est. 1999 *Stock size* Large
Stock Over 25,000 general
antiques, collectables, curios
Open Mon–Sun 10am–4.30pm

⊞ **Yesterdays Antiques**
Contact Mr N Bishop
✉ 86 Grimsby Road, Cleethorpes,
Lincolnshire,
DN35 7DP 🅿
☎ 01472 343020
🄴 n.bishop2@ntlworld.com
Est. 1987 *Stock size* Large
Stock General antiques,
fireplaces a speciality
Open Mon–Sat 9am–5pm or by
appointment
Services Valuations, restoration,
polishing

GAINSBOROUGH

⋗ **Drewery and Wheeldon**
Contact Mr M G Tomson
✉ 124 Trinity Street,
Gainsborough,
Lincolnshire,
DN21 1JD 🅿
☎ 01427 616118 ❶ 01427 811070
🄴 drewery.wheeldon@btconnect.com
Ⓦ www.dreweryandwheeldon.co.uk
Est. 1879
Open Mon–Fri 9am–5.30pm
Sat 9am–12.30pm
Sales General antiques sales,
telephone for details
Catalogues Yes

🏠 **Pilgrims Antiques Centre**
Contact Mr M Wallis
✉ 66a Church Street,
Gainsborough, Lincolnshire,
DN21 2JR 🅿
☎ 01427 810897 ❶ 01427 810897
Est. 1985 *Stock size* Large
No. of dealers 8
Stock General antiques
Open Tues–Sat 10am–4.30pm
closed Wed

⊞ **R M Antiques**
Contact Mr R Maclennan
✉ 4a Tennyson Street,
Gainsborough, Lincolnshire,
DN21 2GJ 🅿
☎ 01427 810624 ❶ 01427 810624
Est. 1984 *Stock size* Large
Stock General antiques
Trade only Yes
Open Mon–Sat 9am–3pm
Services Export

GRANTHAM

⋗ **Golding Young (NAVA)**
Contact Mr Colin Young RICS
✉ The Grantham Auction Rooms,
Old Wharf Road, Grantham,
Lincolnshire,
NG31 7AA 🅿
☎ 01476 565118 ❶ 01476 561475
🄴 enquiries@goldingyoung.com
Ⓦ www.goldingyoung.com
Est. 1900
Open Mon–Fri 9am–5pm
closed 1–2pm
Sales Fortnightly general
antiques sale, bi-monthly
antique and fine art sale
Catalogues Yes

⊞ **Grantham Clocks**
Contact M R Conder
✉ 30 Lodge Way, Grantham,
Lincolnshire,
NG31 8DD 🅿
☎ 01476 561784
Est. 1987 *Stock size* Medium
Stock Clocks
Open By appointment

⊞ **Grantham Furniture
Emporium**
Contact K or J E Hamilton
✉ 4–6 Wharf Road, Grantham,
Lincolnshire,
NG31 6BA 🅿
☎ 01476 562967
Ⓜ 07710 483865
Est. 1976 *Stock size* Large
Stock Victorian–Edwardian and

1920s shipping furniture,
Open Tues–Sun 11am–4pm
closed Wed

⊞ Harlequin Antiques
Contact Tony or Sandra Marshall
⊠ 46 Swinegate, Grantham,
Lincolnshire,
NG31 6RL
☎ 01476 563346
Est. 1995 **Stock size** Medium
Stock General antiques
Open Mon–Sat 9am–5pm
Services Valuations

⌂ Notions Antiques Centre
Contact Mr or Mrs L Checkley
⊠ 1–2a Market Place, Grantham,
Lincolnshire,
NG31 6LQ 🅿
☎ 01476 563603
◍ 07736 677978
🅴 scheckley@fsbdial.co.uk
Est. 1984 **Stock size** Large
No. of dealers 70
Stock General antiques
Open Mon–Fri 10am–5pm Sat
9.30am–5pm Sun 11am–4pm

⋏ Marilyn Swain Auctions (SOFAA)
Contact John Munroe
⊠ The Old Barracks, Sandon
Road, Grantham, Lincolnshire,
NG31 9AS 🅿
☎ 01476 568861 ☏ 01476 576100
Est. 1991
Open Mon–Fri 9am–5.30pm
Sales General antiques
Frequency Fortnightly
Catalogues Yes

⊞ Marcus Wilkinson Jewellers & Antiques (BHI, AHS, NAWCC)
Contact Mr Marcus Wilkinson
⊠ The Time House, 1 Blue Court,
Guildhall Street, Grantham,
Lincolnshire,
NG31 6NJ 🅿
☎ 01476 560400 ☏ 01476 568791
◍ 07966 154590
🅴 info@thetimehouse.com
🆆 www.thetimehouse.com
Est. 1935 **Stock size** Small
Stock Clocks, watches, jewellery
Open Mon–Sat 9.30am–4.30pm
Fairs San Francisco Fall Antique
Show, Los Angeles Spring
Antique Show, London House
and Garden
Services Valuations, restoration,
repairs

GRIMSBY

⊞ Bell Antiques
Contact Mr Victor Hawkey
⊠ 68a Harold Street, Grimsby,
Lincolnshire,
DN32 7NQ 🅿
☎ 01472 695110
Est. 1964 **Stock size** Large
Stock Clocks, music boxes,
barometers
Open By appointment
Fairs Newark, Swinderby
Services Valuations

⋏ Jackson Green & Preston
Contact Mr D Arliss
⊠ New Cartergate, Grimsby,
Lincolnshire,
DN31 1RB 🅿
☎ 01472 311115 ☏ 01472 311114
🅴 auction@jacksongreenpreston.co.uk
🆆 www.jacksongreenpreston.co.uk
Est. 1920
Open By appointment
Sales General household and
antiques sale Fri 10.30am,
viewing Thurs 2.30–7pm at
41–45 Duncombe Street,
Grimsby, DN32 7SG
Frequency Weekly
Catalogues No

HEMSWELL

⊞ Abbey Antiques
Contact Michael Betts
⊠ Hemswell Antique Centre,
Hemswell Cliff, Gainsborough,
Lincolnshire,
DN21 5JT 🅿
☎ 01623 792270 ☏ 01623 490124
◍ 07816210218
Est. 1980 **Stock size** Medium
Stock Antique English furniture,
oriental artefacts
Open By appointment
Services Valuations

⊞ Advena Antiques & Fairs
Contact Alan White
⊠ Building II, Hemswell Antique
Centre, Caenby Corner Estate,
Hemswell Cliff, Gainsborough,
Lincolnshire, DN21 5TJ 🅿
☎ 01427 668389 ☏ 01427 668935
◍ 07713 150510
🅴 advena.antiques@ntlworld.com
Est. 1992 **Stock size** Large
Stock Antique silver, jewellery,
silver plate
Open Mon–Sun 10am–5pm
Services Valuations, repairs

⌂ Astra House Antique Centre
Contact Mr M J Frith
⊠ Old RAF Hemswell,
Nr Caenby Corner,
Hemswell Cliff, Gainsborough,
Lincolnshire,
DN21 5TL 🅿
☎ 01427 668312 ☏ 01427 668312
🅴 astraantiqueshemswell@
btinternet.com
Est. 1992 **Stock size** Large
No. of dealers 50+
Stock General antiques and
collectables including second-
hand items
Open Mon–Sun 10am–5pm
Services Shipping

⊞ Barleycorn Antiques
Contact Shirley or John Wheat
⊠ Hemswell Antiques Centre,
Caenby Corner Estate, Hemswell
Cliff, Gainsborough, Lincolnshire,
DN21 5TW 🅿
☎ 01427 668789
◍ 07850 673965
🆆 www.barleycorn-antiques.co.uk
Est. 1982
Stock Furniture, brass, lighting,
ceramics
Open Mon–Sun 10am–5pm

⌂ Guardroom Antiques
Contact Mr C Lambert
⊠ RAF Station Hemswell,
Gainsborough, Lincolnshire,
DN21 5TL 🅿
☎ 01427 667113
Est. 1993 **Stock size** Large
No. of dealers 50
Stock General antiques including
Victorian and Georgian
furniture, collectables
Open Mon–Sun 10am–5pm or by
appointment
Services Shipping can be arranged

⌂ Hemswell Antique Centres
Contact Robert Miller
⊠ Caenby Corner Estate,
Hemswell Cliff, Gainsborough,
Lincolnshire,
DN21 5TJ 🅿
☎ 01427 668389 ☏ 01427 668935
🅴 info@hemswell-antiques.com
🆆 www.hemswell-antiques.com
Est. 1989 **Stock size** Large
No. of dealers 300
Stock General antiques
Open Daily 10am–5pm
Services Furniture restoration

⊞ Trevor Moss Antiques
Contact Mr T Moss
✉ **Building 1, Hemswell Antique Centre, Caenby Corner Estate, Hemswell, Gainsborough, Lincolnshire, DN21 5TW** 🅟
☎ 01427 668389 ☏ 01427 668935
Est. 1985 *Stock size* Large
Stock General antiques
Open Mon–Sun 10am–5pm
Fairs Newark, Swinderby
Services Restoration

⊞ Second Time Around
Contact Mr Geoff Powis
✉ **Hemswell Antique Centre, Caenby Corner Estate, Hemswell Cliff, Gainsborough, Lincolnshire, DN21 5TJ** 🅟
☎ 01522 543167 or 01427 668389
☏ 07860 679495
Est. 1984 *Stock size* Large
Stock Period longcase and bracket clocks, other clocks 17th–19thC and up to 1940s
Open Mon–Sun 10am–5pm
Services Valuations, restoration

⊞ Smithson Antiques
Contact Skip or Janie Smithson
✉ **Hemswell Antique Centre, Caenby Corner Estate, Hemswell Cliff, Lincolnshire, DN21 5TJ** 🅟
☎ 01754 810265
☏ 07831 399180
Est. 1984 *Stock size* Medium
Stock Victorian kitchen and dairy antiques
Open Daily 10am–5pm

HOLBEACH

⊞ P J Cassidy
Contact Mr P Cassidy
✉ **1 Boston Road, Holbeach, Spalding, Lincolnshire, PE12 7LR** 🅟
☎ 01406 426322
✉ bookscass@aol.com
Est. 1974 *Stock size* Large
Stock Antiquarian books, maps, prints, Lincolnshire topography
Open Mon–Sat 10am–6pm
Services Framing

HORNCASTLE

⊞ G Baker Antiques
Contact Geoffrey or Christine Baker
✉ **16 South Street, Horncastle,**

Lincolnshire, LN9 6DX 🅟
☎ 01507 526553
☏ 07767 216264
Est. 1973 *Stock size* Medium
Stock Period and general furniture
Open Mon–Sat 9am–5pm or by appointment
Fairs Newark, Swinderby
Services Restoration

⊞ Clare Boam
Contact Clare Boam
✉ **22–38 North Street, Horncastle, Lincolnshire, LN9 5DX** 🅟
☎ 01507 522381 ☏ 01507 524202
✉ clareboam@btconnect.com
🌐 www.greatexpectations horncastle.co.uk
Est. 1976 *Stock size* Large
Stock General antiques and collectables
Open Mon–Sat 9am–5pm
Sun 2–4.30pm
Fairs Swinderby

⌂ Drill Hall Antiques Centre
Contact Mrs V Ginn
✉ **The Old Drill Hall, South Street, Horncastle, Lincolnshire, LN9 6EF** 🅟
☎ 01507 525370
Est. 2004 *Stock size* Large
No. of dealers 30
Stock High-quality antiques pre-1949, furniture, pictures, porcelain, silver, jewellery, lighting
Open Mon–Sat 10am–4.30pm
Sun 1–4pm Bank Holidays 11am–4pm

⌂ Great Expectations
Contact Miss M C Boam
✉ **37–43 East Street, Horncastle, Lincolnshire, LN9 6AZ** 🅟
☎ 01507 524202 ☏ 01507 524202
✉ clareboam@btconnect.com
🌐 www.greatexpectations horncastle.co.uk
Est. 1996 *Stock size* Large
No. of dealers 80
Stock General antiques
Open Mon–Sat 9am–5pm
Sun 1–4.30pm and Bank Holidays

⌂ Horncastle Antiques Centre
Contact Mrs P Sims or Mr D Sims
✉ **26 Bridge Street, Horncastle,**

Lincolnshire, LN9 5HZ 🅟
☎ 01507 527777 ☏ 01507 527777
✉ horncastleantiques@hotmail.com
🌐 www.horncastleantiquescentre.com
Est. 1976 *Stock size* Large
No. of dealers over 60
Stock General antiques and collectables
Open Mon–Sat 10am–5pm
Sun 1–5pm
Services Valuations, restoration, shipping

⊞ Lindsay Court Architectural
Contact Mr Lindsay White
✉ **Lindsay Court, Horncastle, Lincolnshire, LN9 5DH** 🅟
☎ 01507 527794
☏ 07768 396117
✉ horncastlestone@aol.com
Est. 1987 *Stock size* Large
Stock Architectural antiques, stoneware, garden statuary salvage, reclaims
Open Tues Thurs–Sat 9.30am–5pm or by appointment
Fairs Newark
Services Export, container packing

⊞ Alan Read
Contact Mr A Read, Liveryman of The Worshipful Company of Furniture Makers
✉ **60 & 62 West Street, Horncastle, Lincolnshire, LN9 5AD** 🅟
☎ 01507 524324/525548
☏ 01507 525548
☏ 07778 873838
Est. 1981 *Stock size* Large
Stock 17th–18thC English furniture and decorative items
Open Tues–Sat 10am–4.30pm closed Wed or by appointment 7 days a week
Services Valuations, bespoke replicas made

⊞ Seaview Antiques
Contact Mr M Chalk
✉ **Stanhope Road, Horncastle, Lincolnshire, LN9 5DG** 🅟
☎ 01507 524524
✉ tracey@seaviewantiques.co.uk
🌐 www.seaviewantiques.co.uk
Est. 1972 *Stock size* Large
Stock General antiques
Open Mon–Sat 9am–5pm
Fairs Newark

⊞ Laurence Shaw Antiques
Contact Laurence Shaw
✉ 77 East Street, Horncastle, Lincolnshire, LN9 6AA ℗
☎ 01507 527638
Est. 1971 **Stock size** Medium
Stock A complete range of general antiques
Open By appointment

KIRTON

⊞ Kirton Antiques (LAPADA)
Contact Alan Marshall
✉ 3 High Street, Kirton, Boston, Lincolnshire, PE20 1DR ℗
☎ 01205 722595 ℗ 01205 722895
⊕ 07860 531600
℮ kirtonantiques@btconnect.com
Est. 1973 **Stock size** Large
Stock Wholesalers and retailers of antiques and related items
Open Mon–Fri 8.30am–5pm
Sat 8.30am–noon or by appointment
Services Valuations, property hire

LINCOLN

⊞ Eric A Bird Jewellers (BHI)
Contact Mr S Thompson
✉ 1 St Mary's Street, Lincoln, Lincolnshire, LN5 7EQ
☎ 01522 520977 ℗ 01522 560586
ⓦ www.eric-a-bird.co.uk
Est. 1959 **Stock size** Medium
Stock Antique and modern clocks, pocket watches, jewellery
Open Tues–Sat 9am–5pm
Services Valuations, restoration and repairs

⊞ C & K Dring
Contact Mr C Dring
✉ 111 High Street, Lincoln, Lincolnshire, LN5 7PY ℗
☎ 01522 540733
Est. 1977 **Stock size** Medium
Stock Victorian and Edwardian inlaid furniture, clocks, music boxes, tinplate toys
Open Mon–Sat 10am–5pm closed Wed
Fairs Newark, Swinderby
Services Valuations

⊞ David J Hansord and Son (BADA, BACA Award Winner 2001)
Contact John Hansord
✉ 6–7 Castle Hill, Lincoln, Lincolnshire, LN1 3AA ℗
☎ 01522 530044 ℗ 01522 530044
⊕ 07831 183511
Est. 1972 **Stock size** Large
Stock 18thC English furniture, works of art and objects
Open Mon–Sat 10am–5pm
Fairs Olympia
Services Valuations, restoration

⊞ Harlequin Gallery (PBFA)
Contact Mrs Anna Cockram
✉ 20–22 Steep Hill, Lincoln, Lincolnshire, LN2 1LT ℗
☎ 01522 522589
℮ harlequin@acockram. fsbusiness.co.uk
Est. 1964 **Stock size** Large
Stock Antiquarian and second-hand books, maps, prints
Open Mon–Sat 10.30am–5.45pm Wed 11am–4.30pm
Services Valuations, antique globe restoration

⌂ Dorrian Lamberts
Contact Mr R Lambert
✉ 64 & 65 Steep Hill, Lincoln, Lincolnshire, LN2 1LR ℗
☎ 01522 545916
Est. 1984 **Stock size** Medium
No. of dealers 17
Stock General antiques
Open Mon–Sat 10am–5pm Sun 11am–4pm in Summer
Services Valuations

➶ Thomas Mawer & Son Ltd
Contact Mr J C Slingsby
✉ Dunston House, Portland Street, Lincoln, Lincolnshire, LN5 7NN ℗
☎ 01522 524984
℮ auctions@thos-mawer.co.uk
ⓦ www.thos-mawer.co.uk
Est. 1864
Open Mon–Thurs 9am–5.30pm Fri 9am–4pm Sat 9am–noon
Sales Victorian and later first Sat of every month, quarterly antiques, regular specialist sales
Catalogues Yes

LONG SUTTON

⊞ Chapel Emporium
Contact Miss B Hill
✉ London Road, Long Sutton, Spalding, Lincolnshire, PE12 9EA ℗
☎ 01406 364808
℮ barbara.hill4@btopenworld.com
Est. 1983 **Stock size** Large
Stock General antiques
Open Tues Sun 10am–5pm
Services Restoration

⌂ Long Sutton Antique and Craft Centre
Contact Colin Witchell
✉ 72–74 London Road, Long Sutton, Spalding, Lincolnshire, PE12 9EB ℗
☎ 01406 362991
Est. 1998 **Stock size** Large
No. of dealers 64
Stock General antiques, collectables and craft
Open Mon–Sat 10.30am–5.30pm Sun 11am–4pm

LOUTH

⌂ The Old Maltings Antique Centre
Contact Mr Norman Coffey
✉ Aswell Street, Louth, Lincolnshire, LN11 9HP ℗
☎ 01507 600366
⊕ 07885 536607
℮ margaret@eastcoast88. freeserve.co.uk
Est. 1979 **Stock size** Large
No. of dealers 20
Stock General antiques, collectables, Victorian–Edwardian furniture
Open Mon–Sat 10am–4.30pm
Services Valuations, restoration

➶ John Taylor's
Contact Mrs A Laverack
✉ The Wool Mart, Kidgate, Louth, Lincolnshire, LN11 9EZ
☎ 01507 611107 ℗ 01507 601280
℮ enquiries@johntaylors.com
ⓦ www.johntaylors.com
Est. 1869
Open Mon–Fri 9am–5.15pm Sat 9am–2pm
Sales General antiques
Frequency Monthly
Catalogues Yes

YORKS & LINCS
LINCOLNSHIRE • STAMFORD

YORKS & LINCS *(vertical margin tab)*

MARKET DEEPING

🏠 **Market Deeping Antiques & Craft Centre**
Contact John Strutt
✉ 50–56 High Street, Market Deeping, Lincolnshire, PE6 8EB 🅿
☎ 01778 380238
Est. 1995 *Stock size* Large
No. of dealers 70
Stock General antiques, collectables, crafts
Open Mon–Sat 10am–5pm Sun 11am–5pm

⊞ **Portland House Antiques**
Contact Mr Cree
✉ 23 Church Street, Market Deeping, Lincolnshire, PE6 8AN 🅿
☎ 01778 347129
Est. 1971 *Stock size* Large
Stock 18thC–early 19thC furniture, pictures and clocks
Open Sat 10am–4pm or by appointment

NETTLEHAM

⊞ **Autumn Leaves**
Contact Mrs Susan Young
✉ Unit 2 Co-op Building, 19 The Green, Nettleham, Lincoln, Lincolnshire, LN2 2NR 🅿
☎ 01522 750779
📧 leaves@onetel.net.uk
🌐 www.abebooks.com/home/autumn_leaves
Est. 1997 *Stock size* Medium
Stock Second-hand books on all subjects
Open Tues–Thurs 9.15am–4.30pm Fri 9.15am–5pm Sat 9.15am–12.30pm
Services Book search

⊞ **Homme de Quimper**
Contact Mr S Toogood
✉ Hillstead, 11 Church Street, Nettleham, Lincoln, Lincolnshire, LN2 2PD 🅿
☎ 01522 753753
📱 07831 773622
📧 steve.toogood@ntlworld.com
🌐 www.hommedequimper.co.uk
Est. 1996 *Stock size* Large
Stock Antique French faïence pottery, 19thC Quimper, Malicome, Desevres, 18thC La Rochelle, Nevers, Rouen, Moustiers, etc
Open Mon–Sun 9am–6pm
Services Valuations, restoration

⊞ **Juke Box World**
Contact Mr S Toogood
✉ Hillstead, 11 Church Street, Nettleham, Lincoln, Lincolnshire, LN2 2PD 🅿
☎ 01522 753753
📧 steve.toogood@ntlworld.com
Est. 1985 *Stock size* Medium
Stock 20thC juke boxes
Open Mon–Sun 9am–6pm
Fairs Ascot Racecourse, Copthorne
Services Valuations, restoration

SCUNTHORPE

🔨 **Canter & Francis**
Contact Mr S J Francis, NAEA
✉ 8 Doncaster Road, Scunthorpe, Lincolnshire, DN15 7RB 🅿
☎ 01724 858855 📠 01724 858855
📧 mail@canterandfrancis.co.uk
🌐 www.canterandfrancis.co.uk
Est. 1947
Open Mon–Fri 9am–5pm
Sales General antiques, household furniture
Frequency Antiques 2–3 a year, general sales every week
Catalogues No

SPALDING

🔨 **R Longstaff & Co**
Contact Mr J A Smith
✉ 5 New Road, Spalding, Lincolnshire, PE11 1BS 🅿
☎ 01775 766766 📠 01775 762289
📧 admin@longstaff.com
🌐 www.longstaff.com
Est. 1770
Open Mon–Fri 9am–6pm Sat 9am–3pm Sun 11am–3pm
Sales General antiques, house clearance
Frequency Bi-monthly
Catalogues No

⊞ **M & M Antiques**
Contact M Dawson
✉ 17a The Crescent, Spalding, Lincolnshire, PE11 1AF 🅿
☎ 01775 766125
📱 07904 157657
Est. 1990 *Stock size* Large
Stock General antiques 1850–1950
Open Mon–Sat 10am–5pm
Fairs Loughborough Art Deco

🔨 **Munton & Russell (ISVA)**
Contact Mr James Smith
✉ 16 Sheep Market, Spalding, Lincolnshire, PE11 1BE 🅿
☎ 01775 722475 📠 01775 769958
🌐 www.muntonandrussell.co.uk
Est. 1964
Open Mon–Fri 9am–6pm
Sales General antiques
Frequency Periodic
Catalogues No

⊞ **Penman Clockcare (BWCMG)**
Contact Mr M Strutt
✉ Unit 4–5, Pied Calf Yard, Sheepmarket, Spalding, Lincolnshire, PE11 1BE 🅿
☎ 01775 714900
📱 07940 911167
📧 strutt@clara.net
🌐 www.antique-clockrepairs.co.uk
Est. 1997 *Stock size* Medium
Stock Antique clocks, watches and jewellery
Open Mon–Fri 9am–5pm Sat 9am–4pm
Services Restoration, full repair service, home calls

⊞ **Spalding Antiques**
Contact Mr John Mumford
✉ 1 Abbey Path, Spalding, Lincolnshire, PE11 1AY 🅿
☎ 01775 713185
Est. 1987 *Stock size* Medium
Stock General antiques, clocks, watches
Open Mon–Sat 10am–5pm

STAMFORD

🔨 **Batemans Auctioneers & Valuers**
Contact Kate Bateman
✉ Broad Street, Stamford, Lincolnshire, PE9 1PX 🅿
☎ 01780 766466 📠 01780 765071
📧 info@batemans-auctions.co.uk
🌐 www.batemans-auctions.co.uk
Open Mon–Fri 10am–5pm
Sales Fine arts, antiques, collectables and general household sales Sat 10.30am, viewing Thurs 10am–5pm Fri 10am–7pm
Frequency Monthly
Catalogues Yes

YORKS & LINCS
LINCOLNSHIRE • STAMFORD

YORKS & LINCS

⊞ The Forge Antiques & Collectables
Contact Tessa Easton
✉ 5 St Mary Street, Stamford, Lincolnshire, PE9 2DE 🅿
☎ 01780 767874
📱 07763 334703
✉ theforgeantiques@fsmail.net
Est. 2000 **Stock size** Large
Stock Furniture, clocks, silver, jewellery, china, glass, textiles
Open Mon–Sat 9.30am–5pm Sun and Bank Holidays 10am–4pm
Fairs Swinderby
Services Search service

⊞ Hunters Interiors (Stamford) Ltd
Contact Jill Hunter
✉ 9a St Mary's Hill, Stamford, Lincolnshire, PE9 2DP 🅿
☎ 01780 757946 📠 01780 757946
📱 07976 796969
✉ huntersinteriors@btopenworld.com
🌐 www.huntersinteriorsof stamford.co.uk
Est. 2000 **Stock size** Small
Stock Furniture, glass, china, ornaments, tapestries, other soft furnishings, 18thC mirrors,
Open Mon–Sat 9am–5.30pm
Services Restoration

⊞ Robert Johnson Coin Co
Contact Mr R Johnson
✉ PO Box 181, Stamford, Lincolnshire, PE9 4XA
📱 01778 561529
✉ rjcoinco@aol.com
Est. 1971 **Stock size** Medium
Stock Greek, Roman, English, hammered and milled coins, medals, banknotes, ancient, English and foreign gold coins, medallions, tokens
Open By appointment only
Fairs Birmingham, York, Stamford
Services Valuations

⊞ Robert Loomes Clock Restoration (BWCG, BHI)
Contact Mr R Loomes
✉ 3 St Leonards Street, Stamford, Lincolnshire, PE9 2HU 🅿
☎ 01780 481319
🌐 www.dialrestorer.co.uk
Est. 1987 **Stock size** Small
Stock Clocks

Open Mon–Fri 9am–5pm
Sat 10am–4pm
Services Restoration

⊞ Graham Pickett Antiques
Contact Mrs H Pickett
✉ 7 High Steet, St Martins, Stamford, Lincolnshire, PE9 2LF 🅿
☎ 01780 481064
📱 07710 936948
✉ graham@pickettantiques. demon.co.uk
🌐 www.pickettantiques.demon.co.uk
Est. 1987 **Stock size** Medium
Stock English and French provincial furniture, beds, silver
Open Mon–Sat 10am–5.30pm
Sun by appointment

⊞ St Georges Antiques
Contact Mr G Burns
✉ 1 St Georges Square, Stamford, Lincolnshire, PE9 2BN 🅿
☎ 01780 754117
📱 07779 528713
Est. 1974 **Stock size** Large
Stock General antiques, furniture
Trade only Yes
Open Mon–Fri 9am–1pm
2–4.30pm

⌂ St Martins Antiques Centre
Contact Peter Light or Tina Higgins
✉ 23a High Street, Stamford, Lincolnshire, PE9 2LF 🅿
☎ 01780 481158 📠 01780 481158
✉ peter@st-martins-antiques.co.uk
🌐 www.st-martins-antiques.co.uk
Est. 1993 **Stock size** Large
No. of dealers 70
Stock General antiques, furniture, porcelain, clocks, jewellery, silver, prints, textiles, lighting, fireplaces, copper, brass, ephemera, upholstered furniture, refurbished antique chairs and sofas
Open Mon–Sat 10am–5pm
Sun 10.30am–5pm
Services Wheelchairs provided

⊞ St Mary's Books & Prints
Contact Mr Tyers
✉ 9 St Mary's Hill, Stamford, Lincolnshire, PE9 2DP

☎ 01780 763033 📠 01780 763033
✉ info@stmarysbookscom
🌐 www.stmarysbooks.com
Est. 1971 **Stock size** Large
Stock Antiquarian, rare and second-hand books, Wisden's Cricketers Almanac a speciality, literature, modern first editions, field sports, leather bindings
Open Mon–Sun 8am–6.30pm
Services Book binding, free valuations, restoration and book search

⊞ St Paul's Street Bookshop (PBFA)
Contact Mr J Blessett
✉ 7 St Paul's Street, Stamford, Lincolnshire, PE9 2BE
☎ 01780 482748 📠 01778 380538
✉ jimblessett@aol.com
Est. 1978 **Stock size** Medium
Stock Antiquarian, rare and second-hand books, specializing in motoring books
Open Mon–Sat 10am–5pm
closed Wed
Services Valuations

⊞ Staniland Booksellers (PBFA)
Contact Mr B J Valentine-Ketchum
✉ 4–5 St Georges Street, Stamford, Lincolnshire, PE9 2BJ
☎ 01780 755800 📠 01780 755800
✉ stanilandbooksellers@ btinternet.com
Est. 1972 **Stock size** Large
Stock Antiquarian, library sets and bindings, rare and second-hand scholarly books, architecture, applied art, art, philosophy, music history, literature, natural history
Open Mon–Sat 10am–1pm
2–5pm
Fairs London Book Fairs
Services Valuations, probate and insurance valuations

⊞ Andrew Thomas
Contact Mr A Thomas
✉ Old Granary, 10 North Street, Stamford, Lincolnshire, PE9 2YN 🅿
☎ 01780 762236 📠 01780 762236
Est. 1969 **Stock size** Large
Stock General antiques and antique painted furniture
Open Mon–Sat 9am–6pm

344

⊞ Undercover Books
Contact Mr T Dobson
✉ 30 Scotgate, Stamford,
Lincolnshire,
PE9 2YQ 🅿
☎ 01780 480989 📠 01780 763963
✉ undercoverbooks@btinternet.com
🌐 www.ukbookworld.com/
members/undercover
Est. 1989 *Stock size* Large
Stock Antiquarian, rare and
second-hand books, law
enforcement a speciality
Open Tues–Sat 10am–5pm

⊞ Vaughan Antiques
(LAPADA)
Contact Mr Barry Vaughan
✉ 45 Broad Street, Stamford,
Lincolnshire,
PE9 1PX 🅿
☎ 01780 765888 📠 01778 342053
📱 07712 657414
✉ vaughanantiques@aol.com
Est. 1994 *Stock size* Large
Stock English furniture, clocks,
decorative items, 17th–19thC
furniture a speciality
Open Mon–Sat 10am–5pm
Fairs NEC, LAPADA

STICKNEY

⊞ B & B Antiques
✉ Main Road,
Stickney, Boston,
Lincolnshire,
PE22 8AD 🅿
☎ 01205 480204
Est. 1970 *Stock size* Medium
Stock General antiques
Open By appointment only

SUTTON BRIDGE

⊞ Old Barn Antiques
Contact Mr Steve Jackson
✉ 48–50 Bridge Road,
Sutton Bridge,
Spalding,
Lincolnshire,
PE12 9UA 🅿
☎ 01406 350435/363371
📠 01406 359158
📱 07956 677228
✉ oldbarnants@aol.com
Est. 1984 *Stock size* Large
Stock Victorian, Edwardian and
1920s furniture
Open Mon–Fri 9am–5pm
Sat 10am–5pm Sun 11am–4pm
Fairs Newark
Services Containers packed

⊞ Old Barn Antiques
Contact Mr Steve Jackson
✉ Holland Lodge, Little Sutton,
Spalding, Lincolnshire,
PE12 9AL 🅿
☎ 01406 363371/350435
📠 01406 359158
📱 07956 677228
✉ oldbarnants@aol.com
Est. 1984 *Stock size* Large
Stock Victorian, Edwardian and
1920s furniture. Trade and
export (warehouse 15,000 square
feet)
Trade only Yes
Open Mon–Fri 9am–5pm Sat
10am–5pm Sun 11am–4pm
Fairs Newark
Services Containers packed

SWINDERBY

⊞ Graham the Hat
Contact Graham Rodwell
✉ Newark Road, Swinderby,
Lincolnshire,
LN6 9HN
☎ 01493 650217 📠 01493 650217
📱 07899 892337
✉ graham@grahamthehat.com
🌐 www.grahamthehat.com
Est. 1997 *Stock size* Large
Stock Collectables
Open By appointment
Fairs Swinderby, Ardingly
Services Trade prices on request

TATTERSHALL

⊞ Wayside Antiques
Contact Mr G Ball
✉ 10 Market Place, Tattershall,
Lincolnshire,
LN4 4LQ 🅿
☎ 01526 342436
Est. 1972 *Stock size* Medium
Stock General antiques
Open By appointment any time

WAINFLEET

⚒ Naylor's Auctions
Contact Ian Naylor
✉ 20 St John's Street, Wainfleet,
Skegness, Lincolnshire,
PE24 4DJ 🅿
☎ 01754 881210 📠 01522 6980006
📱 07932 749334
Est. 1979
Open By appointment
Sales General antiques held
weekly Bargate Green, Boston,
last Sat every month Butterwick

Village Hall 10am, viewing day
prior 4–7pm and from 8am day
of sale
Catalogues No

WALESBY

⊞ Lincolnshire Antiques
and Fine Art
Contact Mr N J Rhodes
✉ White House Farm,
Walesby, Market Rasen,
Lincolnshire,
LN8 3UW 🅿
☎ 01673 838278
📱 07950 271898
Est. 1979 *Stock size* Medium
Stock Quality 17th–19thC oil
paintings and furniture
Open By appointment only

WOODHALL SPA

⊞ M & J Antiques
Contact Mr J Goodyear
✉ Tattershall Road, Woodhall
Spa, Lincolnshire,
LN10 6QJ 🅿
☎ 01526 352140
Est. 1990 *Stock size* Medium
Stock General antiques
Open Flexible

⊞ Underwood Hall
Antiques
Contact G Underwood
✉ 5 The Broadway, Woodhall
Spa, Lincolnshire,
LN10 6ST 🅿
☎ 01526 353815
Est. 1974 *Stock size* Medium
Stock Small furniture,
19th–20thC pottery, porcelain,
silver, jewellery, postcards
Open Mon–Sat 10.30am–4.30pm
Sun 1–4pm or by appointment
Fairs Newark
Services Valuations

⊞ VOC Antiques (LAPADA)
Contact David Leyland
✉ 27 Witham Road, Woodhall
Spa, Lincolnshire,
LN10 6RW 🅿
☎ 01526 352753 📠 01526 352753
✉ djleyland@tinyworld.co.uk
Est. 1975 *Stock size* Medium
Stock Georgian–Victorian
furniture, brass, copper, general
antiques
Open Mon–Sat 9.30am–5.30pm
Sun 2–5pm
Services Valuations, restoration

CO DURHAM

BARNARD CASTLE

⊞ Edward Barrington-Doulby
Contact Mike or Fiona
✉ 23 The Bank, Barnard Castle,
Co Durham,
DL12 8PH 🅿
☎ 01833 630500
Ⓜ 07817 287204
🅴 m.venus@ntlworld.com
Est. 1994 *Stock size* Medium
Stock Furniture, smalls,
hardware, door furniture,
ironmongery, kitchenware
Open Tues–Sat 11am–5pm
Sun 1–5pm

⊞ James Hardy Antiques Ltd
Contact Alan or Amanda Hardy
✉ 12 The Bank, Barnard Castle,
Co Durham,
DL12 8PQ 🅿
☎ 01833 695135 🅖 01833 695135
Ⓜ 07710 162003
🅴 alan@jameshardyantiques.co.uk
🆆 www.jameshardyantiques.co.uk

Est. 1993
Stock 17th–19thC oak, mahogany
period furniture, silver both for
the serious collector and for
special occasion gifts
Open 10am–5pm closed Thurs Sun
Fairs Harrogate
Services Restoration of silver and
furniture

⊞ Kingsley & Co
Contact David Harper
✉ Springwood Cottage,
Barnard Castle, Co Durham,
DL12 9DD 🅿
☎ 01833 650551 🅖 01833 650551
Ⓜ 07711 639035
🅴 sales@kingsleysofas.co.uk
🆆 www.kingsleysofas.co.uk
Est. 2000 *Stock size* Medium
Stock Furniture, smalls, Asian
works of art, restored antique
upholstery, hand-made sofas
Open Mon–Sat 10.30am–5.30pm
Services Valuations, restoration,
upholstery, renovation

⊞ Robson's Antiques
Contact Mr or Mrs Robson
✉ 36 The Bank, Barnard Castle,

Co Durham,
DL12 8PN 🅿
☎ 01833 690157 🅖 01833 638700
Ⓜ 07977 146584
🅴 dale.hunter.robson@virgin.net
🆆 www.robsonsantiques.co.uk
Est. 1975 *Stock size* Large
Stock Fireplaces, Durham quilts,
glass, silver, cutlery, general
antiques
Open Mon–Fri 10am–5.30pm
Sat 10am–6pm Sun 1.30–5pm
Fairs Birmingham Glass Fair,
Newark, Manchester Textile Fair,
NEC
Services Fireplace restoration
and fitting

BISHOP AUCKLAND

⊞ Eden House Antiques
Contact Chris Metcalfe
✉ 10 Staindrop Road, West
Auckland, Bishop Auckland,
Co Durham,
DL14 9JX 🅿
☎ 01388 833013
🅴 chrismetcalfe@aol.com
🆆 www.antiques.co.uk
Est. 1977 *Stock size* Medium
Stock Furniture, clocks, china,
pottery
Open Mon–Sun 10am–6pm
Services Valuations, restoration

⚒ G H Edkins and Son
Contact Denis Edkins
✉ Auckland Auction Rooms,
58 Kingsway, Bishop Auckland,
Co Durham,
DL14 7JF 🅿
☎ 01388 603095 🅖 01388 661239
Ⓜ 07860 321312
Est. 1907
Open Mon–Thurs
9.30am–4.30pm Fri 9.30am–4pm
Sales General antiques
household sale every Thurs,
viewing Wed 9.30am–noon
2–5pm
Catalogues No

CONSETT

⊞ Harry Raine
Contact Mr N C Raine
✉ Kelvinside House,
91 Villa Real Road, Consett,
Co Durham,
DH8 6BL 🅿
☎ 01207 503935
Ⓜ 07758 838328
Est. 1965 *Stock size* Medium

Stock General antiques
Trade only Yes
Open By appointment only

⊞ **Rutherford Interiors**
Contact Karen Rutherford
✉ 80 Medomsley Road, Consett,
Co Durham,
DH8 5HS ♿
☎ 01207 500200 ✆ 01207 500220
Est. 2004 **Stock size** Medium
Stock English and European
furniture, antiques, decorative
items
Open Mon–Sat 9am–5pm
closed Wed

⊞ **Westend Antiques &
Jewellery**
Contact L Newman
✉ 63 Middle Street, Consett,
Co Durham,
DH8 5QG ♿
☎ 01207 582228 ✆ 01207 582228
✉ westendantiques@consett.
btopenworld.com
Est. 1996 **Stock size** Large
Stock General antiques,
jewellery, Roman, medieval
artefacts, bric-a-brac
Open Mon–Sat 9am–5pm
Fairs Newark
Services Valuations, restoration,
clock, watch and pottery repairs

DARLINGTON

⊞ **The Quest Antiques**
Contact Stephen King
✉ 417 North Road, Darlington,
Co Durham,
DL1 3BN ♿
☎ 01325 286156
✉ steveatquest@aol.com
Est. 1981 **Stock size** Medium
Stock Antiques, collectables
1950s–1960s
Open Mon–Sat 1–4pm
Services Valuations

⊞ **Tango Curios**
✉ 3a Houndgate, Darlington,
Co Durham,
DL1 5RL ♿
☎ 01325 465768
✆ 07977 979770
Est. 1986 **Stock size** Large
Stock 20thC decorative arts,
glass, ceramics, metalware,
pictures, furniture
Open Thurs–Sat 5pm 10am–5pm
Fairs Antiques for Everyone, Newark
Services Valuations

DURHAM

⊞ **Capercaillie Antiques**
Contact David Rogers
✉ 25–27 High Street North,
Langley Moor, Durham,
Co Durham,
DH7 8JG ♿
☎ 0191 378 0175
✆ 07930 251116
Est. 1964 **Stock size** Large
Stock Antique furniture
Open Fri 1–4pm Sat 10am–4pm
or by appointment

⊞ **Finley's Finds**
Contact Mr B Finley
✉ 23 Flambard Road, Durham,
Co Durham,
DH1 5HY ♿
☎ 0191 384 1643
Est. 1995
Stock Furniture, china, jewellery
Open Mon–Fri 9am–5pm
Fairs Newark, Swinderby
Services Valuations, house
clearance

⊞ **Old & Gold**
Contact Pam Tracey
✉ 87b Elvet Bridge, Durham,
Co Durham,
DH1 3AG ♿
☎ 0191 386 0728
✆ 07831 362252
Est. 1989 **Stock size** Medium
Stock General antiques
Open Mon–Sun 10am–5pm
Fairs Newark
Services Jewellery repairs

HARTLEPOOL

⊞ **Spring Garden
Furniture & Antiques**
Contact Deborah Herring
✉ 124 Stockton Road,
Hartlepool, Co Durham,
TS25 5AB ♿
☎ 01429 266716 ✆ 01429 266716
Est. 1998 **Stock size** Small
Stock Victorian–Edwardian
furniture, collectables
Open Mon–Sat 10am–5pm
Wed 1.30–5pm
Services Stripping

PETERLEE

⊞ **Emeralds Antiques**
Contact Alan Brown
✉ 1a Seaside Lane,
Easington Colliery, Peterlee,

Co Durham,
SR8 1PF ♿
☎ 0191 523 7320
Est. 1998 **Stock size** Large
Stock General antiques
Open Mon–Sat 9.30am–5pm
Services Valuations, restoration,
house clearance

ST HELEN AUCKLAND

⊞ **Something Different**
Contact Mr Peter Reeves
or Mr Melvin Holmes
✉ 34a Maude Terrace,
St Helen Auckland,
Bishop Auckland, Co Durham,
DL14 9BD ♿
☎ 01388 664366
✆ 07718 391880
✉ melh@bishopauck.freeserve.co.uk
Est. 1980 **Stock size** Large
Stock Memorabilia, militaria,
furniture, clocks, collectables,
silver, lights, decorative items,
carpets, rugs, Continental
antiques
Open Mon–Sat 9.30am–5.30pm
Sun 10am–5pm
Services Valuations, clock
restoration, delivery

WOLSINGHAM

⊞ **Rams Head Antiques**
Contact Keith Thompson
✉ 17 Front Street, Wolsingham,
Bishop Auckland, Co Durham,
DL13 3DF ♿
☎ 01388 526834
Est. 1998 **Stock size** Small
Stock Antique furniture
Open Mon–Sat 11am–5pm

NORTHUMBERLAND

ALNWICK

⊞ **Barter Books**
Contact Stuart Manley
✉ Alnwick Station, Alnwick,
Northumberland,
NE66 2NP ♿
☎ 01665 604888 ✆ 01665 604444
✉ bb@barterbooks.co.uk
🌐 www.barterbooks.co.uk
Est. 1991 **Stock size** Large
Stock Antiquarian and second-
hand books, records, CDs, videos
Open Summer Mon–Sun
9am–7pm winter Mon–Sun
9am–5pm Thurs 9am–7pm
Services Book search, valuations

NORTH EAST
NORTHUMBERLAND • ASHINGTON

⊞ John Smith of Alnwick Ltd
Contact Mr P Smith
✉ West Cawledge Park Gallery, Alnwick, Northumberland, NE66 2HJ 🅿
☎ 01665 604363
Est. 1972 *Stock size* Medium
Stock Country and general antiques, rugs, pictures, furniture
Open Mon–Sun 10am–5pm

⊞ Tamblyn Antiques
Contact Professor Hirst
✉ 12 Bondgate Without, Alnwick, Northumberland, NE66 1PP 🅿
☎ 01665 603024
✉ profbehirst@tamblynant.freeserve.co.uk
Est. 1981 *Stock size* Medium
Stock Small period furniture, ceramics, Finnish, Swedish and Dutch glass
Open Mon–Sat 9.30am–4.30pm
Services Valuations

ASHINGTON

⊞ The Miner's Lamp
Contact Dorothy Kindley
✉ 10a Milburn Road, Ashington, Northumberland, NE63 0HD 🅿
☎ 01670 815327
Est. 1972 *Stock size* Small
Stock General antiques, smalls
Open Mon–Sat 10am–4pm closed Wed

BERWICK-UPON-TWEED

⊞ Dillons Antiques
Contact Tom Dillon
✉ 12–14 Bridge Street, Berwick-upon-Tweed, Northumberland, TD15 1AQ 🅿
☎ 01289 303917
Est. 1999 *Stock size* Small
Stock General antiques
Open Mon–Sat 9am–4pm
Services Valuations, removal service

⊞ James E McDougall
Contact James E McDougall MRICS
✉ St Duthus, 6 Palace Street East, Berwick-upon-Tweed, Northumberland, TD15 1HT 🅿
☎ 01289 330791

✉ james.mcdougall@caucasian-rugs.co.uk
🌐 www.caucasian-rugs.co.uk
Est. 1989 *Stock size* Small
Stock Antique carpets, rugs
Open By appointment
Services Valuations

CHATTON

➹ Jim Railton
Contact Jim Railton
✉ Nursery House, Chatton, Alnwick, Northumberland, NE66 5PY 🅿
☎ 01668 215323 01668 215400
📱 07774 241111
✉ jim@jimrailton.com
🌐 www.jimrailton.com
Est. 1993
Open Mon–Sat 9am–5pm or by appointment
Sales General antiques sale, specializing in country house sales at historic properties
Frequency 4 per annum
Catalogues Yes

CRAMLINGTON

⊞ Granny's Attic
Contact Elizabeth Buhagier
✉ 33 Arlington Grove, Cramlington, Northumberland, NE23 3G2 🅿
☎ 01670 731868 01670 731868
✉ joe.buh@virgin.net
Est. 1987 *Stock size* Large
Stock Antiques, collectables
Open Mon–Sat 10am–5pm
Services Valuations, house clearance

HEXHAM

⊞ Hedley's of Hexham
Contact Mrs P Torday
✉ 3 St Mary's Chare, Hexham, Northumberland, NE46 1NQ 🅿
☎ 01434 602317
✉ hedley@torday96.fsnet.co.uk
Est. 1819 *Stock size* Medium
Stock General antiques, furniture, collectables, china, clocks, Moorcroft
Open Tues–Sat 9.30am–5pm
Services Restoration

⊞ Hencotes Books and Prints (PBFA)
Contact Mrs Penny Pearce
✉ 8 Hencotes, Hexham,

Northumberland, NE46 2EJ 🅿
☎ 01434 605971
✉ enquiries@hencotesbooks.onyx.net.co.uk
Est. 1992 *Stock size* Medium
Stock Antiquarian and second-hand books, specializing in local history, literature, children's books, gardening, cookery
Open Mon–Sat 10.30am–5pm closed Thurs
Fairs Local PBFA, Durham, Newcastle
Services Booksearch

➹ Hexham and Northern Mart
Contact Mr Brian Rogerson
✉ Mart Office, Tyne Green, Hexham, Northumberland, NE46 3SG 🅿
☎ 01434 605444 or 01669 620392 (Rothbury)
📱 07801 862792
✉ furniture@hexhammart.co.uk
🌐 www.hexhammart.co.uk
Est. 1850
Open Mon–Fri 9am–5pm
Sales House clearances, antiques sales (held at Rothbury), viewing 2 days prior to sale
Frequency Every 2 or 3 months
Catalogues No

⊞ Hexham Antiques
Contact John and Dorothy Latham
✉ Unit 10, Acomb Industrial Estate, Acomb, Hexham, Northumberland, NE46 4SA
☎ 01434 603851
Est. 1978 *Stock size* Large
Stock General antiques, collectables, pictures, bric-a-brac
Open Mon Tues Sat 10.30am–4pm or by appointment
Fairs Hexham, Carlisle
Services Picture framing, valuations, house clearance

⊞ Pine Workshop
Contact John Askell
✉ 28 Priestpopple, Hexham, Northumberland, NE46 1PQ 🅿
☎ 01434 601121
Est. 1987 *Stock size* Medium
Stock Antique pine, oak and sycamore
Open Mon–Sat 9am–5pm
Services Kitchen build, bespoke pine

⊞ Priestpopple Books
Contact Mr J B Patterson
✉ 9b Priestpopple, Hexham,
Northumberland,
NE46 1PF
☎ 01434 607773
🅴 priestpopple.books@tiscali.co.uk
Est. 1998 *Stock size* Large
Stock Antiquarian books,
general antiques, militaria,
music, entertainment, art
Open Mon–Sat 9am–5pm
Services Valuations, restoration

🏹 Louis Johnson
Contact John Hayes
✉ 63 Bridge Street, Morpeth,
Northumberland,
NE61 1PQ 🅿
☎ 01670 513025 🅰 01670 503267
🅴 lj@lj-fsbusiness.co.uk
🆆 www.louis-johnson.co.uk
Est. 1955
Open Mon–Fri 9am–5pm
Sales Antiques, fine art and
collectables, cars, motorcycles,
general household. Sale dates
upon application
Catalogues Yes

⊞ Pottery Bank Antiques
Contact Mr Michael Everitt
✉ 43 Bullers Green, Morpeth,
Northumberland,
NE61 1DF 🅿
☎ 01670 516160
🅴 apope@morpethnet.co.uk
🆆 www.morpethnet.co.uk
Est. 1977 *Stock size* Medium
Stock General antiques,
furniture, silver
Open Mon–Sat 11.30am–5.30pm
or by appointment

⊞ Ruperts of Rothbury
Contact Linda Thompson
✉ Townfoot, Rothbury, Morpeth,
Northumberland,
NE65 7SN 🅿
☎ 01669 620350
Est. 2001 *Stock size* Medium
Stock General antiques
Open Sat Sun by appointment
Fairs Newark, Swinderby
Services Picture restoration

⊞ Golfark International
Contact Michael Arkle
✉ 5 Tollgate Crescent,
Rothbury,
Northumberland,
NE65 7RE 🅿
☎ 01669 620487 🅰 01669 620487
📱 07710 693860
🅴 michael@golfark.freeserve.co.uk
Est. 1997 *Stock size* Small
Stock Old golf clubs, bags and
balls, sporting antiques, golfing
memorabilia
Open By appointment

**⊞ Woodside Reclamation
(SALVO)**
Contact Keith Allan
✉ Woodside, Scremerston,
Berwick-upon-Tweed,
Northumberland,
TD15 2SY 🅿
☎ 01289 331211/302658
🅰 01289 330274
🅴 info@redbaths.co.uk
🆆 www.redbaths.co.uk
Est. 1990 *Stock size* Medium
Stock Fireplaces, antique baths,
bathroom ware, doors, timber,
beams, flooring
Open Tues–Sat 9am–5pm
Services Furniture and door
stripping, restoration

⊞ Hamish Dunn Antiques
Contact Mr Dunn
✉ 17 High Street, Wooler,
Northumberland,
NE71 6BU 🅿
☎ 01668 281341 🅰 01668 281341
📱 07940 530123
Est. 1986 *Stock size* Medium
Stock General antiques, second-
hand and antiquarian books
Open Mon–Sat 9am–4.30pm

**⊞ Millers Antiques of
Wooler (LAPADA)**
Contact James Miller
✉ 1–5 Church Street, Wooler,
Northumberland,
NE71 6BZ 🅿
☎ 01668 281500 🅰 01668 282383
📱 07714 332441
🅴 jmiller.antiques@virgin.net
🆆 www.millersantiquesofwooler.com
Est. 1947 *Stock size* Large
Stock Georgian and Victorian
furniture
Open Mon–Fri 9.30am–5pm
Sat Sun by appointment
Fairs DMG Newark

⊞ Oriental Antiques Ltd
Contact Christine Lawler
✉ 45 Castlehill House, Wylam
Manor, Wylam, Northumberland,
NE41 8JG 🅿
☎ 01661 854994 🅰 01661 854994
📱 07879 285926
🅴 christine@orientalantiquesltd.com
🆆 www.orientalantiques.com
Est. 2003 *Stock size* Medium
Stock Oriental furntiure
Trade only Yes
Fairs NEC (autumn)

TYNE AND WEAR

🏹 Boldon Auction Galleries
Contact Mr Hodges
✉ 24a Front Street, East Boldon,
Tyne and Wear,
NE36 0SJ 🅿
☎ 0191 537 2630 🅰 0191 536 3875
🅴 boldon@btconnect.com
🆆 www.boldonauctions.co.uk
Est. 1981
Open Mon–Fri 9am–5pm
Sales General household and
Victorian sales fortnightly
Wed 10am, viewing Sat before
auction 9.30am–12.30pm
Tues before auction 2–6pm,
4 specialist sales annually
including collectables and toys,
style and design 1930–present
day, antiquarian books, antiques
and antique furniture
Catalogues Yes

⊞ Mulroys Antiques
Contact Miss J Mulroy
✉ 24 The Boulevard, Metro Centre,
Gateshead, Tyne and Wear,
NE11 9YL 🅿
☎ 0191 461 1211 🅰 0191 461 1211
Est. 1959 *Stock size* Large
Stock General antiques and
period jewellery
Open Mon–Fri 10am–8pm
Thurs 10am–9pm Sat 9am–7pm
Sun 11am–5pm
Services Valuations, restoration

**⊞ Jane Kirsopp-Reed
Antiques (LAPADA)**
Contact Jane Kirsopp-Reed

⊠ Harewood House,
49 Great North Road, Gosforth,
Newcastle-upon-Tyne,
Tyne and Wear,
NE3 2HH ℗
☎ 0191 284 3202 ❺ 0191 284 3202
❸ info@janekirsoppreedantiques.co.uk
ⓦ www.janekirsoppreedantiques.co.uk
Stock size Large
Stock Early porcelain,
Georgian–Edwardian furniture,
dining and lounge furniture,
English porcelain and glass
Open Mon–Fri 9am–5pm Sat
10am–5pm or by appointment
Fairs Galloway Fairs
Services Restoration

⊞ **The Wooden Betty**
Contact Susan Markall
⊠ Gosforth, Tyne and Wear, NE3 ℗
⑩ 07796 531477
Est. 2000 *Stock size* Small
Stock Period furniture
Open By appointment
Services Restoration

NEWCASTLE-UPON-TYNE

⊞ **Aladdins Architectural
Antiques and Heritage
Workshops (SALVO)**
Contact Mr D Crowley
⊠ 626 Welbeck Road, Walker,
Newcastle-upon-Tyne,
Tyne and Wear,
NE6 4JS ℗
☎ 0191 262 7373
⑩ 07762 527640
❸ dave@architecturalantiques.
fsnet.co.uk or
david.crowley10@ntlworld.com
ⓦ wwwantiquedoorsrestored.com
Est. 1976 *Stock size* Large
Stock General antiques
Open Mon–Sat 10am–6pm
Sun by appointment
Services Valuations, restoration

➢ **Anderson & Garland
(SOFAA)**
Contact Mr A McCoull
⊠ Anderson House,
Crispin Court, New Biggin Lane,
Westerhope, Newcastle-upon-
Tyne, Tyne and Wear,
NE5 1BF
☎ 0191 430 3000 ❺ 0191 430 3001
❸ info@andersongarland.com
ⓦ www.andersongarland.com
Est. 1840
Open Mon–Fri 9am–5.30pm
Sales Fine art sales every 3

months, general antiques sales
fortnightly
Catalogues Yes

⌂ **Antiques Centre**
Contact Chris Parkin
⊠ 142 Northumberland Street,
Newcastle-upon-Tyne,
Tyne and Wear,
NE1 7DQ ℗
☎ 0191 232 9832
❸ timeantiques@talktlk,net
Est. 1983 *Stock size* Large
No. of dealers 13
Stock General antiques,
Art Nouveau, decorative arts,
Arts and Crafts, clocks, watches,
jewellery
Open Mon–Sat 10am–5pm
Services Valuations, restoration,
tea room

⊞ **Attica**
Contact Stephen Pierce
⊠ 2 Old George Yard,
Off Highbridge, Newcastle-
upon-Tyne, Tyne and Wear,
NE1 1EZ ℗
☎ 0191 261 4062
Est. 1983 *Stock size* Medium
Stock Vintage clothing,
1950s–1970s, furniture, decor
Open Mon–Sat 10.30am–5.30pm

➢ **Bonhams**
⊠ 30–32 Grey Street, Newcastle-
upon-Tyne, Tyne and Wear,
NE1 6AE
☎ 0191 233 9930 ❺ 0191 233 9933
ⓦ www.bonhams.com
Open Mon–Fri 9am–5pm
Sales Regional office. Regular
sales held in London and in our
salerooms across the country.
Free auction valuations;
insurance and probate valuations

⊞ **B J Coltman Antiques**
Contact Barry Coltman
⊠ 80 Meldon Terrace, Heaton,
Newcastle-upon-Tyne, Tyne &
Wear,
NE6 5XP ℗
☎ 0191 224 5209
⑩ 077867 077539
Est. 1994 *Stock size* Large
Stock 18th–19thC furniture
Open Mon–Fri 9am–5pm
Services Restoration

⊞ **Corbitt's (ASDA, APS,
BNTA, PTS)**
Contact Mr D McMonagle

⊠ 5 Mosley Street,
Newcastle-upon-Tyne,
Tyne and Wear,
NE1 1YE ℗
☎ 0191 232 7268 ❺ 0191 261 4130
❸ info@corbitts.com
ⓦ www.corbitts.com
Est. 1964 *Stock size* Medium
Stock Stamps, postal history,
coins, medals, autographs
Open Tues–Fri 9am–5pm
Sat 9.30am–4pm
Services Valuations

➢ **Corbitt's**
Contact Mr D McMonagle
⊠ 5 Mosley Street,
Newcastle-upon-Tyne,
Tyne and Wear,
NE1 1YE
☎ 0191 232 7268 ❺ 0191 261 4130
❸ info@corbitts.com
ⓦ www.corbitts.com
Est. 1964
Open Tues–Fri 9am–5pm
Sat 9.30am–4pm
Sales Antique coins, medals,
1 per year. Stamps, history 3 per
year. Cigarette cards, ephemera
1 per year, autographs
Catalogues Yes

⊞ **Owen Humble Antiques
(LAPADA)**
Contact Mr M Humble
⊠ Clayton House,
Walbottle Road, Lemington,
Newcastle-upon-Tyne,
Tyne and Wear,
NE15 9RU ℗
☎ 0191 267 7220 ❺ 0191 267 3377
❸ antiques@owenhumble.com
ⓦ www.owenhumble
antiques.com
Est. 1959 *Stock size* Large
Stock General antiques
Open Mon–Fri by appointment
Sat 10am–1pm
Fairs LAPADA
Services Valuations, restoration,
trade warehouse

⊞ **Intercoin**
Contact Mr Brian
⊠ 103 Clayton Street,
Newcastle-upon-Tyne,
Tyne and Wear,
NE1 5PZ ℗
☎ 0191 232 2064
Est. 1964 *Stock size* Large
Stock Coins, medals, bank notes
Open Mon–Sat 9.30am–4.30pm
Services Valuations

⌂ Little Theatre Antiques Centre

Contact Mr J Bell
✉ Fern Avenue, Jesmond,
Newcastle-upon-Tyne,
Tyne and Wear,
NE2 2RA 🅿
☎ 0191 2094321
📧 john@bennettbell.demon.co.uk
🌐 www.bennett-bell.demon.co.uk
Est. 1993 *Stock size* Large
No. of dealers 13
Stock General antiques, pine
furniture, porcelain, glass,
Arts and Crafts
Open Mon–Sat 10am–5.30pm

➤ Thomas N Miller Auctioneers

Contact Mr A Scott
✉ Algernon Road, Byker,
Newcastle-upon-Tyne,
Tyne and Wear,
NE6 2UN 🅿
☎ 0191 265 8080 📠 0191 265 5050
📧 info@millersauctioneers.co.uk
🌐 www.millersauctioneers.co.uk
Est. 1902
Open Mon–Fri 8.30am–5pm
Sales General antiques,
later furniture, viewing
Sun 10am–noon
Mon Tues 9.30am–4pm
Frequency Weekly
Catalogues No

⊞ Phoenix Design & Antiques

Contact Mrs M Ryle
✉ The Old Monastery,
Blackfriars, Newcastle-upon-
Tyne, Tyne and Wear,
NE1 4XN 🅿
☎ 0191 230 3804
Est. 1984 *Stock size* Small
Stock General antiques
Open Mon–Fri 11.30am–4.30pm
Sat 10.30am–5pm

⊞ Shiners of Jesmond (SALVO)

Contact Mike Nolan or
Brian Gibbons
✉ 81 Fern Avenue, Jesmond,
Newcastle-upon-Tyne,
Tyne and Wear,
NE2 2RA 🅿
☎ 0191 281 6474 📠 0191 281 9041
📱 07708 099722
📧 contactus@shinersofjesmond.com
🌐 www.shinersofjesmond.com
Est. 1983 *Stock size* Large
Stock Internal fittings, antique

doors and door furniture,
antique marble and slate
surrounds, Victorian cast
fireplaces, inserts
Open Mon–Sat 10am–5pm
Sun 11am–2pm
Services Polishing

⊞ Frank Smith Maritime Aviation Books (PBFA)

Contact Alan Parker
✉ 92 Heaton Road, Newcastle-
upon-Tyne, Tyne and Wear,
NE6 5HL 🅿
☎ 0191 265 6333 📠 0191 224 2620
📧 books@franksmith.freeserve.co.uk
Est. 1981 *Stock size* Medium
Stock Antiquarian, rare and
out-of-print books, maritime and
aviation
Open Mon–Fri 10am–4pm
Fairs PBFA
Services Free monthly catalogues
on maritime and aviation

⊞ Graham Smith Antiques (LAPADA)

Contact Mr Graham Smith
✉ 83 Fern Avenue, Jesmond,
Newcastle-upon-Tyne,
Tyne and Wear,
NE2 2RA 🅿
☎ 0191 281 5065 📠 0191 281 5072
📧 gsmithantiques@aol.com
Est. 1973 *Stock size* Medium
Stock Furniture, clocks, smalls
Open Mon–Sat 10am–5pm

⊞ Robert D Steedman (ABA)

Contact Mr David Steedman
✉ 9 Grey Street, Newcastle-
upon-Tyne, Tyne and Wear,
NE1 6EE 🅿
☎ 0191 232 6561
Est. 1907 *Stock size* Medium
Stock Second-hand and
antiquarian books
Open Mon–Fri 9am–5pm
Sat 9am–12.30pm
Fairs Olympia, Edinburgh

⊞ Turnburrys Ltd (SALVO)

✉ 257 Jesmond Road, Newcastle-
upon-Tyne, Tyne and Wear,
NE2 1LB 🅿
☎ 0191 281 1770 📠 0191 240 2569
📧 info@turnburrys.co.uk
🌐 www.turnburrys.co.uk
Est. 1996 *Stock size* Medium
Stock Hardwood flooring,
fireplaces, doors, radiators,
mirrors, bespoke doors, etched

and stained glass
Open Mon–Sat 9am–6pm Sun
11am–3pm
Services Valuations

⊞ Chimney Pieces

Contact Mr T Chester
✉ 98a Howard Street,
North Shields, Tyne and Wear,
NE30 1NA 🅿
☎ 0191 2572118
🌐 www.chimneypieces.co.uk
Est. 1985 *Stock size* Medium
Stock Antique chimney pieces,
architectural antiques, fireplaces
in marble and wood, cast iron,
unusual objects
Open Mon–Sat 10am–5pm
Services Restoration

⊞ Keel Row Books

Contact Bob and Brenda Cook
✉ 11 Fenwick Terrace,
Preston Road, North Shields,
Tyne and Wear,
NE29 0LU 🅿
☎ 0191 296 0664/287 3914
Est. 1980 *Stock size* Large
Stock General antiquarian books,
children's, military,
mountaineering, local history,
cinema a speciality
Open Mon–Sat 10.30am–5pm
Sun 11am–4pm closed Wed
Services Valuations

⊞ Tynemouth Architectural Salvage (SALVO)

Contact Mr Robin Archer
✉ 28 Tynemouth Road,
North Shields, Tyne and Wear,
NE30 4AA 🅿
☎ 0191 296 6070 📠 0191 296 6097
📧 robin@tynemoutharchitectural
salvage.com
🌐 www.tynemoutharchitectural
salvage.co.uk
Est. 1997 *Stock size* Large
Stock Architectural antiques,
architecture, bathrooms
Open Mon–Fri 9am–5pm
Sat 10am–5pm
Fairs Newark
Services Door stripping, restore
cast iron baths

⊞ The Curiosity Shop

Contact Mr G Davies
✉ 16 Frederick Street,
South Shields, Tyne and Wear,

NE33 5EA ℗
☎ 0191 456 5560 ● 0191 427 7597
Ⓜ 07860 219949
ⓔ glenda47@yahoo.co.uk
Est. 1969 *Stock size* Medium
Stock General antiques, Royal
Doulton
Open Mon–Sat 9am–5pm
closed Wed
Fairs Newark
Services Valuations

⊞ **Dolly Domain**
Contact Liz Bonner
✉ 45 Henderson Road,
Simonside, South Shields,
Tyne and Wear,
NE34 9QW ℗
☎ 0191 424 0400/ 0845 6655 667
● 0191 424 0400
ⓔ shop@dollydomain.com
ⓦ www.dollydomain.com
Est. 1991 *Stock size* Large
Stock Dolls and bears
Open Tues–Sat 10am–5pm
Fairs Dolly Domain Fairs

SUNDERLAND

⊞ **Decades**
Contact Judith Richardson
✉ 5b Villette Road, Sunderland,
Tyne & Wear,
SR2 8RH ℗
☎ 0191 565 5142
Est. 1994 *Stock size* Large
Stock General antiques,
furniture, collectables, pottery
Open Mon–Sat 10.30am–4.30pm
closed Wed
Fairs Swinderby, Newark

⊞ **Peter Smith Antiques
(LAPADA)**
Contact Mrs Smith
✉ 12–14 Borough Road,
Sunderland,

Tyne and Wear,
SR1 1EP ℗
☎ 0191 567 3537/514 0008
● 0191 514 2286
Ⓜ 07802 273372
ⓔ petersmithantiques@btinternet.com
ⓦ www.petersmithantiques.co.uk
Est. 1968 *Stock size* Large
Stock General antiques
Open Tues Wed Thurs
10am–4.30pm, Fri Sat 10am–1pm
or by appointment
Services Valuations

TYNEMOUTH

⊞ **Curio Corner**
Contact Mrs S Welton
✉ Units 5 & 6, Land of Green
Ginger, Front Street,
Tynemouth, North Shields,
Tyne and Wear,
NE30 4BP ℗
☎ 0191 296 3316 ● 0191 296 3319
Ⓜ 07831 339906
ⓔ susanwelton@msn.com
ⓦ www.curiocorner.com.uk
Est. 1988 *Stock size* Large
Stock General antique furniture,
lighting, retro furniture
Open Mon–Sat 11am–4.30pm
Fairs Newark

⊞ **Ian Sharp Antiques
(LAPADA, CINOA)**
Contact Mr Ian Sharp
✉ 23 Front Street,
Tynemouth, North Shields,
Tyne and Wear,
NE30 4DX ℗
☎ 0191 296 0656 ● 0191 296 0656
Ⓜ 07850 023689
ⓔ iansharp@sharpantiques.com
ⓦ www.sharpantiques.com
Est. 1988 *Stock size* Medium
Stock Georgian–Edwardian
furniture, pottery

Open Mon–Sat 10am–1pm
1.30–5.30pm or by appointment
Fairs Newark

WASHINGTON

⊞ **Harold J Carr Antiques**
Contact Margaret Carr
✉ Field House, Eastlands,
High Rickleton, Washington,
Tyne & Wear,
NE38 9HQ ℗
☎ 0191 388 6442 ● 0191 388 6442
Est. 1971 *Stock size* Medium
Stock Georgian, Victorian and
later furniture
Open By appointment
Services Shipping

WHITLEY BAY

⊞ **Olivers Bookshop**
Contact Mr John Oliver
✉ 48a Whitley Road, Whitley
Bay, Tyne and Wear,
NE26 2NF ℗
☎ 0191 251 3552
Est. 1986 *Stock size* Medium
Stock Antiquarian, rare and
second-hand books
Open Mon Thurs Fri Sat
11am–5pm
Fairs Tynemouth Book Fair

⊞ **Treasure Chest Antiques**
Contact Mr J Rain
✉ 2a–4 Norham Road, Whitley
Bay, Tyne and Wear,
NE26 2SB ℗
☎ 0191 251 2052
Ⓜ 07808 966611
Est. 1979 *Stock size* Medium
Stock General antiques
Open Mon–Sat 10.30am–4pm
closed 1–2pm
Services House Clearance,
valuation on Saturdays

NORTH WEST

CHESHIRE

ALSAGER

⊞ Trash 'n' Treasure
Contact George G Ogden
✉ 21 Birch Avenue,
Alsager,
Cheshire,
ST7 2QZ 🅿
☎ 01270 873246/872972
Est. 1962 *Stock size* Medium
Stock Furniture, ceramics,
pictures
Open By appointment only
Services Valuations

ALTRINCHAM

⊞ Abacus Books
Contact Mr C Lawton
✉ 24 Regent Road, Altrincham,
Cheshire,
WA14 1RP 🅿
☎ 0161 928 5108
Est. 1979 *Stock size* Medium
Stock Antiquarian and second-
hand books, arts, gardening and
crafts specialities
Open Tue–Sat 10am–5pm
Services Valuations

**⚲ Patrick Cheyne
Auctions**
Contact Mr P Cheyne, RICS
✉ 38 Hale Road, Altrincham,
Cheshire,
WA14 2EX 🅿
☎ 0161 941 4879 ✆ 0161 941 4879
Est. 1982
Open Mon–Fri 10am–5.30pm
Sales Every 2 months Sat
10.30am, viewing Fri 2–4.30pm
6–8pm Sat 9–10.30am. Held at
St Peter's Assembly Rooms, Hale
Catalogues Yes

**⊞ Church Street Antiques
Ltd (LAPADA)**
Contact Mr A Smalley
✉ 4–4a Old Market Place,
Altrincham, Cheshire,
WA14 4NP 🅿
☎ 0161 929 5196 ✆ 0161 929 5196
📱 07768 318661
✉ sales@churchstreetantiques.com
🌐 www.churchstreetantiques.com
Est. 1992 *Stock size* Large
Stock Fine Georgian and
Victorian furniture, art, objets
d'art, carpets, decorative items
Open Mon–Sat 10am–5pm
Sun noon–4pm closed Tues

Fairs Baileys, Coopers, Louise
Walker (Harrogate), Penman
(Chester)
Services Valuations, restoration

⊞ Squires Antiques
Contact Mrs V Phillips
✉ 25 Regent Road, Altrincham,
Cheshire,
WA14 1RX 🅿
☎ 0161 928 0749
Est. 1977 *Stock size* Large
Stock Silver, jewellery, porcelain,

brass, copper, lighting, small fine
furniture
Open Tues–Sat 10am–5pm
closed Wed
Services Valuations

⊞ Village Farm Antiques
Contact Mr Carl Thomason
✉ Village Farm, Station Road,
Dunham Massey, Altrincham,
Cheshire,
WA14 5SA 🅿
☎ 0161 929 4468

Map labels:
Brampton
Carlisle
Cockermouth
Penrith
Workington
Keswick
Whitehaven
Appleby-in-Westmorland
CUMBRIA
Windermere
Kendal
Sedbergh
Grange-over-Sands
Kirkby Lonsdale
Ulverston
Barrow-in-Furness
Carnforth
Morecambe
Isle of Walney
Lancaster
Fleetwood
LANCASHIRE
Clitheroe
Nelson
Blackpool
Burnley
Lytham St. Anne's
Blackburn
Preston
Accrington
Darwen
Southport
Chorley
Rochdale
Ormskirk
Bolton
Oldham
Wigan
Manchester
Salford
GREATER MANCHESTER
Wallasey
MERSEYSIDE
Stockport
Hoylake
Liverpool
Warrington
Cheadle
Marple
Birkenhead
Altrincham
Wilmslow
Heswall
Northwich
Knutsford
Macclesfield
Chester
CHESHIRE
Tarporley
Crewe
Nantwich

(10) 07977 139708
Est. 1987 *Stock size* Large
Stock Wide range of stock
including pine furniture,
architectural antiques, fireplaces,
chaise longues etc
Open Mon–Sun 9am–5pm
Fairs Newark, Swinderby
Services Wood stripping,
upholstery

BARTON

⊞ Derek & Tina Rayment Antiques (BADA, CINOA)
Contact Derek or Tina Rayment
✉ Orchard House, Barton,
Farndon, Cheshire,
SY14 7HT 🅿
☎ 01829 270429   🖷 01829 270893
(10) 07702 922410 or 07860 666629
✉ raymentantiques@aol.com
🌐 www.antique-barometers.com
Est. 1960 *Stock size* Large
Stock Antique barometers
Open By appointment
Fairs Olympia, Chelsea, BADA,
NEC (Jan)
Services Restoration, repairs

BEESTON

⋏ Wright-Manley
Contact Mr W T Witter
✉ Beeston Castle Salerooms,
Beeston Castle, Tarporley,
Cheshire,
CW6 9NZ 🅿
☎ 01829 262150   🖷 01829 261829
✉ wendymiller@wrightmanley.co.uk
🌐 www.wrightmanley.co.uk
Est. 1861
Open Mon–Fri 8.30am–5pm
Sales Victoriana 1st and 3rd
Thurs of month 10.30am,
viewing Wed 10am–6pm.
Quarterly fine art sale
(telephone for details)
Catalogues Yes

CHESTER

⊞ Aldersey Hall Ltd
Contact Anthony Wilding
✉ Aldersey Hall,
47 Northgate Street, Chester,
Cheshire,
CH1 2HQ 🅿
☎ 01244 324885
Est. 1990 *Stock size* Medium
Stock General antiques
Open Mon–Sat 8.30am–5.30pm
Fairs Deco Fair Chester

⊞ Antique Garden
Contact Maria Hopwood
✉ Grosvenor Garden Centre,
Wrexham Road, Belgrave,
Chester, Cheshire,
CH4 9EB 🅿
☎ 01244 629191
(10) 07976 539990
✉ antigard@btopenworld.com
🌐 www.antique-garden.co.uk
Est. 1991 *Stock size* Medium
Stock Gardening antiques
Open Mon–Sun 10am–4.30pm
Services Valuations, shipping

⊞ Antique Scientific Instruments
Contact Charles Tomlinson,
Chester, Cheshire, CH1 🅿
☎ 01244 318395   🖷 01244 318395
✉ charlestomlinson@tiscali.co.uk
Est. 1980
Stock Slide rules, calculators,
early scientific instruments and
drawing equipment,
microscopes, microscope slides
Open By appointment
Services Valuations

⊞ The Antiques Shop
Contact Peter Thornber
✉ 40 Watergate Street, Chester,
Cheshire,
CH1 2LA
☎ 01244 316286
Est. 1987 *Stock size* Medium
Stock Small items, mainly brass,
copper, pewter, Beswick,
Doulton, military badges
Open Mon–Sat 10am–5.30pm
Sun 11am–5pm from Easter to
Christmas
Services Metal repair,
restoration, polishing

⊞ Ask Simon
Contact Mr S Cleveland
✉ 25 Christleton Road, Chester,
Cheshire, CH3 5UF 🅿
☎ 01244 320704
(10) 07815 559431
✉ firstasksimon@aol.com
Est. 1997 *Stock size* Large
Stock Decorative antiques,
domestic paraphernalia, sporting
and farming items, pictures,
collectables, furniture
Open Mon–Sat 10am–5pm
Fairs Ardingly

⋏ Bonhams
✉ New House, 150 Christleton
Road, Chester, Cheshire,

CH3 5TD
☎ 01244 313936   🖷 01244 340028
✉ chester@bonhams.com
🌐 www.bonhams.com
Sales Regional Saleroom.
Regular sales held in London and
in our salerooms across the
country. Free auction valuations;
insurance and probate valuations
Catalogues Yes

⋏ Byrne's Auctioneers
Contact Mr A Byrne MRICS
✉ Booth Mansion, 30 Watergate
Street, Chester, Cheshire,
CH1 2LA 🅿
☎ 01244 312300   🖷 01244 312112
✉ auctions@byrnesauctioneers.co.uk
🌐 www.byrnesauctioneers.co.uk
Est. 1999
Open Mon–Fri 9am–5pm
Sales General sales every 3 weeks
Wed 10am, viewing Mon Tues
prior 10am–pm. Quarterly
antiques sales Wed 11am,
viewing Mon Tues 10am–5pm
Catalogues Yes

⊞ Cameo Antiques
Contact The Manager
✉ 19 Watergate Street, Chester,
Cheshire,
CH1 2LB 🅿
☎ 01244 311467   🖷 01244 311467
Est. 1994 *Stock size* Medium
Stock Silver, jewellery, porcelain,
Moorcroft, Sally Tuffin
Open Mon–Sat 9am–5pm
Services Shipping

⊞ Cestrian Antiques
Contact Mr Malcolm Tice
✉ 28 Watergate Street, Chester,
Cheshire,
CH1 2LA 🅿
☎ 01244 400444
Est. 1993 *Stock size* Large
Stock Small items of furniture,
oak coffers, boxes, silver, glass,
ceramics, longcase clocks, mantel
clocks, wall clocks, pictures,
lighting
Open Mon–Sat 10am–5.30pm or
by appointment Sun evenings
Services Valuations

⊞ D K R Refurbishers
Contact Mr D Wisinger
✉ 26b High Street, Saltney,
Chester, Cheshire,
CH4 8SE 🅿
☎ 01244 680290
Est. 1984 *Stock size* Large

Stock Original pine and oak furniture
Open Mon–Sat 10am–4.30pm Sun noon–4pm
Services Valuations, restoration

⊞ Dollectable
Contact Mo Harding
✉ **53 Lower Bridge Street, Chester, Cheshire, CH1 1RS**
☎ 01244 344888/679195
Est. 1972 *Stock size* Large
Stock Antique dolls
Open Fri noon–5pm Sat 10am–5pm or by appointment
Fairs Kensington, Chelsea, Newark
Services Valuations, restoration

⊞ Farmhouse Antiques
Contact Mrs K Appleby
✉ **23 Christleton Road, Boughton, Chester, Cheshire, CH3 5UF** 🅿
☎ 01244 322478 🖷 01244 322478
📱 07768 645818
📧 progsunited@aol.com
Est. 1973 *Stock size* Large
Stock Wide range of antiques, country furniture, collectables, clocks
Open Mon–Sat 10am–5pm

⊞ Uri Jacobi Oriental Carpet Gallery (LAPADA)
Contact Uri Jacobi
✉ **55–57 Watergate Row, Chester, Cheshire, CH1 2LE** 🅿
☎ 01244 311300 🖷 01244 311300
📱 07973 760722
📧 urijacobi@aol.com
🌐 www.urijacobi.co.uk
Est. 1994 *Stock size* Medium
Stock Contemporary and antique carpets, rugs and tapestries
Open Mon–Sat 9am–5pm
Fairs NEC, LAPADA
Services Valuations, restoration, cleaning

⊞ Jamandic Ltd
Contact Dominic McParland
✉ **22 Bridge Street Row, Chester, Cheshire, CH1 1NN** 🅿
☎ 01244 312822
Est. 1975 *Stock size* Small
Stock General antiques
Open Mon–Fri 9.30am–5.30pm Sat 9.30am–1pm
Services Interior design

⊞ K D Antiques
Contact Mrs D Gillett
✉ **11 City Walls, Chester, Cheshire, CH1 1LD**
☎ 01244 314208
Est. 1997 *Stock size* Medium
Stock Boxes, Staffordshire figures, prints, collectables, glass
Open Mon–Sat 10am–5pm
Fairs Welsh circuit, Manchester G-Mex

⊞ Kayes (LAPADA, NAG)
Contact Mr Nick Kaye
✉ **9 St Michaels Row, Chester, Cheshire, CH1 1EF** 🅿
☎ 01244 327149/343638
🖷 01244 318404
📧 kayesgem@openworld.com
🌐 www.kayeschester.com
Est. 1948 *Stock size* Large
Stock Second-hand, antique and new jewellery and silver
Open Mon–Sat 9.30am–5pm
Services Valuations, restoration

⊞ Lowe and Sons (NAG, BACA Award Winner 2002)
Contact Kevin Parry
✉ **11 Bridge Street Row, Chester, Cheshire, CH1 1PD**
☎ 01244 325850 🖷 01244 345536
📧 lowes.chester@virgin.net
Est. 1770 *Stock size* Large
Stock Antiques, silver, jewellery, decorative arts, Lalique
Open Mon–Sat 9am–5.30pm
Services Restoration

⊞ McLarens Furniture
Contact Jude Leach
✉ **Boughton House, 38 Christleton Road, Chester, Cheshire, CH3 5UE** 🅿
☎ 01244 320774 🖷 01244 314774
Est. 1983 *Stock size* Large
Stock French and Italian furniture
Open Tues–Sat 10am–6pm Sun 11am–5pm

⊞ Moor Hall Antiques
Contact John Murphy
✉ **27 Watergate Row, Chester, Cheshire, CH1 2LE**
☎ 01244 340095
Est. 1993 *Stock size* Medium

Stock 18th–19thC British furniture
Open Mon–Sat 10am–5.30pm

⊞ O'Keeffe Antiques
Contact Mr D O'Keeffe
✉ **2 Christleton Road, Chester, Cheshire, CH3 5UG** 🅿
☎ 01244 311279
📧 okeeffeantiques@ireland.com
Est. 1998 *Stock size* Large
Stock Antique lighting, architectural antiques
Open Tues–Sat 10am–5pm

⊞ The Old Warehouse Antiques
Contact Mrs U O'Donnell
✉ **7–9 Delamere Street, Chester, Cheshire, CH1 4DS** 🅿
☎ 01244 383942
📱 07790 533850
📧 modonnell@xln.co.uk
Est. 1991 *Stock size* Large
Stock Victorian–Edwardian furniture, beds, soft furnishings
Open Mon–Sat 10am–5.30pm
Services Valuations

⊞ Richmond Galleries
Contact Mrs M Armitage
✉ **Watergate Buildings, New Crane Street, Chester, Cheshire, CH1 4JE** 🅿
☎ 01244 317602 🖷 01244 317602
Est. 1974 *Stock size* Large
Stock New and old country pine furniture, decorative items, painted furniture, bespoke service
Open Mon–Sat 9.30am–5pm
Services Bespoke services

⊞ Saltney Restoration Services
Contact Mr J Moore
✉ **50 St Marks Road, Chester, Cheshire, CH4 8DQ** 🅿
☎ 01244 671110 🖷 01244 679722
📱 07713 823383
Est. 1967 *Stock size* Small
Stock Lighting, sanitary ware, furniture, ironware
Open By appointment
Services Restoration

⊞ Second Time Around
Contact Graham Shacklady
✉ **6 Christleton Road, Boughton, Chester, Cheshire,**

CH3 5UG P
☎ 01244 316394 **⊕** 01244 322042
Est. 1979 *Stock size* Large
Stock Georgian, Victorian,
Edwardian furniture, Victorian
burr walnut
Open Mon–Sat 9am–5pm
Fairs Newark
Services Packing, courier, export

⊞ Second Time Around
Contact Graham Shacklady
✉ Staff Yard, 34 Spital Walk,
Boughton, Chester, Cheshire,
CH3 5DB P
☎ 01244 316394 **⊕** 01244 322042
Est. 1979 *Stock size* Large
Stock Georgian–Edwardian
furniture and Victorian
Open Mon–Sat 9am–5pm
Fairs Newark
Services Packing, courier, export

⊞ Stothert Old Books (PBFA)
Contact Mr A Checkley
✉ 4 Nicholas Street, Chester,
Cheshire,
CH1 2NX P
☎ 01244 340756
Ⓜ 07778 137461
Est. 1970 *Stock size* Large
Stock Wide range of antiquarian
and second-hand books
including local history,
topography, natural history,
good illustrated books etc
Open Mon–Sat 10am–5pm
Fairs PBFA, North West Book
Fairs
Services Valuations, book search

⊞ Sweetbriar Gallery (Paperweights) Ltd (Paperweight Collectors Association)
Contact Ray Metcalfe
✉ 56 Watergate Street, Chester,
Cheshire,
CH1 2LA P
☎ 01244 329249 **⊕** 01244 329251
Ⓜ 07860 907532
⊖ sales@sweetbriar.co.uk
Ⓦ www.sweetbriar.co.uk
Est. 1988 *Stock size* Large
Stock Paperweights
Open Mon–Fri 9am–5pm
Fairs Glass Fairs, DMG Fairs
Services Valuations

⊞ Watergate Antiques
Contact Mr A Shindler
✉ Unit 212, Gateway House,

78 Northgate Street, Chester,
Cheshire,
CH1 2LA P
☎ 01244 344516 **⊕** 01244 320350
Ⓜ 0786 0677436
⊖ watergate.antiques@themail.co.uk
Est. 1968 *Stock size* Large
Stock Silver, silver plate, ceramics
Open Mon–Sat 9.30am–5pm
Fairs Newark
Services Restoration, repairs

🏠 Wheatsheaf Antiques Centre
Contact Jeremy Marks
✉ 57 Christleton Road,
Boughton, Chester, Cheshire,
CH3 5UF P
☎ 01244 403743 **⊕** 01244 351713
⊖ info@antiquesonlineuk.com
Ⓦ www.antiquesonlineuk.com
Stock size Large
No. of dealers 7
Stock General antiques
17thC–1930s, books, china,
prints, clocks, silver plate,
vintage clothing
Open Mon–Sat 11am–4pm Sun
noon–4pm or by appointment
Services Shipping

🔨 Whittaker & Biggs (RICS)
Contact Mr J W Robinson
✉ The Auction Room,
Macclesfield Road, Congleton,
Cheshire,
CW12 1NS P
☎ 01260 279858 **⊕** 01260 271629
Ⓦ www.whittakerandbiggs.co.uk
Est. 1931
Open Mon–Fri 9am–5pm
Sales General household
furniture and effects 1st Sat of
month and 2nd and 4th Fri
10am. Antiques, reproduction
and collectables auction 3rd Fri
4pm, viewing evening prior
5–7pm
Frequency Weekly
Catalogues Yes

⊞ Antique & Country Pine
Contact Mr S Blackhurst
✉ 102 Edleston Road, Crewe,
Cheshire,
CW2 7HD P
☎ 01270 258617
Est. 1990 *Stock size* Small

Stock English and Continental
original and stripped pine, hand-
made reproductions
Open Mon–Sat 9.30am–5.30pm
closed Wed

⊞ Copnal Books
Contact Ruth Ollerhead
✉ 18 Meredith Street, Crewe,
Cheshire,
CW1 2PW P
☎ 01270 580470
Est. 1982 *Stock size* Medium
Stock Wide variety of second-
hand, antiquarian and religious
books
Open Mon–Sat 9.30am–4.30pm
Services Valuations

🔨 Coopers Auctioneers
Contact Geoff Cooper
✉ 7 Buxton Road, Disley,
Stockport, Cheshire,
SK12 2DZ P
☎ 01663 765630
Est. 1999
Open Mon–Sat 10am–5.30pm
Sales Antiques, collectables
Frequency Every 4–6 weeks
Catalogues Yes

⊞ Mill Farm Antiques
Contact Mr F Berry
✉ 50–54 Market Street, Disley,
Stockport, Cheshire,
SK12 2DT P
☎ 01663 764045 **⊕** 01663 762690
⊖ enquires@millfarmantiques.
fsbusiness.co.uk
Est. 1971 *Stock size* Medium
Stock Longcase and other clocks,
general antiques, mechanical
music, pianos
Open Mon–Sat 9am–6pm Sun
noon–6pm or by appointment
Services Valuations, restoration
of clocks, mechanical music,
barometers

🏠 Eddisbury Antiques
Contact Sheila Lloyd
✉ 35 Church Street, Frodsham,
Cheshire,
WA6 6PN P
☎ 01928 734477
Ⓜ 07760 104951
⊖ sheila.lloyd8@btopenworld.com
Est. 2003 *Stock size* Medium
No. of dealers 8

Stock Georgian–Edwardian furniture, silver, clocks, jewellery, pictures, ceramics, glass
Open Mon–Sat 10am–5pm
Services Restoration

HALE

⚲ Bonhams
✉ The Stables, 213 Ashley Road, Hale, Cheshire,
WA15 9TB
☎ 0161 927 3822 🌐 0161 927 3824
✉ manchester@bonhams.com
🌐 www.bonhams.com
Open Mon–Fri 9am–5pm
Sales Regional office. Regular sales held in London and in our salerooms across the country. Free auction valuations; insurance and probate valuations

⊞ Porcupine
Contact Ms V Martin
✉ 110 Ashley Road, Hale, Altrincham, Cheshire,
WA14 2UN 🅿
☎ 0161 928 4421
Est. 1982 Stock size Medium
Stock Antique pine, pottery
Open Tues–Sat 9.30am–5.30pm
Sun noon–4pm closed Wed

Key to Symbols

⊞	=	Dealer
⌂	=	Antiques Centre
⚲	=	Auction House
✉	=	Address
🅿	=	Parking
☎	=	Telephone No.
Ⓜ	=	Mobile tel No.
Ⓕ	=	Fax No.
Ⓔ	=	E-mail address
Ⓦ	=	Website address

HATTON

⚲ H & H Classic Auctions Ltd
Contact Simon Hope or Mark Hamilton
✉ Whitegate Farm, Hatton Lane, Hatton, Cheshire,
WA4 4BZ 🅿
☎ 01925 730630 🌐 01925 730830
✉ info@classic-auctions.co.uk

🌐 www.classic-auctions.co.uk
Est. 1993
Open Mon–Fri 9am–5pm
Sales Veteran, vintage, pre-war, classic and collectors' car, motorcycle and automobilia sales. Held at the Pavilion Gardens, Buxton, Derbyshire and other venues around the UK. Automobilia sales Tues noon, viewing from 10am. Car and motorcycle sales Wed 1pm, viewing day before 2–7pm morning of sale from 9am
Catalogues Yes

HUNTINGTON

⊞ Huntington Antiques
Contact Mrs Gregson
✉ 53 Chester Road, Huntington, Cheshire,
CH3 6BS 🅿
☎ 01244 324162
Est. 1994 Stock size Small
Stock Furniture, clocks, paintings
Open Mon–Fri 9am–5.30pm
Services Restoration

KNUTSFORD

⊞ Forest Books of Cheshire
Contact Mrs E Mann
✉ Hartford, Cheshire,
CW8 🅿
☎ 01606 882388
Ⓔ info@forest-books.co.uk
Est. 1996 Stock size Small
Stock Antiquarian, rare, second-hand, new books, pictures, prints
Open By appointment
Fairs Buxton Book Fair

⊞ King Street Antiques
Contact Mrs E L MacDougal
✉ 1 King Street, Knutsford, Cheshire,
WA16 6DW 🅿
☎ 01565 750387
Est. 1993 Stock size Small
Stock Furniture, porcelain, silver
Open Tues–Fri 10.30am–5pm
Sat 10am–5pm closed Wed
Services Valuations

⌂ Knutsford Antique Centre
Contact David McLeod
✉ 113 King Street, Knutsford, Cheshire,
WA16 6EH
☎ 01565 654092

Est. 1996 Stock size Large
No. of dealers 15
Stock General antiques, collectables
Open Tues–Sat 10am–5pm

⊞ The Lemon Tree
Contact Mr S Nelson
✉ 103 King Street, Knutsford, Cheshire,
WA16 6EQ 🅿
☎ 01565 751101 🌐 01565 751101
Est. 1997 Stock size Medium
Stock English country furniture in satin walnut, stripped pine
Open Mon–Sat 10am–5.30pm
Sun noon–5pm

⚲ Frank R Marshall & Co
Contact Mr A Partridge
✉ Marshall House, Church Hill, Knutsford, Cheshire,
WA16 6DH 🅿
☎ 01565 653284 🌐 01565 652341
Ⓜ 07808 483435
Ⓔ antiques@frankmarshall.co.uk
🌐 www.antiques@frankmarshall.co.uk
Est. 1969
Open Mon–Fri 9am–5.30pm closed noon–1pm
Sales General antiques and collectors' sales, 5 per annum, Tues 10am. Fortnightly household sales Tues 10am, viewing Mon 9am-6.30pm
Catalogues Yes

LYMM

⊞ Willowpool Garden Centre & Baron Antiques (LAPADA)
Contact Mrs Roberts
✉ Port of Willow Pool, Burford Lane, Lymm, Cheshire,
WA13 0SH 🅿
☎ 01925 757827 🌐 01925 758101
Ⓔ sales@willowpool.co.uk
🌐 www.willowpool.co.uk
Est. 1964 Stock size Medium
Stock Architectural antiques, decorative arts, salvage and general antiques
Open Mon–Sun 9am–6pm
Fairs Newark, Ardingly
Services Tea shop

MACCLESFIELD

⊞ Gatehouse Antiques
Contact Mr W Livesley
✉ 5–7 Chester Road, Macclesfield,

Cheshire,
SK11 8DG 🅿
☎ 01625 426476 ☏ 01625 426476
ⓦ www.gatehouseantiques.co.uk
Est. 1974 *Stock size* Large
Stock Wide range of antiques
including 18th–20thC furniture,
jewellery, silver, glass, brass,
cooper
Open Mon–Fri 9am–5pm
Wed 9am–1pm Sat 10am–5pm
Services Valuations, restoration,
repairs

⊞ **Derek Hill Antiques**
Contact Mr D Hill
✉ Unit 47, Market Hall,
Grosvenor Centre, Macclesfield,
Cheshire,
SK11 6AR 🅿
☎ 01625 420777
ⓜ 07711 855937
ⓔ hillsantiques@tinyworld.co.uk
ⓦ www.hillsantiques.co.uk
Est. 1969 *Stock size* Large
Stock Collectables, brass, copper,
militaria, jewellery, stamps,
cigarette cards etc
Open Mon–Sat 9am–5.30pm
Services Valuations, jewellery
repairs

⊞ **Mereside Books (PBFA)**
Contact Ms S Laithwaite
✉ 75 Chestergate, Macclesfield,
Cheshire,
SK11 6DG
☎ 01625 425352
Est. 1996 *Stock size* Small
Stock Antiquarian and second-
hand books, local history and
illustrated books a speciality
Open Wed–Sat 10am–5pm
Fairs Cheshire, Buxton

⊞ **Limited Editions**
Contact Charles Fogg
✉ The Barn, Oak Tree Farm,
Knutsford Road, Mobberley,
Cheshire,
WA16 7PU 🅿
☎ 0161 480 1239
ⓔ info@ltd-editions.co.uk
ⓦ www.antique-co.com
Est. 1974 *Stock size* Large
Stock Mostly furniture, especially
dining tables and chairs
Open Thurs–Sat 10am–5.30pm
Sun noon–4pm
Services Restoration, joinery,
polishing, upholstery

NANTWICH

⊞ **Adams Antiques
(BADA, LAPADA)**
Contact Mrs Sandy Summers
✉ Churche's Mansion,
150 Hospital Street, Nantwich,
Cheshire,
CW5 5RY 🅿
☎ 01270 625643 ☏ 01270 625643
ⓜ 07901 855200
ⓔ sandy@adams-antiques.net
ⓦ www.adams-antiques.net
Est. 1970 *Stock size* Large
Stock Early oak, walnut and
country furniture, Welsh
dressers, Mason's Ironstone,
longcase clocks
Open Mon–Sat 10am–5pm
Services Valuations, restoration,
vetting

⊞ **Barn Antiques**
Contact Mr Brian Lee
✉ 8 The Cocoa Yard,
Pillory Street, Nantwich,
Cheshire,
CW5 5BL 🅿
☎ 01270 627770
ⓔ j.lee2@btinternet.com
Est. 1993 *Stock size* Medium
Stock Wide range of china, small
furniture, copper, brass,
collectables including Carlton
ware, Beswick
Open Mon Tues 10am–4pm
Thurs Fri 9.30am–4.30pm
Sat 9.30am–5pm closed
12.30–1.30pm

⊞ **Chapel Antiques**
Contact Mrs D Atkin
✉ 47 Hospital Street, Nantwich,
Cheshire,
CW5 5RL 🅿
☎ 01270 629508
Est. 1983 *Stock size* Medium
Stock Georgian–Victorian
furniture, decorative items,
mirrors
Open Tues–Sat 9.30am–5.30pm
Services Furniture restoration

⊞ **Clock Corner (BHI)**
Contact Mr M Green
✉ 176 Audlem Road, Nantwich,
Cheshire,
CW5 7QJ 🅿
☎ 01270 624481
ⓔ clock.corner@virgin.net
ⓦ www.clockcorner.co.uk
Est. 1975 *Stock size* Large
Stock Antique clocks of all types,

bracket, Vienna, longcase,
mantel etc
Open By appointment
Services Valuations

⊞ **Roderick Gibson**
Contact Mrs R Gibson
✉ 70–72 Hospital Street,
Nantwich, Cheshire,
CW5 5RP 🅿
☎ 01270 625301 ☏ 01270 629603
ⓔ antiques@sfc.co.uk
ⓦ www.sfc.co.uk/antiques
Est. 1975 *Stock size* Medium
Stock Antique and reproduction
furniture, small collectables
Open Mon–Sat 9am–5pm
Services Valuations, probate
service

⊞ **Love Lane Antiques**
Contact Mary Simon
✉ Love Lane, Nantwich,
Cheshire,
CW5 5BH 🅿
☎ 01270 626239
Est. 1982 *Stock size* Medium
Stock General antiques
Open Mon–Sat 10am–5pm
closed Wed

🔨 **Peter Wilson (SOFAA)**
Contact Mr R Stones
✉ Victoria Gallery, Market Street,
Nantwich, Cheshire,
CW5 5DG 🅿
☎ 01270 623878 ☏ 01270 610508
ⓔ auctions@peterwilson.co.uk
ⓦ www.peterwilson.co.uk
Est. 1955
Open Mon–Fri 9am–5.30pm
Sat 9.30am–noon
Sales 2-day sales, 5 per annum,
Wed Thurs 11am, viewing Sun
prior 2–4pm Mon 10am–7pm
Tues 10am–4pm. Uncatalogued
fast weekly sale Thurs 11am,
viewing Wed 10am–7pm
Frequency 40 per annum
Catalogues Yes

NORTHWICH

🏛 **Northwich Antiques
Centre**
Contact Freddie Cockburn
✉ 132 Witton Street, Northwich,
Cheshire,
CW9 5NP 🅿
☎ 01606 47540
ⓜ 07980 645738
ⓦ www.northwichantiques.com
Est. 1999

No. of dealers 7
Stock Period furniture, collectables, china, Moorcroft, Beswick, Doulton
Open Mon–Sun 10am–5pm

PLUMLEY

⊞ Coppelia Antiques
Contact Roy or Valerie Clements
✉ Holford Lodge, Plumley Moor Road, Plumley, near Knutsford, Cheshire, **WA16 9RS**
☎ 01565 722197 ● 01565 722744
ⓦ www.coppeliaantiques.co.uk
Est. 1974
Stock Genuine pre-1800 longcase, bracket, wall clocks, fully restored and guaranteed, Georgian furniture
Open By appointment
Services Restoration

POYNTON

⊞ Recollections
Contact Angela Smith
✉ 69 Park Lane, Poynton, Stockport, Cheshire, **SK12 1RD**
☎ 01625 859373
● 07778 993307
Est. 1984 *Stock size* Medium
Stock Furniture, costume jewellery, decorative china, glass
Open Mon–Sat 10am–5pm
Services House clearance

SANDBACH

⚒ Andrew Hilditch & Son Ltd
Contact Mr T Spencer Andrew
✉ Hanover House, 1a The Square, Sandbach, Cheshire, **CW11 1AP**
☎ 01270 767246 ● 01270 767246
Est. 1866
Open Mon–Fri 9am–5pm closed 12.30–2pm
Sales Quarterly general antiques Wed 10.30am, viewing Mon 10.30am–3pm Tues 10am–3.30pm 7–8.30pm. General sale weekly Wed 10am, viewing Tues 10.30am–3.30pm
Catalogues Yes

⌂ Saxon Cross Antiques Emporium
Contact John Jones
✉ Town Mill, High Street,

Sandbach, Cheshire, **CW11 1AH**
☎ 01270 753005 ● 01270 753005
ⓦ www.saxonantique.co.uk
Est. 1993 *Stock size* Large
No. of dealers 32
Stock Fine antiques from 17th–20thC, porcelain, silver, collectables
Open Mon Tues 10am–4pm Wed Fri Sat 10am–5pm
Services Valuations

TARPORLEY

⌂ Tarporley Antique Centre
Contact Peter Wright
✉ 76 High Street, Tarporley, Cheshire, **CW6 0AT**
☎ 01829 733919
Est. 1991 *Stock size* Large
No. of dealers 10
Stock Pictures, brass, copper, glass, books, furniture
Open Mon–Sat 10am–5pm Sun 11am–4pm

TATTENHALL

⊞ Great Northern Architectural Antiques Co Ltd
Contact Mrs J Devoy
✉ New Russia Hall, Chester Road, Tattenhall, Chester, Cheshire, **CH3 9AH**
☎ 01829 770796 ● 01829 770971
● gnaacoltd@enterprise.net
Est. 1990 *Stock size* Large
Stock Stone, church exteriors, fireplaces, doors, brass ware, sanitary ware, pews, statuary etc
Open Mon–Sun 9.30am–5pm or by appointment
Services Valuations, restoration

WALGHERTON

⌂ Dagfields Crafts & Antiques Centre
Contact Mr I Bennion
✉ Dagfields Farm, Walgherton, Nantwich, Cheshire, **CW5 7LG**
☎ 01270 841336 ● 01270 842604
● contact@dagfields.co.uk
ⓦ www.dagfields.co.uk
Est. 1989 *Stock size* Large
No. of dealers 200
Stock Collectables and furniture

of all periods
Open Mon–Sun 10am–5pm
Services 2 restaurants

WARRINGTON

⊞ Rocking Chair Antiques
Contact Michael Barratt
✉ Unit 3, St Peters Way, Warrington, Cheshire, **WA2 7BL**
☎ 01925 652409 ● 01925 652409
Est. 1976 *Stock size* Large
Stock Victorian–Edwardian bedroom and dining room furniture
Open Mon–Fri 8am–5pm Sat 10am–5pm Sun 11am–4pm
Fairs Swinderby
Services Valuations

WAVERTON

⊞ Antique Exporters of Chester
Contact Mike Kilgannon
✉ Guy Lane Farm, Guy Lane, Waverton, Chester, Cheshire, **CH3 7RZ**
☎ 01829 741001 ● 01829 749204
Est. 1969 *Stock size* Large
Stock 18thC–1930s furniture
Open Mon–Sun 9am–7pm
Services Restoration, shipping

⊞ J Alan Hulme (IMCOS)
Contact Alan Hulme
✉ 52 Mount Way, Waverton, Cheshire, **CH3 7QF**
☎ 01244 336472
● 07774 280871
● alanhulme@pssa.freeserve.co.uk
Est. 1956 *Stock size* Medium
Stock Maps of British Isles 1540–1860, prints of fashion, humour, ornithology, butterflies, flowers 1750–1890, some topographical 1770–1890
Open By appointment
Fairs NEC, Robert Bailey fairs
Services Valuations

⊞ White House Antiques & Stripped Pine
Contact Mrs E Rideal
✉ The White House, Whitchurch Road, Waverton, Chester, Cheshire, **CH3 7PB**
☎ 01244 335063 ● 01244 335098
● rideal@whitehousescientifics.com

Est. 1979 *Stock size* Large
Stock German and English
stripped-pine furniture of all
types
Open Mon–Sat 10am–5pm

WOODFORD

⚲ **Maxwells of Wilmslow
incorporating Dockrees**
Contact Mr M Blackmore FRICS
✉ 133a Woodford Road,
Woodford,
Cheshire,
SK7 1QD 🅿
☎ 0161 439 5182 🖷 0161 439 5182
ⓦ www.maxwell-auctioneers.co.uk
Est. 1989
Open Mon–Fri 9am–5pm
Sales 2 general chattels sales per
month, quarterly antiques sales
Frequency 2 per month
Catalogues Yes

CUMBRIA

ALSTON

⊞ **Alston Antiques**
Contact Mrs J Bell
✉ 10 Front Street, Alston,
Cumbria,
CA9 3SE 🅿
☎ 01434 382129
📱 07876 501929
Est. 1974 *Stock size* Large
Stock Wide range of antiques,
furniture, clocks, barometers,
china, textiles etc
Open Mon–Sat 10am–5pm
Sun 1–5pm closed Tues

APPLEBY IN WESTMORLAND

⊞ **Barry McKay Rare
Books (PBFA)**
Contact Mr B McKay
✉ Kingstone House,
Battlebarrow,
Appleby in Westmorland,
Cumbria,
CA16 6XT 🅿
☎ 017683 52282
ⓔ barry.mckay@britishlibrary.net
Est. 1986 *Stock size* Medium
Stock Antiquarian, second-hand
and new books, specializing in all
aspects of book production and
distribution, some books on
Cumbria and the North
Open Mon–Sat 10am–4pm
preferably by appointment
Services Book search, catalogue

BRAMPTON

⌂ **The Cumbrian Antiques
Centre**
Contact Steve Summerson-
Wright
✉ St Martins Hall, Front Street,
Brampton, Cumbria,
CA8 1NT 🅿
☎ 01697 742515 🖷 01697 742515
ⓔ cumbrianantiques@hotmail.com
Est. 2000 *Stock size* Large
No. of dealers 40
Stock General antiques,
collectables
Open Mon–Sat 10am–5pm
Sun noon–5pm
Services Valuations, house
clearance

⊞ **Moat Antiques**
Contact Carol Irving
✉ 32–34 Main Street, Brampton,
Cumbria,
CA8 1RF 🅿
☎ 01697 741176
Est. 1987 *Stock size* Medium
Stock General antiques
Open Tues–Sat 10.30am–4.30pm
or by appointment

CANONBIE

⊞ **John R Mann Fine
Antique Clocks (MBWCG)**
Contact John Mann
✉ The Clock Showrooms,
Canonbie, Carlisle,
Cumbria,
DG14 0SY 🅿
☎ 01387 371337 🖷 01387 371337
📱 07850 606147
ⓔ jmannclock@aol.com
ⓦ www.johnmannantiqueclocks.co.uk
Est. 1987 *Stock size* Large
Stock Fine antique clocks
Open By appointment
Services Restoration, delivery,
shipping, valuations

CARLISLE

⚲ **Bonhams**
✉ 48 Cecil Street, Carlisle,
Cumbria,
CA1 1NT
☎ 01228 542422 🖷 01228 590106
ⓔ carlisle@bonhams.com
ⓦ www.bonhams.com
Open Mon Tues Thurs Fri
8.30am–1pm 2–5pm
Sales Regional office. Regular
sales held in London and in our

salerooms across the country.
Free auction valuations;
insurance and probate valuations

⊞ **Bookcase**
Contact Mr S Matthews
✉ 17–19 Castle Street, Carlisle,
Cumbria,
CA3 8SY 🅿
☎ 01228 544560 🖷 01228 544775
ⓔ bookcasecarlisle@aol.com
ⓦ www.bookscumbria.com
Est. 1978 *Stock size* Large
Stock Antiquarian, rare and
second-hand books, maps, prints,
classical CDs and LPs, art gallery
Open Mon–Sat 10am–5pm
Services Book search, repairs,
valuations

⌂ **Carlisle Antique Centre**
Contact Mrs W Mitton
✉ Cecil Hall, 46a Cecil Street,
Carlisle, Cumbria,
CA1 1NT 🅿
☎ 01228 536910 🖷 01228 536910
ⓔ wendymitton@aol.com
Est. 1986 *Stock size* Large
No. of dealers 3
Stock Wide range of antiques,
clocks, watches, jewellery, silver,
porcelain
Open Mon–Sat 9am–4pm
Services Restaurant

⊞ **The Eddie Stobart Fan
Club Shop**
Contact Linda Shore
✉ Brunthill Road, Kingstown
Industrial Estate, Carlisle,
Cumbria,
CA3 0EH 🅿
☎ 01228 517800 🖷 01228 517808
ⓔ promotins@eddiestobart.co.uk
ⓦ www.eddiestobart.co.uk
Est. 1996 *Stock size* Medium
Stock Eddie Stobart collection,
die-cast models, clothing,
ceramics, pens, mugs, limited
editions
Open Mon–Fri 9am–5pm Sat
10am–2pm

⊞ **Eddie Stobart
Promotions Ltd**
Contact Bonnie Stephenson
✉ Brunthill Road, Kingstown
Industrial Estate, Carlisle,
Cumbria,
CA3 0EH 🅿
☎ 01228 517800 🖷 01228 517808
ⓔ promotions@eddiestobart.co.uk
ⓦ www.eddiestobart.co.uk

Est. 1993 *Stock size* Large
Stock Eddie Stobart collection,
die-cast models, clothing,
ceramics, pens, limited editions
Open Mon–Fri 8.30am–5.30pm
Sat 10am–2pm
Services Mail-order service with
catalogue

✦ H & H King Ltd
Contact Howard Naylor
✉ Cumbria Auction Rooms,
12 Lowther Street, Carlisle,
Cumbria,
CA3 8DA ℗
☎ 01228 525259 ✆ 01228 597183
✆ cumbriaauctions@Tiscali.co.uk
ⓦ www.cumbriaauctions.com
Est. 1890
Open Mon–Fri 9am–5pm
Sat 9am–noon
Sales Weekly sale of Victorian
and later furniture and effects
Mon. Monthly antiques and
works-of-art sales Mon 9.30am,
viewing Fri 9am–5pm Sat
9am–noon
Catalogues Yes

⊞ Valerie Main Ltd (BADA)
Contact Valerie or David Main
✉ PO Box 92, Carlisle, Cumbria,
CA5 7GD ℗
☎ 01228 711342 ✆ 01228 711341
Ⓜ 07860 679307
✆ valerie.main@btinternet.com
ⓦ www.royalworcester.co.uk
Est. 1986 *Stock size* Large
Stock 20thC English porcelain
Open By appointment
Fairs NEC, Harrogate
Services Shipping

⊞ St Nicholas Galleries Ltd
Contact Mr C Carruthers
✉ 39 Bank Street, Carlisle,
Cumbria,
CA3 8HJ ℗
☎ 01228 544459 ✆ 01228 511015
Est. 1975 *Stock size* Medium
Stock Late Victorian–Edwardian
furniture, watercolours, silver,
silver plate, Doulton figures,
Rolex and Omega watches,
diamond and other jewellery
Open Tues–Sat 10am–5pm
Services Jewellery repairs

✦ Thomson, Roddick & Medcalf Auctioneers
Contact John Thomson

✉ Coleridge House,
Shaddongate, Carlisle,
Cumbria,
CA2 5TU ℗
☎ 01228 528939 ✆ 01228 592128
✆ auctions@thomsonroddick.com
Est. 1880
Sales 10 antiques and collectors'
sales per annum plus specialist
sales of pictures, books, medals,
coins, militaria
Frequency 20 per annum
Catalogues Yes

COCKERMOUTH

⊞ CG's Curiosity Shop
Contact Corrine Ritchie or
Colin Graham
✉ Cocker Bridge,
43 Market Place, Cockermouth,
Cumbria,
CA13 9LT ℗
☎ 01900 824418 or 016973 21108
Ⓜ 07712 206786
✆ cgcuriosity@hotmail.com
Est. 1987 *Stock size* Large
Stock Unusual items, pictures,
militaria, furniture, porcelain,
glass, books, records
Open Mon–Sat 10am–12.45pm
1.45–5pm
Fairs Newark, Swinderby
Services Restoration, house
clearance

⊞ Cockermouth Antiques
Contact Ms E Bell
✉ 5 Station Street, Cockermouth,
Cumbria,
CA13 9QW ℗
☎ 01900 826746
✆ elainebell@aol.com
Est. 1984 *Stock size* Large
Stock Large range of antiques,
ceramics, glass, metalware, silver,
jewellery, books, pictures, textiles
Open Mon–Sat 10am–5pm
closed 1–2pm

⌂ Cockermouth Antiques & Craft Market
Contact Mrs P Gilbert
✉ The Old Courthouse,
Main Street, Cockermouth,
Cumbria,
CA13 9LU ℗
☎ 01900 824346
Est. 1978 *Stock size* Large
No. of dealers 3
Stock Wide range of antiques
including jewellery, china, glass,
postcards, books, ephemera

Open Mon–Sat 10am–5pm
Services Pine stripping and
French polishing

✦ Mitchell's Auction Company (ISVA)
Contact Mr M Wise or Mr K Scott
✉ The Furniture Hall,
47 Station Road, Cockermouth,
Cumbria,
CA13 9PZ ℗
☎ 01900 827800 ✆ 01900 828073
✆ info@mitchellsfineart.com
ⓦ www.mitchellsfineart.com
Est. 1873
Open Mon–Fri 9am–5pm
Sales 5 fine art and antiques
sales per annum Thurs Fri 10am,
weekly general sale
Thurs 9.30am
Catalogues Yes

GRANGE-OVER-SANDS

⊞ Anthemion (BADA, LAPADA)
Contact Jonathan Wood
✉ Cartmel, Grange-over-Sands,
Cumbria,
LA11 6QD ℗
☎ 015395 36295 ✆ 015395 38881
Ⓜ 07768 443757
Est. 1989 *Stock size* Large
Stock Georgian furniture,
decorative items
Open Mon–Sun 10am–5pm
Fairs BADA, LAPADA, Olympia
(June), Harrogate

✦ Gedyes Auctioneers & Estate Agents (NAEA)
Contact Mr N Gedyes
✉ The Auction Centre, Albert
Road, Grange-over-Sands,
Cumbria,
LA11 7EZ ℗
☎ 015395 33366 ✆ 015395 33366
Ⓜ 07740 174537
✆ gedyes@aol.com
Est. 1968
Open Mon–Fri 10am–12.30pm
Sales General and antiques sales
Fri 10am, viewing Thurs 1–6pm
Frequency Monthly
Catalogues No

⊞ Norman Kerr (PBFA)
Contact Mrs H Kerr
✉ Priory Barn, Priest Lane,
Cartmel, Grange-over-Sands,
Cumbria,
LA11 6PX ℗
☎ 015395 36247

NORTH WEST
CUMBRIA • GRASMERE

Est. 1933 *Stock size* Medium
Stock Second-hand and
antiquarian books concerning
art, architecture, travel, natural
history, sport, transport,
engineering
Open By appointment only
Services Valuations

⊞ **Utopia Antiques Ltd**
Contact Mrs J Wilkinson
✉ Yew Tree Barn, High Newton,
Grange-over-Sands,
Cumbria,
LA11 6JP ⓟ
☎ 01539 530065 ✆ 01539 530676
🖃 utopia@utopiaantique.com
🌐 www.utopiaantique.com
Est. 1993 *Stock size* Large
Stock Indian and Asian antique
furniture, handicrafts
Open Mon–Sat 10am–5pm
Sun 11am–5pm
Fairs NEC Furniture Show (Jan)

⊞ **Lakes Craft & Antiques
Gallery**
Contact Joe or Sandra Arthy
✉ 3 Oakbank, Broadgate,
Grasmere, Ambleside,
Cumbria,
LA22 9TA ⓟ
☎ 015394 35037 ✆ 015394 44271
🖃 allbooks@globalnet.co.uk
Est. 1991 *Stock size* Medium
Stock Antiques, craft and gift
items, china, silver, jewellery,
small furniture, antiquarian
books, postcards, cameras etc
Open Mon–Sun March–Nov
9.30am–6pm winter 10am–4pm

⊞ **G K Hadfield (BHI)**
Contact G K Hadfield
✉ Beck Bank, Great Salkeld,
Penrith, Cumbria,
CA11 9LN ⓟ
☎ 01768 870111 ✆ 01768 870111
📱 07968 775694
🖃 gkhadfield@dial.pipex.com
Est. 1966 *Stock size* Large
Stock Clocks, horological books,
clock restoration materials
Open Mon–Sat 9am–5pm or by
appointment
Fairs Specialist clock fairs
Services Gilding, dial restoration,
silvering, book restoration, hand-
cut hands, frets in wood or brass

⊞ **Roadside Antiques**
Contact Mrs K Sealby
✉ Watsons Farm, Greystoke Gill,
Greystoke, Penrith,
Cumbria,
CA11 0UQ ⓟ
☎ 017684 83279
Est. 1988 *Stock size* Large
Stock Antique ceramics, glass,
Staffordshire figures, longcase
clocks, Victorian–Edwardian
furniture, silver, jewellery,
paintings
Open Mon–Sun 10am–6pm
Services Porcelain restoration

⊞ **Dower House Antiques**
Contact Mrs J H Blakemore
✉ 40 Kirkland, Kendal, Cumbria,
LA9 5AD ⓟ
☎ 01539 722778
Est. 1959 *Stock size* Small
Stock 18th–19thC pottery,
porcelain, furniture, pictures
Open By appointment phone
first

⊞ **Granary Collectables**
Contact Mr B Cross
✉ 29 Allhallows Lane, Kendal,
Cumbria,
LA9 4JH ⓟ
☎ 01539 740770
Est. 1998 *Stock size* Medium
Stock Kitchenware, advertising,
stoneware, pottery, collectables,
pictures
Open Tues–Sat 10am–4.30pm

🔨 **Kendal Auction Rooms**
Contact Kevin Kendal
✉ Sandylands Road, Kendal,
Cumbria,
LA9 6EU ⓟ
☎ 01539 733770 ✆ 01539 733770
📱 07713 787509
🖃 info@kendalauctionrooms.co.uk
🌐 www.kendalauctionrooms.co.uk
Est. 1818
Open Mon–Fri 9am–5.30pm
Sales Regular antiques and
collectables, general and
specialist
Frequency See website
Catalogues Yes

⊞ **Kendal Studio Pottery
Antiques**
Contact Mr R Aindow
✉ 2–3 Wildman Street, Kendal,
Cumbria,
LA9 6EN ⓟ
☎ 01539 723291
🖃 robert@aindow.wanadoo.co.uk
Est. 1953 *Stock size* Medium
Stock Oak furniture, art pottery,
maps, prints
Open 10.30am–5pm usually or by
appointment

⊞ **Lakeland Architectural
Antiques**
Contact Mr G Fairclough
✉ 146 Highgate, Kendal,
Cumbria,
LA9 4HW ⓟ
☎ 01539 737147 ✆ 01539 737147
🖃 gordonfairclough@aol.com
🌐 www.architecturalantiques.co.uk
Est. 1987 *Stock size* Medium
Stock Fireplaces, mirrors, lighting
Open Mon–Sat 10am–5pm
Sun by appointment
Services Valuations

⊞ **Sleddall Hall Antiques
Centre**
Contact Mr A Aindow
✉ 5 Wildman Street, Kendal,
Cumbria,
LA9 6EN ⓟ
☎ 01539 723291
🖃 robert@aindow.wannadoo.co.uk
Est. 2005 *Stock size* Medium
Stock Clocks, paintings,
collectables
Open Mon–Sat 10am–5pm
Services Finder

⊞ **Thomond Antiques**
Contact Mr D Masters
✉ 33 Allhallows Lane, Kendal,
Cumbria,
LA9 4JH ⓟ
☎ 01539 736720
🖃 thomondantiques@aol.com
Est. 1998 *Stock size* Medium
Stock China, glass, silver plate,
18th–20thC ceramics
Open Mon–Sat 10am–4.30pm
Services Valuations

⊞ **Utopia Antiques Ltd**
Contact Mrs J Wilkinson
✉ 40 Market Place, Kendal,
Cumbria,
LA9 4TN ⓟ
☎ 01539 722862 ✆ 01539 530676
🖃 utopia@utopiaantique.com
🌐 www.utopiaantique.com
Est. 1993 *Stock size* Large
Stock Indian and Asian antique

furniture, handicrafts
Open Mon–Sat 10am–5pm
Sun 11am–5pm
Fairs NEC Furniture Show (Jan)

KESWICK

⊞ Keswick Bookshop (PBFA)
Contact Ms J Kinnaird
✉ 4 Station Street, Keswick,
Cumbria,
CA12 5HT ℗
☎ 017687 75535
Est. 1994 *Stock size* Medium
Stock Antiquarian and second-hand books, maps, prints
Open Easter–Oct Mon–Sat
10.30am–5pm winter Sat only
advisable to telephone

⊞ Keswick Collectables
Contact Mr M Stainton or
David Lomas
✉ 18 St Johns Street, Keswick,
Cumbria,
CA12 5AS ℗
☎ 017687 74928/75371
Est. 1997 *Stock size* Medium
Stock Collectables, stamps,
books, records, Victoriana,
Beatles memorabilia, oil lamps
Open Mon–Sun 10am–6pm
Services Postal service

⊞ John Young & Son Antiques (LAPADA)
Contact Mr J Young
✉ 12–14 Main Street, Keswick,
Cumbria,
CA12 5JD ℗
☎ 017687 73434 ✆ 017687 73306
Est. 1890 *Stock size* Large
Stock Fine selection of
17th–19thC oak and mahogany
furniture, longcase clocks
Open Mon–Sat 9.30am–5pm

KIRKBY STEPHEN

⊞ The Book House (PBFA)
Contact Mr C Irwin
✉ Town Head, Ravenstonedale,
Kirkby Stephen,
Cumbria,
CA17 4NG ℗
☎ 015396 23634
✉ mail@thebookhouse.co.uk
⊕ www.thebookhouse.co.uk
Est. 1984 *Stock size* Medium
Stock Wide range of general
books, history of technology,
gardening literature, children's

and language
Open Mon–Sat 10am–5pm
closed Tues
Fairs PBFA
Services Catalogues issued

⊞ Haughey Antiques (LAPADA, BACA Award Winner 2003)
Contact D M Haughey
✉ 28–30 Market Street,
Kirkby Stephen,
Cumbria,
CA17 4QW ℗
☎ 017683 71302 ✆ 017683 72423
✉ info@haugheyantiques.co.uk
⊕ www.haugheyantiques.co.uk
Est. 1969 *Stock size* Large
Stock 17th–19thC furniture,
decorative items
Open Mon–Fri 10am–5.30pm Sat
11am–6pm or by appointment
Fairs Olympia (June, Nov),
LAPADA Birmingham (Jan)
Services Valuations, restoration

⊞ David Hill
Contact Mr D Hill
✉ 36 Market Square,
Kirkby Stephen, Cumbria,
CA17 4QT ℗
☎ 017683 371598
Est. 1966 *Stock size* Medium
Stock Small antiques,
kitchenware, collectables,
metalware
Open Thurs–Sat 9.30am–4pm

LONG MARTON

⊞ Ben Eggleston Antiques Ltd
Contact Ben Eggleston
✉ The Dovecote, Long Marton,
Nr Appleby, Cumbria,
CA16 6BJ ℗
☎ 017768 361849 ✆ 01768 361849
✉ ben@beneggglestonantiques.co.uk
⊕ www.beneggglestonantiques.co.uk
Est. 1974 *Stock size* Large
Stock Restored and unrestored
antique pine furniture
Open By appointment
Fairs Newark

NEWBY BRIDGE

⊞ Townhead Antiques (LAPADA)
Contact Mr C P Townley
✉ Townhead, Newby Bridge,
Cumbria,
LA12 8NP ℗

☎ 01539 531321 ✆ 01539 530019
✉ townhead@aol.com
⊕ www.townhead.com
Est. 1960 *Stock size* Large
Stock Wide variety of antiques,
including oak, mahogany,
walnut, rosewood furniture,
porcelain, glass, brass, silver etc
Open Mon–Sat 10am–5pm
evenings and Sun by
appointment
Services Valuations

PENRITH

⊞ Antiques of Penrith
Contact Mrs S Tiffin
✉ 4 Corney Square, Penrith,
Cumbria,
CA11 7PX ℗
☎ 01768 862801
Est. 1953 *Stock size* Large
Stock Varied stock of furniture,
decorative items, collectables
Open Mon–Fri 10am–5pm closed
noon–1.30pm Sat 10am–1pm
closed Wed

⊞ Brunswick Antiques
Contact Mr Martin Hodgson
✉ 8 Brunswick Road, Penrith,
Cumbria,
CA11 7LU ℗
☎ 01768 899338
⊕ 07971 295991
Est. 1987 *Stock size* Medium
Stock 18th–19thC clocks,
furniture, glass, ceramics,
collectables
Open Mon–Sat 10am–4pm
closed Wed
Services Clock repairs

⋌ Penrith Farmers' & Kidd's PLC
Contact Mr M Huddleston
✉ Skirsgill Saleroom,
Skirsgill, Penrith,
Cumbria,
CA11 0DN ℗
☎ 01768 890781 ✆ 01768 895058
✉ info@pfkauctions.co.uk
⊕ www.antiquestradegazette.com/
penrithfarmers
Est. 1876
Open Mon–Fri 9am–5pm
Tues 9am–6pm
Sales General sales of Victoriana
and later furnishings and effects
fortnightly Wed 9.30am, viewing
Tues noon–6pm
Frequency Fortnightly
Catalogues Yes

NORTH WEST

RAUGHTON HEAD

⊞ Cumbria Architectural Salvage (SALVO)
Contact Mr K Temple
✉ Birkshill, Raughton Head, Carlisle, Cumbria, CA5 7DH ♿
☎ 016974 76420 ☻ 016974 76420
Est. 1986 *Stock size* Small
Stock Fireplaces, sanitary ware, oak beams, sandstone flags, doors, radiators, kitchen ranges
Open Mon–Fri 9am–5pm Sat 9am–noon
Services Fireplace restoration

SEDBERGH

⊞ R F G Hollett & Son (ABA)
Contact Mr C G Hollett
✉ 6 Finkle Street, Sedbergh, Cumbria, LA10 5BZ ♿
☎ 01539 620298 ☻ 01539 621396
✉ hollett@sedbergh.demon.co.uk
✇ www.holletts-rarebooks.co.uk
Est. 1960 *Stock size* Large
Stock Wide selection of antiquarian books including natural history, travel, northern topography
Open By appointment
Services Valuations, catalogues

⌂ Sleepy Elephant Books & Artefacts
Contact Mrs A Whittle
✉ 16 Back Lane, Sedbergh, Cumbria, LA10 5AQ ♿
✇ 07967 638503
✉ avrilsbooks@aol.com
Est. 2003 *Stock size* Small
No. of dealers 8 book dealers and 2 antiques deaalers
Stock Second-hand and antiquarian books, general antiques
Open Mon–Sat 10am–5pm Sun noon–5pm (winter open Fri–Mon)
Services Valuations

⊞ Westwood Books Ltd (ABA, PBFA)
Contact Evelyn Westwood
✉ Leisure House, Long Lane, Sedbergh, Cumbria, LA10 5AH ♿
☎ 01539 621233
✉ books@markwestwood.co.uk

Est. 2006 *Stock size* Large
Stock Antiquarian, second-hand and reduced price new books
Open Opening spring 2006, phone for details
Services Coffee shop

⊞ Avril Whittle, Bookseller
Contact Mrs A Whittle
✉ Whittle's Warehouse, 7–9 (Rear) Bainbridge Road, Sedbergh, Cumbria, LA10 5AU ♿
☎ 01539 621770 ☻ 01539 621770
✇ 07967 638503
✉ avrilsbooks@aol.com
Est. 1980 *Stock size* Medium
Stock Scarce, out-of-print and antiquarian books on art, craft and design
Open By appointment
Services Book search, valuations

SHAP

⊞ David A H Grayling (PBFA)
✉ Verdun House, Shap, Penrith, Cumbria, CA10 3NG ♿
☎ 01931 716746 ☻ 01931 716746
✉ graylingbook@fsbdial.co.uk
✇ www.davidgraylingbooks.com
Est. 1972 *Stock size* Medium
Stock Rare, out-of-print and new books on big game, deer, shooting, angling, hunting and natural history
Open By appointment only
Fairs Game fairs
Services Book search, catalogue, mail order, valuations, fine binding

SKELTON

⊞ The Pen & Pencil Gallery
Contact Mrs J Marshall
✉ Church House, Skelton, Penrith, Cumbria, CA11 9TE ♿
☎ 01768 484300
✇ 07720 708181
✉ ppgallery@aol.com
Est. 1995 *Stock size* Large
Stock Vintage and modern fountain pens, writing equipment, pencils, dip pens, inkwells
Open By appointment

Fairs London, Northern, USA pen shows
Services Valuations, repairs

STAVELEY

⊞ Staveley Antiques
Contact Mr J Corry
✉ 27 Main Street, Staveley, Kendal, Cumbria, LA8 9LU ♿
☎ 01539 821393
✇ www.staveleyantiques.co.uk
Est. 1990 *Stock size* Large
Stock Brass and iron beds, French wooden beds, lighting, metalware
Open Mon–Sat 10am–5pm please ring before visiting
Services Metalware restoration

ULVERSTON

⊞ Elizabeth & Son
Contact Mr J Bevins
✉ Market Hall, New Market Street, Ulverston, Cumbria, LA12 7LJ ♿
☎ 01229 582763
Est. 1961 *Stock size* Small
Stock Late 1800–1900s china, glass, jewellery, books
Open Mon–Sat 9am–5pm closed Wed
Services Valuations

WHITEHAVEN

⊞ Michael Moon (PBFA)
Contact Mr M Moon
✉ 19 Lowther Street, Whitehaven, Cumbria, CA28 7AL ♿
☎ 01946 599010 ☻ 01946 599010
Est. 1970 *Stock size* Large
Stock Rare, second-hand and antiquarian books on cinema, history, local history
Open Mon–Sat 9am–5pm closed Wed Jan–Easter
Services Valuations, book search, catalogues (2–3 a year)

GREATER MANCHESTER

ATHERTON

⊞ The Emporium
Contact Mr G Wilson
✉ 486 Blackburn Road, Atherton,

Bolton, Lancashire,
BL1 8PE 🅿
☎ 01204 303090 📠 01204 302299
Est. 1989 *Stock size* Large
Stock Wide variety of second-hand Victorian–Edwardian furniture, china, collectables, glass etc
Open Mon–Sat 9am–5pm
Sun 11am–4pm
Services Valuations

BOLTON

⊞ B J Dawson (BNTA)
Contact Mr P Dawson
✉ 52 St Helens Road, Bolton, Lancashire,
BL3 3NN 🅿
☎ 01204 63732 📠 01204 63732
📱 07801 537412
📧 dawsoncoins@btconnect.com
🌐 historycoin.com
Est. 1966 *Stock size* Large
Stock Ancient coins – Greek, Roman, Byzantine, medallions, old English coins
Open Mon–Fri 9am–5pm
Sat 9am–noon
Fairs London Coin Fair
Services Valuations, lists, medal mounting

⊞ G Oakes & Son
Contact Mr S Hughes
✉ The Courtyard, Hampden Mill, Spring Vale Road, Darwen, Lancashire,
BB3 2ES 🅿
☎ 01254 777144
📱 07774 284609
📧 ycs12@dial.pipex.com
🌐 www.antique-dealeruk.com
Est. 1959 *Stock size* Large
Stock Antiques, Georgian–1920s furniture, shipping furniture, architectural and garden antiques, stained glass windows
Open Mon–Fri 9am–5pm or by appointment
Services Shipping

⊞ Olde Mill Antiques
Contact Paul Morris
✉ Grecian Mill, Fletcher Street, Bolton, Lancashire,
BL3 6NN 🅿
☎ 0800 542 5756 or 01204 528678
📧 julie.porter37@ntlworld.com
Est. 1980 *Stock size* Large
Stock Georgian–Victorian furniture
Open Mon–Fri 9am–5.30pm

Sat Sun 9.30am–4pm
Services Shipping, stripping of satin walnut and pine

BOWDON

⊞ English Garden Antiques
Contact Bill Seddon
✉ The White Cottage, Church Brow, Bowdon, Altrincham, Cheshire,
WA14 2SF 🅿
☎ 0161 928 0854 📠 0161 929 8081
📧 bill@english-garden-antiques.co.uk
🌐 www.english-garden-antiques.co.uk
Est. 1996 *Stock size* Large
Stock English garden antiques including stone troughs, sundials, bird baths, cast-iron urns, staddle stones, gargoyles
Open 10am–5pm confirm by telephone
Services Valuations, restoration, repair, garden security

⊞ French Country Style
Contact Margaret Ernstone
✉ The Old Forge,
7a Church Brow, Bowdon, Cheshire,
WA14 2SF 🅿
☎ 0161 927 9041 📠 0161 927 9041
🌐 www.frenchcountrystyle.co.uk
Est. 2000 *Stock size* medium
Stock French decorative items, furniture, lighting, mirrors
Open Wed–Sat 10am–5pm or by appointment
Services Restoration, delivery

⊞ Richmond Antique Mirrors
Contact Mr J Freeman
✉ The Hollies, Richmond Road, Bowdon, Altrincham, Cheshire,
WA14 2TT 🅿
☎ 0161 928 1229 📠 0161 233 0431
📱 07720 416055
📧 info@richmondantiques.com
🌐 www.richmondantiques.com
Est. 1993 *Stock size* Large
Stock Mirrors including 19thC French and English
Open Tues–Sat noon–6pm or by appointment
Services Valuations, restoration

BREDBURY

⊞ The Old Curiosity Shop
Contact Mrs S Crook
✉ 123 Stockport Road West,

Bredbury, Stockport, Greater Manchester,
SK6 2AN 🅿
☎ 0161 494 9469
Est. 1983 *Stock size* Large
Stock 1920s furniture, barley-twist a speciality, brass, clocks, pottery
Open Mon–Sat 10am–6pm
Sun noon–5pm closed Wed
Services Hand stripping service

BROMLEY CROSS

⊞ Drop Dial Antiques
Contact Irene Roberts
✉ Last Drop Village, Hospital Road, Bromley Cross, Bolton, Lancashire,
BL7 9PZ 🅿
☎ 01204 307186 or 01257 480995
Est. 1974 *Stock size* Medium
Stock Clocks, barometers, boxes, small items of furniture
Open Tues–Sun 12.30–4.30pm closed Mon
Fairs Ripley Castle, Stoneyhurst (Galloway Fairs), Naworth Castle, Duncombe Park
Services Clock and barometer restoration

⊞ Siri Ellis Books (PBFA)
Contact Siri Ellis
✉ Last Drop Village, Hospital Road, Bromley Cross, Bolton, Lancashire,
BL7 9PZ 🅿
☎ 01204 597511
📧 mail@siriellisbooks.co.uk
🌐 www.siriellisbooks.co.uk
Est. 1998 *Stock size* Medium
Stock Antiquarian and second-hand illustrated and children's books
Open Mon–Fri noon–5pm
Sat Sun 10am–5pm
Fairs Buxton, Pudsey, PBFA
Services Free book search

BURY

⊞ Newtons of Bury
Contact Mr Glen Wild
✉ 151 The Rock, Bury, Lancashire,
BL9 0ND 🅿
☎ 0161 764 1863 📠 0161 761 7129
Est. 1900 *Stock size* Medium
Stock Antiques, furniture, china etc
Open Mon–Sat 9am–5pm
Sun noon–4pm except in summer
Services House clearance

NORTH WEST

CHEADLE HULME

⚒ John Arnold & Co
Contact Mr W Bradshaw
✉ Central Salerooms,
15 Station Road, Cheadle Hulme,
Cheshire,
SK8 5AF ♿
☎ 0161 485 2777 ✆ 0161 485 3777
Est. 1865
Open Mon–Fri 10am–4pm
Sales Antiques and general sale
Wed 11am, viewing day prior
11am–4pm day of sale 10–11am
Frequency Weekly
Catalogues No

⊞ Andrew Foott Antiques
Contact Andrew Foott
✉ 4 Claremont Road,
Cheadle Hulme,
Cheshire,
SK8 6EG ♿
☎ 0161 485 3559
Est. 1986 *Stock size* Small
Stock Georgian furniture,
barometers
Open Mon–Fri 9am–5pm
Fairs NEC
Services Restoration

⊞ David Lloyd
Contact David Lloyd
✉ Cheadle Hulme,
Cheshire,
SK8 7DL ♿
☎ 0161 486 6406
✆ 07711 948403
✉ dloyd@onetel.com
Est. 1991 *Stock size* Medium
Stock 18th–20thC silver, silver
plate, flatware
Open By appointment only
Fairs Newark, Staffordshire, NEC
Services Matching flatware for
canteens

FAILSWORTH

**⊞ Failsworth Mill
Antiques**
Contact Mr I Macdonald
✉ Failsworth Mill,
Ashton Road West, Failsworth,
Manchester,
M35 0FD ♿
☎ 0161 684 7440 ✆ 0161 681 7111
✉ oldmailantiques@hotmail.com
Est. 1993 *Stock size* Large
Stock Furniture, small
collectables etc in large
warehouse
Open Mon–Fri 9am–5pm

Sun 10am–4pm
closed Bank Holidays
Services Restoration, export

**🏠 The New Cavern
Antiques & Collectors'
Centre**
Contact Mr Peter Stanley
✉ Failsworth Mill, Ashton Road
West, Failsworth, Manchester,
Lancashire,
M35 0FD ♿
☎ 0161 684 7802
✉ akg21353@aol.com
Est. 1997 *Stock size* Large
No. of dealers 40+
Stock Antiques, collectables,
furniture
Open Mon–Sun 10am–4.30pm
closed Sat
Services Shipping, valuations

**⊞ R J O'Brien & Son
Antiques Ltd**
Contact Mr R O'Brien
✉ Failsworth Mill,
Ashton Road West, Failsworth,
Manchester, Lancashire,
M35 0FD ♿
☎ 0161 688 4414 ✆ 0161 688 4414
✉ obantiques@btinternet.com
🌐 www.antique-exports.com
Est. 1972 *Stock size* Large
Stock Antique furniture
Open Mon–Fri 9am–5pm or by
appointment
Services Container and courier
service

⚒ T L H Auctioneers
Contact Mr Thomas Higham
✉ Unit 5, Victory Industrial
Estate, Mill Street, Failsworth,
Greater Manchester,
M35 0BJ ♿
☎ 0161 688 9099 ✆ 0161 688 9050
✉ sales@tlhauctioneers.co.uk
🌐 www.tlhauctioneers.com
Est. 1994
Open Mon–Sat 9am–5.30pm
Sales Sales weekly Tues 10am,
viewing Mon 2–5.30pm Tues
9–10am, and Sat 10am, viewing
9–10am
Catalogues Yes

HAZEL GROVE

⚒ A F Brock & Co Ltd
Contact Mr A F Brock or
Mrs W Jensen
✉ 269 London Road,
Hazel Grove, Stockport,

Cheshire,
SK7 4PL ♿
☎ 0161 456 5050 ✆ 0161 456 5112
✉ info@afbrock.co.uk
🌐 www.afbrock.co.uk
Est. 1969
Open Mon–Fri 9am–5pm
Sat 9am–4pm closed Wed
Sales 6 coins, jewellery and
antiques sales per year,
telephone for details of sale.
Specialist coin and banknote
sales periodically. Held at the
Acton Court Hotel, Stockport
Catalogues Yes

HEYWOOD

⊞ Heywood Antiques
Contact Mr Norman Marsh
✉ 5 Manchester Road, Heywood,
Lancashire,
OL10 2DZ ♿
☎ 01706 621281
Est. 1989 *Stock size* Medium
Stock Late Victorian, Edwardian
furniture, clocks
Open Mon Wed Fri Sat
9.30am–5pm phone before
visiting
Services Clock repair and
restoration

HINDLEY

**⊞ Wiend Books &
Collectables (PBFA)**
Contact Mr P G Morris
✉ Unit 1, Hindley Business Perk,
Platt Lane, Hindley,
Lancashire,
WN2 3PA ♿
☎ 01942 820500 ✆ 01942 820500
✆ 07976 604203
✉ wiendbooks@lycos.co.uk
🌐 www.wiendbooks.co.uk
Est. 1997 *Stock size* Large
Stock General stock of
antiquarian and second-hand
books, printed collectables,
comics, stamps, programmes,
badges, Wade
Open Mon–Sat 9.30am–5pm
closed Tues
Fairs PBFA
Services Valuations

LEVENSHULME

⊞ Aaron Antiques
Contact Geoffrey Parkinson
✉ Old Town Hall, Stockport
Road, Levenshulme,

Manchester,
M19 3NP 🅿
☎ 01706 366413
Est. 1976 *Stock size* Medium
Stock General antiques
Open Mon–Sat 10.30am–5pm

⌂ **Levenshulme Antiques Village**
Contact Mr Ronald Aston
✉ 965 Stockport Road,
Levenshulme,
Manchester,
M19 3NP 🅿
☎ 0161 256 4644
Est. 1979 *Stock size* Large
No. of dealers 20 in Old Town Hall
Stock Furniture
Open Mon–Sat 10am–5pm
Sun 11am–4pm
Services Restoration, wood stripping, furniture made to order

⊞ **G Long Antiques**
Contact Gladys Long
✉ 811 Stockport Road,
Levenshulme,
Manchester,
M19 3BF 🅿
☎ 0161 224 0845
Est. 1942 *Stock size* Large
Stock General antiques,
18th–19thC furniture
Open Mon–Sat 9am–5pm
Services Valuations, delivery

⊞ **Ross Fireplaces**
Contact Carl Ross
✉ 1024–1028 Stockport Road,
Levenshulme,
Manchester,
M19 3WX 🅿
☎ 0161 224 2550
✉ rossfireplaces@aol.com
Est. 1988 *Stock size* Large
Stock Fireplaces
Open Mon–Sun 10am–4pm
Services Restoration

LITTLEBOROUGH

⊞ **George Kelsall (PBFA)**
Contact Mr B Kelsall
✉ 22 Church Street,
Littleborough,
Lancashire,
OL15 9AA 🅿
☎ 01706 370244
✉ kelsall@bookshop22.fsnet.co.uk
Est. 1979 *Stock size* Large
Stock Mainly second-hand,

modern and antiquarian books
on art, history, reference,
topography of Northern
England, industrial history,
transport, social history
Open Mon 11am–5pm Tues
1–5pm Wed–Sat 10am–5pm
Fairs PBFA (Lancashire, Yorkshire)

⊞ **Nostalgia**
Contact Mr Philip Sunderland
✉ 24 Church Street,
Littleborough,
Lancashire,
OL15 9AA 🅿
☎ 01706 377325
📱 07711 503755
Est. 1994 *Stock size* Medium
Stock General antiques,
furniture, lighting, Victorian
fireplaces
Open Mon–Sat 10.30am–5pm
closed Tues

MANCHESTER

⚒ **Capes, Dunn & Co (ISVA)**
Contact Alison Lakin
✉ 38 Charles Street,
Manchester,
M1 7DB 🅿
☎ 0161 273 1911 📠 0161 273 3474
✉ capesdunn@yahoo.co.uk
🌐 www.ukauctioneers.com
Est. 1826
Open Mon–Fri 9am–5pm
Sales Victorian and later period
furniture and effects Mon noon,
viewing 9.15–11am day of sale.
Specialist sales most Tues noon,
viewing Mon 10am–4pm
Tues 10–noon
Frequency Weekly
Catalogues Yes

⊞ **Empire Exchange**
Contact Mr David Ireland
✉ 1 Newton Street,
Manchester,
M1 1HW 🅿
☎ 0161 236 4445 📠 0161 273 5007
✉ enquiries@empire-uk.com
🌐 www.empire-uk.com
Est. 1986 *Stock size* Large
Stock Collectors' items, old and
new books, toys, football
memorabilia, dolls, teddy bears,
jewellery, military
Open Mon–Sun 9am–7.30pm
Fairs Newark, comic fairs
Services Publishing company,
valuations

⊞ **Kitty Fisher's Finds**
Contact Trish Cunningham
✉ 75 School Lane,
Manchester,
M20 6WN 🅿
☎ 0161 445 1666 📠 0161 445 1666
✉ info@kittyfishersfinds.co.uk
🌐 www.kittyfishersfinds.co.uk
Est. 2003 *Stock size* Medium
Stock Chandeliers, mirrors,
French decorative antiques for
period and contemporary
interiors
Open Tue–Sat 10am–5pm

⊞ **Insitu (SALVO)**
Contact Laurence Green
✉ Talbot Mill, 44 Ellesmere
Street, Manchester,
Lancashire,
M15 4JY 🅿
☎ 0161 839 5525
✉ info@insitumanchester.com
🌐 www.insitumanchester.com
Est. 1984 *Stock size* Large
Stock Complete range of
antiques, fixtures and fittings
Open Mon–Sat 10am–5.30pm
Sun 11am–5pm

⊞ **Secondhand & Rare Books**
Contact Mr E Hopkinson
✉ 1 Church Street,
Manchester,
M4 1PN 🅿
☎ 0161 834 5964 or 01625 861608
Est. 1970 *Stock size* Medium
Stock Antiquarian and second-
hand books, some topography
and special interest
Open Mon–Sat noon–4pm

MARPLE BRIDGE

⊞ **Townhouse Antiques**
Contact Mr Paul Buxcey
✉ 21 Town Street, Marple
Bridge, Stockport, Cheshire,
SK6 5AA 🅿
☎ 0161 427 2228
Est. 1985 *Stock size* Medium
Stock Stripped pine furniture,
carved wood, brass, iron beds,
decorative antiques
Open Mon–Sat 10am–6pm

OLDHAM

⌂ **The Collectors Centre**
Contact Mr I Thorogood
✉ 12a Waterloo Street, Oldham,
Lancashire,

OL1 1SQ 🅿
☎ 0161 624 1365
Est. 1991 *Stock size* Medium
No. of dealers 2
Stock Broad range of collectables
– records, pop memorabilia,
brass, pressed and old English
glass, china, pottery, silver,
videos, toys, etc
Open Mon–Sat 10am–5pm
closed Tues
Services Valuations

⊞ Bob Lees
Contact Mr Bob Lees
✉ 65 George Street, Oldham,
Lancashire,
OL1 1LX 🅿
☎ 0161 628 4693
Est. 1994 *Stock size* Large
Stock General bookshop, second-
hand, some antiquarian, local
history
Open Mon–Sat 10.30am–5.30pm
Fairs Pudsey Book Fair, Buxton
Services Agent for book
rebinding and repair

⊞ Marks Antiques,
Jewellers/Pawnbrokers
Contact Mrs Marks
✉ 16 Waterloo Street, Oldham,
Lancashire,
OL1 1SQ 🅿
☎ 0161 624 5975 ✆ 0161 624 5975
📱 07979 508495
Est. 1970 *Stock size* Medium
Stock Jewellery, pottery, good-
quality furniture
Open Mon–Sat 9.30am–5pm
closed Tues
Fairs Newark
Services Pawnbroker, valuations

PRESTWICH

⊞ Family Antiques
Contact Jean Ditondo
✉ 405–407 Bury New Road,
Prestwich, Manchester,
M25 1AA 🅿
☎ 0161 798 0036
Est. 1984 *Stock size* Large
Stock Antique furniture
Open Mon–Sat 10am–5pm
Fairs Newark, Swinderby
Services Valuations

RADCLIFFE

⊞ Partners Antiques
Contact Mr L Ditondo
✉ Walker Street,

Radcliffe,
Manchester,
M26 1FH 🅿
☎ 0161 796 7095 ✆ 0161 796 7095
📧 luigi.ditondo@btinternet.com
🌐 www.luigi.ditondo@btinternet.com
Est. 1991 *Stock size* Large
Stock Victorian and shipping
furniture
Open Mon–Sun 9am–6pm
Fairs Newark, Ardingly
Services Container service

ROCHDALE

⊞ Antiques & Bygones
Contact Mr K Bonn
✉ 100 Drake Street, Rochdale,
Lancashire,
OL16 1PQ 🅿
☎ 01706 648114
📧 ken.bonn@btopenworld.com
Est. 1983 *Stock size* Medium
Stock Small antique items
including pottery, silver, coins,
medals, jewellery, militaria,
collectables
Open Wed–Sat 10am–3pm

⋏ Central Auction Rooms
Contact Terry Pickering
✉ 4 Baron Street, Rochdale,
Lancashire,
OL16 1SJ 🅿
☎ 01706 646298 ✆ 01706 646298
Est. 1919
Open Mon–Fri 9.30am–4.30pm
Sales General household sales
Tues 2pm, viewing Mon
9.30am–4.30pm. Occasional
antiques and small items Tues
1pm, viewing Mon 9.30am–4pm
Frequency Fortnightly, phone to
check
Catalogues For antique sales

ROMILEY

⊞ Romiley Antiques &
Jewellery
Contact Mr Peter Green
✉ 42 Stockport Road,
Romiley, Stockport,
Cheshire,
SK6 3AA 🅿
☎ 0161 494 6920
📱 07939 668819
Est. 1984 *Stock size* Medium
Stock Antique and second-hand
jewellery, Georgian and Victorian
furniture, pottery, general
antiques, clocks, barometers
Open Thurs Sat 9am–5pm or by

appointment
Services Valuations, house
clearance

ROYTON

⋏ Auction Centre Ltd
Contact Mr M McLaughlin
✉ Edge Lane Street,
Royton, Oldham,
Lancashire,
OL2 6DS 🅿
☎ 0161 338 8698 ✆ 0161 620 5636
📧 auctioncentre@btconnect.com
🌐 www.highamsauctions.com
Est. 1941
Open Mon–Fri 9am–5pm
Sales Regular antiques and
collectors' sales
Frequency Three weeks
Catalogues Yes

SALFORD

⊞ A S Antique Galleries
Contact Audrey Sternshine
✉ 26 Broad Street,
Pendleton, Salford,
Greater Manchester,
M6 5BY 🅿
☎ 0161 737 5938
📧 as@sternshine.demon.co.uk
Est. 1973 *Stock size* Large
Stock Art Nouveau and Art Deco,
bronze and bronze and ivory
figures, lighting, cameo glass,
pewter, ceramics, furniture,
jewellery, silver and general
antiques
Open Thurs–Sat 10am–5.30pm
or by appointment
Services Valuations, restoration,
purchase on commission

STOCKPORT

⊞ Antique Furniture
Warehouse
Contact Mr Juliano
✉ Unit 3–4,
Royal Oak Buildings,
Cooper Street, Stockport,
Cheshire,
SK1 3QJ 🅿
☎ 0161 429 8590 ✆ 0161 480 5375
Est. 1975 *Stock size* Large
Stock Wide range of antiques
Georgian–1940s including
porcelain, English inlay furniture,
decorative items, architectural
antiques, credenzas, walnut and
mahogany bookcases, Dutch
marquetry

NORTH WEST

Open Mon–Sat 10am–4pm
ring before visiting
Services Shipping, packing

⊞ Flintlock Antiques
Contact Mr F Tomlinson
✉ 28–30 Bramhall Lane,
Stockport,
Cheshire,
SK2 6HR ₽
☎ 0161 480 9973
Est. 1968 **Stock size** Medium
Stock Scientific instruments,
telescopes, military items,
paintings, marine models,
furniture
Open Mon–Fri 9am–5pm
Sat 9am–2pm by appointment

⊞ Hole in the Wall
Antiques
Contact Mr A Ledger
✉ 20 Buxton Road,
Heaviley, Stockport,
Cheshire,
SK2 6NU ₽
☎ 0161 476 4013 ❻ 0161 285 2860
❺ paul@antiquesimportexport.
freeserve.co.uk
Est. 1963 **Stock size** Large
Stock 1850–1920 American,
Georgian–Edwardian furniture
Open Mon–Sat 9.30am–5.30pm
or by appointment
Fairs Newark
Services Courier

⊞ Imperial Antiques
(LAPADA)
Contact Alfred Todd
✉ 295 Buxton Road,
Great Moor, Stockport,
Cheshire,
SK2 7NR ₽
☎ 0161 483 3322 ❻ 0161 483 3376
❺ alfred@imperialantiques.com
ⓦ www.imperialantiques.com
Est. 1975 **Stock size** Medium
Stock Oriental antiques,
ceramics, carpets, lighting,
silver, silver plate, French
furniture
Open Mon–Fri 9am–5pm
Fairs NEC
Services Valuations

⊞ Ledger Brothers
Contact Paul or Mark Ledger
✉ 20 Buxton Road (A6),
Heaviley, Stockport,
Cheshire,
SK2 6NU ₽
☎ 0161 476 4013 ❻ 0161 285 2860

❺ paul@antiquesimportexport.
freeserve.co.uk
Est. 1976 **Stock size** Large
Stock French, English, Italian and
American decorative furntiure
Open Mon–Sun 9am–5.30pm

⊞ Manchester Antique
Company
Contact Mr J Long
✉ Mac House,
St Thomas Place, Stockport,
Cheshire,
SK1 3TZ ₽
☎ 0161 355 5566 ❻ 0161 355 5588
❺ sales@manchester-antique.co.uk
ⓦ www.manchester-antique.co.uk
Est. 1969 **Stock size** Large
Stock General antiques, second-
hand and European furniture
Trade only Mainly trade
Open Mon–Fri 8am–5pm
Sat 10am–4pm

⊞ Nostalgia (LAPADA)
Contact Mrs E Durrant
✉ Holland's Mill,
Shaw Heath, Stockport,
Cheshire,
SK3 8BH ₽
☎ 0161 477 7706 ❻ 0161 477 2267
❺ info@nostalgia-uk.com
ⓦ www.nostalgia-uk.com
Est. 1977 **Stock size** Large
Stock Antique fireplaces
1780–1900, sanitary ware
Open Tues–Fri 10am–6pm
Sat 10am–5pm

⊞ Strippadoor
Contact Danny Russell
✉ Victoria Works, Units 2 and 3,
Hempshaw Lane, Stockport,
Cheshire,
SK1 4LG ₽
☎ 0161 477 8980 ❻ 0161 477 6302
Est. 1979 **Stock size** Medium
Stock Antique pine, original
doors and fireplaces
Open Mon–Fri 9am–5.30pm
Sat 10.30am–2.30pm
Services Stripping, leaded light
restoration, ironwork (rimlocks &
handles)

WIGAN

⊞ J W Antiques
Contact William Kenny
✉ 127 Bolton Road, Wigan,
Greater Manchester,
WN4 8AE ₽
☎ 01942 271212

Est. 1996 **Stock size** Large
Stock Leaded windows,
furniture, stone figures, stone
garden benches, cast-iron urns
Open Mon–Sat 9am–5pm
Services Shipping, mostly export
to USA

⊞ John Robinson
Antiques
Contact Mrs E Halliwell
✉ 172–176 Manchester Road,
Higher Ince, Wigan,
Lancashire,
WN2 2EA ₽
☎ 01942 247773 ❻ 01942 824964
Est. 1963 **Stock size** Large
Stock Furniture
Trade only Yes
Open By appointment only
Fairs Newark
Services Wholesale exporters,
mostly shipping furntiure

⊞ Colin de Rouffignac
(BNTA)
Contact Mr C de Rouffignac
✉ 57 Wigan Lane, Wigan,
Lancashire,
WN1 2LF ₽
☎ 01942 237927
Est. 1970 **Stock size** Medium
Stock 18th–early 20thC furniture,
early coins, medals, general
antiques, paintings
Open Mon–Sat 10am–4.30pm
closed Wed
Fairs Tatton
Services Valuations

⊞ Steve's World Famous
Movie Store
Contact Mr S Ellison
✉ 45 Cadogan Drive,
Winstanley, Wigan, Lancashire,
WN3 6JH ₽
☎ 01942 213541 ❻ 01942 213541
❺ movie.store@virgin.net
ⓦ www.worldfamousmovie.com
Est. 1973 **Stock size** Large
Stock Stills, posters, vinyl and CD
soundtracks, books and movie
magazines from 1916 onwards,
other memorabilia, autographs
Open By appointment
Services Free search, mail order,
valuations

WORSLEY

⊞ Northern Clocks
(LAPADA)
Contact Robert or Mary Anne

NORTH WEST
LANCASHIRE • ACCRINGTON

✉ Boothsbank Farm,
Worsley,
Manchester,
M28 1LL **P**
☎ 0161 790 8414
Ⓜ 07970 820258
✉ info@northernclocks.co.uk
Ⓦ www.northernclocks.co.uk
Est. 1997 *Stock size* Medium
Stock Longcase, bracket, wall
clocks
Open Thurs–Sat 10am–5pm
or by appointment
Fairs Antiques for Everyone,
Chester, Buxton
Services Valuations, restoration

LANCASHIRE

ACCRINGTON

⊞ **Alpha Coins & Medals**
Contact Mr P Darlington
✉ 20 Abbey Street,
Accrington,
Lancashire,
BB5 1EB **P**
☎ 01254 395540
Est. 1994 *Stock size* Medium
Stock Post-1800 British coins and
medals
Open Mon–Fri 9.30am–4.30pm

⊞ **Revival**
Contact Mr Ian Smith
✉ 34 Warner Street,
Accrington,
Lancashire,
BB5 1HN **P**
☎ 01254 382316
Est. 1989
Stock size Large
Stock Costume, textiles, jewellery
from 1900–1970s
Open Mon–Sat 10.30am–5pm
closed Wed or by appointment
Fairs Hammersmith Textiles
Services Costume hire

BARTON

⊞ **Kopper Kettle Furniture**
Contact Mr Steve Round
✉ 639 Garstang Road,
Barton, Preston,
Lancashire,
PR3 5DQ **P**
☎ 01772 861064
Est. 1998 *Stock size* Small
Stock Victorian–Edwardian
furniture, some reproduction
Open Mon–Sun 10.30am–5.30pm
closed Fri

BLACKBURN

⊞ **Ancient and Modern
(NAG, OMRS)**
Contact Zac Coles
✉ 17 Newmarket Street,
Blackburn,
Lancashire,
BB1 7DR **P**
☎ 01254 677866 Ⓖ 01254 677866
Est. 1943 *Stock size* Large
Stock Georgian–modern
jewellery, watches, silver, coins,
medals
Open Mon–Sat 9am–5.30pm
Fairs Miami, Bangkok
Services Valuations, restoration

⊞ **Decades (Textile
Society)**
Contact Janet Conroy
✉ 20 Lord Street West,
Blackburn,
Lancashire,
BB2 1JX **P**
☎ 01254 693320
Ⓜ 07939 924794
Est. 1989 *Stock size* Large
Stock Costumes, textiles,
accessories
Open Wed–Sat 11am–5pm or by
appointment
Fairs Anne Zierold fair
Manchester, Textile Association
fair Manchester, Hammersmith
fair London

⊞ **Fieldings Antiques &
Clocks**
Contact Mr Andrew Fielding
✉ 176 Blackburn Road,
Haslingden, Blackburn,
Lancashire,
BB4 5HW **P**
☎ 01254 263358
Ⓜ 07973 698961
Est. 1964 *Stock size* Large
Stock Longcase and other clocks,
period oak furniture, steam
engines, vintage motorcycles, oil
paintings
Open Mon–Fri 9am–5pm phone
first

⊞ **Mitchells Lock Antiques**
Contact Mr S Mitchell
✉ 76 Bolton Road, Blackburn,
Lancashire,
BB2 3PZ **P**
☎ 01254 664663
Ⓜ 07977 856725
Est. 1972 *Stock size* Large
Stock General antiques

Open Mon–Sat 9am–5pm
Fairs Newark, Swinderby, Park
Hall Chorley

BLACKPOOL

⊞ **Ascot Antiques**
Contact Mr C Winwood
✉ 106 Holmefield Road,
Blackpool,
Lancashire,
FY2 9RF **P**
☎ 01253 356383
Est. 1987 *Stock size* Medium
Stock Georgian–Victorian
furniture and oil paintings
Trade only Yes
Open By appointment
Services Valuations

⊞ **Robinsons Timber
Building Supplies Ltd**
Contact Mr A Robinson
✉ 3–7 Boothley Road, Blackpool,
Lancashire,
FY1 3RS **P**
☎ 01253 628826
Est. 1938 *Stock size* Large
Stock Architectural antiques,
doors, floors etc, garden items
Open Mon–Fri 8am–5.30pm
Sat 8am–2pm
Services Timber flooring
restoration

⊞ **B Scott-Spencer**
Contact Mr J Neiman
✉ 228 Church Street, Blackpool,
Lancashire,
FY1 3PX **P**
☎ 01253 294489 Ⓖ 01253 626977
Stock Wide range of general
antiques, jewellery, stamps,
collectables etc
Open Mon–Fri 10am–4pm
telephone for appointment
Services Valuations, repairs,
buying large diamonds

BRETHERTON

⌂ **The Old Corn Mill
Antique Centre**
Contact Mr A Thin
✉ 64 South Road, Bretherton,
Lancashire,
PR26 9AH **P**
☎ 01772 601371 Ⓖ 01772 813599
Est. 1999 *Stock size* Large
No. of dealers 65
Stock Antiques and collectables
Open Mon–Sat 10.30am–5.30pm
Sun 11am–5pm

370

BURNLEY

⊞ Brun-Lea Antiques
Contact Mr John Waite
✉ Unit 1, Elm Street Business Park, Burnley, Lancashire, BB10 1DG 🅿
☎ 01282 413513 📠 01282 832769
📧 jwaite@freenetname.co.uk
🌐 www.antiques-atlas.com
Est. 1973 *Stock size* Large
Stock Period furniture to 1930s
Open Mon–Thurs 8.30am–5.30pm Fri Sat 8.30am–4pm Sun noon–4pm

⊞ Brun-Lea Antiques
Contact Mr John Waite
✉ 3 & 5 Standish Street, Burnley, Lancashire, BB11 1AP 🅿
☎ 01282 432396
📧 jwaite@freenetname.co.uk
🌐 www.antiques-atlas.com
Est. 1973 *Stock size* Large
Stock Edwardian–Victorian furniture
Open Mon–Sat 9am–5pm

⊞ Lonesome Pine Antiques
Contact Mr P Berry
✉ 19 Bank Parade, Burnley, Lancashire, BB11 1UH 🅿
☎ 01282 428415
📱 07791 066983
Est. 1987 *Stock size* Medium
Stock Antique pine furniture, period furniture, reclaimed pine furniture
Open Mon–Sat 9am–5pm
Services Bespoke furniture

BURSCOUGH

⊞ West Lancashire Antiques Export (LAPADA)
Contact Brett Griffiths
✉ Victoria Mill, Victoria Street, Burscough, Lancashire, L40 0SN 🅿
☎ 01704 894634 📠 01704 894486
📱 07759 403036
📧 westlancsantique@btconnect.com
Est. 1969 *Stock size* Large
Stock Antique furniture
Open Mon–Fri 9am–5.30pm Sat Sun 10am–5.30pm
Fairs Swinderby, Newark
Services Shipping, courier service

BURY

🏠 Memories Antique Centre
Contact Mr Huges or Miss Bell
✉ 33–37 Bridge Street, Ramsbottom, Bury, Lancashire, BL0 9AD 🅿
☎ 01706 824122
Est. 1990 *Stock size* Large
No. of dealers 28
Stock Furniture, collectables, brass, pine, oak
Open Mon–Sun 10am–4.30pm

CHARNOCK RICHARD

🏠 Park Hall
Contact Mr David Fletcher
✉ Exhibition Halls, Charnock Richard, Lancashire, PR7 5LP 🅿
☎ 07800 508178 📠 01989 730339
Stock size Medium
No. of dealers 100
Stock General antiques, collectables. General antiques fair held every Sunday. £2 entrance fee
Open Sun 8am–3pm

CLEVELEYS

🪚 Smythes
Contact Mr P Smythe
✉ 174 Victoria Road West, Cleveleys, Lancashire, FY5 3NE 🅿
☎ 01253 852184 📠 01253 854084
📧 smythe@btinternet.com
🌐 www.smythes.net
Est. 1920
Open Mon–Fri 9am–5pm, Sat 9am–noon
Sales Fine art sales
Frequency Every 6–8 weeks
Catalogues Yes

CLITHEROE

⊞ Clitheroe Collectables
Contact Mrs J Spensley
✉ 13 Duck Street, Clitheroe, Lancashire, BB7 1LP 🅿
☎ 01200 422222 📠 01200 422223
📧 sales@clicollect.fsnet.co.uk
🌐 www.clitheroecollectables.co.uk
Est. 1989 *Stock size* Medium

Stock Pottery, Victorian pine furniture
Open Mon–Sat 9am–5pm
Fairs Harrogate
Services Restoration of antique pine

⊞ Past and Present Fireplaces
Contact Mr David Hollings
✉ 22 Whalley Road, Clitheroe, Lancashire, BB7 1AW 🅿
☎ 01200 428678/445373
📱 07779 478716
Est. 1987 *Stock size* Large
Stock Architectural antiques, general antiques, fireplaces, fireplace accessories, fenders etc.
Open Mon–Sat 10.30am–5pm Sun by appointment closed Wed
Fairs Newark, Swinderby
Services Fitting service

⊞ Roundstone Books
Contact Mr J Harding
✉ 29 Moor Lane, Clitheroe, Lancashire, BB7 1BE 🅿
☎ 01200 444242
📧 joharbooks@aol.com
🌐 www.roundstonebooks.co.uk
Est. 1995 *Stock size* Medium
Stock Antiquarian and second-hand books, general stock including alternative medicine, poetry, literature, children's books
Open Tues–Sat 10am–5pm closed Wed
Services Book search

DARWEN

🏠 Belgrave Antiques Centre
Contact Mr M Cooney
✉ Brittania Mill, 136 Bolton Road, Darwen, Lancashire, BB3 1BZ 🅿
☎ 01254 777714
📧 belgraveantiques@aol.com
Est. 1997 *Stock size* Large
No. of dealers 40
Stock Furniture, pottery, Victorian stripped pine, architectural antiques, collectables
Open Tue–Sat 9.30am–5pm Sun 11am–4.30pm
Services Stripping, shipping

NORTH WEST

⊞ K C Antiques (LAPADA)
Contact Mrs K Anderton
✉ 538 Bolton Road, Darwen,
Lancashire,
BB3 2JR ⓟ
☎ 01254 772252
🅔 mickdavies@breathe.mail.net.
Est. 1970 *Stock size* Medium
Stock 18th–19thC furniture and
decorative items
Open Mon–Sat 9am–5.30pm Sun
10am–4pm and by appointment

ECCLESTON

⌂ Bygone Times
Contact Ged Wood
✉ Grove Mill, The Green,
Eccleston, Chorley,
Lancashire,
PR5 5PD ⓟ
☎ 01257 451889 🅕 01257 451090
🅔 ged.wood@virgin.net
🅦 www.bygonetimes.co.uk
Est. 1988 *Stock size* Large
No. of dealers 250 stalls
Stock Antiques, furniture, small
items, collectables, memorabilia
Open Mon–Sun 10am–6pm Wed
10am–8pm

GREAT HARWOOD

**⊞ Benny Charlsworth's
Snuff Box**
Contact Naomi Walsh
✉ 51 Blackburn Road,
Great Harwood, Blackburn,
Lancashire,
BB6 7DF ⓟ
☎ 01254 888550
Est. 1983 *Stock size* Large
Stock Antique furniture,
paintings, pottery, costume
jewellery, linen etc
Open Mon–Fri 10am–1pm
2pm–5pm except Tues and
Sat 10am–12noon
Fairs Newark

**⊞ Jean's Military
Memories**
Contact Mrs J South
✉ 32 Queen Street, Great
Harwood, Blackburn, Lancashire,
BB6 7QQ ⓟ
☎ 01254 877825 🅕 01254 877825
🅜 07710 636069
Est. 1996 *Stock size* Large
Stock Militaria, guns of all types,
edge weaponry 1800–2002
Open Mon–Fri 9am–5pm Sat
9am–4pm or by appointment

HAPTON

⊞ Pipkins Antiques
Contact Maurice Bradley
✉ 5 The Stables, Hapton,
Nr Burnley, Lancashire,
BB12 7LL ⓟ
☎ 07778 265909 🅕 01282 770548
🅔 maurice@pipkins.fsbusiness.co.uk
Est. 1996 *Stock size* Large
Stock Doors, door furniture,
Belfast sinks, general
architectural salvage
Open By appointment

HARLE SYKE

**⌂ Kings Mill Antique
Centre**
Contact Linda Heuer
✉ Unit 6, Kings Mill,
Queen Street, Harle Syke,
Burnley, Lancashire,
BB10 2HX ⓟ
☎ 01282 431953 🅕 01282 839470
🅜 07803 153752
🅔 antiques@kingsmill.demon.co.uk
🅦 www.kingsmill.demon.co.uk
Est. 1996 *Stock size* Large
No. of dealers 30
Stock Antique furniture,
European collectables
Open Mon–Sat 10am–5pm Thurs
10am–7pm Sun 11am–5pm
Services Container service,
courier service, export

HASLINGDEN

⊞ P J Brown Antiques
Contact Mrs K Brown
✉ 8 Church Street, Haslingden,
Rossendale, Lancashire,
BB4 5QU ⓟ
☎ 01706 224888 🅕 01706 224888
🅜 07899 074816
Est. 1979 *Stock size* Medium
Stock Georgian–Edwardian
furniture, small antiques,
advertising items, shop fittings,
old bottles, pot lids
Open Mon–Fri 10am–5.30pm Sat
10am–4pm or by appointment
Fairs Newark

⌂ Holden Wood Antiques
Contact John Ainscough
✉ St Stephens, Grane Road,
Haslingden, Rossendale,
Lancashire,
BB4 4AT ⓟ
☎ 01706 830803
🅔 john@holdenwood.co.uk

🅦 www.holdenwood.co.uk
Est. 1996 *Stock size* Large
No. of dealers 30+
Stock Ceramics, clocks, watches,
paintings, period and country
furniture
Open Mon–Sun 10am–5.30pm
Services Valuations, restoration,
tea rooms

HESKIN GREEN

⌂ Heskin Hall Antiques
Contact Mr Dennis Harrison
✉ Wood Lane, Heskin, Chorley,
Lancashire,
PR7 5PA ⓟ
☎ 01257 452044 🅕 01257 450690
🅔 heskinhall@aol.com
Est. 1995 *Stock size* Large
No. of dealers 65
Stock A complete range of
antiques and collectables
Open Mon–Sun 10am–5.30pm
Services Restoration

HORWICH

⊞ Trains and Diecast
Contact Mr D Brandwood
✉ 138 Wright Street, Horwich,
Bolton, Lancashire,
BL6 7HU ⓟ
☎ 01204 669782 🅕 01204 669782
🅔 david@trainsanddiecast.com
🅦 www.trainsanddiecast.com
Est. 1972 *Stock size* Large
Stock Collectable toys, Dinky, Corgi,
Hornby, Triang, Matchbox etc
Open Mon Thurs Fri 9.30am–5pm
Sat 9.30am–1pm
Services Valuations

KIRKBY LONSDALE

**⊞ Architus Antiques &
Collectables**
Contact Mrs J Pearson
✉ 14 Main Street, Kirkby
Lonsdale, Carnforth, Lancashire,
LA6 2AE ⓟ
☎ 01524 272409
Est. 1994 *Stock size* Medium
Stock Wide range of antiques
and collectables
Open Mon–Sat 10am–5pm
Services Valuations

LANCASTER

**⊞ Anything Old & Military
Collectables**
Contact Mr G H Chambers

✉ **55 Scotforth Road, Lancaster, Lancashire, LA1 4SA** ℗
☎ 01524 69933
Est. 1984 *Stock size* Medium
Stock Militaria including medals, cap badges, edged weapons, uniforms, helmets, Third Reich militaria
Open Wed Sat 1.30–6pm other times by appointment
Services Valuations, medal mounting

⌂ **G B Antiques Centre**
Contact Mr Alan Blackburn
✉ **Lancaster Leisure Park, Wyresdale Road, Lancaster, Lancashire, LA1 3LA** ℗
☎ 01524 844734 ℗ 01524 844735
Est. 1990 *Stock size* Large
No. of dealers 140
Stock Wide range of antiques, collectables
Open Mon–Sun 10am–5pm
Services Café, factory shop

⊞ **Lancastrian Antiques**
Contact Mr S Wilkinson
✉ **70–72 Penny Street, Lancaster, Lancashire, LA1 1XF** ℗
☎ 01524 847004
℮ info@rectorylancs.co.uk
Est. 1981 *Stock size* Medium
Stock General antiques period furniture, porcelain, pottery, paintings
Open Mon–Sat 10am–4.30pm closed Wed
Services Valuations

LONGRIDGE

⊞ **Berry Antiques & Interiors**
Contact Kerry Barnett or Eloise Halsall
✉ **61 Berry Lane, Longridge, Preston, Lancashire, PR3 3NH** ℗
☎ 01772 780476
Est. 2001 *Stock size* Medium
Stock General antiques, collectables
Open Mon–Sat 10am–4pm

⌁ **Henry Holden & Son Ltd**
Contact Mrs S MacCarthy or Mr P McKenna
✉ **Central Salerooms,**

Towneley Road, Longridge, Preston, Lancashire, PR3 3EA ℗
☎ 01772 783274 ℗ 01772 783274
ⓦ www.henryholdenandson.co.uk
Est. 1890
Open Mon–Fri 9.30am–4.30pm
Sales Fortnightly on Sat, household 10am antiques noon, viewing Fri 10am–8pm day of sale 9–10am

LYTHAM ST ANNE'S

⌁ **Lot 3 Auction Hall**
Contact Mr M Mallinson
✉ **3 Kingsway, Lytham St Anne's, Lancashire, FY8 1AB** ℗
☎ 01253 731600 ℗ 01253 731614
℮ enquiries@lot3.co.uk
ⓦ www.lot3.co.uk
Est. 1993
Open Mon–Fri 9am–4.30pm
Sales Antiques, reproductions and collectables every 3rd Wed 9am–2.30pm, viewing Sat 10am–noon Mon–Tues 9am–4pm

⊞ **Windmill Bookshop**
Contact Terry Welsh
✉ **62a Preston Road, Lytham St Anne's, Lancashire, FY8 5AE** ℗
☎ 01253 732485 ℗ 01253 732485
⑩ 07969 846091
Est. 1993 *Stock size* Medium
Stock General stock of antiquarian and second-hand books
Open Mon–Sun 9am–9pm
Fairs Buxton, Pudsey

MORECAMBE

⊞ **Clocktower Antiques**
Contact John Hawthorn-Cardiff
✉ **9 & 11 Queen Street, Morecambe, Lancashire, LA4 5EQ** ℗
☎ 01524 833331
℮ sales@clocktowerantiques.com
ⓦ www.clocktowerantiques.com
Est. 1986 *Stock size* Large
Stock Antique clocks, mixed period furniture
Open Mon–Sun 9am–5pm closed Wed
Services Restoration and repair of clocks, polishing

NELSON

⊞ **Brittons Watches (NAG)**
Contact Mr P Walden or Glen Britton
✉ **4 King Street, Clitheroe, Lancashire, BB7 2EP** ℗
☎ 01200 425555 or 01282 697659
℗ 0870 136 1597
℮ info@brittons-watches.co.uk
ⓦ www.brittons-watches.co.uk
Est. 1969 *Stock size* Large
Stock Quality pre-owned wrist watches from 1920s to present day, antique and quality second-hand jewellery
Open Mon–Sat 10am–5pm
Services Watch and jewellery repairs, valuations

ORMSKIRK

⊞ **Browzaround**
Contact Mrs P Graham
✉ **16 Derby Street West, Ormskirk, Lancashire, L39 3NH** ℗
☎ 01695 576999
Est. 1975 *Stock size* Medium
Stock Pre-war furniture, collectables and antique agricultural tools
Open Tues–Sat 10am–4pm closed Wed
Services Searches

⊞ **Collectors Corner**
Contact Mr B Jermyn
✉ **117 Aughton Street, Ormskirk, Lancashire, L39 3BN** ℗
☎ 01695 577455
⑩ 07710 741250
℮ beaniebob@btinternet.com
Est. 1997 *Stock size* Large
Stock Cigarette cards, Beanie Babies, dolls' houses
Open Wed–Sat 10.30am–5pm
Services Valuations

⊞ **Green Lane Antiques**
Contact Mr J Swift
✉ **Unit B20, Malthouse Business Centre, 48 Southport Road, Ormskirk, Lancashire, L39 1QR** ℗
☎ 01695 580731
ⓦ www.greenlaneantiques.co.uk
Est. 1998 *Stock size* Large
Stock Architectural antiques,

period furniture, clocks, pine etc
Open Mon–Sun 10am–4pm
Services Restoration of clocks

⊞ A Grice
Contact Mr A Grice
✉ **106 Aughton Street, Ormskirk,
Lancashire,
L39 3BS** 🅿
☎ 01695 572007
Est. 1946 **Stock size** Small
Stock Furniture
Open Mon–Sat 10am–5pm
closed Wed
Services Valuations, antique
furniture restoration

PRESTON

⊞ European Fine Arts &
Antiques
Contact Mr Brian Beck
✉ **10 Cannon Street, Preston,
Lancashire,
PR1 3NR** 🅿
☎ 01772 883886 📠 01772 823888
📧 info@european-fine-arts.co.uk
🌐 www.european-fine-arts.co.uk
Est. 1969 **Stock size** Large
Stock Victorian gallery, furniture,
Louis XIV style furniture
Open Mon–Sat 9.30am–5.30pm
or by appointment

⊞ Fine Art Antiques
Contact Mr Mark Pedler
✉ **109 New Hall Lane, Preston,
Lancashire,
PR1 5PB** 🅿
☎ 01772 794010
📱 07883 081887
Est. 1987 **Stock size** Medium
Stock Georgian oak furniture,
bracket and longcase clocks,
barometers, general antiques
Open Mon–Fri 10am–4pm
Fairs Newark, Swinderby,
Shepton Mallet
Services Restoration, chandelier
re-wiring

⊞ David Greenhalgh
Antiques
Contact David Greenhalgh
✉ **Preston Antique Centre,
Horrock's Mill,
New Hall Lane, Preston,
Lancashire,
PL1 5NX** 🅿
☎ 01229 462001
📱 07768 582337
Est. 1960 **Stock size** Medium
Stock General antiques, shipping

goods
Open Mon–Fri 8.30am–5.30pm
Sat 10am–4pm Sun 10am–5pm

⊞ The Odd Chair Company
Contact Sue Cook
✉ **The Studio, Eaves Cottage
Farm, Eaves, Preston,
Lancashire,
PR4 0BH** 🅿
☎ 01772 691777 📠 01772 691888
📧 info@theoddchaircompany.com
🌐 www.theoddchaircompany.com
Est. 1969 **Stock size** Large
Stock 19thC antique chairs, sofas
and decorative furniture
Open Mon–Fri 9am–5pm
Sat by prior arrangement
Fairs Newark, Ardingly
Services Interior design,
upholstery, cabinet making

🏠 Preston Antiques
Centre
Contact Sue Shalloe
✉ **The Mill, New Hall Lane,
Preston,
Lancashire,
PL1 5NX** 🅿
☎ 01772 794498 📠 01772 651694
📧 prestonantiques@talk21.com
🌐 www.prestonantiquescentre.com
Est. 1978 **Stock size** Large
No. of dealers 50
Stock General antiques, clocks,
fine arts, porcelain
Open Mon–Fri 8.30am–5pm
Sat Sun 10am–4pm

⊞ Ribble Reclamation
(SALVO)
Contact Mr Parviz Shahsvov
✉ **Ducie Place, Off New Hall
Lane, Preston,
Lancashire,
PR1 4UJ** 🅿
☎ 01772 794534 📠 01772 794604
📧 joe@ribble-reclamation.com
🌐 www.ribble-reclamation.com
Est. 1977 **Stock size** Large
Stock Garden statuary, arches,
stone flags, lamp posts,
fountains, architectural antiques,
reclaimed building materials
Open Mon–Fri 8am–5pm
Sat 8am–3pm

SABDEN

⊞ Walter Aspinall
Antiques
Contact Mr W Aspinall
✉ **Pendle Antiques Centre,**

Union Mill, Watt Street,
Sabden, Clitheroe,
Lancashire,
BB7 9ED** 🅿
☎ 01282 778642 📠 01282 778643
📧 walter.aspinall@btinternet.com
Est. 1986 **Stock size** Large
Stock General antiques
Victorian–1940s, shipping
furniture, collectables, leaded
windows etc
Open Mon–Thurs 9am–6pm
Fri 9am–5pm Sat 10am–5pm Sun
11am–5pm or by appointment
Services Shipping, restoration,
café

🏠 Pendle Antiques Centre
Ltd
Contact Mr Jason Billington
✉ **Union Mill, Watt Street,
Sabden, Clitheroe,
Lancashire,
BB7 9ED** 🅿
☎ 01282 776311 📠 01282 777642
📧 sales@pendleantiquescentre.co.uk
🌐 www.pendleantiquescentre.co.uk
Est. 1984 **Stock size** Large
No. of dealers 15
Stock Wide range of antiques
including architectural and
shipping wares, bric-a-brac
Open Mon–Sat 10am–5pm
Sun 11am–5pm
Services Shipping

TODMORDEN

⊞ The Border Bookshop
(PBFA, BA)
Contact Mr V H Collinge
✉ **61a Halifax Road, Todmorden,
Lancashire,
OL14 5BB** 🅿
☎ 01706 814721
📧 collinge@borderbookshop.
fsnet.co.uk
🌐 www.borderbookshop.co.uk
Est. 1979 **Stock size** Large
Stock Second-hand books (large
sports section), comics, story
papers 1880–1970
Open Mon–Fri 10am–1pm 2–5pm
Sat 9am–5pm closed Tues
Fairs PBFA
Services Book tokens

⊞ Cottage Antiques
Contact Miss G Slater
✉ **788 Rochdale Road,
Walsden, Todmorden,
Lancashire,
OL14 7UA** 🅿

☎ 01706 813612
ⓦ www.ukcottageantiques.co.uk
Est. 1984 *Stock size* Medium
Stock General pine country
furniture, kitchenware,
collectables, farmhouse-style
items
Open Thurs–Sun 11am–5.30pm
Services Stripping, polishing,
paint finishes, renovations,
custom-built furniture

⊞ Echoes
Contact Mrs P Oldman
✉ 650a Halifax Road,
Eastwood, Todmorden,
Lancashire,
OL14 6DW 🅿
☎ 01706 817505
Est. 1986 *Stock size* Large
Stock Clothing, textiles,
pre-Victorian to late 1950s
Open Wed–Sat 11am–6pm
Sun noon–5pm
Fairs Manchester Textile Fairs
Services Valuations

⊞ Fagin & Co
Contact Mr John Ratcliff
✉ 54 Burnley Road, Todmorden,
Lancashire,
OL14 5EY 🅿
☎ 01706 819499/814773
Ⓜ 07899 774257
ⓔ mrhillside@aol.com
Est. 1994 *Stock size* Medium
Stock General antiques,
collectables, advertising
Open Mon–Sat 10.30am–5pm
closed Tues
Services Valuations

⊞ Re-Collections
Contact Mr Ashleigh Cooper
✉ Sutcliffe House,
137 Halifax Road, Todmorden,
Lancashire,
OL14 5BE 🅿
☎ 01706 818040
Ⓜ 07979 404757
ⓔ mr.ed@freenet.co.uk
Est. 1990 *Stock size* Small
Stock Small furniture, silver,
pottery, collectables, pictures
Open Mon–Sat 10.30am–4pm
Sun noon–4pm
Services Valuations

WHALLEY

⊞ Edmund Davies & Son Antiques
Contact Philip Davies

✉ 32 King Street, Whalley,
Clitheroe, Lancashire,
BB7 9SL 🅿
☎ 01254 823764 ⓕ 01254 823764
Ⓜ 07879 877306
Est. 1960 *Stock size* Medium
Stock Longcase clocks, country
furniture
Open Mon–Sat 10am–5pm
Services Clock and furniture
restoration

MERSEYSIDE

BEBINGTON

⚘ UK Toy & Model Auctions Ltd
Contact Tony Oakes or Barry
Stockton
✉ 46 Wirral Gardens, Bebington,
Wirral, Merseyside,
CH63 3BH 🅿
☎ 01270 841558 ⓕ 01270 841558
Ⓜ 07771 396459
ⓦ www.uktoyauctions.com
Open By appointment
Sales Sales of toys and models
held at the Craxton Wood Hotel,
near Chester, viewings on day of
sale
Frequency 3–4 per year
Catalogues Yes

BIRKENHEAD

⊞ Mistermicawber.Co.Ltd
Contact Mr Barrington
✉ 100 Woodchurch Lane,
Birkenhead, Merseyside,
CH42 9PD 🅿
☎ 0151 608 5445
ⓔ mistermicawber.co@btinternet.com
Est. 1974 *Stock size* Medium
Stock Pre-1930s furniture
Open Mon–Sat 9am–5pm closed
Thurs

BROMBOROUGH

⊞ Full of Beans
Contact Kris Richards
✉ Unit 34, Croft Retail Park,
Dinsdale Road, Bromborough,
Wirral, Merseyside,
CH62 3PY 🅿
☎ 0151 334 6999
ⓦ www.fullofbeanies.com
Est. 1999 *Stock size* Large
Stock Beanie Babies and
accessories
Open Mon–Sat 10am–5pm
Sun Bank Holidays 10.30am–4pm

HESWALL

⊞ The Antique Shop
Contact Mr C Rosenberg
✉ 120–122 Telegraph Road,
Heswall, Wirral, Merseyside,
CH60 0AQ 🅿
☎ 0151 342 1053 ⓕ 0151 342 1053
Est. 1961 *Stock size* Medium
Stock Victorian jewellery, silver,
bric-a-brac, pictures, paintings,
watercolours
Open Fri Sat 10am–5pm
Services Jewellery repairs, silver
repairs, valuations

HOYLAKE

⚘ Kingsley Auctions Ltd
Contact Mr I McKellar
✉ 3–4 The Quadrant,
Hoylake, Wirral,
Merseyside,
CH47 2EE 🅿
☎ 0151 632 5821
Est. 1972
Open Mon–Fri 9am–5pm
closed 1–2pm
Sales General auction sale Tues
10am, viewing Sat 9am–12.30pm
Mon 9am–5pm day of sale
9–10am
Frequency Weekly
Catalogues Yes

⊞ Mansell Antiques & Collectables
Contact Gary Mansell or
David Mansell
✉ Mulberry House,
128–130 Market Street,
Hoylake, Wirral,
Merseyside,
CH47 3BH 🅿
☎ 0151 632 0892 ⓕ 0151 632 6137
ⓦ www.antiquesatlas.com
Est. 1998 *Stock size* Large
Stock 20thC collectables, Art
Deco, Carlton ware, Shelley etc,
Art Nouveau furniture and
lighting
Open Mon–Sat 9am–5pm
closed Wed
Fairs Chester Racecourse
Services Valuations, restoration

⊞ Now and Then
Contact Margaret Hirst
✉ 4 Albert Road,
Hoylake, Wirral,
Merseyside,
CH47 2AB 🅿
☎ 0151 632 0071

NORTH WEST

Est. 1976 *Stock size* Medium
Stock Furniture, collectables,
bric-a-brac
Open Mon–Sun 10am–5pm
closed Wed
Services Valuations

LIVERPOOL

⊞ Antique Cottage
Contact Thomas or Rita Smith
✉ 91 Moss Lane, Liverpool,
Merseyside,
L9 8AQ ℗
☎ 0151 524 0805
📱 07932 495888
✉ rita@dolls96.fsnet.co.uk
Est. 2003 *Stock size* Medium
Stock General antiques, bisque
dolls
Open Mon–Sat 9am–6pm
Fairs Swinderby, Newark

⚒ Cato Crane & Co
Contact Mr J Crane AMATA
✉ 6 and 33–39 Stanhope Street,
Liverpool,
Merseyside,
L8 5RF ℗
☎ 0151 709 5559   📠 0151 707 2454
✉ info@cato-crane.co.uk
🌐 www.cato-crane.co.uk
Est. 1986
Open Mon–Fri 9am–5pm
Sat 9am–1pm or by appointment
Sales Auctions every Tuesday
Thursday including antique
Victorian and 20thC furniture,
collectables and decorative
objects. Quality antiques and
fine art auction every month
Catalogues Yes

⊞ Circa 1900
Contact Mr W Colquhoun
✉ 11–13 Holts Arcade,
India Buildings, Water Street,
Liverpool, Merseyside,
L2 0RR ℗
☎ 0151 236 1282   📠 0151 236 1282
🌐 www.classicartdeco.com
Est. 1996 *Stock size* Large
Stock Art Nouveau, classic Art
Deco, applied arts
Open Mon–Fri 10am–6pm or by
appointment

⚒ Hartley & Co
Contact Mr J Brown
✉ 12–14 Moss Street,
Low Hill, Liverpool,
Merseyside,
L6 1HF ℗

☎ 0151 263 6472/1865
📠 0151 260 3417
Est. 1849
Open Mon–Fri 9am–4.30pm
Sales General household,
antique and reproduction sales
Fri 10.15am, viewing Thurs
9am–4.30pm Fri 9–10.15am.
Merseyside Police lost property
Frequency Fortnightly
Catalogues No

⊞ Liverpool Militaria
Contact Mr Bill Tagg
✉ 17 Cheapside, Liverpool,
Merseyside,
L2 2DY ℗
☎ 0151 236 4404
✉ liverpoolmilitaria@hotmail.com
Est. 1977 *Stock size* Medium
Stock General military antiques
Open Mon–Sat 10.30am–5pm
closed Wed
Fairs Northern Arms & Armour,
International – Birmingham

⊞ Maggs Shipping Ltd
Contact Mr R Webster
✉ 66–68 St Anne Street,
Liverpool, Merseyside,
L3 3DY ℗
☎ 0151 207 2555   📠 0151 207 2555
✉ maggsantiques@compuserve.com
Est. 1971 *Stock size* Large
Stock Restored Georgian-style,
country and pine furniture,
French decorative furniture
Trade only Yes
Open Mon–Fri 9am–5pm
Services Restoration, packing,
shipping

⚒ Outhwaite & Litherland
(SOFAA)
Contact Mr Kevin Whay
✉ Kingsway Galleries,
Fontenoy Street, Liverpool,
Merseyside,
L3 2BE ℗
☎ 0151 236 6561   📠 0151 236 1070
✉ auction@lots.uk.com
🌐 www.lots.uk.com
Est. 1907
Open Mon–Fri 9am–5pm
Sales Antiques sales 4–5 per
annum Wed. Weekly general
household sales Tues 10.30am,
viewing Mon 9am–5pm Tues
9–10.30am. Monthly cavalcade
collectors' sales 1st Tues of
month or day prior to major fine
art and antiques sale
Catalogues Yes

⊞ Pilgrim's Progress
Contact Selwyn Hyams
✉ 1a–3a Bridgewater Street,
Liverpool, Merseyside,
L1 0AR ℗
☎ 0151 708 7515   📠 0151 708 7515
📱 07808 899333
✉ pilgrimsprog@fsbdial.co.uk
🌐 www.pilgrimsprogress.co.uk
Est. 1979 *Stock size* Large
Stock Five floors of mainly
19th and early 20thC furniture
Open Mon–Fri 9am–5pm
Sat 10.30am–1.30pm
Services Valuations, restoration

⊞ Seventeen Antiques
Contact Mr J Brake
✉ 306 Aigburth Road, Liverpool,
Merseyside,
L17 9PW ℗
☎ 0151 727 1717
📱 07712 189604
✉ annebrake@btconnect.com
Est. 1997 *Stock size* Large
Stock Antique pine furniture,
cast-iron fireplaces
Open Mon–Sat 10am–5.30pm
closed Wed
Services Restoration, stripping

⊞ Stefani Antiques
Contact Mrs T Stefani
✉ 497 Smithdown Road,
Liverpool, Merseyside,
L15 5AE ℗
☎ 0151 734 1933/733 4836
📱 07946 646395
Est. 1977 *Stock size* Large
Stock General antiques, pottery,
porcelain, brass, copper,
furniture
Open Mon–Sat 10am–5pm
Services Valuations, restoration

⚒ Turner & Sons (1787)
(NAVA)
Contact Mr Kevin Davies
✉ Century Salerooms,
28–36 Roscoe Street, Liverpool,
Merseyside,
L1 9DW ℗
☎ 0151 709 4005   📠 0151 709 4005
📱 07831 445816
✉ turnersauctions@aol.com
Est. 1787
Open Mon–Fri 9.15am–4.45pm
Sales General household,
antique and commercial sales
Thurs 11am, viewing Wed
9am–4.45pm Thurs 9–11am
Frequency Weekly
Catalogues No

SOUTHPORT

⊞ Birkdale Antiques
Contact John Napp
⊠ 119a Upper Aughton Road,
Southport, Merseyside,
PR8 5NH ▣
☎ 01704 550117
⊚ 07973 303105
⊖ johnnapp@tiscali.co.uk
Est. 1990 *Stock size* Small
Stock French bedroom suites
1820–1900s, chandeliers
Open Tues–Wed
10.30am–5.30pm or by
appointment
Fairs Bingley Hall, Stafford
Services Valuations, restoration

⚲ Bonhams
⊠ Churchtown, Southport,
Merseyside,
PR9 7NE
☎ 01704 507875 ⊙ 01704 507877
⊖ southport@bonhams.com
⊚ www.bonhams.com
Open Mon–Fri 9am–1pm 2–5pm
Sales Regional office. Regular
sales held in London and in our
salerooms across the country.
Free auction valuations;
insurance and probate valuations

⊞ Broadhursts of
Southport Ltd (ABA, PBFA)
Contact Laurens Hardman
⊠ 5–7 Market Street, Southport,
Merseyside,
PR8 1HD ▣
☎ 01704 532064 ⊙ 01704 542009
⊖ litereria@aol.com
Est. 1926
Stock Wide range of scarce and
collectable books
Open Mon–Sat 9am–5.30pm
Fairs Chelsea, Olympia
Services Valuations, restoration,
book search

⊞ King Street Antiques
Contact Mr John Nolan
⊠ 27–29 King Street, Southport,
Merseyside, PR8 1LH ▣
☎ 01704 540084
⊚ 07714 322252
⊚ www.antiquestrade.org
Est. 1969 *Stock size* Large
Stock Antique furniture, interior
design service
Open Mon–Sat 10am–5pm or by
appointment
Services Packing, courier, interior
design

⊞ Molloy's Furnishers
Ltd
Contact Mr S Molloy
⊠ 6–8 St James Street,
Southport, Merseyside,
PR5 5AE ▣
☎ 01704 535204 ⊙ 01704 548101
⊖ sales@molloysfurnishers.co.uk
⊚ www.molloysfurnishers.co.uk
Est. 1976 *Stock size* Medium
Stock Antique shipping,
reproduction furniture
Open Mon–Sat 9am–5.30pm

⊞ Osiris
Contact Mr Paul Wood
⊠ The Royal Arcade,
131a Lord Street, Southport,
Merseyside,
PR8 1PU ▣
☎ 01704 500991/560418
⊚ 07802 818500
Est. 1979 *Stock size* Medium
Stock Art Nouveau and Art Deco
ceramics, Arts and Crafts, glass,
metalware, lighting
Open Mon–Sun 11am–5pm
Fairs Newark
Services Lectures, talks,
valuations

⊞ K A Parkinson Books
Contact K A or J Parkinson
⊠ 359–363 Lord Street,
Southport,
Merseyside,
PR8 1NH ▣
☎ 01704 547016 ⊙ 01704 386416
⊖ tony@parki.co.uk
⊚ www.parki.com
Est. 1972 *Stock size* Large
Stock Antiquarian and second-
hand books, sheet music, maps,
prints, prehistoric, ancient and
medieval antiquities, natural
history items, vinyl records,
autographs, manuscripts
Open Mon–Sat 10am–5pm
Sun 1–5pm
Services Book search

⊞ David M Regan
Contact Mr David Regan
⊠ 25 Hoghton Street,
Southport,
Merseyside,
PR9 0NS ▣
☎ 01704 531266
Est. 1983 *Stock size* Medium
Stock Coins, postcards, medals
Open Mon Wed Fri Sat
10am–5pm
Services Valuations

⌂ Royal Arcade
Contact Ray Parkinson
⊠ 127–131 Lord Street,
Southport, Merseyside,
PR8 1PU ▣
☎ 01704 542087
⊚ www.theroyalarcade.com
Est. 2002 *Stock size* Large
No. of dealers 70
Stock Antiques, collectables,
clocks, mirrors, chandeliers,
jewellery, militaria, Art Deco,
Art Nouveau
Open Mon–Sat 9.30am–5.30pm
Sun 11am–5pm
Services Valuations

⊞ Southport Antiques
Contact Steven Ross
⊠ 19 Market Street, Southport,
Merseyside,
PR8 1HH ▣
☎ 01704 533122
⊚ 07790 551117
⊖ rossblogs1@aol.com
Est. 1997 *Stock size* Large
Stock Victorian–Edwardian
furniture
Open Mon–Sat 9am–5pm
Sun noon–4pm
Fairs Newark, Swinderby
Services Restoration

⊞ The Spinning Wheel
Antiques (iBNS, TPCS)
Contact Roy or Pat Bell
⊠ Royal Arcade Antique Centre,
127–131 Lord Street,
Southport,
Merseyside,
PR8 1PU ▣
☎ 01704 542087
⊚ 07833 314932
⊖ roybell@value-on-line.co.uk
⊚ www.value-on-line.co.uk
Est. 1974 *Stock size* Medium
Stock General collectables, coins,
medals, porcelain, small fine
furniture, clocks, violins,
barometers, dolls, golf
memorabilia etc
Open Mon–Sat 9.30am–5.30pm
Sun 11am–5pm
Fairs Newark, Swinderby

⊞ Tony Sutcliffe Antiques
Contact Anne
⊠ 37a Linaker Street,
Southport,
Merseyside,
PR8 6RP ▣
☎ 01704 537068
⊚ 07860 949516

e tonysutcliffeantiques@
btinternet.com
Est. 1975 *Stock size* Large
Stock General antiques
Open Mon–Fri 8.30am–5pm
Sat Sun by appointment
Fairs Newark, Ardingly

WALLASEY

⊞ **Arbiter**
Contact Mr P Ferrett
⊠ 10 Atherton Street,
New Brighton,
Wallasey,
Merseyside,
CH45 2NY **P**
☎ 0151 639 1159

Est. 1983 *Stock size* Medium
Stock Small objects, 1850–1970
decorative arts, Asian, tribal,
base metal, treen, 20thC prints,
Oriental, Islamic
Open By appointment
Services Valuations

⊞ **Decade Antiques &
Interiors**
Contact A Duffy
⊠ Wallasey, Merseyside,
CH45 **P**
☎ 0151 639 6905
@ 07967 431184
Est. 1974 *Stock size* Medium
Stock Decorative antiques,
textiles, contemporary furniture,

fine art
Open By appointment
Fairs Manchester Textile Fairs

⊞ **Victoria Antiques**
Contact Mr J Collier
⊠ 155–157 Brighton Street,
Wallasey,
Merseyside,
CH44 8DU **P**
☎ 0151 639 0080
@ www.victoriaantiques.co.uk
Est. 1990 *Stock size* Large
Stock Victorian–Edwardian
furniture, longcase clocks
Open Mon–Sat 9.30am–5.30pm
closed Wed
Services Restoration

NORTH WEST

WALES

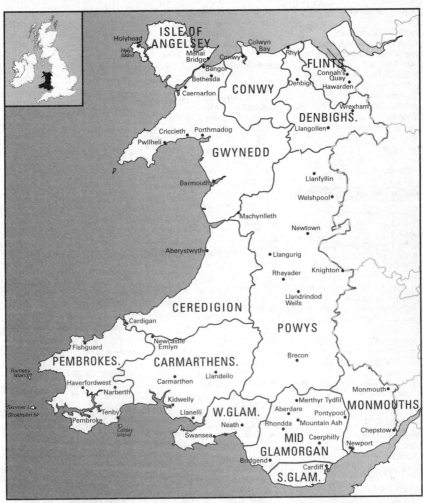

CARMARTHENSHIRE

CARMARTHEN

⊞ **Audrey Bull Antiques**
Contact Jane Bull
✉ 2a Jacksons Lane,
Carmarthen,
Carmarthenshire,
SA31 1QD
☎ 01267 222655
✉ jonathon-bull@lineone.net
Est. 1949 *Stock size* Medium
Stock General antiques,
Georgian–Edwardian furniture,
antique jewellery, silver, porcelain

Open Mon–Sat 9am–5pm
Services Valuations, restoration,
repairs

🔨 **Bonhams**
✉ Napier House,
Spilman Street,
Carmarthen,
Carmarthenshire,
SA31 1JY
☎ 01267 238231 ☎ 02920 727989
✉ carmarthen@bonhams.com
🌐 www.bonhams.com
Open By appointment only
Sales Regional office. Regular
sales held in London and in our

salerooms across the country.
Free auction valuations;
insurance and probate valuations

⊞ **Eynon Hughes**
Contact Eynon Hughes
✉ Mount Antiques Centre,
1 & 2 The Mount, Castle Hill,
Carmarthen, Carmarthenshire,
SA31 1JW 🅿
☎ 01994 427253
Est. 1984 *Stock size* Medium
Stock 18th–20thC furniture,
collectables
Open Mon–Sat 10am–5pm
Services Valuations, restoration

🏠 **The Mount Antiques Centre**
Contact Robert Lickley
✉ 1 & 2 The Mount, Castle Hill, Carmarthen, Carmarthenshire, SA31 1JW 🅿
☎ 01267 220005 ✆ 01267 231286
📱 07855 459572
Est. 1999 *Stock size* Large
No. of dealers 20
Stock Furniture, china, carpets, rugs, mining memorabilia
Open Mon–Sat 10am–5pm Sun 1–3pm
Services Upholstery and furniture restoration

CROSS HANDS

🏛 **C J C Antiques**
Contact John or Caroline Carpenter
✉ Llanllyan Foelgastell, Cross Hands, Carmarthenshire, SA14 7HA 🅿
☎ 01269 831094 ✆ 01269 831094
📧 sales@cjcantiques.co.uk
🌐 www.cjcantiques.co.uk
Est. 1979 *Stock size* Large
Stock Various Victorian items, musical instruments
Trade only Yes
Open By appointment
Services Shipping, valuations

🔨 **Welsh Country Auctions**
Contact Andrew or Bethan Williams
✉ 2 Carmarthen Road, Cross Hands, Llanelli, Carmarthenshire, SA14 6SP
☎ 01269 844428 ✆ 01269 844428
📧 enquires@welshcountry auctions.com
🌐 www.welshcountryauctions.com
Est. 1995
Sales General antiques sale Sat, viewing Fri prior to sale
Frequency Every 2–3 weeks
Catalogues Yes

KIDWELLY

🏛 **Country Antiques (Wales) (BADA, CINOA)**
Contact R Bebb
✉ Castle Mill, Kidwelly, Carmarthenshire, SA17 4UU 🅿
☎ 01554 890534 ✆ 01554 891705
📧 info@welshantiques.com
🌐 www.welshantiques.com

Est. 1969 *Stock size* Large
Stock Welsh oak furniture, pottery, folk art, metalware
Open Tues–Sat 10am–5pm or by appointment
Services Valuations

🏛 **Kidwelly Antiques (BADA, CINOA)**
Contact Mr R Bebb
✉ 31 Bridge Street, Kidwelly, Carmarthenshire, SA17 4UU 🅿
☎ 01554 890328 ✆ 01554 891705
📧 info@welshantiques.com
🌐 www.welshantiques.com
Est. 1969 *Stock size* Large
Stock Georgian–Victorian furniture and accessories
Open Tues–Sat 10am–5pm telephone call advisable

LLANDEILO

🏛 **James Ash Antiques**
Contact James Ash
✉ The Warehouse, Station Road, Llandeilo, Carmarthenshire, SA19 6NG 🅿
☎ 01558 823726/822130
✆ 01558 822130
📧 ashjm@aol.com
Est. 1976 *Stock size* Large
Stock Victorian and Welsh country furniture
Open Mon–Sat 10.30am–5pm or by appointment
Fairs Newark

🔨 **Jones & Llewelyn (NAEA)**
Contact Mrs Ann Rees or Mr Hefin Jones
✉ Llandeilo Auction Rooms, 21 New Road, Llandeilo, Carmarthenshire, SA19 6DE 🅿
☎ 01558 823430 ✆ 01558 822004
📧 enquiries@jonesllewelyn. freeserve.co.uk
🌐 www.jonesllewelyn.freeserve.co.uk
Est. 1948
Open Mon–Fri 9am–5.30pm
Sales General antiques and collectables once a quarter, antiques and effects 2 weekly
Catalogues Yes

🔨 **Bob Jones Prytherch & Co Ltd**
Contact Jonathon Morgan
✉ 50 Rhosmaen Street, Llandeilo, Carmarthenshire,

SA19 6HA 🅿
☎ 01558 822468 ✆ 01558 823712
📧 property@bjpandco.fsb.co.uk
🌐 www.bjpproperty.co.uk
Est. 1996
Open Mon–Fri 9am–5.30pm Sat 9am–1pm
Sales General antiques
Frequency Infrequent
Catalogues No

🏠 **The Works Antiques Centre**
Contact Steve Watts or Jon Storey
✉ Station Road, Llandeilo, Carmarthenshire, SA19 6NH 🅿
☎ 01558 823964
📧 theworks@storeyj.clara.co.uk
🌐 www.works-antiques.co.uk
Est. 2001 *Stock size* Large
No. of dealers 60
Stock General antiques and collectables
Open Tues–Sat 10am–6pm Sun 10am–5pm
Services Restoration

LLANDOVERY

🔨 **Clee Tompkinson & Francis**
Contact Nick Jones
✉ Ty Ocsiwn Tywi Auction House, Llandovery, Carmarthenshire, SA18 2LY 🅿
☎ 01269 591884 or 01550 720440
✆ 01269 595482
📧 ammanford@ctf-uk.com
Est. 1996
Open Mon–Fri 9am–5.30pm Sat 9am–1pm
Sales General antiques
Frequency Monthly
Catalogues No

🏛 **Phillips Antiques and French Polishing (BWCG)**
Contact Philip Wyvill-Bell
✉ 31 High Street, Llandovery, Carmarthenshire, SA20 0DD 🅿
☎ 01550 721355 ✆ 01550 721355
📧 wyvillbell@aol.com
🌐 www.phillips-antiques.com
Est. 1970 *Stock size* Large
Stock Period to Victorian furniture, clocks, porcelain
Open Mon–Sat 10am–5pm
Services Traditional French polishing, restoration

LLANELLI

⊞ Llanelli Antiques
Contact W Knapp
✉ 12 Great Western Crescent, Llanelli, Carmarthenshire, SA15 2RL 🅿
☎ 01554 759448
🌐 diane.knapp@btclick.com
Est. 1962 Stock size Medium
Stock General antiques, Victorian–Edwardian furniture
Open Mon–Sat 10am–1pm
Fairs Newark, Ardingly
Services Valuations, restoration

⊞ Radnedge Architectural Antiques
Contact Julian Cooper
✉ Dafen Inn Row, Llanelli, Carmarthenshire, SA14 8LX 🅿
☎ 01554 755790 🔹 01554 755790
🌐 rantiques@radnedge.fsworld.co.uk
🌐 www.radnedge-arch-antiques.co.uk
Est. 1980 Stock size Large
Stock Architectural antiques, fireplaces, timber, stone
Open Mon–Sat 9am–5pm

LLANWRDA

⊞ Mark Rowan Antiques
Contact Mark Rowan
✉ Garreg Fawr, Porthyrhyd, Llanwrda, Carmarthenshire, SA19 8NY 🅿
☎ 01558 650478 🔹 01558 650712
🌐 sales@markrowan.co.uk
🌐 www.markrowan.co.uk
Est. 1975 Stock size Medium
Stock Country furniture and antiques
Open By appointment only

LLANYBYDDER

⊞ Jen Jones Antiques
Contact Jen Jones
✉ Pontbrendu, Llanybydder, Carmarthenshire, SA40 9UJ 🅿
☎ 01570 480610 🔹 01570 480112
🌐 quilts@jen-jones.com
🌐 www.jen-jones.com
Est. 1971 Stock size Large
Stock Welsh quilts and blankets, small Welsh country antiques
Open Mon–Sat 10am–6pm
Sun by appointment
Fairs BABAADA (March)

NEWCASTLE EMLYN

⊞ The Old Saddler's Antiques
Contact Mr or Mrs Coomber
✉ Bridge Street, Newcastle Emlyn, Carmarthenshire, SA38 9DU 🅿
☎ 01239 711615 (shop hours only)
📱 07971 625113
🌐 dotcoomb@aol.com
Est. 1995 Stock size Large
Stock General antiques, country-style furniture, horse-orientated antiques
Open Mon–Sat 10am–5pm closed Wed
Fairs Carmarthen, Welsh National Antiques Fair

CEREDIGION

ABERYSTWYTH

⊞ The Furniture Cave
Contact P David
✉ 33 Cambrian Street, Aberystwyth, Ceredigion, SY23 1NZ 🅿
☎ 01970 611234 🔹 01970 611234
📱 07816 408871
🌐 thecave@btconnect.com
🌐 www.furniture-cave.co.uk
Est. 1979 Stock size Medium
Stock General antiques and pine
Open Mon–Fri 9am–5pm
Sat 10am–5pm
Fairs Birmingham Antiques Fair
Services Valuations, restoration, repairs

⋏ Lloyd Herbert & Jones
Contact J A Griffiths FRICS
✉ 10 Chalybeate Street, Aberystwyth, Ceredigion, SY23 1HS 🅿
☎ 01970 624328/612559
🔹 01970 617934
🌐 sales@lhj-property.co.uk
🌐 www.lhj-property.co.uk
Est. 1904
Open Mon–Sat 9am–5.30pm
Sales Quarterly general antiques Wed 11am, viewing 9–11am
Catalogues No

⊞ Ystwyth Books (BA)
Contact Mrs H M Hinde
✉ 7 Princess Street, Aberystwyth,

Ceredigion, SY23 1DX
☎ 01970 639479
Est. 1976 Stock size Small
Stock Rare and second-hand books, specializing in Welsh interest
Open Mon–Sat 9.30am–5.15pm

CARDIGAN

⋏ J J Morris
Contact Mr Mal Evans
✉ 5 High Street, Cardigan, Ceredigion, SA43 1HJ 🅿
☎ 01239 612343 🔹 01239 615237
🌐 cardigan@jjmestateagents.co.uk
🌐 www.jjmestateagents.co.uk
Est. 1969
Open Mon–Fri 9am–5.30pm
Sat 9am–noon
Sales General antiques
Frequency Periodic
Catalogues No

LAMPETER

⌂ The Tarrystone
Contact Jennipha Denning
✉ Bristol House, Station Terrace, North Road, Lampeter, Ceredigion, SA48 7HZ 🅿
☎ 01545 570864
📱 07977 938277
🌐 jennipha@thetarrystone.co.uk
Est. 2000 Stock size Medium
No. of dealers 7
Stock Country furniture, tools, lace, linen, period clothing, textiles, stoneware
Open Mon–Sat 9.30am–5pm

LLANDYSUL

⋏ Fred Davies & Co (FNAVA)
Contact Fred Davies
✉ The Square Synod Inn, Llandysul, Ceredigion, SA44 6JA 🅿
☎ 01545 580005 🔹 01545 580006
📱 07831 852511
🌐 admin@synodauctions.co.uk
🌐 www.synodauctions.co.uk
Est. 1992
Open Mon–Fri 9am–5pm
Sat 10am–2pm
Sales General antiques, modern furniture
Frequency Monthly
Catalogues No

CONWY

COLWYN BAY

⊞ Colwyn Books
Contact John Beagan
✉ 66 Abergele Road,
Colwyn Bay, Conwy,
LL29 7PP ℗
☎ 01492 530683
🅔 lindaandjohn@davies-beagan.freeserve.co.uk
Est. 1989 *Stock size* Medium
Stock Antiquarian and second-hand books
Open Mon–Sat 9.30am–5pm
Wed 9.30am–1pm
Services Book search

⊞ Cryers Antiques
Contact Mr Chris Cryer
✉ 14 Bayview Road,
Colwyn Bay, Conwy,
LL29 7PA ℗
☎ 01492 532457
📱 07776 425070
🅔 clairepthomas@zoom.co.uk
Est. 1974 *Stock size* Large
Stock General antiques and collectables
Open Mon–Sat 11am–4.30pm
Fairs Newark, Ardingly, Swinderby
Services Valuations and searches

⊞ North Wales Antiques
Contact Mr F Robinson
✉ 58 Abergele Road,
Colwyn Bay, Conwy,
LL29 7PP ℗
☎ 01492 530521 or 01352 720253 (after 6pm)
Est. 1959 *Stock size* Large
Stock Furniture
Open Mon–Sat 9am–5pm
Fairs Newark
Services House clearance, probate valuations, valuations, furniture shipping

⚲ Rogers Jones & Co
Contact Mr David Rogers Jones
✉ 33 Abergele Road,
Colwyn Bay, Conwy,
LL29 7RU ℗
☎ 01492 532176 🅕 01492 533308
🅔 rogersjones@btconnect.com
🌐 www.rogersjones.co.uk
Est. 1991
Open Mon–Thurs 9am–5pm
Fri 9am–noon
Sales Furniture, ceramics, silver, paintings, collectables last Tues

in month, general and collectables bi-monthly
Catalogues Yes

CONWY

⊞ Bookshop Conwy
Contact P Garnett
✉ 21 High Street,
Conwy,
LL32 8DE ℗
☎ 01492 592137
🌐 bookshopconwy@aol.com
Est. 1975 *Stock size* Medium
Stock Rare and second-hand books
Open Mon–Sun April–Sept closed Sundays in winter

⊞ Castle Antiques
Contact John Nickson
✉ 71 Station Road, Deganwy, Conwy,
LL31 9DF ℗
☎ 01492 583021
Est. 1980 *Stock size* Medium
Stock Georgian–Victorian furniture, oak, mahogany, jewellery, china, silver, paintings, ornaments
Open Mon–Sat 10am–5pm
Services Valuations, shipping

⊞ Paul Gibbs Antiques & Decorative Arts
Contact Paul Gibbs
✉ 25 Castle Street,
Conwy,
LL32 8AY ℗
☎ 01492 593429 🅕 01492 593429
🅔 paul@teapotworld.co.uk
Est. 1959 *Stock size* Medium
Stock Ceramics, glass, decorative arts, focus on teapot design with reference collection open to the public exhibiting 1200 rare and early teapots
Open Mon–Sat 10am–5pm
Fairs Newark
Services Valuations, restoration, repairs

DEGANWY

⊞ Collinge Antiques
Contact Nicky Collinge
✉ 71 Station road, Deganwy, Conwy,
LL31 9DF ℗
☎ 01492 583021 🅕 01492 580022
🅔 sales@collinge-antiques.co.uk
🌐 ww.collinge-antiques.co.uk
Est. 1980 *Stock size* Large

Stock General antiques, Georgian–Edwardian furniture
Open Mon–Sat 9am–5.30pm
Sun 10.30am–4.30pm
Services Restoration, valuations, shipping, upholstery

LLANDUDNO

⊞ 20th Century China & Pottery
Contact Julia Jackson
✉ 18 Mostyn Avenue,
Craig-y-Don,
Llandudno, Conwy,
LL30 1BJ ℗
☎ 01492 650611
🅔 juliajackson@artlovers.co.uk
Est. 2004 *Stock size* Small
Stock China, pottery, porcelain, ornamental ware 1900–1999
Open By appointment
Services Shipping

⊞ Drew Pritchard Ltd (SALVO, BSMGP)
Contact Drew Pritchard or Clive Holland
✉ St George's Church,
Church Walks,
Llandudno, Conwy,
LL30 2HL ℗
☎ 01492 874004 🅕 01492 874003
🅔 enquiries@drewpritchard.co.uk
🌐 www.drewpritchard.co.uk
Est. 1987 *Stock size* Large
Stock Antique stained glass, architectural antiques
Open Mon–Fri 9am–5pm
Sat 10am–4pm
Fairs Newark, SALVO
Services Restoration, commissions

LLANDUDNO JUNCTION

⊞ Collinge Antiques
Contact Nicky Collinge
✉ Old Fyffes Warehouse,
Conwy Road,
Llandudno Junction,
Conwy,
LL31 9LU ℗
☎ 01492 580022 🅕 01492 580022
🅔 sales@collinge-antiques.co.uk
🌐 ww.collinge-antiques.co.uk
Est. 1980 *Stock size* Large
Stock General antiques, Georgian–Edwardian furniture
Open Mon–Sat 9am–5.30pm
Sun 10.30am–4.30pm
Services Restoration, valuations, shipping, upholstery

LLANRWST

⊞ Carrington House Antiques
Contact Richard Newstead
⊠ Ancaster Square, Llanrwst, Conwy,
LL26 0LD 🅿
☎ 01492 642500 📠 01492 642500
🅔 richard@carringtonhouse.co.uk
🅦 www.carringtonhouse.co.uk
Est. 1975 Stock size Medium
Stock Antiques, pine, mahogany and oak furniture
Open Wed–Sun 10.30am–5pm
Services Valuations

⊞ Prospect Books
Contact Mike Dingle
⊠ 10 Trem Arfon, Llanrwst, Conwy,
LL26 0BT 🅿
☎ 01492 640111 📠 01492 640111
🅔 prospectbooks@aol.com
🅦 www.gunbooks.co.uk
Est. 1977 Stock size Small
Stock Rare and second-hand books on weapons
Open By appointment
Fairs Arms Fairs
Services Catalogues

⊞ Snowdonia Antiques
Contact Jeffery Collins
⊠ Bank Building, Station Road, Llanrwst, Conwy,
LL26 0EP 🅿
☎ 01492 640789 📠 01492 640789
📱 07802 503552
Est. 1965 Stock size Medium
Stock Antiques, Welsh dressers, longcase clocks
Open Mon–Sat 9am–5pm
Sun by appointment
Services Restoration

RHOS-ON-SEA

⊞ Bookshop Conwy
Contact P Garnett
⊠ Unit 2 Hadden Court, Penrhyn Avenue, Rhos-on-Sea, Conwy,
LL28 4NH 🅿
☎ 01492 548433
🅔 bookshopconwy@aol.com
Est. 2000 Stock size Medium
Stock Rare and second-hand books
Open Mon–Sun April–September closed Sundays in winter

⊞ Rhos Point Books
Contact Gwyn Morris
⊠ 85 The Promenade, Rhos-on-Sea, Conwy,
LL28 4PR 🅿
☎ 01492 545236 📠 01492 540862
🅔 rhos.point@btinternet.com
🅦 www.rhos.point.btinternet.com
Est. 1984 Stock size Medium
Stock 20,000 antiquarian and second-hand titles, North Wales topography a speciality
Open Mon–Sun 10am–5.30pm
July Aug 10am–9pm
Fairs Ludlow
Services Book search

DENBIGHSHIRE

CHIRK

⊞ Seventh Heaven
⊠ Chirk Mill, Chirk, Wrexham, Denbighshire,
LL14 5BU 🅿
☎ 01691 777622 📠 01691 777313
🅔 requests@seventh-heaven.co.uk
🅦 www.seventh-heaven.co.uk
Est. 1971 Stock size Large
Stock Antique beds, mattresses, bases, bed linen
Open Mon–Sat 9am–5pm
Sun 10am–4pm

FRONCYSYLLTE

⊞ Romantiques Antique Centre
Contact Mr Knight
⊠ The Methodist Chapel, Holyhead Road, Froncysyllte, Llangollen, Denbighshire,
LL20 7RA 🅿
☎ 019691 774567
📱 07778 279614 (day)
🅔 satkin1057@aol.com
🅦 www.romantiques.co.uk
Est. 1993 Stock size Large
Stock Antiques, collectables
Open Mon–Fri 9am–5pm
Sat Sun 11am–4pm
Services Upholstery, restoration of clocks, furniture, barometers

LLANGOLLEN

⚒ Aquaduct Auctions
Contact Mr Knight
⊠ Bryn Seion Chapel, Station Road, Trevor, Llangollen, Denbighshire,
LL20 7TP 🅿
☎ 01691 774567
📱 07778 279614
🅔 satkin1057@aol.com
🅦 www.romantiques.co.uk
Est. 2004
Open Mon–Fri 9am–5pm
Sales Monthly sales of antiques and collectables
Catalogues Yes

⊞ J & R Langford
Contact Mr P C Silverston
⊠ 10 Bridge Street, Llangollen, Denbighshire,
LL20 8PF 🅿
☎ 01978 860182
Est. 1952 Stock size Medium
Stock 18th–19thC Welsh dressers, 18th–early 20thC furniture, china, pictures
Open Tues Fri Sat 9.30am–5pm or by appointment
Services Valuations, probate, insurance

⊞ Passers Buy
Contact Marie Evans
⊠ Oak Street/Chapel Street, Llangollen, Denbighshire,
LL20 8NN 🅿
☎ 01978 860861/757385
Est. 1978 Stock size Medium
Stock Range of furniture, china, brass, ceramics
Open Mon–Sat 1pm–5pm or by appointment closed Thurs
Fairs Anglesey (Gwyn Davis) Fair
Services Doll restoration, doll museum

MARCHWEIL

🏛 Bryn-y-Grog Emporium
Contact Tony David
⊠ Bryn-y-Grog Hall, Marchweil, Wrexham, Denbighshire,
LL13 0SR 🅿
☎ 01978 355555
Est. 2002 Stock size Medium
No. of dealers 30
Stock Antiques, collectables
Open Mon–Sun 10am–5pm

RHUDDLAN

⊞ Downsby Antiques & Collectables
Contact Philip Garratt
⊠ 6 High Street, Rhuddlan, Denbighshire,
LL18 2UB 🅿
☎ 01745 590666
📱 07879 845478
🅔 downsbyantiques@tiscali.co.uk

Est. 2002 *Stock size* Small
Stock General antiques
Open Tues–Sat 10.30am–5.30pm
Fairs Newark, Swinderby
Services Picture framing

RHYL

⊞ **Aquarius**
Contact Mrs Gaynor Williams
⊠ **2 Market Street Street, Rhyl,
Denbighshire,
LL18 1RL** ☒
☎ 01745 332436
Est. 1980 *Stock size* Medium
Stock Period and vintage
clothing, accessories, costume
jewellery, postcards
Open Mon–Sat 10.30am–5pm
winter closed Tues am

RUTHIN

⊞ **Grandpa's Collectables**
Contact Neil Roberts
⊠ **40 Well Street, Ruthin,
Denbighshire,
LL15 1AW** ☒
☎ 01824 705601 ☎ 01824 705601
Est. 1998 *Stock size* Large
Stock Antiques, collectables,
some French furniture
Open Tues–Sat 10am–5pm
Services Delivery

WREXHAM

⋔ **Wingetts Auction
Gallery (NAVA, RICS)**
Contact Richard Hughes
⊠ **29 Holt Street, Wrexham,
Denbighshire,
LL13 8DH** ☒
☎ 01978 353553 ☎ 01978 353264
✉ auctions@wingetts.co.uk
⊕ www.wingetts.co.uk
Est. 1945
Open Mon–Fri 9am–5pm
or by appointment
Sales Fine art, antique and
specialist sales every six weeks.
Victorian–Edwardian furniture
and effects, weekly
Catalogues Yes

DYFED

ABERPORTH

⊞ **Joyce Williams**
Contact Joyce Williams
⊠ **Hurstlands House, Aberporth,
Cardigan, Dyfed,**

SA43 2EN ☒
☎ 01239 810330
⌖ 07974 387004
✉ joyceantiques@btinternet.com
Est. 1972 *Stock size* Small
Stock Small antiques
Open Mon–Sat 9am–5pm or by
appointment

FLINTSHIRE

CONNAH'S QUAY

⋔ **Whitehead & Sons**
Contact Mr T Whitehead
⊠ **264 High Street,
Connah's Quay, Deeside,
Flintshire,
CH5 4DJ** ☒
☎ 01244 818414
⌖ 07771 515395
Est. 1995
Open Mon–Sat 9.30am–5pm
Sales General sales including
antique china, furniture,
household goods, pawnbrokers'
jewellery and regular bailiff's
sales, Tues 6.30pm summer,
Tues 1.30pm winter
Frequency Every Tuesday

HAWARDEN

Capricorn Antiques
Contact Mr K Roberts
⊠ **Ashfield Farm,
Gladstone Way, Hawarden,
Deeside, Flintshire,
CH5 3HE** ☒
☎ 01244 535344
Est. 1987 *Stock size* Large
Stock Early pine and Edwardian
furniture, 1920s stripped oak
Open Mon–Sat 9am–5pm
Sun 11am–4pm
Services Restoration, wood
stripping

⊞ **On The Air Ltd (British
Vintage Wireless Society)**
Contact Steve Harris
⊠ **The Vintage Technology
Centre, The Highway,
Hawarden, Deeside,
Flintshire,
CH5 3DN** ☒
☎ 01244 530300 ☎ 01244 530300
⌖ 07778 767734
✉ info@vintageradio.co.uk
⊕ www.vintageradio.co.uk
Est. 1990 *Stock size* Large
Stock Vintage radios,
gramophones

Open Variable
Fairs NVCF (NEC)
Services Valuations, restoration,
shipping

⊞ **Village Pine Antiques**
Contact Ray Stewart
⊠ **32 Glynne Way,
Hawarden,
Flintshire,
CH5 3NL** ☒
☎ 01244 532211
⌖ 07889 548952
Est. 1980 *Stock size* Medium
Stock Antique pine, smalls
Open Tues–Sat 11am–5pm
Services Valuations, restoration

MOLD

⋔ **J Bradburne-Price & Co**
Contact Mr Roger Griffiths
⊠ **14–16 Chester Street, Mold,
Flintshire,
CH7 1EE** ☒
☎ 01352 753873 ☎ 01352 700071
Est. 1902
Open Mon–Fri 9am–5pm
Sat 9am–noon
Sales Periodic sales of antiques
and modern furniture in Mold
Market
Frequency Infrequent
Catalogues No

NORTHOP

⊞ **Parkview Antiques**
Contact Nic Eastwood
⊠ **High Street, Northop,
Flintshire,
CH7 6BQ** ☒
☎ 01352 840627
Est. 1984 *Stock size* Medium
Stock Pine, oak country furniture
Open Mon–Sat 10am–5pm
Services Restoration, upholstery

SHOTTON

⊞ **Old Bears 4 U**
Contact Paul Slater or Debbie
Horley
⊠ **45 Chester Close, Shotton,
Deeside, Flintshire,
CH5 1AX** ☒
☎ 01244 830066 ☎ 01244 830066
✉ info@oldbears4u.co.uk
⊕ www.oldbears4u.co.uk
Est. 2000 *Stock size* Large
Stock Antique and collectable
bears, animals and accessories
Open By appointment

GWYNEDD

BANGOR

⊞ David Windsor Gallery (IPC, FATG)
Contact Mrs E Kendrick
✉ 173 High Street, Bangor, Gwynedd, LL57 1NU 🅿
☎ 01248 364639 📠 01248 364639
📧 davidwindsorgallery@aol.com
Est. 1970 *Stock size* Medium
Stock 1580–1850 old maps, prints, lithographs, oil paintings, watercolours
Open Mon–Sat 10am–5pm closed Wed
Services Valuations, restoration, framing

BARMOUTH

⌂ Chapel Antiques Centre
Contact Danny Jones or Brenda Evans
✉ High Street, Barmouth, Gwynedd, LL42 IDS 🅿
☎ 01341 281377 📠 01341 281377
📧 jonestheantique@supanet.com
🌐 www.chapelantiqueswales.co.uk
Est. 1993 *Stock size* Medium
No. of dealers 24
Stock General antiques, country furniture, collectables, decorative items
Open Mon–Sun 10.30am–5pm closed Wed out of season
Services Delivery within UK, shipping can be arranged

⊞ Fron House Antiques Decorative Items
Contact Mrs B Howard
✉ Fron House, Jubilee Road, Barmouth, Gwynedd, LL42 1EE 🅿
☎ 01341 280649 📠 01341 280649
📱 07881 471875
Est. 1969 *Stock size* Medium
Stock General antiques, collectables, militaria, nautical antiques
Open Mon–Sun 10am–5pm closed Wed Oct–April
Fairs Swinderby, Newark
Services Credit and debit cards accepted

⊞ Walter Lloyd Jones
Contact V West
✉ High Street, Barmouth, Gwynedd, LL42 1DW 🅿
☎ 01341 281527 📠 01341 280577
📧 staff@w-lloydjones.com
🌐 www.w-lloydjones.com
Est. 1905 *Stock size* Medium
Stock Furniture, china, Gaudy Welsh, cranberry-glass, books
Open Mon–Fri 10am–5pm
Sat 10am–4.30pm winter closed Tues Wed
Services Sales on commission

⚒ Walter Lloyd Jones Saleroom
Contact V West
✉ High Street, Barmouth, Gwynedd, LL42 1DW 🅿
☎ 01341 281527 📠 01341 280577
📧 staff@w-lloydjones.com
🌐 www.w-lloydjones.com
Est. 1905
Open Mon–Fri 10am–5.30pm
Sat 10am–4.30pm winter closed Tues Wed
Sales Irregular sales of antique furniture, smalls, job lots held 3 times a year. Sales on commission at all times

BEAUMARIS

⊞ M Jones A'i Fab Antiques
Contact Merfyn Jones
✉ 42a Castle Street, Beaumaris, Gwynedd, LL58 8BB 🅿
☎ 01248 810624
📱 07778 489496
Est. 1984 *Stock size* Medium
Stock Welsh country furniture, related decorative antiques
Open Mon–Sat 10am–5pm
Services Valuations, restoration

BETHESDA

⊞ A E Morris Books (WBA)
Contact A E Morris
✉ 40 High Street, Bethesda, Bangor, Gwynedd, LL57 3AN 🅿
☎ 01248 602533
Est. 1986 *Stock size* Medium
Stock Rare and second-hand books, antiquarian prints
Open Mon–Sat 10am–5pm

CAERNARFON

⊞ Days Gone By
Contact Sue
✉ 6 Palace Street, Caernarfon, Gwynedd, LL55 1RR
☎ 01286 678010 📠 01286 678554
📧 sue@daysgonebyantiques.co.uk
🌐 www.daysgonebyantiques.co.uk
Est. 1994 *Stock size* Medium
Stock General antiques, period furniture, collectables, jewellery
Open Mon–Sat 9.30am–5.30pm

CRICCIETH

⊞ Capel Mawr Collectors' Centre
Contact Alun Turner
✉ 21 High Street, Criccieth, Gwynedd, LL52 OBS 🅿
☎ 01766 523600
📧 capelmawr@aol.com
Est. 1998 *Stock size* Large
Stock Rare and second-hand books, old postcards, cigarette cards, antiques
Trade only Yes
Open Mid-May–end Sept Mon–Sun winter Tues Thurs–Sat 10am–5pm
Services Mail order

⊞ Criccieth Gallery Antiques
Contact Anita Evans
✉ London House, High Street, Criccieth, Gwynedd, LL52 ORN 🅿
☎ 01766 522836
Est. 1971 *Stock size* Medium
Stock General antiques, antique watches
Open Mon–Sun 9am–5.30pm
Fairs Newark, Mona, Builth Wells
Services Restoration of pottery and porcelain, watch repairs

DOLGELLAU

⊞ Cader Idris Bookshop (WBA)
Contact Barbara or Neil Beeby
✉ 2 Maldwyn House, Finsbury Square, Dolgellau, Gwynedd, LL40 1RF
☎ 01341 421288
Est. 1987 *Stock size* Medium
Stock Antiquarian and second-hand books including Welsh topography
Open Mon–Sat 9.30am–5pm
Wed 9.30am–1pm
Services Book search, valuations

⊞ Cecil Williams Antiques
Contact Cecil Williams
✉ Mervinian House,

Meyrick Street, Dolgellau,
Gwynedd,
LL40 1LN ♿
☎ 01341 421404
Est. 2000 *Stock size* Large
Stock 17th–18thC furniture,
paintings
Open Mon–Sun 9am–5pm
Fairs Chester Race Course

PONTLYFNI

⊞ Sea View Antiques
Contact Mr D Ramsell
✉ Sea View, Pontlyfni,
Caernarfon,
Gwynedd,
LL54 5EF ♿
☎ 01286 660436
⌀ 07990 976562
✉ david@tamsell-
antiques.freeserve.co.uk
Est. 1997 *Stock size* Medium
Stock General antiques,
collectables
Open Mon–Sun noon–6pm

PORTHMADOG

⊞ Huw Williams Antiques
Contact Huw Williams
✉ The Antique Shop,
Madoc Street, Porthmadog,
Gwynedd,
LL49 9NL ♿
☎ 01766 514741 📠 01766 762673
⌀ 07785 747561
✉ huwantiques@aol.com
⌨ www.antiquegunswales.co.uk
Est. 1996 *Stock size* Medium
Stock 17th–19thC antique
weaponry, country furniture,
19th–early 20thC pottery
Open Mon–Sat 10am–5pm
closed Wed
Fairs London Arms Fairs,
Birmingham International Arms
Fair

PWLLDEFAID

⊞ T Evans Antiques
Contact T Evans
✉ Pwlldefaid, Aberdafon,
Pwllheli, Gwynedd,
LL53 8BT ♿
☎ 01758 760215
Est. 1984 *Stock size* Medium
Stock General antiques especially
Welsh country furniture
Open Mon–Sun 9am–5pm
Fairs Carmarthen, Cardiff
Services House clearance

PWLLHELI

⊞ Rodney Adams Antiques
Contact Rodney Adams
✉ Hall Place, 10 Penlan Street,
Pwllheli, Gwynedd,
LL53 5DH ♿
☎ 01758 613173 📠 01758 613173
⌀ 07785 313553
✉ adamsantiques@btconnect.com
⌨ www.rodneyadamsantiques.com
Est. 1960 *Stock size* Large
Stock General antiques, longcase
clocks, early oak furniture
Open Mon–Sat 9am–5pm
Services Valuations, repairs,
restoration

⊞ Penlan Pine
Contact Michael Adams
✉ 7 Penlan Street, Pwllheli,
Gwynedd,
LL53 7DH ♿
☎ 01758 613173 📠 01758 613173
⌀ 07785 313553
Est. 1998 *Stock size* Small
Stock Reproduction and antique
pine furniture
Open Mon–Sat 9am–5pm Thurs
9am–1pm or by appointment
Services Valuations, restoration
and repair

⊞ Period Pine
Contact Allan Stanley
✉ Units 1–3, Bron-y-Berth,
Penrhos, Pwllheli,
Gwynedd,
LL53 7HL ♿
☎ 01758 614343 📠 01758 614100
⌀ 07768 875875
✉ diane@periodpine.freeserve.co.uk
⌨ www.periodpine.com
Est. 1987 *Stock size* Large
Stock General antiques,
complete house furnishings and
interiors, brass beds, lamps
Open Mon–Fri 9am–5pm
Sat Sun 10am–4.30pm
Services Restoration of antiques

ISLE OF ANGLESEY

BEAUMARIS

⊞ The Museum of Childhood Memories
Contact Robert Brown
✉ 1 Castle Street, Beaumaris,
Isle of Anglesey,
LL58 8AP ♿
☎ 01248 712498

⌨ www.aboutbritain.com/museum
ofchildhoodmemories.htm
Est. 1973 *Stock size* Medium
Stock Childhood memorabilia,
tinplate, childhood money boxes,
pottery and glass, gift items
based on museum exhibits
Open Mon–Sat 10.30am–5pm
March–Oct Sun noon–5pm
Services Valuations

HOLYHEAD

⊞ Gwynfair Antiques
Contact Mrs A McCann
✉ 74 Market Street, Holyhead,
Isle of Anglesey,
LL65 1UW ♿
☎ 01407 763740
⌀ 07970 968484
✉ anwenholyhead@aol.com
Est. 1986 *Stock size* Medium
Stock Furniture, jewellery,
ornaments
Open 10.30am–4.30pm
closed Tues Thurs Sun
Services Valuations

LLANERCHYMEDD

⊞ Two Dragons Oriental Antiques
Contact Tony Andrew
✉ 8 High Streett,
Llanerchymedd, Isle of Anglesey,
LL71 8EA ♿
☎ 01248 470204/470100
📠 01248 470040
⌀ 07811 101290
Est. 1979 *Stock size* Large
Stock Antique Chinese country
furniture, signed limited edition
prints by Charles Tunnicliffe
Open By appointment only
Fairs Newark

MENAI BRIDGE

⊞ 41a Antiques
Contact Jack and Jean Harrison
✉ High Street, Menai Bridge,
Gwynedd, LL59 5EF ♿
☎ 01248 713300 📠 01248 852804
⌀ 07710 348892
✉ sales@42a.co.uk
⌨ www.42a.co.uk
Est. 2002 *Stock size* Medium
Stock Period and reproduction
furniture, Chinese, Indian
furniture, prints, paintings
Open Mon–Sat 10.30am–5pm
Wed 10am–1.30pm
Services Restoration

⊞ Better Days
Contact Mr or Mrs Rutter
✉ The Basement, 31 High Street,
Menai Bridge, Gwynedd,
LL59 5EF 🅿
☎ 01248 716657
✉ rosy@betterdaysantiques.co.uk
Est. 1988 Stock size Medium
Stock General antiques
Open Mon–Sat 10.30am–4.30pm
Wed 11am–1pm
Fairs Anglesey
Services House clearance

VALLEY

⊞ Ann Evans (LAPADA)
Contact Mrs Ann Evans
✉ Carna Shop, Station Road,
Valley, Isle of Anglesey,
LL65 3EB 🅿
☎ 01407 741733 ✆ 01407 740109
📠 07753 650376
🌐 www.annevansantiques.com
Est. 1989 Stock size Medium
Stock Welsh dressers,
Staffordshire figures, cranberry
glass, silver, country items,
jewellery
Open Thurs–Sat 10am–4.30pm
Fairs Portmeirion, Gwyn Davies
Services Valuations

MID GLAMORGAN

ABERDARE

⊞ Market Antiques
Contact Mr Toms Glanville
✉ 15 Duke Street, Aberdare,
Mid Glamorgan,
CF44 7ED 🅿
☎ 01685 870242 ✆ 01685 872453
✉ toms@toms.worldonline.co.uk
Est. 1979 Stock size Large
Stock Second-hand and antique
furniture, collectables, china,
glass, pictures etc
Open Mon–Sat 9.30am–5pm
Fairs Abergavenny
Services House clearances

BRIDGEND

⊞ Nolton Antiques & Fine Art
Contact Mr J Gittings
✉ 66 Nolton Street, Bridgend,
Mid Glamorgan,
CF31 3BP 🅿
☎ 01656 667774
✉ gip@welsh-antiques.com
🌐 www.welsh-antiques.com

Est. 1999 Stock size Large
Stock Antique furniture,
ceramics, paintings, clocks,
ephemera, books, stamps,
decorative reproductions
Open Mon–Sat 9.30–4pm
closed Wed
Services Valuations, house
clearance

CAERPHILLY

⊞ G J Gittins & Sons
Contact Mr John Gittins
✉ Caerphilly,
Mid Glamorgan,
CF83
☎ 029 2088 2935
📠 07941 213771
✉ gittinsantiques@supanet.com
Est. 1928 Stock size Medium
Stock General antiques
Open By appointment
Services House clearance

FLEUR-DE-LIS

⊞ Fleur-de-Lis Antiques
Contact Mr Barber
✉ 32 High Street, Fleur-de-Lis,
Blackwood, Gwent,
NP12 3UE 🅿
☎ 01443 835325
📠 07814 554672
Est. 1978 Stock size Large
Stock China, furniture, paintings
Open Mon–Sat 10am–1pm 2–5pm

KENFIG HILL

⊞ J & A Antiques
Contact Mrs J Lawson
✉ 1 Prince Road, Kenfig Hill,
Bridgend, Mid Glamorgan,
CF33 6ED 🅿
☎ 01656 746681
Est. 1991 Stock size Medium
Stock Victorian–Edwardian
china, glass, furniture
Open Mon–Fri 10am–4.30pm
closed Wed Sat 10am–1pm

MERTHYR TYDFIL

⊞ Halfway Trading
Contact Mr J McCarthy
✉ 38 Pontmorlais,
Merthyr Tydfil,
Mid Glamorgan,
CF47 8UN 🅿
☎ 01685 350967
Est. 1995 Stock size Medium
Stock General range of antiques

and new stock
Open Mon–Sat 9am–5pm
Services House clearances

PONTYPRIDD

➴ Pontypridd Auctions Ltd
Contact Mr K Hobbs ARICS
✉ 39a Cefn Lane, Glyncoch,
Pontypridd, Mid Glamorgan,
CF37 3BP 🅿
☎ 01443 403764 ✆ 01443 400734
✉ enquiries@pontyppriddauctions.com
🌐 www.pontypriddauctions.com
Est. 1919
Open Mon–Fri 9am–5pm
Sales Auction Wed 10am,
viewing Tues 2–7pm
Frequency Fortnightly
Catalogues Yes

PORTHCAWL

⊞ Harlequin Antiques
Contact John or Ann Ball
✉ Dock Street, Porthcawl,
Mid Glamorgan,
CF36 3BL 🅿
☎ 01656 785910
📠 07980 837844
Est. 1974 Stock size Medium
Stock General antiques,
antiquarian books, textiles
Open Mon–Sat 10am–4pm
Services Valuations

TONYPANDY

⊞ Jeff's Antiques
Contact Mrs J Howells
✉ 88 Dunraven Street,
Tonypandy, Mid Glamorgan,
CF40 1AP 🅿
☎ 01443 434963
Est. 1976 Stock size Large
Stock Furniture, glass, porcelain,
collectables
Open Mon–Sat 9.30am–5pm
closed Thurs

TREHARRIS

⊞ Treharris Antiques
Contact Mr C Barker or
Mrs Janet Barker
✉ 18 Perrott Street, Treharris,
Mid Glamorgan, CF46 5ER 🅿
☎ 01443 413081
Est. 1971 Stock size Large
Stock Militaria, china, mining
memorabilia, collectable records,
Welsh collectables
Open Always open, ring first

MONMOUTHSHIRE

ABERGAVENNY

⊞ Gingers Trade Antiques
Contact D Edmunds
⊠ Park Road, Abergavenny,
Monmouthshire,
NP7 5TR 🅿
☎ 01873 855073 ❶ 01873 855073
Ⓜ 07980 170982
Est. 1983 *Stock size* Large
Stock Furniture
Open Mon–Sat 10am–5pm
Sun 1–4pm

**⚒ J Straker Chadwick &
Sons**
Contact Mr L H Trumper
⊠ Market Street Chambers,
Market Street, Abergavenny,
Monmouthshire,
NP7 5SD 🅿
☎ 01873 852624 ❶ 01873 857311
🅔 enquiries@strakerchadwick.co.uk
Ⓦ www.strakerchadwick.co.uk
Est. 1872
Open Mon–Fri 9am–12.30pm
1.30pm–5pm Sat
9.30am–12.30pm
Sales General antiques
Frequency Monthly
Catalogues Yes

ABERSYCHAN

⊞ Zig Zags
Contact Simon Edmonds
⊠ Ffrwd Road, Abersychan,
Pontypool, Monmouthshire,
NP4 8PP 🅿
☎ 01495 774982
Est. 1985 *Stock size* Medium
Stock General antiques
Open Tues–Fri 10.30am–5.30pm
Sat 10am–4pm Sun noon–4pm

CHEPSTOW

⊞ Foxglove Antiques
Contact Lesley Brain
⊠ 20 St Mary Street, Chepstow,
Monmouthshire,
NP16 5EW 🅿
☎ 01291 622386
Ⓜ 07949 244611
🅔 foxglovesants@foxglovesants.
free-online.co.uk
Est. 1995 *Stock size* Medium
Stock Antiques and collectables
Open Mon–Sat 10am–5pm closed
Wed
Services Valuations, restoration

MONMOUTH

**⊞ Blestium Antique
Centre**
Contact Brent Watkins
⊠ 9 St Mary's Street, Monmouth,
Monmouthshire,
NP25 3DB
☎ 01600 713999 ❶ 01600 716438
🅔 brent@blestium.co.uk
Ⓦ www.blestium.co.uk
Est. 1999 *Stock size* Large
Stock Furniture, china,
collectables, clocks, silver and
architectural, Georgian oak to
the 1950s
Open Mon–Sat 10am–6pm

⊞ Frost Antiques & Pine
Contact Nick Frost
⊠ 8 Priory Street, Monmouth,
Monmouthshire,
NP25 3BR 🅿
☎ 01600 716687
🅔 nickfrost@frostantiques.com
Ⓦ www.frostantiques.com
Est. 1956 *Stock size* Medium
Stock Pine and country furniture,
Staffordshire figures
Open Mon–Sat 9am–5pm or by
appointment
Services Valuations, restoration

⊞ The House 1860–1925
Contact Nick Wheatley
⊠ 6–8 St James Street,
Monmouth, Monmouthshire,
NP25 3DL 🅿
☎ 01600 772721
🅔 nick@thehouse1860-1925.com
Ⓦ www.thehouse1860-1925.com
Est. 1999 *Stock size* Large
Stock Furniture of the Arts and
Crafts Movement
Open Tues–Sat 11am–5pm or by
appointment
Services Valuations, restoration,
interior design and furnishing

NEWPORT

**⊞ Casnewydd Antiques &
Restoration**
Contact B J Bartlett
⊠ 74b Walford Street, Newport,
Monmouthshire,
NP20 5PG 🅿
☎ 01633 855552
Ⓜ 07855 978773
Est. 2000 *Stock size* Medium
Stock Georgian–Edwardian
furniture, ceramics, paintings,
clocks

Open Mon–Sat 9.15am–5pm
Fairs Newark, Ardingly
Services Valuations, restoration,
shipping

**⊞ Welsh Salvage Co
(SALVO)**
Contact Mr S. Lewis
⊠ Isca Yard, Milman Street,
Newport, Monmouthshire,
NP20 2JL 🅿
☎ 01633 212945 ❶ 01633 213458
🅔 onfo@welshsalvage.co.uk
Ⓦ www.welshsalvage.co.uk
Est. 1984 *Stock size* Large
Stock Fireplaces, fire surrounds,
flagstones, stained glass, path
edging, garden statues,
bathroom fittings, floorboards,
flooring and decorative items
Open Mon–Fri 8.30am–5.30pm
Sat 8.30am–4pm Sun 11am–2pm
Services Restoration, repairs

TINTERN

⊞ Stella Books (PBFA)
Contact Mrs Chris Tomaszewski
⊠ Monmouth Road, Tintern,
Monmouthshire,
NP16 6SE 🅿
☎ 01291 689755 ❶ 01291 689998
🅔 enquiry@stellabooks.com
Ⓦ www.stellabooks.com
Est. 1990 *Stock size* Large
Stock Rare and out-of-print
books, specializing in children's
books and UK topography
Open Mon–Sun 9.30am–5.30pm

⊞ Tintern Antiques
Contact Dawn Floyd
⊠ The Old Bakehouse, Tintern,
Monmouthshire,
NP16 6SE 🅿
☎ 01291 689705 ❶ 01291 689705
🅔 tinternantiques@aol.com

WALES

WALES

PEMBROKESHIRE • PEMBROKE

Est. 1979 *Stock size* Large
Stock General antiques including
china, furniture, jewellery
Open Mon–Sun 10am–5pm or by
appointment

USK

⊞ Bower House Antiques
& Interiors
Contact Janet Cuclesey
✉ 2 Bridge Street, Usk,
Monmouthshire,
NP15 1BG ⓟ
☎ 01291 672810
⓪ 07798 693230
ⓦ www.bowerhouse-antiques.co.uk
Est. 2004 *Stock size* Medium
Stock General antiques, clocks,
furniture, silver, toys, china, glass
Open Mon–Sat 10.30am–5pm or
by appointment
Services House clearance

⊞ Brindley John Ayers
Catalogue of Vintage and
Collectable Fishing Tackle
Contact Mr B J Ayres or
Anne Ayres
✉ Rivermill House,
1 Woodside Court, Usk,
Monmouthshire,
NP15 1SY ⓟ
☎ 01291 672710 ❶ 01291 673464
ⓔ bjayers@vintagefishingtackle.com
ⓦ www.vintagefishingtackle.com
Est. 1988 *Stock size* Large
Stock Antique fishing tackle
Open By appointment
Fairs Newark, Canterbury
Services Catalogues, B & B (for
customers)

PEMBROKESHIRE

CRESSELLY

⚲ RWG Auctions
Contact Russell Weblin-Grimsley
✉ The Old Manse,
Lawrenny Road,
Cresselly,
Pembrokeshire,
SA68 0TB ⓟ
☎ 01646 651427 ❶ 01646 651427
⓪ 07836 774461
Est. 2003
Open Mon–Sat 9am–5pm
Sales General antiques and
collectables sale 2nd Sat of
month at Carew Airfield, Carew,
Nr Tenby, Pembrokeshire.
Catalogues Yes

FISHGUARD

⚲ J J Morris
Contact Mr D A Thomas
✉ 21 West Street, Fishguard,
Pembrokeshire,
SA65 9AL ⓟ
☎ 01348 873836 ❶ 01348 874166
ⓔ fishguard@jjmestateagents.co.uk
ⓦ www.jjmestateagents.co.uk
Est. 1949
Open Mon–Fri 9am–5.30pm
Sat 9am–4pm
Sales General antiques
Frequency About 6 a year
Catalogues No

HAVERFORDWEST

⊞ Dyfed Antiques
Contact Giles Chaplin
✉ The Wesleyan Chapel,
Perrotts Road, Haverfordwest,
Pembrokeshire,
SA61 2JD ⓟ
☎ 01437 760496 ❶ 01437 768285
Est. 1969 *Stock size* Large
Stock General antiques,
architectural salvage, bespoke
furniture
Open Mon–Fri 10am–5pm
Services Advisory and
refurbishment service

⊞ Humphries Antiques
Contact Gary Humphries
✉ 10b Bank Row,
Dew Street, Haverfordwest,
Pembrokeshire,
SA61 1NJ ⓟ
☎ 01437 779208
⓪ 07814 583998
ⓔ gary.humphries5@btinternet.com
Est. 1993 *Stock size* Large
Stock Mainly ceramics, with a
wide range of antiques and
collectables
Open Mon–Fri 10am–4.30pm
Sat 10am–1pm closed Thurs
or by appointment
Fairs Carmarthen, Anglesey
Services Valuations, house
clearance and collecting advice

⊞ Kent House Antiques
Contact Mr Graham Fanstone
✉ Kent House,
15 Market Street,
Haverfordwest, Pembrokeshire,
SA61 1NF ⓟ
☎ 01437 768175
Est. 1988 *Stock size* Medium
Stock General antiques

Open Tues–Sat 10am–4pm
closed Thurs
Services Restoration

NARBERTH

⊞ The Malthouse
Contact P Griffiths or J Wilmot
✉ Back Lane, High Street,
Narberth, Pembrokeshire,
SA67 7AR ⓟ
☎ 01834 860303
Est. 1998 *Stock size* Medium
Stock General antiques, Welsh
country furniture, collectables
Open Mon–Sat 10am–5.30pm
Services Pine stripping

NEWPORT

⌂ Carningli Centre
Contact Mrs Ann Gent
✉ East Street, Newport,
Pembrokeshire,
SA42 0SY ⓟ
☎ 01239 820724
ⓔ info@carningli.co.uk
ⓦ www.carningli.co.uk
Est. 1997 *Stock size* Medium
No. of dealers 10
Stock General antiques, second-
hand books, art gallery
Open Mon–Sat 10am–5.30pm
Services Furniture restoration
and polishing

PEMBROKE

⌂ Pembroke Antiques
Centre
Contact Michael Blake
✉ Wesley Chapel, Main Street,
Pembroke, Pembrokeshire,
SA71 4DE ⓟ
☎ 01646 687017
Est. 1979 *Stock size* Large
Stock General antiques,
Victorian–Edwardian furniture,
china, paintings, ephemera,
postcards
Open Mon–Sat 10am–5pm
Services Repairs, restoration and
valuations

⌂ Pembroke Market
Emporium
Contact Russell Weblin-Grimsley
or Peter Thorpe
✉ Main Street, Pembroke,
Pembrokeshire,
SA71 4DB ⓟ
☎ 01646 686894 ❶ 01646 651427
⓪ 07836 774461

WALES

389

Est. 2003 *Stock size* Medium
No. of dealers 23
Stock Antiques, collectables
Open Mon–Fri 10.30am–5.30pm
Sat 10.30am–5pm

PEMBROKE DOCK

⊞ **Treen Box Antiques**
Contact Mr M D Morris
✉ 61 Bush Street, Pembroke
Dock, Pembrokeshire,
SA72 6AN 🅿
☎ 01646 621800 ● 01646 621800
Ⓜ 07971 636148
● admin@treenbox.fsnet.co.uk
Est. 1990 *Stock size* Large
Stock General antiques, small
upholstered chairs
Open Mon–Sat 9am–5pm or by
appointment
Fairs Ardingly, Stoneleigh
Services Restoration and repair,
upholstery

SAUNDERSFOOT

⊞ **The Strand Antiques &
Collectable**
Contact Paul Lewis
✉ The Strand, Saundersfoot,
Pembrokeshire,
SA68 9EX 🅿
☎ 01834 814545
Est. 2001 *Stock size* Medium
Stock China, glass, jewellery
Open Mon–Sun 9am–6pm
Fairs Saundersfoot Antiques Fair

TEMPLETON

⊞ **Barn Court Antiques**
Contact David Evans
✉ Barn Court, Templeton,
Narberth, Pembrokeshire,
SA67 8SL 🅿
☎ 01834 861224
● info@barncourtantiques.com
Ⓦ www.barncourtantiques.com
Est. 1976 *Stock size* Medium
Stock 18th–19thC fine quality
furniture, china, glass
Open Mon–Sun 10am–5pm
winter closed Mon
Services Valuations, restoration

TENBY

⊞ **Arch House
Collectables**
Contact Jane Williams
✉ St George's Street, Tenby,
Pembrokeshire,

SA70 7JB
☎ 01834 843246
● info@archhousecollectables.co.uk
Ⓦ www.archhousecollectables.co.uk
Est. 1993 *Stock size* Large
Stock Collectables, specializing in
Pendelfin and Peter Fagan
Open Mon–Sat 9.30am–5.30pm

⊞ **Audrey Bull Antiques**
Contact Audrey Bull
✉ 15 Upper Frog Street, Tenby,
Pembrokeshire,
SA70 7JD
☎ 01834 843114
● jonathon-bull@lineone.net
Est. 1949 *Stock size* Medium
Stock General antiques,
Georgian–Edwardian furniture,
antique jewellery, silver, porcelain
Open Mon–Sat 9am–5pm
Sun in summer 11am–4pm
Services Valuations, restorations,
repairs

⊞ **Cofion Books &
Postcards (PTA)**
Contact A Smosarski
✉ Bridge Street, Tenby,
Pembrokeshire,
SA70 7BU 🅿
☎ 01834 845741 ● 01834 843864
● albie@cofin.com
Est. 1987 *Stock size* Large
Stock Second-hand books,
Edwardian postcards, varied
collectables, specializing in
Augustus and Gwen John
publications
Open Mon–Sun 10.30am–5.30pm
Fairs Cardiff Postcard Club
Annual Fair
Services Valuations, book search,
postal approval on postcards

🏠 **Tenby Antiques Centre**
Contact Mrs Thomas
✉ 10 The Green, Tenby,
Pembrokeshire, SA70 8EY 🅿
☎ 01834 849058
Est. 2003 *Stock size* Medium
No. of dealers 8
Stock Period oak, small antiques
Open Mon–Sat 10am–5pm
Sun by appointment

POWYS

BRECON

⊞ **Books, Maps & Prints**
Contact Andrew Wakley
✉ 7 The Struet, Brecon,

Powys,
LD3 7LL 🅿
☎ 01874 622714 ● 01874 622714
Est. 1973 *Stock size* Medium
Stock Books, maps and prints,
antique maps of Wales
Open Mon–Sat 9am–5pm
Wed 9am–1pm
Services Framing

🏠 **The Brecon Antiques
Centre**
Contact Lynton Phillips
✉ 22a High Street, Brecon,
Powys,
LD3 7LA 🅿
☎ 01874 623355
● pheulwen@aol.com
Ⓦ www.antiquedealerswales.com
Est. 1999 *Stock size* Large
No. of dealers 32
Stock Furniture, small antiques
Open Mon–Fri 10am–5pm
Sun 11am–4pm

🔨 **Montague Harris & Co**
Contact John Lewis
✉ 16 Ship Street, Brecon,
Powys,
LD3 9AD 🅿
☎ 01874 623200 ● 01874 623131
● jal@montague-harris.co.uk
Ⓦ www.montague-harris.co.uk
Est. 1900
Open Mon–Fri 9am–5pm
Sat 9am–1pm
Sales General antiques
Frequency Periodically
Catalogues Yes

🔨 **McCartneys**
Contact Chris Jones
✉ 40 High Street, Brecon,
Powys,
LD3 7Ap 🅿
☎ 01874 610990 ● 01874 610991
● brecon@mccartneys.co.uk
Ⓦ www.mccartneys.co.uk
Est. 1949
Open Mon–Fri 9am–5pm
Sat 9.30am–12.30pm
Sales General antiques, furniture
and effects
Frequency Periodically
Catalogues No

🔨 **Pritchard & Partners
(RICS, ISVA)**
Contact MJ Pritchard
✉ 2 The Struet, Brecon,
Powys,
LD3 7LH 🅿
☎ 01874 622261 ● 01874 623020

Est. 1959
Open Mon–Fri 9am–5pm
Sat 9am–noon
Sales Antiques and general effects
Frequency Occasional
Catalogues Yes

BUILTH WELLS

⊞ **Smithfield Antiques**
Contact Suzanne Price
✉ Smithfield Road,
Builth Wells, Powys,
LD2 3AN 🅿
☎ 01982 553022 ✆ 01982 553022
📧 john@smithfieldjoinery.fsnet.co.uk
🌐 www.smithfield-joinery.com
Est. 2000 *Stock size* Medium
Stock General antiques,
fireplaces, oak Welsh dressers
Open Mon–Sat 10am–5pm
closed Wed

CRICKHOWELL

⊞ **Gallop–Rivers
Architectural Antiques**
Contact Mr Gallop
✉ Tyrash, Brecon Road,
Crickhowell, Powys,
NP8 1SF 🅿
☎ 01873 811084 ✆ 01873 811084
📧 enquiries@gallopandrivers.co.uk
🌐 www.gallopandrivers.co.uk
Est. 1988 *Stock size* Large
Stock Antiques, ironmongery,
paving,interior flooring, garden
features, fireplaces, building
materials
Open Mon–Sat 9.30am–5pm

FOUR CROSSES

⊞ **Malthouse Antiques
(Four Crosses) Ltd**
Contact Neville Foulkes
✉ The Old Malthouse,
Pool Road, Four Crosses,
Llanymynech,
Powys,
SY22 6PS 🅿
☎ 01691 830015
📧 info@malthouseantiques.co.uk
🌐 www.malthouseantiques.co.uk
Est. 1983 *Stock size* Large
Stock Pine and country furniture,
architectural effects, doors, cast-
iron windows, baths
Open Mon–Sat 9am–6pm Sun
11am–6pm or by appointment
Services Valuations, restoration
of wooden furniture, baths,
fireplaces

KNIGHTON

🏛 **Offa's Dyke Antique
Centre**
Contact Mr I Watkins or
Mrs H Hood
✉ 4 High Street, Knighton,
Powys,
LD7 1AT 🅿
☎ 01547 528635
Est. 1987 *Stock size* Medium
No. of dealers 10
Stock General antiques, ceramics
Open Mon–Sat 10am–1pm
and 2–5pm
Services House clearance

⊞ **Islwyn Watkins
Antiques**
Contact Mr I Watkins
✉ 4 High Street, Knighton,
Powys,
LD7 1AT 🅿
☎ 01547 520145
Est. 1977 *Stock size* Large
Stock Ceramics and small country
antiques
Open Mon–Sat 10am–1pm 2–5pm
Services Valuations

LLANFYLLIN

⊞ **Galata Coins**
Contact Paul Withers
✉ Old White Lion, Market Street,
Llanfyllin, Powys,
SY22 5BX 🅿
☎ 01691 648765 ✆ 01691 648765
📧 Paul@galata.co.uk
🌐 www.galata.co.uk
Est. 1974 *Stock size* Small
Stock Coins and medals
Open By appointment
Services Valuations

LLANIDLOES

⊞ **The Great Oak Bookshop**
Contact Ross Bozwell or
Karin Reiter
✉ 35 Great Oak Street,
Llanidloes, Powys,
SY18 6BW 🅿
☎ 01686 412959 ✆ 01686 412959
📧 booksales@midwales.com
🌐 www.midwales.com/gob
Est. 1992 *Stock size* Large
Stock Antiquarian, new and
second-hand books
Open Mon–Fri 9.30am–5.30pm
Sat 9.30am–4.30pm
Services Book search, online
bookshop

⊞ **Now & Then**
Contact Mrs J Parker
✉ 2 Long Bridge Street,
Llanidloes, Powys,
ST18 6EE 🅿
☎ 01686 411186
📧 jacqueline@parker7598.
freeserve.co.uk
Est. 2003 *Stock size* Medium
Stock Antique Persian rugs,
carpets, cranberry glass,
collectable ceramics, fine
furniture, clocks
Open Mon–Sat 10am–4.30pm
Fairs Swinderby
Services Restoration, delivery

MACHYNLLETH

⊞ **Dyfi Valley Bookshop
(PBFA, WBA)**
Contact Mr N Beeby
✉ 6 Heol y Doll, Machynlleth,
Powys,
SY20 8BQ 🅿
☎ 01654 703849
📧 beeb@dvbookshop.fsnet.co.uk
🌐 www.abebooks.com/home/
dvbookshop
Est. 1988 *Stock size* Medium
Stock Rare and second-hand
books, specializing in archery,
the Old West, firearms
Open Mon–Sat 9.30am–5pm
Fairs Imperial, Bisley, Trafalgar
Meeting, Bisley
Services Book search, catalogues

⊞ **DYFI Valley Bookshop
(WBA)**
Contact Neil Beeby
✉ 6 Doll Street, Machynlleth,
Montgomeryshire,
SY20 8BQ 🅿
☎ 01654 703849
📧 beeb@dvbookshop.fsnet.co.uk
🌐 www.abebooks.com/home/
dvbookshop
Est. 1988 *Stock size* Medium
Stock Antiquarian and
collectable books
Open Mon–Sat 9.30am–5pm
Services Book search

MONTGOMERY

⊞ **Portcullis Furniture**
Contact Mr John Cox or
Mrs Sally Allen
✉ Snead Farm, Snead,
Montgomery, Powys,
SY15 6EB 🅿
☎ 01588 638077

Ⓜ 07966 188364
Est. 1995 *Stock size* Large
Stock Antique, reproduction and
new furniture, copper, brass,
silver, china, clocks
Open Mon–Sat 10am–5.30pm
Sun 10.30am–4.30pm
Fairs Newark
Services Shipping

NEWBRIDGE ON WYE

⊞ **Newbridge Antiques**
Contact P Allan
✉ **The Old Village Hall,
Newbridge on Wye, Llandrindod
Wells, Powys,
LD1 6LA** 🄿
☎ 01597 860455 ❺ 01597 860655
Est. 1986 *Stock size* Large
Stock General antiques,
furniture, architectural
Open Sat 10am–5pm or by
appointment
Services Valuations, stripping
and restoration

NEWTOWN

🖉 **Morris Marshall & Poole**
Contact Alun Davies
✉ **10 Broad Street, Newtown,
Powys,
SY16 2LZ** 🄿
☎ 01686 625900 ❺ 01686 623783
❺ mmp@newtown.ereal.net
Ⓦ www.morrismarshall.co.uk
Est. 1862
Open Mon–Fri 9am–5pm
Sat 9.30am–2pm
Sales General antiques
Frequency Quarterly
Catalogues Yes

TRECASTLE

🏛 **Trecastle Antique
Centre**
Contact Ro Williams
✉ **Trecastle, Brecon, Powys,
LD3 8UN** 🄿
☎ 01874 638007
Ⓜ 07811 032248
Est. 1996 *Stock size* Large
No. of dealers 10
Stock General antiques
Open Mon–Sun 10am–5pm

WELSHPOOL

⊞ **F E Anderson & Son
(LAPADA)**
Contact Ian Anderson

✉ **5 High Street, Welshpool,
Powys, SY21 7JF** 🄿
☎ 01938 553340 ❺ 01938 590545
Ⓜ 07889 896832
Est. 1842 *Stock size* Large
Stock General antiques,
17th–19thC furniture
Open Mon–Fri 9am–5pm
Sat 9am–2pm
Fairs Olympia, Harrogate,
Birmingham NEC, Kingston
Services Valuations

⊞ **Lamplite Antiques**
Contact Mrs Parks
✉ **2 Boot Street, Welshpool,
Powys, SY21 7SA** 🄿
☎ 01938 555036
Ⓜ 07817 204398
Est. 2000 *Stock size* Large
Stock Country oak furniture, oil
lamps, clocks, general collectables
Open Mon–Sat 8.30am–5pm

SOUTH GLAMORGAN

BARRY

⊞ **Hawkins Brothers
Antiques**
Contact Jeff or Terence Hawkins
✉ **21–23 Romilly Buildings,
Woodham Road, Barry Docks,
South Glamorgan,
CF63 4JE** 🄿
☎ 01446 746561 ❺ 01446 744271
❺ hawkinsbrosantiques@
compuserve.com
Est. 1975 *Stock size* Large
Stock Antique furniture
Open Mon–Sat 9am–5pm
Fairs Newark
Services Restoration

CARDIFF

⊞ **Anchor Antiques
(Wales) Ltd**
Contact B A Brownhill
✉ **The Pumping Station, Penarth
Road, Cardiff, South Glamorgan,
CF11 8TT** 🄿
☎ 029 2023 1308 ❺ 029 2023 2588
Ⓜ 07967 264325
Est. 1989 *Stock size* Large
Stock General antiques, clocks
and ceramics
Open Mon–Sun 9.30am–5.30pm

🖉 **Bonhams**
✉ **7–8 Park Place, Cardiff,
South Glamorgan,
CF10 3DP**

☎ 02920 727980 ❺ 02920 727989
❺ cardiff@bonhams.com
Ⓦ www.bonhams.com
Open Mon–Fri 9am–5.30pm
Sales Regional office. Regular
sales held in London and in our
salerooms across the country.
Free auction valuations;
insurance and probate valuations

⊞ **Capital Bookshop (PBFA)**
Contact Andrew Mitchell
✉ **27 Morgan Arcade, Cardiff,
South Glamorgan,
CF10 1AF**
☎ 029 2038 8423
Est. 1977 *Stock size* Medium
Stock Books, rare and second-
hand including Welsh interest
Open Mon–Sat 10am–5.30pm
Fairs Book fairs, Oxford, Bath

🏛 **Cardiff Antique Centre**
Contact Jane Rowls
✉ **10–12 Royal Arcade, Cardiff,
South Glamorgan,
CF10 1AE** 🄿
☎ 029 2039 8891
Est. 1975 *Stock size* Large
No. of dealers 14
Stock General antiques and
collectables including Welsh
china, jewellery, militaria
Open Mon–Sat 10am–5.30pm
Services Valuations

⊞ **Cardiff Reclamation**
Contact Jeff Evans
✉ **Site 7, Tremorfa Industrial
Estate, Martin Road, Tremorfa,
Cardiff, South Glamorgan,
CF24 5SD** 🄿
☎ 029 2045 8995
Est. 1987 *Stock size* Medium
Stock Architectural antiques,
specializing in fireplaces and
bathrooms
Open Mon–Fri 9am–5pm
Sat 9am–1pm Sun 10am–1pm
Services Bath refinishing, pine
stripping, sandblasting

⊞ **Charleston Antiques**
Contact Steve McDonald
✉ **129 Woodville Road, Cathays,
Cardiff, South Glamorgan,
CF24 4DZ** 🄿
☎ 029 2023 1123
Est. 1970 *Stock size* Large
Stock General antiques
Open Mon–Sat 8am–6pm
Services Valuations, house
clearances

⊞ **Cheapaschips.cc**
Contact Ian Roberts
✉ The Pumping Station,
Penarth Road, Cardiff,
South Glamorgan,
CF11 8TT ▣
☏ 0789 1080714
✉ info@cheapaschips.cc
🖥 www.cheapaschips.cc
Est. 1997 *Stock size* Large
Stock General antiques,
collectables, props for TV and
theatre
Open Mon–Sat 11am–5.30pm
Fairs Newark, Cardiff, Ardingly
Services Valuations

⊞ **Crwys Antiques**
Contact Mr Elfed Caradog
✉ 51 Crwys Road, Cardiff,
South Glamorgan,
CF24 4ND ▣
☏ 029 2022 5318
Est. 1985 *Stock size* Small
Stock General antiques
Open Mon–Sat noon–6pm

⊞ **Hera Antiques**
Contact Neil Richards
✉ 140 Whitchurch Road, Cardiff,
South Glamorgan,
CF14 3LZ ▣
☏ 029 2061 9472
Est. 1987 *Stock size* Large
Stock High-quality furniture,
porcelain and pictures
Open Mon–Sat 10am–5pm
closed Wed
Fairs The Orangery, Margam
Abbey, Port Talbot
Services Restoration, valuations

⌂ **Jacobs Antique Centre**
Contact Mr Cooling
✉ West Canal Wharf, Cardiff,
South Glamorgan,
CF10 5DB ▣
☏ 029 2039 0939 ☏ 029 2037 3587
Est. 1982 *Stock size* Large
No. of dealers 40
Stock General antiques
Open Thurs–Sat 9.30am–5pm
Services Café

⊞ **Keepence Antiques**
Contact Mr Clive Keepence
✉ 32–34 Clare Road, Cardiff,
South Glamorgan,
CF11 6RS ▣
☏ 029 2025 5348
Est. 1969 *Stock size* Medium
Stock Victorian, Edwardian
furniture, shipping goods,

pre 1930's dark oak furniture,
bric-a-brac
Open Mon–Fri 10am–4pm
Sat 10am–2pm

⊞ **Llanishen Antiques**
Contact Mrs J Boalch
✉ 26 Crwys Road, Cardiff,
South Glamorgan,
CF24 4NL ▣
☏ 029 2039 7244
Est. 1982 *Stock size* Medium
Stock General antiques including
19th–20thC furniture
Open Mon–Sat 10am–4pm
Services Restoration

⊞ **Now & Then**
Contact Mr A Williams
✉ 54 Crwys Road, Cardiff,
South Glamorgan,
CF24 4NN ▣
☏ 029 2038 3268 ☏ 029 2065 7629
✉ frongaled50@hotmail.com
Est. 1989 *Stock size* Medium
Stock General antiques
Open Mon–Sat 9am–5pm

⌂ **The Pumping Station**
Contact Mr M A Brownhill
✉ Penarth Road, Cardiff,
South Glamorgan,
CF11 8TT ▣
☏ 029 2022 1085 ☏ 029 2023 2588
☏ 07774 449443
Est. 1989 *Stock size* Large
No. of dealers 35
Stock General antiques, militaria,
model cars, railways
Open Mon–Sun 9.30am–5.30pm
Services Valuations

⊞ **Sambourne House
Antique Pine Ltd**
Contact Tim or Kim Cove
✉ 145 Colchester Avenue,
Cardiff, South Glamorgan,
CF23 9AN ▣
☏ 02920 487823
✉ tkcove34@globalnet.co.uk
🖥 www.sambourne-antiques.co.uk
Est. 1986 *Stock size* Large
Stock Antique and reproduction
pine furniture, smalls, decorative
items
Open Mon–Sun 9am–5pm
Services Hand-built kitchens

⊞ **Tails & The Unexpected
Ltd**
Contact Mark Williams
✉ 10 Victoria Road, Penarth,
South Glamorgan,

CF64 3EF ▣
☏ 029 2070 4499 ☏ 029 2070 4499
☏ 07974 344639
✉ tailsandtheunexpected@
hotmail.com
Est. 1980 *Stock size* Medium
Stock Antique clothing and
accessories
Open By appointment

⊞ **Ty-Llwyd Antiques**
Contact Mr Graham Rowsell
✉ Ty-Llwyd, Lisvane Road,
Lisvane, Cardiff,
South Glamorgan,
CF14 0SF ▣
☏ 029 2075 4109
☏ 07778 117624
✉ ghrowsell@supadsl2.com
Est. 1988 *Stock size* Large
Stock General antiques, clocks
Open By appointment
Services House clearance, clock
repair service

⊞ **Whitchurch Books Ltd
(Welsh Booksellers
Association)**
Contact Gale Canvin
✉ 67 Merthyr Road, Whitchurch,
Cardiff, South Glamorgan,
CF14 1DD ▣
☏ 029 2052 1956 ☏ 029 2062 3599
✉ whitchurchbooks@btconnect.com
🖥 www.ukbookworls.com/
members/gale
Est. 1994 *Stock size* Large
Stock Books, rare and second-
hand, specializing in archaeology
and history
Open Mon–Sat 10am–5.30pm
Fairs Cardiff
Services Mail order catalogues
on archaeology and history

COWBRIDGE

⊞ **Bookstores Wales**
Contact Rob Thomas
✉ 48a Eastgate, Cowbridge,
South Glamorgan,
CF71 7AB ▣
☏ 01446 772929
☏ 07887 605706
Est. 2001 *Stock size* Medium
Stock General antiquarian books,
history, literature, art
Open Mon–Sat 10am–5pm

⊞ **Eastgate Antiques**
Contact Liz Herbert
✉ 6 High Street, Cowbridge,
South Glamorgan,

CF71 7AG P
☎ 01446 775111 ❸ 01446 773505
Est. 1984 *Stock size* Medium
Stock Furniture, silver, jewellery
Open Tues–Sat 10am–1pm
2–5.30pm

🏠 **The Vale of Glamorgan Antique Centre**
Contact Mac Davis
✉ Vale of Glamorgan Antique Centre, 48 Eastgate, Cowbridge, South Glamorgan,
CF71 7AB P
☎ 01446 771190
Est. 1996 *Stock size* Medium
No. of dealers 30
Stock Furniture, china, porcelain, collectables, jewellery, autographs, longcase clocks, Welsh china (Nantgarw & Swansea)
Open Mon–Sat 10am–5pm

WEST GLAMORGAN

CLYDACH

⊞ **Celtic Antique Fireplaces**
Contact Mr R Walker
✉ Unit 13, John Player Industrial Estate, Clydach, Swansea, West Glamorgan,
SA6 5BQ P
☎ 01792 476047 ❸ 01792 476047
Ⓜ 07973 253655
❸ robin-walker@celticfireplaces.co.uk
Ⓦ www.celticfireplaces.co.uk
Est. 1992 *Stock size* Large
Stock Antique fireplaces
Open Wed Sat 10am–2pm or by appointment
Services Renovation

⊞ **Clydach Antiques**
Contact Mr R T Pulman
✉ 83 High Street, Clydach, Swansea, West Glamorgan,
SA6 5LJ P

☎ 01792 843209
Est. 1981 *Stock size* Small
Stock General antiques
Open Mon–Fri 10am–4pm
Services Clock repair

MUMBLES

⊞ **Elizabeth Antiques**
Contact Elizabeth Wickstead
✉ 504 Mumbles Road, Oystermouth, The Mumbles, Swansea, West Glamorgan,
SA3 4BU P
☎ 01792 361909 ❸ 01792 477512
Ⓜ 07831 554351
❸ info@elizabethantiques.com
Ⓦ www.elizabethantiques.com
Est. 1978 *Stock size* Medium
Stock Furniture, jewellery, gifts, Art Deco, movie memorabilia, Titanic, lighting, nautical, golf, retro
Open By appointment

NEATH

⊞ **Neath Market Curios**
Contact Mr R N Cook
✉ General Market, Green Street, Neath, West Glamorgan,
SA11 1DP P
☎ 01639 641775
Est. 1989 *Stock size* Medium
Stock General collectables, medals
Open Tues–Sat 10am–4pm
Services Medal Mounting

SKETTY

⊞ **Sketty Antiques & Gifts**
Contact Mrs Karen Debenedictis
✉ 87 Eversley Road, Sketty, Swansea, West Glamorgan,
SA2 9DE P
☎ 01792 201616
Ⓦ www.skettyantiques.com
Est. 1995 *Stock size* Medium

Stock General antiques, ceramics, furniture, jewellery
Open Tues–Fri noon–4pm
Sat noon–2pm

SWANSEA

⊞ **Booth Antiques**
Contact Jeff and Mary Booth
✉ 798 Brynymor Road, Swansea, West Glamorgan,
SA1 4JE P
☎ 01792 648152
Ⓜ 07799 145524
Est. 1985 *Stock size* Medium
Stock Jewellery, fireplaces
Open Mon–Sat 2–5pm

⊞ **City Antiques**
Contact Mr G Aston
✉ 14 Ticton Arcade, Swansea, West Glamorgan,
SA1 3BE P
☎ 01792 413300
Est. 1970 *Stock size* Large
Stock Victorian–Edwardian Art Deco and amber marcasite jewellery
Open Tues–Sat 10am–4pm
Services Valuations

YSTRADGYNLAIS

⊞ **Penybont Farm Antiques**
Contact Mr I Yankovic
✉ Penybont Farm, Penycae, Ystradgynlais, Swansea, West Glamorgan,
SA9 1SH P
☎ 01639 730620
Est. 1990 *Stock size* Large
Stock General antiques, pine, china
Open Sat Sun 10am–5pm or by appointment
Services Restoration, hand stripping

SCOTLAND

Stornoway
Lewis
Hebrides
Outer

ORKNEY
ISLANDS
Kirkwall
Burwick

Lochmaddy
WESTERN ISLES

Thurso

Wick

Sandness

SHETLAND
ISLANDS

Ullapool

Dornoch

Easter
Ross

Lossiemouth

Fraserburgh

Wester
Ross

Dingwall
Fortrose
Cromarty
Nairn
Elgin

MORAY

Peterhead

Portree

Skye

Inverness

Huntly

HIGHLAND

Glen Mór

Alford

Aberdeen

ABERDEENSHIRE

Newtonmore

Ballater

Stonehaven

Fort
William

Acharacle

Forest of Atholl

ANGUS

Montrose

PERTH &
KINROSS

Meigle

Mull
Oban

ARGYLL
& BUTE

Tyndrum

Dundee

Cairndow

Auchterarder

Perth

St. Andrews

Inveraray

STIRLING

Kinross

Newburgh

FIFE

Ardlussa

Jura

Garelochhead
Heligsburgh

Stirling

Dunfermline

Kirkcaldy

Isle of May

North Berwick

Tarbert

Bute

E.DUMBARTONS.
W. DUMBARTONS.
Greenock
Dumbarton
Glasgow

Falkirk
Cumbernauld

Bo'ness
W. LOTHIAN
Livingston

Edinburgh

Dunbar

E. LOTHIAN

Rothesay
*Gt.
Cumbrae*

RENFREWS.

N. LANARKS.

Dalkeith
MID LOTHIAN

Largs

Hamilton

Irvine
Kilmarnock

Strathaven

Lanark

Peebles

Innerleithen

Kelso

Arran

*Holy
Island*

Troon

S. LANARKSHIRE

Ayr
E. AYRS.
Cumnock

Douglas

SCOTTISH
BORDERS

Melrose
Jedburgh

N. AYRS.

Hawick

Campbeltown

*Sanda
Island*

*Ailsa
Craig*

SOUTH
AYRSHIRE
Girvan

Moffat

Beattock

Thornhill

Langholm

Canonbie

DUMFRIES
AND
GALLOWAY

Dumfries

Stranraer
Glenluce

Wigtown

Castle
Douglas
Kirkcudbright

Port
William

SCOTLAND
ABERDEENSHIRE • ABERDEEN

ABERDEENSHIRE

ABERDEEN

⊞ Bon-Accord Books (PBFA)
Contact Andrew Milne
✉ 69–75 Spital, Aberdeen, Aberdeenshire, AB24 3HX ♿
☎ 01224 643209
✉ bonaccordbooks@btinternet.com
⊕ www.bon-accordbooks.co.uk
Est. 1998 *Stock size* Medium
Stock General and antiquarian books, Scottish, children's and modern topics, first editions
Open Mon–Fri 10.30am–5.30pm Sat 11am–4.30pm closed Wed
Fairs Aberdeen, Glasgow, York, London
Services Postcards, prints, pictures

⊞ Candle Close Gallery
Contact Mrs B Brown
✉ 123 Gallowgate, Aberdeen, Aberdeenshire, AB25 1BU ♿
☎ 01224 624940 ✆ 01224 620548
Est. 1994 *Stock size* Medium
Stock Antique pine, collectors' items, curios
Open Mon–Fri 10am–5.30pm Thurs 10am–7pm Sat 9am–5pm Sun noon–4pm
Fairs Newark

⋗ John Milne Auctioneers (SAA)
Contact Robert Milne
✉ 9 North Silver Street, Aberdeen, Aberdeenshire, AB10 1RJ ♿
☎ 01224 639336 ✆ 01224 645857
✉ info@johnmilne-auctioneers.com
⊕ www.johnmilne-auctioneers.com
Est. 1867
Open Mon–Thur 8.30am–5pm Fri 8.30am–4pm
Sales Weekly general sales Wed 10am, viewing Tues 10am–7pm
Catalogues Yes

⊞ The Odd Lot Antiques
Contact Mr G Mudie
✉ The Georgian House, 18 Adelphi, Union street, Aberdeen, Aberdeenshire, AB11 5BL ♿
☎ 01224 592551 ✆ 01224 592551
⌖ 07771 926736
✉ info@theoddlot.com
⊕ www.theoddlot.com
Est. 1997 *Stock size* Medium
Stock General antiques, furniture, early technology, porcelain, furniture, jewellery, Scottish antiques, curios, books
Open Mon–Sat 10am–5.30pm
Services House clearance

⊞ The Old Aberdeen Bookshop
Contact Mr C Scott-Paul
✉ 140 Spital, Aberdeen, Aberdeenshire, AB24 3JU ♿
☎ 01224 658355
Est. 1996 *Stock size* Medium
Stock Rare and second-hand books
Open Mon–Fri 11am–5.30pm Sat 11am–5pm
Services Valuations

⊞ Rendezvous Gallery Ltd
Contact Mr C D Mead or Mr Andrew Allan
✉ 100 Forest Avenue, Aberdeen, Aberdeenshire, AB15 4TL ♿
☎ 01224 323247 ✆ 01224 323247
✉ info@rendezvousgallery.freeserve.uk
⊕ www.rendezvouz-gallery.co.uk
Est. 1975 *Stock size* Medium
Stock Art Nouveau, Art Deco, Scottish paintings
Open Mon–Sat 10am–6pm

⊞ Thistle Antiques
Contact Mr P Bursill
✉ 28 Esslemont Avenue, Aberdeen, Aberdeenshire, AB25 1SN ♿
☎ 01224 634692
⌖ 07759 429685
⊕ www.thistleantiques.co.uk
Est. 1969 *Stock size* Medium
Stock General antiques, Georgian–Victorian furniture, Art Nouveau lighting
Open Thurs–Fri 10am–4.30pm Sat 10am–1pm

⊞ J R Webb Antiques
Contact J R Webb
✉ 30 Carden Place, Aberdeen, Aberdeenshire, AB10 1UP ♿
☎ 01224 631222
⌖ 07720 771302
Est. 1908 *Stock size* Large
Stock General antiques, jewellery, arms and armour, especially Scottish artefacts and art
Open By appointment only

⊞ Winram's Bookshop
Contact Mrs Margaret Davidson
✉ 32–36 Rosemount Place, Aberdeen, Aberdeenshire, AB25 2XB ♿
☎ 01224 630673 ✆ 01224 630673
Est. 1975 *Stock size* Medium
Stock Rare and second-hand books, especially Scottish topics, postcards, local photographs
Open Mon–Sat 10am–5.30pm Wed 10am–1pm
Fairs Aberdeen
Services Valuations

⊞ Colin Wood Antiques Ltd
Contact Mr C Wood
✉ 25 Rose Street, Aberdeen, Aberdeenshire, AB10 1TX ♿
☎ 01224 643019/644786
✆ 01224 644786
Est. 1969 *Stock size* Medium
Stock General and antique Scottish maps, prints
Open Mon–Sat 10am–5pm

BALLATER

⊞ Deeside Books (PBFA)
Contact Mr B Wayte
✉ The Albert Memorial Hall, Station Square, Ballater, Aberdeenshire, AB35 5QB ♿
☎ 01339 754080 ✆ 01339 754080
✉ deesidebk@aol.com
Est. 1998 *Stock size* Large
Stock Out-of-print and antiquarian books, specializing in Scottish, military, topography and travel, field sports
Open March–Oct Mon–Sat 10am–5pm Sun noon–5pm Nov–March please telephone
Fairs PBFA Ballater, Aberdeen
Services Valuations, book search

⊞ Rowan Antiques & Collectables
Contact Nikki Henderson
✉ Tulchan House, 5–7 Victoria Road, Ballater, Aberdeenshire, AB35 5QQ ♿
☎ 013397 56035 ✆ 013397 56035
✉ nikki.rowan@lineone.net
Est. 1986 *Stock size* Medium
Stock Victorian–1930s furniture, fine and country, jewellery,

porcelain, prints
Open Mon–Sat 10am–5.30pm
Fairs Aberdeen Tree Tops
Services Valuations, shipping

⊞ Treasures of Ballater
Contact Nikki Henderson
⊠ 1 Victoria Road, Ballater,
Aberdeenshire,
AB35 5QQ ▣
☎ 013397 55122 ☻ 013397 56035
☻ nikki.rowan@lineone.net
Est. 1986 **Stock size** Medium
Stock Victorian–1930s furniture,
fine and country, jewellery,
porcelain, prints
Open Mon–Sat 10am–5.30pm
Fairs Aberdeen Tree Tops
Services Valuations, shipping

CLOLA

⌂ Clola Antiques Centre
Contact David Blackburn
⊠ Shannas School, Clola,
MIntlow, Peterhead,
Aberdeenshire,
AB42 5AE ▣
☎ 01771 624584 ☻ 07716 24751
☻ 07836 537188
☻ clolaantiques@aol.com
☻ www.clolaantiquescentre@aol.com
Est. 1989 **Stock size** Large
No. of dealers 6
Stock Furniture, jewellery, china,
glass
Open Mon–Sat 10am–5pm
Sun 11am–5pm
Services Restoration, upholstery

DUNECHT

⊞ Magic Lantern
Contact Mrs J White
⊠ Nether Corskie, Dunecht,
Aberdeenshire,
AB32 7EL ▣
☎ 01330 860678
Est. 1978 **Stock size** Medium
Stock General antiques
Open Telephone call advisable
Services Restoration to china,
furniture

INVERURIE

☄ Thainstone Specialist
Auctions
Contact Mark Barrack or
Zandra Black
⊠ Thainstone Centre, Inverurie,
Aberdeen, Aberdeenshire,
AB51 5XZ ▣

☎ 01467 623770 ☻ 01467 623771
☻ tsa@goanm.co.uk
☻ www.goanm.co.uk
Est. 1942
Open Mon–Fri 9am–5pm
Sales General antiques Tues 6pm
Frequency Monthly
Catalogues Yes

LAURENCEKIRK

☄ James S T Liddle
Contact Mr B Liddle
⊠ The Auction Room,
59 High Street, Laurencekirk,
Aberdeenshire,
AB30 1BH ▣
☎ 01561 377420 ☻ 01561 377420
☻ 07831 475095
☻ barry@liddleantiques.co.uk
☻ www.liddleauctions.co.uk
Est. 1989
Open Mon–Sat 8am–5pm
Sales General furniture sales
Wed evening, viewing Tues
evening and all day Wed.
Quarterly antique sales Sat,
viewing Fri
Frequency Monthly
Catalogues Yes

LONGHAVEN

⊞ Grannie Used To Have
One
Contact Jacqui Harvey
⊠ Sanderling, Longhaven,
Nr Peterhead, Aberdeenshire,
AB42 0NX ▣
☎ 01779 813223 ☻ 01779 813223
☻ 07850 912364
☻ jacqui@grannieusedto.co.uk
☻ www.grannieusedto.co.uk
Est. 1991 **Stock size** Large
Stock Pottery, including Scottish
pottery, porcelain, furniture,
glass, metalware
Open Thurs Fri 1–5pm Sat Sun
11am–5pm or by appointment
Fairs Scone Palace, Perthshire,
Hopetoun House, Edinburgh
Services Valuations

TARLAND

⊞ The Tower Workshops
Contact George Pirie
⊠ Aberdeen Road,
Tarland, Aboyne,
Aberdeenshire,
AB34 4TB ▣
☎ 01339 881154 ☻ 01339 881154
☻ towerworkshops@btinternet.com

☻ www.antiquesagency.co.uk
Est. 1989 **Stock size** Large
Stock Georgian, Victorian &
Edwardian furniture, soft
furnishings, small items,
decorative objects
Open Mon–Sun 11am–5pm
Services Valuations, restoration,
complete house commissions

ANGUS

DUNDEE

☄ Curr & Dewar
Contact S Dewar
⊠ Unit E, 6 North Isla Street,
Dundee, Angus,
DD3 7JQ ▣
☎ 01382 833974 ☻ 01382 835740
☻ enquiries@curranddewar.com
☻ www.curranddewar.com
Est. 1862
Open See sale times or by
appointment
Sales Antiques and quality
furnishings Tues 10am, viewing
Sun 10am–noon Mon 9am–5pm
Tues 9–10am
Frequency Fortnightly
Catalogues Yes

☄ Dundee Philatelic
Auctions (SPTA, PTS, PTA)
Contact Frank Tonelli
⊠ 15 King Street, Dundee,
Angus,
DD1 2JD ▣
☎ 01382 224946 ☻ 01382 224946
☻ dundeephilatelicauctions@
btconnect.com
Est. 1975
Open Mon–Fri 10am–1pm 2–5pm
closed Wed
Sales Stamps, cigarette cards,
coins, banknotes. Public auctions
held at Renfield Centre, 260 Bath
Street, Glasgow
Frequency 4 per annum
Catalogues Yes

☄ B L Fenton & Son
Contact Richard Fenton
⊠ 84 Victoria Road,
Dundee, Angus,
DD1 2NY ▣
☎ 01382 226227
Est. 1919
Open Mon–Fri 9am–4.45pm
Sales Antique furniture, general
auctioneers
Frequency Every Thurs
Catalogues No

⊞ **Neil Livingstone (LAPADA)**
Contact Neil Livingstone
✉ 3 Old Hawkhill, Dundee, Angus, DD1 5EU ℗
☎ 01382 907788 ℮ 01382 229707
℗ 07775 877715
℮ npl@hemscott.net
Est. 1971 *Stock size* Small
Stock Continental works of art and antiques
Open By appointment only

⊞ **Taymouth Architectural Antiques**
Contact Graham Ellis
✉ 49–51 Magdalen Yard Road, Dundee, Angus, DD1 4NF ℗
☎ 01382 666833 ℮ 01382 666833
Est. 1991 *Stock size* Medium
Stock Antique fireplaces, Victorian fixtures and fittings, garden ornaments, antique bathrooms, doors, leaded glass
Open Tues–Sat 9.30am–5.30pm
Fairs Newark, Ardingly
Services Restoration of fireplaces

FORFAR

⊞ **Gow Antiques and Restoration (BAFRA)**
Contact Jeremy Gow
✉ Pitscandly Farm, Forfar, Angus, DD8 3NZ ℗
☎ 01307 465342 ℮ 01307 468973
℗ 07711 416786
℮ jeremy@knowyourantiques.com
℮ www.knowyourantiques.com
Est. 1991 *Stock size* Medium
Stock Furniture
Open Mon–Fri 9am–5pm or by appointment
Fairs SECC Glasgow
Services Restoration, organizes 3-day antique courses

MONTROSE

⊞ **Harper–James**
Contact John Philp
✉ 27 Baltic Street, Montrose, Angus, DD10 8EX ℗
☎ 01674 671307 ℮ 01674 671307
℗ 07970 3055457
℮ antiques@telco4u.net
℮ www.harperjamesantiques.com
Est. 1989 *Stock size* Large
Stock 18th–19thC quality furniture, porcelain, silver

Open Mon–Fri 10am–5pm Sat 10am–4pm or by appointment
Fairs NEC, Aberdeen
Services Restoration, French polishing, modern polishing, upholstery

ARGYLL & BUTE

HELENSBURGH

⊞ **McLaren Books (ABA, PBFA, ILAB)**
Contact George Newlands
✉ 22 John Street, Helensburgh, Argyll & Bute, G84 8BA ℗
☎ 01436 676453 ℮ 01436 673747
℮ george@mclarenbooks.demon.co.uk
℮ www.mclarenbooks.co.uk
Est. 1976 *Stock size* Medium
Stock Rare and second-hand books, especially maritime topics
Open Fri Sat 10am–5pm phone first for other times
Fairs PBFA, ABA book fairs
Services Valuations, books purchased, book search for maritime titles

ROTHESAY

⊞ **Craig Alexander Victorian Shop**
Contact Rachel Hughes
✉ 35 East Princes Street, Rothesay, Isle of Bute, Argyll & Bute, PA20 9DN ℗
☎ 01700 505750
℮ www.isleofbute.com
Est. 1979 *Stock size* Medium
Stock General antiques, jewellery
Open Mon–Sat 9am–5.30pm
Services Jewellery repairs

DUMFRIES & GALLOWAY

CASTLE DOUGLAS

⊞ **Hazel's**
Contact Mrs H Hall
✉ St Andrew Street, Castle Douglas, Dumfries & Galloway, DG7 1EL ℗
☎ 01556 504573 ℮ 01556 504573
℮ www.castledouglas.net
Est. 1989 *Stock size* Large
Stock General antiques
Open Mon–Sat 9.30am–5pm
Services Valuations

DUMFRIES

⊞ **Cargenbank Antiques & Tearooms**
Contact Laurence Hird
✉ Cargen Bank, Dumfries, Dumfries & Galloway, DG2 8PZ ℗
☎ 01387 730303
Est. 1999 *Stock size* Medium
Stock 19thC furniture
Open Mon–Sun winter Thurs–Sun 10am–5pm closed Wed

⊞ **Quarrelwood Art & Antiques**
Contact Oscar van Nieuwenhuizen
✉ Castle Hill, Kirkmahoe, (Kirton), Dumfries, Dumfries & Galloway, DG1 1RD ℗
☎ 01387 710444 ℮ 01387 710088
℗ 07713 643433
℮ oscar@quarrelwoodantiques.com
℮ www.quarrelwoodantiques.com
Est. 1999 *Stock size* Medium
Stock Georgian–Victorian furniture, period jewellery, ceramics, glass, objets d'art
Open By appointment only
Services Valuations, restoration, shipping, advisory service, wedding lists

➢ **Thomson, Roddick & Medcalf**
Contact Sybelle Medcalf
✉ 60 Whitesands, Dumfries, Dumfries & Galloway, DG1 2RS ℗
☎ 01387 279879 ℮ 01387 266236
℮ trmdumfries@btconnect.com
Est. 1899
Open Mon–Fri 9am–5pm
Sales Antiques, fine art, general furnishings
Frequency Weekly
Catalogues Yes

LOCHFOOT

⊞ **Classic Pen Engineering (Writing Equipment Society)**
Contact Mr D Purser
✉ Auchenfranco Farm, Lochfoot, Dumfries, Dumfries & Galloway, DG2 8NZ ℗
☎ 01387 730208 ℮ 01387 730208
℗ 0770 3690843
℮ cpe@auchenfranco.freeserve.co.uk
℮ www.auchenfranco.freeserve.co.uk

Est. 1994
Stock Fountain pens, dip pens, pencils
Open By appointment
Fairs Glasgow Antiques for Everyone, Edinburgh
Services Valuations, restoration

LOCKERBIE

⊞ Cobwebs of Lockerbie Ltd
Contact Irene Beck
✉ 30 Townhead Street, Lockerbie, Dumfries & Galloway, DG11 2AE 🅿
☎ 01576 202554 📠 01576 203737
📧 sales@cobwebsoflockerbie.com
🌐 www.cobwebs-antiques.co.uk
Est. 1993 *Stock size* Large
Stock General antiques and collectables, porcelain, china, mostly Victorian–Edwardian
Open Mon–Sat 9am–5pm

STRANRAER

⚒ Lochyran Furniture Stores
Contact A Patterson
✉ 1 Cairnryan Road, Stranraer, Dumfries & Galloway, DG9 8QJ 🅿
☎ 01776 704442
📧 admin@lochyran.co.uk
🌐 www.lochyran.co.uk
Est. 1994
Sales Antiques, household, silver, etc. sales 1st Sun every month, viewing Fri and Sat
Catalogues Yes but not sent out

WHITHORN

⊞ Priory Antiques
Contact Mary Arnott
✉ 29 George Street, Whithorn, Dumfries & Galloway, DG8 8NS 🅿
☎ 01988 500517
Est. 1988 *Stock size* Medium
Stock General antiques
Open Usually Mon–Sun 10.30am–5pm telephone call advisable
Services Valuations

WIGTOWN

⊞ The Bookshop
Contact Shaun Bythel
✉ 17 North Main Street, Wigtown, Dumfries & Galloway,

DG8 9HL 🅿
☎ 01988 402499 📠 01988 402499
📧 the-bookshop@freeuk.com
🌐 www.the-bookshop.com
Est. 1987 *Stock size* Large
Stock Antiquarian to modern books, specializing in Scottish topics and history
Open Mon–Sat 9am–5pm
Services Publishing

⊞ G C Books Ltd (PBFA)
Contact Mrs Beverly Chadband
✉ Unit 10, Bladnoch Bridge Estate, Wigtown, Newton Stewart, Dumfries & Galloway, DG8 9AB 🅿
☎ 01988 402688 📠 01988 402688
📧 gcbooks@gcbooks.demon.co.uk
Est. 2005 *Stock size* Large
Stock Rare and second-hand books
Open Mon–Sat 10am–5pm
Services Framing

EAST AYRSHIRE

KILMARNOCK

⊞ D & D Programmes
Contact Mr D Stevenson
✉ 49 Titchfield Street, Kilmarnock, Ayrshire, KA1 1QS 🅿
☎ 01563 573316
📧 d-d-programmes@ukf.net
🌐 www.d-d-programmes.ukf.net
Est. 1998 *Stock size* Medium
Stock Football memorabilia
Open Tues–Sat 10am–5pm Fri 10am–8pm
Fairs Glasgow, Alloway
Services Mail-order catalogue available

⊞ Q S Antiques and Cabinetmakers
Contact John Cunningham
✉ Moorfield Industrial Estate, Kilmarnock, Ayrshire, KA2 0DP 🅿
☎ 01563 571071 📠 01563 571055
📧 qsascotland@aol.com
Est. 1982 *Stock size* Large
Stock Victorian–Edwardian furniture
Open Mon–Fri 9am–5.30pm Sat 9am–5pm
Services Pine stripping, paint and varnish removal, Victorian-style solid wood kitchens

EAST LOTHIAN

GULLANE

⊞ Gullane Antiques
Contact Elizabeth Lindsey
✉ 5 Rosebery Place, Gullane, East Lothian, EH31 2AN 🅿
☎ 01620 842994
Est. 1980 *Stock size* Large
Stock General antiques, mixed porcelain, glass, jewellery
Open Mon Tues Fri Sat 10.30am–1pm 2.30–5pm
Fairs Ingelston fair

HADDINGTON

⊞ Yester-Days
Contact Betty Logan
✉ 79 High Street, Haddington, East Lothian, EH41 3ET 🅿
☎ 01620 824543
Est. 1992 *Stock size* Small
Stock Antiques, collectables, small furniture
Open Tues Wed Fri Sat 11am–4.30pm

MUSSELBURGH

⊞ Early Technology
Contact Michael Bennett-Levy
✉ Monkton House, Old Craighall, Musselburgh, East Lothian, EH21 8SF 🅿
☎ 0131 665 5753 📠 0131 665 2839
📱 07831 106768
📧 levy@virgin.net
🌐 www.earlytech.com
Est. 1971 *Stock size* Large
Stock Early electrical and mechanical antiques, clocks, mechanical music
Open By appointment
Services Valuations, restoration, consultancy on collection building

NORTH BERWICK

⊞ Lindsey Antiques
Contact Stephen Lindsey
✉ 49a Kirk Ports, North Berwick, East Lothian, EH39 4HL 🅿
☎ 01620 894114
📱 07761 714791
Est. 1995 *Stock size* Medium

Stock Furniture, ceramics, glass, pictures, etc
Open Mon–Sat 10.30am–5pm closed Thurs

EDINBURGH

EDINBURGH

⊞ Adam Antiques & Restoration
Contact Charles Bergius
✉ 23c Dundas Street, Edinburgh, EH3 6QQ 📮
☎ 0131 556 7555 ● 0131 556 7555
Est. 1983 *Stock size* Medium
Stock 18th–19thC mahogany furniture and associated furnishings
Open Tues–Sat 10.30am–6pm Mon by appointment
Services Restoration

⊞ Armchair Books
Contact Mr D Govan
✉ 72–74 West Port, Edinburgh, EH1 2LE
☎ 0131 229 5927
● armchairbooks@hotmail.com
🌐 www.armchairbooks.co.uk
Stock size Medium
Stock Books, especially Victorian illustrated books
Open Mon–Sun 10am–6pm

➴ Bonhams
✉ 65 George Street, Edinburgh, EH2 2JL
☎ 0131 225 2266 ● 0131 220 2547
● edinburgh@bonhams.com
🌐 www.bonhams.com/edinburgh
Sales Regional Saleroom. Frequent sales including the specialist Scottish sale held once a year. Regular sales held in London and in our salerooms across the country. Free auction valuations; insurance and probate valuations
Catalogues Yes

⊞ Joseph Bonnar Jewellers
✉ 72 Thistle Street, Edinburgh, EH2 1EN 📮
☎ 0131 226 2811 ● 0131 225 9438
● enquiries@josephbonnar.com
Est. 1968 *Stock size* Large
Stock Antique and vintage jewellery
Open Mon–Sat 10.30am–5pm

Services Jewellery repairs and restoration, sourcing stones, restringing, tiara hire

⊞ The Bookworm
Contact Peter Ritchie
✉ 210 Dalkeith Road, Edinburgh, EH16 5DT 📮
☎ 0131 662 4357
Est. 1987 *Stock size* Medium
Stock Second-hand and antiquarian books
Open Mon–Sat 9.30am–5.30pm
Services Valuations, book search

⊞ Bow-Well Antiques
Contact Murdo McLeod
✉ 103 West Bow, Edinburgh, EH1 2JP 📮
☎ 0131 225 3335 ● 0131 226 1259
📱 07710 600431
● murdoch.mcleod@virgin.net
Est. 1979 *Stock size* Large
Stock General and Scottish antiquities
Open Mon–Sat 10am–5pm
Services Shipping

⊞ Broughton Books
Contact Peter Galinsky
✉ 2a Broughton Place, Edinburgh, EH1 3RX 📮
☎ 0131 557 8010
Est. 1971 *Stock size* Medium
Stock Rare and second-hand books
Open Tues–Fri noon–5pm Sat 10.30am–5.30pm

⊞ Cabaret Antiques
Contact Terry Cavers
✉ 37 Grassmarket, Edinburgh, EH1 2HS 📮
☎ 0131 225 8618
Est. 1990 *Stock size* Large
Stock Art Deco, Scottish paperweights, compacts, glass, costume jewellery, ceramics, books
Open Mon–Sun 10.30am–5.30pm
Fairs Mammoth Fairs

⊞ Calton Gallery (BADA)
Contact Andrew Whitfield
✉ 6a Regent Terrace, Edinburgh, EH7 5BM 📮
☎ 0131 556 1010 ● 0131 558 1150
📱 07887 793781
● mail@caltongallery.co.uk
🌐 www.caltongallery.co.uk
Est. 1980 *Stock size* Large
Stock Fine art, Scottish, marine

19th–early 20thC paintings and watercolours
Open By appointment
Services Valuations, restoration

⊞ The Carson Clark Gallery – Scotland's Map Heritage Centre (BCS, IMCOS, SOC)
Contact Paul Clark
✉ 181–183 Canongate, Edinburgh, EH8 8BN 📮
☎ 0131 556 4710 ● 0131 556 4710
● scotmap@aol.com
🌐 www.carson-clark-gallery.co.uk
Est. 1972 *Stock size* Large
Stock Maps and charts, engravings, lithographs
Open Mon–Sat 10.30am–6pm
Services Valuations, appraisals, restoration, repairs, framing, shipping

⊞ D L Cavanagh Antiques
Contact Simon Cavanagh
✉ 49 Cockburn Street, Edinburgh, EH1 1BS 📮
☎ 0131 226 3391
Est. 1972 *Stock size* Large
Stock Coins, medals, silver, jewellery, collectors' items
Open Mon–Sat 11am–5.30pm
Services Valuations

⊞ Bobby Clyde Antiques
Contact Bobby Clyde
✉ 5a Grange Road, Edinburgh, EH9 1UH 📮
☎ 0131 667 6718
Est. 1976 *Stock size* Medium
Stock General antiques, furniture
Open Mon Thurs–Sat 10.30am–5.30pm Sun 1–4pm
Services Stripping, delivery

⊞ Craiglea Clocks (BWCG)
Contact Mr Rafter
✉ 88 Corniston Road, Edinburgh, EH10 5QJ 📮
☎ 0131 452 8568
Est. 1977 *Stock size* Medium
Stock Clocks and barometers
Open Mon–Fri 10am–4pm Sat 10am–1pm
Services Restoration

⊞ Crawford Saleroom
Contact George Duff
✉ 250–252 Leith Walk, Edinburgh,

EH6 5EL ▣
☎ 0131 554 6407 ❻ 0131 337 1422
Est. 1876 *Stock size* Large
Stock Edwardian, Victorian
furniture
Open Mon–Sun 9am–6pm
Services Export

⊞ **Da Capo Antiques**
Contact Nick Carter
✉ 68 Henderson Row,
Edinburgh,
EH3 5BJ ▣
☎ 0131 557 1918
Ⓜ 07786 166570
✉ nickcarter@aol.com
Est. 1977 *Stock size* Medium
Stock 18th–early 20thC furniture,
brass bedsteads, light fittings
Open Tue–Sat noon–6pm
Sun noon–4pm
Services Valuations, restoration

⊞ **Alan Day Antiques
(LAPADA)**
Contact Mr A Day
✉ 25a Moray Place,
Edinburgh,
EH3 6DA ▣
☎ 0131 225 2590
Ⓜ 07860 533922
✉ alanmday@btinternet.com
Ⓦ www.alandayantiques.com
Est. 1973 *Stock size* Medium
Stock General antiques
Trade only Yes
Open By appointment

⊞ **Duncan & Reid**
Contact Mrs Reid
✉ 5 Tanfield, Canon Mills,
Edinburgh,
EH3 5DA ▣
☎ 0131 556 4591
✉ msduncan@ecosse.net
Est. 1979 *Stock size* Medium
Stock 18th–19thC English,
Chinese, Continental ceramics,
glass, decorative objects, second-
hand and antiquarian books
Open Tues–Sat 11am–5pm

⊞ **EASY Edinburgh &
Glasgow Architectural
Salvage Yard (SALVO)**
Contact E Barrass
✉ 31 West Bowling Green Street,
Edinburgh,
EH6 5NX ▣
☎ 0131 554 7077 ❻ 0131 554 3070
✉ enquiries@easy-arch-salv.co.uk
Ⓦ www.easy-arch-salv.co.uk
Est. 1987 *Stock size* Medium

Stock Architectural antiques,
fireplaces, doors, ranges, pews,
Open Mon–Fri 9am–5pm
Sat noon–5pm

⊞ **ECS (ANA)**
Contact Mr T D Brown
✉ 11 West Cross Causeway,
Edinburgh,
EH8 9JW ▣
☎ 0131 667 9095/668 2928
❻ 0131 668 2926
Est. 1977 *Stock size* Large
Stock Antique coins and medals,
stamps, ephemera, cigarette
cards,
Open Mon–Sat 9am–5pm
Fairs Edinburgh
Services Valuations, auctions of
coins and banknotes

⊞ **Donald Ellis Antiques**
Contact Donald Ellis
✉ 7 Bruntsfield Place,
Edinburgh,
EH10 4HN ▣
☎ 0131 229 4720
Est. 1969 *Stock size* Medium
Stock General antiques, clocks
Open Mon–Fri 10am–5pm closed
Wed pm
Fairs Buxton
Services Clock restoration

⊞ **Georgian Antiques
(LAPADA, CINOA)**
Contact John Dixon or
Karen Gray
✉ 10 Pattison Street, Leith,
Edinburgh,
EH6 7HF ▣
☎ 0131 553 7286 ❻ 0131 553 6299
✉ info@georgianantiques.net
Ⓦ www.georgianantiques.net
Est. 1987 *Stock size* Large
Stock Furniture
Open Mon–Fri 8.30am–5.30pm
Sat 10am–2pm
Services Valuations, restoration,
shipping

⊞ **Goodwin's Antiques Ltd**
Contact Mr B Goodwin
✉ 15–16 Queensferry Street,
Edinburgh,
EH2 4QW
☎ 0131 225 4717 ❻ 0131 220 1412
✉ bengoodwin@compuserve.com
Est. 1959 *Stock size* Large
Stock General antiques
Open Mon–Fri 9am–5.30pm
Sat 9am–5pm
Services Valuations, repairs

⊞ **Harlequin Antiques**
Contact Charles Harkness
✉ 30 Bruntsfield Place,
Edinburgh,
EH10 4HJ ▣
☎ 0131 228 9446
Est. 1996 *Stock size* Medium
Stock Clocks
Open Mon–Sat 10am–5pm
Services Clock restoration

⊞ **Hawkins & Hawkins
(BADA)**
Contact Miss Emma Hawkins
✉ 9 Atholl Crescent, Edinburgh,
EH3 8HA ▣
☎ 0131 229 2828 ❻ 0131 229 2128
Ⓜ 07831 093198
✉ emma@emmahawkins.co.uk
Ⓦ www.emmahawkins.demon.co.uk
Est. 1993 *Stock size* Large
Stock Victorian taxidermy,
furniture
Open By appointment
Fairs Olympia
Services Valuations, shipping,
book search

⊞ **Holyrood Architectural
Salvage**
Contact Mr K Fowler
✉ Holyrood Business Park,
146 Duddingston Road West,
Edinburgh,
EH16 4AP ▣
☎ 0131 661 9305 ❻ 0131 656 9404
✉ Ken@has.abel.co.uk
Ⓦ www.holyroodarchitectural
salvage.com
Est. 1993 *Stock size* Large
Stock Period fireplaces, baths,
radiators, panelled doors,
brassware, stained glass
Open Mon–Sat 9am–5pm
Services Restoration of baths

⊞ **Allan K L Jackson**
✉ 67 Causewayside, Edinburgh,
EH9 1QF ▣
☎ 0131 668 4532
Ⓜ 07989 236443
Est. 1974 *Stock size* Medium
Stock General antiques
Open Mon–Sat 10am–5pm
Services House clearance

⊞ **Kaimes Smithy
Antiques**
Contact John Lynch
✉ 79 Howden Hall Road,
Edinburgh,
EH16 6PW ▣
☎ 0131 441 2076

🌐 07973 377198
📧 john@jlynch.freeserve.co.uk
🌐 http://kaimessmithy.mysite.
wannadoo-members.co.uk
Est. 1974 *Stock size* Large
Stock 18th–19thC furniture,
oriental ceramics, glass, clocks,
paintings, curios
Open Tues Wed Fri Sat 1.30–5pm
or by appointment

⊞ Alan Lawson & Son
Contact Mr A Lawson
✉ 181 Causewayside, Edinburgh,
EH9 1PH 🅿
☎ 0131 662 1991
Est. 1974 *Stock size* Medium
Stock General antiques and
reproduction items
Open Mon–Sat 11.30am–5.30pm
Services Valuations, house
clearance

⊞ London Road Antiques
Contact Mr R S Forrest
✉ 15 Earlston Place, Edinburgh,
EH7 5SU 🅿
☎ 0131 652 2790
📧 info@19thC.com
🌐 www.19thC.com
Est. 1979 *Stock size* Large
Stock 19thC furniture, Victorian
and Georgian wares, stripped
pine
Open Mon–Sat 10am–5pm
Sun 1–5pm

⊞ J D Love
Contact Mr J D Love
✉ 15–17 Jane Street,
Edinburgh,
EH6 5HE 🅿
☎ 0131 554 7609 📠 0131 554 7609
🌐 07774 678423
Est. 1967 *Stock size* Medium
Stock General antiques
Open Mon–Fri 9am–4.30pm or by
appointment
Services Valuations

⚲ Lyon & Turnbull (BACA Award Winner 2004)
Contact John Mackie
✉ 33 Broughton Place,
Edinburgh,
EH1 3RR 🅿 📠 0131 557 8668
📧 info@lyonandturnbull.com
🌐 www.lyonandturnbull.com
Est. 1826
Open Mon–Fri 8.30am–5.30pm
Sales Regular sales of fine
antiques, silver and jewellery,
pictures, decorative arts, books,

maps and manuscripts. See
website for details
Catalogues Yes

⊞ J Martinez Antiques
Contact Mr J Martinez
✉ 17 Brandon Terrace,
Edinburgh,
EH3 5DZ 🅿
☎ 0131 558 8720 📠 0131 558 8720
🌐 07836 608090
Est. 1979 *Stock size* Medium
Stock General antiques,
jewellery, clocks
Open Mon–Sat 11am–5pm
Fairs NEC, Ingliston
Services Valuations

⊞ McNaughtan's Bookshop (ABA)
Contact Elizabeth Strong
✉ 3a & 4a Haddington Place,
Edinburgh,
EH7 4AE 🅿
☎ 0131 556 5897 📠 0131 556 8220
📧 mcnbooks@btconnect.com
🌐 www.mcnaughtansbookshop.com
Est. 1957
Stock General antiquarian and
second-hand books including
architecture, children's and
Scottish topics
Open Tues–Sat 9.30am–5.30pm
Fairs ABA
Services Valuations

⊞ Meadow Lamps Gallery
Contact Mr S A Robertson
✉ 48 Warrender Park Road,
Edinburgh,
EH9 1HH 🅿
☎ 0131 221 1212
📧 s4sarok@aol.com
Est. 1900 *Stock size* Medium
Stock Antique lighting
Open Tues Thurs Sat 10am–6pm
Fairs NEC Birmingham, Glasgow
Services Restoration

⊞ Millers Antiques
Contact Mrs S Miller
✉ 187–191 Causewayside,
Edinburgh,
EH9 1PH 🅿
☎ 0131 662 1429 📠 0131 662 4187
Est. 1995 *Stock size* Large
Stock General antiques,
Georgian–Edwardian furniture,
mahogany, oak and pine,
unusual collectables
Open Mon–Sat 10am–5.30pm
Fairs Newark, Swinderby
Services Delivery

⊞ Neilsons Ltd (National Fireplace Association)
Contact Mr & Mrs Neilson
✉ 56 Bankhead Crossway South,
Edinburgh,
EH11 4EP 🅿
☎ 0131 453 5820 📠 0131 453 5820
📧 info@chimneypiece.co.uk
🌐 www.chimneypiece.co.uk
Est. 2003 *Stock size* Large
Stock Antique chimney pieces,
register grates, hob grates,
fenders, fire irons, reproduction
grates, mantels, accessories
Open Tues–Fri 9.30am–5pm
Sat noon–5pm

⊞ Now & Then
Contact Mr D Gordon
✉ 7 & 9 West Cross Causeway,
Edinburgh,
EH8 9JW 🅿
☎ 0131 668 2927 📠 0131 668 2926
🌐 07976 360283
📧 mill@oldtoysandantiques.co.uk
🌐 oldtoysandantiques.co.uk
Est. 1976 *Stock size* Medium
Stock Old toys, antiques,
telephones, old clocks, cameras,
bicycles, automobilia,
railwayana, pre-WW1 office and
domestic equipment, small items
of furniture
Open Tues–Sat 1–5.30pm
Fairs Edinburgh, London
Services Tin toy restoration

⊞ The Old Children's Bookshelf (PBFA)
Contact Shirley Neilson
✉ 175 Canongate, Royal Mile,
Edinburgh,
EH8 8BN 🅿
☎ 0131 558 3411
📧 shirleyocb@aol.com
Est. 1998 *Stock size* Medium
Stock Children's novels, annuals,
prints, comics
Open Mon–Fri 10.30am–5pm
Sat 10am–5pm April–Oct Sun
11am–4.30pm
Fairs PBFA

⊞ The Old Town Bookshop (PBFA)
Contact Ron Wilson
✉ 8 Victoria Street, Edinburgh,
EH1 2HG 🅿
☎ 0131 225 9237 📠 0131 229 1503
🌐 07740 625172
📧 sales@oldtownbookshop.co.uk
🌐 www.oldtownbookshop.co.uk
Est. 1978 *Stock size* Medium

Stock Antiquarian and second-hand books, maps, prints, specializing in antiquarian art books
Open Mon–Sat 10.30am–6pm
Fairs Dublin, London, Edinburgh
Services Valuations, catalogues

⊞ Past & Present (PBFA)
Contact Gary Watt
⊠ 54a Clerk Street, Edinburgh, EH8 9JB ℗
☎ 0131 667 2004 ✆ 0131 667 2004
⊕ 07939 587512
✉ wattg4@aol.com
ⓦ www.past-and-present.co.uk
Est. 1994 *Stock size* Medium
Stock General antiques, antiquarian children's books, Art Deco, Art Deco rings
Open Mon–Fri 10am–5pm Sat 10am–6pm Sun 2–6pm
Fairs Ingliston
Services Valuations, china repair

⊞ Royal Mile Curios
Contact Mr Martin
⊠ 363 High Street, Edinburgh, EH1 1PW ℗
☎ 0131 226 4050
✉ info@antique-jewelry.cc
ⓦ www.antique-jewelry.cc
Est. 1875 *Stock size* Large
Stock Antique and Scottish jewellery
Open Mon–Sun 10.30am–5.30pm

⊞ Royal Mile Gallery
Contact J A Smith
⊠ 272 Canongate, Edinburgh, EH8 8AA ℗
☎ 0131 558 1702
✉ james@royalmilegallery.co.uk
ⓦ www.royalmilegallery.co.uk
Est. 1994 *Stock size* Large
Stock Antiquarian maps, prints
Open Mon–Sat 11.30am–5pm
Services Valuations, framing service

⊞ Samarkand Galleries (LAPADA, CADA, CINOA)
Contact Brian MacDonald
⊠ 16 Howe Street, Edinburgh, EH3 6TD ℗
☎ 0131 225 2010 ✆ 0131 225 2010
✉ howe@samarkand.co.uk
ⓦ www.samarkand.co.uk
Est. 1979 *Stock size* Large
Stock Antique and contemporary rugs from Near East and Central Asia, decorative carpets, nomadic weavings

Open Mon–Sat 10am–6pm Sun 11am–4pm
Fairs HALI Antique Textile Art Fair
Services Search

⊞ James Scott
Contact James Scott
⊠ 43 Dundas Street, Edinburgh, EH3 6QQ ℗
☎ 0131 556 8260
Est. 1964 *Stock size* Medium
Stock General antiques
Open Mon–Sat 11.30am–5pm closed 1–2pm closed Thurs 12.30pm
Services Valuations

⊞ Second Edition
Contact W A Smith
⊠ 9 Howard Street, Edinburgh, EH3 5JP ℗
☎ 0131 556 9403
✉ secondedition@tiscali.co.uk
ⓦ www.secondeditionbookshop.co.uk
Est. 1979 *Stock size* Large
Stock Quality books, militaria, arts, Scottish books
Open Mon–Fri 10.30am–5.30pm Sat 9.30am–5.30pm
Services Valuations, binding

↗ Shapes Fine Art Auctioneers & Valuers
Contact Richard Longwill BA, MRICS
⊠ Bankhead Avenue, Sighthill, Edinburgh, EH11 4BY ℗
☎ 0131 453 3222 ✆ 0131 453 6444
✉ auctionsadmin@shapes auctioneers.co.uk
ⓦ www.shapesauctioneers.co.uk
Est. 1992
Open Mon–Fri 9am–5pm
Sales Fine art and antiques sale 1st Sat of every month 10am, viewing Thur 10am–7pm Fri 10am–4pm
Catalogues Yes

⊞ Still Life
Contact Ewan Lamont
⊠ 54 Candlemaker Row, Edinburgh, EH1 2QE
☎ 0131 225 8524
✉ ewanlamont@mac.com
ⓦ homepage.mac.com/ewan lamont/PhotoAlbum.html
Est. 1984 *Stock size* Large

Stock Portable collectables, china, glass, pictures
Open Mon–Sat noon–5pm

⊞ The Talish Gallery
Contact John Martin
⊠ 168 Canongate, Edinburgh, EH8 8DF ℗
☎ 0131 557 8435
Est. 1969 *Stock size* Large
Stock Small general antiques, Oriental wares, silver
Open Mon–Sat 10am–4pm
Fairs Newark

↗ Thomson, Roddick & Medcalf
Contact Sybelle Medcalf
⊠ The Edinburgh and Lothian Sale Room, 44/3 Hardengreen Business Park, Eskbank, Edinburgh, EH22 3NX ℗
☎ 0131 454 9090 ✆ 0131 454 9191
✉ t.rm@virgin.net
Est. 1999
Open Mon–Fri 9am–5pm
Sales Antiques, fine art, general furnishings, special quarterly sales
Frequency Weekly
Catalogues Yes

⊞ The Thrie Estaits
Contact Peter Powell
⊠ 49 Dundas Street, Edinburgh, EH3 6RS
☎ 0131 556 7084
✉ thethrieestaits@aol.com
Est. 1971 *Stock size* Medium
Stock Unusual antiques, decorative items
Open Tues–Sat 11am–5pm

⊞ Till's Bookshop
Contact Mr R Till
⊠ 1 Hope Park Crescent, Edinburgh, EH8 9NA ℗
☎ 0131 667 0895
✉ tillsbookshop@hotmail.com
Est. 1985 *Stock size* Medium
Stock Literature, fantasy, mystery, humanities, poetry, drama, cinema, general, first editions
Open Mon–Fri noon–7.30pm Sat 11am–6pm Sun noon–5.30pm
Services Valuations

⊞ Trinity Curios
Contact Alan Ferguson
⊠ 4–6 Stanley Road, Edinburgh, EH6 4SG ℗

☎ 0131 552 8481
⑩ 07715 500719
✉ adfer@btinternet.com
Est. 1987 *Stock size* Large
Stock Quality furniture, porcelain, silver, linen, collectables
Open Tues–Fri 10am–5pm Wed Sat noon–6pm Sun 2–5pm

⊞ Unicorn Antiques
Contact N Duncan
✉ 65 Dundas Street, Edinburgh, EH3 6RS
☎ 0131 556 7176
✉ unicorn@ecosse.net
⑩ www.transcotland.com/unicorn
Est. 1969 *Stock size* Small
Stock General antiques, bric-a-brac
Open Mon–Sat 10.30am–6.30pm

⊞ West Port Books
Contact Mr H N Barrott
✉ 145–147 West Port, Edinburgh, EH3 9DD ▣
☎ 0131 229 4431
✉ west@portbooks.freeserve.co.uk
⑩ www.westport.freeserve.co.uk
Est. 1979 *Stock size* Large
Stock Second-hand and antiquarian books, especially fine art books and Indian imports
Open Mon–Tues 10.30am–5.30pm Wed–Sat noon–6pm

⊞ Whytock & Reid
Contact Mr Reid
✉ Sunbury House, Belford Mews, Edinburgh, EH4 3DN ▣
☎ 0131 226 4911 ❶ 0131 226 4595
✉ whytockandreid.com
⑩ www.whytockandreid.com
Est. 1807 *Stock size* Large
Stock Whytock & Reid 19thC furniture, 18thC furniture, rugs, carpets
Open Mon–Fri 9am–5.30pm Sat 10am–2pm
Services Cabinet-making, French polishing

⊞ Richard Wood Antiques
Contact Richard Wood
✉ 66 West Port, Edinburgh, EH1 2LD ▣
☎ 0131 229 6344
Est. 1971 *Stock size* Large
Stock Small silver and Oriental items, collectables
Open Mon–Sat 10am–5pm
Fairs Ingliston Mammoth Fair

FIFE

ABERDOUR

⊞ Antiques & Gifts
Contact Jennifer Graham
✉ 26 High Street, Aberdour, Fife, KY3 0SW ▣
☎ 01383 860523
Est. 1969 *Stock size* Small
Stock General antiques
Open Tues 2–5pm Wed 11am–2.30pm Thurs–Sat 10am–5pm closed 12.30–2pm

CERES

⊞ Ceres Antiques
Contact Evelyn Norrie
✉ 1 The Butts, Ceres, Cupar, Fife, KY15 5NF ▣
☎ 01334 828384
Est. 1969 *Stock size* Medium
Stock General antiques, specializing in linen and lace
Open Mon–Sun 10am–6pm or by appointment
Fairs Newark, Birmingham and Harrogate

DUNFERMLINE

⊞ A K Campbell & Son
Contact Mr A K Campbell
✉ 39 High Street, Dunfermline, Fife, KY12 7DL ▣
☎ 01383 724783
Est. 1977 *Stock size* Medium
Stock Watches
Open Mon–Sat 10am–5pm
Services Valuations, repairs

DYSART

⊞ Second Notions Antiques
Contact Jim Sinclair
✉ 2 Normand Road, Dysart, Kirkcaldy, Fife, KY1 2XJ ▣
☎ 01592 650505 ❶ 01592 573341
⑩ 07977 119787
✉ james@sinclair1155.freeserve.co.uk
⑩ www.secondnotions.co.uk
Est. 1994 *Stock size* Medium
Stock General antiques
Open Mon–Fri noon–4pm Sat 10am–4pm
Fairs Swinderby, Newark
Services Exporting of containers

INVERKEITHING

⊞ Bargain Centre
Contact Hilda Fleming
✉ 3 Boreland Road, Inverkeithing, Fife, KY11 1NK ▣
☎ 01383 416727 ❶ 01383 418054
⑩ www.bargaincentre.com
Est. 1982 *Stock size* Large
Stock General antiques, bric-a-brac, office furniture
Open Mon–Sat 9am–5pm

KIRKCALDY

⊞ A K Campbell & Son
Contact Mr A K Campbell
✉ 262 High Street, Kirkcaldy, Fife, KY1 1LA ▣
☎ 01592 597022
Est. 1977 *Stock size* Medium
Stock General antiques, militaria, furniture, bric-a-brac, postcards, banknotes
Open Mon–Sat 10am–5pm
Services Valuations, house and estate clearance

⊞ A K Campbell & Son
Contact Mr A K Campbell
✉ 277 High Street, Kirkcaldy, Fife, KY1 1JH ▣
☎ 01592 264305/597161
Est. 1977 *Stock size* Medium
Stock Family jewellery including antique jewellery, silver
Open Mon–Sat 10am–5pm
Services Valuations, repairs, goods purchased

⊞ The Golden Past
Contact Fiona Campbell
✉ 90 Rosslyn Street, Kirkcaldy, Fife, KY1 3AD ▣
☎ 01592 653185 ❶ 01592 653185
Est. 1983 *Stock size* Small
Stock General antiques, pine furniture
Open Tues–Sun 10am–5pm

⚒ MD's Auction Ltd
Contact Tommy Stowe or Vicky Cunningham
✉ Unit 15–16, Smeaton Industrial Estate, Hayfield Road, Kirkcaldy, Fife, KY1 2HE ▣
☎ 01592 599969 ❶ 01592 640969
⑩ 07970 737401

@ navatmds@aol.com
W www.mdsauction.co.uk
Est. 1989
Open Mon–Fri 9am–5pm
Sat 10am–1pm
Sales 500 lots, Thurs 6.30pm
Frequency Weekly
Catalogues Yes

MARKINCH

⊞ Squirrel Antiques
Contact Sheila Green
✉ 13 Commercial Street,
Markinch, Fife,
KY7 6DE ℗
☎ 01592 754386 ℮ 01592 754386
Ⓜ 07850 912801
Est. 1984 *Stock size* Medium
Stock General antiques, restored
pine, Scottish pottery
Open Mon–Sat 9am–5pm or by
appointment
Services Valuations

NEWBURGH

⊞ Henderson–Dark Antiques Ltd (LAPADA)
Contact Dawn Dark
✉ 241 High Street, Newburgh,
Fife, KY14 6DY ℗
☎ 01337 840248
℮ hendersondarkantiques@
hotmail.com
W ww.darkantiques.com
Est. 1990 *Stock size* Medium
Stock Good quality 18th–19thC
small items, furniture
Open Mon–Sat 10am–5.30pm
Sun by appointment
Services Valuations, restoration
and shipping

⊞ Newburgh Antiques
Contact Miss D J Fraser
✉ 222 High Street, Newburgh,
Cupar, Fife, KY14 6DZ ℗
☎ 01337 827158
Ⓜ 07850 013191
℮ antiques@wemyssware.net
W www.wemyssware.net
Est. 1989 *Stock size* Small
Stock General antiques, Scottish
pottery
Open By appointment
Services Valuations

NEWPORT-ON-TAY

⊞ Mair Wilkes Books (PBFA)
Contact James Mair

✉ 3 St Marys Lane,
Newport-on-Tay, Fife,
DD6 8AH ℗
☎ 01382 542260 ℮ 01382 542260
℮ mairwilkes.books@zoom.co.uk
Est. 1969 *Stock size* Large
Stock Large selection of rare,
second-hand, antiquarian and
out-of-print books, specializing
in Scottish topics and psychology
Open Tues–Fri 10am–5pm closed
12.30–2pm Sat 10am–5.30pm
Services Valuations, book search

PITTENWEEM

⊞ High Street Antiques
Contact R Clark
✉ 39 High Street,
Pittenweem, Fife,
KY10 2LA ℗
☎ 01333 312870
Ⓜ 07711 300136
Est. 1984 *Stock size* Medium
Stock General antiques, Wemyss
ware
Open Mon–Sun 10.30am–5pm
Services Valuations, goods
purchased

ST ANDREWS

⊞ Bouquiniste
Contact Mrs E A Anderson
✉ 31 Market Street,
St Andrews, Fife,
KY16 9NS ℗
☎ 01334 476724
Est. 1981 *Stock size* Medium
Stock Rare and second-hand
books
Open Mon–Fri 11am–5pm
Sat 10am–5pm Sun 1pm–5pm

⊞ David Brown Gallery
Contact David Brown
✉ 9 Albany Place,
St Andrews, Fife,
KY16 9HH ℗
☎ 01334 477840 ℮ 01334 476915
Est. 1969 *Stock size* Medium
Stock General antiques, Scottish
jewellery, silver, golf memorabilia,
golf prints, paintings
Open Mon–Sat 10am–5pm
Services Valuations, restoration,
jewellery repairs

⊞ A K Campbell & Son
Contact Mr A K Campbell
✉ 84c Market Street,
St Andrews, Fife,
KY16 9PA ℗

☎ 01334 474214
Est. 1977 *Stock size* Medium
Stock Antique jewellery
Open Mon–Sat 10am–5pm
Services Valuations, repairs

⋏ Macgregor Auctions
Contact Mrs Graham
✉ 56 Largo Road,
St Andrews, Fife,
KY16 8RP ℗
☎ 01334 472431 ℮ 01334 479606
Est. 1857
Open Viewing and sale days only
Sales Sale Thurs Fri 10.30am,
viewing day prior 9am–7pm
Frequency Fortnightly
Catalogues Yes

UPPER LARGO

⊞ Waverley Antiques
Contact Dudley StClair
✉ 13 Main Street,
Upper Largo,
Fife,
KY8 6EL ℗
☎ 01333 360437
Est. 1968 *Stock size* Small
Stock General antiques,
furniture, china, etc
Open Mon–Sun 11am–5.30pm

GLASGOW

GLASGOW

⊞ All Our Yesterdays
Contact Susie Robinson
✉ 6 Park Road, Kelvinbridge,
Glasgow,
G4 9JG ℗
☎ 0141 334 7788
℮ antiques@allouryesterdays.
fsnet.co.uk
W www.healingroom.org
Est. 1989 *Stock size* Large
Stock General antiques, mineral
and crystal specimens
Open Flexible Mon–Fri
11am–6pm Sat noon–5.30pm or
by appointment
Services Valuations, search service

⌂ Antiques Centre
Contact Alan Abspure
✉ 188 Woodlands Road,
Charing Cross,
Glasgow,
G36 1LL ℗
☎ 0141 332 5757
Est. 1993 *Stock size* Medium
Stock General antiques,

Victorian–Edwardian
Open Mon–Sun 10am–6pm
Services Valuations, restoration

⊞ The Antiques Warehouse
Contact Maria Mangan
✉ Glasgow, G3
☎ 0141 334 4924 ✆ 0141 334 4924
Est. 1979 **Stock size** Large
Stock General antiques
Open Relocating; phone for details
Services Valuations, restoration and repairs

⋏ Bonhams
✉ 176 St Vincent Street, Glasgow, G2 5SG
☎ 0141 223 8860 ✆ 0141 223 8868
✉ glasgow@bonhams.com
ⓦ www.bonhams.com
Open Mon–Fri 8.30am–5pm
Sales Regional office. Regular sales held in London and in our salerooms across the country. Free auction valuations; insurance and probate valuations

⊞ Broadsword Antiques
Contact Robert Corlett
✉ Studio 6, 99 King Street, Kings Court, Glasgow, G1 5RB Ⓟ
☎ 07967 826362 ✆ 07967 826362
✉ broadswordantiques@tinyworld.com
ⓦ www.militarymaze.com
Est. 1994 **Stock size** Medium
Stock Militaria
Open By appointment

⊞ Browns Clocks
Contact Jim Cairns
✉ 13 Radnor Street, Glasgow, G3 7UA Ⓟ
☎ 0141 334 6308 ✆ 0141 334 6308
✉ james@jcairns.greatxscape.net
Est. 1933 **Stock size** Medium
Stock Longcase clocks
Open Mon–Fri 10am–5pm Sat 10am–1pm
Services Restoration of all antique clocks

⊞ Caledonian Books
Contact Martin or Maureen Smiley
✉ 483 Great Western Road, Glasgow, G12 8HJ Ⓟ
☎ 0141 334 9663 ✆ 0141 334 9663
✉ caledonianbooks@aol.com
ⓦ www.caledonianbooks.co.uk
Est. 1986 **Stock size** Large
Stock Antiquarian and second-hand books
Open Mon–Sat 10.30am–6pm
Services Valuations

⊞ Canning Antiques
Contact Kate
✉ 24–26 Millbrae Road, Langside, Glasgow, G42 9UT Ⓟ
☎ 0141 632 9853 ✆ 0141 632 9853
✉ kate@canning-antiques.com
ⓦ www.canning-antiques.com
Est. 1997 **Stock size** Medium
Stock Wide range of fine Georgian–Edwardian furniture, mirrors, clocks, objets d'art
Open Tues–Sat 10am–5pm, Sun noon–5pm or by appointment
Fairs Antiques for Everyone
Services Restoration

⋏ Collins & Paterson LLP
Contact Robert Paterson or Leonard Kerr
✉ 141 West Regent Street, Glasgow, G2 2SG Ⓟ
☎ 0141 229 1326 ✆ 0141 248 1591
Est. 1848
Open Mon–Fri 9am–4.30pm
Sales General antiques sales Tuesday all day, viewing Monday prior
Frequency Fortnightly

⋏ Arthur E Collins & Son
Contact Leonard Kerr
✉ 141 West Regent Street, Glasgow, G2 2SG
☎ 0141 229 1326 ✆ 0141 248 1591
Est. 1899
Open Mon–Fri 9am–4.30pm
Sales Pawnbroker sales usually Thurs pm, viewing Thurs am
Frequency 1 per week
Catalogues Yes

⊞ Cooper Hay Rare Books (ABA)
Contact Mr C Hay
✉ 182 Bath Street, Glasgow, G2 4HG Ⓟ
☎ 0141 333 1992 ✆ 0141 333 1992
✉ chayrbooks@aol.com
ⓦ www.abebooks.com/home/haybooks
Est. 1984 **Stock size** Medium

Stock Books, prints, specializing in Scottish art and juvenile books
Open Mon–Fri 10am–5.30pm Sat 10am–1pm
Fairs Chelsea, Edinburgh
Services Valuations, book search

⊞ Finnie Antiques Ltd
Contact Bruce Finnie
✉ Showroom, 3B Yorkhill Quay, Glasgow, G3 8QE Ⓟ
☎ 0141 357 5812 ✆ 0141 423 8515
Ⓜ 07973 315460
✉ bruce@finnieantiques.co.uk
ⓦ www.finnieantiques.co.uk
Est. 1980 **Stock size** Medium
Stock Furniture, silver, Arts and Crafts, fireplaces
Open Mon–Fri 10.30am–5pm Sat Sun noon–5pm
Services Valuations, French polishing and waxing

⊞ Flying Dutchman Antiques
Contact Hannie Van Riel
✉ Antiques Warehouse, Glasgow, G3 Ⓟ
☎ 0141 338 6834 ✆ 0141 338 6834
✉ info@fdantiques.com
Est. 1994 **Stock size** Large
Stock General antiques including Continental European furniture
Open Relocating; phone or email for details

⋏ Great Western Auctions
Contact Mrs A Manning
✉ 29–37 Otago Street, Glasgow, G12 8JJ Ⓟ
☎ 0141 339 3290 ✆ 0141 3345650
✉ gwauctions@btconnect.com
ⓦ www.greatwesternauctions.com
Est. 1988
Open Mon–Fri 9am–5pm
Sales General antiques
Frequency Fortnightly
Catalogues Yes

⊞ A D Hamilton Antiques
Contact Jeff Fineman
✉ 7 St Vincent Place, Glasgow, G1 2DW Ⓟ
☎ 0141 221 5423
✉ jefffineman@hotmail.com
ⓦ www.adhamilton.com
Est. 1890 **Stock size** Small
Stock General antiques
Open Mon–Sat 9.30am–5pm

⚒ Kerr & McAlister (SAA)
Contact Mr Thomas McAlister
✉ **140 Niddrie Road, Glasgow,
G42 8QB** 🅿
☎ 0141 423 4271 ☏ 0141 423 7265
🌐 www.kerr-mcalister-auctions.co.uk
Est. 1969
Open Mon–Fri 9am–5pm
Sales Household goods, antique
furniture
Frequency Every Thurs evening,
viewing Thurs 9.30am–5.45pm
Catalogues No

⊞ London Road Emporium
Contact Sarah Urie
✉ **259 London Road, Glasgow,
GP40 1PQ** 🅿
☎ 01415 529898
☏ 07969 256886
Est. 2000 *Stock size* Medium
Stock General antiques
Open Mon–Sun 10am–5pm
Services Valuations

⊞ Lovejoy Antiques
Contact Julie Gallagher
✉ **Antiques Warehouse,
Glasgow,
G3** 🅿
☎ 0141 357 3559 ☏ 0141 357 3559
☏ 07949 651897
✉ julielovejoy@yahoo.co.uk
Est. 1995 *Stock size* Medium
Stock General antiques
Open Relocating; phone or email
for details
Services Polishing, shipping

**⚒ Robert McTear & Co
(IAA)**
Contact Miss Janet Stewart
✉ **Sky Park, 8 Elliot Place,
Glasgow,
G3 8EP** 🅿
☎ 0141 221 4456 ☏ 0141 204 5035
✉ enquiries@mctears.co.uk
🌐 www.mctears.co.uk
Est. 1842
Open Mon–Fri 9am–5pm
Sales Weekly auction of general
antiques on Fri
Catalogues Yes

⊞ Pastimes Vintage Toys
Contact Anne or Gordon Brown
✉ **126 Maryhill Road,
St George's Cross,
Glasgow,
G27 7QS** 🅿
☎ 0141 331 1008
✉ anne@dinkydoll.com
🌐 www.dinkydoll.com

Est. 1976 *Stock size* Medium
Stock Vintage toys, Dinky,
Hornby, dolls' houses, medals,
militaria, small collectables
Open Tues–Sat 9.30am–5.30pm
Services Mail order, valuations

⊞ Tom Pearson
Contact Tom Pearson
✉ **40 Darnley Street, Glasgow,
G42 8PR** 🅿
☎ 0141 429 4411
☏ 07966 362521
Est. 1994 *Stock size* Medium
Stock Georgian, Victorian and
Art Nouveau fireplaces
Open Mon–Fri 10am–6pm
Sat 10am–5pm Sun noon–5pm

⊞ Relics
Contact Steven Currie
✉ **Dowanside Lane,
Glasgow,
G12 9BZ** 🅿
☎ 0141 341 0007
Est. 1989 *Stock size* Medium
Stock General antiques,
collectables including 1960s
Open Mon–Sat 10.30am–6pm
Sun 12.30–6pm
Services Valuations

⊞ R Rutherford
Contact Mrs R Rutherford
✉ **The Victorian Village,
93 West Regent Street,
Glasgow,
G2 2BA** 🅿
☎ 0141 332 9808/0808
☏ 0141 332 9808
Est. 1979 *Stock size* Medium
Stock General antiques, Scottish
agates
Open Mon–Sat 10am–5pm
Services Valuations

**⊞ Samson's Joinery
& Antiques (Scottish
Furniture Makers
Association)**
Contact Ross Samson
✉ **Antiques Warehouse,
Glasgow,
G3**
☎ 0141 632 8681 ☏ 0141 649 6089
☏ 07985 046827
✉ samsons.joinery@virgin.net
🌐 www.samsonsjoinery.co.uk
Est. 1998 *Stock size* Small
Stock Furniture
Open Relocating; phone or email
for details
Services Restoration

**⊞ Saratoga Trunk
Yesteryear Costume
& Textiles**
Contact David McLay
✉ **Fourth Floor, 61 Hyde Park
Street, Glasgow,
G3 8BW** 🅿
☎ 0141 221 4433 ☏ 0141 221 4433
Est. 1976 *Stock size* Large
Stock Vintage clothing,
Victorian–1990s, linens, lace,
costume jewellery, etc
Open Mon–Fri 10.30am–5pm
Fairs Manchester, Birmingham,
Glasgow
Services Valuations, hire to film,
television, theatre productions

**⊞ Jeremy Sniders
Antiques**
Contact Jeremy Sniders
✉ **158 Bath Street, Glasgow,
G2 4TB** 🅿
☎ 0141 332 0043 ☏ 0141 332 5505
✉ jeremysniders@aol.com
🌐 www.jeremysnidersantiques.com
Est. 1981 *Stock size* Medium
Stock General antiques,
Scandinavian antiques,
silverware, jewellery, Georg
Jensen specialist
Open Mon–Sat 9am–5pm
Services Valuations

**⊞ St Lucy Wayside
Antiques**
Contact Joseph Higgins
✉ **56 Battlefield Road,
Lengside, Battlefield,
Glasgow,
G42 9QG** 🅿
☎ 0141 632 3683 ☏ 0141 632 3683
☏ 07946 240252
Est. 2000 *Stock size* Medium
Stock General antiques
Open Mon–Fri 10am–5pm

⊞ Strachan Antiques
Contact Alex Strachan
✉ **40 Darnley Street,
Pollokshields, Glasgow,
G41 2SE** 🅿
☎ 0141 429 4411
☏ 07950 262346
🌐 www.carrickdesign.co.uk/
antiquesite/strachan.html
Est. 1990 *Stock size* Large
Stock Arts and Crafts, Art
Nouveau furniture, small
decorative items
Open Mon–Fri 10am–6pm
Sat 10am–5pm Sun noon–5pm
Fairs SECC Glasgow

⊞ The Studio
Contact Liz McKelvie
✉ DeCourcy's Arcade,
5–21 Cresswell Lane,
Glasgow,
G12 8AA 🅿
☎ 0141 334 8211
📱 07909 742862
✉ lizthestudio@aol.com
🌐 http://www.glasgowwestend.
co.uk/shopping/antiques/studio.html
Est. 1998 *Stock size* Small
Stock Books, small furniture,
ceramics, pictures, glass, textiles,
Glasgow-style Arts and Crafts
and Art Nouveau, Talwin Morris
book bindings
Open Tues–Sat 10am–5.30pm
Sun noon–5pm
Services Shipping, booksearch

**⊞ The Treasure Bunker
Militaria Shop**
Contact Mr K J Andrew
✉ 21 King Street, Merchant City,
Glasgow,
G1 5Q2
☎ 0141 552 8164 📠 0141 552 4651
✉ info@treasurebunker.com
🌐 www.treasurebunker.com
Est. 1985 *Stock size* Large
Stock Military antiques, Battle of
Waterloo–WWII
Open Tues–Sat 11am–5pm
Services Worldwide mail order
catalogue

⊞ Voltaire & Rousseau
Contact Mr J McGonagle
✉ 12–14 Otago Lane, Glasgow,
G12 8PB 🅿
☎ 0141 339 1811
Est. 1971 *Stock size* Large
Stock Rare and second-hand
books
Open Mon–Sat 10am–6pm
Services Valuations

**⊞ Tim Wright Antiques
(LAPADA)**
Contact Judy or Tim Wright
✉ 147 Bath Street, Glasgow,
G2 4SQ 🅿
☎ 0141 221 0364 📠 0141 221 0364
✉ tim@timwright-antiques.com
🌐 www.timwright-antiques.com
Est. 1972 *Stock size* Large
Stock Quality antiques, furniture,
porcelain, glass, bronze, silver,
textiles, samplers
Open Mon–Fri 10am–5pm
Sat 10am–4pm
Services Valuations

HIGHLAND

AULDEARN

⊞ Auldearn Antiques
Contact Roger Milton
✉ Dalmore Manse, Lethen Road,
Auldearn, Nairn, Inverness-shire,
IV12 5HZ 🅿
☎ 01667 453087
📱 07918 100252
✉ rogermiltonrj@aol.com
Est. 1984 *Stock size* Large
Stock General antiques
Open Mon–Sun 9.30am–5.30pm
Services Valuations, restoration
and repairs to wood, metal and
fireplaces

BEAULY

**⊞ Iain Marr (LAPADA,
HADA, Silver Society)**
Contact Iain Marr
✉ 3 Mid Street, Beauly,
Inverness-shire,
IV4 7DP 🅿
☎ 01463 782372 📠 01463 783263
📱 07860 914191
✉ info@iain-marr-antiques.com
🌐 www.iain-marr-antiques.com
Est. 1974 *Stock size* Medium
Stock General antiques
Open Mon–Sat 10.30am–5.30pm
closed 1–2pm closed Thurs
Services Valuations

DINGWALL

**➤ Dingwall & Highland
Marts Ltd (IAA)**
Contact Kenneth MacKay
✉ 15 Tulloch Street, Dingwall,
Ross-shire,
IV15 9JZ 🅿
☎ 01349 863252 📠 01349 865062
✉ dingwallmart@cqm.co.uk
Open Mon–Fri 8am–5pm
Sales General antiques
Frequency Weekly
Catalogues No

DORNOCH

⊞ Castle Close Antiques
Contact George or Joyce McLean
✉ Castle Street, Dornoch,
Highland,
IV25 3SN 🅿
☎ 01862 810405 📠 01862 810405
✉ enquiries@castle-close-
antiques.com
🌐 www.castle-close-antiques.com

Est. 1983 *Stock size* Medium
Stock General antiques,
jewellery, china
Open Mon–Sat 10am–1pm
2–5pm closed Thurs pm

FORTROSE

⊞ Cathedral Antiques
Contact Mrs Patricia MacColl
✉ 45 High Street, Fortrose,
Ross-shire,
IV10 8SU 🅿
☎ 01381 620161
📱 07778 817074
✉ cathant@hotmail.com
Est. 1996 *Stock size* Medium
Stock General antiques,
1780–1920 furniture, ceramics,
silver, glass, decorative objects
Open Fri Sat 10am–5pm or by
appointment
Fairs All Galloway fairs from
Newcastle north
Services Valuations

INVERNESS

⊞ Caledonian Antiques
Contact Claire Watson
✉ 3 Lombard Street, Inverness,
Inverness-shire,
IV1 1QQ
☎ 01463 711100 📠 01320 351346
Est. 1998 *Stock size* Large
Stock Antiques, collectables
Open Mon–Sat 10am–5.30pm
Services Valuations, restoration,
jewellery repairs

➤ Frasers Auctioneers
Contact Mr Davidson
✉ 8a Harbour Road, Inverness,
Inverness-shire,
IV1 1SY 🅿
☎ 01463 232395 📠 01463 233634
Est. 1900
Open Mon–Thurs 9am–5pm
Fri 9am–4pm
Sales General antiques Wed
6pm, viewing Tues and Wed
Frequency Monthly
Catalogues Yes

⊞ Gallery Persia
Contact Gordon MacDonald
✉ Upper Myrtlesfield, Nairnside,
Inverness, Inverness-shire,
IV2 5BX 🅿
☎ 01463 798500 📠 01463 798500
✉ mac@gallerypersia.co.uk
🌐 www.gallerypersia.co.uk
Est. 1989 *Stock size* Medium

Stock Old and antique rugs from Persia, Caucasus, Afghanistan, exemplary modern rugs
Open Mon–Sun by appointment Sat 11am–4pm
Fairs Scottish Game Fair July
Services Restoration, repair, search service. Exhibition held in Spring and Autumn

LANARKSHIRE

LANARK

⊞ Auld Things
Contact Elizabeth Williamson
✉ 14 Broomgate, Lanark, Lanarkshire,
ML11 9EE 🅿
☎ 01555 665822
Est. 1999 *Stock size* Large
Stock Antique furniture, ceramics, glass, jewellery
Open Jan–April Mon–Sat 11am–4pm May–Dec Mon–Sat 10am–5pm
Services Valuations

MORAY

FORRES

⚲ Forres Saleroom
Contact Alexander Morris
✉ Tytler Street, Forres, Moray,
IV36 1EL 🅿
☎ 01309 672422 📠 01309 673339
Est. 1895
Open Mon–Fri 9am–5pm Sat 9am–noon
Sales General antique sales Thurs 6pm, viewing Wed 2–6pm Thurs all day
Frequency Weekly
Catalogues Yes

NORTH AYRSHIRE

ISLE OF ARRAN

⊞ The Stable Antiques
Contact Alistair Linton
✉ Balmichael Visitors Centre, Shiskine Brodick, Isle of Arran, North Ayrshire,
KA27 8DT
☎ 01770 860468
ⓦ www.stableantiques-arran.co.uk
Est. 1984 *Stock size* Medium
Stock General antiques
Open Summer Mon–Sat 10am–5pm Sun noon–5pm

winter Wed–Sat 10am–5pm Sun noon–5pm
Services Furniture restoration

LARGS

⊞ Narducci Antiques
Contact Mr G Narducci
✉ 11 Waterside Street, Largs, North Ayrshire,
KA30 9LW 🅿
☎ 01475 672612 or 01294 461687
📠 01294 470002
ⓜ 07771 577777
ⓔ narducci.antiques@virgin.net
ⓦ www.narducci-antiques.co.uk
Est. 1969 *Stock size* Large
Stock General antiques, Georgian, Victorian, Edwardian furniture
Open Tues Thur Sat 2.30–5.30pm or by appointment
Services Packing, shipping, European haulage

⊞ Nicolson Maps
Contact Malcolm Nicolson
✉ 3 Frazer Street, Largs, North Ayrshire,
KA30 9HP 🅿
☎ 01475 689242 📠 01475 689242
ⓔ nicolsonmaps@btconnect.com
ⓦ www.nicolsonmaps.com
Est. 1979 *Stock size* Medium
Stock General maps and charts
Open Mon–Fri 9am–5pm
Fairs International Map Association
Services Free postal service

PERTH & KINROSS

ABERNYTE

⊞ The Old Church Antiques
Contact George Whitla
✉ The Old Church Scottish Antique and Art Centre, Abernyte, Perth, Perthshire,
PH14 9SJ 🅿
☎ 01828 686642 or 01250 886381
ⓔ enquiries@oldchurchantiques.com
ⓦ www.oldchurchantiques.com
Est. 1999 *Stock size* Medium
Stock Clocks, general antiques, books
Open Mon–Sun 11am–5pm
Services Valuations, clock repairs

⌂ Scottish Antique and Art Centre
Contact Tracy Walsh
✉ Abernyte, Perthshire,

PH14 9SJ 🅿
☎ 01828 686401 📠 01828 686199
ⓔ elaine@scottish-antiques.com
ⓦ www.scottish-antiques.com
Est. 1999 *Stock size* Large
No. of dealers 130
Stock Georgian, Victorian, general antiques and collectables
Open Mon–Sun 10am–5pm
Services Valuations, restoration and repairs, shipping, coffee shop, food hall

AUCHTERARDER

⊞ Ian Burton Antique Clocks (NAWCC, AHS)
Contact Ian Burton
✉ The Antiques Gallery, 125 High Street, Auchterarder, Perthshire,
PH3 1AA 🅿
ⓜ 07785 114800
ⓔ ian@ianburton.com
ⓦ www.ianburton.com
Est. 1974 *Stock size* Large
Stock Antique clocks
Open Mon–Sat 9am–5pm

⊞ K Stanley & Son
Contact Chris Stanley
✉ 20b Townhead, Auchterarder, Perthshire,
PH3 1AH 🅿
☎ 01764 662252 📠 01764 662252
ⓜ 07958 777828
ⓔ ksantique@aol.com
Est. 1956 *Stock size* Medium
Stock General antiques
Open Mon–Sat 10am–5pm Sun noon–5pm

⊞ Times Past Antiques
Contact Andrew or Neil Brown
✉ Broadfold Farm, Auchterarder, Perthshire,
PH3 1DR 🅿
☎ 01764 663166 📠 01764 663166
Est. 1974 *Stock size* Large
Stock Stripped antique pine
Open Mon–Fri 8am–4.30pm Sat Sun 10am–3pm
Services Restoration, stripping, exporting

⊞ Ian Whitelaw Antiques (LAPADA)
Contact Ian Whitelaw
✉ The Loft & Craigrossie Store, Fews, Auchterarder, Perthshire,
PH3 1DG 🅿
☎ 01764 664781 📠 01764 664781
ⓔ ian@ianwhitelawantiques.co.uk

SCOTLAND
PERTH & KINROSS • BLAIRGOWRIE

W www.ianwhitelawantiques.co.uk
Est. 1974 *Stock size* Medium
Stock 18th–19thC furniture
Open Mon–Fri 9am–5pm Sat
10am–5pm or by appointment
Services Valuations, restoration

John Whitelaw & Sons (LAPADA)
Contact Alan Whitelaw
✉ 125 High Street, Auchterarder, Perthshire,
PH3 1AA
☎ 01764 662482 ✆ 01764 663577
M 07836 725558
✉ jwsantique@aol.com
W www.whitelawantiques.com
Est. 1959 *Stock size* Large
Stock General antiques, Georgian furniture
Open Mon–Sat 9am–5pm
Fairs NEC, LAPADA
Services Repairs, restoration

BLAIRGOWRIE

Roy Sim Antiques
Contact Roy Sim
✉ The Granary Warehouse, Lower Mill Street, Blairgowrie, Perthshire,
PH10 6AQ
☎ 01250 873860 ✆ 01250 873860
✉ roy.sim@lineone.net
Est. 1977 *Stock size* Large
Stock Antique furniture, decorative and collectable items, longcase clocks, wall and mantel clocks, copper, brassware
Open Mon–Sat 9am–5.30pm Sun 12.30–5pm

BRIDGE OF EARN

Imrie Antiques & Interiors (LAPADA)
Contact Ian Imrie
✉ Imrie House, Back Street, Bridge of Earn, Perth, Perthshire, PH2 9AE
☎ 01738 812784
Est. 1966 *Stock size* Medium
Stock General antiques
Open Mon–Fri 9am–5pm Sat 9am–1pm
Services Valuations, restoration and repairs

COMRIE

Comrie Antiques
Contact Sylvia Anderson
✉ 2 Commercial Lane,

Comrie, Crieff, Perthshire,
PH6 2DP
☎ 01764 679899/679015
Est. 1999 *Stock size* Small
Stock Period furniture
Open Mon–Sat 10am–5pm
Services Restoration

DUNKELD

Dunkeld Antiques (LAPADA)
Contact David Dytch
✉ Tay Terrace, Dunkeld, Perthshire,
PH8 0AQ
☎ 01350 728832 ✆ 01350 727008
M 07713 074932
✉ sales@dunkeldantiques.com
W www.dunkeldantiques.com
Est. 1986 *Stock size* Large
Stock General antiques, specializing in 18thC–19thC furniture
Open Mon–Sat 10am–5pm Sun noon–5pm

INCHTURE

Inchmartine Fine Art
Contact Paul Stephens
✉ Inchmartine House, Inchture, Perth, Perthshire,
PH14 9QQ
☎ 01828 686412 ✆ 01828 686748
M 07702 190128
✉ fineart@inchmartine.freeserve.co.uk
Est. 1997 *Stock size* Medium
Stock 19th–early 20thC Scottish paintings
Open Mon–Sat 9am–5.30pm
Fairs Buxton, Chester, Narworth, Scone
Services Valuations, cleaning and framing

Inchmartine Restorations
Contact Andrew Stephens
✉ Inchmartine House, Inchture, Perth, Perthshire,
PH14 9QQ
☎ 01828 686412 ✆ 01828 686748
✉ ir@toolbazaar.freeserve.co.uk
W www.toolbazaar.co.uk
Est. 1989 *Stock size* Medium
Stock 18th–19thC furniture
Open Mon–Sat 9am–5.30pm
Fairs Buxton, Gleneagles
Services Valuations and cabinet-making

Inchmartine Tool Bazaar
Contact Andrew Stephens
✉ Inchmartine House, Inchture, Perth, Perthshire,
PH14 9QQ
☎ 01828 686096 ✆ 01828 686748
✉ andrew@toolbazaar.freeserve.co.uk
W www.toolbazaar.co.uk
Est. 1991 *Stock size* Large
Stock Old cabinet-making and woodworking tools
Open Mon–Sat 9am–5.30pm
Fairs Buxton, Scone Palace, SECC Glasgow

C S Moreton Antiques
Contact Paul Stephens
✉ Inchmartine House, Inchture, Perthshire,
PH14 9QQ
☎ 01828 686412 ✆ 01828 686748
M 07702 190128
✉ moreton@inchmartine.freeserve.co.uk
Est. 1854 *Stock size* Medium
Stock Period furniture, Oriental rugs, paintings, objets d'art, old hand tools
Open Mon–Sat 9am–5.30pm
Fairs Buxton, Chester, Narworth, Scone
Services Valuations, restoration and shipping

KILLIN

Maureen H Gauld
Contact Maureen Gauld
✉ Craiglee Main Street, Killin, Perthshire,
FK21 8UN
☎ 01567 820475 ✆ 01567 820605
✉ killingallery@btopenworld.com
W www.killingallery,com
Est. 1973 *Stock size* Medium
Stock Silver, china, glass antiques
Open Mon–Sat 10am–5pm or by appointment

Killin Gallery
Contact J Gauld
✉ Craiglea Main Street, Killin, Perthshire,
FK21 8UN
☎ 01567 820475 ✆ 01567 820605
✉ killingallery@btopenworld.com
W www.killingallery.com
Est. 1994 *Stock size* Medium
Stock Furniture, paintings, etchings
Open Mon–Sat 10am–5pm or by appointment

SCOTLAND

410

MUTHILL

⊞ Upstairs-Downstairs
Contact Elizabeth Richardson
⊠ 18 Drummond Street, Muthill,
Crieff, Perthshire,
PH5 2AN 🅿
☎ 01764 681737
📱 07803 461465
Est. 1996 *Stock size* Small
Stock General antiques,
Victorian, Edwardian, Arts and
Crafts, Art Nouveau, small
furniture items, Continental
glass, golf paraphernalia
Open Mon–Sun 2–5.30pm or by
appointment

PERTH

⊞ Ainslie's Antiques
Contact Robert Ainslie
⊠ Unit 3, Gray Street, Perth,
Perthshire,
PH2 0JH 🅿
☎ 01738 636825
Est. 1959 *Stock size* Large
Stock General antiques including
Victorian and Edwardian
furniture
Trade only Yes
Open Mon–Fri 9am–5pm or by
appointment
Fairs Newark

⊞ Becca Gauldie Antiques & Scribe Books
Contact Becca Gauldie
⊠ The Old School, Glendoick,
Perth, Perthshire,
PH2 7NR 🅿
☎ 01738 860870
📧 becca@gauldie.freeserve.co.uk
Est. 1995 *Stock size* Medium
Stock Scottish country antiques,
large selection of Mauchlinware,
antiquarian and second-hand
books
Open By appoinment only
Fairs NEC, Earls Court, Caroline
Penman

⚲ Lindsay Burns & Co (SAA)
Contact Mr L Burns
⊠ 6 King Street, Perth,
Perthshire,
PH2 8JA 🅿
☎ 01738 633888 📠 01738 441322
📧 lindsayburns@btconnect.com
🌐 www.lburns.co.uk
Est. 1982
Open Mon–Fri 9am–5pm

Sat 9am–noon
Sales General antiques,
household effects bi-weekly
Thurs 10.30am, viewing day prior
to sale
Frequency Bi-weekly
Catalogues Yes

⊞ Design Interiors
Contact Margaret Blane
⊠ 50 South Street, Perth,
Perthshire,
PH2 8PD 🅿
☎ 01738 635360
📧 robert.blane@btconnect.com
Est. 1989 *Stock size* Medium
Stock General antiques and
collectables
Open Mon–Sat 10am–5.30pm
Services China restoration,
picture cleaning, framing

⊞ Alexander S Deuchar & Son
Contact A S Deuchar
⊠ 12 South Street, Perth,
Perthshire,
PH2 8PG 🅿
☎ 01738 626297
📱 07952 639901
Est. 1911 *Stock size* Medium
Stock General antiques
Open Mon–Sat 10am–5pm

⊞ Maurice Dodd Books (PBFA)
Contact Mr R McRoberts
⊠ 1 Burnside Park,
Pitcairnreen, Perth,
Perth & Kinross,
PH1 3BF 🅿
☎ 01738 583100
📧 doddrarebooks@btconnect.com
Est. 1946 *Stock size* Medium
Stock Antiquarian books
including topography, poetry,
the Lake District
Open By appointment only
Fairs Russell Hotel
Services Valuations

⚲ Loves Auction Rooms (SAA, SOFAA)
Contact Mrs E Reid
⊠ 52–54 Canal Street, Perth,
Perthshire,
PH2 8LF 🅿
☎ 01738 633337 📠 01738 629830
📧 enquiries@lovesauctions.co.uk
Est. 1869
Open Mon–Fri 9am–5pm
Sat 9am–noon
Sales Antiques quarterly,

household effects weekly
Frequency Weekly & quarterly
Catalogues Yes (quarterly sales
only)

⊞ Perth Antiques
Contact Robert Blane
⊠ 50 South Street, Perth,
Perthshire,
PH2 8PD 🅿
☎ 01738 440888
📱 07939 196750
📧 robert.blane@btconnect.com
Est. 1998 *Stock size* Large
Stock General antiques,
porcelain, Clarice Cliff, Belleek,
Morecroft, Art Deco pottery,
Monart glass, chintz, jewellery,
painting
Open Mon–Sat 10am–5pm

⊞ Whispers of the Past
Contact Laura Wilson
⊠ 15 George Street, Perth,
Perthshire,
PH1 5JY 🅿
☎ 01738 635472
Est. 1981 *Stock size* Medium
Stock Country antiques
Open Mon–Sat 9.30am–5pm
Jan–Mar closed Wed
Services Interior design

⊞ Yesterdays Today
Contact W MacGregor
⊠ 267 Old High Street, Perth,
Perthshire,
PH1 5QN 🅿
☎ 01738 443534
📱 07713 897793
📧 yesterdaystoday@talk21.com
Est. 1995 *Stock size* Medium
Stock General collectables, coins,
medals, glass, jewellery, silver,
Royal Doulton, Beswick
Open Mon–Sat 9am–5pm
Services Valuations

PITLOCHRY

⊞ Blair Antiques
Contact Duncan Huie
⊠ by Bruar Falls, by Pitlochry,
Perthshire,
PH18 5TW 🅿
☎ 01796 483264
📱 07711 669644
📧 adhuie@aol.com
🌐 www.blairantiques.co.uk
Est. 1976 *Stock size* Medium
Stock General antiques, fine art
Open Mon–Fri 9.30am–5pm
Services Valuations

RAIT

⊞ Edward Bowry
Contact Edward Bowry
✉ Rait Village Antique Centre, Rait, Perth, Perthshire, PH2 7RT ℗
☎ 01821 670318
Est. 1990 *Stock size* Medium
Stock Furniture, old woodworking tools, sporting items
Open By appontment
Services Valuations, restoration and repairs

⊞ Fair Finds Antiques
Contact Lynda Templeman
✉ Rait Village Antiques Centre, Rait, Perth, Perthshire, PH2 7RT ℗
☎ 01821 670379 ℮ 01821 670379
⊕ 07720 394750
⊕ lynda.templeman@btopenworld.com
Est. 1969 *Stock size* Large
Stock Furniture, Wemyss ware, general antiques
Open Mon–Sat 10am–5pm
Sun noon–4.30pm

⊞ Gordon Loraine Antiques
Contact Liane or Gordon Loraine
✉ The Sawmill, Rait Village Antiques Centre, Rait, Perth, Perthshire, PH2 7RT ℗
☎ 01821 670760 ℮ 01821 670760
⊕ 07798 550017
⊕ gordonloraine@supanet.com
Est. 1991 *Stock size* Medium
Stock Good-quality Georgian–Victorian furniture, decorative items, collectables, treen, mauchline ware
Open Mon–Sat 10am–5pm
Sun Sept–Mar noon–4pm

⌂ Rait Village Antiques Centre
Contact Lynda Templeman
✉ Rait, Perth, Perthshire, PH2 7RT ℗
☎ 01821 670379 ℮ 01821 670379
⊕ 07720 394750
⊕ lynda.templeman@btopenworld.com
Est. 1985 *Stock size* Large
No. of dealers 15
Stock Furniture, silver, pottery, porcelain, Wemyss ware, rugs, paintings, jewellery, garden statuary, collectables

Open Mon–Sat 10am–5pm
Sun noon–4.30pm
Services Valuations, restoration, coffee shop

SCONE

⋏ Iain M Smith Auctioneers & Valuers
Contact Iain Smith
✉ Unit 18, Perth Airport Business Park, Scone, Perth, Perthshire, PH2 6NP ℗
☎ 01738 551110 ℮ 01738 551110
⊕ 07836 770664
⊕ imsauctions@beeb.net
⊕ www.iainmsmith.co.uk
Est. 1994
Open Mon–Fri 9am–5pm
Sat 10am–1pm
Sales General antiques, modern furniture
Frequency Weekly
Catalogues No

STANLEY

⊞ Coach House Antiques Ltd (PADA)
Contact John Walker
✉ Charleston, Stanley, Perthshire, PH1 4PN ℗
☎ 01738 828627
⊕ 07710 122244
⊕ johnwalkerantiques@btopenworld.com
Est. 1970 *Stock size* Medium
Stock Period furniture, decorative items, garden items
Open By appointment
Services Valuations, restoration, shipping

RENFREWSHIRE

GREENOCK

⋏ McTear's (SAA, IAA)
Contact Brian Clements
✉ 22 Forsyth Street, Greenock, Renfrewshire, PA16 8DX ℗
☎ 01475 730343 ℮ 01475 726436
⊕ 07767 376642
⊕ enquiries@mctears.co.uk
⊕ www.mctears.co.uk
Est. 1842
Open Mon–Fri 9am–5pm
Sales Monthly sale of antiques, art, weekly sale Victoriana, 3 annual sales of rare whisky
Catalogues Yes

KILBARCHAN

⊞ Gardners 'The Antique Shop' (LAPADA)
Contact George, Robert or David Gardner
✉ Wardend House, Kibbleston Road, Kilbarchan, Johnstone, Renfrewshire, PA10 2PN ℗
☎ 01505 702292 ℮ 01505 702292
⊕ gardantiques@colloquium.co.uk
Est. 1950 *Stock size* Large
Stock General antiques, Georgian–1930s, furniture, porcelain, silver, pictures
Open Mon–Fri 9am–6pm
Sat 10am–5pm
Services Valuations

⊞ McQuade Antiques
Contact Walter McQuade
✉ 7 Shuttle Street, Kilbarchan, Johnstone, Renfrewshire, PA10 2JN ℗
☎ 01505 704249
⊕ 07860 729598
Est. 1967 *Stock size* Medium
Stock General antiques
Open Mon–Fri 10am–5.30pm
Sun 2–5.30pm
Fairs Newark

KILMALCOLM

⊞ Kilmalcolm Antiques
Contact Hilary McLean
✉ Stewart Place, Bridge of Weir Road, Kilmalcolm, Renfrewshire, PA13 4AF ℗
☎ 01505 873149 ℮ 01505 873149
⊕ 07850 126150
Est. 1974 *Stock size* Large
Stock General antiques, Scottish paintings, pottery, Georgian–Victorian furniture
Open Mon–Sat 10am–1pm
2.30–5.30pm
Fairs Hopeton House, Margam

PAISLEY

⊞ Corrigan Antiques
Contact Mr John Corrigan
✉ 23 High Calside, Paisley, Renfrewshire, PA2 6BY ℗
☎ 0141 889 6653 ℮ 0141 848 9700
⊕ 07802 631110
⊕ corriganantiques@talk21.com
Est. 1939 *Stock size* Small
Stock Decorative antiques
Open By appointment only

SCOTTISH BORDERS

COLDSTREAM

⊞ Fraser Antiques
Contact R Fleming
⊠ 65 High Street, Coldstream,
Scottish Borders,
TD12 4DL ⓟ
☎ 01890 882450 ❶ 01890 882451
✉ m13border@aol.com
Est. 1968 *Stock size* Medium
Stock General antiques
Open Tues–Sat 10am–1pm 2–5pm
Services Valuations, restoration

GALASHIELS

⋏ Hall's Auctioneers
Contact Michael Hall
⊠ Ladhope Vale House,
Ladhope Vale, Galashiels,
Scottish Borders,
TD1 1BT ⓟ
☎ 01896 754477 ❶ 01896 754477
Est. 1995
Open Mon–Fri 9am–5pm Sat
9am–noon or by appointment
Sales General antiques and
collectables
Frequency Monthly
Catalogues Yes

INNERLEITHEN

⊞ The Glory Hole
Contact Paul MacNaughton
⊠ 29 High Street, Innerleithen,
Scottish Borders,
EH44 6HA ⓟ
☎ 01896 831306
⓿ 07710 771055
Est. 1996 *Stock size* Medium
Stock General antiques,
specializing in old printing items,
coins
Open Mon–Fri 11am–5pm
closed Tues
Fairs Border fairs

⊞ Keepsakes
Contact Mrs M Maxwell
⊠ 96 High Street,
Innerleithen,
Scottish Borders,
EH44 6HF ⓟ
☎ 01896 831369
⓿ 07773 477291
✉ rmaxwells@keepsakes.
freeserve.co.uk
ⓦ www.website.lineone.
net/~rmaxwell
Est. 1979 *Stock size* Medium

Stock General antiques, dolls,
toys, Art Deco
Open Mon Thurs–Sat
11am–4.30pm
Fairs Ingliston

**⊞ The Last Century
Antiques**
Contact Keith or Gill Miller
⊠ 34 High Street, Innerleithen,
Scottish Borders,
EH44 6HF ⓟ
☎ 01896 831759
✉ last.century@btinternet.com
ⓦ www.lastcenturybooks.com
Est. 1989 *Stock size* Medium
Stock Mostly antiquarian and
out-of-print books, cutlery, glass
Open Mon–Sat 11am–5pm
Fairs Inglestone
Services Valuations

JEDBURGH

**⊞ R & M Turner (Antiques
& Fine Art) Ltd (LAPADA)**
Contact Mr R J Turner or Loraine
⊠ 34–36 High Street, Jedburgh,
Roxburghshire,
TD8 6AG ⓟ
☎ 01835 863445 ❶ 01835 863349
✉ turners.antiques@virgin.net
Est. 1966 *Stock size* Large
Stock Fine art, clocks, furniture,
jewellery, bric-a-brac, porcelain,
reproductions
Open Mon–Fri 9.30am–5.30pm
Sat 10am–5pm
Services Valuations, restoration,
shipping

MELROSE

**⊞ Birch House Antiques at
Michael Vee Design**
Contact Michael Vee
⊠ Birch House, High Street,
Melrose, Scottish Borders,
TD6 9PA ⓟ
☎ 01896 822116 ❶ 01896 682320
⓿ 07761 913349
✉ michael.vee@btinternet.com
ⓦ www.michaelveedesign.com
Est. 1990 *Stock size* Medium
Stock French decorative antiques,
mirrors, garden statuary, urns,
English furniture, lighting
Open Mon–Fri 9am–5pm Sat
9am–3pm

**⊞ Border Country
Furniture**
Contact Denni or Christine Reid

⊠ 2 Palma Place, Melrose,
Scottish Borders,
TD6 9PR ⓟ
☎ 01896 823700 ❶ 01896 823700
⓿ 07929 234752
Est. 1974 *Stock size* Large
Stock General antiques, hand-
made furniture
Open Mon–Sat 10am–5pm
Services Made-to-measure tables
and fireplaces from reclaimed
timbers

⋏ John Swan Ltd
Contact Frank Forrest
⊠ Newtown St Boswells,
Melrose, Scottish Borders,
TD6 0PD ⓟ
☎ 01835 822214 ❶ 01835 823860
✉ stboswells@johnswan.demon.co.uk
Est. 1899
Open Mon–Fri 9am–5pm
Sales General antiques and
house clearance
Catalogues Yes

SHETLAND

LUNNANESS

⊞ Antiques & Collectables
Contact Frank Watt
⊠ Outrabister House,
Lunnaness, Vidlin,
Shetland,
ZE2 9QF ⓟ
☎ 01806 577206 ❶ 01806 577206
⓿ 07884 250336
✉ frank.watt@ntlworld.com
Est. 1994 *Stock size* Large
Stock General antiques and
collectables
Open By appointment
Services Valuations, book search

SOUTH AYRSHIRE

GIRVAN

⊞ Ainslie Books
Contact Mr G Clark
⊠ 1 Glendoune Street, Girvan,
South Ayrshire,
KA26 0AA ⓟ
☎ 01465 715453 ❶ 01465 715453
✉ sales@ainsliebooks.co.uk
ⓦ www.ainsliebooks.co.uk
Est. 1996 *Stock size* Medium
Stock Rare and second-hand
books, specializing in Scottish
and Ayrshire topics
Open Mon–Sat 10am–5pm
Services Book search

SCOTLAND
SOUTH AYRSHIRE • PRESTWICK

⊞ **Clamjamfrey**
Contact Ingrid Powell
✉ 26 Hamilton Street,
Girvan,
South Ayrshire,
KA26 9EY ℗
☎ 01465 715621
✉ clamjam@tiscali.co.uk
ⓦ www.clamjamfrey.com
Est. 1997 *Stock size* Medium
Stock General antiques, Denby
and Poole pottery, 20thC
ceramics, metalware
Open Mon–Sat 10am–5pm
Fairs Edinburgh, Swinderby
Services Valuations

PRESTWICK

⊞ **Crossroads Antiques**
Contact Mr T O'Keeffe
✉ 7 The Cross,
Prestwick,
South Ayrshire,
KA9 1AJ ℗
☎ 01292 474004
Est. 1989 *Stock size* Medium
Stock General antiques, furniture,
china, Scottish paintings
Open Mon–Sat 10.30am–5pm

TROON

⊞ **Tantalus Antiques
(BWCG)**
Contact Iain Sutherland
✉ 79 Templehill, Troon,
South Ayrshire,
KA10 6BQ ℗
☎ 01292 315999
✉ idsantique@aol.com
ⓦ www.tantalusantiques.com
Est. 1997 *Stock size* Medium
Stock General antiques,
furniture, jewellery, clocks,
watches, pictures, paintings,
silverware, ornaments, curios
Open Tues–Sat 10am–5pm or by
appointment
Services Full consultation and
restoration service

SOUTH LANARKSHIRE

HAMILTON

⋏ **L S Smellie & Sons Ltd
(SAA)**
Contact Mr A Smellie
✉ Lower Auchingramont Road,
Hamilton, South Lanarkshire,
ML3 6HW ℗
☎ 01698 282007 ✆ 01698 207473

✉ hamiltonauction@btconnect.com
ⓦ www.hamiltonauctionmarket.co.uk
Est. 1874
Open Mon–Fri 8am–5pm
Sales Weekly general antiques
sale Mon
Catalogues Yes

STRATHAVEN

⊞ **Avondale Antique
Jewellers**
Contact Mrs M Hardie
✉ Unit 3, 11a Green Street,
Strathaven,
South Lanarkshire,
ML10 6AW ℗
☎ 01357 529854
Est. 1997 *Stock size* Large
Stock Antique jewellery
Open Mon–Sat 10.30am–4pm
closed Wed
Fairs Kelvin Hall, Glasgow
Services Valuations, repairs,
restoration of jewellery

WISTON

⊞ **Sunnyside Antiques**
Contact Mark Attwood
✉ Castledykes,
Wiston, Biggar,
South Lanarkshire,
ML12 6HT ℗
☎ 01899 850552 ✆ 01899 850551
⊕ 07798 640629
✉ info@periodantiques.net
ⓦ www.periodantiques.net
Est. 1995 *Stock size* Medium
Stock 17th–19thC period
furniture, longcase clocks
Open Mon–Sun 9am–5pm
Fairs Newark
Services Restoration, shipping

STIRLING

BALTRON

⊞ **Amphora Galleries
Antiques**
Contact Laurie Ruglen,
Bill Robinson
✉ 18 Buchanan Street,
Baltron,
Stirling,
G63 0TT ℗
☎ 01360 440329
Est. 1962 *Stock size* Small
Stock Georgian, Victorian
furniture, porcelain, general
antiques
Open By appointment

BRIDGE OF ALLAN

⊞ **Bridge of Allan Books
(PBFA)**
Contact Andrew Jennings
✉ 2 Henderson Street,
Bridge of Allan, Stirling,
FK9 4HT ℗
☎ 01786 834483 ✆ 01786 834483
✉ books@bridgeofallenbooks.com
ⓦ www.bridgeofallenbooks.com
Est. 1985 *Stock size* Medium
Stock Antiquarian, rare and
second-hand books, prints,
specializing in Scottish and field
sports
Open Mon–Sat 10am–5.30pm
Services Free book search

DOUNE

⊞ **Amphora Galleries
Antiques**
Contact Laurie Ruglen,
Bill Robinson
✉ Scottish Antiques and Arts
Centre, Doune, Stirling,
FK16 6HG ℗
☎ 01786 841203
Est. 2000 *Stock size* Small
Stock Georgian, Victorian
furniture, porcelain, general
antiques
Open Mon–Sun 10am–5pm

⌂ **Scottish Antique and
Arts Centre**
Contact Anne Meikle
✉ Doune,
Stirling,
FK16 6HG ℗
☎ 01786 841203 ✆ 01786 842561
ⓦ www.scottish-antiques.com
Est. 1974 *Stock size* Large
No. of dealers 200
Stock Georgian–Victorian,
general antiques and collectables
Open Mon–Sun 10am–5pm
Services Shipping, coffee shop

FALKIRK

⋏ **Auction Rooms (NAVA)**
Contact Robert Penman
✉ Central Auction Hall,
Bankside, Falkirk,
Stirling,
FK2 7XF ℗
☎ 01324 623000 ✆ 01324 630343
✉ gavel@auctionroomsfalkirk.co.uk
ⓦ www.auctionroomsfalkirk.co.uk
Est. 1989
Open Mon Thurs Fri 9am–5pm

414

Tues 8am–8pm Wed 8am–6pm
Sat 9am–noon
Sales General antiques sales
every Wed evening
Catalogues Yes

GARGUNNOCK

⊞ **Country Home Antiques**
Contact P Christie
✉ Mains Farm,
Gargunnock, Stirling,
FK8 3AY 🅿
☎ 01786 860509 🔱 01786 860509
🔂 gargunnock@aol.com or
antiquestrader@aol.com
🔳 www.scotlandroom.com
Est. 1979 *Stock size* Large
Stock General antiques
Open Mon–Fri 9am–5pm Sat
10am–5pm Sun 12.30–5pm
Services Stripping, waxing,
upholstery, French polishing, full
restoration, shipping

STIRLING

⊞ **Abbey Antiques**
Contact Stuart Campbell
✉ 4 Friars Street, Stirling,
FK8 1HA 🅿
☎ 01786 447840
🔳 07801 692126

Est. 1979 *Stock size* Small
Stock Jewellery, silver, militaria,
paintings, furniture, bric-a-brac
Open Mon–Sat 9am–5pm
Services Valuations

⊞ **Stewart Sales Rooms**
Contact Andrew Penman
✉ 3-6 Kildean Market,
Drip Road, Stirling,
FK9 4AA 🅿
☎ 01786 473414
🔂 thisandthat1@btconnect.com
Est. 1969 *Stock size* Large
Stock General antiques
Open Mon–Sat 10am–5.30pm
Sun 7.30am–3.30pm
Services Valuations, house
clearances

STRATHBLANE

⊞ **What Nots Antiques**
Contact Frank Bruce
✉ 16 Milngavie Road,
Strathblane, Stirling,
G63 9EH 🅿
☎ 01360 770310
Est. 1969 *Stock size* Medium
Stock General antiques, clocks
Open Mon–Sun 9.30am–5pm or
by appointment
Services Landscape painting

WEST LOTHIAN

BO'NESS

🔨 **D J Manning Auctioneers,
Valuers & Appraisers (NAVA)**
Contact Andrew Morgan
✉ Bridgeness Road, Carriden,
Bo'ness, West Lothian,
EH51 9SF 🅿
☎ 01506 827693 🔱 01506 826495
🔂 info@djmanning.co.uk
🔳 www.djmanning.co.uk
Est. 1969
Open Mon–Fri 9am–5pm
Sales Books, general antiques,
collectables
Frequency Quarterly
Catalogues Yes

LINLITHGOW

⊞ **County Antiques**
Contact Mrs Flynn
✉ 30 High Street, Linlithgow,
West Lothian, EH49 7AE 🅿
☎ 01506 671201
Est. 1992 *Stock size* Medium
Stock General antiques, jewellery
Open Mon–Sat 10am–5pm
Fairs Edinburgh
Services Valuations and jewellery
repairs

CHANNEL ISLANDS

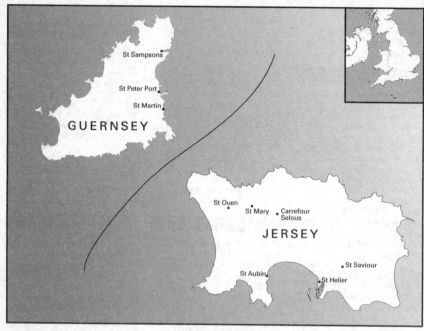

GUERNSEY

ST PETER PORT

⊞ Stephen Andrews Gallery
Contact Stephen Andrews
✉ 5 College Terrace,
The Grange, St Peter Port,
Guernsey,
GY1 2PX 🅿
☎ 01481 710380
Est. 1984 *Stock size* Large
Stock Pottery, porcelain,
furniture, silver
Open Mon–Sat 9.30am–5pm
Fairs Guernsey Antiques Fair

⊞ Channel Islands Galleries Ltd
Contact Geoffrey Gavey
✉ Trinity Square Centre,
Trinity Square,
St Peter Port,
Guernsey,
GY1 ILX 🅿
☎ 01481 723247/247337
✆ 01481 714669
📧 geoff.gavey@cigalleries.f9.co.uk
🌐 www.cigalleries.f9.co.uk
Est. 1970 *Stock size* Medium
Stock Channel Island antique

maps, prints, watercolours,
oil paintings, out-of-print books,
bank notes, coins
Open Mon–Fri 10am–5pm
Sat 10am–1pm
Services Valuations, restoration,
conservation, picture framing

⊞ The Collectors Centre
Contact Andrew Rundle
✉ 1 Sausmarez Street,
St Peter Port, Guernsey,
GY1 2PT 🅿
☎ 01481 725209
Est. 1985 *Stock size* Medium
Stock Antique prints, engravings,
old postcards, coins, bank notes,
memorabilia, stamps
Open Mon–Sat 10.30am–6pm
Services Valuations for
collectables, mail-order, postal
auctions, free catalogue

⊞ W De La Rue Antiques
Contact William de La Rue
✉ 29 Mill Street, St Peter Port,
Guernsey,
GY1 1HG
☎ 01481 723177
Est. 1975 *Stock size* Medium
Stock General antiques,
collectors' items

Open Mon–Sat 10am–12.30pm
2–4pm closed Thurs pm
Services Valuations, buying

⊞ Ann Drury Antiques
Contact Ann Drury
✉ 1 Mansell Street, St Peter Port,
Guernsey,
GY1 1HP
☎ 01481 716193
📱 07781 104304
Est. 1969 *Stock size* Large
Stock 18th–20thC furniture and
decorative antiques
Open Mon–Sat 10am–noon
2–4pm closed Thurs
Fairs Guernsey Antiques Fair
Services Valuations

⊞ Mahogany
Contact Angela Edwards
✉ 7 Mansell Street,
St Peter Port,
Guernsey,
GY1 1HP
☎ 01481 727574 ✆ 01481 727574
Est. 1980 *Stock size* Large
Stock General antiques,
collectables
Open Mon–Sat 10am–12.30pm
2–4pm Thurs closed pm
Fairs Guernsey Antiques Fair

⊞ N St J Paint and Sons Ltd (NAG)
Contact Michael or Paul Paint
⊠ 26 Le Pollet,
St Peter Port,
Guernsey,
GY1 1WQ
☎ 01481 722229 ☏ 01481 710241
✉ paint@guernsey.net
Est. 1947 *Stock size* Large
Stock General antiques, jewellery, silver, objets d'art
Open Mon–Fri 8.45am–5.30pm
Sat 8.45am–5pm
Services Valuations, restoration and repairs (goldsmiths and silversmiths)

⊞ Parasol Antiques
Contact Marianne Barwick
⊠ 2 Contree Mansell,
St Peter Port,
Guernsey,
GY1 1HR 🅿
☎ 01481 710780 ☏ 01481 710780
📱 07781 118715
Est. 1993 *Stock size* Medium
Stock Jewellery, silver, furniture, copper, brass, pictures
Open Mon–Sat 10am–5pm
Thurs 10am–1pm
Fairs Guernsey Antiques Fair
Services Valuations, restoration

ST SAMPSONS

⊞ The Curiosity Shop
Contact Mike Vermeulen
⊠ Commercial Road,
St Sampsons, Guernsey,
GY2 4QP 🅿
☎ 01481 245324
Est. 1978 *Stock size* Medium
Stock General small antiques, collectables, second-hand books
Open Mon–Sat 10am–2pm
closed Thurs
Fairs Guernsey Antiques Fair
Services Framing

⊞ Ray & Scott Ltd (NAG)
Contact M Search
⊠ The Bridge, St Sampsons,
Guernsey,
GY2 4QN 🅿
☎ 01481 244610 ☏ 01481 247843
✉ ray.scott@cwgsy.net
Est. 1962 *Stock size* Large
Stock Fine jewellery, clocks, silver, second-hand watches
Open Mon–Sat 9am–5pm
Fairs Guernsey Antiques Fair, Beau Sejours Fair

Services Valuations, restoration of jewellery, antique clocks, gold and silversmiths

JERSEY

CARREFOUR SELOUS

⊞ David Hick Antiques
Contact David Hick
⊠ Alexandra House,
Carrefour Selous, St Lawrence,
Jersey,
JE3 1GL 🅿
☎ 01534 865965 ☏ 01534 865448
✉ hickantiques@localdial.com
Est. 1974 *Stock size* Large
Stock Furniture, silver, porcelain
Open Wed Fri Sat 9.30am–5pm

ST HELIER

➴ Bonhams
⊠ 39 Don Street, St Helier,
Jersey,
JE2 4TR
☎ 01534 722441 ☏ 01534 759354
✉ jersey@bonhams.com
🌐 www.bonhams.com
Est. 1793
Open Mon–Fri 9am–5pm
Sales Regional office. Regular sales held in London and in our salerooms across the country. The Channel Island Sale is held annually. Free auction valuations; insurance and probate valuations
Catalogues Yes

⊞ Brown's Times Past Antiques
Contact Mick Brown
⊠ La Haie Flearie,
La Rue De Villot, St Martin,
Jersey,
JE3 6BN 🅿
☎ 01534 737090/735264
Est. 1984 *Stock size* Medium
Stock Georgian–Edwardian furniture, ceramics, 19thC pottery and glass
Open Mon–Sat 10am–5pm or by appointment
Services Valuations

⊞ John Cooper Antiques
Contact John Cooper
⊠ 16 Central Market, St Helier,
Jersey,
JE2 4WL
☎ 01534 723600
Est. 1982 *Stock size* Medium
Stock General, mostly small items

including jewellery
Open Mon–Sat 9am–5.30pm
Thurs half day

⊞ David Hick Antiques
Contact David Hick
⊠ 45 Halkett Place, St Helier,
Jersey,
JE2 4WQ 🅿
☎ 01534 721162 ☏ 01534 721162
✉ hickantiques@localdial.com
Est. 1974 *Stock size* Large
Stock Furniture, silver, porcelain
Open Mon–Sat 10am–5pm

⊞ Jersey Coin Company
Contact V or S Dougan
⊠ 26 Halkett Street,
St Helier,
Jersey,
JE2 4WJ
☎ 01534 725743 ☏ 01534 509094
Est. 1965 *Stock size* Medium
Stock Antique coins, bank notes, medals, weapons, militaria books
Open Mon–Sat 9am–5pm
Services Coin valuations

⊞ Peter Le Vesconte Collectables
Contact Peter Le Vesconte
⊠ 62 Stopford Road,
St Helier,
Jersey,
JE2 4LZ 🅿
☎ 01534 732481 ☏ 01534 732481
📱 07797 826292
✉ plvcollectables@jerseymail.co.uk
Est. 1981 *Stock size* Large
Stock Dinky and Corgi toys, mint and boxed toys, militaria (especially WWII), new collectors' toys
Open Mon–Sat 10am–1pm
closed Wed
Fairs Jersey Toy and Phone Card Collectors Fair
Services Toy valuations

⊞ A & R Ritchie
Contact A or R Ritchie
⊠ 7 Duhamel Place,
St Helier,
Jersey,
JE2 4TP 🅿
☎ 01534 873805
Est. 1973 *Stock size* Medium
Stock Collectables, brass, china, glass, toys, silver, jewellery, scent bottles, militaria
Open Mon–Sat 10am–5pm
Services Restoration – militaria and ivory, jewellery

417

CHANNEL ISLANDS
JERSEY • ST MARY

⊞ **Robert's Antiques**
Contact Robert Michieli
⊠ 14 York Street,
St Helier,
Jersey,
JE2 3RQ 🅿
☎ 01534 509071
Ⓜ 07798 876553
Est. 1979 *Stock size* Medium
Stock English silver, porcelain,
jewellery, glass, clocks
Open Mon–Sat 9am–5.30pm or
by appointment
Services Valuations

⊞ **Thomson's Antiques**
Contact Ray or Chris Thomson
⊠ 60 Kensington Place,
St Helier,
Jersey,
JE2 3PA
☎ 01534 723673
Ⓕ 01534 723673
Ⓜ 07797 766806
Est. 1967 *Stock size* Large
Stock General antiques,
furniture
Open Mon–Sat 10am–5pm

⊞ **Thomson's Antiques**
Contact Ray or Chris Thomson
⊠ 10 Waterloo Street, St Helier,
Jersey,
JE2 4WT 🅿
☎ 01534 618673
Ⓜ 07797 826414
Est. 1967 *Stock size* Large
Stock Collectors' items, furniture,
clocks, silver, barometers
Open Mon–Sat 10am–5pm

ST MARY

⊞ **Country House and
Cottage Antiques**
Contact Sarah Johnson
⊠ Rue Esboeufs, St Mary, Jersey,
JE3 3EQ 🅿
☎ 01534 862547
Est. 1984 *Stock size* Large
Stock Georgian–Edwardian, oak,
pine and mahogany furniture,
china, glass, ceramics, silver
Open Mon–Fri 10am–4pm
Sat 9am–1pm
Fairs St Mary's Fair
Services Valuations

ST SAVIOUR

⊞ **Pine for Pine Antiques**
Contact Mrs Brenda Clyde Smith
⊠ Chateau Clairval,
St Saviour,
Jersey,
JE2 7HN 🅿
☎ 01534 737173/724748
Ⓕ 01534 618384
Est. 1974 *Stock size* Medium
Stock Georgian–Edwardian pine
furniture
Open Mon–Fri 10am–4pm
Sat 10am–2pm

TRINITY

⊞ **Park Antiques**
Contact P Cowan
⊠ Trinity, Jersey,
JE3 5HB
☎ 01534 280784
Ⓔ park@itl.net
Est. 1969 *Stock size* Large
Stock English and Continental
furniture
Open Only by appointment

NORTHERN IRELAND

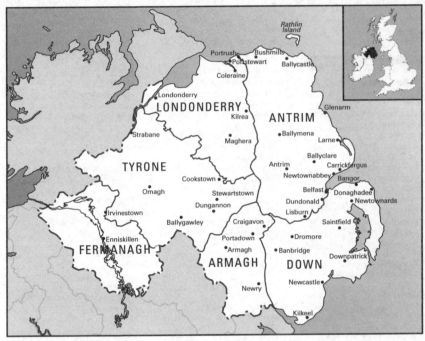

CO ANTRIM

AHOGHILL

⊞ **Once Upon a Time Antiques**
Contact Sean or Ronan McLaughlin
✉ The Old Mill, 2 Parkfield Road, Ahoghill, Co Antrim, BT42 2QF ℗
☎ 028 2587 1244 ✆ 028 2587 1244
📱 07703 360447
✉ ronananrk@aol.com
Est. 1973 *Stock size* Large
Stock Jewellery, furniture, general antiques
Open Mon–Sat 10am–5.30pm
Services Valuations, restoration, coffee shop

ANTRIM

⊞ **David Wolfenden Antiques (LAPADA, IADA)**
Contact David Wolfenden
✉ 219 Lisnevenagh Road, Antrim, BT41 2JT ℗
☎ 028 9442 9498 ✆ 028 9442 9498
📱 07768 128800
✉ antiquewolfirl@aol.com
🌐 www.davidwolfendenantiques.com

Est. 1984 *Stock size* Large
Stock Furniture, general antiques
Open Mon–Sat 10am–6pm
Services Valuations, restoration

BALLINDERRY

⊞ **Ballinderry Antiques**
Contact Mr W Mills
✉ 2 Lower Ballinderry Road, Ballinderry, Upper Lisburn, Co Antrim, BT28 2EP ℗
☎ 028 9265 1046 ✆ 028 9265 1580
🌐 www.ballinderryantiques.com
Est. 1959 *Stock size* Large
Stock Antique furniture, silver
Open Mon–Sat 10am–5.30pm
Fairs Newark
Services Valuations

BALLYCASTLE

⚒ **P J Mcilroy & Son**
Contact Mr Sean Mcilroy FNAEA
✉ 13 Ann Street, Ballycastle, Co Antrim, BT54 6AA ℗
☎ 028 2076 2353 ✆ 028 2076 2126
✉ leo@pjmcilroy.freeserve.co.uk
🌐 www.pjmcilroy.com

Est. 1967
Open Mon–Fri 9am–5.30pm
Sat 10am–12.30pm
Sales General antiques, paintings
Frequency Quarterly
Catalogues Yes

BALLYMENA

⊞ **Angela's Antiques**
Contact Angela McClelland
✉ 75 Wellington Street, Ballymena, Co Antrim, BT43 6AD ℗
☎ 028 2564 1999
Est. 1993 *Stock size* Large
Stock Porcelain, jewellery, furniture, general antiques
Open Mon–Sat 9.30am–5pm

BALLYMONEY

⚒ **McAfee Auctions (IAVI)**
Contact Mr Gerry McAfee
✉ 51 Main Street, Ballymoney, Co Antrim, BT53 6AN ℗
☎ 028 2766 7676 ✆ 028 2766 7666
Est. 1992
Open Mon–Fri 9am–5.30pm
Sat 9.30am–12.30pm

Sales Monthly sales of general antiques. Quarterly specialist Irish art sales
Catalogues Yes

BELFAST

⌂ Archives Antique Centre
Contact Laurence Johnston
✉ 88 Donegal Passage, Belfast, Co Antrim,
BT1 1BX 🅿
☎ 028 9023 2383
Est. 1999 *Stock size* Large
No. of dealers 4
Stock General antiques, collectables, lighting, silver, pub memorabilia
Open Mon–Sat 10.30am–5pm
Services Valuations, brass, and copper restoration

⊞ The Bell Gallery
Contact Nelson Bell
✉ 13 Adelaide Park, Belfast, Co Antrim,
BT9 6FX 🅿
☎ 028 9066 2998 📠 028 9038 1524
📧 bellgallery@btinternet.com
🌐 www.bellgallery.com
Est. 1964 *Stock size* Small
Stock Irish art and contemporary Irish artists, prints, silver, bog oak jewellery, Irish books
Open Mon–Fri 9am–5pm
Services Valuations

⋋ Bloomfield Auctions
Contact Mr George Gribben
✉ 288 Beersbridge Road, Belfast, Co Antrim,
BT5 1DX 🅿
☎ 028 9045 6404
🌐 www.bloomfieldauctions.co.uk
Est. 1991
Open Mon–Fri 10am–5pm
Sales Antiques, fine art, viewing Mon 10am–7pm Tues 10am–6pm
Frequency Every Tues at 6.30pm
Catalogues No

⊞ Bookfinders
Contact Miss Mary Denver
✉ 47 University Road, Belfast, Co Antrim,
BT7 1ND 🅿
☎ 028 9032 8269
Est. 1985 *Stock size* Large
Stock Antiquarian, rare and second-hand books
Open Mon–Sat 10am–5.30pm
Services Book search

⊞ John Carroll Antiques
Contact Vivienne Jackson
✉ Phoenix Gallery, 82 Donegal Pass, Belfast, Co Antrim,
BT7 1BX 🅿
☎ 028 9023 8246
Est. 2000 *Stock size* Large
Stock General antiques, art, 18th–19thC furniture
Open Mon–Fri 10am–5pm and by appointment

⊞ Cellar Antiques
Contact Jonathan Megaw
✉ Belfast Castle, Antrim Road, Belfast, Co Antrim,
BT15 5GR 🅿
☎ 028 9077 6925 ext 31
📠 07977 327788
Est. 1984 *Stock size* Medium
Stock Jewellery, general antiques, collectables
Open Mon–Sat noon–10pm Sun noon–5pm
Services Valuations, restoration and jewellery repairs

⊞ The Collector
Contact William Seawright
✉ 42 Rosscoole Park, Belfast, Co Antrim,
BT14 8JX
☎ 028 9071 0115
📧 billyseawright@ukonline.co.uk
Est. 1964 *Stock size* Large
Stock Antique coins, medals, cigarette cards, postcards, bank notes
Open By appointment and at fairs
Fairs All major fairs in Dublin and Belfast
Services Valuations

⊞ Gormley's Fine Art
Contact Mr Oliver Gormley
✉ 251 Lisburn Road, Belfast, Co Antrim,
BT9 7EN 🅿
☎ 028 9066 3313 📠 028 8225 2797
📧 oliver@gormleys.ie
🌐 www.gormleys.ie
Est. 1989 *Stock size* Large
Stock Contemporary and period oils, watercolours, scupltures and drawings
Open Mon–Sat 9.30am–5.30pm Thurs to 8pm
Fairs Newark
Services Gormley's Fine Art can be viewed in varous locations in Ireland; call for current locations. Valuations

⋋ Morgan's Auctions
Contact Mr Robin Hogg or Fred Adams
✉ 6 Duncrue Crescent, Duncrue Road, Belfast, Co Antrim,
BT3 9BW 🅿
☎ 028 9077 1552 📠 028 9077 4503
Est. 1985
Open Mon–Fri 9am–5pm
Sales General household and antique sale every Tues 11am, viewing Mon 9am–5pm and on the morning of the sale
Catalogues No

⊞ Oakland Antiques
Contact Donald McCluskey
✉ 135 Donegal Pass, Belfast, Co Antrim,
BT7 1DS 🅿
☎ 028 9023 0176 📠 028 9024 8144
📠 07831 176438
📧 sales@oaklandni.com
🌐 www.oaklandni.com
Est. 1975 *Stock size* Large
Stock Georgian–Edwardian furniture, silver, clocks, glass, bronze, spelter, marble, English and Oriental porcelain, oil paintings, watercolours, longcase clocks
Open Mon–Sat 10am–5.30pm
Fairs Ulster Antique and Fine Art Fair
Services Deliveries to anywhere in Northern Ireland

⊞ Past & Present
Contact Trevor or Frances McNally
✉ 58–60 Donegal Pass, Belfast, Co Antrim,
BT7 1BU 🅿
☎ 028 9033 3137 📠 028 9033 3137
Est. 1985 *Stock size* Medium
Stock Edwardian–Victorian furniture, collectables
Open Tues–Sat 10.30am–5pm

⊞ Petite Antiques
Contact Charlie Tosh
✉ 24 Brereton Crescent, Belfast, Co Antrim,
BT8 6QD 🅿
☎ 028 9064 4632
📠 07850 280777
📧 enquiries@petiteantiques.com
🌐 www.petiteantiques.com
Est. 1973 *Stock size* Small
Stock Clocks, porcelain, jewellery
Open Mon–Fri 9am–5pm Sat 9.30am–12.30pm
Services Valuations

NORTHERN IRELAND
CO ANTRIM • GLENGORMLEY

⚲ John Ross & Company (NIAVI)
Contact Mr Daniel Clarke
✉ 37 Montgomery Street, Belfast, Co Antrim, BT1 4NX 🅿
☎ 028 9032 5448 ☏ 028 9033 3642
🖃 info@rossbelfast.com
🌐 www.rossbelfast.com
Est. 1919
Open Mon–Fri 9am–5pm
Sales Quarterly sales of Irish paintings, weekly sales of antiques
Catalogues Yes

⊞ P & B Rowan (IADA)
Contact Peter or Briad Rowan
✉ Carleton House, 92 Malone Road, Belfast, Co Antrim, BT9 5HP 🅿
☎ 028 9066 6448 ☏ 028 9066 3725
🖃 peter@pbrowan.thegap.com
Est. 1973 *Stock size* Large
Stock Antiquarian books
Open By appointment
Fairs Irish Antiques Dealers Fair, PBFA (May/June)
Services Valuations

⊞ Stormont Antiques
Contact Mrs Ann McMurray
✉ 2a Sandown Road, Upper Newtownards Road, Belfast, Co Antrim, BT5 6GY 🅿
☎ 028 9047 2586
🖃 stormontantiques@btconnect.com
Est. 1979 *Stock size* Large
Stock Jewellery, silver
Open Mon–Fri 11.30am–5pm Sat 11.30am–4pm
Services Restoration

BUSHMILLS

⊞ Brian R Bolt Antiques
Contact Brian or Helen Bolt
✉ 88 Ballaghmore Road, Portballintrae, Bushmills, Co Antrim, BT57 8RL 🅿
☎ 028 2073 1129 ☏ 028 2073 1129
📱 07712 579802
🖃 brianbolt@antiques88.freeserve.co.uk
Est. 1979 *Stock size* Medium
Stock Antique and 20thC silver and objects of virtue, decorative arts, antique and 20thC glass, treen, general small items

Open By appointment
Services Valuations, search, worldwide postal service

⊞ Causeway Books
Contact Mr D Speers
✉ 110 Main Street, Bushmills, Co Antrim, BT57 8QD 🅿
☎ 028 2073 2596
Est. 1989 *Stock size* Medium
Stock General second-hand and antiquarian books
Open Mon–Sat 10.30am–5pm

⊞ Dunluce Antiques and Crafts
Contact Mrs Clare Ross
✉ 33 Ballytober Road, Bushmills, Co Antrim, BT57 8UU 🅿
☎ 028 207 31140
🖃 dunluceantiques@btinternet.com
🌐 www.dunlucegallery.com
Est. 1978 *Stock size* Small
Stock General antiques, collectables, Irish art gallery
Open Mon–Thurs 10am–6pm Sat 2–6pm
Services Valuations and porcelain restoration

CARRICKFERGUS

⊞ Robert Christie Antiques (IADA)
Contact Robert Christie
✉ 20 Calhame Road, Ballyclare, Co Antrim, BT39 9NA 🅿
☎ 028 9334 1149 ☏ 028 9334 1149
📱 07802 968846
Est. 1976 *Stock size* Medium
Stock 18th–19thC furniture, clocks, silver and plate, pottery, porcelain
Open Mon–Sat noon–5pm or by appointment
Fairs RDS Fairs, Dublin, Kings Hall, Belfast
Services Valuations

⚲ Lennox Auctions and Valuers
Contact Mr A Lennox
✉ The Basement, 41b Ellis Street, Carrickfergus, Co Antrim, BT38 8AY 🅿
☎ 028 9335 1522 or 028 9337 8527 (pm)
☏ 028 9335 1522
Est. 1987
Open Mon–Fri 9.30am–5pm
Sales Weekly sales Thurs 7pm,

viewing Mon–Thurs 10am–5pm Telephone for details. Periodic house clearance sales
Catalogues No

CARRYDUFF

⚲ Carryduff Auction Group Ltd
Contact Mr Robert Jenkins & Clark McCartney
✉ 10 Comber Road, Carryduff, Co Antrim, BT8 8AM 🅿
☎ 028 9081 3775 ☏ 028 9081 4518
🖃 info@carryduffauctions.co.uk
🌐 www.carryduffauctions.co.uk
Est. 1996
Open Mon–Fri 9am–6pm
Sales General antique sales Tues, viewing Mon, fine art auction first Tuesday in every month
Frequency Two monthly
Catalogues Yes

GLARRYFORD

⊞ Antique Builders Suppliers
Contact Mr Hastings White
✉ 94 Duneoin Road, Drumminning, Glarryford, Co Antrim, BT44 9HH 🅿
☎ 028 2568 5444
📱 07860 675908
🖃 sales@whites-architectural salvage.com
🌐 www.whites-architectural salvage.com
Est. 1983 *Stock size* Large
Stock Architectural salvage, Bangor blue slates, beams, tiles, stained glass windows, chimney pots, weathervanes, hardwood flooring, baths, railway sleepers, red telephone boxes
Open Mon–Sat 7am–11pm
Services Delivery

GLENGORMLEY

⊞ Acorns
Contact Mr P McComb
✉ 4 Portland Avenue, Glengormley, Co Antrim, BT36 5EY 🅿
☎ 028 9080 4100
Est. 1999 *Stock size* Medium
Stock Furniture, general antiques, dolls' houses
Open Mon–Sat 9.30am–5.30pm
Services Local delivery

LARNE

⊞ Bric-A-Brac
Contact Mr J McIlwaine
✉ 4 Riverdale, Larne,
Co Antrim,
BT40 1LB 🅿
☎ 028 2827 5657
Est. 1974 *Stock size* Large
Stock General antiques including
clocks, furniture, oil lamps,
jewellery, paintings
Open Mon–Sat 9am–5.30pm
Tues 9am–2pm

⊞ Cobwebs
Contact Mrs D Knox
✉ 94c Main Street, Larne,
Co Antrim,
BT40 1RE 🅿
☎ 028 2826 7127
Est. 1997
Stock General antiques, clocks,
antique fireplaces, antique pine
Open Mon–Sat 10am–5pm
closed Tues

⋏ Colin Wilkinson and Co (IRRV)
Contact Mr Colin Wilkinson
✉ The Auction Mart,
7 Point Street, Larne,
Co Antrim,
BT40 1HY 🅿
☎ 028 2826 0037 📠 028 2826 0497
Est. 1900
Open Mon–Fri 9.30am–5pm
Sales General antiques,
paintings, silver, porcelain
Frequency Monthly
Catalogues No

LISBURN

⊞ Trevor Falconer Antiques
Contact Trevor Falconer
✉ 51 Bridge Street, Lisburn,
Co Antrim,
BT28 1XZ 🅿
☎ 028 9260 5879
📧 trevor@falconerantiques.freeserve.co.uk
🌐 www.northirishmilitaria.com
Est. 1984 *Stock size* Medium
Stock Medals, militaria
Open Mon–Sat 10am–5pm
Services Restoration of antique
weapons

⊞ Jiri Books
Contact Jim and Rita Swindall
✉ 11 Mill Road, Lisburn,
Co Antrim,
BT27 5TT 🅿
☎ 028 9082 6443 📠 028 9082 6443
📧 jiri.books@dnet.co.uk
Est. 1978 *Stock size* Medium
Stock Largely Irish interest,
second-hand and antiquarian
books
Open By appointment only
Fairs Organizes the Second-hand
and Antiquarian Bookfair (part
of the Belfast Festival)
Services Book searches

⊞ Parvis (IADA)
Contact Parvis or Meriel
Sigaroudinia
✉ Mountain View House,
40 Sandy Lane, Ballyskeagh,
Lisburn, Co Antrim,
BT27 5TL 🅿
☎ 028 9062 1824 📠 028 9062 3311
📱 07801 347358
📧 parvissig@aol.com
🌐 www.parvis.co.uk
Est. 1973 *Stock size* Large
Stock General antiques and fine art
Open By appointment at any time
Fairs IADA Exhibition, Northern
Ireland Antiques Fair
Services Valuations, restoration,
consultancy, own exhibitions

⊞ Van-Lyn Antiques
Contact V or W Hastings
✉ 300 Comber Road, Lisburn,
Co Antrim,
BT27 6TA 🅿
☎ 028 9263 8358
📱 07899 935990
📧 vanlynantiques@aol.com
Est. 1979 *Stock size* Medium
Stock General, antique furniture,
porcelain, brass, glass, books, clocks
Open Mon–Sat 9am–9pm
Fairs Kings Hall, Belfast

NEWTOWNABBEY

⊞ MacHenry Antiques (IADA)
Contact Rupert or Anne
MacHenry
✉ 1–7 Glen Road, Jordanstown,
Newtownabbey, Co Antrim,
BT37 0RY 🅿
☎ 028 9086 2036 📠 028 9085 3281
📱 07831 135226
📧 rupertmachenry@ntlworld.com
Est. 1964 *Stock size* Medium
Stock 18th–19thC furniture,
paintings
Open Fri–Sat 2–7pm or by

appointment
Fairs IADA
Services Valuation for insurance,
probate and family division,
restoration

⋏ Wilson's Auctions (NAVA, IAVI)
Contact Mr Richard Bell
✉ 22 Mallusk Road,
Newtownabbey, Co Antrim,
BT36 4PP 🅿
☎ 028 9034 2626 📠 028 9034 2528
📧 richardbell@wilsonsauctions.com
🌐 www.wilsonsauctions.com
Est. 1964
Open Mon–Fri 9am–6pm
Sales Quarterly sales of Irish art.
Other specialist sales throughout
the year
Frequency Quarterly
Catalogues Yes

PORTRUSH

⊞ Alexander Antiques
Contact Mr David Alexander
✉ 108 Dunluce Road, Portrush,
Co Antrim,
BT56 8NB 🅿
☎ 028 7082 2783 📠 028 7082 2364
📧 sales@alexanderantiques.com
🌐 www.alexanderantiques.com
Est. 1973 *Stock size* Large
Stock Georgian–Edwardian
furniture
Open Mon–Sat 10am–5.30pm
Services Valuations, restoration

⊞ Atlantic Antiques
Contact Mr Samuel Dickie
✉ 22 Portstewart Road, Portrush,
Co Antrim,
BT56 8EQ 🅿
☎ 028 7082 5988
Est. 1997 *Stock size* Medium
Stock General antiques, mostly
ceramics and collectables
Open Mon–Sat 10.30am–5.30pm
Sun 1.30–5.30pm in winter
Mon–Sat 10am–5pm closed Wed

⊞ Kennedy Wolfenden
Contact Miss Eleanor Wolfenden
✉ 86 Main Street, Portrush,
Co Antrim,
BT56 8BN 🅿
☎ 028 7082 2995 📠 028 7082 5587
📱 07831 453038
📧 eleanorwolfenden@hotmail.com
🌐 www.kwauctionsni.co.uk
Est. 1974 *Stock size* Large
Stock Antique furniture,

porcelain, jewellery, silver and paintings
Open Mon–Sat 10am–5.30pm Jul–Aug later
Services Valuations

TOOMEBRIDGE

⊞ Past & Present Antiques
Contact Colin Paul
✉ 21 Hillhead Road, Toomebridge, Co Antrim, BT41 3SF 🅿
☎ 028 7965 9603
📱 07802 657692
Est. 1998 **Stock size** Large
Stock General antiques
Open Tues–Sat 10.30am–5pm
Services Valuations, restoration

CO ARMAGH

ARMAGH

⊞ Craobh Rua Books
Contact Mr James Vallely
✉ 12 Woodford Gardens, Armagh, Co Armagh, BT60 2AZ
☎ 028 3752 6938
📱 07977 476609
✉ Craobh@btinternet.com
Est. 1990 **Stock size** Medium
Stock Books, prints, selection of newspaper prints
Open By appointment only
Fairs The Rare Book Fair, Dublin
Services Catalogue, mail order

CRAIGAVON

⊞ Craigavon Marble Products
Contact Pat McIlduff
✉ 9 Ulster Street Industrial Estate, Lurgan, Craigavon, Co Armagh, BT67 9AN 🅿
☎ 028 3832 6736 📠 028 3832 7764
✉ craigavonmarble@btopenworld.co.uk,
🌐 www.craigavonmarble.co.uk
Est. 2000 **Stock size** Medium
Stock Antique marble, cast iron, wooden fireplaces,
Open By appointment
Services Valuations, restoration

LOUGHGALL

⊞ Huey's Antique Shop
Contact Bill Huey
✉ 45–47 Main Street, Loughgall,

Co Armagh, BT61 8HZ 🅿
☎ 028 3889 1248
📱 07721 844153
✉ billhuey@loughgallantiques.freeserve.co.uk
Est. 1973 **Stock size** Medium
Stock General antiques
Open Mon–Fri 2–6pm Sat 10.30am–6pm

MOIRA

⊞ Four Winds Antiques
Contact MIss Tina Cairns
✉ 96 Main Street, Moira, Co Armagh, BT67 0LH 🅿
☎ 028 9261 2226
📱 07768 292369 (John) or 07713 081748 (Tina)
Est. 1994 **Stock size** Large
Stock Georgian–Edwardian furniture, porcelain, longcase and bracket clocks
Open Mon–Sat 10am–5.30pm or by appointment

PORTADOWN

⚹ Wilson's Auctions Ltd (Portadown) (NAVA, IAVI)
Contact Michael Tomalin
✉ 65 Seagoe Industrial Estate, Portadown, Craigavon, Co Armagh, T63 5QE 🅿
☎ 028 3833 6433 📠 028 3833 6618
✉ michaeltomalin@wilsonsauctions.com
🌐 www.wilsonsauctions.com
Est. 1964
Open Mon–Fri 9am–6pm and on auction nights
Sales Antiques, fine art and disposal auctions Wed 7pm. Advisable to telephone ahead for sale details
Catalogues Yes

CO DOWN

BALLYNAHINCH

⊞ Davidson Books
Contact Mr Arthur Davidson
✉ 34 Broomhill Road, Spa, Ballynahinch, Co Down, BT24 8QD 🅿
☎ 028 9756 2502 📠 028 9756 2502
Est. 1959 **Stock size** Large
Stock Antiquarian books, especially Irish

Open By appointment only
Fairs Annual Belfast Second-hand and Antiquarian Bookfair
Services Valuations

⊞ The French Warehouse
Contact Heather Cowdy
✉ 72 Dunmore Road, Spa, Ballynahinch, Co Down, BT24 8PR 🅿
☎ 02844 839360
✉ frenchwarehouse@nireland.com
🌐 www.french-warehouse.com
Est. 1988 **Stock size** Large
Stock Antique French beds, 19thC French furniture
Open By appointment
Services Shipping

BANGOR

⊞ Annville Antiques
Contact A Chambers
✉ 28 Grays Hill, Bangor, Co Down, BT20 3BB 🅿
☎ 028 9145 2522
Est. 1984 **Stock size** Small
Stock General antiques
Open Mon–Sat 10.30am–4.30pm

⊞ Balloo Moon Antiques
Contact Marie Erwin
✉ Unit 30, Balloo Drive, Bangor, Co Down, BT19 7QY 🅿
☎ 028 9145 6886 📠 028 9145 3183
Est. 1979 **Stock size** Large
Stock General antiques
Open Mon–Sat 10am–5.30pm

DONAGHADEE

⊞ Antiquarian Booksellers
Contact M C McAlister
✉ Prospect House, 4 Millisle Road, Donaghadee, Co Down, BT21 0HY 🅿
☎ 028 9188 2990
✉ rarebooks.phb@btopenworld.com
🌐 www.antiquarianbookslellers.co.uk
Est. 1981 **Stock size** Medium
Stock Antiquarian and out-of-print books, Ireland, travel, fine buildings and natural history specialities
Open Strictly by appointment only

⊞ Phyllis Arnold Gallery Antiques
Contact Ms Phyllis Arnold

✉ **4a Shore Street, Donaghadee,
Co Down,
BT21 0DG** ♿
☎ 028 9188 8199/9185 3322
📠 028 9185 3322
📧 marnold@lowryhill.freeserve.co.uk
🌐 www.irishantiquesandart.com
Est. 1973 *Stock size* Medium
Stock Maps, prints, furniture,
silver, general
Open Wed–Sat 11am–5pm
Services Framing, conservation

⊞ **Blue Dot Antiques**
Contact Sam Parkinson or
Peter Bailie
✉ **4 Parade, Donaghadee,
Co Down,
BT21 0AE** ♿
☎ 028 9188 3436
📱 07775 805362
📧 sam.parkinson@tiscali.co.uk
🌐 www.bluedotantiques.com
Est. 2002 *Stock size* Medium
Stock General antiques,
collectables
Open Mon–Sat 11am–6pm
Sun 2–6pm
Services Valuations

⊞ **Stacks Bookshop**
Contact Mr Jim Tollerton
✉ **67 Comber Road, Dundonald,
Co Down,
BT16 0AE** ♿
☎ 028 9048 6880
🌐 www.stacksonline.co.uk
Est. 1992 *Stock size* Large
Stock Antiquarian Irish, religious,
military and poetry books
Open Mon–Sat 10am–6pm

⊞ **Archway Antiques**
Contact Mrs Boo Hughes
✉ **Hoops Courtyard, Main Street,
Greyabbey, Newtownards,
Co Down,
BT22 2NE** ♿
☎ 028 4278 8889
📱 07703 330900
Est. 1989 *Stock size* Medium
Stock 18th–19thC porcelain,
19thC glass, jewellery, furniture,
silver, kitchenware, linen,
pictures
Open Wed Fri Sat 11am–5pm or
by appointment
Fairs Ulster Antique and Fine Art
Fair, International Fair,

Kings Hall Belfast
Services Valuations, house
clearances

⊞ **Jacquart Antiques**
Contact Mr Dan Uprichard
✉ **37 Tullynagee Road,
Comber, Newtownards,
Co Down,
BT23 5SF** ♿
☎ 028 9752 1109 📠 028 9752 1109
📱 07831 548803
📧 jacquart@nireland.com
🌐 www.jacquart.co.uk
Est. 1992 *Stock size* Large
Stock Imported French antiques,
mainly 19th century furniture
(walnut, oak), mirrors, rare items
Open Mon–Sat 10am–5.30pm or
by appointment
Fairs Ulster Antique and Fine Art
Fair
Services Interior-design item
search

⊞ **Ballyalton House
Architectural Antiques
(SALVO)**
Contact Leonard Cave
✉ **Ballyalton House,
39 Ballyrainey Road,
Newtownards,
Co Down,
BT23 5AD** ♿
☎ 028 9181 3235 📠 028 9181 3235
📧 ballyalton@btconnect.com
🌐 www.ballyalton.freeserve.co.uk
Est. 1993 *Stock size* Large
Stock General architectural
antiques, largest stock of
bathrooms in Ireland. Newly
quarried stone, granite
Open Mon–Fri 8am–6pm
Sat 10am–3pm

➤ **Bangor Auctions**
Contact Mr G Holden-Downes
✉ **11 Greenway Industrial Estate,
Conlig, Newtownards,
Co Down,
BT23 7SU** ♿
☎ 028 9145 0494 📠 028 9127 5993
📧 info@bangorauctions.co.uk
🌐 www.bangorauctions.co.uk
Est. 1991
Open Mon Tues Fri 9am–5pm
Sales General antiques sales
every Thurs 6pm
Catalogues Yes

⊞ **Castle Antiques**
Contact Peter Moore
✉ **6 Regency Manor,
Newtownards, Co Down,
BT23 8ZD** ♿
☎ 028 9181 5710
📱 07989 501666
📧 info@castleantiques.co.uk
🌐 www.castleantiques.co.uk
Est. 1989 *Stock size* Medium
Stock Art Deco ceramics, enamel
signs
Open By appointment only

⊞ **Old Forge Collectables**
Contact David Eynon
✉ **17 Old Forge Crescent,
Newtownards, Co Down,
BT23 8GQ** ♿
☎ 028 91 810422
📱 07743 261487
📧 david.eynon1@btopenworld.com
Est. 1987 *Stock size* Medium
Stock Royal Doulton
Open By appointment
Services Valuations

⊞ **Agar Antiques**
Contact Rosie Agar
✉ **92 Main Street, Saintfield,
Co Down,
BT24 7AB** ♿
☎ 028 9751 1214
Est. 1991 *Stock size* Medium
Stock Victorian furniture,
ceramics, jewellery, Oriental
antiques, Delftware, lighting
Open Tues–Sat 11am–5pm
Services Valuations

⊞ **Antiques at the Stile**
Contact Mr Graham Hancock
✉ **52 Main Street, Saintfield,
Co Down,
BT24 7AB** ♿
☎ 028 9751 0844
📱 07831 587078
📧 antiquesatthestile@ntvinternet.com
🌐 www.antiquesatthestile.com
Est. 1989 *Stock size* Large
Stock Georgian–Edwardian
furniture, clocks, porcelain
Open Tues–Sat 10am–5.30pm or
by appointment
Services Valuations

⊞ **Attic Antiques**
Contact Mr Reuben Doyle
✉ **88 Main Street, Saintfield,
Co Down,
BT24 7AB** ♿

☎ 028 9751 1057
Ⓜ 07803 169799
Est. 1980 *Stock size* Large
Stock General antiques,
jewellery, bric-a-brac, large
selection of stripped pine
Open Mon–Fri 10am–5pm
Sat 10am–5.30pm
Fairs Swinderby
Services Export worldwide,
house clearance

⊞ Attic Pine
Contact Mr Reuben Doyle
✉ 88 Main Street, Saintfield,
Co Down,
BT24 7AB P
☎ 028 9751 1057
Est. 1996 *Stock size* Large
Stock Irish and Continental pine,
reclaimed furniture
Open Mon–Sat 10am–5pm
Services Stripping

⊞ Christine Deane Antiques
Contact Christine Deane
✉ 90 Main Street, Saintfield,
Co Down,
BT24 7AB P
☎ 028 9751 1334
Stock size Medium
Stock Victorian–Edwardian small
pieces of furniture, jewellery,
silver, porcelain
Open Thurs–Sat 10.30am–4.30pm

⊞ Peter Francis Antiques
Contact Mr Peter Francis
✉ 92 Main Street, Saintfield,
Co Down,
BT24 7AD P
☎ 028 9751 1214
Est. 1997 *Stock size* Small
Stock Irish glass, pottery and
Oriental antiques
Open Mon–Sat 11am–5pm
Services Valuations

⊞ Saintfield Antiques & Fine Books
Contact Mr Joseph Leckey
✉ 68 Main Street, Saintfield,
Co Down,
BT24 7AB P
☎ 028 9752 8428 ✆ 028 9752 8428
✉ home@antiquesireland.com
Ⓦ www.antiquesireland.com
Est. 1982 *Stock size* Medium
Stock Porcelain 1750–1850, silver
(especially Georgian), British and
European glass, fine, antiquarian
books

Open Thurs–Sat 11.30–5pm or by
appointment
Fairs All fairs organised by L&M
Fairs Ltd

SEAPATRICK

⊞ Mill Court Antiques
Contact Ms Gillian Close
✉ 99 Lurgan Road, Seapatrick,
Banbridge, Co Down,
BT32 4NE P
☎ 028 4066 2909
Est. 1979 *Stock size* Medium
Stock Furniture, ceramics,
collectables, jewellery
Open Mon–Sat 11.30am–5.30pm
closed Thurs
Services Valuations, restoration

CO FERMANAGH
BALLINAMALLARD

⊞ Ballindullagh Barn
Contact Mr Roy Armstrong
✉ Ballindullagh Barn,
Ballinamallard,
Co Fermanagh,
BT94 2NY P
☎ 028 6862 1802/028 6862 1548
✆ 028 6862 1802
✉ diana@ballindullaghbarn.com
Ⓦ www.ballindullaghbarn.com
Est. 1988 *Stock size* Large
Stock Pine country furniture,
bespoke kitchens oak & pine
Open Mon–Sat 8am–6pm
Services Valuations, restoration

ENNISKILLEN

⊞ Cloughcor House Antiques
Contact Mr Ian Black
✉ 22 Shore Road, Enniskillen,
Co Fermanagh,
BT74 7EF P
☎ 028 6632 4805 ✆ 028 6632 8828
Ⓜ 07774 758827
Est. 1964 *Stock size* Large
Stock Victorian–Edwardian
furniture, European pine, small
silver wares
Open Mon–Sat 9.30am–5.30pm
Services Valuations, restoration
and delivery

TEMPO

⊞ Marion Langham
Contact Marion Langham
✉ Claranagh, Tempo,

Co Fermanagh,
BT94 3FJ
☎ 028 8954 1247
✉ marion@ladymarion.co.uk
Ⓦ www.ladymarion.co.uk
Est. 1982 *Stock size* Large
Stock Belleek, paperweights
Open By appointment
Services Valuations, advice

CO LONDONDERRY
AGHADOWEY

⊞ Sarah Rose Antiques
Contact Mr Jim McCaughey
✉ 51 Ardreagh Road,
Aghadowey, Coleraine,
Co Londonderry,
BT51 4DN P
☎ 028 7086 8722
Est. 1989 *Stock size* Medium
Stock General antiques, pine
Open Sat 10.30am–5.30pm

COLERAINE

⊞ The Forge Antiques
Contact Margaret or Graham
Walker
✉ 24–26 Long Commons,
Coleraine, Co Londonderry,
BT52 1LH P
☎ 028 7035 1339
Est. 1966 *Stock size* Large
Stock Jewellery, silver, porcelain,
furniture, clocks.
Open Mon–Sat 10am–5.30pm
closed Thurs

⊞ Fountain Antique Studios & Workshop
Contact Ms Anne Morton
✉ Fountain Villas,
31 Millburn Road, Coleraine,
Co Londonderry,
BT52 1QT P
☎ 028 703 52260 ✆ 028 703 54268
Ⓜ 07771 525650
✉ info@fountainantiques.co.uk
Est. 1989 *Stock size* Medium
Stock Kitchenware, furniture,
stripped pine, porcelain
Open Mon–Sat 2–5.30pm or by
appointment

KILREA

⊞ Beeswax Antiques
Contact Pat McNeill
✉ 6 Church Street, Kilrea,
Co Londonderry,
BT51 5QU P

☎ 028 2954 1104
Est. 1987 *Stock size* Large
Stock Mahogany and pine furniture, general smalls
Open Mon–Sat 10.30am–5.30pm
Fairs Newark
Services Valuations, restoration

LONDONDERRY

⊞ **Foyle Antiques**
Contact Mr John Helfery
✉ The Old Farmhouse,
16 Whitehouse Road,
Londonderry,
BT48 0NE 🅿
☎ 028 7126 7626 ⊕ 028 7126 7626
⊖ john@foyleantiques.com
⊛ foyleantiques.com
Est. 1984 *Stock size* Large
Stock Antiques and reproduction furniture. Showhouse with 16 furnished period rooms
Open Mon–Sat 10am–6pm
Sun 2–6pm
Services Restoration, upholstery

⊞ **Foyle Books**
Contact Ken Thatcher or A Byrne
✉ 12 Magazine Street,
Londonderry,
BT48 6HH 🅿
☎ 028 7137 2530
⊖ ken@thatcher30.freeserve.uk
Est. 1989 *Stock size* Medium
Stock Antiquarian books, general, books on Derry and Donegal a speciality
Open Mon–Fri 11am–5pm
Sat 10am–5pm
Services Valuations

⊞ **Marcus Griffin Specialists in Silver Jewellery**
Contact Marcus Griffin
✉ 2 London Street, Londonderry,
BT48 6RQ 🅿
☎ 028 7130 9495
Est. 1974 *Stock size* Medium
Stock General antiques, furniture, silver, fossils, objets d'art
Open Mon–Sat 11am–5pm
Fairs Newark

⊞ **The Whatnot**
Contact Ms Margot O'Dowd
✉ 22 Bishop Street, Londonderry,
BT48 6TP 🅿
☎ 028 7128 8333
Est. 1984 *Stock size* Medium
Stock General antiques
Open Mon–Sat 11.30am–5pm

PORTSTEWART

⊞ **Irish Art Group (PTA)**
Contact Michael Hughes
✉ 49 The Promenade,
Portstewart,
Co Londonderry,
BT55 7AE 🅿
☎ 028 7083 4600 ⊕ 028 7083 4600
⊖ michael@irishartgroup.com
⊛ www.irishartgroup.com
Est. 1982 *Stock size* Large
Stock Irish art, prints, collectables, maps, postcards, cigarette cards, fountain pens
Open Mon–Sat 9.30am–1pm 2–5pm
Fairs NEC Spring & Autumn
Services Catalogue (6 times a year)

CO TYRONE

AUGHNACLOY

⊞ **Lucy Forsythe Antiques**
Contact Mr Michael McNamee
✉ The Old Rectory,
24 Carnteel Road, Aughnacloy,
Co Tyrone,
BT69 6DU 🅿
☎ 028 7138 2223
Est. 1992 *Stock size* Small
Stock General antiques
Open Mon–Fri 10am–5.30pm
Thurs 9.30am–1pm

BALLYCOLMAN

⋔ **Melmount Auctions**
Contact Mr Michael McNamee
✉ Unit C, Ballycolman Industrial Estate, Ballycolman,
Co Tyrone,
BT82 9PH 🅿
☎ 028 7138 2223
Est. 1992
Open Mon–Fri 10am–5.30pm
Thurs 9.30am–1pm
Sales General antiques, weekly Thurs, viewing all week
Catalogues No

BALLYGAWLEY

⊞ **Keepers Cottage Antique Irish Pine**
Contact Ann Ross
✉ 101 Kiloleeshill Road,
Ballygawley,
Co Tyrone,
BT70 2HX 🅿
☎ 028 8556 8765

Est. 1987 *Stock size* Medium
Stock Antique Irish pine and country furniture
Open Mon–Sat 9am–5pm
Services Valuations

⊞ **Old Mill Antiques**
Contact Michael and Rose Lippett
✉ The Old Mill,
Tulnavern Road, Ballygawley,
Co Tyrone,
BT70 2HH 🅿
☎ 028 855 67470 ⊕ 028 855 67466
⊕ 07831 866235
⊛ www.oldmillantiques.ulster guide.com
Est. 1970 *Stock size* Large
Stock General antiques
Open Mon–Sat 10am–5.30pm
Fairs Royal Dublin Society Show, King's Hall, Balmoral
Services Valuations

COOKSTOWN

⊞ **Stamp Shop**
Contact Peter McBride
✉ Drumconvis House,
Drumconvis Road, Coagh,
Cookstown,
Co Tyrone,
BT8U 0HF 🅿
☎ 028 8673 7804
⊕ 0780 106 3379
⊖ britishstamp@btinternet.com
Est. 1951 *Stock size* Large
Stock Stamps, medals, postcards, letters
Open By appointment
Services Valuations

MOY

⊞ **Moy Antique Pine**
Contact Mr Barry MacNeice
✉ 12 The Square,
Moy, Dungannon,
Co Tyrone,
BT71 7SG 🅿
☎ 028 8778 9909 ⊕ 028 8778 4895
⊕ 07733 154906
⊖ macneice@fsnet.co.uk
Est. 1974 *Stock size* Large
Stock General antiques
Open Mon–Sat 9am–6pm
Services Freestanding kitchens made with antique wood

⊞ **Moy Antiques**
Contact Mr Lawrence MacNeice
✉ 12 The Square,
Moy, Dungannon,

Co Tyrone,
BT71 7SG 🅿
☎ 028 8778 9909 ● 028 8778 4895
● sales@moyantiques.freeserve.co.uk
Est. 1974 *Stock size* Large
Stock General antique furniture,
garden statues, original marble
fireplaces, pine furniture
Open Mon–Sat 9am–6pm
Fairs Newark, Ardingly
Services Valuations, freestanding
kitchens made with antique
wood

OMAGH

⊞ Gormley's Fine Art
Contact Mr Oliver Gormley
✉ 3–4 Dromore Road, Omagh,
Co Tyrone,
BT78 IRE 🅿
☎ 028 8224 7738 ● 028 8225 2797
● oliver@gormleys.ie
ⓦ www.gormleys.ie
Est. 1989 *Stock size* Large
Stock Contemporary and period
oils, watercolours, scupltures and
drawings
Open Mon–Sat 9.30am–6pm
Thurs to 8pm Sun 2–5.30pm
Fairs Newark
Services Gormley's Fine Art can
be viewed in varous locations in
Ireland; call for current locations.
Valuations

⊞ Kelly Antiques
Contact Mr Louis Kelly
✉ **Mullaghmore House,**

Old Mountfield Road, Omagh,
Co Tyrone,
BT79 7EX 🅿
☎ 028 8224 2314 ● 028 8225 0262
● sales@kellyantiques.com
ⓦ www.kellyantiques.com/
mullaghmorehouse.com
Est. 1936 *Stock size* Large
Stock Period fireplaces,
hardwood furniture, bedroom
suites, tables, chairs, lighting
Open Mon–Fri 10am–7pm
Sat 10am–5pm
Services Restoration, private
auctions. Full-time course in
antique furniture restoration

⊞ Viewback Auctions
Contact Mr G Simpson
✉ 8–10 Jail Square,
Castle Place, Omagh,
Co Tyrone,
BT79 5ER 🅿
☎ 028 8224 6271 ● 028 8224 6271
Ⓜ 07760 275247
● geoff@viewbackantiquesauctins.com
ⓦ www.viewbackantiquesauctions.com
Est. 1979 *Stock size* Large
Stock General antiques
Open Mon–Sat 10am–6pm
Fairs Newark

⚲ Viewback Auctions
Contact Mr G Simpson
✉ 8–10 Castle Place, Omagh,
Co Tyrone,
BT78 5ER 🅿
☎ 028 8224 6271 ● 028 8224 6271
Ⓜ 07760 275247

● viewback@talk21.com
ⓦ www.viewbackantiqueauctions.com
Est. 1979
Open Mon–Sat 10am–6pm
Sales Auctions of household
effects and antiques once a
month or more often.
See website for details

STEWARTSTOWN

⊞ Silversaddle Antiques
Contact Vivian Smith
✉ 1 West Street, Stewartstown,
Co Tyrone,
BT71 5HT 🅿
☎ 028 8773 8088
Est. 1900 *Stock size* Large
Stock Georgian–Edwardian
furniture, clocks, Victorian
chandeliers
Open Mon–Sat noon–6pm
Services Valuations, restoration

⊞ P J Smith (Fair Trades)
Contact Patrick Smith
✉ 1 North Street, Stewartstown,
Co Tyrone,
BT71 5JE 🅿
☎ 028 8773 8071 ● 028 8773 8059
● donryan11@hotmail.com
ⓦ www.antique-fireplaces.com
Est. 1979 *Stock size* Large
Stock Antique fireplaces, stained
glass, beds
Open Mon–Fri 10.30am–1pm
1.40–6pm Thurs until 9pm
Sat 10.30am–6pm
Services Restoration of fireplaces

REPUBLIC OF IRELAND

REPUBLIC OF IRELAND

Carndonagh

DONEGAL

Donegal

NORTHERN
IRELAND

Bundoran

Sligo Manorhamilton

SLIGO

MAYO

Castlebar

Westport

Fenagh

Boyle

LEITRIM

Monaghan

MONAGHAN

Castleblayney

Cavan

CAVAN

Carrickmacross Dundalk

ROSCOMMON

Tuam

Longford

Virginia

LONGFORD

LOUTH

Drogheda

Ceanannus
Mor (Kells)

GALWAY

Galway

Ballinasloe

WESTMEATH

Athlone

Kinnegad

MEATH

Balbriggan

Loughrea

Portumna

OFFALY

Maynooth

DUBLIN

Dublin

Aran
Islands

Gort

Birr

KILDARE

Black
Rock

Dun
Laoghaire

Bray

CLARE

Ennis

LAOIS

WICKLOW

Wicklow

Rathdrum

Freshford

Carlow

Foynes

Limerick

TIPPERARY

Kilkenny

CARLOW

Gorey

LIMERICK

Tipperary

KILKENNY

Tralee

Cahir

Clonmel

WEXFORD

Dingle

Mallow

Fermoy

WATERFORD

Waterford

Wexford

KERRY

CORK

Saltee
Islands

Cahirciveen

Cork

Bantry

Skibbereen

Fastnet Rock

The international dialling code for
the Republic of Ireland is 00353

CO CARLOW

BORRIS

✒ Joe Dunne Auctioneers & Valuers (IAVI)
Contact Joe Dunne
✉ Borris, Co Carlow,
Ireland 🅿
☎ 05997 73191 📠 05997 73536
📧 movehome@dunnesofborris.ie
🌐 www.dunnesofborris.ie
Est. 1984
Open Tues–Sat 9.30am–5pm
Sales Antiques and general household, antiques sales twice yearly
Frequency Every 6 weeks
Catalogues Yes

CO CAVAN

BALLINEA

🎴 F J McAvenues & Son
Contact Dennis McAvenues
✉ 7 Lower Bridge Street, Bellturbet, Co Cavan,
Ireland 🅿
☎ 04995 22204
📧 deninc@eircom.net
Est. 1964 *Stock size* Large
Stock General antiques, furniture, jewellery, silver, clocks
Open Mon–Fri 2–6pm
Sat Sun 11am–5pm
Services Valuations

CO CLARE

CLARECASTLE

🎴 The Antique Loft
Contact Paul Walsh
✉ Barrack Street, Clarecastle, Co Clare,
Ireland 🅿
☎ 065 684 1969 📠 065 684 1969
📧 antiqueloft@eircom.net
Est. 1991 *Stock size* Large
Stock Victorian–Edwardian furniture, collectables, Persian rugs, carpets
Open Mon–Sat 9am–6pm incuding Bank Holidays
Services Valuations, restoration

ENNIS

🎴 Tony Honan
Contact Mr Tony Honan
✉ 14 Abbey Street, Ennis, Co Clare, Ireland

☎ 065 682 8137
Est. 1974 *Stock size* Large
Stock Clocks, oil lamps, jewellery
Open Mon–Sat 10am–6pm

CO CORK

BALLYDEHOB

🎴 Schull Books
Contact Barbara or Jack O'Connell
✉ Ballydehob, Co Cork,
Ireland 🅿
☎ 028 37317 📠 028 37317
📧 schullbooks@eircom.net
🌐 www.schullbooks.com
Est. 1981 *Stock size* Medium
Stock Antiquarian books, second-hand books, military history a speciality
Open June–Sept Mon–Sat 11am–6pm other times by appointment
Fairs All major Irish book fairs
Services Valuations

CASTLETOWNSHEND

🎴 Moylurg Gallery
Contact Timothy MacDermot-Roe
✉ The Mall, Castletownshend, Co Cork,
Ireland 🅿
☎ 028 36396 📠 028 36396
📧 tmdr@eircom.net
Est. 1993 *Stock size* Small
Stock Antique picture frames, oil paintings, watercolours, engravings, prints
Open By appointment June–Sept, late Dec–Early Jan
Services Valuations

CHARLEVILLE

🎴 Fortlands Antiques (IADA)
Contact Mary O'Connor
✉ Fortlands, Charleville, Co Cork,
Ireland 🅿
☎ 063 81295
Est. 1974 *Stock size* Large
Stock Georgian–Victorian furniture, silver, brass, china, objets d'art
Open Mon–Sat 11am–5pm Sun 2–5pm
Fairs Irish Antique Dealers' Fair
Services Valuations, restoration

✒ P J O'Gorman MIPAV Auctioneers (IPAV)
Contact P J O'Gorman

✉ Chapel Street, Charleville, Co Cork,
Ireland 🅿
☎ 063 81407 📠 063 81604
📧 ogormanpj@eirecom.net
Est. 1968
Open Mon–Fri 10am–5.30pm
Sat Sun by appointment
Sales Furniture sales
Frequency Quarterly
Catalogues Yes

CLONAKILTY

🎴 Boyle's Antiques
Contact Joyce Boyle
✉ 35 Ashe Street, Clonakilty, Co Cork,
Ireland 🅿
☎ 02334 222
Est. 1993 *Stock size* Small
Stock Jewellery, silver
Open Mon–Sat 10am–6pm closed Wed Jan–Mar Thurs–Sat only
Services Valuations

CORK

🎴 Antiques & Curios Centre
Contact Liam Hurley
✉ Upper Johns Street, Cork,
Ireland 🅿
☎ 021 427 9995
Est. 1987 *Stock size* Large
Stock Country furniture, general antiques
Open Mon–Sat 10am–5pm

🎴 Georgian Antiques (LAPADA, CINOA, IADA)
Contact Patrick Jones
✉ 21 Lavitts Quay, Cork,
Ireland
☎ 021 427 8153 📠 021 427 9365
📱 0872 563721
📧 info@georgianantiquesltd.com
🌐 www.georgianantiquesltd.com
Est. 1998 *Stock size* Large
Stock 18th–19thC Irish, English and Continental European furniture, decorations
Open Mon–Fri 2–5pm
Sat 10am–5pm
Fairs Irish Antique Dealers' Fair, The Annual Cork Antiques Fair

🎴 Helga's Antiques
Contact Helga McCarthy Cleary or John McCarthy
✉ 7 Cross Street, Cork,
Ireland 🅿
☎ 021 427 0034 📠 021 487 8954
📱 0868 361473

@ helgasantiques@eircom.net
Est. 1994 *Stock size* Large
Stock General antiques,
jewellery, furniture
Open Mon–Sat 10am–5pm or by
appointment
Services Valuations, restoration,
French polishing

⊞ Ann McCarthy
Contact Ann McCarthy
✉ 2 Paul's Lane, Huguenot
Quarter, Cork,
Ireland ℙ
☎ 021 427 3755
Est. 1985 *Stock size* Large
Stock Silver, linen, china, glass, lace
Open Mon–Sat 10am–6pm
Services Valuations

⊞ Mills Antiques
Contact David Coon or Orla Clarke
✉ 3 Paul's Lane, Huguenot
Centre, Cork,
Ireland ℙ
☎ 021 427 3528
@ davidcoon@eircom.net
Est. 1981 *Stock size* Large
Stock General small items, small
furniture, paintings, prints,
objets d'art
Open Mon–Sat 10.30am–6pm
Services Painting and frame
restoration

⊞ Mona's Antiques
Contact Monica Noonan
✉ 79 Oliver Plunkett Street, Cork,
Ireland
☎ 021 427 8171
Est. 1988 *Stock size* Large
Stock Antique jewellery
Open Mon–Sat 11am–6pm

⊞ Noble Antique Fireplaces
Contact James O'Driscoll
✉ Unit 1c, Southside Industrial
Estate, Pouladuff Road, Cork,
Ireland ℙ
☎ 021 432 3477 @ 021 432 3477
Est. 1983 *Stock size* Large
Stock Antiques
Open Mon–Sat 9.30am–5.30pm
Sun by appointment
Services Valuations, restoration

⊞ Diana O'Mahony
Antiques & Jewellery
(IADA, BGA)
Contact Diana or Niamh O'Mahony
✉ 8 Winthrop Street, Cork,
Ireland ℙ
☎ 021 427 6599

Est. 1970 *Stock size* Large
Stock Victorian jewellery,
diamond pieces,
Georgian–Victorian silver, Cork
and Dublin silver, small furniture
Open Mon–Sat 9.30am–5.30pm
Services Valuations, pearl
restringing, remounting

⊞ Stokes Clocks and
Watches Ltd
Contact Philip Stokes
✉ 48 MacCurtain Street, Cork,
Ireland ℙ
☎ 021 455 1195 @ 021 450 9125
@ stokesclocks@eircom.net
Est. 1969 *Stock size* Large
Stock Clocks, watches,
barometers
Open Mon–Fri 9.15am–6pm
Sat 10am–5pm
Services Valuations, restoration,
repairs

⊞ Victoria's Antiques
Contact Ms Frances Lynch
✉ 2 Oliver Plunkett Street, Cork,
Ireland ℙ
☎ 021 427 2752
Est. 1987 *Stock size* Large
Stock Jewellery, silver gifts, small
items of furniture
Open Mon–Sat 9.30am–5.30pm
Services Valuations, restoration

♫ Joseph Woodward &
Sons Ltd (IAVI)
Contact Tom Woodward
✉ 26 Cook Street, Cork,
Ireland ℙ
☎ 021 427 3327 @ 021 427 2891
@ auctions@woodward.ie
ⓦ www.woodward.ie
Est. 1883
Open Mon–Fri 9am–5.30pm
Sales Antiques, paintings, silver,
porcelain. Twice-yearly specialist
Irish silver auctions. Internet
catalogues available
Frequency Monthly
Catalogues Yes

FERMOY

⊞ Country Furniture
Contact Seamus Kirby
✉ Johnstown, Fermoy, Co Cork,
Ireland ℙ
☎ 025 38244 @ 025 38244
ⓜ 0868 126883
@ mkirby@aol.ie
Est. 1990 *Stock size* Large
Stock Antique fireplaces,

pine, salvage
Open Mon–Sat 9am–6pm
Sun 2–6pm other times by
appointment only
Services Pine stripping, house
renovation, kitchens

KINSALE

⊞ Linda's Antiques
Contact Linda or Laura Walsh
✉ Main Street, Kinsale, Co Cork,
Ireland
☎ 021 477 4754 @ 021 477 7582
ⓜ 0872 502467
@ lindasjewellery@eircom.net
Est. 1992
Stock Jewellery, silver, books,
prints, oil paintings, watercolours,
porcelain, objets d'art
Open Mon–Sat 10.30am–5.30pm
Sun 2–6pm
Fairs Cork Antiques Fair

⊞ Trading House
Contact Katarina Runske, Olivier
Bouche or Carole Norman
✉ 54 Main Street, Kinsale, Co Cork,
Ireland ℙ
☎ 021 477 7497 @ 021 477 3517
ⓜ 08724 94722
@ crackpts@iol.ie
Est. 2000 *Stock size* Medium
Stock Furniture
Open Mon–Sat 10am–6pm
Sun 2–6pm

LEAP

⊞ Ovne Antique Stoves
Contact Tom Keane or
Claire Graham
✉ Millside, Dungannon, Leap,
Co Cork,
Ireland ℙ
☎ 028 34917
ⓜ 0868 555635
@ info@ovnestoves.com
ⓦ www.ovnestoves.com
Est. 1990 *Stock size* Medium
Stock Antique stoves from all
around the world 1840–1950
Open Mon–Sat 10am–6pm,
Sun by appointment
Fairs Plan Expo, Royal Dublin Show

MALLOW

⊞ Aidan Foley Antiques
Contact Aidan Foley
✉ Munster House, Doneraile,
Mallow, Co Cork,
Ireland ℙ

REPUBLIC OF IRELAND
CO CORK • MIDLETON

☎ 022 24557 ❻ 022 829 0680
❸ sales@irishcountryhome.com
Ⓦ www.irishcountryhome.com
Est. 1995 *Stock size* Large
Stock Georgian–Victorian
mahogany furniture
Open Mon–Fri 9am–5pm
Services Shipping

⊞ McMahon's Antiques
Contact Mr McMahon
✉ Dromagh, Mallow, Co Cork,
Ireland Ⓟ
☎ 029 78119
Est. 1977 *Stock size* Large
Stock Pre-1940 general antiques
Open Mon–Sat 10am–8pm
Sun noon–8pm

↗ Old Schoolhouse Auction Rooms
Contact Aidan Foley
✉ Main Street, Doneraile,
Mallow, Co Cork,
Ireland Ⓟ
☎ 086 829 0680
Ⓦ www.irishcountryhome.com
Est. 1990
Open Mon–Fri 9am–5pm
Sales Regular general and
antiques auctions
Frequency Monthly
Catalogues Yes

⊞ Schoolhouse Antiques
Contact John Murphy
✉ Main Street, Doneraile,
Mallow, Co Cork
☎ 022 24972 ❻ 087 214 4389
Est. 1990 *Stock size* Large
Stock Antiques, collectables
Open By appointment

MIDLETON

⊞ Rostellan Antiques Ltd
Contact Fran Philpott
✉ Rostellan, Midleton, Co Cork,
Ireland Ⓟ
☎ 021 466 1100
❸ fran6@eircom.net
Est. 1996 *Stock size* Large
Stock General antiques
Open Sat & Sun 2–6pm or by
appointment

CO DONEGAL

BUNDORAN

⊞ Vincent McGowan Antiques
Contact Mr Vincent McGowan

✉ 2–3 Main Street, Bundoran,
Co Donegal,
Ireland Ⓟ
☎ 071 98 41536
Est. 1981 *Stock size* Medium
Stock Georgian–Edwardian
furniture, small items, clocks,
jewellery, Belleek
Open Please call for times
Services Valuations, restoration

CARNDONAGH

⊞ The Bookshop
Contact Mr Michael Herron
✉ Court Place, Pound Street,
Carndonagh, Co Donegal,
Ireland Ⓟ
☎ 074 93 74389 ❻ 074 93 74313
Est. 1987 *Stock size* Large
Stock Irish interest, science,
19thC antiquarian section,
general books
Open Mon–Fri 2–6pm
Sat 11am–6pm Sun 2–6pm
Fairs Annual Belfast Second-
hand and Antiquarian Bookfair
Services Catalogues 4 or 5 a year

DONEGAL

⊞ Sean Thomas Antiques (IADA)
Contact Sean Thomas
✉ Killymard House, Donegal,
Ireland Ⓟ
☎ 07497 35024
❸ killymard@esatclear.ie
Est. 1961 *Stock size* Small
Stock Interesting small items
Open Mon–Sat 10am–6pm
Services Valuations

DUNFANAGHY

⊞ The Gallery
Contact Alan and Moira Harley
✉ Dunfanaghy, Co Donegal,
Ireland Ⓟ
☎ 074 913 6224
Est. 1968 *Stock size* Medium
Stock Silver, brass, Asian
antiques, pottery, porcelain,
jewellery, clocks, old prints, maps
Open Mon–Sat 10am–7pm

CO DUBLIN

BLACKROCK

↗ Adams Blackrock (IAVI)
Contact Ms Martina Noonan
✉ 38 Main Street, Blackrock,

Co Dublin,
Ireland
☎ 01 288 5146 ❻ 01 288 7820
❸ info@adamsblackrock.com
Est. 1947
Open Mon–Fri 9.30am–5.30pm
Sales 20 furniture fine art
auctions per annum, 4 Irish and
continental European paintings
auctions per annum, 4 jewellery
and silver sales per annum,
regular house contents sales
Catalogues Yes

⊞ De Burca Rare Books (IADA, ABA)
Contact Mr Eamon de Burca
✉ Cloonagashel, 27 Priory Drive,
Blackrock, Co Dublin,
Ireland Ⓟ
☎ 01 288 2159 ❻ 01 283 4080
❸ deburca@indigo.ie
Ⓦ www.deburcararebooks.com
Stock Irish antiquarian fine
books, maps, prints, manuscripts
Open Mon–Fri 9am–5.30pm
Sat 10am–1pm
Fairs London and New York book
fairs
Services Mail-order service, book
search, valuations, book binding

⊞ Peter Linden Oriental Rugs and Carpets (IADA)
Contact Mr Peter Linden
✉ 15 George's Avenue,
Blackrock, Co Dublin,
Ireland Ⓟ
☎ 01 288 5875 ❻ 01 283 5616
❸ lindorient@hotmail.com
Ⓦ www.peterlinden.com
Est. 1980 *Stock size* Large
Stock Oriental rugs, carpets,
kilims, tapestries
Open Tues–Sat 10am–5.30pm
Fairs Irish Antique Dealers' Fair
Services Valuations, restoration

⊞ Treasure Chest Antiques
Contact Mr Norman Ludgate
✉ 49 Main Street, Blackrock,
Co Dublin,
Ireland Ⓟ
☎ 01 288 9961
Ⓦ 0872 831027
❸ treasurechest@iol.ie
Est. 1992
Stock Lighting, small furniture,
silver, jewellery, clocks, watches,
general antiques
Open Mon–Fri 11.30am–6.30pm
Sat noon–6pm closed Thurs

DUBLIN

⚒ James Adam
✉ 26 St Stephen's Green, Dublin 2, Ireland 🅿
☎ 01 676 0261 📠 01 662 4725
📧 info@jamesadam.ie
🌐 www.jamesadam.ie
Est. 1887
Open Mon–Fri 9am–5.30pm
closed 1–2pm
Sales Specialist sales throughout the year of Irish art, vintage wine, militaria, toys and ceramics, modern and contemporary art, telephone for details
Catalogues Yes

⊞ Anthony Antiques Ltd (IADA, CINOA)
Contact Jeffrey or Roger Dell
✉ 7 Molesworth Street, Dublin 2, Ireland 🅿
☎ 01 677 7222 📠 01 677 7222
📧 anthonyantiques@oceanfree.net
🌐 www.irelandantiques.com/anthony
Est. 1963 *Stock size* Large
Stock Decorative antique furniture, mirrors, brass, chandeliers
Open Mon–Sat 9am–6pm
Fairs Irish Antique Dealers' Fair

⊞ Antique Prints (IADA, CINOA)
Contact Hugh or Anne Iremonger
✉ 16 South Anne Street, Dublin 2, Ireland 🅿
☎ 01 671 9523 or 01 269 8373
📧 antiqueprints_irl@yahoo.ie
Est. 1969
Stock 17th–20thC prints, maps, books, incunabulae, classical and modern original lithographs
Open Mon–Sat 11am–5pm

⊞ Antique Time
Contact Martin Hennessey
✉ 1 The Hill, Mulhuddart Wood, Dublin 15, Ireland
☎ 01 820 7185
📧 mhenness@hotmail.com
Est. 2001 *Stock size* Medium
Stock Clocks, barometers
Open Tues–Sat 10am–5.30pm
Services Restoration, repair

⊞ Architectural Antiques and Salvage
Contact Mr S Bird or Mr S Flanagan
✉ 31 South Richmond Street, Dublin,

Ireland 🅿
☎ 01 478 4245
🌐 www.arcantiques.ie
Est. 1996 *Stock size* Medium
Stock Architectural salvage, fonts, statues, fireplaces, ecclesiastical items
Open Mon–Sat 10am–6pm

⊞ Architectural Classics
Contact Mr Niall McDonagh
✉ South Gloucester Street, Dublin 2, Ireland 🅿
📠 01 677 3318
📱 086 8207700
📧 info@architecturalclassics.com
🌐 www.architecturalclassics.com
Est. 1986 *Stock size* Large
Stock Antique lighting, door furniture, period fireplaces, garden statuary
Open Mon–Fri 9am–5.30pm
Sat 10am–3pm
Fairs IADA Fairs, Dublin
Services Valuations, restoration

⊞ Christy Bird
Contact Christy Bird or Annette Mulkern
✉ 32 South Richmond Street, Portobello, Dublin 2, Ireland 🅿
☎ 01 475 4049 📠 01 475 8708
📧 paul@christybird.com
🌐 www.christybird.com
Est. 1945 *Stock size* Medium
Stock Antiques, collectables
Open Mon–Sat 10am–6pm

⊞ Lorcan Brereton (IADA)
Contact Mr Diarmuid Brereton
✉ 29 South Anne Street, Dublin 2, Ireland
☎ 01 677 1462 📠 01 677 1125
Est. 1912
Stock Antique and modern jewellery, silver
Open Mon–Sat 9.15am–5.30pm
Fairs IADA
Services Valuations, restoration

⊞ Edward Butler (IADA)
Contact Peter or Elizabeth Bateman
✉ 14 Bachelor's Walk, Dublin 1, Ireland
☎ 01 873 0296 📠 01 873 0296
📱 0872 486916
📧 bateman@iol.ie
🌐 www.edwardbutlerantiques.com
Est. 1850 *Stock size* Medium
Stock Nautical and scientific instruments, 18th–19thC

furniture, paintings, clocks
Open Mon–Fri 11am–4pm or by appointment
Fairs Irish Antique Dealers' Fair

⊞ Cathach Books Ltd (ABA, ILAB)
Contact Mr Enda Cunningham
✉ 10 Duke Street, Dublin 2, Ireland 🅿
☎ 01 671 8676 📠 01 671 5120
📧 cathach@rarebooks.ie
🌐 www.rarebooks.ie
Est. 1964 *Stock size* Medium
Stock Specialists in antiquarian and rare books of Irish interest
Open Mon–Sat 9.30am–5.45pm
Services Valuations

⊞ Caxton Prints (IADA, CINOA)
Contact Ronan Teevan or Liam Fitzpatrick
✉ 63 Patrick Street, Dublin 8, Ireland 🅿
☎ 01 453 0060 📠 01 453 0060
📱 0872 429799
📧 caxton@vodaphone.ie
Est. 1989 *Stock size* Small
Stock Old Masters, 17th–18thC decorative prints
Open Mon–Sat 10.30am–5.30pm
Services Valuations

⊞ Chapters Book and Music Store (BA)
Contact Mr William Kinsella
✉ 108–109 Middle Abbey Street, Dublin 1, Ireland 🅿
☎ 01 872 3297 (books) 01 873 0484 (music) 📠 01 872 3044
📧 chaptersbookandmusicstore@eircom.net
Est. 1983 *Stock size* Large
Stock Antiquarian books, new, bargain, second-hand CDs, Irish music, DVDs, games
Open Mon–Sat 9.30am–6.30pm
Thurs 9.30am–8pm
Sun noon–6.30pm

⊞ Courtville Antiques (IADA, CINOA)
Contact Ms Grainne Pierse
✉ Powerscourt Townhouse Centre, South William Street, Dublin 2, Ireland 🅿
☎ 01 679 4042 📠 01 679 4042
Est. 1964 *Stock size* Large
Stock Victorian and Art Deco jewellery, silver, paintings,

decorative items
Open Mon–Sat 10am–6pm
Fairs Irish Antique Dealers' Fair
Services Commission purchasing

⊞ Delphi Antiques
Contact Mr Declan Corrigan
✉ **Powerscourt Townhouse
Centre, South William Street,
Dublin 2,
Ireland** ℗
☎ 01 679 0331
Est. 1987 **Stock size** Large
Stock Georgian–Edwardian
jewellery, Continental and
European ceramics, Irish Belleek
Open Mon–Sat 10.30am–5.30pm
Services Porcelain restoration

⊞ Michael Duffy Antiques
Contact Mr Michael Duffy
✉ **9–10 Parnell Street, Dublin 1,
Ireland** ℗
☎ 01 872 6928 ❸ 01 872 6928
Ⓜ 0872 562326
Est. 1949 **Stock size** Medium
Stock General Victorian antiques
Open Mon–Sat 10am–5pm

⊞ Euricka Antiques
Contact Alexandra Papadakis
✉ **3 Marks Alley, Francis Street,
Dublin 8,
Ireland** ℗
☎ 01 454 9779
Ⓦ www.euricka-antiques.com
Est. 1990 **Stock size** Small
Stock Furniture and general
antiques
Open Mon–Sat 10am–6pm
Services Restoration

⊞ John Farrington
Antiques (IADA)
Contact Mr John Farrington
✉ **32 Drury Street, Dublin 2,
Ireland** ℗
☎ 01 679 1899
❸ farrington711@hotmail.com
Est. 1979 **Stock size** Large
Stock Fine-quality jewellery,
silver, gilt mirrors
Open Tues–Sat 10.30am–5pm
Fairs Irish Antique Dealers' Fair

⊞ Flanagans Ltd
Contact Brian or Peter Flanagan
✉ **Deerpark Road,
Mount Merrion,
Co Dublin,
Ireland** ℗
☎ 01 288 0218 ❸ 01 288 1336
❸ flandove@iol.ie

Ⓦ www.theflanagan.ie
Est. 1974 **Stock size** Large
Stock Antique pianos, 19thC
furniture, interior design
Open Mon–Sat 10am–6pm
Thurs 10am–9pm
Services Restoration

⊞ Fleury Antiques (IADA)
Contact C or D Fleury
✉ **57 Francis Street, Dublin 8,
Ireland**
☎ 01 473 0878
❸ fleuryantiques@eircom.net
Ⓦ www.fleuryantiques.com
Est. 1979 **Stock size** Large
Stock 18th–19thC furniture,
sculptures, paintings, decorative
objects, porcelain, silver
Open Mon–Sat 9am–6pm

⚲ Herman & Wilkinson
(IAVI)
Contact Mr David Herman
or Mr Ray Wilkinson
✉ **161 Lower Rathmines Road,
Dublin 6,
Ireland** ℗
☎ 01 497 2245 ❸ 01 496 2245
❸ info@hermanwilkinson.ie
Ⓦ www.hermanwilkinson.ie
Est. 1970
Open Mon–Fri 9.30am–5.30pm
Sales Monthly antiques and fine
art sales, Thurs 10am, viewing
Wed 10am–9pm, weekly sales
Thurs
Catalogues Yes

⊞ Patrick Howard
Antiques (IADA)
Contact Patrick Howard
✉ **60 Francis Street, Dublin 8,
Ireland** ℗
☎ 01 473 1126 ❸ 01 473 1126
Ⓜ 0872 331870
❸ antiques@dublin.ie
Ⓦ www.patrickhowardantiques.com
Stock size Large
Stock Decorative arts, furniture,
paintings, prints and lighting
Open Mon–Sat 9.30am–6pm

⊞ The Jewel Casket
(IADA)
Contact Mr Keith Cusack
✉ **17 South Anne Street, Dublin 2,
Ireland**
☎ 01 671 1262
Est. 1989 **Stock size** Large
Stock Antique jewellery, silver,
curios
Open Tues–Sat 9.30am–6pm

⊞ Kevin Jones Antiques
(IADA)
Contact Mr Kevin Jones
✉ **65–66 Francis Street,
Dublin 8,
Ireland** ℗
☎ 01 454 6626
Ⓜ 0876 29790
❸ jonesantiques@eircom.net
Est. 1989 **Stock size** Large
Stock 18th–19thC furniture,
paintings, objets d'art
Open Mon–Sat 10am–5.30pm

⊞ Gerald Kenyon
Antiques (IADA, CINOA)
Contact Mr Gerald A Kenyon
✉ **6 Great Strand Street,
Dublin 1,
Ireland** ℗
☎ 01 873 0625 ❸ 01 873 0882
❸ mark@kenyon-antiques.com
Ⓦ www.kenyon-antiques.com
Est. 1740 **Stock size** Medium
Stock Fine Georgian furniture,
works of art, collectors' items
Open Mon–Fri 9am–6pm
Fairs Irish Antique Dealers' Fair,
Dublin Antiques Fair
Services Interior decoration

⊞ Mitofsky Antiques
(IADA)
Contact Anne Citron
✉ **8 Rathfarnham Road,
Terenure, Dublin 6,
Ireland** ℗
☎ 01 492 0033 ❸ 01 492 0188
❸ info@mintofskyartdeco.com
Ⓦ www.mintofskyartdeco.com
Est. 1994 **Stock size** Large
Stock Art Deco, Art Nouveau,
Arts and Crafts
Open Tues–Sat 10am–5.30pm
Fairs The Kings Hall (Belfast),
IADA

⊞ Neptune Gallery
(IADA, FATG)
Contact Mr Andrew Bonar Law
✉ **41 South William Street,
Dublin 2,
Ireland** ℗
☎ 01 671 5021 ❸ 01 671 5021
❸ abl@nep.ie
Est. 1963 **Stock size** Medium
Stock Irish maps, prints,
watercolours, books
Open Mon–Fri 10am–5.30pm
Sat 10am–1pm
Fairs Irish Antique Dealers' Fair
Services Valuations, framing,
restoration

↗ O'Reillys (IAVI)

Contact Mr Michael Jordan
✉ **126 Francis Street, Dublin 8, Ireland** ℗
☎ 01 453 0311 ℱ 01 453 0226
✉ info@oreillysfineart.com
ⓦ www.oreillysfineart.com
Est. 1952
Open Mon–Fri 9.30am–5pm
Sales Fine jewellery and silverware monthly sale Wed 1pm, viewing Sun noon–4pm Mon Tues 11am–6pm Wed 10am–12.30pm prior to sale
Catalogues Yes

⊞ O'Sullivan Antiques (IADA)

Contact Ms Chantal O'Sullivan
✉ **43–44 Francis Street, Dublin 8, Ireland** ℗
☎ 01 454 1143 ℱ 01 454 1156
ⓜ 0862 543399
✉ info@osullivanantiques.com
ⓦ www.osullivanantiques.com
Est. 1991 *Stock size* Large
Stock 18th–19thC furniture, paintings, mirrors, chandeliers, mantelpieces, garden furniture
Open Mon–Fri 9am–6pm Sat 10am–6pm
Fairs Irish Antique Dealers' Fair
Services Restoration and upholstery

⊞ Rathmines Bookshop (BABI)

Contact Mr James Kinsella
✉ **201 Lower Rathmines Road, Dublin 6, Ireland** ℗
☎ 01 496 1064 ℱ 01 496 1064
Est. 1986 *Stock size* Large
Stock Irish books, first editions
Open Mon–Sat 10am–6pm

⊞ Esther Sexton Antiques (IADA)

Contact Ms Esther Sexton
✉ **51 Francis Street, Dublin 8, Ireland** ℗
☎ 01 473 0909
Est. 1990 *Stock size* Large
Stock Victorian and Edwardian furniture, decorative items
Open Mon–Sat 10.30am–5.30pm
Fairs Irish Antique Dealers' Fair

⊞ The Silver Shop (IADA)

Contact Mr Ian Haslam
✉ **Powerscourt Townhouse Centre, South William Street, Dublin 2,**
Ireland ℗
☎ 01 679 4147 ℱ 01 679 4147
✉ ianhaslam@eircom.net
Est. 1979 *Stock size* Large
Stock 18th–19thC silver, porcelain, portrait miniatures
Open Mon–Sat 11am–6pm
Fairs Irish Antique Dealers' Fair
Services Valuations

⊞ Stokes Books

Contact Mr Stephen Stokes
✉ **19 Market Arcade, South Great George's Street, Dublin 2, Ireland** ℗
☎ 01 671 3584 ℱ 01 671 3181
✉ stokesbooks@oceanfree.net
Est. 1982 *Stock size* Small
Stock General antiquarian. Catalogues available, books on Irish history and literature a speciality
Open Mon–Sat 10.30am–5.30pm
Services Valuations for probate and insurance

⊞ Timepiece Antique Clocks (IADA)

Contact Kevin Chellar
✉ **57–58 Patrick Street, Dublin 8, Ireland** ℗
☎ 01 454 0774 ℱ 01 454 0744
ⓜ 0872 260212
✉ timepieceireland@eircom.net
ⓦ www.timepieceantiqueclocks.com
Est. 1983 *Stock size* Large
Stock 18th–19thC clocks
Open Tues–Sat 10am–5pm
Fairs Irish Antique Dealers' Fair, Burlington Antiques Fair
Services Valuations, restoration

⊞ Jenny Vander

Contact Aidan or Gail Kinsella
✉ **50 Drury Street, Dublin 2, Ireland** ℗
☎ 01 677 0406
Est. 1964 *Stock size* Large
Stock Clothing (including evening dress), 1930s–1950s lace, Victorian–1960s jewellery
Open Mon–Sat 10am–5.30pm

⊞ The Victorian Salvage and Joinery Co Ltd (SALVO)

Contact Mark McDonagh
✉ **South Gloucester Street, Dublin 2, Ireland** ℗
☎ 01 672 7000 ℱ 01 672 7435
ⓜ 0872 551299
✉ vicsalv@indigo.ie
ⓦ www.vicsalv.com
Est. 1999 *Stock size* Large
Stock Reclaimed building materials
Open Mon–Fri 8.30am–5.30 Sat 9am–2pm
Services Valuations, restoration, shipping

⊞ Weir and Sons Ltd

Contact Allan Kilpatrick
✉ **96–99 Grafton Street, Dublin 2, Ireland** ℗
☎ 01 677 9678 ℱ 01 677 7739
✉ weirs@indigo.ie
ⓦ www.weirandsons.com
Est. 1869 *Stock size* Large
Stock Silverware (especially Irish), jewellery, pocket and wrist watches
Open Mon–Sat 9.30am–6pm Thurs 9.30am–8pm
Services Valuations, restoration

⊞ J W Weldon (IADA)

Contact James or Martin Weldon
✉ **55 Clarendon Street, Dublin 2, Ireland** ℗
☎ 01 677 1638 ℱ 01 670 7958
✉ antiques@weldonsofdublin.com
ⓦ www.weldonsofdublin.com
Est. 1900 *Stock size* Large
Stock Irish and diamond jewellery, antique Irish silver and provincial items
Open Mon–Sat 10am–5.30pm
Fairs IADA

↗ Whyte's

Contact Ian Whyte
✉ **38 Molesworth Street, Dublin 1, Ireland** ℗
☎ 01 676 2888 ℱ 01 676 2880
✉ info@whytes.ie
ⓦ www.whytes.ie
Est. 1783
Open Mon–Fri 10am–1pm 2–5.30pm
Sales 4 sales annually of Irish art and collectables
Catalogues Yes

DUN LAOGHAIRE

⊞ James Fenning, Antiquarian Booksellers, (ABA)

Contact Mr James Fenning
✉ **12 Glenview, Rochestown Avenue, Dun Laoghaire, Co Dublin, Ireland** ℗
☎ 01 285 7855 ℱ 01 285 7919
✉ fenning@indigo.ie

Est. 1969 *Stock size* Medium
Stock Antiquarian books
Open By appointment
Services Valuations

⊞ Felix Vink
Contact Felix Vink
⊠ Rear 50 Upper Georges Street,
Dun Laoghaire, Dublin,
Ireland ℙ
☎ 01 230 0900
⓪ 0899 635809
🅔 vinkf@eircom.net
Ⓦ www.mirrorimage.ie
Est. 1990 *Stock size* Medium
Stock Antique mirrors
Trade only Yes
Open By appointment
Fairs Royal Dublin Society
Services Restoration, gilding and
frames

⊞ Naughton's Booksellers
Contact Ms Susan Naughton
⊠ 8 Marine Terrace,
Dun Laoghaire, Co Dublin,
Ireland ℙ
☎ 01 280 4392
🅔 sales@naughtonsbooks.com
Ⓦ www.naughtonsbooks.com
Est. 1978 *Stock size* Medium
Stock Second-hand and
antiquarian books
Open By appointment

⊞ The Old Shop
Contact Ms Siobhan Nugent
⊠ St Michael's Mall,
Dun Laoghaire Shopping Centre,
Co Dublin,
Ireland ℙ
☎ 01 280 9915
Est. 1976 *Stock size* Large
Stock Jewellery, silver, porcelain
Open Mon–Sat 9.30am–6pm

⊞ Through the Looking Glass
Contact Ms Anna Connolly
⊠ 2 Salthill Place, Dun Laoghaire,
Co Dublin,
Ireland ℙ
☎ 01 280 6577
Est. 1989 *Stock size* Large
Stock Mirrors, Georgian furniture
Open Tues–Sat 10.30am–5.30pm
Services Restoration of mirrors

MALAHIDE

⚲ Drums Malahide
Contact Dennis Drum
⊠ New Street,

Malahide,
Co Dublin,
Ireland ℙ
☎ 01 845 2819 ⓕ 01 845 3356
🅔 drumsauc@gofree.indigo.ie
Est. 1974
Open Mon–Fri 9am–5pm
closed 1–2pm
Sales Fine art sales monthly on
Thurs at 7pm, regular fortnightly
mixed household sales Thurs
Catalogues Yes

⊞ Malahide Antique Shop
Contact Mr Frank Donellan
⊠ 14 New Street, Malahide,
Co Dublin,
Ireland ℙ
☎ 01 845 2900
Est. 1974 *Stock size* Large
Stock Jewellery, silver, Georgian
furniture, pictures, porcelain
Open Mon–Sat 10am–5.30pm
closed 1–2pm except Sat
Services Valuations, restoration

SANDYCOVE

⊞ Sandycove Fine Arts (IADA)
Contact Ms Fiona O'Reilly
⊠ 55 Glasthule Road, Sandycove,
Co Dublin,
Ireland ℙ
☎ 01 280 5956
Est. 1993 *Stock size* Medium
Stock Antique furniture,
paintings, china, glass, silver,
silver plate
Open Mon–Sat 10.30am–5.30pm

STILLORGAN

⊞ Beaufield Mews Restaurant, Gardens & Antiques (IADA)
Contact Ms Jill Cox
⊠ Woodlands Avenue,
Stillorgan,
Co Dublin,
Ireland ℙ
☎ 01 288 0375 ⓕ 01 288 6945
⓪ 0872 427360
🅔 beaumews@iol.ie
Ⓦ www.beaufieldmews.com
Est. 1948 *Stock size* Large
Stock Early Irish glass and
porcelain, 18th–19thC small
items of furniture, pictures
Open Tues–Sat 3–9pm Sun 1–5pm
Fairs Irish Antique Dealers' Fair
Services Valuations, award-
winning restaurant on site

CO GALWAY

CLARENBRIDGE

⊞ Clarenbridge Antiques
Contact Mr Martin Griffin
⊠ Limerick Road (N18),
Clarenbridge,
Co Galway,
Ireland ℙ
☎ 091 796522 ⓕ 091 796547
🅔 clarenbridgeantiques@eircom.net
Ⓦ www.clarenbridgeantiques.com
Est. 1981 *Stock size* Large
Stock Irish pine furniture,
country antiques, mahogany and
collectables
Open Summer Mon–Sun winter
Mon–Sat 9am–6pm
Services Pine stripping

CLIFDEN

⊞ Clifden Antiques
Contact Noreen Allen
⊠ Station House, Clifden,
Co Galway,
Ireland ℙ
☎ 095 22230
⓪ 0876 649845
Est. 1999 *Stock size* Medium
Stock 17th–19thC furniture,
contemporary Irish art, general
antiques
Open Mon–Sat 10.30am–6pm or
by appointment
Services Shipping

GALWAY

⊞ Cobwebs (IADA)
Contact Mrs Phyllis MacNamara
⊠ 7 Quay Lane, Galway,
Ireland ℙ
☎ 091 564388 ⓕ 091 564235
⓪ 0872 375745
🅔 cobwebs@eircom.net
Ⓦ www.cobwebsgalway.com
Est. 1972 *Stock size* Large
Stock Antique and fine jewellery
Open Mon–Sat 9.30am–5.30pm
Fairs Irish Antique Dealers Fair

⊞ Tempo Antiques
Contact Frank, Phil or David
Greeley
⊠ 9 Cross Street, Galway,
Ireland ℙ
☎ 091 562282 ⓕ 091 562282
🅔 info@tempoantiques.com
Ⓦ www.tempoantiques.com
Est. 1995 *Stock size* Large
Stock Victorian–Edwardian,

Art Deco antique jewellery, silver, porcelain, collectables
Open Mon–Sat 10am–6pm

⊞ Tolco Antiques
Contact Tom or Breda O'Loughlin
⊠ Headford Road, Galway, Ireland 🅿
☎ 091 751146
Est. 1971 *Stock size* Large
Stock General antiques, collectables
Open Mon–Fri 10am–5pm
Sat 10am–4pm
Services Valuations

⊞ Twice As Nice
Contact Ms Deirdre Grandee
⊠ 5 Quay Street, Galway, Ireland
☎ 091 566332
Est. 1987 *Stock size* Medium
Stock Period clothes, lace, linen, jewellery
Open Mon–Sat 10am–6pm

⊞ The Winding Stair
Contact Mr Val Tyrell
⊠ 4 Mainguard Street, Galway, Ireland 🅿
🖂 tyrell@eircom.net
Est. 1991 *Stock size* Medium
Stock Prints, lighting, furniture, jewellery, collectables, general antiques
Open Mon–Sat 10am–6pm
Services Shipping – small items only

GORT

⊞ Honan's Antiques
Contact Brian or Margaret Honan
⊠ Crowe Street, Gort, Co Galway, Ireland 🅿
☎ 091 631407 🖷 091 631816
🖂 honansantique@eircom.net
🌐 www.honansantiques.com
Est. 1976 *Stock size* Large
Stock Antique pine, clocks, lamps, Victorian fireplaces, advertising signs, mirrors, pub fittings etc
Open Mon–Sat 10am–6pm
Services Pine stripping

MOYCULLEN

⊞ Moycullen Village Antiques (IADA)
Contact Ms Maura Duffy

⊠ Main Street, Moycullen, Co Galway, Ireland 🅿
☎ 091 555303 🖷 091 555303
📱 0868 235976
Est. 1989 *Stock size* Large
Stock Fine Regency–Edwardian furniture, paintings, prints, fine china, silver
Open Mon–Sat 9.45am–5.30pm
Sun 2–5.30pm
Fairs Dublin Horse Show, IADA (Mar, Dec)

CO KERRY

ABBEYDORNEY

⊞ Abbey Antiques
Contact Jerry O'Donovan
⊠ Main Street, Abbeydorney, Co Kerry, Ireland 🅿
☎ 066 7135460
Est. 1989 *Stock size* Large
Stock Victorian fireplaces, Georgian–Edwardian furniture
Open Sun or by appointment

KILLARNEY

⊞ Frameworks (IADA, CINOA)
Contact Katie O'Connell
⊠ 37 New Street, Killarney, Co Kerry, Ireland 🅿
☎ 064 35791 🖷 064 35791
🖂 frameworks@eircom.net
🌐 www.frameworks.ie
Est. 1994 *Stock size* Medium
Stock 19th–20thC furniture, 17th–19thC prints, maps, glass gardenware
Open Mon–Sat 10am–6pm
Fairs Dublin (Sep Mar)
Services Framing

TRALEE

⊞ Lots Furniture, Gifts and Antiques
Contact Margaret Brosnan
⊠ Dingle Road, Tralee, Co Kerry, Ireland 🅿
☎ 066 712 7117 🖷 066 712 7424
🖂 lots@lotsworldwide.com
🌐 www.lotsworldwide.com
Est. 1990 *Stock size* Medium
Stock Victorian furniture, interesting pieces

Open Mon–Fri 9am–6pm
Sat 10am–6pm Sun 2–6pm
Services Restoration

CO KILDARE

MAYMOOTH

⊞ Hugh Cash Antiques
Contact Hugh Cash
⊠ Main Street, Maynooth, Co Kildare, Ireland 🅿
☎ 01 628 5946
📱 0872 434510
Est. 1969 *Stock size* Large
Stock Georgian–Edwardian furniture
Open By appointment only
Services Valuations

CO KILKENNY

BALLYCALLAN

⊞ Edward Comerford Antiques
Contact Edward Comerford
⊠ Ballevan, Ballycallan, Co Kilkenny, Ireland 🅿
☎ 056 776 9384
Est. 2000 *Stock size* Large
Stock General antiques, collectables
Open By appointment

CASTLECOMER

⚒ Mealy's Ltd (IAVI)
Contact Fonsie or George Mealy
⊠ Chatsworth Street, Castlecomer, Co Kilkenny, Ireland 🅿
☎ 056 444 1229/1413
🖷 056 444 1627
🖂 info@mealys.com
🌐 www.mealys.com
Est. 1934
Open Mon–Fri 9am–1pm 2–6pm
Sales 2 antiquarian book auctions per year, viewing days prior to auction. Also fine art sales
Frequency 8 per year
Catalogues Yes

FRESHFORD

⊞ Cass Freshford Antiques
Contact Michael Cass
⊠ Bohercrussia Street, Freshford, Co Kilkenny,

Ireland ℗
☎ 05688 32240
✉ cassantiques@dol.ie
Est. 1966 *Stock size* Medium
Stock Antique furniture
Open Mon–Sat 9am–5pm
Services Restoration

GORESBRIDGE

➹ Michael Donohoe & Sons
Contact Martin Donohoe
✉ Goresbridge, Co Kilkenny, Ireland ℗
☎ 059 977 5145
Est. 1974
Open Mon–Fri 9am–5.30pm
Sales General antiques sales in Feb, April, Aug, Nov
Catalogues Yes

THOMASTOWN

⊞ Tara Antiques
Contact Tom Higginson
✉ Grennan Water Mill, Thomastown, Co Kilkenny, Ireland ℗
☎ 05 677 54077 ✆ 05 677 54077
✉ taraantiques@eircom.net
ⓦ www.taraantiques.ie
Est. 2000 *Stock size* Medium
Stock Georgian–Edwardian furniture, clocks, mirrors
Open Mon–Sat 10.30am–5pm
Services Restoration

CO LAOIS

ABBEYLEIX

⊞ Ireland's Own Antiques
Contact Daniel or Peter Meaney
✉ Main Street, Abbeyleix, Co Laois, Ireland ℗
☎ 050 231348
ⓜ 07717 676131
Est. 1963 *Stock size* Large
Stock General antiques and furniture
Open 10am–8pm or by appointment everyday

CO LAOIS

BALLACOLLA

⊞ Glebe Hall Collectables
Contact Carmel Corrigan-Griffin
✉ Old Killernogh Rectory, Rathmakelly Glebe, Ballacolla,

Co Laois, Ireland ℗
☎ 0502 34105 ✆ 0502 34105
ⓜ 0868 784956
Est. 1980 *Stock size* Large
Stock Pine country furniture, porcelain, linen, paintings, kitchenware, silver plate, books, jewellery
Open Weekends and Bank Holidays by appointment
Services Restoration, tuition

DURROW

➹ Sheppard Irish Auction House (IAVI)
Contact Michael Sheppard
✉ The Square, Durrow, Co Laois, Ireland ℗
☎ 050 236123 ✆ 050 236546
✉ info@sheppards.ie
Est. 1949
Open Mon–Sat 10am–1pm 2–6pm
Sales General antiques, porcelain, furniture, fine arts
Frequency Every 2–3 months
Catalogues Yes

PORTARLINGTON

⊞ McDonnell's Antique Furniture
Contact Ray McDonnell
✉ Cloneyhurke, Portarlington, Co Laois, Ireland ℗
☎ 05024 3304
Est. 1981 *Stock size* Large
Stock Religious furniture, pulpits, pews, statuary, pine and farmhouse furniture
Open Mon–Sat 8am–8pm

CO LEITRIM

CARRICK ON SHANNON

⊞ Trinity Rare Books
Contact Nick or Joanna Kaszuk
✉ Bridge Street, Carrick on Shannon, Co Leitrim
☎ 0719 622144
✉ nickk@iol.ie
ⓦ www.trinityrarebooks.com
Est. 1999 *Stock size* Medium
Stock Antiquarian fine bindings, books, modern first editions
Open Mon–Sat 9.30am–6pm
Services Book search

CO LIMERICK

ADARE

⊞ Carol's Antiques (IADA, CINOA)
Contact Ms Carol O'Connor
✉ Rose Cottage, Main Street, Adare, Co Limerick, Ireland
☎ 061 453 8948 ✆ 061 439 6991
ⓜ 0862 478827
✉ coconnor@indigo.ie
ⓦ www.carolsantiquesadare.com
Est. 1979 *Stock size* Large
Stock Georgian–Victorian furniture, silver, brass, porcelain, objets d'art, jewellery, contemporary Irish art
Open Mon–Sat 9.30am–5.30pm
Fairs Irish Antique Dealers' Fair, Annual Cork Antiques Fair
Services Interior decoration

⊞ Manor Antiques
Contact Mr Simon Quilligan
✉ Main Street, Adare, Co Limerick, Ireland ℗
☎ 061 396515 or 069 64869
ⓜ 0868 365196
Est. 1914 *Stock size* Large
Stock Georgian–Victorian furniture, general antiques
Open Fri Sat 10am–5.30pm or by appointment
Services Shipping

⊞ George Stacpoole (IADA)
Contact Mr George Stacpoole
✉ Main Street, Adare, Co Limerick, Ireland ℗
☎ 061 396409 ✆ 061 396733
✉ stacpool@iol.ie
ⓦ www.georgestacpooleantiques.com
Est. 1962 *Stock size* Medium
Stock Furniture, silver, books, pictures, china, prints
Open Mon–Sat 10am–5.30pm
Fairs IADA
Services Valuations and interior decoration

LIMERICK

⊞ Ann's Antiques
Contact Ann O'Doherty
✉ 32 Mallow Street, Limerick, Ireland ℗
☎ 061 302492 ✆ 061 413035
Est. 1984 *Stock size* Medium

Stock Mid–late Victorian furniture
Open Tues–Fri 11am–5pm or by appointment
Services Valuations, search

⊞ Bygones Antiques
Contact Mr John Costello
✉ **16 Nicholas Street, Limerick, Ireland** ℗
☎ 061 417339
Est. 1979 *Stock size* Medium
Stock Antique pine furniture and beds
Open Mon–Fri 9am–5.30pm half day Sat
Services Pine stripping

⊞ John Gunning Antiques
Contact Mr John Gunning
✉ **2 Castle Street, Limerick, Ireland** ℗
☎ 061 410535
Est. 1970 *Stock size* Large
Stock General antiques
Open Mon–Sat 10am–5pm

⊞ Noonan Antiques
Contact Jim Noonan
✉ **16–17 Ellen Street, Limerick, Ireland** ℗
☎ 061 413861 ☏ 061 413861
⊕ 0872 539165
✉ jandanoonan@eircom.net
Est. 1985 *Stock size* Medium
Stock Antique jewellery, collectables
Open Mon–Sat 10am–5pm

⊞ O'Toole Antiques & Decorative Galleries (IADA)
Contact Noel O'Toole
✉ **Upper William Street, Limerick, Ireland** ℗
☎ 061 414490 ☏ 061 411378
⊕ 0872 550985
✉ noel.o.toole.antiques@oceanfree.net
Est. 1979 *Stock size* Large
Stock 18th–19thC furniture, pictures, fireplaces, mirrors and porcelain
Open Mon–Sat 9.30am–6pm
Fairs IADA
Services Valuations, restoration

⊞ Tess Antiques
Contact Ms Tess Costello
✉ **5 Roches Street, Limerick, Ireland** ℗
☎ 061 416643/399736

Est. 1980 *Stock size* Small
Stock Jewellery, silver, porcelain
Open Tues–Sat 10am–5pm

CO LOUTH
DROGHEDA

⊞ Greene's Antiques Galleries (IADA)
Contact Austin Greene
✉ **Saereve House, Dunany, Co Louth, Ireland** ℗
☎ 041 685 2440
✉ hugo@greenesantiques.com
Est. 1886 *Stock size* Large
Stock 18th–20thC furniture
Open Thurs–Sat 9am–5pm or by appointment

DUNDALK

⊞ Hall's Curio Shop
Contact Margaret or Rory Hall
✉ **9–10 Jocelyn Street, Dundalk, Co Louth, Ireland**
☎ 042 933 4902
Est. 1971 *Stock size* Large
Stock Jewellery, paintings, silver, general
Open Mon–Sat 10am–1pm 2–6pm closed Thurs or by appointment
Services Valuations

CO MAYO
ACHILL SOUND

⊞ Roger Grimes (IADA)
Contact Roger Grimes
✉ **Old Rectory, Achill Sound, Co Mayo, Ireland** ℗
☎ 098 27823 ☏ 098 27823
✉ rogergrimes@eircom.net
Est. 1977
Stock 17th–19thC provincial furniture, metalware, china, pictures, prints, eccentricities
Open Daily in the summer or by appointment
Fairs IADA
Services Valuations

⊞ Vanessa Parker Rare Books (IADA)
Contact Vanessa Parker
✉ **Old Rectory, Achill Sound, Co Mayo, Ireland** ℗

☎ 098 27823 ☏ 098 27823
✉ vanessaparker@eircom.net
Est. 1977
Stock Antiquarian books, folklore, literature, Irish, 19th–20thC children's books, fine bindings
Open Daily in the summer or by appointment
Fairs IADA
Services Valuations, books bought

DUNSHOUGHLIN

⊞ John Duffy Antiques
Contact John Duffy
✉ **Raynestown, Dunshoughlin, Co Mayo, Ireland** ℗
☎ 01 825 0335
Est. 1986 *Stock size* Large
Stock General antiques, fireplaces
Open Mon–Sat 10am–6pm
Services Valuations, restoration

WESTPORT

⊞ Jonathan Beech Antique Clocks (IADA)
Contact Mr Jonathan Beech
✉ **Killeenacoff House, Cloona, Westport, Co Mayo, Ireland** ℗
☎ 098 28688 ☏ 098 28688
⊕ 0872 226247
✉ info@antiqueclocks-ireland.com
⊛ www.antiques-ireland.com
Est. 1984 *Stock size* Medium
Stock Clocks
Open By appointment
Fairs Irish Antique Dealers' Fair, Dublin, Galway, Limerick
Services Valuations, restoration

⊞ Satch Kiely (IADA, LAPADA, CINOA)
Contact Karen Kiely
✉ **Westport Quay, Westport, Co Mayo, Ireland** ℗
☎ 098 25775 ☏ 098 25957
⊕ 08624 81431
✉ satchkielyantiques@eircom.net
Est. 1985 *Stock size* Large
Stock 18th–19thC furniture, Irish and English silver, colonial lamps, fossil bog oak, Killarney furniture, objects
Open Mon–Sat 2–6pm summer noon–5.20pm or by appointment
Fairs Irish Antique Dealers' Fair,

Annual Cork Antiques Fair, Galway and Hunt Museum, Limerick
Services Valuations

⊞ Westport House Antique Shop (IADA)
Contact Earl of Altamont
✉ Westport House, Westport, Co Mayo, Ireland ℗
☎ 098 25430 ☏ 098 25206
✉ info@westporthouse.ie
ⓦ www.westporthouse.ie
Est. 1969 *Stock size* Small
Stock Prints, silver plate, jewellery
Open March–Nov 11.30am–5.30pm or by appointment

CO MEATH
GORMANSTOWN
⊞ Delvin Farm Antiques
Contact J or B McCrane
✉ Gormanstown, Co Meath, Ireland ℗
☎ 01 841 2285 ☏ 01 841 3730
ⓜ 08624 65615
✉ info@delvinfarmpine.com
ⓦ www.delvinfarmpine.com
Est. 1974 *Stock size* Large
Stock Antique country furniture
Open Mon–Sat 9am–5pm

KELLS
⚒ Oliver Usher (IAVI)
Contact Mr Oliver Usher
✉ John Street, Kells, Co Meath, Ireland ℗
☎ 046 92 41097 ☏ 046 92 41097
✉ oliverusher@ireland.com
Est. 1978
Open Mon–Fri 9.30am–5.30pm
Sales Antique and high-class furniture sale Tues 5pm mid month at Kells, viewing Sun 2–6pm Mon 11am–7pm Tues 11am–5pm. Spring and autumn sales at The Conyngham Arms Hotel, Slane. Additional sales at properties around the country, phone for details
Frequency Monthly
Catalogues Yes

⊞ George Williams Antiques (IADA)
Contact George Williams
✉ The Annexe,

Newcastle House, Kilmainhamwood, Kells, Co Meath, Ireland ℗
☎ 04690 52740
ⓜ 0872 529959
✉ gwilliams@eircom.net
ⓦ www.georgian-antiques.com
Est. 1987 *Stock size* Medium
Stock 18th–19thC furniture, paintings
Open By appointment only
Fairs IADA Exhibition, Dublin (Sept)
Services Purchasing on commission, valuations

OLDCASTLE
⚒ Mullen Bros Auctions
Contact Michael Mullen
✉ Oldcastle, Co Meath, Ireland ℗
☎ 049 854 1107 ☏ 049 854 1107
Est. 1962
Open Tues–Fri 10am–6pm
Sales General antiques and household goods 1st Tues of every month 6.30pm, viewing 3 days prior
Catalogues No

CO OFFALY
BIRR
⊞ Ivy Hall Antiques (IADA, CINOA)
Contact Mrs Ena Hoctor
✉ Carrig, Birr, Co Offaly, Ireland ℗
☎ 0509 20148
Est. 1967 *Stock size* Large
Stock 18th–19thC silver, porcelain, furniture, pictures
Open By appointment

EDENDERRY
⊞ Edenderry Architectural Salvage Ltd
Contact Brian Murphy
✉ Monasteroris Industrial Estate, Edenderry, Co Offaly, Ireland ℗
ⓜ 0862 595367
✉ bpmurphy@iol.ie
Est. 1995 *Stock size* Large
Stock Reclaimed flooring, bricks, radiators, doors, baths, sinks, beams, railway sleepers, cobblestones, fireplaces
Open Mon–Fri 9am–5pm

Services Cutting and planing of reclaimed timber beams and flooring

CO SLIGO
SLIGO
⊞ Louis J Doherty & Sons
Contact Louis
✉ Teeling House, Teeling Street, Sligo, Ireland ℗
☎ 071 916 9494 ☏ 071 915 3877
✉ ljdoherty@eircom.net
ⓦ www.irish-antiques.com
Est. 1975 *Stock size* Large
Stock General antiques, Victorian–Edwardian furniture
Open Mon–Sat 9.30am–1pm 2–6pm
Services Valuations

⊞ Georgian Village Antiques
Contact Louis and John Doherty
✉ Castle Street, Sligo, Ireland ℗
☎ 07191 62421 ☏ 07191 69494
✉ ljsvillage@eircom.net
Est. 1976 *Stock size* Medium
Stock Small furniture items, jewellery, porcelain, glass
Open Mon–Sat 10am–6pm
Services Valuations

CO TIPPERARY
BALLINDERRY
⊞ Kilgarvan Antique Centre
Contact Denise Shaw
✉ Kilgarvan Quay, Ballinderry, Nenagh, Co Tipperary, Ireland ℗
☎ 067 22047
✉ deniseshaw27@hotmail.com
Est. 1947 *Stock size* Medium
Stock Georgian antiques, mirrors, general china
Open Mon–Sat 10am–7pm Sun after 3pm Apr–Oct by appointment
Services Restoration of giltwood mirrors and antique furniture, restoration and polishing of wooden and carved furniture

CAHIR
⊞ Abbey Antiques (IADA)
Contact Mr Michael Kennedy
✉ Abbey Street, Cahir,

Co Tipperary,
Ireland ℗
☎ 052 41187 ☏ 052 41187
Ⓜ 0872 728844
✉ celine@antiquesireland.ie
🌐 www.antiquesireland.ie
Est. 1992 *Stock size* Large
Stock Georgian–Edwardian
furniture, French country
furniture, lighting, objets d'art
Open Mon–Sat 10.30am–5.30pm
Services Shipping

⊞ Fleury Antiques (IADA)
Contact C or D Fleury
✉ The Square, Cahir,
Co Tipperary,
Ireland ℗
☎ 052 41226
☏ fleuryantiques@eircom.net
🌐 www.fleuryantiques.com
Est. 1978 *Stock size* Medium
Stock 18th–19thC furniture,
sculptures, paintings, decorative
objects, jewellery, porcelain,
silver
Open Mon–Sat 9am–6pm
Fairs No

CASHEL

⊞ Cashel Antiques
Contact Norah or Joe Barry
✉ Bank Place, Cashel,
Co Tipperary,
Ireland
☎ 062 61319
Est. 1979 *Stock size* Medium
Stock Antique furniture,
jewellery
Open By appointment

⊞ Ladyswell Antiques
& Jewellery
Contact Fiona Bourke
✉ 5 Ladyswell Street, Cashel,
Co Tipperary,
Ireland ℗
☎ 062 61267
Est. 1965 *Stock size* Small
Stock General antiques
Open Mon–Sat 2–6pm
Services Valuations, restoration

CO WATERFORD

WATERFORD

⊞ An Siopa
Contact Maria Halligan
✉ 60 John Street, Waterford,
Ireland ℗
☎ 051 877549 ☏ 051 877549

Est. 1972 *Stock size* Large
Stock Antique jewellery, silver
Open Mon–Sat 9am–6pm
Services Valuations

⋔ City Auction Rooms
(IPAV)
Contact Rody or Ann Keighery
✉ Georges Quay, Waterford,
Ireland ℗
☎ 051 873692 ☏ 051 873692
Est. 1948
Open Mon–Sat 9am–5.30pm
Sales Six-weekly antiques and
general furniture sale Mon 2pm,
viewing Fri Sat Sun noon–6pm
Catalogues Yes

⊞ R J Keighery (IPAV)
Contact Rody or Ann Keighery
✉ 27a William Street, Waterford,
Ireland ℗
☎ 051 873692 ☏ 051 873692
Est. 1948 *Stock size* Large
Stock Antiques, furniture, china,
silver, collectables
Open Mon–Sat 9am–5.30pm
Services Valuations

⊞ The Salvage Shop
Contact Sean Corcoran
✉ Airport Road, Waterford City,
Ireland ℗
☎ 051 873260 ☏ 051 858323
Ⓜ 0872 524657
☏ salvage@iol.ie
🌐 www.bang2000.com
Est. 1991 *Stock size* Large
Stock Architectural salvage and
reclaimed wood furniture
Open Mon–Fri 8am–5.30pm
Sat 10am–3pm
Fairs Beyond the Hall Door
Services Restoration, interior
design

CO WEXFORD

ROSSLARE

⊞ Selskar Antiques
Contact Irene Walker
✉ Poulrankin, Rosslare,
Co Wexford,
Ireland ℗
☎ 053 73967 ☏ 053 73967
Ⓜ 0876 791095
☏ selskarantiques@eircom.net
🌐 www.selskarantiques.biz
Est. 1984 *Stock size* Medium
Stock Antique jewellery, pictures,
fine china, small furniture items,
glass, collectables

Open Mon–Sat noon–6pm
Sun noon–4pm
Fairs O'Donnell Fairs, Wexford
Opera Festival
Services Valuations

WEXFORD

⊞ Forum Antiques
Contact Nora Liddy
✉ Selskar, Wexford,
Ireland ℗
☎ 053 21055
Est. 1996 *Stock size* Medium
Stock Antiquarian books, maps,
prints, china, collectables
Open Mon–Sat 11am–5.30pm
winter telephone first
Fairs National Book Fairs
Services Book valuations

CO WICKLOW

BRAY

⊞ Clancy Chandeliers
(IADA)
Contact Ger, Derek or
Tommy Clancy
✉ Villanova, Ballywaltrim, Bray,
Co Wicklow,
Ireland ℗
☎ 01 286 3460 ☏ 01 286 3460
Ⓜ 0872 428838
☏ info@clancychandeliers.com
🌐 www.clancychandeliers.com
Est. 1989 *Stock size* Large
Stock Period and reproduction
chandeliers, wall lights, hall
lanterns
Open Strictly by appointment
Fairs IADA Exhibition, Dublin
(Sept), IAFAF (Mar)
Services Professional cleaning,
restoration, hanging service

RADHDRUM

⊞ Cathair Books
Contact Mr Eugene Mallon
✉ Pound Brook Lane,
Radhdrum,
Co Wicklow,
Ireland ℗
☎ 040 446939 ☏ 040 446939
☏ cathairbks@eircom.net
🌐 www.abebooks.com/home/
cathair_books
Est. 1974 *Stock size* Medium
Stock Irish-interest books, prints,
maps, postcards
Open Mail order only
Services Valuations

Associated Services

ARCHITECTURAL

Zygmunt Chelminski (UKIC)
Contact Mr Z Chelminski
✉ Studio GE1, 2 Michael Road,
London,
SW6 2AD ▯
☎ 020 7610 9731 ☏ 020 7610 9731
📱 07770 585130
Est. 1993
Services Restoration and conservation of architectural monuments, statues and special effects in marble, granite, stone, terracotta, alabaster, coldstone, iron, bronze, zinc, lead, ormolu, wood, ivory, pietra dura, scagliola, plaster, mother-of-pearl, tortoiseshell, shagreen, amber, onyx, papier-mâché, blue john and semi-precious stones
Open Mon–Fri 10am–5pm appointment advisable

Cleveland Wood Strip
Contact Mr P Stokes
✉ 2 Kensington Road, Oxbridge,
Stockton-on-Tees,
North Yorkshire,
TS18 4DQ ▯
☎ 01642 643033
📱 07980 031169
Est. 1989
Services French polishing, dip and strip, architectural restoration
Open Mon–Sat 10am–5pm but phone first please

Ivo Geikie-Cobb
Contact Mr I Geikie-Cobb
✉ Unit 32, Charterhouse Works,
Eltringham Street,
London,
SW18 1TD ▯
☎ 020 8874 3767 ☏ 020 8874 3767
📱 07761 561569
📧 restore@ivogc.com
🌐 www.ivogc.com
Est. 1991
Services Antique furniture conservation and restoration, gilding, upholstery, re-leathering, French polishing, veneering, architectural restoration
Open Mon–Fri 9.30am–5.30pm

Ivo Geikie-Cobb
Contact Mr I Geikie-Cobb
✉ West Country Workshop,
Ivydene, Semley, Dorset,

SP7 9AU ▯
☎ 01747 830 123 ☏ 01747 830 123
📱 07761 561569
📧 restore@ivogc.com
🌐 www.ivogc.com
Est. 2005
Services Antique furniture conservation and restoration, gilding, upholstery, re-leathering, French polishing, veneering, architectural restoration
Open Mon–Fri 9.30am–5.30pm

Iron Wright
Contact Mr F Sporik
✉ 5 Cranleigh Mews,
Cabul Road, London,
SW11 2QL ▯
☎ 020 7228 2727 ☏ 020 7652 4089
🌐 www.ironwright.co.uk
Est. 1994
Services Repair and restoration of cast-iron fireplaces
Open Mon–Fri 8am–6pm Sat by appointment

Melluish & Davis
Contact Mr J Davis
✉ Unit D (South),
Riding Court Farm,
Riding Court Road, Datchet,
Slough,
SL3 9JU ▯
☎ 01753 582208
📱 07966 247549
📧 meluishdavis@btconnect.com
Est. 1972
Services Restoration and research of marble chimneypieces, sculpture and garden ornaments
Open Mon–Fri 9am–5pm

Salvo
Contact Ruby Kay
✉ PO Box 28080,
London,
SE27 0YZ
☎ 0208 761 2316 ☏ 0208 761 2424
📧 admin@salvoweb.com
🌐 www.salvoweb.com
Est. 1992
Services Salvo networks information on architectural salvage, garden antiques, reclaimed building materials and reproductions. Salvo publishes SalvoEMAILS several times a week, printed *SalvoNEWS* every 3 weeks, *SALVO* magazine intermittently and *The Salvo Guide*

Thistle and Rose
Contact Kim Roberts
✉ 5 Orrock Place, Hawick,
Scottish Borders,
TD9 0HQ ▯
☎ 01450 376928
Est. 2004
Services Restoring and making pine and gesso Adam chimney pieces
Open Mon–Fri 9am–6pm

Gwyn Watkins Stonemason and Architectural Stone Carver
Contact Gwyn Watkins
✉ Stonemason's Shop,
Burghley House, Stamford,
Lincolnshire,
PE9 3JY ▯
☎ 01780 766366
Est. 1988
Services Restoration and repair of garden statuary. Work on listed buildings, repainting, repairing stonework, fireplaces
Open By appointment

BOOKS

Antiquarian Bookcrafts
Contact Des Breen
✉ Craft Centre, Marlay Park,
Dublin 16,
Ireland ▯
☎ 01 494 2834 ☏ 01 494 2811
📧 desbreen@eirecom.net
Est. 1962
Services Book binding, restoration
Open Mon–Fri 7.45am–4.30pm

C & A J Barmby
Contact C Barmby
✉ 140 Lavender Hill, Tonbridge,
Kent,
TN9 2AY
☎ 01732 771590 ☏ 01732 771590
📧 bookpilot@aol.com
Est. 1970
Services Reference books on antiques, display stands, accessories, packaging material
Trade only Yes
Open By appointment

Baron Art
Contact Mr A Baron
✉ 9 and 16 Chapel Yard,
Albert Street, Holt , Norfolk,
NR25 6HG ▯
☎ 01263 713430 ☏ 01263 711670

@ baronholt@aol.com
Est. 2001
Services Restoration of antiquarian books, paintings, ceramics, plus framing
Open Mon–Sat 9am–5pm

The Book Depot
Contact Conrad Wiberg
⊠ 111 Woodcote Avenue,
London,
NW7 2PD
☎ 020 8906 3708
Est. 1980
Services Free book search for any book
Open Mon–Sun 9am–5pm postal business

Brignell Bookbinders
Contact Barry Brignell
⊠ 25 Gwydir Street, Cambridge,
Cambridgeshire,
CB1 2LG ▣
☎ 01223 321280 ☏ 01223 321280
Est. 1982
Services Book binding, repair, presentation of volumes
Open Mon–Thurs 8.30am–4.45pm Fri 8.30am–4pm

Cameron Preservation (IPCRA, IPC, SAPCON)
Contact Mr Elgin Cameron
⊠ Flush Business Centre,
Flush Place, Lurgan,
Co Armagh,
BT66 7DT ▣
☎ 028 3834 3099 ☏ 028 3834 3099
Est. 1993
Services Restoration of art on paper, archives, manuscripts, books, also vellum, parchment, globes
Open Mon–Fri 8.30am–5.15 Sat 8.30am–noon

Fullertons Booksearch
Contact Mr Humphrey Boon
⊠ The Duke's House,
Moorgate Road, Hindringham,
Fakenham, Norfolk,
NR21 0PT ▣
☎ 01420 544088 ☏ 01420 542445
@ fullertons.books@virgin.net
Est. 1991
Services Out-of-print book searching facility. Mail order sales
Open Mon–Fri 9am–5pm

H P Book Finders
Contact Mr Martin Earl

⊠ Mosslaird, Brig O'Turk,
Callander, Scotland,
FK17 8HT ▣
☎ 01877 376377 ☏ 01877 376377
@ martin@hp-bookfinders.co.uk
@ www.hp-bookfinders.co.uk
Est. 1984
Services Book search
Open Mon–Fri 8am–6pm Sat 9am–1pm

F Hutton (Bookbinder) (SOB, Designer Binders)
Contact Felicity Hutton
⊠ Langore House, Langore,
Launceston, Cornwall,
PL15 8LD ▣
☎ 01566 773831
Est. 1985
Services Bookbinding and restoration
Open By appointment

Blair Jeary
Contact Blair Jeary
⊠ The Stable Courtyard,
Burghley House, Stamford,
Lincolnshire,
PE9 3JY ▣
☎ 01780 763725
@ 07834 188601
Est. 1989
Services Restoration and re-binding of antiquarian books
Open By appointment

Meadowcroft Books
Contact Miss Laing
⊠ 21 Upper Bognor Road,
Bognor Regis,
West Sussex,
PO21 1JA ▣
☎ 01243 868614 ☏ 01243 868714
@ enquiries@meadowcroftbooks.demon.co.uk
@ www.meadowcroftbooks.demon.co.uk
Est. 1996
Services Book search
Open By appointment

BUYING SERVICE

Ayuka Ltd
Contact Mune Ota
⊠ Village Farm, Stanford,
Bedfordshire,
SG18 9JQ ▣
☎ 01438 362494 ☏ 01438 228494
@ 07796 804032
@ sales@ayuka.co.uk
@ www.ayuka.co.uk
Services Personal antique buying

service, shipping, advice on buying antiques
Open Mon–Sun 9am–8pm

Cane Chairs Repaired
Contact Paul Boulton
⊠ Dunmayling, High Street,
Burwash, East Sussex,
TN19 7EP ▣
☎ 0800 027 6869 ☏ 01435 882299
@ 07850 943091
@ chairs@btconnect.com
@ www.canechairs.co.uk
Est. 1995
Services Repair of all cane and Lloyd Loom chairs
Open Mon–Fri 8am–6pm

Cane Corner (Basket Makers Association, Devon Rural Skills Trust)
Contact Bridgette Graham
⊠ Behind East Budleigh Garage,
Lower Budleigh, East Budleigh,
Devon,
EX9 7DL ▣
☎ 01395 446616
@ brigitte@canecorner.fsnet.co.uk
@ www.canecorner.co.uk
Est. 1985
Services Antique and modern chairs professionally reseated with split cane and rush, canework on other curiosities restored
Open Mon–Fri 9am–5.30pm hours by chance or appointment

The Cane & Rush Chair Repair Service
Contact R D Nolan
⊠ 156 Horton Hill, Epsom, Surrey,
KT19 8ST ▣
☎ 01372 727063
@ 07961 313933
Est. 1984
Services Cane and rush repair
Open Mon–Fri 7.30am–5pm Sat 8am–noon

Cane Weaving Repairs
⊠ Ely, Cambridgeshire,
CB6 ▣
☎ 0845 330 6336 ☏ 0845 330 6336
Est. 1989
Services Hand-woven cane repair, local delivery and collection of small items
Open By appointment

Caners & Upholders
Contact Steve Warrington
⊠ The Old Beef House,

Stubhampton Manor Farm,
Tarrant Gunville,
Blandford Forum, Dorset,
DT11 8JS ▣
☎ 01258 830300
✉ steven.warrington@virgin.net
Est. 1989
Services Cane and rush repair
and restoration
Open Mon–Fri 9am–5pm or by
appointment

The Chairman of Bearsden (Scottish Furniture Preservation Society)
Contact David Shuttleton
✉ 115a Ayr Road, Newton
Means, Glasgow,
G77 6RF ▣
☎ 0141 639 6005
📱 07814 744229
✉ sales@charlesrennie
mackintosh.co.uk
🌐 www.charlesreniemackintosh.co.uk
Est. 1990
Services Furniture restoration
and upholstery, French polishing,
cabinet-making, bergère suites,
cane and rush seating
Open Mon–Sat 9am–5pm

Former Glory
Contact Tim or Kim Ravenscroft
✉ Ferndown, Dorset,
BH22 ▣
☎ 01202 895859 ✉ 01202 895859
📱 07769 828727
✉ formerglory@btinternet.com
🌐 www.formerglory.co.uk
Est. 1994
Services Cane and rush seating,
furniture restoration. Cane, rush
and restoration material
suppliers
Open By appointment only

Gloucestershire Furniture Hospital
Contact Mr M Deane
✉ Commonfields Farm,
Lower Boulsdon, Newent,
Gloucestershire,
GL18 1JH ▣
☎ 01531 822881 ✉ 01531 822881
📱 07989 993919
✉ doctordeane.gfh@btinternet.com
Est. 1999
Services Antique and modern
furniture repair including
upholstery, caning and French
polishing. Collection service, all
insurance work undertaken
Open Mon–Sat 8am–6pm

Howard Hunt Antiques
Contact Mr H Hunt
✉ The White Hut, Thackhams
Farm, Bottle Lane, Mattingley,
Hook, Hampshire,
RG27 8LJ ▣
☎ 01256 881111 ✉ 01256 881111
Est. 1989
Services Repair and restoration
of furniture, mirrors, porcelain,
upholstery, leathering, gilding,
caning, rushing
Open By appointment

Peter Maitland
Contact Mr P J Maitland
✉ 27 Berkeley Road,
Bishopstone, Bristol,
BS7 8HF ▣
☎ 0117 942 6870
Est. 1990
Services Chair restoration,
caning
Open Mon–Fri 9am–5pm or by
appointment

Andrew A Matthews Restoration (Graduate member of the students section BAFRA)
Contact Mr A A Matthews
✉ Fox House, Gills Hill, Bourn,
Cambridge, Cambridgeshire,
CB3 7TX ▣
📱 07808 590370
Est. 1998
Services Antique restoration and
conservation, cabinet work,
veneering, turning, key-making,
lock repair, polishing, upholstery,
rushing and caning
Open By appointment

Warwick Antique Restorations (UKIC)
Contact Mr R Lawman
✉ 32 Beddington Lane, Croydon,
Surrey,
CR0 4TB ▣
☎ 020 8688 4511
✉ info@warwickantiques.co.uk
🌐 www.warwickantiques.co.uk
Est. 1976
Services Antique clock
restoration, leathering, rushing,
upholstery, caning, brass
Open Tues–Sat 9.30am–5pm

CARPETS & RUGS

Barin Carpets Restoration
Contact H Barin
✉ 57a New King's Road,

London,
SW6 4SE ▣
☎ 020 7731 0546
Est. 1976
Services Cleaning and
restoration of Oriental carpets
and rugs, European tapestries,
Aubussons. Listed by the
conservation unit of The
Museums and Galleries
Commission
Open Mon–Sat 9am–6pm

Keith Bawden (BAFRA)
Contact Keith Bawden
✉ Mews Workshops,
Montpellier Retreat,
Cheltenham, Gloucestershire,
GL50 2XG ▣
☎ 01242 230320 or 01452 863566
Est. 1975
Services Full antique restoration
service of furniture, clocks,
watercolours, jewellery, ceramics
and Oriental carpets, silver,
plating, committed to
conservation and under-
restoring on principle
Open By appointment phone
first

Lannowe Oriental Textiles
Contact Joanna Titchell
✉ Near Bath, Wiltshire
☎ 01225 891487 ✉ 01225 891182
📱 07714 703535
✉ joanna@lannowe.co.uk
Est. 1976
Services Washing, restoration
and conservation of Oriental
carpets, rugs and tapestries
Open By appointment

Michael & Amanda Lewis Oriental Carpets
Contact Amanda Lewis
✉ 8 North Street, Wellington,
Somerset,
TA21 8LT ▣
☎ 01823 667430
✉ rugmike@tesco.net
Est. 1981
Services Restoration, cleaning,
repair to carpets, rugs and flat
weave
Open Tues–Fri 10am–1pm
2–5.30pm Sat by appointment

M & M Restoration
Contact Marina Jezierzanska
✉ Mantel House,
Broomhill Road,
London,

SW18 4JQ ⓟ
☎ 020 8871 5098 ❶ 020 8877 1940
Ⓜ 07949 107611
Est. 1985
Services Restoration and
cleaning of antique tapestries,
carpets, textiles
Open Mon–Fri 9am–6pm

CERAMICS

Carol Basing
Contact Carol Basing
✉ 41 Prospect Road, Sevenoaks,
Kent,
TN13 3UA ⓟ
☎ 01732 456695
Est. 1984
Services Ceramic repair and
restoration
Open By appointment

Grenville Godfrey
Contact Mr G Godfrey
✉ 60 Watts Lane, Eastbourne,
East Sussex,
BN21 2LL ⓟ
☎ 01323 735595
Est. 1997
Services Repair and restoration
of ceramics
Open By appointment

Sarah Peek
Contact Miss S Peek
✉ Redwins, Rear of 6 Preston
Park Avenue, New England
Street, Brighton,
East Sussex,
BN1 6HI ⓟ
☎ 01273 243744 ❶ 07092 393295
❸ conservation@sarahpeek.co.uk
Ⓦ www.sarahpeek.co.uk
Est. 1995
Services Restoration of ceramics,
glass, enamels
Open By appointment

**Helen Warren China
Restoration**
Contact Helen Warren
✉ The Roundhouse, Angley Park,
Cranbrook, Kent,
TN17 2PN ⓟ
☎ 01580 713500
❸ chinarestoration@helenwarren.com
Ⓦ www.helenwarren.com
Est. 1990
Services Ceramic repair and
restoration
Open By appointment

China Repairers
Contact Virginia Baron
✉ The Coach House, King Street
Mews, King Street, London,
N2 8DY ⓟ
☎ 020 8444 3030
Ⓦ www.chinarepairers.co.uk
Est. 1953
Services Ceramic and glass repair.
Tuition available
Open Mon–Thurs 10am–4pm

**The Conservation Studio
(ICOM, IIC, UKIC)**
Contact Mrs F Hayward
✉ 77 Troutbeck, Albany Street,
London,
NW1 4EJ ⓟ
☎ 020 7387 4994 ❶ 020 7387 4994
❸ flu_flo@yahoo.co.uk
Est. 1993
Services Restoration and
conservation of ceramics, glass,
metalwork, ivory and soapstone,
specializing in gilding, painting
on glass and ceramics
Open Mon–Fri 8.30am–4.30pm
Sat by appointment

**Greenwich Conservation
Workshops**
Contact Richard Moy
✉ 22 Nelson Road, London,
SE10 9JB ⓟ
☎ 020 8293 1067
Ⓦ www.spreadeagle.org
Est. 1957
Services Restoration of period
furniture, oil, watercolours,
picture frames, porcelain,
pottery
Open Mon–Sat 10.30am–5.30pm

**Rosemary Hamilton China
Repairs (IDDA)**
Contact Mrs R Hamilton
✉ 44 Moreton Street, London,
SW1V 2PB ⓟ
☎ 020 7828 5018 ❶ 020 7828 1325
❸ rosemary@rosemaryhamilton.co.uk
Est. 1993
Services China repair and
restoration
Open Mon–Fri 9.30am–5.30pm

H J Hatfield and Son
✉ 42 St Michael's Street,
London,
W2 1QP ⓟ
☎ 020 7723 8265 ❶ 020 7706 4562
❸ admin@hjhatfield.com

Ⓦ www.hjhatfield.com
Est. 1834
Services Restoration of furniture,
porcelain, paintings, boulle,
upholstery, lacquerwork,
metalwork, chandeliers, marble
Open Mon–Fri 8am–1pm 2–5pm
(moving soon check via phone or
website before visiting)

**Laurence Mitchell
Antiques (LAPADA)**
Contact Laurence Mitchell
✉ 20 The Mall, 359 Islington
High Street, Islington, London,
N1 0PD
☎ 020 7359 7579
❸ laurence@buymeissen.com
Ⓦ www.buymeissen.com
Est. 1970
Services Restoration of antiques
Open Tues–Fri 10am–5pm Sat
10am–5.30pm

**Q W Conservation (OCS,
UKIC)**
Contact Toby Quartly-Watson
✉ Studio 5 (2nd Floor), Hewlett
House, Havelock Terrace,
London,
SW8 4AS ⓟ
☎ 020 7498 5938 ❶ 020 7498 5938
Ⓜ 07710 355743
❸ stylish.moves@virgin.net
Est. 1991
Services Conservation of
ceramics and related objects
Open Mon–Fri 10am–6pm or by
appointment

**Norman Flynn
Restorations**
Contact Mr N Flynn
✉ 20 Malden Road, Cheam,
Surrey,
SM3 8QF ⓟ
☎ 020 8661 9505
Est. 1972
Services Porcelain, pottery,
enamel restoration
Open Mon–Fri 8.30am–3.30pm

Regency Antiques
Contact R De Santini
✉ Home Cottage, Andrews Hill,
Adversane, Billingshurst,
West Sussex
☎ 01403 780 ❶ 01403 874
Ⓜ 07947 597311
Est. 1978
Services Porcelain and furniture

ASSOCIATED SERVICES
CERAMICS

restoration
Open Mon–Fri 9.30am–5.30pm
by appointment only

Sheila Southwell Studio (BCPAA, IPAA)
Contact Mrs S Southwell
✉ 7 West Street, Burgess Hill, West Sussex, RH15 8NN ℗
☎ 01444 244307
Est. 1969
Services Restoration of ceramics, china, porcelain, earthenware. Commissions accepted for hand-painted, commemorative porcelain for any occasion
Open By appointment

WEST COUNTRY

Addington Studio Ceramic Repairs
Contact Pam Warner
✉ 1 Addington Cottages, Upottery, Honiton, Devon, EX14 9PN ℗
☎ 01404 861519 📠 01404 861308
📧 pam@addingtonstudio.co.uk
🌐 www.addingtonstudio.co.uk
Est. 1991
Services Restoration and conservation of ceramics and glass. Tuition given. Regular London (inside M25) delivery and collection. Supplies for ceramic conservators
Open By appointment

Addington Supplies
Contact Pam Warner
✉ 1 Addington Cottages, Upottery, Honiton, Devon, EX14 9PN ℗
☎ 01404 861519 📠 01404 861308
📧 pam@addingtonstudio.co.uk
🌐 www.addingtonstudio.co.uk
Est. 1991
Services Supplies for ceramic conservators
Open By appointment

Antique China and Porcelain Restoration
Contact Mr Carl Garratt
✉ The Green Willow, Victoria Square, Evercreech, Shepton Mallet, Somerset, BA4 6LL ℗
☎ 01749 831116
Est. 1978
Services Restoration of antique

china, oil paintings and objets d'art
Open By appointment

Boughey Antique Restoration
Contact Dave Boughey
✉ 1 Kniel Cottage, The Quay, Millbrook, Torpoint, Cornwall, PL10 1AN ℗
☎ 01752 829008 📠 01752 829008
📱 07970 540044
Est. 1960
Services Furniture restoration, cabinet-making, porcelain and pottery restoration
Open Mon–Fri 8am–5.30pm or by appointment

Ceramic Restoration Studio
Contact Martina Gray or Emma Organ
✉ Unit 1, 24 Cheap Street, Sherborne, Dorset, DT9 3PX ℗
☎ 01935 813128
Est. 1989
Services Restoration and conservation of ceramics
Open Mon–Fri 10am–12.30pm 1.30pm–4pm or by appointment

China and Glass Restoration
Contact Mrs Susan Birch
✉ The Shoe, Old Hollow, Mere, Warminster, Wiltshire, BA12 6EG ℗
☎ 01747 861703
📧 sukib@onetel.com
Est. 1993
Services China and glass restoration
Open By appointment

Peter Martin Ceramic Restoration
Contact Mr P Martin
✉ 11 Eastbourne Terrace, Westward Ho, Bideford, Devon, EX39 1HG ℗
☎ 01237 421446
📧 pmcr@madasafish.com
Est. 1996
Services Modern and antique ceramic restoration, specializing in decorative pottery and porcelain antiques
Open Strictly by appointment

Reference Works Ltd
Contact Joy or Barry Lamb
✉ 9 Commercial Road, Swanage,

Dorset, BH19 1DF ℗
☎ 01929 424423 📠 01929 422597
📧 sales@referenceworks.co.uk
🌐 www.referenceworks.co.uk
Est. 1984
Services Mail order reference books on pottery and porcelain. Consultants and advisers on British ceramics. Monthly illustrated newsletters and book lists, extensive website. Small range of 18th–20thC pottery, porcelain
Open Mon–Fri 10.30am–4pm Sat 10.30am–1pm or by appointment

EAST

Baron Art
Contact Mr A Baron
✉ 9 and 16 Chapel Yard, Albert Street, Holt , Norfolk, NR25 6HG ℗
☎ 01263 713430 📠 01263 711670
📧 baronholt@aol.com
Est. 2001
Services Restoration of antiquarian books, paintings, ceramics, plus framing
Open Mon–Sat 9am–5pm

Emma Bradshaw Ceramic Restorations (UKIC)
Contact Emma Bradshaw
✉ The Maltings, Station Road, Newport, Essex, CB11 3RN ℗
☎ 01799 542447
Est. 1991
Services Conservation and restoration of bone china, earthenware, porcelain, stoneware, terracotta, early English pottery
Open By appointment

HEART OF ENGLAND

Keith Bawden (BAFRA)
Contact Keith Bawden
✉ Mews Workshops, Montpellier Retreat, Cheltenham, Gloucestershire, GL50 2XG ℗
☎ 01242 230320 or 01452 863566
Est. 1975
Services Full antique restoration service of furniture, clocks, watercolours, jewellery, ceramics and Oriental carpets, silver, plating, committed to conservation and under-

restoring on principle
Open By appointment phone first

The China Repairers
Contact Mrs A Chalmers
✉ 1 Street Farm Workshops, Doughton, Tetbury, Gloucestershire, GL8 8TH 🅿
☎ 01666 503551
Est. 1989
Services China, mirror and picture frame restoration (By Appointment to HRH The Prince of Wales)
Open Mon–Fri 9.30am–4.30pm

China Repairs & Restorations (UKIC)
Contact David Battams
✉ Bletchley, Milton Keynes, Buckinghamshire, MK2 2WR 🅿
📱 07956 832375
✆ david@chinarepairsand restorations.com
🌐 www.chinarepairsand restorations.com
Est. 1998
Services Repair and restoration of china using the latest materials and techniques
Open Mon–Fri 1–5pm

Gray Arts
Contact Mr A Gray
✉ Unit 21b, The Maltings, School Lane, Amersham, Buckinghamshire, HP7 0ET 🅿
☎ 01494 726502 ✆ 01494 726502
📱 07714 274410
Est. 1979
Services Porcelain restoration
Trade only Yes
Open By appointment

Rose Antique Restoration
Contact Nicola Gilbert
✉ 5 Windmill Hill, Princes Risborough, Buckinghamshire, HP27 0EP 🅿
☎ 01844 273517
✆ roserestore@yahoo.com
🌐 www.ceramicrestorers.co.uk
Est. 1976
Services Restoration of china, porcelain, ceramics
Trade only Trade has preference
Open Mon–Thur 9am–5.30pm or by appointment

The Traditional Studio (UKIC)
Contact Viki Green
✉ Welwyn Equestrian Centre, Potters Heath Road, Welwyn, Hertfordshire, AL6 9SZ 🅿
☎ 01707 332084 ✆ 01707 332084
📱 07748 224287
✆ viki@traditionalstudio.fsnet.co.uk
Est. 1997
Services Ceramics, gilded objects, stone, marble sculpture, furniture, lacquer work
Open By appointment

MIDLANDS

Ashdale China Restoration
Contact Mr R Gregory
✉ 19 Boothby Avenue, Ashbourne, Derbyshire, DE6 1EL 🅿
☎ 01335 345965
📱 07961 957530
Est. 1984
Services Repair and restoration
Open By appointment

Roger Hawkins Restoration
Contact R Hawkins
✉ Unit 4, The Old Dairy, Winkburn, Newark, Nottinghamshire, NG22 8PQ 🅿
☎ 01636 636666
📱 07763 780795
Est. 1980
Services Restoration of all types of pottery, porcelain. Tuition given
Open Mon–Fri 9am–5pm

Ravensdale Studios
Contact Mr S Nicholls
✉ 77a Roundwell Street, Tunstall, Stoke-on-Trent, Staffordshire, ST6 5AW 🅿
☎ 01782 836810
✆ restore@ravensdale69.fsnet.co.uk
🌐 www.ravensdalestudios.co.uk
Est. 1988
Services Ceramic restoration
Open Mon–Fri 9am–5pm

Warwick Wright Restoration
Contact Mr S MacGarvey
✉ 19b Wem Business Park, New Street, Wem, Shrewsbury,

Shropshire, SY4 5JX 🅿
☎ 01939 234879
✆ smg2k3@msn.com
Est. 1992
Services Porcelain restoration
Open Mon–Fri 8.30am–4.30pm

YORKSHIRE & LINCOLNSHIRE

Artisan Stock & Business Centre
Contact Mr C Hobs
✉ Enterprise Centre, 70 Brunswick Street, Stockton-on-Tees, Cleveland, TS18 1DW 🅿
☎ 01642 801020 ✆ 01642 391351
Est. 1991
Services Restoration and repair of china and ceramics
Open Mon–Fri 9am–5pm Sat by appointment

Kaleidescope Porcelain and Pottery Restorers
Contact Mr F Roberts
✉ Rose Marie, Main Road, Potterhanworth, Lincoln, Lincolnshire, LN4 2DT 🅿
☎ 01522 793869
Est. 1985
Services Antique repair and restoration, also restoration of modern pieces on request
Open Mon–Fri 9am–7pm Sat 9am–noon

The Pottery & Porcelain Restoration Co
Contact Mr Tom Cosens
✉ 30 Wharf Street, Sowerby Bridge, West Yorkshire, HX6 2AE 🅿
☎ 01422 834828
📱 07817 296381
✆ artrestorers@aol.com
Est. 1990
Services Repair and restoration of all ceramics and spelter, china matching service
Open By appointment only

NORTH WEST

Domino Restorations
Contact Mrs J Hargreaves
✉ c/o G B Antiques Centre, Lancaster Leisure Park, Wyresdale Road, Lancaster, Lancashire, LA1 3LA 🅿

CLOCKS

⊕ 07710 223170
✉ r.j.hargreaves@ic24.net
Est. 1979
Services Porcelain and china restoration, jewellery repair. Repair and restoration of metalware, tortoiseshell and ivory, spelter, bronze
Open By appointment

Monogram Studios
Contact Ryan Adams
✉ 25 Kinsey Street, Congleton, Cheshire,
CW12 1ES ℗
☎ 01260 273957
Est. 1962
Services Pottery and porcelain repair and restoration
Open Mon–Fri 9am–5pm

Porcelain Repairs Ltd
Contact Mr I Norman or Mr A Jones
✉ 240 Stockport Road, Cheadle Heath, Stockport, Cheshire,
SK3 0LX ℗
☎ 0161 428 9599 ☏ 0161 286 6702
✉ porcelain@repairs999.fsnet.co.uk
Est. 1976
Services Repair and restoration of all antique ceramics. Collection and delivery service to central London
Open By appointment only, during office hours

WALES

Ceramic Restoration (GADAR, UKIC)
Contact Lynette Pierce
✉ Woodlands Studio, Glanhafren, Abermule, Montgomery, Powys,
SY15 6NA ℗
☎ 01686 630219
⊕ 07748 868913
Est. 1995
Services China and pottery repair and restoration, figurines a speciality
Trade only Yes
Open By appointment

SCOTLAND

Ellen L Breheny (Accredited Member UKIC)
Contact Ellen L Breheny
✉ 10 Glenisla Gardens, Edinburgh,

EH9 2HR ℗
☎ 0131 667 2620
✉ ellen@breheny.com
Est. 1988
Services Conservation and restoration of ceramics, glass and related materials
Open Mon–Fri 10am–6pm

Renaissance China Restoration
Contact Miss S Harvey
✉ 30 West Annadale Street, Edinburgh,
EH7 4JY ℗
☎ 0131 557 2762
Est. 1984
Services Invisible ceramic restoration
Open Mon–Fri 10am–1pm 2.30–5pm

REPUBLIC OF IRELAND

Glebe Hall Restoration Studios
Contact Carmel Corrigan-Griffin
✉ Old Killernogh Rectory, Rathnakelly Glebe, Ballacolla, Co Laois, Ireland ℗
☎ 0502 34105 ☏ 0502 34105
⊕ 0868 784956
Est. 1980
Services Furniture restoration, gilding, porcelain, ivory, jade
Open By appointment, Sat 11am–4pm

CLOCKS

SOUTH EAST

Neill Robinson Blaxill
Contact Neill Blaxill
✉ 21 St Johns Hill, Sevenoaks, Kent,
TN13 3NX ℗
☎ 01732 454179
ⓦ www.antique-clocks.co.uk
Est. 1980
Services Clock and barometer restoration
Open Mon–Sat 10am–6pm or by appointment

J W Carpenter Antique Clock Restorer (BHI)
Contact John Carpenter
✉ Whitehaven, Sandown Road, Sandwich, Kent,
CT13 9NY ℗
☎ 01304 619787

✉ ticking@onetel.co.uk
Est. 1970
Services Antique clock repair and restoration
Open By appointment

Paul M Read Antique Furniture Restoration
Contact Paul Read
✉ 12b Gaza Trading Estate, Scabharbour Lane, Sevenoaks, Kent,
TN11 8PL ℗
☎ 01732 460022
Est. 1986
Services Full furniture restoration, cabinet-making, marquetry, inlaying, carving, turning, gilding, leather work, full clock restoration service, upholstery, cane and rush seating, traditional French polishing, on-site polishing and specialist wood finishes
Open By appointment

LONDON

Albion Clocks (BHI)
Contact Colin Bent
✉ 4 Grove End, Grove Hill, South Woodford, London,
E18 2LE ℗
☎ 020 8530 5570
✉ colin.bent@btinternet.com
ⓦ www.albionclocks.info
Est. 1963
Services Restoration of clocks and fine furniture, antiquarian horologist
Open Mon–Sun 9am–7pm by appointment

David Ansell (BAFRA, BHI)
Contact David Ansell
✉ 48 Dellside, Harefield, Middlesex,
UB9 6AX ℗
☎ 01895 824648
⊕ 07976 222610
✉ davidansell@btinternet.com
Est. 1990
Services Repair and restoration of clocks
Open Mon–Sun 8.30am–5.30pm or by appointment

William Mansell (BHI, NAG, BWCG)
Contact Bill Salisbury
✉ 24 Connaught Street, London,
W2 2AF ℗

☎ 020 7723 4154 ✆ 020 7724 2273
✉ mail@williammansell.co.uk
ⓦ www.williammansell.co.uk
Est. 1864
Services Repair, restoration and sale of clocks, watches, barometers, barographs
Open Mon–Fri 9am–6pm
Sat 10am–1pm

SOUTH

The Clock-Work-Shop (Winchester) (BHI, AHS)
Contact Mr P Ponsford-Jones
✉ 6a Parchment Street, Winchester, Hampshire, SO23 8AT ℗
☎ 01962 842331 ✆ 01962 878775
ⓜ 07973 736155
ⓦ www.clock-work-shop.co.uk
Est. 1997
Services Restoration of clocks and barometers
Open Mon–Sat 9am–5pm

Stuart Hobbs Antique Furniture Restoration (BAFRA)
Contact Mr S Hobbs
✉ Meath Paddock, Meath Green Lane, Horley, Surrey, RH6 8HZ ℗
☎ 01293 782349 ✆ 01293 773467
Est. 1981
Services Furniture, longcase, bracket clock and barometer restoration
Open By appointment

Horological Workshops (BHI, BADA)
Contact Mr M D Tooke
✉ 204 Worplesdon Road, Guildford, Surrey, GU2 9UY ℗
☎ 01483 576496 ✆ 01483 452212
✉ enquiries@horologicalwork shops.com
ⓦ www.horologicalworkshops.com
Est. 1968
Services Full restoration of antique clocks, watches, barometers
Open Tues–Fri 8.30am–5.30pm
Sat 9am–12.30pm

Gavin Hussey Antique Restoration (BAFRA)
Contact G Hussey
✉ 4 Brook Farm, Clayhill Road, Leigh, Reigate, Surrey,

RH2 8PA ℗
☎ 01306 611634 ✆ 01306 611634
Est. 1994
Services Full restoration of furniture and clocks
Open By appointment

Simon Paterson (BAFRA)
✉ Whitelands, West Dean, Chichester, West Sussex, PO18 0RL ℗
☎ 01243 811900
✉ hotglue@tiscali.co.uk
Est. 1992
Services Repair and restoration of antique furniture and clocks, boulle work, marquetry
Open By appointment

Reeves Restoration at The Coach House Antiques
Contact Paul or Louise Reeves
✉ The Coach House, 60 Station Road, Gomshall, Surrey, GU5 9NP ℗
☎ 01483 203838 ✆ 01483 202999
ⓜ 07774 729325
✉ coach_house.antiques@virgin.net
ⓦ www.coachhouseantiques.com
Est. 1984
Services Antique clock, furniture restoration
Open By appointment

Sundial Antique Clock Service
Contact Mr Peter Mole
✉ 64 The Parade, Brighton Road, Hooley, Coulsdon, Surrey, CR5 3EE ℗
☎ 01737 551991 ✆ 01737 551991
ⓜ 07733 408535
✉ sundialclocks@hooley68.fsnet.co.uk
Est. 1965
Services Barometer and clock restoration, specializing in longcase clock repair
Open By appointment

Surrey Clock Centre
Contact Mr Haw or Mr Ingrams
✉ 3 Lower Street, Haslemere, Surrey, GU27 2NY ℗
☎ 01428 651313
ⓦ www.surreyclockcentre.co.uk
Est. 1968
Services Repair, restoration and sales of clocks and barometers
Open Mon–Tues Thurs–Fri 9am–5pm Wed and Sat 9am–1pm

Tempus Watches (LAPADA)
Contact John Wingate
✉ PO Box 362, Weybridge, Surrey, KT13 8ZF ℗
☎ 01344 874007
✉ enquiries@tempus-watches.co.uk
ⓦ www.tempus-watches.co.uk
Est. 1978
Services Restoration of antique clocks and vintage wristwatches
Open By appointment

Warwick Antique Restorations (UKIC)
Contact Mr R Lawman
✉ 32 Beddington Lane, Croydon, Surrey, CR0 4TB ℗
☎ 020 8688 4511
✉ info@warwickantiques.co.uk
ⓦ www.warwickantiques.co.uk
Est. 1976
Services Antique clock restoration, leathering, rushing, upholstery, caning, brass
Open Tues–Sat 9.30am–5pm

Wheelers (BHI, BWCG)
Contact Mr T P Wheeler
✉ 14–16 Bath Place, Worthing, West Sussex, BN11 3BA ℗
☎ 01903 207656 ✆ 01903 207656
ⓦ www.wheelersclocks.co.uk
Est. 1991
Services Antique clock repair, restoration, sales
Open Mon–Sat 9am–5pm

WEST COUNTRY

M and S Bradbury (BAFRA)
Contact Mr S Bradbury
✉ The Barn, Hanham Lane, Paulton, Bristol, BS39 7PF ℗
☎ 01761 418910
✉ stuart@mandsbradbury.co.uk
ⓦ www.mandsbradbury.co.uk
Est. 1988
Services Clock case restoration
Open Mon–Fri 8am–5pm

David Collyer Antique Restorations
Contact David Collyer
✉ Tunley Farm, Tunley, Bath, Somerset, BA2 0DL ℗
☎ 01761 472727 ✆ 01761 472727
ⓜ 07889 725508
✉ restoration@davidcollyer.com

ⓦ www.davidcollyer.com
Est. 1985
Services Furniture restoration and repair
Open Mon–Fri 9am–5.30pm or by appointment

Merim Restoration
Contact Ian Potts
✉ Bow Street, Langport, Somerset, TA10 9PL 🅿
☎ 01458 252157 🅖 01458 250747
🅔 merimianpots@hotmail.com
Est. 1979
Services Clock restoration, specializing in English longcase
Open Mon–Fri 8am–5pm Sat 8.30am–noon

C Moss Clocks (Worshipful Company of Clocks)
Contact Mr C Moss
✉ 59 Walcot Street, Bath, Somerset, BA1 5BN 🅿
☎ 01225 445892 🅖 01225 445892
🅦 07779 161731
🅔 chris@chrismossclocks.co.uk
ⓦ www.chrismossclocks.co.uk
Est. 1970
Services Clock case restoration, marquetry, parquetry, walnut furniture
Open Mon–Sat 9am–5pm but phone first

Robert P Tandy (BAFRA)
Contact Robert P Tandy
✉ Lake House Barn, Off Colehouse Lane, Kenn, Clevedon, Bristol, BS21 6TQ 🅿
☎ 01275 875014
🅔 robertptandy@hotmail.com
Est. 1987
Services Antique furniture and longcase clock casework restoration
Open Mon–Fri 10am–6pm

Time Restored Ltd (BHI)
Contact J H Bowler-Reed
✉ 20 High Street, Pewsey, Wiltshire, SN9 5AQ 🅿
☎ 01672 563544
ⓦ www.timerestored.co.uk
Est. 1978
Services Restoration of antique clocks, musical boxes and barometers
Open Mon–Fri 10am–6pm

Timecraft Clocks (BHI)
Contact Mr G Smith
✉ Unit 2, 24 Cheap Street, Sherborne, Dorset, DT9 3PX 🅿
☎ 01935 817771 🅖 01935 817771
Est. 1994
Services Clock restoration and repair
Open Tue–Fri 10.30am–5.30pm Sat 10.30am–2pm

Chris Wadge Clocks
Contact Patrick Wadge
✉ 83 Fisherton Street, Salisbury, Wiltshire, SP2 7ST 🅿
☎ 01722 334467
Est. 1985
Services Repair, restoration of antique and modern clocks, 400-day anniversary clocks a speciality
Open Tues–Sat 9am–4pm closed 1–2pm

Antique Renovations
Contact Stephen or Alan Gartland
✉ Unit 1, Lavenham Studios, Brent Eleigh Road, Lavenham, Sudbury, Suffolk, CO10 9PE 🅿
☎ 01787 248511
Est. 1960
Services Repair, cabinet work and French polishing. Recommended by Ercol. Specializing in clock case repair
Open Mon–Fri 8.30am–5pm Sat 9am–1pm

Brian Harris Furniture Restorations (BAFRA, EADA)
Contact Brian Harris
✉ 24 Town Street, Boxsted, Essex, CM6 2LA 🅿
☎ 01371 832832
Est. 1956
Services Antique furniture restoration including carving, gilding, French polishing, inlay work. Also restoration of clocks and barometers
Open Mon–Sat 9am–5pm

Ken Wright (CMBHI)
Contact Keith Wright
✉ 99 Carter Drive,

Collier Row, Romford, Essex, RM5 2PJ 🅿
☎ 01708 767455
Est. 1995
Services Mechanical antique clock repair
Open By appointment

The Barometer Shop (BWCG)
Contact Colin or Verity Jones
✉ 25 New Street, Leominster, Herefordshire, HR6 8DP 🅿
☎ 01568 613652
Est. 1969
Services Supply and restoration of antique mercurial, aneroid barometers, clocks and watches, furniture, ceramics, French polishing, wood finishing, dial painting
Open Mon–Fri 9am–5pm Sat 10am–4pm

Keith Bawden (BAFRA)
Contact Keith Bawden
✉ Mews Workshops, Montpellier Retreat, Cheltenham, Gloucestershire, GL50 2XG 🅿
☎ 01242 230320 or 01452 863566
Est. 1975
Services Full antique restoration service of furniture, clocks, watercolours, jewellery, ceramics and Oriental carpets, silver, plating, committed to conservation and under-restoring on principle
Open By appointment phone first

R Beesly
Contact Mr R Beesly
✉ 41 High Street, Broom, Biggleswade, Bedfordshire, SG18 9NA 🅿
☎ 01767 314918
Est. 1974
Services Cabinet-making, French polishing, clock repair
Open Mon–Sat 8am–6pm or by appointment

Peter Campion Restorations (BAFRA)
Contact Peter Campion
✉ The Old Dairy, Rushley Lane,

Winchcombe, Nr Cheltenham, Gloucestershire, GL54 5JE 🅿
☎ 01242 604403 📠 01242 604403
📧 petercampion@ukonline.co.uk
🌐 www.petercampion.co.uk
Est. 1959
Services Restoration and conservation of furniture, barometers, clock cases. Also cabinet work, inlays, brass, veneering, polishing, furniture designed and made to order
Open Mon–Fri 9am–5.30pm

Gray Arts
Contact Mr A Gray
✉ **Unit 21b, The Maltings, School Lane, Amersham, Buckinghamshire, HP7 0ET** 🅿
☎ 01494 726502 📠 01494 726502
📱 07714 274410
Est. 1979
Services Clock and watch dial restoration
Trade only Yes
Open By appointment

Nick Hansford
Contact Nick Hansford
✉ **Nyth-fa, Llanwrane, Hereford, Herefordshire, HR2 8JE** 🅿
☎ 01981 540460
Est. 1968
Services Clock and watch repair
Open By appointment

Leominster Clock Repairs (BHI)
Contact Ashley Prosser
✉ **Unit 2, The Railway Station, Worcester Road, Leominster, Herefordshire, HR6 8AR** 🅿
☎ 01568 612298
Est. 2000
Services Clock restoration, specializing in longcase clocks
Open Mon–Sat 9am–6pm

Oxford Longcase Clocks
Contact Mr Paul Carroll
✉ **76 Courtland Road, Rose Hill, Oxford, Oxfordshire, OX4 4JB** 🅿
☎ 01865 779660
Est. 1978
Services Clock and barometer repair
Open Mon–Fri 8am–5pm
Sat 8am–noon

Anthony Allen Conservation, Restoration, Furniture and Artefacts (BAFRA, UKIC)
Contact Anthony Allen
✉ **The Old Wharf Workshop, Redmoor Lane, Newtown, High Peak, Derbyshire, SK22 3JL** 🅿
☎ 01663 745274 📠 01663 745274
📧 allen-conservation@tiscali.co.uk
Est. 1970
Services Restoration of clock cases and movements, gilding, marquetry, boulle, upholstery, metalwork, 17th–19thC furniture
Open Mon–Fri 8am–5pm

Barnt Green Antiques (BAFRA)
Contact Phillip Slater
✉ **93 Hewell Road, Barnt Green, Birmingham, West Midlands, B45 8NL** 🅿
☎ 0121 445 4942 📠 0121 445 4942
🌐 www.barntgreenantiques.co.uk
Est. 1977
Services Furniture and longcase clock restoration. All aspects of polishing and finishing including wax and French polishing, marquetry, inlay
Open Mon–Fri 9am–5.30pm
Sat 9am–1pm

Goodacre Engraving (BHI)
Contact John Skeavington
✉ **The Dial House, 120 Main Street, Sutton Bonington, Leicestershire, LE12 5PF** 🅿
☎ 01509 673082 📠 01509 673082
Est. 1948
Services Dial engraving, restoration and clock parts for English longcase and bracket clocks
Open Mon–Sat 9am–5pm telephone for appointment

Richard Higgins Conservation Ltd (BAFRA, UKIC)
Contact Richard Higgins
✉ **The Old School, Longnor, Nr Shrewsbury, Shropshire, SY5 7PP** 🅿
☎ 01743 718162 📠 01743 718022
📧 richardhigginsco@aol.com
Est. 1988

Services Restoration of all fine furniture, clocks, movements, dials and cases, casting, plating, boulle, gilding, lacquerwork, carving, upholstery
Open Mon–Fri 9am–5pm please phone first

James A Jordan (BHI Qualified Member)
Contact Mr J Jordan
✉ **7 The Corn Exchange, Conduit Street, Lichfield, Staffordshire, WS13 6JR** 🅿
☎ 01543 416221
Est. 1988
Services Watch, clock and barometer repairs
Open Mon–Sat 9am–5pm
closed Wed

Upstairs Downstairs Antiques
Contact Mr C Lawrence
✉ **8 Derby Road, Ripley, Derbyshire, DE5 3HR** 🅿
☎ 01773 745201
📱 07885 327753
🌐 www.upstairsdownstairs antiques.co.uk
Est. 1974
Services Furniture restoration, clock repair, French polishing
Open Mon–Sat 10am–4pm

A A Clockcraft (BHI)
Contact Mr D R Peveley
✉ **13 High Street, Bridlington, East Yorkshire, YO16 4PR** 🅿
☎ 01262 602802
🌐 www.aaclockcraft.co.uk
Est. 1984
Services Clock repair and restoration, all periods and all types
Open Mon–Fri 9am–5pm
Sat 10.30am–4.30pm

Antique Clocks (Watch & Clockmakers Guild)
Contact Tom Robinson
✉ **55a Healdfield Road, Castleford, West Yorkshire, WF10 4LJ** 🅿
☎ 01977 516704
📱 07721 092058
Est. 1975
Services Clock restoration
Open By appointment

ASSOCIATED SERVICES
CONSERVATION

Edmund Czajkowski & Son (BAFRA)
Contact Michael Czajkowski
✉ 96 Tor O Moor Road, Woodhall Spa, Lincolnshire, LN10 6SB 🅿
☎ 01526 352895 📠 01526 352895
📧 michael.czajkowski@ntlworld.com
🌐 www.czajkowskiandson.com
Est. 1951
Services Restoration of antique furniture, clocks, barometers
Open Mon–Sat 8.30am–5pm

Robert Loomes Clock Restoration (BWCG, BHI)
Contact Mr R Loomes
✉ 3 St Leonards Street, Stamford, Lincolnshire, PE9 2HU 🅿
☎ 01780 481319
🌐 www.dialrestorer.co.uk
Est. 1987
Services Antique repair and restoration
Open Mon–Fri 9am–5pm or by appointment

Manor House Clocks (BWCMG)
Contact Ken Whitton
✉ The Old Manor House, 1 Rectory Lane, Harlaxton, Grantham, Lincolnshire, NG32 1HD 🅿
☎ 01476 574962
📱 07973 675720
📧 ken@manorhouseclocks.co.uk
Est. 1987
Services Repair of longcase clocks and mercury barometers, valuations
Open By appointment

Philip Oliver of Knaresborough (BHI)
Contact Mr P Oliver
✉ Finkle Street, Knaresborough, North Yorkshire, HG5 8AA 🅿
☎ 01423 868438
Est. 1961
Services Clock repair, restoration
Open Mon–Sat 8am–5.30pm but phone first

J K Speed Antique Furniture Restoration
Contact Mr J Speed
✉ The Workshop, Thornton Road, New York, Lincoln, Lincolnshire, LN4 4YL 🅿

☎ 01205 280313
📱 07734 708672
📧 john@speedthornton19.freeserve.co.uk
Est. 1964
Services Antique repair and restoration, light upholstery, specializing in case repair of longcase clocks, French polishing and all ancillary services
Open Mon–Fri 9am–5.30pm

NORTH WEST

Symon E Boyd Clock Restorer (BHI)
Contact Mr S Boyd
✉ 54 Buxton Road, Disley, Stockport, Cheshire, SK12 2EY 🅿
☎ 01663 763999
Est. 1984
Services Repair and restoration of clocks, barometers, musical boxes and automata
Open By appointment

Llewellyn Clocks
Contact Mr C Llewellyn
✉ 12 Gibson Crescent, Sandbach, Cheshire, CW11 3HW 🅿
☎ 01270 768525
Est. 1976
Services Complete antique clock repair and restoration
Open By appointment only

R S M Antique Restoration
Contact Mr Robin Stone
✉ The Stables, Back Eaves Street, Blackpool, Lancashire, FY1 2HW 🅿
☎ 01253 623839 📠 01253 623839
Est. 1972
Services Antique furniture, clocks, barometer, restoration, marquetry cutting
Open Mon–Fri 9am–6pm

REPUBLIC OF IRELAND

Samuel Elliot
Contact Mr Samuel Elliot
✉ 12 Fade Street, Dublin 2, Ireland 🅿
☎ 01 671 1174
Est. 1961
Services General antique watch restoration
Open Mon–Fri 9.30am–6pm Sat by appointment

CONSERVATION

Graciela Ainsworth (SSCR, UKIC)
Contact Graciela
✉ Unit 4 & 10 Bonnington Mill, 72 Newhaven Road, Edinburgh, EH6 5QG 🅿
☎ 0131 555 1294 📠 0131 467 7080
📧 graciela@graciela-ainsworth.com
Est. 1990
Services Conservation of statues, monuments, stone sculptures, including marble plus plasterwork, carving commissions
Open Mon–Fri 9am–6pm

Archaeological Conservator (ICHAWI, IIC, IPCRA)
Contact Susannah Kelly
✉ 14 Greenmount Lawns, Terenure, Dublin 6
☎ 01 492 7695/01 716 8503
📱 0872 848752
📧 csmchale@gofree.indigo.ie
Est. 1993
Services Conservation of archaeological and historical objects, surveys and environmental reports, studies on conservation facilities
Open Mon–Fri 9am–6pm

Lorna Barnes Conservation (IPCRA, ICOM)
Contact Lorna Barnes
✉ 158 Rialto Cottages, Rialto, Dublin 8, Ireland 🅿
☎ 01 473 6205
📧 barneslorna@hotmail.com
Est. 2000
Services Conservation of glass, ceramic and stone objects, condition surveys, advice on packaging and storage
Open Mon–Fri 9am–6pm

Conservation Letterfrack (UKIC, ICHAWI)
Contact Sven Habermann
✉ Letterfrack, Co Galway, Ireland 🅿
☎ 095 41036 📠 095 41100
📧 info@conservationletterfrack.ie
🌐 www.conservationletterfrack.ie
Est. 1999
Services Conservation and restoration of all historic furniture and related objects, and of historical interiors and

architectural joinery, Museum conservation, cabinet-making, French polishing, veneer work, turning and woodcarving, marquetry, boulle work, metal work repair, pietra dura and marble repair
Open Mon–Fri 9am–5.30pm or by appointment

Roland Haycraft (GADAR)
Contact Mr R Haycraft
✉ The Lamb Arcade, High Street, Wallingford, Oxfordshire, OX10 0BS ℗
☎ 01491 839622
✉ ro@fsbdial.co.uk
⊕ www.juststolen.com
Est. 1980
Services Antique furniture conservation
Open Mon–Fri 9am–5.30pm

Adrian Kennedy (Accredited conservator of ICHAWI, IPCRA, IMA)
Contact Adrian Kennedy
✉ Dublin, Ireland
☎ 01 459 9745 📠 01 459 9745
✉ heritagecare@oceanfree.net
Est. 1998
Services Conservation and restoration of museum, folk-life and religious-type objects dating from the archaeological period to 20thC
Open By appointment

Kings Gallery (FATG)
Contact Sandra Christian
✉ 28 Palace Street, Canterbury, Kent, CT1 2DZ ℗
☎ 01227 786986 📠 01227 780532
⊕ www.kingsgallery.co.uk
Est. 1993
Services Restoration, framing, including tapestries, gilding, conservation, original art
Open Mon–Sat 9am–5.45pm

Leather Conservation Centre (UKIC, SSCR)
Contact Jan Beaumont
✉ University College Campus, Boughton Green Road, Moulton Park, Northampton, Northamptonshire, NN2 7AN ℗
☎ 01604 719766 📠 01604 719649
✉ lcc@northampton.ac.uk
⊕ www.leatherconservation.org
Est. 1978

Services Internships for leather conservation
Open Mon–Fri 8.30am–5pm

London Stone Conservation (SPAB)
Contact Florian Kirchertz
✉ 42 Sekforde Street, Finsbury, London, EC1R 0AH ℗
☎ 020 7251 0592 📠 020 7251 0592
📱 07876 685470
✉ lsc@londonstoneconservation.com
⊕ www.londonstone conservation.co.uk
Est. 2004
Services Conservation and restoration of ancient buildings, monuments, masonry, stone carving, letters
Open By appointment

George Monger
Contact Mr G Monger
✉ Unit 6, The Barn, Glebe Farm Industrial Units, Onehouse, Stowmarket, Suffolk, IP14 3HL ℗
☎ 01449 677900 📠 01449 674803
📱 07703 441265
✉ geomcons@tinyworld.co.uk
Est. 1995
Services Conservation and restoration, including social and industrial history and ethnography of pieces
Open By appointment

Plowden and Smith Ltd (MGR)
Contact Sarah Giles
✉ 190 St Ann's Hill, London, SW18 2RT ℗
☎ 020 8874 4005 📠 020 8874 7248
✉ info@plowden-smith.com
⊕ www.plowden-smith.com
Est. 1966
Services Repair and restoration of paintings, furniture, stone, metalwork, decorative arts, object mounting, exhibitions
Open Mon–Fri 9am–5pm

Robert Pye Antiques Restoration & Conservation of Fine Period Furniture
Contact Robert Pye
✉ Tuxwell Farm, Spaxton, Bridgwater, Somerset, TA5 1DF ℗
☎ 01278 671833 📠 01278 671803
✉ robpyeantiques@breathe.com

⊕ www.pyeantiquerestoration. freewebspace.com
Est. 2001
Services Restoration and conservation
Open Mon–Fri 8.30am–6pm
Sat Sun by appointment

Q W Conservation (OCS, UKIC)
Contact Toby Quartly-Watson
✉ Studio 5 (2nd Floor), Hewlett House, Havelock Terrace, London, SW8 4AS ℗
☎ 020 7498 5938 📠 020 7498 5938
📱 07814 687213
✉ stylish.moves@virgin.net
Est. 1991
Services Conservation and restoration of stone sculpture
Open Mon–Fri 10am–6pm or by appointment

Gordon Richardson
Contact Gordon Richardson
✉ 36 Silverknowes Road, Edinburgh, EH4 5LG ℗
☎ 0131 312 7959
Services Conservation and restoration of paintings, pictures, prints, drawings, globes, scientific instruments, silverware, metalware, military artefacts, ships' models, decorative objects
Open By appointment

Textile Conservation (UKIC)
Contact Fiona Hutton
✉ Ivy House Farm, Wolvershill Road, Banwell, Somerset, BS29 6LB ℗
☎ 01934 822449
✉ fiona@textileconservation.co.uk
Est. 1989
Services Textile conservation
Open Mon–Fri 9am–5pm

Textile Conservation Consultancy (IIC)
Contact Sheila Landi or Liz Clemence
✉ The Stable Courtyard, Burghley House, Stamford, Lincolnshire, PE9 3JY ℗
☎ 01780 480188 📠 01780 480188
✉ sheilalandi@textileconservation consultancy.co.uk
⊕ www.textileconservation consultancy.co.uk

CONSULTANCY

Est. 1992
Services Conservation and repair of all textile objects
Open By appointment

Voitek Conservation of Works of Art (IPC)
Contact Mrs E Sobczynski
✉ 9 Whitehorse Mews, Westminster Bridge Road, London, SE1 7QD ♿
☎ 020 7928 6094 ● 020 7928 6094
✆ voitekcwa@btinternet.com
Est. 1972
Services Conservation of prints, drawings, watercolours, maps, conservation mounting and project planning. Conservation of sculpture, marble, terracotta, wood
Open By appointment

CONSULTANCY

A D Antiques
Contact Alison Davey
✉ PO Box 2407, Woodseaves, Stafford, Staffordshire, ST15 8WY
Ⓜ 07811 783518
✆ alison@adantiques.com
Ⓦ www.adantiques.com
Est. 1997
Services Advice on interior decoration and private decorative arts collections. Collections purchased. Buys on commission at auction
Open By appointment

Jocelyn Chatterton
Contact Jocelyn Chatterton
✉ PO Box 36812, London, WC1H 9ZQ
☎ 020 7837 7317
Ⓜ 07798 804853
✆ jocelyn@cixi.demon.co.uk
Ⓦ www.cixi.demon.co.uk
Est. 1997
Services Professional lecturer and textile consultant: Chinese social history and antique textiles
Open By appointment

Tim Corfield Professional Antiques Consultant
Contact Tim Corfield
✉ Beechcroft, Buckholt Road, Broughton, Stockbridge, Hampshire, SO2J 8DA ♿
☎ 01794 301141 ● 01794 301141

Ⓜ 07798 881383
✆ daniel@corefieldmorris.com
Ⓦ www.corfieldmorris.com
Est. 1992
Services Advising clients on purchases at auction or in the trade
Open By appointment

Craftsman Antiques
Contact Mark Haines
✉ 25 Bridget Drive, Sedbury, Chepstow, Monmouthshire, NP16 7AR ♿
☎ 01291 625145 ● 01291 625145
Ⓜ 07836 634712
✆ mark@oakden.co.uk
Ⓦ www.antiquekitchenalia.com
Est. 1968
Services Consultancy for kitchenware, providing information, books, films etc from the Stone Age to the present day
Open Mon–Sun 9am–5pm

Georgiana Antiques & Interiors
Contact Julie George
✉ Cambrian House, Frankton, Ellesmere, Shropshire, SY12 9HE ♿
☎ 01691 690307
Ⓜ 07745 373568
Est. 2003
Services Interior design consultations and commisions to find antiques for the home, also has a small stock of general antiques for the home
Open Flexible hours call for an appointment

IDS Valuation Consultants (BWCG)
Contact Iain Sutherland
✉ 79 Templehill, Troon, Ayrshire, KA10 6BQ ♿
☎ 01292 315999
Est. 1995
Services Valuations and full consultation service
Open Mon–Sat 9.30am–5.30pm or by appointment

Robert Kleiner & Co Ltd (BADA, CINOA)
Contact Robert Kleiner or Jane de Hurtig
✉ 30 Old Bond Street, London, W1S 4AE ♿
☎ 020 7629 1814 ● 020 7629 1239

✆ robert.kleiner@virgin.net
Est. 1989
Services Advice on purchase and sale of Chinese works of art, jades, porcelain, snuff bottles, valuations of collections. Specialist in Chinese snuff bottles.
Open Mon–Fri 9.30am–5.30pm

David C E Lewry (BAFRA, Woodwork Fellowship)
Contact Mr D Lewry
✉ Wychelms, 66 Gorran Avenue, Peel Common, Gosport, Hampshire, PO13 0NF ♿
☎ 01329 286901 ● 01329 289964
Ⓜ 07785 766844
Est. 1979
Services Consultancy on furniture restoration
Open By appointment

Michael Lipitch Ltd (BADA)
Contact Mr M Lipitch
✉ Mayfair, PO Box 3146, London, EN4 0BP ♿
Ⓜ 07730 954347
✆ michaellipitch@hotmail.com
Est. 1960
Services Specialist advice on forming collections of 18thC fine furniture and objects
Open By appointment

Magic Lanterns
Contact J A Marsden
✉ By George, 23 George Street, St Albans, Hertfordshire, AL3 4ES ♿
☎ 01727 865680
Est. 1987
Services Lighting consultancy for period houses
Open Mon–Fri 10am–5pm Sat 10am–5.30pm Sun 1–5pm

DISPLAY EQUIPMENT

Arcade Arts Ltd
Contact Mr K Hewitt or Monika Wengraf-Hewitt
✉ 25 West Hill Road, London, SW18 1LL ♿
☎ 020 8265 2564 ● 020 8874 2982
Est. 1997
Services Makers of display stands, repair and renovation of art objects

Open By appointment

C & A J Barmby
Contact C Barmby
✉ **140 Lavender Hill, Tonbridge, Kent, TN9 2AY**
☎ 01732 771590 **❶** 01732 771590
✉ bookpilot@aol.com
Est. 1970
Services Reference books on antiques, display stands, accessories, packaging material
Trade only Yes
Open By appointment

BJK Sales
Contact Christopher Edwards
✉ **Unit 8–9, Apollo Business Centre, Trundleys Road, London, SE8 5JE** 🅿
☎ 020 8692 2325 or 020 8691 5284
❶ 020 8694 2391
✉ bjksales@bjkshopequipment.co.uk
Ⓦ www.bjkshopequipment.co.uk
Est. 1974
Services Showcases, towers, counters and tabletop displays
Open Mon–Fri 10am–5.30pm

Turn On Lighting
Contact Janet Holdstock
✉ **116–118 Islington High Street, Camden Passage, Islington, London, N1 8EG** 🅿
☎ 020 7359 7616 **❶** 020 7359 7616
Est. 1976
Services Display lighting
Open Tues–Fri 10am–6pm Sat 9.30am–4.30pm

DOCUMENTATION AND PROVENANCE

DIVA (Digital Inventory and Visual Archive) (GADAR)
Contact Mr R Haycraft
✉ **The Lamb Arcade, High Street, Wallingford, Oxfordshire, OX10 0BS** 🅿
☎ 01491 839622
✉ diva@fsbdial.co.uk
Ⓦ www.just-stolen.com
Est. 1980
Services Museum-quality archive documentation, recorded on CD or printed, for insurance, probate, inheritance division and provenance history, plus, if property is stolen, world-wide

publicity on two websites. For collectors of all valuable objects
Open Mon–Fri 9am–5.30pm

ENAMEL

Mark Newland Enamel Restorer
Contact Mr M Newland
✉ **1 Whitehouse Way, Southgate, London, N14 7LX** 🅿
☎ 020 8361 0429
Est. 1982
Services Restoration of enamelled jewellery and objets d'art
Open By appointment

FLOORS

Holland & Welsh
Contact Michael Nap
✉ **Unit 13, Riverside Park, Treforest Industrial Estate, Pontypridd, Mid Glamorgan, CF37 5TG** 🅿
☎ 01443 660255 **❶** 01443 660651
Est. 1997
Services Supply and installation of antique flooring
Open Mon–Fri 9am–5pm
Sat Sun 9.30am–1.30pm

FRAMES

Baron Art
Contact Mr A Baron
✉ **9 and 16 Chapel Yard, Albert Street, Holt, Norfolk, NR25 6HG** 🅿
☎ 01263 713430 **❶** 01263 711670
✉ baronholt@aol.com
Est. 2001
Services Framing and restoration of antiquarian books, paintings, ceramics
Open Mon–Sat 9am–5pm

Berkeley Framing (FATG)
Contact David Gethyn-Jones
✉ **16–18 High Street, Berkeley, Gloucestershire, GL13 9BJ** 🅿
☎ 01453 811513 **❶** 01453 511616
Ⓜ 07802 911894
✉ berkeley.framing@tesco.net
Est. 1956
Services Picture framing
Open Mon–Sun 9.30am–5.30pm

Burghley Fine Art Conservation Ltd
Contact Mike Cowell

✉ **The Stable Courtyard, Burghley House, Stamford, Lincolnshire, PE9 3JY** 🅿
☎ 01780 762155 **❶** 01780 762155
Est. 1977
Services Restoration of oil paintings and picture frames
Open By appointment

The China Repairers
Contact Mrs A Chalmers
✉ **1 Street Farm Workshops, Doughton, Tetbury, Gloucestershire, GL8 8TH** 🅿
☎ 01666 503551
Est. 1989
Services China, mirror and picture frame restoration (By Appointment to HRH The Prince of Wales)
Open Mon–Fri 9.30am–4.30pm

Courtyard Restoration
Contact Shaun Butler or Cosi Sarkar
✉ **2 Parkfield Road, Aghoghill, Co Antrim, BT42 2QS** 🅿
☎ 028 2587 8875
✉ c.sarkar@btinternet.co.uk
Est. 1995
Services Furniture restoration, French polishing, re-carving, veneer repair, picture frame restoration
Open Mon–Sat 10am–5.30pm

Greenwich Conservation Workshops
Contact Richard Moy
22 Nelson Road, London, SE10 9JB 🅿
☎ 020 8293 1067
Ⓦ www.spreadeagle.org
Est. 1957
Services Restoration of period furniture, oil, watercolours, picture frames, porcelain, pottery
Open Mon–Sat 10.30am–5.30pm

Huddersfield Picture Framing Co.
Contact Miss P Ward
✉ **15 Greenfield Road, Holmfirth, Huddersfield, West Yorkshire, HD9 2LA** 🅿
☎ 01484 687598 **❶** 01484 687598
Est. 1979
Services Picture framing

Open Wed–Fri 10am–6pm
Sat 10am–1pm Sat or by
appointment

Inglenook Fine Arts (FATG)
Contact Gerry Bagshaw
✉ Greenend Gallery,
Greenend, Whitchurch,
Shropshire,
SY13 1AA **P**
☎ 01948 665422 ℮ 01948 665422
🅔 info@inglenookfinearts.co.uk
🅦 www.inglenookfinearts.com
Est. 1985
Services Picture restoration,
framing
Open Mon–Sat 9.30am–5pm
Wed closed 1pm

Inglenook Fine Arts (FATG)
Contact Jill Bagshaw
✉ 31 Pillory Street, Nantwich,
Cheshire,
CW5 5BQ **P**
☎ 01270 611188
🅔 info@inglenookfinearts.co.uk
🅦 www.inglenookfinearts.com
Est. 1993
Services Picture restoration,
framing
Open Mon–Sat 9.30am–5pm
Wed closed 1pm

Kings Gallery (FATG)
Contact Sandra Christian
✉ 28 Palace Street,
Canterbury,
Kent,
CT1 2DZ **P**
☎ 01227 786986 ℮ 01227 780532
🅦 www.kingsgallery.co.uk
Est. 1993
Services Restoration, framing,
including tapestries, gilding,
conservation, original art
Open Mon–Sat 9am–5.45pm

Looking Glass of Bath (IIC)
Contact Anthony Reed
✉ 93–96 Walcot Street, Bath,
Somerset,
BA1 5BG **P**
☎ 01225 461969 ℮ 01225 316191
🅜 07831 323878
🅔 info@lookingglassofbath.co.uk
🅦 www.lookingglassofbath.co.uk
Est. 1968
Services Restoration of mirrors,
picture frames, regilding,
carving, manufacturer and

supplier of antique mirror glass,
paper and oil restoration
Open Mon–Sat 9am–6pm

Douglas McLeod Period Frames
Contact Suzie McLeod
✉ 44 Trinity Street, Salisbury,
Wiltshire,
SP1 2BD **P**
☎ 01722 337565 ℮ 01722 337565
Est. 1982
Services Restoration of old
frames, picture restoration,
carving, gilding, lacewing
framing
Open Mon–Fri 9am–5pm
Sat 10am–4pm

Renaissance
Contact Mr Peter Cross
✉ 11 Enterprise Close, Croydon,
Surrey,
CR0 3RZ **P**
☎ 020 8664 9686 ℮ 020 8664 9737
Est. 1996
Services Furniture and frame
repair and restoration
Open Mon–Fri 10am–6.30pm

RSB Antiques
Contact Richard Baker
✉ 30 Dover Road, Walmer, Deal,
Kent,
CT14 7JW **P**
☎ 01304 374082
🅔 richardsbaker@yahoo.co.uk
Est. 1985
Services Restoration and
cleaning of pictures and
18th–19thC gilt frames
Open By appointment

Saracen Antiques Ltd
Contact Mr C Mills
✉ Upton Downs Farm, Burford,
Oxfordshire,
OX18 4LY **P**
☎ 01993 822987
🅔 cmills6702@aol.com
Est. 1996
Services Furniture restoration,
frames and upholstery
Open Mon–Sat 9am–5.30pm

Vigi Sawdon
Contact Vigi Sawdon
✉ 79–81 Ledbury Road, London,
W11 2AG **P**
☎ 020 7229 9321 ℮ 020 7229 2033
🅜 07859 896383
🅔 sawdon@aol.com
🅦 www.vigisawdon.co.uk

Est. 1994
Services Gilding and restoration
of old wooden, gesso and
composite mirrors, architectural
pieces, frames. Also provides
French and Italian paint effects,
trompe l'oeil, marble, bamboo
Open By appointment

FURNITURE

SOUTH EAST

T M Akers Antique Restoration Ltd (BAFRA)
Contact Tim Akers
✉ 39 Chancery Lane, Beckenham,
Kent,
BR3 2NR **P**
☎ 020 8650 9179
🅜 07768 948421
🅔 enquiries@akersofantiques.co.uk
🅦 www.akersofantiques.co.uk
Est. 1985
Services Period antique furniture
restoration
Open Mon–Fri 9am–5pm

Ashdown Antiques Restoration
Contact Robert Hale
✉ Old Forge Farm,
Old Forge Lane, Horney
Common, Uckfield, East Sussex,
TB22 3EL **P**
☎ 01825 713003
🅔 roberthale2@yahoo.com
Est. 1975
Services Furniture restoration,
painting, gilding, marquetry,
inlay work
Open Mon–Sat 9am–6pm or by
appointment

The Barn
Contact Mr Burgess
✉ North Street, Rotherfield,
Crowborough, East Sussex,
TN6 3NA **P**
☎ 01892 852060
Est. 1979
Services Furniture restoration
Open By appointment

Bespoke Furniture
Contact Mr M McEwan
✉ Ladwood Farm, Acrise,
Folkestone, Kent,
CT18 8LL **P**
☎ 01303 893635
Est. 1994
Services Restoration of antique
furniture. Traditional or

contemporary individual pieces of furniture made to order
Open Mon–Fri 8.30am–5pm Sat 9am–2pm Sun by appointment

Bigwood Restoration
Contact Mr S Bigwood
✉ Bigwood Antiques, High Street, Brasted, Kent, TN16 1JA ℗
☎ 01959 564458
✉ sales@bigwoodantiques.com
🌐 www.bigwoodantiques.com
Est. 1984
Services Complete restoration of all antique furniture
Open Mon–Sat 10am–5pm Sun noon–4pm

Kevin Birch Antique Furniture Restorers (BAFRA)
Contact Kevin Birch
✉ Unit 2, Service House, 61–63 Rochester Road, Aylesford, Kent, ME20 7BS ℗
☎ 01622 790080 📠 01622 790080
✉ kevin@kbirch.fsbusiness.co.uk
🌐 www.kevinbirch.co.uk
Est. 1993
Services Furniture restoration, French polishing and upholstery
Open Mon–Fri 8.30am–5pm

Brass Foundry Castings Ltd (BAFRA)
Contact Raymond Konyn
✉ PO Box 151, Westerham, Kent, TN16 1YF
☎ 01959 563863 📠 01959 561262
✉ info@brasscastings.co.uk
🌐 www.brasscastings.co.uk
Est. 1979
Services Cast brass period fittings
Open Mon–Sun 9am–5pm; online and mail order only

Brightling Restoration
Contact D White
✉ Little Worge Farm, Brightling, Robertsbridge, East Sussex, TN32 5HN ℗
☎ 01424 838424 📠 01424 838681
✉ brtrest@aol.com
Est. 2000
Services Restoration of English and Continental furniture
Open Mon–Fri 8am–4.30pm

Brown and Harman
Contact Steven Harman
✉ Broyle Place Farm, Ringmer, Lewes, East Sussex,

BN8 5SD ℗
☎ 01273 814588 📠 01273 814589
✉ brownandharman@virgin.net
Est. 1982
Services Bespoke furniture
Open Mon–Fri 8.30am–5pm

Christy Antique Restoration (GADAR)
Contact Stephen Christy
✉ The Oast, Hurst Farm, Mountain Street, Chilham, Canterbury, Kent, CT4 8DH ℗
☎ 01227 730924 📠 01304 613585
✉ info@christyantiques.co.uk
🌐 www.christyantiques.co.uk
Est. 1989
Services Restoration of furniture and upholstery, gilding, French polishing
Open Mon–Fri 9am–4pm

Benedict Clegg (BAFRA)
Contact Mr Benedict Clegg
✉ Rear of 20 Camden Road, Tunbridge Wells, Kent, TN1 2PY
☎ 01892 548095
Est. 1987
Services Antique furniture repair and restoration
Open Mon–Fri 9am–5pm

W H Earles
Contact Mr W H Earles
✉ 60 Castle Road, Tankerton, Whitstable, Kent, CT5 2EA ℗
☎ 01227 264346
Est. 1978
Services English, Continental and most period furniture restoration and papier-mâché
Open Mon–Fri 8.30am–6pm

Extreme Conservation
Contact Dennis Buggins
✉ Unit 8, Hurst Farm, Mountain Street, Chilham, Canterbury, Kent, CT4 8DH ℗
☎ 01227 738084 📠 01227 732508
✉ den.bug@zen.co.uk
🌐 www.extremearchitectural.co.uk
Est. 1977
Services Restoraton of furniture, lighting and gilding
Open By appointment

Farm Cottage Antiques
Contact Mrs Lynn Winder
✉ Basement, 6a Claremont Road,

Seaford, East Sussex, BN25 2AY ℗
☎ 01323 896766 📠 01323 894982
📱 07765 292253
Est. 1995
Services Furniture restoration
Open Mon–Fri 9am–1pm or by appointment

Glassenbury Country Furniture Ltd
Contact Clive Cowell
✉ Iden Green, Goudhurst, Cranbrook, Kent, TN17 2PA ℗
☎ 01580 212022
Est. 1985
Services Repair and restoration, makes on commission
Open Mon–Fri 8.30am–5.30pm Sat by appointment

T C Hinton
Contact T C Hinton
✉ The Board Stores, Spencer Mews, Rear of 20 Camden Rd, Tunbridge Wells, Kent, TN1 2PY ℗
☎ 01892 547515 📠 01892 547515
Est. 1979
Services Restoration and conservation of antique furniture, French polishing, gilding, painted furniture, antique paint effects
Open Mon–Fri 9am–1pm 2–5.30pm

R G Jones
Contact R G Jones
✉ 1 Brickfield Cottage, Bilting, Ashford, Kent, TN25 4ER ℗
☎ 01233 812849
Est. 1985
Services Antique restoration, gilding
Open Mon–Fri 9am–4pm

George Justice
Contact Jonathon Thompsett
✉ 12a Market Street, Lewes, East Sussex, BN7 2NB ℗
☎ 01274 474174
✉ geo.justice@virgin.net
🌐 www.lewesartisans.com
Est. 1910
Services Furniture restoration, cabinet-making, French polishing, furniture wax retailer
Open Mon–Fri 8am–5pm

ASSOCIATED SERVICES
FURNITURE

R Lindsell
Contact R Lindsell
✉ 2b Southwood Road,
Ramsgate, Kent,
CT11 0AA 🅿
☎ 01843 588845/ 293551
Est. 1973
Services Furniture repair and
restoration, French polishing
Open Mon–Fri 11am–7pm

**Timothy Long Restoration
(BAFRA, Conservation
Register)**
Contact Timothy Long
✉ St John's Church, London
Road, Dunton Green, Sevenoaks,
Kent,
TN13 2TE 🅿
☎ 01732 743368 📠 01732 742206
📧 info@timlong.co.uk
🌐 www.timlong.co.uk
Est. 1978
Services Antique furniture
restoration, marquetry, boulle,
clock cases, upholstery, cabinet
work and polishing
Open Mon–Fri 8am–5pm

Park View Antiques
Contact Patrick Leith-Ross
✉ High Street, Durgates,
Wadhurst, East Sussex,
TN5 6DE 🅿
☎ 01892 740264 📠 01892 740264
📱 07970 202036
📧 leithross@btconnect.com
🌐 www.parkviewantiques
Est. 1985
Services Furniture restoration
Open By appointment

Phillburys
Contact Mr G C Rattenbury
✉ Unit 2, Udimore Workshop,
School Lane, Udimore, Rye,
East Sussex,
TN31 6AS 🅿
☎ 01797 222361
Est. 1982
Services Restoration of antique
furniture
Open Mon–Sat 8am–6pm

Marco Pitt (BADA)
Contact Mr Marco Pitt
✉ New England House,
New England Street, Brighton,
East Sussex,
BN1 4GH 🅿
📱 07814 492976
📧 marco.pitt@ntlworld.com
🌐 www.russianfurniture

restoration.co.uk
Est. 1978
Services Complete furniture
restoration, specializing in
Russian, French, European pieces
Open Mon–Fri 9am–6pm Sat
9am–1pm

Potter Antiques (GADAR)
Contact Victor Potter
✉ The Old Milking Parlour,
Mile Oak Farm, 524 Mile Oak
Road, Portslade, Brighton,
East Sussex,
BN41 2RF 🅿
☎ 01273 423730 📠 01273 418853
📱 07768 274461
📧 cvpotter@aol.com
🌐 www.craftsmen-in-wood.com
Est. 2001
Services Repair and restoration
of furniture, wooden items,
architectural woodwork, carving,
marquetry, inlay, turning,
gilding, caning, upholstery.
Specialists in replacement of
desk and writing slope leathers,
baize surfaces and repolishing of
ebonized items
Open Wed–Fri 10am–5.30pm

**Paul M Read Antique
Furniture Restoration**
Contact Paul Read
✉ 12b Gaza Trading Estate,
Scabharbour Lane,
Sevenoaks,
Kent,
TN11 8PL 🅿
☎ 01732 460022
Est. 1986
Services Full furniture
restoration, cabinet-making,
marquetry, inlaying, carving,
turning, gilding, leather work,
full clock restoration service,
upholstery, cane and rush
seating, traditional French
polishing, on-site polishing and
specialist wood finishes
Open By appointment

**Restore-It (Folkestone)
Ltd**
Contact Roger Keeling
✉ 69 Tontine Street, Folkestone,
Kent,
CT20 1JR
☎ 01303 223726
Est. 1999
Services Furniture restoration
and polishing
Open Mon–Fri 9.30am–5.30pm

T Straw Restoration
Contact Mr T Straw
✉ Ladwood Farm, Acrise,
Folkestone, Kent,
CT18 8LL 🅿
☎ 01303 894001
Est. 1989
Services Antique furniture
restoration
Open Mon–Fri 8am–6pm but
phone first

V Stringer
Contact Mr Victor Stringer
✉ Unit 5, Acorn House,
The Broyle, Ringmer, Lewes,
East Sussex,
BN8 5NN 🅿
☎ 01273 814434 📠 01273 814434
📱 07791 274171
📧 vsp47@hotmail.com
Est. 1989
Services Antique restoration,
reproduction polishers, furniture
makers
Open Mon–Fri 8am–6pm
Sat 8am–noon

Temple Jones Restoration
Contact Mr E or
Miss B Temple Jones
✉ Caspers House, Heathfield
Road, Burwash Common,
East Sussex,
TN19 7LT 🅿
☎ 01435 883130 📠 01435 883130
📱 07802 415138
📧 temple-jones@talk21.com
Est. 1996
Services Restoration and
conservation work to period
antique furniture
Open By appointment

**Tony's Antique Services
Ltd**
Contact Tony King
✉ 85 Seaside Road, Eastbourne,
East Sussex,
BN21 3PL
☎ 01323 733776 📠 01323 733776
📱 07752 201786
Est. 1977
Services Furniture restoration,
export, search service
Open Tues–Sat 10am–5pm
Mon by appointment

**Richard Tozer Furniture
workshop**
Contact Richard Tozer
✉ Unit 3, Wembdon Business
Centre, Bower Road, Smeeth,

Ashford, Kent,
TN25 6SZ 🅿
☎ 01303 813824 📠 01303 813824
📱 07818 032088
✉ asjanandruth@hotmail.com
Est. 1987
Services All aspect of restoration
undertaken
Open By appointment

LONDON

Abeam Antiques
Contact Joseph Yousif
✉ **159 Carr Road, Northolt,
Middlesex,
UB5 4RE** 🅿
☎ 020 8426 8857
Est. 1994
Services Furniture, lighting
restoration, repair
Open By appointment

J Abrahart
Contact Mr J Abrahart
✉ **62a Valetta Road, London,
W3 7TN** 🅿
☎ 020 8746 7260
Est. 1955
Services Antique furniture repair
and restoration, French polishing
Open By appointment

G Albanese
Contact Mr G Albanese
✉ **Unit 3a, 100 Rosebery Avenue,
London,
E12 6PS** 🅿
☎ 020 8471 5417
Est. 1978
Services Antique restoration and
cabinet-making
Trade only Yes
Open Mon–Fri 7am–5pm

Albion Clocks (BHI)
Contact Colin Bent
✉ **4 Grove End, Grove Hill,
South Woodford, London,
E18 2LE** 🅿
☎ 020 8530 5570
✉ colin.bent@btinternet.com
🌐 www.albionclocks.com.info
Est. 1963
Services Restoration of clocks
and fine furniture, antiquarian
horologist
Open Mon–Sun 9am–7pm please
phone first

Antique Restorers &
Cabinet Makers Ltd
Contact Barry Howells

or John Eagle
✉ **7a Tynemouth Terrace,
Tynemouth Road, Tottenham,
London,
N15 4AP** 🅿
☎ 020 8808 7965 📠 020 8801 5313
📱 07956 970924
Est. 2005
Services 18th–19thC antique
furniture restoration,
leatherwork, gilding, marquetry
and copy brasswork, copy chair
making, cabinet-making, replica
work
Open Mon–Thurs 7am–3.30pm
Fri 7am–1.30pm

Ballantyne Booth Ltd
(UKIC)
Contact Miss H Mark or
Mr Scott Bowram
✉ **Wendover House, 2a
Wendover Road, London,
NW10 4RT** 🅿
☎ 020 8965 2777 📠 020 8965 2777
Est. 1983
Services Cabinet work,
veneering, glazing, carving,
polishing, upholstery, aerial
conservation and restoration
Open Mon–Fri 9am–5.30pm

Bell House Restoration Ltd
Contact Mr R Humphrey
✉ **20–22 Beardell Street, London,
SE19 1TP** 🅿
☎ 020 8761 9002 📠 020 8761 9012
📱 07771 801269
✉ bellhouserestore@aol.com
Est. 1984
Services Antique furniture
restoration, gilding, polishing,
colouring, turning, veneering,
restoration abroad, simulation
Open Mon–Fri 8am–5pm

A J Brett & Co
Contact Mr Negri or
Mrs Chesworth
✉ **168 Marlborough Road,
London,
N19 4NP** 🅿
☎ 020 7272 8462 📠 020 7272 5102
✉ ajbrett@aol.com
🌐 www.ajbrett.co.uk
Est. 1960
Services Furniture restoration,
gilding, upholstery
Open Mon–Fri 7.30am–3.30pm

Carlsson Antique
Contact Mr Fell
✉ **Arch No 28, Popes Grove,**

Strawberry Hill, Twickenham,
Middlesex,
TW1 4JW 🅿
☎ 020 8893 9834
📱 07941 918277
Est. 2000
Services Furniture restoration,
French polishing, cabinet-
making, wood turning, carving,
bespoke carpentry
Open Mon–Fri 10am–6pm

The Collector's Workshop
Contact Mr B Brannan
✉ **Unit 11, The Peacock Estate,
20/22 White Hart Lane, London,
N17 8DT** 🅿
☎ 020 8808 1920 📠 020 8808 1920
📱 07778 754754
✉ enquiries@collectorsworkshop.co.uk
🌐 www.collectorsworkshop.co.uk
Est. 1968
Services Antique furniture repair
and restoration, upholstery,
carving, gilding, leather desk
lining, dummy book spines
Open Mon–Sat 7am–4pm please
phone first

The Craftsman's Joint
Contact Mrs Jo Hollis
✉ **173 Kingston Road, London,
SW19 1LH** 🅿
☎ 020 8545 0655 📠 020 8395 4566
✉ craftsmansjoint@aol.com
Est. 1991
Services Furniture restoration,
cabinet-making, French
polishing, upholstery, caning,
leatherwork
Open Mon–Fri 9.30am–5.30pm
Sat 9am–3pm closed Wed or by
appointment

Crawford Antiques
Contact Mr Rama
✉ **87 Cricklewood Lane, London,
NW2 1HR** 🅿
☎ 020 8450 3660
Est. 1969
Services Antique repair and
French polishing
Open Mon–Sat 9am–6pm

Hannerle Dehn
Contact Hannerle Dehn
✉ **Studio 4, Southam Street,
London,
W10 5PP** 🅿
☎ 020 8964 0599 📠 020 7602 1192
📱 07798 623715
✉ robinersligh@freeserve.co.uk
Est. 1978

Services Restoration of 18th–19thC lacquered and gilded, painted and decorated furniture
Open Mon–Fri 7.30am–5pm or by appointment

Dyson Furniture
Contact Nick Dyson
✉ Eel Pie Boatyard, Eel Pie Island, Twickenham, Middlesex, TW1 3DY
☎ 020 8891 5309
Est. 1992
Services Complete furniture repair and restoration, turning, marquetry, inlay work, cabinet-making
Open Mon–Fri 10am–6pm

Elizabeth Street Antiques and Restoration Services
Contact Mr Naik
✉ 35 Elizabeth Street, London, SW1W 9RP P
☎ 020 7730 6777
⓪ 07973 909257
📧 info@elizabethstreetantiques.com
🌐 www.elizabethstreetantiques.com
Est. 1993
Services Antique restoration, marquetry, French polishing, upholstery
Open Mon–Sat 8am–7pm

Fens Restoration and Sales
Contact Mrs M Saville
✉ 46 Lots Road, London, SW10 0QF P
☎ 020 7352 9883
Est. 1979
Services Repair and restoration of furniture, stripping
Open Mon–Fri 9am–5pm
Sat by appointment

Mark Finamore
Contact Mark Finamore
✉ 63 Orford Road, Walthamstow, London, E17 9NJ P
☎ 020 8521 9407
Est. 1981
Services General antiques service, gilding, furniture restoration and conservation
Open Mon–Fri 10.30am–6pm or Sat by appointment

Ivo Geikie-Cobb
Contact Mr I Geikie-Cobb
✉ Unit 32, Charterhouse Works,

Eltringham Street, London, SW18 1TD P
☎ 020 8874 3767 📠 020 8874 3767
⓪ 07761 561569
📧 restore@ivogc.com
🌐 www.ivogc.com
Est. 1991
Services Antique furniture conservation and restoration, gilding, upholstery, re-leathering, French polishing, veneering, architectural restoration
Open Mon–Fri 9.30am–5.30pm

Greenwich Conservation Workshops
Contact Richard Moy
22 Nelson Road, London, SE10 9JB P
☎ 020 8293 1067
🌐 www.spreadeagle.org
Est. 1957
Services Restoration of period furniture, oil, watercolours, picture frames, porcelain, pottery
Open Mon–Sat 10.30am–5.30pm

H J Hatfield and Son
✉ 42 St Michael's Street, London, W2 1QP P
☎ 020 7723 8265 📠 020 7706 4562
📧 admin@hjhatfield.com
🌐 www.hjhatfield.com
Est. 1834
Services Restoration of furniture, porcelain, paintings, boulle, upholstery, lacquerwork, metalwork, chandeliers, marble
Open Mon–Fri 8am–1pm 2–5pm (moving soon check via phone or website before visiting)

Hornsby Furniture Restoration Ltd
Contact Mr M Gough
✉ 35 Thurloe Place, London, SW7 2HJ P
☎ 020 7225 2888 📠 020 7838 0235
📧 sales@antiqueous.com
🌐 www.hornsbyfurniture.com
Est. 1890
Services Antique furniture restoration including gilding, cabinet-making, upholstery, bespoke furniture, French polishing, caning
Open Mon–Fri 8am–5.30pm
Sat 9am–12.30pm

Kantuta
Contact Mrs N Wright
✉ 1d Gleneagle Road, London, SW16 6AX P
☎ 020 8677 6701
Est. 1986
Services Upholstery and furniture restoration
Open Mon–Sat 10am–6pm

Magical Restorations
Contact Mr F Hussain
✉ 4 Wilson Walk, off Prebend Gardens, London, W4 1TP P
☎ 020 8741 3799 📠 020 8741 3799
⓪ 07956 681655
📧 enquiries@magical-restorations.com
🌐 www.magical-restorations.com
Est. 1997
Services Furniture repair and restoration, carving, gilding, French polishing
Open Mon–Fri 9am–5pm

Martin Murray Antiques (TVADA)
Contact Martin Murray
✉ 2 Baronsmere Road, East Finchley, London, N2 9QB P
☎ 020 8883 0755
⓪ 07970 625359
📧 martin@martin97.wanadoo.co.uk
Est. 1997
Services Furniture repair and restoration, French polishing
Open By appointment

M Merritt
Contact Mr M Merritt
✉ 8 Brightfield Road, London, SE12 8QF P
☎ 020 8852 7577
Est. 1983
Services Antique furniture restoration, cabinet-making, veneering
Open Mon–Fri 9am–5pm or by appointment

Minerva Antiques
Contact Jonathan Atkins
✉ 90 Royal Hill, Greenwich, London, SE10 8RT P
☎ 020 8691 2221
📧 antiquerestoration.co.uk
🌐 www.minerva-antiques.co.uk
Est. 1986
Services On line replacement of

table and desk top leathers
Open Tues–Sat 10am–6pm
Sun 11am–5pm

Laurence Mitchell Antiques (LAPADA)
Contact Laurence Mitchell
✉ 20 The Mall, 359 Islington High Street, Islington, London, N1 0PD
☎ 020 7359 7579
✉ laurence@buymeissen.com
🌐 www.buymeissen.com
Est. 1970
Services Restoration of antiques
Open Tues–Fri 10am–5pm
Sat 10am–5.30pm

Richard G Phillips Ltd
Contact Mr R G Phillips
✉ 95–99 Shernhall Street, London, E17 9HS ℗
☎ 020 8509 9075 📠 020 8509 9077
Est. 1984
Services Antique furniture restoration. Also manufactures classical English furniture and decorative four-poster beds
Open By appointment

Piers Furniture Repair Workshop
Contact Mr P Tarrant-Willis
✉ The Old Air Raid Shelter, Athlone Street, London, NW5 4LN ℗
☎ 020 7209 5824
Est. 1990
Services Antique furniture repair and restoration, French polishing
Open By appointment

Plowden and Smith Ltd (MGR)
Contact Sarah Giles
✉ 190 St Ann's Hill, London, SW18 2RT ℗
☎ 020 8874 4005 📠 020 8874 7248
✉ info@plowden-smith.com
🌐 www.plowden-smith.com
Est. 1966
Services Repair and restoration of paintings, furniture, stone, metalwork, decorative arts, object mounting, exhibitions
Open Mon–Fri 9am–5pm

R M W Restorations
Contact Mr R Mark-Wardlaw
✉ Unit B08, Acton Business Centre, School Road,

London, NW10 6TD ℗
☎ 020 8965 2938 📠 020 8965 2938
Est. 1986
Services Antique furniture repair and restoration, traditional and modern finishes, insurance work, cabinet work, French polishing
Open Mon–Fri 10am–6pm

Regency Restoration
Contact Mrs E Ball
✉ 72 Ingot Place, London, SW8 43NS
☎ 020 7622 5275 or 020 782 84268
Est. 1987
Services Restoration of 18th–19thC mirrors, picture frames, English and Continental painted and gilded furniture, architectural gilding, church interiors, polychrome sculpture, lacquerwork, oil paintings, carving
Open Mon–Fri 9.30am–5.30pm

Sears
Contact Mr D Foster
✉ 79 Ashby Mews, Brockley, London, SE4 1TB ℗
☎ 020 8694 9911 📠 020 8694 9911
Est. 1975
Services Furniture restoration
Open Mon–Fri 8am–4pm

Michael Slade
Contact M Slade
✉ 42 Quernmore Road, London, N4 4QP ℗
☎ 020 8341 3194
📱 07813 377029
✉ mikeslade@ntl.com
Est. 1984
Services Antique repair and restoration, furniture making, upholstery, French polishing, furniture sales
Open Mon–Fri 10am–6pm please telephone first

H A Smith & Son
Contact Mr A Smith
✉ 36a Nelson Road, Harrow on the Hill, Harrow, Middlesex, HA1 3ET ℗
☎ 020 8864 2335 📠 020 8864 2335
Est. 1920
Services Antique and modern furniture restoration, repair and upholstery
Open Mon–Fri 9am–6pm
Sat 10am–2pm

Solomon
Contact Solomon
✉ 49 Park Road, London, N8 8SY ℗
☎ 020 8341 1817 📠 020 8341 1817
✉ solomon@solomonantiques.fsnet.co.uk
Est. 1981
Services Restoration, upholstery, polishing
Open Mon–Sat 9am–6pm

Titian Studio (BAFRA, UKIC)
Contact Rodrigo Titian
✉ 32 Warple Way, Acton, London, W3 0DJ ℗
☎ 020 8222 6600 📠 020 8749 2220
✉ info@titianstudios.co.uk
🌐 www.titianstudios.co.uk
Est. 1965
Services Restoration of gilding and lacquering, French polishing, caning, cabinet-making
Open Mon–Fri 8am–5.30pm

M Tocci
Contact Mr M Tocci
✉ Unit 4, 81 Southern Row, London, W10 5AL ℗
☎ 020 8960 4826
Est. 1978
Services Gilding, painted furniture restoration, lacquer on furniture and decorations
Open Mon–Fri 7.30am–4.30pm

SOUTH

A Dunn
Contact Mr A Dunn
✉ Rear of 128 Sheen Road, Richmond, Surrey, TW9 1UR ℗
☎ 020 8948 7032
Est. 1974
Services Furniture repair and restoration
Open Mon–Fri 8am–5.30pm

Aggeby's
Contact Andrew Agg
✉ Charlwood Place, Norwood Hill Road, Charlwood, Surrey, RH6 0EB ℗
☎ 01293 863700
Est. 2001
Services Furniture restoration
Open Mon–Fri 9am–6pm or by appointment

ASSOCIATED SERVICES
FURNITURE

Allen Avery Interiors
Contact Paul Avery
✉ No 1 High Street, Haselmere,
Surrey,
GU27 2AG ▣
☎ 01428 643883 ✆ 01428 656815
Est. 1970
Services Restoration
Open Mon Tues Thurs Fri
9am–1pm 2.15–5pm Wed
Sat 9am–1pm

Antique Restorers
Contact Mr W Barker
✉ 2 Station Approach,
Stoneleigh, Epsom,
Surrey,
KT19 0QZ ▣
☎ 020 8393 9111
Est. 1980
Services Upholstery, French
polishing, furniture repair, cane
and rush seating.
Open Mon–Fri 9.30am–4.30pm

Ben Norris & Co (BAFRA)
Contact Colin Bell
✉ Unit 8 Orchard Business Park,
Cottismore Farm, Newbury,
Berkshire,
RG20 4SY ▣
☎ 01635 297950 ✆ 01635 299851
Ⓜ 07887 637678
Est. 1980
Services Restoration of antique
furniture and gilding,
reproduction cabinet-making,
furniture made to order
Open Mon–Fri 8.30am–5pm

A E Booth and Son
Contact David or Ann Booth
✉ 300 Hook Road, Hook,
Chessington, Surrey,
KT9 1NY ▣
☎ 020 8397 7675 ✆ 020 8397 7675
Est. 1934
Services Restoration of antique
and modern reproduction
furniture including polishing and
upholstery
Open By appointment

Clive Bristow Antiques
Contact Mr Clive Bristow
✉ Lydgate, Seale Lane, Seale,
Farnham, Surrey,
GU10 1LF ▣
☎ 01252 782775
Est. 1971
Services French polishing, fine
antique furniture restoration
Open By appointment

The Cabinet Repair Shop
Contact Mrs M H Embling
✉ Woodlands Farm, Blacknest
Road, Blacknest, Alton,
Hampshire,
GU34 4BQ ▣
☎ 01252 794260 ✆ 01252 793084
Ⓦ www.dsembling.co.uk
Est. 1984
Services Restoration of antique
and modern furniture, insurance
claim work
Open Mon–Fri 8am–5pm Sat by
appointment

**Peter Casebow Ltd
(BAFRA)**
Contact Mr P Casebow
✉ Pilgrims Mill Lane, Worthing,
West Sussex,
BN13 3DE ▣
☎ 01903 264045
Ⓔ pcasebow@hotmail.com
Est. 1987
Services Restoration of period
furniture including square-piano
restoration
Open By appointment

**B Castle (Exhibitor of the
Royal Academy & Mall
Gallery)**
Contact Mr B Castle
✉ 2 Charmandean Road,
Worthing, West Sussex,
BN14 9LB ▣
☎ 01903 239702
Est. 1982
Services Antique repair and
restoration of small furniture,
decorative items, woodcarver
Open Mon–Sat by appointment

**Alan Cooper Antique
Restorations**
Contact Alan Cooper
✉ Unit 7, Park Farm, Hundred
Acre Lane, Wivelsfield Green,
Haywards Heath, West Sussex,
RH17 7RU ▣
☎ 01273 890017
Est. 1973
Services Antique repair, French
polishing, restoration
Open Mon–Fri 8am–3pm

**Copperwheat Restoration
(RICS)**
Contact Carole Copperwheat
✉ Rear of Pascall Atkey,
29–30 High Street, Cowes,
Isle of Wight,
PO31 7RX ▣

☎ 01983 281011
Ⓜ 07720 399670
Est. 1985
Services Antique furniture repair,
restoration, commissions
Open Any time by prior
telephone call

Corwell
Contact Mr S Corbin
✉ Unit 6, Amners Farm,
Burghfield, Reading, Berkshire,
RG30 3UE ▣
☎ 0118 983 3404 ✆ 0118 983 3404
Ⓔ info@corwell.co.uk
Ⓦ www.corwell.co.uk
Est. 1989
Services Antique restoration,
cabinet-making
Open Mon–Fri 9am–5pm
Sat 9am–2pm

Davenports Antiques
Contact Mr C Height
✉ Unit 5, Woodgate Centre,
Oak Tree Lane, Woodgate,
Chichester, West Sussex,
PO20 6GU ▣
☎ 01243 544242
Ⓜ 07745 985628
Ⓔ height@btinternet.com
Est. 1980
Services Antique furniture
restoration
Open Mon–Fri 8.30am–6pm

Sonia Demetriou
Contact Sonia Demetriou
✉ 2 Elbridge Farm Buildings,
Chichester Road, Bognor Regis,
West Sussex,
PO21 5EG ▣
☎ 01243 842235 ✆ 01243 842235
Ⓔ sondem@intelynx.net
Ⓦ www.art-scope.co.uk
Est. 1977
Services Restoration of antique
painted furniture and objets
d'art
Open Mon–Fri 9.30am–6pm
Sat by appointment

R G Dewdney
Contact Mr R G Dewdney
✉ Norfolk Road, South
Holmwood, Dorking, Surrey,
RH5 4LA ▣
☎ 01306 888174 ✆ 01306 742636
Ⓔ regdewdney@btconnect.com
Est. 1968
Services General antique repair
and restoration, leatherwork
Open Mon–Fri 9am–6pm

Downland Furniture Restoration
Contact Mr S Macintyre
✉ **Wepham Farmyard, Wepham, Arundel, West Sussex, BN18 9EA** 🅿
☎ 01903 883387
📱 07713 104818
Est. 1984
Services Furniture restoration and conservation
Open Mon–Fri 9am–5pm or by appointment

K Edwards Antiques
Contact Mr K Edwards
✉ **Unit 6, Annington Commercial Centre, Annington Road, Steyning, West Sussex, BN44 3WA** 🅿
☎ 01903 814300
✉ kedwa31024@aol.com
Est. 1988
Services Restoration
Open Mon–Fri 8am–5pm

Richard Elderton
Contact R C Elderton
✉ **Home Farm, Mill Lane, Hawkley, Liss, Hampshire, GU33 6NU** 🅿
☎ 01420 538374
✉ woodman@cix.co.uk
🌐 www.cix.co.uk/~woodman/
Est. 1976
Services Antique furniture restoration, new bespoke solid wood furniture, metalworking repair, woodturning
Open Mon–Fri 9am–5pm or by appointment

G and R Fraser-Sinclair (BAFRA)
Contact Mr G Fraser-Sinclair
✉ **Haysbridge Farm, Brickhouse Lane, South Godstone, Godstone, Surrey, RH9 8JW** 🅿
☎ 01342 844112 ☏ 01342 844112
Est. 1978
Services General restoration of 18thC furniture
Open Mon–Fri 8am–5.30pm

A D Gardner
Contact Mr Gardner
✉ **2a East Road, Reigate, Surrey, RH2 9EX** 🅿
☎ 01737 222430
Est. 1969
Services Antique repair and restoration, fine French

polishing, caning, leathering, upholstery
Open Mon–Fri 8.30am–5.30pm

Simon Gooding
Contact Simon Gooding
✉ **Unit 1b, Dorotay Farm, Haselmere, Surrey, GU27 2DQ** 🅿
☎ 01428 651072
📱 07770 630068
Est. 1984
Services Furniture restoration, French polishing, leather desk tops
Open Mon–Fri 8am–5pm

Goodwood Furniture Restoration (BAFRA)
Contact Bruce Neville
✉ **21 Richmond Road, Westerton, Chichester, West Sussex, PO18 0PQ** 🅿
☎ 01243 778614
📱 07719 778079
✉ bruce@goodwoodrestoration.co.uk
🌐 www.goodwoodrestoration.co.uk
Est. 1991
Services Antique furniture restoration, cabinet-making
Open Mon–Sat 8.30am–5.30pm

G J Hall, Antique Furniture Restoration
Contact Mr G J Hall
✉ **Unit 1, Rear of Longreach, Branshill Road, Eversley, Hampshire, RG27 0PS** 🅿
☎ 01189 737001
📱 07711 846712
✉ garyh29@hotmail.com
Est. 1984
Services Restoration and conservation of fine antique furniture, copy chair making, French polishing, insurance work, design commissions
Open Mon–Fri 9.30am–5.30pm

Hedgecoe & Freeland Ltd (LAPADA)
Contact Justin Freeland
✉ **Rowan House, 21 Burrow Hill Green, Chobham, Woking, Surrey, GU24 8QP** 🅿
☎ 01276 858206 ☏ 01276 857352
📱 07771 953870
✉ hedgecoefreeland@aol.com
🌐 www.hedgecoefreeland.com
Est. 1969
Services Cabinet-making,

polishing, upholstery, metalwork, gilding, lacquerwork and paintwork
Open Mon–Fri 8am–5pm

Stuart Hobbs Antique Furniture Restoration (BAFRA)
Contact Mr S Hobbs
✉ **Meath Paddock, Meath Green Lane, Horley, Surrey, RH6 8HZ** 🅿
☎ 01293 782349 ☏ 01293 773467
Est. 1981
Services Furniture, longcase, bracket clock and barometer restoration
Open By appointment

Howard Hunt Antiques
Contact Mr H Hunt
✉ **The White Hut, Thackhams Farm, Bottle Lane, Mattingley, Hook, Hampshire, RG27 8LJ** 🅿
☎ 01256 881111 ☏ 01256 881111
Est. 1989
Services Repair and restoration of furniture, mirrors, porcelain, upholstery, leathering, gilding, caning, rushing
Open By appointment

Gavin Hussey Antique Restoration (BAFRA)
Contact G Hussey
✉ **4 Brook Farm, Clayhill Road, Leigh, Reigate, Surrey, RH2 8PA** 🅿
☎ 01306 611634 ☏ 01306 611634
Est. 1994
Services Full restoration of furniture and clocks
Open By appointment

David C E Lewry (BAFRA, Woodwork Fellowship)
Contact Mr D Lewry
✉ **Wychelms, 66 Gorran Avenue, Peel Common, Gosport, Hampshire, PO13 0NF** 🅿
☎ 01329 286901 ☏ 01329 289964
📱 07785 766844
Est. 1979
Services Consultancy on furniture restoration
Open By appointment

John Lloyd (BAFRA)
✉ **Bankside Farm, Jacobs Post, Ditchling Common, West Sussex,**

RH15 0SJ 🅿
☎ 01444 480388 🅕 01444 480388
📱 07941 124772
📧 info@lloydjohnfinefurniture.co.uk
🌐 www.johnlloydfinefurniture.co.uk
Est. 1989
Services Complete repair and
restoration of period,
reproduction and modern
furniture, short courses on care
and repair of antiques and
gilding
Open Mon–Fri 8.30am–5.30pm

Carlos Lopez & Son
Contact Mr C Lopez
✉ 151 London Road, Burgess Hill,
West Sussex,
RH15 8LH 🅿
☎ 01444 243176
Est. 1977
Services Antique furniture
restoration and hand-made chair
copying
Open Mon–Fri 9am–1pm 2–6pm
Sat 9am–1pm

Lush Restoration
Contact Mr M Lush
✉ 64d Old Milton Road,
New Milton, Hampshire,
BH25 6DX 🅿
☎ 01425 629680
Est. 1992
Services Repair and restoration,
upholstery
Open Mon–Fri 8am–1pm 2–5pm

Lymington Restoration
Contact Mr M Cooper
✉ Fairlea House, 110–112 Marsh
Lane, Lymington, Hampshire,
SO41 9EE 🅿
☎ 01590 677558 🅕 01590 677558
Est. 1996
Services Restoration of antique
furniture, gilding, upholstery
Open Mon–Fri 9am–5pm

Malcolm Morrisen, Antique Furniture Restorer
Contact Malcolm Morrisen
✉ Old Post Office Cottage,
East Ilsley, Newbury, Berkshire,
RG20 7LF 🅿
☎ 01635 281349
📱 07990 880717
Est. 2003
Services Antique furniture
restoration and conservation
Open Mon–Fri 9am–5pm by
appointment

Timothy Naylor Antiques (BAFRA)
Contact T Naylor
✉ 24 Bridge Road, Chertsey,
Surrey,
KT16 8JN 🅿
☎ 01932 567129 🅕 01932 564948
📧 tim@timothynaylor.com
🌐 www.timothynaylor.com
Est. 1988
Services Georgian and Regency
furniture restoration
Open Mon–Fri 8.30am–5pm

New Forest Antique Restoration Ltd
Contact Piers Paterson
✉ 23 Bridge Street,
Fordingbridge, Hampshire,
SP6 1AH 🅿
☎ 0845 2305123
📧 info@restorer.net
🌐 www.restorer.net
Est. 1995
Services Furniture restoration,
upholstery, bespoke hand-made
furniture
Open Mon–Fri 8am–5pm or by
appointment

Simon Paterson (BAFRA)
✉ Whitelands, West Dean,
Chichester, West Sussex,
PO18 0RL 🅿
☎ 01243 811900
📧 hotglue@tiscali.co.uk
Est. 1992
Services Repair and restoration
of antique furniture and clocks,
boulle work, marquetry
Open By appointment

K S Pawlowski
Contact K S Pawlowski
✉ 37 High Street, Turner
Dumbrell Workshops, Ditchling,
Hassocks, West Sussex,
BN6 8SY 🅿
☎ 01273 846003 🅕 01273 846003
📧 pawlowski@ditchling.fsnet.co.uk
Est. 1983
Services Conservation and
restoration of antique furniture
Open By appointment

Eva-Louise Pepperall
Contact E Pepperall
✉ Dairy Lane Cottage, Walberton,
Arundel, West Sussex,
BN18 0PT 🅿
☎ 01243 551282
📧 evalouisepepperall@hotmail.com
🌐 www.pepperall.com

Est. 1977
Services Restoration of antique
furniture, gilding, japanning
Open By appointment

Mr Pickett's
Contact Mr M Pickett
✉ The Lifestyle Centre,
Bosham Roundabout, Delling
Lane, Bosham, Nr Chichester,
West Sussex,
PO18 8NN 🅿
☎ 01243 574573 🅕 01243 574573
📱 07779 997012
📧 info@mrpicketts.co.uk
🌐 www.mrpicketts.co.uk
Est. 1991
Services Paint stripping, sanding,
waxing, full restoration, bespoke
items made to order from
reclaimed pine
Open By appointment

Albert Plumb Furniture Co (BAFRA)
Contact Mrs S Plumb
✉ Itchenor Green, Chichester,
West Sussex,
PO20 7DA 🅿
☎ 01243 513700
📧 apfco@supanet.com
Est. 1977
Services Antique furniture
restorers and upholsterers.
Bespoke cabinet-makers
Open Mon–Fri 8.30am–6.30pm or
by appointment

D Potashnick
Contact Mr D Potashnick
✉ 7 The Parade, 73 Stoats Nest
Road, Coulsdon, Surrey,
CR5 2JJ 🅿
☎ 020 8660 8403
Est. 1969
Services Restoration of furniture
Open Mon–Fri 9am–5pm or by
appointment

Vincent Reed Furniture
Contact Vincent
✉ 103a Keymer Road, Keymer,
Hassocks, West Sussex,
BN6 8QL 🅿
☎ 01273 845678
📱 07815 751005
📧 info@vincentreed.com
🌐 www.vincentreed.co.uk
Est. 1992
Services 17th–18thC furniture
restoration
Open Mon–Fri 9am–5pm
Sat 10am–4pm

Reeves Restoration at the Coach House Antiques
Contact Paul or Louise Reeves
✉ The Coach House, 60 Station Road, Gomshall, Surrey, GU5 9NP 🅿
☎ 01483 203838 ✆ 01483 202999
📱 07774 729325
📧 coach_house.antiques@virgin.net
🌐 www.coachhouseantiques.com
Est. 1984
Services Antique clock, furniture restoration
Open By appointment

Regency Antiques
Contact R De Santini
✉ Home Cottage, Andrews Hill, Adversane, Billingshurst, West Sussex
☎ 01403 780 ✆ 01403 874
📱 07947 597311
Est. 1978
Services Porcelain and furniture restoration
Open Mon–Fri 9.30am–5.30pm by appointment only

Renaissance
Contact Mr Peter Cross
✉ 11 Enterprise Close, Croydon, Surrey, CR0 3RZ 🅿
☎ 020 8664 9686 ✆ 020 8664 9737
Est. 1996
Services Furniture and frame repair and restoration
Open Mon–Fri 10am–6.30pm

Restore
Contact Mr G R Fisher or Mrs S Fisher
✉ Restore/Taggs Boat Yard, 44 Summer Road, Thames Ditton, Surrey, KT7 0QQ 🅿
☎ 020 8398 4703
📱 07970 186769
📧 info@restoreltd.co.uk
🌐 www.restoreltd.co.uk
Est. 1999
Services Antique furniture restoration, sales of antique and contemporary design furniture
Open Mon–Fri 9am–5pm

Robinson Restorations
Contact Mr Nick Robinson
✉ Unit 8, Seven House, 34–38 Town End, Caterham, Surrey, CR3 5UG 🅿
☎ 01883 330111
📱 07970 255053

Est. 1896
Services Antique restoration, French polishing
Open Mon–Fri 8am–6pm Sat 10am–4pm

David A Sayer Antique Furniture Restorer (BAFRA, Furniture History Society, Regional Furniture Society)
Contact David Sayer
✉ Courtlands, Park Road, Banstead, Surrey, SM7 3EF 🅿
☎ 01737 352429 ✆ 01737 373255
📱 07775 636009
Est. 1985
Services Comprehensive repair, restoration and conservation service of English and Continental furniture
Open Mon–Fri 8am–6pm

Michael Schryver Antiques
Contact Mr M Schryver
✉ The Granary, 10 North Street, Dorking, Surrey, RH4 1DN 🅿
☎ 01306 881110 ✆ 01306 876168
📧 michael.schryver@virgin.net
Est. 1971
Services 18thC furniture restoration
Open Mon–Fri 8.30am–5.30pm or by appointment

Andrew Sharp Antique Restoration Ltd
Contact Mr A Sharp
✉ Unit 1, Forest Villa Courtyard, Lyndhurst Road, Brockenhurst, Hampshire, SO42 7RL 🅿
☎ 01590 622577
Est. 1996
Services Sale and restoration of Georgian–Victorian furniture
Open Mon–Sat 9am–5.30pm

Surrey Restoration Ltd (AFRA)
Contact Mark Grady
✉ Highway Farm, Horsley Road, Downside, Cobham, Surrey, KT11 3JZ 🅿
☎ 01932 868883 ✆ 01483 268285
📱 07711 635484
📧 emcghee@surreyrestoration.freeserve.co.uk
Est. 1994
Services Antique furniture

restoration, interior wooden panelling of period houses
Open Mon–Sat 8.30am–6.30pm

Sussex Woodcraft
Contact Mr Waters
✉ 15 Drayton Cottages, Drayton Lane, Drayton, Chichester, West Sussex, PO20 2EW 🅿
☎ 01243 788830
Est. 1937
Services Cabinet-making and restoration
Open Mon–Fri 8am–5pm

T S Restorations
Contact T Street
✉ 13 Blatchford Close, Horsham, West Sussex, RH13 5RG 🅿
☎ 01403 273766
Est. 1989
Services Antique repair and restoration
Open Mon–Fri 8am–5pm

Roy Temple Polishing
Contact Mr R Temple
✉ Unit 15, Sheeplands Farm, Twyford Road, Wargrave, Reading, Berkshire, RG10 8DL 🅿
☎ 01189 402211 or 01628 660106
✆ 01189 402211
Est. 1996
Services Furniture repair and restoration, polishing, leathering
Open Mon–Sat 9am–5pm

The Traditional Restoration Company Ltd
Contact Ms Thompson
✉ The Coach House, Dorney Court, Dorney, Windsor, Berkshire, SL4 6QL 🅿
☎ 01628 660708
🌐 www.traditionalrestoration.co.uk
Est. 1991
Services Restoration of 18th–19thC furniture, carving, upholstery, metalwork
Open Mon–Fri 8am–5.30pm (but phone first) weekends by appointment

Troke, Terry
Contact T Troke
✉ 22 Fairview Road, Hungerford, Berkshire, RG17 0BT 🅿
☎ 01488 683310

Est. 1975
Services Antique furniture repair and restoration
Open By appointment

G Williams
Contact Graham Williams
✉ The Builders Yard, Church Street, Betchworth, Surrey, RH3 7DN ▣
☎ 01737 843266
Est. 1975
Services General restoration, desk-top leathering, gold tooling, French polishing
Open Mon–Fri 9am–6pm Sat 10am–2pm

Wotruba & Son
Contact Mr F F Wotruba
✉ Clump Workshops, Bassett Green Road, Chilworth, Southampton, Hampshire, SO16 3NF ▣
☎ 023 8076 6411
📱 07887 712401
✉ f.f.wotruba@btinternet.com
Est. 1995
Services Antique restoration, including upholstery, polishing, veneering, boulle work, wood turning
Open Mon–Fri 10am–5pm Sat 10am–noon or by appointment

WEST COUNTRY

Antique Restoration (Furniture History Society, NACF)
Contact George Judd
✉ East Farm, Winterbourne Gunner, Salisbury, Wiltshire, SP4 6EW ▣
☎ 01980 610576/611828
Est. 1975
Services Antique furniture, porcelain and painting restoration, cabinet-making, upholstery, metalwork, leatherwork, gilding
Open Mon–Fri 9am–7pm Sat by appointment

David Battle Antique Furniture Restoration and Conservation (BAFRA)
Contact David Battle
✉ Brightley Pound, Umberleigh, Devon, EX37 9AL ▣
☎ 01769 540483
✉ david@brightley.clara.net

🌐 brightley.clara.net
Est. 1984
Services Comprehensive service for English and Continental period furniture
Open By appointment

Boughey Antique Restoration
Contact Dave Boughey
✉ 1 Kniel Cottage, The Quay, Millbrook, Torpoint, Cornwall, PL10 1AN ▣
☎ 01752 829008 ☏ 01752 829008
📱 07970 540644
Est. 1960
Services Furniture restoration, cabinet-making, porcelain and pottery restoration
Open Mon–Fri 8am–5.30pm or by appointment

Bowen & Lucas Antique Restoration
Contact Mr J Bowen or Mr Lucas
✉ Unit 2, Alexandra Court, Yeovil, Somerset, BA21 5AL ▣
☎ 01935 474446
📱 07866 384606
Est. 1984
Services Furniture restoration, French polishing, carving, cabinet-making
Open Mon–Sat 8.30am–5pm

M and S Bradbury (BAFRA)
Contact Mr S Bradbury
✉ The Barn, Hanham Lane, Paulton, Bristol, BS39 7PF ▣
☎ 01761 418910
✉ stuart@mandsbradbury.co.uk
🌐 www.mandsbradbury.co.uk
Est. 1988
Services Furniture restoration including clock cases
Open Mon–Fri 8am–5pm

Lawrence Brass
Contact Lawrence Brass
✉ Apple Studio, Bath, Somerset, BA1 5YX ▣
☎ 01225 852222
🌐 www.lawrencebrass.com
Est. 1973
Services Antique furniture restoration
Open Mon–Sat 9am–5pm

J E Cadman
Contact Mr Cadman
✉ 15 Norwich Road,

Bournemouth, Dorset, BH2 5QZ ▣
☎ 01202 290973
Est. 1901
Services Antique restoration, mostly furniture
Open Mon–Fri 9am–5pm

Castle House Antique Restoration Ltd (BAFRA)
Contact Mr Michael Durkee
✉ Castle House, Units 1 and 3, Bennetts Field Estate, Wincanton, Somerset, BA9 9DT ▣
☎ 01963 33884 ☏ 01963 31278
Est. 1975
Services Antique furniture restoration and conservation
Open Mon–Fri 8.30am–5pm

Christopher Cole
Contact Mr C Cole
✉ The Workshop, 36 Claude Avenue, Oldfield Park, Bath, Somerset, BA2 1AG ▣
☎ 01225 310298 ☏ 01225 310298
📱 07890 824042
Est. 1994
Services Antique furniture restoration, carving, turning, French polishing
Open Mon–Fri 8.30am–7pm

David Collyer Antique Restorations
Contact David Collyer
✉ Tunley Farm, Tunley, Bath, Somerset, BA2 0DL ▣
☎ 01761 472727 ☏ 01761 472727
📱 07889 725508
✉ Restoration@davidcollyer.com
🌐 www.davidcollyer.com
Est. 1985
Services Furniture restoration and repair
Open Mon–Fri 9am–5.30pm or by appointment

W J Cook (BAFRA)
Contact W J Cook
✉ High Trees, Savernake Forest, Near Marlborough, Wiltshire, SN8 4NE ▣
☎ 01672 513017 ☏ 01672 514455
✉ wjcook@btconnect.com
🌐 www.antiquerestoration.uk.com
Est. 1963
Services Furniture polishing, restoration, upholstery, gilding
Open By appointment

Mark Coray Fine Antique Furniture Restoration (BAFRA)
Contact Mark Coray
⊠ The Coach House Workshops, Ford Street, Wellington, Somerset, TA21 9PG 🅿
☎ 01823 663766
📱 07979 245524
🌐 www.markcoray.co.uk
Est. 1996
Services All antique furniture restoration, gilding, furniture made to order
Open By appointment

Coryndon (BAFRA)
Contact N G Coryndon or David Lewis
⊠ Rainscombe Farm Buildings, Oare, Marlborough, Wiltshire, SN8 4HZ 🅿
☎ 01672 562581 📠 01672 563995
📧 mail@coryndon.co.uk
Est. 1964
Services General restoration of furniture, gilding, paint finishes. Collection and delivery
Open Mon–Fri 8.30am–4.30pm

D M Antique Restoration
Contact Mr D Pike
⊠ Purn Farm, Bridgewater Road, Bleadon, Weston-super-Mare, Somerset, BS24 0AN 🅿
☎ 01934 811120
Est. 1983
Services Restoration of furniture and chests of drawers
Open Mon–Fri 8am–5pm

Rocco d'Ambrosio
Contact Mr or Mrs R Crees
⊠ 94 Benedict Street, Glastonbury, Somerset, BA6 9EZ 🅿
☎ 01458 831541/ 01278 722234
Est. 1969
Services Furniture restoration, French polishing, upholstery restoration
Open Mon–Fri 9am–6pm or by appointment

M L Davis
Contact Mr M L Davis
⊠ Rear of 1079 Christchurch Road, Bournemouth, Dorset, BH7 6BQ 🅿
☎ 01202 434684
Est. 1987

Services Full restoration of furniture, brass cleaning
Open Mon–Fri 8.30am–5.30pm or by appointment

Christopher John Douglas
Contact Mr C J Douglas
⊠ Befferlands Farm Workshop, Berne Lane, Charmouth, Bridport, Dorset, DT6 6RD 🅿
☎ 01297 561120
📱 07989 161019
Est. 1975
Services Restoration of antique furniture, old pine, Art Deco
Open Mon–Fri 9am–5.30pm

Dudley & Spencer
Contact John Spencer or Ray Dudley
⊠ Unit 21, Signal Way, Central Trading Estate, Swindon, Wiltshire, SN3 1PD 🅿
☎ 01793 535394 📠 01793 535394
Est. 1980
Services Furniture restoration, upholstery, leather tops
Open Mon–Fri 7am–5pm

A A Eddy & Son
Contact Mr K Eddy or Mr M Eddy
⊠ 1a Elphinstone Road, Peverell, Plymouth, Devon, PL2 3QQ 🅿
☎ 01752 787138 📠 01752 789013
📱 07980 615471
Est. 1889
Services Full repair and restoration, French polishing. Free estimates and advice in the Plymouth area
Open Mon–Fri 7.30am–5pm

Esox Antique Restoration
Contact Mr B Elston
⊠ 1 Henderbarrow Cottages, Holwill, Beaworthy, Devon, EX21 5TW 🅿
☎ 01409 221873 📠 01409 221873
📱 07967 283602
📧 esoxantiques@btopenworld.com
Est. 1987
Services Full furniture restoration, French polishing
Open Mon–Sun 9am–5pm but phone first

Former Glory
Contact Tim or Kim Ravenscroft
⊠ Ferndown, Dorset, BH22 🅿

☎ 01202 895859 📠 01202 895859
📱 07769 828727
📧 formerglory@btinternet.com
🌐 www.formerglory.co.uk
Est. 1994
Services Cane and rush seating, furniture restoration. Cane, rush and restoration material supplies
Open By appointment only

Ivo Geikie-Cobb
Contact Mr I Geikie-Cobb
⊠ West Country Workshop, Ivydene, Semley, Dorset, Sp7 9AU 🅿
☎ 01747 830 123 📠 01747 830 123
📱 07761 561569
📧 restore@ivogc.com
🌐 www.ivogc.com
Est. 2005
Services Antique furniture conservation and restoration, gilding, upholstery, re-leathering, French polishing, veneering, architectural restoration
Open Mon–Fri 9.30am–5.30pm

Gilboys Ltd
Contact Mr S Gilboys
⊠ Hole Farm, The Old Stable, Buckfastleigh, Devon, TQ11 0LA 🅿
☎ 01803 762763 📠 01803 762763
📱 07753 858454
📧 simon@gilboys.entadsl.com
🌐 www.gilboys.co.uk
Est. 1992
Services Restoration, French polishing, modern furniture finishes (dining room table heatproofing). Maker of replacement doors, silver soldering, brass repairs
Open Mon–Fri 8.30am–5pm

John Hamblin
Contact John or Mark
⊠ Unit 6, 15 Oxford Road, Penmill Trading Estate, Yeovil, Somerset, BA21 5HR 🅿
☎ 01935 471154 📠 01935 471154
📱 07889 281659
Est. 1981
Services Antique furniture restoration, French polishing, cabinet-making
Open Mon–Sat 9am–5pm

Hart's Antiques
Contact Mr M Hart
⊠ Nanscawen,

FURNITURE

Prideaux Road,
St Blazey, Par, Cornwall,
PL24 2SR 🄿
☎ 01726 816389
🅜 07816 122730
Est. 1985
Services Antique furniture
restoration including upholstery,
gilding and lacquerwork
Open Mon–Sat 9am–6pm

Philip Hawkins Furniture (BAFRA)
Contact Mr P Hawkins
✉ Glebe Workshop, Semley,
Shaftesbury, Dorset,
SP7 9AP 🄿
☎ 01747 830830 🄵 01747 830830
🄴 hawkinssemley@hotmail.com
Est. 1987
Services Restoration and
replication of antique furniture
Open Mon–Fri 9am–5pm or by
appointment

Bruce Isaac
Contact Mr Bruce Isaac
✉ Crown Works, 114a Rodden
Road, Frome, Somerset,
BA11 2AW 🄿
☎ 01373 453277 🄵 01373 830849
🅜 07711 399165
Est. 1990
Services Furniture restoration
Open Mon–Fri 8am–5pm

Mike Keeley
Contact Mike Keeley
✉ 205 Old Church Road,
Clevedon, Somerset,
BS21 7UD 🄿
☎ 01275 873418
🄴 mikeandsheila@blueyonder.co.uk
Est. 1980
Services General repair to
antique furniture, specializing in
dining furniture
Open By appointment
Mon–Fri 9am–5pm

Market Place Antiques Restorations
Contact Martin Bryan Turner
✉ Nuttaberry Works,
Nuttaberry Industrial Estate,
Bideford East, Bideford,
Devon,
EX39 4DU 🄿
☎ 01237 476628
Est. 1984
Services Antique furniture
restoration
Open By appointment

Alf McKay
Contact Mr A McKay
✉ Manor Barn, Hewish,
Crewkerne, Somerset,
TA18 8QT 🄿
☎ 01460 78916 🄵 01460 78916
🅜 07720 810750
🄴 info@cabinet-maker.biz
🅦 www.cabinet-maker.biz
Est. 1972
Services Restoration, cabinet-
maker of traditional furniture
Open By appointment

Rod Naylor
Contact Angela Naylor
✉ 208 Devizes Road, Hilperton,
Trowbridge, Wiltshire,
BA14 7QP 🄿
☎ 01225 754497 🄵 01225 754497
🄴 rod.naylor@virgin.net
🅦 www.rodnaylor.com
Est. 1970
Services Restoration of antique
wood carvings, supplies replicas
of hard-to-find items and
materials for caddies, boxes,
desks etc, cabinet-making,
supplier of power carving
machinery and tools
Open By appointment only

Newmans (BAFRA)
Contact Tony Newman
✉ Tithe Barn, Crowcombe,
Somerset,
TA4 4AQ 🄿
🅜 07717 682027
🄴 tony@cheddon.fsnet.co.uk
Est. 1991
Services All types of restoration
Open Sun–Mon 9am–5pm or by
appointment

Oakfield Cabinet Makers
Contact Mr X Haines
✉ Unit 8, Mount Pleasant,
Offwell, Honiton, Devon,
EX14 9RN 🄿
☎ 01404 46858 🄵 01404 46858
🄴 enquiries@oak-field.co.uk
🅦 www.oak-field.co.uk
Est. 1989
Services Cabinet-making and
restoration
Open Mon–Fri 7.30am–6pm
Sat 9am–1pm

Ottery Antique Restorers (BABAADA, LAPADA)
Contact Mr C James
✉ Wessex Way,
Wincanton Business Park,

Wincanton, Somerset,
BA9 9RR 🄿
☎ 01963 34572 🄵 01963 34572
🅜 07770 923955
🄴 charles@otteryantiques.co.uk
🅦 www.otteryantiques.co.uk
Est. 1986
Services Furniture restoration
Open Mon–Fri 8am–5.30pm Sat
9.30am–1pm

Park Lane Restoration
Contact Matthew Channell
✉ Unit 2, Marston Park Lane,
St Clement, Truro,
Cornwall,
TR1 1SX 🄿
☎ 01872 223944
🅜 07765 448594
Est. 1984
Services 18th–19thC furniture
restoration, cabinet veneering,
stripping and French polishing.
Fire, flood, shipping damage
insurance work
Open Mon–Fri 8am–6pm

Alexander Paul Restorations
Contact Dave Steele
✉ Fenny Bridges, Honiton,
Devon,
EX14 3BG 🄿
☎ 01404 850881
🅜 07815 291470
🄴 dave@alexanderpaulantiques.com
🅦 www.alexanderpaulantiques.com
Est. 2000
Services Full restoration
including French polishing,
turning, veneering
Open Mon–Fri 9am–5.30pm
Sat 10am–4pm

R L Peploe
Contact Mr Peploe
✉ 18 Hughenden Road, Clifton,
Bristol,
BS8 2TT 🄿
☎ 0117 923 9349
Est. 1986
Services Cabinet work, gilding,
carving, general finishing
Open Mon–Fri 9am–5pm

Piers Pisani Antiques
Contact Mr Piers Pisani
✉ The Old Chapel,
Marston Road, Sherborne,
Dorset,
DT9 4BL 🄿
☎ 01935 815209 🄵 01935 815209
🅜 07973 373753

@ pp@pierspisani.com
W www.pierspisani.com
Est. 1987
Services Full furniture
restoration, cabinet-making
Open Mon–Sat 10am–5pm

Richard S Powell Antique Restorer & Cabinet Maker
Contact Richard S Powell
✉ 3 Puddles Lane, Coate,
Devizes, Wiltshire,
SN10 3LF ♿
☎ 01380 860892
📱 07881 934383
W www.antiqueandfurniture
restoration-devizes.co.uk
Est. 1982
Services English furniture
restoration, cabinet-maker,
restoration of interior woodwork
Open By appointment

Robert Pye Antiques Restoration & Conservation of Fine Period Furniture
Contact Robert Pye
✉ Tuxwell Farm, Spaxton,
Bridgwater, Somerset,
TA5 1DF ♿
☎ 01278 671833 📠 01278 671803
@ robpyeantiques@breathe.com
W www.pyeantiquerestoration.
freewebspace.com
Est. 2001
Services Restoration and
conservation
Open Mon–Fri 8.30am–6pm
Sat Sun by appointment

Revival
Contact Mr B Gould
✉ South Road, Timsbury, Bath,
Somerset,
BA3 1LD ♿
☎ 01761 472255 📠 01761 472255
Est. 1979
Services Antique restoration,
upholstery, French polishing
Open Mon–Fri 7am–4.30pm

Philip A Ruttleigh Antiques incorporating Crudwell Furniture
Contact Philip Ruttleigh
✉ Odd Penny Farm, Crudwell,
Wiltshire,
SN16 9SJ ♿
☎ 01285 770970
📱 07989 250077
W www.crudwellfurniture.co.uk
Est. 1989

Services Furniture restoration
Open Mon–Fri 9am–5pm or by
appointment

F B Sadowski
Contact Mr Sadowski
✉ Unit 2, Plot 1a,
Rospeath Estate, Crowlas,
Penzance, Cornwall,
TR20 8DU ♿
☎ 01736 741083
@ feliks@restorefurniture.fsnet.co.uk
Est. 1903
Services Furniture restoration.
Repairs including boulle work,
marquetry
Open Mon–Fri 10.30am–5pm

Graham Sparks Restoration
Contact Mr Graham Sparks
✉ Unit 63, Tone Mill, Tonedale,
Wellington, Somerset,
TA21 0AB ♿
☎ 01823 663636 📠 01823 667393
@ gsparksrestoration@yahoo.co.uk
Est. 1979
Services Furniture restoration,
upholstery, cabinet-making
Open Mon–Fri 8am–6pm
Sat 8am–1pm

St Thomas Antiques
Contact Ken Holdsworth
✉ 74 St Thomas Street, Wells,
Somerset,
BA5 2UZ ♿
☎ 01749 672520
Est. 1969
Services Repair, repolishing
Open Mon–Fri 10am–4pm
closed Wed

Robert P Tandy (BAFRA)
Contact Robert P Tandy
✉ Lake House Barn,
Off Colehouse Lane, Kenn,
Clevedon, Bristol,
North Somerset,
BS21 6TQ ♿
☎ 01275 875014
@ robertptandy@hotmail.com
Est. 1987
Services Antique furniture and
longcase clock casework
restoration
Open Mon–Fri 10am–6pm

John Thorpe Fine Furniture
Contact Mr John Thorpe-Dixon
✉ Bruno House, 5a Treburley
Industrial Estate, Launceston,

Cornwall,
PL15 9PU ♿
☎ 01579 371175
Est. 1990
Services Antique furniture
restoration, cabinetry,
refinishing. London and all areas
West
Open Mon–Fri 9am–5pm

Edward Venn Antiques Restorations
Contact Edward Venn
✉ Unit 3, 52 Long Street,
Williton, Taunton, Somerset,
TA4 4QU ♿
☎ 01984 632631
W www.vennantiquerestoration.co.uk
Est. 1978
Services Furniture and clock
restoration, valuations,
upholstery, reproductions
Open Mon–Fri 10am–5pm or by
appointment

Brian Walker
Contact Brian Walker
✉ Westwood, Dinton Road,
Fovant, Salisbury, Wiltshire,
SP3 5JW ♿
☎ 01722 714370 📠 01722 714853
Est. 1972
Services Furniture restoration
and maker
Open Mon–Fri 8am–6pm
Sat by appointment

Westmoor Furniture
Contact Gary Male
✉ Units 8–9, Walronds Park,
Isle Brewers, Taunton, Somerset,
TA3 6QP ♿
☎ 01460 281535
Est. 1994
Services Antique restoration and
repair, custom-made furniture
and kitchens
Open Mon–Fri 9am–6pm

N D Whibley Restorations
Contact Mr Whibley
✉ 1166 Ringwood Road,
Bear Cross, Bournemouth,
Dorset,
BH11 9LG ♿
☎ 01202 575167
Est. 1975
Services Polishing and
restoration of furniture,
Georgian and Victorian clock
cases, medical cases, scientific
instrument cases
Open By appointment

Wood 'n' Things
Contact Mr William Page
✉ The Old Coach House, Station Road, Shirehampton, Bristol, BS11 9TX 🅿
☎ 0117 938 2004
Ⓜ 07780 607919 (Mon–Fri)
Est. 1982
Services Furniture restoration, cabinet-making, French polishing
Open Mon–Fri 9am–6pm advisable to call first

EAST

Abbey Antique Restorers
Contact Mr David Carter
✉ Coxford Abbey Farmhouse, Coxford, King's Lynn, Norfolk, PE31 6TB 🅿
☎ 01485 528043
Est. 1969
Services Conservation and restoration of antique furniture
Open Mon–Sun 9am–6pm please phone first

Roger Allan
Contact Mr R Allan
✉ The Old Red Lion, Bedingfield, Eye, Suffolk, IP23 7LQ 🅿
☎ 01728 628491
Est. 1973
Services Picture restorer, furniture restorer
Trade only Yes
Open By appointment

Antique Renovations
Contact Stephen or Alan Gartland
✉ Unit 1, Lavenham Studios, Brent Eleigh Road, Lavenham, Sudbury, Suffolk, CO10 9PE 🅿
☎ 01787 248511
Est. 1960
Services Repair, cabinet work and French polishing. Recommended by Ercol. Specializing in clock case repair
Open Mon–Fri 8.30am–5pm Sat 9am–1pm

Antique Restorations
Contact Terry Wheeler
✉ Unit 2 & 3, Bench Barn Farm, Clare, Sudbury, Suffolk, CO10 8HQ 🅿
☎ 01787 277635
Est. 1978
Services Furniture restoration,

commissions to make one-off pieces
Open Mon–Fri 9am–5pm please phone first

M Barrett Restoration
Contact Mr M Barrett
✉ Unit 7, Warbraham Farm, Heath Road, Burwell, Cambridge, Cambridgeshire, CB5 0AP 🅿
☎ 01638 741700 📠 01638 741700
Est. 1987
Services Pre-1940s furniture restoration
Open Mon–Fri 8.30am–5pm

Clive Beardall Restoration Ltd (BAFRA)
Contact Mr Clive Beardall
✉ 104b High Street, Maldon, Essex, CM9 5ET 🅿
☎ 01621 857890 📠 01621 850753
📧 info@clivebeardall.co.uk
🌐 www.clivebeardall.co.uk
Est. 1982
Services Specializing in period furniture restoration, traditional hand French polishing, wax polishing, upholstery, marquetry, carving, gilding, leather desk-lining, rush and cane seating, decorative finishes, bespoke cabinet-making, valuations
Open Mon–Fri 8am–5.30pm Sat 9am–2pm

K W Box
Contact Mr K W Box
✉ The Workshop, Upper Street, Stratford St Mary, Colchester, Essex, CO7 6JN 🅿
☎ 01206 322673
Est. 1985
Services 17th–early 19thC furniture restoration and one-off cabinet-making to order. 25 years experience
Open Mon–Fri 8am–6pm Sat 8am–1pm

Bradshaw Fine Wood Furniture Ltd
Contact Andrew Hurley
✉ Unit 12, Clovelly Works, Chelmsford Road, Rawreth, Wickford, Essex, SS11 8SY 🅿
☎ 01268 571414 📠 01268 571314
📧 andy@bwfw.co.uk
🌐 www.bwfw.co.uk

Est. 1988
Services French polishing, furniture restoration and repair work
Open Mon–Fri 8am–6pm

The Cabinet Maker
Contact Gary Fitzjohn
✉ Unit 23, Boleness Road, Wisbech, Cambridgeshire, PE13 2RB 🅿
☎ 01945 475635 📠 01945 475635
Ⓜ 07813 391481
Est. 1997
Services Bespoke furniture manufacturers
Open Mon–Fri 8.30am–5pm

Clare Hall Co
Contact Mr M Moore
✉ The Barns, Clare Hall, Clare, Sudbury, Suffolk, CO10 8PJ 🅿
☎ 01787 278445 📠 01787 278803
Est. 1960
Services Restoration of all antiques including polishing and upholstery. Replicas of antique globes and four-poster beds
Open By appointment

Steven J Cotterell
Contact Steven Cotterell
✉ 72 Springfield Road, Somersham, Ipswich, Suffolk, IP8 4PQ 🅿
☎ 01473 831530
Ⓜ 07733 291705
📧 somersham.flyer@yahoo.co.uk
Est. 1975
Services French polishing, furniture restoration and painting
Open Mon–Sat 7.30am–6pm

Michael Dolling (BAFRA)
Contact Mr Michael Dolling
✉ Church Farm, Barns, Glandford, Holt, Norfolk, NR25 7JR 🅿
☎ 01263 741115 📠 01953 718658
Est. 1984
Services General furniture restoration and repair
Open Mon–Fri 9am–5pm

A Dunn & Son
Contact Mr R Dunn
✉ 8 Wharf Road, Chelmsford, Essex, CM2 6LU 🅿
☎ 01245 354452 📠 01245 494991
📧 info@adunnandson.co.uk

Ⓦ www.adunnandson.com
Est. 1896
Services Antique furniture
restoration
Open Mon–Fri 8am–6pm
Sat by appointment

Essex Reupholstery Services
Contact Mr S T Richardson
✉ **49 Chestnut Grove, Southend on Sea, Essex, SS2 5HG**
☎ 01702 464775 📠 01702 305684
Est. 1987
Services Restoration of antique furniture, paddings, upholstery
Open Mon–Fri 8am–5pm

Forge Studio Workshops
Contact Mr D Darton
✉ **Stour Street, Manningtree, Essex, CO11 1BE** 🅿
☎ 01206 396222 📠 01206 396222
Est. 1979
Services Antique furniture restoration
Open Mon–Fri 8.30am–5.30pm
Sat 8.30am–1pm

Furse Restoration
Contact Mr Fred Furse
or Mr Andrew Furse
✉ **Unit 15 Beechcroft, Damases Lane, Boreham, Chelmsford, Essex, CM3 3AL** 🅿
☎ 01245 466744 📠 01245 466744
📧 andrew@furserestoration.co.uk
Ⓦ www.furserestoration.co.uk
Est. 1993
Services Antique restoration, bespoke cabinet-making, French polishing, veneer design and pressing
Open Mon–Fri 8am–6pm
Sat 9am–1pm

Michael Goater Restoration (BAFRA)
Contact Michael Goater
✉ **15 Red Barn Yards, Thornham Magna, Eye, Suffolk, IP23 8HH** 🅿
☎ 01379 788722
📧 michaelgoater@primex.co.uk
Ⓦ www.michaelgoater.co.uk
Est. 1987
Services Full restoration and conservation of 18th–19thC furniture
Open Mon–Sun 9am–6pm

P Godden
Contact Mr P Godden
✉ **32 Darcy Road, Old Heath, Colchester, Essex, CO2 8BB** 🅿
☎ 01206 790349
Est. 1962
Services Antique furniture restoration
Open Mon–Sat 9am–5pm

Haig & Hosford
Contact Mr J Hosford
✉ **Unit 3, 42 Feering Hill, Colchester, Essex, CO5 9NH** 🅿
☎ 01376 571502
Est. 1981
Services French polishing, antique restoration
Open Mon–Fri 8.30am–5pm
Sat 8.30am–1pm and by appointment

Brian Harris Furniture Restorations (BAFRA, EADA)
Contact Brian Harris
✉ **24 Town Street, Boxsted, Essex, CM6 2LA** 🅿
☎ 01371 832832
Est. 1956
Services Antique furniture restoration including carving, gilding, French polishing, inlay work. Also restoration of clocks and barometers
Open Mon–Sat 9am–5pm

Hyde Antique & Reproduction Furniture
Contact Neil Hyde
✉ **Unit 5, Ashwellthorpe Industrial Estate, Norwich, Norfolk, NR16 1ER** 🅿
☎ 01508 481888 📠 01508 481888
📱 07970 526975
Est. 1999
Services Restoration of 18thC oak furniture, manufacture of replica furniture
Open Mon–Sat 8am–5.30pm

Jeff Ingall
Contact Mr J Ingall
✉ **33 Hillside Road, Southminster, Essex, CM0 7AL** 🅿
☎ 01621 772686
Est. 1989

Services Antique furniture restoration, furniture maker
Open Mon–Sun 9am–6pm

S Layt
Contact Mr S Layt
✉ **Unit 5, New Cut, Wellington Street, Newmarket, Suffolk, CB8 0HT** 🅿
☎ 01638 668388
Est. 1999
Services Antique furniture restoration, French polishing
Open Mon–Fri 9am–5.30pm

Lomas Pigeon & Co Ltd (BAFRA, AMU)
Contact Mr W A J Pigeon
✉ **37 Beehive Lane, Chelmsford, Essex, CM2 9TQ** 🅿
☎ 01245 353708 📠 01245 355211
📧 wpigeon@compuserve.com
Ⓦ www.lomas-pigeon.co.uk
Est. 1938
Services Upholstery, antique restoration, French polishing, cabinet-making
Open Mon–Fri 10am–4pm
Sat 9am–noon closed Wed

Maisey Restoration
Contact Mr Steve Maisey
✉ **Townsell Bridewell Street Estate, Bridewell Street, Clare, Sudbury, Suffolk, CO10 8OD** 🅿
☎ 01787 277000
Est. 1991
Services Repair, restoration and French polishing
Open Mon–Fri 8am–5pm

Andrew A Matthews Restoration (Graduate member of the students section BAFRA)
Contact Mr A A Matthews
✉ **Fox House, Gills Hill, Bourn, Cambridge, Cambridgeshire, CB3 7TX** 🅿
📱 07808 590370
Est. 1998
Services Antique restoration and conservation, cabinet work, veneering, turning, key-making, lock repair, polishing, upholstery, rushing and caning
Open By appointment

R J McPhee
Contact Mr R J McPhee
✉ **20 Muspole Street, Norwich,**

Norfolk,
NR3 1DJ 🅿
☎ 01603 667701 📠 01603 667701
📧 r.mcphee@jrmcabinetmaker.co.uk
Est. 1980
Services 17th–18thC fine antique
furniture restoration
Open Mon–Fri 8am–1pm 2–5pm
Sat by appointment

Peter Norman Antiques
Contact Mr Tony Marpole
✉ 55 North Street, Burwell,
Cambridge, Cambridgeshire,
CB5 0BA 🅿
☎ 01638 616914
📧 amarpole@aol.com
Est. 1977
Services General antique
restoration, woodwork, caning,
upholstery, relining and restoring
oils
Open Mon–Sat 9am–5.30pm
prior warning best

The Old Coach House
Contact David Burrough
✉ Church Hill, Starston,
Harleston, Norfolk,
IP2 9PT 🅿
☎ 01379 852123
Est. 1990
Services Furniture restoration,
French polishing, carving,
stripping
Open Mon–Sat 9am–5pm

Mark Peters Antiques Ltd
Contact Mr M Peters
✉ Green Farm Cottage,
Oak Road, Thurston,
Bury St Edmunds,
Suffolk,
IP31 3SN 🅿
☎ 01359 230888
📧 mark@markpetersantiques.com
Est. 1977
Services Furniture restoration
Open Mon–Fri 8am–5pm
Sat 9am–noon

Ludovic Potts
Restorations (BAFRA)
Contact Mr Ludovic Potts
✉ Elm Tree Barns, Elm Tree Farm,
Parnell Road, Guyhirn,
Cambridgeshire,
PE13 4AQ 🅿
☎ 01353 741537
📱 07889 341671
📧 mail@restorers.co.uk
🌐 www.restorers.co.uk
Est. 1986

Services Modern and antique
furniture restoration
Open By appointment

Prust & Sons Antique
Furniture Restoration
Contact Mr Prust
✉ 9 West Road, Westcliff-on-Sea,
Essex,
SS0 9AU
☎ 01702 345972 📠 01702 391093
📧 sales@prust.co.uk
🌐 www.prust.co.uk
Est. 1987
Services Antique furniture
restoration
Open Mon–Sat 8.30am–5.30pm
Sun 10am–3pm

Richard Anthony Rush
Antiques
Contact Mr R Rush
✉ Unit 5, Penny Corner,
Farthing Road, Ipswich, Suffolk,
IP1 5AP 🅿
☎ 01473 464609 📠 01473 464609
📱 07939 220041
📧 admin@antiques.eu.com
🌐 www.antiques.eu.com
Est. 1997
Services Restoration, repair of
18thC furniture, gilding,
upholstery
Open Mon–Fri 8am–6pm
Sat 8am–1.30pm

Richard's Polishing
Contact Mr R Bufton
✉ Bentley Road, Weeley Heath,
Clacton on Sea, Essex,
CO16 9DP 🅿
☎ 01255 831539 📠 01255 831539
📱 07712 873864
📧 sos@sos.uk.com
🌐 www.sos.uk.com
Est. 1979
Services Antique restoration, all
polish finishes
Open Mon–Fri 9am–5pm

Robert's Antiques
Contact Graham Bettany
✉ The Barn, South Street,
Risby, Bury St Edmunds,
Suffolk,
IP28 6QU 🅿
☎ 01284 811440 📠 01284 811726
📧 info@robertsantiques.co.uk
🌐 www.robertsantiques.co.uk
Est. 1978
Services French polishing
Open Tues–Fri 8.30am–5pm
Sat Sun noon–4pm

D J Short
Contact Mr D Short
✉ The Stables, High Street,
Horseheath, Cambridge,
Cambridgeshire,
CB1 6QN 🅿
☎ 01223 891983
Est. 1969
Services Antique furniture
restoration
Open Mon–Fri 9am–5pm
Sat 9am–1pm

R J Smith Restoration
Contact Mr R J Smith
✉ Unit 1, 4 Hepworth Road,
Barningham, Bury St Edmonds,
Suffolk,
IP31 1BP 🅿
☎ 01284 704894
📱 07759 930678
Est. 1991
Services Repair and restoration of
Georgian–Edwardian furniture,
French polishing, upholstery
Open Mon–Sat 8.30am–5.30pm

R A Surridge
Contact Mr R Surridge
✉ The Barn, Thistledown,
Latchingdon Road, Cold Norton,
Chelmsford, Essex,
CM3 6HR 🅿
☎ 01621 828036 📠 01621 828036
Est. 1978
Services Antique restoration and
cabinet-maker
Open Mon–Fri 8am–5pm

Teywood Ltd
Contact Mr K Cottee
✉ East Gores Farm, Salmons
Lane, Coggeshall, Essex,
CO6 1RZ 🅿
☎ 01376 563025 📠 01376 563025
📧 teywoodfurniture@aol.com
Est. 1984
Services Antique furniture
restoration and cabinet-maker
Open Mon–Fri 9am–5pm

R Tidder Antique
Furniture Restoration
Contact Richard Tidder
✉ Unit 22, Grainge Road
Industrial Estate,
Southend-on-Sea, Essex,
SS2 5DD 🅿
☎ 01702 600464
📧 richardtidder@aol.com
Est. 1988
Services Furniture restoration
Open Mon–Fri 9am–6pm

Paul Waldmann Woodwork (Conservation Unit)
Contact Mr P Waldmann
✉ 41 Norfolk Street, Cambridge, Cambridgeshire, CB1 2LD 🅿
☎ 01223 314001
📱 07740 167055
✉ pm.waldmann@ntlworld.com
Est. 1982
Services Antique furniture restoration, cabinet-making
Open By appointment

Whitfield Restoration
Contact Mr J Palmer
✉ London Road, Cockford, Colchester, Essex, CO6 1LG 🅿
☎ 01206 213212
📱 07803 044229
Est. 1990
Services Antique furniture restoration, cabinet-making, French polishing
Open Mon–Sat 9am–5pm

Robert Williams (BAFRA)
Contact Mr Robert Williams
✉ 32 Church Street, Willingham, Cambridge, Cambridgeshire, CB4 5HT 🅿
☎ 01954 260972
Est. 1980
Services Restoration of carving, ivory, mother of pearl, bonework, papier-mâché, tortoiseshell, weapons. Also cabinet-maker and locksmith
Open Mon–Fri 9am–5pm Sat Sun by appointment

HEART OF ENGLAND

A C Restorations
Contact Mr Adrian Clark
✉ Unit 9d, Quickbury Farm, Hatfield Heath Road, Sawbridgeworth, Hertfordshire, CM21 9HY 🅿
☎ 01279 721583
📱 07905 156976
Est. 1993
Services Furniture restoration, polishing, leather lining, carving, general services
Open Mon–Fri 9am–5.30pm

A & P French Polishers
Contact Ashley Pert
✉ Aylesbury, Buckinghamshire
☎ 01296 482233   📠 01296 482233
📱 07793 741143
✉ ashleypert@frenchpolisher.com
🌐 www.frenchpolisher.com
Est. 2001
Services French polishing
Open By appointment

Antique and Modern Restoration by Richard Parsons
Contact Mr R Parsons
✉ 85 Pondcroft Road, Knebworth, Hertfordshire, SG3 6DE 🅿
☎ 01438 812200
Est. 1980
Services Antique and modern furniture restoration, French polishing
Open By appointment

Antique Restoration & Polishing
Contact Mr M P Wallis
✉ 1 The Row, Hawridge, Chesham, Buckinghamshire, HP5 2UH 🅿
☎ 01494 758172   📠 01494 758701
✉ peckandgaz@yahoo.co.uk
Est. 1968
Services General antique furniture restoration and polishing
Open By appointment

Keith Bawden (BAFRA)
Contact Keith Bawden
✉ Mews Workshops, Montpellier Retreat, Cheltenham, Gloucestershire, GL50 2XG 🅿
☎ 01242 230320 or 01452 863566
Est. 1975
Services Full antique restoration service of furniture, clocks, watercolours, jewellery, ceramics and Oriental carpets, silver, plating, committed to conservation and under-restoring on principle
Open By appointment phone first

R Beesly
Contact Mr R Beesly
✉ 41 High Street, Broom, Biggleswade, Bedfordshire, SG18 9NA 🅿
☎ 01767 314918
Est. 1974
Services Cabinet-making, French polishing, clock repair
Open Mon–Sat 8am–6pm or by appointment

Belmont House Antiques
Contact Michael Mastrolasca
✉ Belmont House, 77 Bedford Road, Willington, Bedfordshire
☎ 01234 838750
📱 07771 829709
✉ belmonthouse77@aol.com
Est. 1987
Services Antique furniture restoration
Open Mon–Sat 9am–5pm

Andy Briggs
Contact Andy Briggs
✉ 35 Rack End, Standlake, Oxfordshire, OX29 7FA 🅿
☎ 01865 301705
📱 07977 936882
Est. 1991
Services Restoration and conservation of town and country furniture, cabinet-making, items bought and sold, copies of stolen items made
Open By appointment

Peter Campion Restorations (BAFRA)
Contact Peter Campion
✉ The Old Dairy, Rushley Lane, Winchcombe, Nr Cheltenham, Gloucestershire, GL54 5JE 🅿
☎ 01242 604403   📠 01242 604403
✉ petercampion@ukonline.co.uk
🌐 www.petercampion.co.uk
Est. 1959
Services Restoration and conservation of furniture, barometers, clock cases. Also cabinet work, inlays, brass, veneering, polishing, furniture designed and made to order
Open Mon–Fri 9am–5.30pm

Charnwood Antiques (EADA)
Contact Mr Nigel Hoy
✉ Unit 2e, The Maltings, Station Road, Sawbridgeworth, Hertfordshire, CM21 9JX 🅿
☎ 01279 600562
📱 07957 551899
Est. 1988
Services Cabinet-maker, antique furniture restoration, upholstery, cabinet lining, French polishing
Open Tues–Fri 10am–5pm Sat Sun 11am–5pm

Chess Antique Restorations
Contact Mr T Chapman
✉ 85 Broad Street, Chesham, Buckinghamshire, HP5 3EF ℗
☎ 01494 783043 ☏ 01494 791302
✆ chessrest@aol.com
Ⓦ www.chessantiquerestorations.co.uk
Est. 1969
Services All cabinet work, hand finishing, upholstery, ceramics, metalwork, picture restoration, traditional polishing
Open Mon–Fri 9am–5pm

N A Copp
Contact Nigel Copp
✉ Red Lane, Tewkesbury, Gloucestershire, GL20 5BQ ℗
☎ 01684 293935
Est. 1984
Services Restorer of antique furniture, maker of kitchens, general cabinet making
Open Mon–Fri 8.30am–5.30pm

Martin Coulborn Restorations Ltd
Contact Mr M Coulborn
✉ Canterbury House, Bridge Road, Frampton on Severn, Gloucestershire, GL2 7HE ℗
☎ 01452 740334
Est. 1978
Services Antique furniture restorer, maker of replica 18thC-style furniture
Open Mon–Fri 9am–1pm 2–5pm, please telephone before visiting

Robert H Crawley (BAFRA)
Contact Mr R Crawley
✉ The Studio, 16 Boston Road, Hanwell, London, W7 3TB ℗
Ⓜ 07710 240956
✆ restorarinmail@yahoo.co.uk
Est. 1979
Services Antique furniture restoration
Open Mon–Fri 8.30am–4.30pm

D H R Ltd (BAFRA, UKIC)
Contact Mr David Hordern
✉ 8–10 Lea Lane, Thame Road, Long Crendon, Aylesbury, Buckinghamshire, HP18 9RN ℗
☎ 01844 202213 ☏ 01844 202214
Est. 1985

D M E Restorations Ltd (BAFRA)
Contact Jonathon Cannell
✉ 11 Church Street, Ampthill, Bedfordshire, MK45 2PL ℗
☎ 01525 405819
Ⓜ 07789 955884
Ⓦ www.dmerestorations.com
Est. 1986
Services Restoration and conservation of antique furniture
Open Mon–Fri 8am–5pm or by appointment

Deerstalker Antiques
Contact Mr or Mrs Eichler
✉ 28 High Street, Whitchurch, Buckinghamshire, HP22 4JT ℗
☎ 01296 641505
Est. 1978
Services Restoration of furniture pre-1850
Open Tue Wed Thurs Sat 10am–5.30pm or by appointment

Dovetail Restoration
Contact Mr Robert Askham
✉ Home Farm, Ardington, Wantage, Oxfordshire, OX12 8PD ℗
☎ 01235 833614 ☏ 01235 833110
Est. 1973
Services Antique and modern furniture restoration
Open Mon–Fri 8.30am–5.30pm Sat by appointment

J W Eaton
Contact Mr J Eaton
✉ The Barn, Tupsley Court Farm, Hampton Dene Road, Hereford, Herefordshire, HR1 1UX ℗
☎ 01432 354344
Ⓜ 07866 500667
Est. 1990
Services General antique restoration
Open Mon–Fri 9am–5pm

Forum Antiques
Contact Mr Weston Mitchell
✉ Springfield Farm, Perrott's Brook, Cirencester, Gloucestershire, GL7 7DT ℗
☎ 01285 831821
✆ enquiries@westonmitchell.com
Ⓦ www.westonmitchell.com
Est. 1985
Services Restoration of antique furniture
Open By appointment only

Gloucestershire Furniture Hospital
Contact Mr M Deane
✉ Commonfields Farm, Lower Boulsdon, Newent, Gloucestershire, GL18 1JH ℗
☎ 01531 822881 ☏ 01531 822881
Ⓜ 07989 993919
✆ doctordeane.gfh@btinternet.com
Est. 1999
Services Antique and modern furniture repair including upholstery, caning and French polishing. Collection service, all insurance work undertaken
Open Mon–Sat 8am–6pm

Ian Gray Antique Restoration
Contact Ian Gray
✉ The Stables, Park Farm, Great Hampden, Great Missenden, Buckinghamshire, HP16 9RD ℗
☎ 01494 488560 ☏ 01494 488560
Ⓦ www.iangrayrestoration.co.uk
Est. 1993
Services Furniture restoration, French polishing
Open Mon–Fri 8am–5.30pm

Robert Gripper Restoration
Contact Mr R Gripper
✉ Manor Barn, Manor Farm, Ascott-under-Wychwood, Chipping Norton, Oxfordshire, OX7 6AL ℗
☎ 01993 831960 ☏ 01993 830395
✆ robgripper@aol.com
Est. 1982
Services Antique furniture restoration, modern insurance work
Open Mon–Fri 9am–5pm

Roland Haycraft (GADAR)
Contact Mr R Haycraft
✉ The Lamb Arcade, High Street, Wallingford, Oxfordshire, OX10 0BS ℗
☎ 01491 839622
✆ ro@fsbdial.co.uk
Ⓦ www.juststolen.com

Est. 1980
Services Antique furniture conservation, restoration and bespoke cabinet-making
Open Mon–Fri 9am–5.30pm

Alan Hessel (BAFRA)
Contact Mr A Hessel
✉ The Old Town Workshop, St George's Close, Moreton-in-Marsh, Gloucestershire, GL56 0LP 🅿
☎ 01608 650026 📠 01608 650026
📱 07860 225608
Est. 1975
Services Restoration of fine 17th–19thC furniture
Open Mon–Fri 8.30am–5pm or by appointment

John Hulme
Contact Mr J Hulme
✉ 11a High Street, Chipping Norton, Oxfordshire, OX7 5AD 🅿
☎ 01608 641692 📠 01608 641692
Est. 1980
Services Antique furniture restoration and conservation
Open Mon–Fri 7.30am–6pm

Icknield Restorations
Contact Simon Pallister
✉ Icknield Farm, Tring Road, Dunstable, Bedfordshire, LU6 2JX 🅿
☎ 01525 222883
Est. 1994
Services Antique furniture restoration
Open Mon–Fri 9.30am–6pm

Ipsden Woodcraft
Contact Mr M Small
✉ The Post Office, The Street, Ipsden, Wallingford, Oxfordshire, OX10 6AG 🅿
☎ 01491 680262
Est. 1981
Services Antique furniture restoration
Open Mon–Fri 8am–6pm

J R Jury & Son
Contact Mr Ken Jury
✉ Springfields, Cobhall Common, Allensmore, Hereford, Herefordshire, HR2 9BJ 🅿
☎ 01432 279108
Est. 1974

Services Antique furniture restoration, French polishing
Open Mon–Fri 8am–5pm

Robert Lawrence-Jones
Contact Robert Lawrence-Jones
✉ Frogmarsh Mill, South Woodchester, Stroud, Gloucestershire, GL5 5ET 🅿
☎ 01453 872817
Est. 1980
Services Cabinet-making, furniture restoration
Open Mon–Fri 9am–5pm but phone first

E C Legg and Son
Contact Mr C Legg
✉ 3 College Farm Buildings, Tetbury Road, Cirencester, Gloucestershire, GL7 6PY 🅿
☎ 01285 650695
Est. 1903
Services Furniture restoration, carving, rushing, leather laying
Open Mon–Fri 9am–5pm Sat 9am–noon

Clive Loader Restorations
Contact Mr C Loader
✉ Stables Workshop, Lodge Cottage, High Street, Shipton under Wychwood, Oxfordshire, OX7 6DG 🅿
☎ 01993 832727
Est. 1984
Services Antique furniture restoration
Open Mon–Fri 8am–5pm

M K Restorations
Contact Mr M Knight
✉ Unit 8e4, Quickbury Farm, Hatfield Heath Road, Sawbridgeworth, Hertfordshire, CM21 9HY 🅿
☎ 01279 726664
📱 07939 438587
✉ mk-restorations@talk21.com
Est. 1992
Services Antique furniture restoration, specializing in veneering and inlay work
Open Mon–Sat 9am–6.30pm

Miracle Finishing
Contact Mr C Howes or Mr A Howes
✉ The Cottage, Woodhall Farm, Hatfield, Hertfordshire, AL9 5NU 🅿

☎ 01707 270587 📠 01707 270587
📱 07803 397133/ 07790 696631
Est. 1992
Services Furniture restoration, French polishing, upholstery, pine stripping
Open Mon–Fri 8.30am–5pm

J Moore Restorations
Contact Mr J Moore
✉ College Farm House Workshops, Chawston Lane, Chawston, Bedford, Bedfordshire, MK44 3BH 🅿
☎ 01480 214165
✉ john@moorerestorations.freeserve.co.uk
🌐 www.jmooreantiques.co.uk
Est. 1975
Services All aspects of furniture restoration, particularly period furniture
Open Mon–Fri 9am–5pm

Clive Payne (BAFRA, LAPADA)
Contact Clive Payne
✉ Unit 11, Langstone Priory Workshops, Station Road, Kingham, Oxfordshire, OX7 6UP 🅿
☎ 01608 658856 📠 01608 658856
📱 07801 088363
✉ clive.payne@virgin.net
🌐 www.clivepayne.co.uk
Est. 1986
Services Antique furniture restoration, specializing in country furniture and Georgian mahogany
Open Mon–Fri 9am–5pm

Charles Perry Restorations Ltd (BAFRA)
Contact John Carr
✉ Praewood Farm, Hemel Hempstead Road, St Albans, Hertfordshire, AL3 6AA 🅿
☎ 01727 853487 📠 01727 846668
✉ johncarr@cperryrestorations.co.uk
Est. 1986
Services Anything associated with antique furniture restoration including carving, gilding, caning and upholstery
Open Mon–Fri 8.30am–5.30pm

Nathan Polley Antique Restoration
Contact Mr N Polley
✉ The Barn,

Upton Grove,
Tetbury Upton, Tetbury,
Gloucestershire,
GL8 8LR 🅟
☎ 01666 504997
📱 07977 263236
Est. 1995
Services Repair and restoration
Open Mon–Fri 8am–6.30pm
Sat 8am–4pm

Alan J Ponsford Antique Restorations
Contact Alan Ponsford
✉ Decora, Northbrook Road,
Gloucester, Gloucestershire,
GL4 3DP 🅟
☎ 01452 307700
Est. 1962
Services Restoration
Open Mon–Fri 8am–5pm

R J Poynter
Contact Mr R Poynter
✉ Lyndhurst, Westland Green,
Little Hadham, Ware,
Hertfordshire,
SG11 2AF 🅟
☎ 01279 842395
📧 richjane@ntlworld.com
Est. 1984
Services Antique furniture
restoration
Open Mon–Fri 10am–5pm
Sat by appointment only

Saracen Antiques Ltd
Contact Mr C Mills
✉ Upton Downs Farm, Burford,
Oxfordshire,
OX18 4LY 🅟
☎ 01993 822987
📧 cmills6702@aol.com
Est. 1996
Services Furniture restoration,
frames and upholstery
Open Mon–Sat 9am–5.30pm

Smith, James
Contact Mr J Smith
✉ Wisteria Studio,
Wharf Road, Shillingford,
Oxfordshire,
OX10 7EW 🅟
☎ 01865 858650
📱 07745 406175
📧 info@furniture-restorers.co.uk
🌐 www.furniture-restorers.co.uk
Est. 1994
Services Antique furniture
restoration, conservation of
original finishes
Open Mon–Fri 9am–5.30pm

Sunningend Joiners and Cabinet Makers Ltd
Contact Mr R J Duester
✉ Industrial Estate, Station
Road, Bourton-on-the-Water,
Cheltenham, Gloucestershire,
GL54 2EP 🅟
☎ 01451 820761 ☎ 01451 810671
📧 sunningend@aol.com
Est. 1972
Services Joinery, cabinet-making,
antique furniture restoration
Open Mon–Thurs 8am–5pm
Fri 8am–4pm

Timber Restorations (Guild of Master Craftsmen)
Contact Mr S Shannon
✉ Hyde Hall Barn, Sandon,
Buntingford, Hertfordshire,
SG9 0RU 🅟
☎ 01763 274849 ☎ 01763 274849
📱 07973 748644
📧 info@timberrestorations.co.uk
🌐 www.timberrestorations.co.uk
Est. 1997
Services Spray lacquering, French
polishing, furniture repair,
caustic and non-caustic stripping,
wax polishing, furniture sales,
leather top inlay
Open Mon–Sat 9am–5pm

Christopher Tombs
Contact Mr C G Tombs
✉ Unit 45, Northwick Business
Centre, Blockley, Moreton-in-
Marsh, Gloucestershire,
GL56 9RF 🅟
☎ 01386 700085
📱 07778 655965
Est. 1994
Services English furniture
restoration
Open Mon–Fri 8am–5pm

Truman & Bates
Contact Mr P Truman
✉ Classic Works, Station Road,
Hook Norton, Banbury,
Oxfordshire,
OX15 5LS 🅟
☎ 01608 730433
Est. 1961
Services Restoration of antique
furniture, French polishing
Open Mon–Fri 8am–5pm

P M Welch
Contact Zoe Greenhalgh
✉ Unit 4 Bourton Link, Bourton
Industrial Park, Bourton-on-the-
Water, Gloucestershire,
GL5 2HQ 🅟
☎ 01451 810800 ☎ 01451 810666
📧 pmwelch@tiscali.co.uk
🌐 www.antiques-restorers.com
Est. 1969
Services Restoration of English
and Continental furniture
Open Mon–Fri 7.45am–5.30pm
Sat 7.45am–noon

Richard J Young Antiques Restorer
Contact Richard Young
✉ 5 Macaroni Wood, Eastleach,
Cirencester, Gloucestershire,
GL7 3NF 🅟
☎ 01367 850587
📧 richardyoung.restorer@virgin.net
Est. 1980
Services Restoration of furniture
and in-house wood
Open By appointment

MIDLANDS

Abbey Restorations
Contact Allan Standing
✉ Darley Abbey Mills,
Darley Abbey, Derbyshire,
DE22 1DZ 🅟
☎ 01332 344547
Est. 1974
Services Restoration of furniture,
upholstery
Open Mon–Fri 8.30am–5.30pm
Sat 8.30am–noon

Anthony Allen Conservation, Restoration, Furniture and Artefacts (BAFRA, UKIC)
Contact Anthony Allen
✉ The Old Wharf Workshop,
Redmoor Lane, Newtown,
High Peak, Derbyshire,
SK22 3JL 🅟
☎ 01663 745274 ☎ 01663 745274
📧 allen-conservation@tiscali.co.uk
Est. 1970
Services Restoration of
17th–19thC furniture, gilding,
marquetry, boulle, upholstery,
metalwork, clock cases and
movements
Open Mon–Fri 8am–5pm

The Antiques Workshop
Contact Mr Paul Burrows
✉ 68 Yoxall Road, Solihull,
West Midlands,
B90 3RP 🅟
☎ 0121 744 1744

Ⓜ 07860 168078
Est. 1988
Services Furniture restoration
Open Mon–Sat 9am–5pm

Barnt Green Antiques (BAFRA)
Contact Phillip Slater
✉ 93 Hewell Road, Barnt Green, Birmingham, West Midlands, B45 8NL ℙ
☎ 0121 445 4942 ℱ 0121 445 4942
ⓦ www.barntgreenantiques.co.uk
Est. 1977
Services Furniture and longcase clock restoration. All aspects of polishing and finishing including wax and French polishing, marquetry, inlay
Open Mon–Fri 9am–5.30pm Sat 9am–1pm

Belle Vue Restoration
Contact Mr Peter Grady
✉ 19 Belle Vue Road, Shrewsbury, Shropshire, SY3 7LN ℙ
☎ 01743 272210
ⓦ www.bellevue-restoration.co.uk
Est. 1984
Services Antique furniture restoration
Open Mon–Fri 7.30am–4.30pm

S C Brown
Contact Mr S C Brown
✉ 53 Melton Road, Birmingham, West Midlands, B14 7ET ℙ
☎ 0121 441 1479
Est. 1981
Services Antique furniture restoration, furniture designed and made
Open Mon–Sat 8am–5.30pm

Jacob Butler – Period Joinery Specialist
Contact Jacob Butler
✉ The Chapel, Main Street, Matlock, Derbyshire, DE4 4LQ ℙ
☎ 01629 822170/825640
ℯ jacob@owdman.co.uk
ⓦ www.jowdman.co.uk
Est. 1987
Services Repair and restoration of period joinery and furniture
Open By appointment

Byethorpe Furniture
Contact J Gelsthorpe
✉ Shippen Rural Business Centre,

Church Farm, Barlow, Derbyshire, S18 7TR ℙ
☎ 0114 289 9111 ℱ 0114 289 9111
ⓦ www.byethorpe.com
Est. 1995
Services Antique restoration, maker of bespoke furniture
Open Mon–Sat 9.30am–5.30pm

Cameo Antiques
Contact Mrs S Hinton
✉ 3 Liverpool Road East, Church Lawton, Stoke-on-Trent, Staffordshire, ST7 3AQ ℙ
☎ 01782 772555
Est. 1985
Services Complete repair and restoration of furniture, stripping
Open Mon–Fri 9am–6pm Sat 9am–4pm

Comfort Solutions
Contact Miss Jo MacDonald or Miss Susan Robinson
✉ 57 Berry Hedge Lane, Winshall, Burton-On-Trent, Staffordshire, DE15 0DP ℙ
☎ 01283 741234 ℱ 071283 741234
ℯ sales@comfort-solutions.co.uk
ⓦ www.comfort-solutions.co.uk
Est. 1997
Services Repair, restoration and upholstery
Open Mon–Fri 9am–5pm

K Davenport Interiors Ltd
Contact Mr M Davenport
✉ The Queens Yard, Madac Place, Beatrice Street, Oswestry, Shropshire, SY11 1QJ ℙ
☎ 01691 652293 ℱ 01691 652293
Ⓜ 07885 817026
ⓦ www.kdavenportinteriors.co.uk
Est. 1965
Services Upholstery and restoration of antique furniture
Open Mon–Fri 8.30am–5pm

Ian Dewar
Contact Mr Ian Dewar
✉ 55 Whateleys Drive, Kenilworth, Warwickshire, CV8 2GY ℙ
☎ 01926 856767
Ⓜ 07984 272880
ℯ jdewar6885@aol.com
Est. 1989

Services Antique furniture restoration, French polishing
Open Mon–Fri 8.30am–5.30pm

Joyce Ellis
Contact Joyce Ellis
✉ Yew Tree Farm, Stratford Road, Wootton Wawen, Solihull, West Midlands, B95 6BY ℙ
☎ 01564 795401
Ⓜ 07712 126048
ℯ info@legrenantiques.com
ⓦ www.legrenantiques.com
Est. 1989
Services General restoration, specializing in French beds and farmhouse tables
Open Tues–Sun 9am–5.30pm

T J Gittins
Contact Mr T J Gittins
✉ The Old Barn, Nagington Grange, Childs Ercall, Market Drayton, Shropshire, TF9 2TW
☎ 01952 840409
Services Antique furniture restoration
Open By appointment

Guy Goodwin Restoration
Contact Mr Guy Goodwin
✉ 1a St John's, Warwick, Warwickshire, CV34 4NE ℙ
☎ 01926 407409 ℱ 01926 407409
Est. 1979
Services Antique furniture restoration
Open Mon–Fri 9am–5.30pm

Grantham Workshops Cabinet Makers
Contact Peter Grantham
✉ 51a–57 Union Street, Kettering, Northamptonshire, NN16 9DA ℙ
☎ 01536 411461 ℱ 01536 392239
ℯ info@grantham-workshops.co.uk
ⓦ www.grantham-workshops.co.uk
Est. 1979
Services Conservation and restoration of antique furniture. Veneer and inlay replacement, French polishing and colouring
Open Mon–Fri 9am–5.30pm

Laila Gray
Contact Laila Gray
✉ 25 Welford Road, Kingsthorpe, Northamptonshire, NN2 8AQ ℙ

☏ 07941 263236
Est. 1984
Services Antique furniture restoration, French polishing
Open By appointment

Heritage Antiques
Contact M Nelms
✉ Unit 2, Trench Farm, Tilley Green, Wem, Shropshire, SY4 5PJ **▣**
☎ 01939 235463 **✆** 01939 235416
✉ heritageantiques@btconnect.com
⊕ www.heritageantiques.co.uk
Est. 1988
Services Furniture restoration
Open Mon–Fri 9am–5pm Sat by appointment

Richard Higgins Conservation Ltd (BAFRA, UKIC, BHI)
Contact Richard Higgins
✉ The Old School, Longnor, Nr Shrewsbury, Shropshire, SY5 7PP **▣**
☎ 01743 718162 **✆** 01743 718022
☏ 07838 188427
✉ richardhigginsco@aol.com
Est. 1988
Services Restoration of all fine furniture, clocks, movements, dials and cases, casting, plating, boulle, gilding, lacquerwork, carving, period upholstery, tortoiseshell and ivory
Open Mon–Fri 8am–6pm

L J Holmes Antique Furniture Restoration
Contact Mr L J Holmes
✉ The Old Stables Workshop, Cowsden, Upton Snodsbury, Worcestershire, WR7 4NX **▣**
☎ 01905 381892
Est. 1983
Services Furniture restoration
Open Mon–Fri 9am–5pm

Hope Antiques
Contact Mr D White
✉ The Coach House, Spring Croft, Hartwell Lane, Rough Close, Stoke-on-Trent, Staffordshire, ST3 7NG **▣**
☎ 01782 399022 **✆** 01782 399022
☏ 07762 392712
✉ hopeantiques@btintenet.com
Est. 1986
Services Repair and restoration of furniture, French polishing,

pine stripping, inlay work. Country oak furniture made to order (from wood no less than 150 years old)
Open Mon–Sat 8am–6pm

John Hubbard Antique Restoration & Conservation (LAPADA, CINOA)
Contact John Hubbard
✉ Castle Ash, Birmingham Road, Blakedown, Worcestershire, DY10 3JE **▣**
☎ 01562 701020 **✆** 01562 700001
✉ jphubbard@aol.com
Est. 1968
Services Furniture restoration, French polishing, desktop leathers, upholstery
Open By appointment Mon–Fri 9am–5.30pm

Kings of Loughborough
Contact Mr A King
✉ 5 Oliver Road, Loughborough, Leicestershire, LE11 2BZ **▣**
☎ 01509 556162 **✆** 01509 556159
Est. 1971
Services Repair, restoration and cabinet-making
Open By appointment

Lincoln Restorations
Contact Andrew Lincoln
✉ 54 Mill Road, High Heath, Pelsall, Walsall, West Midlands, WS4 1BS **▣**
☎ 01922 693999
⊕ www.lincolnrestorations.co.uk
Est. 1986
Services Full antique furniture restoration
Open Mon–Fri 8.30am–6pm

Charles Lowe & Sons Ltd
Contact Richard Lowe
✉ 37–40 Churchgate, Loughborough, Leicestershire, LE11 1UE **▣**
☎ 01509 212554
Est. 1846
Services Furniture restoration, French polishing, valuation
Open Mon–Fri 9am–5.30pm

Mackenzie & Smith (UKIC)
Contact Mr Tim Smith
✉ 4 The Bullring, Ludlow, Shropshire, SY8 1AD **▣**
☎ 01584 877133

Est. 1998
Services Antique furniture 17th–19thC restoration, clock case restoration
Open Mon–Fri 9am–5pm

Malvern Studios (BAFRA, UKIC, NCCR)
Contact Jeff Hall
✉ 56 Cowleigh Road, Malvern, Worcestershire, WR14 1QD **▣**
☎ 01684 574913 **✆** 01684 569475
✉ malvern.studios@btinternet.com
⊕ www.malvernstudios.co.uk
Est. 1961
Services Restoration of any form of furniture and panelling, including ivory boulle, gilding, tortoiseshell, black lacquer, chinoiserie, satinwood, hand-painted cameos
Open Mon Tues Thurs 9am–5.15pm Fri Sat 9am–4.45pm

Nigel Mayall
Contact Mr N Mayall
✉ 114 Richmond Road, Bewdley, Worcestershire, DY12 2BQ **▣**
☎ 01299 401754
☏ 07815 120501
✉ frenchpolishers@nigelmayall. demon.co.uk
Est. 1989
Services High-class French polishing, repair, minor restoration, re-leathering, veneer repair, repair and restoration of panelling and staircases, delivery and collection service, free estimates
Open Mon–Fri 10am–6pm please phone first

Melbourne Hall Furniture Restorers
Contact Mr N Collumbell
✉ Old Saw Mill Craft Centre, Melbourne Hall, Melbourne, Derby, Derbyshire, DE73 8EN **▣**
☎ 01332 864131
☏ 07718 108166
Est. 1982
Services Repair and restoration, French polishing
Open By appointment

Middleton Antiques (BAFRA)
Contact Mr S Herberholz
✉ Middleton Hall, Middleton,

**Tamworth, Staffordshire,
B78 2AE** ▣
☎ 01827 282858
📱 07973 151681
Est. 1997
Services Complete repair and
restoration of antique furniture
including metalwork, turning,
upholstery, carving, caning,
gilding, porcelain restoration
Open Wed–Sun 11am–5pm

K Needham Restoration Ltd

Contact Kevin Needham
✉ Hollyhouse Barn, Bakewell
Road, Rowsley, Derbyshire,
DE4 2EB ▣
☎ 01629 735455 📠 01629 735455
📧 needham@talktalk.net
🌐 www.needhamrestorations.co.uk
Est. 1993
Services Repair and restoration
Open Mon–Sat 9am–5pm

Painswick Antiques

✉ 6 Churchgate, Retford,
Nottinghamshire,
DN22 6PQ ▣
☎ 01777 706278
Est. 1977
Services Repair and restoration
Open Mon–Sat 9am–6pm

Perkins Stockwell and Co Ltd

Contact Mr J Stockwell
✉ 12 Abbey Gate, Leicester,
Leicestershire,
LE4 0AB ▣
☎ 01162 516501 📠 01162 510697
📧 perkinsstockwell@btconnect.com
Est. 1760
Services Repair and restoration
of furniture
Open Mon–Fri 7am–4pm

John Reed and Son Upholsterers (AMU)

Contact Mr J Reed or Mr T Reed
✉ 141 Regent Street, Kettering,
Northamptonshire,
NN16 8QQ ▣
☎ 01536 510584 📠 01536 510584
📧 johnreed.andson@lineone.net
🌐 www.johnreedandson
upholsterers.com
Est. 1972
Services Repair, restoration,
upholstery, French and spray
polishing
Open Mon–Thurs 8am–5.30pm
Fri 8am–noon

Regency Furniture Restoration

Contact Mr M Houghton
✉ 29 St Kenelm's Avenue,
Halesowen, West Midlands,
B63 1DW ▣
☎ 0121 550 8356 📠 0121 550 8356
Est. 1997
Services Antique furniture
restoration and cabinet-making,
French polishing
Open Mon–Fri 8am–5pm or by
appointment

Renaissance Antiques

Contact Mr S Macrow
✉ 18 Marshall Lake Road,
Shirley, Solihull,
West Midlands,
B90 4PL ▣
☎ 0121 745 5140
Est. 1979
Services Antique furniture
restoration
Open Mon–Sat 9am–5pm

Tim Ross-Bain

Contact Mr T Ross-Bain
✉ Halford Bridge, Fosse Way,
Halford, Shipston-on-Stour,
Warwickshire,
CV36 5BN ▣
☎ 01789 740778 📠 01789 740778
📧 info@rossbain.com
🌐 www.rossbain.com
Est. 1979
Services Antique furniture
restoration, interior decoration
and repair, cabinet-making
Open 24 hours by appointment

Sealcraft

Contact Mr P M Sealey
✉ 107 New Road, Bromsgrove,
Worcestershire,
B60 2LJ ▣
☎ 01527 872677
Est. 1995
Services Antique restoration and
repair, French polishing
Open By appointment

Anthony Smith

Contact Mr A Smith
✉ Perton Court Farm,
Jenny Walkers Lane,
Wolverhampton, West Midlands,
WV6 7HB ▣
☎ 01902 380303 📠 01902 380303
Est. 1969
Services Antique and quality
furniture restoration
Open Mon–Fri 8.30am–5pm

J A Snelson

Contact Mr J A Snelson
✉ Jennett Tree Farm,
Jennett Tree Lane, Callow End,
Worcestershire,
WR2 4UA ▣
☎ 01905 831887
📱 07734 357794
Est. 1984
Services Fine antique
restoration, French polishing,
cabinet work
Open Mon–Fri 9am–5pm
Sat 9am–noon

J W Stevens and Son

Contact Mr M J Stevens
✉ 61 Main Street, Lubenham,
Market Harborough,
Leicestershire,
LE16 9TF ▣
☎ 01858 463521
Est. 1947
Services Antique furniture
restoration
Open By appointment only

Swans Antiques and Interiors

Contact Mr Tom Scott
✉ 17 Mill Street, Oakham,
Rutland,
LE15 6EA ▣
☎ 01572 724364 📠 01572 755094
📱 07860 304084
📧 info@swansofoakham.co.uk
🌐 www.swansofoakham.co.uk
Est. 1984
Services Full restoration service,
cabinet makers
Open Mon–Sat 9am–5.30pm
Sun by appointment

Ed Thomas Old Country Pine

Contact Mr E Thomas
✉ 22 Old Hednesford Road,
Cannock, Staffordshire,
WS11 6LD ▣ 📠 01543 506731
📱 07966 243477
📧 edthomasoldcountrypine
@lycos.co.uk
Est. 1981
Services Made-to-measure pine
furniture using only old original
pine.
Open Mon–Sat 9am–5.30pm

Treedale Antiques

Contact Mr G Warren
✉ Pickwell Lane, Little Dalby,
Melton Mowbray,
Leicestershire,

ASSOCIATED SERVICES
FURNITURE

LE14 2XB P
☎ 01664 454535 ☏ 01572 757521
Est. 1968
Services 17th–18thC furniture
restoration
Open Mon–Sat 9am–5pm Sun by
appointment

**Upstairs Downstairs
Antiques**
Contact Mr C Lawrence
✉ 8 Derby Road, Ripley,
Derbyshire,
DE5 3HR P
☎ 01773 745201
Ⓜ 07885 327753
Ⓦ www.upstairsdownstairs
antiques.co.uk
Est. 1974
Services Furniture restoration,
clock repair, French polishing
Open Mon–Sat 10am–4pm

**Richard Walker – Antique
Restoration**
Contact Mr R Walker
✉ 302 Via Gellia Mills,
Via Gellia Road, Bonsall,
Matlock, Derbyshire,
DE4 2AJ P
☎ 01629 825791
Est. 1992
Services Furniture repair and
restoration
Open By appointment

**Wizzards Furniture
Restorers**
Contact Mr Hayes
✉ The Old Stables,
Meadow Lane, Nottingham,
Nottinghamshire,
NG2 3HQ P
☎ 0115 986 7484 ☏ 0115 986 7484
Est. 1994
Services Furniture repair and
restoration, stripping, French
polishing
Open Mon–Fri 8.30am–5pm or by
appointment

Wood Restorations
Contact Mr Peter Wood
✉ Eastfield Farm,
Crick Road, Rugby,
Warwickshire,
CV23 0AB P
☎ 01788 822253 ☏ 01788 822253
Ⓔ peter.wood31@btopenworld.com
Est. 1969
Services Antique furniture
restoration
Open By appointment

**Anthony James Beech
Furniture Conservation &
Restoration (BAFRA, UKIC)**
Contact Anthony Beech
✉ The Stable Courtyard,
Burghley House, Stamford,
Lincolnshire,
PE9 3JY P
☎ 01780 481199 ☏ 01780 481199
Ⓦ www.furnitureconservation.co.uk
Est. 1997
Services Furniture restoration
Open By appointment

Adrian J Black
Contact Mr A J Black
✉ 7 Eastfield Avenue, Scartho,
Grimsby, Lincolnshire,
DN33 2PD P
☎ 01472 824823
Est. 1968
Services Antique furniture repair
and restoration
Open By appointment

Cleveland Wood Strip
Contact Mr P Stokes
✉ 2 Kensington Road, Oxbridge,
Stockton-on-Tees, North Yorkshire,
TS18 4DQ P
☎ 01642 643033
Ⓜ 07980 031169
Est. 1989
Services French polishing, dip
and strip, architectural
restoration
Open Mon–Sat 10am–5pm but
please phone first

Kenneth F Clifford
Contact Mr K Clifford
✉ 29 St Aubyn's Place, York,
North Yorkshire,
YO24 1EQ P
☎ 01904 635780
Est. 1982
Services Antique repair and
restoration
Open By appointment

D A Copley
Contact Mr D A Copley
✉ 54a New Lane, Siddal, Halifax,
West Yorkshire,
HX3 9AL P
☎ 01422 351854
Est. 1949
Services Antique repair and
restoration, French polishing
Open Mon–Fri 8am–5pm
Sat 8am–noon

**Edmund Czajkowski & Son
(BAFRA)**
Contact Michael Czajkowski
✉ 96 Tor O Moor Road,
Woodhall Spa,
Lincolnshire,
LN10 6SB P
☎ 01526 352895 ☏ 01526 352895
Ⓔ michael.czajkowski@ntlworld.com
Ⓦ www.czajkowskiandson.com
Est. 1951
Services Restoration of antique
furniture, clocks, barometers
Open Mon–Sat 8.30am–5pm

R D Dunning
Contact Mr R Dunning
✉ Scaife Cottage,
Gate Helmsley, York,
North Yorkshire,
YO41 1NE P
☎ 01759 371961
Est. 1972
Services Antique furniture repair
and restoration
Open Mon–Fri 9am–6pm or by
appointment

Easingwold Antiques
Contact Jane Fish
✉ 108 Long Street, Easingwold,
North Yorkshire,
YO61 3HX P
☎ 01347 822977
Ⓜ 07968 088705 or 07977 108907
Est. 2003
Services Restoration of wooden
furniture
Open Tues–Sat 10am–5pm

Fishlake Antiques
Contact Fiona Trimmingham
✉ Vine Cottage,
Haygreen Corner, Fishlake,
South Yorkshire,
DN7 5LA P
☎ 01302 841411
Est. 1979
Services Furniture restoration
Open Sun 1–4pm or by
appointment

Furniture Revivals
Contact Michael Edwards
✉ Yeadon, Leeds,
LS19 P
Ⓜ 07831 817845
Ⓔ enquiries@furniturerevivals.co.uk
Ⓦ www.furniturerevivals.co.uk
Est. 1991
Services Furniture restoration,
upholstery
Open By appointment

ASSOCIATED SERVICES
FURNITURE

Hunters Interiors (Stamford) Ltd
Contact Jill Hunter
✉ 9a St Mary's Hill, Stamford, Lincolnshire, PE9 2DP 🅿
☎ 01780 757946 🖷 01780 757946
📱 07976 796969
✉ huntersinteriors@btopenworld.com
🌐 www.huntersinteriorsof stamford.co.uk
Est. 2000
Services Antique furniture restoration
Open Mon–Sat 9am–5.30pm

Park Antiques
Contact Brian O'Connell
✉ 2 North View, Menston, Ilkley, West Yorkshire, LS29 6JU 🅿
☎ 01943 872392
📱 07811 034123
🌐 www.parkantiques.com
Est. 1980
Services Furniture restoration
Open Wed–Fri 10.30am–4.30pm Sat 9.30am–5.30pm Sun noon–5pm

Period Furniture Ltd (LAPADA)
Contact Mrs S Worrall
✉ Moorside, Tockwith, York, North Yorkshire, YO26 7QG 🅿
☎ 01423 358399 🖷 01423 359050
🌐 www.antique-furniture.co.uk
Est. 1985
Services Antique repair and restoration, sales of Georgian–Art Deco furniture, bespoke furniture makers
Open Mon–Fri 8am–5pm Sat 9am–5pm Sun 10am–4pm

A G Podmore & Son
Contact Andrew or David Podmore
✉ North Minster Business Park, Northfield Lane, Poppleton, York, North Yorkshire, YO26 6QU 🅿
☎ 01904 799800 🖷 01904 799801
🌐 www.agpodmore.co.uk
Est. 1968
Services Conservation and restoration of antique furniture, French polishing, wax finishing, specializing in clock cases, pianos, desks, repolishing and restoration of panelling and staircases
Open Mon–Fri 8.30am–5pm

K J Sarginson Fine Furniture (UKIC)
Contact Mr K Sarginson
✉ The Joinery, Escrick Grange, Stillingfleet Road, Escrick, York, North Yorkshire, YO19 6EB 🅿
☎ 01904 728202 🖷 01904 728202
Est. 1991
Services Antique restoration and repair of fine furniture. Dining tables a speciality
Open Mon–Fri 8.15am–5.30pm or by appointment

Gerald Shaw
Contact Mr M G Shaw
✉ Jansville, Quarry Lane, Harrogate, North Yorkshire, HG1 3HR 🅿
☎ 01423 503590
Est. 1956
Services Repair and restoration of antique furniture
Open By appointment

Tony Smart Restorations
Contact Tony Smart
✉ Low Barn, Glebe Farm, Lund, Beverley, East Yorkshire, YO25 9TT 🅿
☎ 01377 217438
Est. 1971
Services General fine furniture restoration
Open Mon–Fri 9am–5pm

David South (HADA)
Contact James South or David South
✉ 15 High Street, Pateley Bridge, North Yorkshire, HG3 5AP 🅿
☎ 01423 712022 🖷 01423 712412
✉ sales@davidsouth.co.uk
🌐 www.davidsouth.co.uk
Est. 1985
Services Restoration of upholstered furniture, French polishing
Open Mon–Sat 9am–5.30pm

J K Speed Antique Furniture Restoration
Contact Mr J Speed
✉ The Workshop, Thornton Road, New York, Lincoln, Lincolnshire, LN4 4YL 🅿
☎ 01205 280313
📱 07761 242219
✉ john@speedthornton19. freeserve.co.uk

Est. 1964
Services Antique repair and restoration, light upholstery, specializing in case repair of longcase clocks
Open Mon–Fri 9am–5.30pm

Spires Restoration
Contact Mr G Bexon
✉ 32 Upgate, Louth, Lincolnshire, LN11 9ET 🅿
☎ 01507 600707 🖷 01507 602588
📱 07866 230725
Est. 1994
Services Repair and restoration of furniture
Open Mon–Fri 8am–5pm or by appointment

Tomlinson Antiques (LAPADA)
Contact Sarah Worrall
✉ Moorside, Tockwith, York, North Yorkshire, YO26 7QG 🅿
☎ 01423 358833 🖷 01423 358188
✉ info@antique-furniture.co.uk
🌐 antique-furniture.co.uk
Est. 1977
Services Repair and restoration of furniture, bespoke manufacturing service
Trade only Mon–Fri; retail club at weekends
Open Mon–Fri 8am–5pm Sun 10am–4pm

Neil Trinder (BAFRA)
Contact Mr N Trinder
✉ Burrowlee House, Broughton Road, Sheffield, South Yorkshire, S6 2AS 🅿
☎ 0114 285 2428
✉ neiltrinder@yahoo.co.uk
Est. 1985
Services Furniture restoration including gilding, upholstery, marquetry
Open By appointment

Westway Pine
Contact Mr J Dzierzek
✉ Carlton Lane, Helmsley, York, YO62 5HB 🅿
☎ 01439 771399 🖷 01439 771401
📱 07890 319325
✉ westway.pine@btopenworld.com
Est. 1986
Services Antique reproductions
Open Mon Wed–Fri 9am–5pm Sat 10am–5pm Sun 1–5pm

B D Whitham
Contact Mr B D Whitham
✉ 1 South View Cottage,
Draughton, Skipton,
North Yorkshire,
BD23 6EF 🅿
☎ 01756 710422
Est. 1984
Services Repair and restoration,
upholstery
Open Mon–Fri 9am–6pm and by
appointment

Nigel Wright
Contact Mr N Wright
✉ Unit 106, JC Albyn Complex,
Burton Road, Sheffield,
South Yorkshire,
S38 BZ 🅿
☎ 0114 272 1127
Est. 1983
Services Complete repair and
restoration of antique furniture,
veneering, inlays, French
polishing, colouring, etc
Open By appointment

NORTH EAST

G M Athey
Contact Mr Athey
✉ Corner Shop, Narrowgate,
Alnwick, Northumberland,
NE66 1JQ 🅿
☎ 01665 604229
Ⓜ 07836 718350
🅔 mathey@alancom.net
Est. 1982
Services Full restoration, French
polishing, upholstery. Deals in
Georgian and Victorian furniture
and china
Open Mon–Sat 8am–4.30pm

B J Coltman Restoration
Contact Barry
✉ 80 Meldon Terrace, Heaton,
Newcastle-upon-Tyne,
Tyne & Wear,
NE6 5XP 🅿
☎ 0191 224 5209
Ⓜ 07786 7077539
Est. 1994
Services Furniture restoration,
French polishing, cabinet work
Open Mon–Fri 8am–5pm

Richard Pattison
Contact Richard Pattison
✉ Unit 4, New Kennels,
Blagdon Estate, Seaton Burn,
Newcastle-upon-Tyne,
Tyne and Wear,

NE13 6DB 🅿
☎ 01670 789888
Est. 1977
Services Traditional antique
furniture restoration
Open Mon–Sat 9am–5pm

Richard Zabrocki & Son
Contact Mr I Zabrocki
✉ Hoults Estate, Walker Road,
Newcastle-upon-Tyne,
Tyne & Wear,
NE6 1AB 🅿
☎ 0191 265 5989
Est. 1949
Services Repair and restoration
of antique furniture
Open By appointment

NORTH WEST

Antique Furniture Restoration & Conservation (BAFRA, UKIC)
Contact Eric Smith
✉ The Old Church, Park Road,
Darwen, Lancashire,
BB3 2LD 🅿
☎ 01254 776222
Ⓜ 07977 811067
🅔 ericsmith@restorations.ndo.co.uk
🕊 www.bafra.org.uk
Est. 1965
Services Furniture restoration
Open Mon–Sun 9am–7pm please
phone first

K Bennett
Contact Mr Keith Bennett
✉ Oak House Farm, Wycollar,
Colne, Lancashire,
BB8 8SY 🅿
☎ 01282 866853
Est. 1973
Services Antique furniture
restoration
Open By appointment

Steve Blackwell French Polishers
Contact Mr S Blackwell
✉ Ley Print, Unit 3, Leyland Lane,
Preston, Lancashire,
PR25 1UT 🅿
☎ 01772 459735 🅕 01772 459735
Ⓜ 07929 170114
Est. 1989
Services Full antique furniture
restoration service and modern
finishes
Open Mon–Thurs 8am–5pm Fri
8am–4.30pm

M Bradley
Contact Mr M Bradley
✉ 25a Oxford Road,
Waterloo, Crosby, Merseyside,
L22 8QE 🅿
☎ 0151 920 5511
Est. 1969
Services Antique furniture
restoration, French polishing,
repair, upholstery repair
Open Mon–Fri 9am–5pm
Sat 9am–noon

Chester Antiques Restoration Ltd
Contact Mike Green
✉ Unit 4, White Lane Depot,
Christelton, Chester,
Cheshire,
CH3 6AH 🅿
☎ 01244 332796
Ⓜ 07830 169671
Est. 1983
Services Restoration of antique
furniture, French polishing
Open Mon–Fri 9am–5pm
Sat 9am–1.30pm

Michael Clayton French Polisher
Contact Mr M Clayton
✉ The Workshop,
Lestrange Street, Cleethorpes,
Lancashire,
BU35 7HS 🅿
☎ 01472 602795
Est. 1979
Services French polishing
Open By appointment

Cottage Antiques
Contact Angelica Slater
✉ 788 Rochdale Road, Walsden,
Todmorden, Lancashire,
OL14 7UA 🅿
☎ 01706 813612 🅕 01706 813612
Ⓜ 07773 798032
🕊 www.ukcottageantiques.co.uk
Services Stripping, polishing,
renovations, paint finishes,
custom-built furniture
Open Tues–Sun 9.30am–5.30pm

A Grice
Contact Mr A Grice
✉ 106 Aughton Street, Ormskirk,
Lancashire,
L39 3BS 🅿
☎ 01695 572007
Est. 1984
Services Furniture restoration
Open Wed Sat 1.30–6pm or by
appointment

Hamilton Antique Restoration
Contact Mr C Sayle
✉ 1a Orry Place, Douglas, Isle of Man
☎ 01624 662483
Est. 1989
Services Complete furniture repair and restoration service, upholstery
Open By appointment

Michael Holroyd Restorations
Contact Mr M Holroyd
✉ Pendle Antique Centre, Union Mill, Watt Street, Sabden, Clitheroe, Lancashire, BB7 9ED 🅿
☎ 01282 771112
📱 07711 011465
✉ antiquesrestorer@tiscali.co.uk
Est. 1996
Services Complete repair and restoration service including spray finish, wax finish, French polishing, cabinet-making and veneering, traditional upholstery
Open Mon–Fri 8am–5pm
Sat by appointment

Hopkins Antique Restoration
Contact Mr Mark Hopkins
✉ Unit 1, Excelsior Works, Charles Street, Heywood, Lancashire, OL10 2HW 🅿
☎ 01706 620549
Est. 1987
Services Antique furniture restoration, French polishing, cabinet-making
Open Mon–Sat 9am–5pm

J Kershaw Fine Furniture Restoration
Contact Mr J Kershaw
✉ Unit 10, Normans Hall Farm, Shrigley Road, Pott Shrigley, Macclesfield, Cheshire, SK10 5SE 🅿
☎ 01625 560808 📠 01625 560808
Est. 1985
Services Full repair and restoration service including French polishing, inlay work, marquetry, lacquerwork
Open By appointment

Peter Lawrenson
Contact Margaret Lawrenson
✉ Brook Cottage,

Scronkey Pilling, Preston, Lancashire, PR3 6SQ 🅿
☎ 01253 790671
Est. 1984
Services Furniture restoration
Open By appointment

Macdonalds Restoration
Contact Mr A Macdonald
✉ Unit 203, Jurby Industrial Estate, Ramsey, Isle of Man, IM7 3BB 🅿
☎ 01624 897648
Est. 1980
Services Traditional antique and modern furniture repair and restoration, cabinet-making
Open Mon–Sun 8am–6pm

Mansion House Antiques
Contact Mr Andrew Smith
✉ 11 Hand Lane, Leigh, Lancashire, WN7 3LP 🅿
☎ 01942 605634
Est. 1995
Services Antique furniture restoration
Open By appointment

Pilgrim's Progress
Contact Selwyn Hyams
✉ 1a–3a Bridgewater Street, Liverpool, Merseyside, L1 0AR 🅿
☎ 0151 708 7515 📠 0151 708 7515
🌐 www.pilgrimsprogress.co.uk
Est. 1979
Services Cabinet-making, French polishing, traditional upholstery
Open Mon–Fri 9am–5pm
Sat 10.30am–1.30pm

R S M Antique Restoration
Contact Mr Robin Stone
✉ The Stables, Back Eaves Street, Blackpool, Lancashire, FY1 2HW 🅿
☎ 01253 623839 📠 01253 623839
Est. 1972
Services Antique furniture, clocks, barometer, restoration, marquetry cutting
Open Mon–Fri 9am–6pm

T N Richards
Contact Mr D Richards
✉ Hamilton Place, Chester, Cheshire, CH1 2BH 🅿
☎ 01244 320241
Est. 1975

Services Complete repair and restoration service
Open By appointment

R J H Rimmel
Contact Mr R J H Rimmel
✉ 3 Newton Bank Cottages, Newton Hall Lane, Mobberley, Cheshire, WA16 7LB 🅿
☎ 01565 873847
Est. 1974
Services Full furniture restoration service, special commissions and church work undertaken
Open By appointment

Seventeen Antiques
Contact Mr J Brake
✉ 306 Aigburth Road, Liverpool, Merseyside, L17 9PW 🅿
☎ 0151 727 1717
📱 07712 189604
🌐 www.seventeenantiques.gbr.cc
Est. 1997
Services Furniture restoration, stripping
Open Mon–Sat 10am–5.30pm closed Wed

Treen Antiques (UKIC, RFS, FHS)
Contact Simon Feingold
✉ Treen House, 72 Park Road, Prestwich, Greater Manchester, M25 0FA 🅿
☎ 0161 720 7244 📠 0161 720 7244
📱 07973 471185
✉ simonfeingold@hotmail.com
Est. 1990
Services Collection management, valuations, conservation
Open By appointment

J D Worrall (Conservation)
Contact Mr J Worrall
✉ Unit 4a, The Old Brickworks, Pott Shrigley, Stockport, Cheshire, SK6 7HX 🅿
☎ 01663 733817
📱 07970 074381
✉ john@restorer.fsbusiness.co.uk
🌐 www.jdworrrall.co.uk
Est. 1997
Services Complete antique repair and restoration including upholstery, carving, gilding, veneer, inlay, cabinet work and French polishing
Open By appointment

ASSOCIATED SERVICES
FURNITURE

WALES

Antique Restorations (BAFRA)
Contact Mr A Smith
✉ Crug-y-deri, Llandissilio, Pembrokeshire, SA66 7JJ ▣
☎ 01437 563334
✉ antiquerestore@aol.com
Est. 1987
Services Restorers of painted and decorated furniture. Specialists in Oriental lacquering, japanning, gilding
Open Mon–Fri 9am–4.30pm or by appointment

Iain Ashcroft Furniture
Contact Mr Iain Ashcroft
✉ Ty Canol Farm, Sunbank, Llangollen, Denbighshire, LL20 7UL ▣
☎ 01978 860392
✉ ianashcroft@virgin.net
ⓦ www.ianashcroft.co.uk
Est. 1987
Services Antique furniture, restoration, carving, inlaying
Open Mon–Fri 9am–5pm

D J Gravell
Contact D J Gravell
✉ Unit 5, Aber Court, Ferryboat Close Enterprise Park, Morrison, Swansea, West Glamorgan, SA6 8QN ▣
☎ 01792 310202 ✆ 01792 310202
✉ jgravell@universalwood finishers.co.uk
ⓦ www.universalwoodfinishers.co.uk
Est. 1989
Services Antique furniture repair and restoration
Open Mon–Fri 8.30am–5.30pm Sat 9–11am

B G Jones
Contact B G Jones
✉ Cwmbwri Honey Farm, Ferryside, Carmarthenshire, SA17 5TW ▣
☎ 01267 267318
✉ beegeejay2003@yahoo.co.uk
Est. 1986
Services Antique repair and restoration of furniture
Open Mon–Fri 9am–5pm please phone first

Parkview Antiques
Contact Nic Eastwood
✉ High Street, Northop,

Flintshire, CH7 6BQ ▣
☎ 01352 840627
Est. 1984
Services Furniture restoration
Open Mon–Sat 10am–5pm

Pastiche
Contact Mr S Pesticcio
✉ 15 Duxford Close, Llandaff, Cardiff, South Glamorgan, CF5 2PR ▣
☎ 02920 566759
Est. 1975
Services Period and traditional restoration and redecoration of Victorian furniture and property
Open By appointment

Phillips Antiques and French Polishing (BWCG)
Contact Philip Wyvill-Bell
✉ 31 The High Street, Llandovery, Carmarthenshire, SA20 0DD ▣
☎ 01550 721355 ✆ 01550 721355
✉ wyvillbell@aol.com
Est. 1970
Services Restoration, polishing
Open Mon–Sat 10am–5pm

Phoenix Conservation.com (BAFRA, UKIC)
Contact Hugh Haley
✉ Selwyn Forge, Tenby Road, St Clears, Carmarthenshire, SA33 4JP ▣
☎ 01994 232109
✉ phoenixconservation@hotmail.com
ⓦ www.phoenixconservation.com
Est. 1992
Services Antique furniture conservation and repair
Open By appointment

T N Richards
Contact Mr D Richards
✉ Caergynog, Llanbedr, Gwynedd, LL45 2PL ▣
☎ 01341 241485
Est. 1974
Services Complete repair and restoration service
Open By appointment

Snowdonia Antiques
Contact Jeffery Collins
✉ Bank Building, Station Road, Llanrwst, Conwy Valley, LL26 0EP ▣
☎ 01492 640789 ✆ 01492 640789

ⓜ 07802 503552
Est. 1965
Services Antique repair and restoration
Open Mon–Sat 9am–5pm Sun by appointment

St Helens Restoration
Contact Jo McCarthy
✉ 87–88 St Helens Avenue, Swansea, West Glamorgan, SA1 4NN ▣
☎ 01792 465240 ✆ 01792 467788
✉ admin@sthelensrestoration.co.uk
ⓦ www.sthelensrestoration.co.uk
Est. 1979
Services Antique repair and restoration, upholstery, French polishing
Open Mon–Fri 9am–5pm Sat 9.30am–1pm

SCOTLAND

Adam Antiques & Restoration
Contact Charles Bergius
✉ 23c Dundas Street, Edinburgh, EH3 6QQ ▣
☎ 0131 556 7555 ✆ 0131 556 7555
Est. 1983
Services Quality repair to 18th–19thC furniture. Sales of 18th–19thC, mainly mahogany furniture and associated furnishings
Open Tues–Sat 10.30am–6pm Mon by appointment

Antique Furniture Restoration
Contact David Carson
✉ 108c Causewayside, Edinburgh, EH9 1PU ▣
☎ 0131 667 1067
ⓜ 07779 824543
✉ carsonantrest@btopenworld.com
Est. 1994
Services Repair and restoration of all old and antique furniture
Open Mon–Fri 10am–6pm Sat 10am–2pm

The Chairman of Bearsden (Scottish Furniture Preservation Society)
Contact David Shuttleton
✉ 115a Ayr Road, Newton Means, Glasgow, G77 6RF ▣
☎ 0141 639 6005

☎ 07814 744229
✉ sales@charlesrennie
mackintosh.co.uk
⊕ www.charlesrennie
mackintosh.co.uk
Est. 1990
Services Furniture restoration
and upholstery, French polishing,
cabinet-making, bergère suites,
cane and rush seating
Open Mon–Sat 9am–5pm

Chisholme Antiques
Contact Kim Roberts
✉ 5 Orrock Place, Hawick,
Scottish Borders,
TD9 0HQ ♿
☎ 01450 376928
Est. 1979
Services Antique repair and
restoration of furniture, cabinet-
making
Open Mon–Fri 9am–6pm

Chylds Hall Fine Furniture Restoration
Contact Stephen Pickering
✉ Old Dairy Cottage,
Upper Stepford, Dunscore,
Dumfries & Galloway,
DG2 0JP ♿
☎ 01387 820558 ✆ 01387 280558
Est. 1991
Services Fine furniture
restoration, period paint finish
restoration, French polishing
Open By appointment only

Douglas & Kay
Contact Mr P Kay
✉ c/o YWC,
40 Rogart Street,
Glasgow,
G40 2AA ♿
☎ 0141 556 5564
☎ 07974 494618
Est. 1948
Services Repair and restoration
of furniture, French polishing
Open By appointment

Roland Gomm
Contact Roland Gomm
✉ 65 Constitution Street,
Edinburgh,
EH6 7AF ♿
☎ 0131 467 5525
☎ 07947 179774
Est. 1986
Services French polishing,
restoration of fine antique
furniture
Open By appointment

Gow Antiques and Restoration (BAFRA)
Contact Jeremy Gow
✉ Pitscandly Farm, Forfar,
Angus,
DD8 3NZ ♿
☎ 01307 465342 ✆ 01307 468973
☎ 07711 416786
✉ jeremy@knowyourantiques.com
⊕ www.knowyourantiques.com
Est. 1991
Services Specialists in restoration
of European furniture,
17th–18thC marquetry
Open Mon–Fri 9am–5pm or by
appointment

Inchmartine Restorations (BAFRA)
Contact Andrew Stephens
✉ Inchmartine House, Inchture,
Perth, Perthshire,
PH14 9QQ ♿
☎ 01828 686412 ✆ 01828 686748
✉ ir@toolbazaar.freeserve.co.uk
⊕ www.toolbazaar.co.uk
Est. 1989
Services Restoration of antique
furniture pre-1840
Open Mon–Sat 9am–5.30pm

Sherman Upholstery
Contact Jim Sherman
✉ Blairdaff Street, Buckie,
Morayshire,
AB56 1PT ♿
☎ 01542 834680 ✆ 01542 834680
☎ 07703 881903
✉ linda@sherman73.freeserve.co.uk
Est. 1956
Services Antique repair,
restoration, upholstery
Open Mon–Fri 8.30am–4.30pm

The Tower Workshops
Contact George Pirie
✉ Aberdeen Road, Tarland,
Aboyne, Aberdeenshire,
AB34 4TB ♿
☎ 01339 811544 ✆ 01339 811544
⊕ www.antiquesagency.co.uk
Est. 1989
Services Antique restoration
including house interiors
Open Mon–Sun 11am–5pm

Graham Watson
Contact Mr G Watson
✉ The Workshop,
Mill Wynd, Greenlaw,
Scottish Borders,
TD10 6UA ♿
☎ 01361 810770/810593

Est. 1996
Services Furniture restoration,
French polishing
Open Mon–Sat 8am–5pm

NORTHERN IRELAND

Antique Services
Contact David Hosgood
✉ 288 Beersbridge Road, Belfast,
Co Antrim,
BT5 5DY ♿
☎ 028 9020 3933
Est. 1984
Services Restoration, re-polishing
Open Mon–Fri 8am–5pm

Courtyard Restoration
Contact Cosi Shaker or
Shaun Butler
✉ The Old Mill, 2 Parkfield Road,
Ahogill, Ballymena,
Co Antrim,
BT42 2QS ♿
☎ 028 2587 8875
☎ 07967 144784
Est. 1996
Services Restoration of furniture,
frame repair, re-carving
Open Mon–Sat 10am–5pm

Crozier Antique Furniture Restoration
Contact Mr Peter Crozier
✉ 39 Tassagh Road, Keady,
Co Armagh,
BT60 3TU ♿
☎ 028 3753 8242
Est. 1986
Services Restoration
Open Mon–Fri 9am–6pm or by
appointment

J Davies Restorations
Contact Jonathan Davies
✉ Rear of 23 Coleraine Road,
Portstewart, Co Londonderry,
BT55 7HP ♿
☎ 028 7083 3851
Est. 1989
Services Furniture restoration,
polishing
Open Mon–Fri 9am–5pm

Kelly Antiques
Contact Mr Louis Kelly
✉ Mullaghmore House,
Old Mountfield Road, Omagh,
Co Tyrone,
BT79 7EX ♿
☎ 028 8224 2314 ✆ 028 8225 0262
✉ sales@kellyantiques.com
⊕ www.kellyantiques.com

Est. 1936
Services Restoration, private bi-annual auctions. International Centre of Excellence for conservation, heritage and restoration. Full-time course in restoration techniques
Open Mon–Fri 10am–7pm
Sat 10am–5pm

Peter Williams
Contact Peter Williams
✉ 25 Ballykeigle Road, Comber, Co Down, BT23 5SD 🅿
☎ 028 9752 8360 ✆ 028 9752 8360
Est. 1983
Services Furniture restoration
Open By appointment

REPUBLIC OF IRELAND

Conservation Letterfrack (UKIC, ICHAWI)
Contact Sven Habermann
✉ Letterfrack, Co Galway, Ireland 🅿
☎ 095 41036 ✆ 095 41100
✉ info@conservationletterfrack.ie
🌐 www.conservationletterfrack.ie
Est. 1999
Services Conservation and restoration of all historic furniture and related objects, and of historical interiorsand architectural joinery, Museum conservation, cabinet-making, French polishing, veneer work, turning and woodcarving, marquetry, boulle work, metal work repair, pietra dura and marble repair
Open Mon–Fri 9am–5.30pm or by appointment

Euricka Antiques
Contact Alexandra Papadakis
✉ 3 Marks Alley, Francis Street, Dublin 8, Co Dublin, Ireland
☎ 01 454 9779
🌐 www.euricka-antiques.com
Est. 1990
Services Furniture restoration
Open Mon–Sat 10am–6pm

E Fitzpatrick (GADAR)
Contact E Fitzpatrick
✉ 17 Sidney Park, Wellington Road, Cork, Ireland 🅿
☎ 021 450 3084
Est. 1989

Services Repair and restoration of antique furniture
Open By appointment

Paul Geoghegan (National Guild of Craftsmen)
Contact Paul Geoghegan
✉ 9 Elmcastle Park, Kilmanagh, Dublin 24, Co Dublin, Ireland 🅿
☎ 01 451 4362
Ⓜ 08765 22769
Est. 1970
Services Furniture restoration, collecton and delivery service
Open By appointment

Glebe Hall Restoration Studios
Contact Carmel Corrigan-Griffin
✉ Old Killernogh Rectory, Rathnakelly Glebe, Ballacolla, Co Laois, Ireland 🅿
☎ 0502 34105 ✆ 0502 34105
Ⓜ 0868 784956
Est. 1980
Services Furniture restoration, gilding, porcelain, ivory, jade
Open By appointment
Sat 11am–4pm

Val Hughes (IPCRA)
Contact Mr Val Hughes
✉ 132 Arden Vale, Tullamore, Co Offaly, Ireland 🅿
☎ 0506 22600
Est. 1990
Services Conservation and restoration of antique and fine furniture
Open Mon–Sat 8.30am–6pm

Stephen McDonnell (BAFRA)
Contact Mr McDonnell
✉ 2 Anglesea Lane, Dun Laoghaire, Co Dublin, Ireland 🅿
☎ 01 280 7077 ✆ 01 284 2268
Ⓜ 0863 363537
Est. 1994
Services Furniture restoration, traditional finishing, French polishing, cabinet repair
Open Tues–Sat 9am–5.30pm

Michael O'Connell
Contact Michael O'Connell
✉ Clodagh, Crookstown, Cork, Co Cork, Ireland 🅿

☎ 021 733 6450
🌐 www.mandboconnell@yahoo.co.uk
Est. 1908
Services Furniture restoration, French polishing, cabinet-making
Open By appointment

Des Petrie
Contact Des Petrie
✉ Rosserk, Killala, Co Mayo, Ireland 🅿
☎ 09 632162/632632
Ⓜ 0866 021730
Est. 1985
Services Furniture restoration
Open Mon–Fri 9am–6pm

A Restoration Centre
Contact Kevin O'Reilly
✉ 6 The Pines, Grange Road, Rathfarnham, Dublin 16, Co Dublin, Ireland
☎ 01 280 1635
Ⓜ 08727 06565
Est. 1978
Services Furniture restoration
Open By appointment

Sealey Furnishings
Contact Ron
✉ MG Business Park, Galway Road, Tuam, Co Galway, Ireland 🅿
☎ 09 328661 ✆ 09 328661
✉ sales@sealeyfurnishings.com
🌐 www.sealeyfurnishings.com
Est. 1975
Services Furniture restoration, upholstery
Open Mon–Sat 10am–5.30pm

GILDING

2 K Carving (CGLI)
Contact Saena Ku
✉ 42 Sekforde Street, Finsbury, London, EC1R 0AH 🅿
☎ 020 7251 0592 ✆ 020 7251 0592
Ⓜ 07788 143219
Est. 2000
Services Antique restoration, woodcarving. gilding and wood conservation
Open By appointment

Anthony Allen Conservation, Restoration, Furniture and Artefacts (BAFRA, UKIC)
Contact Anthony Allen
✉ The Old Wharf Workshop,

**Redmoor Lane, Newtown,
High Peak, Derbyshire,
SK22 3JL** 📠
☎ 01663 745274 ✆ 01663 745274
✉ allen-conservation@tiscali.co.uk
Est. 1970
Services Restoration of
17th–13thC furniture, gilding,
marquetry, boulle, upholstery,
metalwork, clock cases and
movements
Open Mon–Fri 8am–5pm

Peter Binnington (BAFRA, Society of Gilders)
Contact Mr Peter Binnington
✉ Barn Studio, Botany Farm,
East Lulworth, Wareham, Dorset,
BH20 5QH 📠
☎ 01929 400224 ✆ 01929 400744
✉ nicepatina@aol.com
Est. 1979
Services Gilding, specialist in
verre églomisé
Open By appointment

A J Brett & Co
Contact Mr Negri or
Mrs Chesworth
✉ 168 Marlborough Road,
London,
N19 4NP 📠
☎ 020 7272 8462 ✆ 020 7272 5102
✉ ajbretts@aol.com
🌐 www.ajbrett.co.uk
Est. 1960
Services Furniture restoration,
gilding, upholstery
Open Mon–Fri 7.30am–3.30pm

Christy Antique Restoration (GADAR)
Contact Stephen Christy
✉ The Oast, Hurst farm,
Mountain Street , Chilham,
Canterbury, Kent,
CT4 8DH 📠
☎ 01227 730924 ✆ 01304 613585
✉ info@christyantiques.co.uk
🌐 www.christyantiques.co.uk
Est. 1989
Services Restoration of furniture
and upholstery, gilding, french
polishing
Open Mon–Fri 9am–4pm

W J Cook (BAFRA)
Contact Mr B Cook
✉ High Trees, Savernake Forest,
SW11 3JS 📠
☎ 020 7736 5329
✉ wjcook@btconnect.com
🌐 www.antiquerestoration.uk.com

Est. 1963
Services Furniture polishing,
restoration, upholstery, gilding
Open By appointment

Alison Cosserat
Contact Miss Alison Cosserat
✉ 13f Tonedale Mills, Tonedale,
Wellington, Somerset,
TA21 0AW 📠
☎ 01823 665279
📱 07989 465427
Est. 1997
Services Gold leaf specialist
Open Mon–Fri 10am–6pm

Extreme Conservation
Contact Dennis Buggins
✉ Unit 8, Hurst Farm,
Mountain Street, Chilham,
Canterbury, Kent,
CT4 8DH 📠
☎ 01227 738084 ✆ 01227 732508
✉ den.bug@zen.co.uk
🌐 www.extremearchitectural.co.uk
Est. 1977
Services Restoraton of furniture ,
lighting and gilding
Open By appointment

Michael Ferris
Contact Mr M Ferris
✉ Rose Cottage, Chapel Lane,
South Cockerington, Louth,
Lincolnshire,
LN11 7EB 📠
☎ 01507 327463 ✆ 01507 327463
Est. 1979
Services Antique repair,
restoration, gilding, re-gilding
Open By appointment

Mark Finamore
Contact Mark Finamore
✉ 63 Orford Road,
Walthamstow, London,
E17 9NJ 📠
☎ 020 8521 9407
Est. 1981
Services General antiques
service, gilding, furniture
restoration and conservation
Open Mon–Fri 10.30am–6pm or
Sat by appointment

Glebe Hall Restoration Studios
Contact Carmel Corrigan-Griffin
✉ Old Killernogh Rectory,
Rathnakelly Glebe, Ballacolla,
Co Laois,
Ireland 📠
☎ 0502 34105 ✆ 0502 34105

📱 0868 784956
Est. 1980
Services Furniture restoration,
gilding, porcelain, ivory, jade
Open By appointment
Sat 11am–4pm

R G Jones
Contact R G Jones
✉ 1 Brickfield Cottage, Bilting,
Ashford, Kent,
TN25 4ER 📠
☎ 01233 812849
Est. 1985
Services Antique restoration,
gilding
Open Mon–Fri 9am–4pm

Looking Glass of Bath (IIC)
Contact Anthony Reed
✉ 93–96 Walcot Street, Bath,
Somerset,
BA1 5BG 📠
☎ 01225 461969 ✆ 01225 316191
📱 07831 323878
✉ info@lookingglassofbath.co.uk
🌐 www.lookingglassofbath.co.uk
Est. 1968
Services Restoration of mirrors,
picture frames, gilding, carving,
manufacturers and supplier of
antique mirror glass, paper and
oil restoration
Open Mon–Sat 9am–6pm

Master Gilder (UKIC, The Gilding Society)
Contact Prakash Brinicombe
✉ 158 Kenmare Road, Knowle,
Bristol,
BS4 1PH
☎ 0117 949 5956 ✆ 0117 949 5956
📱 07881 634222
✉ prakash@mastergilder.com
🌐 www.mastergilder.com
Est. 1978
Services Gold-leaf restoration,
invisible repair and matching
existing giltwork, conservation
and new work
Open By appointment

Regency Restoration
Contact Mrs E Ball
✉ Arch 72, Ingate Place,
London,
SW8 3NS 📠
☎ 020 7622 5275 or 020 7828 4268
Est. 1987
Services Restoration of
18th–19thC mirrors, picture
frames, English and Continental

ASSOCIATED SERVICES
GLASS

painted and gilded furniture,
architectural gilding, church
interiors, polychrome sculpture,
lacquerwork, oil paintings,
carving
Open Mon–Fri 9.30am–5.30pm

Vigi Sawdon
Contact Vigi Sawdon
✉ 79–81 Ledbury Road,
London,
W11 2AG ▣
☎ 020 7229 9321 ✆ 020 7229 2033
📱 07859 896383
📧 sawdon@aol.com
🌐 www.vigisawdon.co.uk
Est. 1994
Services Gilding and restoration
of old wooden, gesso and
composite mirrors, architectural
pieces, frames. Also provides
French and Italian paint effects,
trompe l'oeil, marble, bamboo
Open By appointment

Sussex Gilding
Contact Mark Cashmen
✉ 59 Rodmell Avenue, Saltdean,
Brighton, East Sussex,
BN2 8PG ▣
☎ 01273 304890
📱 07775 742934
📧 sussexgilding@aol.com
🌐 www.sussexgilding.com
Est. 1992
Services Restoration of gilding
and carving, overmantels and
mirrors commissioned to order
Open By appointment

Titian Studio (BAFRA, UKIC)
Contact Rodrigo Titian
✉ 32 Warple Way, Acton,
London,
W3 0DJ ▣
☎ 020 8222 6600 ✆ 020 8749 2220
📧 info@titianstudios.co.uk
🌐 www.titianstudios.co.uk
Est. 1965
Services Restoration of gilding
and lacquering, French polishing,
caning, cabinet-making
Open Mon–Fri 8am–5.30pm

M Tocci
Contact Mr M Tocci
✉ Unit 4, 81 Southern Row,
London,
W10 5AL ▣
☎ 020 8960 4826
Est. 1978
Services Gilding, painted

furniture restoration, lacquer on
furniture and decorations
Open Mon–Fri 7.30am–4.30pm

GLASS

F W Aldridge Ltd
Contact Miss Angela Garwood
✉ Unit 3, St Johns Industrial
Estate, Dunmow Road, Takeley,
Essex,
CM22 6SP ▣
☎ 01279 874000 ✆ 01279 874002
📧 angela@fwaldridge.abel.co.uk
🌐 www.fwaldridgeglass.com
Est. 1926
Services Repair and restoration
of glass, supply of Bristol glass
for antique and modern table
silverware, all glass and silver
restoration
Open Mon–Fri 9am–5.30pm

Peter Binnington (BAFRA, Society of Gilders)
Contact Mr Peter Binnington
✉ Barn Studio, Botany Farm,
East Lulworth, Wareham,
Dorset,
BH20 5QH ▣
☎ 01929 400224 ✆ 01929 400744
📧 nicepatina@aol.com
Est. 1979
Services Gilding, specialist in
verre églomisé
Open By appointment

Ellen L Breheny (Accredited Member UKIC)
Contact Ellen L Breheny
✉ 10 Glenisla Gardens,
Edinburgh,
EH9 2HR ▣
☎ 0131 667 2620
📧 ellen@breheny.com
Est. 1988
Services Conservation and
restoration of ceramics, glass and
related materials
Open Mon–Fri 10am–6pm

China and Glass Restoration
Contact Mrs Susan Birch
✉ The Shoe, Old Hollow, Mere,
Warminster, Wiltshire,
BA12 6EG ▣
☎ 01747 861703
📧 sukib@onetel.com
Est. 1993
Services China and glass
restoration
Open By appointment

China Repairers
Contact Virginia Baron
✉ The Coach House, King Street
Mews, King Street, London,
N2 8DY ▣
☎ 020 8444 3030
🌐 www.chinarepairers.co.uk
Est. 1953
Services Ceramic and glass repair.
Tuition available
Open Mon–Thurs 10am–4pm

The Conservation Studio (ICOM, IIC, UKIC)
Contact Mrs F Hayward
✉ 77 Troutbeck, Albany Street,
London,
NW1 4EJ ▣
☎ 020 7387 4994 ✆ 020 7387 4994
📧 flu_flo@yahoo.co.uk
Est. 1993
Services Restoration and
conservation of ceramics, glass,
metalwork, ivory and soapstone,
specializing in gilding, painting
on glass and ceramics
Open Mon–Fri 8.30am–4.30pm
Sat by appointment

Facets Glass Restoration
Contact Mrs K Moore
✉ 107 Boundary Road, London,
E17 8NQ ▣
☎ 020 8520 3392 ✆ 020 8520 3392
📱 07778 758304
📧 repairs@facetsglass.co.uk
🌐 www.facetsglass.co.uk
Est. 1996
Services Antique glass
restoration including supply of
blue glass liners for table
silverware, re-bristling hair
brushes, cutlery restoration, flute
and trumpet stopper suppliers
Open By appointment

Looking Glass of Bath (IIC)
Contact Anthony Reed
✉ 93–96 Walcot Street, Bath,
Somerset,
BA1 5BG ▣
☎ 01225 461969 ✆ 01225 316191
📱 07831 323878
📧 info@lookingglassofbath.co.uk
🌐 www.lookingglassofbath.co.uk
Est. 1968
Services Restoration of mirrors,
picture frames, regilding,
carving, manufacturers and
supplier of antique mirror glass,
paper and oil restoration
Open Mon–Sat 9am–6pm

Martyn Pearson Glass
Contact Martyn Pearson
✉ The Stables Craft Centre, Halfpenny Green Vineyard, Tom Lane, Bobbington, Staffordshire, DY7 5EP 🅿
☎ 01384 221399 ⊙ 01384 221399
📠 07951 305617
Est. 1995
Services Glass cutting, engraving and repair
Open Thurs–Tues 11am–5pm

Sarah Peek
Contact Miss S Peek
✉ Redwins, Rear of 6 Preston Park Avenue, New England Street, Brighton, East Sussex, BN1 6HI 🅿
☎ 01273 243744 ⊙ 07092 393295
🅴 conservation@sarahpeek.co.uk
🅆 www.sarahpeek.co.uk
Est. 1995
Services Restoration of ceramics, glass, enamels
Open By appointment

Red House Glasscrafts
Contact Mrs J Oakley or B Taylor
✉ Ruskin Glass Centre, Wollaston Road, Amblecote, Stourbridge, West Midlands, DY8 4HE 🅿
☎ 01384 399460 ⊙ 01384 399460
📠 07901 522277
Est. 1987
Services Repair and restoration of antique crystal
Open Mon–Fri 9am–5pm Sat 10am–4pm

The Traditional Studio (UKIC)
Contact Viki Green
✉ Welwyn Equestrian Centre, Potters Heath Road, Welwyn, Hertfordshire, AL6 9SZ 🅿
☎ 01707 332084 ⊙ 01707 332084
📠 07748 224287
🅴 viki@traditionalstudio.fsnet.co.uk
Est. 1997
Services Glass restoration
Open By appointment

GRAMOPHONES & RADIOS

Philip Knighton (The Gramophone Man) (RETRA)
Contact Philip Knighton

✉ Bush House, 17b South Street, Wellington, Somerset, TA21 8NR 🅿
☎ 01823 661618 ⊙ 01823 661618
🅴 gramman@msn.com
Est. 1981
Services Supplies and restores gramophones, early wirelesses, sells 78rpm records
Open Tues–Sat 10am–5pm closed Mon

Talking Point Antiques
Contact Mr Paul Austwick
✉ 66 West Street, Sowerby Bridge, West Yorkshire, HX6 3AP 🅿
☎ 01422 834126
🅴 tpagrams@aol.com
Est. 1985
Services Repair, refurbishment and restoration of wind-up gramophones
Open Thurs Fri Sat 10.30am–5.30pm and by appointment

The Wireless Works
Contact Rob Rusbridge
✉ 27 Fore Street, Bugle, St Austell, Cornwall, PL26 8PA 🅿
☎ 01726 852200 ⊙ 01726 852200
🅴 rob@wirelessworks.co.uk
🅆 www.wirelessworks.co.uk
Est. 1995
Services Radio, gramophone and antique electronics repair, restoration, rebuilding and trading
Open By appointment

INLAY WORK

Anita Marquetry Ltd
Contact Howard Sansome
✉ Unit 5-7, Ddole Enterprise Park, Llandrindod Wells, Powys, LD1 6DF 🅿
☎ 01597 825505 ⊙ 01597 824484
🅴 lear@marquetry.co.uk
🅆 www.marquetry.co.uk
Est. 1990
Services Veneer, marquetry, inlays restored
Open Mon–Fri 9am–5pm

Antique Restorers Ltd & Cabinet Makers Ltd
Contact Barry Howells or John Eagle
✉ 7a Tynemouth Terrace, Tynemouth Road, Tottenham,

London, N15 4AP 🅿
☎ 020 8808 7965 ⊙ 020 8801 5313
📠 07956 970924
Est. 2005
Services 18th–19thC antique furniture restoration, leatherwork, gilding, marquetry and copy brasswork, copy chair making
Open Mon–Thurs 7am–3.30pm Fri 7am–1.30pm

Castle House (BAFRA)
Contact Mr Michael Durkee
✉ Castle House, Units 1 and 3, Bennetts Field Estate, Wincanton, Somerset, BA9 9DT 🅿
☎ 01963 33884 ⊙ 01963 31278
Est. 1975
Services Antique furniture restoration and conservation
Open Mon–Fri 8.30am–5pm

Dyson Furniture
Contact Nick Dyson
✉ Eel Pie Boatyard, Eel Pie Island, Twickenham, Middlesex, TW1 3DY
☎ 020 8891 5309
Est. 1992
Services Complete furniture repair and restoration, turning, marquetry, inlay work, cabinet-making
Open Mon–Fri 10am–6pm

M K Restorations
Contact Mr M Knight
✉ Unit 8e, Quickbury Farm, Hatfield Heath Road, Sawbridgeworth, Hertfordshire, CM21 9HY 🅿
☎ 01279 726664
📠 07939 438587
🅴 mk-restorations@talk21.com
Est. 1992
Services Antique furniture restoration, specializing in veneering and inlay work
Open Mon–Sat 9am–6.30pm

Paul Waldmann Woodwork (Conservation Unit)
Contact Mr P Waldmann
✉ 41 Norfolk Street, Cambridge, Cambridgeshire, CB1 2LD 🅿
☎ 01223 314001
📠 07740 167055
🅴 pm.waldmann@ntlworld.com
Est. 1982

ASSOCIATED SERVICES
JEWELLERY

Services Antique furniture restoration, cabinet-making
Open By appointment

JEWELLERY

Aladdin's Cave
Contact Roberta Spencer
✉ 19 Queen's Arcade, Leeds, West Yorkshire, LS1 6LF 🅿
☎ 0113 245 70903
✉ robertajspencer@hotmail.com
Est. 1985
Services Jewellery repair, valuations
Open Mon–Sat 10am–5pm

Keith Bawden (BAFRA)
Contact Keith Bawden
✉ Mews Workshops, Montpellier Retreat, Cheltenham, Gloucestershire, GL50 2XG 🅿
☎ 01242 230320 or 01452 863566
Est. 1975
Services Full antique restoration service of furniture, clocks, watercolours, jewellery, ceramics and Oriental carpets, silver, plating, committed to conservation and under-restoring on principle
Open By appointment phone first

Berkshire Antiques Co Ltd
Contact Mr Sutton
✉ 42 Thames Street, Windsor, Berkshire, SL4 1PR 🅿
☎ 01753 830100
✉ b.antiques@btconnect.com
🌐 www.jewels2go.co.uk
Est. 1981
Services Jewellery repair
Open Mon–Sat 10.30am–5.30pm Sun by appointment

Bicks Jewellers & Antiques
Contact Mr Morris
✉ 5 Montpellier Walk, Cheltenham, Gloucestershire, GL50 1SD 🅿
☎ 01242 524738 ☎ 01242 524738
Est. 1895
Services Jewellery restoration and repair
Open Tues–Sat 10am–4pm

Domino Restorations
Contact Mrs J Hargreaves
✉ c/o G B Antiques Centre,

Lancaster Leisure Park, Wyresdale Road, Lancaster, Lancashire, LA1 3LA 🅿
📱 07710 223170
✉ r.j.hargreaves@ic24.net
Est. 1979
Services Porcelain and china restoration, jewellery repair. Repair and restoration of metalware, tortoiseshell and ivory, spelter, bronze
Open By appointment

Mark Newland Enamel Restorer
Contact Mr M Newland
✉ 1 Whitehouse Way, Southgate, London, N14 7LX 🅿
☎ 020 8361 0429
Est. 1982
Services Restoration of enamelled jewellery and objets d'art
Open By appointment

Barry Papworth (NAG)
Contact Steve Park
✉ 28 St Thomas Street, Lymington, Hampshire, SO41 9NE 🅿
☎ 01590 676422
Est. 1978
Services Restoration of jewellery and silver. Workshop on site
Open Mon–Sat 9.15am–5.15pm

B M Witmond (Freeman of the Goldsmiths Company)
Contact Barry Witmond
✉ The Stable Courtyard, Burghley House, Stamford, Lincolnshire, PE9 3JY 🅿
☎ 01780 480868 ☎ 01780 480866
📱 07774 870513
✉ silversmiths@bmwitmond.co.uk
🌐 www.bmwitmond.co.uk
Est. 1976
Services Manufacture and restoration of tortoiseshell, restoration of ivory and English and Continental plate, jewellery and flatware, jewellery manufacture
Open By appointment

LEATHER

Antique Leather Dressing
Contact Val Pringle
✉ PO Box 67, Langport,

Somerset, TA10 9WJ
☎ 01458 241816
📱 07947 277833
✉ sales@antiqueleatherdressing.co.uk
🌐 www.antiqueleatherdressing.co.uk
Est. 2003
Services Leather dressing products, including Pecard
Open Please telephone or e-mail

Antique Leathers (LAPADA)
Contact Jackie Crisp
✉ Unit 2, Bennetts Field Trading Estate, Wincanton, Somerset, BA9 9DT 🅿
☎ 01963 33163 ☎ 01963 33164
✉ info@antique-leathers.co.uk
🌐 www.antique-leathers.co.uk
Est. 1965
Services Hand-dyed leatherwork on desk tops, gold tooling, traditional upholstery, leather chair repair and restoration, bookshelf edging
Open Mon–Fri 9.30am–5pm

Antique Restorers & Cabinet Makers Ltd
Contact Barry Howells or John Eagle
✉ 7a Tynemouth Terrace, Tynemouth Road, Tottenham, London, N15 4AP 🅿
☎ 020 8808 7965 ☎ 020 8801 5313
📱 07956 970924
Est. 2005
Services 18th–20thC antique furniture restoration, leatherwork, gilding, marquetry and copy brasswork, copy chair making
Open Mon–Thurs 7am–3.30pm Fri 7am–1.30pm

J Crisp
Contact Mr J Crisp
✉ 96 Hillway, Highgate, London, N6 6DP 🅿
☎ 020 8340 0668 ☎ 020 8340 0668
Est. 1979
Services Loose leather services, traditional upholstery, French and leather polishing, table liners, leather gilding
Open Mon–Fri 10am–6pm by appointment

R G Dewdney
Contact Mr R G Dewdney
✉ Norfolk Road,

South Holmwood, Dorking,
Surrey,
RH5 4LA ▣
☎ 01306 888174 📠 01306 742636
✉ regdewdney@btconnect.com
Est. 1968
Services Leatherwork, general
antique repair and restoration
Open Mon–Fri 9am–6pm

**Director Furniture
Leathergilders**
Contact Mrs M Taylor or
Mrs P A Rowe
✉ 39 Severn Stoke, Worcester,
Worcestershire,
WR8 9JA ▣
☎ 01905 371339
Est. 1984
Services Replacement leather
desk and table linings, hand-
coloured and antiqued, hand-
gilded in the traditional method
to customer's specifications. Full
grainhide or skiver
Open By appointment

**Leather Conservation
Centre (UKIC, SSCR)**
Contact Jan Beaumont
✉ University College Campus,
Boughton Green Road,
Moulton Park,
Northampton,
Northamptonshire,
NN2 7AN ▣
☎ 01604 719766 📠 01604 719649
✉ lcc@northampton.ac.uk
🌐 www.leatherconservatin.org
Est. 1978
Services Conservation and
restoration of leather objects,
research, training and
information for leather and
leather conservation
Open Mon–Fri 8.30am–5pm
please phone first

The Manor Bindery Ltd
Contact Philip Bradburn
✉ Calshot Road, Fawley,
Southampton,
Hampshire,
SO45 1BB ▣
☎ 02380 894488 📠 02380 899418
✉ manorbindery@btconnect.com
🌐 www.manorbindery.co.uk
Est. 1976
Services Desk and table top
leathering, edging. Supplier of
leather-bound books and false
books for display
Open Mon–Fri 8am–5pm

**Norwich Antique
Restoration**
Contact John Harvey
✉ Unit 2, Half Moon Way,
Norwich, Norfolk,
NR2 4EB ▣
☎ 01603 762504 📠 01603 762504
📱 07990 585999
✉ tee@leatherdesks.com
Est. 1973
Services Leather and desk tops,
French polishing
Open Mon–Sat 9am–5pm

**Stanstead Abbotts
Leathers**
Contact Mrs L Ray
✉ Hedges, Commonside Road,
Harlow, Essex,
CM18 7EY ▣
☎ 01279 453914 📠 01279 432295
Est. 1981
Services Table liners
Open Mon–Fri 9am–5.30pm

Woolnough (AC) Ltd
Contact Mr A Cullen
✉ Unit 7, Parmiter Industrial
Estate, Parmiter Street, Bethnal
Green, London,
E2 9HZ ▣
☎ 020 8980 9813 📠 020 8980 9814
Est. 1885
Services Desk top leathering,
leather upholstery, bookshelf
edging, chairback embossing and
distressed hand-stained leather
upholstery
Open Mon–Fri 7am–3.30pm

LIGHTING

A B C Restoration Ltd
Contact Chris Christofi
✉ Unit 23a,
Rosebury Industrial Park,
Rosebury Avenue, Tottenham
Hale, London,
N17 9SR ▣
☎ 020 8880 9697 📠 020 8801 4618
Est. 1999
Services Restoration, repair of
lighting, chandliers, bronzing on
metalwork, clocks
Open Mon–Fri 8.30am–5.30pm or
by appointment

Abeam Antiques
Contact Joseph Yousif
✉ 159 Carr Road, Northolt,
Middlesex,
UB5 4RE ▣
☎ 020 8426 8857

Est. 1994
Services Furniture, lighting
restoration, repair
Open By appointment

George & Peter Cohn
Contact Peter Cohn
✉ Unit 21, 21 Wren Street,
London,
WC1X 0HF ▣
☎ 020 7278 3749
Est. 1947
Services Experts in restoration
and cleaning of crystal
chandeliers, repair, restoration
and electrification of antique
light fittings
Open Mon–Fri 9.30am–4pm

Dernier and Hamlyn Ltd
✉ Unit 5, Croydon Business
Centre, 214 Purley Way,
Croydon, Surrey,
CR0 4XG ▣
☎ 020 8760 0900 📠 020 8760 0955
✉ info@dernier-hamlyn.com
🌐 www.dernier-hamlyn.com
Est. 1888
Services Traditional and
contemporary bespoke lighting
specialists, manufacturing and
restoration. Holders of royal
warrant for manufacture and
restoration to HM Queen
Open Mon–Fri 9am–5pm

Extreme Conservation
Contact Dennis Buggins
✉ Unit 8, Hurst Farm,
Mountain Street, Chilham,
Canterbury,
Kent,
CT4 8DH ▣
☎ 01227 738084 📠 01227 732508
✉ den.bug@zen.co.uk
🌐 www.extremearchitectural.co.uk
Est. 1977
Services Restoraton of furniture ,
lighting and gilding
Open By appointment

Magic Lanterns
Contact J A Marsden
✉ By George,
23 George Street, St Albans,
Hertfordshire,
AL3 4ES ▣
☎ 01727 865680
Est. 1987
Services Lighting consultancy for
period houses
Open Mon–Fri 10am–5pm
Sat 10am–5.30pm Sun 1–5pm

David Malik & Son Ltd
Contact Sara Malik
✉ 5 Metro Centre,
Britannia Way, Park Royal,
London,
NW10 7PA 🅿
☎ 020 8965 4232 🖷 020 8965 2401
Est. 1950
Services Chandelier, wall bracket,
candelabra restoration, re-
wiring, gilding
Open Mon–Fri 9am–5pm

**The Old Barn (Lighting
Association)**
Contact Geoff Day
✉ Foxhole Farm, London Road,
Hertford Heath, Hertford,
Hertfordshire,
SG13 7NR 🅿
Est. 1990
Services Lighting restoration, re-
wiring chandeliers and
components
Open By appointment

J N Preedy
Contact Jon Preedy
✉ Hereford House,
55 Station Road, Billingshurst,
West Sussex,
RH14 9SE 🅿
☎ 01403 785379 🖷 01403 785379
Est. 1995
Services Electrical re-wiring for
antiques only, chandeliers,
converting vases, lamps
Open By appointment

Sargeant Restorations
Contact David and Ann Sargeant
✉ 26 London Road, Sevenoaks,
Kent,
TN13 1AP 🅿
☎ 01732 457304 🖷 01732 457688
📱 07771 553632
Est. 1989
Services Restoration of all light
fittings, lustres, candelabra
Open Tues–Sat 9am–5.30pm
closed Wed

Turn On Lighting
Contact Janet Holdstock
✉ 116–118 Islington High Street,
Camden Passage, Islington,
London,
N1 8EG 🅿
☎ 020 7359 7616 🖷 020 7359 7616
Est. 1976
Services Display lighting
Open Tues–Fri 10am–6pm Sat
9.30am–4.30pm

David Turner Workshops
Contact Mr D Turner
✉ 24 Tottenham Road, London,
N1 4BZ 🅿
☎ 020 7241 5400 🖷 020 7241 5416
📧 mo@davidturner.uk.com
Est. 1987
Services Repair and restoration
of metalwork, lighting,
decorative antiques, small-scale
bespoke lighting commissions
Open Mon–Fri 9.30am–6pm

Woodall & Emery Ltd
Contact Mrs Chinn
✉ Haywards Heath Road,
Balcombe, Haywards Heath,
West Sussex,
RH17 6PG 🅿
☎ 01444 811608
📧 enquiries@woodallandemery.co.uk
🌐 www.woodallandemery.co.uk
Est. 1860
Services Restoration and sale of
antique and decorative lighting
Open Tues–Sat 10am–5pm

LOCKS AND KEYS

Blackstage
Contact David Benford
✉ The Old Stable, Catton Hall,
Catton, Swadlincote, Derbyshire,
DE12 8LN 🅿
☎ 0870 220 0494 🖷 0870 220 0987
📱 07896 637021
📧 mail@blackstage.co.uk
🌐 www.Blackstage.co.uk
Est. 2002
Services Restoration,
reproduction of locks and keys
for furniture, clocks, doors and
windows
Open Mon–Fri 9am–4pm

Lock & Key Centre
Contact Robert Evans
✉ 18 Queen Street, Aylesbury,
Buckinghamshire,
HP20 1LU 🅿
☎ 0800 559 3995
📧 admin.lockandkey@btconnect.com
🌐 www.lockandkeycentre.co.uk
Est. 2001
Services Key cutting specialists
Open Mon–Fri 8.30am–5pm
Sat 8.30am–1pm

**Andrew A Matthews
Restoration (Graduate
member of the students
section BAFRA)**
Contact Mr A A Matthews

✉ Fox House, Gills Hill, Bourn,
Cambridge, Cambridgeshire,
CB3 7TX 🅿
📱 07808 590370
Est. 1998
Services Antique restoration and
conservation, cabinet work,
veneering, turning, key-making,
lock repair, polishing, upholstery,
rushing and caning
Open By appointment

MARBLE

**Conservation Letterfrack
(UKIC, ICHAWI)**
Contact Sven Habermann
✉ Letterfrack, Co Galway,
Ireland 🅿
☎ 095 41036 🖷 095 41100
📧 info@conservatinletterfrack.ie
🌐 www.conservationletterfrack.ie
Est. 1999
Services Conservation and
restoration of all historic
furniture and related objects,
and of historical interiors and
architectural joinery, Museum
conservation, cabinet-making,
French polishing, veneer work,
turning and woodcarving,
marquetry, boulle work, metal
work repair, pietra dura and
marble repair
Open Mon–Fri 9am–5.30pm or by
appointment

H J Hatfield and Son
✉ 42 St Michael's Street,
London,
W2 1QP 🅿
☎ 020 7723 8265 🖷 020 7706 4562
📧 admin@hjhatfield.com
🌐 www.hjhatfield.com
Est. 1834
Services Restoration of furniture,
porcelain, paintings, boulle,
upholstery, lacquerwork,
metalwork, chandeliers, marble
Open Mon–Fri 8am–1pm 2–5pm
(moving soon check via phone or
website before visiting)

Rimmer Restoration
Contact Mr J S Rimmer
✉ 14 Hastings Place, Lytham,
Lancashire,
FY8 5LZ 🅿
☎ 01253 794521
📧 johnrimmer@btinternet,com
Est. 1987
Services Marble restorer
Open By appointment

Vigi Sawdon
Contact Vigi Sawdon
✉ 79–81 Ledbury Road, London, W11 2AG ℗
☎ 020 7229 9321 ✆ 020 7229 2033
📱 07859 896383
✉ sawdon@aol.com
🌐 www.vigisawdon.co.uk
Est. 1994
Services Gilding and restoration of old wooden, gesso and composite mirrors, architectural pieces, frames. Also provides French and Italian paint effects, trompe l'oeil, marble, bamboo
Open By appointment

MARQUETRY

Anthony Allen Conservation, Restoration, Furniture and Artefacts (BAFRA, UKIC)
Contact Anthony Allen
✉ The Old Wharf Workshop, Redmoor Lane, Newtown, High Peak, Derbyshire, SK22 3JL ℗
☎ 01663 745274 ✆ 01663 745274
✉ allen-conservation@tiscali.co.uk
Est. 1970
Services Restoration of 17th–19thC furniture, gilding, marquetry, boulle, upholstery, metalwork, clock cases and movements
Open Mon–Fri 8am–5pm

Anita Marquetry Ltd
Contact Howard Sansome
✉ Unit 5-7, Ddole Enterprise Park, Llandrindod Wells, Powys, LD1 6DF ℗
☎ 01597 825505 ✆ 01597 824484
✉ lear@marquetry.co.uk
🌐 www.marquetry.co.uk
Est. 1990
Services Veneer, marquetry, inlays restored
Open Mon–Fri 9am–5pm

Castle House (BAFRA)
Contact Mr Michael Durkee
✉ Castle House, Units 1 and 3, Bennetts Field Estate, Wincanton, Somerset, BA9 9DT ℗
☎ 01963 33884 ✆ 01963 31278
Est. 1975
Services Antique furniture restoration and conservation
Open Mon–Fri 8.30am–5pm

A Dunn & Son
Contact Mr R Dunn
✉ 8 Wharf Road, Chelmsford, Essex, CM2 6LU ℗
☎ 01245 354452 ✆ 01245 494991
✉ info@adunnandson.co.uk
🌐 www.adunnandson.com
Est. 1896
Services Makers of marquetry and boulle
Open Mon–Fri 8am–6pm
Sat by appointment

Dyson Furniture
Contact Nick Dyson
✉ Eel Pie Boatyard, Eel Pie Island, Twickenham, Middlesex, TW1 3DY
☎ 020 8891 5309
Est. 1992
Services Complete furniture repair and restoration, turning, marquetry, inlay work, cabinet-making
Open Mon–Fri 10am–6pm

Gow Antiques and Restoration (BAFRA)
Contact Jeremy Gow
✉ Pitscandly Farm, Forfar, Angus, DD8 3NZ ℗
☎ 01307 465342 ✆ 01307 468973
📱 07711 416786
✉ jeremy@knowyourantiques.com
🌐 www.knowyourantiques.com
Est. 1991
Services Specialists in restoration of European furniture, 17th–18thC marquetry
Open Mon–Fri 9am–5pm or by appointment

R S M Antique Restoration
Contact Mr Robin Stone
✉ The Stables, Back Eaves Street, Blackpool, Lancashire, FY1 2HW ℗
☎ 01253 623839 ✆ 01253 623839
Est. 1972
Services Antique furniture, clocks, barometer, restoration, marquetry cutting
Open Mon–Fri 9am–6pm

METAL

A B C Restoration Ltd
Contact Chris Christofi
✉ Unit 23a, Rosebury Industrial Park, Rosebury Avenue, Tottenham Hale, London, N17 9SR ℗
☎ 020 8880 9697 ✆ 020 8801 4618
Est. 1999
Services Restoration, repair of lighting, chandeliers, bronzing on metalwork, clocks
Open Mon–Fri 8.30am–5.30pm or by appointment

Antique Renovating
Contact Philip Lennon
✉ 43 Bent Street, Cheetham Hill, Greater Manchester, M8 8NW ℗
☎ 0161 834 8000
Est. 1963
Services Restoration of silver, goldware, brass, copperware, polish, lacquer
Open Mon–Fri 7.30am–4.30pm

John Armistead Restorations
Contact Mr John Armistead
✉ Malham Cottage, Bellingdon, Chesham, Buckinghamshire, HP5 2UR ℗
☎ 01494 758209 ✆ 01494 758209
✉ j.armistead@ntlworld.com
🌐 www.john-armistead-restorations.co.uk
Est. 1979
Services Repair and restoration of all antique metalwork including casting, replacement of missing parts, lighting
Open Mon–Fri 9am–5pm

Bold as Brass Polishers
Contact James Taylor
✉ Unit 13, Visicks Works, Perranarworthal, Truro, Cornwall, TR3 7NR ℗
☎ 01872 864207
Est. 1994
Services Brass, copper, stainless steel and aluminium polishing
Open Please phone before visiting

Brass Foundry Castings Ltd (BAFRA)
Contact Raymond Konyn
✉ PO Box 151, Westerham, Kent, TN16 1YF ℗
☎ 01959 563863 ✆ 01959 561262
✉ info@brasscastings.co.uk
🌐 www.brasscastings.co.uk
Est. 1979
Services Lost-wax castings of period details
Open Mon–Sun 9am–5pm; online and mail order only

Brass & Wood Still Looking Good
Contact Marcus Lee-Adams
✉ Unit 3046,
**20 Deacon Street, Leicester,
Leicestershire,
LE2 7EF** 🄿
☎ 07973 294622
📧 brassandwood.stilllookinggood
@btinternet.com
Est. 2000
Services Metal restoration
Open By appointment

Bristol Restoration Workshop
Contact Mr Hall
✉ **8 Devon Road, Bristol,
BS5 9AD** 🄿
☎ 0117 954 2114 📠 0117 954 2114
📧 bristolrestoration@virgin.net
Est. 1979
Services Metalware restoration and repair
Open Mon–Fri 8am–5pm

Michael Brook Antique Metal Restoration (BAFRA)
Contact Mr M Brook
✉ **London,
SE5**
☎ 020 7708 0467 📠 020 7708 0467
📧 michaelbrook@antiquemetal
restoration.co.uk
🌐 www.antiqueconservation.co.uk
Est. 1988
Services Antique metal restoration, specializing in ormolu cleaning and repair, patination of fine bronzes and English and French metalwork, especially Matthew Boulton. Listed in the Conservation Register
Open By appointment

The Conservation Studio (ICOM, IIC, UKIC)
Contact Mrs F Hayward
✉ **77 Troutbeck, Albany Street,
London,
NW1 4EJ** 🄿
☎ 020 7387 4994 📠 020 7387 4994
📧 flu_flo@yahoo.co.uk
Est. 1993
Services Restoration and conservation of ceramics, glass, metalwork, ivory and soapstone, specializing in gilding, painting on glass and ceramics
Open Mon–Fri 8.30am–4.30pm
Sat by appointment

Devon Metalcraft Ltd (incorporating Suffolk Brass)
Contact Trevor Ford
✉ **2 Victoria Way, Exmouth,
Devon,
EX8 1EW**
☎ 01395 272846 📠 01395 276688
📱 07860 927177
📧 info@devonmetalcrafts.co.uk
🌐 www.devonmetalcrafts.co.uk
Est. 1982
Services Supplies replica cast brass handles from catalogue, make one-off copies of handles to specification
Trade only Yes
Open Mon–Fri 8am–5pm or by appointment

Domino Restorations
Contact Mrs J Hargreaves
✉ **c/o G B Antiques Centre,
Lancaster Leisure Park,
Wyresdale Road, Lancaster,
Lancashire,
LA1 3LA** 🄿
📱 07710 223170
📧 r.j.hargreaves@ic24.net
Est. 1979
Services Porcelain and china restoration, jewellery repair. Repair and restoration of metalware, tortoiseshell and ivory, spelter, bronze
Open By appointment

Richard Elderton
Contact R C Elderton
✉ **Home Farm, Mill Lane,
Hawkley, Liss, Hampshire,
GU33 6NU** 🄿
☎ 01420 538374
📧 woodman@cix.co.uk
🌐 www.cix.co.uk/~woodman/
Est. 1976
Services Antique furniture restoration, new bespoke solid wood furniture, metalworking repair, woodturning
Open Mon–Fri 9am–5pm or by appointment

E Hansen
Contact Mr E Hansen
✉ **103 Priory Road, Hungerford,
Berkshire, RG17 0AW** 🄿
☎ 01488 684772
📱 07885 511986
📧 epgerdes-hans@amserve.net
Est. 1985
Services Metal restoration
Open Mon–Fri 9am–6pm

Rupert Harris Conservation (IIC, UKIC, NACF, SPAB, ICOM)
Contact Cathy Brown
✉ **Unit 5c, 1 Fawe Street,
London,
E14 6PD** 🄿
☎ 020 7987 6231/7515 2020
📠 020 7987 7994
📧 enquiries@rupertharris.com
🌐 www.rupertharris.com
Est. 1982
Services Conservation and restoration of fine metalwork and sculpture
Trade only Yes
Open By appointment

Shawlan Antiques (LAPADA)
Contact Mr Shawn Parmakis
✉ **415a Whitehorse Road,
Thornton Heath, Surrey,
CR7 8SD** 🄿
☎ 020 8684 5082 📠 020 8684 5082
📱 07889 510253
Est. 1974
Services Metal restoration, foundry work, patination, gilding, chasing
Open Mon–Sat 9am–8pm

David Turner Workshops
Contact Mr D Turner
✉ **24 Tottenham Road, London,
N1 4BZ** 🄿
☎ 020 7241 5400 📠 020 7241 5416
📧 mo@davidturner.uk.com
Est. 1987
Services Repair and restoration of metalwork, lighting, decorative antiques, small-scale bespoke lighting commissions
Open Mon–Fri 9.30am–6pm

University of Central England School of Jewellery
Contact Frank Cooper
✉ **Vittoria Street, Birmingham,
B1 3PA**
☎ 0121 248 4582 📠 0121 248 4587
📧 frank.cooper@uce.ac.uk
🌐 www.uce.ac.uk/web2/biad
Est. 1890
Services Comprehensive product replication facilities including 3D laser scanning, rapid prototyping (CAD/CAM), casting, and surface finishing including anodizing for reproduction of small 3D items and interactive display
Open Mon–Fri 9.30am–5pm

MILITARIA

The Queen's Shilling
Contact Mrs A Wolf
✉ 87 Commercial Road, Poole,
Dorset,
BH14 0JD 🅿
☎ 01202 723335
Est. 1986
Services Medal mounting, sew-on blazer badges for uniforms, sells memorabilia, medal framing
Open Mon–Fri 10am–4.30pm
Sat 10am–1pm Wed closed

Chris Rollason Home Counties Medal Services
Contact Mr C Rollason
✉ 53 Bodiam Crescent,
Hampden Park, Eastbourne,
East Sussex,
BN22 9HQ 🅿
☎ 01323 506012
Est. 1979
Services Full-size medals restored and mounted to wear or in frame or case. Miniature dress medals supplied and mounted. Regimental ties, blazer badges, buttons, medal accessories also supplied
Open Mon–Fri 9am–5pm

Ian Whitmore
Contact Ian Whitmore
✉ Hinckley,
Leicestershire,
LE10
☎ 01455 444789
🅔 i.whitmore@ntlworld.com
🅦 www.beam.to/restorer
Est. 1979
Services Specialist gunmaking, restoration of arms and armour
Open By appointment

Robert Williams (BAFRA)
Contact Mr Robert Williams
✉ 32 Church Street,
Willingham, Cambridge,
Cambridgeshire,
CB4 5HT 🅿
☎ 01954 260972
Est. 1980
Services Restoration of carving, ivory, mother-of-pearl, bonework, papier-mâché, tortoiseshell, weapons. Also cabinet-maker and locksmith
Open Mon–Fri 9am–5pm
Sat Sun by appointment

MUSICAL INSTRUMENTS

Cambridge Pianola Company and J V Pianos
Contact Tom Poole
✉ The Limes, High Street,
Landbeach,
Cambridgeshire,
CB4 8DR 🅿
☎ 01223 861348 🅖 01223 441276
🅔 ftpoole@talk21.com
🅦 www.cambridgepianola company.co.uk
Est. 1972
Services Restoration, transport and tuning of pianos
Open By appointment

Peter Casebow (BAFRA)
Contact Mr P Casebow
✉ Pilgrims Mill Lane, Worthing,
West Sussex,
BN13 3DE 🅿
☎ 01903 264045
🅜 07790 339602
🅔 pcasebow@hotmail.com
Est. 1987
Services Restoration of period furniture including square-piano restoration
Open By appointment

A Frayling-Cork (BAFRA)
Contact Mr A Frayling-Cork
✉ 2 Mill Lane, Wallingford,
Oxfordshire,
OX10 0DH 🅿
☎ 01491 826221
Est. 1979
Services Antique furniture repair, restoration, French polishing, metal fittings, specializing in musical instruments
Open By appointment 24hr answerphone

Peter Goodfellow
Contact Peter Goodfellow
✉ Ivybank Croft,
Lochiepots Road,
Miltonduff, Elgin,
Moray,
IV30 8WL 🅿
☎ 01343 545045
🅔 peter@goodfellowviolins.com
🅦 www.goodfellowviolins.com
Est. 1996
Services Restoration of classic and modern violins, violas, cellos. Provides appraisal, valuation, makes new instruments
Open By appointment

Michael Parfett
Contact Mr M Parfett
✉ Unit 1e, 9 Queens Yard,
White Post Lane, London,
E9 5EN 🅿
☎ 020 8985 5882 🅖 020 8985 5882
🅜 07811 435221
🅦 www.michaelparfett.com
Est. 1990
Services Keyboard musical instrument restoration, also harps and stringed instruments, lacquerwork, gilding
Open By appointment

Guinevere Sommers-Hill Violins
Contact Guinevere Sommers-Hill
✉ The Arbery Centre,
Market Place, Wantage,
Oxfordshire,
OX12 8AB 🅿
☎ 01235 770094 🅖 01235 770094
🅔 sommershill@yahoo.com
Est. 2001
Services Violin restoration and repair, bow work, also makes new violins
Open Mon–Fri 9.30am–5pm
Sat 9.30am–12.30pm

ORIENTAL

E & C Royall
Contact Mr C Royall
✉ 10 Waterfall Way,
Medbourne, Market
Harborough, Leicestershire,
LE16 8EE 🅿
☎ 01858 565744
🅔 royall@telco4u.net
Est. 1981
Services Repair and restoration
Open Mon–Fri 9am–5pm or by appointment

PACKERS AND SHIPPERS

Adam Crease Shipping Ltd (BIFA)
Contact Adam Crease or Malcolm Heaton
✉ Unit 15, The Heathrow Estate,
The Parkway, Hounslow,
Middlesex,
TW4 6NQ
☎ 020 8759 6089 🅖 020 8754 7472
🅔 adam@adamcreaseshipping.com
🅦 www.adamcreaseshipping.com
Est. 2003
Services Shipping of fine art and

antiques to the USA: packing, air, sea and road services, storage and installation
Open Mon–Fri 8am–6pm

Good Moves Ltd
Contact Christine Vibert
✉ PO Box 113, Minden Place, St Helier, Jersey,
JE4 2QF 🅿
☎ 01534 769086 📠 01534 769538
✉ admin@goodmoves.co.je
Services Ship anywhere to and from Jersey and Guernsey
Open Mon–Fri 9am–5pm

Rolands Antiques
Contact Marion
✉ Firs Farm, The Square, Thurnby, Leicestershire,
LE7 0PX 🅿
☎ 0116 241 2732 📠 0116 243 1271
✉ rolands@wheadon4792.fsbusiness.co.uk
Est. 1973
Services Collection, packing and shipping of antiques
Open Mon–Fri 9am–5pm

Michael Allcroft Antiques
Contact Michael Allcroft
✉ 203 Buxton Road, Newtown, Disley, Stockport, Cheshire,
SK12 2RA 🅿
☎ 01663 744014 📠 01663 744014
📱 07798 781642
✉ allcroft@aol.com
Est. 1986
Services Packing and export to foreign countries, Victorian-Edwardian English oak and walnut plus mahogany ideal for the Japanese/Korean market
Open Tues–Thurs 11am–5pm Sat 11am–5pm or by appointment

Anglo Pacific International plc. Fine Art Division (LAPADA)
Contact Nick Simmons
✉ Units 1 & 2, Bush Industrial Estate, Standard Road, London,
NW10 6DF 🅿
☎ 020 8838 8008 📠 020 8453 0225
✉ antiques@anglopacific.co.uk
🌐 www.anglopacific.co.uk
Est. 1977
Services Packing, shipping and international removals. Also valuations and restoration
Open Mon–Fri 8.30am–5.30pm

Antique Transport Services
Contact Mr Kennedy
✉ 14 Holmfield Avenue, Bournemouth, Dorset,
BH7 6SF
☎ 01202 482265 📠 01202 482265
📱 07850 477466
✉ billyk6@msn.com
Est. 1989
Services Removal and transportation of fine antiques and art
Open Mon–Fri 9am–6pm

Robert Boys Shipping
Contact Robert Boys
✉ North London Freight Centre, York Way, Kings Cross, London,
N1 0AU 🅿
☎ 020 7837 4806 📠 020 7837 4815
✉ info@robertboysshipping.co.uk
Est. 1989
Services Shipping, packing, forwarding
Open Mon–Fri 8am–6pm

Davies Turner Worldwide Movers Ltd
Contact Olivia Ricordini
✉ 49 Wates Way, Mitcham, Surrey,
CR4 4HR
☎ 0207 622 4393 📠 0207 720 3897
✉ antiques@daviesturner.co.uk
🌐 www.daviesturner.com
Est. 1870
Services Packing, shipping of antiques and fine art throughout the world
Open Mon–Fri 8am–5pm

Derbyshire Removals
Contact Michael Powell
✉ Butterley Cottage, Butterley Lane, Ashover, Derbyshire,
S45 0JU 🅿
☎ 01629 582762/01246 202289
📱 07774 422561
Est. 1987
Services Removal service of antique and fine furniture, packing
Open Ring anytime

Alan Franklin Transport Ltd
Contact Alan Franklin
✉ 26 Blackmoor Road, Verwood, Dorset,
BH31 6BB
☎ 01202 826539 📠 01202 827337

✉ aft@afteurope.co.uk
🌐 www.alanfranklintransport.co.uk
Est. 1975
Services Specialist carriers of antiques and fine art world-wide
Open Mon–Fri 8.30am–5.30pm

Gander & White Shipping Ltd (BADA, LAPADA)
Contact Mr Oliver Howell
✉ Unit 1, St Martins Way, London,
SW17 0JH 🅿
☎ 020 8971 7171 📠 020 8946 8062
✉ info@ganderandwhite.com
🌐 www.ganderandwhite.com
Est. 1933
Services Packing and shipping
Open Mon–Fri 9am–5.30pm

Hedleys Humpers (LAPADA, BADA, BIFA, BAR, IATA)
✉ 3 St Leonards Road, London,
NW10 6SX 🅿
☎ 020 8965 8733 📠 020 8965 0249
✉ mg@hedleyshumpers.com
🌐 www.hedleyshumpers.com
Est. 1973
Services Door-to-door delivery by road, sea and air of single items to full container loads. Arrange collection, export, packing, insurance and all export and customs paperwork on customers' behalf
Open Mon–Fri 8am–6pm

International Furniture Exporters Ltd
Contact Iris Mitchell
✉ Old Cement Works, South Heighton, Newhaven, East Sussex,
BN9 0HS 🅿
☎ 01273 611251 📠 01273 611574
🌐 www.asweb.co.uk/ife
Est. 1990
Services Furniture exporters
Open Mon–Fri 7am–6pm

Kuwahara Ltd (LAPADA, HHGFAA)
Contact Mr S Kuwahara
✉ 6 McNicol Drive, London,
NW10 7AW 🅿
☎ 020 8963 1100 📠 020 8963 0100
✉ info@kuwahara.co.uk
🌐 www.kuwahara.co.uk
Est. 1983
Services Fine art packing and shipping, door-to-door transport

around the world by land,
air or sea
Trade only Yes
Open Mon–Fri 9am–5.30pm

C & N Lawrence
Contact Mr N Lawrence
✉ 7 Church Walk, Brighton Road,
Horley, Surrey,
RH6 7EE 🅿
☎ 01293 783243
Est. 1983
Services Removals, shipping,
packing for antiques trade
Trade only Yes
Open Mon–Fri 9am–5pm

Lockson Services Ltd (LAPADA, BIFA)
Contact Bob King
✉ Unit 1, Heath Park Industrial
Estate, Freshwater Road,
Chadwell Heath, Essex,
RM8 1RX 🅿
☎ 020 8597 2889 📠 020 8597 5265
📱 07831 621428
📧 enquiries@lockson.co.uk
🌐 www.lockson.co.uk
Est. 1943
Services Packers and shippers
Open Mon–Fri 8am–6pm

John Morgan and Sons (FIDI, OMNI, BAR, BAR Overseas Group, HHGFAA)
Contact Mr William Morgan
✉ Removal House,
30 Island Street, Belfast,
Co Antrim,
BT4 1DH 🅿
☎ 028 9073 2333 📠 028 9045 7402
📧 info@morganremovals.com
🌐 www.morganremovals.com
Est. 1915
Services Specialist antique
removals and local, worldwide
household removals
Open Mon–Fri 9am–5.30pm

PDQ Air Freight/Art Move (LAPADA, CINOA, GTA, BIFA, IATA, FIATA, AIMSS)
✉ Unit 4, Court 1, Challenge
Road, Ashford, Middlesex,
TW15 1AX 🅿
☎ 01784 243695 📠 01784 242237
📧 artmove@pdq.uk.com
🌐 www.pdq.uk.com
Est. 1983
Services Packing and shipping,
fair logistics, hand-carry couriers,
bonded warehouse
Open Mon–Fri 9am–5.30pm

Seabourne Mailpack Worldwide Ltd (LAPADA)
Contact Paul Reuby or
Becky Moyce
✉ Unit 13, Saxon Way, Moor
Lane, West Drayton, Middlesex,
UB7 0LW 🅿
☎ 020 8897 3888 📠 020 8322 1701
📧 info@seabourne-mailpack.com
🌐 www.seabourne-mailpack.com
Est. 1962
Services Export packing and
world wide delivery of fine art,
antiques, furniture
Open Mon–Fri 9am–6pm

The Shipping Company
Contact Matt Walton
✉ Bourton Industrial Park,
Bourton-on-the-Water,
Cheltenham, Gloucestershire,
GL54 2HQ 🅿
☎ 01451 822451 📠 01451 810985
📱 07971 425978
📧 enquiries@theshipping
companyltd.com
🌐 www.theshippingcompanyltd.com
Est. 1998
Services Packing and shipping of
antiques worldwide
Open Mon–Fri 9am–6pm
telephone mobile at other times

Sterling Art Services
Contact Oliver Reed
✉ Unit 5, Cypress Court,
Harris Way, Sunbury-on-Thames,
Middlesex,
TW16 7EL 🅿
☎ 01932 771442 📠 01932 771443
📧 sales@sterlingartservices.co.uk
🌐 www.sterlingartservices.co.uk
Est. 2000
Services Specialists packers and
shippers of fine art and antiques
Open Mon–Fri 9am–5pm

Stevens Antiques & Office Removals
Contact Steven McCarrol
✉ 255 Lochburn Road, Glasgow,
G20 0QQ
☎ 0141 332 9797
📱 07778 742150
Est. 1994
Services Antiques removal
service
Open By appointment

A J Williams Shipping (LAPADA)
Contact Jan Ottway
✉ Unit 32, Westfield Trading

Estate, Radstock, Bath
☎ 01761 413976 📠 01761 410868
📧 ajw_4@hotmail.com
Est. 1977
Services Packing and shipping of
antiques and fine art worldwide
Open Mon–Fri 9am–5.30pm or by
appointment

PAINTED FURNITURE

Antique Restorations (BAFRA)
Contact Mr A Smith
✉ Crug-y-deri, Llandissilio,
Pembrokeshire,
SA66 7JJ 🅿
☎ 01437 563334
📧 antiquerestore@aol.com
Est. 1987
Services Restorers of painted and
decorated furniture. Specialists
in Oriental lacquering,
japanning, gilding
Open Mon–Fri 9am–4.30pm or by
appointment

Steven J Cotterell
Contact Steven Cotterell
✉ 72 Springfield Road,
Somersham, Ipswich, Suffolk,
IP8 4PQ 🅿
☎ 01473 831530
📱 07733 291705
📧 somersham.flyer@yahoo.co.uk
Est. 1975
Services French polishing,
furniture restoration and
painting
Open Mon–Sat 7.30am–6pm

Hannerle Dehn
Contact Hannerle Dehn
✉ Studio 4, Southam Street,
London,
W10 5PP 🅿
☎ 020 8964 0599 📠 020 7602 1192
📱 07798 623715
📧 robinersligh@freeserve.co.uk
Est. 1978
Services Restoration of
18th–19thC lacquered and
gilded, painted and decorated
furniture
Open Mon–Fri 7.30am–5pm or by
appointment

Sonia Demetriou
Contact Sonia Demetriou
✉ 2 Elbridge Farm Buildings,
Chichester Road, Bognor Regis,
West Sussex,
PO21 5EG 🅿

ASSOCIATED SERVICES
PAPER

☎ 01243 842235 📠 01243 842235
📧 sondem@intelynx.net
🌐 www.art-scope.co.uk
Est. 1977
Services Restoration of antique painted furniture and objets d'art
Open Mon–Fri 9.30am–6pm
Sat by appointment

T C Hinton
Contact T C Hinton
✉ The Board Stores, Spencer Mews, Rear of 20 Camden Rd, Tunbridge Wells, Kent,
TN1 2PY 🅿
☎ 01892 547515 📠 01892 547515
Est. 1979
Services Restoration and conservation of antique furniture, French polishing, gilding, painted furniture, antique paint effects
Open Mon–Fri 9am–1pm 2–5.30pm

M Tocci
Contact Mr M Tocci
✉ Unit 4, 81 Southern Row, London,
W10 5AL 🅿
☎ 020 8960 4826
Est. 1978
Services Gilding, painted furniture restoration, lacquer on furniture and decorations
Open Mon–Fri 7.30am–4.30pm

PAPER

Cameron Preservation (IPCRA, IPC, SAPCON)
Contact Mr Elgin Cameron
✉ Flush Business Centre, Flush Place, Lurgan, Co Armagh,
BT66 7DT 🅿
☎ 028 3834 3099 📠 028 3834 3099
Est. 1993
Services Restoration of art on paper, archives, manuscripts, books, also vellum, parchment, globes
Open Mon–Fri 8.30am–5.15
Sat 8.30am–noon

Voitek Conservation of Works of Art (IPC)
Contact Mrs E Sobczynski
✉ 9 Whitehorse Mews, Westminster Bridge Road, London,
SE1 7QD 🅿
☎ 020 7928 6094 📠 020 7928 6094
📧 voitekcwa@btinternet.com
Est. 1972

Services Conservation and restoration of marble, stone, terracotta, wood
Open By appointment

PAPIER MACHE

Zygmunt Chelminski (UKIC)
Contact Mr Z Chelminski
✉ Studio GE1, 2 Michael Road, London,
SW6 2AD 🅿
☎ 020 7610 9731 📠 020 7610 9731
📱 07770 585130
Est. 1993
Services Restoration and conservation of architectural monuments, statues and special effects in marble, granite, stone, terracotta, alabaster, coldstone, iron, bronze, zinc, lead, ormolu, wood, ivory, pietra dura, scagliola, plaster, mother-of-pearl, tortoiseshell, shagreen, amber, onyx, papier-mâché, blue john and semi-precious stones
Open Mon–Fri 10am–5pm appointment advisable

W H Earles
Contact Mr W H Earles
✉ 60 Castle Road, Tankerton, Whitstable, Kent,
CT5 2EA 🅿
☎ 01227 264346
Est. 1978
Services English, Continental and most period furniture restoration and papier-mâché
Open Mon–Fri 8.30am–6pm

Robert Williams (BAFRA)
Contact Mr Robert Williams
✉ 32 Church Street, Willingham, Cambridge, Cambridgeshire,
CB4 5HT 🅿
☎ 01954 260972
Est. 1980
Services Restoration of carving, ivory, mother-of-pearl, bonework, papier-mâché, tortoiseshell, weapons. Also cabinet-maker and locksmith
Open Mon–Fri 9am–5pm
Sat Sun by appointment

PICTURE RESTORATION

Roger Allan
Contact Mr R Allan
✉ The Old Red Lion, Bedingfield,

Eye, Suffolk,
IP23 7LQ 🅿
☎ 01728 628491
Est. 1973
Services Picture restorer, furniture restorer
Trade only Yes
Open By appointment

Antique China and Porcelain Restoration
Contact Mr Carl Garratt
✉ The Green Willow, Victoria Square, Evercreech, Shepton Mallet, Somerset,
BA4 6LL 🅿
☎ 01749 831116
Est. 1978
Services Restoration of antique china, oil paintings and objets d'art
Open By appointment

Baron Art
Contact Mr A Baron
✉ 9 and 16 Chapel Yard, Albert Street, Holt , Norfolk,
NR25 6HG 🅿
☎ 01263 713430 📠 01263 711670
📧 baronholt@aol.com
Est. 2001
Services Restoration of antiquarian books, paintings, ceramics, plus framing
Open Mon–Sat 9am–5pm

Keith Bawden (BAFRA)
Contact Keith Bawden
✉ Mews Workshops, Montpellier Retreat, Cheltenham, Gloucestershire,
GL50 2XG 🅿
☎ 01242 230320 or 01452 863566
Est. 1975
Services Full antique restoration service of furniture, clocks, watercolours, jewellery, ceramics and Oriental carpets, silver, plating, committed to conservation and under-restoring on principle
Open By appointment phone first

Burghley Fine Art Conservation Ltd
Contact Mike Cowell
✉ The Stable Courtyard, Burghley House, Stamford, Lincolnshire,
PE9 3JY 🅿

☎ 01780 762155 ✆ 01780 762155
Est. 1977
Services Restoration of oil paintings and picture frames
Open By appointment

Glebe Hall Restoration Studios
Contact Carmel Corrigan-Griffin
✉ Old Killernogh Rectory, Rathnakelly Glebe, Ballacolla, Co Laois, Ireland ▣
☎ 0502 34105 ✆ 0502 34105
📱 0868 784956
Est. 1980
Services Furniture restoration, gilding, porcelain, ivory, jade
Open By appointment, Sat 11am–4pm

Greenwich Conservation Workshops
Contact Richard Moy
22 Nelson Road, London, SE10 9JB ▣
☎ 020 8293 1067
🌐 www.spreadeagle.org
Est. 1957
Services Restoration of period furniture, oil, watercolours, picture frames, porcelain, pottery
Open Mon–Sat 10.30am–5.30pm

H J Hatfield and Son
✉ 42 St Michael's Street, London, W2 1QP ▣
☎ 020 7723 8265 ✆ 020 7706 4562
✉ admin@hjhatfield.com
🌐 www.hjhatfield.com
Est. 1834
Services Restoration of furniture, porcelain, paintings, boulle, upholstery, lacquerwork, metalwork, chandeliers, marble
Open Mon–Fri 8am–1pm 2–5pm (moving soon check via phone or website before visiting)

Inglenook Fine Arts (FATG)
Contact Jill Bagshaw
✉ 31 Pillory Street, Nantwich, Cheshire, CW5 5BQ ▣
☎ 01270 611188
✉ info@inglenookfinearts.co.uk
🌐 www.inglenookfinearts.com
Est. 1993
Services Picture restoration, framing
Open Mon–Sat 9.30am–5pm Wed closed 1pm

Inglenook Fine Arts (FATG)
Contact Gerry Bagshaw
✉ Greenend Gallery, Greenend, Whitchurch, Shropshire, SY13 1AA ▣
☎ 01948 665422 ✆ 01948 665422
✉ info@inglenookfinearts.co.uk
🌐 www.inglenookfinearts.com
Est. 1985
Services Picture restoration, framing
Open Mon–Sat 9.30am–5pm Wed closed 1pm

Plowden and Smith Ltd (MGR)
Contact Sarah Giles
✉ 190 St Ann's Hill, London, SW18 2RT ▣
☎ 020 8874 4005 ✆ 020 8874 7248
✉ info@plowden-smith.com
🌐 www.plowden-smith.com
Est. 1966
Services Repair and restoration of paintings, furniture, stone, metalwork, decorative arts, object mounting, exhibitions
Open Mon–Fri 9am–5pm

Regency Restoration
Contact Mrs E Ball
✉ Arch 72, Ingate Place, London, SW8 3NS ▣
☎ 020 7622 5275 or 020 7828 4268
Est. 1987
Services Restoration of 18th–19thC mirrors, picture frames, English and Continental painted and gilded furniture, architectural gilding, church interiors, polychrome sculpture, lacquerwork, oil paintings, carving
Open Mon–Fri 9.30am–5.30pm

RSB Antiques
Contact Richard Baker
✉ 30 Dover Road, Walmer, Deal, Kent, CT14 7JW ▣
☎ 01304 374082
✉ richardsbaker@yahoo.co.uk
Est. 1985
Services Restoration and cleaning of pictures and 18th–19thC gilt frames
Open By appointment

Siracusa Paintings Ltd
Contact Alyson Lawrence
✉ Lev Antiques Ltd, 97a Kensington Church Street, London, W8 7LN ▣
☎ 020 7727 9248
📱 07768 470473
✉ alyson@richardlawrence.co.uk
Est. 1984
Services Restoration of 17th–20thC oil paintings
Open Tues–Sat 10.30am–5.45pm or by appointment

Andrew Wheeler (IOC)
Contact Andrew Wheeler
✉ 3 Wapping Road, Harbourside, Bristol, BS1 4BH ▣
☎ 0117 942 3003
✉ andrewwheeler123@yahoo.co.uk
🌐 www.fine-art-on-paper-restoration.co.uk
Est. 1970
Services Restoration of fine prints, watercolours, drawings
Open Mon–Fri 9am–5pm but phone first

PINE

Christopher John Douglas
Contact Mr C J Douglas
✉ Befferlands Farm Workshop, Berne Lane, Charmouth, Bridport, Dorset, DT6 6RD ▣
☎ 01297 561120
📱 07989 161019
Est. 1975
Services Restoration of antique furniture, old pine, Art Deco
Open Mon–Fri 9am–5.30pm

Oldwoods Furniture
Contact Sid Duck
✉ Unit 4, Colston Yard, Colston Street, Bristol, BS1 5BD ▣
☎ 0117 929 9023
Est. 1980
Services Furniture repair and restoration, buying and selling
Open Mon–Fri 9am–5pm but phone first

The Pine Mine
Contact Mr Caspian Crewe-Read
✉ 100 Wandsworth Bridge Road, London, SW6 2TF ▣
☎ 020 7736 1092 ✆ 020 7736 5283

@ pinemine@hotmail.com
Est. 1972
Services Country furniture and
antique pine repair and
restoration, bespoke furniture
maker
Open Mon–Sat 9.30am–5.30pm
Sun 11am–4pm

Ed Thomas Old Country Pine
Contact Mr E Thomas
✉ 22 Old Hednesford Road,
Cannock, Staffordshire,
WS11 6LD ℗ ☎ 01543 506731
Ⓜ 07966 243477
@ edthomasoldcountrypine@
lycos.co.uk
Est. 1981
Services Made-to-measure pine
furniture using only old original
pine.
Open Mon–Sat 9am–5.30pm

Wood Be Good
Contact Dennis Langford or
John Ball
✉ 1 Jarrow Road, London,
SE16 3JR ℗
☎ 020 7232 2639 ℗ 020 8657 6610
Ⓜ 07831 657357
@ john.rw.ball@bluewonder.co.uk
Est. 1984
Services Pine furniture repair
and restoration, pine stripping
Open Mon–Fri 7am–5pm but
phone first

PLASTERWORK

Seamas O'Heocha Teoranta (IPCRA, Irish Georgian Society, An Taisce, Dublin Civic Trust)
Contact Seamas O'Heocha
✉ Corbally, Barna, Galway,
Ireland ℗
☎ 091 590256 ℗ 091 590256
Ⓜ 0872 581150
@ info@seamasoheochateo.com
Ⓦ www.soheochateo.com
Est. 1987
Services Ornate plasterwork
restoration and conservation,
contractors and consultants
Open Mon–Fri 9am–6pm or by
appointment

Taylor Pearce Restoration Services Ltd (UKIC)
Contact Mr K Taylor
✉ Fishers Court, Besson Street,
London,

SE14 5AF ℗
☎ 020 7252 9800 ℗ 020 7277 8169
@ admin@taylorpearce.co.uk
Est. 1985
Services Sculpture, conservation
and restoration of stone, bronze,
plaster and terracotta. By
appointment to HM Queen
Open By appointment

RUGS AND CARPETS

The Rug Studio
Contact Rachel Bassill
✉ First floor, Building A,
Oriental Carpet Centre,
105 Eade Road, London,
N4 1TJ ℗
☎ 020 8977 4403
@ info@therugstudio.co.uk
Ⓦ www.therugstudio.co.uk
Est. 1994
Services Rug cleaning,
restoration, bespoke, valuation,
duplication, hire service
Open Mon–Sat by appointment

SCIENTIFIC

The Barometer Shop (BWCG)
Contact Colin or Verity Jones
✉ 25 New Street, Leominster,
Herefordshire,
HR6 8DP ℗
☎ 01568 613652
Est. 1969
Services Supply and restoration
of antique mercurial, aneroid
barometers, clocks and watches,
furniture, ceramics, French
polishing, wood finishing, dial
painting
Open Mon–Fri 9am–5pm
Sat 10am–4pm

Nationwide Barometers
Contact David Newton
✉ 16 New Street, Honiton,
Devon,
EX14 1EY ℗
☎ 01404 47466 ℗ 01404 47466
Ⓦ www.barometerparts.co.uk
Est. 2004
Services Barometer parts
suppliers, scientific glass blowers
Open Mon–Fri 9am–5pm
Sat 9am–3pm closed Thurs

Gordon Richardson
Contact Gordon Richardson
✉ 36 Silverknowes Road,
Edinburgh,

EH4 5LG ℗
☎ 0131 312 7959
Services Conservation and
restoration of paintings, pictures,
prints, drawings, globes,
scientific instruments, silverware,
metalware, military artefacts,
ships' models, decorative objects
Open By appointment

Russell Scientific Instruments Ltd
Contact Edward Allen
✉ Rash's Green Industrial Estate,
Dereham, Norfolk,
NR19 1JG ℗
☎ 01362 693481 ℗ 01362 698548
@ sales@russell-scientific.co.uk
Ⓦ www.russell-scientific.co.uk
Est. 1862
Services Restoration of antique
barometers, barographs,
meteorological equipment,
thermometers
Open Mon–Fri 9am–4pm

Weather House Antiques
Contact Kym Walker
✉ Foster Clough, Hebden Bridge,
West Yorkshire,
HX7 5QZ ℗
☎ 01422 882808/886961
(workshop) ℗ 01422 882808
Ⓜ 07801 071710
@ kymwalker@btinternet.com
Est. 1986
Services Barometer restoration
Open By appointment only

SCULPTURE

Graciela Ainsworth (SSCR, UKIC)
Contact Graciela
✉ Unit 4 & 10 Bonnington Mill,
72 Newhaven Road, Edinburgh,
EH6 5QG ℗
☎ 0131 555 1294 ℗ 0131 467 7080
@ graciela@graciela-ainsworth.com
Est. 1990
Services Conservation of statues,
monuments, stone sculptures,
including marble plus
plasterwork, carving commissions
Open Mon–Fri 9am–6pm

Rupert Harris Conservation (IIC, UKIC, NACF, SPAB, ICOM)
Contact Cathy Brown
✉ Unit 5c, 1 Fawe Street,
London,
E14 6PD ℗

☎ 020 7987 6231/7515 2020
☎ 020 7987 7994
✉ enquiries@rupertharris.com
🌐 www.rupertharris.com
Est. 1982
Services Conservation and restoration of fine metalwork and sculpture
Trade only Yes
Open By appointment

Taylor Pearce Restoration Services Ltd (UKIC)
Contact Mr K Taylor
✉ Fishers Court, Besson Street, London, SE14 5AF 🅿
☎ 020 7252 9800 ☎ 020 7277 8169
✉ admin@taylorpearce.co.uk
Est. 1985
Services Sculpture, conservation and restoration of stone, bronze, plaster and terracotta. By appointment to HM Queen
Open By appointment

Voitek Conservation of Works of Art (IPC)
Contact Mrs E Sobczynski
✉ 9 Whitehorse Mews, Westminster Bridge Road, London, SE1 7QD 🅿
☎ 020 7928 6094 ☎ 020 7928 6094
✉ voitekcwa@btinternet.com
Est. 1972
Services Conservation of sculpture, marble, terracotta, wood
Open By appointment

SEARCH SERVICE

Antique Finder
Contact Linda Chapple
✉ Boxhurst, Sandhurst, Cranbrook, Kent, TN18 5PE 🅿
☎ 01580 850219
✉ linda.boxhurst@virgin.net
📱 07979 957359
Est. 1995
Services Finds antiques
Open By appointment

Jonathan Brearley Antiques
Contact Jonathan Brearley
✉ 17 High Street, Linton, Swadlincote, Derbyshire, DE12 6QL 🅿
☎ 01283 763233
📱 07973 862040

✉ jbrearley@aol.com
Est. 1995
Services Search service for individuals and companies extending to items to create an Edwardian or Regency room
Open Mon–Sat 9am–6pm

Era Vintage Boutique
Contact Donna Kettlewell
✉ 1 Victoria Road, Saltaire, West Yorkshire, BD13 3LA 🅿
☎ 01274 598777
✉ info@eravintage.fsbusiness.co.uk
🌐 www.cissieandbertha.com
Est. 1991
Services Sourcing 1920s–1970s textiles, home furnishings, jewellery, clothing
Open Mon–Sun noon–5pm

ukauctioneers.com
Contact Eileen McCarthy
✉ The Old Hare and Hounds, 24 Old Wrexham Road, Chester, Cheshire, CH4 7HS
☎ 01244 680587
📱 07860 123421
✉ info@ukauctioneers.com
🌐 www.ukauctioneers.com
Est. 1998
Services Search facility and on-line commission bidding
Open Mon–Fri 9am–5pm

SILVER

F W Aldridge Ltd
Contact Miss Angela Garwood
✉ Unit 3, St Johns Industrial Estate, Dunmow Road, Takeley, Essex, CM22 6SP 🅿
☎ 01279 874000 ☎ 01279 874002
✉ angela@fwaldridge.abel.co.uk
🌐 www.fwaldridgeglass.com
Est. 1926
Services Repair and restoration of glass, supply of Bristol glass for antique and modern table silverware, all glass and silver restoration, plating and repair service
Open Mon–Fri 9am–5.30pm

Antique Renovating
Contact Philip Lennon
✉ 43 Bent Street, Cheetham Hill, Greater Manchester, M8 8NW 🅿
☎ 0161 834 8000

Est. 1963
Services Restoration of silver, goldware, brass, copperware, polish, lacquer
Open Mon–Fri 7.30am–4.30pm

Keith Bawden (BAFRA)
Contact Keith Bawden
✉ Mews Workshops, Montpellier Retreat, Cheltenham, Gloucestershire, GL50 2XG 🅿
☎ 01242 230320 or 01452 863566
Est. 1975
Services Full antique restoration service of furniture, clocks, watercolours, jewellery, ceramics and Oriental carpets, silver, plating, committed to conservation and under-restoring on principle
Open By appointment phone first

Barry Papworth (NAG)
Contact Steve Park
✉ 28 St Thomas Street, Lymington, Hampshire, SO41 9NE 🅿
☎ 01590 676422
Est. 1978
Services Restoration of jewellery and silver. Workshop on site
Open Mon–Sat 9.15am–5.15pm

B M Witmond (Freeman of the Goldsmiths Company)
Contact Barry Witmond
✉ The Stable Courtyard, Burghley House, Stamford, Lincolnshire, PE9 3JY 🅿
☎ 01780 480868 ☎ 01780 480866
📱 07774 870513
✉ silversmiths@bmwitmond.co.uk
🌐 www.bmwitmond.co.uk
Est. 1976
Services Manufacture and restoration of tortoiseshell, restoration of ivory and English and Continental plate, jewellery and flatware, jewellery manufacture
Open By appointment

STONEWORK

Lorna Barnes Conservation (IPCRA, ICOM)
Contact Lorna Barnes
✉ 158 Rialto Cottages, Rialto, Dublin 8,

ASSOCIATED SERVICES
STRIPPING

Ireland 🅿
☎ 01 473 6205
📧 barneslorna@hotmail.com
Est. 2000
Services Conservation of glass, ceramic and stone objects, condition surveys, advice on packaging and storage
Open Mon–Fri 9am–6pm

Zygmunt Chelminski (UKIC)
Contact Mr Z Chelminski
✉ **Studio GE1, 2 Michael Road, London,**
SW6 2AD 🅿
☎ 020 7610 9731 📠 020 7610 9731
📱 07770 585130
Est. 1993
Services Restoration and conservation of architectural monuments, statues and special effects in marble, granite, stone, terracotta, alabaster, coldstone, iron, bronze, zinc, lead, ormolu, wood, ivory, pietra dura, scagliola, plaster, mother-of-pearl, tortoiseshell, shagreen, amber, onyx, papier-mâché, blue john and semi-precious stones
Open Mon–Fri 10am–5pm appointment advisable

London Stone Conservation (SPAB)
Contact Florian Kirchertz
✉ **42 Sekforde Street, Finsbury, London,**
EC1R 0AH 🅿
☎ 020 7251 0592 📠 020 7251 0592
📱 07876 685470
📧 lsc@londonstoneconservation.com
🌐 www.londonstone conservation.co.uk
Est. 2004
Services Conservation and restoration of ancient buildings, monuments, masonry, stone carving, letters
Open By appointment

Plowden and Smith Ltd (MGR)
Contact Sarah Giles
✉ **190 St Ann's Hill, London,**
SW18 2RT 🅿
☎ 020 8874 4005 📠 020 8874 7248
📧 info@plowden-smith.com
🌐 www.plowden-smith.com
Est. 1966
Services Repair and restoration of paintings, furniture, stone,

metalwork, decorative arts, object mounting, exhibitions
Open Mon–Fri 9am–5pm

Q W Conservation (OCS, UKIC)
Contact Toby Quartly-Watson
✉ **Studio 5 (2nd Floor), Hewlett House, Havelock Terrace, London,**
SW8 4AS 🅿
☎ 020 7498 5938 📠 020 7498 5938
📱 07814 687213
📧 stylish.moves@virgin.net
Est. 1991
Services Conservation and restoration of stone sculpture
Open Mon–Fri 10am–6pm or by appointment

Taylor Pearce Restoration Services Ltd (UKIC)
Contact Mr K Taylor
✉ **Fishers Court, Besson Street, London,**
SE14 5AF 🅿
☎ 020 7252 9800 📠 020 7277 8169
📧 admin@taylorpearce.co.uk
Est. 1985
Services Sculpture, conservation and restoration of stone, bronze, plaster and terracotta. By appointment to HM Queen
Open By appointment

Voitek Conservation of Works of Art
Contact Mr W Sobczynski
✉ **9 Whitehorse Mews, Westminster Bridge Road, London,**
SE1 7QD 🅿
☎ 020 7928 6094 📠 020 7928 6094
📧 voitekcwa@btinternet.com
Est. 1972
Services Conservation and restoration of marble, stone, terracotta, wood
Open By appointment

Gwyn Watkins Stonemason and Architectural Stone Carver
Contact Gwyn Watkins
✉ **Stonemason's Shop, Burghley House, Stamford, Lincolnshire,**
PE9 3JY 🅿
☎ 01780 766366
Est. 1988
Services Restoration and repair of garden statuary. Work on

listed buildings, repainting, repairing stonework, fireplaces
Open By appointment

STRIPPING

Acorn Antique Interiors
Contact Brian or Margaret
✉ **Eddystone Road, Wadebridge, Cornwall,**
PL27 7AL 🅿
☎ 01208 812815
Est. 1982
Services Paint stripping
Open Mon–Sat 9am–5pm

Back to the Wood
Contact Mr J Davis
✉ **Country House,**
251 Uxbridge Road, Rickmansworth, Hertfordshire,
WD3 2DP 🅿
☎ 01923 222943
📱 07976 297008
🌐 www.hertsdoorstripping.co.uk
Est. 1981
Services Pine stripping, Victorian–Edwardian fireplaces a speciality
Open Mon–Sat 10am–5pm

E Carty
Contact Mr E Carty
✉ **51 Trinity Street, Gainsborough, Lincolnshire,**
DN21 1JF 🅿
☎ 01427 614452
📱 07733 474895 or 07929 973657
Est. 1976
Services Stripping and restoration
Open Mon–Sat 10am–6pm

Chemicals Ltd
Contact John Foster
✉ **Southport, Merseyside,**
PR8 5LF 🅿
☎ 01704 890800 📠 01704 890900
📧 sales@paramose.com
🌐 www.paintstripper.com
Est. 1982
Services Original and water washable strippers, Paramose stripping machines, restoration materials
Open Mon–Fri 9am–5pm phone first for directions

Chiltern Strip & Polish
Contact Mr B Black
✉ **Kitchener Works, Kitchener Road, High Wycombe, Buckinghamshire,**

HP11 2SJ 🅿
☎ 01494 438052
Est. 1986
Services Non-caustic stripping, repair and repolishing. Sale of antique furniture
Open Mon–Fri 9am–5pm Sat 9am–noon

Cleveland Wood Strip
Contact Mr P Stokes
✉ 2 Kensington Road, Oxbridge, Stockton-on-Tees, North Yorkshire, TS18 4DQ 🅿
☎ 01642 643033
📱 07980 031169
Est. 1989
Services French polishing, dip and strip, architectural restoration
Open Mon–Sat 10am–5pm but phone first please

Cottage Antiques
Contact Angelica Slater
✉ 788 Rochdale Road, Walsden, Todmorden, Lancashire, OL14 7UA 🅿
☎ 01706 813612 📠 01706 813612
📱 07773 798032
🌐 www.ukcottageantiques.co.uk
Services Stripping, polishing, renovations, paint finishes, custom-built furniture
Open Tues–Sun 9.30am–5.30pm

The Door Stripping Company Ltd
Contact Mr B Findley
✉ 32 Main Road, Renishaw, Sheffield, South Yorkshire, S21 3UT 🅿
☎ 01246 435521
Est. 1984
Services Pine stripping, non-caustic restoration of furniture
Open Mon–Fri 9am–5pm Sat–Sun 11am–2pm

Holme Valley Warehouse
Contact Paula Moss or Michael Silkstone
✉ 11 Westgate, Honley, Holmfirth, Huddersfield, West Yorkshire, HD9 1AA 🅿
☎ 01484 667915 📠 01484 667915
Est. 1995
Services Pine stripping and restoration
Open Mon–Sun 10am–5pm

Miracle Stripping
Contact Mr C Howes or Mr A Howes
✉ The Cottage, Woodhall Farm, Hatfield, Hertfordshire, AL9 5NU 🅿
☎ 01707 270587 📠 01707 270587
📱 07790 696631/ 07790 696631
Est. 1992
Services Stripping of doors, cast-iron fireplaces etc
Open Mon–Fri 8.30am–5pm

Myriad
Contact Karen Montlake
✉ 48–54 Milford Street, Salisbury, Wiltshire, SP1 2BP 🅿
☎ 01722 413595/718203 (evenings)
📠 01722 416395
📧 enquiries@myriad-antiques.co.uk
🌐 www.myriad-antiques.co.uk
Est. 1994
Services Paint and varnish stripping of furniture and doors, caustic and non-caustic processes, full restoration
Open Mon–Sat 9.30am–5pm Sun by appointment

Mr Pickett's
Contact Mr M Pickett
✉ The Lifestyle Centre, Bosham Roundabout, Delling Lane, Bosham, Nr Chichester, West Sussex, PO18 8NN 🅿
☎ 01243 574573 📠 01243 574573
📱 07779 997012
📧 info@mrpicketts.co.uk
🌐 www.mrpicketts.co.uk
Est. 1991
Services Paint stripping, sanding, waxing, full restoration, bespoke items made to order from reclaimed pine
Open By appointment

Popes Farm Antique Pine & Stripping
Contact Peter Thompson
✉ Popes Farm, Windmill Hill, Hailsham, East Sussex, BN27 4RS 🅿
☎ 01323 832159
📧 peter@popesfarm.co.uk
🌐 www.popesfarm.co.uk
Est. 1973
Services Pine stripping
Open Mon–Fri 8.30am–5pm Sat 8.30am–4pm

Salisbury Stripping Co
Contact Karen Montlake
✉ 48–54 Milford Street, Salisbury, Wiltshire, SP1 2BP 🅿
☎ 01722 413595/718203 (evenings)
📠 01722 416395
📧 enquiries@myriad-antiques.co.uk
🌐 www.myriad-antiques.co.uk
Est. 1994
Services Paint and varnish stripping of furniture and doors, caustic and non-caustic processes, full restoration
Open Mon–Sat 9.30am–5pm Sun by appointment

Strip and Polish
Contact David Vale
✉ Unit 24, Lye Valley Industrial Estate, Lye, Stourbridge, West Midlands, DY9 8HX 🅿
☎ 01384 891777 📠 01384 892174
📱 07790 312379
📧 stripandpolish@hotmail.com
Est. 1999
Services Repair and restoration, French polishing, upholstery and paint finishing
Open Mon–Fri 9am–5pm weekend by arrangement

Strip Easy Ltd
Contact R Belfield
✉ Godleton Farm, Silver Street, Sway, Lymington, Hampshire, SO41 6DJ 🅿
☎ 0203 8033 2293
Est. 1978
Services Restoration pine furniture, paint stripping
Open Mon–Sat 9am–5pm

Strip It Ltd
Contact Mr Panton
✉ 109–111 Pope Street, Birmingham, West Midlands, B13 3AG 🅿
☎ 0121 243 4000
🌐 www.stripit.biz
Est. 1983
Services Stripping furniture, restoration
Open Mon–Sat 8am–5.30pm

The Stripper
Contact Mr K Pinder
✉ Sneaton Lane, Ruswarp, Whitby, North Yorkshire, YO22 5HL 🅿

ASSOCIATED SERVICES
SUPPLIERS

☎ 01947 820035/880966
Est. 1995
Services Stripping of furniture, doors, furniture, renovation
Open Mon–Fri 8am–6pm Sat 8am–noon

The Stripping Store
Contact Jeff Low
✉ 10 Backcauseway Street, Parkhead, Glasgow, G32 5HE 🅿
☎ 0141 550 8195
⑩ 07733 305145
Est. 1997
Services Hand stripping of period and traditional furniture
Open Mon–Sat 10am–6pm

Strippit
Contact Mr Sage
✉ 212 High Street, Herne Bay, Kent, CT6 5AX 🅿
☎ 01227 741759
Services Pine stripping service
Open Mon–Sat 10am–5pm closed Thurs pm

Timber Restorations
Contact Mr S Shannon
✉ Hyde Hall Barn, Sandon, Buntingford, Hertfordshire, SG9 0RU 🅿
☎ 01763 274849 ☎ 01763 274849
⑩ 07973 748644
🄴 info@timberrestorations.co.uk
⑩ www.timberrestorations.co.uk
Est. 1997
Services Spray lacquering, French polishing, furniture repair, caustic and non-caustic stripping, wax polishing, furniture sales, leather top inlay
Open Mon–Sat 9am–5pm

Windsor Antiques
Contact Mr G Henderson
✉ Rosemary Farm, Rosemary Lane, Castle Hedingham, Halstead, Essex, CO9 3AJ 🅿
☎ 01787 461653
Est. 1981
Services Door and furniture stripping
Open By appointment

York Vale (GADAR)
Contact Mr Evely
✉ Unit 6a, Victoria Farm, Water Lane, York, North Yorkshire, YO30 6PQ 🅿

☎ 01904 690561
🄴 yorkvale@hotmail.com
Est. 1984
Services Pine stripping, antique repair and restoration, new hand-made kitchens
Open Mon–Fri 9am–5.30pm Sat 9am–2.30pm

SUPPLIERS

Addington Supplies
Contact Pam Warner
✉ 1 Addington Cottages, Upottery, Honiton, Devon, EX14 9PN 🅿
☎ 01404 861519 ☎ 01404 861308
🄴 pam@addingtonstudio.co.uk
⑩ www.addingtonstudio.co.uk
Est. 1991
Services Supplies for ceramic conservators
Open By appointment

Antique Leather Dressing
Contact Val Pringle
✉ PO Box 67, Langport, Somerset, TA10 9WJ
☎ 01458 241816
⑩ 07947 277833
🄴 sales@antiqueleatherdressing.co.uk
⑩ www.antiqueleatherdressing.co.uk
Est. 2003
Services Leather dressing products, including Pecard
Open Please telephone or e-mail

C & A J Barmby
Contact C Barmby
✉ 140 Lavender Hill, Tonbridge, Kent, TN9 2AY
☎ 01732 771590 ☎ 01732 771590
🄴 bookpilot@aol.com
Est. 1970
Services Reference books on antiques, display stands, accessories, packaging material
Trade only Yes
Open By appointment

Richard Barry Southern Marketing Ltd
Contact Mr Richard Fill
✉ Unit 1–2, Chapel Place, North Street, Portslade, Brighton, East Sussex, BN41 1DR 🅿
☎ 01273 419471 ☎ 01273 421925
🄴 sales@richardbarry.co.uk
⑩ www.richardbarry.co.uk
Est. 1978

Services Suppliers to the antiques trade of all wood-finishing materials
Open Mon–Fri 8am–5pm

Brass Foundry Castings Ltd (BAFRA)
Contact Raymond Konyn
✉ PO Box 151, Westerham, Kent, TN16 1YF
☎ 01959 563863 ☎ 01959 561262
🄴 info@brasscastings.co.uk
⑩ www.brasscastings.co.uk
Est. 1979
Services Cast brass period fittings
Open Mon–Sun 9am–5pm; online and mail order only

Chemicals Ltd
Contact John Foster
✉ Southport, Merseyside, PR8 5LF 🅿
☎ 01704 890800 ☎ 01704 890900
🄴 sales@paramose.com
⑩ www.paintstripper.com
Est. 1982
Services Original and water washable strippers, Paramose stripping machines, restoration materials
Open Mon–Fri 9am–5pm phone first for directions

Classic Finishes
Contact Mark Baker
✉ 140–146 Oak Street, Norwich, Norfolk, NR3 3BP 🅿
☎ 01603 760374 ☎ 01603 660477
⑩ www.classicfinishes.co.uk
Est. 1987
Services Restoration materials, advice, specialist paints, French and wax polishes
Open Mon–Fri 8.30am–5pm Sat 9am–1pm

Devon Metalcraft Ltd (incorporating Suffolk Brass)
Contact Trevor Ford
✉ 2 Victoria Way, Exmouth, Devon, EX8 1EW
☎ 01395 272846 ☎ 01395 276688
⑩ 07860 927177
🄴 info@devonmetalcrafts.co.uk
⑩ www.devonmetalcrafts.co.uk
Est. 1982
Services Supplies replica cast brass handles from catalogue, make one-off copies of handles to specification

Trade only Yes
Open Mon–Fri 8am–5pm or by appointment

Former Glory
Contact Tim or Kim Ravenscroft
✉ Ferndown, Dorset, BH22 🅿
☎ 01202 895859 ℻ 01202 895859
✉ formerglory@btinternet.com
🌐 www.formerglory.co.uk
Est. 1994
Services Cane and rush seating, furniture restoration. Cane, rush and restoration material supplies
Open By appointment only

Mach Upholstery
Contact Oliver Hubbard
✉ No 1 Londonderry Terrace, Machynlleth, Powys, SY20 8BG 🅿
☎ 01654 703568 ℻ 01654 703840
Est. 1994
Services Upholstery supplies
Open Mon–Fri 9am–5.30pm

Rod Naylor
Contact Angela Naylor
✉ 208 Devizes Road, Hilperton, Trowbridge, Wiltshire, BA14 7QP 🅿
☎ 01225 754497 ℻ 01225 754497
✉ rod.naylor@virgin.net
🌐 www.rodnaylor.com
Est. 1970
Services Restoration of antique wood carvings, supplies replicas of hard-to-find items and materials for caddies, boxes, desks etc, cabinet-making, supplier of power carving machinery and tools
Open By appointment only

John Penny Antique Services
Contact Mr J Penny
✉ Unit 10, City Industrial Park, Southern Road, Southampton, Hampshire, SO15 0HA 🅿
☎ 023 8023 2066 ℻ 023 8021 2129
Est. 1981
Services Suppliers of furniture restoration materials
Open Mon–Fri 9am–5pm
Sat 9am–12.30pm

TAXIDERMY

Heads 'n' Tails (Guild of Taxidermists)
Contact David McKinley

✉ Wivelscombe, Somerset, TA4 🅿
☎ 01984 623097 ℻ 01984 624445
✉ mac@taxidermyuk.com
🌐 www.taxidermyuk.com
Est. 1981
Services Taxidermy, natural history specimens
Open By appointment

TEXTILES

Jocelyn Chatterton
Contact Jocelyn Chatterton
✉ PO Box 36812, London, WC1H 9ZQ
☎ 020 7837 7317
🕾 07798 804853
✉ jocelyn@cixi.demon.co.uk
🌐 www.cixi.demon.co.uk
Est. 1997
Services Professional lecturer and textile consultant: Chinese social history and antique textiles
Open By appointment

Kings Gallery (FATG)
Contact Sandra Christian
✉ 28 Palace Street, Canterbury, Kent, CT1 2DZ 🅿
☎ 01227 786986 ℻ 01227 780532
🌐 www.kingsgallery.co.uk
Est. 1993
Services Restoration, framing, including tapestries, gilding, conservation, original art
Open Mon–Sat 9am–5.45pm

Lannowe Oriental Textiles
Contact Joanna Titchell
✉ Near Bath, Wiltshire
☎ 01225 891487 ℻ 01225 891182
🕾 0771 470 3535
✉ joanna@lannowe.co.uk
Est. 1976
Services Washing, restoration and conservation of Oriental carpets, rugs and tapestries
Open By appointment

M & M Restoration
Contact Mrs M Druet
✉ Mantel House, Broomhill Road, London, SW18 4JQ 🅿
☎ 020 8871 5098 ℻ 020 8877 1940
🕾 07850 310104
Est. 1985
Services Restoration and cleaning of antique tapestries, carpets and textiles
Open Mon–Fri 9am–6pm

The Restoration Studio
Contact Ela
✉ 63 Jeddo Road, London, W12 9EE 🅿
☎ 020 8740 4977
🕾 07711 157644
🌐 www.restorationstudio.co.uk
Est. 1987
Services Restoration of tapestries, needlework, embroidery, Aubussons
Open Mon–Fri 10am–5pm

The Textile Conservancy Co Ltd (UKIC)
Contact Alexandra Seth-Smith ACR
✉ Pickhill Business Centre, Smallhythe Road, Tenterden, Kent, TN30 7LZ 🅿
☎ 01580 761600 ℻ 01580 761600
✉ alex@textile-conservation.co.uk
🌐 www.textile-conservation.co.uk
Est. 1997
Services Cleaning, repair, condition reports of historic textiles, costumes, tapestries, rugs. Advice on preventative conservation, storage, display, mounting
Open Mon–Fri 9am–6pm by appointment

Textile Conservation (UKIC)
Contact Fiona Hutton
✉ Ivy House Farm, Wolvershill Road, Banwell, Somerset, BS29 6LB 🅿
☎ 01934 822449
✉ fiona@textileconservation.co.uk
Est. 1989
Services Textile conservation
Open Mon–Fri 9am–5pm

Textile Conservation Consultancy (IIC)
Contact Sheila Landi or Liz Clemence
✉ The Stable Courtyard, Burghley House, Stamford, Lincolnshire, PE9 3JY 🅿
☎ 01780 480188 ℻ 01780 480188
✉ sheilalandi@textileconservationconsultancy.co.uk
🌐 www.textileconservationconsultancy.co.uk
Est. 1992
Services Conservation and repair of all textile objects
Open By appointment

TOYS

Berkshire Antiques Co Ltd
Contact Mr Sutton
✉ 42 Thames Street, Windsor, Berkshire, SL4 1PR ℙ
☎ 01753 830100
✉ b.antiques@btconnect.com
ⓦ www.jewels2go.co.uk
Est. 1981
Services Antique dolls' hospital
Open Mon–Sat 10.30am–5.30pm
Sun by appointment

Haddon Rocking Horses
Contact Paul Stollery
✉ 5 Telford Road, Clacton-on-Sea, Essex, CO15 4LP ℙ
☎ 01255 424745 ❺ 01255 475505
✉ millers@haddonrockinghorses.co.uk
ⓦ www.haddonrockinghorses.co.uk
Est. 1971
Services Restorers and manufacturers of rocking horses
Open Mon–Thurs 8am–5pm Fri 8am–1pm

Recollect The Dolls Hospital
Contact Paul Jago
✉ 17 Junction Road, Burgess Hill, West Sussex, RH15 0HR ℙ
✉ dollshopuk@aol.com
Est. 1973
Services Complete restoration service for all dolls
Open Tues–Fri 10am–4pm Sat 10am–1pm or by appointment

Stevenson Brothers (British Toymakers Guild)
Contact Mark Stevenson or Sue Russell
✉ The Workshop, Ashford Road, Bethersden, Ashford, Kent, TN26 3AP ℙ
☎ 01233 820363 ❺ 01233 820580
✉ sales@stevensonbros.com
ⓦ www.stevensonbros.com
Est. 1982
Services Restoration of rocking horses and children's pedal cars
Open Mon–Fri 9am–6pm
Sat 10am–1pm

The Toy Works
Contact Paul Commander
✉ Holly House, Askham, Penrith, Cumbria, CA10 2PG ℙ
☎ 01931 712077 ❺ 01931 712077
✉ info@thetoyworks.co.uk
ⓦ www.thetoyworks.co.uk
Est. 1985
Services Restoration of old toys, dolls' houses, rocking horses, teddy bears
Open Wed–Sat 9am–5pm
Sun 11am–4pm

TUITION

Addington Studio Ceramic Repairs
Contact Pam Warner
✉ 1 Addington Cottages, Upottery, Honiton, Devon, EX14 9PN ℙ
☎ 01404 861519 ❺ 01404 861308
✉ pam@addingtonstudio.co.uk
ⓦ www.addingtonstudio.co.uk
Est. 1991
Services Restoration and conservation of ceramics and glass. Tuition given. Regular London (inside M25) delivery and collection. Supplies for ceramic conservators
Open By appointment

Buckinghamshire Chilterns University College
Contact Rowena Robertson
✉ Faculty of Design, Queen Alexandra Road, High Wycombe, Buckinghamshire, HP11 2JZ ℙ
☎ 01494 522141 ❺ 01494 461196
✉ desenq@bcuc.ac.uk
ⓦ www.bcuc.ac.uk/design
Est. 1993
Services BA Hons course in furniture conservation and restoration, HND in furniture studies
Open Mon–Fri 9am–5.30pm

Jocelyn Chatterton
Contact Jocelyn Chatterton
✉ PO Box 36812, London, WC1H 9ZQ
☎ 020 7837 7317
ⓜ 07798 804853
✉ jocelyn@cixi.demon.co.uk
ⓦ www.cixi.demon.co.uk
Est. 1997
Services Professional lecturer and textile consultant: Chinese social history and antique textiles
Open By appointment

China Repairers
Contact Virginia Baron
✉ The Coach House, King Street Mews, King Street, London, N2 8DY ℙ
☎ 020 8444 3030
ⓦ www.chinarepairers.co.uk
Est. 1953
Services Ceramic and glass repair. Tuition available
Open Mon–Thurs 10am–4pm

The Chippendale International School of Furniture (SSCR)
Contact Mr Anselm Fraser
✉ Myreside, Gifford, Haddington, East Lothian, EH41 4JA ℙ
☎ 01620 810680 ❺ 01620 810701
✉ info@chippendale.co.uk
ⓦ www.chippendale.co.uk
Est. 1982
Services International school of furniture, professional training of people to design, make and restore furniture
Open Mon–Fri 7.30am–5pm

Glebe Hall Restoration Studios
Contact Camel Corrigan-Griffin
✉ Old Killernogh Rectory, Rathnakelly Glebe, Ballacolla, Co Laois, Ireland ℙ
☎ 0502 34105 ❺ 0502 34105
ⓜ 0868 784956
Est. 1980
Services Courses and workshops held on care and conservation of fine and decorative arts and antiquities. Saturday morning clinics by appointment
Open By appointment Sat 11am–4pm

Gow Antiques and Restoration (BAFRA)
Contact Jeremy Gow
✉ Pitscandly Farm, Forfar, Angus, DD8 3NZ ℙ
☎ 01307 465342 ❺ 01307 468973
ⓜ 07711 416786
✉ jeremy@gowantiques.co.uk
ⓦ www.knowyourantiques.com
Est. 1991
Services Three-day Antique Furniture Recognition Courses. For dates and further information please telephone
Open Mon–Fri 9am–5pm or by appointment

Roger Hawkins Restoration

Contact R Hawkins
✉ Unit 4, The Old Dairy, Winkburn, Newark, Nottinghamshire, NG22 8PQ
☎ 01636 636666
Est. 1980
Services Restoration of all types of pottery, porcelain. Tuition given
Open Mon–Fri 9am–5pm

Leather Conservation Centre (UKIC, SSCR)

Contact Jan Beaumont
✉ University College Campus, Boughton Green Road, Moulton Park, Northampton, Northamptonshire, NN2 7AN 🅿
☎ 01604 719766 ✆ 01604 719649
🔵 lcc@northampton.ac.uk
🌐 www.leatherconservation.org
Est. 1978
Services Internships for leather conservation
Open Mon–Fri 8.30am–5pm

John Lloyd (BAFRA)

✉ Bankside Farm, Jacobs Post, Ditchling Common, West Sussex, RH15 0SJ 🅿
☎ 01444 480388 ✆ 01444 480388
📱 07941 124772
🔵 info@lloydjohnfinefurniture.co.uk
🌐 www.johnlloydfinefurniture.co.uk
Est. 1989
Services Complete repair and restoration of period, reproduction and modern furniture, short courses on care and repair of antiques and gilding
Open Mon–Fri 8.30am–5.30pm

Robert Mucci

Contact Mr Robert Mucci
✉ 68 High Street, Hastings, TN34 3EW
☎ 01424 445340
Est. 1990
Services Lectures on non-European art
Open By appointment

Mullaghmore House Enterprises

Contact Mr Louis Kelly
✉ Mullaghmore House, Old Mountfield Road, Omagh, Co Tyrone,

BT79 7EX 🅿
☎ 028 8224 2314 ✆ 028 8225 0262
🔵 mullaghmorehouse@aol.com
🌐 www.mullaghmorehouse.com
Est. 1936
Services International college offering residential courses on restoration techniques
Open Mon–Fri 10am–7pm
Sat 10am–5pm

Simmons & Miles

Contact Stephen Simmons or Helen Miles
✉ Le Gué Besnard, 61140 Juvigny-sous-Andaine, Orne, France 🅿
☎ 00 33 2 33 38 40 48
🔵 france@simmondsandmiles.co.uk
🌐 www.simmonsandmiles.co.uk
Est. 1988
Services One-to-one tuition in antique furniture restoration
Open By appointment

University of Central England School of Jewellery

Contact Dawn Meaden-Johnson
✉ Vittoria Street, Birmingham, B1 3PA
☎ 0121 248 4582 ✆ 0121 248 4582
🔵 dawn.meaden-johnson@uce.ac.uk
🌐 www.uce.ac.uk/web2/biad
Est. 1890
Services An annual short-course programme taught by practitioners. Hands-on workshop-based tuition appropriate to small-scale metalwork and jewellery, e.g. laser welding, casting and workshop techniques
Open Mon–Thurs 9.30am–3pm

West Dean College

Contact Gemma Hall
✉ West Dean, Chichester, West Sussex, PO18 0QZ 🅿
☎ 01243 818299 ✆ 01243 818291
🔵 diplomas@westdean.org.uk
🌐 www.westdean.org.uk
Est. 1971
Services Courses on the conservation and restoration of books, furniture, fine metalwork, ceramics, buildings, interiors and sites
Open By appointment

The Wiston Project School

Contact Mr N Wears
✉ The Old School, Wiston,

Haverfordwest, Pembrokeshire, SA62 4PS 🅿
☎ 01437 731579
Est. 1988
Services School of furniture making
Open By appointment

Peter Young Auctioneers

Contact Mr P Young
✉ Barnby Memorial Hall, Blyth, Worksop, Nottinghamshire, DN10 4RQ 🅿
☎ 01777 816609
📱 07801 079818
🔵 beaconhillside@btopenworld.com
🌐 www.peteryoungauctioneers.co.uk
Est. 1961
Services Regular timetable of antiques lectures for local further education groups, plus antiques visits, excursions and holidays
Open Mon–Fri 9.30am–5.30pm

UPHOLSTERY

SOUTH EAST

Kevin Birch Antique Furniture Restorers (BAFRA)

Contact Kevin Birch
✉ Unit 2, Service House, 61–63 Rochester Road, Aylesford, Kent, ME20 7BS 🅿
☎ 01622 790080 ✆ 01622 790080
🔵 kevin@kbirch.fsbusiness.co.uk
🌐 www.kevinbirch.co.uk
Est. 1993
Services Furniture restoration, French polishing and upholstery
Open Mon–Fri 8.30am–5pm

The Chair Repair Workshop

Contact Keith Woodcock or Cecilia Hall
✉ The Corner Shop, 1–3 North Street, New Romney, Kent, TN28 8DW 🅿
☎ 01797 364374 ✆ 01797 364374
Est. 2002
Services Upholstery
Open Mon–Fri 8.30am–5pm
Sat 9am–1pm

M L Connor

Contact Michael Connor
✉ Unit 6, Granville Road, Maidstone, Kent,

ASSOCIATED SERVICES
UPHOLSTERY

ME14 2BJ 🅿
☎ 01622 762866 📠 01622 762866
Est. 1955
Services Upholstery restoration
Open By appointment

Deal Upholstery Services
Contact Mr P E Cavanagh
✉ 116 Downs Road, Walmer, Deal, Kent,
CT14 7TF 🅿
☎ 01304 372297
Est. 1988
Services Antique and modern upholstery, loose covers
Open Mon–Fri 9am–5pm

Norris of Blackheath
Contact Paul Norris
✉ Dimpleshaven, Pett Road, Pett, East Sussex,
TN35 4HE 🅿
☎ 01424 812129
🌐 www.norris-of-blackheath-upholstery.co.uk
Est. 1945
Services Upholstery, free estimates, pick-up and delivery
Open Mon–Fri 8am–6pm

T J Upholstery
Contact Mr Tim Jenner
✉ Unit One, Hill House Farm, High Street, Wadhurst, East Sussex,
TN5 6AA 🅿
☎ 01892 784417
📱 07867 672707
Est. 1979
Services Traditional upholstery
Open Mon–Fri 8am–6pm but phone first

LONDON

W J Cook (BAFRA)
Contact Mr B Cook
✉ High Trees, Savernake Forest, SW11 3JS 🅿
☎ 020 7736 5329
📧 wjcook@btconnect.com
🌐 www.antiquerestoration.uk.com
Est. 1963
Services Furniture polishing, restoration, upholstery, gilding
Open By appointment

J Crisp
Contact Mr J Crisp
✉ 96 Hillway, Highgate, London, N6 6DP 🅿
☎ 020 8340 0668 📠 020 8340 0668
Est. 1979

Services Loose leather services, traditional upholstery, French and leather polishing, table liners, leather gilding
Open Mon–Fri 10am–6pm by appointment

Elizabeth Street Antiques and Restoration Services
Contact Mr Naik
✉ 35 Elizabeth Street, London, SW1W 9RP 🅿
☎ 020 7730 6777
📱 07973 909257
📧 info@elizabethstreetantiques.com
🌐 www.elizabethstreetantiques.com
Est. 1993
Services Antique restoration, marquetry, French polishing, upholstery
Open Mon–Sat 8am–7pm

Kantuta
Contact Mrs N Wright
✉ 1d Gleneagle Road, London, SW16 6AX 🅿
☎ 020 8677 6701
Est. 1986
Services Upholstery and furniture restoration
Open Mon–Sat 10am–6pm

Solomon
Contact Solomon
✉ 49 Park Road, London, N8 8SY 🅿
☎ 020 8341 1817 📠 020 8341 1817
📧 solomon@solomonantiques.fsnet.co.uk
Est. 1981
Services Restoration, upholstery, polishing
Open Mon–Sat 9am–6pm

SOUTH

A and R Upholstery
Contact Matthew Smith
✉ 78 Robin Hood Way, Winnersh, Wokingham, Berkshire,
RG41 5JM 🅿
☎ 014915 179015, 0118 978 8573 or 01635 827414
Est. 1990
Services Upholstery, custom-made headboards
Open Mon–Fri 9am–5pm

Antique Restorers
Contact Mr W Barker
✉ 2 Station Approach, Stoneleigh, Epsom, Surrey,

KT19 0QZ 🅿
☎ 020 8393 9111
Est. 1980
Services Upholstery, French polishing, furniture repair, cane and rush seating.
Open Mon–Fri 9.30am–4.30pm

Dee Cee Upholstery (AMU)
Contact Mr D A Caplen
✉ 502 Portswood Road, Portswood, Southampton, Hampshire,
SO17 3SP 🅿
☎ 023 8055 5888 📠 023 8067 6761
📧 enquiries@deeceeupholstery.co.uk
🌐 www.deeceeupholstery.co.uk
Est. 1978
Services Traditional upholstery specialist, all upholstery and DIY supplies
Open Mon–Thurs 8am–5.30pm Fri 8am–5pm Sat 9am–1pm or by appointment

A D Gardner
Contact Mr Gardner
✉ 2a East Road, Reigate, Surrey, RH2 9EX 🅿
☎ 01737 222430
Est. 1969
Services Antique repair and restoration, fine French polishing, caning, leathering, upholstery
Open Mon–Fri 8.30am–5.30pm

Hartley Upholstery and Antique Restorations
Contact Paul Bligh
✉ Unit 2, Priors Farm, Reading Road, Mattingley, Hook, Hampshire,
RG27 8JU 🅿
☎ 0118 932 6567 📠 0118 932 6567
Est. 1984
Services Upholstery, French polishing and cabinet work. Commissions undertaken
Open Mon–Sat 9am–5pm or by appointment

Hedgecoe & Freeland Ltd (LAPADA)
Contact Justin Freeland
✉ Rowan House, 21 Burrow Hill Green, Chobham, Woking, Surrey,
GU24 8QP 🅿
☎ 01276 858206 📠 01276 857352
📱 07771 953870
📧 hedgecoefreeland@aol.com
🌐 www.hedgecoefreeland.com

Est. 1969
Services Cabinet-making, polishing, upholstery, metalwork, gilding, lacquerwork and paintwork
Open Mon–Fri 8am–5pm

Hythe Reupholstery Service
Contact Mr G Batchelor
✉ 51 Hollybank Crescent, Hythe, Southampton, Hampshire, SO45 5FZ 🅿
☎ 02380 845727
Est. 1988
Services Upholstery and reconditioning of furniture
Open Mon–Fri 9am–5.30pm
Sat 9am–1pm

King & Eastland Upholsterers
Contact Kevin Eastland
✉ 60 Queen Street, Horsham, West Sussex, RH13 5AD 🅿
☎ 01403 275149 📠 01403 275149
🌐 www.kingandeastland.com
Est. 1992
Services Traditional upholstery
Open Mon–Fri 8am–5pm
Sat 8am–noon

Lush Restoration
Contact Mr M Lush
✉ 64d Old Milton Road, New Milton, Hampshire, BH25 6DX 🅿
☎ 01425 629680
Est. 1992
Services Repair and restoration, upholstery
Open Mon–Fri 8am–1pm 2–5pm

Lymington Restoration
Contact Mr M Cooper
✉ Fairlea House, 110–112 Marsh Lane, Lymington, Hampshire, SO41 9EE 🅿
☎ 01590 677558 📠 01590 677558
Est. 1996
Services Restoration of antique furniture, gilding, upholstery
Open Mon–Fri 9am–5pm

A H Smith & Son
Contact Mr M Smith
✉ 3, 6 & 7 The Parade, Old Lodge Lane, Purley, Surrey, CR8 4DG 🅿
☎ 020 8660 1211
Est. 1949
Services Upholstery, French

polishing, antique repair
Open Mon–Fri 9am–5pm
Sat 9am–1pm but phone first

Suite Dreams Upholstery
Contact Len Double
✉ Larkwhistle Cottage, Christmas Hill, Sutton Scotney, Winchester, Hampshire, SO21 3ET 🅿
☎ 01962 885630 📠 01962 885630
📱 07860 843691
Est. 1991
Services Traditional and modern upholstery, loose covers a speciality
Open Mon–Sat 9am–6pm but phone for directions

WEST COUNTRY

Rocco d'Ambrosio
Contact Mr or Mrs R Crees
✉ 94 Benedict Street, Glastonbury, Somerset, BA6 9EZ 🅿
☎ 01458 831541/ 01278 722234
Est. 1969
Services Furniture restoration, French polishing, upholstery restoration
Open Mon–Fri 9am–6pm or by appointment

Daniel Fox Upholstery
Contact Mr D Fox
✉ Goulds Farm, Nethercott, Braunton, Devon, EX33 1HT 🅿
☎ 01271 815998
Est. 1994
Services Upholstery
Open Mon–Fri 9am–5pm

Russell Hudson Upholsterer
Contact Mr R Hudson
✉ Unit 2e, Riverside Business Park, Riverside Road, Bath, Somerset, BA2 3DW 🅿
☎ 01225 400003
📧 russell.hudson@virgin.net
Est. 1985
Services Antique upholstery
Open Mon–Fri 8.30am–5.30pm

M J R Upholstery (Guild of Master Craftsmen)
Contact Mr M J Rowbrey
✉ Unit 7, Cornishway South, Galmington Trading Estate, Taunton, Somerset,

TA1 5NQ 🅿
☎ 01823 338793
Est. 1988
Services Upholstery
Open Mon–Fri 9am–5pm

Wincanton Antiques
Contact Tony or Clare
✉ London House, 12 High Street, Wincanton, Somerset, BA9 9JL 🅿
☎ 01963 32223
Est. 1997
Services Upholstery
Open Mon–Sat 9.30am–5pm

EAST

Decorcraft Upholsterers (AU)
Contact Mr A Wise
✉ Sand Acre, Elmham Drive, Nacton, Ipswich, Suffolk, IP10 0DG 🅿
☎ 01473 659396 📠 01473 659396
Est. 1975
Services Upholstery
Open Mon–Sat 9am–6pm

Essex Reupholstery Services
Contact Mr S T Richardson
✉ 49 Chestnut Grove, Southend on Sea, Essex, SS2 5HG
☎ 01702 464775 📠 01702 305684
Est. 1987
Services Restoration of antique furniture, paddings, upholstery
Open Mon–Fri 8am–5pm

Lomas Pigeon & Co Ltd (BAFRA, AMU)
Contact Mr W A J Pigeon
✉ 37 Beehive Lane, Chelmsford, Essex, CM2 9TQ 🅿
☎ 01245 353708 📠 01245 355211
📧 wpigeon@compuserve.com
🌐 www.lomas-pigeon.co.uk
Est. 1938
Services Upholstery, antique restoration, French polishing, cabinet-making
Open Mon–Fri 10am–4pm
Sat 9am–noon closed Wed

Ludovic Potts Restorations (BAFRA)
Contact Mr Ludovic Potts
✉ Elm Tree Barns, Elm Tree Farm, Penell Road, Guyhirn, Cambridgeshire,

PE13 4AQ ☎
☎ 01353 741537
📱 07889 341671
✉ mail@restorers.co.uk
🌐 www.restorers.co.uk
Est. 1986
Services Modern and antique furniture restoration
Open By appointment

Robert's Antiques
Contact Graham Bettany
✉ The Barn, South Street, Risby, Bury St Edmunds, Suffolk, IP28 6QU ☎
☎ 01284 811440 ☎ 01284 811726
✉ info@robertsantiques.co.uk
🌐 www.robertsantiques.co.uk
Est. 1978
Services Restoration of upholstery, French polishing
Open Mon–Fri 8.30am–5pm Sat–Sun noon–4pm but phone first

R J Smith Restoration
Contact Mr R J Smith
✉ Unit 1, 4 Hepworth Road, Barningham, Bury St Edmonds, Suffolk, IP31 1BP ☎
☎ 01284 704894
📱 07759 930678
Est. 1991
Services Repair and restoration of Georgian–Edwardian furniture, French polishing, upholstery
Open Mon–Sat 8.30am–5.30pm

HEART OF ENGLAND

Camden Re-Upholstery
Contact John Camden
✉ Askett Works, 51 High Street, Princes Risborough, Buckinghamshire, HP27 0AE ☎
☎ 01844 344877
Est. 1968
Services Upholstery and upholstery restoration
Open Any time ring first

Churchill Upholstery
Contact David Matthews
✉ Unit 1, Mount Farm, Junction Road, Churchill, Chipping Norton, Oxfordshire, OX7 6NP ☎
☎ 01608 658139 ☎ 01608 658139
📱 07957 355114
Est. 1986

Services Antique upholstery and soft furnishings
Open Mon–Fri 8am–5pm

Cottage Upholstery (Guild of Traditional Upholsterers)
Contact Gregory Cupitt-Jones
✉ Unit 6, Manor Farm, Nettlebed, Henley-on-Thames, Oxfordshire, RG9 5DA ☎
☎ 01491 642167
📱 07885 813558
✉ workshop@cottageupholstery.co.uk
🌐 www.cottageupholstery.co.uk
Est. 1994
Services Traditional upholstery of antique and period furniture
Open Mon–Fri 8.30am–5.30pm Sat by appointment

Andrew & Philip Leach
Contact Andrew or Philip Leach
✉ The Railway Station, Worcester Road, Leominster, Herefordshire, HR6 8AR ☎
☎ 01568 616404
Est. 1982
Services Upholstery, loose covers
Open Mon–Fri 8.30am–5.30pm

Saracen Antiques Ltd
Contact Mr C Mills
✉ Upton Downs Farm, Burford, Oxfordshire, OX18 4LY ☎
☎ 01993 822987
✉ cmills6702@aol.com
Est. 1996
Services Furniture restoration, frames and upholstery
Open Mon–Sat 9am–5.30pm

MIDLANDS

Abbey Restorations
Contact Allan Standing
✉ Darley Abbey Mills, Darley Abbey, Derbyshire, DE22 1DZ ☎
☎ 01332 344547
Est. 1974
Services Restoration of furniture, upholstery
Open Mon–Fri 8.30am–5.30pm Sat 8.30am–noon

Anthony Allen Conservation, Restoration, Furniture and Artefacts (BAFRA, UKIC)

Contact Anthony Allen
✉ The Old Wharf Workshop, Redmoor Lane, Newtown, High Peak, Derbyshire, SK22 3JL ☎
☎ 01663 745274 ☎ 01663 745274
✉ allen-conservation@tiscali.co.uk
Est. 1970
Services Restoration of clock cases and movements, gilding, marquetry, boulle, upholstery, metalwork, 17th–19thC furniture
Open Mon–Fri 8am–5pm

K Davenport Interiors Ltd
Contact Mr M Davenport
✉ The Queens Yard, Madac Place, Beatrice Street, Oswestry, Shropshire, SY11 1QJ ☎
☎ 01691 652293 ☎ 01691 652293
📱 07885 817026
🌐 www.kdavenportinteriors.co.uk
Est. 1965
Services Upholstery and restoration of antique furniture
Open Mon–Fri 8.30am–5pm

Imperial Upholstery
Contact Mr Nigel Scattergood
✉ Unit 1 Tutbury Mill Mews, Lower High Street, Tutbury, Burton-on-Trent, Staffordshire, DE13 9LU ☎
☎ 01283 521117
📱 07968 372824
🌐 www.imperialupholstery.co.uk
Est. 1993
Services Upholstery, antique restoration, French polishing
Open Tues–Fri 9am–5pm Sat 9am–1pm

John Reed and Son Upholsterers (AMU)
Contact Mr J Reed or Mr T Reed
✉ 141 Regent Street, Kettering, Northamptonshire, NN16 8QQ ☎
☎ 01536 510584 ☎ 01536 510584
✉ johnreed.andson@lineone.net
🌐 www.johnreedandson upholsterers.com
Est. 1972
Services Repair, restoration, upholstery, French and spray polishing
Open Mon–Thurs 8am–5.30pm Fri 8am–noon

P Woodcock & Co
Contact Mr Paul Day
✉ 56a Salop Road, Oswestry,

Shropshire,
SY11 2RQ P
☎ 01691 653317 or 0800 542 0008
🖷 01691 679724
📧 chairsbydays@hotmail.com
🌐 www.chairsbydays.co.uk
Est. 1954
Services Upholstery and
restoration of antique furniture,
manufacturer of reproduction
antiques
Open Mon–Fri 7.15am–5pm
Sat 9am–4pm

YORKSHIRE & LINCOLNSHIRE

Furniture Revivals
Contact Michael Edwards
✉ Yeadon, Leeds,
LS19 P
🖷 07831 817845
📧 enquiries@furniturerevivals.co.uk
🌐 www.furniturerevivals.co.uk
Est. 1991
Services Furniture restoration,
upholstery
Open By appointment

Paul Rawcliffe Upholstery Services
Contact Mr P Rawcliffe
✉ Unit 10, New Enterprise
Centre, Humber Bank South,
South Quay, Grimsby,
Lincolnshire,
DN31 3SD P
☎ 01472 251732 🖷 01472 251732
🖷 07709 651002
Est. 1989
Services Repair, restoration of
antique furniture, French polishing
Open Mon–Fri 8am–5pm

David South (HADA)
Contact James South or
David South
✉ 15 High Street, Pateley Bridge,
North Yorkshire,
HG3 5AP P
☎ 01423 712022 🖷 01423 712412
📧 sales@davidsouth.co.uk
🌐 www.davidsouth.co.uk
Est. 1985
Services Restoration of
upholstered furniture, French
polishing
Open Mon–Sat 9am–5.30pm

NORTH EAST

G M Athey
Contact Mr Athey
✉ Corner Shop, Narrowgate,

Alnwick, Northumberland,
NE66 1JQ P
☎ 01665 604229
🖷 07836 718350
📧 mathey@alancom.net
Est. 1982
Services Full restoration, French
polishing, upholstery. Deals in
Georgian and Victorian furniture
and china
Open Mon–Sat 8am–4.30pm

NORTH WEST

E Callister
Contact Mr E Callister
✉ 24 Lark Lane, Liverpool,
Merseyside,
L17 8US P
☎ 0151 727 5679
Est. 1964
Services Upholstery, French
polishing
Open Mon–Fri 9am–5pm
Sat 9am–noon

Hamilton Antique Restoration
Contact Mr C Sayle
✉ 1a Orry Place, Douglas,
Isle of Man
☎ 01624 662483
Est. 1989
Services Complete furniture
repair and restoration service,
upholstery
Open By appointment

J E Hatcher & Son
Contact Mr C Hatcher
✉ 121a Victoria Road West,
Cleveleys, Thornton Cleveleys,
Lancashire,
FY5 3LA P
☎ 01253 853162
Est. 1946
Services Traditional upholstery
Open Mon–Fri 8.30am–5.30pm
Sat 8.30am–11am

Richard Higgins Conservation Ltd (BAFRA, UKIC)
Contact Richard Higgins
✉ The Old School, Longnor,
Nr Shrewsbury, Shropshire,
SY5 7PP P
☎ 01743 718162 🖷 01743 718022
📧 richardhigginsco@aol.com
Est. 1988
Services Restoration of all fine
furniture, clocks, movements,
dials and cases, casting, plating,

boulle, gilding, lacquerwork,
carving, upholstery
Open Mon–Fri 9am–5pm
please phone first

Michael Holroyd Restorations
Contact Mr M Holroyd
✉ Pendle Antique Centre,
Union Mill, Watt Street, Sabden,
Clitheroe, Lancashire,
BB7 9ED P
☎ 01282 771112
🖷 07711 011465
📧 antiquesrestorer@tiscali.co.uk
Est. 1996
Services Complete repair and
restoration service including
spray finish, wax finish, French
polishing, cabinet-making and
veneering, traditional upholstery
Open Mon–Fri 8am–5pm Sat by
appointment

Pilgrim's Progress
Contact Selwyn Hyams
✉ 1a–3a Bridgewater Street,
Liverpool, Merseyside,
L1 0AR P
☎ 0151 708 7515 🖷 0151 708 7515
🌐 www.pilgrimsprogress.co.uk
Est. 1979
Services Cabinet-making, French
polishing, traditional upholstery
Open Mon–Fri 9am–5pm
Sat 10.30am–1.30pm

WALES

Cliff Amey & Son (AMU)
Contact Cliff Amey
✉ 12 Clive Road, Canton, Cardiff,
South Glamorgan,
CF5 1HJ P
☎ 02920 233462 🖷 02920 233462
📧 dennis.amey@talk21.com
Est. 1951
Services Upholstery
Open Mon–Fri 8am–5pm

Mach Upholstery
Contact Oliver Hubbard
✉ No 1 Londonderry Terrace,
Machynlleth, Powys,
SY20 8BG P
☎ 01654 703568 🖷 01654 703840
Est. 1994
Services Upholstery supplies
Open Mon–Fri 9am–5,30pm

S M Upholstery Ltd
Contact P Morgan
✉ 212a Whitchurch Road,

ASSOCIATED SERVICES
VALUERS

Cardiff, South Glamorgan,
CF14 3NB 🅿
☎ 029 2061 7579 🖷 029 2061 7579
🅴 sales@smfoam.co.uk
Est. 1974
Services Traditional upholstery
Open Mon–Fri 9.30am–1pm
2–5pm Sat 9.30am–1pm

SCOTLAND

**The Chairman of Bearsden
(Scottish Furniture
Preservation Society)**
Contact David Shuttleton
✉ 115a Ayr Road,
Newton Means, Glasgow,
G77 6RF 🅿
☎ 0141 639 6005
🖷 07814 744229
🅴 sales@charlesrennie
mackintosh.co.uk
🅦 www.charlesrennie
mackintosh.co.uk
Est. 1990
Services Furniture restoration
and upholstery, French polishing,
cabinet-making, bergère suites,
cane and rush seating
Open Mon–Sat 9am–5pm

Just Chairs
Contact Mr R Kerr
✉ 18/2 Sunnyside Lane,
Just off Easter Road,
Edinburgh,
EH7 5RA 🅿
☎ 0131 652 0320
Est. 1984
Services Traditional upholstery,
antique chairs (restored) bought
and sold
Open Mon–Fri 8.30am–5pm

Sherman Upholstery
Contact Jim Sherman
✉ Blairdaff Street, Buckie,
Morayshire,
AB56 1PT 🅿
☎ 01542 834680 🖷 01542 834680
🖷 07703 881903
🅴 linda@sherman73.freeserve.co.uk
Est. 1956
Services Antique repair,
restoration, upholstery
Open Mon–Fri 8.30am–4.30pm

W M Stark
Contact William Stark
✉ 88 Peddie Street, Dundee,
Tayside,
DD1 5LT 🅿
☎ 01382 660040

Est. 1977
Services Upholstery, re-covering
Open Mon–Fri 8am–4.30pm

REPUBLIC OF IRELAND

**The Complete Upholstery
Centre**
Contact Kevin Meldrum
✉ Step Lane, Barrack Street,
Cork, Co Cork,
Ireland 🅿
☎ 021 496 3186 🖷 021 496 3186
Est. 1976
Services Antique upholstery
service
Open Mon–Fri 9am–1pm
2–5.30pm

Sealey Furnishings
Contact Ron
✉ MG Business Park,
Galway Road, Tuam, Co Galway,
Ireland 🅿
☎ 09 328661 🖷 09 328661
🅴 sealey@eircom.net
🅦 www.sealeyfurnishings.com
Est. 1975
Services Furniture restoration,
upholstery
Open Mon–Sat 10am–5.30pm

VALUERS

Alpine Antiques
Contact Mr Carney
✉ 15 Sharples Avenue,
Astley Bridge, Bolton,
Greater Manchester,
BL1 7HB 🅿
☎ 01204 303364
Services Valuation of antiques
Open By appointment

**David Ford & Associates
(LAPADA)**
Contact David Ford
✉ Christmas Pie Popse,
Green Lane East, Wanborough,
Normandy, Guildford, Surrey,
GU32 2JL 🅿
☎ 01483 810230 🖷 01483 810230
🖷 07770 687553
🅴 davidnford@hotmail.com
Est. 1965
Services Valuation of antiques
and fine art
Open By appointment

**IDS Valuation Consultants
(BWCG)**
Contact Iain Sutherland
✉ 79 Templehill, Troon,

Ayrshire,
KA10 6BQ 🅿
☎ 01292 315999
Est. 1995
Services Valuations and full
consultation service
Open Mon–Sat 9.30am–5.30pm
or by appointment

**Lennox Auctions and
Valuers**
Contact Mr A Lennox
✉ The Basement, 41b Ellis Street,
Carrickfergus, Co Antrim,
BT38 8AY 🅿
☎ 028 9335 1522 or 028 9337 8527
(pm) 🖷 028 9335 1522
Est. 1987
Services Valuations on porcelain
and glass
Open Mon–Fri 9.30am–5pm

Lovers of Blue and White
Contact Andrew Pye
✉ Steeple Morden, Royston,
Hertfordshire,
SG8 0RN 🅿
☎ 01763 853800 🖷 01763 853700
🅴 china@blueandwhite.com
🅦 www.blueandwhite.com
Est. 1995
Services Valuation and
identification of British transfer
ware, 1780–present day
Open By appointment

**Nicholas Somers &
Company Chartered Arts
and Antiques Surveyor**
Contact Nicholas Somers, FRICS,
FRSA, FIAVI
✉ 45b Lurline Gardens,
Battersea, London,
SW11 4DD 🅿
☎ 020 7627 1248 🖷 020 7622 9587
🖷 07836 698889
Est. 1990
Services Insurance valuations
and sales advice for antiques,
fine art and chattels. Expert
witness work. Offices in Bath
Open By appointment

**Sotheby's (International
Auctioneers)**
Contact William Montgomery
✉ The Estate Office, Grey Abbey,
Newtownards, Co Down,
BT22 2QA 🅿
☎ 028 4278 8668 🖷 028 4278 8652
🅴 william.montgomery@sothebys.com
🅦 www.sothebys.com
Est. 1979

Services Sotheby's Northern Ireland office provides free valuations of antiques for sale by auction. Insurance valuations can be arranged, and advice given on buying, selling and restoration. Free transport of goods for auction is provided to Sotheby's in England
Open By appointment only

Weller King (ARVA)
Contact Christopher King
✉ Church House,
Old London Road, Coldwaltham, Pulborough, West Sussex,
RH20 1LF 🅿
☎ 01798 874380 🖷 01798 873731
📱 07796 174381
🄴 info@wellerking.com
🆆 www.wellerking.com
Est. 1993
Services Insurance and probate valuations, personal and confidential help and advice with the sale of antiques, fine art, jewellery, expert witness work
Open Mon–Fri 9am–5pm

WEB DESIGN

Sellingantiques.co.uk
Contact David Wilshaw
✉ Office 49, The Maltings, Royden Road, Stanstead Abbots, Ware, Hertfordshire,
SG12 8HG
☎ 0870 922 0488
🄴 contact@sellingantiques.co.uk
🆆 www.sellingantiques.co.uk
Est. 2002
Services Professional websites designed specially for antique dealers
Open Mon–Fri 9am–5.30pm

WOOD & WOOD CARVING

2 K Carving (CGLI)
Contact Saena Ku
✉ 42 Sekforde Street, Finsbury, London,
EC1R 0AH 🅿
☎ 020 7251 0592 🖷 020 7251 0592
📱 07788 143219
Est. 2000
Services Antique restoration, woodcarving, gilding and wood conservation
Open By appointment

Richard Barry Southern Marketing Ltd
Contact Mr Richard Fill
✉ Unit 1–2, Chapel Place, North Street, Portslade, Brighton, East Sussex,
BN41 1DR 🅿
☎ 01273 419471 🖷 01273 421925
🄴 sales@richardbarry.co.uk
🆆 www.richardbarry.co.uk
Est. 1978
Services Suppliers to the antiques trade of all wood-finishing materials
Open Mon–Fri 8am–5pm

B Castle (Exhibitor of the Royal Academy & Mall Gallery)
Contact Mr B Castle
✉ 2 Charmandean Road, Worthing, West Sussex,
BN14 9LB 🅿
☎ 01903 239702
Est. 1982
Services Antique repair and restoration of small furniture, decorative items, woodcarver
Open Mon–Sat by appointment

Classic Finishes
Contact Mark Baker
✉ 140—46 Oak Street, Norwich, Norfolk,
NR3 3BP 🅿
☎ 01603 760374 🖷 01603 660477
🆆 www.classicfinishes.co.uk
Est. 1987
Services Colour matching service for wood
Open Mon–Fri 8.30am–5pm
Sat 9am–1pm

Christopher Cole
Contact Mr C Cole
✉ The Workshop,
36 Claude Avenue, Oldfield Park, Bath, Somerset,
BA2 1AG 🅿
☎ 01225 310298 🖷 01225 310298
📱 07890 824042
Est. 1994
Services Antique furniture restoration, carving, turning, French polishing
Open Mon–Fri 8.30am–7pm

J D P Restorations
Contact Mr Payne
✉ 6 Denbigh Close, Tonteg, Pontypridd, Mid Glamorgan,

CF38 1HB 🅿
☎ 01443 204170
Est. 1980
Services Antique wood restoration
Open Mon–Fri 9am–6pm

Rod Naylor
Contact Angela Naylor
✉ 208 Devizes Road, Hilperton, Trowbridge, Wiltshire,
BA14 7QP 🅿
☎ 01225 754497 🖷 01225 754497
🄴 rod.naylor@virgin.net
🆆 www.rodnaylor.com
Est. 1970
Services Restoration of antique wood carvings, supplies replicas of hard-to-find items and materials for caddies, boxes, desks, cabinet-making, supplier of power carving machinery and tools
Open By appointment only

Q W Conservation (OCS, UKIC)
Contact Toby Quartly-Watson
✉ Studio 5 (2nd Floor), Hewlett House, Havelock Terrace, London,
SW8 4AS 🅿
☎ 020 7498 5938 🖷 020 7498 5938
📱 07814 687213
🄴 stylish.moves@virgin.net
Est. 1991
Services Conservation and restoration of wood sculpture
Open Mon–Fri 10am–6pm or by appointment

WRITING

Classic Pen Engineering (Writing Equipment Society)
Contact Mr D Purser
✉ Auchenfranco Farm, Lochfoot, Dumfries, Dumfries & Galloway,
DG2 8NZ 🅿
☎ 01387 730208 🖷 01387 730208
📱 07703 690843
🄴 cpe@auchenfranco.freeserve.co.uk
🆆 www.auchenfranco.freeserve.co.uk
Est. 1994
Services Complete refurbishment of writing instruments. Sales and valuations of fountain pens, dip pens and pencils
Open By appointment

Fairs

The Fairs section is divided into two parts. The first part gives an
alphabetical list of fair organizers, while the second lists in date order
antiques fairs that will take place in the UK and Ireland throughout 2006.
Every effort has been made to ensure that this information is correct
at the time of going to press. However it is highly recommended that
you telephone to confirm the details are still as stated. You may also
discover that the event organizer has several additional events,
which could not be included at the time of going to press. If you would
like your fair(s) to be included in next year's directory, please inform us
by October 1st 2006. (FWC = Free with Card).

Abbey Fairs
Contact Nick Cox
✉ PO Box 7482,
Nottingham,
NG16 2ZQ
☎ 01773 770422
🖃 abbeyfairs@yahoo.co.uk
🌐 www.abbeyfairs.com
Fairs Art Deco Fairs in London,
Warwick, Twickenham, Battersea
and Kelam Hall, Newark

Adams Antiques Fairs
Contact Matthew Adams
☎ 020 7254 4054
🌐 www.adams-antiques-fairs.co.uk
Fairs Brocante and Decorative
Living Show and Frock Me! at
Kensington Town Hall. Adams
Antiques Fairs at Kensington
Town Hall and the Royal
Horticultural Hall, London, 'Turn
Out Your Attic', Battersea Arts
Centre

Albany Fairs
Contact Robert Davison
☎ 0191 584 2934
📱 07976 619009
🖃 enquiries@albanyfairs.com
🌐 www.albanyfairs.com
Fairs Albany Fairs at Ullswater,
Cumbria, Moffatt, Dumfriesshire
and St Andrews, Fife

**The Antiquarian
Booksellers Association**
✉ Sackville House,
40 Piccadilly,
London,
W1J 0DR
☎ 020 7439 3118 📠 020 7439 3119
🖃 info@aba.org.uk
🌐 www.aba.org.uk
Fairs The Antiquarian Book Fair
(London) and the Chelsea and
Edinburgh Book Fairs

Antique Arms Fairs Ltd
Contact Margaret
✉ PO Box 355, Hereford,
Herefordshire,
HR1 9XE 🅿
☎ 01432 355416 📠 01432 371767
🖃 info@antiquearmsfairsltd.co.uk
🌐 www.antiquearmsfairsltd.co.uk
Fairs London Antiques Arms
Fairs, Hotel Ibis London Earls
Court

**The Antique Dealers Fair
Ltd**
Contact Ingrid Nilson

✉ PO Box 119,
Cranbrook, Kent,
TN18 5WB
☎ 01797 252030
Fairs The LAPADA Antiques &
Fine Art Fair

Antique Forum Group
☎ 01782 393660 📠 01782 393357
🖃 info@antiqueforumgroup.com
🌐 www.antiqueforumgroup.com
Fairs Big Brum, Birmingham,
Antiques Festivals, Trentham
Gardens, and Uttoxeter 2-day
Antiques Fair. Please phone for
details. Also Antiques and
Collectors Market, every Tuesday
(8am–3pm), Newcastle-under-
Lyme

**Antiques & Collectors
World**
✉ PO Box 129,
Tadworth, Surrey,
KT20 5YR
☎ 01737 812989
📱 07802 768364
🖃 orchard.cottage@clara.co.uk
Fairs Antiques & Collectors Fairs,
Goodwood Racecourse

Antiques Fairs Ireland
Contact Joan Murray
✉ PO Box 5057,
Dublin 2, Ireland
☎ 00353 167 08295
📱 00 353 (0) 8726 7607
🖃 antiquesfairsireland@esatclear.ie
🌐 www.antiquesfairsireland.com
Fairs Antiques Fairs in Dublin.

Arun Fairs
Contact Stephanie Clark
☎ 01903 734112
📱 07774 852622
Fairs Arun Antiques Fairs at
Rustington and Worthing,
West Sussex

B+T Toy Fairs
Contact Brian Kelly
✉ 24 Albert Road,
Glenageary,
Co Dublin,
Ireland
☎ 00 353 (0) 1 2803008
🖃 briana.kelly@rte.ie
🌐 www.dublintoyandtrainfair.com
Fairs Dublin Toy and Train Fair

BABAADA
✉ 280 High Street,
Batheaston, Bath,

BA1 7RA
☎ 01225 851466 📠 01225 851120
🖃 bathdecorativefair@ukonline.co.uk
🌐 www.babaada.com/antique_fair.htm
Fairs Bath Annual Decorative &
Antiques Fair

Robert Bailey Fairs Ltd
✉ PO Box 1110,
Brentwood,
Essex,
CM14 4SE
☎ 01277 214677 📠 01277 214550
🖃 admin@baileyfairs.co.uk
🌐 www.baileyfairs.co.uk
Fairs Antiques fairs at Knutsford,
Harrogate Seaford College,
Petworth, Buxton Autumn
Antiques and Hatfield House,
Hertfordshire

The Battersea Pen Home
Contact Simon Gray or
Sean Lovell
✉ PO Box 6128,
Epping,
CM16 4GG
☎ 0870 900 1888
🖃 info@penhome.co.uk
Fairs The London Pen Show

Beckett Antiques Fairs
Contact Alan Mycock
☎ 0114 289 0656
Fairs Beckett Antiques Fairs at
Doncaster and York Racecourses

Bentley Grice Promotions
☎ 01424 845174
Fairs Antiques and Collectors
Fairs in Hastings, East Sussex

Best of Fairs
Contact Tom Burt
✉ Churchgate Barn,
Churchgate, Glomsford,
Sudbury, Suffolk,
CO10 7QE
☎ 01787 280306
Fairs The Best of Fairs, Copdock,
near Ipswich and Long Melford

**Biggleswade Antiques
Fairs**
Contact Mary and Philip Hall
✉ Field View,
Poplar Close, Roxton,
Bedfordshire
☎ 01234 871449 📠 01234 871449
📱 07778 789917
Fairs Biggleswade Antiques Fairs
at Biggleswade and Kempston,
Bedfordshire and Huntingdon

Lynne & Richard Bonehill
Contact Richard and Lynne Bonehill
✉ The Bosuns Nest, Carthew Way, St Ives, Cornwall, TR26 1RJ
☎ 01736 793213
✉ richard@bonehill3.freeserve.co.uk
ⓦ www.bonehill3.freeserve.co.uk
Fairs Lostwithiel Antiques & Bygones Fairs

Bowman Antiques Fairs Ltd
Contact Helen Bowman or Ben Wray
✉ PO Box 64, Shipley, West Yorkshire, BD17 7YA
☎ 07071 284333 ☏ 07071 284334
Ⓜ 07889 828288
✉ info@antiquesfairs.com
ⓦ www.antiquesfairs.com
Fairs Stafford Bingley Hall Giant 3-Day Antiques Fairs

Boxford Books & Fairs
Contact Ken McLeod
✉ 3 Firs Farm Cottage, Boxford, Colchester, Suffolk, CO10 5NU Ⓟ
☎ 01787 210810 ☏ 01473 823187
Est. 1981
Fairs Suffolk Books Market, Long Melford

British Antique Dealers Association
Contact Lucie Evans
✉ 20 Rutland Gate, London, SW7 1BD
☎ 020 7589 6108 ☏ 020 7581 9083
✉ enq@bada-antiques-fair.co.uk
ⓦ www.bada-antiques-fair.co.uk
Fairs The BADA Antiques and Fine Art Fair, London

British Numismatic Trade Association Ltd
Contact General Secretary
✉ PO Box 2, Rye, East Sussex, TN31 7WE
☎ 01797 229988 ☏ 01797 229988
✉ bnta@lineone.net
ⓦ www.bnta.net
Est. 1978
Fairs Coinex and other coin and medal fairs, London

Margaret Browne Fairs
☎ 0208 874 3622
Fairs Quality Antiques Fairs in Dorking, Surrey

Brunel Clock & Watch Fair
Contact Carol Barnes
✉ PO Box 273, Uxbridge, Middlesex, UB9 4LP
☎ 01895 834694 ☏ 01895 832904
Fairs Brunel Clock & Watch Fairs, Brunel University, Uxbridge (please phone for details) and Midland Clock & Watch Fairs

Buxton Book Fair
Contact Mrs S Laithwaite
☎ 01625 425352
Fairs Buxton Book Fairs

Mark Carter Militaria & Medal Fairs
Contact Mark Carter
✉ PO Box 470, Slough, SL3 6RR
☎ 01753 534777
✉ markgcarter@onetel.com
Fairs Mark Carter Militaria & Medal Fairs, Bristol, Aldershot and Stratford-upon-Avon

Castle Antique Fairs NI
Contact Peter Moore
✉ 15 Hawthron Hill, Newtownards, Co Down, BT23 8ET
☎ 028 9181 5710 ☏ 028 9181 5710
Ⓜ 07989 501666
✉ info@castleantiques.co.uk
ⓦ www.castleantiques.co.uk
Fairs Antiques fairs at Templepatrick, Lissanoure Castle (between Ballymena and Ballymoney) and Newtownards, Northern Ireland

Clarion Events Ltd
Contact Jessica Curtis or Clementine Musson
✉ Olympia Exhibition Halls, London, W14 8UX
☎ 0870 126 1726
✉ olympia-antiques@clarion events.com
ⓦ www.halifair.com or www.olympia-antiques.com
Fairs HALI Fair - Carpets, Textiles & Tribal Art (contact Rachel Dopwney Diaz 0207 970 4600), the Fine Art Design & Antiques Fair and the Summer and Winter Fine Art & Antiques Fairs (contact Cementine Musson), all at Olympia, London

Clarion Events–NEC Ltd
Contact Fran Foster
✉ NEC House, Birmingham, B40 1NT
☎ 0121 767 2744 ☏ 0121 767 3535
ⓦ www.antiquesforeveryone.co.uk
Fairs The National Fine Art & Antiques Fair, NEC, Birmingham, and Antiques for Everyone, Birmingham, Glasgow and London

Crispin Fairs
Contact Mrs P Wyatt
✉ 43 Tintern Crescent, Coley Park, Reading, Berkshire, RG1 6HB Ⓟ
☎ 0118 950 2960
Est. 1981
Fairs Crispin Fairs at Wokingham, Berkshire and Hartley Wintney, Hampshire (phone for details)

Cross County Fairs Ltd
Contact Mr Lionel Parker
☎ 01474 834120
Fairs Cross County Fairs, Effingham Park, West Sussex

Graham Davey
Contact Graham Davey
☎ 01603 758252
✉ graham@v21.me.uk

Don Davidson
Contact Don Davidson
✉ Burford Terrace, Burford Road, Chipping Norton, Oxfordshire, OX7 5EF
☎ 01608 641870
Ⓜ 07796 671650
Fairs Chipping Norton Toy Fair

Davidson Monk Fairs
Contact Linda Monk
✉ PO Box 201, Croydon, Surrey, CR9 7AQ Ⓟ
☎ 020 865 64583 ☏ 020 865 64583
Est. 1987
Fairs Coin fairs at the Drury's Hotel, Great Russell Street, London WC1

Dennis Jewellery
Contact Dennis O'Sullivan
☎ 01202 669061 ☏ 01202 669061
Ⓜ 07736 42431
Fairs Antique & Collectors Fairs,

Poole. Also Avonbridge Antqiues & Collectors' Market, every Tuesday, United Reform Church Hall, Fisherton Street, Salisbury, 8am–2pm

Devon County Antiques Fairs
⊠ The Glebe House, Bow, Devonshire, EX17 6DB
☎ 01363 82571 ✆ 01363 82312
✉ dcaf@antiques-fairs.com
⬤ www.antiques-fairs.com
Fairs Devon County Antiques Fairs at Exeter, Yeovil, Matford, Salisbury and Wadebridge phone or see website for full details)

DMG Antiques Fairs
⊠ PO Box 100, Newark, Nottinghamshire, BG24 1DJ 🅿
☎ 01636 702326
⬤ www.dmgantiquefairs.com
Est. 1998
Fairs Newark International Antiques & Collectors Fair, Detling International Antiques & Collectors Fair, Shepton Mallet Antiques & Collectors Fair, Ardingly International Antiques & Collectors Fair, Ardingly Sunday Antiques & Collectors Fair, Newmarket International Antiques & Collectors Fair and Malvern International Antiques & Collectors Fair

Dolly Domain Fairs
Contact Liz and David Bonner
⊠ 45 Henderson Road, Simonside, South Shields, Tyne & Wear, NE34 9QW 🅿
☎ 0191 424 0400 ✆ 0771 309 1523
⬤ 07713 091523
✉ fairs@dollydomain.com
⬤ www.dollydomain.com
Fairs Leeds Doll & Teddy Fair

Dualco Promotions
☎ 0161 283 1255 or 0161 766 2012
⬤ www.dualco.co.uk
Fairs Antique and Collectors' Fairs in Bury, Oldham, Preston and Bolton, Lancashire and Leeds, Halifax, Barnsley and Cleckheaton, Yorkshire

E W Services
Contact David Smith
⊠ PO Box 56,

Wellingborough, Northamptonshire, NN8 1SF
☎ 01933 225674
✉ david.smith34@ntlworld.com
⬤ www.ewsfairs.com
Fairs International Pottery and Ceramics Fair, National Glass Fair and Art Deco Fair at St Albans. See website for other events

East Preston Festival Fair
☎ 01903 771161
Fairs Antique and Collectables fair in March, June and October at East Preston Village Hall, West Sussex

Bob Evans Fairs
⊠ Ashtrees, Kirby Bellars, Melton Mowbray, Leicestershire, LE14 2DU
☎ 01664 812627 ✆ 01664 813727
Fairs 2-day Peterborough Festival of Antiques. Bob Evans Fairs at Coventry, Hereford, Hinckley, Kettering and Peterborough

Fair Antiques
Contact Mr Duncan Wats
☎ 01162 404411
Fairs East Berkshire Antiques Fair, near Maidenhead

Fat Cat Fairs
Contact Andy & Sheila Briggs
☎ 01865 301705
⬤ 07977 936882
✉ andy@fatcatfairs.co.uk
⬤ www.fatcatfairs.co.uk
Fairs Fat Cat Fairs, Burford, Oxfordshire and Lechlade-on-Thames, Gloucestershire and Abingdon, Oxfordshire

Felix Fairs
Contact Mr Willmers
⊠ 16 Beach Road West, Portishead, Bristol, BS20 7HR 🅿
☎ 01275 842480
Est. 1989
Fairs Monthly antiques fairs in Bristol (please phone for details)

Four In One Promotions
Contact Mrs Hitchman
☎ 0121 360 3649 ✆ 0121 360 3649
⬤ 07802 536636
✉ fourinonepromotions@btinternet.com
Fairs Mammoth Antiques &

Collectors Fairs, Castle Donington, Debyshire, Edinburgh and Kelso, Scottish Borders (please phone for details)

Freya Antiques Fairs
☎ 01508 489252
⬤ 07799 401067
✉ freyaantiques@yahoo.com
⬤ www.antiquesbarn.co.uk
Fairs Freya Antiques Fairs at Banham, Haddiscoe, Loddon, Worstead, Swaffham and Norwich, Norfolk and at Brandon, Suffolk (please phone for details)

Galloway Antiques Fairs
⊠ Halston Lodge, 88 Cornwall Road, Harrogate, North Yorkshire, HG1 2NG 🅿
☎ 01423 522122 ✆ 01423 522122
⬤ 07966 528725
✉ susan@gallowayfairs.co.uk
⬤ www.gallowayfairs.co.uk
Fairs Galloway Antiques Fairs. Please phone for full details of venues and dates

Gemsco Promotions
Contact Rodney Weeks
⊠ Wheelwrights Cottage, Harrow Piece, Maulden, Bedford, Bedfordshire, MK45 2DG
☎ 01525 402596
⬤ 07771 570814
Fairs Antiques Fairs in Luton, Silsoe, Great Missenden and Cheshunt

Grandma's Attic
☎ 01590 677687 ✆ 01590 677687
⬤ 07850 263406
⬤ www.grandmasattic.co.uk
Fairs Antiques Fairs in Hampshire, Dorset and Wiltshire. See website for details

Grenadiers
⊠ 102 Sydenham Road, London, SE26 5JX
☎ 020 8659 1588
⬤ 07887 571337
✉ enquiries@grenadiers.co.uk
Fairs Hildenborough Militaria Fair, Hildenborough, Kent. Phone for details

Grosvenor Exhibitions Ltd
Contact Roger Cooling
⊠ 21 High Street, Spalding,

Lincolnshire,
PE11 1TX
☎ 01775 767400 🖶 01775 713125
Fairs The Great Northern
International Antiques &
Collectors Fair

Harrogate Antique & Fine Art Fair Ltd

Contact Louise Walker
✉ **Prioryfield House,
20 Canon street, Taunton,
Somerset,
TA1 1SW**
☎ 01823 323363 🖶 01823 271072
📧 info@harrogateantique.com
🌐 www.harrogateantiquefair.com
Fairs The Harrogate Antique &
Fine Art Fair

Harvey Management Services Ltd

Contact Patricia and
Ralph Harvey
☎ 020 7624 5173
📧 fairs@decorativefair.com
🌐 www.decorativefair.com
Fairs The Decorative Antiques
and Textiles Fair, Battersea Park,
London in WInter, Spring and
Autumn (dates for the Spring
Fair are not yet fixed)

Jan Hicks

Contact Jan Hicks
✉ **1 Leverton Cottages,
Chilton Foliat, Hungerford,
Berkshire,
RG17 0TA**
☎ 01488 683986 🖶 01488 683986
📱 07770 230686
🌐 www.antiquesandaudacity.com
Fairs Antiques & Audacity, Losely
Park, near Guildford, Surrey

Hinchingbrooke Fairs

☎ 01638 662104 🖶 01638 668571
📱 07710 489169
📧 ken@kencharity.com
🌐 www.hinchingbrookefairs.co.uk
Fairs Hinchingbrooke House
Antiques Fair in the ancestral
home of the Cromwell family
and the Earls of Sandwich, near
Huntingdon in January, August,
October and December (phone
for full details)

Hoyles Promotions

✉ **PO Box 40, St Annes,
Lancashire,
FY8 2JR**
☎ 01253 782828 🖶 01253 714715

📧 info@hoylespromotions.co.uk
🌐 www.hoylespromotions.co.uk
Est. 1975
Fairs Antique and Collectors
Fairs, Southport and and
Blackpool (Please phone to check
dates for the Collectors Market
in Blackpool Winter Gardens)

Hyson Fairs Ltd

Contact Sheila Hyson
☎ 01647 231459
🌐 www.hysonfairsltd.co.uk
Fairs Antiques & Collectors' Fairs
and Antiques & Fleamarkets,
Exmouth, Antiques &
Fleamarkets, Holsworthy, Devon
and Charity Antiques &
Collectors' Fairs, Chagford,
Devon. Please phone for details

IPM Promotions

✉ **130/132 Brent Street,
London,
NW4 2DR**
☎ 020 8202 9080 or 020 8203 1500
🖶 020 8203 7031
📧 bloomsbury@memories
postcards.co.uk
🌐 www.memoriespostcards.co.uk
/blomsbury.hym
Fairs Bloomsbury Postcard &
Collectors Fairs, London

Ipswich Antiques & Collectables Fair

Contact Vicky Roberts-Barber
☎ 01473 688201
Est. 1977
Fairs Ipswich Antiques &
Collectables Fairs, Copdock,
near Ipswich

J Fairs

Contact J Gibbons
✉ **23 Kestrel Crescent, Brackley,
NN13 6SX**
☎ 01280 703454
Fairs Antique & Collectors Fairs,
Berkhamsted (phone for details)

J & K Fairs

Contact K Hasnip
✉ **3 South View, Humberston,
Lincolnshire**
☎ 01472 813281
Est. 1981
Fairs J & K Fairs, Lincolnshire
Showground

Jaguar Fairs Ltd

✉ **PO Box 158, Derby,
DE21 5ZA**

☎ 01332 831404 🖶 01332 831404
🌐 www.jaguarfairs.com
Fairs Antiques in the Park at
Kedleston Hall, Derbyshire and
Sandringham Royal Estate,
Norfolk. Also The Giant
Wetherby Racecourse and Derby
University Antiques Fairs. See
website for dates

Janba Fairs

Contact Barry Phillips
✉ **PO Box 1, Wisbech,
Cambridgeshire,
PE13 4QJ**
☎ 01945 870160 or 07860 517048
🖶 01945 870660
📧 janba@supanet.com
🌐 www.janba.supanet.com
Fairs Janba Fairs, St Ives,
Cambridgeshire and Camfairs,
Hertford

Jiri Books

Contact Jim or Rita Swindall
☎ 028 9082 6443
Est. 1982
Fairs Annual Belfast Book Fair

Kibworth Exhibitions Ltd

Contact Duncan Watts
✉ **Unit 5, Saddington Lodge,
Shearsby Road, Saddington,
Leicestershire,
LE8 0SE**
☎ 0116 240 4411 🖶 0116 240 4411
📱 07973 423030
📧 enquiries@shellscheme.co.uk
Fairs East Berks Antique Fairs

LAPADA

✉ **535 Kings Road,
Chelsea, London,
SW10 0SZ**
☎ 020 7823 3511 🖶 020 7823 3522
📧 lapada@lapada.co.uk
🌐 www.lapada.co.uk
Fairs
LAPADA@TheRoyalAcademy,
London. Also the LAPADA
Autumn Antiques and Fine Art
Fair, Cheltenham, organised by
The Antique Dealers Fair Ltd

Allen Lewis Fairs

Contact Allen Lewis
✉ **64 Lower Blandford Road,
Broadstone, Dorset,
BH18 8NY**
☎ 01202 604306 🖶 01202 604306
📱 07768 285970
📧 allen.lewis@btconnect.com
Fairs The Antique Dealers Fair of

Wales, Margam Park, West Glamorgan and Ruthin Scholl and The Portmeirion Antiques Fair, Portmeirion Village, Gwynedd

Lomax Antiques Fairs
Contact Liz Allport
☎ 01603 737631 ☐ 01603 737631
Ⓜ 07747 843074
ⓔ info@lomaxantiquesfairs.co.uk
ⓦ www.lomaxantiquesfairs.co.uk
Fairs The North Norfolk Fine Art & Antiques Fair, Burnham Market, The Langley Park Spring Antiques Fair, Loddon, Norfolk and The East Anglian Antiques Dealers Fair, Loddon, Norfolk

London Ceramics Fairs
Contact Fred Hynes
☎ 01303 258635 ☐ 01303 258635
Fairs London Ceramic Fairs, Lancaster Gate, London

London Map Fairs
ⓔ info@londonmapfairs.com
ⓦ www.londonmapfairs.com
Est. 1980
Fairs London Map Fairs at the Rembrandt Hotel, London and the International Map Fair, Olympia, London

M & S Fairs
Contact Jim Mansfield
☎ 01223 233059
Ⓜ 07960 102889
Fairs M & S Antiques & Collectors Fairs, Meldreth and Cottenham, near Cambridge (please phone for details)

David Maggs
Contact David Maggs
✉ Yew Tree Cottage, Whipsnade, Bedfordshire, LU6 2LG
☎ 01582 872514
Fairs Monthly fairs at Bushey Hall School, Bushey, Hertfordshire

Magnum Antiques Fairs
Contact Stewart Watt
✉ Old Vicarage, Stoke Row, Henley-on-Thames, Oxfordshire, RG9 5RB
☎ 01491 681009
Fairs Magnum Antiques Fairs, Midhurst, West Sussex and Winchester

Marcel Fairs
☎ 020 8950 1844
Fairs Marcel Fairs in and around London (phone for full details)

Midas Fairs
Contact Joy Alder
✉ PO Box 175, Beaconsfield, Buckinghamshire, HP9 1UL
☎ 01494 674170
ⓦ www.midas_antiques_fairs.co.uk
Fairs Midas Fairs, Beaconsfield, Buckinghamshire

Millennium Fairs
✉ 9 Binyon Gardens, Taverham, Norwich, Norfolk, NR8 6SR
☎ 01603 868575
Fairs Antiques and Collectables Fairs in East Anglia. Phone for dates and details

Monmouthshire County Council
Contact Geoffrey Harris
✉ Markets Office, Town Hall, Cross Street, Abergavenny, Monmouthshire, NP7 5HD
☎ 01873 735845
ⓔ geoffharris@monmouthshire.gov.uk
ⓦ www.abergavennymarket.co.uk
Fairs Abergavenny Antiques & Collectors Fairs. Toy and TrainFair in May. Also Fleamarket every Wednesday 6am–4pm, Market Hall, Abergavenny

Newcomen Fairs Ltd
Contact Graham Wilson
✉ Elsecar Antique Centre, Elsecar Heritage Centre, Wath Road, Barnsley, South Yorkshire, S74 8HJ Ⓟ
☎ 01226 744425 ☐ 01226 361561
Ⓜ 07712 834895
ⓔ sales@elsecarantiques.co.uk
ⓦ www.elsecarantiques.co.uk
Est. 2001
Fairs Newcomen Fairs, Elsecar, South Yorkshire

Northern Clock & Watch Fairs
☎ 01691 831162 ☐ 01691 839203
ⓔ fairs@oswatch.fsnet.co.uk

Fairs Northern Clock & Watch Fairs, Haydock Park Racecourse, Merseyside. Also a fair at Newark

Louis O'Sullivan
Contact Louis O'Sullivan
☎ 00 353 1 285 9294
Fairs International Irish Antiques and Fine Art Fair, Royal Dublin Society, Dublin, Ireland

Oakleigh Leisure Ltd
Contact John Aitchison
✉ Oakley Antiques Fairs, Old Tithe Hall, Start Hill, Near Bishop's Stortford, Hertfordshire, CM22 7TF
☎ 01279 871110 ☐ 01279 870844
ⓔ olltd@aol.com
Fairs Antiques and Collectables Fair Chingford, Essex and Bishop's Stortford

The Old Brig
Contact Ann Young
✉ 33 Great King Street, Edinburgh, EG3 6QR
☎ 0131 556 6728 ☐ 0131 556 6728
Fairs The Highland Antiques Fair and The Old Brig Antique & Collectors' Fairs, The Highland Conference Centre, Nairn, Inverness

Pantheon Fairs Ltd
Contact Clare Dorrell
✉ 3a Charlotte Street, Perth, Scotland, PH1 5LW
☎ 01738 446534 ☐ 01738 451388
Ⓜ 07779 297931
ⓔ antiques@cdorrell.fsworld.com
Fairs The Fine Antiques Fairs of Scotland, Hopetoun House, South Queensferry, near Edinburgh and The Goodwood House Fine Antiques Fairs, Chichester, West Sussex

Paraphernalia Fairs
Contact Jill Robinson
☎ 01305 860012 ☐ 01305 824862
Fairs Paraphernalia Fairs, Lyndhurst, New Forest, Hampshire

Penman Antiques Fairs
Contact Caroline Penman
✉ Widdicombe, Bedford Place, Uckfield,

East Sussex,
TN22 1LW
☎ 0870 350 2442 🖷 0870 350 2443
📱 07774 850044
📧 info@penman-fairs.co.uk
🌐 www.penman-fairs.co.uk
Fairs Penman Antiques Fairs at
Kensington Town Hall, London,
Petersfield, Chester, Chelsea Old
Town Hall, London, Lindfield,
Hove, Sherborne and Petersfield

Pig & Whistle Promotions
Contact Lindy Berkman
☎ 020 8883 7061
📧 info@pigandwhistle
promotions.com
🌐 www.allypally-uk.com
Fairs Alexandra Palace Antique &
Collectors Fairs, London

Pre-empt Events
Contact Anita Bott
✉ 16 Garden Road,
Sundridge Park,
Bromley, Kent,
BR1 3LX
☎ 020 8290 1888 🖷 020 8290 1888
📧 info@vintagefashionfairs.com
Fairs Battersea Vintage Fashion
Fairs, Lavender Hill, London

Prospect Promotions
Contact Mrs S Mather
✉ Primrose Cottage,
Howards Lane, Eccleston,
St Helens,
WA10 5QD
☎ 01744 750606 🖷 01744 750606
📧 sandracca@aol.com
🌐 www.creativecrafts-
online.co.uk
Fairs Antique & Collectors Fair,
Wilmslow, Cheshire

Provincial Booksellers Fairs Association
✉ 16 Melbourn Street,
Royston,
Hertfordshire,
SG8 7BZ
☎ 01763 248400 🖷 01763 248921
📧 info@pbfa.org
🌐 www.pbfa.org
Fairs Antiquarian book fairs
throughout the UK

Scotfairs
Contact R M Torrens
✉ PO Box 5339,
Crieff, Perthshire,
PH7 3YL
☎ 01764 654555 🖷 01764 654340

Fairs Scotfairs Antique and
Collectors Fairs, Ayr, Edinburgh,
Glasgow and Stirling (please
phone for details)

Simmons Gallery
Contact Frances Simmons
✉ PO Box 104,
Leytonstone, London,
E11 1ND
☎ 020 8989 8097
📧 Lcf@simmonsgallery.co.uk
🌐 www.simmonsgallery.co.uk
Fairs London Coin Fair,
Bloomsbury, London

Specialist Glass Fairs Ltd
Contact Patricia Hier
☎ 01260 271975
📧 info@glassfairs.co.uk
🌐 www.glassfairs.co.uk
Fairs The Original National Glass
Collectors Fairs

Arthur Swallow Fairs
Contact Mr J Ball
☎ 01298 27493/73188
📱 07860 797200
Fairs The International Antiques
& Collectors Fairs at RAF
Swinderby

Take Five Fairs
Contact John Slade
✉ 417a Chertsey Road,
Whitton, Twickenham,
Middlesex,
TW2 6LS
☎ 020 8894 0218
📱 07904 171137
🌐 www.antiquefairs.co.uk
Fairs Antiques & Collectables
Fairs, Grand Glass Fairs and Art
Nouveau/Deco Fairs, Woking,
Surrey and Bristol

Towy Antiques Fairs
Contact Robert and Carol Pugh
✉ PO Box 24,
Carmarthen,
SA31 1YS
☎ 01267 236569 🖷 01267 220444
📱 027885 333845
📧 towyfairs@btopenworld.com
🌐 www.towy-fairs.co.uk
Fairs Carmarthen and Cowbridge
Antiques Fairs

Trident Exhibitions
Contact Louisa Pridham
✉ West Devon Business Park,
Tavistock, Devon,
PL19 9DP

☎ 01822 614671 🖷 01822 614818
📧 louisa.pridham@trident-
exhibitions.co.uk
🌐 www.buxtonantiquesfair.co.uk
Fairs The Buxton Antiques Fair

TVADA
☎ 01993 882420
📧 tamesis@tvada.co.uj
🌐 www.tvada.co.uk
Fairs Thames Valley Antiques
Fairs; spring at the Bluecoat
School, Sonning-on-Thames,
Reading and autumn at Radley
College, Oxford (please phone
for details)

Unicorn Fairs Ltd
Contact David Fletcher
✉ PO Box 30, Hereford,
Herefordshire,
HR2 8SW
☎ 07800 508178
Fairs Buxton Antique &
Collectors Fairs. Also Antiques
and Collectors Fair every Sunday
8am–3pm at the Exhibition Halls,
Park Hall, Charnock Richard,
Lancashire, off the A49, behind
the M6 Charnock Richard services
– follow the Camelot signs – free
parking and refreshments

V&A Fairs
✉ Holly Bank Cottage, Forden,
Nr Welshpool, Powys,
SY21 8LT
☎ 01938 580438
📧 vandafairs@talk21.com
🌐 www.vandafairs.com
Fairs V&A Antique & Collectors
Fairs, Nantwich, Cheshire,
Stretton, near Warrington,
Cheshire, and Bridgnorth,
Shropshire

Virgo Fairs
☎ 01765 620563
📱 07950 621395
Fairs Antiques and Collectors
fairs in Ripley, North Yorkshire

Wessex Antiques Fairs
Contact Jo Wanford
☎ 01278 789568
📧 gerry.wanford@virgin.net
Fairs Wessex Antiques Fairs,
Taunton, Churchill and Weston-
super-Mare, Somerset

West Country Fairs
Contact Fred Wilcox
✉ PO Box 2603,

FAIRS: ORGANIZERS
CONTACT DETAILS

Wells, Somerset,
BA5 2YL
☎ 01749 677049 ✆ 01749 677049
Fairs Antiques & Collectors Fairs
in Weymouth and Sherbourne,
Dorset and Wells, Somerset

West Midland Antique Fairs
Contact Nick Fletcher
✉ PO Box 134,
Shrewsbury,
Shropshire,
SY1 1ZZ 🅿
☎ 01743 271444
📧 mail@staffordantiquesfairs.co.uk
🌐 www.staffordantiquesfairs.co.uk
Est. 1973
Fairs Stafford Antiques Fair.
Please phone for details

Wilton House
Contact Sandra Piper
✉ Wilton House, Wilton,
Salisbury, Wiltshire, SP2 0BJ
☎ 01722 746720 ✆ 01722 744447
📧 tourism@wiltonhouse.com
🌐 www.wiltonhouse.com
Fairs 29th Annual Antique Fair at
Wilton House

Winter Fairs
Contact Diana Ives
☎ 01753 685098 or 020 8950 3690
Fairs Winter Fairs (previously
Magna Carta Fayres), Windsor,
Berkshire

Wonder Whistle Enterprises
Contact Alan and Ludi Kipping
✉ 1 Ritson Road,

London,
E8 1DE 🅿
☎ 020 7249 4050 ✆ 020 7249 5060
📧 alan&ludi@ww-antique-
fairs.demon.co.uk
🌐 www.ww-antique-
fairs.demon.co.uk
Fairs Sandown Park Antique &
Collectors Fairs. Please phone to
confirm dates

Ann Zierold Fairs
☎ 01824 750500
📧 enquiries@annzieroldfairs.co.uk
🌐 www.annzieroldfairs.co.uk
Fairs Antiques, Art Deco, textile
and glass fairs in Liverpool,
Loughborough (please check
provisional dates), Chester and
Leeds

FOR FAIR ORGANIZERS SEE PAGE 518

JANUARY

1

Antiques and Collectors Fair
Organizer Virgo Fairs
Location Ripley,
North Yorkshire
Details Phone for details

Arun Antiques Fair
Organizer Arun Fairs
Location Woodland Centre,
Woodland Avenue,
Rustington, West Sussex,
off A259 ▣
Est. 1995
Entrance fee 75p
Details 40 stalls of antiques and
collectables

Bob Evans Fair
Organizer Bob Evans Fairs
Location Leisure Centre,
Coventry Road, Hinckley,
Leicestershire
(tel. 01455 610011) ▣
Est. 1972
Open 9.30am–4.30pm
Details 120 stalls

Collectamania
Organizer West Country Fairs
Location Weymouth Pavilion,
The Esplanade, Weymouth,
Dorset ▣
Open Trade 9am public 10am–4pm
Entrance fee Trade FWC public
£1 Seniors 80p
Details Antiques and collectables.
75 Stands. Refreshments

Cross County Fairs
Organizer Cross County Fairs Ltd
Location Effingham Park,
West Sussex ▣
Est. 1990
Open 9am–4.30pm
Entrance fee £2

**Ipswich Antiques
& Collectables Fairs**
Organizer Ipswich Antiques &
Collectables Fair
Location The County Hotel,
Copdock, near Ipswich,
Suffolk ▣
Est. 1977
Open 9am–5pm
Entrance fee £1.25
Details Ipswich Antiques &
Collectables Fairs, Copdock,
near Ipswich

Magnum Antiques Fair
Organizer Magnum Antiques Fairs
Location River Park Leisure
Centre, Gordon Road,
Winchester, Hampshire ▣
Est. 1993
Open 9.30am–4pm
Entrance fee £1.50
Details 160 stands of antiques
and collectables

The Best of Fairs
Organizer Best of Fairs
Location Village Hall, Copdock,
near Ipswich, Suffolk (opposite
Moat House Hotel) ▣
Est. 1979
Open 10am–4pm
Details 55 stands. Dateline c1970.
No repro or seconds

**V&A Antique & Collectors
Fair**
Organizer V&A Fairs
Location The Civic Hall,
Nantwich, Cheshire ▣
Est. 2000
Open Trade (FWC) 8.30–10am
public 10am–4.30pm
Details 65+ stands, refreshment
facilities, disabled facilities

1–2

Hingchingbrook Fair
Organizer Hinchingbrooke Fairs
Location Hinchingbrooke House,
Near Huntingdon
Details Hinchingbrooke House
Antiques Fair in the ancestral
home of the Cromwell family
and the Earls of Sandwich

Janba Fair
Organizer Janba Fairs
Location Burgess Hall, St Ivo
Leisure Centre, St Ives,
Cambridgeshire ▣
Est. 1978
Open 10am–4pm (trade FWC) 9am
Entrance fee £1.10 senior 80p
accompanied children under 16 free

2

**Bloomsbury Postcard
& Collectors Fair**
Organizer IPM Promotions
Location Royal National Hotel,
Bedford Way, London WC1 ▣
Open 9am–4.30pm
Early entry 8am
Entrance fee £1

Details 120 stands of postcards,
printed ephemera, autographs,
programmes, photos, cigarette
cards, postal history etc

5

**Antique Collectors Flea
Market**
Organizer Paraphernalia Fairs
Location Lyndhurst Community
Centre, New Forest, Hampshire
Open 9.30am–4.30pm
Details 41 stalls

6–8

Robert Bailey Fair
Organizer Robert Bailey Fairs Ltd
Location Tatton Park, Knutsford,
Cheshire ▣
Open Fri 1–6pm Fri Sat
11am–6pm Sun 11am–5pm
Entrance fee £5
Details 50 dealers, vetted and
datelined

7

Antiques and Fleamarket
Organizer West Country Fairs
Location The Memorial Hall,
Digby Road, Sherborne, Dorset ▣
Open 10am–4pm
Entrance fee Free
Details 45 stands

Suffolk Books Market
Organizer Boxford Books & Fairs
Location Long Melford

7–8

**Devon County Antiques
Fair**
Organizer Devon County
Antiques Fairs
Location Devon County
Showground, Westpoint ▣
Open Sat 11am–5pm Sun 10am -
4pm Early entry Sat 10am
Entrance fee Sat £4.50 Sun 10am
£3.50 1pm £3.00 Children under
16 free Early entry £6
Details Up to 500 stands

8

Antique & Collectors Fair
Organizer Blooms A1 Events
Location The Racecourse,
Beverley, East Riding of Yorkshire ▣
Est. 2000

FAIRS: CALENDAR
JANUARY

Open 9am–4pm
Entrance fee £1
Details 70 stands

Antiques & Collectables Fair
Organizer Take Five Fairs
Location Woking Leisure Centre, Kingfield Road, Woking, Surrey
Open 8.30am–4pm
Entrance fee £2
Details 175 stalls

Bob Evans Fair
Organizer Bob Evans Fairs
Location Leisure Centre, Holmer Road, Hereford (tel. 01432 278178) ⬛
Est. 1974
Open 9.30am–4.30pm
Details 200 stalls

Deco Fair
Organizer Ann Zierold Fairs
Location Marriott Hotel South, Speke Aerodrome, Liverpool

J & K Fair
Organizer J & K Fairs
Location Lincolnshire Showground, A15 north of Lincoln ⬛
Est. 1981
Open 9am–4pm
Entrance fee £1 concessions 70p children under 14 free

Lostwithiel Antiques & Bygones Fair
Organizer Lynne & Richard Bonehill
Location The Community Centre, Lostwithiel, Cornwall, on A390 ⬛
Est. 1989
Open 10.30am–4.30pm
Entrance fee 25p
Details 40 dealers, antiques, bric-a-brac, books, postcards, stamps, jewellery, silver, collectables
Trade only 9.30am FWC

Malvern International Antiques & Collectors Fair
Organizer DMG Antiques Fairs
Location Three Counties Showground, Malvern, Worcestershire ⬛
Est. 1997
Open 8.30am–5pm
Entrance fee 8.30am £4 10am £2.50
Details Up to 200 exhibitors

Midas Antiques Fair
Organizer Midas Fairs
Location Bellhouse Hotel,

Beaconsfield, Buckinghamshire ⬛
Open 10.30am–5pm
Entrance fee £1.50 children (6–16) 50p children under 6 free
Details Quality dateline stands

V&A Antiques & Collectors Fair
Organizer V&A Fairs
Location Park Royal Hotel, Stretton, Nr Warrington, Cheshire (M56 junction 10) ⬛
Est. 2000
Open Trade (FWC) 8.30–10am public 10am–4.30pm
Details 100 stands, refreshment facilities, disabled facilities. Please note that this venue will be closed for two months at some point during the year. Please check with organisers

10–11

Ardingly International Antiques & Collectors Fair
Organizer DMG Antiques Fairs
Location South of England Showground, Ardingly, West Sussex ⬛
Est. 1997
Open Tues10am–6pm Wed 8am–4pm
Entrance fee Tues £20 (includes Wed entry) Wed £5
Details Up to 1700 exhibitors

13–15

The Antique Dealers Fair of Wales
Organizer Allen Lewis Fairs
Location The Orangery, Margam Park, South Wales, West Glamorgan ⬛
Est. 1984
Open 10am–5pm
Entrance fee £3.50 accompanied children under 16 free
Details Fully stand-fitted quality dateline fair featuring full-time antique dealers

The Great Northern International Antiques & Collectors Fair
Organizer Grosvenor Exhibitions Ltd
Location The Great Yorkshire Showground, Harrogate (A661 Harrogate–Wetherby Road) ⬛
Est. 1985
Open Fri 10.30am–5pm Sat Sun 9.30am–5pm

Entrance fee Fri £4 Sat Sun £5
Details About 400 exhibitors
Trade only Fri 8am (£10)

West London Antiques & Fine Art Fair
Organizer Penman Antiques Fairs
Location Kensington Town Hall, Hornton Street, London W8
Est. 1976
Open Thurs noon–8pm Fri Sat 10.30am–6pm Sun 10.30am–5pm
Entrance fee £4
Details 70–85 stands, the best of furniture, arts and artefacts from the past 300 years

14

Antiques and Collectors Fair
Organizer West Country Fairs
Location The Town Hall, Market Square, Wells, Somerset ⬛
Est. 1992
Open 10am–4pm
Entrance fee Free
Details 25 stands. One of the region's busiest Saturday fairs in England's 'smallest city'

14–15

Detling International Antiques & Collectors Fair
Organizer DMG Antiques Fairs
Location Kent County Showground, Detling, Nr Maidstone, Kent ⬛
Est. 1998
Open Sat 8.30am–5pm Sun 10am–4pm
Entrance fee Sat 8.30am £6 Sat 10am Sun £4.50
Details Up to 500 exhibitors

Weekend Antiques Festival
Organizer Antique Forum Group
Location Trentham Gardens (Junction 15, M6) ⬛
Est. 1974
Open 10am–5pm
Entrance fee Free
Details A beautiful setting for an antiques festival (provisional dates)

15

Alexandra Palace Antique & Collectors Fair
Organizer Pig & Whistle Promotions

Location The Great Hall, Alexandra Palace, Wood Green, London N22 🅿
Est. 1970
Open Trade 10am public 11am–5pm
Entrance fee Trade £6 with card public £5
Details London's largest antiques fair with over 700 stands and a substantial amount of furniture

Biggleswade Antiques Fair
Organizer Biggleswade Antiques Fairs
Location Weatherley Centre, Biggleswade, Bedfordshire
Open 9.30am–4.30pm

Bob Evans Fair
Organizer Bob Evans Fairs
Location The Cresset, Bretton Centre, Peterborough (tel. 01733 265705) 🅿
Est. 1974
Open 9.30am–4.30pm
Details 160 stalls

Mark Carter Militaria & Medal Fair
Organizer Mark Carter Militaria & Medal Fairs
Location The Princes Hall, Princes Way, Aldershot, Hampshire GU 11 1NX 🅿
Est. 1988
Open Trade 9.30am public 10.30am–2.30pm
Entrance fee £2 trade preview £3.50
Details 100+ tables of quality militaria, medals and military books

Quality Antiques Fair
Organizer Margaret Browne Fairs
Location Dorking, Surrey

Silhouette Fair
Organizer Fat Cat Fairs
Location The Guildhall, Abbey Close, Abingdon, Oxfordshire, OX14 3JE
Est. 1972
Open 9am–4pm
Entrance fee £1
Details 70 stalls. Good refreshments available

Winter Fair
Organizer Winter Fairs
Location Windsor Girls School, Imperial Road, Windsor,

Berkshire 🅿
Open 10am–4.30 pm
Details Antiques Fair

16

Coin Fair
Organizer Davidson Monk Fairs
Location Drury's Hotel, Great Russell Street, London WC1
Est. 1990
Open 9.30am–2.30pm
Entrance fee £2
Details Coin fair including antiquities and medallions

18–22

The National Fine Arts and Antiques Fair
Organizer Clarion Events–NEC Ltd
Location NEC, Birmingham 🅿
Open Wed 11am–8pm Thurs–Sun 11am–6pm
Entrance fee £10

20–22

Shepton Mallet Antiques & Collectors Fair
Organizer DMG Antiques Fairs
Location Royal Bath and West Showground, Shepton Mallet, Somerset 🅿
Est. 1997
Open Sat 8.30am–9.30pm (early entrance 7.30 am) Sun 10am–4pm
Entrance fee Fri £10 Sat 8.30am £7.50 Sat 9.30am Sun £5
Details Up to 600 exhibitors
Trade only Fri 1–5pm

21

Antiques and Collectables Fair
Organizer Oakleigh Leisure Ltd
Location Assembly Hall, The Green, Station Road, Chingford, London E4 🅿
Est. 1978
Open 10.30am–4pm
Entrance fee £1 adults 70p concessions under 16 free
Details Up to 80 stalls

Camfair
Organizer Janba Fairs
Location Castle Hall, Hertford 🅿
Est. 1979
Open 10am–4.30pm

Entrance fee £1.10 senior 90p accompanied children under 16 free
Details 1930 dateline

22

Adams Antiques Fair
Organizer Adams Antiques Fairs
Location Lindley Hall, Royal Horticultural Hall, Elverton Street (off Vincent Square) Victoria, London SW1
Est. 1971
Open 10am–4.30pm
Entrance fee £3 accompanied children under 16 free
Details The longest-running Sunday fair in London. All manner of antiques

Antique & Collectors Fair,
Organizer Prospect Promotions
Location Wilmslow Leisure Centre, Wilmslow, Cheshire

Antiques and Collectables Fair
Organizer Oakleigh Leisure Ltd
Location Rhode's Art Centre, South Road, Bishop's Stortford, Herfordshire 🅿
Est. 1978
Open 10.30am–4pm
Entrance fee £1 adults 70p concessions under 16 free

Antiques Fairs Ireland
Organizer Antiques Fairs Ireland
Location Tara Towers Hotel, Merrion Road, Dublin 4
Details Provisional date (check by phone or see website)

Biggleswade Antiques Fair
Organizer Biggleswade Antiques Fairs
Location Addison Centre, Kempton, Bedfordshire
Open 9.30am–4.30pm

Bloomsbury Postcard & Collectors Fair
Organizer IPM Promotions
Location Royal National Hotel, Bedford Way, London WC1
Details See Bloomsbury Postcard & Collectors Fair 2 Jan

Bushey Hall School
Organizer David Maggs
Location Bushey Hall School,

London Road, Bushey,
Hertfordshire ▣
Open 9am–3pm
Entrance fee £1
Details 100–120 stalls

Deco Fair
Organizer Ann Zierold Fairs
Location County Stand, Chester
Racecourse

Fat Cat Fairs
Organizer Fat Cat Fairs
Location Burford School,
Burford, Oxfordshire (on A40 to
Cheltenham) ▣
Open 9am–4pm
Entrance fee 75p
Details 46 stalls. Good
refreshments available

M & S Fair
Organizer M & S Fairs
Location Meldreth Village Hall,
10 miles south of Cambridge,
2 miles north of Royston
(just off A10)

**V&A Antique & Collectors
Fair**
Organizer V&A Fairs
Location The Community Hall,
Low Town (on A442), Bridgnorth,
Shropshire ▣
Est. 2000
Open Trade (FWC) 8.30–10am
public 10am–4.30pm
Details 25 stands, refreshment
facilities, disabled facilities

Wessex Antiques Fairs
Organizer Wessex Antiques Fairs
Location Winter Gardens
Pavilion, Weston-super-Mare
Est. 1988
Open 10am–4.30pm
Entrance fee £1
Details Antiques and collectables

24–29

**The Decorative Antiques
and Textiles Fair**
Organizer Harvey Management
Services Ltd
Location The Marquee, Battersea
Park, London
Est. 1985
Open First day noon–8pm then
11am–8pm Sat 11am–7pm
Sun 11am–6pm
Entrance fee £8 including
catalogue

Details Around 100 dealers.
Decorative items, antiques,
modern classics, art and textiles

26

**V&A Antique & Collectors
Fair**
Organizer V&A Fairs
Location The Civic Hall,
Nantwich, Cheshire
Details See V&A Antique &
Collectors Fair 1 Jan

27–29

**The International
Antiques & Collectors Fair
at RAF Swinderby**
Organizer Arthur Swallow Fairs
Location RAF Swinderby, A46
between Newark and Lincoln ▣
Open Fri 7am–5pm Sat Sun
8am–5pm
Entrance fee Fri trade day £10,
Sat Sun £4
Details Over 2000 stands

28

Antique & Collectors Fair
Organizer Dennis Jewellery
Location The Holy Angels Church,
Lilliput Road, Poole, Dorset ▣
Est. 1997
Open 9am–4pm
Entrance fee 50p
Details 17 stands, jewellery,
china, books, postcards, linen, etc

**Antiques and Collectors
Fair**
Organizer West Country Fairs
Location The Town Hall, Market
Square, Wells, Somerset
Details See Antiques and
Collectors Fair 14 Jan

28–29

**Buxton Antique
& Collectors Fair**
Organizer Unicorn Fairs Ltd
Location Pavilion Gardens,
Buxton, Derbyshire ▣
Est. 1977
Open 9am–5pm
Entrance fee £2 Seniors £1.50
Details 100 stalls

The Best of Fairs
Organizer Best of Fairs
Location The Old School, Lower

Green, Long Melford, Suffolk ▣
Est. 1979
Open 10am–4pm
Details 50+ stalls. Dateline c1970.
No repro or seconds

29

Arun Antiques Fair
Organizer Arun Fairs
Location Charmandean Centre,
Worthing, Wes Sussex ▣
Est. 1995
Entrance fee £1
Details Antiques and collectables

Deco Fair
Organizer Ann Zierold Fairs
Location Loughborough Town Hall

Marcel Fair
Organizer Marcel Fairs
Location Berkhamsted Sports
Hall, Hertfordshire

FEBRUARY

2

**Antique Collectors Flea
Market**
Organizer Paraphernalia Fairs
Location Lyndhurst Community
Centre, New Forest, Hampshire
Details See Antique Collectors
Flea Market 5 Jan

2–4

**Newark International
Antiques & Collectors Fair**
Organizer DMG Antiques Fairs
Location Newark & Notts
Showground, Newark ▣
Est. 1997
Open Thurs noon–6pm Fri
8am–5pm Sat 9am–4pm
Entrance fee Thurs £20 (includes
Fri) Fri £10 (includes Sat) Sat £5
Details Up to 4000 exhibitors
Trade only See website for discounts

3–5

Robert Bailey Fair
Organizer Robert Bailey Fairs Ltd
Location Pavilions of Harrogate,
Great Yorkshire Showground ▣
Open Fri 1–6pm Fri Sat
11am–6pm Sun 11am–5pm
Entrance fee £5
Details 80 dealers, vetted and
datelined

4

Antiques and Fleamarket
Organizer West Country Fairs
Location The Memorial Hall,
Digby Road, Sherborne, Dorset
Details See Antiques and
Fleamarket 7 Jan

Devon County Antiques Fair
Organizer Devon County
Antiques Fairs
Location Matford Centre,
Devon ▣
Open 10am–4.30pm Early entry
9am
Entrance fee £2.50 Children
under 16 free Early entry £3.50
Details Several hundred stands,
both inside and out

5

Antiques Fairs Ireland
Organizer Antiques Fairs Ireland
Location Castleknock Hotel,
Porterstown Road,
Castleknock,
Dublin 15

Arun Antiques Fair
Organizer Arun Fairs
Location Woodland Centre,
Woodland Avenue, Rustington,
West Sussex, off A259
Details See Arun Antiques Fair 1 Jan

Battersea Vintage Fashion Fairs
Organizer Pre-empt Events
Location Battersea Art Centre,
Lavender Hill, London SW11 ▣
Est. 2003
Open 9.30am–4.30pm early entry
9am (£2.50)
Entrance fee £4 students £2.50
with card
Details An Aladdin's Cave of
beautiful unique pieces. The
perfect haunt for individuals
looking for one-offs or for
research purposes

Cross County Fairs
Organizer Cross County Fairs Ltd
Location Effingham Park, West
Sussex
Details See Cross County Fairs 1 Jan

Dublin Toy and Train Fair
Organizer B+T Toy Fairs
Location Clontarf Castle Hotel,

Castle Avenue, Clontarf, Dublin 3
Open 10am–5pm
Details Toy and train fair

Fat Cat Fairs
Organizer Fat Cat Fairs
Location New Memorial Hall,
Lechlade-on-Thames,
Gloucestershire ▣
Open 9am–4pm
Entrance fee 75p
Details Good refreshments
available

Fleamarket
Organizer West Country Fairs
Location Weymouth Pavilion,
The Esplanade, Weymouth,
Dorset ▣
Open 10am–4pm
Entrance fee Trade FWC public
£1 Seniors 80p
Details Antiques and collectables.
75 Stands. Refreshments

Ipswich Antiques & Collectables Fairs
Organizer Ipswich Antiques &
Collectables Fair
Location The County Hotel,
Copdock, near Ipswich, Suffolk
Details See Ipswich Antiques &
Collectables Fairs 1 Jan

Magnum Antiques Fair
Organizer Magnum Antiques Fairs
Location Grange Centre, Bepton
Road, Midhurst, West Sussex ▣
Est. 1993
Open 9.30am–4pm
Entrance fee £1
Details 100 stands of antiques
and collectables

Mark Carter Militaria & Medal Fair
Organizer Mark Carter Militaria
& Medal Fairs
Location Yate Leisure Centre,
Kennedy Way, Yate, Bristol ▣
Est. 1988
Open Trade 9.30am public
10.30am–2.30pm
Entrance fee £2 trade preview
£3.50
Details 100+ tables of quality
militaria, medals and military books

The Best of Fairs
Organizer Best of Fairs
Location Village Hall, Copdock,
near Ipswich, Suffolk
Details See The Best of Fairs 1 Jan

10–12

Stafford Bingley Hall Giant 3-Day Antiques Fair
Organizer Bowman Antiques
Fairs Ltd
Location Bingley Hall, County
Showground, Stafford ▣
Est. 1978
Open 10am–5pm
Entrance fee £4 seniors £3
children under 16 free
Details Long-established quality
antiques fair with 420 stands
including 100 furniture stands
Trade only Fri 8.30am Sat 9.30am
(£5)

The Petersfield Antiques Fair
Organizer Penman Antiques Fairs
Location The Festival Hall,
Petersfield, Hampshire ▣
Est. 1973
Open Fri Sat 10.30am–6pm
Sun 10.30am–5pm
Details 43 exhibitors with
traditional and affordable vetted
antiques

11

Antiques and Collectables Fair
Organizer Oakleigh Leisure Ltd
Location Assembly Hall, The
Green, Station Road, Chingford,
London E4
Details See Antiques and
Collectables Fair 21 Jan

Antiques and Collectors Fair
Organizer West Country Fairs
Location The Town Hall, Market
Square, Wells, Somerset
Details See Antiques and
Collectors Fair 14 Jan

London Coin Fair
Organizer Simmons Gallery
Location Holiday Inn, Coram
Street, London WC1 ▣
Est. 1977
Open 9.30am–5pm (last entry
3.30pm)
Entrance fee £4.00
Details Largest specialist UK
numismatic show, over 70 dealers

Suffolk Books Market
Organizer Boxford Books & Fairs
Location Long Melford

FAIRS: CALENDAR
FEBRUARY

11–12

61st Luton Antiques Fair
Organizer Gemsco Promotions
Location Putteridge Bury House,
Hitchin Road, Luton LU2 8LE
(off A505) ▣
Est. 1975
Open Sat 11am–5pm
Sun 10am–5pm
Details Dateline fair, restaurant

12

Antique & Collectors Fair
Organizer Blooms A1 Events
Location The Racecourse,
Beverley, East Riding of Yorkshire
Details See Antique & Collectors
Fair 8 Jan

Antiques & Collectables Fair
Organizer Take Five Fairs
Location Woking Leisure Centre,
Kingfield Road, Woking, Surrey
Details See Antiques &
Collectables Fair 8 Jan

Art Deco Fair
Organizer Abbey Fairs
Location North triline Suite,
Twickenham Rugby Ground,
Twickenham, Middlesex ▣
Est. 2001
Open 10am–4pm
Entrance fee £2.50
Details Art Deco and early post-
war design

Biggleswade Antiques Fair
Organizer Biggleswade Antiques
Fairs
Location Kimbolton Castle,
Huntingdon
Open 10am–4.30pm

Bob Evans Fair
Organizer Bob Evans Fairs
Location Sports Connexion,
Ryton on Dunsmore, Coventry
(tel. 02476 306155) ▣
Est. 1974
Open 9.30am–4.30pm
Details 300 stalls

**Lostwithiel Antiques
& Bygones Fair**
Organizer Lynne & Richard
Bonehill
Location The Community Centre,
Lostwithiel, Cornwall, on A390
Details See Lostwithiel Antiques
& Bygones Fair 8Jan

**Malvern International
Antiques & Collectors Fair**
Organizer DMG Antiques Fairs
Location Three Counties
Showground, Malvern,
Worcestershire
Details See Malvern International
Antiques & Collectors Fair 8 Jan

Midas Antiques Fair
Organizer Midas Fairs
Location Bellhouse Hotel,
Beaconsfield, Buckinghamshire
Details See Midas Antiques
Fair 8 Jan

Northern Clock & Watch Fair
Organizer Northern Clock &
Watch Fairs
Location Haydock Park
Racecourse, Merseyside ▣
Est. 1997
Open 9am–3pm
Entrance fee 9am £5 10.30am £2

**V&A Antique & Collectors
Fair**
Organizer V&A Fairs
Location Park Royal Hotel,
Stretton, Nr Warrington,
Cheshire (M56 junction 10)
Details See V&A Antique &
Collectors Fair 8 Jan

17–19

**The Chester Antiques
& Fine Art Show**
Organizer Penman Antiques Fairs
Location The County Grandstand,
Chester Racecourse, Chester ▣
Est. 1990
Open Fri Sat 10.30am–6pm
Sun 10.30am–5pm
Details 60 stands, furniture, art &
artefacts, mainly pre-1900, a few
modern paintings

18

Camfair
Organizer Janba Fairs
Location Castle Hall, Hertford
Details See Camfair 21 Jan

19

**Abergavenny Antiques
& Collectors Fairs**
Organizer Monmouthshire
County Council
Location Abergavenny Market
Hall, Abergavenny,
Monmouthshire
Details See Abergavenny
Antiques & Collectors Fairs 15 Jan

Adams Antiques Fair
Organizer Adams Antiques Fairs
Location Kensington Town Hall,
Hornton Street,
(Off Kensington High St.),
London W8 ▣
Details See Adams Antiques Fair
22 Jan at the Horticultural Hall
for all other details

**Antiques and Collectables
Fair**
Organizer Oakleigh Leisure Ltd
Location Rhode's Art Centre,
South Road, Bishop's Stortford,
Herfordshire
Est. 1978
Details See Antiques and
Collectables Fair 22 Jan

Antiques Fairs Ireland
Organizer Antiques Fairs Ireland
Location Clontarf Castle, Castle
Ave, Clontarf, Dublin D3

Art Deco Fair
Organizer Abbey Fairs
Location The Grand Hall, Art
Centre, Lavender Hill, Battersea,
London SW11
Open 10am–4pm
Entrance fee £3
Details Art Deco Fair

Biggleswade Antiques Fair
Organizer Biggleswade Antiques
Fairs
Location Weatherley Centre,
Biggleswade, Bedfordshire
Details See Biggleswade Antique
Fair 15 Jan

**Bloomsbury Postcard
& Collectors Fair**
Organizer IPM Promotions
Location Royal National Hotel,
Bedford Way, London WC1
Details See Bloomsbury Postcard
& Collectors Fair 2 Jan

Bob Evans Fair
Organizer Bob Evans Fairs
Location Leisure Village,
Thurston Drive, Kettering,
Northamptonshire
(tel. 01536 414141) ▣
Est. 1974
Open 9.30am–4.30pm
Details 300 stalls

Buxton Book Fair
Organizer Buxton Book Fair
Location Pavilion Gardens, Buxton, Derbyshire **P**
Est. 1982
Open 10am–4.30pm
Entrance fee £1
Details 80 dealers

Chipping Norton Toy Fair
Organizer Don Davidson
Location Chipping Norton School, Burford Road (A361), Chipping Norton, Oxfordshire **P**
Est. 1990
Open 10.30am–3pm
Details Collectors' toy and train fair. 20 dealers

J & K Fair
Organizer J & K Fairs
Location Lincolnshire Showground, A15 north of Lincoln
Details See J & K Fair 8 Jan

Quality Antiques Fair
Organizer Margaret Browne Fairs
Location Dorking, Surrey

Silhouette Fairs
Organizer Fat Cat Fairs
Location The Guildhall, Abbey Close, Abingdon, Oxfordshire, OX14 3JE
Details See Silhouette Fairs 15 Jan

Winter Fair
Organizer Winter Fairs
Details See Winter Fair 15 Jan

21

Sandown Park Antiques Fairs
Organizer Wonder Whistle Enterprises
Location Sandown Park Racecourse, Portsmouth Road, Esher, Surrey **P**
Open Noon–5pm Early trade 11am
Entrance fee £3 Early £4
Details The largest indoor weekly fair in the South

24–26

Galloway Antiques Fair
Organizer Galloway Antiques Fairs
Location Sonyhurst College, Hurst Green, Nr Clitheroe, Lancs
Open 10.30am–5pm

25

Antique & Collector's Fair
Organizer Hoyles Promotions
Location Southport Floral Hall, Southport, Merseyside **P**
Est. 1975
Open Trade 8.30–9.30am public 9.30am–4pm
Entrance fee £2 early £1.50 concessions trade FWC
Details In the recently renovated Floral hall, easy disabled access

Antique & Collectors Fair
Organizer Dennis Jewellery
Location The Holy Angels Church, Lilliput Road, Poole, Dorset
Details See Antique & Collectors Fair 28 Jan

Art Deco Fair
Organizer Take Five Fairs
Location Brunel Train Shed, Templemeads Station, Bristol **P**
Open 9.30am–4pm
Entrance fee £3

25–26

Detling International Antiques & Collectors Fair
Organizer DMG Antiques Fairs
Location Kent County Showground, Detling, Nr Maidstone, Kent
Details See Detling International Antiques & Collectors Fair 14–15 Jan

International Pottery and Ceramics Fair 'Feats of Clay'
Organizer E W Services
Location The Alban Arena Theatre, Civic Centre, St Albans, Hertfordshire **P**
Est. 2005
Open Sat 10am–5pm Sun 10am–3pm
Entrance fee £2.50
Details Studio pottery

Janba Fair
Organizer Janba Fairs
Location Burgess Hall, St Ivo Leisure Centre, St Ives, Cambridgeshire
Details See Janba Fair 1–2 Jan

The Best of Fairs
Organizer Best of Fairs
Location The Old School, Lower Green, Long Melford, Suffolk
Details See The Best of Fairs 28–29 Jan

26

Antique & Collectors Fair,
Organizer Prospect Promotions
Location Wilmslow Leisure Centre, Wilmslow, Cheshire

Antiques & Collectors Fair
Organizer Bentley Grice Promotions
Location The Mermaid, Sackville Hotel, De La Warr Parade, Bexhill-on-Sea, East Sussex **P**
Entrance fee £1
Details Bar, restaurant

Art Deco Fair
Organizer Abbey Fairs
Location The Heritage Motor Centre Gaydon, Warwick (Junction 12 M40) **P**
Est. 1992
Open 9am–4pm
Entrance fee £3
Details Art Deco

Biggleswade Antiques Fair
Organizer Biggleswade Antiques Fairs
Location Addison Centre, Kempton, Bedfordshire
Details See Biggleswade Antique Fair 22 Jan

Bob Evans Fair
Organizer Bob Evans Fairs
Location The Cresset, Bretton Centre, Peterborough (tel. 01733 265705)
Details See Bob Evans Fair 15 Jan

Bushey Hall School
Organizer David Maggs
Location Bushey Hall School, London Road, Bushey, Hertfordshire
Details See Bushey Hall School 22 Jan

Fat Cat Fairs
Organizer Fat Cat Fairs
Location Burford School, Burford, Oxfordshire (on A40 to Cheltenham)
Details See Fat Cat Fairs 22 Jan

M & S Fair
Organizer M & S Fairs
Location Meldreth Village Hall, 10 miles south of Cambridge, 2 miles north of Royston (just off A10)

Wessex Antiques Fairs
Organizer Wessex Antiques Fairs
Location Winter Gardens
Pavilion, Weston-super-Mare
Details See Wessex Antiques Fair
22 Jan

28–1 MARCH

**Ardingly International
Antiques & Collectors Fair**
Organizer DMG Antiques Fairs
Location South of England
Showground, Ardingly,
West Sussex
Details See Ardingly
International Antiques &
Collectors Fair 10–11 Jan

MARCH

1–6

**Fine Art, Design
& Antiques Fair**
Organizer Clarion Events Ltd
Location Olympia Exhibition
Centre, London P
Est. 1994
Open Telephone for details
Entrance fee £10 single £16 double
Details The rich variety of specialist
stock will appeal to collectors and
curators while connoisseurs and
private buyers will find something
unique. An exceptional choice of
antique furniture and fine art is
for sale. Preview night 28 Feb

2

**Antique Collectors Flea
Market**
Organizer Paraphernalia Fairs
Location Lyndhurst Community
Centre, New Forest, Hampshire
Details See Antique Collectors
Flea Market 5 Jan

3–5

29th Annual Antique Fair
Organizer Wilton House
Location Wilton House, Wilton,
Salisbury P
Est. 1977
Open 10am–5pm
Entrance fee £4.50
Details Antiques and collectables

**The Portmeirion Antiques
Fair**
Organizer Allen Lewis Fairs

Location Portmeirion Village,
Gwynedd, North Wales off A487 P
Est. 1980
Open 10am–5pm
Entrance fee Free please apply
for invitation
Details Fully stand-fitted quality
dateline fair featuring full-time
antique dealers

4

Antiques and Fleamarket
Organizer West Country Fairs
Location The Memorial Hall,
Digby Road, Sherborne, Dorset
Details See Antiques and
Fleamarket 7 Jan

Frock Me!
Organizer Adams Antiques Fairs
Location Chelsea Town Hall,
King's Road, Chelsea, London SW3
Est. 2003
Open 10am–5.30pm
Entrance fee £3 accompanied
children under 16 free, students
with valid card £1.50
Details The fashion and
accessories event for Central
London. Vintage costume, period
fashion, modern design, hats,
fans, gloves, shoes, jewellery and
accessories

4–5

**3rd South Herts Antiques
Fair**
Organizer Gemsco Promotions
Location Theobalds Park,
Cheshunt, Herts (off Lieutenant
Ellis Way) P
Est. 2005
Open Sat 11am–5pm
Sun 10am–5pm
Details Datelined event

**Buxton Antique
& Collectors Fair**
Organizer Unicorn Fairs Ltd
Location Pavilion Gardens,
Buxton, Derbyshire
Details See Buxton Antique &
Collectors Fair 28–29 Jan

Devon County Antiques Fair
Organizer Devon County
Antiques Fairs
Location Devon County
Showground, Westpoint
Details See Devon County
Antiques Fair 7–8 Jan

5

Arun Antiques Fair
Organizer Arun Fairs
Location Woodland Centre,
Woodland Avenue, Rustington,
West Sussex, off A259
Details See Arun Antiques Fair 1 Jan

Bob Evans Fair
Organizer Bob Evans Fairs
Location Leisure Centre,
Coventry Road, Hinckley,
Leicestershire (tel. 01455 610011)
Details See Bob Evans Fair 1 Jan

Cross County Fairs
Organizer Cross County Fairs Ltd
Location Effingham Park,
West Sussex
Details See Cross County Fairs 1 Jan

Deco Fair
Organizer Ann Zierold Fairs
Location Royal Armouries, Leeds,
West Yorkshire

Fat Cat Fairs
Organizer Fat Cat Fairs
Location New Memorial Hall,
Lechlade-on-Thames,
Gloucestershire
Details See Fat Cat Fairs 5 Feb

Fleamarket
Organizer West Country Fairs
Location Weymouth Pavilion,
The Esplanade, Weymouth, Dorset
Details See Fleamarket 5 Feb

**Ipswich Antiques
& Collectables Fairs**
Organizer Ipswich Antiques &
Collectables Fair
Location The County Hotel,
Copdock, near Ipswich, Suffolk
Details See Ipswich Antiques &
Collectables Fairs 1 Jan

M & S Fair
Organizer M & S Fairs
Location Cottenham Village College,
north of Cambridge (on B1049)

**Mark Carter Militaria
& Medal Fair**
Organizer Mark Carter Militaria
& Medal Fairs
Location Stratford Leisure &
Visitor Centre, Stratford-upon-
Avon, Warwickshire P
Est. 1997
Open Trade 9.30am public

10.30am–2.30pm
Entrance fee £2 trade preview £3 accompanied children free
Details 90 tables of quality militaria, medals and military books

The Best of Fairs
Organizer Best of Fairs
Location Village Hall, Copdock, near Ipswich, Suffolk
Details See The Best of Fairs 1 Jan

Turn Out Your Attic
Organizer Adams Antiques Fairs
Location Battersea Arts Centre, Lavender Hill, London SW11
Est. 2005
Open 11am–5pm
Details Attic sales in the Grand Hall – toys, retro, records, posters, comics, jewellery, postcards, bric-a-brac, CDs, books, furniture, antiques and collectables!

6

Suffolk Books Market
Organizer Boxford Books & Fairs
Location Long Melford

8–11

Bath Annual Decorative & Antiques Fair
Organizer BABAADA
Location The Pavilion, North Trade Road, Bath 🅿
Est. 1989
Open Wed trade day Thurs Fri Sat public opening
Entrance fee £2 or email for complimentary tickets
Details BABAADA members and invited guests, Restaurant and bar on site

9–12

Robert Bailey Fair
Organizer Robert Bailey Fairs Ltd
Location Tatton Park, Knutsford, Cheshire
Details See Robert Bailey Fair 6–8 Jan

10–12

The Great Northern International Antiques & Collectors Fair
Organizer Grosvenor Exhibitions Ltd
Location The Great Yorkshire Showground, Harrogate (A661 Harrogate–Wetherby Road)
Details See The Great Northern International Antiques & Collectors Fair 13–15 Jan

11

Antiques and Collectors Fair
Organizer West Country Fairs
Location The Town Hall, Market Square, Wells, Somerset
Details See Antiques and Collectors Fair 14 Jan

Camfair
Organizer Janba Fairs
Location Castle Hall, Hertford
Details See Camfair 21 Jan

Suffolk Books Market
Organizer Boxford Books & Fairs
Location Long Melford

11–12

Carmarthen Antiques & Collectors' Fair
Organizer Towy Antiques Fairs
Location United Counties Showground, Carmarthen 🅿
Est. 1994
Open 10am–5pm
Details Antiques and collectables

12

Alexandra Palace Antique & Collectors Fair
Organizer Pig & Whistle Promotions
Location The Great Hall, Alexandra Palace, Wood Green, London N22
Details See Alexandra Palace Antique & Collectors Fair 15 Jan

Antique and Collectables Fair
Organizer East Preston Festival Fair
Location East Preston Village Hall, West Sussex
Entrance fee 50p

Antique & Collectors Fair
Organizer Blooms A1 Events
Location The Racecourse, Beverley, East Riding of Yorkshire
Details See Antique & Collectors Fair 8 Jan

Antiques & Collectables Fair
Organizer Take Five Fairs
Location Woking Leisure Centre, Kingfield Road, Woking, Surrey
Details See Antiques & Collectables Fair 8 Jan

Bob Evans Fair
Organizer Bob Evans Fairs
Location Leisure Centre, Holmer Road, Hereford (tel. 01432 278178)
Details See Bob Evans Fair 8 Jan

Grand Glass Fair
Organizer Take Five Fairs
Location Woking Leisure Centre, Kingfield Road, Woking, Surrey 🅿
Open 9.30am–4pm
Entrance fee £3

J & K Fair
Organizer J & K Fairs
Location Lincolnshire Showground, A15 north of Lincoln
Details See J & K Fair 8 Jan

Lostwithiel Antiques & Bygones Fair
Organizer Lynne & Richard Bonehill
Location The Community Centre, Lostwithiel, Cornwall, on A390
Details See Lostwithiel Antiques & Bygones Fair 8 Jan

Midas Antiques Fair
Organizer Midas Fairs
Location Bellhouse Hotel, Beaconsfield, Buckinghamshire
Details See Midas Antiques Fair 8 Jan

V&A Antique & Collectors Fair
Organizer V&A Fairs
Location Park Royal Hotel, Stretton, Nr Warrington, Cheshire (M56 junction 10)
Details See V&A Antique & Collectors Fair 8Jan

17

St Patrick's Day Antiques & Collectors Fair
Organizer Castle Antique Fairs NI
Location Templeton Hotel, Templepatrick, Northern Ireland 🅿
Est. 1989
Open Noon–9pm
Entrance fee £2.50 accompanied children free
Details 37 dealers

17–19

Galloway Antiques Fair
Organizer Galloway Antiques Fairs
Location Naworth Castle, Brampton, Nr Carlisle, Cumbria
Open 10.30am–5pm

Stafford Bingley Hall Giant 3-Day Antiques Fair
Organizer Bowman Antiques Fairs Ltd
Location Bingley Hall, County Showground, Stafford
Details See Stafford Bingley Hall 10–12 February

18

Coin Fair
Organizer Davidson Monk Fairs
Location Drury's Hotel, Great Russell Street, London WC1
Details See Coin Fair 14 Jan

19

Abergavenny Antiques & Collectors Fairs
Organizer Monmouthshire County Council
Location Abergavenny Market Hall, Abergavenny, Monmouthshire
Details See Abergavenny Antiques & Collectors Fairs 15 Jan

Adams Antiques Fair
Organizer Adams Antiques Fairs
Location Kensington Town Hall, Hornton Street, (Off Kensington High St.), London W8 ♿
Details See Adams Antiques Fair 22 Jan at the Horticultural hall for all other details

Antiques & Collectors Fair
Organizer West Country Fairs
Location Weymouth Pavilion, The Esplanade, Weymouth, Dorset ♿
Est. 1998
Open 10am–4.30pm
Entrance fee £1 seniors 80p accompanied children under 12 free
Details 80 stands. Antiques and collectables, small furniture and thousands of postcards. Refreshments

Antiques Fairs Ireland
Organizer Antiques Fairs Ireland
Location Tara Towers Hotel, Merrion Road, Dublin 4
Details Provisional date (check by phone or see website)

Biggleswade Antiques Fair
Organizer Biggleswade Antiques Fairs
Location Weatherley Centre, Biggleswade, Bedfordshire
Details See Biggleswade Antique Fair 15 Jan

Chiswick Art Deco Fair
Organizer Abbey Fairs
Location Chiswick Town Hall, Heathfield Terrace, London W4 ♿
Est. 1988
Open 10am–4pm
Entrance fee £2
Details Art Deco Fair plus some 20thC

Malvern International Antiques & Collectors Fair
Organizer DMG Antiques Fairs
Location Three Counties Showground, Malvern, Worcestershire
Details See Malvern International Antiques & Collectors Fair 8 Jan

Quality Antiques Fair
Organizer Margaret Browne Fairs
Location Dorking, Surrey

Silhouette Fairs
Organizer Fat Cat Fairs
Location The Guildhall, Abbey Close, Abingdon, Oxfordshire, OX14 3JE
Details See Silhouette Fairs 15 Jan

The Old Brig Antique & Collectors' Fair
Organizer The Old Brig
Location Newton Hotel, Nairn, Inverness
Est. 1974
Open 11am–4.30pm
Entrance fee £1

Winter Fair
Organizer Winter Fairs
Details See Winter Fair 15 Jan

22

Big Brum
Organizer Antique Forum Group
Location St Martin's Market (The Rag), Edgbaston Street
Details See Big Brum Morning Antiques Fair 18 Jan

22–28

The BADA Antiques and Fine Art Fair
Organizer British Antique Dealers Association
Location The Duke of York Square, Chelsea, London SW3 ♿
Est. 1993
Open Opens daily at 11am
Entrance fee Single entry £10 Double entry £15. All tickets include a BADA Annual Handbook and one re-entry pass per person
Details Approximately 100 dealers, members of the British Antique Dealers Association, selling art and antiques

24–25

Peterborough Festival of Antiques
Organizer Bob Evans Fairs
Location East of England Showground, Peterborough (tel. 01733 234451)
Details 1700 stalls

The Edinburgh Book Fair
Organizer Antiquarian Booksellers Association
Location The Assembly Rooms, George Street, Edinburgh
Est. 2000
Open Fri noon–7pm Sat 11am–5pm
Entrance fee Free
Details Antiquarian Books

24–26

Kings Road Antiques Fair
Organizer Penman Antiques Fairs
Location Chelsea Old Town Hall, Kings Road, London SW3
Est. 2005
Open Fri Sat 10.30am–6pm Sun 11am–5pm

Shepton Mallet Antiques & Collectors Fair
Organizer DMG Antiques Fairs
Location Royal Bath and West Showground, Shepton Mallet, Somerset
Details See Shepton Mallet Antiques & Collectors Fair 20–22 Jan

25

Antique & Collectors Fair
Organizer Dennis Jewellery
Location The Holy Angels Church, Lilliput Road, Poole, Dorset
Details See Antique & Collectors Fair 28 Jan

Antiques and Collectables Fair
Organizer Oakleigh Leisure Ltd

Location Assembly Hall, The Green, Station Road, Chingford, London E4
Details See Antiques and Collectables Fair 21 Jan

Leeds Doll & Teddy Fair
Organizer Dolly Domain Fairs
Location Pudsey Civic Hall, New Pudsey, Leeds, West Yorkshire P
Open 10.30am–4pm
Entrance fee Adults £3 children 50p
Details The 25th year of the fair

25–26

Antiques and Collectors Fair
Organizer Virgo Fairs
Location Ripley, North Yorkshire
Details Phone for details

The Best of Fairs
Organizer Best of Fairs
Location The Old School, Lower Green, Long Melford, Suffolk
Details See The Best of Fairs 28–29 Jan

Galloway Antiques Fair
Organizer Galloway Antiques Fairs
Location Lynford Hall, Nr Thetford, Norfolk
Open 10.30am–5pm

26

Antiques & Collectors Fair
Organizer Bentley Grice Promotions
Location The Mermaid, Sackville Hotel, De La Warr Parade, Bexhill-on-Sea, East Sussex
Details See Antiques & Collectors Fair 26 Feb

Arun Antiques Fair
Organizer Arun Fairs
Location Charmandean Centre, Worthing, West Sussex
Details See Arun Antiques Fair 29 Jan

Bloomsbury Postcard & Collectors Fair
Organizer IPM Promotions
Location Royal National Hotel, Bedford Way, London WC1
Details See Bloomsbury Postcard & Collectors Fair 2 Jan

Bushey Hall School
Organizer David Maggs
Location Bushey Hall School,

London Road, Bushey, Hertfordshire
Details See Bushey Hall School 22 Jan

Buxton Book Fair
Organizer Buxton Book Fair
Location Pavilion Gardens, Buxton, Derbyshire
Est. 1982
Details See Buxton Book Fair 19 Feb

Deco Fair
Organizer Ann Zierold Fairs
Location Loughborough Town Hall

Fat Cat Fairs
Organizer Fat Cat Fairs
Location Burford School, Burford, Oxfordshire (on A40 to Cheltenham)
Details See Fat Cat Fairs 22 Jan

V&A Antique & Collectors Fair
Organizer V&A Fairs
Location The Community Hall, Low Town (on A442), Bridgnorth, Shropshire
Details See V&A Antique & Collectors Fair 22 Jan

Wessex Antiques Fairs
Organizer Wessex Antiques Fairs
Location Winter Gardens Pavilion, Weston-super-Mare
Details See Wessex Antiques Fair 22 Jan

30

V&A Antique & Collectors Fair
Organizer V&A Fairs
Location The Civic Hall, Nantwich, Cheshire
Details See V&A Antique & Collectors Fair 1 Jan

31–2 APRIL

Albany Fairs
Organizer Albany Fairs
Location Pooley Village Hall, Ullswater, Cumbria
Est. 1980
Open 10am–4.30pm
Details Antiques and collectables

Galloway Antiques Fair
Organizer Galloway Antiques Fairs
Location Fettes College, Edinburgh, Scotland
Open 10.30am–5pm

The International Antiques & Collectors Fair at RAF Swinderby
Organizer Arthur Swallow Fairs
Location RAF Swinderby, A46 between Newark and Lincoln
Details See The International Antiques & Collectors Fair at RAF Swinderby 27–29 Jan

APRIL

1

Antiques and Fleamarket
Organizer West Country Fairs
Location The Memorial Hall, Digby Road, Sherborne, Dorset
Details See Antiques and Fleamarket 7 Jan

Devon County Antiques Fair
Organizer Devon County Antiques Fairs
Location Matford Centre, Devon
Details See Devon County Antiques Fair 4 Feb

1–2

Buxton Antique & Collectors Fair
Organizer Unicorn Fairs Ltd
Location Pavilion Gardens, Buxton, Derbyshire
Details See Buxton Antique & Collectors Fair 28–29 Jan

2

Arun Antiques Fair
Organizer Arun Fairs
Location Woodland Centre, Woodland Avenue, Rustington, West Sussex, off A259
Details See Arun Antiques Fair 1 Jan

Battersea Vintage Fashion Fairs
Organizer Pre-empt Events
Location Battersea Art Centre, Lavender Hill, London SW11
Details See Battersea Vintage Fashion Fairs 5 Feb

Cross County Fairs
Organizer Cross County Fairs Ltd
Location Effingham Park, West Sussex
Details See Cross County Fairs 1 Jan

APRIL

Fat Cat Fairs
Organizer Fat Cat Fairs
Location New Memorial Hall,
Lechlade-on-Thames,
Gloucestershire
Details See Fat Cat Fairs 5 Feb

**Ipswich Antiques
& Collectables Fairs**
Organizer Ipswich Antiques &
Collectables Fair
Location The County Hotel,
Copdock, near Ipswich,
Suffolk
Details See Ipswich Antiques &
Collectables Fairs 1 Jan

J & K Fair
Organizer J & K Fairs
Location Lincolnshire Showground,
A15 north of Lincoln
Details See J & K Fair 8 Jan

M & S Fair
Organizer M & S Fairs
Location Cottenham Village College,
north of Cambridge (on B1049)

Magnum Antiques Fair
Organizer Magnum Antiques Fairs
Location Grange Centre, Bepton
Road, Midhurst, West Sussex
Details See Magnum Antiques
Fair 5 Feb

Northern Clock & Watch Fair
Organizer Northern Clock &
Watch Fairs
Location Haydock Park
Racecourse, Merseyside
Details See Northern Clock &
Watch Fair 12 Feb

The Best of Fairs
Organizer Best of Fairs
Location Village Hall, Copdock,
near Ipswich, Suffolk
Details See The Best of Fairs 1 Jan

**The International Art
Deco – Art Nouveau – Arts
& Crafts Fair**
Organizer Abbey Fairs
Location Kelham Hall,
Kelham, Newark,
Nottinghamshire P
Est. 2004
Open 9.30am–4pm
Entrance fee £3 Early trade £4
Details Art Deco, Arts and Crafts,
Art Nouveau, early post-war
design
Trade only 8–9.30am

4

Sandown Park Antiques Fairs
Organizer Wonder Whistle
Enterprises
Location Sandown Park Racecourse,
Portsmouth Road, Esher, Surrey
Details See Sandown Park
Antiques Fairs 21 Feb

6

**Antique Collectors Flea
Market**
Organizer Paraphernalia Fairs
Location Lyndhurst Community
Centre, New Forest, Hampshire
Details See Antique Collectors
Flea Market 5 Jan

6–8

**Newark International
Antiques & Collectors Fair**
Organizer DMG Antiques Fairs
Location Newark & Notts
Showground, Newark
Details See Newark International
Antiques & Collectors Fair 2–4 Feb

6–9

Antiques for Everyone
Organizer Clarion Events–NEC Ltd
Location NEC, Birmingham
Details Details as for National
Fine Arts and Antiques 18– 22 Jan

8

Antiques and Collectors Fair
Organizer West Country Fairs
Location The Town Hall, Market
Square, Wells, Somerset
Details See Antiques and
Collectors Fair 14 Jan

Suffolk Books Market
Organizer Boxford Books & Fairs
Location Long Melford

9

Antique & Collectors Fair
Organizer Blooms A1 Events
Location The Racecourse,
Beverley, East Riding of Yorkshire
Details See Antique & Collectors
Fair 8 Jan

**Antiques and Collectables
Fair**
Organizer Oakleigh Leisure Ltd

Location Rhode's Art Centre,
South Road, Bishop's Stortford,
Herfordshire
Est. 1978
Details See Antiques and
Collectables Fair 22 Jan

Antiques & Collectables Fair
Organizer Take Five Fairs
Location Woking Leisure Centre,
Kingfield Road, Woking,
Surrey
Details See Antiques &
Collectables Fair 8 Jan

Art Deco Fair
Organizer Abbey Fairs
Location The Grand Hall, Art
Centre, Lavender Hill, Battersea,
London SW11
Details See Art Deco Fair 19 Feb

Chipping Norton Toy Fair
Organizer Don Davidson
Location Chipping Norton
School, Burford Road (A361),
Chipping Norton, Oxfordshire
Details See Chipping Norton Toy
Fair 19 Feb

London Map Fair
Organizer London Map Fairs
Location Rembrandt Hotel,
South Kensington,
London
Est. 1980
Open 10.30am–5pm

**Lostwithiel Antiques
& Bygones Fair**
Organizer Lynne & Richard
Bonehill
Location The Community Centre,
Lostwithiel, Cornwall, on A390
Details See Lostwithiel Antiques
& Bygones Fair 8 Jan

Midas Antiques Fair
Organizer Midas Fairs
Location Bellhouse Hotel,
Beaconsfield,
Buckinghamshire
Details See Midas Antiques Fair
8 Jan

**V&A Antique & Collectors
Fair**
Organizer V&A Fairs
Location Park Royal Hotel,
Stretton, Nr Warrington,
Cheshire (M56 junction 10)
Details See V&A Antique &
Collectors Fair 8 Jan

FAIRS: CALENDAR

FAIRS: CALENDAR

11–12

Ardingly International Antiques & Collectors Fair
Organizer DMG Antiques Fairs
Location South of England Showground, Ardingly, West Sussex
Details See Ardingly International Antiques & Collectors Fair 10–11 Jan

14–15

Albany Fairs
Organizer Albany Fairs
Location Pooley Village Hall, Ullswater, Cumbria
Est. 1980
Details See Albany Fairs 31 Mar–2 Aprs

Devon County Antiques Fair
Organizer Devon County Antiques Fairs
Location Royal Cornwall Showground, Wadebridge, Cornwall 🅿
Open Sun 11am–5pm Mon 10am–4.30pm Early Entry Sun 10am
Entrance fee Sun £3.50 Mon £2.50 Early entry £4 Children under 16 free
Details 250 inside stands and many outside pitches

14–17

Galloway Antiques Fair
Organizer Galloway Antiques Fairs
Location Cranleigh School, Cranleigh, Surrrey
Open 10.30am–5pm

15–16

Antiques and Collectors Fair
Organizer Virgo Fairs
Location Ripley, North Yorkshire
Details Phone for details

Weekend Antiques Festival
Organizer Antique Forum Group
Location Trentham Gardens (Junction 15, M6) 🅿
Est. 1974
Open 10am–5pm
Entrance fee Free
Details A beautiful setting for an antiques festival

15–17

The 6th North Norfolk Fine Art & Antiques Fair
Organizer Lomax Antiques Fairs
Location Sussex Barn, Burnham Market, Norfolk, PE31 8JY 🅿
Est. 2000
Open 15th 11am–6pm 16th 10.30am–6pm 17h 10.30am–5pm
Details Fine art and antiques

16

Abergavenny Antiques & Collectors Fairs
Organizer Monmouthshire County Council
Location Abergavenny Market Hall, Abergavenny, Monmouthshire
Details See Abergavenny Antiques & Collectors Fairs 15 Jan

Biggleswade Antiques Fair
Organizer Biggleswade Antiques Fairs
Location Weatherley Centre, Biggleswade, Bedfordshire
Details See Biggleswade Antique Fair 15 Jan

Silhouette Fairs
Organizer Fat Cat Fairs
Location The Guildhall, Abbey Close, Abingdon, Oxfordshire, OX14 3JE
Details See Silhouette Fairs 15 Jan

The Old Brig Antique & Collectors' Fair
Organizer The Old Brig
Location The Highland Conference Centre, Nairn , Inverness
Details See The Old Brig Antique & Collectors' Fair 19Mar

Winter Fair
Organizer Winter Fairs
Details See Winter Fair 15 Jan

16–17

Janba Fair
Organizer Janba Fairs
Location Burgess Hall, St Ivo Leisure Centre, St Ives, Cambridgeshire
Details See Janba Fair 1–2 Jan

Wessex Antiques Fairs
Organizer Wessex Antiques Fairs
Location Winter Gardens Pavilion, Weston-super-Mare
Details See Wessex Antiques Fair 22 Jan

17

Antique & Collectors Fair,
Organizer Prospect Promotions
Location Wilmslow Leisure Centre, Wilmslow, Cheshire

Antiques & Collectors Fair
Organizer Antiques & Collectors World
Location Goodwood Racecourse, near Chichester, West Sussex 🅿
Open Trade 6.30am public 9am–3pm
Entrance fee Trade with card £5 7–9am public 9am–1.30pm £3 with concessions 2–4pm £2 no concessions
Details 250 stalls inside, 350 pitches outside

Antiques & Collectors Fair
Organizer Bentley Grice Promotions
Location The Mermaid, Sackville Hotel, De La Warr Parade, Bexhill-on-Sea, East Sussex
Details See Antiques & Collectors Fair 26 Feb

Art Nouveau/Deco Fair
Organizer Take Five Fairs
Location Woking Leisure Centre, Kingfield Road, Woking, Surrey 🅿
Open 9am–4pm
Entrance fee £2.50
Details 200 stalls

Bob Evans Fair
Organizer Bob Evans Fairs
Location Leisure Village, Thurston Drive, Kettering, Northamptonshire (tel. 01536 414141)
Details See Bob Evans Fair 19 Feb

Malvern International Antiques & Collectors Fair
Organizer DMG Antiques Fairs
Location Three Counties Showground, Malvern, Worcestershire
Details See Malvern International Antiques & Collectors Fair 8 Jan

Mammoth Antiques and Collectors Fair
Organizer Castle Antique Fairs NI

FAIRS: CALENDAR
APRIL

Location Lissanoure Castle,
Loughguille, between Ballymena
and Ballymoney, Northern
Ireland **P**
Est. 1989
Open 11am–7pm
Entrance fee £3 accompanied
children free
Details 45 dealers

Quality Antiques Fair
Organizer Margaret Browne
Fairs
Location Dorking, Surrey

21–23

Albany Fairs
Organizer Albany Fairs
Location Pooley Village Hall,
Ullswater,
Cumbria
Est. 1980
Details See Albany Fairs 31
Mar–2 Apr

22

Antique & Collector's Fair
Organizer Hoyles Promotions
Location Southport Floral Hall,
Southport, Merseyside
Details See Antique & Collector's
fair 22 Feb

Antique & Collectors Fair
Organizer Dennis Jewellery
Location The Holy Angels Church,
Lilliput Road, Poole,
Dorset
Details See Antique & Collectors
Fair 28 Jan

Antiques and Collectables
Fair
Organizer Oakleigh Leisure Ltd
Location Assembly Hall,
The Green, Station Road,
Chingford, London E4
Details See Antiques and
Collectables Fair 21 Jan

22–23

Detling International
Antiques & Collectors Fair
Organizer DMG Antiques Fairs
Location Kent County
Showground, Detling,
Nr Maidstone, Kent
Details See Detling International
Antiques & Collectors Fair
14–15 Jan

23

Antiques Fairs Ireland
Organizer Antiques Fairs Ireland
Location Clontarf Castle,
Castle Ave, Clontarf, Dublin D3

Biggleswade Antiques Fair
Organizer Biggleswade Antiques
Fairs
Location Addison Centre,
Kempton, Bedfordshire
Details See Biggleswade Antique
Fair 22 Jan

Bloomsbury Postcard
& Collectors Fair
Organizer IPM Promotions
Location Royal National Hotel,
Bedford Way, London WC1
Details See Bloomsbury Postcard
& Collectors Fair 2 Jan

Bushey Hall School
Organizer David Maggs
Location Bushey Hall School,
London Road, Bushey,
Hertfordshire
Details See Bushey Hall School
22 Jan

Buxton Book Fair
Organizer Buxton Book Fair
Location Pavilion Gardens,
Buxton, Derbyshire
Est. 1982
Details See Buxton Book Fair
19 Feb

Fat Cat Fairs
Organizer Fat Cat Fairs
Location Burford School,
Burford, Oxfordshire (on A40 to
Cheltenham)
Details See Fat Cat Fairs 22 Jan

M & S Fair
Organizer M & S Fairs
Location Meldreth Village Hall,
10 miles south of Cambridge,
2 miles north of Royston
(just off A10)

Mark Carter Militaria
& Medal Fair
Organizer Mark Carter Militaria
& Medal Fairs
Location The Princes Hall,
Princes Way, Aldershot,
Hampshire
GU11 1NX
Details See Mark Carter Militaria
& Medal Fair 15 Jan

27

V&A Antique & Collectors
Fair
Organizer V&A Fairs
Location The Civic Hall,
Nantwich, Cheshire
Details See V&A Antique &
Collectors Fair 1 Jan

27–1 MAY

Harrogate Antique & Fine
Art Fair
Organizer Harrogate Antique &
Fine Art Fair Ltd
Location Harrogate International
Centre **P**
Est. 1974
Open Thurs Fri 11am–8pm Sat
Sun 11am–6pm Mon 11am–5pm
Entrance fee £6 including
catalogue
Details Antiques and fine art

28–29

Albany Fairs
Organizer Albany Fairs
Location Pooley Village Hall,
Ullswater, Cumbria
Est. 1980
Details See Albany Fairs 31
Mar–2 Apr

The 78th London Antique
Arms Fair
Organizer Antique Arms Fairs Ltd
Location Hotel Ibis, Earls Court,
London **P**
Est. 1968
Open Sat 9am–6pm Sun
9am–1pm
Entrance fee Sat 9am £15 (can be
prebooked – covers both days)
Sat afternoon Sun £7 per day
Details The oldest antique arms
fair in the country

28–30

Galloway Antiques Fair
Organizer Galloway Antiques Fairs
Location The Old Swan Hotel,
Swan Road, Harrogate, North
Yorkshire
Open 10.30am–5pm

29–30

11th Mid Beds Antiques Fair
Organizer Gemsco Promotions
Location Silsoe Conference

538

Centre (Cranfield University), Silsoe, Bedfordshire, MK45 4DT (off A6) **P**
Est. 2001
Open Sat 11am–5pm
Sun 10am–5pm
Details Dateline fair, restaurant

Devon County Antiques Fair
Organizer Devon County Antiques Fairs
Location Devon County Showground, Westpoint
Details See Devon County Antiques Fair 7–8 Jan

The Best of Fairs
Organizer Best of Fairs
Location The Old School, Lower Green, Long Melford, Suffolk
Details See The Best of Fairs 28–29 Jan

29–1 MAY

East Berkshire Antiques Fair
Organizer Kibworth Exhibitions Ltd
Location Berkshire College of Agriculture, Hall Place, Burchetts Green, Maidenhead
Details 50 dealers. Quality event

Lindfield Antiques Fair
Organizer Penman Antiques Fairs
Location King Edward Hall, Lindfield, West Sussex **P**
Est. 1973
Open Sat 2–6pm Sun Mon 10am–5pm
Details Traditional and affordable vetted antiques

30

Adams Antiques Fair
Organizer Adams Antiques Fairs
Location Kensington Town Hall, Hornton Street, (Off Kensington High St.), London W8 **P**
Details See Adams Antiques Fair 22 Jan at the Horticultural hall for all other details

Bob Evans Fair
Organizer Bob Evans Fairs
Location Sports Connexion, Ryton on Dunsmore, Coventry (tel. 02476 306155)
Details See Bob Evans Fair 12 Feb

Deco Fair
Organizer Ann Zierold Fairs
Location County Stand, Chester Racecourse

Marcel Fair
Organizer Marcel Fairs
Location Berkhamsted Sports Hall, Hertfordshire

30–1 MAY

Wessex Antiques Fairs
Organizer Wessex Antiques Fairs
Location Winter Gardens Pavilion, Weston-super-Mare
Details See Wessex Antiques Fair 22 Jan

MAY

1

Abergavenny Toy and Train Collectors Fair
Organizer Monmouthshire County Council
Location Abergavenny Market Hall, Abergavenny, Monmouthshire **P**
Est. 2006

Antiques & Collectors Fair
Organizer Antiques & Collectors World
Location Goodwood Racecourse, near Chichester, West Sussex
Details Antiques & Collectors Fair 17 Apr

Antiques & Collectors Fair
Organizer Bentley Grice Promotions
Location The Mermaid, Sackville Hotel, De La Warr Parade, Bexhill-on-Sea, East Sussex
Details See Antiques & Collectors Fair 26 Feb

Art Nouveau/Deco Fair
Organizer Take Five Fairs
Location Harlequins' Stadium, Chertsey Road, Twickenham, Middlesex

Bob Evans Fair
Organizer Bob Evans Fairs
Location The Cresset, Bretton Centre, Peterborough (tel. 01733 265705)
Details See Bob Evans Fair 15 Jan

J & K Fair
Organizer J & K Fairs
Location Lincolnshire Showground, A15 north of Lincoln
Details See J & K Fair 8 Jan

Newtonards Antiques & Collectors Fair
Organizer Castle Antique Fairs NI
Location Queens Hall, West Street, Newtownards, Northern Ireland **P**
Est. 1992
Open 11am–5pm
Entrance fee £2 donation to cancer research (accompanied children free)
Details 34 dealers

Quality Antiques Fair
Organizer Margaret Browne Fairs
Location Dorking, Surrey

V&A Antique & Collectors Fair
Organizer V&A Fairs
Location The Civic Hall, Nantwich, Cheshire
Details See V&A Antique & Collectors Fair 1 Jan

4

Antique Collectors Flea Market
Organizer Paraphernalia Fairs
Location Lyndhurst Community Centre, New Forest, Hampshire
Details See Antique Collectors Flea Market 5 Jan

4–7

LAPADA@TheRoyalAcademy
Organizer LAPADA
Location The Royal Academy, 6 Burlington Gardens, London
Est. 2005
Details LAPADA's new flagship fair will include some 80 members of LAPADA, who will exhibit a wide range of paintings, furniture, jewellery, silver, glass and other works of art

5

Turn Out Your Attic
Organizer Adams Antiques Fairs
Location Battersea Arts Centre, Lavender Hill, London SW11
Est. 2005
Details See Turn Out Your Attic 5 Mar

5-7

Albany Fairs
Organizer Albany Fairs
Location Pooley Village Hall,
Ullswater, Cumbria
Est. 1980
Details See Albany Fairs
31 Mar–2 Apr

Shepton Mallet Antiques & Collectors Fair
Organizer DMG Antiques Fairs
Location Royal Bath and West
Showground, Shepton Mallet,
Somerset
Details See Shepton Mallet
Antiques & Collectors Fair
20–22 Jan

6

Frock Me!
Organizer Adams Antiques Fairs
Location Chelsea Town Hall,
King's Road, Chelsea,
London SW3
Details See Frock Me! 4 Mar

7

Ardingly Sunday Antiques & Collectors Fair
Organizer DMG Antiques Fairs
Location South of England
Showground, Ardingly,
West Sussex **P**
Open 8am–10pm
Entrance fee £5
Details Up to 350 stalls of
antiques and collectables

Arun Antiques Fair
Organizer Arun Fairs
Location Woodland Centre,
Woodland Avenue,
Rustington, West Sussex, off
A259
Details See Arun Antiques Fair
1 Jan

Cross County Fairs
Organizer Cross County Fairs Ltd
Location Effingham Park,
West Sussex
Details See Cross County Fairs 1 Jan

Fat Cat Fairs
Organizer Fat Cat Fairs
Location New Memorial Hall,
Lechlade-on-Thames,
Gloucestershire
Details See Fat Cat Fairs 5 Feb

Ipswich Antiques & Collectables Fairs
Organizer Ipswich Antiques &
Collectables Fair
Location The County Hotel,
Copdock, near Ipswich,
Suffolk
Details See Ipswich Antiques &
Collectables Fairs 1 Jan

M & S Fair
Organizer M & S Fairs
Location Cottenham Village
College, north of Cambridge
(on B1049)

Mark Carter Militaria & Medal Fair
Organizer Mark Carter Militaria
& Medal Fairs
Location Yate Leisure Centre,
Kennedy Way, Yate, Bristol
Details See Mark Carter Militaria
& Medal Fair 5 Feb

The Best of Fairs
Organizer Best of Fairs
Location Village Hall, Copdock,
near Ipswich, Suffolk
Details See The Best of Fairs 1 Jan

10-14

The 42nd Buxton Antiques Fair
Organizer Trident Exhibitions
Location Pavilion Gardens,
Buxton, Derbyshire **P**
Est. 1964
Open Please telephone for details
Details Traditional datelined fair.
General antiques and
collectables

12-14

The Great Northern International Antiques & Collectors Fair
Organizer Grosvenor Exhibitions
Ltd
Location The Great Yorkshire
Showground, Harrogate (A661
Harrogate–Wetherby Road)
Details See The Great Northern
International Antiques &
Collectors Fair 13–15 Jan

13

Antiques and Collectables Fair
Organizer Oakleigh Leisure Ltd

Location Assembly Hall,
The Green, Station Road,
Chingford, London E4
Details See Antiques and
Collectables Fair 21 Jan

Suffolk Books Market
Organizer Boxford Books & Fairs
Location Long Melford

13-14

Carmarthen Antiques & Collectors' Fair
Organizer Towy Antiques Fairs
Location United Counties
Showground, Carmarthen
Details See Carmarthen Antiques
Fair 11–12 March

14

Alexandra Palace Antique & Collectors Fair
Organizer Pig & Whistle
Promotions
Location The Great Hall,
Alexandra Palace, Wood Green,
London N22
Details See Alexandra Palace
Antique & Collectors Fair 15 Jan

Antiques & Collectables Fair
Organizer Take Five Fairs
Location Woking Leisure Centre,
Kingfield Road, Woking, Surrey
Details See Antiques &
Collectables Fair 8 Jan

Lostwithiel Antiques & Bygones Fair
Organizer Lynne & Richard
Bonehill
Location The Community Centre,
Lostwithiel, Cornwall, on A390
Details See Lostwithiel Antiques
& Bygones Fair 8 Jan

Midas Antiques Fair
Organizer Midas Fairs
Location Bellhouse Hotel,
Beaconsfield, Buckinghamshire
Details See Midas Antiques Fair
8 Jan

The Old Brig Antique & Collectors' Fair
Organizer The Old Brig
Location The Highland
Conference Centre, Nairn,
Inverness
Details See The Old Brig Antique
& Collectors' Fair 19 Mar

V&A Antique & Collectors Fair
Organizer V&A Fairs
Location Park Royal Hotel, Stretton, Nr Warrington, Cheshire (M56 junction 10)
Details See V&A Antique & Collectors Fair 8 Jan

16

Sandown Park Antiques Fairs
Organizer Wonder Whistle Enterprises
Location Sandown Park Racecourse, Portsmouth Road, Esher, Surrey
Details See Sandown Park Antiques Fairs 21 Feb

17

Big Brum
Organizer Antique Forum Group
Location St Martin's Market (The Rag), Edgbaston Street
Details See Big Brum Morning Antiques Fair 18 Jan

19–21

Albany Fairs
Organizer Albany Fairs
Location Pooley Village Hall, Ullswater, Cumbria
Est. 1980
Details See Albany Fairs 31 Mar–2 Apr

19–22

Antiques & Audacity
Organizer Jan Hicks
Location Arundel Castle, West Sussex **P**

Est. 2005
Open Fri 10am–7pm Sat 10am–6.30pm Sun 10am–5.30pm
Entrance fee £5
Details Antiques, contemporary art and design

20

Antiques and Collectors Fair
Organizer West Country Fairs
Location The Town Hall, Market Square, Wells, Somerset
Details See Antiques and Collectors Fair 14 Jan

Camfair
Organizer Janba Fairs
Location Castle Hall, Hertford
Details See Camfair 21 Jan

Coin Fair
Organizer Davidson Monk Fairs
Location Drury's Hotel, Great Russell Street, London WC1
Details See Coin Fair 14 Jan

21

Abergavenny Antiques & Collectors Fairs
Organizer Monmouthshire County Council
Location Abergavenny Market Hall, Abergavenny, Monmouthshire
Details See Abergavenny Antiques & Collectors Fairs 15 Jan

Adams Antiques Fair
Organizer Adams Antiques Fairs
Location Kensington Town Hall, Hornton Street, (Off Kensington High St.), London W8 **P**

Details See Adams Antiques Fair 22 Jan at the Horticultural hall for all other details

Antiques and Collectables Fair
Organizer Oakleigh Leisure Ltd
Location Rhode's Art Centre, South Road, Bishop's Stortford, Herfordshire
Est. 1978
Details See Antiques and Collectables Fair 22 Jan

Antiques & Collectors Fair
Organizer West Country Fairs
Location Weymouth Pavilion, The Esplanade, Weymouth, Dorset
Details See Antiques & Collectors Fair 19 Mar

Art Deco Fair
Organizer Abbey Fairs
Location Twickenham Rugby Ground, Twickenham, Middlesex
Details See Art Deco Fair 12 Feb

Battersea Vintage Fashion Fairs
Organizer Pre-empt Events
Location Battersea Art Centre, Lavender Hill, London SW11
Details See Battersea Vintage Fashion Fairs 5 Feb

Biggleswade Antiques Fair
Organizer Biggleswade Antiques Fairs
Location Weatherley Centre, Biggleswade, Bedfordshire
Details See Biggleswade Antique Fair 15 Jan

Bushey Hall School
Organizer David Maggs
Location Bushey Hall School,

THE ANNUAL
Buxton ANTIQUES FAIR
10TH – 14TH May 2006
The Pavilion Gardens
Buxton, Derbyshire

Traditional paintings and watercolours · Antique furniture · Jewellery · Ceramics
Objets d'art · Silver · Glass · Clocks and barometers · Bronzes · Maps and prints

www.buxtonantiquesfair.co.uk

London Road, Bushey,
Hertfordshire
Details See Bushey Hall School
22 Jan

Dublin Toy and Train Fair
Organizer B+T Toy Fairs
Location Clontarf Castle Hotel,
Castle Avenue, Clontarf,
Dublin 3
Details See Dublin Toy and Train
Fair 5 Feb

**National Glass Collectors
Fair**
Organizer Specialist Glass Fairs Ltd
Location The Heritage Motor
Centre
Details Please see website details

Silhouette Fairs
Organizer Fat Cat Fairs
Location The Guildhall,
Abbey Close, Abingdon,
Oxfordshire, OX14 3JE
Details See Silhouette Fairs 15 Jan

**V&A Antique & Collectors
Fair**
Organizer V&A Fairs
Location The Community Hall,
Low Town (on A442),
Bridgnorth,
Shropshire
Details See V&A Antique &
Collectors Fair 22 Jan

Winter Fair
Organizer Winter Fairs
Details See Winter Fair 15 Jan

26–28

**The International
Antiques & Collectors Fair
at RAF Swinderby**
Organizer Arthur Swallow Fairs
Location RAF Swinderby, A46
between Newark and Lincoln
Details See The International
Antiques & Collectors Fair at RAF
Swinderby 27–29 Jan

26–29

**The Antique Dealers Fair
of Wales**
Organizer Allen Lewis Fairs
Location The Orangery,
Margam Park, South Wales,
West Glamorgan
Details See The Antique Dealers
Fair of Wales 13–15 Jan

27

Antique & Collectors Fair
Organizer Dennis Jewellery
Location The Holy Angels Church,
Lilliput Road, Poole, Dorset
Details See Antique & Collectors
Fair 28 Jan

27–28

Antiques and Collectors Fair
Organizer Virgo Fairs
Location Ripley, North Yorkshire
Details Phone for details

The Best of Fairs
Organizer Best of Fairs
Location The Old School,
Lower Green, Long Melford,
Suffolk
Details See The Best of Fairs
28–29 Jan

27–29

**The 14th Langley Park
Spring Antiques Fair**
Organizer Lomax Antiques Fairs
Location Langley Park School,
Loddon, Norfolk,
NR14 6BJ ℗
Est. 1990
Open 27th noon–6pm 28th
10.30am–6pm 29th 10.30am–5pm
Details Datelined antiques

28

Antiques Fairs Ireland
Organizer Antiques Fairs Ireland
Location Tara Towers Hotel,
Merrion Road, Dublin 4
Details Provisional date (check by
phone or see website)

Arun Antiques Fair
Organizer Arun Fairs
Location Charmandean Centre,
Worthing, West Sussex
Details See Arun Antiques Fair
29 Jan

Best of British
Organizer Abbey Fairs
Location The Heritage Motor
Centre Gaydon, Warwick
(Junction 12 M40) ℗
Est. 1992
Open 1am–4pm
Entrance fee £8 on the day (to
include entry to all attractions
including the motor museum)

£5 if purchased in advance from
Abbey Fairs
Details Antiques and collectors'
fair

**Bloomsbury Postcard
& Collectors Fair**
Organizer IPM Promotions
Location Royal National Hotel,
Bedford Way, London WC1
Details See Bloomsbury Postcard
& Collectors Fair 2 Jan

Buxton Book Fair
Organizer Buxton Book Fair
Location Pavilion Gardens,
Buxton, Derbyshire
Est. 1982
Details See Buxton Book Fair 19 Feb

Fat Cat Fairs
Organizer Fat Cat Fairs
Location Burford School,
Burford, Oxfordshire (on A40 to
Cheltenham)
Details See Fat Cat Fairs 22 Jan

28–29

Janba Fair
Organizer Janba Fairs
Location Burgess Hall, St Ivo
Leisure Centre, St Ives,
Cambridgeshire
Details See Janba Fair 1–2 Jan

Wessex Antiques Fairs
Organizer Wessex Antiques Fairs
Location Winter Gardens
Pavilion, Weston-super-Mare
Details See Wessex Antiques Fair
22 Jan

29

Antique & Collectors Fair,
Organizer Prospect Promotions
Location Wilmslow Leisure
Centre, Wilmslow, Cheshire

Antiques & Collectors Fair
Organizer Antiques & Collectors
World
Location Goodwood Racecourse,
near Chichester, West Sussex
Details Antiques & Collectors Fair
17 Apr

Antiques & Collectors Fair
Organizer Bentley Grice
Promotions
Location The Mermaid, Sackville
Hotel, De La Warr Parade,

FOR FAIR ORGANIZERS SEE PAGE 518

Bexhill-on-Sea, East Sussex
Details See Antiques & Collectors
Fair 26 Feb

Art Nouveau/Deco Fair
Organizer Take Five Fairs
Location Woking Leisure Centre,
Kingfield Road, Woking, Surrey
Details See Art Nouveau/Deco
Fair 17 Apr

Bob Evans Fair
Organizer Bob Evans Fairs
Location Sports Connexion,
Ryton on Dunsmore, Coventry
(tel. 02476 306155)
Details See Bob Evans Fair 12 Feb

Malvern International Antiques & Collectors Fair
Organizer DMG Antiques Fairs
Location Three Counties
Showground, Malvern,
Worcestershire
Details See Malvern
International Antiques &
Collectors Fair 8 Jan

Quality Antiques Fair
Organizer Margaret Browne Fairs
Location Dorking, Surrey

JUNE

1

Antique Collectors Flea Market
Organizer Paraphernalia Fairs
Location Lyndhurst Community
Centre, New Forest, Hampshire
Details See Antique Collectors
Flea Market 5 Jan

1–3

Newark International Antiques & Collectors Fair
Organizer DMG Antiques Fairs
Location Newark & Notts
Showground, Newark
Details See Newark International
Antiques & Collectors Fair 2–4 Feb

2–4

Robert Bailey Fair
Organizer Robert Bailey Fairs Ltd
Location Seaford College,
Petworth, West Sussex **P**
Open Fri 1–6pm Sat 11am–6pm
Sun 11am–5pm
Entrance fee £5

3

Devon County Antiques Fair
Organizer Devon County
Antiques Fairs
Location Matford Centre, Devon
Details See Devon County
Antiques Fair 4 Feb

3–4

Buxton Antique & Collectors Fair
Organizer Unicorn Fairs Ltd
Location Pavilion Gardens,
Buxton, Derbyshire
Details See Buxton Antique &
Collectors Fair 28–29 Jan

4

Arun Antiques Fair
Organizer Arun Fairs
Location Woodland Centre,
Woodland Avenue, Rustington,
West Sussex, off A259
Details See Arun Antiques Fair
1 Jan

Cross County Fairs
Organizer Cross County Fairs Ltd
Location Effingham Park,
West Sussex
Details See Cross County Fairs
1 Jan

Fat Cat Fairs
Organizer Fat Cat Fairs
Location New Memorial Hall,
Lechlade-on-Thames,
Gloucestershire
Details See Fat Cat Fairs 5 Feb

Ipswich Antiques & Collectables Fairs
Organizer Ipswich Antiques &
Collectables Fair
Location The County Hotel,
Copdock, near Ipswich, Suffolk
Details See Ipswich Antiques &
Collectables Fairs 1 Jan

M & S Fair
Organizer M & S Fairs
Location Cottenham Village
College, north of Cambridge (on
B1049)

Magnum Antiques Fair
Organizer Magnum Antiques Fairs
Location Grange Centre,
Bepton Road, Midhurst,

West Sussex
Details See Magnum Antiques
Fair 5 Feb

The Best of Fairs
Organizer Best of Fairs
Location New Village Hall,
Copdock, near Ipswich, Suffolk
Details See The Best of Fairs 1 Jan

8–11

ABA Centenary Antiquarian Book Fair
Organizer Antiquarian
Booksellers Association
Location Olympia,
London **P**
Est. 1959
Open Thurs 4pm–9pm, Fri
11am–7pm, Sat 11am–6pm,
Sun 11am–5pm
Entrance fee Thurs £15 and then
£10 (or £15 double) including a
fair guide
Details Antiquarian book fair.
All tickets also allow entry to the
Olympia Fine Arts and Antqiues
Fair and the HALI Textile and
Carpet Fair, which run concurrently

9

London Map Fair
Organizer London Map Fairs
Location Olympia 2,
Conference Centre **P**
Est. 1980
Open Fri noon–7pm Sat
10am–6pm
Entrance fee Free
Details London Map Fairs at the
Rembrandt Hotel, London and
the International Map Fair,
Olympia, London

9–11

Galloway Antiques Fair
Organizer Galloway Antiques Fairs
Location Duncombe Park,
Helmsley, North Yorkshire
Open 10.30am–5pm

9–18

HALI Fair - Carpets, Textiles & Tribal Art
Organizer Clarion Events Ltd
Location The National Hall,
Olympia, Gallery Level **P**
Est. 1998
Open Please phone for information

Entrance fee Please phone for information
Details The rarest and most precious textile and tribal art from around the world. Preview 8 Jun

Summer Fine Art & Antiques Fair
Organizer Clarion Events Ltd
Location Olympia Exhibition Centre, London P
Est. 1973
Open Phone for details
Entrance fee £10 single £16 double
Details The rich variety of specialist stock will appeal to collectors and curators while connoisseurs and private buyers will find something unique. An exceptional choice of antique furniture and fine art is for sale. Preview night 8 Jun

10

Antiques and Collectors Fair
Organizer West Country Fairs
Location The Town Hall, Market Square, Wells, Somerset
Details See Antiques and Collectors Fair 14 Jan

London Coin Fair
Organizer Simmons Gallery
Location Holiday Inn, Coram Street, London WC1
Details See London Coin Fair 11 Feb

11

Lostwithiel Antiques & Bygones Fair
Organizer Lynne & Richard Bonehill
Location The Community Centre, Lostwithiel, Cornwall, on A390
Details See Lostwithiel Antiques & Bygones Fair 8 Jan

Midas Antiques Fair
Organizer Midas Fairs
Location Bellhouse Hotel, Beaconsfield, Buckinghamshire
Details See Midas Antiques Fair 8 Jan

V&A Antique & Collectors Fair
Organizer V&A Fairs
Location Park Royal Hotel, Stretton, Nr Warrington,

Cheshire (M56 junction 10)
Details See V&A Antique & Collectors Fair 8 Jan

15

Chiswick Art Deco Fair
Organizer Abbey Fairs
Location Chiswick Town Hall, Heathfield Terrace, London W4
Details See Chiswick Art Deco Fair 19 Mar

16–18

Stafford Bingley Hall Giant 3-Day Antiques Fair
Organizer Bowman Antiques Fairs Ltd
Location Bingley Hall, County Showground, Stafford
Details See Stafford Bingley Hall 10–12 February

17

Antique & Collector's Fair
Organizer Hoyles Promotions
Location Southport Floral Hall, Southport, Merseyside
Details See Antique & Collector's fair 22 Feb

Antiques and Collectables Fair
Organizer Oakleigh Leisure Ltd
Location Assembly Hall, The Green, Station Road, Chingford, London E4
Details See Antiques and Collectables Fair 21 Jan

Camfair
Organizer Janba Fairs
Location Castle Hall, Hertford
Details See Camfair 21 Jan

17–18

Albany Fairs
Organizer Albany Fairs
Location Pooley Village Hall, Ullswater, Cumbria
Est. 1980
Details See Albany Fairs 31 Mar–2 Apr

The St Albans Art Deco Fair
Organizer E W Services
Location The Alban Arena Theatre, Civic Centre, St Albans, Hertfordshire P
Est. 2004

Open Sat 10am–5pm Sun 10am–4pm
Entrance fee £3
Details Specialist Art Deco fair, 100 tables plus furniture

18

Abergavenny Antiques & Collectors Fairs
Organizer Monmouthshire County Council
Location Abergavenny Market Hall, Abergavenny, Monmouthshire
Details See Abergavenny Antiques & Collectors Fairs 15 Jan

Adams Antiques Fair
Organizer Adams Antiques Fairs
Location Kensington Town Hall, Hornton Street, (Off Kensington High St.), London W8 P
Details See Adams Antiques Fair 22 Jan at the Horticultural hall for all other details

Antique and Collectables Fair
Organizer East Preston Festival Fair
Location East Preston Village Hall, West Sussex
Entrance fee 50p

Antiques Fairs Ireland
Organizer Antiques Fairs Ireland
Location Clontarf Castle, Castle Ave, Clontarf, Dublin D3

Biggleswade Antiques Fair
Organizer Biggleswade Antiques Fairs
Location Weatherley Centre, Biggleswade, Bedfordshire
Details See Biggleswade Antique Fair 15 Jan

Fleamarket
Organizer West Country Fairs
Location Weymouth Pavilion, The Esplanade, Weymouth, Dorset
Details See Fleamarket 5 Feb

Newmarket International Antiques & Collectors Fair
Organizer DMG Antiques Fairs
Location Rowley Mile Racecourse, Newmarket, Suffolk P
Est. 1997
Open 8am–4pm
Entrance fee 8am £6 10am £3.50
Details Up to 250 exhibitors

Quality Antiques Fair
Organizer Margaret Browne Fairs
Location Dorking, Surrey

Silhouette Fairs
Organizer Fat Cat Fairs
Location The Guildhall, Abbey Close, Abingdon, Oxfordshire, OX14 3JE
Details See Silhouette Fairs 15 Jan

The Old Brig Antique & Collectors' Fair
Organizer The Old Brig
Location The Highland Conference Centre, Nairn, Inverness
Details See The Old Brig Antique & Collectors' Fair 19 Mar

Winter Fair
Organizer Winter Fairs
Details See Winter Fair 15 Jan

23–24

Albany Fairs
Organizer Albany Fairs
Location Town Hall, Moffat, Dumfriesshire
Est. 1980
Open 10am–4.30pm
Details Antiques and collectables

23–25

Galloway Antiques Fair
Organizer Galloway Antiques Fairs
Location Blair Castle, Blair Atholl, Pitlochry, Scotland
Open 10.30am–5pm

24

Antique & Collectors Fair
Organizer Dennis Jewellery
Location The Holy Angels Church,

Lilliput Road, Poole, Dorset
Details See Antique & Collectors Fair 28 Jan

Suffolk Books Market
Organizer Boxford Books & Fairs
Location Long Melford

24–25

Antiques and Collectors Fair
Organizer Virgo Fairs
Location Ripley, North Yorkshire
Details Phone for details

The Best of Fairs
Organizer Best of Fairs
Location The Old School, Lower Green, Long Melford, Suffolk
Details See The Best of Fairs 28–29 Jan

25

Bloomsbury Postcard & Collectors Fair
Organizer IPM Promotions
Location Royal National Hotel, Bedford Way, London WC1
Details See Bloomsbury Postcard & Collectors Fair 2 Jan

Bushey Hall School
Organizer David Maggs
Location Bushey Hall School, London Road, Bushey, Hertfordshire
Details See Bushey Hall School 22 Jan

Fat Cat Fairs
Organizer Fat Cat Fairs
Location Burford School,

Burford, Oxfordshire (on A40 to Cheltenham)
Details See Fat Cat Fairs 22 Jan

Malvern International Antiques & Collectors Fair
Organizer DMG Antiques Fairs
Location Three Counties Showground, Malvern, Worcestershire
Details See Malvern International Antiques & Collectors Fair 8 Jan

Mark Carter Militaria & Medal Fair
Organizer Mark Carter Militaria & Medal Fairs
Location Stratford Leisure & Visitor Centre, Stratford-opon-Avon, Warwickshire
Details See Mark Carter Militaria & Medal Fair 5 Mar

Turn Out Your Attic
Organizer Adams Antiques Fairs
Location Battersea Arts Centre, Lavender Hill, London SW11
Est. 2005
Details See Turn Out Your Attic 5 Mar (note that this may be held on 9 July)

Wessex Antiques Fairs
Organizer Wessex Antiques Fairs
Location Winter Gardens Pavilion, Weston-super-Mare
Details See Wessex Antiques Fair 22 Jan

28

Big Brum
Organizer Antique Forum Group
Location St Martin's Market

(The Rag), Edgbaston Street
Details See Big Brum Morning
Antiques Fair 18 Jan

29

V&A Antique & Collectors Fair
Organizer V&A Fairs
Location The Civic Hall,
Nantwich, Cheshire
Details See V&A Antique &
Collectors Fair 1 Jan

JULY

1

Antiques and Fleamarket
Organizer West Country Fairs
Location The Memorial Hall,
Digby Road, Sherborne, Dorset
Details See Antiques and
Fleamarket 7 Jan

1–2

Devon County Antiques Fair
Organizer Devon County
Antiques Fairs
Location Devon County
Showground, Westpoint
Details See Devon County
Antiques Fair 7–8 Jan

2

Arun Antiques Fair
Organizer Arun Fairs
Location Woodland Centre,
Woodland Avenue, Rustington,
West Sussex, off A259
Details See Arun Antiques Fair
1 Jan

Battersea Vintage Fashion Fairs
Organizer Pre-empt Events
Location Battersea Art Centre,
Lavender Hill, London SW11
Details See Battersea Vintage
Fashion Fairs 5 Feb

Cross County Fairs
Organizer Cross County Fairs Ltd
Location Effingham Park,
West Sussex
Details See Cross County Fairs
1 Jan

Fat Cat Fairs
Organizer Fat Cat Fairs
Location New Memorial Hall,

Lechlade-on-Thames,
Gloucestershire
Details See Fat Cat Fairs 5 Feb

Ipswich Antiques & Collectables Fairs
Organizer Ipswich Antiques &
Collectables Fairs
Location The County Hotel,
Copdock, near Ipswich, Suffolk
Details See Ipswich Antiques &
Collectables Fairs 1 Jan

J & K Fair
Organizer J & K Fairs
Location Lincolnshire Showground,
A15 north of Lincoln
Details See J & K Fair 8 Jan

Northern Clock & Watch Fair
Organizer Northern Clock &
Watch Fairs
Location Haydock Park
Racecourse, Merseyside
Details See Northern Clock &
Watch Fair 12 Feb

The Best of Fairs
Organizer Best of Fairs
Location New Village Hall,
Copdock, near Ipswich, Suffolk
Details See The Best of Fairs 1 Jan

6

Antique Collectors Flea Market
Organizer Paraphernalia Fairs
Location Lyndhurst Community
Centre, New Forest, Hampshire
Details See Antique Collectors
Flea Market 5 Jan

7–9

Albany Fairs
Organizer Albany Fairs
Location Pooley Village Hall,
Ullswater, Cumbria
Est. 1980
Details See Albany Fairs
31 Mar–2 Apr

Galloway Antiques Fair
Organizer Galloway Antiques Fairs
Location Alnwick Castle,
Alnwick, Northumberland
Open 10.30am–5pm

Hove Antiques & Fine Art Fair
Organizer Penman Antiques Fairs
Location Hove Town Hall,

East Sussex
Est. 1973
Open Fri Sat 11am–6pm
Sun 11am–5pm
Details Traditional and affordable
vetted antiques and fine art

Robert Bailey Fair
Organizer Robert Bailey Fairs Ltd
Location Tatton Park, Knutsford,
Cheshire
Details See Robert Bailey Fair
6–8 Jan

8–9

Carmarthen Antiques & Collectors' Fair
Organizer Towy Antiques Fairs
Location United Counties
Showground, Carmarthen
Details See Carmarthen Antiques
Fair 11–12 March

9

Deco Fair
Organizer Ann Zierold Fairs
Location Loughborough Town Hall
Details Provisional date

Lostwithiel Antiques & Bygones Fair
Organizer Lynne & Richard Bonehill
Location The Community Centre,
Lostwithiel, Cornwall, on A390
Details See Lostwithiel Antiques
& Bygones Fair 8 Jan

Midas Antiques Fair
Organizer Midas Fairs
Location Bellhouse Hotel,
Beaconsfield, Buckinghamshire
Details See Midas Antiques Fair
8 Jan

Turn Out Your Attic
Organizer Adams Antiques Fairs
Location Battersea Arts Centre,
Lavender Hill, London SW11
Est. 2005
Details See Turn Out Your Attic 5
Mar (note that this may be held
on 25 Jun)

V&A Antique & Collectors Fair
Organizer V&A Fairs
Location Park Royal Hotel,
Stretton, Nr Warrington,
Cheshire (M56 junction 10)
Details See V&A Antique &
Collectors Fair 8 Jan

11–13

The Highland Antiques Fair
Organizer The Old Brig
Location The Highland Conference Centre, Nairn, Inverness 🅿
Est. 1984
Open 11am–4.30pm
Entrance fee £3

12–15

Albany Fairs
Organizer Albany Fairs
Location Victory Memorial Hall, St Andrews, Fife
Open 10am–4.30pm
Details Antiques and Collectables

14–16

Shepton Mallet Antiques & Collectors Fair
Organizer DMG Antiques Fairs
Location Royal Bath and West Showground, Shepton Mallet, Somerset
Details See Shepton Mallet Antiques & Collectors Fair 20–22 Jan

15

Antiques and Collectors Fair
Organizer West Country Fairs
Location The Town Hall, Market Square, Wells, Somerset
Details See Antiques and Collectors Fair 14 Jan

Coin Fair
Organizer Davidson Monk Fairs
Location Drury's Hotel, Great Russell Street, London WC1
Details See Coin Fair 14 Jan

15–16

Buxton Book Fair
Organizer Buxton Book Fair
Location Pavilion Gardens, Buxton, Derbyshire
Est. 1982
Details See Buxton Book Fair 19 Feb

Weekend Antiques Festival
Organizer Antique Forum Group
Location Trentham Gardens (Junction 15, M6)
Details See Weekend Antiques Festival 15–16 Apr

16

Abergavenny Antiques & Collectors Fairs
Organizer Monmouthshire County Council
Location Abergavenny Market Hall, Abergavenny, Monmouthshire
Details See Abergavenny Antiques & Collectors Fairs 15 Jan

Adams Antiques Fair
Organizer Adams Antiques Fairs
Location Kensington Town Hall, Hornton Street, (Off Kensington High St.), London W8 🅿
Details See Adams Antiques Fair 22 Jan at the Horticultural hall for all other details

Antiques & Collectors Fair
Organizer West Country Fairs
Location Weymouth Pavilion, The Esplanade, Weymouth, Dorset
Details See Antiques & Collectors Fair 19 Mar

Biggleswade Antiques Fair
Organizer Biggleswade Antiques Fairs
Location Weatherley Centre, Biggleswade, Bedfordshire
Details See Biggleswade Antique Fair 15 Jan

Quality Antiques Fair
Organizer Margaret Browne Fairs
Location Dorking, Surrey

Silhouette Fairs
Organizer Fat Cat Fairs
Location The Guildhall, Abbey Close, Abingdon, Oxfordshire, OX14 3JE
Details See Silhouette Fairs 15 Jan

17

Frock Me!
Organizer Adams Antiques Fairs
Location Chelsea Town Hall, King's Road, Chelsea, London SW3
Details See Frock Me! 4 Mar

18–19

Ardingly International Antiques & Collectors Fair
Organizer DMG Antiques Fairs
Location South of England Showground, Ardingly, West Sussex
Details See Ardingly International Antiques & Collectors Fair 10–11 Jan

21–22

Albany Fairs
Organizer Albany Fairs
Location Pooley Village Hall, Ullswater, Cumbria
Est. 1980
Details See Albany Fairs 31 Mar–2 Apr

Albany Fairs
Organizer Albany Fairs
Location Town Hall, Moffat, Dumfriesshire
Details See Albany Fairs 23–24 Jun

21–23

The Great Northern International Antiques & Collectors Fair
Organizer Grosvenor Exhibitions Ltd
Location The Great Yorkshire Showground, Harrogate (A661 Harrogate–Wetherby Road)
Details See The Great Northern International Antiques & Collectors Fair 13–15 Jan

22

Camfair
Organizer Janba Fairs
Location Castle Hall, Hertford
Details See Camfair 21 Jan

22–23

Buxton Antique & Collectors Fair
Organizer Unicorn Fairs Ltd
Location Pavilion Gardens, Buxton, Derbyshire
Details See Buxton Antique & Collectors Fair 28–29 Jan

Detling International Antiques & Collectors Fair
Organizer DMG Antiques Fairs
Location Kent County Showground, Detling, Nr Maidstone, Kent
Details See Detling International Antiques & Collectors Fair 14–15 Jan

23

Antiques Fairs Ireland
Organizer Antiques Fairs Ireland
Location Tara Towers Hotel,
Merrion Road, Dublin 4
Details Provisional date (check by
phone or see website)

**Bloomsbury Postcard
& Collectors Fair**
Organizer IPM Promotions
Location Royal National Hotel,
Bedford Way, London WC1
Details See Bloomsbury Postcard
& Collectors Fair 2 Jan

Bushey Hall School
Organizer David Maggs
Location Bushey Hall School,
London Road, Bushey,
Hertfordshire
Details See Bushey Hall School
22 Jan

Fat Cat Fairs
Organizer Fat Cat Fairs
Location Burford School,
Burford, Oxfordshire (on A40 to
Cheltenham)
Details See Fat Cat Fairs 22 Jan

**The Old Brig Antique
& Collectors' Fair**
Organizer The Old Brig
Location The Highland Conference
Centre, Nairn, Inverness
Est. 1984
Details See The Old Brig Antique
& Collectors' Fair 19 Mar

**V&A Antique & Collectors
Fair**
Organizer V&A Fairs
Location The Community Hall,
Low Town (on A442), Bridgnorth,
Shropshire
Details See V&A Antique &
Collectors Fair 22 Jan

Wessex Antiques Fairs
Organizer Wessex Antiques Fairs
Location Winter Gardens
Pavilion, Weston-super-Mare
Details See Wessex Antiques Fair
22 Jan

27

**V&A Antique & Collectors
Fair**
Organizer V&A Fairs
Location The Civic Hall,
Nantwich, Cheshire
Details See V&A Antique &
Collectors Fair 1 Jan

27–30

Antiques for Everyone
Organizer Clarion Events–NEC Ltd
Location Earls Court, London ⓟ
Open Thurs 11am–8pm Fri–Sun
11am–6pm
Entrance fee £10

28

Arun Antiques Fair
Organizer Arun Fairs
Location Charmandean Centre,
Worthing, West Sussex
Details See Arun Antiques Fair
29 Jan

28–30

Albany Fairs
Organizer Albany Fairs
Location Pooley Village Hall,
Ullswater, Cumbria
Est. 1980
Details See Albany Fairs 31
Mar–2 Apr

**The International
Antiques & Collectors Fair
at RAF Swinderby**
Organizer Arthur Swallow Fairs
Location RAF Swinderby, A46
between Newark and Lincoln
Details See The International
Antiques & Collectors Fair at RAF
Swinderby 27–29 Jan

29

Antique & Collectors Fair
Organizer Dennis Jewellery
Location The Holy Angels Church,
Lilliput Road, Poole, Dorset
Details See Antique & Collectors
Fair 28 Jan

29–30

Antiques and Collectors Fair
Organizer Virgo Fairs
Location Ripley,
North Yorkshire
Details Phone for details

The Best of Fairs
Organizer Best of Fairs
Location The Old School,
Lower Green, Long Melford,
Suffolk
Details See The Best of Fairs
28–29 Jan

30

Art Deco Fair
Organizer Abbey Fairs
Location Kelham Hall,
Kelham, Newark,
Nottinghamshire
Entrance fee
Details See The International Art
Deco – Art Nouveau – Arts &
Crafts Fair Fair 2 April

Marcel Fair
Organizer Marcel Fairs
Location Berkhamsted Sports
Hall, Hertfordshire

AUGUST

3

**Antique Collectors Flea
Market**
Organizer Paraphernalia Fairs
Location Lyndhurst Community
Centre, New Forest, Hampshire
Details See Antique Collectors
Flea Market 5 Jan

3–5

**Newark International
Antiques & Collectors Fair**
Organizer DMG Antiques Fairs
Location Newark & Notts
Showground, Newark
Details See Newark International
Antiques & Collectors Fair 2–4 Feb

5

Devon County Antiques Fair
Organizer Devon County
Antiques Fairs
Location Matford Centre,
Devon
Details See Devon County
Antiques Fair 4 Feb

Suffolk Books Market
Organizer Boxford Books & Fairs
Location Long Melford

6

Arun Antiques Fair
Organizer Arun Fairs
Location Woodland Centre,
Woodland Avenue,

FOR FAIR ORGANIZERS SEE PAGE 518

Rustington, West Sussex,
off A259
Details See Arun Antiques Fair
1 Jan

Cross County Fairs
Organizer Cross County Fairs Ltd
Location Effingham Park,
West Sussex
Details See Cross County Fairs
1 Jan

Fat Cat Fairs
Organizer Fat Cat Fairs
Location New Memorial Hall,
Lechlade-on-Thames,
Gloucestershire
Details See Fat Cat Fairs 5 Feb

Magnum Antiques Fair
Organizer Magnum Antiques Fairs
Location Grange Centre, Bepton
Road, Midhurst, West Sussex
Details See Magnum Antiques
Fair 5 Feb

The Best of Fairs
Organizer Best of Fairs
Location Village Hall, Copdock,
near Ipswich, Suffolk
Details See The Best of Fairs 1 Jan

11–13

Stafford Bingley Hall Giant 3-Day Antiques Fair
Organizer Bowman Antiques
Fairs Ltd
Location Bingley Hall, County
Showground, Stafford
Details See Stafford Bingley Hall
10–12 February

13

Bushey Hall School
Organizer David Maggs
Location Bushey Hall School,
London Road, Bushey,
Hertfordshire
Details See Bushey Hall School
22 Jan

J & K Fair
Organizer J & K Fairs
Location Lincolnshire Showground,
A15 north of Lincoln
Details See J & K Fair 8 Jan

Lostwithiel Antiques & Bygones Fair
Organizer Lynne & Richard Bonehill
Location The Community Centre,

Lostwithiel, Cornwall, on A390
Details See Lostwithiel Antiques
& Bygones Fair 8 Jan

Mark Carter Militaria & Medal Fair
Organizer Mark Carter Militaria
& Medal Fairs
Location Yate Leisure Centre,
Kennedy Way, Yate, Bristol
Details See Mark Carter Militaria
& Medal Fair 5 Feb

Midas Antiques Fair
Organizer Midas Fairs
Location Bellhouse Hotel,
Beaconsfield, Buckinghamshire
Details See Midas Antiques Fair
8 Jan

Newmarket International Antiques & Collectors Fair
Organizer DMG Antiques Fairs
Location Rowley Mile
Racecourse, Newmarket, Suffolk
Details See Newmarket Antiques
& Collectors Fair 18 Jun

V&A Antique & Collectors Fair
Organizer V&A Fairs
Location Park Royal Hotel,
Stretton, Nr Warrington,
Cheshire (M56 junction 10)
Details See V&A Antique &
Collectors Fair 8 Jan

16

Big Brum
Organizer Antique Forum Group
Location St Martin's Market
(The Rag), Edgbaston Street
Details See Big Brum Morning
Antiques Fair 18 Jan

18–20

Albany Fairs
Organizer Albany Fairs
Location Pooley Village Hall,
Ullswater, Cumbria
Est. 1980
Details See Albany Fairs 31
Mar–2 Apr

Albany Fairs
Organizer Albany Fairs
Location Pooley Village Hall,
Ullswater, Cumbria
Est. 1980
Details See Albany Fairs 31
Mar–2 Apr

Sherborne Antiques Fair
Organizer Penman Antiques Fairs
Location Digby Hall,
Hound Street, Sherborne,
Dorset
Est. 1973
Open Fri noon– 8pm
Sat 10.30am–6pm
Sun 10.30am–5pm
Details Traditional and
affordable vetted antiques

19–20

6th Annual Giant Weymouth Fleamarket
Organizer West Country Fairs
Location Weymouth Pavilion,
The Esplanade, Weymouth,
Dorset P
Open Trade 9am public
10am–5pm
Entrance fee £1 seniors 80p
accompanied children under
12 free
Details 80+ stands of collectables
and antiques. Refreshments

20

Abergavenny Antiques & Collectors Fairs
Organizer Monmouthshire
County Council
Location Abergavenny Market
Hall, Abergavenny,
Monmouthshire
Details See Abergavenny
Antiques & Collectors Fairs 15 Jan

Ardingly Sunday Antiques & Collectors Fair
Organizer DMG Antiques Fairs
Location South of England
Showground, Ardingly,
West Sussex
Details See Ardingly Sunday
Antiques & Collectors Fair 7 May

Silhouette Fairs
Organizer Fat Cat Fairs
Location The Guildhall, Abbey
Close, Abingdon, Oxfordshire,
OX14 3JE
Details See Sihouette Fairs 15 Jan

The Old Brig Antique & Collectors' Fair
Organizer The Old Brig
Location The Highland Conference
Centre, Nairn, Inverness
Details See The Old Brig Antique
& Collectors' Fair 19 Mar

FAIRS: CALENDAR
SEPTEMBER

24–25

Devon County Antiques Fair
Organizer Devon County Antiques Fairs
Location Royal Cornwall Showground, Wadebridge, Cornwall **P**
Open Fri 11am–5pm Sat 10am–4.30pm Early Entry Fri 10am
Entrance fee Fri £3.50 Sat £2.50 Early entry £4 Children under 16 free
Details 250 inside stands and many outside pitches

25–26

Albany Fairs
Organizer Albany Fairs
Location Town Hall, Moffat, Dumfriesshire
Details See Albany Fairs 23–24 Jun

25–28

Galloway Antiques Fair
Organizer Galloway Antiques Fairs
Location Rookesbury Park, Wickham, Hampshire
Open 10.30am–5pm

26

Antique & Collectors Fair
Organizer Dennis Jewellery
Location The Holy Angels Church, Lilliput Road, Poole, Dorset
Details See Antique & Collectors Fair 28 Jan

Antiques and Collectors Fair
Organizer West Country Fairs
Location The Town Hall, Market Square, Wells, Somerset
Details See Antiques and Collectors Fair 14 Jan

Camfair
Organizer Janba Fairs
Location Castle Hall, Hertford
Details See Camfair 21 Jan

26–27

Antiques and Collectors Fair
Organizer Virgo Fairs
Location Ripley, North Yorkshire
Details Phone for details

26–28

Buxton Antique & Collectors Fair
Organizer Unicorn Fairs Ltd
Location Pavilion Gardens, Buxton, Derbyshire
Details See Buxton Antique & Collectors Fair 28–29 Jan

The Best of Fairs
Organizer Best of Fairs
Location The Old School, Lower Green, Long Melford, Suffolk
Details See The Best of Fairs 28–29 Jan

27

Antiques Fairs Ireland
Organizer Antiques Fairs Ireland
Location Clontarf Castle, Castle Ave, Clontarf, Dublin D3

Bloomsbury Postcard & Collectors Fair
Organizer IPM Promotions
Location Royal National Hotel, Bedford Way, London WC1
Details See Bloomsbury Postcard & Collectors Fair 2 Jan

27–28

Janba Fair
Organizer Janba Fairs
Location Burgess Hall, St Ivo Leisure Centre, St Ives, Cambridgeshire
Details See Janba Fair 1–2 Jan

Wessex Antiques Fairs
Organizer Wessex Antiques Fairs
Location Winter Gardens Pavilion, Weston-super-Mare
Details See Wessex Antiques Fair 22 Jan

28

Antique & Collectors Fair,
Organizer Prospect Promotions
Location Wilmslow Leisure Centre, Wilmslow, Cheshire

Antiques & Collectors Fair
Organizer Antiques & Collectors World
Location Goodwood Racecourse, near Chichester, West Sussex
Details Antiques & Collectors Fair 17 Apr

Antiques & Collectors Fair
Organizer Bentley Grice Promotions
Location The Mermaid, Sackville Hotel, De La Warr Parade, Bexhill-on-Sea, East Sussex
Details See Antiques & Collectors Fair 26 Feb

Bob Evans Fair
Organizer Bob Evans Fairs
Location Leisure Centre, Coventry Road, Hinckley, Leicestershire (tel. 01455 610011)
Details See Bob Evans Fair 1 Jan

Buxton Book Fair
Organizer Buxton Book Fair
Location Pavilion Gardens, Buxton, Derbyshire
Est. 1982
Details See Buxton Book Fair 19 Feb

Malvern International Antiques & Collectors Fair
Organizer DMG Antiques Fairs
Location Three Counties Showground, Malvern, Worcestershire
Details See Malvern International Antiques & Collectors Fair 8 Jan

Mammoth Antiques and Collectors Fair
Organizer Castle Antique Fairs NI
Location Lissanoure Castle, Loughguille, between Ballymena and Ballymoney, Northern Ireland
Details See Mammoth Antiques and Collectors Fair 17 Apr

Quality Antiques Fair
Organizer Margaret Browne Fairs
Location Dorking, Surrey

V&A Antique & Collectors Fair
Organizer V&A Fairs
Location The Civic Hall, Nantwich, Cheshire
Details See V&A Antique & Collectors Fair 1 Jan

SEPTEMBER

1–3

Galloway Antiques Fair
Organizer Galloway Antiques Fairs
Location Naworth Castle, Brampton, Nr Carlisle, Cumbria
Open 10.30am–5pm

The Great Northern International Antiques & Collectors Fair
Organizer Grosvenor Exhibitions Ltd
Location The Great Yorkshire Showground, Harrogate (A661 Harrogate–Wetherby Road)
Details See The Great Northern International Antiques & Collectors Fair 13–15 Jan

2

Antiques and Fleamarket
Organizer West Country Fairs
Location The Memorial Hall, Digby Road, Sherborne, Dorset
Details See Antiques and Fleamarket 7 Jan

Frock Me!
Organizer Adams Antiques Fairs
Location Chelsea Town Hall, King's Road, Chelsea, London SW3
Details See Frock Me! 4 Mar

2–3

Detling International Antiques & Collectors Fair
Organizer DMG Antiques Fairs
Location Kent County Showground, Detling, Nr Maidstone, Kent
Details See Detling International Antiques & Collectors Fair 14–15 Jan

Devon County Antiques Fair
Organizer Devon County Antiques Fairs
Location Devon County Showground, Westpoint
Details See Devon County Antiques Fair 7–8 Jan

3

Adams Antiques Fair
Organizer Adams Antiques Fairs
Location Lindley Hall, Royal Horticultural Hall, Elverton Street (off Vincent Square) Victoria, London SW1
Details See Adams Antiques Fair 22 Jan

Antiques Fairs Ireland
Organizer Antiques Fairs Ireland
Location Castleknock Hotel, Porterstown Road, Castleknock, Dublin 15

Art Deco Fair
Organizer Abbey Fairs
Location The Heritage Motor Centre Gaydon, Warwick (Junction 12 M40)
Details See Art Deco Fair 26 Feb

Arun Antiques Fair
Organizer Arun Fairs
Location Woodland Centre, Woodland Avenue, Rustington, West Sussex, off A259
Details See Arun Antiques Fair 1 Jan

Bob Evans Fair
Organizer Bob Evans Fairs
Location Sports Connexion, Ryton on Dunsmore, Coventry
Details See Bob Evans Fair 12 Feb

Chipping Norton Toy Fair
Organizer Don Davidson
Location Chipping Norton School, Burford Road (A361), Chipping Norton, Oxfordshire
Details See Chipping Norton Toy Fair 19 Feb

Cross County Fairs
Organizer Cross County Fairs Ltd
Location Effingham Park, West Sussex
Details See Cross County Fairs 1 Jan

Fat Cat Fairs
Organizer Fat Cat Fairs
Location New Memorial Hall, Lechlade-on-Thames, Gloucestershire
Details See Fat Cat Fairs 5 Feb

Fleamarket
Organizer West Country Fairs
Location Weymouth Pavilion, The Esplanade, Weymouth, Dorset
Details See Fleamarket 5 Feb

Ipswich Antiques & Collectables Fairs
Organizer Ipswich Antiques & Collectables Fair
Location The County Hotel, Copdock, near Ipswich, Suffolk
Details See Ipswich Antiques & Collectables Fairs 1 Jan

J & K Fair
Organizer J & K Fairs
Location Lincolnshire Showground, A15 north of Lincoln
Details See J & K Fair 8 Jan

M & S Fair
Organizer M & S Fairs
Location Cottenham Village College, north of Cambridge (on B1049)

Mark Carter Militaria & Medal Fair
Organizer Mark Carter Militaria & Medal Fairs
Location The Princes Hall, Princes Way, Aldershot, Hampshire GU11 1NX
Details See Mark Carter Militaria & Medal Fair 15 Jan

Northern Clock & Watch Fair
Organizer Northern Clock & Watch Fairs
Location Haydock Park Racecourse, Merseyside
Details See Northern Clock & Watch Fair 12 Feb

The Best of Fairs
Organizer Best of Fairs
Location Village Hall, Copdock, near Ipswich, Suffolk
Details See The Best of Fairs 1 Jan

5–6

Ardingly International Antiques & Collectors Fair
Organizer DMG Antiques Fairs
Location South of England Showground, Ardingly, West Sussex
Details See Ardingly International Antiques & Collectors Fair 10–11 Jan

7

Antique Collectors Flea Market
Organizer Paraphernalia Fairs
Location Lyndhurst Community Centre, New Forest, Hampshire
Details See Antique Collectors Flea Market 5 Jan

7–10

Robert Bailey Fair
Organizer Robert Bailey Fairs Ltd
Location Tatton Park, Knutsford, Cheshire
Details See Robert Bailey Fair 6–8 Jan

8–10

Albany Fairs
Organizer Albany Fairs
Location Pooley Village Hall,

551

Ullswater, Cumbria
Est. 1980
Details See Albany Fairs 31
Mar–2 Apr

The Antique Dealers Fair of Wales
Organizer Allen Lewis Fairs
Location The Orangery,
Margam Park, South Wales,
West Glamorgan
Details See The Antique Dealers
Fair of Wales 13–15 Jan

The Petersfield Antiques Fair
Organizer Penman Antiques Fairs
Location The Festival Hall,
Petersfield, Hampshire
Details See Petersfield Antiques
Fair 10–12 February

9

Antique & Collector's Fair
Organizer Hoyles Promotions
Location Southport Floral Hall,
Southport, Merseyside
Details See Antique & Collector's
fair 22 Feb

Antiques and Collectors Fair
Organizer West Country Fairs
Location The Town Hall, Market
Square, Wells, Somerset
Details See Antiques and
Collectors Fair 14 Jan

Coin Fair
Organizer Davidson Monk Fairs
Location Drury's Hotel,
Great Russell Street,
London WC1
Details See Coin Fair 14 Jan

Suffolk Books Market
Organizer Boxford Books & Fairs
Location Long Melford

10

Abergavenny Antiques & Collectors Fairs
Organizer Monmouthshire
County Council
Location Abergavenny Market Hall,
Abergavenny, Monmouthshire
Details See Abergavenny
Antiques & Collectors Fairs 15 Jan

Bob Evans Fair
Organizer Bob Evans Fairs
Location The Cresset,

Bretton Centre, Peterborough
(tel. 01733 265705)
Details See Bob Evans Fair 15 Jan

Chiswick Art Deco Fair
Organizer Abbey Fairs
Location Chiswick Town Hall,
Heathfield Terrace,
London W4
Details See Chiswick Art Deco
Fair 19 Mar

Lostwithiel Antiques & Bygones Fair
Organizer Lynne & Richard Bonehill
Location The Community Centre,
Lostwithiel, Cornwall, on A390
Details See Lostwithiel Antiques
& Bygones Fair 8 Jan

Midas Antiques Fair
Organizer Midas Fairs
Location Bellhouse Hotel,
Beaconsfield, Buckinghamshire
Details See Midas Antiques Fair
8 Jan

V&A Antique & Collectors Fair
Organizer V&A Fairs
Location Park Royal Hotel,
Stretton, Nr Warrington,
Cheshire (M56 junction 10)
Details See V&A Antique &
Collectors Fair 8 Jan

15–16

Albany Fairs
Organizer Albany Fairs
Location Town Hall, Moffat,
Dumfriesshire
Details See Albany Fairs 23–24 Jun

15–24

100th Chelsea Antiques Fair
Organizer Penman Antiques Fairs
Location Chelsea Old Town Hall,
Kings Road, Chelsea,
London SW3
Est. 1950
Open Check website for times
Details Traditional antiques fair
with quality period furniture and
stylish artefacts

16

Camfair
Organizer Janba Fairs
Location Castle Hall, Hertford
Details See Camfair 21 Jan

Newtonards Antiques & Collectors Fair
Organizer Castle Antique Fairs NI
Location Queens Hall, West
Street, Newtownards, Northern
Ireland
Details See Newtonards Antiques
& Collectors Fair 1 May

16–17

Antiques Fair
Organizer Allen Lewis Fairs
Location Ruthin School, Ruthin,
Denbighshire ℗
Open 10am–5pm
Entrance fee £2 accompanied
children under 16 free
Details Fully stand-fitted quality
dateline fair featuring full-time
antique dealers. Phone for details

Carmarthen Antiques & Collectors' Fair
Organizer Towy Antiques Fairs
Location United Counties
Showground, Carmarthen
Details See Carmarthen Antiques
Fair 11–12 March

17

Alexandra Palace Antique & Collectors Fair
Organizer Pig & Whistle
Promotions
Location The Great Hall,
Alexandra Palace, Wood Green,
London N22
Details See Alexandra Palace
Antique & Collectors Fair 15 Jan

Antiques and Collectables Fair
Organizer Oakleigh Leisure Ltd
Location Rhode's Art Centre,
South Road, Bishop's Stortford,
Herfordshire
Est. 1978
Details See Antiques and
Collectables Fair 22 Jan

Antiques Fairs Ireland
Organizer Antiques Fairs Ireland
Location Tara Towers Hotel,
Merrion Road, Dublin 4
Details Provisional date (check by
phone or see website)

Biggleswade Antiques Fair
Organizer Biggleswade Antiques
Fairs
Location Weatherley Centre,

Biggleswade, Bedfordshire
Details See Biggleswade Antique
Fair 15 Jan

Bob Evans Fair
Organizer Bob Evans Fairs
Location Leisure Village,
Thurston Drive, Kettering,
Northamptonshire
(tel. 01536 414141)
Details See Bob Evans Fair 19 Feb

Dublin Toy and Train Fair
Organizer B+T Toy Fairs
Location Clontarf Castle Hotel,
Castle Avenue, Clontarf,
Dublin 3
Details See Dublin Toy and Train
Fair 5 Feb

**Malvern International
Antiques & Collectors Fair**
Organizer DMG Antiques Fairs
Location Three Counties
Showground, Malvern,
Worcestershire
Details See Malvern
International Antiques &
Collectors Fair 8 Jan

Quality Antiques Fair
Organizer Margaret Browne Fairs
Location Dorking, Surrey

Silhouette Fairs
Organizer Fat Cat Fairs
Location The Guildhall,
Abbey Close, Abingdon,
Oxfordshire,
OX14 3JE
Details See Silhouette Fairs 15 Jan

**The Old Brig Antique
& Collectors' Fair**
Organizer The Old Brig
Location The Highland
Conference Centre, Nairn,
Inverness
Details See The Old Brig Antique
& Collectors' Fair 19 Mar

Winter Fair
Organizer Winter Fairs
Details See Winter Fair 15 Jan

20

Big Brum
Organizer Antique Forum Group
Location St Martin's Market
(The Rag), Edgbaston Street
Details See Big Brum Morning
Antiques Fair 18 Jan

22–24

Albany Fairs
Organizer Albany Fairs
Location Pooley Village Hall,
Ullswater, Cumbria
Est. 1980
Details See Albany Fairs 31
Mar–2 Apr

**Shepton Mallet Antiques
& Collectors Fair**
Organizer DMG Antiques Fairs
Location Royal Bath and West
Showground, Shepton Mallet,
Somerset
Details See Shepton Mallet
Antiques & Collectors Fair
20–22 Jan

23–24

**Antiques and Collectors
Fair**
Organizer Virgo Fairs
Location Ripley, North Yorkshire
Details Phone for details

**Buxton Antique
& Collectors Fair**
Organizer Unicorn Fairs Ltd
Location Pavilion Gardens,
Buxton, Derbyshire
Details See Buxton Antique &
Collectors Fair 28–29 Jan

The Best of Fairs
Organizer Best of Fairs
Location The Old School, Lower
Green, Long Melford, Suffolk
Details See The Best of Fairs
28–29 Jan

Weekend Antiques Festival
Organizer Antique Forum Group
Location Trentham Gardens
(Junction 15, M6)
Details See Weekend Antiques
Festival 15–16 Apr

24

Arun Antiques Fair
Organizer Arun Fairs
Location Charmandean Centre,
Worthing, West Sussex
Details See Arun Antiques Fair
29 Jan

Biggleswade Antiques Fair
Organizer Biggleswade Antiques
Fairs
Location Addison Centre,

Kempton, Bedfordshire
Details See Biggleswade Antique
Fair 22 Jan

Bushey Hall School
Organizer David Maggs
Location Bushey Hall School,
London Road, Bushey,
Hertfordshire
Details See Bushey Hall School
22 Jan

Buxton Book Fair
Organizer Buxton Book Fair
Location Pavilion Gardens,
Buxton, Derbyshire
Est. 1982
Details See Buxton Book Fair
19 Feb

Deco Fair
Organizer Ann Zierold Fairs
Location Royal Armouries, Leeds,
West Yorkshire

Fat Cat Fairs
Organizer Fat Cat Fairs
Location Burford School,
Burford, Oxfordshire (on A40 to
Cheltenham)
Details See Fat Cat Fairs 22 Jan

**V&A Antique & Collectors
Fair**
Organizer V&A Fairs
Location The Community Hall,
Low Town (on A442), Bridgnorth,
Shropshire
Details See V&A Antique &
Collectors Fair 22 Jan

Wessex Antiques Fairs
Organizer Wessex Antiques Fairs
Location Winter Gardens
Pavilion, Weston-super-Mare
Details See Wessex Antiques Fair
22 Jan

24–25

**The 77th London Antique
Arms Fair**
Organizer Antique Arms Fairs Ltd
Location Hotel Ibis, Earls Court,
Londonn
Details See 76th London Antique
Arms Fair 28–29 April

28

**V&A Antique & Collectors
Fair**
Organizer V&A Fairs

Location The Civic Hall, Nantwich, Cheshire
Details See V&A Antique & Collectors Fair 1 Jan

29–30

Coinex
Organizer British NumismaticTrade Association Ltd
Location London
Est. 1978
Details Annual fair organised by the BNTA, coins, banknotes, medals. Please phone for details of location, fees and opening hours

Peterborough Festival of Antiques
Organizer Bob Evans Fairs
Location East of England Showground, Peterborough (tel. 01733 234451)
Details See Peterborough Festival of Antiques 24–25 Mar

29–1 OCTOBER

Stafford Bingley Hall Giant 3-Day Antiques Fair
Organizer Bowman Antiques Fairs Ltd
Location Bingley Hall, County Showground, Stafford
Details See Stafford Bingley Hall 10–12 February

29–2 OCTOBER

Robert Bailey Fair
Organizer Robert Bailey Fairs Ltd
Location Pavilions of Harrogate, Great Yorkshire Showground
Details See Robert Bailey Fair 3–5 Feb

29–3 OCTOBER

Harrogate Antique & Fine Art Fair
Organizer Harrogate Antique & Fine Art Fair Ltd
Location Harrogate International Centre
Details Harrogate Antique & Fine Art Fair 27 Apr–1 May

30

Antique & Collectors Fair
Organizer Dennis Jewellery
Location The Holy Angels Church,

Lilliput Road, Poole, Dorset
Details See Antique & Collectors Fair 28 Jan

OCTOBER

1

Adams Antiques Fair
Organizer Adams Antiques Fairs
Location Kensington Town Hall, Hornton Street, (Off Kensington High St.), London W8 🄿
Details See Adams Antiques Fair 22 Jan at the Horticultural hall for all other details

Arun Antiques Fair
Organizer Arun Fairs
Location Woodland Centre, Woodland Avenue, Rustington, West Sussex, off A259
Details See Arun Antiques Fair 1 Jan

Cross County Fairs
Organizer Cross County Fairs Ltd
Location Effingham Park, West Sussex
Details See Cross County Fairs 1 Jan

Deco Fair
Organizer Ann Zierold Fairs
Location Loughborough Town Hall
Details Provisional date

Fat Cat Fairs
Organizer Fat Cat Fairs
Location New Memorial Hall, Lechlade-on-Thames, Gloucestershire
Details See Fat Cat Fairs 5 Feb

Fleamarket
Organizer West Country Fairs
Location Weymouth Pavilion, The Esplanade, Weymouth, Dorset
Details See Fleamarket 5 Feb

Ipswich Antiques & Collectables Fairs
Organizer Ipswich Antiques & Collectables Fair
Location The County Hotel, Copdock, near Ipswich, Suffolk
Details See Ipswich Antiques & Collectables Fairs 1 Jan

M & S Fair
Organizer M & S Fairs
Location Cottenham Village College, north of Cambridge (on B1049)

Magnum Antiques Fair
Organizer Magnum Antiques Fairs
Location Grange Centre, Bepton Road, Midhurst, West Sussex
Details See Magnum Antiques Fair 5 Feb

Mark Carter Militaria & Medal Fair
Organizer Mark Carter Militaria & Medal Fairs
Location Yate Leisure Centre, Kennedy Way, Yate, Bristol
Details See Mark Carter Militaria & Medal Fair 5 Feb

The Best of Fairs
Organizer Best of Fairs
Location Village Hall, Copdock, near Ipswich, Suffolk
Details See The Best of Fairs 1 Jan

3

Sandown Park Antiques Fairs
Organizer Wonder Whistle Enterprises
Location Sandown Park Racecourse, Portsmouth Road, Esher, Surrey
Details See Sandown Park Antiques Fairs 21 Feb

3–8

The Decorative Antiques and Textiles Fair
Organizer Harvey Management Services Ltd
Location The Marquee, Battersea Park, London
Details See The Decorative Antiques and Textiles Fair 24–29 Jan

5

Antique Collectors Flea Market
Organizer Paraphernalia Fairs
Location Lyndhurst Community Centre, New Forest, Hampshire
Details See Antique Collectors Flea Market 5 Jan

6–8

Albany Fairs
Organizer Albany Fairs
Location Pooley Village Hall, Ullswater, Cumbria
Est. 1980
Details See Albany Fairs 31 Mar–2 Apr

Galloway Antiques Fairr
Organizer Galloway Antiques Fairs
Location Stansted House, Rowlands Castle, Hampshire
Open 10.30am–5pm

The International Antiques & Collectors Fair at RAF Swinderby
Organizer Arthur Swallow Fairs
Location RAF Swinderby, A46 between Newark and Lincoln
Details See The International Antiques & Collectors Fair at RAF Swinderby 27–29 Jan

7

Devon County Antiques Fair
Organizer Devon County Antiques Fairs
Location Matford Centre, Devon
Details See Devon County Antiques Fair 4 Feb

8

Antique & Collectors Fair
Organizer Blooms A1 Events
Location The Racecourse, Beverley, East Riding of Yorkshire
Details See Antique & Collectors Fair 8 Jan

Antique and Collectables Fair
Organizer East Preston Festival Fair
Location East Preston Village Hall, West Sussex
Entrance fee 50p

Antiques & Collectables Fair
Organizer Take Five Fairs
Location Woking Leisure Centre, Kingfield Road, Woking, Surrey
Details See Antiques & Collectables Fair 8 Jan

Art Deco Fair
Organizer Abbey Fairs
Location Kelham Hall, Kelham, Newark, Nottinghamshire
Entrance fee
Details See The International Art Deco – Art Nouveau – Arts & Crafts Fair Fair 2 April

Bob Evans Fair
Organizer Bob Evans Fairs
Location Leisure Centre, Holmer Road, Hereford (tel. 01432 278178)
Details See Bob Evans Fair 8 Jan

J & K Fair
Organizer J & K Fairs
Location Lincolnshire Showground, A15 north of Lincoln
Details See J & K Fair 8 Jan

London Map Fair
Organizer London Map Fairs
Location Rembrandt Hotel, South Kensington, London
Details See London Map Fair 9 Apr

Lostwithiel Antiques & Bygones Fair
Organizer Lynne & Richard Bonehill
Location The Community Centre, Lostwithiel, Cornwall, on A390
Details See Lostwithiel Antiques & Bygones Fair 8 Jan

Midas Antiques Fair
Organizer Midas Fairs
Location Bellhouse Hotel, Beaconsfield, Buckinghamshire
Details See Midas Antiques Fair 8 Jan

The London Pen Show
Organizer The Battersea Pen Home
Location Kensington Town Hall, London P
Open 10am–5pm
Entrance fee £5 (£20 from 8am)
Details Sponsored by Conway Stewart Ltd

Turn Out Your Attic
Organizer Adams Antiques Fairs
Location Battersea Arts Centre, Lavender Hill, London SW11
Est. 2005
Details See Turn Out Your Attic 5 Mar

V&A Antique & Collectors Fair
Organizer V&A Fairs
Location Park Royal Hotel, Stretton, Nr Warrington, Cheshire (M56 junction 10)
Details See V&A Antique & Collectors Fair 8 Jan

12–14

Newark International Antiques & Collectors Fair
Organizer DMG Antiques Fairs
Location Newark & Notts Showground, Newark
Details See Newark International Antiques & Collectors Fair 2–4 Feb

13–15

Robert Bailey Fair
Organizer Robert Bailey Fairs Ltd
Location Pavilion Gardens, Buxton, Derbyshire P
Open Fri 1–6pm Sat 11am–6pm Sun 11am–5pm
Entrance fee £5
Details 50 dealers, vetted and datelined

14

Antiques and Collectors Fair
Organizer West Country Fairs
Location The Town Hall, Market Square, Wells, Somerset
Details See Antiques and Collectors Fair 14 Jan

Leeds Doll & Teddy Fair
Organizer Dolly Domain Fairs
Location Pudsey Civic Hall, New Pudsey, Leeds, West Yorkshire
Details See Leeds Doll & Teddy Fair 25 Mar

Winter Fair
Organizer Winter Fairs
Details See Winter Fair 15 Jan

14–15

62nd Luton Antiques Fair
Organizer Gemsco Promotions
Location Putteridge Bury House, Hitchin Road, Luton LU2 8LE (off A505)
Details See 61st Luton Antiques Fair 11–12 Feb

15

Abergavenny Antiques & Collectors Fairs
Organizer Monmouthshire

FAIRS: CALENDAR
OCTOBER

County Council
Location Abergavenny Market Hall, Abergavenny, Monmouthshire
Details See Abergavenny Antiques & Collectors Fairs 15 Jan

Antiques & Collectors Fair
Organizer West Country Fairs
Location Weymouth Pavilion, The Esplanade, Weymouth, Dorset
Details See Antiques & Collectors Fair 19 Mar

Antiques Fairs Ireland
Organizer Antiques Fairs Ireland
Location Clontarf Castle, Castle Ave, Clontarf, Dublin D3

Art Deco Fair
Organizer Abbey Fairs
Location The Grand Hall, Art Centre, Lavender Hill, Battersea, London SW11
Details See Art Deco Fair 19 Feb

Biggleswade Antiques Fair
Organizer Biggleswade Antiques Fairs
Location Weatherley Centre, Biggleswade, Bedfordshire
Details See Biggleswade Antique Fair 15 Jan

Bob Evans Fair
Organizer Bob Evans Fairs
Location Leisure Centre, Coventry Road, Hinckley, Leicestershire
Details See Bob Evans Fair 1 Jan

Malvern International Antiques & Collectors Fair
Organizer DMG Antiques Fairs
Location Three Counties Showground, Malvern, Worcestershire
Details See Malvern International Antiques & Collectors Fair 8 Jan

Quality Antiques Fair
Organizer Margaret Browne Fairs
Location Dorking, Surrey

Silhouette Fairs
Organizer Fat Cat Fairs
Location The Guildhall, Abbey Close, Abingdon, Oxfordshire, OX14 3JE
Details See Silhouette Fairs 15 Jan

The Old Brig Antique & Collectors' Fair
Organizer The Old Brig
Location The Highland Conference Centre, Nairn, Inverness
Details See The Old Brig Antique & Collectors' Fair 19 Mar

18
Big Brum
Organizer Antique Forum Group
Location St Martin's Market (The Rag), Edgbaston Street
Details See Big Brum Morning Antiques Fair 18 Jan

19–22
The LAPADA Antiques & Fine Art Fair
Organizer The Antique Dealers Fair Ltd
Location Cheltenham Racecourse, Cheltenham, Gloucestershire 🅿
Est. 2004
Open Thur 11am–8pm Fri Sat 11am–6pm Sun 11am–5pm
Entrance fee £10
Details Showcase for members of LAPADA, with 90 stands

20–22
Albany Fairs
Organizer Albany Fairs
Location Pooley Village Hall, Ullswater, Cumbria
Est. 1980
Details See Albany Fairs 31 Mar–2 Apr

22
Antiques and Collectables Fair
Organizer Oakleigh Leisure Ltd
Location Rhode's Art Centre, South Road, Bishop's Stortford, Herfordshire
Est. 1978
Details See Antiques and Collectables Fair 22 Jan

Biggleswade Antiques Fair
Organizer Biggleswade Antiques Fairs
Location Kimbolton Castle, Huntingdon
Details See Biggleswade Antiques Fair 12 Feb

Bushey Hall School
Organizer David Maggs
Location Bushey Hall School, London Road, Bushey, Hertfordshire
Details See Bushey Hall School 22 Jan

Buxton Book Fair
Organizer Buxton Book Fair
Location Pavilion Gardens, Buxton, Derbyshire
Est. 1982
Details See Buxton Book Fair 19 Feb

Deco Fair
Organizer Ann Zierold Fairs
Location County Stand, Chester Racecourse

Fat Cat Fairs
Organizer Fat Cat Fairs
Location Burford School, Burford, Oxfordshire (on A40 to Cheltenham)
Details See Fat Cat Fairs 22 Jan

M & S Fair
Organizer M & S Fairs
Location Meldreth Village Hall, 10 miles south of Cambridge, 2 miles north of Royston (just off A10)

Mark Carter Militaria & Medal Fair
Organizer Mark Carter Militaria & Medal Fairs
Location Stratford Leisure & Visitor Centre, Stratford-upon-Avon, Warwickshire
Details See Mark Carter Militaria & Medal Fair 5 Mar

Wessex Antiques Fairs
Organizer Wessex Antiques Fairs
Location Winter Gardens Pavilion, Weston-super-Mare
Details See Wessex Antiques Fair 22 Jan

23
Suffolk Books Market
Organizer Boxford Books & Fairs
Location Long Melford

26
V&A Antique & Collectors Fair
Organizer V&A Fairs
Location The Civic Hall,

Nantwich, Cheshire
Details See V&A Antique &
Collectors Fair 1 Jan

27–29

East Berkshire Antiques Fair
Organizer Kibworth Exhibitions Ltd
Location Berkshire College of
Agriculture, Hall Place,
Burchetts Green,
Maidenhead
Details 50 dealers. Quality event

Galloway Antiques Fair
Organizer Galloway Antiques Fairs
Location Sonyhurst College,
Hurst Green, Nr Clitheroe, Lancs
Open 10.30am–5pm

**The 15th East Anglian
Antique Dealers Fair**
Organizer Lomax Antiques Fairs
Location Langley Park School,
Loddon, Norfolk, NR14 6BJ ◻
Est. 1990
Open 27th noon–6pm 28th
10.30am–6pm 29th 10.30am–5pm
Details Datelined antiques

**The Chester Antiques
& Fine Art Show**
Organizer Penman Antiques Fairs
Location The County Grandstand,
Chester Racecourse,
Chester ◻
Open Thurs evening preview,
then Fri Sat 10.30am–6pm
Sun 10.30am–5pm
Details 60 stands, furniture, art &
artefacts, mainly pre-1900, a few
modern paintings

28

Antique & Collector's Fair
Organizer Hoyles Promotions
Location Southport Floral Hall,
Southport, Merseyside
Details See Antique & Collector's
fair 22 Feb

Antique & Collectors Fair
Organizer Dennis Jewellery
Location The Holy Angels Church,
Lilliput Road, Poole, Dorset
Details See Antique & Collectors
Fair 28 Jan

Camfair
Organizer Janba Fairs
Location Castle Hall, Hertford
Details See Camfair 21 Jan

28–29

Antiques and Collectors Fair
Organizer Virgo Fairs
Location Ripley, North Yorkshire
Details Phone for details

**Detling International
Antiques & Collectors Fair**
Organizer DMG Antiques Fairs
Location Kent County
Showground, Detling,
Nr Maidstone, Kent
Details See Detling International
Antiques & Collectors Fair 14–15 Jan

The Best of Fairs
Organizer Best of Fairs
Location The Old School, Lower
Green, Long Melford, Suffolk
Details See The Best of Fairs
28–29 Jan

29

Antiques & Collectors Fair
Organizer Bentley Grice Promotions
Location The Mermaid, Sackville
Hotel, De La Warr Parade,
Bexhill-on-Sea, East Sussex
Details See Antiques & Collectors
Fair 26 Feb

Art Nouveau/Deco Fair
Organizer Take Five Fairs
Location Woking Leisure Centre,
Kingfield Road, Woking, Surrey
Details See Art Nouveau/Deco
Fair 17 Apr

**Battersea Vintage Fashion
Fairs**
Organizer Pre-empt Events
Location Battersea Art Centre,
Lavender Hill, London SW11
Details See Battersea Vintage
Fashion Fairs 5 Feb

Bob Evans Fair
Organizer Bob Evans Fairs
Location Leisure Village,
Thurston Drive, Kettering,
Northamptonshire
(tel. 01536 414141)
Details See Bob Evans Fair 19 Feb

Chipping Norton Toy Fair
Organizer Don Davidson
Location Chipping Norton
School, Burford Road (A361),
Chipping Norton, Oxfordshire
Details See Chipping Norton Toy
Fair 19 Feb

30

Marcel Fair
Organizer Marcel Fairs
Location Berkhamsted Sports
Hall, Hertfordshire

31–1 NOVEMBER

**Ardingly International
Antiques & Collectors Fair**
Organizer DMG Antiques Fairs
Location South of England Show-
ground, Ardingly, West Sussex
Details See Ardingly International
Antiques & Collectors Fair 10–11 Jan

NOVEMBER

2

**Antique Collectors Flea
Market**
Organizer Paraphernalia Fairs
Location Lyndhurst Community
Centre, New Forest, Hampshire
Details See Antique Collectors
Flea Market 5 Jan

3–5

Albany Fairs
Organizer Albany Fairs
Location Pooley Village Hall,
Ullswater, Cumbria
Est. 1980
Details See Albany Fairs
31 Mar–2 Apr

Robert Bailey Fair
Organizer Robert Bailey Fairs Ltd
Location Hatfield House,
Hatfield, Hertfordshire ◻
Open Sat 11am–6pm
Sun 11am–5pm
Entrance fee £5
Details 50 dealers, vetted and
datelined

**The Great Northern
International Antiques
& Collectors Fair**
Organizer Grosvenor Exhibitions Ltd
Location The Great Yorkshire
Showground, Harrogate (A661
Harrogate–Wetherby Road)
Details See The Great Northern
International Antiques &
Collectors Fair 13–15 Jan

**The Portmeirion Antiques
Fair**
Organizer Allen Lewis Fairs

Location Portmeirion Village, Gwynedd, North Wales off A487
Entrance fee
Details See The Portmeirion Antiques Fair 3–5 Mar

4

Antiques and Fleamarket
Organizer West Country Fairs
Location The Memorial Hall, Digby Road, Sherborne, Dorset
Details See Antiques and Fleamarket 7 Jan

London Coin Fair
Organizer Simmons Gallery
Location Holiday Inn, London Bloomsbury, Coram Street, London WC1
Details See London Coin Fair 11 Feb

4–5

Buxton Antique & Collectors Fair
Organizer Unicorn Fairs Ltd
Location Pavilion Gardens, Buxton, Derbyshire
Details See Buxton Antique & Collectors Fair 28–29 Jan

Devon County Antiques Fair
Organizer Devon County Antiques Fairs
Location Devon County Showground, Westpoint
Details See Devon County Antiques Fair 7–8 Jan

5

Adams Antiques Fair
Organizer Adams Antiques Fairs
Location Lindley Hall, Royal Horticultural Hall, Elverton Street (off Vincent Square) Victoria, London SW1
Details See Adams Antiques Fair 22 Jan

Annual Christmas Fleamarket
Organizer West Country Fairs
Location Weymouth Pavilion, The Esplanade, Weymouth, Dorset P
Open Trade 9am public 10am–4pm
Entrance fee £1 Seniors 80p
Details Antiques and collectables. 80 Stands. Refreshments

Arun Antiques Fair
Organizer Arun Fairs
Location Woodland Centre, Woodland Avenue, Rustington, West Sussex, off A259
Details See Arun Antiques Fair 1 Jan

Cross County Fairs
Organizer Cross County Fairs Ltd
Location Effingham Park, West Sussex
Details See Cross County Fairs 1 Jan

Deco Fair
Organizer Ann Zierold Fairs
Location Royal Armouries, Leeds, West Yorkshire

Fat Cat Fairs
Organizer Fat Cat Fairs
Location New Memorial Hall, Lechlade-on-Thames, Gloucestershire
Details See Fat Cat Fairs 5 Feb

Ipswich Antiques & Collectables Fairs
Organizer Ipswich Antiques & Collectables Fair
Location The County Hotel, Copdock, near Ipswich, Suffolk
Details See Ipswich Antiques & Collectables Fairs 1 Jan

J & K Fair
Organizer J & K Fairs
Location Lincolnshire Showground, A15 north of Lincoln
Details See J & K Fair 8 Jan

M & S Fair
Organizer M & S Fairs
Location Cottenham Village College, north of Cambridge (on B1049)

Mark Carter Militaria & Medal Fair
Organizer Mark Carter Militaria & Medal Fairs
Location The Princes Hall, Princes Way, Aldershot, Hampshire GU11 1NX
Details See Mark Carter Militaria & Medal Fair 15 Jan

The Best of Fairs
Organizer Best of Fairs
Location New Village Hall, Copdock, near Ipswich, Suffolk
Details See The Best of Fairs 1 Jan

6–12

Winter Fine Art & Antiques Fair
Organizer Clarion Events Ltd
Location Olympia Exhibition Centre, London P
Est. 1992
Open Phone for details
Entrance fee £10 single £16 double
Details The rich variety of specialist stock will appeal to collectors and curators while connoisseurs and private buyers will find something unique. An exceptional choice of antique furniture and fine art is for sale

7

Devon County Antiques Fair
Organizer Devon County Antiques Fairs
Location Matford Centre, Devon
Details See Devon County Antiques Fair 4 Feb

Sandown Park Antiques Fairs
Organizer Wonder Whistle Enterprises
Location Sandown Park Racecourse, Portsmouth Road, Esher, Surrey
Details See Sandown Park Antiques Fairs 21 Feb

10–12

Galloway Antiques Fair
Organizer Galloway Antiques Fairs
Location Scone Palace, Perth, Scotland
Open 10.30am–5pm

·11

24th Annual Belfast Book Fair
Organizer Jiri Books
Location Wellington Park Hotel, Malone Road, Belfast P
Est. 1982
Open 10am–5pm
Entrance fee £2 concessions £1
Details 35 dealers exhibiting from NI, ROI and GB, much Irish interest stocks

12

Antique & Collectors Fair
Organizer Blooms A1 Events
Location The Racecourse,

FOR FAIR ORGANIZERS SEE PAGE 518

Beverley, East Riding of Yorkshire
Details See Antique & Collectors
Fair 8 Jan

Bob Evans Fair
Organizer Bob Evans Fairs
Location The Cresset,
Bretton Centre, Peterborough
(tel. 01733 265705)
Details See Bob Evans Fair 15 Jan

Chiswick Art Deco Fair
Organizer Abbey Fairs
Location Chiswick Town Hall,
Heathfield Terrace, London W4
Details See Chiswick Art Deco
Fair 19 Mar

Deco Fair
Organizer Ann Zierold Fairs
Location Loughborough Town Hall
Details Provisional date

Lostwithiel Antiques & Bygones Fair
Organizer Lynne & Richard
Bonehill
Location The Community Centre,
Lostwithiel, Cornwall, on A390
Details See Lostwithiel Antiques
& Bygones Fair 8 Jan

Malvern International Antiques & Collectors Fair
Organizer DMG Antiques Fairs
Location Three Counties
Showground, Malvern,
Worcestershire
Details See Malvern
International Antiques &
Collectors Fair 8 Jan

Midas Antiques Fair
Organizer Midas Fairs
Location Bellhouse Hotel,
Beaconsfield, Buckinghamshire
Details See Midas Antiques Fair
8 Jan

National Glass Collectors Fair
Organizer Specialist Glass Fairs Ltd
Location The Heritage Motor
Centre
Details Please see website details

Turn Out Your Attic
Organizer Adams Antiques Fairs
Location Battersea Arts Centre,
Lavender Hill, London SW11
Est. 2005
Details See Turn Out Your Attic
5 Mar

V&A Antique & Collectors Fair
Organizer V&A Fairs
Location Park Royal Hotel,
Stretton, Nr Warrington,
Cheshire (M56 junction 10)
Details See V&A Antique &
Collectors Fair 8 Jan

15

Big Brum
Organizer Antique Forum Group
Location St Martin's Market (The
Rag), Edgbaston Street
Details See Big Brum Morning
Antiques Fair 18 Jan

17–19

Shepton Mallet Antiques & Collectors Fair
Organizer DMG Antiques Fairs
Location Royal Bath and West
Showground, Shepton Mallet,
Somerset
Details See Shepton Mallet
Antiques & Collectors Fair
20–22 Jan

18

Antiques and Collectors Fair
Organizer West Country Fairs
Location The Town Hall, Market
Square, Wells, Somerset
Details See Antiques and
Collectors Fair 14 Jan

Camfair
Organizer Janba Fairs
Location Castle Hall, Hertford
Details See Camfair 21 Jan

Frock Me!
Organizer Adams Antiques Fairs
Location Chelsea Town Hall,
King's Road, Chelsea, London
SW3
Details See Frock Me! 4 Mar

18–19

12th Mid Beds Antiques Fair
Organizer Gemsco Promotions
Location Silsoe Conference
Centre (Cranfield University),
Silsoe, Bedfordshire, MK45 4DT
(off A6)
Details See 11th Mid Beds
Antiques Fair 29–30 Apr

Weekend Antiques Festival
Organizer Antique Forum Group
Location Trentham Gardens
(Junction 15, M6)
Details See Weekend Antiques
Festival 15–16 Apr

19

Abergavenny Antiques & Collectors Fairs
Organizer Monmouthshire
County Council
Location Abergavenny Market Hall,
Abergavenny, Monmouthshire
Details See Abergavenny
Antiques & Collectors Fairs 15 Jan

Alexandra Palace Antique & Collectors Fair
Organizer Pig & Whistle Promotions
Location The Great Hall,
Alexandra Palace, Wood Green,
London N22
Details See Alexandra Palace
Antique & Collectors Fair 15 Jan

Antiques and Collectables Fair
Organizer Oakleigh Leisure Ltd
Location Rhode's Art Centre,
South Road, Bishop's Stortford,
Herfordshire
Est. 1978
Details See Antiques and
Collectables Fair 22 Jan

Antiques Fairs Ireland
Organizer Antiques Fairs Ireland
Location Tara Towers Hotel,
Merrion Road, Dublin 4
Details Provisional date (check by
phone or see website)

Biggleswade Antiques Fair
Organizer Biggleswade Antiques
Fairs
Location Weatherley Centre,
Biggleswade, Bedfordshire
Details See Biggleswade Antique
Fair 15 Jan

Bob Evans Fair
Organizer Bob Evans Fairs
Location Sports Connexion,
Ryton on Dunsmore, Coventry
(tel. 02476 306155)
Details See Bob Evans Fair 12 Feb

Dublin Toy and Train Fair
Organizer B+T Toy Fairs
Location Clontarf Castle Hotel,

FAIRS: CALENDAR
DECEMBER

Castle Avenue, Clontarf, Dublin 3
Details See Dublin Toy and Train
Fair 5 Feb

Northern Clock & Watch Fair
Organizer Northern Clock &
Watch Fairs
Location Haydock Park
Racecourse, Merseyside
Details See Northern Clock &
Watch Fair 12 Feb

Quality Antiques Fair
Organizer Margaret Browne Fairs
Location Dorking, Surrey

Silhouette Fairs
Organizer Fat Cat Fairs
Location The Guildhall, Abbey
Close, Abingdon, Oxfordshire,
OX14 3JE
Details See Sihouette Fairs 15 Jan

**The Old Brig Antique
& Collectors' Fair**
Organizer The Old Brig
Location The Highland Conference
Centre, Nairn, Inverness
Details See The Old Brig Antique
& Collectors' Fair 19 Mar

Winter Fair
Organizer Winter Fairs
Details See Winter Fair 15 Jan

23–26

Antiques for Everyone
Organizer Clarion Events–NEC Ltd
Location Earls Court, London
Details See Antiques for
Everyone 18–22 Jan

24–26

**The International
Antiques & Collectors Fair
at RAF Swinderby**
Organizer Arthur Swallow Fairs
Location RAF Swinderby, A46
between Newark and Lincoln
Details See The International
Antiques & Collectors Fair at RAF
Swinderby 27–29 Jan

25

Antique & Collector's Fair
Organizer Hoyles Promotions
Location Southport Floral Hall,
Southport, Merseyside
Details See Antique & Collector's
fair 22 Feb

Antique & Collectors Fair
Organizer Dennis Jewellery
Location The Holy Angels Church,
Lilliput Road, Poole, Dorset
Details See Antique & Collectors
Fair 28 Jan

Suffolk Books Market
Organizer Boxford Books & Fairs
Location Long Melford

25–26

Janba Fair
Organizer Janba Fairs
Location Burgess Hall, St Ivo
Leisure Centre, St Ives,
Cambridgeshire
Details See Janba Fair 1–2 Jan

The Best of Fairs
Organizer Best of Fairs
Location The Old School, Lower
Green, Long Melford, Suffolk
Details See The Best of Fairs
28–29 Jan

26

Antiques & Collectors Fair
Organizer Bentley Grice
Promotions
Location The Mermaid, Sackville
Hotel, De La Warr Parade,
Bexhill-on-Sea, East Sussex
Details See Antiques & Collectors
Fair 26 Feb

Art Deco Fair
Organizer Abbey Fairs
Location Battersea Town Hall
Details See Art Deco Fair 19 Feb

Arun Antiques Fair
Organizer Arun Fairs
Location Charmandean Centre,
Worthing, West Sussex
Details See Arun Antiques Fair
29 Jan

Biggleswade Antiques Fair
Organizer Biggleswade Antiques
Fairs
Location Addison Centre,
Kempton, Bedfordshire
Details See Biggleswade Antique
Fair 22 Jan

Bob Evans Fair
Organizer Bob Evans Fairs
Location Leisure Centre, Holmer
Road, Hereford (tel. 01432 278178)
Details See Bob Evans Fair 8 Jan

Bushey Hall School
Organizer David Maggs
Location Bushey Hall School,
London Road, Bushey,
Hertfordshire
Details See Bushey Hall School
22 Jan

Buxton Book Fair
Organizer Buxton Book Fair
Location Pavilion Gardens,
Buxton, Derbyshire
Est. 1982
Details See Buxton Book Fair
19 Feb

Fat Cat Fairs
Organizer Fat Cat Fairs
Location Burford School, Burford,
Oxfordshire (on A40 to Cheltenham)
Details See Fat Cat Fairs 22 Jan

**V&A Antique & Collectors
Fair**
Organizer V&A Fairs
Location The Community Hall,
Low Town (on A442), Bridgnorth,
Shropshire
Details See V&A Antique &
Collectors Fair 22 Jan

Wessex Antiques Fairs
Organizer Wessex Antiques Fairs
Location Winter Gardens
Pavilion, Weston-super-Mare
Details See Wessex Antiques Fair
22 Jan

30

**V&A Antique & Collectors
Fair**
Organizer V&A Fairs
Location The Civic Hall,
Nantwich, Cheshire
Details See V&A Antique &
Collectors Fair 1 Jan

DECEMBER

2

Coin Fair
Organizer Davidson Monk Fairs
Location Drury's Hotel, Great
Russell Street, London WC1
Details See Coin Fair 14 Jan

2–3

**Buxton Antique
& Collectors Fair**
Organizer Unicorn Fairs Ltd

Location Pavilion Gardens, Buxton, Derbyshire
Details See Buxton Antique & Collectors Fair 28–29 Jan

3

Antique & Collectors Fair
Organizer Blooms A1 Events
Location The Racecourse, Beverley,
East Riding of Yorkshire
Details See Antique & Collectors Fair 8 Jan

Antiques Fairs Ireland
Organizer Antiques Fairs Ireland
Location Castleknock Hotel, Porterstown Road, Castleknock, Dublin 15

Art Deco Fair
Organizer Abbey Fairs
Location The Heritage Motor Centre Gaydon, Warwick (Junction 12 M40)
Details See Art Deco Fair 26 Feb

Arun Antiques Fair
Organizer Arun Fairs
Location Woodland Centre, Woodland Avenue, Rustington, West Sussex, off A259
Details See Arun Antiques Fair 1 Jan

Cross County Fairs
Organizer Cross County Fairs Ltd
Location Effingham Park, West Sussex
Details See Cross County Fairs 1 Jan

Fat Cat Fairs
Organizer Fat Cat Fairs
Location New Memorial Hall, Lechlade-on-Thames, Gloucestershire
Details See Fat Cat Fairs 5 Feb

Ipswich Antiques & Collectables Fairs
Organizer Ipswich Antiques & Collectables Fair
Location The County Hotel, Copdock, near Ipswich, Suffolk
Details See Ipswich Antiques & Collectables Fairs 1 Jan

Magnum Antiques Fair
Organizer Magnum Antiques Fairs
Location Grange Centre, Bepton

Road, Midhurst, West Sussex
Details See Magnum Antiques Fair 5 Feb

Mark Carter Militaria & Medal Fair
Organizer Mark Carter Militaria & Medal Fairs
Location Yate Leisure Centre, Kennedy Way, Yate, Bristol
Details See Mark Carter Militaria & Medal Fair 5 Feb

Quality Antiques Fair
Organizer Margaret Browne Fairs
Location Dorking, Surrey

The Best of Fairs
Organizer Best of Fairs
Location Village Hall, Copdock, near Ipswich, Suffolk
Details See The Best of Fairs 1 Jan

Turn Out Your Attic
Organizer Adams Antiques Fairs
Location Battersea Arts Centre, Lavender Hill, London SW11
Est. 2005
Details See Turn Out Your Attic 5 Mar

7

Antique Collectors Flea Market
Organizer Paraphernalia Fairs
Location Lyndhurst Community Centre, New Forest, Hampshire
Details See Antique Collectors Flea Market 5 Jan

7–9

Newark International Antiques & Collectors Fair
Organizer DMG Antiques Fairs
Location Newark & Notts Showground, Newark
Details See Newark International Antiques & Collectors Fair 2–4 Feb

8

Antiques & Collectables Fair
Organizer Take Five Fairs
Location Woking Leisure Centre, Kingfield Road, Woking, Surrey
Details See Antiques & Collectables Fair 8 Jan

8–10

Robert Bailey Fair
Organizer Robert Bailey Fairs Ltd
Location Pavilions of Harrogate, Great Yorkshire Showground
Details See Robert Bailey Fair 3–5 Feb

Stafford Bingley Hall Giant 3-Day Antiques Fair
Organizer Bowman Antiques Fairs Ltd
Location Bingley Hall, County Showground, Stafford
Details See Stafford Bingley Hall 10–12 February

9–10

Carmarthen Antiques & Collectors' Fair
Organizer Towy Antiques Fairs
Location United Counties Showground, Carmarthen
Details See Carmarthen Antiques Fair 11–12 Mar

10

Adams Antiques Fair
Organizer Adams Antiques Fairs
Location Kensington Town Hall, Hornton Street, (Off Kensington High St.), London W8 🅿
Details See Adams Antiques Fair 22 Jan at the Horticultural hall for all other details

Antiques & Collectors Fair
Organizer West Country Fairs
Location Weymouth Pavilion, The Esplanade, Weymouth, Dorset
Details See Antiques & Collectors Fair 19 Mar

Antiques Fairs Ireland
Organizer Antiques Fairs Ireland
Location Clontarf Castle, Castle Ave, Clontarf, Dublin D3

Battersea Vintage Fashion Fairs
Organizer Pre-empt Events
Location Battersea Art Centre, Lavender Hill, London SW11
Details See Battersea Vintage Fashion Fairs 5 Feb

Bushey Hall School
Organizer David Maggs
Location Bushey Hall School,

London Road, Bushey, Hertfordshire
Details See Bushey Hall School
22 Jan

J & K Fair
Organizer J & K Fairs
Location Lincolnshire Showground,
A15 north of Lincoln
Details See J & K Fair 8 Jan

London Map Fair
Organizer London Map Fairs
Location Rembrandt Hotel,
South Kensington, London
Details See London Map Fair 9 Apr

**Lostwithiel Antiques
& Bygones Fair**
Organizer Lynne & Richard
Bonehill
Location The Community Centre,
Lostwithiel, Cornwall, on A390
Details See Lostwithiel Antiques
& Bygones Fair 8 Jan

M & S Fair
Organizer M & S Fairs
Location Cottenham Village
College, north of Cambridge
(on B1049)

**Malvern International
Antiques & Collectors Fair**
Organizer DMG Antiques Fairs
Location Three Counties
Showground, Malvern,
Worcestershire
Details See Malvern International
Antiques & Collectors Fair 8 Jan

Midas Antiques Fair
Organizer Midas Fairs
Location Bellhouse Hotel,
Beaconsfield, Buckinghamshire
Details See Midas Antiques Fair
8 Jan

**The Old Brig Antique &
Collectors' Fair**
Organizer The Old Brig
Location The Highland Conference
Centre, Nairn, Inverness
Details See The Old Brig Antique
& Collectors' Fair 19 Mar

**V&A Antique & Collectors
Fair**
Organizer V&A Fairs
Location Park Royal Hotel,
Stretton, Nr Warrington,
Cheshire (M56 junction 10)
Details See V&A Antique &
Collectors Fair 8 Jan

14

**V&A Antique & Collectors
Fair**
Organizer V&A Fairs
Location The Civic Hall,
Nantwich, Cheshire
Details See V&A Antique &
Collectors Fair 1 Jan

16

Camfair
Organizer Janba Fairs
Location Castle Hall, Hertford
Details See Camfair 21 Jan

17

**Abergavenny Antiques
& Collectors Fairs**
Organizer Monmouthshire
County Council
Location Abergavenny Market
Hall, Abergavenny,
Monmouthshire
Details See Abergavenny
Antiques & Collectors Fairs 15 Jan

Biggleswade Antiques Fair
Organizer Biggleswade Antiques
Fairs
Location Weatherley Centre,
Biggleswade,
Bedfordshire
Details See Biggleswade Antique
Fair 15 Jan

Buxton Book Fair
Organizer Buxton Book Fair
Location Pavilion Gardens,
Buxton, Derbyshire
Est. 1982
Details See Buxton Book Fair
19 Feb

Silhouette Fairs
Organizer Fat Cat Fairs
Location The Guildhall, Abbey
Close, Abingdon, Oxfordshire,
OX14 3JE
Details See Silhouette Fairs 15 Jan

Wessex Antiques Fairs
Organizer Wessex Antiques Fairs
Location Winter Gardens
Pavilion, Weston-super-Mare
Details See Wessex Antiques Fair
22 Jan

Winter Fair
Organizer Winter Fairs
Details See Winter Fair 15 Jan

26

**Boxing Day Antique
& Collector's Fair**
Organizer Hoyles Promotions
Location The Empress Ballroom,
Blackpool P
Est. 1978
Details Traditional Boxing Day
Fair, drawing dealers and
collectors from all over the UK

28

Art Nouveau/Deco Fair
Organizer Take Five Fairs
Location Woking Leisure Centre,
Kingfield Road, Woking,
Surrey
Details See Art Nouveau/Deco
Fair 17 Apr

Bob Evans Fair
Organizer Bob Evans Fairs
Location Leisure Village,
Thurston Drive, Kettering,
Northamptonshire
(tel. 01536 414141)
Details See Bob Evans Fair 19 Feb

30

Antique & Collectors Fair
Organizer Dennis Jewellery
Location The Holy Angels Church,
Lilliput Road, Poole, Dorset
Details See Antique & Collectors
Fair 28 Jan

Bob Evans Fair
Organizer Bob Evans Fairs
Location Sports Connexion,
Ryton on Dunsmore, Coventry
(tel. 02476 306155)
Details See Bob Evans Fair 12 Feb

30–31

**Buxton Antique
& Collectors Fair**
Organizer Unicorn Fairs Ltd
Location Pavilion Gardens,
Buxton, Derbyshire
Details See Buxton Antique &
Collectors Fair 28–29 Jan

The Best of Fairs
Organizer Best of Fairs
Location The Old School,
Lower Green, Long Melford,
Suffolk
Details See The Best of Fairs
28–29 Jan

Indexes

In the Index of Specialists and the General Index, shops and businesses beginning with a forename are listed alphabetically by surname: thus R G Archer Books is listed under A and Michael Saffell Antiques appears under S.

The county in which a city, town or village has been placed in the Directory is also given In the Index of Place Names. Note that this is not always the county given in the address that forms part of the entry.

KEY TO MEMBER ORGANIZATIONS

In order to make the information in this book more concise we have used the following abbreviations where applicable.

ABA	Antiquarian Booksellers' Association
ADA	Antique Dealers' Association
ADDA	Art Deco Dealers' Association
AFRA	Antique Furniture Repairers Association
AHS	Antiquarian Horological Society
AIMSS	Airfreight Industry Minimum Security Standards
AMU	Association Master Upholsterers
ANA	American Numismatic Association
APS	American Philatelic Society
ARVA	Association of Regional Valuers & Auctioneers
ASDA	American Stamp Dealers' Association
ASVA	Association of Society of Valuers & Auctioneers
AU	Association of Upholsterers
BA	Booksellers' Association
BABAADA	Bath & Bradford on Avon Antique Dealers' Association
BABI	Booksellers' Association of Britain & Ireland
BACA	British Antiques and Collectables Awards
BADA	British Antique Dealers' Association
BAFRA	British Antique Furniture Restorers' Association
BAR	British Association of Removers
BCCA	British Cheque Clearers Association
BCPAA	British China & Porcelain Artists' Association
BCS	British Cartographic Society
BGA	British Gemologists' Association
BHI	British Horological Institute
BIFA	British International Freight Association
BJA	British Jewellers' Association
BNTA	British Numismatic Trade Association
BSMGP	British Society of Master Glass Painters
BWCG	British Watch & Clockmakers' Guild
CAAV	Central Association of Agricultural Valuers
CADA	Cotswold Antique Dealers' Association
CC	Clockmakers' Company
CGLI	City & Guilds of London Institute
CINOA	Confédération Internationale des Négociants en Oeuvres d'Art
CLPGS	City of London Phonograph & Gramophone Society
CMBHI	Craft Member of the British Horological Institute
CPADA	Camden Passage Antique Dealers' Association
CPTA	Camden Passage Traders' Association
DADA	Dorking Antique Dealers' Association
DGA	Diamond member of the Gemmological Association

EADA	Essex Antique Dealers' Association
ESoc	Ephemera Society
FAAV	Full Member of the Association of Agricultural Valuers
FATG	Fine Art Trade Guild
FGA	Fellow of the Gemological Association of Great Britain
FHS	Federation of the Swiss Watch Industry
FIATA	International Federation of Freight Forwarders Associations
FIDI	Fédération Internationale des Déménageurs Internationaux
FNAVA	Federation of National Auctioneers & Valuers
FSVA	Fellow of the Society of Valuers & Auctioneers
GADAR	Guild of Antique Dealers & Restorers
GAGTL	Gemmological Association and Gem Testing Laboratory of Great Britain
GCS	Golf Collectors' Society (GB, USA)
GIA	Gemological Institute of America
GTA	Gun Traders' Association
HADA	Hudson Antique Dealers' Association
HHGFAA	Household Goods Forwarders of America
IAA	Institute of Antiques Auctioneers
IADA	Irish Antique Dealers' Association
IADAA	International Association of Dealers in Ancient Art
IAMA	The International Antiquarian Map Sellers' Association
IAPN	International Society of Professional Numismatists
IATA	International Air Transport Association
IAVI	Irish Auctioneers & Valuers Institute
IBNS	International Bank Note Society
IBSS	International Bond and Share Society
ICHAWI	Institute for the Conservation of Historic & Artistic Works in Ireland
ICOM	International Council of Museums (Committee for Conservation)
IDDA	Interior Decorators' & Designers' Association
IIC	International Institute for Conservation of Historic & Artistic Work
ILAB	International League of Antiquarian Booksellers
IMA	Irish Museums Association
IMCOS	International Map Collectors' Society
IMTA	International Map Trade Association
IOC	Institute of Conservation
IPAA	International Porcelain Artists' Association
IPAV	Institute of Professional Auctioneers & Valuers

KEY TO MEMBER ORGANIZATIONS

IPC	Institute of Paper Conservation	**PNG**	Professional Numismatists' Guild
IPCRA	Irish Professional Conservators' & Restorers' Association	**PTA**	Postcard Traders' Association
		PTS	Philatelic Traders' Society
IPG	Independent Publishers Guild	**RADS**	Registered Antique Dealers' Association
IRRV	Institute of Revenues, Ratings & Valuation		
ISVA	Incorporated Society of Valuers & Auctioneers	**RETRA**	Radio, Electrical and Television Retailers' Association
		RFS	Royal Forestry Society
ITA	Islington Trading Association	**RICS**	Royal Institute of Chartered Surveyors
KCSADA	Kensington Church Street Antique Dealers' Association	**RWHA**	Royal Warrant Holders' Association
		SAA	Scottish Association of Auctioneers
LAPADA	London & Provincial Antique Dealers' Association	**SAADA**	Sherborne Art & Antique Dealers' Association
LJAJDA	London & Japan Antique Jewellery Dealers' Association	**SAPCON**	South African Paper Conservation Group
LSVA	London Silver Vaults Association	**SIS**	Scientific Instrument Society
MAPH	Member of the Association of Professional Horologists	**SLAD**	Society of London Art Dealers
		SMA	Society of Motor Auctions
MBHI	Member of British Horological Society	**SOB**	Society of Book Binders
MBWCG	Member of British Watch & Clockmakers' Guild	**SOC**	Society of Cartographers
		SOFAA	Society of Fine Art Auctioneers
MGR	Museums and Galleries Register	**SPAB**	Society for the Protection of Ancient Buildings
NACF	National Art Collections Fund		
NAEA	National Art Education Association	**SPTA**	Scottish Philatelic Traders' Association
NAG	National Association of Goldsmiths	**SSA**	Sussex Saleroom Association
NAVA	National Association of Auctioneers & Valuers	**SSBA**	Stony Stratford Business Association
		SSCR	Scottish Society for Conservation & Restoration
NAWCC	National Association of Watch & Clock Collectors		
NCCR	National Council for Conservation and Restoration	**TADA**	Tetbury Antique Dealers' Association
		TCS	Tennis Collectors' Society
NIAVI	Northern Ireland Auctioneers & Valuers Institute	**TPCS**	Torquay Pottery Collectors' Club
		TRADA	Timber Research and Development Association
NPA	National Pawnbrokers Association		
OCS	Oriental Ceramic Society	**TVADA**	Thames Valley Antique Dealers' Association
OMNI	Overseas Moving Network International		
		UACC	Universal Autograph Collectors' Club
OMRS	Order Medals Research Society	**UKIC**	United Kingdom Institute for Conservation
OMSA	Orders and Medals Society of America		
PAADA	Petworth Art & Antique Dealers' Association	**WADA**	Warwick Antique Dealers Association
PADA	Portobello Antique Dealers' Association	**WBA**	Welsh Booksellers' Association
PBFA	Provincial Book Fair Association	**WKADA**	West Kent Antique Dealers' Association

INDEX OF ADVERTISERS

The Brackley Antique Cellar	281	Oxford Street Antique Centre	279
Dukeries Antiques Centre	285	Station Mill Antiques Centre	263
Fat Cat Fairs	545	Top Banana	*back jacket*
The Irish Antique Dealers Association	431	Trident Exhibitions Ltd	541
Brian Loomes	325		

INDEX OF SPECIALISTS
ADVERTISING

ADVERTISING

Castle Antiques 424

ANTIQUE TINS
Michael Saffell Antiques 182

AERONAUTICA

Aviation Antiques & Collectables 28

ANCIENT ART

Aaron Gallery 85

ANTIQUITIES

The Emporium Antiques Centre Too 21
Helios Gallery 181
Valued History 203

ANCIENT EGYPTIAN
Seaby Antiquities 94
Rupert Wace Ancient Art Ltd 96

ROMAN & MEDIEVAL ARTEFACTS
Westend Antiques & Jewellery 347

ARCHITECTURAL

Antique Builders Suppliers 421
Au Temps Perdu 184
Auldearn Antiques 408
Ballyalton House Architectural
   Antiques 424
CASA 64
Cast From The Past 174
Cast Offs 307
Cox's Architectural Salvage Yard Ltd 242
Cumbria Architectural Salvage 364
M R Dingle 155
Dismantle & Deal Direct 233
Dorset Reclamation 171
Drummonds Architectural
   Antiques Ltd 138
Drummonds Architectural
   Antiques Ltd 72
EASY Edinburgh & Glasgow
   Architectural Salvage Yard 401
Ecomerchant Ltd 34
Edenderry Architectural Salvage Ltd 440
The Emporium 317
Frome Reclamation 189
The Golden Past 404
Great Northern Architectural
   Antiques Co Ltd 359
Heritage Reclamation 256
Heritage Reclamations 228
Holyrood Architectural Salvage 401
Lakeland Architectural Antiques 362
LASSCO RBK 61
LASSCO St Michael's 49
Lindsay Court Architectural 341
MDS Ltd 306
Minchinhampton Architectural
   Salvage Co 238

Mongers Architectural Salvage 215
Nottingham Architectural Antiques
   & Reclamation 289
Olliff's Architectural Antiques 185
Petals in the Warehouse 126
Retrouvius Architectural
   Reclamation 61
Ribble Reclamation 374
The Salvage Shop 441
Taymouth Architectural Antiques 398
Tynemouth Architectural Salvage 351
The Victorian Salvage and Joinery
   Co Ltd 435
Walcot Reclamation Ltd 183
J R Webb Antiques 396
Wells Reclamation Company 192
Willesden Green Architectural
   Salvage 61
Willowpool Garden Centre & Baron
   Antiques 357
Woodside Reclamation 349

BATHROOM FITTINGS
Alscot Bathroom Company 308
Cardiff Reclamation 392
Catchpole and Rye 37
Thomas Crapper & Co 303

CHURCH FURNISHINGS
Antique Church Furnishings 141
Architectural Antiques and Salvage 433
Chancellors Church Furnishings 141
McDonnell's Antique Furniture 438

DOOR FURNITURE
Chloe Alberry 103
Memento 136
Christopher Preston Ltd 82
Shiners of Jesmond 351

DOORS
Aladdins Architectural Antiques and
   Heritage Workshops 350
Dyfed Antiques 389
LASSCO Warehouse 80
Pipkins Antiques 372
Strippadoor 369

FIREPLACES
Abacus Fireplaces 318
Adrian Ager 158
Ampthill Antiques Emporium 230
Architectural Rescue 62
The Architectural Stores 42
Brighton Architectural Salvage 13
Cardiff Reclamation 392
Celtic Antique Fireplaces 394
Chesney's Antique Fireplaces 82
Craigavon Marble Products 423
John Duffy Antiques 439
Dyfed Antiques 389
Hearth & Home 18
Lindsay Architectural Antiques 306
Malthouse Antiques (Four Crosses)
   Ltd 391
Mill Antiques 318
Neilsons Ltd 402

Nostalgia 369
Original Architectural Antiques
   Co Ltd 240
Past and Present Fireplaces 371
Pine-Apple Antiques 318
Shiners of Jesmond 351
P J Smith (Fair Trades) 427
St Julien 322
Tom Pearson 407
The Victorian Fireplace 31
Ward's Antiques 62
Westland and Co 49
Yesterdays Antiques 339

FLAGSTONES
Abergavenny Reclamation 254

FLOORING
Abergavenny Reclamation 254
Ashridge Antique Flooring 256
Howard's Reclamation 143
LASSCO Flooring 61

GARDEN ORNAMENTS/STATUARY
The Architectural Emporium 27
Architectural Heritage 240

GOTHIC ITEMS
Robert Mills Architectural Antiques 185

HEARTH ITEMS
Granary Antiques 282

IRONWORK
Rococo Antiques & Interiors 284

MANTELS
Westland and Co 49

MARBLE
Bonstow and Crawshay Antiques 180

STAINED GLASS
Architectural Artefacts 227
Dalton Antiques 308
Drew Pritchard Ltd 382
Gatehouse Workshops 288
Robert Mills Architectural Antiques 185

STOVES
Ovne Antique Stoves 430

TELEPHONE BOXES
James Fuller and Son 203

ARMS & ARMOUR

Peter Finer 301
Michael German Antiques Ltd 99
The Lanes Armoury 14
Michael D Long Ltd 288
M J M Antiques 118
Quillon Antiques of Tetsworth 266
St Pancras Antiques 145
West Street Antiques 135
Huw Williams Antiques 386

INDEX OF SPECIALISTS
BOOKS

ARMOUR
Arbour Antiques Ltd 303
Peter Dale Ltd 66

ARMS
Sporting Antiques 44

JAPANESE SWORDS
Garth Vincent Antique Arms and
  Armour 338

ASIAN WORKS OF ART

Antik West Oriental Art & Antiques 98
Gregg Baker Asian Art 98
Sebastiano Barbagallo Antiques 75, 103
David Bowden Chinese and Japanese
  Art 87
Brandt Oriental Antiques 87
Paul Champkins Oriental Art 88
Glade Antiques 235
Anita Gray 90
Grays Antique Market 90
Gerard Hawthorn Ltd 90
Catherine Hunt Oriental Antiques 238
Imperial Antiques 369
Indigo 77, 196
J A N Fine Art 100
Peter Johnson 154
Peter Kemp 100
Jeremy Mason 69
Phoenix Oriental Art 52
Rossi & Rossi Ltd 94
Shiraz Antiques 94

19THC JAPANESE IMARI
Brown & Kingston 71

CENTRAL ASIA
Artique 247

CERAMICS
Guest and Gray 90
Roger Keverne Ltd 91
Rankin Conn Oriental Antiques 78

CHINESE ART
Eskenazi Ltd 89
S Marchant & Son 101
Priestley and Ferraro 70

EARLY CHINESE LACQUER
Brian Harkins 67

EAST ASIAN ART & ARCHAEOLOGY
Hanshan Tang Books 84

JAPANESE
Barry Davies Oriental Art 98
MCN Antiques 106

JAPANESE PAINTING
Brian Harkins 67

JAPANESE WOODCUT PRINTS
Japanese Gallery Ltd 51, 100

NETSUKE
Adèle De Havilland 88

NORITAKE
Dragonlee Collectables 38

AUTOGRAPH LETTERS. MANUSCRIPTS

Bertram Rota Ltd 111

BAROMETERS

Antique Barometer & Clock Shop 294
The Antique Barometer Company 49
Antique Barometers 204
Antique Time 433
The Barometer Shop 253
Barometer World 165
Baskerville Antiques 147
N F Bryan-Peach Antiques 280, 286
Cobwebs 422
Andrew Foott Antiques 366
Knole Barometers 189
Derek & Tina Rayment Antiques 354
Derek Roberts Antiques 42
Summersons 305
Time in Hand 303
Alan Walker 119

BOOKS

Adam & Eve Books 80
Addyman Annexe 250
Duncan M Allsop 304
Archive Books and Music 57
Armstrong's Books
  & Collectables 307
Bath Old Books 180
Beaumont Travel Books 62
Bon-Accord Books 396
Books & Bygones 179
Books & Maps 172
Bookstores Wales 393
Richard Booth's Bookshop Ltd 250
Bouquiniste 405
Bridport Old Bookshop 174
Broadhursts of Southport Ltd 377
Steven Burak Books 107
The Castle Book Shop 207
Countryside Books 117
Craobh Rua Books 423
The Dartmoor Bookshop Ltd 158
G David 202
davidleesbooks.com 251
Deeside Books 396
The Earlsfield Bookshop 85
Faversham Interiors 34
Steven Ferdinando 190
David Ferrow 215
Simon Finch Norfolk 216
Fisher & Sperr 54
Paul Foster Books 84
Robert Frew Ltd 89
Major Iain Grahame 221
Hall's Bookshop 43
Peter Hames 159

Adrian Harrington 99
Peter Herington Antiquarian
  Bookseller 73
G Heywood Hill Ltd 90
Horsham Bookshop 146
Jiri Books 422
Jonkers Ltd 264
George Kelsall 367
Kim's Bookshop 145
Robert Kirkman Ltd 231
E W Marchpane Ltd 111
New, Secondhand & Antiquarian
  Books 178
Colin Page Antiquarian Books 15
Pedlar's Pack Books 171
Phoenix Books 188
Piccadilly Rare Books 26
The Pocket Bookshop 166
Poor Richard's Books 223
Bernard Quaritch Ltd 94
Rainbow Books 15
H Rowan 173
P & B Rowan 421
Second Edition 403
Bernard J Shapero Rare Books 94
Shipwreck Brightlingsea's Antique
  and Collectables Centre 206
Sleepy Elephant Books
  & Artefacts 364
Clive Smith 208
Staniland Booksellers 344
Robert D Steedman 351
Stothert Old Books 356
Stride & Son 145
Christine Swift Books 33
Taikoo Books Ltd 330
Tetbury Old Books 248
Richard Thornton Books 56
Till's Bookshop 403
Unsworths Booksellers Ltd 108
R G Watkins 191
Whitchurch Books Ltd 393
Nigel Williams Rare Books 112

ACADEMIC, SCHOLARLY, BINDINGS, SETS, 1ST EDITIONS
Jericho Books 265

AFRICA
Heritage Books 131
Yesterdays Books 174

ANTIQUES
Hay Cinema Bookshop 251
Ian K Pugh Books 313

ARCHERY
Dyfi Valley Bookshop 391

ARCHITECTURE
Richard Axe Books 320
Camden Books 181
Helmsley Antiquarian & Secondhand
  Books 322
The Old Town Bookshop 402
Janette Ray Rare Books 329

INDEX OF SPECIALISTS
BOOKS

ART
Biblion Ltd 87
Bookshop Conwy 382
Brighton Books 13
Caledonian Books 406
Thomas Heneage Art Books 68
West Port Books 404

ARTS & HUMANITIES
Howes Bookshop Ltd 19

ASIAN
Fine Books Oriental Ltd 108

ATLASES
Altea Maps and Books 86

AVIATION
CCB Aviation Books and Prints 31
Patterson Liddle 182

BELLRINGING
Church Green Books 267

BINDINGS
A & Y Cumming Ltd 21

BOOK PRODUCTION/DISTRIBUTION
Barry McKay Rare Books 360

CANALS
Patterson Liddle 182

CHILDREN'S
Books Bought and Sold Ltd 135
Bookshop Conwy 383
The Canterbury Book Shop 30
Siri Ellis Books 365
W A Howe 176
Minstergate Bookshop 329
The Old Children's
  Bookshelf 402
Peakirk Bookshop 204
Rose's Books 252
Keith A Savage 227
Stella Books 388
Treasure Trove Books 278

CINEMA
Inprint 246
Keel Row Books 351
Michael Moon 364

COLLECTABLE
Paton Books 258

CORNWALL
Bonython Bookshop 156
Just Books 157
New Street Books 154

COUNTRY PURSUITS, COUNTRYSIDE
Books Galore 188
The Old Hall Bookshop 281

CRICKET
Hambleton Books 327
Christopher Saunders 243
St Mary's Books & Prints 344

DECORATIVE ARTS
Potterton Books 326

DETECTIVE FICTION
Murder & Mayhem 252
Treasure Trove Books 278

DORSET TOPOGRAPHY
Antique Map and Bookshop 177

EARLY PRINTED
Thomas Thorp 260

EROTICA
Paper Pleasures 190

FIELD SPORTS
The Barn Book Supply 198
David A H Grayling 364
Hereward Books 204
R E and G B Way 221

FILM & TELEVISION
Yorkshire Relics 335

FINE & ANTIQUARIAN
Saintfield Antiques & Fine Books 425

FIRST EDITIONS
Biblion Ltd 87
A & Y Cumming Ltd 21

FOREIGN
Voltaire & Rousseau 408

GIRLS SCHOOL STORIES
The Haunted Bookshop 202

GLOUCESTERSHIRE & WORCESTERSHIRE
Bookworms of Evesham 311

HAMPSHIRE
Book Academy 138

THOMAS HARDY
Antique Map and Bookshop 177

HEALTH & WELL-BEING
Circle Books 184

G A HENTY
Antique Map and Bookshop 177

HEREFORD & WORCESTER
Lechmere Antiquarian Books 312

HISTORICAL FICTION
Boris Books 129

HISTORY
Circle Books 184

Clevedon Books 187

HISTORY OF SCIENCE
Mair Wilkes Books 405

HORSERACING
Byrkley Books Ltd 296

ILLUSTRATED
Nicholas Goodyer 54
Vanessa Parker Rare Books 439

IRISH INTEREST
Antiquarian Booksellers 423
The Bookshop 432
Cathach Books Ltd 433
Cathair Books 441
Davidson Books 423
Foyle Books 426
Stacks Bookshop 424
Stokes Books 435
Trinity Rare Books 438

JUDAICA
Henry Pordes Books Ltd 111

KENT TOPOGRAPHY
Marrin's Bookshop 35

LAKE DISTRICT
Maurice Dodd Books 411

LAW ENFORCEMENT
Undercover Books 345

LEATHER BINDINGS
Any Amount of Books 108
McConnell Fine Books 33

C S LEWIS
Daeron's Books 236

LINCOLNSHIRE TOPOGRAPHY
P J Cassidy 341

LITERATURE
Addyman Books 250
I D Edrich 48
R A Gekoski Booksellers 108
Jarndyce Antiquarian
  Booksellers 108
The Winchester Bookshop 130

LOCAL HISTORY
Abacus Gallery 299
Bookshop Conwy 382
Mereside Books 358
Michael Moon 364

MARITIME
All Books 210
Brazenhead Ltd 213
Fisher Nautical 149
McLaren Books 398
Frank Smith Maritime Aviation
  Books 351

MEDICAL
Patrick Pollak Rare Books 167

MILITARY
The Bookworm 400
Invicta Bookshop 119
Schull Books 429

MODERN LANGUAGES
Marijana Dworski Books 251

MOTORING
St Paul's Street Bookshop 344

MUSIC
The Chichester Bookshop 144
Hancock & Monks 251
The Malvern Bookshop 312
Travis & Emery Music Bookshop 112

MYSTICAL
Watkins Books Ltd 112

NATURAL HISTORY
Chelsea Gallery 80
A & T Gibbard 17
Nicholas Goodyer 54
David A H Grayling 364
The Old Hall Bookshop 281
Russell Rare Books 74

NORFOLK
The Angel Bookshop 217

NORTHERN TOPOGRAPHY
R F G Hollett & Son 364

ORIENTAL, EUROPEAN CERAMICS
Lion Fine Arts & Books 251

ORNITHOLOGY
Isabelline Books 152

PHOTOGRAPHY
Photo Books International 108

POETRY
Bookfinders 420

PRE-1700
P J Hilton Books 110

PRIVATE PRESS
Besley's Books 220

ARTHUR RACKHAM
Goldsworth Books and Prints 142

RAILWAY
Bookshop Conwy 383
Patterson Liddle 182

REFERENCE BOOKS ON MAPS & CARTOBIBLIOGRAPHIES
Tooley, Adams and Co 267

RELIGION
Beckham Books 228
Copnal Books 356
Kyrios Books 285

RUPERT BEAR
The Exchange 171

RUSSIAN
Anthony C Hall 114

SCIENCE & TECHNOLOGY
Austwick Hall Books 319
Clevedon Books 187
The Eagle Bookshop 231
Patrick Pollak Rare Books 167
Rogers Turner Books 63

SCOTTISH TOPICS
Ainslie Books 413
The Bookshop 399
Cooper Hay Rare Books 406
Mair Wilkes Books 405
McNaughtan's Bookshop 402
Voltaire & Rousseau 408

SHERLOCK HOLMES
The Black Cat Bookshop 277

SPAIN, HISPANIC STUDIES
Paul Orssich 80

SPORTING
Rare Books & Berry 190
Windmill Bookshop 373

SUFFOLK
Blake's Books 228

SUSSEX TOPOGRAPHY
Bookworms of Shoreham 149

TEXTILES
Avril Whittle, Bookseller 364

THEOLOGY
John Thornton 82

TOLKIEN
Daeron's Books 236

TOPOGRAPHY
Kemp Booksellers 318
The Old Hall Bookshop 281
The Petersfield Bookshop 126
West Country Old Books 170

TRANSPORT
Simon Lewis Transport Books 240

TRAVEL
Allens 270
Altea Maps and Books 86
ATLAS 86
Marijana Dworski Books 251
Reg & Philip Remington 258
Peter Rhodes Books 127

Russell Rare Books 74

VICTORIAN & EDWARDIAN THEATRE
J C Books 219

VICTORIAN ILLUSTRATED
Armchair Books 400

WELSH INTEREST
Rhos Point Books 383
Ystwyth Books 381

WEST COUNTRY INTEREST
Exeter Rare Books 161
Honiton Old Book Shop 164

WWI & WWII
M & M Baldwin 311
Marrin's Bookshop 35

YORKSHIRE TOPOGRAPHY
Grove Rare Books 319
Helmsley Antiquarian & Secondhand Books 322

BOXES

Mostly Boxes 116

LIMOGES BOXES
Michael's Boxes 92

MONEY BOXES
Collectors Old Toy Shop 335
The Museum of Childhood Memories 386

TEA CADDIES
Gerald Mathias 74
June and Tony Stone Fine Antique Boxes 23

TORTOISESHELL
Bazaar Boxes 256

TREEN
Newsum Antiques 250

TUNBRIDGE WARE
Dreweatt Neate Tunbridge Wells Salerooms 43

BREWERIANA

Pub Paraphernalia UK Ltd 64

BUTTONS

The Button Queen Ltd 88
Old Button Shop 176

CARPETS & RUGS

Belgrave Carpet Gallery Ltd 65
Essie Carpets 89
Gallery Persia 408

INDEX OF SPECIALISTS
CARS & AUTOMOBILIA

Gideon Hatch Rugs & Carpets 82
Uri Jacobi Oriental Carpet
 Gallery 355
Michael & Amanda Lewis Oriental
 Carpets and Rugs 192
Mayfair Carpet Gallery Ltd 61, 69
James E McDougall 348
Desmond and Amanda North 33
Polonaise Gallery 80
The Rug Gallery 278
Sabera Trading Oriental Carpets &
 Rugs 58
Samarkand Galleries 403
Anthony Thompson Ltd 107

ORIENTAL
Abington Books 223
Peter Linden Oriental Rugs and
 Carpets 432
Lindfield Galleries 146
Parvis 422

CARS & AUTOMOBILIA
H & H Classic Auctions Ltd 357
Yesterdays Components Ltd 207

BROOKLANDS BADGES
C A R S (Classic Automobilia and
 Regalia Specialists) 14

CARVINGS

IVORY
A and E Foster Ltd 263

CERAMICS
Black Sheep Antiques 24
Aurea Carter 76
Caterham Clearance Centre 133
Cohen & Cohen 98
Collectors Corner 24
Dreweatt Neate 116
Gabor Cossa Antiques 202
Julian Eade 268
Jonathan Horne 99
Offa's Dyke Antique Centre 391
Pantiles Collectables 43
Quay Antiques & Collectables 25
Richard Scott Antiques 216
Thomond Antiques 362
B & T Thorn and Son 160
Tudor House Antiques 292
Sally Turner Antiques 237

18THC ENGLISH PORCELAIN
Law Fine Art Ltd 115

19TH–20THC
Richard Winterton Auctioneers and
 Valuers 296

20THC DECORATIVE ARTS
Paul Gibbs Antiques & Decorative
 Arts 382

ART DECO
Tango Art Deco & Antiques 305

BESWICK
Barn Antiques 358
Box of Porcelain 175
DDM Auction Rooms 339

BOW
Brian Haughton Antiques 90

CHELSEA
Brian Haughton Antiques 90

CHILDREN'S PLATES
Rene Nicholls 196

CHINESE
Antiquus 187

CLARICE CLIFF
AJC Antiquities 41
Banana Dance Ltd 82
Malcolm Bord 109
The Old Curiosity Shop 167
Castle Antiques 424
Clarice Cliff Ltd 123
Eskdale Antiques 328
Nolton Antiques & Fine Art 387
Riverside Antiques 303

COMMEMORATIVE
Hope & Glory 99
Leons Militaria 51

GAUDY WELSH
Grandpa's Collectables 384

HUMMEL
Fleur-de-Lis Antiques 387

MEISSEN
Yvonne Adams Antiques 244
Brian Haughton Antiques 90
London Antique Gallery 100
Mario's Antiques 106
Laurence Mitchell Antiques 447, 463
www.buymeissen.com 53

NAMED CERAMICS
Malcolms No 1 Auctioneers
 & Valuers 326

ORIENTAL
R & G McPherson Antiques 101

ROCKINGHAM
Holly Farm Antiques 333

ROYAL DOULTON
DDM Auction Rooms 339
Fleur-de-Lis Antiques 387
Old Forge Collectables 424

ROYAL DOULTON FIGURINES
Bart and Julie Lemmy 169

SOUTH DEVON TORQUAY WARE
The Spinning Wheel Antiques 377

SUSIE COOPER
Banana Dance Ltd 82

CHANNEL ISLANDS
Channel Islands Galleries Ltd 416

CINEMA
Steve's World Famous Movie Store 369

CLOCKS
A & C Antique Clocks 183
About Time Antiques 170
Rodney Adams Antiques 386
Antique Barometer & Clock Shop 294
Antique Clocks 334
Antique Clocks 453
Antique Clocks by Patrick Thomas 134
Antique Time 433
Antiques in Baslow 272
Ashby Antiques 276
The Barbers Clock 314
Baskerville Antiques 147
Jonathan Beech Antique Clocks 439
Bell Antiques 340
Eric A Bird Jewellers 342
Bower House Antiques & Interiors 389
Bric-A-Brac 422
N F Bryan-Peach Antiques 280, 286
Ian Burton Antique Clocks 409
D Card 115
John Carlton-Smith 66
Carnegie Paintings & Clocks 171
Charles Antiques 280
Chelsea Clocks and Antiques 104
Chobham & Eton Antique Clocks 116
Churchill Clocks 147
City Clocks 48
Bryan Clisby 124
The Clock Clinic Ltd 84
Clock Corner 358
The Clock House 132
The Clock Shop 128
The Clock Shop 300
The Clock Workshop 115
The Clockshop 142
Clocktower Antiques 373
The Clock-Work-Shop (Winchester) 129
Coach House Antiques 19
Cobwebs 422
Country Clocks 259
John Cowderoy Antiques Ltd 16
Craiglea Clocks 400
Roger A Davis Antiquarian
 Horologist 137
Derbyshire Clocks 275
Gavin Douglas 105
Dreweatt Neate Bristol Salerooms 184
Drop Dial Antiques 365
Leigh Extence Antique Clocks 163
Fieldings Antiques & Clocks 370

Jeffrey Formby Antiques 242
Four Winds Antiques 423
Robin Fowler Period Clocks 338
Frosts of Clerkenwell Ltd 48
Gaby's Clocks and Things 41
Gardiner Houlgate 195
Grandfather Clock Shop 245
Grantham Clocks 339
Alexandra Gray Antiques &
    Decorative Ideas 126
Gutlin Clocks & Antiques 77
G K Hadfield 362
Gerald Hampton 175
Roy C Harris 296
Heywood Antiques 366
Tony Honan 429
Horological Workshops 138
Bernard G House Longcase Clocks 192
House of Clocks 230
It's About Time 213
Kembery Antique Clocks Ltd 181
Roger Lascelles Clocks 85
Laurel Bank Antiques 329
Keith Lawson Antique Clocks 219
Brian Loomes 324
Robert Loomes Clock
    Restoration 344
G E Marsh (Antique Clocks) Ltd 129
J Martinez Antiques 402
F J McAvenues & Son 429
Montpellier Clocks 238
The Old Church Antiques 409
The Old Clock Shop 44
The Old Village Clock Shop 130
Samuel Orr 148
Pendulum of Mayfair 93
Penman Clockcare 343
Petite Antiques 420
Phillips Antiques and French
    Polishing 380
Derek Roberts Antiques 42
Neill Robinson Blaxill 450
Roderick Antique Clocks 101
Second Treasures 35
Shrewsbury Clock Shop 295
Something Different 347
St Lucy Wayside Antiques 407
Time and Motion 316
Time in Hand 303
Timecraft Clocks 178
Timecraft Clocks 452
Timepiece Antique Clocks 435
W F Turk Fine Antique Clocks 85
Ty-Llwyd Antiques 393
Village Clocks 226
Chris Wadge Clocks 199
What Nots Antiques 415
Marcus Wilkinson Jewellers &
    Antiques 340
Mick & Fanny Wright 242

18TH–EARLY 19THC FRENCH
Jillings 243

19TH–20THC
Collectors Choice 165

ANNIVERSARY/400 DAY
David Ansell 113

AUSTRO-HUNGARIAN
Campbell and Archard 40

DECORATIVE
Woodward Antique Clocks 239

DIAL
Leominster Clock Repairs 253

EXTERIOR PUBLIC CLOCKS
Stokes Clocks and Watches Ltd 430

LANTERN CLOCKS
W.F. Bruce Antique Clocks 21

LONGCASE
Craig Barfoot Clocks 263
Browns Clocks 406
The Essence of Time 298
Farmhouse Antiques 355
Fishlake Antiques 331
Jester Antiques 248
Leominster Clock Repairs 253
John R Mann Fine Antique
    Clocks 360
Mill Farm Antiques 356
Northern Clocks 369
P A Oxley Antique Clocks &
    Barometers 194
Second Time Around 341
Allan Smith 199
Chris Wilde Antiques 322

WALL AND MANTEL
Jester Antiques 248

COINS, BANKNOTES & MEDALS
Alpha Coins, Banknotes
    & Medals 370
A H Baldwin and Son 109
E J & C A Brooks 206
B J Dawson 365
Clive Dennett 217
Dix Noonan Webb 88
Gannochy Coins, Banknotes
    & Medals 202
Lockdale Coins Ltd 224
R & J Coins 212
J Smith 330
Sterling Coins, Banknotes
    & Medals 174
World Coins 31

ANCIENT & MEDIEVAL COINS
Classical Numismatic Group Inc. 88
David M Regan 377

BANKNOTES
Michael Coins 101
Colin Narbeth and Son 111
West Essex Coin Investments 123

BRITISH & GERMAN MEDALS
Raymond D Holdich 110

CAMPAIGN MEDALS
Burgate Antiques 30

COINS
Aarons Coins 191
Brigantia Ltd 329
Antiques & Bygones 368
Birmingham Coins 306
Coincraft 108
Collectors Forum 211
Format Coins 306
Intercoin 350
R W Jeffery 154
Jersey Coin Company 417
Robert Johnson Coin Co 344
Knightsbridge Coins 69
C J Martin Coins Ltd 56
World Coins 31

MEDALS
Dixon's Medals 317
Dutton & Smith Medals
    & Badges 287
Neate Militaria & Antiques 228
Yeovil Collectors Centre 193

OLD ENGLISH COINS
David M Regan 377
Studio Coins 129

TUDOR & STUART COINS
Roderick Richardson 217

COLLECTABLES
Ad-Age Antique Advertising 36
R G Cave & Sons Ltd 292
Collectables 163
D'Eyncourt Antiques 133
Glebe Hall Collectables 438
The Old Forge Antiques 27
Special Auction Services 119

20THC
Tagore Ltd 95

AMERICAN
Trails End Collectables Ltd 206

BEATRIX POTTER FIGURES
The Collector 187

FOUNTAIN PENS, DIP PENS, PENCILS
Classic Pen Engineering 398

PENS
The Pen & Pencil Gallery 364

POT LIDS
Rob Gee 169

SCI-FI
Suffolk Sci-fi Fantasy 224

COMMEMORATIVES

Antique and Collectors' Centre Diss 214
The Commemorative Man 176
Special Auction Services 119

COUNTRY HOUSE SALES

Jim Railton 348

CUTLERY

Portobello Antique Store 106

DECORATIVE ARTS

35 The Goffs 16
A D Antiques 300
Abstract/Noonstar 98
Acme Inc. 12
Aesthetics 71
Artemis Decorative Arts Ltd 98
Victor Arwas Gallery 86
Aspidistra Antiques 282
Corrigan Antiques 412
Decorative Antiques 291
Dreweatt Neate Bristol Salerooms 184
Editions Graphiques 88
The Gooday Gallery 139
Mitofsky Antiques 434
Sylvia Powell Decorative Arts 58
Pruskin Galleries 101
Puritan Values at the Dome 227
Fizzy Warren Decorative Antiques 129

1930S
Bexley Antiques and Interiors 28

20THC
Paul Gibbs Antiques & Decorative
Arts 382

ART DECO
Antiques & Interiors 217
Art Deco Originals/Muir Hewitt 334
Baron Art 216
Camel Art Deco 50
Ciancimino Ltd 66
La Belle 155
Alexander von Moltke 69
Omega Decorative Arts 211
Zeitgeist Antiques 97
Tango Curios 347

ART NOUVEAU
Emporium Antiques 39
Past & Present 420

ART NOUVEAU JEWELLERY
Tadema Gallery 53
Zeitgeist Antiques 97

ARTS & CRAFTS
Art Furniture 57
Emporium Antiques 39
Hill House Antiques & Decorative
Arts 73

Peter Hoare Antiques 43
Paraphernalia 272
Past & Present 420
Paul Reeves 101
Valmar Antiques 212

COTSWOLD ARTS & CRAFTS
David Pickup 261

GLASGOW STYLE
The Studio 408

JAMES POWELL
(WHITEFRIARS) GLASS
Ruskin Decorative Arts 245

LIBERTY
Jag Applied and Decorative Arts 100

MIRRORED ART DECO
FURNITURE
B and T Antiques Ltd 103

SCULPTURE
A S Antique Galleries 368

DESIGN

BRITISH POST-WAR
Twinkled 19

**FRENCH, AMERICAN,
1930–70**
Original Vintage Costume Jewellery
227, 272

ELECTRICAL &
MECHANICAL

CAMERAS
Stuart Heggie 30
Jessop Classic Photographic 108

EARLY TELEVISION
Early Technology 399

RADIOS
On The Air Ltd 384

STEAM, MODEL
ENGINEERING

Dreweatt Neate Honiton
Salerooms 163

TELEPHONES
Candlestick & Bakelite 37
Deja Vu Antiques 294

EPHEMERA

The Autograph Collectors Gallery 287
The Border Bookshop 374
Corinium Auctions 239
François 17
Star Signings 112

**ARTIST-DESIGNED POSTERS
1920–51**
Rennies Seaside Modern 108

AUTOGRAPHS
Tony Young Autographs 16

CIGARETTE CARDS
Bumbles 132
ECS 401
London Cigarette Card
Company Ltd 191
Marcel Cards 256
Murray Cards (International) Ltd 59

POSTCARDS
Archway Antiques 275
Brighton Postcard Shop 13
Carlton Antiques 312
Cofion Books & Postcards 390
The Collector 420
Foley Furniture 312
Memories 59
Step Back In Time 15
UK Old Postcards Ltd 29

POSTERS
Big Screen Collectables 27
Dodo 59
The Witch Ball 112

TRADING CARDS
Cards Inc 259
London Cigarette Card
Company Ltd 191
Murray Cards (International) Ltd 59

VANITY FAIR CARTOONS
Notions Antiquaria 111

YORKSHIRE POSTCARDS
Mike Fineron Cigarette Cards &
Postcards 329

FANS

L and D Collins 72

FRENCH ANTIQUES

Frantique 323

FURNITURE

3 Church Street Antiques 277
Alexander Antiques 422
Angel Antiques 147
Anthemion 361
Antique Furniture Warehouse 368
The Antique Shop 54
Antique Warehouse 62
The Antiques Warehouse 140
Apollo Antiques Ltd 304
Arcane Antiques Centre 258
Armstrong Antiques 320
Rodney Arthur Classics 149
Chris Baron Antiques 71

M G Bassett Pine & Decorative Items 270
Bayliss Antiques 292
Clive Beardall Restoration Ltd 210
Berg Brothers Ltd 104
Berry Antiques 242
Bishops Furniture Stores 65
H Blairman & Sons Ltd 87
G D Blay Antiques 133
Border Country Furniture 413
Julia Boston Antiques 76
Botting & Berry 19
C R Boumphrey 167
M J Bowdery 138
Brambridge Antiques 124
Breakspeare Antiques 247
Bristol Trade Antiques 184
Brun-Lea Antiques 371
F G Bruschweiler Antiques Ltd 211
Philip Buddell Antiques 157
Audrey Bull Antiques 379
Burton Antiques 296
Edward Butler 433
Ian Caldwell 141
Canonbury Antiques
Carrington House Antiques 383
Ronald G Chambers — Fine Antiques 147
Chateaubriand Antiques 16
The Chest of Drawers 247
Chest of Drawers Ltd 50
Chesterfield Antiques 306
John Clay Antiques 76
Cleall Antiques 148
Clifden Antiques 436
Collins Antiques 259
B J Coltman Antiques 350
Comberton Antiques & Interiors 203
Comrie Antiques 410
J and M Coombes 134
Coopers Furniture 297
Corfield Potashnick 85
Marc Costantini Antiques 76
Cottage Antiques 225
Cottage Antiques 274
Barry Cotton Antiques 117
Thomas Coulborn and Sons 309
Country House and Cottage Antiques 418
Cross Hayes Antiques 195
Crown Antiques 17
Cryers Antiques 382
D K R Refurbishers 354
Christine Deane Antiques 425
Louis J Doherty & Sons 440
English and Continental Antiques 222
English Rose Antiques 207
Eton Antiques 116
Eynon Hughes 379
Farrelly Antiques 236
Anthony Fell Antiques & Works of Art 216
Brian Fielden 58
Filsham Farmhouse Antiques 26
Flower House Antiques 41
Forge Interiors 23
Forum Antiques 240

Four Winds Antiques 423
Frameworks 437
Franklin Antiques 117
French Treasures 24
Jim Gallie Antiques 206
Michael Gander 257
Gavantiques 136
Georgian House Antiques 262
John Gilbert Antiques 325
A Grice 374
Hamilton Antiques 228
Bob Harrison Antiques 277
J Hartley Antiques Ltd 140
Kenneth Harvey Antiques 81
Hatherleigh Antiques 162
Heritage Antiques 145
Brian L Hills 271
Robert Hirschhorn 62
Christopher Hodsoll Ltd 68
Hugh Cash Antiques 437
Hunters Interiors (Stamford) Ltd 344
Ireland's Own Antiques 438
Isabella Antiques 200
Peter Johnson 154
Peter Jones/PJ2 69
Jubilee Antiques 219
Kaimes Smithy Antiques 401
Roger King Antiques 118
Kings Cottage Antiques 302
David M Lancefield Antiques 40
Latchford Antiques 238
Laurel Bank Antiques 329
The Lemon Tree 357
Lennox Cato Antiques 33
Levenshulme Antiques Village 367
Lithgow Sons & Partners 327
David Loveday Antiques
Ludovic Potts Antiques 203
Alexander Lyall Antiques 225
MacHenry Antiques 422
Magic Lantern 397
McBains Antiques 161
Richard Midwinter Antiques 293
Milton Antiques & Restoration 171
Minerva Antiques 63, 97
John Nash Antiques and Interiors 252
F B Neill 208
New England House Antiques 259
Newark Antiques Warehouse Ltd 287
Michael Norman Antiques 20
Now and Then 375
Old Barn Antiques 345
The Old Coach House 215
The Old Cottage Antiques 48
The Old Malthouse 118
The Old Maltings Antique Centre 342
The Old Steam Bakery 155
Oola Boola Antiques London 65
Orientation Antiques 81
Oxford Street Antique Centre 278
P & R Antiques Ltd 224
Park Antiques 418
Park Lane Antiques 217
Parkways Antiques 191
Partners Antiques 368
Pelham Galleries Ltd 93
Phoenix Trading 208

Graham Pickett Antiques 344
Polly's Parlour 197
Quality Furniture Warehouse 58
Radnor House Antiques 152
Randolph Antiques 223
Recollections 359
Regent Antiques 54
Reindeer Antiques Ltd 101, 283
Richmond Hill Antiques 140
Rogers & Co 79
Rostellan Antiques Ltd 432
Seaview Antiques 341
Second Time Around 355, 356
Selwoods Antiques 191
Shaston Antiques 177
Sitting Pretty Antiques 228
Spurrier-Smith Antiques 270
Staithe Antiques 213
Stalham Antique Gallery 219
J Stamp & Sons 279
The Stores 208
Jane Strickland & Daughters 165
Sutton Valence Antiques 41
Tara Antiques 438
Martin Taylor Antiques 310
Thistlethwaite Antiques 326
S and S Timms Antiques Ltd 232
Tomlinson Antiques 328
Tower Antiques 175
Tower Bridge Antiques 61
Richard Tozer Furniture Workshop 27
Treedale Antiques 290
Trudi's Treasures 16
P & K Turner Auctions 296
Sally Turner Antiques 237
Upstairs Downstairs 241
Warren Antiques 225
Waterfall Antiques 255
The Waterloo Trading Co 53
Anthony Welling 140
Westville House Antiques 191
Whitchurch Antique Centre 294
Ian Whitelaw Antiques 409
T G Wilkinson Antiques Ltd 149
David Wolfenden Antiques 419
The Wooden Betty 350
Yesteryears 170

17THC ENGLISH
J H S Antiques Ltd 270

17TH–18THC ENGLISH
Alan Read 341

17TH–18THC ITALIAN
Cura Antiques 104

17TH–18THC OAK
Early Oak 323

17TH–19THC
Amors of Evenley 281
Antiques and Fine Art Ltd 154
Roger Grimes 439

18THC
Dunkeld Antiques 410

INDEX OF SPECIALISTS
FURNITURE

18THC ENGLISH
John Keil Ltd 73
Brian Rolleston Antiques Ltd 101
Turpins Antiques 118
Witney Antiques 268

18THC WALNUT, MAHOGANY
Nicholas Abbott 124

18TH–19THC
John Anthony 132
Barnt Green Antiques 310
E W Cousins & Son 225
Nicholas Fowle Antiques 218
G Long Antiques 367
Charles Lumb & Sons Ltd 321
Mr Richard Anthony Rush Antiques 224
Stocks and Chairs 177
Vaughan Antiques 345
Wayside Antiques 274

18TH–19THC CONTINENTAL
Blender Antiques 261

18TH–19THC ENGLISH
Northiam Antiques 23

18TH–19THC MAHOGANY
James Hardy Antiques Ltd 346
C. Fredericks and Son 99
John Heather 229
Michael Hughes 73
Michael Lipitch Ltd 91
Michael Lipitch Ltd 456
Scottish Antique and Arts Centre 414
Serendipity 253
Taurus Antiques 36

19THC
Adrian Alan Ltd 86
Lugley Antiques and Interiors 130
Moat Antiques 360
Wargrave Antiques 120

19THC FRENCH BEDROOM FURNITURE
Swans Antiques and Interiors 290

19THC MAHOGANY
Thakeham Furniture 149

19TH–20THC
Hilary Batstone Antiques 65

ARTS & CRAFTS
Samson's Joinery & Antiques 407

BARLEY TWIST
The Old Curiosity Shop 365

BEDROOM
Antique Bed Company 123
The Antique Bed Shop 208
The Antique Brass Bedstead Co Ltd 208
The Bed Workshop 184
Bedsteads 184
Bedsteads 180

French House Antiques 77
La Maison 47
Manor Farm Antiques 266
Pugh's Antiques 165
Seventh Heaven 383
Staveley Antiques 364
The Suffolk Antique Bed Centre 224
Upstairs & Downstairs Antiques 276
Valentina Antique Beds 20
The Victorian Brass Bedstead Co 145
Works of Iron 337

BENTWOOD CHAIRS
Robert Whitfield 63

BILLIARD ROOM
Billiard Room Antiques 187

BOOKCASES
Canning Antiques 406

CAMPAIGN & MILITARY
Christopher Clarke Antiques 244

CHAIRS
Antique English Windsor Chairs 262
Chris Baylis Country Chairs 268
The Chair Set 268
Cheddar Antiques & Upholstery 187
Failsworth Mill Antiques 366
Kantuta 84
Limited Editions 358
The Odd Chair Company 374
The Odd Chair Company 81

CHESTS-OF-DRAWERS
Amors of Evenley 281
Waterfall Antiques 183

CHINESE
Nicholas Grindley 63
The Richard Harvey Collection Ltd 303
Orient Expressions Ltd 78
Shanxi Ltd 80
Snap Dragon 74
Two Dragons Oriental Antiques 386

CHURCH FURNISHINGS
Page Antiques 298

COLONIAL
Alderson 246

CONTEMPORARY DESIGNER
Solomon 55

CONTINENTAL
Birdie Fortescue Antiques 77
Mallett at Bourdon House Ltd 92
The Pine Furniture Store 259

COUNTRY
The Antiques Warehouse 226
Christopher Peters Antiques 305
Cobweb Antiques 161
Early Oak 323
G W Ford & Son Ltd 271

Granary Pine 194
Jan Hicks Antiques 117, 248
Charles Lowe & Sons Ltd 278
Malthouse Antiques 135
Red Lion Antiques 148
Mark Seabrook Antiques 204

COUNTRY OAK
Cellar Antiques 322

COUNTRY PINE
Best Secondhand Centre 273

DECORATIVE
Phoenix 178
Tapestry Antiques 239
Decorative Antiques 76

DESKS
Canning Antiques 406
Dorking Desk Shop 135
D J Green Antiques 271

DINING
Amors of Evenley 281
Antiquarius 230
Brook Farm Antiques 293
Canning Antiques 406
W J Casey Antiques 304
Coopers of Ilkley 336
Dycheling Antiques 145
Michael W Fitch Antiques 40
Freshfords Fine Art 189
Andy Gibbs 254
Hill Farm Antiques 118
Limited Editions 358
Pantiles Spa Antiques 43

EARLY ENGLISH WALNUT
St Ouen Antiques 257

EARLY OAK
Herbert G Gasson 24
Peter Norden Antiques 248

EAST EUROPEAN OLD PINE
Chorley-Burdett Antiques 172

ENGLISH
Apollo Galleries 44
Avon Antiques 193
Callingham Antiques Ltd 147
Chorley-Burdett Antiques 172
Geary Antiques 338
Hare's Antiques Ltd 240
W R Harvey & Co (Antiques) Ltd 268
M Lees & Son 315
Peter Lipitch Ltd 73
Mallett & Son (Antiques) Ltd 92
Mauleverer Antiques 319
Noel Mercer Antiques 225
Moxhams Antiques 194
Quinneys of Warwick 305
Patrick Sandberg Antiques 101
Stair & Company Ltd 95
Suffolk House Antiques 229

INDEX OF SPECIALISTS
FURNITURE

ENGLISH & WELSH OAK 17THC
Day Antiques 247

FARMHOUSE TABLES
Simon Coleman Antiques 83

FRENCH
Deja Vu Antiques 210
French House Antiques 329
David Litt Antiques 230
Martin Quick Antiques 291
Trading House 430

FRENCH BEDS
The French Warehouse 423

FRENCH COMMODES & ARMOIRES
The Decorator Source 247

FRENCH COUNTRY
Appley Hoare Antiques 68
Hugo Austin Antiques 139
Christopher's Antiques 136
Jan Hicks Antiques 117, 248

FRENCH FARMHOUSE TABLES
Country Brocante 192
Denzil Grant 222

FRENCH PAINTED
Pop Antiques 233

FRUITWOOD
Graham Price Antiques Ltd 20
Sieff 248

GEORGE II ARCHITECTURAL FURNITURE
Edward Hurst Antiques 195

GEORGIAN
Aura Antiques 324
Peter Clark Antiques 306
Corfield Ltd 125
Dorchester Antiques 263
J Green & Son 279
Hera Antiques 393
G A Hill Antiques 29
R N Myers & Son 320
Prichard Antiques 250
Shardlow Antiques 276
R S Wilson & Son 320

GEORGIAN MAHOGANY
Christopher Buck Antiques 39
Kingsley & Co 346

GEORGIAN–VICTORIAN
Frantiques of Devizes 195
Kidwelly Antiques 380
Phoenix Trading Company – South Yorkshire 330
Wheatsheaf Antiques Centre 356

GILTWOOD
Clifford Wright Antiques Ltd 75

GLASS
Dreweatt Neate 116

JAPANESE
Brigsy's Antique Centre 35
Tansu 334

LACQUER
Alan Read 341

LARGE
Fair Finds Antiques 412

LIBRARY
Michael W Fitch Antiques 40

LINEN PRESSES
Waterfall Antiques 183

MAHOGANY
G W Ford & Son Ltd 271

MODERN ACCESSORIES
Heath-Bullocks 137

OAK
Beedham Antiques Ltd 117
Douglas Bryan 32
Keith Hockin Antiques 245
Paul Hopwell Antiques 284
Huntington Antiques Ltd 245
In Period Antiques 250
Charles Lowe & Sons Ltd 278
Malthouse Antiques 135
Alan Read 341
Mark Seabrook Antiques 204
Stuart Interiors Antiques Ltd 189
Westway Pine 323

ORIENTAL
Oriental Antiques Ltd 349
Ridgeway Antiques 213

PAINTED
Gilbert and Dale 189
Old Bus Station Antiques Ltd 281
Phoenix Antiques 44
Simpsons 298

PINE
A B Period Pine 285
Acorn Antique Interiors 157
Annterior Antiques 166
Antique & Country Pine 356
Antique & Design 30
Attic Pine 425
Mick Burt (Antique Pine) 338
Bygones Antiques 439
Capricorn Antiques 384
Charlotte's Barn 281
Chimney Mill Galleries 221
Cottage Farm Antiques 237
Country Pine Trading Co 296
Delvin Farm Antiques 440

The Dragon 168
Ben Eggleston Antiques Ltd 363
Flourish Farm Antiques 275
Friargate Pine Co Ltd 274
Goodwin's Home & Garden 234
Hardy Country 176
Hardy's Antiques 223
Harlequin Antiques 288
Heathfield Antiques 216
Holt Antique Centre 216
Millgate Antiques 327
North Wilts Exporters 194
The Old Pine Shop 205
One Step Back 221
Partners in Pine 207
Pastorale Antiques 22
Penlan Pine 386
Pennsylvania Pine Company 158
Mr Pickett's 144
Pine and Things 303
Pine for Pine Antiques 418
Pine Workshop 348
Porcupine 357
Q S Antiques and Cabinetmakers 399
Quorn Pine 280
Sambourne House Antique Pine Ltd 199, 393
Seventeen Antiques 376
Snapdragon 168
Times Past Antiques 409
Townhouse Antiques 367
Up Country Ltd 44
Westway Pine 323

REGENCY
Hera Antiques 393

RUSSIAN
Antoine Chenevière Fine Arts Ltd 88
Mark Ransom Ltd 70

RUSTIC
Candle Close Gallery 396

SITTING ROOM
Antiquarius 230

SMALL
Roger Lamb Antiques and Works of Art 245

SOFT/UPHOLSTERED
Leek Antiques Centre (Barclay House) 297
Squirrel Antiques 405

SWEDISH
Filippa & Co 67

TABLES
Failsworth Mill Antiques 366

UNFITTED KITCHENS
Christopher Peters Antiques 305

VICTORIAN
Ann's Antiques 438
Magnolia House Antiques 168
Nichols Antique Centre 332

VICTORIAN BALLOON BACK DINING CHAIRS
Paul Ward Antiques 333

VICTORIAN–EDWARDIAN
Grantham Furniture Emporium 339
Riro D Mooney 203
The Old Bakery Antiques Ltd 260

WALNUT
Richard Courtney Ltd 72
In Period Antiques 250
Alan Read 341

WARDROBES
Canning Antiques 406
Waterfall Antiques 183

WELSH
Adams Antiques 358
James Ash Antiques 380
Collinge Antiques 382
Collinge Antiques 382
T Evans Antiques 386
Michael Rowland Antiques 245

WELSH COUNTRY
M Jones A'i Fab Antiques 385

WELSH OAK
Country Antiques (Wales) 380

WHYTOCK & REID
Whytock & Reid 404

WOODEN
Robinsons Timber Building Supplies Ltd 370

GARDENING ANTIQUES
Antique Garden 354
Matthew Eden 195
Flaxton Antique Gardens 320
Jon Fox Antiques 242
Juro Farm and Garden Antiques 314
Romantiques 155

STATUARY
Phoenix Trading Co 82

GLASS
Antique Glass 180
Bell Antiques 163
Christine Bridge Antiques 83
Charis 169
The Coach House Antique Centre 30
Delomosne & Son Ltd 197
Frank Dux Antiques 181

Peter Francis Antiques 425
Nassirzadeh Antiques 101
Offa's Dyke Antique Centre 391
Perth Antiques 411
Tamblyn Antiques 348
Tombland Antiques Centre 218
Upstairs–Downstairs 411
Brian Watson Antique Glass 217
Mark J West 85

18TH–19THC DRINKING GLASSES
Jasmin Cameron 71
Jeanette Hayhurst 99
H S C Fine Arts Ltd 324

19THC
Vintage Antiques Centre 305

19THC CONTINENTAL
Alexia Amato Antiques 71

COLOURED
Andrew Lineham Fine Glass 105

CRANBERRY
Grimes House Antiques & Fine Art 242
Sandra Wallhead 272

EARLY IRISH
Beaufield Mews Restaurant, Gardens & Antiques 436

ENGLISH DRINKING GLASSES
Somervale Antiques 190

ENGLISH PRESSED GLASS 1930S
Clarice Cliff Ltd 123

LALIQUE
R Arantes 50

MID-CENTURY DESIGN
Mid 20th Century 119

NORTH EAST & VICTORIAN
Robson's Antiques 346

PERFUME BOTTLES
Lynda Brine Antiques 180
J Lawrence 271
Le Boudoir 180

SCANDINAVIAN
Boldon Auction Galleries 349
Alexe Stanion Antiques 70

WHITEFRIARS
The Country Seat 264

HANDBAGS
Linda Bee 86
Eat My Handbag Bitch 109

HATS
Tails & The Unexpected Ltd 393

HAT BLOCKS
Blockheads 282

HAT PINS
Sandra Wallhead 272

ICONS
Iconastas Russian Works of Art 68
Mark Gallery 96

IRISH ART
Whyte's 435

JADE
Adèle De Havilland 88

JEWELLERY
Abbey Antiques 415
Emmy Abe Antiques
Advena Antiques & Fairs 340
Aladdin's Cave 336
An Siopa 441
Ancient and Modern 370
Antiques 19
Antiques by Jules Ltd 86
Arts Decoratifs 211
Belmont 109
Benjamin Jewellery 57
Joseph Bonnar Jewellers 400
Booth Antiques 394
Buckingham Antiques 322
Audrey Bull Antiques 379
A K Campbell & Son 404, 405
Chapel Place Antiques 42
City Antiques 394
Cobra & Bellamy 66
Courtville Antiques 433
Sandra Cronan Ltd 88
Edge 72
Eldreds Auctioneers and Valuers 167
Elisabeth's Antiques Ltd 89
Gem Antiques 36
Glydon and Guess 138
Grays Antique Market 90
Anthony Green Antiques 110
Green's Antique Galleries 99
Hancocks and Co (Jewellers) Ltd 90
Harvey & Gore 68
Henley Street Antique Centre 303
Horton 139
Johnson Walker Ltd 91
John Joseph 91
Kemps 192
Keystone Antiques 277
Lev Antiques Ltd 100
Linda's Antiques 430
The Little Gem 295
E P Mallory and Son Ltd 182

Massada Antiques 92
McKenna & Co 74
Moira 93
Richard Ogden Ltd 93
O'Reillys 435
Penman Clockcare 343
Rare Jewellery Collections Ltd 94
Royal Mile Curios 403
Russell Lane Antiques 304
Searle & Co Ltd 49
Skellgate Curios 325
Spectrum 95
Spectrum Fine Jewellery Ltd 12
Stormont Antiques 421
Tempo Antiques 436
Miwa Thorpe 74
Timgems Jewellers 218
Tintern Antiques 388
Sally Turner Antiques 237
Vinci Antiques 96
J R Webb Antiques 396
J W Weldon 435
What Now Antiques 273
Whichcraft Jewellery 213
Marcus Wilkinson Jewellers
& Antiques 340
Wimpole Antiques 96

AMBER
Hallmark Antiques 90

ART NOUVEAU
Tadema Gallery 53

COSTUME JEWELLERY

Hirst Antiques 105
Mermaid Vintage 143

CUFFLINKS
The Cufflink Shop 72

DIAMOND
Bicks Jewellers & Antiques 238
M & A Kaae 91

ENGAGEMENT RINGS
Hallmark Jewellers 14

ETHNIC & GEMSTONE
Leolinda 51

FRENCH
Trianon Antiques Ltd 95

GEMSTONE
Punzi 22

HAND-MADE
Hirsh London 49, 91

SCOTTISH
Bow-Well Antiques 400

VICTORIAN
Matthew Foster 89
Marie Antiques 60

KITCHENWARE

Bread & Roses 247, 292
Cottage Collectibles 247
Sheila Hyson 169

JELLY MOULDS
Appleby Antiques 103

LIGHTING

Annie's Attic 301
Chris Baron Antiques 71
Bedouin Antiques 150
Berg Brothers Ltd 104
Blackwood Cowell Antiques 97
Collectable Furniture 80
Delomosne & Son Ltd 197
Denton Antiques 99
Dernier and Hamlyn Ltd 493
Exeter Antique Lighting 161
The Façade 57
Hector Finch Lighting 76
Hanworth House Antiques & Interiors 231
The Lamp Gallery 140
Magic Lanterns 258
Manor Antiques and Interiors 232
Meadow Lamps Gallery 402
Mill Lane Antiques 213
Number 38 169
O'Keeffe Antiques 355
Odeon Lighting 297
Paraphernalia 272
Period Style Lighting 113
Post House Antiques 132
Saltney Restoration Services 355
W Sitch (Antique) Co Ltd 94
Stiffkey Lamp Shop 219
Laurence Tauber Antiques 141
Jeanne Temple Antiques 236
Thornleigh Trading Antique
Lighting 155
Wilkinson PLC 62, 96

1960S
More Than Just Furniture 80

ALABASTER LIGHTS
Charles Edwards 76

CHANDELIERS
Artefact 75
Birkdale Antiques 377
George & Peter Cohn 493
Mrs M.E. Crick Chandeliers 98
Decor Antique Chandeliers 99
French Country Style 365
Gutlin Clocks & Antiques 77
Malthouse Antiques 291
Rainbow Antiques 78

DISPLAY
Turn On Lighting 53

**EARLY ELECTRIC, GAS
CONVERSION**
Sarah Scott Antiques 333

LAMPS
Ann Quested Antiques 175

OIL LAMPS
Lamplite Antiques 392
Tiffins Antiques 123

PARAFFIN LAMPS
Laurens Antiques 46

TABLE LAMPS
Memento 136

LUCITE

Ashton Gower Antiques 244

MAGAZINES & NEWSPAPERS

Book and Comic Exchange 104

COMICS
Automattic Comics 195
The Border Bookshop 374
Comic Book Postal Auctions Ltd 57
Comic Connections 260
Wonderworld 174

**COMICS & ANNUALS
1930–80**
30th Century Comics 84

MAGAZINES
Tilleys Vintage Magazine Shop 333

NEWSPAPERS
Craobh Rua Books 423

MAPS & PRINTS

Altea Maps and Books 86
Antique Map & Print Gallery 311
Baynton–Williams 142
The Carson Clark Gallery – Scotland's
Map Heritage Centre 400
Leoframes 14
Michael Lewis Gallery 186
Marrin's Bookshop 35
Melnick House Antiques 115
Neptune Gallery 434
Old Maps 143
Oldfield Gallery 128
Royal Mile Gallery 403
Sanders of Oxford 266
Christine Swift Books 33
Town Prints 226
David Windsor Gallery 385

1550–1850
The Witch Ball 16

CARICATURES
G J Saville 335

COUNTY MAPS
Gillmark Map Gallery 257

DERBYSHIRE MAPS
J Dickinson Maps & Prints 271

GEORGIAN & REGENCY PRINTS
Isaac and Ede 68

MAPS
Faversham Interiors 34
Hereford Map Centre Ltd 252
Simon Hunter Antique Maps 20
The Map House 74
Nicolson Maps 409
Jonathan Potter Ltd 93
G J Saville 335
Colin Wood Antiques Ltd 396

PRINTS
Antique Prints 433
Big Screen Collectables 27
Classic Prints 72
Craobh Rua Books 423
Trowbridge Gallery 16, 79

REFERENCE BOOKS ON MAPS, CARTOBIBLIOGRAPHIES
Tooley, Adams and Co 267

SPORTING PRINTS
Pickwick Gallery 303

SUFFOLK
Claude Cox Books 224

MARITIME
Bookshop Conwy 382
Dreweatt Neate Bristol Salerooms 184
Gillian Gould Antiques 58, 110
Langfords Marine Antiques 81
Marine Instruments 152

NAVAL ITEMS
Cobwebs 127
Nautical Antique Centre 179

MEMORABILIA
MANUSCRIPTS
Argyll Etkin Ltd 86
Bernard Quaritch Ltd 94

MINING
The Mount Antiques Centre 380

MR PUNCH
Mr Punch's Antique Market 177

TITANIC, OCEAN LINERS
Henry Aldridge & Son 15

TRANSPORT
Paperchase 231

METALWARE
Coach House Antiques Ltd 412
W A Pinn & Sons 212

BRASS DOOR FURNITURE
Christopher Preston Ltd 82

COPPER, BRASS, PEWTER
Golden Cross Antiques 18

MILITARIA
Antiques & Bygones 368
Anything Old & Military Collectables 372
Blunderbuss Antiques 87
Bosley's Military Auctioneers 235
Casque and Gauntlet Militaria 136
Chelsea Military Antiques 72
Coldstream Military Antiques 235
Collectors Corner 24
Trevor Falconer Antiques 422
Grenadiers 65, 314
Peter Hancock 145
Ickleton Antiques 211
Jean's Military Memories 372
Just Military Ltd 332
M & R Lankshear Antiques 175
Liverpool Militaria 376
Pastimes 185
The Pumping Station 393
Q & C Militaria 239
The Treasure Bunker Militaria Shop 408
Treharris Antiques 387
Wallis & Wallis 22
Ware Militaria Auctions 259

ETHNIC WEAPONS
Broadsword Antiques 406

THIRD REICH
The Old Brigade 283

UNIFORMS
Broadsword Antiques 406
Laurence Corner 57

WWII
Boscombe Militaria 172

MIRRORS
Adrian Ager 158
Antique Mirrors 297
Antiques & Decor 141
Hilary Batstone Antiques 65
Chelsea Antique Mirrors 66
Hanworth House Antiques & Interiors 231
Housepoints 30
Overmantels 83
Richmond Antique Mirrors 365
Jane Strickland & Daughters 165
Tara Antiques 438
Through The Looking Glass 102
Felix Vink 436

FRENCH
Julian Antiques 146

GESSO ORNAMENTS
Kilgarvan Antique Centre 440

GILDED
Ashton Gower Antiques 244

GILTWOOD
Ossowski 69

MERCURY MIRROR PLATES
Looking Glass of Bath 181

MUSIC
Lisa Cox Music 161
Evans Emporium 163

GRAMOPHONES & RECORDS
Chris Baker Gramophones 40
Talking Point Antiques 338

GUITARS
Vintage & Rare Guitars (Bath) Ltd 183
Vintage & Rare Guitars (London) 112

INSTRUMENTS
C J C Antiques 380
Gardiner Houlgate 195
Rosina Antiques 120

JUKE BOXES
Juke Box World 343

MECHANICAL MUSIC
DecoGraphic Collectors Gallery 142
Keith Harding's World of Mechanical Music 243

MUSIC BOXES
Mayflower Antiques 106
Vanbrugh House Antiques 246
Vincent Freeman Antiques 51
Sandra Wallhead 272

PIANOS
Cambridge Pianola Company and J V Pianos 204
R R Limb Antiques 286
Miss Elany 286
Music Room Antiques 232
Piano Export 186
Pianos Galore 22

PRINTED
Browsers Bookshop 152
Travis & Emery Music Bookshop 112

RECORDS
Yorkshire Relics 335

STRING INSTRUMENTS
J and A Beare Ltd 86
Turner Violins 285, 306, 337

WIND INSTRUMENTS
Toot-Sweet 337
Windworld 307

MUSIC MEMORABILIA

THE BEATLES
More Than Music 17

OBJETS D'ART

Peter Johnson 154

ORMOLU

Yellow Lantern Antiques 20

PAPERWEIGHTS

Sweetbriar Gallery
  (Paperweights) Ltd 356
Wealth of Weights 19

SCOTTISH
Cabaret Antiques 400

PICTURES

Carnegie Paintings & Clocks 171
Thomas Coulborn and Sons 309
David Duggleby Fine Art 326
Eastbourne Fine Art 17
Graham Gallery 119
Kings Gallery 30
Northallerton Auctions Ltd 324
Sally Turner Antiques 237

19THC YORKSHIRE PAINTINGS
Bennetts Antiques
  & Collectables Ltd 319

20THC
Rupert Cavendish Antiques 76
John Nicholson Fine Art
  Auctioneers 137

BIRKET FOSTER
Laurence Oxley Ltd 121

**BRITISH AVANT-GARDE ART
1930–50**
Peter Nahum at the Leicester
  Galleries 69

BRITISH MARINE
Calton Gallery 400

ETCHINGS
Killin Gallery 410

FOLK ART
Robert Young Antiques 83

FOREIGN VIEWS
Grosvenor Prints 110

FRAMES
Moylurg Gallery 429

IRISH ART
Dunluce Antiques and Crafts 421

IRISH ART
George Williams Antiques 440

MARINE
Dreweatt Neate Bristol Salerooms 184
Colin de Rouffignac 369

OIL PAINTINGS
Fieldings Antiques & Clocks 370

PORTRAITS
Grosvenor Prints 110

PRE-RAPHAELITES
Peter Nahum at the Leicester
  Galleries 69

ROYAL ACADEMICIANS
Michael Wood Fine Art 167

RUSSIAN
John Nicholson Fine Art
  Auctioneers 137

SCOTTISH
Calton Gallery 400

SPORTING
Grosvenor Prints 110

ST IVES & NEWLYN SCHOOLS
Michael Wood Fine Art 167

VICTORIAN
Oliver Charles Antiques Ltd 147
Peter Nahum at the Leicester
  Galleries 69

VICTORIAN WATERCOLOURS
Turner & Sons (1787) 376

WEST COUNTRY
Dreweatt Neate Honiton Salerooms 163

PORCELAIN

Bampton Gallery 159
C and B Antiques 255
Davies Antiques 80
Lauries Antiques 144
MCN Antiques 106
Wellington Gallery 60

18TH–19THC
Mere Antiques 169

18THC ENGLISH
T C S Brooke 220
Roderick Jellicoe 100
Law Fine Art Ltd 115

18THC ENGLISH FIGURES
David & Sally March Antiques 185

18THC EUROPEAN
E and H Manners 100

ASIAN
Colin D Monk 101

BEATRIX POTTER
Box of Porcelain 175

BRITISH TRANSFER WARE
Lovers of Blue and White 258

CHINESE
Fleurdelys Antiquités 105
Santos 102
Jorge Welsh 102

CHINESE ARMORIAL
Heirloom & Howard Ltd 200

CHINESE EXPORT
Geoffrey Waters Ltd 102

COALPORT
Milestone Antiques 298

DISCONTINUED DENBIGH
Folly Four Antiques & Collectables 126

ENGLISH
Stockspring Antiques 102

ENGLISH 18THC
Albert Amor 65

GOSS & CRESTED
The Goss & Crested China Club 124

ORIENTAL
Artemesia 121
Robert Morgan Antiques 177

ROYAL CROWN DERBY
Friargate Antiques Company 274

SOUVENIR CHINA
The Crested China Co 317

WORCESTER
Bygones by the Cathedral 314
Brian Haughton Antiques 90
Philip Serrell Auctioneers & Valuers
  313, 315
Simon Spero 102

WORCESTER (FIRST PERIOD)
Moor Antiques 158

POTTERY

Burslem Antiques and Collectables 299
Harrison's 299
Lauries Antiques 144
Libra Antiques 100
Potteries Antique Centre 299
Potteries Specialist Auctions 300

ART
John Lewis 338

BLUE & WHITE
Sue Norman 74
Doug Pye 272

BRITISH
Islwyn Watkins Antiques 391

CATS
Cat Pottery 217

CREAMWARE
Polly Pallister 106

DELFTWARE
Moxhams Antiques 194

DENBY
Clamjamfrey 414
Mansfield Antique Centre 286
Shirley May 272

ENGLISH BLUE PRINTED 1780–1900
Gillian Neale Antiques 233

FRENCH FAIENCE
Homme de Quimper 343

MAJOLICA
Nicolaus Boston Antiques 310
Britannia 87

MALING WARE
Decades 352
Ian Sharp Antiques 352

MASON'S IRONSTONE
Winson Antiques 264

MCINTYRE
Rumours Decorative Arts 52

MOORCROFT
AJC Antiquities 41
The Neville Pundole Gallery 31
The Old Curiosity Shop 167
Porchester Antiques 186
Rumours Decorative Arts 52

PENDELFIN
Arch House Collectables 390

POLITICAL & ROYAL COMMEMORATIVES
Roger DeVille Antiques 271

POOLE
Clamjamfrey 414
Poole Pottery China Matching
Service 173

PRATTWARE
Malthouse Antiques 245

SCOTTISH
Grannie Used To Have One 397
Magic Lantern 397

STAFFORDSHIRE
Frost Antiques & Pine 388
Graylings Antiques 197
Park Antiques 337
Serendipity 33

STAFFORDSHIRE FIGURES
Aarons Antiques 191
Castle Antiques 209
Staffordshire Pride 165

STUDIO
Tremayne Applied Arts 156

SUNDERLAND LUSTREWARE
Ian Sharp Antiques 352

TORQUAY WARE
Corner Shop Antiques and Gallery 151

VICTORIAN STAFFORDSHIRE
Crows Auction Gallery 134

WEMYSS
Newburgh Antiques 405
Rogers de Rin 74

POWDER COMPACTS
Sue Wilde 167

RAILWAYANA
Dreweatt Neate Honiton Salerooms 163
Solent Railwayana Auctions 129
Yesteryear Railwayana 38

REGIONAL ANTIQUES
DORSET BUTTONS
Old Button Shop 176

FRENCH
Bristol Brocante 184

REPRODUCTIONS
British Antique Replicas 144

ROCKS & MINERALS
BLUE JOHN, ASHFORD MARBLE
Michael Pembery Antiques 272

SCIENTIFIC INSTRUMENTS
Victor Burness Antiques 61
Country Life Antiques 244
Grimes Militaria 185
David J Hansord and Son 342
Mike Read Antique Sciences 153
Eric Tombs 135

BAROGRAPHS
Barometer World 165

BINOCULARS
Marine 292
Quicktest 259

GLOBES
Arthur Middleton Ltd 56
Trevor Philip & Son Ltd 70

MEDICAL
Branksome Antiques 176

METEOROLOGICAL
Richard Twort 193

MICROSCOPES, PHARMACEUTICAL ANTIQUES
Ganymede Antiques 280

SLIDE RULES
Antique Scientific Instruments 354

TELESCOPES
Odin Antiques 15

SCULPTURE
Brian L Hills 271

ANIMALIER
Victor Franses Gallery 67

BERGMAN VIENNA BRONZES
Farthings 165

EUROPEAN
Daniel Katz Ltd 91

SEWING
Variety Box 44

CURTAIN FURNITURE
Cottage Antiques 270

DORSET BUTTONS
Old Button Shop 176

SEWING MACHINES
Vintage Sewing Machines 139

SILVER
Advena Antiques & Fairs 340
Alicia Antiques 267
Argenteus Ltd 109
Atlam Sales and Service 103
Paul Bennett 86
Daniel Bexfield Antiques 86
John Bull (Antiques) Ltd 87
Barbara Cattle 329
Chapel Place Antiques 42
Adrian Cohen Antiques 72
Paul Daniel 109
Reginald Davis (Oxford) Ltd 265
D & B Dickinson 181
Bryan Douglas 109
R Feldman Ltd Antique Silver 109

I Franks 109
Gardiner Houlgate 195
Angelo Gibson 73
Jonathan Green Antiques 198
Keystone Antiques 277
Koopman Rare Art (London) Ltd 110
David M Lancefield Antiques 40
J Lawrence 271
Leona Levine Silver Specialist 218
Sanda Lipton 91
Lowe and Sons 355
E P Mallory and Son Ltd 182
C and T Mammon 111
Marks Antiques 92
Iain Marr 408
Mussenden & Sons, GB 173
Jeffrey Neal & Lynn Bloom 111
Not Just Silver 142
Otter Antiques 164
Payne and Son
    (Goldsmiths) Ltd 266
Percy's Ltd 111
R E Porter 173
Douglas Roberts Antiques 256
Schredds of Portobello 107
Searle & Co Ltd 49
Silstar Antiques Ltd 111
Silver and Plate Centre 52
The Silver Shop 435
B Silverman 102
Jack Simons Antiques Ltd 111
Skellgate Curios 325
Stephen Kalms Antiques 110
S & J Stodel 112
Stormont Antiques 421
Styles Silver 118
Tempo Antiques 436
Miwa Thorpe 74
Sally Turner Antiques 237
William Walter Antiques Ltd 112
Warwick Antique Centre 305

18THC
ADC Heritage Ltd 85
Mary Cooke Antiques Ltd 84

BOXES
Corner House Antiques 241

CHESTER
Kayes 355

CUTLERY
Langfords 110

EARLY 20THC
Hedingham Antiques 211

EARLY SPOONS
Henry Willis (Antique Silver) 178

EXETER
D Lovell 169

FLATWARE
Hamiltons 110
Nat Leslie Ltd 111

GEORG JENSEN
The Silver Fund Ltd 70
Jeremy Sniders Antiques 407

GEORGIAN
James Hardy & Co 73

IRISH
M P Levene Ltd 79
Nicholas Shaw Antiques 149
Weir and Sons Ltd 435

PHOTOGRAPH FRAMES
Hayman & Hayman 73

SCOTTISH
Nicholas Shaw Antiques 149

SCOTTISH PROVINCIAL
Thomson, Roddick
    & Medcalf 398, 403

SHEFFIELD PLATE
David Foord-Brown Antiques 145

SPORT & PASTIMES
Beer Collectables 159
Books & Collectables Ltd 202
Dickins Auctioneers 234
Dreweatt Neate Marlborough
    Saleroom 196
Evans and Partridge 128
Nick Potter Ltd 94
Sporting Antiques 44
Windmill Bookshop 373
World of Sport 18
Wot-a-Racket 33

ANGLING
Neil Freeman Angling Auctions 107

BILLIARDS & SNOOKER
Academy Billiard Company 141
Sir William Bentley Billiards 117

CANES & WALKING STICKS
Geoffrey Breeze Antique Canes 247
Michael German Antiques Ltd 99

CHESS SETS
S Millard Antiques 182

CRICKET
K Faulkner 121, 185
Football in Focus (2001) Ltd 18

CRICKET MEMORABILIA
J W McKenzie Ltd 136

FISHING TACKLE
Brindley John Ayers Catalogue of
    Vintage and Collectable Fishing
    Tackle 389

FOOTBALL
Brentside Programmes 205

D & D Programmes 399
Football in Focus (2001) Ltd 18

GOLF
David Brown Gallery 405

MEMORABILIA
Golfark International 349

SPORTING ANTIQUES
Mullock & Madeley 295
Warwick Auctions 307

PRINTS
Manfred Schotten Antiques 261

STAMPS
Boscombe Stamp Company 172
ECS 401
Stamp Shop 426

STATUARY
BRONZE
Apollo Galleries 44

TANTALUSES
Barham Antiques 104

TAXIDERMY
Get Stuffed 51
Penybont Farm Antiques 394
Alexis F J Turner Antiques 136

TEXTILES
Antique Textiles and Lighting 180
Bijou Art 32
Margaret Callaghan 14
Clifton Hill Textiles 184
Sheila Cook Textiles 104
Decades 370
Marilyn Garrow Fine Textile Art 226
Joss Graham Orientals 67
The Green Room 223
Lewis Antiques & Interiors 200
Betty Lovell 169
Lunn Antiques Ltd 78, 105
Past Caring 216
Catherine Shinn Decorative
    Textiles 239
Peta Smyth Antique Textiles 70
The Snug 158
Susannah 183
Tails & The Unexpected Ltd 393
Textile-Art: The Textile Gallery 95

1940S–50S CLOTHING
The Girl Can't Help It 60

19THC SAMPLERS
The Forge Antiques & Collectables 344

INDEX OF SPECIALISTS
TOOLS

AUBUSSON TAPESTRY
Chelsea Antique Rug Gallery 72

BED & TABLE LINEN
Jane Sacchi Linens Ltd 82

CHINESE
Linda Wrigglesworth Ltd 96

COSTUME AND CLOTHING
Bizarre! 168
Marion Bowen Vintage Clothes 22
Echoes 375
Old Hat Vintage & Classic Clothing 78
St Martins Antiques Centre 344
Jenny Vander 435
Vintage to Vogue 183
Wardrobe 16
Wartime Wardrobe 274

DURHAM QUILTS
Robson's Antiques 346

EUROPEAN 18THC & EARLIER
Robin Haydock Rare Textiles 73

LACE
Ceres Antiques 404
Portland House Antiques and
    Collectables 165

LINEN
Ceres Antiques 404
Easingwold Antiques 320

SAMPLERS
Erna Hiscock 105

TAPESTRIES
Joanna Booth 71
C John Ltd 91

WELSH QUILTS
Jen Jones Antiques 381

TOOLS

Cottage Antiques 270
Woodville Antiques 35

LETTERPRESS PRINTING
The Glory Hole 413

WOODWORKING
Old Tools Feel Better! 169
David Stanley Auctions 279
The Tool Shop 227
Trinder's Fine Tools 222

TOYS, DOLLS & BEARS

Acme Toy Company 305
B & D Collectors' Toys 38
Basically Bears 21

Boldon Auction Galleries 349
Boscombe Toy Collectors 172
Collectors Corner 144
Abbey Models 172
Antique Toys 163
DecoGraphic Collectors
    Gallery 142
S Millard Antiques 182
Mimi Fifi 106
Now & Then 402
Pastimes 178
Retrobuy 278
Trains and Diecast 372
Unique Collections of
    Chipstead 133
Vectis Auctions Ltd 327
Wallis & Wallis 22
Wheels of Steel 96

BISQUE DOLLS
Antique Cottage 376

DOLLS
Dollectable 355
Dolly Domain 352
Little Paws 293
Recollect The Dolls Hospital 144
Sue Pearson Antique Dolls & Teddy
    Bears 15
The Shrubbery 179
Upstairs Downstairs 196

DOLLS' HOUSES, FURNITURE
Acorns 421
Hobday Toys 235

KÖSEN ANIMALS
Bears Galore 24

MINIATURE TOYS
Jeffrey Neal & Lynn Bloom 111

MODELS
DDM Auction Rooms 339

ROCKING HORSES
Ann's Antiques 299
Stevenson Brothers 27

STEIFF
Bears Galore 24
Bearly Trading of London 64
Dollyland 56
Off World 235
Park House Antiques 245
Peter Le Vesconte Collectables 417
Teddy Bears of Witney 268

TEDDY BEARS
Baba Bears 13
Bears 'n' Bunnies 28
Bears on the Square 292
Little Paws 293
Sue Pearson Antique Dolls & Teddy
    Bears 15

TEDDY HOSPITAL
Bee Antiques 29

TIN TOYS
Collectors Dream 16

TRAINS
The Vintage Toy & Train Shop 167

TRIBAL ART

Goodrich House Antiques 231

WATCHES

Atlam Sales and Service 103
Chamade Antiques 104
Samuel Elliot 454
Frosts of Clerkenwell Ltd 48
Anthony Green Antiques 110
Harpers Jewellers Ltd 329
Penman Clockcare 343
Pieces of Time 93
Tempus Watches 115
Marcus Wilkinson Jewellers
    & Antiques 340

COVENTRY POCKET
Mortimers Curios 302

VINTAGE ROLEX
I Ehrnfeld 56

WRISTWATCHES
Brittons Watches 373
Sugar Antiques 53

WINE ANTIQUES

Robin Butler 222
Malthouse Antiques 245

CORKSCREWS
Kaizen International Ltd 38
Christopher Sykes 232

WOODCARVINGS

ORNAMENTAL TURNING
Early Technology 399

WORKS OF ART

C and L Burman 87
Dreweatt Neate 116
Pelham Galleries Ltd 93

GERMAN & AUSTRIAN
Villa Grisebach Art Auctions 58

IMPERIAL RUSSIAN
Shapiro & Co. 94

A

Abbey Dore, Herefordshire 250
Abbeydorney, Co Kerry 437
Abbeyleix, Co Laois 438
Aberdare, Mid Glamorgan 387
Aberdeen, Aberdeenshire 396
Aberdour, Fife 404
Aberford, West Yorkshire 333
Abergavenny, Monmouthshire 388
Abernyte, Perth & Kinross 409
Aberporth, Dyfed 384
Abersychan, Monmouthshire 388
Aberystwyth, Ceredigion 381
Abinger Hammer, Surrey 131
Accrington, Lancashire 370
Achill Sound, Co Mayo 439
Acle, Norfolk 213
Adare, Co Limerick 438
Aghadowey, Co Londonderry 425
Ahoghill, Co Antrim 419
Alcester, Warwickshire 301
Aldeburgh, Suffolk 220
Aldermaston, Berkshire 115
Aldershot, Hampshire 121
Alford, Lincolnshire 338
Alfreton, Derbyshire 269
Allington, Lincolnshire 338
Almondsbury, Gloucestershire 237
Alnwick, Northumberland 347
Alport, Derbyshire 269
Alresford, Hampshire 121
Alsager, Cheshire 353
Alston, Cumbria 360
Alton, Hampshire 121
Altrincham, Cheshire 353
Amersham, Buckinghamshire 233
Ampthill, Bedfordshire 230
Andover, Hampshire 121
Antrim, Co Antrim 419
Appleby in Westmorland,
 Cumbria 360
Appledore, Kent 27
Ardingly, West Sussex 142
Armagh, Co Armagh 423
Arundel, West Sussex 142
Ascot, Berkshire 115
Ascott-Under-Wychwood,
 Oxfordshire 260
Ash, Hampshire 122
Ash Vale, Hampshire 122
Ashbourne, Derbyshire 269
Ashburton, Devon 158
Ashby de la Zouch, Leicestershire 276
Ashford, Kent 27
Ashington, Northumberland 348
Ashmore Green, Berkshire 115
Ashtead, Surrey 132
Ashurst, Kent 27
Askrigg, North Yorkshire 319
Aston Clinton, Buckinghamshire 233
Aston Subedge, Gloucestershire 237
Atcham, Shropshire 290
Atherton, Greater Manchester 364

Auchterarder, Perth & Kinross 409
Aughnacloy, Co Tyrone 426
Auldearn, Highland 408
Austwick, North Yorkshire 319
Avebury, Wiltshire 193
Axminster, Devon 159
Aylesbury, Buckinghamshire 233
Aylesby, Lincolnshire 338
Aylsham, Norfolk 213

B

Bagshot, Surrey 132
Baildon, West Yorkshire 333
Bakewell, Derbyshire 270
Balcombe, East Sussex 12
Balcombe, West Sussex 143
Ballacolla, Co Laois 438
Ballater, Aberdeenshire 396
Ballinamallard, Co Fermanagh 425
Ballinderry, Co Antrim 419
Ballinderry, Co Tipperary 440
Ballinea, Co Cavan 429
Ballycallan, Co Kilkenny 437
Ballycastle, Co Antrim 419
Ballycolman, Co Tyrone 426
Ballydehob, Co Cork 429
Ballygawley, Co Tyrone 426
Ballymena, Co Antrim 419
Ballymoney, Co Antrim 419
Ballynahinch, Co Down 423
Balsham, Cambridgeshire 201
Baltron, Stirling 414
Bamford, Derbyshire 272
Bampton, Devon 159
Banbury, Oxfordshire 260
Bangor, Co Down 423
Bangor, Gwynedd 385
Barham, Kent 27
Barlow, Derbyshire 272
Barlow, South Yorkshire 330
Barmouth, Gwynedd 385
Barnard Castle, Co Durham 346
Barnet, Hertfordshire 255
Barnham, West Sussex 143
Barnsley, South Yorkshire 330
Barnstaple, Devon 159
Barnt Green, Worcestershire 310
Barry, South Glamorgan 392
Barton, Lancashire 370
Barton, Cheshire 354
Basford, Staffordshire 295
Basildon, Essex 205
Basingstoke, Hampshire 122
Baslow, Derbyshire 272
Bath, Somerset 179
Batley, West Yorkshire 334
Battle, East Sussex 12
Battlesbridge, Essex 205
Beaconsfield, Buckinghamshire 233
Beauly, Highland 408
Beaumaris, Gwynedd 385
Beaumaris, Isle of Anglesey 386
Bebington, Merseyside 375

Beccles, Suffolk 220
Beckenham, Kent 27
Bedale, North Yorkshire 319
Bedford, Bedfordshire 231
Beer, Devon 159
Beeston, Cheshire 354
Beeston, Nottinghamshire 285
Belfast, Co Antrim 420
Bells Yew Green, Kent 27
Belper, Derbyshire 273
Belton, Lincolnshire 338
Bembridge, Isle of Wight 130
Benenden, Kent 27
Benfleet, Essex 206
Bentley, South Yorkshire 330
Bere Regis, Dorset 171
Berkeley, Gloucestershire 237
Berkhamsted, Hertfordshire 255
Berwick-upon-Tweed,
 Northumberland 348
Betchworth, Surrey 132
Bethersden, Kent 27
Bethesda, Gwynedd 385
Beverley, East Riding of Yorkshire 316
Bewdley, Worcestershire 310
Bexhill-on-Sea, East Sussex 12
Bexley, Kent 28
Bicester, Oxfordshire 260
Biddenden, Kent 28
Bideford, Devon 159
Bidford-on-Avon, Warwickshire 301
Biggin Hill, Kent 28
Biggleswade, Bedfordshire 231
Billingshurst, West Sussex 143
Bilsington, Kent 28
Birchington, Kent 28
Birkenhead, Merseyside 375
Birmingham, West Midlands 305
Birr, Co Offaly 440
Bishop Auckland, Co Durham 346
Bishops Castle, Shropshire 290
Bishops Waltham, Hampshire 122
Bisley, Gloucestershire 237
Bitton, Somerset
Blackburn, Lancashire 370
Blackford, Somerset 183
Blackpool, Lancashire 370
Blackrock, Co Dublin 432
Blairgowrie, Perth & Kinross 410
Blandford Forum, Dorset 171
Bletchingley, Surrey 132
Blewbury, Oxfordshire 260
Bloxham, Oxfordshire 260
Bluewater, Kent 28
Bobbersmill, Nottinghamshire 285
Bodicote, Oxfordshire 261
Bognor Regis, West Sussex 144
Bolton, Greater Manchester 365
Bolton Abbey, North Yorkshire 319
Bo'ness, West Lothian 415
Boroughbridge, North Yorkshire 319
Borris, Co Carlow 429
Boscastle, Cornwall 151
Bosham, West Sussex 144

INDEX OF PLACE NAMES

C

Boston, Lincolnshire 339
Botley, Hampshire 122
Bourne, Lincolnshire 339
Bourne End, Buckinghamshire 234
Bournemouth, Dorset 172
Bourton-on-the-Water,
   Gloucestershire 237
Bovey Tracey, Devon 160
Bowdon, Greater Manchester 365
Brackley, Northamptonshire 280
Bradford, West Yorkshire 334
Bradford-on-Avon, Wiltshire 193
Bradwell, Derbyshire 273
Bramley, Surrey 132
Brampton, Cumbria 360
Brancaster Staithe, Norfolk 213
Brasted, Kent 28
Bray, Co Wicklow 441
Brecon, Powys 390
Bredbury, Greater Manchester 365
Brentwood, Essex 206
Bretherton, Lancashire 370
Brewood, Staffordshire 295
Bridge of Allan, Stirling 414
Bridge of Earn, Perth & Kinross 410
Bridgend, Mid Glamorgan 387
Bridgnorth, Shropshire 291
Bridgwater, Somerset 183
Bridlington, East Riding of
   Yorkshire 317
Bridport, Dorset 174
Brierley Hill, West Midlands 307
Brigg, Lincolnshire 339
Brightlingsea, Essex 206
Brighton, East Sussex 13
Brinklow, Warwickshire 301
Brinkworth, Wiltshire 194
Bristol, Somerset 183
Brixham, Devon 160
Broad Hinton, Wiltshire 194
Broadstairs, Kent 29
Broadway, Worcestershire 310
Brockenhurst, Hampshire 122
Brockham, Surrey 132
Bromborough, Merseyside 375
Bromham, Bedfordshire 231
Bromley, Kent 29
Bromley Cross, Greater
   Manchester 365
Bromsgrove, Worcestershire 311
Brook, Hampshire 122
Broomfield, Essex 206
Bruton, Somerset 186
Buckingham, Buckinghamshire 234
Budby, Nottinghamshire 285
Bude, Cornwall 151
Budleigh Salterton, Devon 160
Builth Wells, Powys 391
Bundoran, Co Donegal 432
Bungay, Suffolk 221
Buntingford, Hertfordshire 255
Bures, Suffolk 221
Burford, Oxfordshire 261
Burgess Hill, West Sussex 144

Burlton, Shropshire 291
Burnham Market, Norfolk 213
Burnham-on-Sea, Somerset 186
Burnley, Lancashire 371
Burrough Green, Suffolk 221
Burscough, Lancashire 371
Burstall, Essex 206
Burton-on-Trent, Staffordshire 296
Burwash, East Sussex 16
Burwell, Cambridgeshire 201
Bury, Lancashire 371
Bury, Greater Manchester 365
Bury St Edmunds, Suffolk 221
Bushey, Hertfordshire 255
Bushmills, Co Antrim 421
Buxton, Derbyshire 273

C

Caernarfon, Gwynedd 385
Caerphilly, Mid Glamorgan 387
Cahir, Co Tipperary 440
Callington, Cornwall 151
Callington, Devon 160
Calne, Wiltshire 194
Calstock, Cornwall 151
Cambridge, Cambridgeshire 201
Camelford, Cornwall 151
Campsey Ash, Suffolk 221
Cannock, Staffordshire 296
Canonbie, Cumbria 360
Canterbury, Kent 30
Cardiff, South Glamorgan 392
Cardigan, Ceredigion 381
Carlisle, Cumbria 360
Carmarthen, Carmarthenshire 379
Carndonagh, Co Donegal 432
Carrefour Selous, Jersey 417
Carrick on Shannon, Co Leitrim 438
Carrickfergus, Co Antrim 421
Carryduff, Co Antrim 421
Carshalton, Surrey 132
Cashel, Co Tipperary 441
Castle Cary, Somerset 187
Castle Donington, Derbyshire 273
Castle Douglas, Dumfries
   & Galloway 398
Castlecomer, Co Kilkenny 437
Castleford, West Yorkshire 334
Castleton, Derbyshire 273
Castletownshend, Co Cork 429
Caterham, Surrey 133
Cattedown, Devon 160
Caversham, Berkshire 115
Cawthorne, South Yorkshire 330
Ceres, Fife 404
Chacewater, Cornwall 151
Chalfont St Giles,
   Buckinghamshire 234
Chalford, Gloucestershire 238
Chalgrove, Oxfordshire 262
Chard, Somerset 187
Charlestown, Cornwall 152
Charleville, Co Cork 429

Charlton Kings, Gloucestershire 238
Charlwood, Surrey 133
Charnock Richard, Lancashire 371
Chatham, Kent 31
Chatteris, Cambridgeshire 203
Chatton, Northumberland 348
Chawston, Bedfordshire 231
Cheadle, Staffordshire 296
Cheadle Hulme,
   Greater Manchester 366
Cheam, Surrey 133
Cheddar, Somerset 187
Chelmsfield, Essex 207
Chelmsford, Essex 207
Cheltenham, Gloucestershire 238
Chepstow, Monmouthshire 388
Cherhill, Wiltshire 194
Chertsey, Surrey 133
Chesham, Buckinghamshire 234
Chester, Cheshire 354
Chesterfield, Derbyshire 273
Chichester, West Sussex 144
Chilcompton, Somerset 187
Chilham, Kent 31
Chilton, Oxfordshire 262
Chinnor, Oxfordshire 262
Chippenham, Wiltshire 194
Chipping Camden,
   Gloucestershire 239
Chipping Norton, Oxfordshire 262
Chipping Sodbury, Somerset 187
Chipstead, Surrey 133
Chirk, Denbighshire 383
Chislehurst, Kent 31
Chittering, Cambridgeshire 203
Chobham, Surrey 133
Chorleywood, Hertfordshire 256
Christchurch, Dorset 175
Christian Malford, Wiltshire 195
Church Stretton, Shropshire 291
Cirencester, Gloucestershire 239
Clare, Suffolk 222
Clarecastle, Co Clare 429
Clarenbridge, Co Galway 436
Cleethorpes, Lincolnshire 339
Cleobury Mortimer,
   Worcestershire 311
Clevedon, Somerset 187
Cleveley, Oxfordshire 263
Cleveleys, Lancashire 371
Clifden, Co Galway 436
Cliftonville, Kent 32
Clitheroe, Lancashire 371
Clola, Aberdeenshire 397
Clonakilty, Co Cork 429
Clowne, Derbyshire 274
Clydach, West Glamorgan 394
Clyst Honiton, Devon 160
Coalville, Leicestershire 276
Cobham, Surrey 134
Cockermouth, Cumbria 361
Cocking, West Sussex 145
Codford, Wiltshire 195
Coggeshall, Essex 207

Colchester, Essex 207
Coldstream, Scottish Borders 413
Coleford, Gloucestershire 240
Coleraine, Co Londonderry 425
Coltishall, Norfolk 214
Colwyn Bay, Conwy 382
Colyton, Devon 160
Combe Martin, Devon 160
Comberton, Cambridgeshire 203
Compton, Surrey 134
Comrie, Perth & Kinross 410
Congleton, Cheshire 356
Connah's Quay, Flintshire 384
Consett, Co Durham 346
Conwy, Conwy 382
Cookham, Berkshire 116
Cookstown, Co Tyrone 426
Coombe Bissett, Wiltshire 195
Cork, Co Cork 429
Corsham, Wiltshire 195
Cosford, Shropshire 291
Coulsdon, Surrey 134
Coventry, West Midlands 307
Cowbridge, South Glamorgan 393
Cowes, Isle of Wight 130
Coxheath, Kent 32
Coxley, Somerset 187
Craigavon, Co Armagh 423
Cramlington, Northumberland 348
Cranborne, Dorset 175
Cranbrook, Kent 32
Cranleigh, Surrey 134
Craven Arms, Shropshire 292
Crawley, Hampshire 122
Crediton, Devon 160
Cresselly, Pembrokeshire 389
Crewe, Cheshire 356
Crewkerne, Somerset 187
Criccieth, Gwynedd 385
Crickhowell, Powys 391
Cromer, Norfolk 214
Cromford, Derbyshire 274
Cross Hands, Carmarthenshire 380
Cross Hills, West Yorkshire 334
Crowborough, East Sussex 16
Crowcombe, Somerset 188
Croydon, Surrey 134
Crudwell, Wiltshire 195
Cuckfield, West Sussex 145
Cullompton, Devon 161
Cutsdean, Gloucestershire 240

D

Dagnall, Hertfordshire 256
Danbury, Essex 207
Darlington, Co Durham 347
Dartford, Kent 32
Dartmouth, Devon 161
Darwen, Lancashire 371
Daventry, Northamptonshire 281
Deal, Kent 33
Debden, Essex 207
Debenham, Suffolk 222

Deddington, Oxfordshire 263
Deganwy, Conwy 382
Denby Dale, West Yorkshire 334
Denham, Buckinghamshire 235
Derby, Derbyshire 274
Dereham, Norfolk 214
Desborough, Northamptonshire 281
Devizes, Wiltshire 15
Dingwall, Highland 408
Disley, Cheshire 356
Diss, Norfolk 214
Ditchling, West Sussex 145
Ditton Priors, Shropshire 292
Dolgellau, Gwynedd 385
Donaghadee, Co Down 423
Donegal, Co Donegal 432
Donnington, Berkshire 116
Dorchester, Dorset 175
Dorchester on Thames,
   Oxfordshire 263
Dorking, Surrey 134
Dornoch, Highland 408
Doune, Stirling 414
Dover, Kent 33
Downham Market, Norfolk 214
Driffield, East Riding of Yorkshire 317
Drinkstone, Suffolk 222
Drogheda, Co Louth 439
Droitwich Spa, Worcestershire 311
Dublin, Co Dublin 433
Dudley, West Midlands 307
Duffield, Derbyshire 274
Dulverton, Somerset 188
Dumfries, Dumfries & Galloway 398
Dun Laoghaire, Co Dublin 435
Dunchurch, Warwickshire 301
Dundalk, Co Louth 439
Dundee, Angus 397
Dundonald, Co Down 424
Dunecht, Aberdeenshire 397
Dunfanaghy, Co Donegal 432
Dunfermline, Fife 404
Dunkeld, Perth & Kinross 410
Dunshoughlin, Co Mayo 439
Dunstable, Bedfordshire 231
Dunster, Somerset 188
Durham, Co Durham 347
Durrow, Co Laois 438
Duxford, Cambridgeshire 203
Dysart, Fife 404

E

Earlswood, Warwickshire 301
Easingwold, North Yorkshire 320
East Boldon, Tyne & Wear 349
East Cosham, Hampshire 122
East Hagbourne, Oxfordshire 263
East Molesey, Surrey 135
East Peckham, Kent 33
East Pennard, Somerset 188
Eastbourne, East Sussex 16
Eastcote, Middlesex 113
Eastleigh, Hampshire 123

Eccleshall, Staffordshire 296
Eccleston, Lancashire 372
Edenbridge, Kent 33
Edenderry, Co Offaly 440
Edinburgh, Edinburgh 400
Egerton, Kent 33
Eggington, Bedfordshire 231
Elham, Kent 34
Ellesmere, Shropshire 292
Ely, Cambridgeshire 203
Emsworth, Hampshire 123
Enfield, Middlesex 113
Ennis, Co Clare 429
Enniskillen, Co Fermanagh 425
Epsom, Surrey 136
Eridge Green, Kent 34
Erith, Kent 34
Esher, Surrey 136
Eton, Berkshire 116
Evenley, Northamptonshire 281
Eversley, Hampshire 123
Evesham, Worcestershire 311
Ewell, Surrey 136
Exeter, Devon 161
Exminster, Devon 162
Exmouth, Devon 162
Exning, Suffolk 222
Eye, Suffolk 222

F

Failsworth, Greater Manchester 366
Fairford, Gloucestershire 241
Fakenham, Norfolk 215
Falkirk, Stirling 414
Falmouth, Cornwall 152
Fareham, Hampshire 123
Faringdon, Oxfordshire 264
Farnborough, Hampshire 123
Farnham, Surrey 136
Farningham, Kent 34
Farnsfield, Nottinghamshire 285
Faversham, Kent 34
Featherstone, West Yorkshire 334
Felixstowe, Suffolk 223
Fermoy, Co Cork 430
Fernhurst, Surrey 137
Fifield, Berkshire 117
Finchingfield, Essex 208
Finedon, Leicestershire 277
Finedon, Northamptonshire 282
Finningham, Suffolk 223
Fishguard, Pembrokeshire 389
Fishlake, South Yorkshire 331
Flaxton, North Yorkshire 320
Fleur-de-Lis, Mid Glamorgan 387
Flore, Northamptonshire 282
Folkestone, Kent 34
Fordham, Cambridgeshire 203
Fordingbridge, Hampshire 123
Forest Row, East Sussex 18
Forfar, Angus 398
Forres, Moray 409
Fortrose, Highland 408

Four Crosses, Powys 391
Four Elms, Kent 35
Fowey, Cornwall 152
Framlingham, Suffolk 223
Freshford, Co Kilkenny 437
Freshford, Somerset 189
Freshwater, Isle of Wight 130
Frinton-on-Sea, Essex 208
Frodsham, Cheshire 356
Frome, Somerset 189
Froncysyllte, Denbighshire 383
Furness Vale, Derbyshire 274

G

Gainsborough, Lincolnshire 339
Galashiels, Scottish Borders 413
Galway, Co Galway 436
Gargrave, North Yorkshire 320
Gargunnock, Stirling 415
Gateshead, Tyne & Wear 349
Gillingham, Dorset 176
Girvan, South Ayrshire 413
Glarryford, Co Antrim 421
Glasgow, Glasgow 405
Glastonbury, Somerset 189
Glemsford, Suffolk 223
Glengormley, Co Antrim 421
Glossop, Derbyshire 274
Gloucester, Gloucestershire 241
Godalming, Surrey 137
Golden Cross, East Sussex 18
Gomshall, Surrey 137
Goole, East Riding of Yorkshire 317
Goresbridge, Co Kilkenny 438
Goring on Thames, Berkshire 117
Gormanstown, Co Meath 440
Gort, Co Galway 437
Gosforth, Tyne & Wear 349
Gosport, Hampshire 123
Gotham, Nottinghamshire 285
Goudhurst, Kent 35
Grampound, Cornwall 152
Grange-Over-Sands, Cumbria 361
Grantham, Lincolnshire 339
Grasmere, Cumbria 362
Gravesend, Kent 35
Grays, Essex 208
Great Baddow, Essex 208
Great Bookham, Surrey 137
Great Dunmow, Essex 208
Great Harwood, Lancashire 372
Great Salkeld, Cumbria 362
Great Waltham, Essex 208
Great Yarmouth, Norfolk 215
Greenock, Renfrewshire 412
Greyabbey, Co Down 424
Greystoke, Cumbria 362
Grimsby, Lincolnshire 340
Grimston, Leicestershire 277
Gringley on the Hill,
   Nottinghamshire 285
Guestling, East Sussex 18
Guildford, Surrey 137

Guisborough, North Yorkshire 320
Gullane, East Lothian 399
Guyhirn, Cambridgeshire 203

H

Hacheston, Suffolk 223
Haddenham, Cambridgeshire 204
Haddington, East Lothian 399
Hadleigh, Suffolk 223
Hadlow Down, East Sussex 18
Hagley, West Midlands 308
Hailsham, East Sussex 18
Hainault, Essex 208
Hale, Cheshire 357
Halesowen, West Midlands 308
Halesworth, Suffolk 224
Halifax, West Yorkshire 334
Hallow, Worcestershire 311
Halstead, Essex 208
Hamilton, South Lanarkshire 414
Hamstreet, Kent 35
Hapton, Lancashire 372
Harefield, Middlesex 113
Harle Syke, Lancashire 372
Harleston, Norfolk 215
Harlow, Essex 209
Harpole, Northamptonshire 282
Harriseahead, Staffordshire 296
Harrogate, North Yorkshire 320
Hartlepool, Co Durham 347
Hartley Wintney, Hampshire 124
Harwich, Essex 209
Haslemere, Surrey 138
Haslingden, Lancashire 372
Hassocks, West Sussex 145
Hastings, East Sussex 19
Hatch End, Middlesex 113
Hatherleigh, Devon 162
Hatton, Cheshire 357
Hatton, Warwickshire 301
Haverfordwest, Pembrokeshire 389
Havering-atte-Bower, Essex 209
Hawarden, Flintshire 384
Hawes, North Yorkshire 322
Haworth, West Yorkshire 335
Hayfield, Derbyshire 275
Hayle, Cornwall 152
Hay-on-Wye, Herefordshire 250
Hazel Grove, Greater Manchester 366
Headley, Hampshire 124
Heanor, Derbyshire 275
Heathfield, East Sussex 19
Hebden Bridge, West Yorkshire 335
Hele, Devon 162
Helensburgh, Argyll & Bute 398
Helmsley, North Yorkshire 322
Helston, Cornwall 152
Hemel Hempstead, Hertfordshire 256
Hemswell, Lincolnshire 340
Henfield, West Sussex 146
Henley-in-Arden, Warwickshire 301
Henley-on-Thames, Oxfordshire 264
Henlow, Bedfordshire 231

Hereford, Herefordshire 252
Herne Bay, Kent 35
Hertford, Hertfordshire 256
Heskin Green, Lancashire 372
Heswall, Merseyside 375
Hexham, Northumberland 348
Heywood, Greater Manchester 366
High Halden, Kent 35
High Wycombe, Buckinghamshire 235
Highbridge, Hampshire 124
Hinckley, Leicestershire 277
Hindhead, Surrey 138
Hindley, Greater Manchester 366
Hingham, Norfolk 215
Hinton St George, Somerset 189
Hitchin, Hertfordshire 257
Hoby, Leicestershire 277
Holbeach, Lincolnshire 341
Holland-on-Sea, Essex 209
Holmfirth, West Yorkshire 335
Holsworthy, Devon 162
Holt, Norfolk 215
Holyhead, Isle of Anglesey 386
Holywood, Co Down 424
Honiton, Devon 163
Honley, West Yorkshire 335
Horley, Surrey 138
Horncastle, Lincolnshire 341
Horndean, Hampshire 124
Hornsea, East Riding of Yorkshire 317
Horsham, West Sussex 146
Horwich, Lancashire 372
Houghton, West Sussex 146
Hove, East Sussex 20
Howden, East Riding of Yorkshire 318
Hoylake, Merseyside 375
Huddersfield, West Yorkshire 336
Hull, East Riding of Yorkshire 318
Hungerford, Berkshire 117
Hunston, West Sussex 146
Huntingdon, Cambridgeshire 204
Huntington, Cheshire 357
Hurst Green, East Sussex 20
Hurstpierpoint, West Sussex 146
Hythe, Kent 35

I

Ilchester, Somerset 189
Ilford, Essex 209
Ilkeston, Derbyshire 275
Ilkley, West Yorkshire 336
Ilmington, Warwickshire 301
Ilminster, Somerset 189
Impington, Cambridgeshire 204
Inchture, Perth & Kinross 410
Ingatestone, Essex 209
Innerleithen, Scottish Borders 413
Inverkeithing, Fife 404
Inverness, Highland 408
Inverurie, Aberdeenshire 397
Ipswich, Suffolk 224
Ironbridge, Shropshire 292
Isle of Arran, North Ayrshire 409

Islip, Northamptonshire 282
Iver, Buckinghamshire 235
Ixworth, Suffolk 225

J

Jedburgh, Scottish Borders 413

K

Keighley, West Yorkshire 336
Kells, Co Meath 440
Kelvedon, Essex 209
Kempsford, Gloucestershire 241
Kendal, Cumbria 362
Kenfig Hill, Mid Glamorgan 387
Keston, Kent 36
Keswick, Cumbria 363
Kettering, Northamptonshire 282
Kibworth, Leicestershire 277
Kidderminster, Worcestershire 311
Kidwelly, Carmarthenshire 380
Kilbarchan, Renfrewshire 412
Killamarsh, South Yorkshire 331
Killarney, Co Kerry 437
Killin, Perth & Kinross 410
Killinghall, North Yorkshire 323
Kilmalcolm, Renfrewshire 412
Kilmarnock, East Ayrshire 399
Kilrea, Co Londonderry 425
Kimbolton, Cambridgeshire 204
King's Lynn, Norfolk 216
Kingham, Oxfordshire 264
Kingsbridge, Devon 165
Kingsclere, Berkshire 118
Kingston-upon-Thames, Surrey 138
Kington, Herefordshire 252
Kinsale, Co Cork 430
Kirkby in Ashfield,
  Nottinghamshire 285
Kirkby Lonsdale, Lancashire 372
Kirkby Stephen, Cumbria 363
Kirkcaldy, Fife 404
Kirton, Lincolnshire 342
Knaresborough, North Yorkshire 323
Knighton, Powys 391
Knole, Somerset 189
Knowle, West Midlands 308
Knutsford, Cheshire 357

L

Lampeter, Ceredigion 381
Lanark, Lanarkshire 409
Lancaster, Lancashire 372
Landbeach, Cambridgeshire 204
Langenhoe, Essex 209
Langford, Nottinghamshire 286
Langport, Somerset 190
Largs, North Ayrshire 409
Larne, Co Antrim 422
Launceston, Cornwall 152
Laurencekirk, Aberdeenshire 397
Lavenham, Suffolk 225

Lealholm, North Yorkshire 323
Leamington Spa, Warwickshire 302
Leap, Co Cork 430
Leavesden, Hertfordshire 257
Lechlade, Gloucestershire 241
Leckhampstead, Berkshire 118
Ledbury, Herefordshire 252
Leeds, West Yorkshire 336
Leek, Staffordshire 297
Leicester, Leicestershire 277
Leigh-on-Sea, Essex 209
Leighton Buzzard, Bedfordshire 232
Leiston, Suffolk 225
Lelant, Cornwall 153
Leominster, Herefordshire 253
Lepton, West Yorkshire 337
Letchworth Garden City,
  Hertfordshire 257
Levenshulme, Greater
  Manchester 366
Lewes, East Sussex 21
Leyburn, North Yorkshire 323
Lichfield, Staffordshire 298
Limerick, Co Limerick 438
Lincoln, Lincolnshire 342
Lindfield, West Sussex 146
Linlithgow, West Lothian 415
Lisburn, Co Antrim 422
Liskeard, Cornwall 153
Liss, Hampshire 125
Little Horstead, East Sussex 22
Little Waltham, Essex 210
Littleborough, Greater
  Manchester 367
Littlebourne, Kent 36
Littlehampton, West Sussex 147
Liverpool, Merseyside 376
Llandeilo, Carmarthenshire 380
Llandovery, Carmarthenshire 380
Llandudno, Conwy 382
Llandudno Junction, Conwy 382
Llandysul, Ceredigion 381
Llanelli, Carmarthenshire 381
Llanerchymedd, Isle of Anglesey 386
Llanfyllin, Powys 391
Llangollen, Denbighshire 383
Llanidloes, Powys 391
Llanrwst, Conwy 383
Llanwrda, Carmarthenshire 381
Llanybydder, Carmarthenshire 381
Lochfoot, Dumfries & Galloway 398
Lockerbie, Dumfries & Galloway 399
London
  East 47
  North 49
  South 61
  West 85
Londonderry, Co Londonderry 426
Long Eaton, Nottinghamshire 286
Long Marston, Warwickshire 302
Long Marton, Cumbria 363
Long Melford, Suffolk 225
Long Sutton, Lincolnshire 342
Long Wittenham, Oxfordshire 265

Longhaven, Aberdeenshire 397
Longridge, Lancashire 373
Longtown, Herefordshire 254
Looe, Cornwall 153
Lostwithiel, Cornwall 153
Loughborough, Leicestershire 278
Loughgall, Co Armagh 423
Loughton, Essex 210
Louth, Lincolnshire 342
Lower Stondon, Bedfordshire 232
Lowestoft, Suffolk 226
Lubenham, Leicestershire 278
Ludlow, Shropshire 292
Lunnaness, Shetland 413
Luton, Bedfordshire 232
Lydeard St Lawrence, Somerset 190
Lyme Regis, Dorset 176
Lyminge, Kent 36
Lymington, Hampshire 125
Lymm, Cheshire 357
Lyndhurst, Hampshire 125
Lyneham, Wiltshire 196
Lynton, Devon 165
Lytchett Minster, Dorset 176
Lytham St Anne's, Lancashire 373

M

Macclesfield, Cheshire 357
Machynlleth, Powys 391
Maidstone, Kent 36
Malahide, Co Dublin 436
Maldon, Essex 210
Mallow, Co Cork 430
Malmesbury, Wiltshire 196
Maltby, South Yorkshire 331
Malton, North Yorkshire 323
Malvern, Worcestershire 312
Manchester, Greater Manchester 367
Maningford Bruce, Wiltshire 196
Manningtree, Essex 211
Mansfield, Nottinghamshire 286
Manton, Rutland 289
Marazion, Cornwall 153
Marchweil, Denbighshire 383
Margate, Kent 36
Market Deeping, Lincolnshire 343
Market Drayton, Shropshire 293
Market Harborough,
  Leicestershire 278
Market Weighton, East Riding of
  Yorkshire 318
Markinch, Fife 405
Marlborough, Wiltshire 196
Marlesford, Suffolk 226
Marlow, Buckinghamshire 235
Marple Bridge, Greater
  Manchester 367
Marsham, Norfolk 217
Martlesham, Suffolk 226
Martock, Somerset 190
Masham, North Yorkshire 324
Matlock, Derbyshire 275
Mattingley, Hampshire 126

Maymooth, Co Kildare 437
Melbury Osmond, Dorset 176
Melbury Sampford, Dorset 176
Melksham, Wiltshire 197
Melrose, Scottish Borders 413
Melton Mowbray, Leicestershire 279
Menai Bridge, Isle of Anglesey 386
Menston, West Yorkshire 337
Mere, Wiltshire 197
Merstham, Surrey 138
Merthyr Tydfil, Mid Glamorgan 387
Merton, Devon 165
Mevagissey, Cornwall 153
Mexborough, South Yorkshire 331
Middle Aston, Oxfordshire 265
Middleham, North Yorkshire 324
Middleton, Suffolk 226
Midgham, Berkshire 118
Midhurst, West Sussex 147
Midleton, Co Cork 432
Midsomer Norton, Somerset 190
Milford-on-Sea, Hampshire 126
Milton Keynes, Buckinghamshire 235
Minchinhampton,
   Gloucestershire 242
Minehead, Somerset 190
Mobberley, Cheshire 358
Modbury, Devon 165
Moira, Co Armagh 423
Mold, Flintshire 384
Monkton, Devon 165
Monmouth, Monmouthshire 388
Montgomery, Powys 391
Montrose, Angus 398
Morecambe, Lancashire 373
Moreton-in-Marsh,
   Gloucestershire 242
Morpeth, Northumberland 349
Mortimer, Berkshire 119
Moy, Co Tyrone 426
Moycullen, Co Galway 437
Much Wenlock, Shropshire 293
Mulbarton, Norfolk 217
Mumbles, West Glamorgan 394
Musselburgh, East Lothian 399
Muthill, Perth & Kinross 411

Nailsworth, Gloucestershire 243
Nantwich, Cheshire 358
Narberth, Pembrokeshire 389
Nayland, Suffolk 226
Neath, West Glamorgan 394
Needham Market, Suffolk 227
Nelson, Lancashire 373
Nettleham, Lincolnshire 343
New Malden, Surrey 139
New Mills, Derbyshire 275
New Milton, Hampshire 126
Newark, Nottinghamshire 286
Newbridge on Wye, Powys 392
Newburgh, Fife 405
Newbury, Berkshire 119

Newby Bridge, Cumbria 363
Newcastle Emlyn,
   Carmarthenshire 381
Newcastle-upon-Tyne,
   Tyne & Wear 350
Newenden, Kent 37
Newent, Gloucestershire 243
Newhaven, East Sussex 22
Newnham, Gloucestershire 243
Newport, Essex 211
Newport, Isle of Wight 130
Newport, Monmouthshire 388
Newport, Pembrokeshire 389
Newport, Shropshire 293
Newport Pagnell,
   Buckinghamshire 235
Newport-on-Tay, Fife 405
Newton Abbot, Devon 165
Newtown, Powys 392
Newtownabbey, Co Antrim 422
Newtownards, Co Down 424
Norbury, Shropshire 293
North Aston, Oxfordshire 265
North Berwick, East Lothian 399
North Cave, East Riding of
   Yorkshire 318
North Cheriton, Somerset 190
North Petherton, Somerset 190
North Shields, Tyne & Wear 351
North Walsham, Norfolk 217
North Wraxall, Wiltshire 197
Northallerton, North Yorkshire 324
Northampton, Northamptonshire 283
Northfleet, Kent 37
Northiam, East Sussex 23
Northleach, Gloucestershire 243
Northmoor, Oxfordshire 265
Northop, Flintshire 384
Northwich, Cheshire 358
Norton, Gloucestershire 244
Norton, North Yorkshire 324
Norwich, Norfolk 217
Nottingham, Nottinghamshire 287
Nuneaton, Warwickshire 302
Nutley, East Sussex 23

Oakham, Rutland 290
Ockbrook, Derbyshire 276
Ockley, Surrey 139
Okehampton, Devon 166
Old Bedhampton, Hampshire 126
Oldbury, West Midlands 308
Oldcastle, Co Meath 440
Oldham, Greater Manchester 367
Olney, Buckinghamshire 236
Omagh, Co Tyrone 427
Orford, Suffolk 227
Ormskirk, Lancashire 373
Orpington, Kent 37
Osgathorpe, Leicestershire 279
Ossett, West Yorkshire 337
Oswestry, Shropshire 293

Otford, Kent 37
Otley, West Yorkshire 338
Oundle, Northamptonshire 283
Oxford, Oxfordshire 265
Oxted, Surrey 139

Padstow, Cornwall 154
Paignton, Devon 166
Paisley, Renfrewshire 412
Pangbourne, Berkshire 119
Par, Cornwall 154
Pateley Bridge, North Yorkshire 324
Patrington, East Riding of
   Yorkshire 318
Peacehaven, East Sussex 23
Peakirk, Cambridgeshire 204
Peasenhall, Suffolk 227
Pembroke, Pembrokeshire 389
Pembroke Dock, Pembrokeshire 390
Penistone, South Yorkshire 331
Penkridge, Staffordshire 298
Penn, Buckinghamshire 236
Penrith, Cumbria 363
Penryn, Cornwall 154
Penzance, Cornwall 154
Pepard, Oxfordshire 266
Pershore, Worcestershire 313
Perth, Perth & Kinross 411
Peterborough, Cambridgeshire 204
Peterlee, Co Durham 347
Petersfield, Hampshire 126
Pett, East Sussex 23
Petts Wood, Kent 37
Petworth, West Sussex 147
Pevensey, East Sussex 23
Pewsey, Wiltshire 198
Pickering, North Yorkshire 324
Pitlochry, Perth & Kinross 411
Pittenweem, Fife 405
Pluckley, Kent 37
Plumley, Cheshire 359
Plymouth, Devon 166
Plympton, Devon 167
Polegate, East Sussex 23
Polesworth, Warwickshire 302
Polperro, Cornwall 155
Pontlyfni, Gwynedd 386
Pontrilas, Herefordshire 254
Pontypridd, Mid Glamorgan 387
Poole, Dorset 176
Porlock, Somerset 190
Portadown, Co Armagh 423
Portarlington, Co Laois 438
Porthcawl, Mid Glamorgan 387
Porthmadog, Gwynedd 386
Portrush, Co Antrim 422
Portsmouth, Hampshire 126
Portstewart, Co Londonderry 426
Potterspury, Northamptonshire 283
Potton, Bedfordshire 232
Poynton, Cheshire 359
Prees Heath, Shropshire 294

Preston, Lancashire 374
Prestwich, Greater Manchester 368
Prestwick, South Ayrshire 414
Puckeridge, Hertfordshire 257
Puddletown, Dorset 177
Pudsey, West Yorkshire 338
Pulborough, West Sussex 149
Pwlldefaid, Gwynedd 386
Pwllheli, Gwynedd 386
Pymore, Dorset 177

Q

Queen Camel, Somerset 190
Queniborough, Leicestershire 279
Quorn, Leicestershire 280

R

Radcliffe, Greater Manchester 368
Radhdrum, Co Wicklow 441
Radstock, Somerset 190
Rainham, Kent 38
Rait, Perth & Kinross 412
Ramsbury, Wiltshire 198
Ramsey, Cambridgeshire 204
Ramsgate, Kent 38
Raughton Head, Cumbria 364
Raveningham, Norfolk 218
Rayleigh, Essex 211
Reading, Berkshire 119
Redbourn, Hertfordshire 257
Redditch, Worcestershire 313
Redhill, Surrey 139
Redruth, Cornwall 155
Reepham, Norfolk 219
Reigate, Surrey 139
Retford, Nottinghamshire 289
Rhos-on-Sea, Conwy 383
Rhuddlan, Denbighshire 383
Rhyl, Denbighshire 384
Richmond, North Yorkshire 325
Richmond, Surrey 139
Rickmansworth, Hertfordshire 258
Ringstead, Norfolk 219
Ringwood, Hampshire 127
Ripley, Derbyshire 276
Ripley, Surrey 140
Ripon, North Yorkshire 325
Risby, Suffolk 227
Robin Hood's Bay, North
  Yorkshire 325
Rochdale, Greater Manchester 368
Rochester, Kent 38
Rolvenden, Kent 39
Romford, Essex 211
Romiley, Greater Manchester 368
Romsey, Hampshire 127
Rosslare, Co Wexford 441
Ross-on-Wye, Herefordshire 254
Rothbury, Northumberland 349
Rotherfield, East Sussex 23
Rotherham, South Yorkshire 331
Rothesay, Argyll & Bute 398

Rothley, Leicestershire 280
Rottingdean, East Sussex 23
Royston, Hertfordshire 258
Royton, Greater Manchester 368
Rugby, Warwickshire 302
Rugeley, Staffordshire 299
Ruislip, Middlesex 113
Runfold, Surrey 140
Rushden, Northamptonshire 283
Ruthin, Denbighshire 384
Ryde, Isle of Wight 131
Rye, East Sussex 24

S

Sabden, Lancashire 374
Saffron Walden, Essex 211
Saintfield, Co Down 424
Salford, Greater Manchester 368
Salisbury, Wiltshire 198
Saltaire, West Yorkshire 338
Saltburn-by-the-Sea, North
  Yorkshire 325
Sandbach, Cheshire 359
Sandgate, Kent 39
Sandiacre, Nottinghamshire 289
Sandown, Isle of Wight 131
Sandwich, Kent 40
Sandycove, Co Dublin 436
Saundersfoot, Pembrokeshire 390
Sawbridgeworth, Hertfordshire 258
Saxmundham, Suffolk 227
Scarborough, North Yorkshire 326
Scone, Perth & Kinross 412
Scratby, Norfolk 219
Scremerston, Northumberland 349
Scunthorpe, Lincolnshire 343
Seaford, East Sussex 25
Seagrave, Leicestershire 280
Seal, Kent 40
Seapatrick, Co Down 425
Seaton, Devon 167
Sedbergh, Cumbria 364
Sedlescombe, East Sussex 25
Selby, North Yorkshire 326
Semley, Dorset 177
Sessay, North Yorkshire 326
Settle, North Yorkshire 326
Sevenoaks, Kent 40
Shaftesbury, Dorset 177
Shanklin, Isle of Wight 131
Shap, Cumbria 364
Shardlow, Derbyshire 276
Sheffield, South Yorkshire 331
Shefford, Bedfordshire 232
Shenton, Warwickshire 302
Shepton Mallet, Somerset 191
Sherborne, Dorset 177
Sherburn-in-Elmet, North
  Yorkshire 326
Shere, Surrey 140
Sheringham, Norfolk 219
Shifnal, Shropshire 294
Shipston-on-Stour, Warwickshire 303

Shipton Bellinger, Hampshire 127
Shoreham by Sea, West Sussex 149
Shotton, Flintshire 384
Shrewsbury, Shropshire 294
Sible Hedingham, Essex 211
Sidmouth, Devon 167
Silverstone, Northamptonshire 283
Sissinghurst, Kent 40
Sittingbourne, Kent 41
Skelton, Cumbria 364
Sketty, West Glamorgan 394
Skipton, North Yorkshire 327
Sleights, North Yorkshire 327
Sligo, Co Sligo 440
Slingsby, North Yorkshire 327
Slough, Berkshire 120
Snape, Suffolk 227
Snitterfield, Warwickshire 303
Snodland, Kent 41
Soham, Cambridgeshire 204
Solihull, West Midlands 308
Somerton, Somerset 191
Sonning-on-Thames, Berkshire 120
South Benfleet, Essex 212
South Brent, Devon 167
South Holmwood, Surrey 141
South Molton, Devon 167
South Shields, Tyne & Wear 351
South Woodham Ferrers, Essex 212
Southam, Gloucestershire 244
Southampton, Hampshire 127
Southend-on-Sea, Essex 212
Southport, Merseyside 377
Southsea, Hampshire 128
Southwold, Suffolk 227
Sowerby Bridge, West Yorkshire 338
Spalding, Lincolnshire 343
Sproughton, Suffolk 228
St Albans, Hertfordshire 258
St Andrews, Fife 405
St Columb, Cornwall 155
St Helen Auckland, Co Durham 347
St Helier, Jersey 417
St Ives, Cambridgeshire 205
St Ives, Cornwall 156
St Just, Cornwall 156
St Just-in-Roseland, Cornwall 156
St Leonards-on-Sea, East Sussex 26
St Mary, Jersey 418
St Neots, Cambridgeshire 205
St Peter Port, Guernsey 416
St Sampsons, Guernsey 417
St Saviour, Jersey 418
Stafford, Staffordshire 299
Staines, Middlesex 113
Staithes, North Yorkshire 327
Stalham, Norfolk 219
Stamford, Lincolnshire 343
Standlake, Oxfordshire 266
Stanley, Perth & Kinross 412
Stansted Mountfitchet, Essex 212
Stanton upon Hine Heath,
  Shropshire 295
Staplecross, East Sussex 26

Staveley, Cumbria 364
Steventon, Oxfordshire 266
Stewartstown, Co Tyrone 427
Steyning, West Sussex 149
Stickney, Lincolnshire 345
Stiffkey, Norfolk 219
Stillorgan, Co Dublin 436
Stirling, Stirling 415
Stockbridge, Hampshire 128
Stockbury, Kent 41
Stockport, Greater Manchester 368
Stockton-on-Tees, North Yorkshire 327
Stoke sub Hamdon, Somerset 191
Stoke-on-Trent, Staffordshire 299
Stokesley, North Yorkshire 327
Stony Stratford, Buckinghamshire 236
Storrington, West Sussex 149
Stourbridge, West Midlands 308
Stourpaine, Dorset 178
Stowmarket, Suffolk 228
Stow-on-the-Wold,
  Gloucestershire 244
Stranraer, Dumfries & Galloway 399
Stratford-upon-Avon,
  Warwickshire 303
Strathaven, South Lanarkshire 414
Strathblane, Stirling 415
Streat, West Sussex 149
Stroud, Gloucestershire 246
Sudbury, Suffolk 228
Sunderland, Tyne & Wear 352
Surbiton, Surrey 141
Sutton Bridge, Lincolnshire 345
Sutton Coldfield, West Midlands 309
Sutton Valence, Kent 41
Sutton-in-Ashfield,
  Nottinghamshire 289
Swadlincote, Derbyshire 276
Swaffham, Norfolk 219
Swanage, Dorset 178
Swansea, West Glamorgan 394
Swinderby, Lincolnshire 345
Swindon, Wiltshire 199

Tacolneston, Norfolk 219
Tadcaster, North Yorkshire 327
Tadworth, Surrey 141
Tamworth, Staffordshire 300
Tarland, Aberdeenshire 397
Tarporley, Cheshire 359
Tattenhall, Cheshire 359
Tattershall, Lincolnshire 345
Taunton, Somerset 191
Tavistock, Devon 168
Tedburn St Mary, Devon 168
Teddington, Middlesex 113
Teignmouth, Devon 168
Temple Cloud, Somerset 192
Templeton, Pembrokeshire 390
Tempo, Co Fermanagh 425
Tenby, Pembrokeshire 390
Tenterden, Kent 41

Tetbury, Gloucestershire 246
Tetsworth, Oxfordshire 266
Tewkesbury, Gloucestershire 249
Teynham, Kent 42
Thame, Oxfordshire 267
Thames Ditton, Surrey 141
Thaxted, Essex 212
Thirsk, North Yorkshire 327
Thomastown, Co Kilkenny 438
Thornton, East Riding of
  Yorkshire 318
Thornton-le-Dale, North
  Yorkshire 327
Thrapston, Northamptonshire 284
Thurcroft, South Yorkshire 333
Thurmaston, Leicestershire 280
Ticehurst, East Sussex 26
Tiddington, Warwickshire 304
Tideford, Cornwall 156
Timsbury, Somerset 192
Tintagel, Cornwall 156
Tintern, Monmouthshire 388
Tiverton, Devon 168
Tockwith, North Yorkshire 328
Todmorden, Lancashire 374
Tonbridge, Kent 42
Tonypandy, Mid Glamorgan 387
Toomebridge, Co Antrim 423
Topsham, Devon 168
Torquay, Devon 170
Totnes, Devon 171
Tottenhill, Norfolk 219
Towcester, Northamptonshire 284
Tralee, Co Kerry 437
Trecastle, Powys 392
Treharris, Mid Glamorgan 387
Tring, Hertfordshire 259
Tringford, Hertfordshire 259
Trinity, Jersey 418
Troon, South Ayrshire 414
Truro, Cornwall 156
Tunbridge Wells, Kent 42
Turners Hill, West Sussex 150
Tutbury, Staffordshire 300
Twickenham, Middlesex 114
Twyford, Berkshire 120
Tynemouth, Tyne & Wear 352
Tytherleigh, Devon 171

Uckfield, East Sussex 26
Uffculme, Devon 171
Ulverston, Cumbria 364
Upminster, Essex 212
Upper Largo, Fife 405
Upper Poppleton, North
  Yorkshire 328
Uppingham, Rutland 290
Upton-upon-Severn,
  Worcestershire 314
Usk, Monmouthshire 389
Uttoxeter, Staffordshire 300
Uxbridge, Middlesex 114

Valley, Isle of Anglesey 387
Ventnor, Isle of Wight 131
Veryan, Cornwall 157

Waddesdon, Buckinghamshire 236
Wadebridge, Cornwall 157
Wadhurst, East Sussex 26
Wainfleet, Lincolnshire 345
Walesby, Lincolnshire 345
Walgherton, Cheshire 359
Wall under Heywood, Shropshire 295
Wallasey, Merseyside 378
Wallingford, Oxfordshire 267
Walmer, Kent 44
Walsall, West Midlands 309
Walton-on-Thames, Surrey 141
Ware, Hertfordshire 259
Wareham, Dorset 178
Warfield, Berkshire 120
Wargrave, Berkshire 120
Warminster, Wiltshire 199
Warrington, Cheshire 359
Warton, Warwickshire 304
Warwick, Warwickshire 304
Washington, Tyne & Wear 352
Watchet, Somerset 192
Waterford, Co Waterford 441
Watford, Hertfordshire 259
Watton, Norfolk 219
Wavendon, Buckinghamshire 236
Waverton, Cheshire 359
Wednesbury, West Midlands 309
Weedon, Northamptonshire 284
Wellingborough,
  Northamptonshire 284
Wellington, Somerset 192
Wells, Somerset 192
Wells-next-the-Sea, Norfolk 220
Welshpool, Powys 392
Wendover, Buckinghamshire 236
Wentworth, South Yorkshire 333
West Bridgford, Nottinghamshire 289
West Byfleet, Surrey 141
West Grinstead, West Sussex 150
West Haddon, Northamptonshire 284
West Malling, Kent 44
West Ruislip, Middlesex 114
West Wickham, Kent 44
West Yatton, Wiltshire 200
Westbury-on-Trym, Somerset 192
Westcliff-on-Sea, Essex 213
Westerham, Kent 44
Westgate-on-Sea, Kent 45
Weston-super-Mare, Somerset 193
Westport, Co Mayo 439
Wetherby, West Yorkshire 338
Wexford, Co Wexford 441
Weybridge, Surrey 141
Weymouth, Dorset 179
Whaley Bridge, Derbyshire 276

Whalley, Lancashire 375
Wheathampstead, Hertfordshire 259
Wheatley, Oxfordshire 267
Whitbourne, Worcestershire 314
Whitby, North Yorkshire 328
Whitchurch, Buckinghamshire 237
Whitehaven, Cumbria 364
Whithorn, Dumfries & Galloway 399
Whitley Bay, Tyne & Wear 352
Whitstable, Kent 45
Whitwick, Leicestershire 280
Wickham, Hampshire 129
Wickwar, Gloucestershire 249
Wigan, Greater Manchester 369
Wigston, Leicestershire 280
Wigtown, Dumfries & Galloway 399
Wilstead, Bedfordshire 232
Wilton, Wiltshire 200
Wimborne, Dorset 179
Wincanton, Somerset 193
Winchcombe, Gloucestershire 249
Winchester, Hampshire 129
Windmill Hill, East Sussex 26
Windsor, Berkshire 120
Winslow, Buckinghamshire 237

Wisbech, Cambridgeshire 205
Wisborough Green, West Sussex 150
Wiston, South Lanarkshire 414
Withernsea, East Riding of
  Yorkshire 319
Witney, Oxfordshire 267
Wittersham, Kent 46
Wiveliscombe, Somerset 193
Woburn, Bedfordshire 232
Woking, Surrey 142
Wokingham, Berkshire 121
Wolferton, Norfolk 220
Wolsingham, Co Durham 347
Wolverhampton, West Midlands 309
Woodbridge, Suffolk 228
Woodford, Cheshire 360
Woodford Green, Essex 213
Woodhall Spa, Lincolnshire 345
Woodseaves, Staffordshire 300
Woodstock, Oxfordshire 268
Wooler, Northumberland 349
Woolhampton, Berkshire 121
Woolpit, Suffolk 229
Wooten Wawen, Warwickshire 305
Worcester, Worcestershire 314

Worsley, Greater Manchester 369
Worthing, West Sussex 150
Wotton-under-Edge,
  Gloucestershire 250
Wraysbury, Middlesex 114
Wrexham, Denbighshire 384
Writtle, Essex 213
Wroxham, Norfolk 220
Wylam, Northumberland 349
Wymeswold, Leicestershire 280
Wymondham, Norfolk 220
Wymondham, Leicestershire 280
Wymondham, Norfolk 220

Y

Yarm, North Yorkshire 328
Yarmouth, Isle of Wight 131
Yarnton, Oxfordshire 268
Yealmpton, Devon 171
Yeovil, Somerset 193
York, North Yorkshire 328
Yoxall, Staffordshire 300
Yoxford, Suffolk 229
Ystradgynlais, West Glamorgan 394

0–9

2 K Carving 515, 488
20th Century China & Pottery 382
20th Century Marks 44
21st Century Antics 198
22 Broad Street 253
269 Antiques 75
275 Antiques 75
291, London 75
3 Church Street Antiques 277
30th Century Comics 84
35 The Goffs 16
41a Antiques 386
51 Antiques 103
6a Antiques 23
75 Portobello Road 103
88 Antiques 102

A

A & C Antique Clocks, Bristol 183
A & C Antiques & Collectables, Hatch
   End 113
A & P French Polishers 475
A A Clockcraft 453
A and R Upholstery 510
A B C Restoration Ltd 493, 495
A B Period Pine 285
A C Restorations 475
A D Antiques 300, 456
A D Carpets 61
A H Antiques & House Clearance 286
A J's Antiques 331
A S Antique Galleries 368
A645 Trading Post 334
AA Antiques 47
Aaron Antiques, Levenshulme 366
Aaron Antiques, Tunbridge Wells 42
Aaron Gallery, London 85
David Aaron, London 85
Aarons Antiques, Taunton 191
Aarons Coins, Taunton 191
Abacus, York 328
Abacus Books, Altrincham 353
Abacus Fireplaces, Thornton 318
Abacus Gallery, Stoke-on-Trent 299
Abbas Antiques 177
Abbey Antique Restorers 472
Abbey Antiques, Abbeydorney 437
Abbey Antiques, Cahir 440
Abbey Antiques, Hemswell 340
Abbey Antiques, Ramsey 204
Abbey Antiques, Stirling 415
Abbey Antiques, Whitby 328
Abbey Auctions, Leeds 336
Abbey Bears, Looe 153
Abbey Fairs, Nottingham 518
Abbey Galleries, Bath 179
Abbey Models, Bournemouth 172
Abbey Restorations 478, 512
Abbeydale Antiques 331
A Abbott Antiques, Ipswich 224
Jaki Abbott, London 71
Nicholas Abbott, Hartley Wintney 124
Abbotts Auction Rooms, Campsey
   Ash 221
Abeam Antiques 461, 493
Aberford Interiors 333

Abergavenny Reclamation 254
Abington Books 223
About Time Antiques 170
J Abrahart 461
Abstract/Noonstar 98
Academy Billiard Company 141
Acanthus Antiques & Collectables 287
Acme Inc., Bexhill-on-Sea 12
Acme Toy Company, Birmingham 305
Acorn Antique Interiors, Wadebridge
   157, 504
Acorn Antiques, Dulverton 188
Acorn Antiques, London 64
Acorn Antiques, Sheffield 331
Acorn Antiques, Worthing 150
Acorn Antiques & Collectors Centre,
   Sawbridge 258
Acorns, Glengormley 421
Acres Fine Art Auctioneers
   & Valuers 309
Ad-Age Antique Advertising 36
Adam & Eve Books 80
Adam Antiques & Restoration,
   Edinburgh 400, 486
James Adam, Dublin 433
Adams Antiques, Nantwich 358
Rodney Adams Antiques, Pwllheli 386
Yvonne Adams Antiques, Stow-on-
   the-Wold 244
Adams Antiques Fairs 518
Adams Arts & Antiques Ltd,
   Tunbridge Wells 42
Henry Adams Auctioneers,
   Chichester 144
Adams Auctions, Burnham-on-Sea 186
Adams Blackrock, Blackrock 432
Norman Adams Ltd, London 71
ADC Heritage Ltd 85
Addington Antiques, Reading 119
Addington Studio Ceramic Repairs
   448, 508
Addington Supplies 448, 506
Addyman Annexe 250
Addyman Books 250
Philip Adler Antiques 246
Admiral Vernon Antiques Market 103
Advena Antiques & Fairs,
   Hemswell 340
Advena Antiques & Fairs, York 328
Aesthetics 71
Afford Decorative Antiques 304
After Noah 49, 65, 71
Agar Antiques, Saintfield 424
Adrian Ager, Ashburton 158
Aggeby's 463
Ainslie Books, Girvan 413
Ainslie's Antiques, Perth 411
Graciela Ainsworth 454, 502
AJC Antiquities, Snodland 41
T M Akers Antique Restoration Ltd 458
Aladdin's Cave, Leeds 336, 492
Aladdins Antiques, Bournemouth 172
Aladdins Architectural Antiques and
   Heritage Workshops, Newcastle-
   upon-Tyne 350
Adrian Alan Ltd 86
G Albanese 461
Albany Antiques, Birmingham 305
Albany Antiques, Hindhead 138

Albany Fairs 518
Chloe Alberry 103
Alberts of Kensington 113
Albion Clocks, London 48, 450, 461
Albion House Antiques,
   Bovey Tracey 160
Albion House Antiques, Turners Hill 150
Alchemy Antiques 246
Alcove Antiques 192
Aldersey Hall Ltd 354
Alderson 246
Henry Aldridge & Son, Devizes 15
F W Aldridge Ltd, Takely 490, 503
Aldridges of Bath, Bath 179
Alexander Antiques, Portrush 422
Craig Alexander Victorian Shop 398
Alexandria Antiques 13
Alfies Antique Market 59
Alfreton Antique Centre 269
Alice's 103
Alicia Antiques 267
All Books 210
All Our Yesterdays, Glasgow 405
All Our Yesterdays, Sandwich 40
Roger Allan 472, 500
Michael Allcroft Antiques 275, 498
Allen Avery Interiors 464
Anthony Allen Conservation,
   Restoration, Furniture and
   Artefacts 453, 478, 488, 495
Allens 270
Duncan M Allsop 304
Alpha Coins & Medals 370
Alpine Antiques 514
Alscot Bathroom Company 308
Alston Antiques 360
Altea Maps and Books 86
Amadeus Antiques 42
Alexia Amato Antiques 71
Amber Antiques, Caversham 115
Amber Antiques, Southampton 127
Ambrose Auctioneers & Valuers 210
Rocco d'Ambrosio 469, 511
The American Comic Shop 31
The Amersham Auction Rooms 233
Cliff Amey & Son 513
Amhuerst Auctions 41
Albert Amor, London 65
Amors of Evenley, Evenley 281
Richard Amos Antiques 34
Amphora Galleries Antiques,
   Baltron 414
Amphora Galleries Antiques,
   Doune 414
Ampthill Antiques and Collectables 230
Ampthill Antiques Emporium 230
Amwell Auctions 259
An Siopa 441
Anchor Antiques (Wales) Ltd,
   Cardiff 392
Anchor Antiques Ltd, London 108
Ancient & Modern, Chippenham 194
Ancient and Modern, Blackburn 370
Ancient and Oriental Ltd 277
Anderson & Garland, Newcastle-
   upon-Tyne 350
F E Anderson & Son, Welshpool 392
Anderson Antiques, Saltburn-by-the-
   Sea 325

Andipa Gallery 71
Paul Andrews Antiques, London 80
Stephen Andrews Gallery, St Peter
  Port 416
Angel Antiques, Petworth 147
Angel Antiques, Redditch 313
The Angel Bookshop,
  North Walsham 217
Angela's Antiques 419
Anglo Pacific International plc. Fine
  Art Division 498
Anita Marquetry Ltd, Llandrindod
  Wells 491, 495
Anita's Antiques, Plymouth 166
Annie's Antiques, Farnham 136
Annie's Attic, Brinklow 301
Annie's Vintage Costume and
  Textiles, London 49
Anno Domini Antiques 65
Ann's Antiques, Limerick 438
Ann's Antiques, Stoke-on-Trent 299
Annterior Antiques 166
Annville Antiques 423
David Ansell, Harefield 113, 450
Anthea's Antiques 103
Anthemion 361
Anthony Antiques Ltd, Dublin 433
John Anthony, Bletchingley 132
Antics 144
Antik West Oriental Art & Antiques 98
Antiquarian Bookcrafts, Dublin 444
Antiquarian Booksellers,
  Donaghadee 423
The Antiquarian Booksellers
  Association 518
Antiquarius, Ampthill 230
Antiquarius Antique Centre, London 71
Antiquated 147
Antique & Country Pine 356
Antique & Design 30
Antique & Modern Fireplaces 238
Antique and Collector's Centre,
  Scarborough 326
Antique and Collectors' Centre Diss 214
Antique and Modern Restoration by
  Richard Parsons 475
Antique and Second Hand Traders 339
Antique Arms Fairs Ltd 518
Antique Barometer & Clock Shop,
  Shrewsbury 294
The Antique Barometer Company,
  London 49
Antique Barometers, Ramsey 204
Antique Bed Company, Emsworth 123
The Antique Bed Shop, Halstead 208
Antique Boutique, Leeds 336
The Antique Brass Bedstead Co Ltd,
  Great Baddow 208
Antique Builders Suppliers,
  Glarryford 421
The Antique Cellar, Warwick 304
The Antique Centre at Olney, Olney 236
Antique Chair Shop, Norwich 217
Antique Chairs and Museum,
  Launceston 152
Antique China and Porcelain
  Restoration, Shepton Mallet 448, 500
Antique Church Furnishings, Walton-
  on-Thames 141

Antique Clocks, Castleford 334, 453
Antique Clocks by Patrick Thomas,
  Dorking 134
Antique Cottage, Liverpool 376
The Antique Dealers Fair Ltd 518
Antique English Windsor Chairs,
  Chipping Norton 262
Antique Enterprises, Romsey 127
Antique Exporters of Chester,
  Waverton 359
Antique Finder, Cranbrook 503
Antique Forum Group 518
Antique Furniture Restoration,
  Edinburgh 486
Antique Furniture Restoration &
  Conservation, Darwen 484
Antique Furniture Warehouse,
  Stockport 368
Antique Garden, Chester 354
Antique Glass, Bath 180
Antique Interiors, Twickenham 114
Antique Leather Dressing, Langport
  492, 506
Antique Leathers, Wincanton 492
The Antique Loft, Clarecastle 429
Antique Map & Print Gallery,
  Hallow 311
Antique Map and Bookshop,
  Puddletown 177
Antique Mart, Richmond 139
Antique Mirrors, Leek 297
Antique Prints, Dublin 433
Antique Renovating, Cheetham Hill
  495, 503
Antique Renovations, Lavenham
  452, 472
Antique Restoration, Salisbury 468
Antique Restoration & Polishing,
  Chesham 475
Antique Restorations, Sudbury 472,
  486, 499
Antique Restorers, Epsom 464, 510
Antique Restorers & Cabinet Makers
  Ltd, London 461, 491, 492
The Antique Rooms, Maldon 210
Antique Scientific Instruments,
  Chester 354
Antique Services, Belfast 487
The Antique Shop & Collectables,
  Godalming 137
The Antique Shop, Heswall 375
The Antique Shop, London 54
The Antique Shop, Newnham 243
The Antique Store, Leek 297
The Antique Tea Shop, Hereford 252
Antique Textiles and Lighting, Bath 180
Antique Time, Dublin 433
Antique Toys, Honiton 163
The Antique Trader at the Millinery
  Works, London 49
Antique Transport Services,
  Bournemouth 498
The Antique Wardrobe Company,
  Windsor 120
Antique Warehouse, London 62
Antiques, Hastings 19
Antiques, Marazion 153
Antiques & Bygones, Rochdale 368
Antiques & Collectables, Lunnaness 413

Antiques & Collectors Market,
  Beckenham 27
Antiques & Collectors World,
  Tadworth 518
Antiques & Curios, Oakham 290
Antiques & Curios, Worcester 314
Antiques & Curios Centre, Cork 429
Antiques & Curios Shop,
  Peterborough 204
Antiques & Decor, Weybridge 141
Antiques & Interiors, Norwich 217
Antiques & Pine Shop, New Mills 276
Antiques @ The George, Burford 261
Antiques Across the World,
  Nottingham 287
Antiques Adventure, Coventry 307
Antiques and Country Living,
  Frome 189
Antiques and Country Pine,
  Crewkerne 187
Antiques and Fine Art Ltd,
  Penzance 154
Antiques and Gifts, Downham
  Market 214
Antiques and Things, London 75
Antiques at Cranbrook 32
Antiques at Heritage, Woodstock 268
Antiques at the Stile, Saintfield 424
Antiques at Wendover 236
Antiques by Jules Ltd, London 86
Antiques Centre, Glasgow 405
Antiques Centre, Newcastle-upon-
  Tyne 350
The Antiques Centre York 328
Antiques Consultant, London 48
The Antiques Exchange, London 61
Antiques Fairs Ireland 518
Antiques in Baslow 272
Antiques Little Shop, Barnet 255
Antiques Loft, Cromford 274
Antiques of Bloxham 260
Antiques of Penrith 363
Antiques of Sherborne 177
Antiques of Wimbledon 85
Antiques on High Ltd, Oxford 265
The Antiques Shop Bruton 186
The Antiques Shop, Chester 354
Antiques Warehouse, Buxton 273
Antiques Warehouse & Restoration,
  Uxbridge 114
The Antiques Warehouse Ltd,
  Bristol 183
The Antiques Warehouse, Glasgow 406
The Antiques Warehouse,
  Marlesford 226
The Antiques Warehouse, Runfold 140
The Antiques Warehouse,
  Worcester 314
Antiques Within, Leek 297
The Antiques Workshop, Solihull 478
Antiquiteas, Brockenhurst 122
Antiquities, Arundel 142
Antiquus, Castle Cary 187
Antiquus, London 65
Anvil Antiques, Hartley Wintney 124
Anvil Antiques, Leek 297
Anvil Books, Halesowen 308
Any Amount of Books 108

Anything Goes 55
Anything Old & Military Collectables 372
Apollo Antiques Ltd, Warwick 304
Apollo Galleries, Westerham 44
The Apple Market 109
Appleby Antiques 103
Appleton Eves Ltd 121
Roger Appleyard Ltd 331
Jess Applin 201
Apter– Fredericks Ltd 71
Aquaduct Auctions 383
Aquarius, Rhyl 384
Aquarius Antiques, Leeds 336
Aquarius Books, Market Harborough 278
R Arantes 50
Arbiter 378
Arbour Antiques Ltd 303
Arbras Gallery 103
Arcade Arts Ltd 456
Arcadia Antiques & Interiors, Bristol 184
Arcadia Antiques Centre 317
Arcane Antiques Centre 258
Arch House Collectables 390
Archaeological Conservator 454
Architectural Antiques and Salvage, Dublin 433
Architectural Artefacts, Southwold 227
Architectural Classics, Dublin 433
The Architectural Emporium, Ashurst 27
Architectural Heritage, Cutsdean 240
Architectural Rescue, London 62
The Architectural Stores, Tunbridge Wells 42
Architus Antiques & Collectables 372
Archive Books and Music, London 57
Archives Antique Centre, Belfast 420
Archway Antiques, Greyabbey 424
Archway Antiques, Matlock 275
C Arden Bookseller 250
Argenteus Ltd 109
Argyll Etkin Ltd 86
Aristocratz 184
The Ark Angel 247
Nicholas Arkell Antiques Ltd 134
Armchair Books 400
The Armoury of St James 65
Armstrong Antiques, Harrogate 320
Armstrong's Books & Collectables, Coventry 307
John Arnold & Co, Cheadle Hulme 366
Phyllis Arnold Gallery Antiques, Donaghadee 423
Sean Arnold Sporting Antiques, London 96
Arrow Auctions 313
Art and Antiques, Eton 116
Art Deco Originals/Muir Hewitt, Halifax 334
Art Furniture, London 57
Art Nouveau Lighting, Tetbury 247
Art Nouveau Originals, Broadway 310
Artefact 75
Artemesia, Alresford 121
Artemis Decorative Arts Ltd 98

Rodney Arthur Classics 149
Artique 247
Artisan Stock & Business Centre 449
Arts Decoratifs 211
Artworks Sculpture Gallery 40
Arun Fairs 518
Arundel Antiques Centre 142
The Arundel Bookshop 142
Arundel Bridge 142
Victor Arwas Gallery 86
Ascent Auction Galleries 26
Ascot Antiques, Blackpool 370
Asenbaum Fine Arts Ltd 107
James Ash Antiques 380
Ashbourne Antiques Ltd 269
Ashby Antiques 276
Ashcombe Coach House Antiques 146
Iain Ashcroft Furniture 486
Ashdale China Restoration 449
Ashdown Antiques Restoration 26, 458
Ashe Antiques Warehouse 222
Ashridge Antique Flooring 256
Ashton Gower Antiques, Stow-on-the-Wold 244
Ashton's Antiques, Brighton 13
Asian Art.co.uk Ltd 163
Ask Simon 354
Aspidistra Antiques 282
Walter Aspinall Antiques 374
Assembly Antiques Centre 180
Astoria Art Deco 209
Astra House Antique Centre 340
Athelstan's Attic 196
G M Athey 484, 513
Atique, Boscastle 151
Atique, Tintagel 156
Atlam Sales and Service 103
Atlantic Antiques 422
ATLAS 86
Attic Antiques, Saintfield 424
Attic Pine, Saintfield 425
The Attic, Chesham 234
The Attic, Newton Abbot 165
Attica, Newcastle-upon-Tyne 350
Atticus Books, Grays 208
Au Temps Perdu 184
Auction Centre Ltd, Royton 368
The Auction House Bridport, Bridport 174
Auction Rooms, Falkirk 414
Audrey Bull Antiques, Carmarthen 379
Audrey Bull Antiques, Tenby 390
Auld Things 409
Auldearn Antiques 408
Aura Antiques 324
Hugo Austin Antiques 139
Austwick Hall Books 319
The Autograph Collectors Gallery 287
Autolycus 290
Automattic Comics 195
Autumn Leaves 343
Avebury Antiques 193
Aviation Antiques & Collectables 28
Avon Antiques, Bradford-on-Avon 193
Avon House Antiques, Kingsbridge 165
Avondale Antique Jewellers, Strathaven 414
Richard Axe Books 320

Axminster Auctions 159
Aytac Antiques 86
Ayuka Ltd 445

B

B & B Antiques, Stickney 345
B & D Collectors' Toys, Ramsgate 38
B and T Antiques Ltd, London 103
B+T Toy Fairs 518
Baba Bears 13
BABAADA 518
Back 2 Wood, Appledore 27
Back in Time, London 55
Back to Front, Buxton 273
Back to the Wood, Rickmansworth 504
Baddow Antique Centre 208
Badgers Books 150
Baggins Book Bazaar 38
Baggott Church Street Ltd 244
Duncan J Baggott 244
Bagham Barn Antiques 31
The Baildon Furniture Co Ltd 334
Robert Bailey Fairs 518
Baileys, Holsworthy 162
A Bainbridge & Co 114
Henry Baines, Tunbridge Wells 42
G Baker Antiques, Horncastle 341
Gregg Baker Asian Art, London 98
Chris Baker Gramophones, Sandwich 40
J & J Baker, Lavenham 225
T Baker, Langford 286
A H Baldwin and Son, London 109
M & M Baldwin, Cleobury Mortimer 311
Ball & Claw Antiques, Tetbury 247
David Ball Antiques, Leighton Buzzard 232
Ballantyne Booth Ltd 461
Ballinderry Antiques 419
Ballindullagh Barn 425
Balloo Moon Antiques 423
Ballyalton House Architectural Antiques 424
Bamfords, Matlock 275
Bamfords Auctioneers & Valuers, Derby 274
Bampton Gallery 159
Banana Dance Ltd 82
Banbury Antiques Centre 260
Bangor Auctions 424
Simon Banks Antiques 282
Banners Collectors & Antiques Centre 331
Kate Bannister Antiques 50
Bar Bookstore (The Antiquary Ltd) 326
Sebastiano Barbagallo Antiques 61, 75, 103
Barbara's Antiques and Bric-a-Brac 117
The Barbers Clock, Worcester 314
Barbers Fine Art Auctioneers (West Sussex Estate Agents, Surveyors and Auctioneers), Woking 142
Barbican Antique Centre 166
Barclay Antiques 265
Eddy Bardawil 98
Barden House Antiques 42
Craig Barfoot Clocks 263
Bargain Box, Luton 232

Bargain Centre, Inverkeithing 404
Barham Antiques 104
Barin Carpets Restoration 446
Barkham Antiques Centre 121
Robert Barley 76
Barleycorn Antiques 340
C & A J Barmby 444, 457, 506
Barmouth Court Antique Centre 332
Barn Antique Centre,
  Long Marston 302
Barn Antiques, Nantwich 358
Barn Antiques, Pulborough 149
Barn Antiques, Rolvenden 39
The Barn, Crowborough 458
The Barn Antiques, Barnstaple 159
The Barn Antiques, Letchworth
  Garden City 257
The Barn at Bilsington, Bilsington 28
The Barn Book Supply, Salisbury 198
Barn Court Antiques, Templeton 390
Barnaby's of Battle 12
R A Barnes Antiques, Bicester 260
Lorna Barnes Conservation, Dublin
  454, 503
Jane Barnes Antiques and Interiors,
  Honiton 163
Barnet Bygones 255
Barnett Antiques 144
Barnstaple Auctions 159
Barnt Green Antiques, Barnt Green
  310, 453, 479
The Barometer Shop, Leominster 253,
  452, 502
Barometer World, Merton 165
Chris Baron Antiques, London 71
Baron Art, Holt 215, 216, 444, 448,
  457, 500
R F Barrett Rare Books, Matlock 275
M Barrett Restoration,
  Cambridge 472
David Barrington, Brasted 28
Edward Barrington-Doulby, Barnard
  Castle 346
Barrow Lodge Antiques 183
Richard Barry Southern Marketing
  Ltd, Brighton 506, 515
Barry's Antiques, Great Yarmouth 215
Barter Books 347
Basically Bears 21
Carol Basing 447
Baskerville Antiques 147
M G Bassett Pine & Decorative
  Items 270
Batemans Auctioneers & Valuers 343
Eric Bates & Sons Ltd 220
Bath Antiques Online 180
Bath Old Books 180
Hilary Batstone Antiques 65
Batten's Jewellers 174
The Battersea Pen Home 518
David Battle Antique Furniture
  Restoration and Conservation,
  Umberleigh 468
Battle Antiques Centre 12
Battlesbridge Antiques Centre 205
Battlesbridge Antiques Lighting 206
Keith Bawden 446, 448, 452, 475,
  492, 500
H C Baxter & Sons 84

Bay Tree Antiques 200
Chris Baylis Country Chairs,
  Woodstock 268
Bayliss Antiques, Ludlow 292
Matthew Bayly Antiques 187
Baynton-Williams 142
George Bayntun 180
Bazaar Boxes, Hertford 256
Bazar, London 102
BBM Jewellery, Coins & Antiques 311
BBR Auctions 330
Beacon Antiques 336
Bear Essentials, Basildon 205
The Bear Shop – Truro, Truro 156
Bear Steps Antiques, Shrewsbury 294
Clive Beardall Restoration Ltd 210, 472
J and A Beare Ltd 86
Bearly Trading of London 64
Bearne's 161
Bears 'n' Bunnies, Bluewater 28
Bears Galore, Rye 24
Bears on the Square, Ironbridge 292
Peter Beasley 34
Beau Nash Antiques 42
Beaufield Mews Restaurant, Gardens
  & Antiques 436
Beaumont Travel Books 62
John Beazor & Sons Ltd 201
James Beck Auctions 215
Beckett Antiques Fairs 518
Beckham Books 228
Beckwith and Son incorporating
  Hertford Antiques 256
The Bed Workshop, Bristol 184
Bedale Antiques 319
Bedouin Antiques 150
Bedsteads, Bath 180
Bedsteads, Bristol 184
Bee Antiques, Broadstairs 29
Linda Bee, London 86
Jonathan Beech Antique Clocks,
  Westport 439
Anthony James Beech Furniture
  Conservation & Restoration,
  Stamford 482
Beech House 332
Beedham Antiques Ltd 117
The Beehive 37
Beer Collectables 159
R Beesly 452, 475
Beeswax Antiques 425
Behind the Boxes – Art Deco 65
Paul Beighton Auctioneers Ltd 333
Robert Belcher Antiques 311
Belgrave Antiques Centre, Darwen 3
Belgrave Carpet Gallery Ltd,
  London 65
Bell Antiques, Grimsby 340
Bell Antiques, Honiton 163
Bell Antiques, Romsey 127
Bell Antiques, Twyford 120
The Bell Gallery, Belfast 420
Bell House Restoration Ltd,
  London 461
Bell Passage Antiques, Wickwar 249
Belle Vue Restoration 479
La Belle 155
C Bellinger Antiques 255
John Bellman Ltd 150

Belmont, London 109
Belmont House Antiques,
  Willington 475
Belmont Jewellers, Erith 34
Below Stairs of Hungerford 117
Ben Norris & Co 464
Benchmark Antiques 174
Benjamin Jewellery 57
Bennett and Kerr Books,
  Steventon 266
Alan Bennett Ltd, Truro 156
K Bennett 484
Paul Bennett, London 86
Bennetts Antiques & Collectables Ltd,
  Bedale 319
Sir William Bentley Billiards,
  Hungerford 117
Bentley's Fine Art Auctioneers,
  Cranbrook 32
Bentley Grice Promotions 518
Benton Fine Art and Antiques 242
Berg Brothers Ltd 104
Berkeley Antiques, Winchcombe 249
Berkeley Framing 457
Berkeley House Antiques, Westgate-
  on-Sea 45
Berkeley Market 237
Berkshire Antiques Co Ltd, Windsor
  120, 492, 508
Berry Antiques, Moreton-in-Marsh 242
Berry Antiques & Interiors,
  Longridge 373
Berry Street Bookshop,
  Wednesbury 309
Bertie's 85
Besley's Books 220
Bespoke Furniture 458
Best of Fairs 518
Best Secondhand Centre 273
Better Days 387
Beverley 59
Bewdley Antiques 310
Daniel Bexfield Antiques 86
Bexhill Museum 12
Bexley Antiques and Interiors 28
Biblion Ltd 87
Bicks Jewellers & Antiques 238, 492
Biddle & Webb Ltd 306
Bidford Antiques & Collectables 301
Big Screen Collectables 27
Edward Bigden Fine Art 222
Biggleswade Antiques Fairs 518
Paula Biggs, Moreton-in-Marsh 242
Paula Biggs, Stow-on-the-Wold 244
Paula Biggs, Tetbury 247
Bigwood Auctioneers Ltd 304
Bigwood Restoration 459
Bijou Art 32
Billiard Room Antiques 187
Bingley Antiques, Haworth 335
Robert Bingley Antiques, Oakham 290
Peter Binnington 489, 490
Kevin Birch Antique Furniture
  Restorers, Aylesford 459, 509
Birch House Restoration at Michael Vee
  Design, Melrose 413
John Bird Antiques, Petworth 147
Eric A Bird Jewellers, Lincoln 342
Christy Bird, Dublin 433

Birkdale Antiques 377
The Birmingham Antique Centre 306
Birmingham Coins 306
Bishopgate Antiques 329
Bishops Furniture Stores 65
Bishopston Books 184
Bizarre, London 59
Bizarre!, Topsham 168
BJK Sales 457
BK Art & Antiques 244
The Black Cat Bookshop, Leicester 277
Black Cat Trading & Antiques,
   Ringwood 127
Black Country Auctions 307
Black Dog Antiques 221
Black Sheep Antiques 24
Adrian J Black 482
Blackstage 494
Blackwater Pine Antiques 156
Steve Blackwell French Polishers,
   Preston 484
Blackwell's Rare Books, Oxford 265
Blackwood Cowell Antiques 97
Blair Antiques 411
H Blairman & Sons Ltd 87
Blake's Books 228
Blanchard Ltd, Marlborough 196
Blanchard Ltd, London 66
Neill Robinson Blaxill 450
Neill Robinson Blaxill 40, 450
G D Blay Antiques 133
Blender Antiques 261
Blenheim Antiques 241
Blestium Antique Centre 388
Blewbury Antiques 260
Blockheads 282
N Bloom and Son (1912) Ltd 66
Bloomfield Auctions 420
Blue Dot Antiques 424
Bluebells 151
Blunderbuss Antiques 87
John Bly, London 66
John Bly, Tring 259
Blyburgate Antiques 220
Clare Boam 341
Boar's Nest Trading 314
Bogan House Antiques 171
Bold as Brass Polishers 495
Boldon Auction Galleries 349
Brian R Bolt Antiques 421
Bon-Accord Books 396
Bond Street Antiques, Cromer 214
The Bond Street Antiques Centre,
   London 87
Lynne & Richard Bonehill 519
The Bones Lane Antiques Centre 206
Bonhams,
   Banbury 260
   Bath 180
   Bedale 319
   Cambridge 201
   Cardiff 392
   Carlisle 360
   Carmarthen 379
   Chester 354
   Edinburgh 400
   Glasgow 406
   Guildford 137
   Hale 357

Henley-On-Thames 264
Honiton 163
Hove 20
Ipswich 224
Knowle 308
Leeds 336
London 79, 87
Market Harborough 278
Newcastle-Upon-Tyne 350
Oxford 265
Par 154
Reepham 219
Retford 289
Sevenoaks 40
Southport 377
St Helier 417
Tetbury 247
Whitstable 45
Winchester 129
Joseph Bonnar Jewellers 400
Bonnons Antique Glass 123
Bonstow and Crawshay Antiques 180
Bonython Bookshop 156
Book Academy, Hindhead 138
Book and Comic Exchange, London 104
The Book Bug, Hitchin 257
The Book Depot, London 445
The Book House, Kirkby Stephen 363
The Book Jungle,
   St Leonards-on-Sea 26
The Book Palace, London 64
The Book Passage, Bridgnorth 291
The Book Shop, Cambridge 202
Bookbarn Ltd, Temple Cloud 192
Bookbox, Stow-on-the-Wold 244
Bookcase, Carlisle 360
Bookends, Emsworth 123
Bookends of Fowey 152
Bookfinders, Belfast 420
Bookman's Halt, St Leonards-on-Sea 26
Bookmark Children's Books, Broad
   Hinton 194
The Bookmark, Rainham 38
Books & Bygones, Weymouth 179
Books & Collectables Ltd,
   Cambridge 202
Books & Maps, Bournemouth 172
Books Afloat, Weymouth 179
Books Bought and Sold Ltd, East
   Molesey 135
Books Etc., Cromer 214
Books Galore, Crewkerne 188
Books, Maps & Prints, Brecon 390
Bookshop Conwy, Conwy 382
Bookshop Conwy, Rhos-on-Sea 383
The Bookshop on the Heath Ltd,
   London 62
The Bookshop, Carndonagh 432
The Bookshop, Coventry 307
The Bookshop, Wigtown 399
Bookstores Wales, Cowbridge 393
Bookworld, Oswestry 293
Bookworm, Holland-on-Sea 209
The Bookworm, Edinburgh 400
Bookworms of Evesham 311
Bookworms of Shoreham 149
A E Booth and Son, Chessington 464
Booth Antiques, Swansea 394
Joanna Booth, London 71

Richard Booth's Bookshop Ltd 250, 251
Malcolm Bord 109
The Border Bookshop, Todmorden 374
Border Country Furniture, Melrose 413
Boris Books 129
Boscombe Militaria 172
Boscombe Stamp Company 172
Boscombe Toy Collectors 172
Bosley's Military Auctioneers 235
Julia Boston Antiques, London 76
Nicolaus Boston Antiques,
   Broadway 310
Bosworth Antiques 302
Botting & Berry 19
Le Boudoir 180
Boughey Antique Restoration 448, 468
Boulton & Cooper Fine Art 323
C R Boumphrey 167
Bouquiniste 405
Bourbon Hanby Antique Centre 71
J H Bourdon-Smith Ltd 66
Bourne End Antiques Centre 234
Bourne End Auction Rooms 234
Bourne Mill Antiques, Farnham 136
Bourton Bears 261
Bow Windows Bookshop 21
David Bowden Chinese and Japanese
   Art 87
M J Bowdery 138
Bowen & Lucas Antique Restoration,
   Yeovil 468
Marion Bowen Vintage Clothes,
   Newhaven 22
Bowen, Son & Watson, Ellesmere 292
Bower House Antiques & Interiors 389
Bowhouse Antiques 117
Bowman Antiques Fairs Ltd,
   Shipley 519
Michael J Bowman, Newton Abbot 166
Edward Bowry 412
Bow-Well Antiques 400
Box of Porcelain, Dorchester 175
K W Box, Colchester 472
Boxford Books & Fairs 519
Symon E Boyd Clock Restorer,
   Stockport 454
Patrick Boyd-Carpenter and Howard
   Neville, London 87
Boyle's Antiques 429
Robert Boys Shipping 498
Boz Books 251
The Brackley Antiques Cellar 280
J Bradburne-Price & Co 384
Roger Bradbury Antiques,
   Coltishall 214
M and S Bradbury, Bristol 451, 468
M Bradley, Crosby 484
Robert Bradley Antiques, Salisbury 198
Bradley's Past and Present Shop,
   Petworth 147
Emma Bradshaw Ceramic
   Restorations, Newport 448
Bradshaw Fine Wood Furniture Ltd,
   Wickford 472
Bradwell Antiques Centre 273
Braemar Antiques 82
John Bragg Antiques, Lostwithiel 153
Bragge & Sons, Rye 24
Brambridge Antiques 124

Augustus Brandt Antiques, Petworth 147
Brandt Oriental Antiques, London 87
Branksome Antiques 176
Steve Vee Bransgrove Collectables 189
Brass and Wood Still Looking Good, Leicester 277, 496
Brass Foundry Castings Ltd, Westerham 459, 495, 506
Lawrence Brass, Bath 180, 468
Brazenhead Ltd 213
Bread & Roses, Ludlow 292
Bread & Roses, Tetbury 247
Breakspeare Antiques 247
Jonathan Brearley Antiques, Swadlincote 503
Brearley's Antiques Corner Curios, Burton-on-Trent 296
The Brecon Antiques Centre 390
Geoffrey Breeze Antique Canes 247
Ellen L Breheny 450, 490
Brentside Programmes 205
Lorcan Brereton 433
A J Brett & Co, London 461, 489
James Brett Ltd, Norwich 217
Brewery House Antiques & Collectables 276
Bric-A-Brac 422
Christine Bridge Antiques, London 83
Bridge Garage Antiques, Sedlescombe 25
Bridge House Antiques & Interiors, Hungerford 117
Bridge of Allan Books 414
Bridgnorth Antiques Centre 291
Bridport Old Bookshop 174
Brigantia Ltd, York 329
F E A Briggs Ltd, Brook 122
F E A Briggs Ltd, London 104
Andy Briggs, Standlake 475
Brightling Restoration 459
Brighton Architectural Salvage 13
Brighton Books 13
Brighton Flea Market 13
Brighton Lanes Antique Centre 13
Brighton Postcard Shop 13
Brightwells 253
Brignell Bookbinders 445
Brigsy's Antique Centre 35
Brindley John Ayers Catalogue of Vintage and Collectable Fishing Tackle 389
Lynda Brine Antiques 180
Bristol Bookbarn 184
Bristol Brocante 184
Bristol Restoration Workshop 496
Bristol Trade Antiques 184
Bristow and Garland, Fordingbridge 123
Clive Bristow Antiques, Farnham 464
Britannia 87
British Antique Dealers Association 519
British Antique Replicas, Burgess Hill 144
British Numismatic Trade Association 519
Brittons Watches 373
Brixham's King Street Rooms 160

Tony Broadfoot Antiques 13
Broadhursts of Southport Ltd 377
Broadstairs Antiques and Collectables 29
Broadsword Antiques 406
Broadway Bears at the Bindery 310
Brocante Antiques 196
A F Brock & Co Ltd 366
Michael Brook Antique Metal Restoration, London 496
Brook Farm Antiques, Norbury 293
T C S Brooke, Wroxham 220
E J & C A Brooks, Benfleet 206
Broughton Books 400
David Brower 98
Browgate Antiques 333
Brown & Kingston, London 71
Brown and Harman, Ringmer 459
Alasdair Brown, London 80
S C Brown, Birmingham 479
P J Brown Antiques, Haslingden 372
Stephen Brown Antiques, Twyford 120
David Brown Gallery, St Andrews 405
I and J L Brown Ltd, Hereford 252
I and J L Brown Ltd, London 76
Margaret Browne Fairs 519
B Browning & Son 314
Browns Antiques, London 64
Browns Clocks, Glasgow 406
Brown's Times Past Antiques, St Helier 417
Browsers, Exmouth 162
Browsers Barn, Wadhurst 26
Browsers Bookshop, Falmouth 152
Browzaround 373
W.F. Bruce Antique Clocks, Lewes 21
Steven B Bruce Auctioneers Ltd, Bidford-on-Avon 301
W. Bruford 16
Brunel Clock & Watch Fairs 519
Brun-Lea Antiques 371
Brunswick Antiques 363
F G Bruschweiler Antiques Ltd 211
Brushwood Antiques 264
Douglas Bryan, Cranbrook 32
N F Bryan-Peach Antiques, Wymeswold 280
N F Bryan-Peach Antiques, Newark 286
Bryn-y-Grog Emporium 383
Christopher Buck Antiques, Sandgate 39
Buck House Antique Centre, Beaconsfield 233
Buckies 202
Buckingham Antiques, Helmsley 322
Buckingham Antiques Centre Ltd 234
Buckinghamshire Chilterns University College 508
Wayne Buckner Antiques 122
Philip Buddell, Truro 156
Philip Buddell Antiques, Truro 157
John Bull (Antiques) Ltd 87
Bullring Antiques 251
Bumbles 132
Peter Bunting 269
Steven Burak Books 107
Alison Burdon 76
Burford Antiques Centre 261
Burgate Antiques 30

Burgess Farm Antiques 129
Burghley Fine Art Conservation Ltd 457, 500
C and L Burman 87
Victor Burness Antiques 61
The Burnham Model & Collectors Shop 186
Lindsay Burns & Co 411
David E Burrows Antiques 279
Burslem Antiques and Collectables 299
Burstow & Hewett 12
Mick Burt (Antique Pine) 338
Ian Burton Antique Clocks, Auchterarder 409
Burton Antiques, Burton-on-Trent 296
Burwell Auctions 204
Bury & Hilton 297
Robert Bush Antiques 209
Bushwood Antiques 257
Butchers Antiques 152
Butchoff Interiors 98
Edward Butler, Dublin 433
R Butler, Pangbourne 119
Robin Butler, Clare 222
Roderick Butler, Honiton 163
Jacob Butler – Period Joinery Specialist, Matlock 479
The Button Queen Ltd 88
C J Button-Stephens Antiques 163
Buxton Book Fair 519
Byethorpe Antiques 330
Byethorpe Furniture 479
Bygone Days, Daventry 281
Bygone Times, Eccleston 372
Bygones, Burford 261
Bygones Antiques, Limerick 439
Bygones by the Cathedral, Worcester 314
Bygones of Worcester 314
Bygones Reclamation (Canterbury) Ltd, Canterbury 30
Byrkley Books Ltd 296
Byrne's Auctioneers 354

C

C A R S (Classic Automobilia and Regalia Specialists) 14
C and B Antiques 255
C J C Antiques 380
Cabaret Antiques 400
The Cabinet Maker, Wisbech 472
The Cabinet Repair Shop, Alton 464
Cader Idris Bookshop 385
J E Cadman 468
Ian Caldwell 141
Caledonia Antiques, Bristol 184
Caledonian Antiques, Inverness 408
Caledonian Books, Glasgow 406
Margaret Callaghan 14
Callingham Antiques Ltd 147
E Callister 513
Calne Antiques 194
Calton Gallery 400
Calverley Antiques 42
Cambridge Fine Art, Bakewell 270
Cambridge House Antiques, Birmingham 306

Cambridge Pianola Company and J V Pianos, Landbeach 204, 497
Cambs Antique Centre, Cambridge 202
Camden Books, Bath 181
Camden Passage Antiques Market, London 50
Camden Re-Upholstery, Princes Risborough 512
Camel Art Deco 50
Cameo, Midgham 118
Cameo Antiques, Chester 354
Cameo Antiques, Stoke-on-Trent 479
Cameron Preservation, Lurgan 445, 500
Jasmin Cameron, London 71
Camilla's Bookshop 16
A K Campbell & Son, Dunfermline 404
Kirkcaldy 404
St Andrews 405
Campbell and Archard, Seal 40
Peter Campbell Antiques, Melksham 197
Peter Campion Restorations 452, 475
Candle Close Gallery, Aberdeen 396
Candle Lane Books, Shrewsbury 294
Candlestick & Bakelite 37
The Cane & Rush Chair Repair Service, Epsom 445
Cane Chairs Repaired, Burwash 445
Cane Corner, East Budleigh 445
Cane Weaving Repairs, Ely 445
Caners & Upholders, Blandford Forum 445
M D Cannell 218
Canning Antiques 406
Elizabeth Cannon Antiques 207
Canonbury Antiques 59
Canter & Francis 343
The Canterbury Auction Galleries 30
Canterbury Bears 36
The Canterbury Book Shop 30
Canute Antiques 144
Capel Mawr Collectors' Centre 385
Capercaillie Antiques 347
Capes, Dunn & Co 367
Capital Antiques Ltd, London 61
Capital Bookshop, Cardiff 392
Patric Capon 29
Capricorn Antiques 384
D Card 115
Cardiff Antique Centre 392
Cardiff Reclamation 392
Cards Inc 259
Mervyn Carey 27
Cargenbank Antiques & Tearooms 398
Carlisle Antique Centre 360
Carlsen's Antiques and Fine Arts, Lymington 125
Carlsson Antique, Twickenham 461
Carlton Antiques, Malvern 312
Carlton Hollis Ltd, Harrogate 320
John Carlton-Smith, London 66
Carnegie Paintings & Clocks 171
Carningli Centre 389
Carol's Antiques 438
J W Carpenter Antique Clock Restorer, Sandwich 450
Steve Carpenter, Wisbech 205

Harold J Carr Antiques 352
Carrington House Antiques, Llanrwst 383
Carringtons Antiques, Milford-on-Sea 126
John Carroll Antiques 420
Carryduff Auction Group Ltd 421
The Carson Clark Gallery – Scotland's Map Heritage Centre 400
David Carstairs 189
Cartels Auctioneers and Valuers 132
Mark Carter Militaria & Medal Fairs, Slough 519
Aurea Carter, London 76
E Carty 504
CASA 64
Case & Dewing 214
Peter Casebow Ltd 464, 497
W J Casey Antiques 304
Hugh Cash Antiques 437
Cashel Antiques 441
Jack Casimir Ltd 104
Casnewydd Antiques & Restoration 388
Casque and Gauntlet Militaria 136
Cass Freshford Antiques 437
Cassidy Antiques and Restorations, Warminster 199
P J Cassidy, Holbeach 341
Cast From The Past 174
Cast Offs 307
B Castle, Worthing 464, 515
Castle Antique Centre Ltd, Westerham 45
Castle Antiques, Conwy 382
Castle Antiques, Leigh-on-Sea 209
Castle Antiques, Newtownards 424
Castle Antiques, Nottingham 287
Castle Antiques, Orford 227
Castle Antiques, Warwick 304
Castle Antiques Ltd, Deddington 263
Castle Antiques Warehouse, Stoke-on-Trent 299
The Castle Book Shop, Colchester 207
Castle Books, Poole 176
Castle Close Antiques, Dornoch 408
Castle Galleries, Salisbury 198
Castle Gate Antiques, Helmsley 322
Castle Gibson, London 50
Castle Hill Books, Kington 252
Castle House Antique Restoration Ltd, Wincanton 468, 491, 495
Castle Reclamation, Martock 190
Castlegate Antique Centre 286
Cat Pottery 217
Catchpole and Rye 37
Caterham Clearance Centre 133
Cathach Books Ltd 433
Cathair Books 441
Cathay Antiques 287
Cathedral Antiques, Fortrose 408
Cathedral Antiques, Rochester 38
Lennox Cato Antiques, Edenbridge 33
Cato Crane & Co, Liverpool 376
The Cats Whiskers Antiques 196
Barbara Cattle 329
Causeway Books 421
D L Cavanagh Antiques 400
R G Cave & Sons Ltd, Ludlow 292

Cave's, Northampton 283
Cavendish Antiques & Collectors Centre, York 329
Rupert Cavendish Antiques, London 76
Cavendish Fine Art, Sonning-on-Thames 120
Cawthorne Antique and Collectors Centre 330
Caxton Prints 433
CCB Aviation Books and Prints 31
Cedar Antiques Centre Ltd, Hartley Wintney 124
Cedar Antiques Ltd, Hartley Wintney 124
Cellar Antiques, Belfast 420
Cellar Antiques, Hawes 322
Celtic Antique Fireplaces 394
Central Auction Rooms, Rochdale 368
Century Fine Arts 125
Ceramic Restoration Studio, Sherborne 448, 450
Ceramics International, Stoke-on-Trent 299
Ceres Antiques, Ceres 404
Cestrian Antiques 354
CG's Curiosity Shop 361
Chacewater Antiques 151
The Chair Repair Workshop, New Romney 509
The Chair Set, Woodstock 268
The Chairman of Bearsden 446, 486, 514
La Chaise Antiques 244
Chaldon Books and Records 133
Chalkwell Auctions Ltd 210
E Chalmers Hallam 127
Chamade Antiques 104
Ronald G Chambers – Fine Antiques 147
Paul Champkins Oriental Art 88
Chancellors Church Furnishings 141
Chancery Antiques Ltd 50
Chandlers Antiques 242
Channel Islands Galleries Ltd 416
Chapel Antiques, Glossop 274
Chapel Antiques, Nantwich 358
Chapel Antiques Centre, Barmouth 385
Chapel Antiques Centre, Sheffield 332
Chapel Emporium, Long Sutton 342
Chapel Place Antiques, Tunbridge Wells 42
Chapel Street Arcades, Penzance 154
Michael Chapman Antiques, Finedon 282
Peter Chapman Antiques and Restoration, London 50
Chappells Antiques Centre, Bakewell 270
Chapter & Verse Booksellers, Rye 24
Chapter House Books, Sherborne 178
Chapters Book and Music Store, Dublin 433
Chard Antiques Centre 187
Charing Cross Markets 109
Charis 169
Charles Antiques, Whitwick 280
Daniel Charles Antiques, Ashbourne 270

Oliver Charles Antiques Ltd, Petworth 147
Charles Town Trading, Charlestown 152
Charleston Antiques, Cardiff 392
Charlotte's Barn 281
Benny Charlsworth's Snuff Box 372
Charlton House Antiques 50
Charnwood Antiques 475
Chateaubriand Antiques 16
Chattels 175
Jocelyn Chatterton 456, 507, 508
Chaucer Bookshop 30
Cheapaschips.cc 393
Checkley Interiors 299
Cheddar Antiques & Upholstery 187
Cheffins 202
Zygmunt Chelminski 444, 500, 504
Chelsea Antique Mirrors 66
Chelsea Antique Rug Gallery 72
Chelsea Clocks and Antiques 104
Chelsea Galleries 104
Chelsea Gallery 80
Chelsea Military Antiques 72
Cheltenham Antique Market 238
Chemicals Ltd 504, 506
Antoine Chenevière Fine Arts Ltd 88
Robert Cheney Antiques, Finedon 282
Peter Cheney Auctioneers and Valuers, Littlehampton 147
Cherry Antiques 256
Chertsey Antiques 133
Cherub Antiques 132
Chesney's Antique Fireplace Warehouse 56, 82
Chess Antique Restorations 476
Chess Antiques 235
The Chest of Drawers, Tetbury 247
Chest of Drawers Ltd, London 50
Chester Antiques Restoration Ltd 484
Chesterfield Antiques, Birmingham 306
Chesterfield Antiques Centre 273
G & J Chesters 302
Chevertons of Edenbridge Ltd 33
Cheyne Antiques, London 76
Patrick Cheyne Auctions, Altrincham 353
Cheyne Galleries, Twickenham 114
Chichester Antiques Centre 144
The Chichester Bookshop 144
The Children's Bookshop 251
Chiltern Strip & Polish 504
Chimney Mill Galleries, Bury St Edmunds 221
Chimney Pieces, North Shields 351
China and Glass Restoration, Warminster 448, 490
China Repairers, London 447, 490, 508
The China Repairers, Tetbury 449, 457
China Repairs & Restorations, Milton Keynes 449
The Chippendale International School of Furniture 508
Chippenham Auction Rooms 194
Chipping Norton Antique Centre 262
Chisholme Antiques 487
Chislehurst Antiques 31
Chiswick and West Middlesex Auctions 97

The Chiswick Fireplace Co 97
Chiswick Park Antiques 97
Chloe Antiques 150
Chobham & Eton Antique Clocks 116
Choice Antiques 199
Chorley–Burdett Antiques 172
Chris's Crackers 190
Robert Christie Antiques, Carrickfergus 421
Judith Christie, Tiverton 168
Christie's, London 66
Christie's South Kensington 79
W J Christophers, Canterbury 30
Christopher's Antiques, Farnham 136
Christy Antique Restoration, Canterbury 459, 489
Church Green Books, Witney 267
Church Hill Antique Centre Ltd, Lewes 21
Church House Antiques, Weybridge 141
Church Street Antiques, London 59
Church Street Antiques Ltd, Altrincham 353
Church Street Gallery, Shipston-on-Stour 303
Churchgate Auctions Ltd 277
Churchill Clocks, Midhurst 147
Churchill Upholstery, Chipping Norton 512
Churchside Antiques 318
Chylds Hall Fine Furniture Restoration 487
Ciancimino Ltd 66
Cider Press Antiques Centre 191
Cindy's Antiques 39
Circa 1900, Liverpool 376
CIRCA Antiques & Art, Stony Stratford 236
Circle Books 184
Cirencester Arcade 239
City Antiques, Swansea 394
City Antiques Ltd, Rochester 38
City Auction Rooms, Waterford 441
City Clocks, London 48
Claire's Collectables 172
Clamjamfrey 414
Clancy Chandeliers 441
Clare Antiques Warehouse 222
Clare Hall Co 472
Claremont Antiques 26
Clarenbridge Antiques 436
Clarence House Antiques 192
Clarendon Books 278
Clarion Events Ltd 519
Clarion Events-NEC Ltd 519
Peter Clark Antiques, Birmingham 306
Christopher Clarke Antiques, Stow-on-the-Wold 244
Clarke Gammon Wellers Auctioneers & Valuers, Guildford 147
Classic Bindings, London 66
Classic Finishes, Norwich 506, 515
The Classic Library, London 81
Classic Pen Engineering, Lochfoot 398, 515
Classic Pictures, Bournemouth 172
Classic Prints, London 72

Classical Numismatic Group Inc., London 88
Classique Antiques, South Benfleet 212
John Clay Antiques 76
Michael Clayton French Polisher 484
Cleall Antiques 148
Clee Tompkinson & Francis 380
Cleethorpes Collectables 339
Clegg & Son, Goole 317
Benedict Clegg, Tunbridge Wells 459
Clementines Antiques 45
Clevedon Books 187
Clevedon Salerooms 187
Cleveland Wood Strip 444, 482, 505
Clewlow Antiques 328
Clifden Antiques 436
Clarice Cliff Ltd 123
Cliffe Antiques Centre 21
Clifford Antiques, London 54
Kenneth F Clifford, York 482
Clifton Hill Textiles, Bristol 184
Bryan Clisby 124
Clitheroe Collectables 371
Clobber 172
The Clock Clinic Ltd, London 84
Clock Corner, Nantwich 358
The Clock House, Carshalton 132
The Clock Shop, Southsea 128
The Clock Shop, Tutbury 300
The Clock Workshop, Caversham 115
The Clockshop, Weybridge 142
Clocktower Antiques, Morecambe 373
The Clock-Work-Shop (Winchester) 129, 451
Cloisters Antiques 203
Clola Antiques Centre 397
Cloud Cuckoo Land, London 50
Cloud Cuckoo Land, Mevagissey 153
Cloughcor House Antiques 425
Clydach Antiques 394
Clyde Antiques, Patrington 318
Bobby Clyde Antiques, Edinburgh 400
The Coach House, Lydeard St Lawrence 190
The Coach House Antique Centre, Canterbury 30
Coach House Antiques, Hastings 19
The Coach House Antiques, Gomshall 137
Coach House Antiques Ltd, Stanley 412
Coach House Books, Pershore 313
Coalville Pine & Antiques 276
The Cobbled Yard 56
Cobra & Bellamy 66
Cobweb Antiques, Cullompton 161
Cobweb Books, Thornton-le-Dale 327
Cobwebs, Galway 436
Cobwebs, Holt 216
Cobwebs, Larne 422
Cobwebs, Southampton 127
Cobwebs Antiques and Collectables, Bembridge 130
Cobwebs of Lockerbie Ltd 399
Cockermouth Antiques 361
Cockermouth Antiques & Craft Market 361
Cockrell Antiques 141
Cofion Books & Postcards 390
Cohen & Cohen, London 98

Adrian Cohen Antiques, London 72
George & Peter Cohn 493
Coinage Hall Antique Centre 157
Coincraft 108
Coins and Bullion 109
Coldstream Military Antiques 235
Christopher Cole 468, 515
Sibyl Colefax & John Fowler 88
Simon Coleman Antiques 83
T V Coles 204
Collectable Adge, Calstock 151
Collectable Furniture, London 80
Collectable Interiors, Warminster 199
Collectables, Honiton 163
Collectables, Nostalgia and Militaria, Warwick 304
The Collector, Belfast 420
The Collector, Clevedon 187
The Collector's Workshop, London 461
Collectors Carbooks, Silverstone 283
Collectors Centre, Walsall 309
The Collectors Centre, Oldham 367
The Collectors Centre, St Peter Port 416
Collectors Choice, Modbury 165
Collectors Corner, Chichester 144
Collectors Corner, Chippenham 194
Collectors' Corner, Little Waltham 210
Collectors Corner, Ormskirk 373
Collectors Corner, Rye 24
Collectors Corner, Truro 157
Collectors Corner, Watford 259
Collectors Dream, Eastbourne 16
Collectors Fair, Upminster 212
Collectors Forum, Romford 211
Collectors Gallery, Shrewsbury 294
Collectors Old Toy Shop, Halifax 335
Collectors Place, Shrewsbury 294
The Collectors' Shop, Norwich 217
Collectors World, Nottingham 287
Collectors' World, Cromer 214
Collinge & Clark, London 108
Collinge Antiques, Deganwy 382
Collinge Antiques, Llandudno Junction 382
L and D Collins, London 72
Collins & Paterson LLP, Glasgow 406
Arthur E Collins & Son, Glasgow 406
J Collins & Son, Bideford 159
J. Collins & Son Fine Art, Bideford 159
Collins Antiques, Wheathampstead 259
Colliton Antique Centre 175
David Collyer Antique Restorations 451, 468
B J Coltman Antiques 350, 484
Colton Antiques 209
Colwyn Books 382
Colyton Antique Centre 160
Comberton Antiques & Interiors 203
Edward Comerford Antiques 437
Comfort Solutions 479
Comic Book Postal Auctions Ltd, London 57
Comic Connections, Banbury 260
The Commemorative Man 176
Commotions Antique, Electric & Turret Clocks 160
The Complete Upholstery Centre 514
Compton Mill Antique Emporium 297

Comrie Antiques 410
M L Connor 509
Conquest House Antiques, Canterbury 30
Rosemary Conquest, London 50
Conservation Letterfrack 454, 488, 494
The Conservation Studio 447, 490, 496
W J Cook, Marlborough 468, 489, 510
Stephen Cook Antiques Ltd, Broadway 310
Sheila Cook Textiles, London 104
Mary Cooke Antiques Ltd, London 84
Sandy Cooke Antiques, Long Melford 225
Cookham Antiques 116
Coombe Antiques, New Malden 139
J and M Coombes, Dorking 134
Cooper and Tanner Chartered Surveyors, Frome 189
Alan Cooper Antique Restorations, Haywards Heath 464
John Cooper Antiques, St Helier 417
Cooper Fine Arts, Brasted 28
Cooper Hay Rare Books, Glasgow 406
Coopers Auctioneers, Disley 356
Coopers Furniture, Leek 297
Coopers of Ilkley, Ilkley 336
David J Cope 296
D A Copley 482
Copnal Books, Crewe 356
N A Copp 476
Coppelia Antiques 359
Copper Kettle Antiques Centre 243
Copperhouse Gallery 152
Copperwheat Restoration 130, 464
Mark Coray Fine Antique Furniture Restoration 469
Corbitt's 350
Corfield Ltd, Lymington 125
Corfield Potashnick, London 85
Tim Corfield Professional Antiques Consultant, Stockbridge 456
Corinium Auctions 239
Cork Brick Antiques & Gallery 221
Cornell Books Ltd 249
Laurence Corner, London 57
Corner Antiques, Worthing 150
Corner Cupboard Curios, Cirencester 239
Corner Farm Antiques, Newport 293
Corner House Antiques, Lechlade 241
Corner Shop Antiques and Gallery, Camelford 151
Cornucopia 335
Corrigan Antiques 412
Corry's Antiques 278
Corve Street Antiques 292
Corwell 464
Coryndon 469
Alison Cosserat 489
Marc Costantini Antiques 76
Costume Jewellery 14
Cotham Antiques 184
The Cotswold Auction Co, Cheltenham 238
Cirencester 240
Gloucester 241
Cotswold Home & Garden, Chipping Norton 262

Cotswold Pine, Middle Aston 265
The Cottage, Gloucester 241
Cottage Antiques, Bakewell 270
Cottage Antiques, Derby 274
Cottage Antiques, Glossop 275
Cottage Antiques, Long Melford 225
Cottage Antiques, Todmorden 374, 484, 505
Cottage Antiques and Lulu's, Cliftonville 32
Cottage Collectables, Holt 216
Cottage Collectibles, East Pennard 188
Cottage Collectibles, Eccleshall 296
Cottage Collectibles, Tetbury 247
Cottage Farm Antiques, Aston Subedge 237
Cottage Style Antiques, Rochester 38
Cottage Upholstery, Nettlebed 512
Cottees of Wareham, Wareham 178
Steven J Cotterell 472, 499
Barry Cotton Antiques 117
Thomas Coulborn and Sons, Sutton Coldfield 309
Martin Coulborn Restorations Ltd, Frampton on Severn 476
Count House Antiques 157
Country & Town Antiques, Bagshot 132
Country Antiques & Interiors, Uffculme 171
Country Antiques (Wales), Kidwelly 380
Country Brocante, Wells 192
Country Clocks, Tring 259
Country Collections, Wheatley 267
Country Collector, Pickering 324
Country Furniture, Fermoy 430
Country Home Antiques, Gargunnock 415
Country Homes and Antiques, Uttoxeter 300
Country House and Cottage Antiques, St Mary 418
Country House Antiques, Rickmansworth 258
Country Life Antiques, Stow-on-the-Wold 244
Country Life Interiors, Berkhamsted 255
Country Life Interiors, Bushey 255
Country Living Antiques, Callington 151
Country Markets Antiques & Collectables, Chilton 262
Country Pine Trading Co, Cheadle 296
Country Rustics, Compton 134
The Country Seat, Henley-on-Thames 264
Country Ways, Rye 24
Countryside Books 117
County Antiques 415
Courthouse Antiques Centre 332
Richard Courtney Ltd 72
Courts Miscellany 253
Courtville Antiques 433
Courtyard Antiques, Brasted 28
Courtyard Books, Glastonbury 189
Courtyard Collectables, St Ives 156
Courtyard Curios, Maidstone 36

Courtyard Restoration, Ahoghill 457, 487
E W Cousins & Son 225
John Cowderoy Antiques Ltd 16
Claude Cox Books, Ipswich 224
Lisa Cox Music, Exeter 161
Cox's Architectural Salvage Yard Ltd, Moreton-in-Marsh 242
Peter Crabbe Antiques 202
Crafts Nouveau 55
Craftsman Antiques, Chepstow 456
The Craftsman's Joint, London 461
Stuart Craig, London 88
Julia Craig, London 104
Craigavon Marble Products 423
Craiglea Clocks 400
Brian and Caroline Craik Ltd 181
Cranglegate Antiques 219
Craobh Rua Books 423
Thomas Crapper & Co 303
Crawford Antiques, London 461
Crawford Saleroom, Edinburgh 400
Robert H Crawley 476
Adam Crease Shipping Ltd 497
Creek Antiques 62
Crescent Road Antiques 43
Crest Collectables 16
The Crested China Co 317
Crewkerne Antiques 188
Criccieth Gallery Antiques 385
Mrs M.E. Crick Chandeliers 98
M & A Cringle 213
J Crisp 492, 510
Madeline Crispin Antiques, London 57
Crispin Fairs, Reading 519
Criterion Auctioneers, London 50
Criterion Riverside Auctions, London 82
Peter A Crofts 205
Sandra Cronan Ltd 88
The Crooked Window 188
Cross County Fairs Ltd 519
Cross Hayes Antiques 195
Crossroads Antiques 414
Crown Antiques, Eastbourne 17
Crown Arcade, London 104
Crown Jewellers of Harrogate 320
Crows Auction Gallery, Dorking 134
The Crows Nest, Weymouth 179
Croydon Coin Auctions 134
Crozier Antique Furniture Restoration 487
Mary Cruz Antiques 181
Crwys Antiques 393
Cryers Antiques 382
The Cufflink Shop 72
Cullompton Old Tannery Antiques 161
Cumbria Architectural Salvage, Raughton Head 364
The Cumbrian Antiques Centre, Brampton 360
A & Y Cumming Ltd 21
Cundalls 323
Cura Antiques 104
Curborough Hall Farm Antiques Centre 298
The Curio Cafe and Antiques, Newark 286

Curio Corner, Tynemouth 352
Curio Corner, Whitby 328
CurioCity, Southend-on-Sea 212
Curios, Ventnor 131
Curiosity Corner, Guisborough 320
Curiosity Shop, Alfreton 269
The Curiosity Shop, South Shields 351
The Curiosity Shop, St Sampsons 417
The Curiosity Shop on the Quay, Weymouth 179
Curiosity Too, Great Yarmouth 215
Curiouser & Curiouser 149
Curr & Dewar 397
Cutcrew Antiques 156
Edmund Czajkowski & Son 454, 482

D

D & D Programmes 399
D H R Ltd 476
D K R Refurbishers, Chester 354
D M Antique Restoration 469
D M E Restorations Ltd 476
Da Capo Antiques 401
Clifford and Roger Dade 141
Daeron's Books 236
John Daffern Antiques 321
Dagfields Crafts & Antiques Centre 359
Oscar Dahling Antiques 134
Dairy House Antiques 177
John Dale Antiques, London 104
Dale House, Moreton-in-Marsh 242
Peter Dale Ltd, London 66
Dalkeith Auctions Bournemouth 172
Dalton Antiques 308
Danbury Antiques 207
The Dandelion Clock 18
Andrew Dando, Bradford-on-Avon 193
Paul Daniel 109
Dann Antiques Ltd 197
The Dartmoor Bookshop Ltd 158
M W Darwin & Son 319
K Davenport Interiors Ltd, Oswestry 479, 512
Davenports Antiques, Chichester 464
Graham Davey 519
Davey & Davey 176
G David 202
davidleesbooks.com 251
Davidson Antiques, London 59
Carlton Davidson Antiques, London 50
Don Davidson, Chipping Norton 519
Davidson Books, Ballynahinch 423
Davidson Monk Fairs, Croydon 519
Fred Davies & Co, Llandysul 381
Edmund Davies & Son Antiques, Whalley 375
Davies Antiques, London 80
Peggy Davies Ceramics, Stoke-on-Trent 299
Barry Davies Oriental Art, London 98
J Davies Restorations, Portstewart 487
Davies Turner Worldwide Movers Ltd, Mitcham 498
Davies, White & Perry, Newport 293
Davies, White & Perry, Shifnal 294

M L Davis, Bournemouth 469
Reginald Davis (Oxford) Ltd, Oxford 265
Roger A Davis Antiquarian Horologist, Great Bookham 137
Andrew Davis Antiques, Richmond 139
Stephanie Davison Antiques 271
B J Dawson 365
Day Antiques, Tetbury 247
Alan Day Antiques, Edinburgh 401
Days Gone By 385
DDM Auction Rooms 339
M & J De Albuquerque 267
De Burca Rare Books 432
De Danann Antiques Centre 175
Adèle De Havilland 88
W De La Rue Antiques 416
Deal Upholstery Services 510
Christine Deane Antiques 425
Deans Antiques 76
Debden Antiques 207
Debenham Antiques 222
Deborah Paul 294
Decade Antiques & Interiors, Wallasey 378
Decades, Blackburn 370
Decades, Sunderland 352
Decodream 134
DecoGraphic Collectors Gallery 142
Decor Antique Chandeliers 99
Decorative Antiques, Bishops Castle 291
Decorative Antiques, London 76
Decorative Arts, Brighton 14
Decorative Arts, London 57
The Decorator Source 247
Decorcraft Upholsterers 511
Decors, Deal 33
Decorum, Arundel 143
Deddington Antique Centre 263
Dee Cee Upholstery 510
Dee, Atkinson and Harrison 317
Deerstalker Antiques 237, 476
Deeside Books 396
Hannerle Dehn 461, 499
Deja Vu Antiques, Leigh-on-Sea 210
Deja Vu Antiques, Shrewsbury 294
Deja-Vu Antiques & Books, Lostwithiel 153
Delomosne & Son Ltd 197
Delphi Antiques 434
Delvin Farm Antiques 440
Sonia Demetriou 464, 499
Heather Denham Antiques, Petworth 148
Denham's, Horsham 146
Clive Dennett 217
Denning Antiques 137
Dennis Jewllery 519
Guy Dennler Antiques & Interiors 168
Denton Antiques 99
Derbyshire Clocks 275
Derbyshire Removals 498
Dernier and Hamlyn Ltd 493
A S Derrick 274
Derwentside Antiques 273
Design Explosion, Southsea 128
The Design Gallery, Westerham 45

Design Interiors, Perth 411
Designer Classics, Enfield 113
Alexander S Deuchar & Son 411
Deva Antiques 124
Roger DeVille Antiques 271
Devon CountyAntique Fairs 520
Devon Metalcraft Ltd 496, 506
Ian Dewar 479
R G Dewdney 464, 492
D'Eyncourt Antiques 133
Diamond Mills & Company 223
Dickens Curios 208
Alastair Dickenson Ltd, London 66
Dickins Auctioneers, Buckingham 234
D & B Dickinson, Bath 181
J Dickinson Maps & Prints,
    Bakewell 271
Dickinson's Antiques Ltd,
    Gargrave 320
Robert Dickson and Lesley Rendall
    Antiques 72
Didier Aaron (London) Ltd 67
Didier Antiques 99
Dillons Antiques 348
M R Dingle 155
Dingly Dell Antiques
    & Collectables 134
Dingwall & Highland Marts Ltd 408
The Dining Room Shop 83
Director Furniture Leathergilders 493
Dismantle & Deal Direct 233
Diss Antiques & Interiors 214
Eric Distin Auctioneers & Chartered
    Surveyors 160
DIVA (Digital Inventory and Visual
    Archive) 457
Dix Noonan Webb 88
Dixon's Medals 317
Dix-Sept Antiques 228
DMG Antiques Fairs 520
Graham Dobinson Antiques 124
Maurice Dodd Books 411
Dodo 59
Gudrun Doel 169
The Dog House 309
Louis J Doherty & Sons 440
Dollectable 355
Michael Dolling 472
Dolly Domain 352
Dolly Domain Fairs 520
Dollyland 56
Dolphin Quay Antique Centre,
    Emsworth 123
Dolphin Square Antiques, Dorking 135
Domani Antique
    & Contemporary 169
Dome Antiques 55
Domino Restorations 449, 492, 496
Gary Don Antiques 337
Don's Den 309
Michael Donohoe & Sons 438
The Door Stripping Company Ltd
    332, 505
Dorchester Antiques 263
The Dorchester Bookshop 175
Dorking Desk Shop 135
Dorking House Antiques 135
Dorothy's Antiques 219
Dorridge Antiques, Warwick 304

Dorridge Antiques & Collectables
    Centre, Solihull 308
Dorset Reclamation 171
Bryan Douglas, London 109
Christopher John Douglas,
    Charmouth 469, 501
Gavin Douglas, London 105
Douglas & Kay, Glasgow 487
Dovetail Interiors of Bedale 319
Dovetail Restoration, Wantage 476
Dower House Antiques 362
Downland Furniture Restoration 465
Downlane Hall Antiques 43
Downsby Antiques & Collectables 383
A E Dowse & Son 332
Dragon Antiques, Harrogate 321
Dragon Antiques, Kettering 282
The Dragon, South Molton 168
Dragonlee Collectables, Rochester 38
Dragons Hoard, St Ives 156
Draycott Books 239
Drew Pritchard Ltd 382
Dreweatt Neate,
    Bristol Salerooms 184, 195
    Eastbourne Salerooms 17
    Donnington 116
    Godalming Salerooms 137
    Honiton Salerooms 163
    Marlborough Saleroom 196
    Tunbridge Wells Salerooms 43
Drewery and Wheeldon 339
Drill Hall Antiques Centre 341
C & K Dring 342
Drop Dial Antiques 365
Druet Antiques 67
Drummonds Architectural Antiques
    Ltd, Hindhead 138
Drummonds Architectural Antiques
    Ltd, London 72
Drums Malahide 436
Ann Drury Antiques 416
Dualco Promotions 520
Dudley & Spencer 469
John Duffy Antiques,
    Dunshoughlin 439
Michael Duffy Antiques, Dublin 434
David Duggleby Fine Art 326
Hy Duke & Son 175, 176
Dukeries Antiques Centre 285
Duncan & Reid 401
Dundee Philatelic Auctions 397
Dunkeld Antiques 410
Dunluce Antiques and Crafts 421
A Dunn, Richmond 463
A Dunn & Son, Chelmsford 472, 495
Hamish Dunn Antiques, Wooler 349
Joe Dunne Auctioneers & Valuers,
    Borris 429
R D Dunning 482
K W Dunster Antiques 113
Durham House 245
Durrants Auction Rooms 220
Dutton & Smith Medals & Badges 287
Frank Dux Antiques 181
Marijana Dworski Books 251
Dycheling Antiques 145
Dyfed Antiques 389
Dyfi Valley Bookshop 391
Peter Dyke at The Old Bakery 29

Dynasty Antiques 176
Dyson & Son, Clare 222
Dyson Furniture, Twickenham 462,
    491, 495

E

E K Antiques 282
E W Services 520
Julian Eade 268
The Eagle Bookshop 231
W H Earles 459, 500
The Earlsfield Bookshop 85
Early Oak, Knaresborough 323
Early Technology, Musselburgh 399
Earnshaw Antiques 332
Easingwold Antiques 320, 482
East Preston Festival Fair 520
Eastbourne Antiques Market 17
Eastbourne Auction Rooms 17
Eastbourne Fine Art 17
Eastbourne Pine 17
Eastcote Bookshop 113
Easter Antiques 123
Eastgate Antiques 393
EASY Edinburgh & Glasgow
    Architectural Salvage Yard 401
Eat My Handbag Bitch 109
J W Eaton 476
Eccles Road Antiques 82
Echoes 375
Eclectic Antiques and Interiors,
    London 72
Eclectica, London 51
Eclectica Interiors, Ashbourne 270
Eclectique, Exeter 161
Ecomerchant Ltd 34
ECS 401
The Eddie Stobart Fan Club Shop 360
Eddie Stobart Promotions Ltd 360
Eddisbury Antiques 356
A A Eddy & Son 469
Charles Ede Ltd 88
Matthew Eden, Corsham 195
Eden House Antiques, Bishop
    Auckland 346
Edenderry Architectural
    Salvage Ltd 440
Edge 72
Editions Graphiques 88
G H Edkins and Son 346
David Edmonds Indian Furniture 97
I D Edrich 48
L Edscer 156
Charles Edwards, London 76
Peter Edwards, London 88
K Edwards Antiques, Steyning 465
Ben Eggleston Antiques Ltd 363
I Ehrnfeld 56
Elden Antiques 338
Richard Elderton 465, 496
Eldreds Auctioneers and Valuers 167
Elham Antiques 34
J G Elias Antiques Ltd 132
Elisabeth's Antiques Ltd, London 89
Elizabeth & Son, Ulverston 364
Elizabeth Antiques, Mumbles 394
Elizabeth R Antiques,
    East Molesey 136

Elizabeth Street Antiques and Restoration Services, London 67, 462, 510
Ellenor Hospice Care Shop, Otford 37
Ellenor Hospice Projects, Bexley 28
Samuel Elliot, Dublin 454
Elliott's, Petworth 148
Joyce Ellis, Solihull 479
Donald Ellis Antiques, Edinburgh 401
Siri Ellis Books, Bromley Cross 365
Richard Ellory Furniture 338
Elm Hill Antiques 217
ELR Auctions Ltd 332
Elsecar Antiques Centre 330
Elvisly Yours 57
Emanouel Corporation (UK) Ltd 89
Emeralds Antiques 347
Garry M Emms and Co Ltd 215
Empire Exchange 367
The Emporium, Atherton 364
The Emporium, Bridlington 317
Emporium Antiques, Sandgate 39
The Emporium Antiques Centre Too, Lewes 21
The Emporium Antiques Centre, Lewes 21
L'Encoignure 81
Endeavour Books 328
English and Continental Antiques, Eye 222
Toby English Antiquarian & Secondhand Bookshop, Wallingford 267
English Garden Antiques, Bowdon 365
English Heritage, Bridgnorth 291
English Rose Antiques, Coggeshall 207
Enhancements 14
The Enterprise Collectors Market 17
Era Vintage Boutique 503
Escolme House Antiques 276
Eskdale Antiques, Sleights 327
Eskdale Antiques, Whitby 328
Eskenazi Ltd, London 89
John Eskenazi Ltd, London 89
Esox Antique Restoration 469
The Essence of Time 298
Essex Reupholstery Services 473
Essex Reupholstery Services 511
Essie Carpets 89
Etcetera Antiques, Seaton 167
Etceteras, Bakewell 271
Eton Antiques, E 116
Euricka Antiques 434, 488
European Accent 186
European Fine Arts & Antiques 374
Ann Evans, Valley 387
Evans and Partridge, Stockbridge 128
T Evans Antiques, Pwlldefaid 386
Evans Emporium, Honiton 163
Bob Evans Fairs 520
Evergreen Antiques & Interiors 155
Eversley Barn Antiques 123
Ewbank Fine Art Auctioneers 142
The Exchange 171
Exeter Antique Lighting 161
Exeter Rare Books 161
Exeter's Antiques Centre on the Quay 161
Exning Antiques & Interiors 222

Expectations 155
Expressions 294
Leigh Extence Antique Clocks, Honiton 163
Extence Antiques, Teignmouth 168
Extreme Conservation 459, 493, 499

F

Nicole Fabre French Antiques 76
The Façade 57
Facets Glass Restoration 490
Fagin & Co, Todmorden 375
Fagins Antiques, Hele 162
Failsworth Mill Antiques 366
Fair Antiques, Maidenhead 520
Fair Finds Antiques, Rait 412
Fakenham Antiques Centre 215
Trevor Falconer Antiques 422
Falstaff Antiques 39
Family Antiques 368
Famously Yours Ltd 28
Fandango 51
Fanny's Antiques 119
Farleigh Antiques 32
Farm Cottage Antiques, Seaford 459
Farm House Antiques, King's Lynn 216
Farmhouse Antiques, Chester 355
Farningham Pine 34
Farrelly Antiques 236
John Farrington Antiques 434
Farthing, Yarm 328
Farthings, Lynton 165
Farthings, Rottingdean 23
Fat Cat Fairs 520
Fauconberges 221
K Faulkner, Bristol 185
K Faulkner, Wokingham 121
Faversham Interiors 34
Keith Fawkes 58
R Feldman Ltd Antique Silver 109
Felix Fairs 520
Feljoy Antiques 51
Anthony Fell Antiques & Works of Art 216
Fellows & Sons 306
James Fenning, Antiquarian Booksellers, 435
Fens Restoration and Sales 462
B L Fenton & Son 397
Fenwick & Fenwick Antiques 310
Steven Ferdinando 190
The Ferret (Friday Street Antiques Centre) 264
Michael Ferris 489
David Ferrow 215
Brian Fielden 58
Fieldings Antiques & Clocks 370
Fieldstaff Antiques 38
The Fifteenth Century Bookshop 21
Filibuster & Booth Ltd 332
Filippa & Co 67
Filsham Farmhouse Antiques 26
Mark Finamore 462, 489
Finan and Co 197
Finch Antiques, Sandgate 39
Hector Finch Lighting, London 76
Simon Finch Norfolk, Holt 216
Simon Finch Rare Books, London 89

Finchingfield Antiques Centre 208
Fine Art Antiques, Preston 374
Fine Books Oriental Ltd, London 108
Fine Pine Antiques, Totnes 171
Finedon Antiques Ltd 282
Peter Finer 301
Mike Fineron Cigarette Cards & Postcards 329
Finishing Touches 274
Finley's Finds 347
Finnie Antiques Ltd 406
Fisher & Sperr, LOndon 54
Fisher Nautical, Streat 149
Kitty Fisher's Finds, Manchester 367
Fisherton Antiques Market 198
Fishlake Antiques 331, 482
Michael W Fitch Antiques 40
E Fitzpatrick 488
Flagstaff Antiques 130
Flagstones Pine and Country Furniture 279
Flanagans Ltd 434
Flaxton Antique Gardens 320
A Fleming (Southsea) Ltd 128
Fleur-de-Lis Antiques, Fleur-de-Lis 387
Fleur de Lys Antiques & Collectables, Hay-on-Wye 251
Fleurdelys Antiquités, London 105
Fleury Antiques, Cahir 441
Fleury Antiques, Dublin 434
Flintlock Antiques 369
Flourish Farm Antiques 275
Flower House Antiques 41
Flying Duck Enterprises 62
Flying Dutchman Antiques 406
Norman Flynn Restorations 447
Focus on the Past 185
Aidan Foley Antiques, Mallow 430
Foley Furniture, Malvern 312
Foley House Antiques, Malvern 312
The Folkestone Stamp and Collectors Shop 34
Folly Four Antiques & Collectables 126
David Foord-Brown Antiques 145
Football in Focus (2001) Ltd 18
Andrew Foott Antiques 366
David Ford & Associates, Guildford 514
G W Ford & Son Ltd, Bakewell 271
Forest Antique Centre, Lyndhurst 125
Forest Books of Cheshire, Knutsford 357
Forest House Antiques, New Milton 126
The Forge Antiques & Collectables, Stamford 344
The Forge Antiques, Coleraine 425
Forge Interiors, Rotherfield 23
Forge Studio Workshops, Manningtree 473
Format Coins 306
Jeffrey Formby Antiques 242
Former Glory, Ferndown 446, 469, 507
Former Glory, Gosport 123
Forres Saleroom 409
Birdie Fortescue Antiques 77
Fortlands Antiques 429
Forum Antiques, Cirencester 240, 476
Forum Antiques, Wexford 441
Foss Gate Books 329
Matthew Foster, London 89

Michael Foster, London 72
W A Foster, London 97
Graham Foster Antiques,
  Hurstpierpoint 146
Paul Foster Books, London 84
A and E Foster Ltd, Cleveley 263
Fosters Antiques Centre,
  Rotherham 331
Fountain Antique Studios &
  Workshop, Coleraine 425
Fountain Antiques, Honiton 163
Four in One Promotions 520
Four Winds Antiques 423
Fourways Antiques 287
Nicholas Fowle Antiques, Norwich 218
A and J Fowle, London 84
Robin Fowler Period Clocks 338
Jon Fox Antiques,
  Moreton-in-Marsh 242
Fox Cottage Antiques, Stow-on-the-
  Wold 245
Daniel Fox Upholstery, Braunton 511
Foxglove Antiques 388
Foxhole Antiques 20
Foyle Antiques 426
Foyle Books 426
Frameworks 437
Diane France Antiques 141
Peter Francis Antiques 425
François 17
N & I Franklin, London 67
Franklin Antiques, Hungerford 117
Alan Franklin Transport Ltd,
  Verwood 498
I Franks, London 109
J A L Franks and Co, London 67
Victor Franses Gallery 67
Frantique, Knaresborough 323
Frantiques of Devizes 195
Fraser Antiques, Coldstream 413
Fraser's Autographs, London 110
Frasers Auctioneers, Inverness 408
G and R Fraser-Sinclair, Godstone 465
A Frayling-Cork 497
C. Fredericks and Son 99
Freeman and Lloyd Antiques,
  Sandgate 39
Neil Freeman Angling Auctions,
  London 107
Vincent Freeman Antiques, London 51
French & Country Living, Wetherby 338
French Country Style, Bowdon 365
French House Antiques, London 77
French House Antiques, York 329
French Lavender, Kidderminster 311
French Treasures, Rye 24
The French Warehouse,
  Ballynahinch 423
Charles French, Eastbourne 17
Freshfords Fine Art 189
Robert Frew Ltd 89
Freya Antiques Fairs 520
Freya Books and Antiques 219
Friargate Antiques Company 274
Friargate Pine Co Ltd 274
Friend or Faux 221
Frome Reclamation 189
Fron House Antiques Decorative
  Items 385

Frost Antiques & Pine, Monmouth 388
Frosts of Clerkenwell Ltd, London 48
Fritz Fryer Antique Lighting 254
Fulham Antiques 77
Full of Beans 375
James Fuller and Son 203
Fullertons Booksearch 445
Funnye Olde Worlde 291
Furness Vale Antiques 274
The Furniture Barn, Market
  Harborough 279
The Furniture Cave, Aberystwyth 381
Furniture Revivals, Leeds 482, 513
The Furniture Trading Co, Botley 122
Furniture Vault, London 51
Furse Restoration 473
Jonathan Fyson Antiques 261

G

G B Antiques Centre 373
G C Books Ltd 399
Gabor Cossa Antiques 202
Gaby's Clocks and Things 41
Gainsborough House 249
Galata Coins 391
Galerie, Newark 286
Gallerie Antiques, Hainault 208
Gallerie Veronique, Enfield 113
Gallery 1930, London 60
The Gallery, Dunfanaghy 432
Gallery 23 Antiques,
  Chalfont St Giles 234
Gallery Kaleidoscope incorporating
  Scope Antiques, London 59
Gallery of Antique Costume &
  Textiles, London 96
Gallery Persia, Inverness 408
Jim Gallie Antiques 206
Gallimaufry 311
Gallop– Rivers Architectural
  Antiques 391
Galloway Antiques Fairs 520
Gander & White Shipping Ltd,
  London 498
Michael Gander, Hitchin 257
Gannochy Coins and Medals 202
Ganymede Antiques 280
Garden Art, Hungerford 117
Garden House Antiques, Yoxford 229
Gardiner Houlgate, Corsham 195
John Gardiner, Somerton 191
Richard Gardner Antiques,
  Petworth 148
A D Gardner, Reigate 465, 510
Gardners 'The Antique Shop',
  Kilbarchan 412
Gargrave Gallery 320
John Garner Antiques 290
Garrard Antiques 292
Marilyn Garrow Fine Textile Art 226
Garth Antiques 321
Herbert G Gasson 24
Gatehouse Antiques, Macclesfield 357
Gatehouse Workshops,
  Nottingham 288
Gateway Antiques 261
Gathering Moss 54
Maureen H Gauld 410

Becca Gauldie Antiques & Scribe
  Books 411
Peter Gaunt 89
Gavantiques 136
Geary Antiques 338
Gedyes Auctioneers & Estate
  Agents 361
Rob Gee 169
Ivo Geikie-Cobb 444, 462, 469
R A Gekoski Booksellers 108
Gem Antiques, Maidstone 36
Gem Antiques, Sevenoaks 40
Gems, Chichester 144
Gensco Promotions 520
Lionel Geneen Ltd 173
Gentry Antiques 155
Paul Geoghegan 488
George House, Whaley Bridge 276
George Street Antique Centre,
  Bath 181
George Street Antiques Centre,
  Hastings 19
Georgian Antiques, Cork 429
Georgian Antiques, Edinburgh 401
Georgian House Antiques, Chipping
  Norton 262
The Georgian Rooms, Bridlington 317
Georgian Village Antiques, Sligo 440
Georgiana Antiques & Interiors,
  Ellesmere 292, 456
Michael German Antiques Ltd 99
Get Stuffed 51
A & T Gibbard 17
David Gibbins, Woodbridge 228
Stanley Gibbons Auctions Ltd,
  London 110
Andy Gibbs, Ross-on-Wye 254
Christopher Gibbs Antiques,
  London 67
Paul Gibbs Antiques & Decorative
  Arts, Conwy 382
Angelo Gibson, London 73
Roderick Gibson, Nantwich 358
Nicholas Gifford-Mead 67
Gilbert and Dale, Ilchester 189
David Gilbert Antiques, Sandgate 39
John Gilbert Antiques, Robin Hood's
  Bay 325
Gilboys Ltd 469
The Gilded Lily Jewellery Ltd 89
Gildings 279
Gabrielle de Giles, Sandgate 39
John Giles, Petworth 148
G and F Gillingham Ltd 58
Gillmark Map Gallery 257
Annabelle Giltsoff 199
Giltwood Gallery 238
Gingers Trade Antiques 388
The Ginnel Antique Center 321
The Girl Can't Help It 60
G J Gittins & Sons, Caerphilly 387
T J Gittins, Market Drayton 479
Glade Antiques 235
Martin Gladman Second-hand
  Books 54
Glassdrumman 43
Glassenbury Country Furniture Ltd 459
Glebe Hall Collectables 438, 450, 488,
  489. 501,508

The Globe Antiques & Art Centre 163
The Glory Hole, Innerleithen 413
The Glory Hole, Sandiacre 289
Glossop Antique Centre 275
Gloucester Antiques Centre 241
Gloucester Road Bookshop 79
Gloucestershire Furniture Hospital
    446, 476
Glydon and Guess 138
Michael Goater Restoration 473
P Godden 473
Grenville Godfrey 447
Godleton Barn Antiques 125
Godson & Coles 73
Pamela Godwin 84
Golden Cross Antiques 18
Golden Oldies, Penkridge 298
The Golden Past, Kirkcaldy 404
Golding Young 339
Goldmark Gallery 290
Gaby Goldscheider 130
Goldsmith & Perris 60
Goldsworth Books and Prints 142
Golfark International 349
Roland Gomm 487
Good Day Antiques and Decor 126
Good Fairy Antique Market 105
Good Golly Bear Dolly 36
Good Moves Ltd 498
The Good Olde Days 276
Goodacre Engraving 453
The Gooday Gallery 139
Richard Goodbrey Antiques 223
Goodbye To All That 303
Peter Goodfellow 497
Simon Gooding 465
Goodrich House Antiques 231
Pamela Goodwin, Tunbridge Wells 43
Guy Goodwin Restoration,
    Warwick 479
Goodwins, Ilford 209
Goodwin's Antiques Ltd,
    Edinburgh 401
Goodwin's Home & Garden,
    Buckingham 234
Goodwood Furniture Restoration 465
Nicholas Goodyer 54
Ora Gordon, London 60
Gordon's Medals, London 89
Gormley's Fine Art, Belfast 420
Gormley's Fine Art, Omagh 427
Gorringes,
    Bexhill-On-Sea 13
    Lewes 21
    Tunbridge Wells 43
    Worthing 150
The Goss & Crested China Club 124
Gillian Gould Antiques 58, 110
Government House Quality Antique
    Lighting 249
Gow Antiques and Restoration 398,
    487, 495, 508
Graham Gallery, Reading 119
The Graham Gallery, London 89
Joss Graham Orientals, London 67
Graham the Hat, Swinderby 345
Major Iain Grahame, Bures 221
Granary Antiques, Flore 282
Granary Antiques, Thrapston 284

The Granary Antiques, Nuneaton 302
Granary Collectables, Kendal 362
Granary Pine, Bradford-on-Avon 194
Grandfather Clock Shop 245
Grandma's Attic, Lymington 520
Grandma's Attic, Walmer 44
Grandpa's Collectables 384
Grange Antiques, Rottingdean 24
Grange Antiques Ltd,
    Milton Keynes 235
Grannie Used To Have One,
    Longhaven 397
Granny's Attic, Cramlington 348
Granny's Attic, Ramsgate 38
Granny's Attic, Veryan 157
Granny's Cupboard Antiques,
    Wisbech 205
Denzil Grant, Drinkstone 222
Andrew Grant Fine Art Auctioneers,
    Worcester 314
Grantham Clocks 339
Grantham Furniture Emporium 339
Grantham Workshops Cabinet
    Makers 479
Graus Antiques 90
D J Gravell 486
Anita Gray, London 90
Laila Gray, Kingsthorpe 479
Ian Gray Antique Restoration, Great
    Missenden 476
Alexandra Gray Antiques &
    Decorative Ideas, Portsmouth 126
Gray Arts, Amersham 449, 453
David A H Grayling, Shap 364
Graylings Antiques, Marlborough 197
Grays Antique Market, London 90
Grays Antiques, Worcester 314
Great Expectations 341
Great Grooms of Dorking 135
Great Grooms of Hungerford 117
Great Malvern Antiques 312
Great Northern Architectural
    Antiques Co Ltd 359
The Great Oak Bookshop 391
Great Western Auctions 406
Ron Green, Towcester 284
J Green & Son, Queniborough 279
Anthony Green Antiques, London 110
D J Green Antiques, Bakewell 271
Jonathan Green Antiques,
    Salisbury 198
The Green Antiques & Collectables,
    Westerham 45
Sally Green Designs,
    Hartley Wintney 124
The Green Dragon, Seaton 167
Green Dragon Antiques and Crafts
    Centre, Wincanton 193
Green Lane Antiques, Ormskirk 373
The Green Room, Framlingham 223
Green's Antique Galleries, London 99
Greene's Antiques Galleries,
    Drogheda 439
David Greenhalgh Antiques 374
Greens of Cheltenham Ltd 238
Greenslade Taylor Hunt Fine Art 191
Jonathan Greenwall Antiques 39
Colin Greenway Antiques 268
Greenwich Auctions Partnership 62

Greenwich Conservation Workshops
    447, 457, 462, 501
Greenwich Gallery 63
Judy Greenwood Antiques 77
Henry Gregory 105
Grenadiers, London 65, #520
Grenadiers, Worcester 314
Le Grenier Antiques 305
Gresham Books 188
Grey-Harris & Co 185
Greystoke Antiques 178
A Grice 374, 484
Griffin Antiques, Ely 203
Griffin Antiques, Enfield 113
Simon Griffin Antiques Ltd, London 90
Marcus Griffin Specialists in Silver
    Jewellery, Londonderry 426
Griffith & Partners Ltd 108
Roger Grimes, Achill Sound 439
Grimes House Antiques & Fine Art,
    Moreton-in-Marsh 242
Grimes Militaria, Bristol 185
Nicholas Grindley 63
Robert Gripper Restoration 476
Grosvenor Chambers Restoration,
    Plymouth 166
Grosvenor Exhibitions Ltd,
    Spalding 520
Grosvenor House Interiors,
    Beaconsfield 234
Grosvenor Prints, London 110
Grounds & Co 205
The Grove Antique Centre,
    Honiton 164
Grove Rare Books, Bolton Abbey 319
Guardroom Antiques 340
Nicolas Guedroitz Ltd 67
Guest and Gray, London 90
Lynn Guest Antiques, Retford 289
Claire Guest at Thomas Goode & Co.
    Ltd, London 90
Guinevere Antiques Ltd 77
Gullane Antiques 399
Bernard Gulley Antiques 231
John Gunning Antiques 439
Gutlin Clocks & Antiques 77
Gwynfair Antiques 386

H & H Classic Auctions Ltd 357
H L B Antiques 175
H P Book Finders 445
H R W Antiques Ltd 77
H S C Fine Arts Ltd 324
Hackney House Antiques 272
Haddon Rocking Horses 508
G K Hadfield 362
Hadji Baba Ancient Art Ltd 90
Hadlow Down Antiques 18
Haig & Hosford 473
David Hakeney Antiques 316
Halcyon Days 49
Halfway Trading 387
Halifax Antique Centre 335
Anthony C Hall, Twickenham 114
G J Hall, Antique Furniture
    Restoration, Eversley 465
Hall's Bookshop, Tunbridge Wells 43

Hallidays, North Petherton 190
Hallidays, Taunton 191
Hallidays (Fine Antiques) Ltd,
    Dorchester on Thames 263
Hallmark Antiques, London 90
Hallmark Jewellers, Brighton 14
Hall's Auctioneers, Galashiels 413
Hall's Curio Shop, Dundalk 439
Halls Fine Art Auctions,
    Shrewsbury 294
Hambleton Books 327
John Hamblin 469
Peter Hames 159
Ross Hamilton (Antiques) Ltd,
    London 67
Hamilton Antique Restoration,
    Douglas 485, 513
Hamilton Antiques, Woodbridge 228
A D Hamilton Antiques, Glasgow 406
Rosemary Hamilton China Repairs,
    London 447
Hamiltons, London 110
Jeffery Hammond Antiques 253
Hampstead Antique and Craft
    Emporium 58
Gerald Hampton, Christchurch 175
Hampton Antiques, Northampton 283
The Hampton Court Emporium, East
    Molesey 136
Peter Hancock, Chichester 145
Hancock & Monks, Hay-on-Wye 251
Hancocks and Co (Jewellers) Ltd,
    London 90
J Hanlon Antiques 337
E Hansen, Hungerford 496
Hansen Chard Antiques, Pershore 313
Nick Hansford 453
Hanshan Tang Books 84
David J Hansord and Son 342
Hanworth House Antiques
    & Interiors 231
Harbour Traders Ltd 206
Keith Harding's World of Mechanical
    Music 243
James Hardy & Co, London 73
James Hardy Antiques Ltd, Barnard
    Castle 346
Hardy Country, Melbury Osmond 176
Hardy's Antiques, Hacheston 223
Hardy's Collectables,
    Bournemouth 173
Hare's Antiques Ltd 240
Brian Harkins 67
Harlequin Antiques, Edinburgh 401
Harlequin Antiques, Grantham 340
Harlequin Antiques, Nottingham 288
Harlequin Antiques, Porthcawl 387
Harlequin Gallery, Lincoln 342
Harley Antiques 195
Harmers of London Stamp
    Auctioneer Ltd 97
Harold's Place 98
Martin and Dorothy Harper Antiques,
    Bakewell 271
Harper– James, Montrose 398
Harpers Jewellers Ltd, York 329
Harpurs of Oundle, Oundle 283
Adrian Harrington 99
Roy C Harris, Burton-on-Trent 296

Montague Harris & Co, Brecon 390
Harris Antiques, Thaxted 212
John Harris Antiques and
    Restorations, Petworth 148
Rupert Harris Conservation, London
    496, 502
Brian Harris Furniture Restorations,
    Boxsted 452, 473
Harris Lindsay, London 68
Harris's Arcade, London 105
Bob Harrison Antiques, Hinckley 277
Harrison's, Stoke-on-Trent 299
Harrogate Antique and Fine Art Fair
    Ltd 521
Hart & Rosenberg, London 105
Rosemary Hart, London 51
Hart's Antiques, Par 469
Hartley & Co, Liverpool 376
J Hartley Antiques Ltd, Ripley 140
Andrew Hartley Fine Arts, Ilkley 336
Hartley Upholstery and Antique
    Restorations, Hook 510
W R Harvey & Co (Antiques) Ltd,
    Witney 268
Harvey & Gore, London 68
Kenneth Harvey Antiques, London 81
Patricia Harvey Antiques, London 60
The Richard Harvey Collection Ltd,
    Shipston-on-Stour 303
Harvey Management Services Ltd,
    London 521
Elizabeth Harvey-Lee, North Aston 265
Harwich Antiques Centre 209
Haslam & Whiteway 99
Hastings Antiques Centre 26
Bradley Hatch Jewellers, Wroxham 220
Gideon Hatch Rugs & Carpets,
    London 82
J E Hatcher & Son 513
Simon Hatchwell Antiques 81
H J Hatfield and Son 447, 462, 494, 501
Hatherleigh Antiques 162
Roderick Haugh 77
Haughey Antiques 363
Brian Haughton Antiques 90
The Haunted Bookshop 202
Havelocks Pine and Antiques 321
Havenplan Ltd 331
Barry L Hawkins, Downham Market 215
Hawkins & Hawkins, Edinburgh 401
Brian Hawkins Antiques, London 48
Hawkins Brothers Antiques, Barry 392
Philip Hawkins Furniture,
    Shaftesbury 470
Roger Hawkins Restoration, Newark
    449, 509
Hawkridge Books 273
Hawleys 318
Gerard Hawthorn Ltd 90
Hay Antique Market 251
Hay Cinema Bookshop 251
Hay on Wye Booksellers 251
Roland Haycraft 455, 476
Robin Haydock Rare Textiles 73
Jeanette Hayhurst 99
Hayman & Hayman 73
Roger Haynes Antique Finder 297
Anthony Hazeldine Oriental
    Carpets 241

Hazel's 398
Headrow Antiques 337
Heads 'n' Tails 507
Heanor Antiques Centre 275
Heape's 186
Hearth & Home 18
Mike Heath Antiques, Newport 130
Heath-Bullocks, Godalming 137
Heathcote Antiques 334
John Heather 229
Heathfield Antiques 216
Hedgecoe & Freeland Ltd 465, 510
Hedingham Antiques 211
Hedleys Humpers, London 498
Hedley's of Hexham 348
Stuart Heggie 30
Heirloom & Howard Ltd,
    West Yatton 200
Heirloom Antiques, Chichester 145
Heirloom Antiques, Rye 24
Heirlooms, Worcester 314
Heirlooms Antique Jewellers &
    Silversmiths, Wareham 179
Helena's Collectables 140
Helga's Antiques 429
Helios and Co, Weedon 284
Helios Gallery, Bath 181
Helmsley Antiquarian & Secondhand
    Books 322
The Helston Bookworm 152
Hemswell Antique Centres 340
Hencotes Books and Prints 348
Henderson– Dark Antiques Ltd 405
Thomas Heneage Art Books 68
Henfield Antiques and Home 146
Martin Henham 53
Henley Antique Centre 264
Henley Antiques & Collectables
    Centre 301
Henley Street Antique Centre 303
Hera Antiques 393
Marcelline Herald Antiques 116
Heraldry Today 198
Hereford Antique Centre 252
Hereford House Interiors,
    Billingshurst 143
Hereford Map Centre Ltd 252
Hereward Books 204
Peter Herington Antiquarian
    Bookseller 73
Heritage Antique Centre,
    Berkhamsted 255
Heritage Antiques, Chichester 145
Heritage Antiques, Margate 36
Heritage Antiques, Wem 480
Heritage Books, Ryde 131
Heritage Reclamation, Hemel
    Hempstead 256
Heritage Reclamations,
    Sproughton 228
Herman & Wilkinson 434
Hermitage Antiques, Honiton 164
Hermitage Antiques PLC, LOndon 68
H W Heron & Son Ltd 300
The Herts & Essex Antique Centre 258
Heskin Hall Antiques 372
Alan Hessel 477
Hexham and Northern Mart 348
Hexham Antiques 348

Heywood Antiques 366
G Heywood Hill Ltd, London 90
David Hick Antiques, Carrefour
　Selous 417
David Hick Antiques, St Helier 417
Jan Hicks, Hungerford 521
Jan Hicks Antiques, Fifield 117
Jan Hicks Antiques, Tetbury 248
Jenny Hicks Beach, London 82
Richard Higgins Conservation Ltd,
　Longnor 480, 453, 513
The Higgins Press, Lostwithiel 153
High Peak Antiques, Bamford 272
High Street Antiques, Bisley 237
High Street Antiques, Pittenweem 405
High Street Antiques, Solihull 308
High Street Books, Honiton 164
High Street Retro Centre, Hastings 19
Andrew Hilditch & Son Ltd,
　Sandbach 359
Hilditch Auctioneers, Malmesbury 196
Claudia Hill, Beaconsfield 234
David Hill, Kirkby Stephen 363
Frank Hill & Son, Patrington 318
Derek Hill Antiques, Macclesfield 358
G A Hill Antiques, Brasted 29
Hill Farm Antiques,
　Leckhampstead 118
Hill House Antiques & Decorative
　Arts, London 73
Brian L Hills 271
P J Hilton Books 110
Hinchinbrooke Fairs 521
Nigel Hindley 77
Hingstons of Wilton 200
David Hinton Antiques, Rotherfield 23
T C Hinton 459, 500
Robert Hirschhorn 62
Hirsh London 49, 91
Hirst Antiques 105
Erna Hiscock 105
Hitchcox's Antiques 262
The Hive 202
Appley Hoare Antiques, London 68
Peter Hoare Antiques, Tunbridge
　Wells 43
Stuart Hobbs Antique Furniture
　Restoration, Horley 451, 465
John Hobbs Ltd, London 68
Hobbs Parker, Ashford 27
Hobday Toys 235
Keith Hockin Antiques 245
William Hockley Antiques 148
Philip Hodge Antiques 218
Ian Hodgkins & Co Ltd 246
Christopher Hodsoll Ltd 68
Henry Holden & Son Ltd,
　Longridge 373
Holden Wood Antiques,
　Haslingden 372
Raymond D Holdich 110
Hole in the Wall Antiques 369
Holland & Welsh 457
R F G Hollett & Son 364
Holloway's 260
Holly Farm Antiques 333
Holme Valley Warehouse 335, 505
Brian and Lynn Holmes, London 99
D Holmes, Wadebridge 157

L J Holmes Antique Furniture
　Restoration, Upton Snodsbury 480
Andy Holmes Books, Nottingham 288
Holmes Ltd, London 91
Holmfirth Antiques 335
Holmwood Antiques 141
Michael Holroyd Restorations 485, 513
Holt Antique Centre 216
Holt Antique Gallery 216
Holt's, Wolferton 220
Holyrood Architectural Salvage 401
Home & Colonial Antique Centre 255
Homme de Quimper 343
Tony Honan, Ennis 429
Honan's Antiques, Gort 437
Honeycombe Antiques 223
Honeypot Antiques 137
Honiton Antique Centre 164
Honiton Old Book Shop 164
Honley Antiques & Pine 335
Hope & Glory, London 99
Hope Antiques, Stoke-on-Trent 480
Hopkins Antique Restoration 485
J R Hopper & Co 319
Paul Hopwell Antiques 284
Horncastle Antiques Centre 341
Jonathan Horne 99
Horners Auctioneers, Acle 213
Horners Auctioneers,
　North Walsham 217
Hornsby Furniture Restoration Ltd 462
R Hornsey & Sons, Market
　Weighton 318
Hornsey Auctions Ltd, London 55
Hornsey's of Ripon 325
Horological Workshops 138, 451
Horseshoe Antiques 261
Horsham Bookshop 146
Horton 139
Hotspur Ltd 68
Houghton Antiques 204
The House 1860– 1925 388
The House Hospital 83
Bernard G House Longcase Clocks 192
The House of Christian 122
House of Clocks 230
The House of Edgebaston 306
The House of Elliott 256
House of Mirrors 77
The House That Jack Built 156
House Things Antiques 277
Housepoints 30
John Howard, Woodstock 268
Patrick Howard Antiques, Dublin 434
The Howard Gallery, Dorking 135
Howard's Reclamation, Barnham 143
Howards of Moreton-in-Marsh 243
Christopher Howe Antiques,
　London 68
W A Howe, Poole 176
Ernest Howes, Abbey Dore 250
Howes Bookshop Ltd, Hastings 19
Hoyles Promotions 521
John Hubbard Antique Restoration &
　Conservation, Blakedown 480
Hubbard's Antiques, Ipswich 224
Huddersfield Picture Framing
　Co. 335, 457
Hudson Bay Antiques, Carshalton 132

Hudson Bay Trading Co Antiques,
　London 84
Russell Hudson Upholsterer, Bath 511
Huey's Antique Shop 423
Geoffrey Hugall 232
Eynon Hughes, Carmarthen 379
Michael Hughes, London 73
Val Hughes, Tullamore 488
David Hughes Antiques, Weston-
　super-Mare 193
P J Hughes Antiques, Worcester 314
J Alan Hulme, Waverton 359
John Hulme, Chipping Norton 477
Humberts 237
Mac Humble Antiques, Bradford-on-
　Avon 194
Owen Humble Antiques, Newcastle-
　upon-Tyne 350
Humbleyard Fine Art 105
Dudley Hume 14
Humphrey– Carrasco 68
Humphries Antiques 389
Hungerford Arcade 118
Hungry Ghost 237
Howard Hunt Antiques, Hook 446, 465
Catherine Hunt Oriental Antiques,
　Cheltenham 238
Simon Hunter Antique Maps, Hove 20
Hunters Antiques, Peacehaven 23
Hunters Interiors (Stamford) Ltd,
　Stamford 344, 483
Huntingdon Trading Post 204
Huntington Antiques 357
Huntington Antiques Ltd, Stow-on-
　the-Wold 245
Hunts Pine 329
Anthony Hurst, Woodbridge 229
Edward Hurst Antiques, Coombe
　Bissett 195
Gavin Hussey Antique Restoration
　451, 465
Hutchison Antiques and Interiors 209
F Hutton (Bookbinder) 445
Hyde Antique & Reproduction
　Furniture 473
Hyperion Auction Centre 205
Sheila Hyson 169
Hyson Fairs Ltd 521
Hythe Reupholstery Service 511

I

Ibbett Mosely 40
Ickleton Antiques 211
Icknield Restorations 477
Iconastas Russian Works of Art 68
IDS Valuation Consultants 456
IDS Valuation Consultants 514
Imperial Antiques, Hull 318
Imperial Antiques, Stockport 369
Imperial Upholstery,
　Burton-on-Trent 512
Imrie Antiques & Interiors 410
In My Room 14
In Period Antiques 250
In Retrospect 37
Inch's Books 324
Inchmartine Fine Art 410
Inchmartine Restorations 410, 487

Inchmartine Tool Bazaar 410
Indigo, London 77
Indigo, Maningford Bruce 196
Jeff Ingall 473
D D & A Ingle 288
Inglenook Antiques, Harpole 282
Inglenook Antiques, Northampton 283
Inglenook Antiques, Ramsbury 198
Inglenook Fine Arts, Nantwich 458, 501
Inglenook Fine Arts, Whitchurch
    458, 501
Raymond P Inman 20
Inprint 246
Inside Out 46
Insitu 367
Intercoin 350
Intercol 54
Interiors and Antiques 150
International Furniture
    Exporters Ltd 498
Invicta Bookshop 119
Iona Antiques 99
IPM Promotions 521
Ipsden Woodcraft 477
Ipswich Antiques & Collectables
    Fair 521
Ireland's Own Antiques 438
Irish Art Group 426
Iron Wright 444
Isaac and Ede, London 68
Bruce Isaac, Frome 470
Isabella Antiques, Warminster 200
Isabelline Books, Falmouth 152
It's About Time 213
John Ives 114
Ivy Hall Antiques 440

J

J & A Antiques 387
J & K Fairs 521
J A N Fine Art 100
J C Books 219
J D P Restorations 515
J F F Militaria & Fire Brigade
    Collectables 126
J Fairs 521
J H S Antiques Ltd 270
J N Antiques 257
J S Auctions 261
J W Antiques 369
Jack's 174
A E Jackson, Chesham 235
Allan K L Jackson, Edinburgh 401
Jackson Green & Preston, Grimsby 340
Jackson-Grant Antiques, Teynham 42
Jacob & His Fiery Angel, Padstow 154
Uri Jacobi Oriental Carpet Gallery,
    Chester 355
Lionel Jacobs, Richmond 139
Jacobs and Hunt Fine Art
    Auctioneers, Petersfield 126
Jacobs Antique Centre, Cardiff 393
Jacquart Antiques 424
Jadis Antiques Ltd 181
Jaffray Antiques 197
Jag Applied and Decorative Arts 100
Jaguar Fairs 521
Jamandic Ltd 355

Anthony James & Son Ltd, London 73
Brian James Antiques, Shrewsbury 294
James of St Albans, St Albans 258
Janba Fairs 521
Janic Antiques 300
Japanese Gallery Ltd 51, 100
Jardinique 121
Jarndyce Antiquarian Booksellers 108
JBN Vanos Trading 128
Jean's Military Memories 372
Blair Jeary 445
Jeff's Antiques 387
R W Jeffery, Penzance 154
Jefferys, Lostwithiel 153
Robin Jeffreys, Topsham 169
Roderick Jellicoe 100
Jeremy & Westerman,
    Nottingham 288
Jeremy Ltd, London 69
Jericho Books 265
Jersey Coin Company 417
John Jesse 102
Jessop Classic Photographic 108
Jester Antiques 248
Francis Jevons 64
The Jewel Casket 434
S & H Jewell Ltd 141
Jillings 243
Jiri Books 422, 521
Joan's Antiques 147
C John Ltd 91
Louis Johnson, Morpeth 349
Peter Johnson, Penzance 154
Arthur Johnson & Sons,
    Nottingham 288
Martin D Johnson Antiques,
    Seaford 25
Robert Johnson Coin Co, Stamford 344
Johnson Walker Ltd, London 91
Johnsons Antiques, Castle Cary 187
Johnsons Antiques Ltd, Leek 297
Jonathan Charles Antiques 297
B G Jones 486
Leon Jones, Ludlow 293
R G Jones, Ashford 459, 489
M Jones A'i Fab Antiques,
    Beaumaris 385
Jones and Jacob Ltd, Henley-on-
    Thames 264
Jones & Llewelyn, Llandeilo 380
Christopher Jones Antiques, Flore 282
Christopher Jones Antiques,
    London 77
Jen Jones Antiques, Llanybydder 381
Kevin Jones Antiques, Dublin 434
Peter Jones/PJ2, London 69
Bob Jones Prytherch & Co Ltd,
    Llandeilo 380
Howard Jones, The Silver Shop,
    London 100
Jonkers Ltd 264
James A Jordan, Lichfield 298, 453
Jordans Antique Centre, Hemel
    Hempstead 256
Jordans of Rottingdean 24
John Joseph 91
Journeyman Antique Centre 136
JT's Curios & Antiques 338
Jubilee Antiques, Tottenhill 219

Jubilee Hall Antiques Centre,
    Lechlade 241
Desmond Judd Auctioneers 32
Juke Box World 343
Julian Antiques 146
Junk and Disorderly, Mulbarton 217
The Junk Box, London 63
Junktion Antiques 339
Juro Farm and Garden Antiques 314
J R Jury & Son 477
Just a Second 85
Just Books 157
Just Chairs 514
Just Desks 60
Just Military Ltd 332
George Justice 459

K

K C Antiques 372
K D Antiques 355
K L M & Co 337
M & A Kaae 91
Kaimes Smithy Antiques 401
Kaizen International Ltd 38
Kaleidescope Porcelain and Pottery
    Restorers 449
Stephen Kalms Antiques 110
Kantuta 84, 462, 510
Katharine House Gallery 197
Daniel Katz Ltd 91
Kayes 355
Kear of Kennington Antiques 63
Keel Row Books 351
Mike Keeley 470
Keepence Antiques 393
Keepers Cottage Antique Irish
    Pine 426
Keepsakes 413
R J Keighery 441
H W Keil Ltd, Broadway 311
John Keil Ltd, London 73
Kellow Books 262
Kelly Antiques 427, 487
George Kelsall 367
Kembery Antique Clocks Ltd 181
Peter Kemp, London 100
Kemp Booksellers, Howden 318
Kemps, Westbury-on-Trym 192
Kendal Auction Rooms 362
Kendal Studio Pottery Antiques 362
Adrian Kennedy, Dublin 455
Kennedy Carpets, London 54
Kennedy Wolfenden, Portrush 422
Ken's Paper Collectables 235
Kent Auction Galleries Ltd,
    Folkestone 34
Kent House Antiques,
    Haverfordwest 389
Kentdale Antiques 34
Gerald Kenyon Antiques 434
Kerr & McAlister, Glasgow 407
Norman Kerr, Grange-over-Sands 361
J Kershaw Fine Furniture
    Restoration 485
Keshishian 69
Kessler Ford Antiques 158
Keswick Bookshop 363
Keswick Collectables 363

Carol Ketley Antiques, London 57
Sophie Ketley Antiques, London 73
Roger Keverne Ltd 91
Key Antiques 262
Keymer Son & Co Ltd 29
Keys 213
Keystone Antiques 277
Kibworth Exhibitions Ltd 521
Kibworth Pine Co 277
Kidderminster Antique Centre 312
Kidderminster Market Auctions 312
George Kidner 125
Kidwelly Antiques 380
Satch Kiely 439
Kilgarvan Antique Centre 440
Killin Gallery 410
Kilmalcolm Antiques 412
Kilnsea Antiques 318
Kim's Bookshop 145
Kimber & Son 312
King & Eastland Upholsterers, Horsham 511
Ann King Antique Clothes, Bath 181
John King, London 69
John King, Much Wenlock 293
Margaret King, Wymondham 220
Roger King Antiques, Hungerford 118
H & H King Ltd, Carlisle 361
King Street Antiques, Knutsford 357
King Street Antiques, Southport 377
King Street Curios, Melksham 197
Kings Antiques, Southsea 128
Kings Cottage Antiques, Leamington Spa 302
King's Court Galleries, Dorking 135
King's Court Galleries, LOndon 77
Kings Gallery, Canterbury 30, 455, 458, 507
Kings Mill Antique Centre, Harle Syke 372
Kings of Loughborough 480
Kingsley & Co, Barnard Castle 346
Kingsley Auctions Ltd, Hoylake 375
The Kingston Antiques Centre 138
Kingsway House Antiques 164
Kington Antiques 252
Graham Kirkland 78
Robert Kirkman Ltd 231
Jane Kirsopp-Reed Antiques 349
Kirton Antiques 342
Kitch22 130
Kleanthous Antiques Ltd 105
Robert Kleiner & Co Ltd 456
Philip Knighton (The Gramophone Man) 491
Knights Sporting Auctions 218
Knightsbridge Coins 69
Knole Barometers 189
Bertram Knoller 139
Knutsford Antique Centre 357
Kolekt 337
Koopman Rare Art (London) Ltd 110
Kopper Kettle Furniture 370
L & E Kreckovic 78
Krypton Komics 56
Kuwahara Ltd 498
Kyrios Books 285

L P Furniture 309
Laburnum Antiques & Interiors 177
The Lacquer Chest 100
Lacy Scott & Knight 221
Ladyswell Antiques & Jewellery 441
Lake Antiques, Sandown 131
Lakeland Architectural Antiques, Kendal 362
Lakes Craft & Antiques Gallery, Grasmere 362
Roger Lamb Antiques and Works of Art, Stow-on-the-Wold 245
The Lamb Arcade, Wallingford 267
Raymond Lambert, Woodbridge 229
Lambert and Foster, Tenterden 41
Dorrian Lamberts, Lincoln 342
Lambrays 157
Lamont Antiques Ltd 63
The Lamp Gallery 140
Lamplite Antiques 392
Lancastrian Antiques 373
David M Lancefield Antiques 40
Rupert Landen Antiques 119
W H Lane & Son, Fine Art Auctioneers and Valuers, Penzance 154
Lane Antiques, Stockbridge 128
Russell Lane Antiques, Warwick 304
The Lanes Armoury, Brighton 14
Philip Laney 312
Langford Antiques, Southsea 128
J & R Langford, Llangollen 383
Langfords, London 110
Langfords Marine Antiques, London 81
Marion Langham 425
Langton's Antiques & Collectables 332
Lankester Antiques & Books 211
M & R Lankshear Antiques 175
Lannowe Oriental Textiles 446, 507
Lansdown Antiques 248
The Lantern Shop Gallery 167
Lantiques 148
LAPADA 521
Roger Lascelles Clocks 85
Judith Lassalle 51
LASSCO Flooring 61
LASSCO RBK 61
LASSCO St Michael's 49
LASSCO Warehouse 80
The Last Century Antiques 413
Latchford Antiques 238
Laurel Bank Antiques 329
Laurens Antiques 46
John Laurie Antiques Ltd, London 51
Lauries Antiques, Bognor Regis 144
Lavender and Linen, Langenhoe 209
D S Lavender Antiques Ltd, London 91
Joseph Lavian 54
Law Fine Art Ltd 115
C & N Lawrence, Horley 499
J Lawrence, Bakewell 271
F G Lawrence and Son, Redhill 139
Lawrence Books, Newark 286
Lawrence Fine Art Auctioneers Ltd, Crewkerne 188
Bob Lawrence Gallery, London 69

Robert Lawrence-Jones, Stroud 477
Lawrences Auctioneers Ltd, Bletchingley 132
Peter Lawrenson 485
E M Lawson and Co, East Hagbourne 264
Alan Lawson & Son, Edinburgh 402
Keith Lawson Antique Clocks, Scratby 219
Lawton's Antiques 34
David Lays 154
S Layt 473
David Lazarus Antiques 124
Peter Le Vesconte Collectables 417
Andrew & Philip Leach 512
Leather Conservation Centre 455, 493, 509
Lechlade Arcade 242
Lechmere Antiquarian Books 312
Ledger Brothers 369
Leek Antiques Centre (Barclay House) 297
Bob Lees, Oldham 368
M Lees & Son, Worcester 315
E C Legg and Son, Cirencester 477
Legg of Dorchester, Bere Regis 171
Leicester Antiques Warehouse 278
The Leicester Antiques Warehouse 280
Leiston Trading Post 225
Bart and Julie Lemmy 169
The Lemon Tree 357
Lennard Antiques 212
Lennox Auctions and Valuers 421, 514
Leoframes 14
Leolinda 51
Leominster Antique Centre 253
Leominster Antique Market 253
Leominster Clock Repairs 253, 453
Leons Militaria 51
Le-Potier 206
Les and Gary's 213
Nat Leslie Ltd 111
Lev Antiques Ltd 100
M P Levene Ltd 79
Levenshulme Antiques Village 367
Leona Levine Silver Specialist 218
Lewes Antique Centre 22
Lewes Book Centre 22
Lewes Flea Market 22
John Lewis, Saltaire 338
M & D Lewis, London 105
Lewis Antiques & Interiors, Warminster 200
Allen Lewis Fairs, Broadstone 521
Michael Lewis Gallery, Bruton 186
Michael & Amanda Lewis Oriental Carpets and Rugs, Wellington 192, 446
Simon Lewis Transport Books, Coleford 240
David C E Lewry 456, 465
Leyburn Antiques Centre 323
Libra Antiques 100
Libritz Stamps 256
James S T Liddle 397
Lights, Camera, Action 288
R R Limb Antiques 286
Limited Editions 358

GENERAL INDEX

M

Lincoln Restorations 480
Lincolnshire Antiques and Fine Art 345
Linda's Antiques 430
Linden & Co (Antiques) Ltd,
London 111
Linden Antique Prints, Westerham 45
Linden House Antiques,
Leominster 254
Linden House Antiques, Stansted
Mountfitchet 212
Peter Linden Oriental Rugs and
Carpets, Blackrock 432
Lindfield Galleries 146
Lindsay Architectural Antiques,
Birmingham 306
Lindsay Court Architectural,
Horncastle 341
R Lindsell 460
Lindsey Antiques 399
Andrew Lineham Fine Glass 105
Linen & Lace 335
Lion Fine Arts & Books,
Hay-on-Wye 251
Lion House Antiques Ltd,
Burstall 206
Lion Street Books, Hay-on-Wye 251
Michael Lipitch Ltd, London 91, 456
Peter Lipitch Ltd, London 73
Sanda Lipton 91
Liscious Interiors 266
Lisseters Antiques 260
Lister Haigh 319
Lita Kaye Antiques 125
Gordon Litherland 296
Lithgow Sons & Partners 327
David Litt Antiques 230
Roger Little Antique Pottery 266
The Little Gem 295
Little Paws 293
Little River Oriental Antiques 74
The Little Shop 25
Little Theatre Antiques Centre 351
Liverpool Militaria 376
Neil Livingstone 398
Llanelli Antiques 381
Llanishen Antiques 393
Llewellyn Clocks 454
Lloyd Herbert & Jones 381
Walter Lloyd Jones, Barmouth 385
Walter Lloyd Jones Saleroom,
Barmouth 385
David Lloyd, Cheadle Hulme 366
John Lloyd, Ditchling Common
465, 509
Lloyds International Auction Galleries
Ltd, London 85
Clive Loader Restorations 477
Lochyran Furniture Stores 399
Lock & Key Centre 494
Lockdale Coins Ltd, Ipswich 224
Lockdale Coins Ltd, Lowestoft 226
Locke & England 302
Lockson Services Ltd 499
Lodge and Thomas 157
Lomas Pigeon & Co Ltd 473, 511
Lomax Antiques Fairs 522
London Antique Gallery 100
London Cigarette Card Company Ltd,
Somerton 191

London House Antique Centre,
Moreton-in-Marsh 243
London House Antiques,
Westerham 45
London Map Fairs 522
London Road Antiques, Edinburgh 402
London Road Emporium, Glasgow 407
London Stone Conservation 455, 504
Lonesome Pine Antiques 371
Stephen Long, London 81
G Long Antiques, Levenshulme 367
Michael D Long Ltd, Nottingham 288
Long Melford Antiques Centre 225
Timothy Long Restoration,
Sevenoaks 460
Long Street Antiques, Tetbury 248
Long Sutton Antique and Craft
Centre 342
Michael Longmore and Trianon
Antiques Ltd 91
R Longstaff & Co 343
Looking Back 161
Looking Glass of Bath 181, 458,
489, 490
The Looking Glass, Bourton-on-the-
Water 237
Robert Loomes Clock Restoration,
Stamford 344, 454
Brian Loomes, Pateley Bridge 324
Carlos Lopez & Son 466
Gordon Loraine Antiques 412
Alan Lord Antiques, Chilham 31
Alan Lord Antiques, Hythe 35
Kelly Lordan 48
Lot 3 Auction Hall,
Lytham St Anne's 373
Lots Furniture, Gifts and Antiques,
Tralee 437
Lots Road Galleries, London 81
Loughborough Antiques Centre 278
Love Lane Antiques, Nantwich 358
J D Love, Edinburgh 402
David Loveday Antiques 81
Lovejoy Antiques 407
Betty Lovell, Topsham 169
D Lovell, Topsham 169
Lovers of Blue and White, Royston
258, 514
Loves Auction Rooms, Perth 411
Lowe and Sons, Chester 355
Charles Lowe & Sons Ltd,
Loughborough 278, 480
Lowestoft Auction Rooms 226
Lucy Forsythe Antiques 426
Ludlow Antique Beds
& Fireplaces 293
Lugley Antiques and Interiors 130
Charles Lumb & Sons Ltd 321
Luna 288
Lunn Antiques Ltd 78, 105
Lush Restoration 466, 511
Alexander Lyall Antiques 225
Lye Antique Furnishings 308
Lyme Regis Antique & Craft
Centre 176
Lymington Antique Centre 125
Lymington Restoration 466, 511
Lyndhurst Antique Centre 126
Lyon & Turnbull 402

M

M & C Cards 241
M & C Stamps 241
M & J Antiques 345
M & M Antiques 343
M & M Restoration 446, 507
M & S Fairs 522
M B G Antiques 286
M G R Exports 186
M J M Antiques 118
M J R Upholstery 511
M K Restorations 477, 491
Macdonalds Restoration 485
Macgregor Auctions 405
Mach Upholstery 507, 513
MacHenry Antiques 422
Mackenzie & Smith 480
Maddermarket Antiques 218
David Maggs 522
Maggs Bros Ltd, London 92
Maggs Shipping Ltd, Liverpool 376
Magic Lantern, Dunecht 397
Magic Lanterns, St Albans 258,
456, 493
Magical Restorations 462
Magnolia House Antiques 168
Magnum Antiques Fairs, 522
Magpie, Hinckley 277
Magpie Antiques, Long Melford 225
The Magpie's Nest, Ringwood 127
Magpies Collectables Gifts &
Antiques, Cliftonville 32
Magus Antiques 60
Mahogany 416
Mah's Antiques 100
Valerie Main Ltd 361
Mair Wilkes Books 405
Maisey Restoration 473
La Maison, Bourne End 234
La Maison, London 47
Peter Maitland 446
Malahide Antique Shop 436
Malcolms No 1 Auctioneers
& Valuers 326
David Malik & Son Ltd 494
The Mall Antiques Arcade 52
Mallams, Bicester 260
Mallams, Cheltenham 238
Mallams, Oxford 266
Mallett & Son (Antiques) Ltd 92
Mallett at Bourdon House Ltd 92
E P Mallory and Son Ltd 182
The Malthouse, Narberth 389
Malthouse Antiques, Bridgnorth 291
Malthouse Antiques, Dorking 135
Malthouse Antiques, Stow-on-the-
Wold 245
Malthouse Antiques (Four Crosses)
Ltd, Four Crosses 391
Malthouse Antiques Centre,
Alcester 301
Malthouse Arcade, Hythe 35
The Malvern Bookshop, Malvern 312
Malvern Studios 480
Malvern Studios, Malvern 312
C and T Mammon 111
Manchester Antique Company,
Stockport 369

Manchester House Antiques, Chipping Norton 262
Caira Mandaglio 106
Mandarin Gallery 37
John R Mann Fine Antique Clocks 360
E and H Manners 100
D J Manning Auctioneers, Valuers & Appraisers 415
Manor Antiques, Adare 438
Manor Antiques, Bournemouth 173
Manor Antiques and Interiors, Wilstead 232
The Manor Bindery Ltd, Southampton 493
Manor Farm Antiques, Pepard 266
Manor Farm Antiques, Standlake 266
Manor House Clocks, Grantham 454
William Mansell, London 450
Mansell Antiques & Collectables, Hoylake 375
F C Manser & Son Ltd 295
Mansfield Antique Centre 286
Mansion House Antiques 485
Mantle Antiques 327
The Map House, London 74
Map World, London 92
Maple Antiques 141
Marcel Cards 256
Marcel Fairs 522
Marcet Books 63
David & Sally March Antiques 185
S Marchant & Son 101
E W Marchpane Ltd 111
Mariad Antiques 74
Marie Antiques 60
Marine, Craven Arms 292
Marine Instruments, Falmouth 152
Mario's Antiques 106
Mark Gallery 96
Market Antiques, Aberdare 387
Market Deeping Antiques & Craft Centre 343
Market Place Antiques Restorations, Bideford 470
Market Row Antiques & Collectables, Saffron Walden 211
Marks Antiques, London 92
Marks Antiques, Jewellers/Pawnbrokers, Oldham 368
The Marlborough Parade Antique Centre 197
Marlborough Rare Books Ltd, London 92
Marlenes 185
Marlow Antiques Centre 235
Edward Marnier Antiques 198
Iain Marr 408
Marrin's Bookshop 35
Marryat Antiques Ltd 140
G E Marsh (Antique Clocks) Ltd 129
Frank R Marshall & Co, Knutsford 357
Marshall Buck and Casson, Bury St Edmunds 221
Tony Martin, Looe 153
Martin & Pole, Wokingham 121
Peter J Martin and Son, Eton 116
Robin Martin Antiques, London 106
Peter Martin Ceramic Restoration, Bideford 448

C J Martin Coins Ltd, London 56
David Martin-Taylor Antiques, London 78
J Martinez Antiques 402
Martlesham Antiques 226
Jeremy Mason 69
Massada Antiques 92
Roy Massingham Antiques 29
Master Gilder 489
Gerald Mathias 74
Mathy's Emporium 319
Matlock Antiques & Collectables 275
Christopher Matthews, Harrogate 321
Andrew A Matthews Restoration, Cambridge 446, 473, 494
Maud's Attic 224
Mauleverer Antiques 319
Matthew Maw 323
Thomas Mawer & Son Ltd 342
Maxey & Son 205
Maxwells of Wilmslow incorporating Dockrees 360
Ann May, London 78
May and Son, Shipton Bellinger 127
Greta May Antiques, Tonbridge 42
Nigel Mayall 480
Mayfair Carpet Gallery Ltd 61, 69
Mayfair Gallery Ltd 92
Mayflower Antiques 106
Mark Maynard 78
McAfee Auctions 419
F J McAvenues & Son 429
McBains Antiques 161
Ann McCarthy 430
McCartneys, Brecon 390
McCartneys, Ludlow 293
McConnell Fine Books 33
Theresa McCullough Ltd 83
Joy McDonald Antiques 83
Stephen McDonnell, Dublin 488
McDonnell's Antique Furniture, Portarlington 438
James E McDougall 348
Vincent McGowan Antiques 432
P J Mcilroy & Son 419
Barry McKay Rare Books, Appleby in Westmorland 360
Alf McKay, Crewkerne 470
McKenna & Co 74
J W McKenzie Ltd 136
McLaren Books, Helensburgh 398
McLarens Furniture, Chester 355
Douglas McLeod Period Frames 458
McMahon's Antiques 432
MCN Antiques 106
McNally Antiques 134
McNaughtan's Bookshop 402
R J McPhee 473
R & G McPherson Antiques 101
McQuade Antiques 412
Robert McTear & Co, Glasgow 407
McTear's, Greenock 412
James McWhirter 81
MD's Auction Ltd 404
MDS Ltd 306
Margaret Mead Antiques 195
Meadow Lamps Gallery 402
Meadowcroft Books 445
Mealy's Ltd 437

Medina Gallery, Barnstaple 159
Medina Gallery, Bideford 160
Megarry's Antiques 209
Melbourne Antiques & Interiors, London 64
Melbourne Hall Furniture, Derby 274
Melbourne Hall Furniture Restorers, Derby 480
Melford Antiques Warehouse 225
Mellors & Kirk 288
Melluish & Davis 444
Melmount Auctions 426
Melnick House Antiques 115
Melton's 92
Memento 136
Memories, Ashburton 158
Memories, London 59
Memories, Rochester 39
Memories, Tenterden 41
Memories, Weedon 284
Memories Antique Centre, Bury 371
Memories Antiques, Bramley 132
Memory Lane, Bognor Regis 144
Memory Lane, Nottingham 288
Memory Lane, Petts Wood 37
Memory Lane Antiques, Great Bookham 137
Memory Lane Antiques, Lower Stondon 232
Memory Lane Antiques, Ripley 276
Memory Lane Antiques, Stourbridge 309
Noel Mercer Antiques 225
Merchant House Antiques, Honiton 164
Merchant House Antiques, Ipswich 224
Mere Antiques 169
Mereside Books 358
Merim Restoration 452
Merlin Antiques 248
Mermaid Vintage 143
M Merritt 462
Metro Retro 52
Mews Antique Emporium, Holt 216
The Mews Antique Market, London 92
Sarah Meysey-Thompson Antiques 229
Giuseppe Miceli 283
Judith Michael, London 57
Michael Coins, London 101
Michael's Boxes, London 92
Mid 20th Century 119
Mid Sussex Auctions Ltd 12
Midas Fairs 522
Middle of the Road 64
Middleham Antiques 324
Middleton Antiques 480
Arthur Middleton Ltd, London 56
Bobbie Middleton, Tetbury 248
Richard Midwinter Antiques 293
Milestone Antiques, Easingwold 320
Milestone Antiques, Lichfield 298
Milford Secondhand Services 137
Mill Antiques, Hull 318
Mill Court Antiques, Seapatrick 425
Mill Farm Antiques, Disley 356
Mill House Antiques, Goudhurst 35

Mill Lane Antiques, Woodford Green 213
S Millard Antiques 182
Millennium Fairs 522
Thomas N Miller Auctioneers, Newcastle-upon-Tyne 351
Miller Services, Seagrave 280
Robert Miller 80
Millers Antiques, Edinburgh 402
Millers Antiques Ltd, Ringwood 127
Millers Antiques of Wooler 349
Timothy Millett Ltd 64
Millgate Antiques 327
Mills Antiques, Cork 430
Mrs Mills' Antiques Etc., Ely 203
Robert Mills Architectural Antiques, Bristol 185
John Milne Auctioneers 396
Mary Milnthorpe & Daughters 326
Milton Antiques & Restoration 171
Frank Milward 119
Mimbridge Antiques and Collectables 133
Mimi Fifi 106
Minchinhampton Architectural Salvage Co 238
The Miner's Lamp 348
Minerva Antiques 63, 97, 462
Ministry of Pine 192
Minster Books 179
Minstergate Bookshop 329
Mint Antiques 24
Mint Arcade 24
Miracle Finishing 477
Miracle Stripping 505
Felix Vink 436
Miscellany Antiques, Malvern 313
Miss Elany, Long Eaton 286
Mistermicawber.Co.Ltd 375
Mrs Mitchell, Coxley 187
Laurence Mitchell Antiques, London 447, 463
Mitchell's Auction Company, Cockermouth 361
Mitchells Lock Antiques, Blackburn 370
Mitofsky Antiques 434
Moat Antiques 360
Modern and Antique Fire Arms 173
Moira 93
Mole Hall Antiques 220
Molloy's Furnishers Ltd 377
Mollycoddles Collectables 19
Alexander von Moltke 69
Mona's Antiques 430
Monarch Antiques 26
George Monger, Stowmarket 455
Mongers Architectural Salvage, Hingham 215
Colin D Monk 101
Monmouthshire County Council 522
Monogram Studios 450
Montpellier Clocks, Cheltenham 238
Montpellier Mews Antique Market, Harrogate 321
Michael Moon 364
Riro D Mooney 203
Eric T Moore, Hitchin 257
Moore, Allen & Innocent, Cirencester 240

Moor Antiques, Ashburton 158
Moor Hall Antiques, Chester 355
John Moore Antiques, Chawston 231
Marcus Moore Antiques, Stanton upon Hine Heath 295
J Moore Restorations, Bedford 477
Walter Moores & Son, Towcester 284
Walter Moores & Son, Woburn 232
Patrick Moorhead Antiques 14
Mora & Upham Antiques 78
More Than Just Furniture 80
More Than Music 17
C S Moreton Antiques 410
William Morey & Son 177
John Morgan and Sons, Belfast 499
Elizabeth Morgan Antiques, Bexhill-on-Sea 13
Robert Morgan Antiques, Semley 177
Morgan's Auctions, Belfast 420
Michel André Morin 52
Patrick & Gillian Morley, Warwick 305
Robert Morley & Co Ltd, London 64
Morphets of Harrogate 321
Ian Morris, Chesterfield 273
J J Morris, Cardigan 381
J J Morris, Fishguard 389
Maureen Morris, Saffron Walden 211
Peter Morris, Bromley 29
A E Morris Books, Bethesda 385
Morris Bricknell, Ross-on-Wye 254
Morris Marshall & Poole, Newtown 392
Malcolm Morrisen, Antique Furniture Restorer 466
Jan Morrison 185
Mortimers, Exeter 162
Mortimers Curios, Leamington Spa 302
David Morton 212
Moseley Emporium 307
Bruce Moss Antiques, Dorking 135
Trevor Moss Antiques, Hemswell 341
C Moss Clocks, Bath 182, 452
Moss End Antiques Centre, Warfield 120
Sydney L Moss Ltd, London 93
Mostly Boxes 116
The Mount Antiques Centre 380
Mount Pleasant Antiques Centre 318
The Movie Shop 218
Moxhams Antiques 194
Moy Antique Pine 426
Moy Antiques 426
Moycullen Village Antiques 437
Moylurg Gallery 434
Mr Punch's Antique Market 177
Robert Mucci 509
Mullaghmore House Enterprises 509
Mullen Bros Auctions 440
Mullock & Madeley 295
Mullucks Wells 208
Mulroys Antiques 349
Munton & Russell 343
Murder & Mayhem 252
Martin Murray Antiques 462
Murray Cards (International) Ltd 59
The Museum of Childhood Memories 386
Musgrave Bickford Antiques 160

Music Room Antiques 232
Mussenden & Sons, GB 173
R N Myers & Son 320
Myriad, Salisbury 198, 505
Myriad Antiques, London 106
Mytton Antiques 290

N

Peter Nahum at the Leicester Galleries 69
Nakota Antiques 19
Nan Leith's Brocanterbury 31
Nanbooks 326
Napier House Antiques 228
Colin Narbeth and Son 111
Narducci Antiques 409
John Nash Antiques and Interiors 252
Nassirzadeh Antiques 101
Nationwide Barometers 502
Naughton's Booksellers 436
Nautical Antique Centre 179
Timothy Naylor Antiques 466
Rod Naylor, Trowbridge 470, 507, 515
Naylor's Auctions, Wainfleet 345
Jeffrey Neal & Lynn Bloom, London 111
Neal Sons & Fletcher, Woodbridge 229
Gillian Neale Antiques, Aylesbury 233
Justin Neales Antiques & Interiors, Alcester 301
Neales Auctioneers, Nottingham 288
Neate Militaria & Antiques 228
Neath Market Curios 394
Andrew Nebbett Antiques 60
Needfull Things Ltd 324
A & A Needham, Buxton 273
K Needham Restoration Ltd, Rowsley 481
Needles Antique Centre 25
C Negrillo Antiques and Jewellery 74
F B Neill 208
Neilsons Ltd 402
Neptune Gallery 434
D M Nesbit & Co 128
Howard Neville 43
The New Cavern Antiques & Collectors' Centre 366
The New Curiosity Shop 55
New England House Antiques 259
New Forest Antique Restoration Ltd 466
New Street Antique and Craft Centre, Plymouth 166
New Street Books, Penzance 154
New, Secondhand & Antiquarian Books 178
Newark Antiques Centre 286
Newark Antiques Warehouse Ltd 287
Newbridge Antiques 392
Newburgh Antiques 405
Newbury Salvage Ltd 119
Newcomen Fairs 522
Newhampton Road Antiques 309
Newhaven Flea Market 23
Mark Newland Enamel Restorer 457, 492
Newmans 188, 470
Newsum Antiques 250

Newtons of Bury 365
John Nicholas Antiques Ltd 81
Rene Nicholls 196
Nichols Antique Centre 332
John Nicholson Fine Art Auctioneers, Fernhurst 137
Nicolson Maps, Largs 409
Nightingale Antiques and Craft Centre 44
Ingrid Nilson 37
Nimbus Antiques 276
Nimmo & Spooner 78
No. One Castlegate Antiques 287
No 24 of Frinton 208
No. 9 Antiques 309
Noah's 188
Noble Antique Fireplaces 430
Nolton Antiques & Fine Art 387
Nooks and Crannies 131
Noonan Antiques 439
John Noott Galleries 311
Norah's Antique Shoppe 120
Peter Norden Antiques 248
Norfolk Antiques 218
Sue Norman, London 74
Michael Norman Antiques, Hove 20
Peter Norman Antiques, Burwell 201, 474
Norman D Landing Militaria, Bournemouth 173
Norris of Blackheath, London 62
Norris of Blackheath, Pett 23, 510
Desmond and Amanda North 33
North Devon Antiques Centre 159
North Laine Antiques & Flea Market 14
North London Auctions 55
North Shropshire Reclamation and Antique Salvage 291
North Wales Antiques 382
North Wilts Exporters 194
Northallerton Auctions Ltd 324
Northcote Road Antiques Market 83
Northern Antiques Co 324
Northern Clock & Watch Fairs 522
Northern Clocks 369
Northfleet Hill Antiques 37
Northiam Antiques 23
Northwich Antiques Centre 358
Norton Heath Antiques & Collectables 207
Norwich Antique Restoration 493
Norwich Auction Rooms 218
Nostalgia, Littleborough 367
Nostalgia, Stockport 369
Not Just Silver 142
Notions Antiquaria, London 111
Notions Antiques Centre, Grantham 340
Nottingham Architectural Antiques & Reclamation 289
Notts Pine 190
Now & Then, Cardiff 393
Now & Then, Dunchurch 301
Now & Then, Edinburgh 402
Now and Then, Hoylake 375
Now & Then, Llanidloes 391
Now & Then Antiques, Selby 326
Number 6, Chinnor 262

Number 19, London 52
Number 20, Chipping Norton 262
Number 38, Topsham 169
Nutley Antiques 23
Simon Nutter and Thomas King-Smith 245

O

O'Briens Antiques 336
Michael O'Connell 488
P J O'Gorman MIPAV Auctioneers 429
Seamas O'Heocha Teoranta 502
O'Keeffe Antiques 355
Louis O'Sullivan 522
O'Sullivan Antiques Ltd 275
G Oakes & Son 365
Oakfield Cabinet Makers 470
Oakland Antiques 420
Oakleigh Leisure 522
Oaks & Partners 161
Oaktree Antiques 278
Oasis 15
Obelisk Antiques 200
R J O'Brien & Son Antiques Ltd 366
Octavia Antiques 148
The Odd Chair Company, Preston 374
The Odd Chair Company, London 81
The Odd Lot Antiques 396
Odeon Lighting 297
Odiham Auction Sales 126
Odin Antiques 15
O'Donnell Antiques 267
Odyssey Fine Arts Ltd 69
Of Special Interest 55
Off the Wall 256
Off World 235
Offa's Dyke Antique Centre 391
Richard Ogden Ltd 93
Old & Gold 347
The Old Aberdeen Bookshop 396
Old Amersham Auctions 233
The Old Bakery Antiques, Woolhampton 121
The Old Bakery Antiques, Wymondham 280
The Old Bakery Antiques Ltd, Wheathampstead 260
Old Bank Antiques, Elham 34
Old Bank Antiques Centre, Bath 182
The Old Barn, Hertford 494
Old Barn Antiques, Compton 134
Old Barn Antiques, Sutton Bridge 345
Old Barn Antiques, Windsor 120
Old Barn Antiques, Sutton Bridge 345
Old Bears 4 U 384
Old Book Shop 309
The Old Brewery Antiques 229
The Old Brig 522
The Old Brigade 283
Old Bus Station Antiques Ltd 281
Old Button Shop 176
Old Chapel Antiques & Collectables Centre 300
The Old Chemist Shop Antique Centre 202
The Old Children's Bookshelf 402
The Old Church Antiques 409
The Old Cinema 97

The Old Clock Shop 44
The Old Coach House 215, 474
Old Colonial 44
The Old Cop Shop 170
The Old Corn Mill Antique Centre 370
Old Corner House Antiques 46
The Old Cornstore Antiques Centre 143
The Old Cottage Antiques 48
The Old Curiosity Shop, Bredbury 365
The Old Curiosity Shop, King's Lynn 216
The Old Curiosity Shop, Sidmouth 167
The Old Custom House 155
Old English Pine 40
Old Field Antiques 336
The Old Forge Antiques, Appledore 27
Old Forge Collectables, Newtownards 424
Old Friendship Antiques 335
The Old Granary Antique Centre 216
The Old Hall Bookshop 281
Old Hat Vintage & Classic Clothing 78
The Old House (Antiques China Glass) Ltd 25
The Old Ironmongers Antiques Centre 242
Old Lodge Farm Antiques 307
The Old Malthouse, Hungerford 118
The Old Maltings Antique Centre, Louth 342
Old Maps 143
Old Merchant's House Antiques Centre & Victorian Tearoom 254
The Old Mill, London 62
Old Mill Antique Centre, Bridgnorth 291
Old Mill Antiques, Ballygawley 426
The Old Mint House 23
Old Mother Hubbard 243
The Old Palace Antiques 153
The Old Pine Shop 205
The Old Rope Works 197
The Old Saddler's Antiques 381
The Old School Antiques, Penryn 154
The Old School Rooms Antiques, Wincanton 193
Old Schoolhouse Auction Rooms, Mallow 432
The Old Shoe Box 254
The Old Shop 436
The Old Steam Bakery 155
The Old Tackle Box 32
Old Talbot Gallery 324
The Old Toll House 315
Old Tools Feel Better! 169
The Old Town Antiques Centre, Eastbourne 17
The Old Town Bookshop, Edinburgh 402
Old Town Hall Antique & Collectors Centre, Needham Market 227
Old Town Hall Antiques, Falmouth 152
The Old Trinket Box 113
The Old Village Clock Shop 130
The Old Warehouse Antiques 355
Old World Trading Co 78

Olde Hoxton Curios 52
Olde Mill Antiques 365
Olden Days 153
Oldfield Gallery 128
Oldnautibits 190
Oldwoods, Bristol 185
Oldwoods Furniture, Bristol 501
Patrick Oliver Antiques,
    Cheltenham 239
Philip Oliver of Knaresborough 454
Olivers, Sudbury 228
Olivers Bookshop, Whitley Bay 352
Olliff's Architectural Antiques 185
Diana O'Mahony Antiques &
    Jewellery 430
Omega Decorative Arts 211
On The Air Ltd 384
On the Hill Antiques 299
Once Removed 273
Once Upon A Time, Truro 157
Once Upon a Time Antiques,
    Ahoghill 419
One Step Back 221
Online Antiques 130
Onslow Auctions Ltd 178
Ooh-La-La 55
Oola Boola Antiques London 65
O'Reillys 435
Orient Expressions Ltd 78
Oriental Antiques Ltd 349
The Orientalist, Bath 182
The Orientalist, London 59
Orientation Antiques 81
Origin Modernism 52
Original Architectural Antiques Co
    Ltd 240
Original Old Pine Furniture 18
Original Vintage Costume Jewellery,
    Bakewell 272
Original Vintage Costume Jewellery,
    Snape 227
Samuel Orr 148
Paul Orssich 80
M G Osborne 226
Osiris 377
Ossowski 69
O'Sullivan Antiques 435
Otford Antique and Collectors
    Centre 37
Othellos 210
O'Toole Antiques & Decorative
    Galleries 439
Otter Antiques, Honiton 164
Otter Antiques, Long Wittenham 265
Ottery Antique Restorers Ltd
    193, 470
Out In The Sticks 211
Out of Time 52
Outhwaite & Litherland 376
Anthony Outred Antiques Ltd 197
Overmantels 83
Ovne Antique Stoves 430
Owlets 35
Oxford Furniture Warehouse 266
Oxford Longcase Clocks 453
Oxford Street Antique Centre 278
P A Oxley Antique Clocks &
    Barometers, Cherhill 194
Laurence Oxley Ltd, Alresford 121

P

P & R Antiques Ltd 224
The Packhouse Antiques Centre 140
Colin Page Antiquarian Books,
    Brighton 15
Page Antiques, Leek 298
Kevin Page Oriental Art Ltd,
    London 52
Painswick Antiques 481
N St J Paint and Sons Ltd 417
Pairs Antiques Ltd 69
Palace Antiques 136
Polly Pallister 106
Dermot & Jill Palmer Antiques 15
Palmers Green Antiques Centre 56
Pandora's Box 171
Pantheon Fairs Ltd 522
Pantiles Antiques, Tunbridge Wells 43
Pantiles Collectables,
    Tunbridge Wells 43
Pantiles Spa Antiques, Tunbridge
    Wells 43
Paper Pleasures 190
Paperchase 231
Barry Papworth 125, 492, 513
Parade Antiques 166
Paraphernalia, Bakewell 272
Paraphernalia, Lostwithiel 153
Paraphernalia, Sheffield 333
Paraphernalia Fairs, Perth 522
Parasol Antiques 417
Michael Parfett 497
Paris Antiques, Ampthill 230
Paris-Art, Leigh-on-Sea 210
Park Antiques, Menston 337, 483
Park Antiques, Trinity 418
Park Hall, Charnock Richard 371
Park House Antiques, Stow-on-the-
    Wold 245
Park Lane Antiques,
    North Walsham 217
Park Lane Restoration, Truro 470
Park View Antiques, Wadhurst 26, 460
Vanessa Parker Rare Books 439
Parkins 133
K A Parkinson Books 377
Parkview Antiques 384, 486
Parkways Antiques 191
Parlour Farm Antiques 240
Ian Parmiter 128
Partners Antiques, Radcliffe 368
Partners in Pine, Coggeshall 207
Timothy Partridge Antiques 17
Parvis 422
Passageway Antiques 143
Passers Buy 383
Passiflora 295
Past & Present, Belfast 420
Past & Present, Bentley 330
Past 'n' Present, Christchurch 175
Past & Present, Edinburgh 403
Past & Present, Hingham 215
Past & Present, Letchworth Garden
    City 257
Past & Present, Okehampton 166
Past and Present, Risby 227
Past & Present Antiques,
    Toombridge 423

Past and Present Fireplaces,
    Clitheroe 371
Past Caring 216
Past Present Toys 56
Past Sentence 41
Pastiche 486
Pastime Antiques & Collectables,
    Christchurch 175
Pastimes, Bristol 185
Pastimes, Sherborne 178
Pastimes Vintage Toys, Glasgow 407
Pastorale Antiques 22
Simon Paterson 451, 466
Paton Books 258
Patricks Antiques 300
Patterson Liddle 182
Pattinsons Galleries, Canterbury 31
Richard Pattison, Newcastle-upon-
    Tyne 484
Alexander Paul Antiques 164
Alexander Paul Restorations 470
M Pauw Ltd 78
Pavilion 18
K S Pawlowski 466
Clive Payne, Kingham 477
George A Payne & Son Ltd,
    Bournemouth 173
Payne and Son (Goldsmiths) Ltd,
    Oxford 266
G Payne Antiques, Nuneaton 302
PDQ Air Freight/Art Move 499
W & H Peacock 231
Peakirk Bookshop 204
Pearman Antiques & Interiors 287
Pearse Lukies Ltd 213
Tom Pearson, Glasgow 407
Sue Pearson Antique Dolls & Teddy
    Bears, Brighton 15
Martyn Pearson Glass,
    Bobbington 491
Pearsons Auction Rooms,
    Andover 121
Peasenhall Art & Antiques
    Gallery 227
Pedlar's Pack Books 171
Sarah Peek 447, 491
Pelham Galleries Ltd 93
Michael Pembery Antiques 272
Pembroke Antiques Centre 389
Pembroke Market Emporium 389
The Pen & Pencil Gallery 364
Pendle Antiques Centre Ltd 374
Pendulum of Mayfair 93
Penistone Pine & Antiques 331
Penlan Pine 386
Penman Antiques Fairs 522
Penman Clockcare 343
Penn Barn 236
Pennard House Antiques 188
Pennies Antiques, Clyst Honiton 160
Pennies Antiques, Exeter 162
Pennies Antiques, Topsham 170
Pennsylvania Pine Company 158
John Penny Antique Services 507
Penny Farthing Antiques,
    Swindon 199
Pennyfarthing Antiques, Boston 339
Pennyfarthing Antiques,
    Dartmouth 161

Pennyfarthing Antiques, Lymington 125
Penrith Farmers' & Kidd's PLC 363
Penybont Farm Antiques 394
Penzance Rare Books 155
R L Peploe 470
Eva-Louise Pepperall 466
Pepys Antiques 27
Percy's Ltd 111
Period Fireplaces 185
Period Furniture Ltd, York 483
Period Furniture Showrooms, Beaconsfield 234
Period Piano Company 28
Period Pine 386
Period Style Lighting 113
Periplus Books 236
Perkins Stockwell and Co Ltd 481
Perry & Phillips, Bridgnorth 291
Charles Perry Restorations Ltd, St Albans 477
Perryhill Antiques 138
Perth Antiques 411
Petals in the Warehouse 126
Paul M Peters, Harrogate 321
Christopher Peters Antiques, Warwick 305
Mark Peters Antiques Ltd, Bury St Edmunds 474
The Petersfield Bookshop 126
Petite Antiques 420
Des Petrie 488
Petworth Antique Centre & Market 148
John M Peyto & Co Ltd 37
Phantique 162
Trevor Philip & Son Ltd, London 70
Philips Traditional Bathrooms, Bobbersmill 285
Phillburys 460
Phillips Antiques and French Polishing, Llandovery 380, 486
Elaine Phillips Antiques Ltd, Harrogate 321
Phillips Brothers, Snitterfield 303
Richard G Phillips Ltd, London 463
Ronald Phillips Ltd, London 93
S J Phillips Ltd, London 93
Phillips of Hitchin Antiques Ltd 257
Phipps & Pritchard 312
Phoenix, Sherborne 178
Phoenix Antiques, Fordham 203
Phoenix Antiques, Tunbridge Wells 44
Phoenix Books, Crewkerne 188
Phoenix Conservation.com, St Clears 486
Phoenix Design & Antiques, Newcastle-upon-Tyne 351
Phoenix Fireplaces, Battlesbridge 206
Phoenix Furniture, Wallingford 267
Phoenix Oriental Art, London 52
Phoenix Trading, Frinton-on-Sea 208
Phoenix Trading Co, London 82
Phoenix Trading Company – South Yorkshire, Bentley 330
Photo Books International 108
Piano Export 186
Pianos Galore 22
Piccadilly Antiques, Bath 182

Piccadilly Rare Books, Ticehurst 26
Picfair Antiques 328
Pickering and Chatto, London 93
Pickering Antique Centre 324
Pickering Antique Centre (Hawthorn House Antiques) 325
Graham Pickett Antiques 344
Mr Pickett's 144, 466. 505
Paul Pickford Antiques 275
David Pickup 261
Pickwick Gallery 303
Pieces of Time 93
Piers Furniture Repair Workshop 463
Pig & Whistle Promotions 523
The Pig Sty 20
Piggeries Pine 259
Pilgrim Antiques, Honiton 164
Pilgrim Antiques Centre, Ampthill 230
Pilgrim's Progress, Liverpool 376, 485, 513
Pilgrims Antique Centre, Dorking 135
Pilgrims Antiques Centre, Gainsborough 339
Pillars Antiques 196
Pine & Period Furniture, Grampound 152
Pine and Things, Shipston-on-Stour 303
Pine Antiques, Olney 236
The Pine Barn, Crawley 122
The Pine Cellars, Winchester 129
Pine for Pine Antiques, St Saviour 418
The Pine Furniture Store, Watford 259
The Pine Mine, London 501
A Pine Romance, London 55
Pine Workshop, Hexham 348
Pine-Apple Antiques, Hull 318
Pineapple House, Alresford 121
W A Pinn & Sons 212
Pipkins Antiques 372
Piers Pisani Ltd Antiques 178, 470
Nicholas S Pitcher Oriental Art 93
Marco Pitt 460
Places and Spaces 75
Planet Bazaar 49
Plestor Barn Antiques 125
Plowden and Smith Ltd 455, 463, 501, 504
Albert Plumb Furniture Co 466
Plumridge Antiques 131
Plymouth Auction Rooms 160
Plympton Antiques 164
The Pocket Bookshop 166
Pod Interior Style 125
A G Podmore & Son 483
The Poison Dwarf 289
Pokesdown Antique Centre 173
Patrick Pollak Rare Books 167
Nathan Polley Antique Restoration 477
Polly's Parlour 197
Polmorla Bookshop 158
Poloantiques 70
Polonaise Gallery 80
Alan J Ponsford Antique Restorations 478
Pontypridd Auctions Ltd 387

Pooks Transport Bookshop 280
Pool Auctions 155
Poole Pottery China Matching Service 173
Poor Richard's Books 223
Pop Antiques 233
Tony Popek Antiques 327
Popes Farm Antique Pine & Stripping 26, 505
Porcelain Repairs Ltd 450
Porch House Antiques 248
Porchester Antiques 186
Porcupine 357
Henry Pordes Books Ltd 111
Porlock Antiques and Gallery Ltd 190
Portcullis Furniture 391
R E Porter 173
Portland Antiques & Curios, West Bridgford 289
Portland Books, Leamington Spa 302
Portland House Antiques, Market Deeping 343
Portland House Antiques and Collectables, Honiton 165
Portobello Antique Store 106
Portobello Studios 106
Post House Antiques 132
D Potashnick 466
Potter Antiques, Portslade 460
Jonathan Potter Ltd, London 93
Nick Potter Ltd, London 94
Potteries Antique Centre, Stoke-on-Trent 299
Potteries Specialist Auctions, Stoke-on-Trent 300
Potterton Books 326
The Pottery & Porcelain Restoration Co, Sowerby Bridge 449
Pottery Bank Antiques, Morpeth 349
The Pottery Buying Centre, Basford 295
Ludovic Potts Antiques 203, 474, 511
H W Poulter & Son 82
Richard S Powell Antique Restorer & Cabinet Maker, Devizes 471
Sylvia Powell Decorative Arts, London 58
R J Poynter 478
George Pragnell The Jeweller 303
J N Preedy 494
Pre-empt Events 523
John Prestige Antiques 160
Preston Antiques Centre 374
Antony Preston Antiques, Stow-on-the-Wold 245
Christopher Preston Ltd, London 82
Prestwood Antiques 270
Graham Price Antiques Ltd 20
Prichard Antiques 250
W D Priddy Antiques, Chichester Furniture Warehouse 145
Pride & Joy Antiques 186
Priestley and Ferraro 70
Priestpopple Books 349
Princess Antique Centre 295
Principia Fine Art 118
Priors Reclamation 292
Priory Antiques, Whithorn 399

Priory Antiques & Collectables, Orpington 37
Priory Books, Malvern 313
Pritchard & Partners, Brecon 390
Edward Pritchard Antiques & 20thC Furniture, Market Harborough 279
Promenade Antiques & Books 313
Prospect Books, Llanrwst 383
Prospect Promotions, St Helens 523
Proudfoot Antiques 237
Provincial Booksellers Fairs Association 523
Pruskin Galleries 101
Prust & Sons Antique Furniture 213, 474
Pub Paraphernalia UK Ltd 64
H J Pugh and Co, Ledbury 253
Ian K Pugh Books, Pershore 313
Pugh's Antiques, Monkton 165
Pullman Gallery Ltd 70, 94
The Pumping Station 393
The Neville Pundole Gallery 31
Punzi 22
Puritan Values at the Dome 227
The Purple Antique Shop Centre 301
Doug Pye, Bakewell 272
John Pye & Sons Ltd, Nottingham 289
Robert Pye Antiques Restoration & Conservation of Fine Period Furniture, Bridgwater 455, 471

Q

Q & C Militaria 239
Q S Antiques and Cabinetmakers 399
Q W Conservation 447, 455, 504, 515
Quality Furniture Warehouse 58
Bernard Quaritch Ltd 94
Quarrelwood Art & Antiques 398
Quay Antiques & Collectables, Rye 25
The Quay Centre, Topsham 170
Quay Court Antiques, St Ives 205
The Quay Gallery Antiques Emporium, Exeter 162
Quayside Antiques, Rye 25
Quayside Antiques, Shrewsbury 295
Queen Street Antique Centre 146
The Queen's Shilling 497
The Quest Antiques 347
Ann Quested Antiques 175
Martin Quick Antiques 291
Quicktest 259
Quiet Street Antiques, Bath 182
The Quiet Woman Antiques Centre, Chipping Norton 263
Quill Antiques 33
Quillon Antiques of Tetsworth 266
Liz Quilter 233
Quinneys of Warwick 305
Quinto Bookshop 111
Quorn Pine 280

R

R & J Coins 212
R M Antiques 339
R M W Restorations 463
R S M Antique Restoration 454, 485, 495

Radio Days 61
Radnedge Architectural Antiques 381
Radnor House Antiques 152
Raffety & Walwyn Ltd 101
Jim Railton 348
Rainbow Antiques, London 78
Rainbow Books, Brighton 15
Harry Raine 346
Rait Village Antiques Centre 412
Rams Head Antiques 347
Alan Ramsey Antiques 327
Randolph Antiques 223
Randtiques 120
Piers Rankin, London 52
George Rankin Coin Co Ltd, London 47
Rankin Conn Oriental Antiques, London 78
Mark Ransom Ltd 70
Rare Books & Berry 190
Rare Jewellery Collections Ltd 94
Rathmines Bookshop 35
Ravensdale Studios 449
Paul Rawcliffe Upholstery Services 513
Rawlinsons 173
Ray & Scott Ltd, St Sampsons 417
Janette Ray Rare Books, York 329
Derek & Tina Rayment Antiques 354
Michael Rayner Bookseller 239
Alan Read, Horncastle 341
Paul M Read Antique Furniture Restoration, Sevenoaks 450, 460
Mike Read Antique Sciences, Lelant 153
Reading Collectors Centre 119
Recollect The Dolls Hospital, Burgess Hill 144, 508
Recollections, Poynton 359
Re-Collections, Todmorden 375
Recollections Antiques, London 58
Record Detector 47
The Red House Antiques Centre, York 329
Red House Glasscrafts, Stourbridge 491
Red Lion Antiques, Petworth 148
Red Lion Antiques Market, London 106
The Red Teapot Arcade 106
Reed & Son, Saffron Walden 211
John Reed and Son Upholsterers, Kettering 481, 512
Vincent Reed Furniture, Hassocks 145, 466
Reel Poster Gallery 97
Reeman Dansie 207
Reeves & Son, Hastings 19
Reeves Restoration at The Coach House Antiques, Gomshall 451, 467
Paul Reeves 101
Reference Works Ltd 448
David M Regan 377
Regency Antiques, Billingshurst 447, 467
Regency Furniture Restoration, Halesowen 481
Regency Restoration, London 463, 489, 501

Regent Antiques 54
Reigate Galleries 139
Reindeer Antiques Ltd, London 101
Reindeer Antiques Ltd, Potterspury 283
Relic Antiques, London 79
The Relic Antiques Trade Warehouse, London 57
Relics, Glasgow 407
Relics, Wadebridge 158
Reg & Philip Remington 258
Renaissance, Croydon 458, 467
Renaissance, Sherborne 178
Renaissance Antiques, Solihull 481
Renaissance China Restoration, Edinburgh 450
Rendells 158
Rendezvous Gallery Ltd 396
Renishaw Antique & Pine Centre 333
Rennies Seaside Modern 108
A Restoration Centre, Dublin 488
The Restoration Studio, London 507
Restore, Thames Ditton 467
Restore-It (Folkestone) Ltd 460
Retrobuy 278
Retrouvius Architectural Reclamation 61
Revival, Accrington 370
Revival, Bath 471
Revival, Bradford-on-Avon 194
Revival, Keighley 336
C H & D M Reynolds 325
Isobel Rhodes, Woodbridge 229
Peter Rhodes Books, Southampton 127
Rhos Point Books 383
Ribble Reclamation 374
Richard Anthony Rush Antiques 474
David Richards & Sons, London 94
Richard's Polishing, Clacton on Sea 474
T N Richards, Chester 485
T N Richards, Llanbedr 486
Richards Son & Murdoch, Redruth 155
Gordon Richardson, Edinburgh 455, 502
Roderick Richardson, King's Lynn 217
Richardson Antiques Ltd, Leek 298
Richmond Antique Mirrors, Bowdon 365
Richmond Galleries, Chester 355
Richmond Hill Antiques 140
Ridgeway Antiques 213
J and M Riley 146
R J H Rimmel 485
Rimmer Restoration 494
Ringstead Village Antique & Collectors Centre 219
Rin-Tin-Tin 15
Ripping Yarns 55
The Risby Barn Antique Centre 227
A & R Ritchie 417
Riverbank Gallery Ltd, Petworth 148
Riverside Antiques, Stratford-upon-Avon 303
Riverside Antiques Centre, Sawbridgeworth 258
Sue Rivett Antiques 215

Roadside Antiques 362
Robert's Rumble, Hastings 19
Roberts & Mudd Antiques, Leek 298
Robert's Antiques, St Helier 418, 474, 512
Tyrone R Roberts, Dereham 214
Derek Roberts Antiques, Tonbridge 42
Douglas Roberts Antiques, Chorleywood 256
Stephen Roberts (Auctioneer) Ltd, Watton 219
Leon Robertson Antiques 154
John Robinson Antiques, Wigan 369
Robinson Restorations, Caterham 467
Robinsons Timber Building Supplies Ltd, Blackpool 370
Robson's Antiques 346
Rocking Chair Antiques, Warrington 359
Rocking Horse Antique Market, Ardingly 142
Rocking Horse Elite, South Woodham Ferrers 212
Rococo Antiques & Interiors 284
Roderick Antique Clocks 101
John Roe Antiques 282
Rogers & Co, London 79
Rogers Antiques Gallery, London 107
Rogers de Rin, London 74
Rogers Jones & Co, Colwyn Bay 382
Rogers Turner Books, London 63
Roland Gallery, Bath 182
Rolands Antiques, Thurnby 498
Chris Rollason Home Counties Medal Services 497
Brian Rolleston Antiques Ltd 101
John Rolph 226
Roman Painted House 33
Romantiques, Redruth 155
Romantiques Antique Centre, Froncysyllte 383
de Romes 334
Romiley Antiques & Jewellery 368
Ronsons 244
Rose Antique Restoration, Princes Risborough 449
Rose Antiques, Ashbourne 270
Rosebery Fine Art Ltd 65
Rosemary & Time 267
Rose's Books 252
Rosina Antiques 120
John Ross & Company, Belfast 421
Charles Ross Fine Art Auctioneers, Woburn 232
Ross Fireplaces, Levenshulme 367
Ross Old Books and Print Shop, Ross-on-Wye 254
Tim Ross-Bain 481
Rossi & Rossi Ltd 94
Ross-on-Wye Antique Gallery 255
Rostellan Antiques Ltd 432
Bertram Rota Ltd 111
Rother Reclamation 35
Colin de Rouffignac 369
Roundstone Books 371
H Rowan, Bournemouth 173
P & B Rowan, Belfast 421

Rowan Antiques & Collectables, Ballater 396
Mark Rowan Antiques, Llanwrda 381
S H Rowland, Chelmsford 207
Michael Rowland Antiques, Stow-on-the-Wold 245
Rowley Fine Art 203
Royal Arcade, Southport 377
Royal Mile Curios, Edinburgh 403
Royal Mile Gallery, Edinburgh 403
Royal Standard Antiques, Cowes 130
E & C Royall 497
RSB Antiques, Deal 33, 458, 501
Ruegavarret Ltd 206
The Rug Gallery, Leicester 278
The Rug Studio, London 54, 502
Rugeley Antique Centre 299
Rule's Antiques 120
Simon & Penny Rumble Antiques 203
Rumours Decorative Arts 52
Ruperts of Rothbury 349
Mr Richard Anthony Rush Antiques 224
Ruskin Decorative Arts 245
Russell Rare Books, London 74
Russell Scientific Instruments Ltd, Dereham 502
Nicky Russell, Topsham 170
R Rutherford, Glasgow 407
Marlene Rutherford Antiques, Chesterfield 274
Rutherford Interiors, Consett 347
Rutland Antiques Centre, U 290
Philip A Ruttleigh Antiques, Crudwell 195, 471
RWG Auctions 389
Ryde Antiques 131
Rye Auction Galleries 25
Rye Old Books 25

S

S & J Antiques 309
S M Upholstery Ltd 513
S W Antiques 313
Sabera Trading Oriental Carpets & Rugs 58
Sabre Sales 128
Jane Sacchi Linens Ltd 82
F B Sadowski 471
Michael Saffell Antiques 182
Saffron Walden Antiques Centre 211
Saffron Walden Auctions 211
Sage Antiques & Interiors 140
Sainsburys Antiques Ltd 173
Saintfield Antiques & Fine Books 425
Salisbury Antiques Market 199
Salisbury Antiques Warehouse Ltd 199
Salisbury Stripping Co 505
N P and A Salt Antiques 333
F D Salter, Clare 222
Nicholas Salter Antiques, London 48
Salters Bookshelf 'The Bookshelf at the Top', Kingsbridge 165
Saltney Restoration Services 355
The Salvage Shop 441
Salvo 444
Samarkand Galleries 403

Sambourne House Antique Pine Ltd, Cardiff 393
Sambourne House Antique Pine Ltd, Swindon 199
Anthony Sampson, Dulverton 188
Alistair Sampson Antiques Ltd, London 94
Samson's Joinery & Antiques, Glasgow 407
Patrick Sandberg Antiques 101
Sandby Fine Art 54
Sanders of Oxford 266
Sandgate Passage 40
Sandycove Fine Arts 436
Sandy's Antiques 174
Santos 102
Saracen Antiques Ltd 458, 478, 512
Sarah Rose Antiques 425
Saratoga Trunk Yesteryear Costume & Textiles 407
Sargeant Restorations 494
K J Sarginson Fine Furniture 483
Sasha 228
Christopher Saunders, Newnham 243
Charles Saunders Antiques, London 74
Keith A Savage 227
G J Saville 335
Vigi Sawdon 458, 490, 495
Saxon Cross Antiques Emporium 359
David A Sayer Antique Furniture Restorer 467
Scarborough Perry Fine Arts 20
Scarlett Antiques 272
Scarthingwell Auction Centre 327
Christine Schell 74
Schoolhouse Antiques, Chipping Camden 239
Schoolhouse Antiques, Mallow 432
T Schotte Antiques 227
Manfred Schotten Antiques 261
Schredds of Portobello 107
Michael Schryver Antiques 467
Schull Books 429
Scotfairs 523
Francis Scott, Driffield 317
James Scott, Edinburgh 403
Richard Scott Antiques, Holt 216
Sarah Scott Antiques, Sheffield 333
Scottish Antique and Art Centre, Abernyte 409
Scottish Antique and Arts Centre, Doune 414
B Scott-Spencer 370
Sea View Antiques 386
Seabourne Mailpack Worldwide Ltd 499
Mark Seabrook Antiques, Kimbolton 204
Seabrook Antiques, Glemsford 223
Seaby Antiquities 94
Seaford House Antiques 243
Arthur Seager Antiques 246
Sealcraft 481
Sealey Furnishings 488, 514
M G Seaman & Daughter 302
Seaquel Antiques & Collectors Market 18
Searle & Co Ltd 49

Sears 463
Seaview Antiques 341
Second Edition, Edinburgh 403
Second Notions Antiques, Dysart 404
Second Time Around, Hemswell 341
Second Time Around, Hornsea 317
Second Time Around, Chester 355
Second Time Around, Chester 356
Second Treasures, Folkestone 35
Secondhand & Rare Books,
    Manchester 367
The Second-Hand Bookshop,
    Oxted 139
Secondhand Department,
    Broadstairs 29
Secondhand Land, Ash 122
Joel Segal Books 170
M & D Seligman 58
Sellingantiques.co.uk 515
Selskar Antiques 441
Selwoods Antiques 191
Semley Auctioneers 177
Serendipity, Deal 33
Serendipity, Ledbury 253
Serendipity Antiques,
    Huddersfield 336
Philip Serrell Auctioneers & Valuers,
    Malvern 313
Philip Serrell Auctioneers & Valuers,
    Worcester 315
Seventeen Antiques 376, 485
Seventh Heaven 383
Esther Sexton Antiques 435
The Shambles 158
Shanklin Auction Rooms 131
Shanxi Ltd 80
Bernard J Shapero Rare Books 94
Shapes Fine Art Auctioneers &
    Valuers 403
Shapiro & Co. 94
Shardlow Antiques 276
Andrew Sharp Antique Restoration
    Ltd, Brockenhurst 467
Ian Sharp Antiques, Tynemouth 352
Shaston Antiques 177
Gerald Shaw, Harrogate 483
John Shaw Antiques Ltd,
    Rotherham 331
Laurence Shaw Antiques,
    Horncastle 342
Nicholas Shaw Antiques,
    Petworth 149
Shawlan Antiques 496
R Shelton 275
C B Sheppard & Son, Sutton-in-
    Ashfield 289
Sheppard Irish Auction House,
    Durrow 438
Sherbrook Selectables 160
Shere Antiques Centre 140
Sherman Upholstery 487, 514
D W Sherwood Ltd 283
Shine's Antiques and Collectables 18
Shiners of Jesmond 351
Catherine Shinn Decorative
    Textiles 239
The Shipping Company 499
Shipwreck Brightlingsea's Antique
    and Collectables Centre 206

Shiraz Antiques 94
Shirley May 272
Shiver Me Timbers 155
G S Shobrook and Co incorporating
    Fieldens 167
D J Short 474
Shortmead Antiques 231
Shrewsbury Antique Centre 295
Shrewsbury Clock Shop 295
The Shrubbery 179
Sidmouth Collectables 167
Sieff 248
Sigma Antiques 325
Silstar Antiques Ltd 111
Silver and Plate Centre, London 52
The Silver Fund Ltd, London 70
The Silver Shop, Dublin 435
B Silverman 102
Silversaddle Antiques 427
Silvesters 28
Michael Sim, Chislehurst 32
Roy Sim Antiques, Blairgowrie 410
Simmons & Miles, Orne, France 509
J C Simmons & Son, Saltburn-by-the-
    Sea 326
Simmons Gallery, London, 523
Jack Simons Antiques Ltd, London 111
Simon's Books, Somerton 191
Suzie Simons, London 79
Simply Oak 231
John Simpson, York 330
Simpsons, Leek 298
Sims Reed Ltd 70
Siracusa Paintings Ltd 501
Sissinghurst Antiques Gallery 40
W Sitch (Antique) Co Ltd 94
Sitting Pretty Antiques 228
Sivyer's 13
Skellgate Curios 325
Sketty Antiques & Gifts 394
Skipton Antiques & Collectors
    Centre 327
Justin F Skrebowski Prints 107
Michael Slade 463
Sleddall Hall Antiques Centre 362
Sleepy Elephant Books & Artefacts 364
Tony Smart Restorations 483
L S Smellie & Sons Ltd 414
Allan Smith, Swindon 199
Anthony Smith, Wolverhampton 481
Clive Smith, Great Dunmow 208
J Smith, York 330
James Smith, Shillingford 478
Royden Smith, Lichfield 298
Smith & Smith Designs (Driffield) Ltd,
    Driffield 317
A H Smith & Son, Purley 511
H A Smith & Son, Harrow 463
David Smith Antiques, Manton 289
Graham Smith Antiques, Newcastle-
    upon-Tyne 351
Peter Smith Antiques,
    Sunderland 352
Keith Smith Books, Ledbury 253
P J Smith (Fair Trades),
    Stewartstown 427
Francis Smith Ltd, London 82
Frank Smith Maritime Aviation
    Books, Newcastle-upon-Tyne 351

John Smith of Alnwick Ltd 348
R J Smith Restoration, Bury St
    Edmunds 474, 512
Iain M Smith Auctioneers & Valuers,
    Scone 412
Smithfield Antiques 391
Smiths the Rink Ltd 322
Smithson Antiques 341
Peta Smyth Antique Textiles 70
Smythes 371
Snap Dragon, London 74
Snapdragon, South Molton 168
Tim Snell Antiques 182
J A Snelson 481
Jeremy Sniders Antiques 407
Snooper's Paradise 15
Snowdonia Antiques 383, 486
The Snug 158
Soames Country Auctioneers 265
Sodbury Antiques 187
R Solaimany 94
Soldiers of Rye 25
Solent Railwayana Auctions 129
Solomon 55, 463, 510
Nicholas Somers & Company
    Chartered Arts and Antiques
    Surveyor 514
Somerton Antique Centre 191
Somervale Antiques 190
Something Different 347
Something Else Antiques 122
Somlo Antiques Ltd 70
Guinevere Sommers-Hill Violins 497
Soo San 79
Sotheby's 95, 514
Sotheby's South 143
Henry Sotheran Ltd 95
Source 182
South Coast Collectables,
    Eastbourne 18
South Street Antiques, Axminster 159
David South, Pateley Bridge 324,
    483, 513
Southdown House Antique
    Galleries 29
Southern Independent
    Auctions Ltd 15
Southgate Auction Rooms 56
Southport Antiques 377
Sheila Southwell Studio 448
Spalding Antiques 343
Graham Sparks Restoration 192, 471
Special Auction Services 119
Specialised Postcard Auctions 240
Specialist Glass Fairs Ltd 523
Spectrum, London 95
Spectrum Fine Jewellery Ltd,
    Battle 12
J K Speed Antique Furniture
    Restoration 454, 483
A and J Speelman Ltd 95
Ken Spelman 330
Martin Spencer-Thomas 162
Simon Spero 102
The Spinning Wheel Antiques 377
Spires Restoration 483
Lorraine Spooner Antiques Ltd 284
Sport and Star Autographs,
    Basildon 205

Sport and Star Autographs,
London 49
Sporting Antiques, Tunbridge
Wells 44
Stephen Sprake Antiques 79
Spread Eagle Antiques 63
Spread Eagle Books 63
Spring Garden Furniture
& Antiques 347
Spurrier-Smith Antiques 270
Squires Antiques, Altrincham 353
Squires Antiques, Faversham 34
The Squirrel Antique & Collectors
Centre, Basingstoke 122
Squirrel Antiques, Chichester 145
Squirrel Antiques, Markinch 405
Squirrels, Brockenhurst 122
St Clements Antiques 266
St Crispin Antiques & Collectors
Centre 316
St Georges Antiques 344
St Giles Old Pine Company 234
St Helens Restoration 486
St James Antiques 313
St James Street Antiques 166
St Julien 322
St Just Bygones 156
St Leonard's Antiques and Craft
Centre 166
St Lucy Wayside Antiques 407
St Martins Antiques Centre 344
St Mary's Books & Prints,
Stamford 344
St Mary's Chapel Antiques,
Devizes 196
St Nicholas Galleries Ltd 361
St Ouen Antiques 257
St Pancras Antiques 145
St Paul's Street Bookshop 344
St Petersburg Collection Ltd 95
St Thomas Antiques 471
Stable Antiques, Pickering 325
Stable Antiques, Storrington 149
Stable Antiques at Houghton 146
The Stable Antiques, Isle of Arran 409
Stable Doors, Hailsham 18
Stablegate Antiques 27
The Stables, Long Melford 226
The Stables Antique Centre,
Hatton 301
John Stacey & Sons 210, 216
Stacks Bookshop 424
George Stacpoole 438
The Staffordshire Knot, Whitby 328
Staffordshire Pride, Honiton 165
The Staffs Bookshop, Lichfield 298
Staines Antiques 114
Stair & Company Ltd 95
Staithe Antiques, Brancaster
Staithe 213
Staithes Antiques 327
Stalham Antique Gallery 219
J Stamp & Sons, Market
Harborough 279
Stamp and Hobbies, Gravesend 35
Stamp Shop, Cookstown 426
Stanfords 213
Staniland Booksellers 344
Alexe Stanion Antiques 70

K Stanley & Son, Auchterarder 409
David Stanley Auctions,
Osgathorpe 279
Stanstead Abbotts Leathers 493
Star Gallery, Lewes 22
Star Gallery 2, Lewes 22
Star Signings 112
W M Stark 514
Station Mill Antiques Centre 263
Staveley Antiques 364
steam-models.uk.com 269
Robert D Steedman 351
Stefani Antiques 376
Stella Books 388
Step Back In Time 15
Steppes Hill Farm Antiques 41
Stepping Stones 323
Sterling Art Services, Subury-on-
Thames 499
Sterling Books,
Weston-super-Mare 193
Sterling Coins and Medals,
Bournemouth 174
J W Stevens and Son, Market
Harborough 481
Stevens Antiques & Office Removals,
Glasgow 499
Stevenson Brothers, Bethersden
27, 508
Steve's World Famous Movie
Store 369
Stewart Sales Rooms 415
Stiffkey Lamp Shop 219
Still Life 403
Stirling Antiques 131
Stockbridge Antiques Centre 129
Stocks and Chairs, Poole 177
Stocks Pine, Bexhill-on-Sea 13
Stockspring Antiques 102
S & J Stodel 112
William H Stokes, Cirencester 240
Stokes Books, Dublin 435
Stokes Clocks and Watches Ltd,
Cork 430
June and Tony Stone Fine Antique
Boxes 23
Stony Stratford Antiques 236
The Stores 208
Storeys Ltd 112
Stormont Antiques 421
Stothert Old Books 356
Stow Antiques 246
Strachan Antiques 407
J Straker Chadwick & Sons 388
Strand Antiques, London 98
The Strand Antiques & Collectable,
Saundersfoot 390
Strand Quay Antiques, Rye 25
Stratford Antiques and Interiors 304
Stratford Antiques Centre 304
T Straw Restoration 460
J Streamer 210
Stretton Antiques Market 291
Jane Strickland & Daughters 165
Stride & Son 145
V Stringer 460
Strip and Polish, Stourbridge 505
Strip Easy Ltd, Lymington 505
Strip It Ltd, Birmingham 505

Strippadoor, Stockport 369
The Stripper, Whitby 505
The Stripping Store, Glasgow 506
Strippit, Herne Bay 506
M A Stroh Bookseller 48
Stuart Interiors Antiques Ltd 189
The Studio, Glasgow 408
Studio 101, Eton 116
Studio Antiques, Bromley 29
Studio Bookshop, Brighton 15
Studio Coins, Winchester 129
Stuff & Nonsense 235
Sturmans Antiques 322
Styles Silver 118
The Suffolk Antique Bed Centre 224
Suffolk House Antiques 229
Suffolk Sci-fi Fantasy 224
Sugar Antiques 53
Suite Dreams Upholstery 511
Summers Antiques, Polegate 23
Summers Davis Antiques Ltd,
Wallingford 267
Summersons 305
Sunderlands Sale Rooms 252
Sundial Antique Clock Service,
Coulsdon 451
Sundial Antiques, Amersham 233
Sunningend Joiners and Cabinet
Makers Ltd 478
Sunnyside Antiques 414
Supatra 121
Surrey Antiques, Horley 138
Surrey Clock Centre, Haslemere 451
Surrey Restoration Ltd, Cobham 467
R A Surridge 474
Susannah 183
Sussex Gilding, Brighton 490
Sussex Woodcraft, Chichester 467
Tony Sutcliffe Antiques 377
Sutton Valence Antiques,
Maidstone 36
Sutton Valence Antiques 41
Suzette Antiques 25
Spencer Swaffer 143
Marilyn Swain Auctions 340
Arthur Swallow Fairs 523
The Swan at Tetsworth 266
Swan Gallery Antiques, Burford 262
John Swan Ltd, Melrose 413
Swans Antiques and Interiors,
Oakham 290, 481
Sweetbriar Gallery (Paperweights)
Ltd 356
Sweetings Antiques Belper 273
Christine Swift Books, Egerton 33
K W Swift, Ludlow 293
Swiss Cottage Furniture 337
E Swonnell Ltd 95
G E Sworder & Sons 212
Sydenham Antiques Centre 65
Christopher Sykes, Woburn 232
William Sykes & Son, Holmfirth 335
Symonds Salvage Ltd 28

T J Upholstery 510
T L H Auctioneers 366
T S Restorations 467

Tadema Gallery 53
Tagore Ltd 95
Taikoo Books Ltd 330
Tails & The Unexpected Ltd 393
Take Five Fairs 523
Talbot Walk Antique Centre 140
The Talish Gallery 403
Talisman 176
The Talking Machine 59
Talking Point Antiques 338, 491
Tamblyn Antiques, Alnwick 348
Tamlyn and Son, Bridgwater 183
Robert P Tandy 452, 471
Tango Art Deco & Antiques,
    Warwick 305
Tango Curios, Darlington 347
Tankerton Antiques 46
Tansu 334
Tantalus Antiques 414
Tapestry Antiques, Cheltenham 239
Tapestry Antiques, Hertford 257
Chris Tapsell Antiques 53
Tara Antiques, London 60
Tara Antiques, Thomastown 438
Tarka Books, Barnstaple 159
Tarporley Antique Centre 359
Lorraine Tarrant Antiques,
    Ringwood 127
Tarrant Street Antique & Collectors
    Centre, Arundel 144
The Tarrystone 381
Tattersalls 290
Laurence Tauber Antiques 141
Taunton Antiques Market 192
Taurus Antiques 36
Tavistock Furniture Store 168
Peter Taylor and Son, Leavesden 257
Martin Taylor Antiques,
    Wolverhampton 310
Michael J Taylor Antiques,
    Sheffield 333
Pam Taylor Antiques, London 107
Louis Taylor Fine Art Auctioneers,
    Stoke-on-Trent 300
Taylor Pearce Restoration Services
    Ltd, London 502, 503, 504
Taylor's Collectables, Truro 157
Taylors, Ashburton 158
John Taylor's, Louth 342
Taylor-Smith Antiques, Westerham 45
Taymouth Architectural Antiques 398
Tea and Antiques 223
Tea Gowns & Textiles 254
Teddy Bears of Witney 268
Telephone Lines Ltd 239
Jeanne Temple Antiques,
    Wavendon 236
Temple Jones Restoration, Burwash
    Common 460
Roy Temple Polishing, Wargrave 467
Tempo Antiques, Galway 436
Tempus Watches, Ascot 115, 451
Tenby Antiques Centre 390
Tennants Auctioneers, Harrogate 322
Tennants Auctioneers, Leyburn 323
Tenterden Antique & Silver Vaults 41
Tenterden Antiques Centre 41
Tess Antiques 439
Tetbury Old Books 248

Tewkesbury Antiques Centre 249
Textile Conservation, Banwell 455, 507
The Textile Conservancy Co Ltd,
    Tenterden 507
Textile Conservation Consultancy,
    Stamford 455, 507
Textile-Art: The Textile Gallery,
    London 95
Teywood Ltd 474
Thainstone Specialist Auctions 397
Thakeham Furniture 149
Thanet Antiques & Marine
    Paraphernalia Ltd 38
The Theatre Antiques Centre 223
Themes and Variations 107
Thistle and Rose, Hawick 444
Thistle Antiques, Aberdeen 396
Thistlethwaite Antiques, Settle 326
Andrew Thomas, Stamford 344
Sean Thomas Antiques, Donegal 432
Philip Thomas Design, London 107
Ed Thomas Old Country Pine,
    Cannock 481, 502
Thomond Antiques 362
John Thompson, Tunbridge Wells 44
Jósef Thompson,
    Saltburn-by-the-Sea 326
M and A C Thompson,
    Wymondham 220
John Thompson Antiques,
    Knaresborough 323
Anthony Thompson Ltd, London 107
Thompsons Auctioneers,
    Killinghall 323
Thomson, Roddick & Medcalf,
    Dumfries 398
    Edinburgh 403
    Carlisle 361
Thomson's Antiques, St Helier 418
B & T Thorn and Son 160
Thornleigh Trading Antique
    Lighting 155
John Thornton, London 82
Thornton & Linley,
    Knaresborough 323
Richard Thornton Books, London 56
Thorntons of Harrogate 322
Thomas Thorp, Wheathampstead 260
Miwa Thorpe, London 74
John Thorpe Fine Furniture,
    Launceston 471
The Thrie Estaits 403
Thrift Cottage Antiques 221
Through the Looking Glass, Dun
    Laoghaire 436
Through The Looking Glass,
    London 102
Kate Thurlow and David Alexander
    Antiques 83
Thurmaston Antiques Centre 280
R Tidder Antique Furniture
    Restoration 474
Tiffins Antiques 123
Tilleys Vintage Magazine Shop 333
Till's Bookshop 403
Timber Restorations, Buntingford
    478, 506
Timbers Antiques & Collectables,
    Lavenham 225

Time and Motion, Beverley 316
Time in Hand, Shipston-on-Stour 303
Time Restored Ltd, Pewsey 198, 452
Timecraft Clocks, Sherborne 178, 452
Timepiece Antique Clocks, Dublin 435
Timepiece Antiques, Teignmouth 168
Times Past, Buntingford 255
Times Past Antiques,
    Auchterarder 409
Times Past Antiques, Eton 116
Timgems Jewellers 218
S and S Timms Antiques Ltd 232
Tin Tin Collectables 60
Tina's Antiques 195
The Tinder Box 300
Tindley & Chapman 112
Tinkers Pine Stripping & Antiques 154
Tintern Antiques 388
Titian Studio 463, 490
Titus Omega 53
Toad Hall Antique Centre 20
Tobias & The Angel 84
Toby Jug Collectables, Deal 33
Tobys,
    Exminster 162
    Newton Abbot 166
    Torquay 170
M Tocci 463, 490, 500
Todd & Austin Antiques & Fine Art,
    Winchester 129
Todd's Antiques, Launceston 152
Tolco Antiques, Galway 437
Tom Tom 112
Tom's Clock Shop 286
Tombland Antiques Centre 218
Tombland Bookshop 218
Christopher Tombs, Moreton-in-
    Marsh 478
Eric Tombs, Dorking 135
Tomlinson Antiques 328, 483
Tony's Antique Services Ltd 18, 460
The Tool Shop 227
Tooley, Adams and Co 267
Toot-Sweet 337
Rupert Toovey & Co 149
Top Banana Antiques Malls 248, 249
Top Drawer Antiques 270
Top Hat Antiques 289
Totteridge Gallery 207
Tower Antiques, Cranborne 175
Tower Bridge Antiques, London 61
Tower House Decorative Antiques,
    Almondsbury 237
The Tower Workshops, Tarland 397, 487
Town and Country Antiques
    Centres 338
Town Hall Antiques 233
Town House 47
Town Prints 226
Townhead Antiques 363
Townhouse Antiques 367
Townsend Bateson 249
Townsford Mill Antiques Centre 209
James Townshend Antiques 183
Towy Antiques Fairs 523
The Toy Works 508
Toynbee-Clarke Interiors Ltd 95
Richard Tozer Furniture Workshop
    27, 460

Trade Antiques Centre 22
Traders Antiques and Country Pine Centre 121
Trading House, Kinsale 430
The Trading Post Antique Centre, Tytherleigh 171
The Traditional Restoration Company Ltd, Windsor 467
The Traditional Studio, Welwyn 449, 491
Traditions, Pulborough 149
Trafalgar Bookshop 15
Trails End Collectables Ltd 206
Trains and Diecast 372
Trash 'n' Treasure 353
Travers Antiques 57
Travis & Emery Music Bookshop 112
The Treasure Bunker Militaria Shop, Glasgow 408
The Treasure Chest, Weymouth 179
Treasure Chest Antiques, Blackrock 432
Treasure Chest Antiques, Whitley Bay 352
The Treasure Chest Books, Felixstowe 223
Treasure Trove Books, Leicester 278
Treasure World, London 48
Treasures, Four Elms 35
Treasures of Ballater 397
The Treasury, Lewes 22
Trecastle Antique Centre 392
Tredantiques 162
Treedale Antiques, Oakham 290, 481
Treen Antiques, Prestwich 485
Treen Box Antiques, Pembroke Dock 390
Treharris Antiques 387
Tremayne Applied Arts 156
Trianon Antiques Ltd 95
Trident Exhibitions 523
Neil Trinder, Sheffield 483
Trinder's Fine Tools, Clare 222
Trinity Curios, Edinburgh 403
Trinity Rare Books, Carrick on Shannon 438
Triton Gallery 239
Troke, Terry 467
Trouvailles 36
Trowbridge Gallery, Crowborough 16
Trowbridge Gallery, London 79
Irene S Trudgett Collectables 129
Trudi's Treasures 16
Truman & Bates 478
Tudor House, Stow-on-the-Wold 246
Tudor House Antiques, Christchurch 175
Tudor House Antiques, Halesowen 308
Tudor House Antiques, Ironbridge 292
Tudor House Antiques and Collectables, Henley-on-Thames 264
Tudor Rose Antique Centre, Petworth 149
W F Turk Fine Antique Clocks, London 85
Turks Head Antiques, Eton 116
Turn On Lighting 53, 457, 494

Turnburrys Ltd 351
Malcolm Turner, Norwich 218
Turner & Sons (1787), Liverpool 376
R & M Turner (Antiques & Fine Art) Ltd, Jedburgh 413
Alexis F J Turner Antiques, East Molesey 136
Sally Turner Antiques, Wendover 237
P & K Turner Auctions, Cannock 296
P & K Turner Auctions, Earlswood 301
Turner Violins, Beeston 285
Birmingham 307
Leeds 337
David Turner Workshops 494, 496
Turpins Antiques 118
Tussie Mussies 41
TVADA 523
Twice As Nice 437
The Twickenham Antiques Warehouse 114
Twinkled 19
Two Dragons Oriental Antiques 386
Richard Twort 193
Twyford Antiques Centre, Evesham 311
Stow-on-the-Wold 246
Matthew Tyler Antiques 226
Ty-Llwyd Antiques 393
Tynemouth Architectural Salvage 351

U

UK Old Postcards Ltd 29
UK Toy & Model Auctions Ltd 375
ukauctioneers.com 503
Andrew R Ullmann Ltd 49
Undercover Books 345
Underwood Hall Antiques 345
Unicorn Antiques 404
Unicorn Fairs Ltd 523
Unique Collections of Chipstead 133
Uniques 31
University of Central England School of Jewellery 496, 509
Robin Unsworth Antiques, Olney 236
Unsworths Booksellers Ltd, London 108
Up Country Ltd 44
Upstairs & Downstairs Antiques, Ripley 276
Upstairs Downstairs, Devizes 196
Upstairs Downstairs, Gloucester 241
Upstairs-Downstairs, Muthill 411
Upstairs Downstairs, Torquay 170
Upstairs Downstairs Antiques, Ripley 453, 482
Oliver Usher 440
Utopia Antiques Ltd, Grange-over-Sands 362
Kendal 362
Utter Clutter, Leominster 254

V

V&A Fairs 523
Vale Antiques, Easingwold 320
Vale Antiques, London 102
The Vale of Glamorgan Antique Centre 394

Valelink Ltd 15
Valentina Antique Beds 20
Valley Auctions 36
Valmar Antiques 212
Valued History 203
Jan Van Beers Oriental Art 96
Vanbrugh House Antiques 246
Jenny Vander 435
Vane House Antiques 53
Geoffrey Van-Hay Antiques 138
Van-Lyn Antiques 422
Variety Box 44
Vaughan Antiques 345
Vectis Auctions Ltd 327
The Venerable Bead 170
Edward Venn Antiques Restorations 471
T Vennett-Smith Auctioneers and Valuers 285
Ventnor Antiques Centre 131
Ventnor Junction 131
Vicar Lane Antique Centre 317
Victoria Antiques, London 48
Victoria Antiques, Saltaire 338
Victoria Antiques, Wadebridge 158
Victoria Antiques, Wallasey 378
Victoria House, Bedford 231
The Victorian Brass Bedstead Co 145
Victorian Chairman 174
Victorian Dreams 124
The Victorian Fireplace 31
The Victorian Salvage and Joinery Co Ltd 435
Victoriana Antiques and Kents Jewellers 162
Victoria's Antiques, Cork 430
Viewback Auctions 427
Vigo Carpet Gallery 96
Villa Grisebach Art Auctions 58
Village Antiques, Batley 334
Village Antiques, Cheam 133
Village Antiques, Cobham 134
Village Antiques Aldermaston 115
Village Books, Dereham 214
Village Clocks, Long Melford 226
Village Farm Antiques, Altrincham 353
The Village Market Antiques, Weedon 284
Village Pine Antiques, Hawarden 384
Garth Vincent Antique Arms and Armour, Allington 338
Vincents of Clifton, Bristol 186
Vinci Antiques 96
Vintage & Rare Guitars (Bath) Ltd 183
Vintage & Rare Guitars (London) 112
Vintage Antiques Centre, Warwick 305
Vintage Jewels, Westerham 45
Vintage Sewing Machines, Ockley 139
Vintage to Vogue, Bath 183
The Vintage Toy & Train Shop, Sidmouth 167
Virginia 107
Virgo Fairs 523
G Viventi 61
VOC Antiques 345
Voitek Conservation of Works of Art 456, 500, 503, 504

Voltaire & Rousseau 408
Volume One Books and Records 174
Vortex Books 108
S Vye 170

W

Rupert Wace Ancient Art Ltd 96
Geraldine Waddington Books and
  Prints 283
Valerie Wade 74
Chris Wadge Clocks 199, 452
A E Wakeman and Sons Ltd 168
Walcot Reclamation Ltd 183
Waldegrave Antiques 113
Paul Waldmann Woodwork
  (Conservation Unit) 475, 491
Patrick Waldron Antiques 240
Alan Walker, Newbury 119
Brian Walker, Salisbury 471
Richard Walker – Antique
  Restoration, Matlock 482
Walker, Barnett & Hill, Cosford 291
Walker Galleries, Harrogate 322
The Walking Stick Shop 143
E F Wall 229
Sandra Wallhead 272
Wallis & Wallis 22
John Walsh & Co. 337
William Walter Antiques Ltd,
  London 112
J D and R M Walters, Rolvenden 39
Walton & Hipkiss 308
Nigel Ward & Co, Pontrilas 254
Ward and Chowen Auction Rooms,
  Tavistock 168
Paul Ward Antiques, Sheffield 333
Ward's Antiques, London 62
Wardrobe 16
Ward-Thomas Antiques 201
Ware Militaria Auctions 259
Wargrave Antiques 120
Warminster Antique Centre 200
W W Warner Antiques 29
Jimmy Warren, Littlebourne 36
Leigh Warren, London 79
Warren Antiques, Leiston 225
Helen Warren China Restoration,
  Cranbrook 447
Fizzy Warren Decorative Antiques,
  Stockbridge 129
Robert A Warry Auctioneer,
  Blandford Forum 172
Wartime Wardrobe 274
Warwick Antique Centre 305
Warwick Antique Restorations
  446, 451
Warwick Auctions 307
The Warwick Leadlay Gallery,
  London 63
Warwick Wright Restoration,
  Wem 449
Waterfall Antiques, Bath 183
Waterfall Antiques, Ross-on-Wye 255
Watergate Antiques 356
The Waterloo Trading Co 53
Geoffrey Waters Ltd 102
Waterside Antiques 203
R G Watkins, Stoke sub Hamdon 191

Islwyn Watkins Antiques,
  Knighton 391
Watkins Books Ltd, London 112
Gwyn Watkins Stonemason and
  Architectural Stone Carver,
  Stamford 444, 504
Watling Antiques 32
Graham Watson, Greenlaw 487
Brian Watson Antique Glass,
  Marsham 217
Gordon Watson Ltd, London 75
L D Watts 183
Waverley Antiques 405
R E and G B Way, Burrough Green 221
Ways Auction House, Ryde 131
Ways Bookshop,
  Henley-on-Thames 264
Wayside Antiques, Duffield 274
Wayside Antiques, Tattershall 345
Wealth of Weights 19
Weather House Antiques 502
Paul Weatherell Antiques 321
Trude Weaver 107
J R Webb Antiques, Aberdeen 396
Webb Fine Arts, Winchester 129
S J Webster-Speakman 227
Weedon Antiques 284
Mike Weedon, London 53
Weir and Sons Ltd 435
Peter K Weiss 112
P M Welch 47
J W Weldon 435
Weller & Dufty Ltd, Birmingham 307
Weller King, Pulborough 515
Wellers Auctioneers, Chertsey 133
Anthony Welling 140
Wellington Gallery 60
Wells Antique Centre 220
Wells Auction Rooms 192
Wells Reclamation Company 192
Welsh Country Auctions 380
Welsh Salvage Co 388
Jorge Welsh 102
Wentworth Arts, Crafts
  & Antiques 331
Wessex Antiques 178
Wesley J West & Son, Potton 232
Wessex Antiques Fairs 523
Mark J West 85
West Country Fairs 523
West Country Old Books 170
West Dean College 509
West Essex Antiques 209
West Essex Coin Investments 123
West Lancashire Antiques Export 371
West Midland Antique Fairs 524
West Midlands Collectors Centre 310
West of England Auctions 170
West Port Books 404
West Street Antiques, Dorking 135
West Street Antiques, Haslemere 138
Westend Antiques & Jewellery 347
Westenholz Antiques Ltd 70
Westgate Auctions 45
Westland and Co 49
Westminster Group Antique
  Jewellery 96
Westmoor Furniture 471
Westport House Antique Shop 440

Westville House Antiques 191
Westway Pine, Helmsley 323, 483
Westwood Books Ltd,
  Hay-on-Wye 252
  Sedbergh 364
Westwood House Antiques 249
Tim Wharton 258
What-Not Antiques, Chobham 133
What-Not-Shop Antiques,
  Stowmarket 228
What Nots Antiques, Strathblane 415
What Now Antiques, Buxton 273
Whatever Comics,
  Canterbury 31
  Maidstone 36
The Whatnot, Londonderry 426
Wheatsheaf Antiques Centre 356
Andrew Wheeler, Bristol 501
Wheelers, Worthing 150, 451
Wheels of Steel 96
N D Whibley Restorations 471
Whichcraft Jewellery 213
Whispers of the Past 411
Whitchurch Antique Centre 294
Whitchurch Books Ltd 393
D P White, Ramsbury 198
E & B White, Brighton 16
M & M White Antiques and
  Reproduction Centre, Reigate 139
White Elephant Antique and
  collectables, Leicester 278
White House Antiques & Stripped
  Pine, Waverton 359
Whitehead & Sons 384
Whiteladies Antiques
  & Collectables 186
John Whitelaw & Sons 410
Ian Whitelaw Antiques 409
Whitemoors Antique Centre 302
Whitestone Farm Antiques 145
Robert Whitfield, London 63
Whitfield Restoration, Colchester 475
B D Whitham 484
Ian Whitmore 497
Whittaker & Biggs 356
Avril Whittle, Bookseller 364
Whyte's 435
Whytock & Reid 404
Wick Antiques 125
Wickersley Antiques 287
Wickham Square Gallery 123
Wiend Books & Collectables 366
Wild Goose Antiques 165
Sue Wilde, Sidmouth 167
Chris Wilde Antiques, Harrogate 322
Wilfords 284
David J Wilkins 58
N I Wilkinson, Bakewell 272
Colin Wilkinson and Co, Larne 422
T G Wilkinson Antiques Ltd,
  Petworth 149
Marcus Wilkinson Jewellers &
  Antiques, Grantham 340
Wilkinson PLC, London 62, 96
S J. Willder Antiques 308
Willesden Green Architectural
  Salvage 61
William Antiques, Ascott-under-
  Wychwood 260

Williams & Watkins Auctioneers Ltd, Ross-on-Wye 255
John Williams Antique & Collectables, Warwick 305
Cecil Williams Antiques, Dolgellau 385
George Williams Antiques, Kells 440
Huw Williams Antiques, Porthmadog 386
Nigel Williams Rare Books, London 112
A J Williams Shipping, Bath 499
G Williams, Betchworth 468
Joyce Williams, Aberporth 384
Peter Williams, Comber 488
Robert Williams, Canbridge 475, 497, 500
Henry Willis (Antique Silver) 178
Willowpool Garden Centre & Baron Antiques 357
Willroy Antiques Centre 202
Peter Wilson, Nantwich 358
R S Wilson & Son, Boroughbridge 320
O F Wilson Ltd, London 75
Wilsons Antiques, Worthing 150
Wilson's Auctions, Newtownabbey 422
Wilson's Auctions Ltd (Portadown), Portadown 423
Agnes Wilton, London 53
Wilton House, Salisbury 524
The Wimborne Emporium 179
Wimpole Antiques 96
Wincanton Antiques 193, 511
The Winchester Bookshop 130
P F Windibank 135
The Winding Stair 437
Windle & Co 334
Windmill Antiques, Stafford 299
Windmill Bookshop, Lytham St Anne's 373
Windsor & Eton Antiques Centre 116
Windsor Antiques 506
David Windsor Gallery, Bangor 385
Windsor House Antiques Centre, Moreton-in-Marsh 243
Windsor House Antiques Ltd, London 96
Windworld 307
Wingetts Auction Gallery 384
Winram's Bookshop 396
Winslow Antique Centre 237
Winson Antiques, Kingham 264
Alan Winson Antiques, Burton-on-Trent 296
Dominic Winter Book Auctions 199
Winter Fairs 524
Richard Winterton Auctioneers and Valuers, Burton-on-Trent 296
Wintertons Ltd, Lichfield 298
Winton Antiques 265
The Wireless Works 491
Mary Wise & Grosvenor Antiques 102
Wish Barn Antiques 25
The Wiston Project School 509
The Witch Ball, Brighton 16
The Witch Ball, London 112
Withers of Leicester, Hoby 277
B M Witmond 492, 503

Witney Antiques 268
Wizpan China & Collectables 311
Wizzards Furniture Restorers 482
Thos Wm Gaze & Son 214
Woburn Abbey Antiques Centre 233
David Wolfenden Antiques 419
D Wombell & Son 328
Wonder Whistle Enterprises 524
Wonderworld 174
Dale Wood & Co, Batley 334
Wood 'n' Things, Wolverhampton 310, 472
Colin Wood Antiques Ltd, Aberdeen 396
Richard Wood Antiques, Edinburgh 404
Wood Be Good, Croydon 134, 502
Michael Wood Fine Art, Plymouth 167
Wood Pigeon, London 83
Wood Restorations, Rugby 482
Woodage Antiques 53
Woodall & Emery Ltd, Balcombe 143, 494
Woodbridge Gallery 229
P Woodcock & Co, Oswestry 512
Woodcock House Antiques, Impington 204
The Wooden Betty, Gosforth 350
Wooden Heart, Stoke-on-Trent 300
Woodford Auctions 48
Woodmans House Antiques 290
Wood's Antiques, Lynton 165
Woods Wharf Antiques Market, Haslemere 138
Woodside Reclamation 349
Woodstock Antiques 337
Woodville Antiques 35
Joseph Woodward & Sons Ltd, Cork 430
Woodward Antique Clocks, Cheltenham 239
Woolley and Wallis Salisbury Salerooms Ltd 199
Woolnough (AC) Ltd 493
Worcester Antiques Centre 315
Worcester Medal Service Ltd 311
The Works Antiques Centre 380
Works of Iron 337
World Coins 31
World of Sport 18
World War Books 44
Worlds Apart 334
World's End Bookshop 75
J D Worrall (Conservation) 485
Worthing Auction Galleries Ltd 150
Wot-a-Racket 33
Wotruba & Son 468
Wotton Auction Rooms Ltd 250
Wratten Antique & Craft Mews 32
Linda Wrigglesworth Ltd 96
Ken Wright, Romford 452
Mick & Fanny Wright, Minchinhampton 242
Nigel Wright, Sheffield 484
Tim Wright Antiques, Glasgow 408
Clifford Wright Antiques Ltd, London 75

Gary Wright Antiques Ltd, Moreton-in-Marsh 243
Wright-Manley, Beeston 354
www.antiques.co.uk 70
www.buymeissen.com 53
Stephen Wycherley 307
Wymondham Antique Centre 220
Wyrardisbury Antiques 114
Wyseby House Books 118

X

Ximenes Rare Books Inc 241

Y

Yarmouth Antiques and Books 131
Yarnton Antique Centre 268
Year Dot 337
Yellow Lantern Antiques 20
Yeovil Collectors Centre 193
Yesterday and Today, Sutton-in-Ashfield 289
Yester-Days, Haddington 399
Yesterdays Antiques, Cleethorpes 339
Yesterdays Books, Bournemouth 174
Yesterdays Components Ltd, Chelmsfield 207
Yesterdays Today, Perth 411
Yester-Year, Iver 235
Yesteryear Railwayana, Ramsgate 38
Yesteryears, Topsham 170
Yew Tree, Woburn 233
Yew Tree Antiques Warehouse, Wiveliscombe 193
Yiju 44
York Antiques Centre 330
York Gallery Ltd, London 53, 79
York House (Antiques), Richmond 325
York Vale Antiques 330, 506
Yorkshire Relics 335
Youll's Antiques 118
Michael Young, London 53
Young & Son, London 60
John Young & Son Antiques, Keswick 363
Robert Young Antiques, London 83
Richard J Young Antiques Restorer, Cirencester 478
Peter Young Auctioneers, Gringley on the Hill 285, 509
Tony Young Autographs, Brighton 16
R M Young Bookseller, South Molton 168
Yoxall Antiques & Fine Arts 308
Ystwyth Books 381

Z

Richard Zabrocki & Son 484
Zany Lady 293
Zeitgeist Antiques 97
Ann Zierold Fairs 524
Zig Zags 388

MILLER'S

Antiques Shops, Fairs & Auctions in the UK & Ireland 2007

ENTRY FORM

Please return a signed copy of this form to: Miller's Publications (Directory 2007), The Cellars, High Street, Tenterden, Kent TN30 6BN or fax to 01580 766100.

Name of Business: ....

Type of Entry *(Dealer/Auction House/Market or Centre/Associated Service)*: ....

Contact Name: ....

Street: ....

Town: .... County: .... Postcode: ....

Address for mailing *(if different from above)*: ....

....

Telephone: .... Fax: .... Mobile: ....

Email: .... Web address: ....

Trade only *(Yes/No)*: .... Parking nearby *(Yes/No)*: ....

Member of: .... Established: ....

Opening/Office hours: ....

Dealers only

Principal Stock: ....

If a Specialist Dealer, please give speciality *(one only)*: ....

Services offered *(Valuation/Restoration/Shipping/Book Search)*: ....

....

Exhibitor at which fairs? *(two only)*: ....

Quantity of stock held *(Small/Medium/Large)*: ....

Auction Houses only

Sale details: ....

Catalogues *(Yes/No)*: .... Frequency of main sale: ....

Markets/Centres only

Number of stalls/shops/dealers: ....

Associated Service only

Specialist area: ....

Services offered: ....

I agree that the above data may be included in the 2007 and future editions of Miller's Antiques Shops, Fairs & Auctions in the UK & Ireland. I further acknowledge that it is my responsibility to keep this information up to date and agree to inform Octopus Publishing Group Ltd (OPG) of any changes to it.

Signature: _____ Name: _____ Date: _____

Paragraph A: We Octopus Publishing Group Ltd (OPG) wish to share the information you have provided with our business partners for promotional and product development purposes, via a range of media including web sites and digital television. If you do not wish us to use your information in this way, then please tick here: q

If you no longer want to be included in the above publication or if you have any queries concerning the personal information held about you, please contact: Valerie Lewis, Miller's Publications, The Cellars, High Street, Tenterden, Kent TN30 6BN.